Picturing Hegel

Picturing Hegel

An Illustrated Guide to Hegel's *Encyclopaedia Logic*

Julie E. Maybee

LEXINGTON BOOKS
A division of
ROWMAN & LITTLEFIELD PUBLISHERS, INC.
Lanham • Boulder • New York • Toronto • Plymouth, UK

Published by Lexington Books
A division of Rowman & Littlefield Publishers, Inc.
A wholly owned subsidiary of The Rowman & Littlefield Publishing Group, Inc.
4501 Forbes Boulevard, Suite 200, Lanham, Maryland 20706
http://www.lexingtonbooks.com

Estover Road, Plymouth PL6 7PY, United Kingdom

British Library Cataloguing in Publication Information Available

Library of Congress Cataloging-in-Publication Data

Maybee, Julie E., 1965–
Picturing Hegel : an illustrated guide to Hegel's Encyclopaedia logic / Julie E. Maybee.
p. cm.
Includes bibliographical references and index.
ISBN 978-0-7391-1615-9 (cloth : alk. paper) — ISBN 978-0-7391-1616-6 (pbk. : alk. paper)
eISBN: 978-0-7391-3979-0
1. Hegel, Georg Wilhelm Friedrich, 1770–1831. Wissenschaft der Logik. 2. Logic, Modern—19th century. I. Title.
B2942.Z7M39 2009
160—dc22

2009014534

Printed in the United States of America

Dedication

For my parents,
Marida and Warren

the determinate animal —
i.e. the animal

Contents

Acknowledgments xi
Introduction xiii

1. Entering the Gallery: Hegel's Overall Project and the Project of the *Logic*

I. The Skepticism of Hume and Kant 1
II. Reason Overgrasps Reality 7
III. Essential, Necessary Universals 16
IV. Reason Drives Itself: Semantics and Syntax 19
V. Hegel's Argument 25
VI. Hegel's Overall Project 31
VII. The Conceptual and Semantic Project of the *Logic* 32
VIII. The Syntactic Project of the *Logic* 34

2. The Doctrine of Being

I. Introduction 45

II. The Doctrine of Quality 51

Being 51 • Nothing 51 • Becoming 53 • Being-there 55 • Being-in-itself 58 • Limit 64 • Spurious Infinity 67 • Being-for-itself or Genuine Infinity 71 • Repulsion or Negative Relation 78 • Attraction 83

III. The Doctrine of Quantity 88

Pure Quantity or Quantity in General 88 • Quantum or Quantity as There 89 • Number or Developed Quantum 90 • Extensive and Intensive Magnitude 91 • Degree 92 • Ratio 95

IV. The Doctrine of Measure 99

Immediate Measure 100 • The Measureless 102 • Transition to Essence 107

V. Wrap Up Being: Comments on Syntax 113

3. The Doctrine of Essence

I. Introduction 121

II. Essence as the Ground of Existence 131

Identity 131 • Immediate Distinction 133 • Likeness and Unlikeness 137 • Positive and Negative 142 • Distinction "In Itself" 145 • Transition to Ground 147 • Ground 151 • Transition to Existence 154 • Existence 156 • Thing 159 • Properties 161 • Matters 163 • Thing as Form 165 • One Matter 166 • Thing as One Form 168 • Matter and Form Fall Apart 169 • Transition to Appearance 172

III. The Doctrine of Appearance 175

Appearance 175 • World of Appearance 176 • Content and Form: Law of Appearance 181 • Content and Form: External Form 183 • External Content 184 • Transition to Relationship 185 • Immediate Relationship: Whole and Parts 187 • Force and Utterance 189 • Transition to Inner and Outer 196 • Inner and Outer 198 • Transition to Actuality 209

IV. The Doctrine of Actuality 212

Immediate Actuality 214 • Possibility 215 • Contingency and Chance 217 • Transition to Condition 221 • Condition 224 • Real Possibility 230 • The Condition as a Totality 232 • The Matter (*Sache*) Itself and The Activity of Necessity 235 • External Necessity 243 • The Necessary 250 • Absolute Relationship 258 • Immediate Substance and Substantiality 264 • Substance as Cause 269 • The Effect as a Substance 274 • Transition to Reciprocal Action 278 • Reciprocal Action 281 • Transition to the Concept 290

V. Wrap Up Essence: Comments on Syntax 303

4. The Doctrine of the Concept

I. Introduction 315

II. The Doctrine of the Subjective or Formal Concept 323

Universality 324 • Particularity 326 • Singularity 328 • The Three Moments Cannot Be Held Apart 333 • Universality as Identity, Particularity as Distinction, Singularity as Ground 335 • The Concept Utters 337 • Transition to the Judgment 338

The Stages of Judgment
The Judgment 341 • Abstract Judgment 344 • Qualitative Judgment: Immediate Judgment or Judgment of Thereness 348 • The (Simply) Negative Qualitative Judgment 349 • Transition to the Empty Qualitative Judgment of Identity and the Negatively Infinite Qualitative Judgment 350 • The Empty Qualitative Judgment of Identity 352 • Negatively Infinite Qualitative Judgment 354 • The Judgment of Reflection: Singular Judgment of Reflection 358 • Particular Judgment of Reflection 361 • Universal Judgment of Reflection 363 • Transition to the Judgment of Necessity 365 • The Judgment of Necessity: Categorical Judgment of Necessity 366 • Hypothetical Judgment of Necessity 367 • Disjunctive Judgment of Necessity 369 • The Judgment of the Concept: Assertoric Judgment or the Immediate Judgment of the Concept 371 • Problematic Judgment of the Concept 372 • Apodictic Judgment of the Concept 373 • Transition to the Syllogism 375

The Stages of Syllogism
Immediate Syllogism or Formal Syllogism of the Understanding 378 • The First Figure of Qualitative Syllogism or Syllogism of Thereness 381 • The SL-Development for Qualitative Syllogism 384 • The Second Figure of Qualitative Syllogism (from SL) 385 • The Third Figure of Qualitative Syllogism (from SL) 390 • The EL-Development for Qualitative Syllogism: The Second Figure of Qualitative Syllogism 395 • The Third Figure of Qualitative Syllogism (from EL) 396 • Comparing the EL- and SL-Developments of Qualitative Syllogism 397 • The Quantitative or Mathematical Syllogism 406 • The Syllogism of Reflection 408 • The Syllogism of Allness: The First Figure of the Syllogism of Reflection 409 • The Syllogism of Induction: The Second Figure of the Syllogism of Reflection 411 • Syllogism of Analogy: The Third Figure of the Syllogism of Reflection 413 • The Syllogism of Necessity 416 • Categorical Syllogism: The First Figure of the Syllogism of Necessity 416 • Hypothetical Syllogism: The Second Figure of the Syllogism of Necessity 421 • Disjunctive Syllogism: The Third Figure of the Syllogism of Necessity 427 • Transition to the Object 433

III. The Doctrine of the Object 435

The Object 436 • Transition to Mechanism 438 • Formal Mechanism 441 • Non-indifferent Mechanism 443 • Absolute Mechanism 451 • Transition to

Chemism 458 • Chemism 461 • Transition to Purpose 466 • Abstract Purpose 470 • Subjective, Immediate, External or Finite Purpose 475 • First Moment of Purpose Realizing Itself 477 • Second Moment of Purpose Realizing Itself 483 • Third Moment of Purpose Realizing Itself 486 • Realized Purpose 489 • Transition to Idea 494

IV. The Doctrine of the Idea 504

Immediate Idea or Life 507 • The First Process of Life: Living-ness Inside Itself 511 • The Second Process: Living-ness Against Inorganic Nature 514 • The Third Process: Living-ness as the Genus-in-itself 516 • The Process of the Genus 522 • Transition to Cognition 525 • Cognition Generally 535 • Theoretical Cognition, Cognition as Such, or Understanding 545 • The Analytic Method of Cognition 549 • The Synthetic Method of Cognition 550 • The Synthetic Moment of Universality: Definition 552 • The Synthetic Moment of Particularity: The Universal Specified and Divided 553 • The Synthetic Moment of Singularity: Theorem, or the Universal in Its Concrete Singularity 557 • Transition to Willing 562 • Finite Willing 563 • Spurious Infinity of Finite Willing 570 • Absolute or Speculative Idea 574 • The Beginning of the Speculative Method: Being, the Immediate 584 • The Progression of the Speculative Method 589 • Immediate Absolute Idea as Nature 598

V. Wrap up Concept: Comments on Syntax 602

VI. Epilogue: Hegel's Materialism, Optimism, and Faith 607

References 611
Index 613

Acknowledgments

This book has been a part of my life for a number of years. Many people have provided valuable assistance and input, though I take full responsibility for the book's contents. The seeds of the book were planted while I was an undergraduate at Carleton University in Ottawa, Ontario, when Prof. Béla Egyed drew one diagram on the board representing Hegel's claim in the *Encyclopaedia Logic* that philosophy is a "circle of circles" (§15)—a diagram much like figure 1.2. Prof. Egyed also insisted that Hegel's system could only be properly understood through the logic. I have been told that it was unusual to encounter the logic in any form in an undergraduate (and even sometimes a graduate) class at that time, and I am grateful to Béla for sparking my interest. I am also grateful to Béla for a comment he made not long after I started attending Cornell University as a graduate student. I called him at his office to complain about the analytic philosophy that dominated my new department. "Ah, it will be good for you," Béla said. "You will learn to speak both languages."

Several students at the University of Kansas—where I first developed a series of diagrams to help explain certain sections of the logic—convinced me that the diagrams were pedagogically useful and encouraged me to publish them in some form. One student even offered to reproduce the diagrams using a computer program. Among these students were Stephen Ferguson and John McClendon. John—whose long years of scholarship before enrolling in the Ph.D. program at KU made something of a mockery of any claim on my part to be his "professor"—continued to encourage me to write and complete the manuscript as years passed. In many ways, John has been a mentor and role model for me.

A few years after joining Lehman College, City University of New York, Prof. William Pohle encouraged me to begin writing the book in earnest and provided valuable comments on several early drafts. Reading e-mails from and writing e-mails to Bill on my Blackberry from the bathroom at Rusk Rehabilitation Institute kept me sane. Bill can understand in a way few others can what it is like to lose a child. I am indebted to Bill not only for his help with the book, but for much else as well.

Prof. Allen Wood also reviewed early hand-written drafts of the diagrams as well as several later drafts of chapters, and has been an especially important source of support, encouragement and feedback on the manuscript. In Allen, I found the perfect person to follow up on Béla's advice: someone who is not only a wonderful and fair commenter, mentor and role model, but who also speaks "both languages."

I am indebted to José Muñiz, a young philosopher and former undergraduate student at Lehman, without whose helpful comments, gentle encouragement and hard work as the manuscript's typesetter, this book would never have been finished. José is now a promising graduate student, but he has become successful in many ways since he first started working on the manuscript.

My daughter, Leyna, has seen the most change in her life over the time that I have been writing this book. An aneurysm and resulting brain injury at the age of 12—which partly explains why this book took me so long to finish—almost killed her, and certainly changed her life. But I am happy to say that she came back far enough to pester me and accuse me once again of being "obsessed" with the manuscript. I am grateful to Leyna for coming back at all, and for the constancy of her pestering—a reminder that, while things have changed, much has also remained the same. When some doors close, they blow open others.

My son, Kellen, had to grow up quickly and learn to carry the burden of two children. He has turned into a fine young man while I have been writing this book. I am grateful to him for his strength and sense of humor, even if he wanted nothing whatever to do with Hegel.

My husband, Roosevelt, has never wanted much to do with Hegel, either. He was an analytic philosopher. But I am grateful for the other kinds of support he provided while I worked on the manuscript. I thank him for putting up with nearly round-the-clock typesetting work during the completion of the manuscript as well as with my failures to live up to some family responsibilities during times when work on the manuscript was more intense. I am also grateful for those times when I needed, not just a friend, but an attorney, which he had the foresight to become.

I am grateful to Eric "Eagle-eye" Campbell, who provided invaluable proofreading and made several humorous title suggestions, which I am sure occurred to him during moments of frustration with the manuscript. Prof. Patricia Thompson gave me the idea for the title, *Picturing Hegel*. Others also provided important professional support. I wish to thank Sophia Diamantis-Fry (who was at the other end of numerous e-mail exchanges from various rehabilitation hospitals, and without whom I would not have been able to survive), Prof. Richard Mendelsohn, Dean Marlene Gottlieb, and Prof. Andrew McLaughlin.

The book is dedicated to my parents, Warren and Marida Maybee, without whom I would not be at all, and certainly would not be who I am. I am grateful to them for more than I can say.

Introduction

Pictures may be worth a thousand words everywhere else, but they are worth so much more when the thousand words they are replacing are Hegel's. In this book I use pictures, or diagrams, to illuminate the step-by-step development of one of G.W.F. Hegel's difficult discussions of logic. The illustrations help to unveil key aspects of his logic that have not been well explicated before, thereby shining new light on the subject matter that Hegel himself came increasingly during his lifetime to see as the proper introduction to his philosophical system (Pinkard 2000, 341).

Why study Hegel's logic today? Aside from a historical interest in Hegel's work, there are two main reasons why scholars should still be interested in Hegel's logic. First, the logic offers complex and penetrating definitions of many of Western philosophy's most central and enduring concepts: universality, reason, cause, thing, property, and appearance, just to name a few. Hegel's definitions are worth studying not only because they illuminate the meanings of these terms, but also because they exhibit many of the assumptions that are hidden behind the way these terms have commonly been defined in the history of Western philosophy. Hegel considered himself an encyclopedic culmination of Western philosophy. To some degree he succeeded—at least his work manages in large part to summarize beautifully many of the presuppositions of traditional Western philosophy. As a result, we ignore him at our peril. There is a sense in which we have to go through Hegel to get past ourselves.

Second, Hegel's logic is not the standard logic that we teach and learn in schools today. Hegel offered an alternative model of logic that he would have argued is more scientific than the formalistic logics we study now. In the end, we may not come to think that his model is best, but our devotion to our own logic is all the weaker if we fail to engage the challenges posed by his.

Many commentaries on Hegel's logic have been hostile. The view has often been (as I once heard a colleague of mine quip) that the phrase "Hegel's logic" is an oxymoron. The joke suggests that Hegel's so-called logic is not logical at all, but is a jumble of random moves from one step to the next. Even many commentators who have admired Hegel's work have thrown up their hands when it comes to his logic. Some say that Hegel cheated from time to time to get the transitions that he wanted. Some have given in to the charge that much of Hegel's logic is arbitrary. Others have dismissed Hegel's logic as incurably metaphysical, since it requires importing ontological or empirical material (material that is extra-logical, from outside logic, or not provided by logic itself) to move from some steps to the next. Some of these criticisms are rooted in part in the model of logic that Hegel rejected—an issue I will return to shortly. Even so, they suggest that Hegel's logic is so different from what has traditionally been considered logic that it should not count as logic at all. Unfortunately, even writers who have been sympathetic to Hegel's logic have done little to mollify these criticisms. While sympathetic commentators do a better job of making Hegel's transitions from one step to the next seem plausible, the logic still feels like a stroll in the park: there is little sense in these commentaries that we have been forced or driven to subsequent logical steps (at least once you pass the first three stages). In this book, I explore with some precision the degree to which we are driven from stage to stage in Hegel's logic. By emphasizing this drivenness, I try not only to justify Hegel's very strong claim that his logic is characterized by necessity (see, for example, *The Encyclopaedia Logic*, Remarks to §§12, 42, 87 and 88, and the third Addition to §24), but also to answer the charge that his logic is not logical. By answering this charge, I hope to rehabilitate Hegel's logic—as well as his definitions of concepts—for serious consideration.

Hegel's claim that his logic is driven by necessity should not be surprising. Necessity—the sense of being forced to logical conclusions—is the hallmark of what has passed and continues to pass for "logic" in the history of Western philosophy. Arguments are logical when conclusions *must* follow from premises, or when we are *driven* to conclusions by premises—terms that capture the idea of necessity. Without that necessity, we have, not a logic, but a stroll in the park or a Sunday drive. The diagrams that I use do a particularly good job of illuminating to what degree Hegel made good on his claim that he was offering a logic, rather than a stroll in the park—even a stroll in the park that makes sense. The diagrams reveal that Hegel's claim to have offered a genuine logic is stronger than previously thought. Of course, even in contemporary formal logic, each step in a proof is not generated by necessity. Sometimes there are different paths to the same conclusion: logical operations or transitions can be in different orders, and different combinations of logical rules or operations can generate the same conclusion. Hegel's logic should therefore not be disqualified if each and every step is not driven by necessity from the previous step. For Hegel, necessity is the idea that, when all the conditions are present, then the conclusion or matter must follow (see §147 in the *Encyclopaedia Logic*). This definition leaves open the possibility that, as in contemporary logic, some conditions—or steps—could come in different orders, and each individual step would not necessarily have to follow from the previous step. Still, the comparison with contemporary logic suggests that, for Hegel's logic to qualify as "logical" in the standard sense, there must be periodic conclusions or steps to which we are driven, or that do follow necessarily from some set of previous steps. I try to show that, although Hegel's logic is different from contemporary logic, it is more logical in this standard sense than most critics have thought.

The legitimacy of using diagrams to flesh out logic has received support in the work of some modern logicians—though they did not have Hegel's kind of logic in mind. Jon Barwise and John Etchemendy, for example, designed a computer program called *Tarski's World*, which teaches university students the basics of modern logic using diagrams depicting simple, geometrical objects—such as pyramids and cubes—in three-dimensional space (Barwise and Etchemendy 1991). Barwise and Etchemendy have argued that the success of this and other programs used for teaching logic has forced them to reconsider the nature of reasoning itself. In particular, it convinced them that diagrams and visual representations in general can be legitimate constituents of proofs (Barwise and Etchemendy 1990). They have even suggested that theories of logic will have to change to accommodate the types of reasoning people use when working with diagrams and other forms of visual representation. Indeed, Barwise and Etchemendy suggest, using visualization in reasoning is pervasive. Practitioners in science and engineering disciplines use systems for visualizing information to problem solve. Traditional logic has ignored such visual sources of information, however, focusing instead on sentences as the basic building blocks for reasoning. Observing how their students used diagrams in *Tarski's World* to solve logic problems, however, convinced Barwise and Etchemendy that the exclusive focus on sentences was mistaken. Reasoning can involve both sentences and information provided in various types of diagrams. Indeed, they suggest, diagrams can play a crucial and independent role in reasoning processes that cannot be captured by sentences. Hence, traditional, sentence-based theories of logic will need to be replaced by a richer theory of inference that includes the use of both diagrams and language (Barwise and Etchemendy 1998). Like modern logic, Hegel's logic is particularly well suited to visual representation.

Readers who are familiar with Hegel's work may be worried by my use of diagrams or pictures. Hegel was critical of the sort of thinking that has often been translated into English as "picture-thinking." For Hegel, "picture-thinking," or *Vorstellung*, is the kind of thinking we employ when we imagine something or call something before our minds in everyday life. When we ordinarily think of a "dog," for example, we conjure up some image of a dog in our minds. It might be the image of a border collie, or of a beloved mutt from our childhood. Although there is a genuine, philosophical concept lurking behind or within such picture-thoughts, these picture-thoughts muddy things because they include various sorts of empirical elements. If our image of a "dog" looks like a border collie, for example, our thought includes a particular size, color and body-shape that does not belong to the genuine concept of "dog" as such. The genuine concept of "dog" refers to all dogs, and so cannot include references to particular colors, sizes or body-shapes, given the wide range of colors and so on that dogs come in. In addition, our image or representation of "dog" may have various feelings attached to it—animus or love, for example—which are also extraneous to the concept of "dog" as such. As Hegel suggests in the *Encyclopaedia Logic*, picture-thoughts are metaphors for concepts. Philosophy's job is to replace such metaphorical images or representations with genuine, philosophical concepts (or *Begriffe*) that leave out the extraneous empirical and emotional content (§3).

Although I employ pictures or diagrams in the effort to understand and explain Hegel's logic clearly, my use of illustrations does not invoke this sort of metaphorical picture-thinking. The spare, geometrical designs I offer have very little empirical content. Unless readers have particularly bad memories of elementary school mathematics, I doubt they will conjure too many emotions either. Concepts are usually portrayed as circles or ovals ("bubbles"), for example, processes are depicted by arrows; and although there is some empirical content in the idea that a concept is a bubble, I think that empirical content is arid enough not to divert the reader from the underlying conceptual points.

It might be argued, however, that diagrams will still count as representational thought, or *Vorstellung*, insofar as they are signs. The diagrams may not include much empirical content, but they are still signs, and, for Hegel, symbols and signs are representational thought or *Vorstellung* and therefore less than properly philosophical. Signs and symbols are mid-way between the types of thoughts that are mixed with sensible material and the properly philosophical concepts that belong to pure thought. On this view, even if the diagrams are spare, because they are signs, they still belong to the type of thinking that Hegel would regard as not properly philosophical. Hence diagrams should not be used.

There are two interpretations of this argument. The first suggests that we should not use diagrams to understand or learn about Hegel's logic because diagrams belong to the kind of representational thought that Hegel rejected as not properly philosophical. This interpretation rejects the use of the diagrams as a pedagogical device because they are too representational. The implication of this interpretation of the objection is that only non-representational, written language can be used to inspire properly philosophical thought.

As John Burbidge has suggested, however, written language—words on a page—are signs too. One must always rearticulate the signs on the page (words) by thinking past them to the meaning (Burbidge 1981, 15). We do not get anything out of a book by staring at the words. We move through the words to the thought. Indeed, for Hegel, the best signs were ones that disappeared, which is why he preferred the spoken word to the written. Signs that disappear do a better job than do static or fixed signs of forcing the mind to pay attention to the thought, rather than to the sign itself. The sounds of words are signs too, but because the sounds disappear, the listener has no choice but to move beyond the signs to the meaning itself—or lose the thought (Burbidge 1981, 14-15). Burbidge suggests that our ability to read written words has become so rote or mechanical that we no longer really see them as signs. We move beyond the written word automatically, and seem to pass almost immediately to the meanings of the words and to our own activity of comprehension and thought (Burbidge 1981, 18). The automatic nature of reading allows our minds to roam free over the thoughts, which allows written words to inspire the kind of activity necessary for philosophical thought. Although this process is automatic, words on a page are still signs. While the diagrams I offer are signs, then, their use is as legitimate as is the use of the signs of standard, written language. They are, we might say, another written language. Once the "grammar" of the diagrams is learned, the reader will be able to see past them to the meanings themselves, and thought will be able to roam free—and philosophically—over the concepts and meanings signified by the diagrams. From a pedagogical point of view, then, the diagrams are no worse than written language. They may even be better: although the diagrams are static, they emphasize the dynamic nature of Hegel's logic by depicting conceptual movement (spatially) through the use of arrows.

I do not think Hegel would object to geometrical illustrations being used as pedagogical devices. His own lectures were filled with illustrations and examples drawn from ordinary life that he used to try to help his students grasp his philosophical points. Picture-thinking or *Vorstellung* confuses, hides and covers up properly conceptual thought. So long as examples—or diagrams—illuminate concepts, they would not detract or distract us from what Hegel considers the proper subject matter of philosophy.

So far I have shown only that the diagrams are a legitimate way of learning about Hegel's logic, just as words on a page are a legitimate way of coming to understand the logic. Barwise's and Etchemendy's work suggests a second interpretation of the objection I outlined above, however. Perhaps I want to make a stronger claim for the diagrams than the first interpretation suggests. Perhaps I want to say, not just that the diagrams are a legitimate pedagogical device for learning about Hegel's logic, but rather that they are essential to the logic itself—not just to understanding the logic, but to the inferential processes of the logic itself. Think of mathematics. To what degree are the signs in a mathematical solution part of the mathematical inference? Are mathematical diagrams—of parallel lines or of a geometrical object, for instance—part of mathematical reasoning itself, or are they pedagogical tools that make it easier for novices to learn to think through to the pure, mathematical thoughts? I agree with Barwise and Etchemendy that there are visual and diagrammatic reasoning processes that cannot be captured in sentences and that a comprehensive logic will have to account for these processes. I do not want to claim, however, that the inferential processes in Hegel's logic are examples of this sort of reasoning. The inferential moves in Hegel's logic can be conceived without diagrams. The diagrams are not essential to, or part of, the inferential processes outlined by Hegel. For many of us, however, the diagrams might be crucial—if not essential—to our ability to learn the inferential processes of the logic. The written signs or diagrams in mathematical proofs may not be part of the thought of the mathematical solution (and more power to the one who can think the solution without the signs!), but most of us would never grasp the solution without the help of the mathematical signs. Similarly, I want to say that the diagrams I offer are not part of the inferential processes of the logic—and more power to the one who can learn to think the logic without them! But thinking the thoughts is much easier with the help of the signs (or diagrams).

Moreover, the diagrams offer a new window into Hegel's work. They illuminate elements of Hegel's logic that, in my view, have never been clearly explicated before. They do a particularly good job of illuminating the logical syntax Hegel employs. Syntax is the connective tissue between logical steps. It has the same basic function that we think the syntax of a sentence has. In grammar, "syntax" refers to the collection of rules or patterns that determine how we can string words together into meaningful sentences. In logic, "syntax" refers to the rules or patterns that determine how we can string concepts or claims together into good arguments. Syntactic rules are supposed to be in some sense necessary. Just as breaking the rules or patterns of syntax in language renders language unintelligible, so breaking the rules or patterns of syntax in logical arguments makes those arguments invalid. If the rules of syntax are observed, the conclusion follows necessarily from the earlier steps in the argument. Proper syntax gives logical arguments their necessity.

The lack of a clearly explicated syntax is what makes Hegel's logic seem like an oxymoron or a stroll in the park. For Hegel, logic is largely about rational concepts (we will see why this is so in Chapter One). It involves tracing the step-by-step development of concepts of rationality. The syntax of Hegel's logic is the patterns or types of inferences that he uses to move from one concept to the next. In the diagrams, I present a pictorial "grammar" that cuts through Hegel's tortured and laborious writing and reveals the syntactic structures that comprise the logical movement from one conceptual stage to the next. The diagrams reveal several repeating syntactic patterns that dominate Hegel's logic. Because Hegel uses the same basic syntactic moves throughout his philosophy, understanding these patterns opens the door to the argumentative structure of all of Hegel's works. Moreover, as we will see, the popular belief that Hegel's logic employs one basic syntactic pattern—namely a pattern that involves the assertion of a "thesis," followed by the assertion of something that is opposed to that thesis in some way (the "antithesis"), followed by the assertion of something that unites or combines the thesis and antithesis (the "synthesis")—is best set aside as a poor way of describing the syntax of Hegel's logic.

An example will show how the diagrams reveal the syntax—and hence the necessity—of Hegel's logic. Hegel's idea of logical necessity is in large part a concept of exhaustion: in many places, a next step or stage of logical reasoning is necessary because there is nothing more that can be said about the elements or concepts that are currently in play. Once everything has been said about the current conceptual elements, thought has exhausted them, and so must, of necessity, move on to another concept. In these places, the next stage is necessitated by the fact that thought has exhausted all other possibilities. We will see the beauty of this account of necessity in Chapter One during the logical development of one portion of the Doctrine of Quantity, for instance. The following quick diagrams depict the four logical stages of Quantum, Number, Extensive and Intensive Magnitude, and Degree. Most of the diagrams I offer are more complicated than these quick sketches (I also offer fuller diagrams for these four stages in Chapter One). But these quick sketches show that the two quantitative concepts of "one" and "many" take turns occupying all possible positions in the diagrams for these four stages. There are two logical elements at play in these stages: (1) an outer boundary, which represents the whole, and (2) two internal "bits" (to use a modern, quantitative-sounding term) that are the same as each other and that together make up the whole. The sketches depict these elements as a divided bubble, where the bubble's outer boundary is the whole, and the inner two sections are its bits:

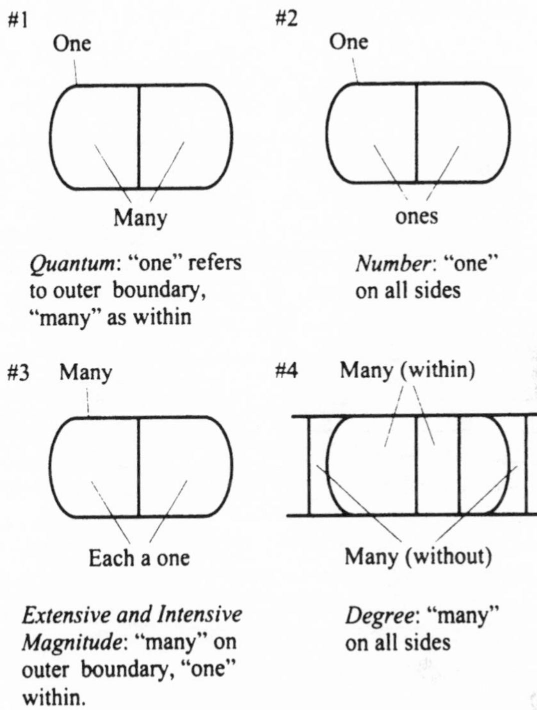

Figure I.1

By the end of the four stages, the concepts "one" and "many" have been exhausted. They have each designated both the outer boundary and inner bits at the same time (#2, #4), and the outer boundary only or the inner bits while the other term designated the other element (#1, #3). There are no more elements for "one" and "many" to designate, and, because the two internal bits are the same (a logical conclusion established before these stages), no more possible ways in which they can apply to the current elements. The concepts of "one" and "many" have been exhausted. The next stage of Immediate Measure necessarily requires bringing in another logical concept, namely, "quality." The "new" concept will not really be new, however. It will only be new to this context. Another important component of Hegel's syntactic definition of necessity is that any concept brought in must be implied by or already used in earlier steps, although it is only drawn out fully (as a kind of momentary conclusion) in the new stage (see, for example, the Remark to §88 in the *Encyclopaedia Logic*). This second component of the definition of logical necessity will show that those critics who have suggested that Hegel's logic brings in elements beyond or outside of logic's own resources are also mistaken.

The syntactic patterns of Hegel's logic, however, are only part of the story. For Hegel, logic should develop the *contents*, as well as the syntactic forms, of truthful claims and arguments. One of the truisms of contemporary propositional and predicate logics is that syntactic rules preserve truth. Hegel argued that these sorts of formalistic logics pay attention to the *form* of judgments or arguments, but do not pay enough attention to the *content* of judgments or arguments (see his Remark to §162 in the *Encyclopaedia Logic*, for example). Formalistic logics exemplify the classic rule of computer programming: garbage in, garbage out. If the content plugged into the syntax is true, then the content reached in the conclusion using the syntactic rules will be true too: truth will be preserved through the logical steps. If the content plugged into the syntax is false, then the content of the conclusion is likely to be false too: garbage in, garbage out.

For Hegel, a "logic" that is concerned merely with the form of truth but does not say anything about the contents of truthful forms is inadequate (again, see his Remark to §162 in the *Encyclopaedia Logic*). His logic aims to address the contents of truthful judgments and arguments by defining concepts and their relationships with one another in a way that shows how they can be combined into meaningful forms. This aim requires his logic to be much more concerned with semantics—the meanings and meaning-relationships of concepts—than are formalistic logics. The diagrams reveal the meanings of the logical concepts Hegel discusses, along with the syntactic relationships between stages. The diagrams provide a snapshot: they literally "picture" the semantic meanings of concepts such as "being," "number," "degree," "existence," "thing," "substance," and so on. The diagrams therefore solve one of the most difficult challenges faced by those who comment on Hegel's work. In particular, commentators must constantly struggle to find some way of explaining Hegel's texts that does not simply obscure his obscure thought and writing in another layer of obscure concepts and terms. The diagrams cut through his conceptually dense writing and make the meanings of his concepts more accessible to readers not already familiar with Hegel's philosophical terminology. Moreover, the diagrams help to show that the meanings are generated by a logical syntax, so that Hegel does not appeal to extra-logical elements to define his concepts.

The diagrams reveal, for example, how he wants to define the concept of determination—that is, what it means to be determined in some particular way, or to have a character. This concept plays a crucial role throughout Hegel's works. We will see that Hegel offers several accounts of determination in his logic, culminating in a highest definition, which is that having a character or being determined involves self-consciously determining oneself in relation to an other that one recognizes and embraces as oneself, where the "other" is the course of our whole lives (see the stage entitled "The Progression of the Speculative Method" in Chapter Four). Since this account of determination involves self-consciousness, it is relevant only to those things in the world that are self-conscious. Lower accounts of what it means to be determined will be properly applied to non-conscious, physical stuff. For Hegel, non-conscious physical stuffs are what they are in relation to their others too. In one lower stage, for example, physical stuffs are determined by others that limit them, in the way that my computer is determined in part by the fact that this desk limits it. In a later stage, stuffs may get their characters by being the same as their others, in the way that a dog is defined as a dog insofar as it is the same as all the other individual dogs in the world. The mutually defining relationship between dogs makes them dogs. The concept or quality that captures their relationship—let's call it "dogness"—comes to have a definition of its own by capturing the sameness of the dogs, but also by being separated from the dogs as individual dogs. The concept of "dogness" relates each collie, English hound and so on, but is not *merely* the collection of those individual dogs. It has a definition as a quality apart from or independent of those individual dogs, and to that degree "repulses" the individual dogs, to use Hegel's language. "Dogness" has a character as a quality, then, by both grasping the sameness of the individual dogs and also being independent of the dogs as individuals.

In a still later stage, the identities of things in the world are fixed by an "other" that is even less dependent on what the physical world is like. Individual apples, bananas and so on, for example, are all "fruit." "Fruit" fixes their identities. It defines them, even though individual apples, pears and so on are so different from one another. For Hegel, "fruitness" is a more sophisticated identity than "dogness" because "dogness" is still a quality that is there in the world. "Dogness" depends on the nature of individual dogs for its being or nature. It is defined by the given character that individual dogs *have in common*. "Fruitness," however, as an identity, is not dependent on the given character or being of items in the same way. If someone offered you a tray of cherries, pears and raisins, for example, and you were under the impression that "fruit" has being in the world, you would refuse the cherries and so on because they are not "fruit." But, of course, you do not expect to see "fruit" on the tray, because you know that "fruit" has no individual being in the world (see the Remark to §13 in the *Encyclopaedia Logic*). There is no specific, given character in the world that is "fruit." Instead, "fruit" is associated with a wide variety of given characters. As we go through Hegel's logic, we will see that it develops and defends increasingly more sophisticated (semantic) definitions of determination, as well as how those definitions apply to things and to concepts such as "quality," "property," and "existence." The diagrams illuminate this semantic project—a project in which, as former President Bill Clinton might put it, Hegel's logic defines what the meaning of "is" is.

Hegel's logic also defines the syntactic meanings of "is," by exploring what "is" can mean when it is used as a connector in logical sentences such as "A is B." Part of the meaning of "is" will be determined by the syntactic relationship between A and B that is asserted by the word "is." Hegel explores these issues in the "Doctrine of the Concept." The diagrams illuminate these syntactic meanings of "is" as well.

Although I have so far treated syntax and semantics separately, this discussion of Hegel's notion of determination demonstrates that, as with many oppositions in Hegel's philosophy, it is ultimately impossible to hold syntax and semantics apart. Just as the oppositions "form and content," and "quality and quantity," for example, are impossible to separate in an absolute way, Hegel's logic suggests, so semantics and syntax ultimately intertwine. The distinctions are useful to a certain degree, but cannot be sustained permanently. In general, for Hegel, to be determined in a particular way, or have a character, is to be in a certain sort of relationship with some "other." Logical concepts are defined or get their characters by having certain sorts of relationships with other concepts. These relationships are syntactic—they constitute the connections between the logical elements. The concept of "being," for example, is at one point defined in relation to an other, a "nothing," which is later defined as the limit of "being." Here "being" gets its definition as a concept by having a certain sort of logical relationship with an "other" concept ("nothing" or "limit") in the chain of logical steps. It is, in other words, defined syntactically. It gets its meaning, or semantics through syntax.

At the same time, on the other side, syntax becomes semantics. Various syntactic patterns that appear in Hegel's logic—such as the ones captured by the perhaps infamous terms "in itself," "for itself," and "in and for itself"—are defined by the logical development and hence come to have meanings. "In-itselfness" is the character that a concept has when it is defined as a separate concept against an "other." In the most basic logical sense, "for-itselfness" describes a concept that arises as the "negation of the negation," or as a concept that stops a process of negation between two logical elements. A negation process between logical elements occurs when one element has an identity or is determined only by passing into its other, and the other, in turn, is determined only by passing into its other. The negation process is the endless flipping back and forth between the one element and the other that is spawned when we try to fix the identities of each of the two logical elements. A concept that is "for itself" negates or stops this negation process by embracing both elements and their process of negation for its character or contents. A "for itself" concept is thus a new concept that is defined by the two elements and their whole process of negation. Because the new concept is defined by the whole process, those elements and their negation belong to its contents, and so are not an "other" for it. The whole process *is* or *constitutes* the new concept. The elements that it embraces are not an "other" for the "for itself" concept because they define it, they are what it is or belong to its character or contents. As a result, the concept that is "for itself" is not negated. It does not pass into an "other." It stops or negates the negation process. In Hegel's terms, it is the negation of the negation (see the stage of "Being-for-itself" in Chapter Two).

One of Hegel's most important examples of a "for itself" concept is the concept of consciousness. As conscious beings, we are each a "for itself." Our consciousnesses include a constant fluctuation in conscious awareness. My consciousness, for instance, is filled with a vision of this computer. But then I turn my head and it is filled with a vision of the window and then the other wing of my building. Thus, the contents of our conscious awarenesses are constantly in flux, or being negated. But this process is not an "other" for us: it just is us, it defines what we are as conscious beings. Moreover, our consciousnesses remain what they are through this flux of conscious awareness, and so they stop this negation process. Each of our consciousnesses is a whole that embraces the negation process of conscious awareness for its definition. We are each a "for itself," and the constant negation process of our conscious awareness is for-each-of-us. To put it logically, a "for itself" is a one that includes the negation process (the process is its definition or identity), and the negation process is for-it. As we will see, consciousness—as well as self-consciousness—are two forms of "being" or "is" that Hegel's logic defines as types of "for itself" concepts.

"In-itselfness" and "for-itselfness" are *syntactic concepts*—a term that intertwines syntax and semantics. They are syntactic patterns that come to have meanings as concepts because they are elements of Hegel's syntax that are repeated over and over. The diagrams reveal the semantics of these and other syntactic concepts by depicting the steps in which they occur. Because Hegel uses these same syntactic concepts throughout all of his works, these diagrams help to uncover the arguments of Hegel's other books.

The intertwined nature of syntax and semantics can be seen in the important syntactic concept I have already discussed briefly above, namely, the concept of necessity. In semantic terms, the concept of necessity refers to the essence of something. In this sense, necessity is closely tied to Hegel's conception of determination or identity. The essence of something is the "whatever-it-is" without which the something would not be what it is. Drawing on the "fruit" example discussed above, the necessary concept or essence of an apple would be the definition or determination without which an apple would not be what it is. An apple is a "fruit," that is the essential and necessary *kind* of thing that it is. The essential determination of something is its highest, most sophisticated definition.

In syntactic terms, the concept of necessity captures the idea that logical steps in a process of syntactic development must follow from earlier ones—that there is a kind of algorithmic imperative that drives us from stage to stage and does not allow us to veer off in other directions. Again, this is the sense in which, in contemporary logic, we say that a conclusion follows "necessarily" from the premises. We are required or forced to draw that conclusion.

For Hegel, these syntactic and semantic accounts of necessity intertwine. Semantic necessity is fixed through a syntactic process. The essential (i.e. necessary) identity or definition of something is determined through a syntactic process of development. For living things, the syntactic process of development is the process of life itself (see the stages of Life in Chapter Four). The essences of concepts are determined through a syntactic process as well. The highest definition (i.e. semantic necessity) of a concept is reached through a process that involves developing syntactic relationships between concepts. The semantically necessary definition or determination comes at the end of a chain of logical moves. This necessary definition is "highest" because it is the last definition in a logical series that has already tried out several definitions along the way. Indeed, as we'll see, the "highest" definition absorbs the earlier ones. The term "highest" is thus a syntactic term indicating that we have taken a concept as far in the logical (syntactic) process as it can go, and have defined it as fully as we can. We thus home in on the semantically necessary definition of a concept through a syntactically necessary process of logical development. At the end of the syntactic process is a semantic definition of a concept which is necessary or essential in both the syntactic and semantic senses.

It is the intertwined nature of syntax and semantics that distinguishes Hegel's logic from more formalistic, contemporary logics. Contemporary logics are almost exclusively concerned with syntax. Unlike Hegel, who, as mentioned, thought logic should develop both truthful forms (syntax) and truthful meanings (semantics), contemporary logics suppress the semantic element by simply stipulating the meanings of central logical terms. The meanings of logical operators such as "and," "or," and "if . . . then," are stipulated by a list of syntactic rules of derivation. In propositional logic—which is based on propositions or sentences—letters such as "P" and "Q" stand for sentences that are simply assumed to be meaningful. Moreover, every occurrence of "P" or "Q" is assumed to have the same meaning as every other occurrence of the same letter in the same argument or context. Contemporary prepositional logic is more semantically complicated, since it permits the parsing of sentences into smaller units. Letters such as "F" and "G" are used to stand for functions. These functions are applied to variables—represented by letters such as "x" and "y." Thus the logical sentence "if Fx then Gx" (this should be read "if F at x, then G at x" or "if x is F, then x is G" and is represented symbolically as: $Fx \rightarrow Gx$) might mean something like "if x is a frog, then x is green." Here again, however, the combinations of the function and the variable are simply assumed to be meaningful, just as the letter "P" and other letters were assumed to be meaningful sentences in propositional logic. Not every sentence is meaningful, however. Even the simple sentence "x is green" is only meaningful if we presuppose that we know what "is" means.

There is no attempt in these logics, however, to spell out what semantic elements a sentence or function/variable combination must have to be meaningful. Thus, the assumptions of meaningfulness suppress a serious engagement with semantic issues. Just as Gregorian chants simplify rhythm so that they can play with musical tonality, while avant-garde jazz suppresses tonality so that it can play with rhythm and timbre, contemporary logics stipulate and suppress semantics so that they can play with syntax. The semantic element cannot go away completely, however—logical connectives and variables still have to *mean something*. But the question of how they mean—or what they would have to be like to be meaningful at all—is set aside, so that attention can be lavished on syntactic issues. Because meanings are stipulated, however, these logics are open to the charge that they are not properly scientific in Hegel's old-fashioned sense of the term. A proper *science* of logic should not be making assumptions about central logical elements. Again, in prepositional logic, for instance, the form "Fx" stands for "x is F." But what is the force of the "is" here? As we will see more fully in Hegel's logic, there are many different ways for something to "be" something—there are many different meanings of "is." Former President Clinton was surely right that the rationality or truth of a claim or argument does in fact depend in part on what the meaning of "is" is. Hegel's emphasis on defining the logical meaning of "is" and other terms requires him to do some metaphysics—as he admits (see for example the *Encyclopaedia Logic*, Remark to §9). A proper science of logic, Hegel would argue, should develop and explore the implications (for logic and truth) of all these meanings.

Indeed, Hegel distinguished his own logic from both the traditional Aristotelian logic and the modern logic of his day, which he argued were overly formal precisely because they ignore the meanings that concepts have, insofar as concepts are defined in relation to each other (*Encyclopaedia Logic* remarks to §162 and §82), and not just in relation to things in the world. To take a simple example from early in Hegel's logic, the concept of "becoming" is defined in relation to the concepts of both "being" and "nothing." As a general concept, "becoming" describes the process of flipping back and forth between "being" and "nothing:" "to become" is to go from "is" to "nought," or from "nought" to "is." When an apple, for instance, becomes red, it changes from not-red to red. When it becomes brown as it rots, it goes from red to not-red, or not-brown to brown. When it grows on a tree and becomes an apple in the first place, it goes from being nothing to being. The concept of "becoming" is defined in relation to the concepts of "being" and "nothing" by embracing them both, and it has this meaning without ever having to be applied to the physical world of things. "Becoming" has a definition or content, and so is concrete, as Hegel says (*Encyclopaedia Logic* remark to §82), not because it is filled up with things from the world, but because it is defined by other concepts, or because its definition includes or refers to other concepts.

There is thus a disagreement between Hegel and devotees of more formalistic logics over the role that semantics should play in logic. This disagreement gives rise in part to the criticism against Hegel that his logic is not really logical. Those who are looking for an exclusively syntactic logic will not be satisfied by Hegel's logic. There is a syntax to Hegel's logic, as we will see, but there is also no denying that Hegel's logic is driven by semantic issues as well. Sometimes the movement from one stage to the next is driven by the meanings of the logical elements that are in play, rather than by purely syntactic considerations. Those who think logic should be driven exclusively by syntax—those who are devoted to a logic in which the semantic element is suppressed—will find Hegel's logic unsatisfactory, just as Hegel found the formalistic logics unsatisfactory. It remains an open question, in my view, about which model is best—a question we will surely never solve until we engage more fully with Hegel's logic. As I try to show in this book, Hegel is a formidable opponent.

The book I outline primarily is Hegel's *Encyclopaedia Logic*, which is the introduction to the encyclopedia of his whole philosophy, the *Encyclopaedia of the Philosophical Sciences* (1817). The *Encyclopaedia Logic* was written for classroom use, and contains numbered sections that were used as a prelude to class discussion. Hegel sometimes supplemented these sections with extra paragraphs. These extra paragraphs are generally referred to as "Remarks," and are identified by the number of the section to which they belong, followed by the letter "R." So, for example, the Remark to §104 is referred to as "§104R." Many sections have no Remarks. Most editions of the *Encyclopaedia Logic* also contain extra paragraphs drawn from several of Hegel's students' transcriptions of his lectures. These paragraphs are generally referred to as "Additions," and are identified by the number of the section to which they belong, followed by the letter "A." Many sections have no Additions, but some have more than one Addition, in which case the Additions are numbered. So the second Addition to §24 is referred to as "§24A2," for example. Although the editors who added the Additions made every attempt to remain faithful to Hegel's lectures, because these paragraphs were not written by Hegel, they are not regarded as having the same authority as the other paragraphs, which contain Hegel's own published writing. To the degree that the Additions can be trusted, however, they contain many examples that often help to clarify Hegel's numbered sections.

Because the *Encyclopaedia Logic* is a textbook, Hegel did not regard it as a stand-alone work, but only as a classroom tool to be supplemented by lectures (see, for example, the first paragraph of Hegel's foreword to the third [1830] edition of the *Encyclopaedia Logic*). Still, there are a few reasons to prefer it to his much longer, book-form discussion of logic contained in the *Wissenschaft der Logik*, or *Science of Logic*, which was published in three volumes from 1812–1816. Hegel was working on a revised version of the *Wissenschaft* when he died in 1831, but he only managed to finish revisions to the first volume (which were published in 1832). The *Encyclopaedia Logic*, which he revised twice—once in 1827 and again 1830—therefore represents the last time Hegel visited the entire topic of logic. Because the *Encyclopaedia Logic* contains the Additions, it is also sometimes easier to understand than the longer work. Moreover, the focus on the *Encyclopaedia Logic* instead of the *Wissenschaft* is justified by a renewed interest in the former which has been made possible in the English-speaking world by the publication in 1991 of a textually faithful translation by T. F. Geraets, W. A. Suchting and H. S. Harris. I lean on their translation—widely available through Hackett Press—in many places throughout this analysis.

It might be argued that I should focus on the *Wissenschaft* or *Science of Logic* because it is Hegel's most detailed and hence most sophisticated treatment of logic. The *Encyclopaedia* is more useful for my purposes, however. It offers a stripped-down version of the logical development with little fanfare. Since the *Encyclopaedia* was a textbook, Hegel focused the work on only the essential logical moves. Because my goal in this book is to trace the syntax of Hegel's logic as precisely as possible, I want to focus on the essential steps, without the fanfare. As a result, although there are some places where I consider the *Wissenschaft* or *Science of Logic*, I give preference to the *Encyclopaedia*, especially since it was—for the most part—Hegel's last word on logic.

In Chapter One, I introduce Hegel's overall project and the place of logic within that project for the benefit of those who are not already familiar with Hegel's work. This first chapter relies heavily on Hegel's philosophical relationship with one of his greatest influences, Immanuel Kant. Kant's work largely provides the lens through which Hegel's project can be seen more clearly and makes more sense. However, no previous knowledge of Kant or other historical philosophers is required to understand these introductory descriptions, since I have tried to be careful to explain historical views, as well as Hegel's, in a way that would make sense to someone coming to these works for the first time.

Chapters Two, Three and Four are organized around Hegel's *Encyclopaedia Logic* itself. The Logic actually begins with two "Prefaces" and a "Foreword" (corresponding to each of three editions), an "Introduction," and a long "Preliminary Conception" in which Hegel introduces his views in relation to the history of philosophy. The logical argument itself begins with the section called the "Doctrine of Being," which develops logical concepts and relationships relevant to grasping things that have being in the world. Chapter Two covers this subdivision of the Logic. Chapter Three covers the next subdivision, the "Doctrine of Essence," which develops logical concepts and relationships that are essences or are essential. The final subdivision, the "Doctrine of the Concept," is covered in Chapter Four. It focuses primarily on the logically connective relationships that are used to string concepts together with other concepts and into meaningful forms of judgment and argument. The "Doctrine of the Concept" completes Hegel's *Encyclopaedia Logic*—though it will lead on to new topics of discussion for other books in the whole *Encyclopaedia*—and Chapter Four completes the journey of picturing Hegel's logic.

Chapter One

Entering the Gallery: Hegel's Overall Project, and the Project of the *Logic*

Even though Hegel came to think of logic as the best way to introduce his philosophical system, readers will have difficulty understanding his philosophy without some basic background knowledge of the historical context of Hegel's work, his overall project, and how he thought logic fit into that project. Historically, Hegel wanted to rescue scientific knowledge from the skepticism that he saw in his philosophical predecessors. If those philosophers could not show us how to use our reason to gain knowledge about the world, that was only because they had the wrong account of the nature of reason. Hegel's project is largely an attempt to redefine the nature of our reason or rationality so that we can show once and for all that it is capable of providing us with knowledge. Because his logic spells out the account of reason that he wants to propose, it is the centerpiece of his system. In this chapter, I explain this background for those who have no familiarity with Hegel or with any of the philosophers who influenced his views. This discussion should make it easier to understand what Hegel is doing in the *Encyclopaedia Logic,* when we dive into the details of picturing his logic in Chapter Two and beyond.

I. The Skepticism of Hume and Kant

Hegel's logic is part of a long conversation in the history of Western philosophy about the nature of rationality, but it also belongs to a particular historical moment in that conversation. Understanding Hegel's historical moment requires going back a couple of steps in that history. I will start with the naïve view, which dominated the Scientific Revolution in Europe. We will then look briefly at the work of the 18th century, British skeptic David Hume (1711–1776). From Hume we will move to look at the work of the 18th century, German philosopher Immanuel Kant (1724–1804), who tried to answer or correct Hume's skepticism. Hegel's philosophy is in part a response to Kant's work. Indeed, Hegel once said that he grew up on Kant's philosophy (Pinkard 2000, 339). For Hegel, Kant's correction to Hume was still too skeptical, and so he sought to correct the skepticism he found in Kant in his own work.

I will be telling the story about Hume, Kant and Hegel largely through Kant's and Hegel's eyes. We will look at Hume's philosophy from Kant's perspective, so that I will be interpreting what Hume said through Kant's eyes. I will then tell the story of Kant's philosophy largely from Hegel's perspective, so that I will be interpreting what Kant said through Hegel's eyes. What did Kant take his project to be in relation to Hume's work? And what did Hegel take his project to be in relation to Kant's work? I want to focus on how Kant thought he was responding to Hume, rather than on interpretive debates about what Hume actually said, and I want to look at what Hegel took himself to be doing in response to Kant, rather than at interpretive debates about whether Hegel understood Kant's work correctly.

According to the naïve view of science that had its roots in the ancient Greek philosopher Aristotle and the Scientific Revolution, we can have fairly direct knowledge of the physical world. To gain knowledge, we simply look around us and pull the world into our heads, so to speak. Our knowledge about the world is a copy, or mirror, of what the world is like. Of course, naïve science recognized that we have to pursue or work for our knowledge—we have to perform experiments to learn things, for instance, we have to look hard at things, sometimes using special instruments. But the basic idea about how we gain knowledge was fairly straightforward. We perform experiments, observe the world, and then form ideas in our heads that reflect, copy, or mirror what we "discovered" about the world in our experiments and observations.

Hume challenged naïve science's description of how we gain knowledge. As Kant saw it, Hume's work showed that we cannot justify naïve science's assumption that our ideas in our heads correspond to, or copy, the world. Think of our idea of cause, for instance. According to our usual concept of cause, when one event is the cause of another, those two events have a special connection with one another. In particular, they are connected in such a way that when the first event happens (the cause) the other event must also happen (the effect). Notice the emphasis on the word "must" here: the concept of cause suggests that there is a necessary connection between these two events, such that, when the cause is present, the effect must necessarily follow. Thus, we have an idea in our heads—the idea of "cause"—according to which there is a necessary connection between the cause and the effect. Since naïve science assumes that our ideas are copies of what the world is like, it would have assumed that this idea of cause, too, copies what causes are like out there in the world.

As Kant saw it, however, Hume's work correctly showed that this concept of cause cannot possibly be a copy of what the real world is like. No matter how many experiments we do, or observations we make, nothing in our experience of the real world justifies this idea that a cause and an effect are necessarily connected to one another. We may see two events happen next to each other many times over: one kind of event happens, and then the other kind of event happens. We may see this association over and over. But no matter how much sensory evidence we have for this association, none of it justifies our idea that there is a necessary causal relation between the two events. Neither our sensory evidence nor our reasoning about this sensory evidence can prove that there is a necessary connection between cause and effect. We never observe any special causal connection between the two events, nor can we infer that one exists using our reasoning.[1] Hume had showed that, since we do not observe the causal necessity in our experience of the world, our idea of cause must be generated by us, and not by the world that we are observing. There is nothing in our experience of the world itself which our idea about the necessary connection between cause and effect copies. Our idea of the necessary connection goes beyond what we are entitled to conclude from our observations of the real world.

Kant thought that Hume's argument drives us to a skeptical conclusion about the status of scientific knowledge: it suggests that our claims to have causal knowledge of the world cannot be justified by scientific observations and experimentation. Our concept of cause is a basic scientific concept. We make claims all the time about things in the world being causes or effects of other things in the world. If Hume is right, for Kant, none of these claims count as knowledge. If there is nothing in the world that copies our concept of cause, then our claims to have found "causes" in the world are unjustified, and therefore cannot be said to count as knowledge. It follows that we do not really know anything we claim to know about causes in science—our claims that plate movements in the earth cause earthquakes, that earthquakes cause tsunamis and so on. If "cause" is something that we simply make up—if it is not out there in the real world, but is only in our heads—then no amount of observation or experimentation will give us knowledge of causal processes in the real world.

Kant was unsatisfied with such a skeptical conclusion. He wanted to establish a firm, rational foundation for our scientific knowledge. Kant also could not accept the solution to skepticism that Hume had proposed. Hume had suggested that the idea of causal necessity was generated by our own imaginations as a response to our experiences of repeatedly associated events. Our concept of cause is a kind of imaginary thought that grows out of custom or habit. Once we've seen one event associated with another event often enough, we assume or suppose that the events must necessarily be connected together as cause and effect. For Kant, however, the suggestion that our cherished notion of causal necessity might be nothing but habit or custom was unacceptable. He wanted to provide some kind of proof that our concept of causal necessity had more scientific validity than Hume's claim that it was grounded in custom or habit seemed to suggest (see *Critique of Pure Reason*, B5, B19-20). Science and knowledge are supposed to be grounded in reason, not in imagination, no matter how well "confirmed" that imagination might be by the repetition of experience. Hume had broken the connection between reason and science or knowledge, and had therefore undermined the idea that we have any scientific knowledge at all. Kant wanted to reestablish that we have scientific knowledge of the world by redrawing the connection between reason and knowledge.

Kant's own solution to Hume's skepticism involved pursuing what Kant described as a Copernican revolution in philosophy (*Critique of Pure Reason*, Bxvi). Nicolas Copernicus (1473–1543) was the Polish astronomer who first suggested that the earth revolves around the sun, rather than the other way around. Copernicus's proposal was revolutionary because the common belief in Europe at the time was that the sun revolved around the earth. Kant proposed a solution to Hume's problem similar to the Copernican revolution in astronomy. Hume's problem grew out of assumptions made by naïve science. The naïve view of science assumed that the world is the source our ideas or knowledge. For naïve science, we gain knowledge of the world by pulling it in. We observe things about the world (such as the law of gravity, for example) and then we come to have ideas in our minds that correspond to or copy that world (our idea of "the law of gravity," for example). We simply use our reason or rationality to copy things we discover about the world. Our reason or rationality provides us with knowledge because of what the world is like. For Kant, Hume had shown that this theory of how we gain knowledge does not work. Our idea of "cause" does not correspond to or copy what the world is like because (as Hume had shown, for Kant) it is made up by us. We do not have any knowledge of causes, based on what the world is like, because we have no reason to think that our world is like what our idea says it is. Kant proposed a philosophical theory that flipped the assumption made by naïve science. Instead of supposing that we have knowledge because of what the world is like, Kant suggested that we have knowledge because of what *we* are like. Instead of saying that, for the purposes of our knowledge, we revolve around the world, Kant proposes that, when it comes to our knowledge, the world revolves around us. Our reason or rationality provides us with knowledge not because of what the world is like, but because of what we are like.

Kant argued that we humans, because we are rational creatures, share a cognitive structure with one another that makes our experiences regular and gives us knowledge. Our knowledge is grounded by this intersubjectively shared structure in us, rather than by the world. It's because each of us, as rational human beings, shares this cognitive structure that our experiences are fairly regular from one time to the next and that we agree with one another in our judgments about the world. The intersubjectivity of our experiences—the agreement between us—makes our observations "objective" enough to count as knowledge. Thus, Kant reestablished the connection between reason and objective knowledge that Hume had broken, but instead of grounding that connection in what the world is like, he grounds it in what we are like—in our cognitive, or rational, mental structure.

For the naïve view of science, there are two senses of "objectivity." Kant uses only one of these senses to ground his claim that a shared cognitive structure of rationality in us can provide us with knowledge. If a drunk person reports seeing a pink elephant, there are two reasons that could be offered for why the "observation" is merely subjective, rather than objective. First, the observation is subjective, rather than objective, because there is no elephant out there. In other words, the observation is merely subjective because there is no real object out there in the world that the person is observing. It would be "objective" if there were a real object out there in the world.

A second meaning of the word "objective" grows out of the question "how do we know there is no pink elephant out there?" We know there is no pink elephant out there because *no one else sees* the elephant. This answer reveals a second reason why the drunken person's observation is subjective: the observation is subjective because no one else shares it. It would be objective if it were shared by others. Thus, there are two elements built into the traditional Western conception of objectivity: something is objective if it is really out there, and something is objective if it is shared by others. These two senses of objectivity are connected to one another, of course: we share our experiences of real objects because those real objects are out there in the world.

Kant uses the second sense of objectivity to claim that our shared cognitive structure can give us knowledge. For Kant, Hume's work forces us to give up the first sense of objectivity altogether. Our theories of scientific causes cannot be objective in the sense that they are out there in the world because—as Hume showed us—the necessary connection between cause and effect cannot be found out there in the world. But we can still use the second sense of "objectivity" to ground our claim to have knowledge. Scientific theories can still be objective because they are *intersubjective*, they are shared by other rational beings. We have knowledge, then, because our experiences are regular and shared with other rational human beings. Keep in mind, however, that, for Kant, this intersubjectivity is explained by what we are like—namely, again, that we share a rational, cognitive structure that constitutes our experience of the world—and not—as naïve science had claimed—by what the world is like.

Kant's solution to Hume's problem has a problem of its own that Hegel would try to correct. Kant was forced to admit that his view led to the conclusion that our knowledge is still limited in a certain way. Because our shared rationality structures the way we see the world, for Kant, we still cannot know what the world is like in itself, outside of—or beyond—our experience of it. The way we see the world, and what the world is like in itself, beyond us, may well be two very different matters. We cannot get outside of our mental structures to see what the world would be like on its own. Our knowledge is only of what the world is like for a rational human being, and does not extend to what the world is like in itself. Thus, Kant had to admit that, according to his theory, there may be plenty that we know, but there is also a leftover world-in-itself, or "Thing-in-itself" (*Ding an sich*), about which we can know nothing (see, e.g. *Critique of Pure Reason*, Bxxv-xxvi).

Thus, while Kant succeeds in reestablishing the connection between reason and knowledge that he thought Hume had broken, knowledge is still limited in Kant's theory. Our scientific claims are no longer grounded in the imagination of causes and effects, as they were for Hume (according to Kant), but in our rationality. However, we have knowledge only about our (rational, human) experience of the world, and not about what the world is like in itself or on its own, as it might be seen from outside of our rational, cognitive structures. For Hegel, Kant's theory improperly restricts our knowledge. He rejected the implication of Kant's theory that we can know nothing about the Thing-in-itself, or what the world is like outside of our cognitive structure (see, e.g. §44 in the *Encyclopaedia Logic*),[2] and he intended his project to respond to this view.

How does Hegel respond to Kant's problem? How does Hegel try to show that we have knowledge not only of our human world of experience, but also of the world itself? This question is especially pressing because Hegel accepted Kant's Copernican revolution to a certain degree. Hegel agrees with Kant that we have knowledge of the world because of what we are like, namely, because of our reason or rationality. So how, for Hegel, can we get out of our heads, so to speak, to the world as it is in itself? The short answer to this question is that, for Hegel, our reason or rationality gives us knowledge of the world in itself because the same rationality or reason that is in us is *in the world itself*. Kant is wrong to think that reason or rationality is only in us human beings, in our consciousnesses (§§43-44). We can use our reason or rationality to have knowledge of the Thing-in-itself because the world just is, in itself, reason. The very same rationality that is in us is in the world, as its own defining principle. Rationality shapes and determines the nature of the world itself. "Being," or the being of the world, to use some technical jargon for a moment, just is "Thought." Rationality is in, or overlaps, reality itself. Rationality determines reality, makes reality understandable, and that is why we can understand reality with our rationality. The world is, in itself, rational.

Hegel expresses the view that rationality overlaps the world with the German verb *übergreifen*, which is literally translated into English as "overgrasp." I follow Geraets, Suchting and Harris, who use the word "overgrasp" in their translation of the *Encyclopaedia Logic* (1991). The English word "overlap," which is the best ordinary English word to use in this context, does not capture the connection that Hegel wants to draw between rationality's being in the world and the world's understandability. Rationality overlaps the world, but it does so in a way that makes the world graspable, that understands and stands under, so to speak, the world. Rationality, overgrasps reality in this sense: it defines, determines, informs, stands under, understands, and is in the world itself. Hence, for Hegel, our rational ideas about the world correspond to the world as it is in itself because our rational consciousnesses reflect the very same rationality that deter-mines what the world in itself is like.

II. Reason Overgrasps Reality

Hegel's claim that reason overgrasps reality has roots in the views of the ancient Greeks. The Greeks suggested that our ability to grasp the world is explained by *nous*—by an immaterial, overlapping, principle of rationality. Hegel acknowledged his debt to the ancient Greek concept of *nous* when he praised Anaxagoras (c. 500/499–428/7BC) for introducing the concept of *nous* and for recognizing for the first time in the history of philosophy that thought or mind is the fundamental principle of the universe (*Lectures on the History of Philosophy* 1983, vol. 1, 102, 171, 183). Since thought generally is defined by rationality, the *nous*, thought or rationality that is in the world is the same sort of thought or rationality that is in us. For Anaxagoras, we can understand the world because the very same rationality or *nous* that is in us is in the world. Again, the world is, in itself, rational.

The Pythagoreans translated this view into a certain model of how to understand the world. For them, mathematics is the purest and most exemplary form of rationality, both in us and in the world itself. They claimed that the cosmos was in some sense "made of" numbers, and was in that sense (at least mathematically) inherently rational. For the Pythagoreans, harmony in the world was an expression of this inherent, mathematical rationality. Thus, hearing harmonious sounds or music involved "really" hearing numbers, and the harmony in the rotational patterns of the various planetary spheres were also an expression of the mathematical rationality of the world. Since rationality is built into the world in this way, understanding the world involves simply "recognizing," or, in the case of the Pythagoreans, "listening" to the (numerical) harmony of the world.[3]

The idea that reason or rationality defines the world is often taken to be the central claim of the philosophical view called idealism. According to idealism, thought or rationality is the primary element that determines the nature of the world. Some idealists, such as the 18th century, British philosopher, Bishop George Berkeley (1685–1753), deny that there is any physical matter at all. For Berkeley, for instance, all there is is ideas. There is no physical world. The world of our experience is nothing but ideas. However, a philosopher does not have to go as far as Berkeley did—does not have to deny that there is a physical or material world—to be considered an idealist. So long as rationality or reason is the primary causal and defining force over the physical world, the view has traditionally been characterized as idealistic. By contrast, if matter is the primary causal and defining force over ideas, thought or rationality, the view has traditionally been characterized as materialistic. For an idealist, thoughts cause things to happen in the world. For a materialist, matter or the physical world is independent of thought or ideas and causally primary. Things that happen in the world cause thoughts *in us*. I emphasize the words "in us" because it typically follows from the materialist's belief in the primacy of matter (being) over thought—or from the materialist's view that things in the world are the primary cause of thought—that thought, reason or rationality is only in us rational, human beings. Of course, we can "put" our thought or reason into the physical world, when we design or make things such as chairs, works of art, computers, tools and so on. Still, according to this view, there is no thought or reason in the natural, "dumb" physical world of rocks and dirt itself.

Hegel's view that reason or rationality is in the world itself and "overgrasps" that world has led him to be classified as an idealist. Although Hegel does not deny the existence of a physical or material world, as Berkeley did, he seems to privilege ideas or rational universals over the empirical or physical world of matter. Rationality is in the world itself in the sense that it characterizes and helps to determine what happens in the world. Capital-"R" Rationality or Reason is a giant, completed conceptual system that "overgrasps" the physical world in the sense that it defines the nature of that physical world and has causal effects on what happens in the world. Hegel's famous—or perhaps infamous—concept of the "Absolute" is the thought of the whole, conceptual system of Reason or Rationality taken together with its expression in the physical world. The physical world just is the expression of Rationality or Reason. And the "Absolute" is the thought of the whole conceptual system of Reason or Rationality taken together with its "being" or expression in the physical, material world. Notice that the Absolute is itself a thought—a big-Idea, or an "Idea" with a capital-"I." It is the thought of Reason, or the whole conceptual system, "overgrasping"—defining and shaping—the physical world. It is the thought of the whole process of Reason as expressed into reality. Because Hegel suggests that the Absolute or big Idea is the primary cause of what happens in the real world, he is classified as an idealist.

Of course, the Absolute Idea is not a thought that any of us mere mortals can have. None of us can think of the whole, completed process of Reason expressed into the world. A lot of the process happened before we were born and (we hope) a lot more of it will happen after each of us dies. Since each of us mere mortals has access only to a small slice of the whole process of Reason overgrasping the world, none of us can have the thought of the whole process as a completed process. For Hegel, the Absolute is God. Only an eternal God—outside of time and therefore outside of the world's (temporal) process of development—could have the thought of the world's process of development as a completed process. Nevertheless, for Hegel, God's reason is our reason too. God's rationality is our rationality too. The rationality that is in us is the same rationality that God has, and that God expresses into the world. Indeed, for Hegel, our human history is part of the process through which God's capital-"R" Reason is expressed into reality. Our reason is the same Reason that is in the world. The world's rationality is our rationality, and that is why we can have knowledge of what the world is like in itself.

As we go through the development of Hegel's logic, I will examine from time to time the degree to which I think Hegel's logic supports the traditional claim that Hegel is an idealist. I will suggest that Hegel's logic has some characteristics usually associated with materialism rather than idealism. I will not be the first person, certainly, to read Hegel somewhat materialistically. The 19th century Christian, Danish philosopher, Søren Kierkegaard (1813–1855), for instance, accused Hegel of being a pantheist (see, for example, Kierkegaard 1992, VI, 122-3). According to pantheism, the world just is God, or, put the other way around, God just is the world. Kierkegaard's charge that Hegel is a pantheist suggests a materialistic reading of Hegel's concept of the Absolute. If the Absolute is God, and if the Absolute expresses itself in the world, as Hegel suggests, then Hegel's God is in the world. Indeed, Hegel's God is in the world so completely, for Kierkegaard, that there is no longer room for a god conceived of as a spiritual entity beyond or independent of the physical world. Hegel's conception of the Absolute leads to a pantheistic conception of God (see, for example, Kierkegaard 1992, VI, 226-7, 95, 87). Kierkegaard's charge interprets Hegel's view materialistically because it accuses Hegel of turning God into a physical or material object, namely, into this world. For Kierkegaard, Hegel's God is no longer a spirit or Idea, but matter. If Kierkegaard's charge that Hegel is a pantheist is right—if Hegel's philosophy truly implies that the Absolute or God just is the physical world of matter—then Hegel cannot be much of an idealist. My own view is that, although Kierkegaard's charge is unfair (see Chapter Four, Section VI), Hegel is more of a materialist than is usually believed.

Hegel's materialistic elements are highlighted in part in the claim that the world is rational or that Reason is in the world, which can be contrasted with the views of Plato (c. 428–348 BC). The ancient Greek philosopher, Plato, privileged rational universals or concepts (ideas)—the Forms—over the material or physical world. Indeed, he thought of the physical world as so imperfect and messy that he exiled the rational concepts or Forms to another realm. To say that reason is in the world would be to say that things in the world have the relevant rational concepts in them. A chair would have the rational concept of "chair" in it, for instance, or a human being would have the rational concept of "human" in him or her. In the messy physical world, however, there are chairs that do not work and men and women die. If existing chairs really copied the rational concept of chair, then all chairs would work; and if people really copied the universal concept of "human," then they would never be able to be not-human. A broken chair is not a "chair" anymore: it is a "not-chair." If a chair really had the rational concept of chair in it, then it would remain a chair. Similarly, if humans really had the rational concept of human in them, then they would never die and become not-human. The world is messy because chairs and humans fall apart and die. Since chairs fall apart and humans die, the rational concepts of chair and human are not in the chair or human, and, hence, are not in the world at all. The Forms or rational concepts must be in another world or in a separate realm—the realm of the Forms. While things in the world do not have rational concepts in them, they are still connected to the rational concepts. They can have their identities, or be what they are, only because they have a relationship with those concepts. A chair can be a chair, for instance, because it is an (admittedly imperfect) copy of the rational concept of chair. Things in the world get their identities by participating in the Forms, by being imperfect copies of the Forms or rational concepts. Thus the rational concepts are primary in relation to material things in the world. They define or characterize things in the world, and things in the world could not be what they are without the rational concepts of Forms (see, e.g. Plato, *Parmenides*, 131-135a). (It is unclear whether Plato would agree that there are forms of things such as chairs and humans (*Parmenides* 130c), but he would agree that chairs and humans participate in forms such as beauty and justice (*Parmenides* 130e-131).

The primacy of the Forms also shaped Plato's epistemological views, or his views about the nature of human knowledge. To have knowledge is to grasp the rational concepts. To know what a human is, for instance, is to know the rational concept of "human." To know what a human is is to know the whatever-it-is that makes a human "human." The rational concept or Form of "human" is universal: it captures the whatever-it-is that all individual humans have that makes them "human" as such. Knowledge of the human requires knowing the universal, rational concept or Form of human. How do we come to know that universal, rational concept? You might think that the best way to know the universal, rational concept of "human" would be to look at a lot of individual human beings and draw some conclusions about what they have in common. But, for Plato, things in the world are such poor copies of the concepts that we cannot use them to grasp the universal, rational concepts. For Plato, there's no point in studying individual good things, for instance, to learn about the nature of "goodness" as a rational concept. We can gain knowledge of "goodness" only by reason, or only by using our rationality to access the separate world of the universal, rational concepts (ideas) or Forms. This is the conclusion pointed at by Plato's famous parable of the cave (*Republic*, Book 7, 514-516b).

There are two assumptions that explain why Plato exiled his rational universals to another realm and privileged the ideal. The world is a messy place. Things break, they come in and out of existence, and are imperfect. But a certain model of rationality, not just a claim about the world, also accompanies the conclusion that the Forms or rational universals cannot be in the world. For Plato, rational universals are supposed to capture the essence of things. Again, the rational universal of "human," for instance, would be the characteristic—whatever-it-is—that all humans share, or the whatever-it-is that makes humans human. The essence of humans doesn't change just because humans die, or because humans are imperfect. The essence of humans is always just what it is. It is unchanging. Thus, Plato's view that the Forms cannot be in this world grows out of not only the assumption that the world is messy, but also out of the assumption that rational universals are constant, unchanging, static or fixed.

Against this model, Hegel recovers the physical world for reason. Plato was right, of course, that the physical world is a messy place. Unlike Plato, however, Hegel links the messy physical world back to reason by redefining reason. He offers a new conception of rationality that sees rationality itself as not constant, static or unchanging, but as containing contradictions and change, and so as capable of overlapping or overgrasping (*übergreifen*) the messiness, the comings and goings, the imperfections of the physical world. This is the sort of rationality envisioned by Hegel's famous dialectics: a messy rationality for a messy world. Reason and the physical world overlap each other, for Hegel, because they are both messy. They are both *dialectical*. The dialectics of opposites takes place in the physical world when humans die and become the opposite "not-human," and chairs break and become the opposite "not-chair." Dialectics happens both at the level of reality—in the messy, physical world—and at the level of thought—in rationality itself, now conceived of as itself dialectical. Dialectical reason overlaps a dialectical world. In Hegel's dialectics, *everything* contains contradiction, opposition or negation.

In philosophy, dialectics is usually defined as a certain sort of process of thought or reason. The idea that thought or reason is dialectical also has its roots in the ancient Greek philosophers. Plato and his teacher, Socrates, are generally regarded as the first dialectical philosophers because they saw philosophy as a dialectical process. For them, we come to know things through a dialogue in which an interlocutor suggests a thesis and the teacher—Socrates himself—would raise examples or thoughts which oppose the thesis just suggested. This process is a process of reasoning that is supposed to lead the interlocutor to have better knowledge of the topic at hand. Thus, reason or rationality and coming to know things is a dialectical process of opposites in which a person's thesis is put up against opposed views in order to give rise to a better or more developed thesis or claim, or to better knowledge.

In Hegel, the dialectical nature of reason is transformed from a process that occurs between people into a process that takes place between the concepts themselves. For him, rational concepts develop dialectically in relation to one another, without the need for any human dialogue. As we will see more fully in Section VII, the logic traces this dialectical development for only a certain or restricted set of concepts, namely, for those concepts that are, as Hegel puts it, "behind the back of consciousness, so to speak" (§25R). Whereas the *Phenomenology* tells the story of the dialectical development of conscious awareness, the logic tells the story of the dialectical development of concepts that consciousness is not directly aware of. As I will argue later, these concepts are non-empirical concepts, such as the concept of cause, that are "behind the back" of consciousness in the sense that they are concepts that consciousness does not directly think about in ordinary life, but presupposes in the down-to-earth empirical concepts with which consciousness is primarily concerned.

Hegel's dialectical conception of reason allows his reason to overgrasp the messiness of the world—a messiness which, for Hegel, is really nothing but a second level of dialectical development. For Hegel, what Plato regarded as the imperfection of the world is a dialectical development that takes place in reality. I will discuss the nature of this dialectical development more fully in Section VIII, but Hegel's suggestion is that the messiness of change in the physical world is simply a reflection of Reason itself, which is now defined dialectically rather than statically as Plato had done. Reason itself is defined by a messy interplay of opposites and contradiction that stands under and understands the messiness of the physical world of reality, which is nothing but a dialectical process that reflects the dialectical nature of Reason itself.

Hegel's view that dialectics is both in thought and in reality helps to show how his philosophy may be read somewhat materialistically. Since the messiness of the physical world is a reflection of the dialectics of Reason, then the dialectics of Reason is out there in the physical, material or real world. Of course, this view does not yet imply what the materialist wants to hold, namely that reality is self-generating and self-subsistent in relation to thought, or that reality is the primary cause of thought. Hegel does not deny that reality is self-generating, independent, and causal in relation to thought, however. As we will see, his logic recognizes that there is a dialectic of reality which causes thought to work to grasp the changes in reality. Even at the end of the logic, I will argue, the self-generating, independent dialectic of reality is never overcome. Although there is still a sense, for Hegel, in which Reason is the first cause, I will argue that Hegel's logic envisions an interplay between reality and thought that respects the independent and causally self-generating elements of reality in its relationship with thought.

We can now see more precisely how Hegel will attempt to overcome what he takes to be the limited nature of Kant's account of knowledge. Remember that, according to Kant, we can have knowledge only of the world of experience, because our reason shapes the way we experience the world, and we cannot get out of our heads to see what the world would be like on its own. Hegel's answer to Kant is very close to the ancient Greek philosopher Aristotle's response to Plato's view. Aristotle (384–322 BC) had argued that, contrary to his teacher Plato's views, the world is graspable not because it is an imperfect copy of perfect rationality that is "somewhere" else or in another realm, but because rationality is in the world itself. The Forms are not in some other realm, but in this world, and define or identify things as what they are. The Forms are in-forms: they inform the world itself. Thus, the Form of "animal" is in the individual animal itself. Universal reason is in the world itself.

Like Aristotle, Hegel suggests that the world is graspable because it has rationality in it as its very own defining principle. When we see a dog and identify it as an animal, we are not just applying some concept of ours to it. That would be Kant's view, namely, that our ideas and concepts are only in us human beings. On the contrary, Hegel suggests, there is something about the dog, too, that identifies it as an animal. The dog itself must live up to some concept, some defining principle, that makes it an animal and not some other kind of thing. That defining principle would be the universal concept "animal," or the rational principle of "animality"—the universal that makes all animals what they are as animals. Hence, the rational universal or concept of animal is not just in us, but is, as Aristotle had thought, in the dog itself. And it is only insofar as things live up to such rational concepts at all that they have what identity they have. As Hegel apparently put it in one lecture, "'to be an animal,' the kind considered as the universal, pertains to the determinate animal [i.e. the dog] and constitutes its determinate essentiality. If we were to deprive a dog of its animality we could not say what it is" (§24A1). Rationality, to say it again, overgrasps reality. It is in reality and makes reality what it is. Rationality informs and shapes reality by giving things their characters.

Of course, Plato, too, had said that things in the world can be what they are or have their identity only to the degree that they participate in or are imperfect copies of the rational concepts or Forms. Unlike Plato, however, Hegel can take the additional (Aristotelian) step of claiming that the rational concepts are in things themselves because of his dialectical conception of both the world and reason. Plato was right that the world is messy, but he was wrong to think of reason as unchanging, stiff, and static. Once Hegel defines reason as dialectical, and characterizes the world's messiness as dialectical, he can, like Aristotle, put reason back into the world. And once reason is back in the world, Hegel can overcome Kant's skepticism. For Hegel, we can know what the world is really like because both the world and our reason are dialectical in the same way.

However, to say that reason is in the world is not to say that it is nothing else besides the world. Plato's impulse to exile the Forms to another realm was motivated by a distinction between the ideal (reason) and the real (the physical world) that Hegel also tries to maintain. While ideal, rational concepts are in the world, there is also a sense in which they are not in the world, for Hegel. Although the universal "animal" belongs to the individual dog itself, and not to some other realm, that ideal or universal is not merely a material principle. Plato was right to insist that the universals are not themselves material or physical.

Let me take an example drawn from one of Hegel's Remarks in the *Encyclopaedia Logic* to illustrate the point. Ordinary life shows us quite clearly the proper status of the universal "fruit," Hegel suggests. Someone who thought that "fruit" was a material or physical item and wanted "fruit," would reject cherries, pears and raisins offered on a tray because none of those are "fruit" (§13R). However, we understand that "fruit" is a concept that is not a material something that can be had or touched in the physical world, but is available to or can be grasped only through thought. The universal or concept of fruit is in the pears, cherries and so on, but it is also not in them in the sense that when you reach for a cherry, you are not taking hold of "fruit" itself.

Of course, even to talk of "cherries," "pears" and "raisins" is already to employ universals too. We cannot really eat "cherry" either. We can only eat this singular item, this one thing in front of us that we identify with the universal "cherry." As Hegel apparently put it in a lecture employing the example of "animal" discussed above, "'animal as such' cannot be pointed out; only a definite animal can ever be pointed at" (§20A1). As a result, the concept of "cherry" is already a universal too, but the point is easier to make with "fruit" because we do not use "fruit" to refer to definite, singular items the way we do with the words "cherry," "apple" and other such universals. We use the expression "a piece of" fruit, and the phrase "a piece of" makes clear that we are eating a singular item that is identified with the concept "fruit." But because we say we eat "an apple," it seems as if "apple" refers to the singular item, even though it, too, is a universal. We eat only the singular item—the "this" here in front of us—not the universal. Hence, for Hegel, universals in general—"fruit," "apple," "cherry" and so on—are not in the material, physical world in an immediate way. They are not something you can immediately touch physically, or eat. They are in the world or material, but they are not merely material. They are ideal (spiritual) and belong to thought, even though they are also in, inform and shape material reality.[4]

Hegel tries to capture the relationship between the ideal and the real, material, or physical world in his *Philosophy of Right* with the sentence "[w]hat is rational, is actual, and what is actual, is rational" ("Preface," see Hegel 1991, 20; Hegel 1967, 10). In a Remark to §6 of the *Encyclopaedia Logic,* Hegel makes clear that he does not mean by this claim that everything that exists in the world is completely rational. The world contains, he says, both contingency—or accident and chance—as well as actuality. An "actuality" is an existing item that lives up to, or fulfills its concept. Thus, actual items are rational because they live up to their proper rational concepts, or universals. But that does not mean that the world does not contain many things that fail to live up to their concepts. "Who is not smart enough," Hegel says, "to be able to see around him quite a lot that is not in fact how it ought to be?" (§6R). A broken hammer, for example, would be an existing item, but it would not be an actuality, because, since it is broken, it does not live up to its concept as a hammer. The broken hammer is therefore a contingent existence, and while it is certainly there in the world, it is not rational, and hence not "actual," in Hegel's sense. Philosophy, Hegel says, is not concerned with such contingent items, however, but with "the Idea" (§6R), with the rational concepts or universals themselves and with their expressions in the world. Philosophy is concerned with actuality—with the rational universals and the degree to which they are instantiated in the world.

Hegel's conception of actuality is closely connected to his conception of truth. He distinguishes between correctness and truth. Correctness captures the more ordinary sense of "truth." It points to the agreement between a statement or representation about something, and the content of the associated experience. So, to use Hegel's own examples, the statements "the rose is red" and "so-and-so is ill" are correct if they agree with the content of our experience of the world (i.e. the rose is indeed red, the person is indeed ill). But such statements cannot be true, according to Hegel's conception of truth (§172R, §172A). The redness of the rose does not make a rose a rose, i.e. it does not get at the concept of a rose. Plenty of roses, after all, are not red. Hence, being red is not part of the universal, rational concept of rose, and therefore cannot be true in Hegel's sense. For Hegel, a true statement or concept lives up to or exemplifies its universal, rational concept. Like his concept of actuality, Hegel's concept of truth grows out of the idea that rationality overgrasps the world. Something in the world is true to the degree that it lives up to or is overgrasped by the appropriate universal, rational concept.

Hegel's conceptions of truth and actuality can be illustrated by an example Hegel uses from time to time in the *Encyclopaedia Logic*. There may be lots of people we call friends, but a true friend is only one whose actions live up to the universal, rational concept of friendship (§24A2). We distinguish, for instance, between "fair-weather" friends and true or actual friends. As the old blues singers will tell you, a fair-weather friend is your friend when your pocket is full, but as soon as your pocket is empty, that "friend" is gone. A real friend, by contrast, is someone who remains your friend even when your pocket is empty. Such a person is a friend who really lives up to the concept of friendship, and so is, as we would say, a true or actual friend. Thus, the way we often think about friendship echoes Hegel's conceptions of truth and actuality. We think a true or actual friend is someone who properly lives up to the concept of friendship. For Hegel, truth and actuality are always about living up to the relevant concept.

Hegel's suggestion that the actual is rational and vice versa also expresses a teleological theory. For Hegel, rationality not only makes the world what it is or defines things in the world, it also guides the world. It actively overgrasps reality in the sense that it is the moving principle of the world. Reason creatively informs, and actively shapes reality. Defining concepts are active in the sense that they set the goals or drive things not only toward their ends in the literal sense (death, deterioration), but also toward their ideal or excellence. Thus, the concept of "friend" not only captures the truth of friendship, but it sets the goal of friendship. Individual friends strive to be, not just fair-weather friends, but true friends, actual friends or friends that fully live up to the concept of friendship. Human beings strive to be, not just human, but true or actual human beings, or human beings who fully live up to the concept of being human. Humans strive to live up to the concept of human insofar as they strive to be as rational and ethical as they can. The concept of human sets the bar of excellence to which people try to rise. Similarly, rose bushes aim at producing, not just roses, but excellent roses that fully live up to the concept of rose, and so on. As we saw above, Hegel's claim is that the rationality that overgrasps reality is not static. Reason drives the world teleologically by setting the goals or purposes of things. The universal, rational concepts set the level of excellence toward which things strive. For Hegel, contingent items or events are only the world's superficial outer rind or appearance (§6R), as he says, whereas rationality is the world's inner principle. This metaphor expresses his teleological idea that rationality guides the world insofar as things in the world aim at or strive to live up to their concepts, even though many of them, for contingent reasons, fall short. Thus, the universal, rational concepts not only define items as what they (truly) are, they also express what those items' goals or purposes are.

If the individual universal, rational concepts are the moving principle of individual things, then Rationality as a whole, with a capital "R"—which is the whole system of rational, universal concepts—is the moving principle of the whole world. Insofar as Rationality overgrasps the whole world, it also expresses the world's aim. Rationality is the power in the world; it is the ultimate purpose of the whole world. To say that Rationality is the teleological end or purpose of the whole world is to say that the world is, over time, becoming more and more rational. The world is progressing toward an ever better fulfillment of rationality. It is slowly fulfilling its rational purpose. When Hegel says that the rational is actual and the actual is rational, he does not mean that that the existing world is currently completely rational. However, he does think that the world is becoming more rational—more actual, more true—all the time. Rationality as the whole system of rational concepts not only describes the world, it powers the world, it drives the world as the world's own purpose.

III. Essential, Necessary Universals

Underpinning Hegel's view that universals such as "animal" overgrasp animals themselves is a particular understanding of the term "universal." Hegel distinguishes between several different ways of conceiving of universals, and the early course of the logic can be seen, in part, as an argument for a third and higher definition, which he regards as superior to the earlier two. The simplest (and, for Hegel, lowest) definition of universals sees universals as a label for a kind of mathematical set. On this view, the universal "apple" would simply be the set of all apples, for example, and the universal "red" would be the set of all red things. The universal "apple" would be the community of all apples; the universal "red" would be the community of all red things. Hegel calls this account of universals the "communality" form of universality (*Encyclopaedia Logic,* §20R), and he regards it as inadequate. In §20R, he says it is an "external" form of universality, largely because it cannot explain why certain items should be put into certain sets. Why do this item (an apple) and this item over here (another apple), but not this item here (a banana) belong in the set "apple"? The communality account of universals requires that we human beings—from the outside, i.e. externally—put the items into those community baskets. It makes no reference to the items themselves—i.e. to their internal natures—to explain why the items belong in the baskets. The *Encyclopaedia Logic* provides an argument for abandoning the communality definition of universals in the "Doctrine of Being," since the progression from one stage to the next will force us to leave this definition behind.

A second definition of universals that Hegel distinguishes corrects for the problem in the communality definition. The second definition of universals explains why items belong together in the baskets, groups or sets: it says that the things in the set or basket belong together because they share some quality (or qualities) in common. This is the *"commonality"* definition of universals, a term that draws on Hegel's comment that a universal may refer to what things "have in common" (§20R), and on an Addition in which Hegel apparently distinguished his own view of universals from one according to which universality is "interpreted merely as something held in common" (§24A1). The term "com-

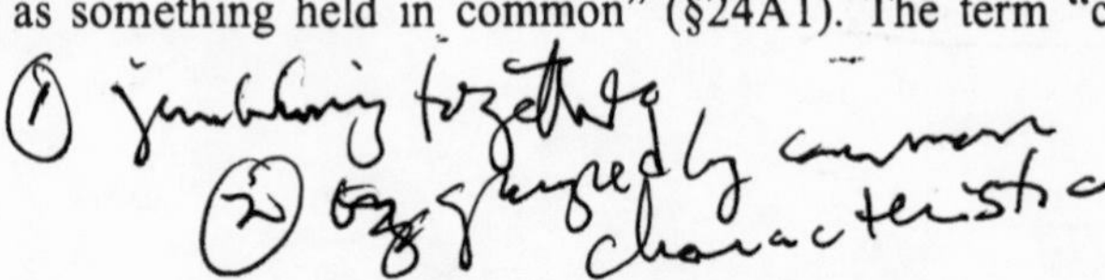

monality" fits this account of universals well, because it highlights the fact that this account of universals involves picking out the shared or common qualities that explain why items belong in the relevant baskets or sets. Individual dogs are all in the basket for "dog," for instance, because they share certain characteristics in common, which are captured by the concept of "dog."

This commonality definition improves on the communality definition. In the communality definition, the things in the sets or baskets have merely an "external" relationship with one another. Their relationship with one another is "external" in the sense that they do not glue themselves together. Again, the communality definition cannot explain why the items in the set are in the same basket, which implies that an outside or external force—we human beings, for instance—must group the items together. Under the commonality definition, however, the natures of the items themselves hold the items together in the set. Individual dogs are held together in the set "dog" by their own natures or characteristics, so that they no longer need an external force to hold them together. The commonality definition is thus more "internal," rather than external, because it makes use of the "internal" qualities or characteristics of things to group them together. What the things have in common places them in their particular baskets. The items no longer have a merely external relationship with one another: they are related together by virtue of their own natures, and not merely because some external force holds them together.

The trouble with the commonality definition of universals, for Hegel, is that it does not yet get to the heart of universality. According to the commonality definition, the universal "human," for instance, would be something like a summary of the common characteristics that humans share. But this account violates Hegel's basic idealism: his commitment to the view that universals, concepts or ideas are the primary force behind reality. For Hegel, ideals or concepts define reality, they make reality what it is, and are the goals toward which things in the world strive. The commonality account reverses the priority of the ideal and the real. It suggests that the real gives rise to the ideal, since it suggests that the concept "human" is generated by summarizing what individual humans have in common. The commonality definition also suggests that the ideal or concept is tied to, or rooted in, the real. Since individual humans come first, on this account, and since they give rise to the universal "human," that universal depends on individual humans for its nature. On this account, the nature of the individual humans gives the universal "human" its character. Such an account, however, would undermine Hegel's attempt to overcome what he regards as Kant's unacceptable skepticism. If the real gives rise to the ideal, and if our filters shape how we experience the world, then Kant would be right to say that we cannot know what the world is like in itself, since we cannot get out of our heads or out from behind our filters to see what the world would be like on its own. Hegel thinks he can overcome Kant's skepticism by showing that our concepts, our reason, is in the world itself. He can make good on his argument only if he can show that our rational concepts—which belong to Reason itself—are in the world and make the world what it is, and he can show that our concepts make the world what it is only if concepts give rise to the real. For Hegel, then, the proper definition of universals will be one that sees universals as essentially defining concepts that are not ultimately tied to any particular reality. Universals are the essences of things. These essences are the sorts of universals that are the power behind and that drive the world.

The move from one definition of universal to the next absorbs the earlier definitions. The communality definition saw a universal as a set or group (community). The commonality definition also sees a universal as a set or group, but it adds the idea that the things have something in common. Similarly, defining universals as essences also absorbs the earlier two definitions. A universal is still a group, set or community of things. It also groups things that have something in common—though what they have in common will be more restricted under the essential account than it would be under the commonality account. For instance—and Hegel himself apparently used this example—all human beings have earlobes and so having earlobes might be a common characteristic included in the universal "human" as defined under the commonality account. However, having earlobes does not capture the defining element that makes humans human (see *Encyclopaedia Logic,* §175A). An essential universal will capture the defining nature of a thing. Hence, while earlobes might be included when the universal "human" is defined according to the commonality account, they will not be included when the universal "human" is defined according to the essential account of universals. Thus, although an essential universal will point toward what things have in common, the characteristics it points toward are more restricted than they would be under the commonality account of the universal. Nevertheless, the essential definition of universals still absorbs the two earlier definitions.

It also adds to them. Again, essential universals pick out what is essential to and necessary in things (see §39): they point toward the whatever-it-is without which a thing would not be what it is. That whatever-it-is is essential to, or necessary to, the thing because the thing could not be what it is without the whatever-it-is. Again, the universal "human" would point toward whatever-it-is that makes humans human, and without which a human would not be human. That whatever-it-is is necessary to the human because the human could not be what it is without the whatever-it-is. For Hegel, then, there is an essential and necessary connection between universals and their individual instances. This necessity is missing from the commonality definition, and explains why the commonality definition, while better than the communality definition, must also be set aside as the last word in universals.

Thus the rationality that overgrasps the world is an essential rationality, a necessary rationality, a rationality without which the world would not be what it is. Reason is the essential and necessary identity of the world. This necessary rationality is also, for Hegel, what the world aims at, what its purposes are, and what the world is slowly coming to instantiate more precisely through its history. Thus reason is the essential and necessary purpose of the world.

IV. Reason Drives Itself: Semantics and Syntax

Hegel's concept of reason is necessary in two senses. It is necessary, first, in the sense that it overgrasps the identity and serves as the purposes of the world. It is semantically necessary: it defines things in the world, or gives them their identity or meaning. And it is teleologically necessary to the world in the sense that it drives the world to its various purposes. Reason is also necessary in a second sense, however, namely in a syntactical sense. Reason is dialectical, which means that reason undergoes a process of logical development on its own account. It is syntactically necessary. This second sense in which reason is necessary will be crucial to Hegel's argument against Kant's skepticism. Kant's skepticism derives in part from his assumption that rationality is only in us, only in our human heads. Hegel's ability to show that reason follows out its own process of dialectical development will help him to show why reason is not dependent on us, why it is in fact independent even of us.

The claim that reason or rationality develops necessarily and dialectically on it own has roots in the work of Kant, and, in particular, in Kant's concept of reason. Kant had divided human rationality into two elements: the understanding and reason. The understanding is the faculty that is responsible for organizing and regularizing our sensory experiences of the world. Kant regarded it as the primary faculty of human knowledge, since it largely provides the universal structure that, as we saw earlier, guarantees the objectivity of our experiences and, hence, makes knowledge of the world of experience possible. Reason's job is to coordinate the concepts or categories of the understanding in the process of developing a completely unified conceptual system, and it performs this job independently of the world of experience. Reason follows out necessary conceptual implications independently of how those concepts might apply to the world of experience. Reason drives itself by going where the universals take it.

Hegel adopts this idea of an independently driven rationality. But whereas Kant thought that reason was liable to lead us astray—since it was liable to make knowledge claims that could not be confirmed by experience and therefore should be kept under check by the understanding—Hegel liberates reason from the tyranny of the understanding. Instead of following Kant's assumption that reason is only in us Hegel uses Kant's suggestion that reason develops a unified conceptual system on its own to argue that reason is not only our reason, but the reason of the world itself. If, as Kant says, human reason drives necessarily on its own account toward systemic, conceptual unity (see *Critique of Pure Reason*, A323/B380), then it does not need us—or our heads—to drive it. Reason develops a unified, conceptual system independently even of us.

For Kant, reason's job is to coordinate the concepts of the understanding by following out conceptual implications in a way that produces greater and greater conceptual unity. Kant thought that reason would do this by using a long chain of syllogisms. A syllogism is a general, logical form of argument into which various concepts can be plugged. An example of a syllogism that Kant gives is: "All men are mortal, Caius is a man, therefore Caius is mortal" (*Critique of Pure Reason*, A322/B378-9). Another example he gives can be written as: Everything composite is alterable, bodies are composite, therefore bodies are alterable (*Critique of Pure Reason*, A330-1/B387). Kant suggests that reason's coordinating process involves working toward totality—or "allness"—for each concept that it takes up (*Critique of Pure Reason*, A322/B379, A326/B383). Reason uses the syllogism to establish universal rules that unify concepts under larger and more-encompassing concepts. In the first example, for instance, reason would be working on the concept of "mortality." It would be trying to move toward totality for the concept of "mortality." In the example, reason would so far have used this syllogism to work toward the totality of "mortality" by establishing the universal rule "all men are mortal" (see *Critique of Pure Reason*, A330/B386-7). This rule coordinates the concepts "men" and "mortality" by determining that the concept of "mortality" contains the totality of the other concept or namely "all men." The rule thus begins to tell us what items belong in the totality "mortality": so far, "all men" belong to "mortality." In the other example, reason is also beginning to tell us which items belong to the concept in question there. Reason is beginning to fill up the concept, as a basket, with items that belong to it. In this second example, the concept in question is "alterability," and reason would have worked toward establishing totality for "alterability," so far, by showing that "alterability" contains all composite things. Reason has used the syllogism to establish the rule "everything composite is alterable." These rules move from a less-encompassing concept to a larger, more encompassing concept. The rule "all men are mortal" shows that "man" is a less encompassing concept than "mortality" because "all men" fit under the concept of mortality. Similarly, "composite" fits within "alterable" since everything composite is alterable, according to the rule.

The concepts "mortality" and "alterability" are not completed, however. Their baskets are not yet full of all the things that belong to them. All men may belong in the basket "mortality," and everything composite may belong in the basket "alterability," but there are other things, too, that belong in those baskets. Other animals besides all men, for example, are also mortal, but the extension of "mortality" is limited so far to all men, and the extension of "alterability" is limited so far to everything composite. Therefore, each concept's extension has only been established in relation to a certain condition. Their baskets have been filled up only under a certain condition. The basket for "mortality" has things in it only insofar as those things are men, and "alterability" has things in its basket only insofar as they are alterable. Reason has full baskets for the concepts "man" and "composite," because it is now dealing with all men and everything composite, but it does not yet have full baskets for "mortality" and "alterability" in these examples. Kant's idea is that reason's drive toward totality or completeness would lead it to generate additional syllogisms. Reason would aim to fill up the baskets of all the concepts it dealt with. Hence, in our examples, reason's drive toward totality would eventually push it on to further syllogisms to fill the baskets or to establish totality for "mortality" and "alterability."

Notice that, in developing its totalities, reason would go beyond what can be established by the faculty of the "understanding"—in Kant's technical sense that we saw above—which he distinguished from the faculty of reason. The faculty of the understanding keeps its eyes on the world of experience. It therefore cannot really make any claims about "all men" or "everything composite." After all, none of us, with our understandings, has experienced "all men," for example, nor *could* we experience "all men." We have not been around the whole time "men" have existed, and more "men" will exist after we're gone. The faculty of reason's claim that "all men are mortal" therefore goes beyond what could possibly be established by anybody's understanding.

The chain of syllogisms proceeds in both directions: (1) on the side of the ever-smaller and less-encompassing concepts—the conditions (in our examples, "man" and "composite" are the conditions)—or (2) on the side of the ever-increasing unity and comprehensiveness. Kant called (1) the descending series of syllogisms, or the episyllogisms, and (2) the ascending series of syllogisms, or the prosyllogisms (*Critique of Pure Reason*, A381/B388, A336-7/B394):

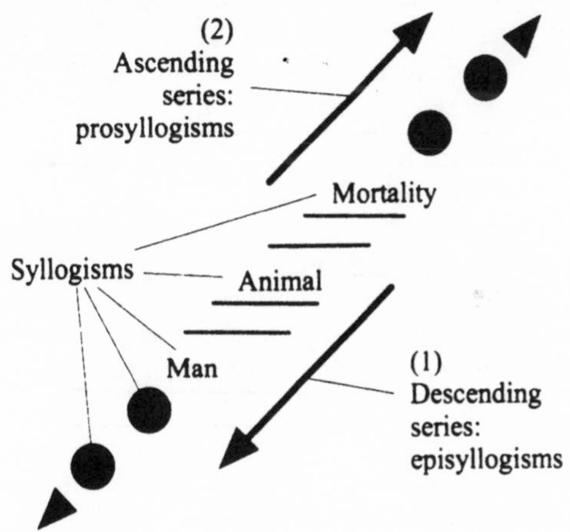

Figure 1.1

Since reason is concerned with unity and totality, it will be concerned primarily with (2), the prosyllogisms that lead to increasing unity or comprehensiveness. However, because reason goes beyond what the understanding can do, the understanding cannot supply the increasingly comprehensive universals that will be needed for the prosyllogisms. Instead, reason would have to create new concepts for the prosyllogisms on its own. Moreover, because the province of the understanding is experience, as the prosyllogisms take reason beyond the understanding, reason would go beyond experience as well. Therefore, some of the concepts that reason generates would be transcendental in the sense that they could not be applied to experience at all. In following out the prosyllogisms, then, reason would produce its own transcendental ideas, as Kant called them, or concepts that went beyond what could be applied to the world of experience (see *Critique of Pure Reason*, A337/B394). Kant calls this concept-creating reason what has been translated as "speculative" reason (see, e.g. *Critique of Pure Reason*, Bxx-xxi, A327/B384). Reason "speculates"—it creates its own ideas.

Kant thought that our reason would continue to follow out such prosyllogisms until it landed on a concept that was completely comprehensive. Such a completely comprehensive or all-encompassing universal would be unconditioned. As an all-encompassing universal, it would contain all of the conditions—all "men," for instance, everything "mortal," everything "composite," everything "alterable" and so on—and there would therefore be no conditions, or concepts outside of it that it did not include. The universal would also be completely independent. The concept "mortal" applies only to things under certain conditions—i.e. things defined as "man," for instance, or, even once it is extended further, as "animal." These limiting conditions are something that the concept of "mortality" depends on. The concept of "mortality" needs the concept of "man" to define at least some of the things to which it applies. "Mortality" is a more-encompassing concept than the concept of "man," but it depends on the concept of "man" to gather up some of the things to which it applies. "Mortality" depends on the presence of those other conditions for its own ability to apply to things. There would be no such dependent relationship for an all-encompassing universal, however, because there would be no concepts that it did not contain. It would include everything, and so would not need other concepts to pick out which things it should include and which things it should not. There would be no concepts or conditions outside of it at all on which it would depend. It would be all-encompassing, whole and complete, with no conditions outside of it. It would be unconditioned in the sense of being independent of any conditions. Kant therefore conceives of an unconditioned universal as both all-inclusive and independent. This unconditioned universal—the Unconditioned—is the precursor to Hegel's Absolute.

So far we have seen that Kant conceives of self-driving reason as a principle of thought that coordinates concepts, generates concepts, aims at ever increasing comprehensiveness, and, ultimately, aims at unconditioned totality. Added to this list is a feature drawn from Kant's story about how reason is supposed to accomplish these tasks. As we have seen, for Kant, reason performs these tasks through a process of logically necessary development—in his case, the process of following out necessary syllogisms. These features, taken together, capture Kant's vision of how reason drives itself. Hegel adopts the general outlines of Kant's conception of reason, but he also departs from Kant's view in a few important ways.

Hegel adopts Kant's view, to begin with, that reason is self-driving, concept-generating and driving toward ever-increasing comprehensiveness. He even adopts Kant's term for describing such a concept-generating reason—the term traditionally translated as "speculative." As in Kant's view, Hegel's adoption of these features will lead his notion of reason to be conceptual, or concerned with concepts. In Hegel's hands, however, reason will also involve semantics, or the meanings of concepts. For Hegel, the concepts that reason will generate as it progresses toward ever-increasing comprehensiveness are essential universals, universals that are necessary and make items in the world what they are. Moreover, such essential universals are teleological: they express not only what objects are, but the goals or purposes of objects, what objects strive to be. Spelling out these goals for a universal will require Hegel to involve the meanings of those concepts. Again, a "true" friend is someone who lives up to the essential concept of friendship. The essential concept of "friendship" must therefore include a particular meaning or semantic content that would separate a "true" friend from a merely so-called friend. To be an essential friend is therefore to live up to a particular meaning of the concept of "friendship."

Hegel's emphasis on meanings departs from Kant's definition of reason in an important respect, however. Hegel envisions reason's self-development as a process of defining the meanings of concepts in relation to one another, rather than in relation to the world of things, which was the pattern in Kant's view. For Kant, reason's process of self-development through the prosyllogisms still had its eyes on the things in the world. The syllogisms drew in things from the world to fill up the universals' baskets. For Hegel, however, while concepts do overgrasp or inform things in the world, reason's conceptual process of self-development makes little reference to those things. Hegel's reason follows out its own necessary development, independently of how the concepts apply to the world of things. Moreover, Kant's idea that reason develops by filling up conceptual baskets invokes a notion of universals that is too close to the communality definition that Hegel rejects. The communality definition of universals defined a universal as nothing more than a set or basket of some type of thing. Like the communality definition, Kant seems to define reason's universal concepts as completed sets of all the things that belong in their baskets. This view sees universals as defined by the items that fill them up. Kant's prosyllogisms seemed to be aimed at "all-ness" in this full-basket sense. For Hegel, however, this definition reverses the proper relationship between the world and rational universals. As we saw in the Introduction and again in the discussion of Hegel's idealism above, Hegel views reason as primary, and the world as secondary. Reason's universals define the world, and not the other way around. Hence, reason's self-development process must be independent of, and prior to, things in the world. In his view, then, conceptual universals define themselves in relation to each other, rather than in relation to the world of things. His vision of reason's self-development therefore stays at the level of concepts. Each concept develops out of earlier concepts, and their meanings are all fixed by their places in the development, and their relationships to each other. Hegel does not see the concepts as baskets that are defined by being filled up with things. Hegel agrees with Kant that reason undergoes a process of development, but he rejects Kant's model according to which universals develop in relation to things in the world.

Hegel thus adopts, but also revises, Kant's vision of reason's conceptual development.

There are still other features of Kant's view that Hegel adopts—and revises—however. In addition to accepting Kant's ideas that reason is concept-generating and aims at increasing comprehensiveness, Hegel also adopts Kant's idea that reason's drive toward increasing comprehensiveness eventually lands on an unconditioned totality. For Hegel, however, there can be only one unconditioned totality, or overarching universal, outside of which there is nothing. Kant's unconditioned concept is not alone, since in addition to the unconditioned concept generated by reason, there is the world-in-itself, or Thing-in-itself, about which we can know nothing. Kant's view falls short of making the unconditioned concept truly unconditioned, because it suggests that there is this world, this "Thing-in-itself," outside of reason. A truly unconditioned concept that has no conditions outside of it must include the world itself. Otherwise the world would condition the unconditioned, and the unconditioned would no longer be unconditioned. This argument provides another incentive for Hegel's views that the world itself must be overgrasped by reason and that reason is not just in us. If Reason is to succeed in being unconditioned—Absolute—it must be in the world or include the world itself. Moreover, Reason is not just a spiritual or conscious principle that is in us, it is the spiritual or conscious principle of the world itself, and hence is outside of and independent of our (human) thought. Hegel's Absolute is the one, highest, all-encompassing, unconditioned, conceptual, universal principle.

There is another way in which Hegel's conception of reason both accepts and yet departs from Kant's view. Hegel accepts Kant's suggestion that reason develops through a necessary logical process, but the syntactic process Hegel envisions is a far cry from the syllogistic one outlined by Kant. The term "syntax" describes the way in which items are connected with one another. Grammatical devices in sentences, for example—devices that combine or link the words of a sentence—are a sentence's "syntax." Similarly, in contemporary propositional and predicate logics, the rules that link one logical step with the next are the argument's "syntax." Take the following argument from propositional logic as an example: (1) "if P is true, then Q is true," (2) "P is true;" (3) "therefore Q is true." The syntactic device used in this argument-form, which is called *modus ponens*, is the rule that spells out under what conditions we are logically entitled to remove the "if . . . then" connector. It says we can remove the "if . . . then" connector from the conclusion of the argument because the second premise says that the statement after the "if" in the "if" clause is true (the "if" clause is "if P is true" and the second premise asserts that "P is true"). Once the statement in the "if" clause is asserted, we are entitled to assert the statement that follows the "then" in the "then" clause (the "then" clause is "then Q is true," and what follows it is the statement "Q is true"). This rule allows us to conclude simply "Q is true," and so to get rid of the "if . . . then" connector that we had in the first premise. So, for example, if one premise is "if it rains the streets get wet," and "it rains" is the second premise, then we can conclude "the streets are wet." Our conclusion eliminates the "if . . .then" connector. This rule is the syntactic rule that explains how the conclusion which lacks the "if . . . then" connector—namely, "therefore Q is true"—is linked to the two premises—"if P is true, then Q is true" and "P is true." It links or connects the conclusion to the two premises.

Kant argues that following out his syllogisms would involve a similarly syntactic, logical derivation. The lines of the syllogisms will all be linked to one another by rules of logical derivation that are the connective tissue of the whole string of syllogisms. Because this logical derivation involves following strict rules, for Kant, the process of "following" would be necessary: the next logical steps would be required by the earlier ones. So long as the logic is correct, the conclusions of the syllogisms would follow necessarily from the premises, and the premises would be logically required by the conclusions (see *Critique of Pure Reason*, A332/B389). The ideas or concepts that reason created would be logically required by the same syntactic development.

This syntactic process explains how reason is syntactically necessary. Reason is necessary because it creates necessary concepts as it develops through logical steps that necessitate one another. Hegel's reason, too, will employ a syntactic process of logically necessary development. Steps in reason's concept-generating process will necessitate, further steps. However, the syntax Hegel relies on in his notion of a self-developing, concept-creating reason is completely different from Kant's. Hegel replaces Kant's use of the syllogism with conceptual dialectics. Dialectics captures the necessary, syntactic process of development that reason undergoes in its movement toward the unconditioned, both in thought, and in the world which it overgrasps (see Section VIII).

V. Hegel's Argument

I have roughly defined Hegel's notion of reason and why it leads him to suggest that reason overgrasps or informs the world. I have also argued that his view that reason overgrasps the world may be more plausible than might be thought. I have said little about his argument, however. Hegel argues for his view by outlining the process of reason that Kant had pointed at, but never developed. Whereas Kant merely tells us *that* reason aims at an unconditioned concept through a syllogistic, logical process, Hegel attempts to *outline* the step-by-step logical process which derives the unconditioned concept. Hegel's logic is different from Kant's, as I suggested in the last section. Nevertheless, Hegel outlines, step by step, reason's self-driving development toward the unconditioned. His argument for his claim that reason overgrasps the world is this outline—the whole dialectical story about how reason develops its all-encompassing unconditioned.

To see why the whole dialectical story amounts to Hegel's argument for his view that reason overgrasps the world, think again of Kant. Hegel's claim that rationality overgrasps reality is a denial of Kant's claim that there is a world-in-itself, or Thing-in-itself, beyond rationality. If reason overgrasps reality, then there is nothing, or no-thing, outside of reason's grasp, and that means there would be no Thing-in-itself outside of reason's grasp either. The idea of the Thing-in-itself implies that there is a way of grasping the world that goes beyond reason, and which could never be reached with rationality. For Kant, our concepts are like filters that we use to grasp the thing, and the Thing-in-itself is the unfiltered thing. As Hegel remarks in the *Encyclopedia Logic*, from one point of view the Thing-in-itself is really an empty nothing, or an object without concept, because it is the dead abstraction that remains after we remove all experienced consciousness. Since the world of appearance or experience contains everything that belongs to experience, the Thing-in-itself contains nothing. The thing-in-it-self is really just what is not-experienced, since what we do experience, contains, for Kant, all of our possible experiences (see §44R). So, on the one hand, the Thing-in-itself seems to be an empty object, an object to which no concepts can be applied. But, on the other hand, Hegel suggests, the Thing-in-itself is also supposed (for Kant) to be what is most real and true. Compared to the Thing-in-itself, the world of appearance is just how the thing appears to us, and not what it is in itself, or what it is really like. Of course, Kant would reject Hegel's characterization of the Thing-in-itself as an empty object—it is a something, it's just a something that we cannot grasp. As soon as Kant says it's a something (and not empty), however, Hegel would argue, then Kant has admitted that the Thing-in-itself has some determination or other, or has some character or other, which suggests that there is something there which could be grasped, even if we cannot grasp it. In that case, there must be a "vision," a possible grasping, of the unfiltered thing—a point of view for grasping the unfiltered thing—though, of course, that point of view could not be entertained by any beings (like us, according to Kant) who require their own filters for grasping things. Because, for Kant, grasping or determining involves thought or concepts, Kant's notion of the Thing-in-itself ultimately implies that there must be concepts or determinations which are beyond our rationality but that could characterize or grasp the Thing-in-itself—that there is a conceptual point of view from which the world as it is in itself could be grasped. Kant's view thus implies that there are concepts, or understanding, beyond the grasp of our rationality, that there is a way of grasping the world that is beyond our rationality. This is what Hegel denies.[5]

Hegel can argue against Kant's claim that there is an unknown Thing-in-itself, then, by showing that, as reason goes through its process of development, it covers all possible concepts—that there are no possible conceptual paths that reason did not take. That means, first of all, that there must be no forks on the road of necessary conceptual development which would force reason to choose one path and leave another unexplored. There must, second of all, be no extraneous tributaries to that road, or no stray incoming paths from alternate sources, which would again imply the existence of a conceptual path that reason had not itself explored. If there are no possible conceptual paths that reason did not take, then there would be no concepts left out of reason's repertoire that could be used to grasp the world in a way different from the way reason does grasp it. There would be no conceptual points of view not already explored by reason itself. Hegel can show that there are no paths that reason did not take if he succeeds in showing that reason's process of development is necessary and complete, and only if he can do this for the whole process of development. Indeed, Hegel says, philosophy, which, as we will see in a moment, tells the story of developing reason, is a whole that circles back upon itself (§15), and this circling-back helps to demonstrate the truth of the philosophical project. Only the totality or the whole system can in the end demonstrate that Kant was wrong. For, only the whole system can show that there are no left-out conceptual points of view from which the world could be grasped in a way different from the way reason grasps it. If, at the end of the process of necessary development, reason circles back to the starting point, then that helps to show that the process of development was complete, and hence, that there were no concepts left out of the development—so long, of course, as Hegel succeeds in showing us that the process of development has in fact been necessary.

Hegel has to show, then, that during the whole dialectical story of reason's development, there is nothing coming in from outside sources, or from outside reason's own resources—no backward paths or tributaries left unexplored by reason—and that there are no forks in reason's forward development that force it to leave a conceptual path unexplored—no forward paths left unexplored by reason. Only if he can do this for a completed system will he have shown that reason has explored every conceptual path, and therefore, that there is no left-over concept that reason did not explore that could be used to grasp the world in a way different from the way in which reason grasps it. Hegel therefore has to go over the complete outline of reason's necessary process of development before he can accomplish this proof. That is why only the whole system can be seen as the proof of, or the truth of, Hegel's philosophical project. At the end of this proof, Hegel's Absolute—his unconditioned universal—would satisfy one meaning of "unconditioned" that we saw in the discussion of Kant's notion of reason in Section IV, namely, "unconditioned" in the sense of having no concepts outside of it. Notice that, in showing that reason relies on no outside sources, Hegel will also have contributed to his argument for the view that reason develops on its own account, and by its own power.

Hegel's argument that the process of development is complete and leaves no concepts out will also serve as a defense of his claim that reason aims at the second sense of "unconditioned" that we saw above, namely, unconditioned in the sense of all-encompassing. If Hegel succeeds in showing that, as reason goes through its process of development, it generates increasingly larger concepts, then there's the hope that, when we get to the end of the process, the final universal is complete and leaves no concept out. For only if the concepts are indeed becoming increasingly inclusive could the final concept be all-inclusive, such that it covers all possible conceptual bases, and there are no conceptual bases that reason does not cover that could be used to grasp the world in a way different from the way in which reason grasps it. Once again, however, we will only be able to tell if Hegel's Absolute or universal unconditioned is indeed all-inclusive once we have gone through the entire outline to see if the concepts he outlines are indeed increasingly inclusive.

Hegel's claim that his philosophy is presuppositionless (§1) is closely tied to his goal of deriving the Absolute or universal unconditioned. Hegel's philosophy is supposed to be presuppositionless in the sense that it does not make any assumptions about logic—about the list of logical concepts, or the rules of logical inference. However, he will succeed in showing that his philosophy is presuppositionless only if he succeeds in generating the Absolute or universal unconditioned. For only if Hegel derives the all-inclusive unconditioned—outside of which there is nothing, including no stray concepts—will he have shown that his philosophy does not presuppose anything. If there were any stray concepts left out of the derivation, Hegel's philosophy would have made a presupposition, namely, to exclude that concept. And only if the Absolute or unconditioned includes all possible logical inferences will Hegel have shown that his philosophy makes no assumptions about the rules of logic. For if there were an inference that were left out of the unconditioned, then Hegel's logic would have made an assumption; namely, to exclude that inference.

As Hegel makes clear in the *Encyclopaedia Logic*, however, his claim that philosophy must be presuppositionless does not mean that the individual philosopher coming to his work must be completely ignorant or completely lack interest in the ideas and concepts. Philosophers bring to the table, of course, some familiarity with their topic and some interest in it. Nonetheless, Hegel suggests, philosophy must defend the concepts or universals it employs by showing that those concepts are truly rational. It must derive the concepts it claims are the rational ones, and that means it must show how reason generates its concepts necessarily from one stage to the next (§1). If philosophy succeeds in outlining reason's necessary conceptual development, and if it succeeds in demonstrating how reason develops the promised unconditioned, then it will be presuppositionless, as Hegel claims. It will be presuppositionless for the same reason that the universal it describes is unconditioned. For if the unconditioned universal that philosophy describes is truly all-encompassing, then there will be no conditions outside of it, no concepts or inferences outside of it. And if there are no concepts or inferences outside of it, then there would be no assumptions that the philosophy that describes it presupposes. Thus the philosophical system which describes the unconditioned would be presuppositionless.

Hegel says that his presuppositionless philosophical system "presents itself as a circle of circles" (§15). Just as the whole philosophical system circles back on itself, so each subjectmatter within the philosophical system circles back on itself. We can think of the whole system as a description of one universal—the Absolute, or unconditioned universal—through a discussion of the different subject matters of philosophy:[6]

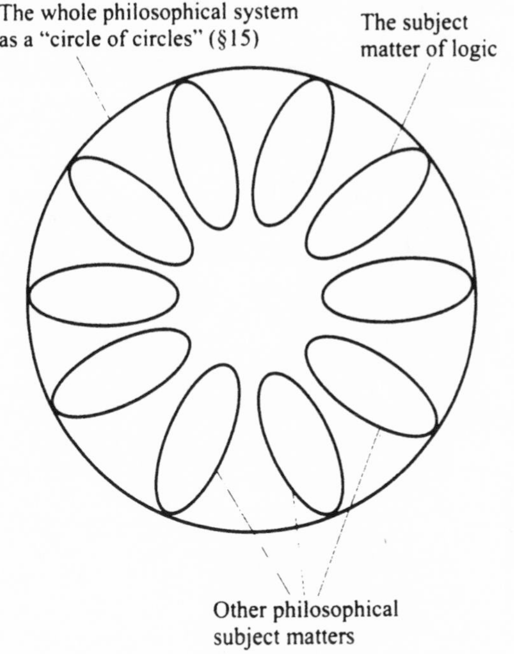

Figure 1.2

Each subject matter is complete in the sense that it circles back upon itself, and the whole, too, circles back on itself. And each subject matter reflects some portion of the whole, unconditioned universal or "Idea," as Hegel puts it (§15).

The unconditioned universal, which the philosophical system describes, can also be depicted as a different sort of "circle of circles." As Hegel's argument against Kant's notion of the unconditioned suggests (see Section IV), to be truly unconditioned, this one universal will, (1) have the world as its own activity. The world will therefore be its object. It will also (2) have the entire system of concepts that overgrasp the world within it as well. It will have the system of concepts as its object as well. The unconditioned is thus a universal that has within it as its object both the whole world and the entire system of concepts. In the diagrams I offer, the unconditioned universal will look like this:

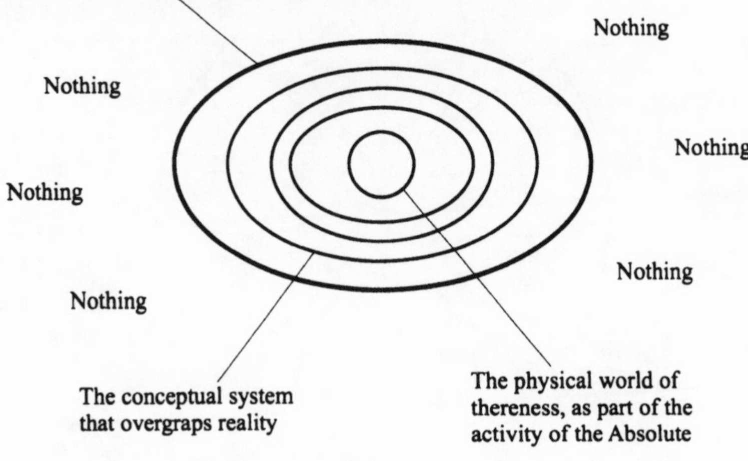

Figure 1.3

We will see more precisely the nature of the unconditioned or Absolute at the end of the logic, but the basic idea is that the unconditioned, all-encompassing universal will have within it a further bunch of circles representing everything else (the world and the entire conceptual system), and outside of which there is nothing.

I have deliberately underplayed Hegel's religious views because I believe that Hegel's project can be largely understood without reference to religion. As I mentioned above, Søren Kierkegaard actually accused Hegel of proposing a philosophy that is devoid of religion. But of course, Hegel's final view, as we will see at the end of the logic, is that rationality—because it is thought, or a conscious principle—cannot just be floating around by itself. It must be someone's thought, some rational entity's rationality. It is God's rationality, God's consciousness. The Absolute is an Absolute Spirit, an unconditioned consciousness. God is rationality—the rational, unconditioned universal that has both the whole conceptual system and the physical world of experience within it as its object. And God's rational activity is our world of experience.

Hegel's argument seems boastful, and, on the face of it, it is certainly a tall order. He has to show that each step is necessitated, and that the project as a whole covers all the conceptual bases. Part of our job in picturing the logic will be to see how well he makes his case—at least in logic, since the topic of logic is not the end of Hegel's argument. The diagrams reveal that Hegel is much more successful in making his case than has often been thought. While his claim is boastful, it does not imply that he knows everything, or that there is no room for future growth in human knowledge. Hegel is famous for having claimed that history had reached its goal with the modern Europe of his day (*Lectures on the History of Philosophy* 1983, vol. 3, 551-2). He meant that human beings' awareness of the system of rational concepts had become complete enough for humans to be able to derive dialectically—and hence prove—the overgrasping nature of rationality. The claim does not entail, however, that there is no space for growth in human knowledge. Humans will still argue, for example, about which rational concepts best describe some worldly phenomenon, and new experiences will yet have to be grasped. Hegel simply denies that there is anything—any Thing-in-itself—which we could never grasp with our rationality. Hegel denies Kant's claim that there could be a Thing-in-itself about which we could in principle never know. Every experience belongs to the world, Hegel would say, and as such it is fully graspable with the rationality we have, even if we do not yet grasp it.

VI. Hegel's Overall Project

We can now describe Hegel's overall project. For Hegel, the world is rationality's expression, and is developing toward an ever greater and more perfect expression of reason. As a result, everything in the world—from human individuals, to human civilizations, to human political, social, economic institutions, to the natural world itself—everything expresses the overarching principle and development of rationality itself. The disciplines of knowledge, then, should aim at understanding all the ways in which reason unfolds in the world. The *Philosophy of Right*, traces the unfolding of reason in the field of "right" or ethics. The natural sciences study the unfolding of reason in the natural world. The study of history looks at the unfolding of reason in human history, and at how human civilizations have (supposedly) become more rational over the years. Unlike the natural world, however, humans express the development of rationality at two levels. For the natural world, the development of reason just happens to it. But for humans, rationality is also something of which they can be aware. For humans are not just things in the world, they are self-consciously aware, rational things in the world (see, e.g. *Encyclopaedia Logic* §24A1). Hence there is an additional story to be told for rational consciousnesses, namely, a story about a developing, ever-greater self-conscious awareness of the unfolding of reason. This is the story contained in the *Phenomenology of Spirit*, which traces types of conscious awareness from the simplest and least rational, to the most rational. The whole collection of projects, taken together, is Hegel's complete argument for the view that he has grasped the all-encompassing universal, and that he has visited every possible universal concept in every subject-matter or every field of knowledge along the way. If each of his projects succeeds in making each of its cases for its limited field, then the whole collection succeeds in making the argument against Kant and for the view that rationality overgrasps all of reality.

Thus, every one of Hegel's works is an attempt to grasp the unfolding of reason as it occurs in some particular realm of knowledge, be it human history, ethics, natural science, or phenomenology (conscious awareness). Each one tells a dialectical story about self-developing reason in relation to some particular subject-matter. The development of the subject-matter creates and determines, as it goes along, the concepts that are at issue in any particular work. In every case, the same syntactic devices, the same dialectics, are used in the unfolding story that Hegel tells. That is why logic, which outlines the range of syntactic devices for dialectics, underpins all of Hegel's works.

VII. The Conceptual and Semantic Project of the *Logic*

Like every one of Hegel's works, the logic tells a story about the dialectical development of a range of concepts that belongs within the all-encompassing, unconditioned universal. Hegel hints at the range of concepts logic concerns when he says it is about essential universals that are "pure" and "abstract." Logic is the science of the "pure Idea," or of the all-encompassing universal (what he is calling the "Idea") as abstract thought (*Encyclopaedia Logic*, §19). In a lecture, Hegel apparently also described the business of logic as having to do with "pure thought" or with "pure thought-determinations" (§24A2). A "thought-determination" is a universal concept of the sort we saw above (see §24A1). For Hegel, a pure or abstract concept is one that has no empirical content from the world of experience. This idea, too, has its roots in Kant's philosophy. Many of the concepts that will appear in the Logic are concepts that correspond to Kant's so-called categories of the understanding (Kant 1950 [1783], 51). Indeed, it is striking just how closely Hegel's concepts in the "Doctrine of Being" and "Doctrine of Essence" follow Kant's table of categories. It is almost as if Hegel begins in the "Doctrine of Being" with Kant's categories of quality (reality, negation, limitation) and then moves to Kant's concepts of quantity (unity/measure, plurality/magnitude, totality/whole) while the "Doctrine of Essence" outlines Kant's concepts of modality (possibility, existence, necessity), and then moves to Kant's concepts of relation (substance, cause, community)—although Kant had listed quantity before quality, and relation before modality. Moreover, Hegel's "Doctrine of the Concept" closely mirrors Kant's logical table of judgments. The fit is not exact—Hegel has more concepts overall than Kant does—but the general outline of these sections of Hegel's logic is very close to Kant's tables.[7] Kant had conceived of his categories as part of the basic structure of rational consciousness that organizes and regularizes our experiences of the world. The categories are traditional logical concepts that Kant had suggested belong to the "filter" through which we experience the world. Because Kant conceived of these categories as preceding experience, as coming prior to experience, he, like Hegel (see §42A3), suggested that they lacked empirical content. Empirical content comes from the world of experience, and hence must come after experience. However, Hegel's use of the logical concepts goes beyond Kant's categories. Hegel belonged to a tradition of immediate post-Kantian philosophers who had criticized Kant for appealing to the logical concepts represented by the categories without properly justifying the choice of, and use of, those concepts. Philosophers such as Karl Leonard Reinhold (1758–1823), Johannes Schultze (1786–1869) and Johann Gottlieb Fichte (1762–1814) had accused Kant of uncritically presupposing the traditional list of logical concepts. They tried in their own philosophies to correct for Kant's failing. Hegel, too, belongs to this post-Kantian tradition.

Many concepts are not pure or abstract, but are mixed with empirical content. A comparison Hegel makes between the business of the logic and the project of the *Phenomenology of Spirit* will illuminate what a universal concept without any empirical content might be like. The *Phenomenology* tells the story of the dialectical development of types of consciousness from the most simple, or as Hegel describes it in the *Encyclopaedia Logic*, the most "immediate" to the most rational, which is the type of consciousness of "philosophical science" (§25R). Because the *Phenomenology* deals with consciousness, it has to do with awareness, with what different levels of rational, conscious awareness would feel like to the one who had that level of conscious awareness. Hegel says that, unlike the *Phenomenology*, the development of the subject matter of logic takes place "behind the back of consciousness, so to speak" (§25R). I think he means that, while the *Phenomenology* tells the story of what the various types of rational consciousness are aware of, the *Encyclopaedia Logic* tells a story about abstract universals that consciousness is not directly aware of.

What abstract universal concepts would be elements of consciousness that consciousness would not be aware of? The universal concepts that logic is concerned with are the tools of consciousness. They are concepts that consciousness uses, without being aware of it. Because consciousness is awareness, consciousnesses going about the business of ordinary life will be primarily aware of experience. They will therefore be filled or occupied with ordinary, experiential, empirical contents, and, as a result, will be concerned primarily with concepts that have experiential elements mixed in. But such empirical concepts will include or presuppose more basic concepts that lack empirical content.

Take, for example, the concept of "earthquake," which a rational consciousness might use as it engages with the world. "Earthquake" is often defined in terms of the elements that cause it. An earthquake is the effect of shifting plates in the earth, which are its cause. An earthquake just is the result of shifting plates in the earth. The concept "earthquake" thus presupposes the concepts of "cause" and "effect." As Hume had shown, however (according to the Kantian tradition to which Hegel was responding), the notion of "cause" cannot be generated by experience, or by observation and reasoning. Hence, it must be provided purely by thought, and precede experience. The notion of "cause" is a non-empirical concept presupposed by the concept of "earthquake." Because consciousness is filled with the experiential concept of "earthquake," however, it is not really aware of the underlying, non-empirical notion of "cause." It presupposes the notion of "cause," without really being aware of it. For Hegel, then, logic has the job of dialectically developing and defining these and other non-empirical concepts that are "behind the back" of consciousness, but are the universal concepts presupposed by the empirical concepts with which consciousness is primarily concerned.

Because Hegel belonged to the post-Kantian tradition that had criticized Kant for having presupposed the categories, Hegel tried to justify his concepts by deriving them in a syntactic process of logical development. This derivation project leads Hegel to have a much longer list of logical concepts than Kant had proposed. Hegel also thought his list was more complete, more comprehensive, than Kant's (he thought his list was completely comprehensive [see §42R]). Hegel's longer and more comprehensive list of logical concepts is derived through the syntactic project.

VIII. The Syntactic Project of the *Logic*

For Hegel, then, logic develops universal concepts that lack empirical content themselves, but are the presuppositions of ordinary, experiential consciousness. To use an inexact metaphor for a moment, they are the building blocks upon which the more empirical concepts depend. But it is not enough to have building blocks. Besides the bricks that we use to construct our buildings, we also need the mortar to hold them together. The logic also concerns itself with the development of the mortar, or with the connective tissue of rational thought, as well as with the bricks. This connective tissue is its syntax. The syntax of Hegel's logic shows how reason can move from one concept to another concept that is connected or linked to it. It lays out the various syntactic devices that reason uses as it necessarily moves from one concept to the next in its development toward the unconditioned, all-encompassing, universal or Absolute. As mentioned above, Hegel's notion of syntax is captured by his notion of dialectics. In addition to developing the basic conceptual building blocks, then, logic has the job of developing the basic syntactic devices of dialectics. This job is what makes understanding the logic so crucial to understanding the rest of Hegel's works.

We have already seen something of the nature of dialectics in section I and in the description of Hegel's overall project in the last section. The discussion of Kant's notion of reason revealed that the dialectical process creates or generates concepts, and that the concepts it generates are increasingly comprehensive. We will see examples of how the dialectical process that Hegel envisions generates concepts as we go through the logic, but we can begin to see why the concepts it generates would become increasingly comprehensive by returning for a moment to the three definitions of "universal" discussed in Section III. Recall that I suggested that the definition of universal as a concept of commonality included, but also added to, the idea contained in the lower definition of universal as communality, or as a set term. The commonality definition replaced, but also absorbed, the earlier definition. Similarly, I suggested, Hegel's definition of the universal as necessary and essential included, but also added to, both of those two lower definitions. It replaced, but also absorbed, the two earlier definitions. This relationship between earlier and later concepts demonstrates one of Hegel's central syntactic concepts—the concept captured by the German verb *aufheben*. According to Hegel, as we go through the dialectical stages of the logic—or of any one of his works—as we progress from lower, less rational stages to higher and more rational ones—the later stages do not simply replace earlier ones, they also subsume or absorb the earlier stages. Hegel uses the German verb *aufheben* to express this double-meaning—to replace and absorb or subsume at the same time. The German term *aufheben*, as Hegel apparently remarked in one of his lectures, means both "to clear away" or "cancel," and "to preserve" (§96A).

There has been a great deal of controversy about how to translate *aufheben*, in light of the fact that there is no English equivalent for the technical, logical sense in which Hegel wants to use the term to mean both to cancel and to preserve. Geraets and Harris (over the objection of Suchting) translate it as "sublate," a tradition which began in the late nineteenth century (according to Suchting: see Geraets et al. 1991, xxv). Although Suchting makes a good case for using the English word "suspend" to translate the technical uses of *aufheben* (Geraets et al. 1991, xxv-xxvi), I will follow Geraets and Harris, and the tradition, and use the term "sublate" for *aufheben*.

For Hegel, then, dialectical development involves *Aufhebung* or sublation. Later stages cancel the earlier stages in the sense that earlier stages are shown to be inadequate, and therefore cannot be left to stand on their own accounts. At the same time, the later stages still have the earlier stages within them—they build on top of one another. This pattern of development is crucial to Hegel's notion of dialectics, and to his idea that there is an overall, all-encompassing, unconditioned universal. The unconditioned universal is supposed to be the universal that contains everything else or is completely comprehensive. Hegel's idea that later stages always absorb earlier stages helps to defend this claim.

As mentioned in the Introduction, one of the other jobs of syntax is to specify the connective patterns or rules according to which concepts and judgments may be linked together into meaningful claims and arguments. The third section of his Logic—the "Doctrine of the Concept"—takes up this task. Kant, too, had included a set of rules that were supposed to perform the same role in his conception of the underlying structure of rationality. His notion of the understanding included a set of rules or concepts for linking judgments—what he called the "logical table of judgments" (Kant 1950 [1783], 50).

Some of the other central components of Hegel's dialectics can be illuminated through a comparison with Plato's view (see Section II), and, in particular, to the reason why Plato exiled rational universals or the Forms to another realm. Plato exiled universals to a separate realm because of the world's imperfection and flux. Many things in the world are imperfect: they break, decay, degenerate, come and go out of existence. Hegel agrees that the world is indeed a messy place. Things in the world often do not live up to their concepts. But they have what identity they have because they do live up to their concepts at least partially, even if they are imperfect. There are imperfect flashlights, and imperfect friends. Moreover, things do change. A living person dies, a rock is crushed and so on. Once again, Hegel would say, it is rationality that accounts for these changes—for the rock that, no longer living up to the concept of "rock," becomes "sand," for example. Everyone knows the world is a messy place. Plato exiled his rational universals to another realm not just because of what he thought the world was like, but also because of what he thought reason must be like (see section I). Rationality itself, he assumed, must be constant and unchanging, static and fixed. For Hegel, Plato's assumption can be rejected by pairing the messy world with a new conception of rationality that is not constant, static and unchanging, but contains its own moving principle, contradictions and change, and so is capable of overgrasping the messiness, the comings and goings, the imperfections of the world. This is the sort of rationality envisioned in Hegel's dialectics.

Kant had argued that reason's self-driving activity will lead it into a dialectical process that produces contradictions. Kant thought that reason would produce four such contradictions or "antinomies," as they are traditionally called. Here are the four contradictions, which Kant put in the form of a thesis and antithesis: (1) (thesis) that the world has, in terms of time and space, a beginning or limit; and (antithesis) that it does not; (2) (thesis) that everything in the world consists of simple elements; and (antithesis) that it does not, that everything in the world is composite; (3) (thesis) that there are free causes in the world, such as the motivation to freely act in a rational and moral manner; and (antithesis) that there are no such free causes, but only mechanistic natural or physical causes; and (4) (thesis) that there is some necessary being in the series of world events; or (antithesis) that there is no such necessary being, indeed nothing necessary in the world, so that everything in the series of world events is contingent (Kant 1950 [1783], 87).

A more detailed look at one of these antinomies as an example will illuminate why Kant thought reason would generate these contradictions as well as the solution he proposed. The antinomy I will focus on here is (1) above: the claim that the world has a limit and the claim that it does not have such a limit, but is infinite. Suppose reason completes the series of prosyllogisms envisioned by Kant that covers all the concepts that we use to describe our experience of and knowledge about the world. For Kant, reason would then have generated a series of increasingly large concepts up to an unconditioned concept of the whole world. Kant argued that, once reason generates this unconditioned, it can look at it in two different ways that will lead it to draw two contradictory conclusions about the nature of the world. Such an unconditioned concept of the world would take the form of a universal that overarches a whole series of syllogisms involving conditioned concepts. As I will explain more fully in a moment, Kant argues that reason can see this unconditioned concept either as (1) the series of syllogisms, or as (2) the overarching conceptual totality:

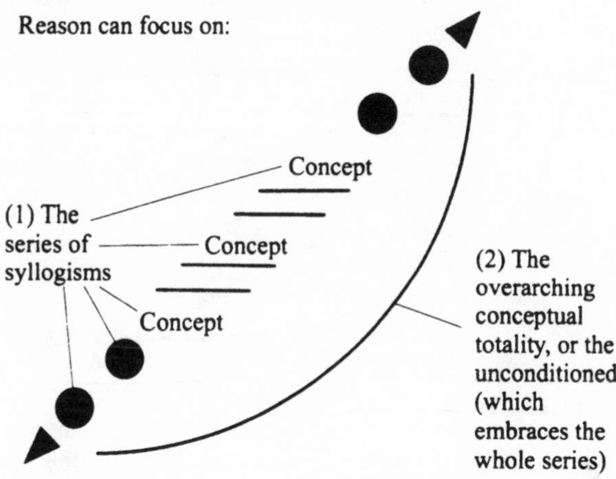

Figure 1.4

The trouble is that each of these visions will lead to a conclusion about the nature of the world which contradicts the conclusion produced by the other vision. Because Kant thought that reason is entitled to see the unconditioned in either of these two ways, he thought reason was equally entitled to draw both of these contradictory conclusions. Reason is dialectical, for Kant, because it leads on its own account to these contradictory conclusions.

Let me now spell out more fully the two different visions of the unconditioned that, according to Kant, lead reason to the two contradictory conclusions. On the one hand, if reason sees the unconditioned merely as a series of syllogisms, it will focus on the conditioned or dependent nature of the concepts in these syllogisms. In other words, it will focus on the unconditioned as a step-by-step, logical series, and hence on the way in which each step in the series is dependent on the earlier steps. It will then see the world as a series of dependent elements. Because every element in the world would be dependent, in this view, there would be no independent element which could serve as the beginning of such a series, and reason would see the series as one that ran on indefinitely. In that case, reason will conclude that the world has no beginning, and runs on indefinitely.

On the other hand, however, reason can focus on the unconditioned as the overarching totality. It can see the unconditioned as a complete chunk, or as a chunk that is not conditioned by, or dependent on, anything outside of it. On this view, because the unconditioned has no conditions outside of it, it is independent. In this case, reason will see the unconditioned as an independent end-point of the series of syllogisms—as the first member of the series, or the independent beginning of the series. Reason will therefore see the unconditioned as the beginning of the world, or the limit of the world, and will conclude that the world has a beginning or limit, and hence does not run on indefinitely (*Critique of Pure Reason*, A417-18, B445-6).

Because reason is inclined to be dialectical in this way, or to lead on its own account to such contradictory conclusions, Kant argued that reason must be kept in check by the understanding. We can avoid the contradiction, Kant suggested, by simply reminding ourselves that in drawing this conclusion reason has gone beyond the understanding, and hence beyond what can properly be called knowledge. None of our understandings can draw conclusions about the whole world, because none of us has experienced or can experience the whole world. Hence these conclusions cannot be applied to the world of our experience, and so cannot be called knowledge. The contradictions vanish, then, once we realize that, while reason draws these conclusions on its own account, these conclusions cannot be applied to the world of experience. Only those conclusions that fall within the purview of the understanding can properly be considered conclusions that apply to the world of experience, and hence knowledge (see Kant 1950 [1783], 95; *Critique of Pure Reason*, A506/B534).

Kant's idea that reason produces antinomies or contradictions on its own was turned into a principle of logical development, before Hegel, by Fichte. Fichte called his own method of logical development the "synthetic procedure" (Fichte 1982 [1794], 111). When reason generates the sort of contradiction described by Kant's antinomies, Fichte suggested, the contradiction can be resolved by the introduction of a new concept into a new judgment which allows us to interpret the earlier contradictory judgments in a way that resolves the contradiction. The introduction of the new concept into the next judgment is necessary to make sense of the judgments and categories that had led to the original contradiction. In traditional Western philosophy, the term "logic" captures a kind of causal connection between elements of thought or judgments. Just as there is supposed to be a necessary connection between a cause and an effect, the term "logic" is supposed to capture the idea that there is a necessary connection between thoughts or judgments such that one thought or judgment leads necessarily to the next. Fichte's suggestion that the introduction of the new concept and judgment is necessary allows him to characterize the move as a logical one in this traditional, quasi-causal sense.

Fichte's method of logical development is introduced in the early parts of the *Science of Knowledge*. Fichte suggested that the science of knowledge begins with the absolute self. This beginning leads to a counter-positing or counter-assertion, namely to the not-self (I will not explain how these two judgments arise, for Fichte). These two judgments—the self and the not-self—contradict one another. Two elements of this contradiction will help us to see how the contradiction can be resolved, however. First, the not-self can be counterposed to the self only if the self is still in some sense posited in the background. That not-self is opposed to the self presupposes that the self is still there to be opposed. Moreover, two things are opposed to one another in relation to some shared respect, or to some respect in which they are alike. That respect provides the key to resolving their contradiction (Fichte 1982 [1794], 111). The contradiction between the self and not-self is resolved, according to Fichte, by introducing the concept of divisibility (Fichte 1982 [1794], 110). The concept of divisibility allows us to resolve the contradiction between the self and not-self by defining the self and not-self as divisions of one self. That new one self is the respect or element that both the original self and not-self share. Once we see the original self and not-self as aspects of one self, then the self and not-self can both be true or asserted at the same time. A book, for instance, can be both red and not-red at the same time if we see these two judgments as references to different aspects of the book: the cover and the pages, for instance. Thus, the contradiction between the original self and the not-self is resolved because both are true or can be asserted at the same time. Moreover, the introduction of the new concept—in this case, the concept of divisibility—is logically justified because it allows us to make sense of the two earlier judgments that, though contradictory, had each been logically justified on their own accounts.

Fichte's synthetic method of logical development can be described with the classical "thesis-antithesis-synthesis" model often ascribed to Hegel. The original judgment is the "thesis," the contradictory judgment would be the "antithesis," and the judgment which resolves the contradiction and introduces the new concept would be the "synthesis." Indeed, Fichte himself used the terms "thetic" judgment—the original assertion, understood as identical to itself and not opposed to anything else (Fichte 1982 [1794], 114)—antithesis, and synthesis to characterize his own model of logical development. Hegel, by contrast, never uses these terms to characterize his method.[8] That Hegel never uses this terminology even though he was certainly familiar with it from both Fichte's and Schelling's work and could have chosen to use it—shows that Hegel did not think that the model applied to his own method of logical development.

Nevertheless, Hegel was clearly influenced by Fichte's synthetic method. For one thing, Fichte's method suggests a way of getting reason past Kant's antinomies. For Kant, reason must be stopped at the door of contradiction, and should not pass beyond that door. The understanding keeps reason in check by reminding reason that to go beyond the door of contradiction introduced by the antinomies would lead reason beyond experience itself, and hence into territory where reason has no jurisdiction. Fichte's method opens the door: it provides a way for reason to justifiably tread into territory beyond the door of contradiction without becoming unreasonable.

Moreover, reason's move beyond the door of contradiction, for Fichte, is not only justified, but is also justified in the strongest sense: it is necessary, it is justified logically. Without the new concept and new judgment all the judgments and concepts that had led to the contradiction would themselves become logically unjustified. In standard logic, a judgment that leads to a contradiction is shown to be false or untrue. For Fichte, however, reason is driven necessarily to resolve the contradiction in order to make sense of and hence retroactively justify the development of reason up to that point. Fichte's synthetic method thus introduces a new way of thinking about logical development that Hegel adopts. Fichte broadens the definition of logical method to include a successive process of resolving contradiction and oppositions.

Whereas Fichte saw the logical development of reason—as had Kant—as largely a process of judgments, however, Hegel reconceives the logical process as one belonging largely to rational concepts themselves. Because Kant had thought of reason's process of development as syllogistic, he centered his model of reason's development in the judgment: judgments such as "everything composite is alterable," for instance, or "all men are mortal." Although Fichte's method of logical development adds the introduction of new concepts—such as the concept of divisibility, as we have just seen—his method is largely still centered in the judgment. Fichte characterizes the original self, for instance, as the judgment or proposition "A is A," or "A = A." He defines the not-self with the proposition "not-A is not equal to A." Fichte also defines the self which resolves the contradiction between the original self and the not-self as a proposition, namely, the proposition "A in part = not-A, and vice versa." Hegel, by contrast, places the contradiction within rational concepts themselves. For Hegel, every rational concept contains contradiction as part of its definition. Moreover, the contradiction within a concept is resolved, not by a new judgment, as it was for Fichte—even if that new judgment included a new concept as well—but by the introduction of a new concept or the redefinition of the concept in question. Hegel's logical development is centered in concepts, rather than judgments.

Hegel uses the contradiction or opposition that he suggests is within rational concepts themselves to make reason itself messy. His view that reason is messy, as I suggested in Section II, is what allows him to overcome the tension between a perfect rationality and an imperfect world that had led Plato to exile reason to a separate realm. For Hegel, both the rational concepts themselves and everything in the world that the concepts overgrasp contain oppositions (§48R, §48A). The opposition and contradiction within rational concepts themselves makes it possible for those concepts to be in the world and to overgrasp the contradiction and opposition that is the messiness of the world.

As I suggested in Section II, we can imagine Plato offering an argument to justify exiling the Forms or rational concepts to a separate realm. Take the concept of "human" again, for instance. If the rational universal or the Form of "human" were really in an individual human, then that human would always be a human, and hence would never die. That human would never become "not-human" in any way. We all can see quite plainly, however, that individual human beings do die. Hence they can be at best poor imitations, or imperfect copies of the rational universal or concept of "human." Hegel answers this argument by suggesting that the process of dying is not only in humans themselves, but also in the concept "human" that overgrasps them. Plato's imagined argument assumes that the conceptual universal "human" is fixed and static. Kant showed us, however, that reason is in fact dialectical—its own self-driving activity leads to contradictions. Although Kant had the wrong model of how reason develops—through syllogisms—and offered a flawed solution to reason's dialectical nature, Hegel might say, Kant's view that reason itself is dialectical provides the key to responding to Plato's argument. Reason's dialectical nature allows it to contain contradictions and oppositions and therefore overgrasp a messy world.

If we say, for instance, that the concept of "human" is fixed and unmoving, or contains only the positive elements of "human," then a human who dies and hence includes negativity or the not-human elements would not properly instantiate the concept of "human." At best, he or she would be imperfect, as Plato's imagined argument claims. In fact, however, it is not just the existing human, but also the concept of "human" itself that contains negation, Hegel argued. Plato's model treats "human" as if it is a static, purely positive concept, so that only a human who never died would live up to that concept. The properly rational view, however, is that the true definition of the concept of "human" includes negativity. It contains its negation within it, so that a human being's mortality is part of the very concept of what it is to be human. A human being is not a human who then has mortality attached to him or her as an accident. Rather, to be a human is just to be a human that is mortal. A human's nothingness is thus part of both his or her reality and his or her ideality, definition or concept as "human" (§81A1, see also §92A). Rational concepts themselves contain negation, opposition or contradiction.

This idea is defended in the "Doctrine of Being" in the logic. There, Hegel suggests that every concept and everything in the world contains its negation within it. He uses the concept translated as "Being-in-itself" to capture the basic idea of reality. Everything that has a character is a Being-in-itself. The concept of Being-in-itself is defined in relation to its negation or other. It has a character by being connected to its negation as part of its own definition. Moreover, every Being-in-itself in reality, too, is defined, or gets what character it has, by having negation as part of its definition. Hence, both the concept "human" and real humans, too, contain their own negation or (in the case of the real human beings) their deaths within them. The concepts and realities include their negation within them as part of their definition or determination. The "not-human" defines not only the concept but real human beings too. Having negation within them is what gives them a rudimentary determination or character at all. Concepts and human beings are something at all because they contain negation.

Because "negation" is such an unspecified term, there are several ways something gets its character or is defined by "negation." First, concepts are defined by negation as a general account of how things are differentiated from one another. I can tell there is a computer on my desk here, because the computer only extends so far. It is stopped by this other thing, the desk. The desk is opposed to it. Hence the computer is defined by, or limited by, the desk. It gets its identity as a singular item in opposition to the desk. This opposition appears in the concept of computer as a contradiction: the concept of computer has its negation within it in the sense that it gets its identity or limit in opposition to the "not-computer." "Computer" gets what character it has by containing its opposition—the "not-computer"—within it. In the example, the desk would be the "not-computer" which helps to define the computer as what it is. Hence, not only the reality, but the ideality or concepts themselves contain oppositions or contradictions. Notice that, if there were not such oppositions in reality, then we would be unable to distinguish one item from the next. Reality would consist of one whole block of indistinguishable [blank]. I use a blank here because this block would have no character, no distinguishing characteristics. We would be unable to say what it is. Just as reality requires negation for things to be defined, so concepts or ideality require negation for them to be defined.

"Negation" is also a reference to death and destruction. Everything in the finite world of ordinary stuff in our everyday lives is a "Being-there," and so is defined in a way that includes negation. But things are not just defined against other things outside of them that are not-them, as they were in the example of the computer above. Rather, as we saw in the "humans are mortal" example, things have their nothingness within them in a way that forecasts a change in the quality of the thing involved. Everything is bound, one way or another, to be negated. Everything changes into an opposition. Living things die, rocks are ground into sand, a book mildews to nothing and so on. We can see these processes as living fulfillment of the basic fact that, for Hegel, all Being-theres contain contradiction: they are something and also nothing. As mortal, a human being is both human and "not-human," a rock is rock and "not-rock," a book is book and "not-book." The nebulousness of the term "negation" leaves open how these changes might occur—dying, being ground up, mildewing etc. are all processes that bring to fruition the conceptual truth of things, namely, that their very determinations contain "negation." It's because the concepts themselves contain negation that we see these sorts of processes of death and decay in the natural world.

Finally, the nebulousness of "negation" also allows Hegel to use his notion of Being-there to capture the physical motion of things. To return to an example Hegel apparently used in a lecture, a planet has its principle of nothing or "negation" in it, and this negation is exhibited when it moves (§81A1). The movement is a fulfillment of the contradiction that is at the heart of the planet's very definition or concept as a "planet," which also includes negation: planet-over-here is also not-planet-over-here. As planet-over-there it fulfills its conceptual, ideal or inherent negation or contradiction. Planet-over-here brings its otherness or opposition into existence as planet-over-there. Reason's dialectical nature allows concepts to account for physical motion, and shows that reason really is, as I put it earlier, the moving principle of the world.

Thus, for Hegel, reason is dialectical. It contains contradictions insofar as its concepts contain opposition within them, and this opposition allows reason to overgrasp a messy world of contradiction, opposition and change.

Dialectical reason contains three moments: (1) the moment of the understanding, (2) the dialectical or negatively rational moment, and (3) the speculative, or positively rational moment (§§79-82). The moment of the understanding is the moment of fixity, and mirrors the kind of rationality that Kant had in mind. It is the moment when rationality fixes on things and says what they are. It is the moment that allows things to have a character, even though they are bound to change. It is the moment that says the rock is a rock, or the man is a man. The dialectical moment or negatively rational moment is the moment at which the moment of fixity falls apart. It is Kant's dialectical moment—the moment during which reason comes to its contradictions. It is the moment involved in the argument imagined for Plato above—the moment during which reason realizes that the man is also bound to be not-man or to die. Finally, the speculative or positively rational moment is the moment at which reason fixes on the result of this process—a new moment, during which reason overgrasps both of the earlier moments. The speculative moment is the moment during which reason understands, for example, that the concept "man" overgrasps a man with his mortality, that the concept "planet" overgrasps a planet with its motion, and so on (§§79-82).

As we go through the process of development in the logic, each of these moments will come into play. Some conceptual stopping points will be a moment of fixity, in which reason fixes on the nature of something. Some moments will be moments of negation, in which reason judges that the something is bound to be negated. And some conceptual stopping points will be moments of speculation, which include both of the earlier sides. These three moments describe the development process of dialectical reason in general terms. To see more of what dialectics is like, however, we will simply have to dive in to the process of development itself, which we do in Chapter Two.

Notes

1. See any edition of Hume's *An Enquiry Concerning Human Understanding* (1748), Section 6.

2. References to the *Encyclopaedia Logic* will henceforth appear simply as parenthetical section references—such as "(§44)" or "(§24A1)"—without mentioning the *Encylopaedia*. References to the *Science of Logic* will be specifically indicated.

3. I am grateful to William Pohle for this example (and for many other suggestions).

4. The German word "*Geist*" (spirit) or "*geistlich*" (spiritual) is notoriously difficult to translate into English. Although it can mean "ghost" and "spirit" in the more supernatural sense, it also refers to much more earthly matters—to mind, intellect, intelligence, wit, morale (as in the French "*esprit*" ["*esprit de corps*," for example]) and imagination. For Hegel, because the rational universals are in things themselves, they are not merely physical, but they are certainly not supernatural either. They are thoughts, concepts, not supernatural beings.

5. Hegel will ultimately offer an additional argument against Kant's concept of the Thing-in-itself during the course of the logic. Hegel is able to attack Kant's Thing-in-itself, as we've seen here, because Kant's view implies that the Thing-in-itself is not just

an unfiltered thing, but the real thing, the true thing—in contrast with our experience, which is of mere appearance. Kant's Thing-in-itself has another implied attribute, however, that Hegel also uses to attack Kant's view. The Thing-in-itself is supposed to be the force behind the mere appearance: it, as Thing-in-itself, pushes out the appearances that we experience. In other words, Kant's Thing-in-itself is supposed to produce—in some sense—the appearances that we experience through our filters. This implication gives Hegel another angle of attack against Kant's Thing-in-itself, which we will encounter in his discussion of the concepts of force and utterance, which I take up in Chapter Three.

6. I owe this diagram of the "circle of circles" to Béla Egyed, who drew it for the class when I was an undergraduate at Carleton University in Ottawa, Ontario, and who may well have planted the seed for the idea that the rest of the logic could be diagramed as well.

7. I am grateful to Allen Wood for pointing out this parallel between Kant's categories and Hegel's logical concepts.

8. Gustav E. Mueller reaches the same conclusion and traces the history of the "myth" that Hegel employed the "thesis-antithesis-synthesis" logical triad in "The Hegel Legend of 'Thesis-Antithesis-Synthesis'" (1958).

Chapter Two
The Doctrine of Being

I. Introduction

In this chapter, we begin the journey of "picturing" Hegel's logic. Picturing his logic will show that Hegel's logic is a real logic, driven by necessity from steps to conclusions. As I suggested in Chapter One, while contemporary logic is centered around claims or propositions, Hegel's logic is centered around concepts. We will be able to see the step-by-step development of the logic in what we might call the "grammar" of the diagrams. In the diagrams, concepts are typically represented by circles or what I will call "bubbles"; and processes or logical actions are represented by arrows. Often, a concept will be represented by a combination of bubbles and arrows. The diagrams reveal the systematic way in which concepts and processes are introduced by Hegel, as bubbles and arrows are added to the diagrams bit by bit. Each diagram develops into the next diagram with the addition of some small move. The step-by-step development is particularly evident in this chapter, because the concepts we will be working with—and the diagrams needed to represent them—will be fairly simple. We will see Hegel develop several logical moves that he will reuse periodically throughout the logic. We will also begin to see what sort of necessity drives us from stage to stage. Because the diagrams bring out the systematic, necessary development of the logic, they literally allow us to "picture" the logic of Hegel's logic.

The "Doctrine of Being" outlines the logical concepts that are "behind the back" (see Chapter One, Section VII) of the world of immediate being. They are "behind the back" of the world of immediate being because the concepts introduced in this section of the logic are presupposed by our ordinary judgments about the world we experience around us. One of the concepts introduced in this section, for instance, is the concept of "degree." Although we may not talk very much about the concept of degree, it is "behind the back" of many of the things we do talk about. When we talk about temperature, for instance, we presuppose that we understand what it means for something to have a certain degree. "Degree" is a quantitative concept—since it has to do with numerical relationships—that is presupposed by our ordinary judgments about temperature. Because the concept of "degree" is presupposed by the concept or subject of temperature, we could also say that it is "behind the back" of our judgments about temperature. "Being" is Hegel's term for the ordinary world of sense experience, hence the "Doctrine of Being" introduces and defines concepts that are "behind the back" of our judgments about the ordinary, sensory world in the way in which the concept of "degree" is "behind the back" of our judgments about temperature.

Hegel divides this section of the logic into three types of logical concepts: concepts that are "behind the back" of our judgments about the qualities of things, concepts that are "behind the back" of our judgments about the quantities of things, and concepts that involve a combination of both quality and quantity. These three types of concepts give this first section of the logic three subsections: the "Doctrine of Quality," the "Doctrine of Quantity," and the "Doctrine of Measure." Hegel uses the term "measure" to refer to concepts in which quality and quantity are combined. When we make judgments about "ice," for instance, we are making judgments that presuppose a certain combination of quality and quantity. "Ice" is water that is hard—and hence has a certain quality—because it is at a certain degree of temperature—and hence presupposes a certain quantity (namely, the quantity or degree of temperature).

Hegel draws many of the concepts that appear in this section of the logic from his understanding of the early history of philosophy, particularly the Presocratic philosophers. As we saw in Chapter One, Hegel held that the history of human beings is a history of coming to understand reason better and better. The history of philosophy in particular tells the story of how humans have come to understand more and more fully the basic concepts of reason—i.e. logic. Thus, for Hegel, the historical development of philosophy roughly parallels the development of logic, even if some logical stages are absent from the history of philosophy. As he puts it, "though the development of Philosophy in history must correspond to the development of logical philosophy, there will still be passages in it [logical philosophy] which are absent in historical development" (*Lectures on the History of Philosophy* 1983, vol. 1, 302).

Hegel shared the widely held belief among Western philosophers of the modern era that the history of philosophy began with the Presocratics. In particular, according to Hegel, philosophy began with the Presocratic philosopher Thales (*Lectures on the History of Philosophy* 1983, vol. 1, 178)). Because the Presocratics come in the beginning of philosophy, and because, for Hegel, the history of philosophy traces the story of the development of logic, many of the concepts in the beginning of the logic correspond to concepts Hegel found in the Presocratics. Hegel credits the Eleatic philosophers, for example, and particularly Parmenides, with introducing the concepts of Being (as the truth and abstract universal), and of non-being or Nothing (*Lectures on the History of Philosophy* 1983, vol. 1, 282, 301-2). According to Parmenides, reality or the world is a unified whole with no motion or change in it. It is a One Being. Motion would require something to move into "the void" or nothing, but by definition the void or nothing cannot exist. Therefore, motion is impossible.

Hegel credits Heraclitus with introducing the concept of Becoming (*Lectures on the History of Philosophy* 1983, vol. 1, 283, 302). Heraclitus suggested that the world is constantly in flux, changing, or becoming. Notice that Parmenides actually wrote after Heraclitus and took himself to be criticizing Heraclitus. In the logic, however, as we'll see, the concepts of "Being" and "Nothing" come before the concept of "Becoming." Thus, there is apparently another way in which the history of philosophy does not map neatly on to the course of the logic. Not only are there some gaps or missing concepts from the history of philosophy, as Hegel suggested in the quotation above, but also concepts are apparently sometimes developed out of logical order in the history of philosophy. The philosopher who introduced the concept of "Becoming" came before the one who introduced the concepts of "Being" and "Nothing."

Hegel credits the Presocratic philosopher Leucippus for introducing the concept of Being-for-itself, and of the One as a Being-for-itself (*Lectures on the History of Philosophy* 1983, vol. 1, 302). Leucippus tried to reestablish the legitimacy of change, motion and the multiplicity of the world—which was called into question by Parmenides and Zeno of Elea—by suggesting that combinations of atoms or unchanging beings produce the higher-level changes that we see in the world. Whereas Parmenides had simply rejected the multiplicity of the world in favor of its unity or Being, we can see Leucippus' philosophy as an attempt to sort out the puzzles of "the one and the many" posed by the apparent fact that the world contains both unity and multiplicity at the same time. Occasionally, the parallels between Hegel's understanding of the Presocratics and of logic will help us to explain these early sections of the logic, and in those cases I will make use of these parallels in my explanations.

The unconditioned as a set of bubbles:

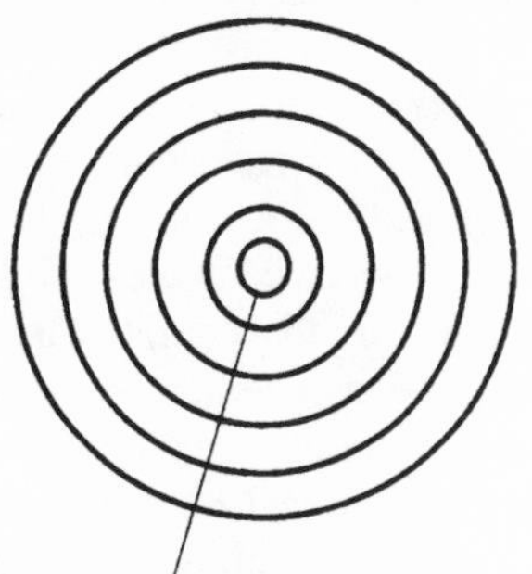

The beginning of the logic: the simplest and emptiest concept

Figure 2.1

To see how Hegel opens his logic, we must keep in mind where he wants the logic to end up. As we saw in Chapter One, Hegel is trying to develop the unconditioned—the all-encompassing concept that contains everything else, and outside of which there is nothing (see Chapter One, Section V). That unconditioned will be Reason itself, which, for Hegel, overgrasps everything else. In the "grammar" of the diagrams, we can think of the unconditioned as a big bubble containing all other possible bubbles within it

We can also think of Reason

three-dimensionally as a funnel. If you look at it from the top it will look like the diagram above, but if you look at it from the side, it would look like a funnel, with the simplest concept at the bottom point of the funnel, and Reason itself, as the all-encompassing concept, at the mouth of the funnel. We could then picture Reason three-dimensionally like this:

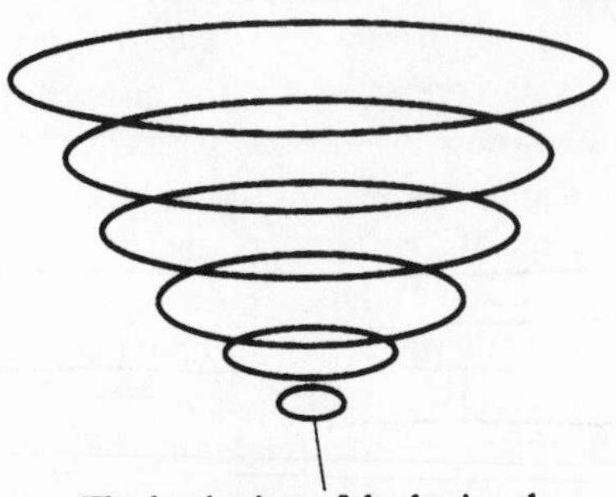

Figure 2.2

The logic only develops a certain subset of the concepts of Reason, namely, the concepts that have to do with logic. There are other concepts that are developed in other subject matters (see Chapter One, Section VII). Nevertheless, the logic has the same basic structure that the rest of the project has. Like the whole project, we can picture it two-dimensionally as a big bubble with a bunch of smaller bubbles in it or, three-dimensionally, as a funnel with the simplest concept at the bottom and the largest, logical concept at the mouth of the funnel.

Hegel begins his logic with the smallest or simplest bubble, with the point of the funnel. Because the highest concept of logic encompasses all other logical concepts, Hegel could have begun his discussion anywhere. Middle and mid-sized bubbles would already presuppose the bubbles they have in them. Later rings in the funnel presuppose the earlier rings. If Hegel started with a middle bubble, so long as the smaller bubbles it contained were properly understood, he could begin to develop the rest of the logical process there. Hegel apparently suggested in one lecture, for example, that it would have been especially attractive to begin with the concept of "the Concept," since it is the unity and the truth of the two main earlier concepts, the concept of "Being," which is covered in the "Doctrine of Being," and the concept of "Essence," which is covered in the "Doctrine of Essence" (§159A). (The concept of "the Concept" is developed in the third subdivision of the Logic, namely, the "Doctrine of the Concept.") Because "the Concept" is the unity of "Being" and "Essence," however, it contains the complex bubbles of "Being" and "Essence" within it. As Hegel suggests, as soon as he defined "the Concept" as the unity of "Being" and "Essence," he would have to explain what "Being" and "Essence" are. Without the developed logical background that he supplies in earlier parts of the logic, more than likely we would employ inappropriate definitions for these concepts drawn from ordinary, representational thought (see §159A). Such definitions would contain emotional or empirical elements that would be irrelevant to a proper philosophical understanding (see the Introduction). Beginning with the simplest, emptiest concept allows Hegel to develop and define earlier concepts so that later concepts, such as the concept of "the Concept," will be properly understood (see §159A).

Because Hegel begins his logic with the smallest concept at the point of the funnel, the image of the funnel illustrates the entire course of the logic. The course of the logic will involve moving from ring to ring or bubble to bubble from the simplest concept at the point of the funnel to the largest concept at the mouth of the funnel. This image is a bit simplistic, but it is worth keeping in mind as an overall, approximate picture of the logical development.

For Hegel, the simplest concept lacks a content, character or determination. To be determined or to have a determination is simply to have a character. Something is determined when it has some quality or character, or when some quality or character can be ascribed to it. The simplest concept, for Hegel, lacks a quality, character or determination, however. The bubble and funnel diagrams illustrate this idea because they depict the smallest and simplest bubble as empty. As the innermost bubble, it contains no other bubbles. A concept that is determined or has a character, by contrast, would be depicted as a bubble with something inside it. The emptiness of the bubble for the simplest concept represents the idea that the simplest concept has no content: since the bubble is empty, it is empty of character or content. Later concepts, by contrast, are defined or get their characters by including concepts that have appeared earlier during the logical process of development. As we move up the funnel toward the highest concept, the bubbles are defined by the smaller bubbles that we have passed; bigger bubbles are defined by the smaller bubbles that they contain. Since the smallest bubble has no bubbles within it, however, it lacks a content. As we will see, the first concept gets what character or definition it has, Hegel says, not from what it is like, but from "what is meant."

Because later concepts contain earlier concepts that define them, Hegel says that these later concepts are concrete—a sense of concreteness which he distinguishes from our ordinary understanding of concreteness. We generally think of concreteness as having to do with the real, physical world. A subject matter such as philosophy is abstract because it deals only with concepts, whereas psychology or biology are more concrete because they apply to the real world. For similar reasons, we usually think of sensation as concrete—because it deals with the physical world—and conceptual thought as abstract (see §85A). For Hegel, however, concepts are themselves concrete, because they have the earlier concepts to define them. Concepts are "filled up," to use the bubble metaphor for a moment, with the other concepts that define them, and hence are not abstract or empty. In one of his lectures, for example, he apparently described the concept of "Becoming"—which is the third concept we will meet in the "Doctrine of Being"—as the first genuinely concrete concept (§88A). As we will see, "Becoming" relies on the two earlier concepts that precede it for its character. Those two earlier concepts define it and hence make it concrete.

Although there can only be one smallest bubble, it is defined by two concepts, which give rise to the two separate stages that open Hegel's logic. First, the empty, smallest bubble is "Being." "Being" is the concept of this empty bubble taken as, or treated as, having presence. But because the bubble lacks a content (it is empty), however, it can also be taken as, or treated as, nothing, or as absence. Something with no content or character can be just as much nothing as it is something. "Nothing" is thus the second concept that may be applied to the simplest, empty bubble. With the concepts of "Being" and "Nothing" to start us off, the development of the "Doctrine of Being" begins.

In the "Doctrine of Being," the primary dialectical relationship that concepts have with one another involves "passing over into another" (§84). Concepts are defined by passing into their others. In the diagrams, this passing-into is represented by one-way arrows. But the logical relationships that emerge in the "Doctrine of Being" are more complex than this simple characterization suggests. We will review at the end of this chapter some of the dominant logical relationships—or syntactic patterns—that emerge.

I will be giving the different stages names: "Being," "Nothing," "Spurious Infinity," "Number," "Degree," "Ratio," and so on. Many of the names of stages are drawn directly from Hegel's text. In many places, Hegel describes some logical process, says that the result "is" some term or concept—such as "becoming," "being-there, "limit," and so on—and highlights the term. In §88, for instance, he describes a way in which "Being" and "Nothing" can be taken to be a unity, and then says "this unity is *becoming*" (emphasis his). In cases like this, I have named the logical stage after the term or concept that Hegel himself has highlighted. Indeed, wherever possible, I have used Hegel's own terms or concepts to name the stages. These names are important, because Hegel chooses them purposely to suggest that he is providing definitions of the concepts in question. The stage of "Number" in the "Doctrine of Quantity," for instance, is not only a stage in the logic but is also supposed to provide a logical definition of the concept of number. Hegel intends his logic to provide what he takes to be the correct definitions of many traditional philosophical concepts. The terms and concepts that he associates with individual stages of the logic often tell us what concept he takes himself to be defining in that particular stage. Sometimes, however, Hegel provides no clear indication in his text for which particular concept or term he is defining. In those cases, I have provided my own name for a stage, but I always draw on Hegel's text for the name that I use.

Note that, for both simplicity and brevity, I will not put quotation marks around the names of concepts that define stages of the logic from now on: the stage and concept of "Being" will become Being, for example. Readers will be able to recognize the names of stages by the use of capital letters. I will also remove quotation marks from references to the titles of Hegel's sections and sub-sections: the "Doctrine of Being" will become the Doctrine of Being, for example.

II. The Doctrine of Quality

Being

Figure 2.3

Being is the concept of bare presence. It includes no determinations of any kind, and therefore has no nature, or qualities of any sort. I represent it with a dashed line at this point because it has as of yet no content, quality or character, and hence is not really an "entity" at all, but only a shadow, so to speak.

Nothing

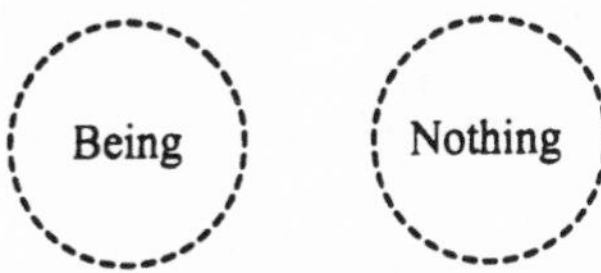

Figure 2.4

Because Being has no character, determination, quality, or nature, it is just as much Nothing as it is Being. This second concept is logically implied by or generated out of the thought of Being by considering the nature of Being more precisely. The concept of Nothing is not a completely new idea, but rather a conclusion drawn about the concept of Being. Both Being and Nothing have the same empty content, since neither has any determinations. The only difference between them is what is meant (§87). Being is meant as pure presence, Nothing is meant as pure absence. Nothing, too, is an empty shadow, and is represented in the diagram with a dashed outline.

Hegel is providing what he takes to be the proper logical definition of the philosophical concepts of being and nothing. The basic, logical definition of the term Being is bare presence, and of Nothing is bare absence. Hegel credits the Presocratic philosopher Parmenides for having introduced these concepts (see the Introduction to this chapter). Parmenides suggested that the world is One Being, with no motion or change in it. Parmenides distinguished that world from "the void" or nothing, which, as nothing, cannot exist. If the world is a solid chunk with no change or motion in it, however, Hegel is suggesting, then it has no character, no qualities, no determination. A chunk with no distinctions in it has no distinction, character, determination. It is an indistinguishable chunk, which is simply taken to be present, and is opposed only to an indistinguishable chunk which is taken to be nothing or absent. Parmenides' One Being and void correspond to the way he has defined the concepts of Being or Nothing here.

The term translated as "meant" is the German verb "*meinen*." "*Meinen*" means "to mean." But it also means "to opine." In the history of Western philosophy, opinion is often contrasted with knowledge, where knowledge has an objective basis, while opinion is regarded as subjective guesswork that has no objective basis at all. Hegel's use of the term "*meinen*" thus suggests both that the difference between Being and Nothing is what is meant, and that the ascription of this difference has no objective basis, or no basis in the nature of the logical terms themselves. And in fact, the character of the two concepts really is the same: they both lack character, or lack a content. Thus, there is no difference in character between the two concepts on which the distinction between Being and Nothing could be based. The distinction between them lacks a foundation in the nature of the concepts themselves, and Hegel's use of the term "*meinen*" draws our attention to this fact.

With Being and Nothing, the speculative process of reason has generated its first contradiction or opposition (see Chapter One, Section VIII for a discussion of the role contradiction plays in Hegel's logic, as well as discussion of the understanding and the dialectical moment). When the understanding tried to fix the definition of Being, Being was just as much Nothing, and the dialectical moment generated the concept of Nothing. The understanding is the faculty of reason that is responsible for fixing the characters or definitions of things (see the Introduction to the book). When the understanding tried to fix the character of Being, Being had no character, and so was just as much Nothing as it was Being. Reason thus generates the first pair of contradictory or opposed concepts.

We have now said all we can about each concept on its own. But the concepts remain undefined. Neither Being nor Nothing has a determination, character, definition or content. Since the goal of logic is to understand or define logical concepts, the course of the logic has hit an impasse with our current logical strategy. There is nothing more that can be said about each of these concepts by itself. We have exhausted the strategy of defining them each on their own. Because the goal of logic has not yet been achieved, however, we are driven to say more, to move beyond this logical impasse.

There is only one way in which the logic can move forward from this point: it must characterize the two concepts together. Being and Nothing are both the same empty thought with a difference merely in what is meant. Because neither Being nor Nothing has a content, their content cannot be combined into a new concept. Instead, they can be put together in the same thought only as a concept of the same, one, empty concept, first taken one way—as presence (Being)—then taken the other way—as absence (Nothing)—then taken the first way again—as presence—and so on. Thus, the logic can proceed only by generating the thought of an endless flipping back and forth between an empty concept taken as presence, and the same empty concept taken as absence. This is precisely how Hegel will define Becoming in the next stage.

We are beginning to get a glimpse of what Hegel means when he promises that the movement from step to step in his logic is necessary. We will characterize this necessity more precisely as we go along, and we will have to see if Hegel can make good on his promise throughout the logical development. However, the move from Being to Nothing to Becoming suggests that his concept of necessity is in large part a concept of exhaustion. When the logical elements in play have been exhausted under one strategy, then a new strategy must be found to move forward. Here, the logic began by defining Being and Nothing each on their own. When that strategy was exhausted, however—when there was nothing further that could be said about Being and Nothing on their own—a logical impasse was reached. A new strategy has to be found to move forward. The new strategy involves characterizing Being and Nothing together, rather than each by itself. This new strategy is necessary because all other options under the old strategy have been exhausted while the goal of defining the logical concepts has not yet been achieved. Moreover, the particular strategy introduced is necessitated as the only possible way of moving forward. There are only two elements in play: Being and Nothing. Each has been completely defined on its own, so that strategy is finished. Moreover, again, neither Being nor Nothing have a character or content, so their characters cannot be combined to form a new concept. Instead, all that can be done is to think of the same empty concept that is at the heart of both of them, first meant as presence (Being) and then meant as absence (Nothing). Hence, the next step follows necessarily as the only remaining option when other options have all been exhausted (see §88R1).

Becoming

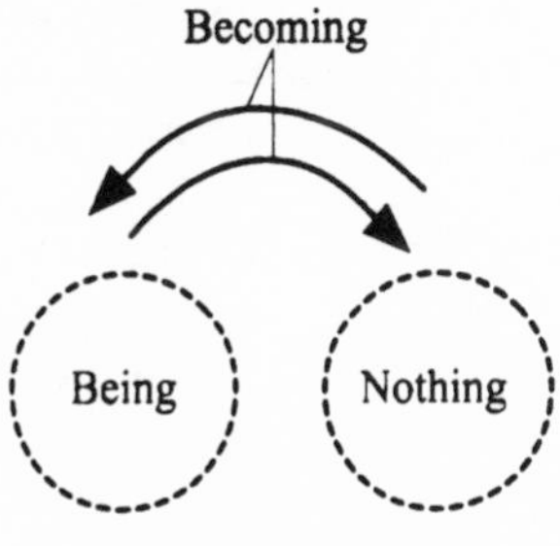

Figure 2.5

Becoming is the concept that captures the only way of thinking about Being and Nothing taken together. Being and Nothing are both the same empty thought taken one way, as presence, and then the other, as absence. Becoming is the concept of a flipping-back-and-forth process between the same empty thought taken as presence and the same empty thought taken as absence. It is the concept of bare presence (Being) becoming bare absence (Nothing)—the process of passing-away—and of bare absence (Nothing) becoming bare presence (Being)—the process of coming to be—and vice versa. It is the thought of flipping back and forth between Being and Nothing.

Hegel credits the Presocratic philosopher Heraclitus with having introduced the concept of Becoming (see the Introduction to this chapter). Hegel's concept of Becoming is a concept of constant flux without stasis: to Become is to be constantly flipping back and forth between Being and Nothing. It is not clear that Heraclitus actually held that the world is constantly in flux, and therefore not clear that Hegel has interpreted him fairly. Heraclitus may have held, instead, that there are higher levels of stasis that grow out of flux—in the way that a river is a kind of stasis that depends on the constant movement of water. Hegel's concept of Becoming, however, is a concept of constant flux, even if Heraclitus did not conceive of the world in that way. It is opposed to Parmenides' claim that the world was a constant stasis

Hegel apparently suggested that the concept of Becoming is the first *concrete* concept in the logic (§88A). Being and Nothing are abstract concepts, rather than concrete ones. Becoming is the first concrete concept because, unlike Being and Nothing, it has a determination or character. It is defined by the concepts of Being and Nothing—they give it the conceptual character that it has. When I first began drawing Hegel's logic, I drew Becoming as a bubble, with Being and Nothing as smaller bubbles within it, in an attempt to follow out the metaphorical idea that concepts are concrete because they are "filled" with earlier concepts. However, depicting Becoming as a bubble with Being and Nothing in it would be misleading. For, although Becoming does have what character it has because of Being and Nothing, it is not a static concept—which depicting it as a bubble might suggest. Rather, Becoming is a process—the process of going back and forth between Being and Nothing—that is better represented with arrows. To become is to go from nothing to being. A person becomes, for example, when he or she goes from nothing to being, or is born. To become is also to go from being to nothing. A person also becomes, for example, when he or she dies, and thereby goes from Being to Nothing. In general, to become is to undergo a process: a process of going from nothing to being, or being to nothing. Moreover, Hegel himself cautions us that Becoming is not a genuine unity (§88R4), by which he means that Becoming does not sublate (in his technical sense of *aufheben*) Being and Nothing—it does not swallow them up or replace them as a higher-order concept. Being and Nothing remain independent of Becoming. Indeed, as we'll see in the next step, Being and Nothing reassert their independence from Becoming right away. Because Becoming as a concept is a process and never absorbs Being and Nothing, it is better depicted as arrows, rather than as a bubble that contains Being and Nothing. Still, Becoming is a concrete concept in the sense that it has a character or definition, which it gets from the fact that its definition piggy-backs on, and hence includes, the concepts of Being and Nothing.[1]

Because Becoming involves an endless process of flipping back and forth between Being and Nothing, it is unstable. To become is, on the one hand, to go from Nothing to Being, but once the process is over, the concept that grasps the situation is Being, not Becoming. To become is also, on the other hand, to go from Being to Nothing, but once the process is over, the concept needed to grasp the situation is Nothing, not Becoming. Becoming never gets to be the defining concept of either moment of stasis. It defines the process, but it never defines the end of the process. Over the course of the process of Becoming, there is no stasis, no moment of conceptual fixity: the *process* is defined by *both* "is" (Being) and "is-not" (Nothing). The *moment of stasis*, by contrast, is defined *either* by the "is" (Being) or by the "is-not" (Nothing). Thus, in the moment of stasis, Becoming itself dies out or disappears (§89A). The end of a process of becoming is never Becoming itself, but always Being or Nothing.

Nevertheless, the process of Becoming has had an impact on Being and Nothing. It has changed the definitions of Being and Nothing—a change that we draw out in the next stages. The process of flipping back and forth between Being and Nothing implies that Being and Nothing are *connected* with one another. The next several stages draw out the implications of this new-found connection for each of the bubbles involved, and so we now turn our attention back to the individual bubbles, which are still independent but also now connected with one another.[2]

Being-there

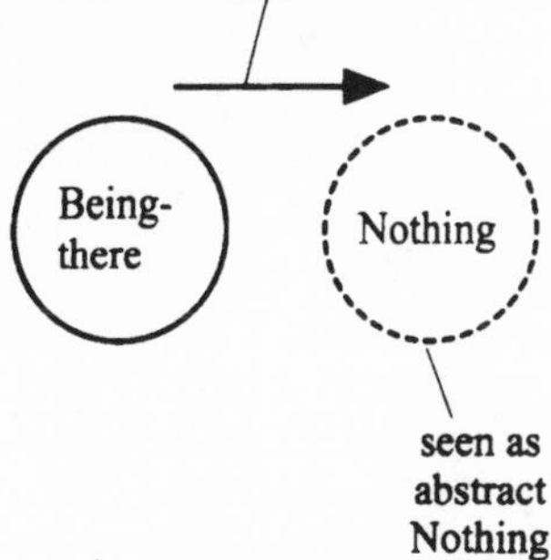
Being-there is Being that is posited as or characterized by negation (§92) or Nothing. It is defined in terms of its ability to become Nothing
Being-there
Nothing
seen as abstract Nothing

Figure 2.6

One side of the process of Becoming now comes into view, namely the process of passing-away, or of going from Being to Nothing. We draw out the logical implications of the movement of passing-away, or of going from Being to Nothing. (We will see later why this process has to come into view first, before the process of coming to be, or of going from Nothing to Being.) In the process of Becoming, the concept of Being was connected to the concept of Nothing when it turned out that Being could become Nothing. So we now have to go back to redefine Being to take account of this connection. Being-there is Being now defined as a Being-that-could-become-nothing. Being-there is a presence that can pass into nothing—a something that is alterable as such, or whose quality is this mutability. Being-there is Being now defined as what-could-be-nothing. It expresses Hegel's basic idea that something can be there only in relation to nothing. The concept of Being-there thus draws out and captures the definition of Being that was implied by the last stage. Because it draws out the implications of the last stage, it is logically implied by that last stage. Being-there is Being that is posited as, or taken as, Nothing, which is to say that Being-there is defined in terms of its ability to become Nothing. Moreover, because Being-there is now thought of as something with a character or determination of its own (§90), I have given its bubble a solid outline.

This is Hegel's first account of a concept of determination. Being now has a rudimentary character—or quality—that allows it to at least be there. The type of determination that Being-there has is that it has a quality.

With Being-there we see the first occurrence of a common syntactic pattern in Hegel's logic: something that is at first hinted at, but cannot yet be posited or grasped because it does not yet have a character on its own, later becomes a solid, independent concept by taking on a character of its own. So Being first appeared as concept without a real character (which I represented by making its bubble dashed), but now, as Being-there, is truly there or posited because it has a character of its own (which I represent by making its bubble solid).

Hegel says that Being-there is the genuine unity of Being and Nothing, though it is a one-sided unity (§88R4). Being-there unifies Being and Nothing because being able to pass into Nothing gives Being a new definition that is now genuinely defined as presence. Something is genuinely present when its absence is a real possibility for it. Before, Being was merely meant or supposed presence. Now, however, Being-there defines genuine presence or thereness because it could be Nothing. Moreover, Being-there has a rudimentary determination or character. It is Being that now has enough of a character to at least be there: Being-there as a concept has a character because it could be nothing. Because the Being-side is now defined in a way that involves the concept of Nothing, it is no longer independent of Nothing. But the unity achieved by Being-there is a one-sided unity, since Nothing is still "an outsider" for it. Being-there *could be* Nothing, but that does not mean that it is in fact Nothing: its being Nothing is merely an abstract possibility for it. Being-there and Nothing thus remain independent concepts because of the one-sidedness of the unity achieved by Being-there. The diagram depicts this independence because Being-there and Nothing remain separate bubbles in this stage.

Being-there expresses Hegel's idea that determination or definition is rooted in negation. In general, to be there—to have enough of a character or determination to be there—is to be able to be nothing. To be there—to have any character at all—is to be able to have none. Being-there is a basic concept of determination: it is a basic concept of having a character, quality or determination. Moreover, it gets this definition, or is determined as a concept, by the same process that it says determines everything else. Put another way, syntax is semantics: the logical process both produces Being-there (syntactically) and defines what it means (semantically) as a concept. Being-there itself, as a concept, is determined by the presence of and its ability to be Nothing, or negation; and it means or says that everything or anything, in general, is determined by the ability to be Nothing. Everything is determined through negation (see §91A). How Being-there is defined is how it says everything else is defined too. This marriage between syntax and semantics will extend throughout the logic: the logical processes that give rise to a concept (syntax) also define what the concept means (semantics) as a concept.

Hegel uses the concept of "thereness," which is introduced by Being-there, throughout his work to characterize a "givenness" or determinate (defined, characterized) presence in the finite world of experience. Therenesses are "immediate" in the sense that they are simply found there—they could just as well be nothing, be absent, or not be there. We will see the sort of "givenness" or "thereness" that we have here again, for example, in the stage of Immediate Measure below, which, as immediate, also involves an accidental, "found" connection between, in that case, quality and quantity. When we come upon a chair, for example, we may "find" from an immediate point of view that it has the quality "yellow"—its yellowness is simply given to immediate experience. Because the quality is simply "found" to be there, it is immediate.

Hegel distinguishes such "given" qualities from qualities that have a more intimate connection to the items to which they are supposed to belong because those qualities are part of the concept of the item in question. Qualities that are merely given have an undetermined or accidental connection to the items to which they are supposed to be attached. The yellowness, for example, has no special connection to the chair. The yellowness could be absent—the chair could be red. The yellowness is merely "found" to be on the chair, but has no special connection to the concept of chair. It is attached to the chair in an "immediate" way. Other qualities of the chair, however, such as its legs—though perhaps not an essential quality (there are chairs without legs)—do have a more intimate connection to the concept of "chair." Having legs is more bound-up with the concept of what a chair is: a chair must have some way of "standing," we might say (even bleacher "chairs" that have no legs but are designed to sit directly on the benches have a mechanism that prevents them from rolling backward when you lean against the back, for example) and that is the conceptually necessary function that the legs perform. Whereas the chair has no particular connection to its yellowness, the chair's legs are bound to the concept of the chair itself. The yellowness is a being-there, but the chair's legs represent a higher level of quality, because the connection between the chair and the legs is more intimate. The legs are conceptually bound to the chair. This type of quality—quality that is tied to the concept of the thing—will be developed later.

In the next stage, we draw out the implications of the other side of Becoming, namely the movement of coming-to-be, or of going from the side of absence to presence, or from Nothing to Being-there (since Being has now become Being-there). For logical reasons, the process of coming-to-be had to be considered after the movement of passing away. Unlike the concept of Nothing, the concept of Being cannot be the end or result of a process of becoming. When something passes away, it can become abstract nothing, but something cannot become abstract being. To come-to-be is to come-to-be something in particular, that is, something with a character or determination. The end or result of a process of coming-to-be is always a something—and a something always has a character, a determination. Being is not a something, since it has no determination or character. That's why Being had to be redefined as Being-there before we could consider the process of coming-to-be. Only a Being-there (determinate Being)—and not Being—can be the end of a process of coming-to-be. Coming-to-be is a movement that logically can only apply after Being has become Being-there. Therefore, Hegel had to consider passing-away and coming-to-be in the order in which he does: passing-away had to come before coming-to-be.

So far I have offered one diagram per concept. In the next stage, however, I offer two diagrams for one concept. In some cases, I will offer three or more diagrams per concept. The trouble is that some of Hegel's official concepts contain logical moves that are too complex to represent in a single diagram. The next stage of Being-in-itself, for example, contains a couple of logical moves that can be more clearly represented by two diagrams instead of one. One diagram would have been overly complicated. In this and other cases like it, I stick to the name of a stage given by Hegel's text, but divide up my pictorial representation of the concept into separate diagrams for pictorial convenience. As a result, some stages, such as the next, have more than one diagram associated with them.

Being-in-itself

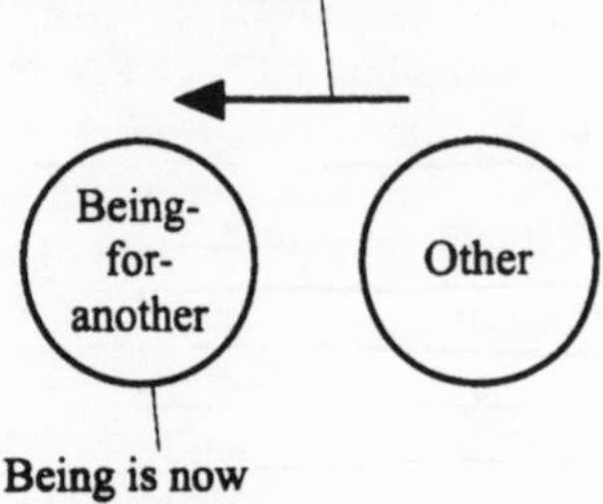
Nothing has Being-there as its negation, so it is determined too: it is determined as the absence of Being-there (or of determinate presence), i.e. as an other.
Being-for-another
Other
Being is now defined by its relation with the Other: it is Being-for-another

Figure 2.7

Nothing has a negation too, however. It has Being-there as its negation. Since having a negation is what gives something a determination or character, Nothing has a character now too (which I represent by giving it a solid-lined bubble). Nothing is not abstract Nothing or abstract absence anymore. It's an absence with a character. In fact, its character is that it's the absence of Being-there, i.e. it's the absence of a determinate presence (which is what Being-there is). Being-there was a determinate thereness (that-there) which could have been abstract Nothing (i.e. gone, where "gone" is abstract absence). Now that Nothing has an identity of its own, it is not just abstract, any-old absence. Instead, it's the absence of Being-there, i.e. of the specific thereness that Being-there has. So if Being-there has yellowness as its given thereness, for example, then Nothing is now determined as the absence of yellow, i.e. other-than-yellow. There are a lot of qualities that are other-than-yellow. Similarly, there are a lot of qualities that are "other" than the quality that Being-there has. So the "other" here is a general sort of other, i.e. otherness-in-general.

Being-there changes too, however. It is no longer a Being-there, or an individualized Being with thereness (a Being with a quality). As the negation of otherness-in-general, Being-there becomes the Being of otherness-in-general. It is Being-for-other, or Being-for-another (*Sein-für-Anderes*). Being the "other" of a general "other" (otherness-in-general) changes Being-there in another way as well. After all, what sort of Being-there is the other of otherness-in-general? Answer: only a generalized Being-there, or Being-thereness in general, has otherness-in-general for its other. As Hegel points out, Being-for-another is an expanse of Being-thereness (§91). The expanse of determinate Being is the other of otherness-in-general.

This stage adds two new incremental steps to the logical development. First, Nothing is redefined in response to the redefinition of Being to Being-there in the last stage: Nothing becomes otherness-in-general. Second, once Nothing is redefined as otherness-in-general, the "other" to which otherness-in-general is opposed must be redefined again. So the side of Being or presence is redefined once again from Being-there to Being-for-another, which is the expanse or realm of Being-thereness. Each incremental logical move is necessitated by the previous step.

My interpretation of the meaning of Being-for-another here reinforces John Burbidge's decision to translate *Dasein* (which Geraets et al. translate as Being-there) as "a being" (Burbidge 1981, 42). Burbidge's translation has useful implications in English. Hegel is moving conceptually from an individualized determinate being (*Dasein*) to a generalized determinate being, or the realm or expanse of determinate being-ness (which comes into view here as *Sein-für-Anderes* and is fully developed later as Being-in-itself). Unfortunately, the term "Being-there" does not make the individualistic implications of *Dasein* clear, whereas Burbidge's translation of *Dasein* as "a being" does.[3]

Although the two sides are defined in relation to one another, they are still distinct from one another, which is represented here by the fact that the two bubbles are still separate. They are each defined by the other side, but they still have only an external connection with one another so that each is outside of the other. Neither side has absorbed the other into its own definition. They are connected, but separate. Later on in the logic, concepts will be connected to other concepts in a way that means that they will not remain separate anymore: concepts will absorb other concepts, which I will depict by putting the bubbles for some concepts *inside* the bubbles for other concepts. Since neither the Being-side nor the Nothing-side of the logical process has absorbed the other side here, however, I continue to depict the two bubbles as separate from one another. We will see how the logical process of absorption works later on.

In this stage we see another syntactic pattern that will be repeated elsewhere in the logic. A concept meant to apply to an individual later embraces or refers to a realm or expanse. In Chapter Two, for example, the concept of Appearance at first refers to individual appearances, but later becomes the whole World of Appearance. The same thing has happened here: a being or a Being-there has become the realm of Beingness-for-other. At this point, the syntactic movement is conceptually important. Thereness is always individualized. Only individual things have being-thereness. If someone offered us a plate of apples, we can never take "apple," we can only ever take *an* apple. An apple is there only as an individual. A being has thereness, but for-anotherness is the quality of the whole expanse of Being-thereness. The expanse of thereness has the general characteristic of being-there-for-an-other, or of Being-for-another. To be there, in general, is to be for another. Therefore, Being-for-anotherness does indeed apply to the whole expanse of Being-there, as Hegel suggests (§91).

Hegel uses the concept of "*for another*" throughout his works. Items in the finite world of being are "for another." In general, determinate beings in the finite world point toward their others, or imply the presence of an other. It is this "pointing-toward-another" feature of determinate being which gives it a character. Otherwise, Being would be a whole expanse of indeterminable presence.

Imagine a kind of indeterminate space. If we wave our hands generally in the air, and imagine that there are no individual spatial items that we can pick out, we get an idea of what indeterminate space would be like for the visual field. Indeterminate space would be empty air-space. Determining that space—filling it up with spatial objects that give it a character—points beyond itself. This printer, for example, which determines some of the space in front of me, points beyond itself. Its determination as spatially limited implies that there is an "other" outside of it, namely, the space that is not-the-printer. The printer's space is determined in relation to an other outside of it which is not-the-determination. Determinate being has the same general feature. As soon as being is determined, it points beyond itself to an other. This general characteristic of determinate being is captured by the concept of for-anotherness. Of course, we have to be careful with spatial examples at this point, since space is a quantitative concept, and we have not yet logically developed the quantitative concepts (see Hegel 1969, 110). From a qualitative point of view—which is where we are now—indeterminate presence would be an expanse of presence for which we could not pick out any qualities—no color, texture or qualitative characterization of any sort.

Determinate beings are also "for another" in a third way, however, that is more closely related to our usual understanding of "reality." The full nature of reality will be developed in the next diagram, but for-anotherness is a vital piece. We distinguish between mere intentions and intentions that have become realities (as Hegel remarks, §91A). When do intentions become realities? Answer: when they can be experienced by others, when they are out there, available to others. Genuine realities are always available for others. They are, to put it logically, *for another*. This sense of for-anotherness will be crucially important in other places in Hegel's works. In the so-called master-slave dialectic of the *Phenomenology*, for example, for-anotherness drives the early stages of development. Ignoring, for a moment, what a being-for-itself is (which will be taken up in the logic shortly), Hegel begins by defining a self-consciousness as a being-for-itself. But self-consciousness does not just want to be a "being-there" kind of being-for-itself. A self-consciousness that is merely there (as in the stage of Being-there) is potentially alterable—it could be not-self-consciousness. So it has not yet proven that it is indeed a self-consciousness. To do that, it has to prove that it is a self-consciousness out there in reality somehow. Because self-consciousness is "in the head" or is thought, it is not immediately visible from the outside. So to be real, self-consciousness has to make its inner character visible in the real world out there. It wants to be a *real* being-for-itself—not just a thought-of being-for-itself—and that means that it has to put itself as being-for-itself out there into reality. To be a real self-consciousness, it cannot just be a self-consciousness in its head, so to speak. It has to be an out-there self-consciousness—the kind of self-consciousness that others can "see" or experience as well. To make itself a real self-consciousness or being-for-itself, then, it must make its being-for-itselfness into something that is *for another*. It has to turn its being-for-itselfness into something that can be experienced by others. It has to begin the process of becoming objective or putting itself out-there.

Ultimately, of course, for Hegel, to be really real it must not only be a being-for-itself that *can* be experienced by others, it must be a being-for-itself that is *in fact* experienced by others. A self-consciousness is in fact out there when it is recognized as a self-consciousness by others who are capable of recognizing a self-consciousness, which is to say, by other self-consciousnesses. For, only if the "other" does succeed in seeing the self-consciousness *as a self-consciousness* has the self-consciousness truly succeeded in putting itself out-there or making itself objective. Being in objective space requires not only that the self-consciousness make itself *for another*, but also that the "other" succeeds in reading it and identifying it as a self-consciousness. Objectivity requires two processes: becoming for-another, and recognition. That is why a being-for-itself or self-consciousness will be a genuine self-consciousness, for Hegel, only in the presence of an other (self-consciousness) that *recognizes* it as a self-consciousness. Only if an other can and does acknowledge that it is a genuine self-consciousness or being-for-itself can a self-consciousness really be a self-consciousness or being-for-itself (see the *Phenomenology*, §§177-79, 186-7). Still, reality's requirement that something be out there, or for-another, before it can be considered real is what drives self-consciousness to demonstrate its being-for-itselfness—to put itself out there as a being-for-itself—in the beginning of the master-slave dialectic. To be a real self-consciousness is to be, first of all, for-another.

This discussion of the master-slave dialectic in the *Phenomenology* shows how an understanding of the logic can help to illuminate the progress of Hegel's other works. Without this underlying logical description, it is hard to see in the *Phenomenology* why the two self-consciousnesses at the beginning of the master-slave dialectic are driven to fight one another. There is nothing necessary or automatic in Hegel's suggestion that when two self-consciousnesses meet they must fight one another in a battle to the death. We are left wondering why they do not just make friends, or cooperate. Hegel's explanation for why they must battle at that point in the development of consciousness is that the battle is motivated by the logical process of becoming "for another." Their battle is the result of a first attempt to put their self-consciousnesses out-there, to make themselves objective by making their self-consciousnesses for-another. The desire to be for-another leads each of them to try to dominate the other, to make the other into an expression of themselves.

In the next two stages, we draw out the logical implications of the full, two-way process of Becoming for both the side of presence and that of absence.

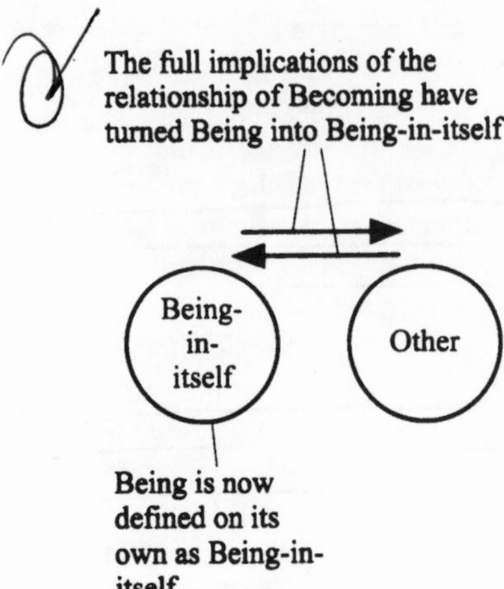
The full implications of the relationship of Becoming have turned Being into Being-in-itself
Being-in-itself
Other
Being is now defined on its own as Being-in-itself

Figure 2.8

We now look back to the side of Being, and try to say what it is—not from the point of view of the side of absence (Other)—but from the point of view of the side of presence, given that both sides of Becoming have now returned. What looked like Being-for-otherness from the point of view of absence becomes—from the point of view of presence—the whole realm of determinate being, or determinate-being-in-general. The kind of Being that has otherness-in-general as its other is Being-in-general, or the general concept of being determined. So Being-in-itself is the general concept of being determined, or having a quality. Because we are talking about determination as it applies to every determinate being, we are no longer talking about any particular quality or thereness, such as yellowness. Being-in-itself is the quality in general of "being as what it is." Not everything has yellowness, but everything does have the quality of being what it is. Moreover, this is just what we mean by determination and quality as general concepts: when we fix on what something is, we have determined its quality. To be determined is to have the quality of being what it is, or to have a quality (in general). Being-in-itself is the concept of quality as such (§91).

Being-in-itself is also the general concept of *reality* (§91). All reality has presence (as in the stage of Being), individualized thereness (as in Being-there), for-anotherness (as in Being-for-another), and, in general, in-itselfness or quality (as in Being-in-itself). Thus, while Being-in-itself introduces a new definition for the presence-side of the opposition, the new definition absorbs or includes the earlier definitions. Being-in-itself includes the presence (Being), thereness (Being-there) and for-anotherness (Being-for-another) that belonged to the earlier definitions of Being. The diagrams illustrate this absorption well, because the diagram for Being-in-itself includes the very same elements that were in Being and Being-there: it includes the Being-bubble (and Being and Being-there were just earlier definitions of the Being-bubble). At the same time, Being-in-itself offers a new definition that also moves beyond the earlier definitions. It moves beyond earlier definitions in the sense that it includes additional elements that they did not include. In the diagram, Being-in-itself includes both of the arrows that were introduced in the process of Becoming, while neither Being nor Being-there included those elements.

The move to Being-in-itself thus demonstrates Hegel's syntactic concept of *aufheben* or sublation (see Chapter One, Section VIII). The German verb *aufheben* means both to cancel and to preserve. In general, the diagrams depict *aufheben* well, because they build on one another. Later diagrams include some of the same bubbles or arrows that we had in earlier stages, but they also add new bubbles or arrows that were not included in the earlier stages. The move to Being-in-itself is an example of *aufheben* or sublation because Being-in-itself has both cancelled and preserved the earlier stages. It preserves earlier stages by including the elements that defined those earlier stages. But it also cancels those earlier stages by suggesting that the earlier definitions were inadequate and had to be revised. Being-in-itself cancels the concept of Being by suggesting that the concept of Being no longer stands as the last word on the topic of "being." The necessity that drives us from stage to stage cancels the earlier definitions of concepts by showing that they cannot stand as the last word.

As with the idea of "thereness" that is behind the concept of Being-there, and "for-anotherness," which is behind Being-for-another, Hegel also uses the idea of "*in-itselfness*," which is behind the concept of Being-in-itself, throughout his works. In general, in-itselfness captures the character that makes something what it is (see §125A) when it is taken by itself, even though it has been defined in relation to something that is its other. That the something can be defined on its own gives it an air of independence. The "in-itselfness" of something is the definition or character that something has when the something is considered by itself, independently of the "other," even though the "other" plays a role in its definition. In-itselfness is thus a one-sided point of view. Although otherness or negation helps to define the "in-itselfness" of something, that otherness is treated as outside of the something, as something the something can live without, so to speak. To define the "in-itselfness" of something is to treat it as if it can have its definition on its own, even though it has the definition it has only because of its other. Everything is "what it is" on its own. The "what it is" of anything seems to attach to the something by itself, and makes the something capable of being what it is on its own, even though the something is what it is only because there are other things that are its other, or that are other than it is. When something is determined "in itself," we treat it as if it can be what it is on its own, even though it would not be what it is without its other. We treat a (yellow) apple, for instance, as if it can be what it is on its own, even though it would not be what it is without its "other(s)"—redness, bananas, wood blocks or what have you. As Hegel apparently suggested, the side of negation is shrouded, or, we might say, hidden, within Being-in-itself (§91A). We pretend in-itselfness is merely positive, and not at all negative (§91A). Every determinate quality in general implies its own absence or otherness, but we think of the something one-sidedly as independent of that otherness. Again, we focus on the "what it is" of the something *in itself*, on what defines the something in itself, and not on the otherness without which the something would not be what it is. The apparent independence of in-itselfness is depicted in the diagram for Being-in-itself because Being-in-itself is still a separate bubble from its Other, and so still seems to be capable of being separate from, or independent of, its Other.

Limit

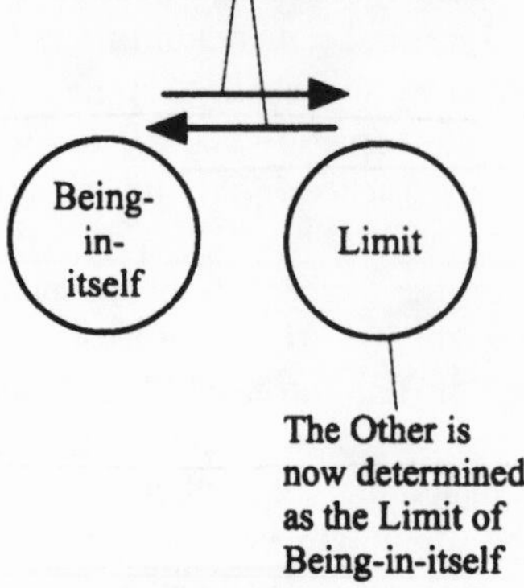
The implications of the relationship of Becoming are now drawn out for the side of absence
Being-in-itself
Limit
The Other is now determined as the Limit of Being-in-itself

Figure 2.9

We now draw out the implications of the full process of Becoming for the side of absence. What is the "other" of Being-in-itself? Being-in-itself is the general concept of being-determined, having a quality, or being real. Everything that is determined or is what it is has its Limit as its other to define it. A general characteristic of determination is that things cease to be what they are at their Limit (Rinaldi 1992, 151). The other of this desk in front of me, for instance, is everything beyond its limit (floor, chair, grayness, etc.). In other words, everything that is other than this desk limits this desk. The desk is limited by everything other than itself. The same is true for the realm or expanse of determinate being (Being-in-itself): everything that is other than determinate being is its Limit. Thus, the other of the general concept of quality is Limit. To be real is to be limited. Being-in-itself has Limit as its other.

The longer *Wissenschaft der Logik* or *Science of Logic* discusses a number of additional concepts between Being-there and Being-in-itself that do not appear in the *Encycopaedia Logic*: Determination (*Bestimmung*), Constitution (*Beschaffenheit*), Ought-to-be (*Sollen*) and Restriction (*Schranke*) (Hegel 1969, 122-4, 131). These additional concepts can be understood as more precise characterizations or descriptions of the processes represented by the arrows in the diagrams. The arrows represent the processes of Becoming, which are reappearing between—and hence having an effect on—Being and Nothing and their various more developed definitions. Here are diagrams depicting these additional concepts:

In Becoming, this arrow represented the process of passing-away, but since the process is now included in the definition of Being and gives Being what character it has (as Being-there), the process itself can be defined as a process of **Determination**. The arrow also depicts the idea that Nothing is Being-there's destination (another translation for *Bestimmung* [Rinaldi 1992, 149])

Being-there Nothing

The process of coming-to-be in the relationship of Becoming now becomes **Constitution**. The Other constitutes the side of presence, or makes presence what it is, because the side of presence is now defined by the Other as Being-for-another

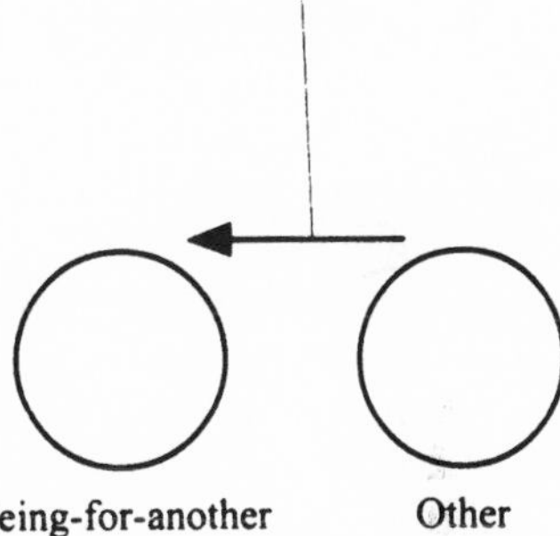

Being-for-another is now defined as Being-in-itself, which is Being that is supposed to be capable of being defined by itself or on its own. So now the two arrows represent the idea that, while Being-in-itself is supposed to be in-itself, it **Ought to be** more [Burbidge 1981, 52] because it is also for another.

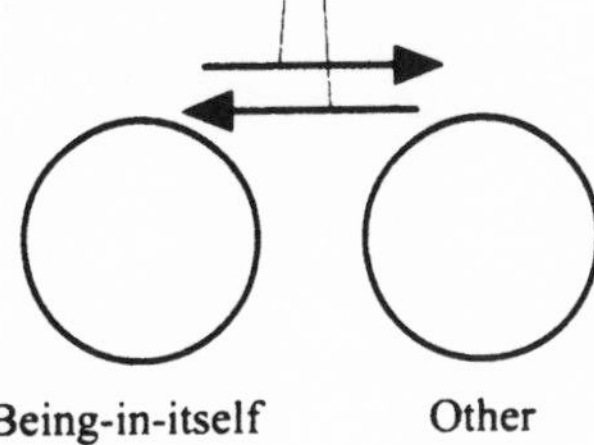

While Being-in-itself ought to be more, it is restricted by its Limit. Put another way, Limit is its **Restriction.** Limit is also its barrier (which is another translation of *Schranke* [Rinaldi 1992, 149])

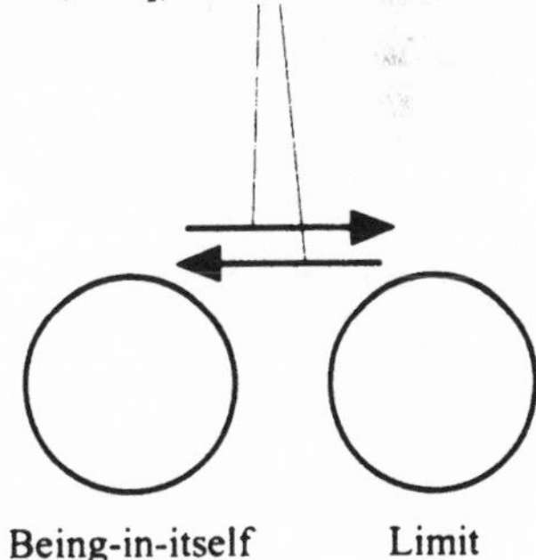

Figure 2.10

With Being-in-itself, something in reality is defined as not only alterable (which came into view in Being-there), but also finite, or limited, as Hegel suggests (§92). The type of being that reality has is one that is defined both by alterability (the ability to change) and finitude (being limited). Hegel's view is that getting sick (change), being born and dying (finitude) do not belong to humans only as accidents, but rather are part of the very concept of humanity. To be human is to be a human who changes and is mortal (§81A1, §92A; see also Chapter One, Section VIII above). Everything in reality has change and coming-to-be and passing-away as part of its very concept.

With the concept of Limit, we have come to another stage in which the current logical strategy has been exhausted. With Being-in-itself and Limit we have said everything we can say about the logical elements we have in play so far. We have three elements in play: the side of presence (the Being-side), the side of absence (the Nothing-side), and the process of Becoming between them. We have now finished defining both the Being-side and the Nothing-side in light of the full, logical implications of the effect that the process of Becoming had on them: each side has now been defined in light of both the processes of coming-to-be and passing-away. The diagrams illustrate this exhaustion because, as the presence of the two arrows suggest, the definitions of both Being-in-itself and Limit take into account both processes that we saw in Becoming. We have thus exhausted the logical elements we currently have in play, and so must, necessarily, find a fresh way of looking at what we have to move forward.

The new logical strategy will grow out of what has been developed to this point. While drawing out the implications of the process of Becoming, each side was defined by reference to its other, which grew out of the fact that the process of Becoming involves passing from one side to the other. The elements in play also exhibit the instability that Becoming had, however. Becoming was unstable because it was characterized as a process of flipping back and forth between Being and Nothing. Becoming never succeeded in characterizing a moment of stasis, but was constantly in flux. With Being-in-itself and Limit, we have generated another back-and-forth process. Being-in-itself can be what it is only by reference to its Limit; and Limit can be what it is only by reference to Being-in-itself. Each side is what it is by reference to its other. Limit is just as "otherable" (Harris 1983, 103) as Being-in-itself is. Neither side can be fixed or defined without passing into the other side. This characteristic of "otherability" or flipping back and forth, is drawn out in the next stage and points the way toward a new way of defining the elements in play. Hidden within this stage is the kernel of the idea that will produce the new strategy.

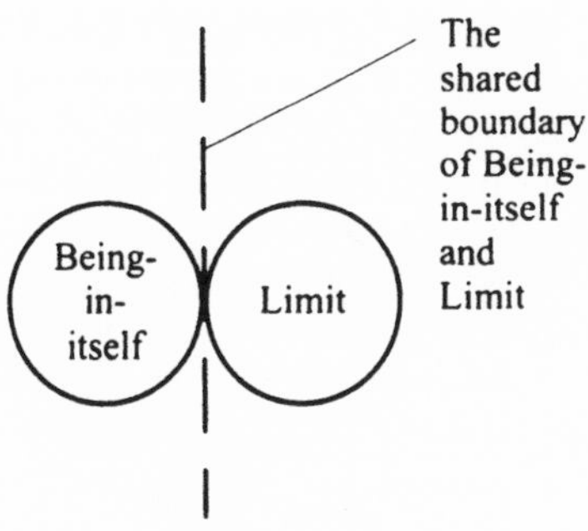

Figure 2.11

Limit and Being-in-itself are both defined by the very same boundary. The very same boundary that Limits Being-in-itself limits Limit. Being-for-itself and Limit thus share something, or have something *in common*. This shared element will point the way toward the new strategy.

Spurious Infinity

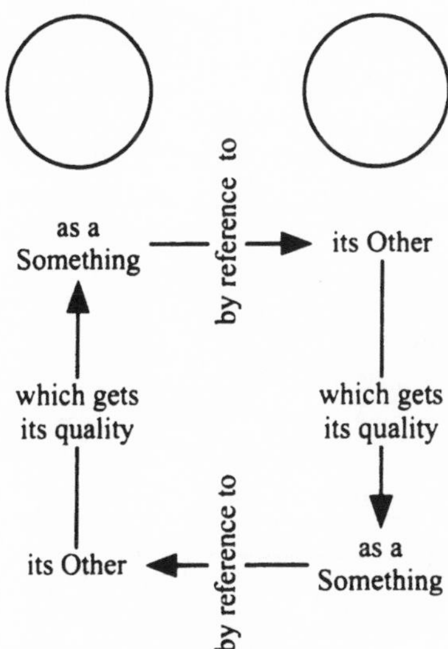

Figure 2.12

We thought we had a something (on the side of presence) that was defined by reference to its other (on the side of absence). But we now notice that the other is also a something defined by reference to *its* other. The Limit is what it is by reference to Being-in-itself: it is the limit *of* Being-in-itself. Thus, just as Being-in-itself was defined by reference to its other, so its other (Limit) is defined by reference to *its* other. As soon as we try to fix the character or definition of Being-in-itself we must refer to its other, Limit; but to fix the definition or character of Limit, we must refer to its other too, or to Being-in-itself. We can also characterize this stage as a process of passing over: as soon as we try to fix the definition of Being-in-itself we pass over into, or have to use, the concept of Limit; but as soon as we try to fix the definition of Limit we pass over into, or have to use, the concept of Being-in-itself again. Being-in-itself and Limit are thus both somethings, or have a character or definition, only by reference to or by passing into their others. Being-in-itself is a something by reference to or by passing into its other, and the other (Limit) is a something by reference to *its* other, which is a something by reference to its other, which is a something by reference to its other . . . and so on endlessly. We have the same kind of endless back-and-forth process that we had between Being and Nothing in Becoming, except that now we have an endless back-and-forth process between somethings and their others. Thus, something (reading the diagram clockwise from left to right) becomes or can be what it is, or gets its quality as a something, by reference to or by passing into its other, which, in turn, gets its quality as (and so becomes) a something by reference to its other, which, of course, gets its quality as (and so becomes) a something by reference to its other and so on. We are flipping back and forth between the two bubbles: something is what it is by reference to or by passing into its other, which is a something by reference to or by passing into its other, and so on, infinitely.

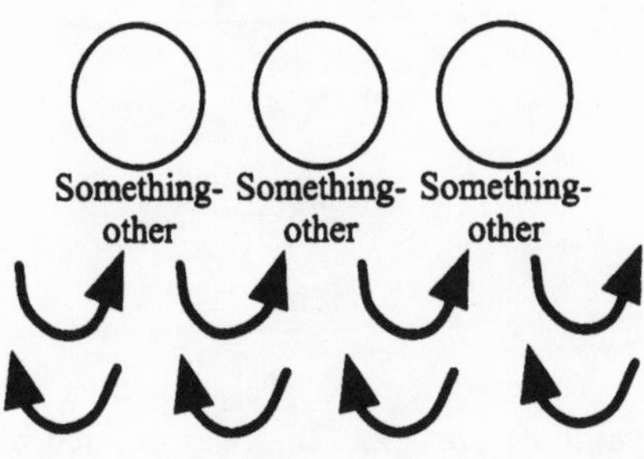

Figure 2.13

Since we ordinarily think of infinite processes linearly, rather than circularly, we can recast this process as an endless process that runs on linearly in both directions. Everything is a something (or has a quality) only by reference to or by passing into its other. Every something is a something by reference to or by passing into an other, or is a something-other. The endless, back-and-forth process in the last diagram is also an endless running-on process of something-others: one something is a something by reference to or by passing into its other, which is a something by reference to *its* other, which is a something by reference to *its* other and so on. Because we are still in the realm of reality (see Being-in-itself), everything in reality is a something-other.

For Hegel, an endless flipping or running-on process is a bad infinity, an infinity with which the logic cannot rest. The logical process cannot end with a spurious or bad infinity. It is driven, necessarily, to bring the infinity to a halt. The logic is the story of the rational generation of logical concepts and moves. It is an account of how Reason generates the concepts and syntax of logic. As we saw in Chapter One, Hegel draws his conception of reason from Kant. For Kant, rational thought includes both the faculty of the understanding and the faculty of speculative reason, which generates concepts on its own. Although Hegel has a more dialectical conception of speculative reason than Kant does, he adopts Kant's suggestion that rational thought includes both of these abilities: the ability to understand things, and the ability to generate new concepts (see Chapter One, Section VIII). For Hegel, understanding something requires fixing that thing's definition. The faculty of the understanding is responsible for moments of stasis, for moments in which the character or definition of something is established on its own; moments in which something can be taken to be what it is by itself (§80). The understanding's domain is thus in-itselfness. Although in-itselfness is one-sided in the sense that it emphasizes presence (even though the presence points toward the absence), it is a necessary part of reason. To be rational is at least in part to understand things, and to understand things is to be able to say what they are or to fix the definitions of things. Because reason is always in part about understanding things, there is a logical need to fix the definitions or characters of things. That means that there will always be a need to return to moments of stasis or fixity in which the definitions of things can be fixed, and hence to move beyond endless processes of bad infinity. The understanding must get its due.

This need to understand things, to return to moments of fixity or stasis, applies not only to understanding things generally, but also to understanding the logical concepts. The logic must fix or determine the definitions of logical concepts. Fixing or understanding the definitions of concepts, however, requires being able to say what a concept means. As a result, the logical process that generates these meanings must continuously return to moments of stasis or fixity in which the definitions of concepts can be determined. The logic cannot rest with endless infinities. It must find a way to return to moments of stasis, to moments of stability in which the definitions of concepts can be fixed, even if a spurious infinity is never quite extinguished. The faculty of reason allows us to achieve a new moment of stasis by generating a concept that can take account of or include both sides of a process of spurious infinity.

At this point in the logic, we are trying to fix or define a concept of quality—or a basic concept of having a character—for the finite world of being. The driving question of the Doctrine of Quality is "what (quality) is it?" The understanding cannot answer this question if it is too busy flipping back and forth (or running on) endlessly. The understanding has generated an endless contradiction which will prevent it from accomplishing its own goal. It will be unable to fix the definitions of these concepts under the conditions it has now generated. In the diagram depicting spurious infinity as a process of flipping back and forth, when we try to fix the identity of one side, we are sent to the other side, and then when we try to fix its identity, we are sent off again to the other side, and so on. In the diagram depicting spurious infinity as a linear process, when we try to fix what one something is, we are sent to the next something, and then when we try to fix what this next something is, we are sent to still a next something, and so on. Under these conditions, the question "what (quality) is it?" is never answered. We never succeed in explaining what holds up the Earth, for instance, by listing an endless series of supports: the Earth is held up by an elephant, which is held up by a bear, which is held up by a . . . and so on, endlessly. This explanation can never be finished, so that the answer to the question "what holds up the Earth?" is never answered. Similarly, the definition of a concept can never be finished and hence fixed by an infinite progress. The definition of quality will be fixed only if the spurious infinity can be stopped—which it will be, in the next, crucially important move.

Since the understanding gives rise to the spurious infinity that defines finitude, it has produced a contradiction: the understanding produces a concept of infinity defined by finiteness, or an infinity of finiteness.

Hegel calls this sort of endless flipping or running-on infinity *negative* or *spurious infinity* (§94), and he regards it as a false infinity. It is the sort of infinity that belongs only to logical concepts about the finite world and to the finite world of limited things themselves. Just as Being-in-itself is defined only by reference to its other—Limit—every something in the finite world is defined by reference to its other, to its limit, too. Being-in-itself is a finite concept that grasps the finite world. The limited nature of Being-in-itself and of finite things produces the spurious infinity: because finite things and Being-in-itself as a concept are limited, they are defined only by reference to their others. The attempt to define Being-in-itself and finite things necessarily drives us to the thought of their others, their limits.

Not only has the logic reached a logically untenable situation that prevents it from being able to achieve the goal of defining the concepts in question, but it has also exhausted the current logical strategy. We have been employing a logical strategy that tries to define each of the concepts on its own. The fact that this strategy has produced a logically unsatisfactory spurious infinity shows that the strategy has been exhausted. There is nothing more we can do to define the concepts if we continue to focus on defining each of the concepts on its own. We had the same logical situation after the stages of Being and Nothing. Once we had finished completely defining Being and Nothing each on its own, there was nothing more we could say about each of them. At the same time, both concepts remained undefined. Since the goal of logic is to define concepts, we had to find a new logical strategy to succeed in defining the concepts at hand. Similarly, here, we must find a new logical strategy if we are to break out of the logical impasse produced by the spurious infinity and to succeed in defining the concepts at hand. The strategy we will turn to is implied by this stage. While the spurious infinity fails to define the concepts, it does tell us something about those concepts. It tells us that the two concepts are necessarily connected to one another. The new logical strategy will involve exploring the connection between the two concepts. We made the same logical move after the stage of Nothing: since we could no longer say anything about the concepts of Being and Nothing each on their own, we went on to explore the connection between them in the stage of Becoming.

The seeds of Hegel's resolution of spurious infinities are suggested by the Presocratic philosopher Heraclitus. Heraclitus is supposed to have said that, although the waters of a river are in constant flux, the river itself stays the same, so that we step and do not step into the same river (Kirk et al. 1983, 195).[4] Indeed, the existence of the river depends on the constant flow of water. Thus, the river is a higher level of stasis that includes the constant flux of the water. Like Heraclitus, Hegel's logic overcomes the constant flux of spurious infinities by moving to a higher level of stasis. In a finite infinity, something is always in opposition to its other—it is limited by its other—but in a genuine infinity, something remains "at home with itself in its other," as Hegel apparently put it in a lecture, or comes "to itself in its other" (§94A). To see what these phrases

are supposed to mean, however, we must see how Hegel generates such a genuine infinity in the next stages of the logic.

Being-for-itself or Genuine Infinity

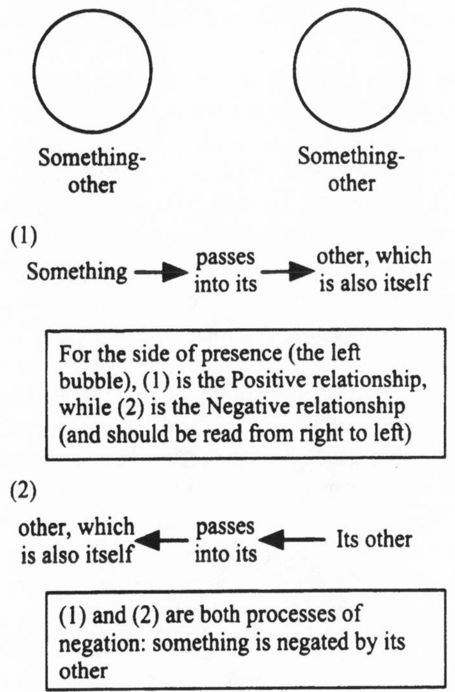

Figure 2.14

Both sides now have the same definition, character or quality—they are both defined as something-others or have the same quality as something-others. Because they are both the same, when one something-other passes into its other, it is passing into another something-other. So when each side passes into its other, it is actually passing into *itself*. This is the *positive* way of putting their connection. The *negative* way of characterizing their connection is to say of each side that its other passes into *its* other (the negation passes into its negation).

Thus, the two sides are now the same in two ways: in terms of what we might think of as their internal definition (as something-others), and in terms of how they are defined by their connection to on another. They have the same definition as something-others, insofar as each is defined on its own (i.e. "in itself"), but they also have the same sort of connection to each other. Each is connected to its other in such a way that, when it passes into its other, it passes into itself. They are therefore the same as one another both in the "in itself" sense and in terms of their connection. A desk, for instance, is what it is in opposition to its other (the computer), but the computer is what it is in opposition to its other (the desk). They are both something-others—somethings that are what they are by passing into their others—and have the same kind of connection with one another—their definitions both point toward the other.

We can characterize both the positive and the negative way of putting their connection using the concept of *negation*. The negative connection (the negation [the other] passing into its negation [its other]) is a process of negation: when the other passes into its other, it is negated. The positive connection (a something-other can be defined as a something only by passing into its other) is also a process of negation: when the something-other passes over into its other it is negated. Hence, the passing-into process in general is a process of negation. Both the passing-over process of the something-other and the passing-over process of its other (which is also a something-other) are processes of negation. Indeed, the whole process of spurious infinity is a process of negation. Each something-other can be what it is only by being negated and passing into its other, which is also itself (since they are both the same as something-others—this is the positive connection). Similarly, the other something-other, too, can be what it is only by being negated and passing into its other, which is itself (since the two sides are the same as something-others—this is the negative connection). So we have one process of endless negation, in which the left side is negated, and passes into the right side, and then the right side is negated, and passes into the left side, and so on.

There must be some way of negating all this negating, of stopping the whole negation process. The process of negation has defined both sides as the same one sort of thing, namely, a-something-that-is-"what-it-is"-by-passing-into-its-other. Since both elements have the same quality of being "what it is," the quality of being "what it is" can no longer be used to distinguish them. The desk and the computer both have the quality of being "what it is" (the desk is what it is, the computer is what it is) so that quality no longer distinguishes the elements as individuals. To grasp what the elements are—which is the goal of reason—we must shift our attention away from Being-in-itself and Limit as individual concepts. The whole negation process thus spawns a new thought, namely, the thought of the quality of the two sides. The two sides are a "one" insofar as they have the same character. Being-for-itself is the thought of both of the something-others as One. Because Being-for-itself grasps both sides as a One, it is a thought that stops the negation or passing-over process of the something-others. It grasps all of the logical elements currently in play—i.e. both of the something-others and their connection to one another—and so does not have an other. Because Being-for-itself has no "other," it cannot undergo a process of negation or pass into an other. Hence, Being-for-itself cannot be negated. It stops the negation process. Being-for-itself is the negation of the negation (§95).

Being-for-itself, which will be depicted in the next diagram, is a genuine infinity, for Hegel, because it abides on its own while having activity within it. A genuine infinity is the independent and free item that abides or remains what it is while having a process of negation (running on or flipping) within it. A genuine infinity is thus a thought that captures the running-on or endless-flipping process of false infinity. It is a stabilized thought that captures a negation process of false infinity, without passing over or negating on its own account. Like Heraclitus's river, Being-for-itself is a concept that piggy-backs on and stabilizes a constant process of flux. Because the new thought or Being-for-itself is stabilized, and does not pass over or is not negated, it negates the negation process. Again, it is the negation of the negation.

Being-for-itself is a new thought generated by the something-others' passing-over process of negation. It is the thought of the connectedness of the something-others, of their oneness. It gathers up the something-others.

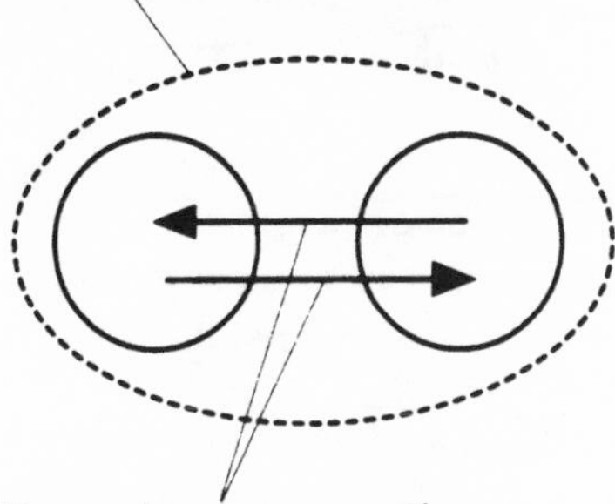

Being-for-itself is coming into view as a new kind of presence, a single One that is the something-others taken together. Notice that the One stops the running on or flipping process between the something-others because it absorbs their process and does not have any other of its own to pass into. It is the negation of the negation: it negates or stops the something-others' process of negation
The passing-over or negation processes between the something-others (the Positive and Negative relationships)

Figure 2.15

Being-for-itself can be taken in two ways that grow out of the earlier stages of presence and absence. (1) First, Being-for-itself appears under the banner of presence, or Being, which makes no reference to the negation side or to Nothing. Taken this way, Being-for-itself is the thought of the something-others taken together as qualitatively connected, or of the quality that the something-others share. Under this banner, Being-for-itself is a One that captures what we can think of as the positive character of the something-others, namely, their quality. Being-for-itself is the (One) whole expanse of the something-others. Because Being-for-itself is just the thought of the quality of the something-others, it does not yet have a character of its own. Since it lacks a character of its own, I represent it with a dashed outline at this point (cf. Being and Nothing above).

(2) Second, however, Being-for-itself appears under the banner of absence, negation, or Being-there. The concept of Being-there made reference to the side of negation or Nothing. Taken this way, the One is defined not only by the positive character of the something-others, but also by their negative character as well, or by the process of negation that they undergo. The process of negation between the something-others defines them as separate from one another, keeps them apart. Because they are the same as one another in terms of their quality or character, they would be defined qualitatively as one single quality without the process of negation to define them as separated. When the One includes their process of negation, then, it captures their separation. Under the banner of absence, the One is the thought of the something-others as separate items gathered together into a set. It is the set of something-others.

Because Being-for-itself includes both the something-others and their whole process of negation within it, it includes all of the logical elements currently in play. There is, at the moment, no "other" or negation outside of it. Although the something-others are still in play, they are not the One's other, since they are included in the One's definition. They are only for-the-One: because the One gathers them up, they have their thereness only for it. They make the One what it is, and so are not "other" for it. Being-for-itself has no "other" into which it could pass, and so does not itself pass over. It negates or stops the passing-over process. It is the negation of the process of negation, or the *negation of the negation*. Being-for-itself is a new kind of Being or presence that absorbs a process of flux, in the same way that Heraclitus's river is a new kind of presence that absorbs the flux of the water into a new level of stability.

Being-for-itself is the most rudimentary account of *ideality* (§95R) or of conceptual *universality*. Reality is about out-thereness—having thereness in public space, or being there for another. Being-for-itself takes a step away from the thereness of reality toward the ideality or universality of thought. Hegel offers three definitions of universality in the Doctrine of Being. This stage develops the most rudimentary definition, which I called the communality definition of universals (see also Chapter One, Section III). According to the communality account of universals, a universal is a term that gathers the "what it is" of something-others. In this early stage of Being-for-itself, a universal is the set or group of items that are qualitatively connected to one another insofar as they each have the character of being "what it is." Being-for-itself is the expanse of being that has the character of being "what it is." This sort of universality is rudimentary because it is still tied to thereness. As Hegel puts it, Being-for-itself is an ideality that has reality (§95R). The "what it is" of the something-others is the thereness of those something-others, or the way in which they have their thereness. Because Being-for-itself gathers up their "what it is," it includes their thereness in its definition. It is defined from below by the thereness of the something-others. Being-for-itself thus includes the quality of finite "thereness" that belongs to the something-others. Nevertheless, because it is a group-term (i.e. a universal), it is still one step away from reality, and one step closer to ideality or thought. Gathering items out there into a set or group is an activity of thought. Somethings become a set or an expanse of being only in thought. Because Being-for-itself is defined from the bottom-up by the character of the something-others, however, it does not yet have a definition of its own, separate from the definition it gets from the something-others. I have therefore depicted it with a dashed outline in the diagram.

Like the concepts of Being-there and Being-in-itself, the concept of Being-for-itself introduces an element that will return repeatedly during the course of the logic. "For-itselfness" is a type of universality that is always associated with multiplicity and with overcoming the "otherness" of opposition. Because Being-for-itself embraces its other, it is not opposed, limited, constricted by that other in the way that Being-in-itself and Limit were limited, opposed or constricted by each other. To use some of the language Hegel uses later, a "for itself" concept abides or remains at home with itself through the comings and goings of what it embraces, or in the face of an underlying instability. The lack of limitation or constriction and the stability over and above an underlying instability define for-

itselfness as a *genuine infinity*. To be genuinely or truly infinite is to be unlimited, unconstricted, and to abide through and over an underlying, unstable multiplicity. Throughout the logic, we will continue to encounter moments and processes of for-itselfness, but the basic definition of for-itselfness is introduced here in Being-for-itself.

As Hegel apparently pointed out in a lecture (§96A), one of the most important kinds of for-itselfness is the "I" or consciousness—a type of being that will be defined in Chapter Four. Consciousness is a kind of "for itself" because it is both a multiplicity and is defined by an "other" that is not really an other. Consciousness is a universal in the sense of being a group-term. An individual person's consciousness is a set of individual conscious experiences. Although a consciousness is constantly in flux, with new sensible and conscious contents at every moment (new thoughts, new visual, auditory, olfactory input and so on), it is still a One that gathers up all those individual states. It is a collection or group of individual, momentary conscious experiences. Although consciousness is defined in relation to an "other"—namely the individual conscious experiences that make it up—that "other" is not really "other," or not alien. The consciousness as a whole includes or embraces that "other," and so is not limited, constricted or opposed by that other in the way that Being-in-itself, for instance, was limited and opposed by Limit. Moreover, a consciousness abides or remains at home with itself through the comings and goings of its other. Although a consciousness's conscious awareness has a constantly fluctuating content, the consciousness itself remains what it is as a One throughout the comings and goings of conscious awareness. Indeed, it is in part the constant fluctuation of the "other" of consciousness that makes it alive, or a spirit, rather than a dead head, so to speak (see §96A). We will examine Hegel's concept of spirit more fully in Chapter Four.

Hegel says that, insofar as Being-for-itself is related to itself, or considered on its own, it is an immediacy (§96). The concept of immediacy is another important concept throughout Hegel's logic. An *immediacy*, for Hegel, is always an independent, seemingly self-subsisting something, that does not yet have an "other" or moment of negation, and that is defined, at least in part, by given or "found" content. Hegel uses the term to characterize not only concepts—which is the subject matter of the logic—but things in the world as well. A rock, for instance, is an immediacy because it is something we simply "find" in the world, or is given to us in the world of experience, and seems to be able to subsist on its own, without help from us or any other "other." Being-for-itself is an immediate concept in this same sense. The givenness or immediacy of a concept is rooted in the degree to which a concept is connected to thereness. Being-for-itself is stable and seemingly self-subsistent because it has no "other" or moment of negation and does not itself pass over. But it is still defined by given or "found" content because it depends on the thereness or given character of the something-others for its definition. Being-for-itself is being defined from the bottom up: it is a set-term that merely gathers up the something-others. The character of Being-for-itself is thus given to it by the given nature of the something-others in the set, or by whatever character the something-others in the set happen to have. Whenever we return throughout the logic to a stage of immediacy, or to "Immediate" this or "Immediate" that, Hegel has this same logical description in mind. In the stage of Immediate Measure below, for example, the "measure" is given or found. A measure is a unity of quality and quantity. Ice, for instance, is an Immediate Measure. It is discreet, self-subsistent, and its character is simply given by or found in experience. Ice just happens to be hard in a certain range of temperatures. Its quality and quantity are simply found out there or given.

Immediacy characterizes not only concepts, but also logical relationships. Sometimes, the connections or relationships between concepts can also be "found" or given. These connections tend to be loose and undefined. In the stage of Immediate Measure, for example, not only are the quantity and quality given or found, but their unity or connection is also given: they are just "found" together. There is nothing about the concept of water or temperature which requires water to freeze or get hard (the quality) at a certain temperature (the quantity). That water freezes at a certain temperature is simply a given fact about the world, something we "found" out there in the world of experience. The concept of ice includes this given or found connection between the hard quality of water and a quantity of temperature. Both the character of ice as well as the connection between the quantity and quality are simply given or found. Because that connection is simply found, it is loose and undefined. The concept of ice does not define and cannot explain why the hard quality of the water corresponds to the particular quantity of temperature that it does.

At the moment, Being-for-itself has a similarly immediate connection with the something-others that it gathers. Being-for-itself would have a defined connection with the something-others if it played a role in gathering the something-others together. However, at the moment, Being-for-itself does not pull the something-others together. The something-others are defined as the same as one another based on their own connection to one another—namely, the passing-over process that they have with one another—not because of what Being-for-itself is like as a concept. Being-for-itself does not do the work of connecting the something-others together. It simply gathers up their pre-established sameness. It "finds" their sameness, their connection. Because Being-for-itself as a concept does no work for the something-others, it has a merely external connection with them. If we think of the set of humans as a basket full of humans, for instance, what holds the humans together is the external basket, but there is no necessary connection between the universal "human" as a set-term and the humans in the basket. The set-term "human" does not explain why the humans belong together in the set. Nor does it define or capture the connection that the humans have to one another. A universal of communality is merely a name for the external basket. Ultimately, of course, Hegel will offer an account of universality that defines the connections between concepts in a necessary or essential way (see §39).

Hegel contrasts immediacy with *mediatedness*. Something that is immediate seems to be able to subsist on its own, without reference to any "other." Something that is *mediated*, however, cannot be what it is without its other. The concept of quantity, for instance, will turn out to be mediated: a bit of quantity can be a "bit" only in relation to another bit of quantity that limits it. The original "bit" needs the other "bit" to succeed in having its own characters as a "bit." We will revisit the concepts of immediacy and mediation in the stage of Degree (in the Doctrine of Quantity) below, where the two categories intertwine.

Although we progressed logically from reality to ideality, because we are progressing from lower to higher stages of thought, the fact that ideality has been introduced after the concept of reality shows that ideality is a higher stage of thought. Even though ideality has been developed out of the concept of reality, it would be wrong to conclude that ideality is dependent on or derived from reality. In the next stage, the logical process demonstrates that the opposite is true: reality is dependent on ideality, and ideality is the truth of reality (§96A). The logical process will show that we cannot grasp the world of being, the world of experience, with the concepts of reality by themselves. Reason drives us, necessarily, to ideality. As we saw in Spurious Infinity, we could not grasp or characterize "somethings" in reality without getting ourselves into an endless running-on or flipping back-and-forth process that prevented us from truly defining what was before us. Only by bringing in ideality—a new, stable concept of Being-for-itself—can we grasp or characterize the nature of reality itself. The introduction of ideality was necessitated by the attempt to grasp reality. Ideality overgrasps reality. Reality would not be what it is without ideal concepts to characterize it. Ideality makes reality what it is (see Chapter One, Section II). Ideality is logically necessary for grasping reality. Of course, ideality includes reality in its definition too. The contents of conscious awareness (reality) give a consciousness (ideality) its life. Reality gives ideality its life, its activity, insofar as reality is sublated within ideality (§96A).

So far, I have been giving the stages of the logic names that Hegel provides in his text. Hegel does not really give the next few stages specific names. These moves chronicle the stages of the One and the many, which are the concepts we will now use to develop the connection between Being-for-itself (the One) and the something-others (the many) more precisely. Because Hegel does not provide clear indications of the names that he would give to these stages, I have used his text to choose what seem to be appropriate names for the next few stages (Repulsion, etc.).

Repulsion, or Negative Relation

The One gets its character or definition as an independent entity by *repulsing* the many, which are also itself. The many are the One—they make it up (in the diagram they are inside it)—so when the One repulses the many it repulses itself as the many

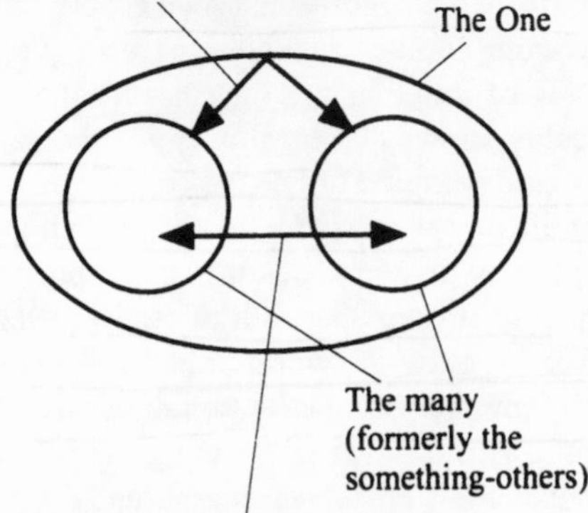

I have now replaced the two arrows representing the passing-over process between the many (formerly the something-others) with one double-sided arrow

Figure 2.16

In the last stage, Being-for-itself was defined as a gathering-term or set-term for the something-others. It was the concept of the "what it is" of the something-others taken together as a One. The One can be a set-term for the something-others, however, only if the something-others are defined as separate from one another, or as more than one item. The something-others must be many. Recall from the stage of Spurious Infinity that the many are engaged in a process of passing into one another—a process that, in that stage, defined them as the same. If the many are completely the same as one another, however, then they would be only one item, and would no longer be a set, or more than one item. So if the something-others are to remain a set of items—the many—they must be distinguished from one another, or must be defined as separate from one another. In the stages of Being-in-itself and Limit, the passing-over process that defined the two inside bubbles as the same was defined as a process of negation. There, the passing-over process defined the two inside bubbles—which in that stage were defined as Being-in-itself and Limit—as different from one another. That element of negation returns here: the passing-over process between the something-others is now defined as a process of mutual negation. That process makes the something-others more than one thing or many. To use Hegel's anthropomorphic language, through that process, the something-others repulse one another, or hold themselves apart. Their process of reciprocal exclusion (§97) makes them many.

For Hegel, something can have a character or determination only if it includes negation or nothing in its definition (see Being-there). Because neither Being nor Nothing included negation in their definitions, for instance, they had no character or determination. Being-for-itself also had no independent character in the last stage because it was defined in purely positive terms as the qualitative sameness of the something-others. Now negation has come back into the picture, however, because the many are defined by negation. The One—which gathers up the many—is therefore also defined by negation. That means that the One begins to have a character or be defined of its own as well.

Indeed, the One *must* come to have a character of its own. Now that the many are holding themselves apart, they no longer gather themselves up, so to speak, as they did in Spurious Infinity when their passing-over process defined them as the same. In Being-for-itself, the One did not have the function of gathering up the things in the set. The passing-over process of the many defined the many as the same. The process of the many did the work of holding the many together as a set. Now that the many have defined themselves as separate from one another, however, they can remain a set only if the One does the work of gathering them up. So to remain the One of the many, the One must take on the function of gathering up the many, or of defining the many as connected to one another in a set. When the One takes on this new function—a function the many no longer have—the One begins to have a character of its own. This new function gives the One a definition that the many do not share. It separates the definition of the One from that of the many. Because the One now has a determination or definition of its own, I represent it with a solid outline in the diagram (cf. the stage of Being-there).

So what function, exactly, does the One now have in relation to the many? We know this function must succeed in gathering up the many. The many are separated from one another, so the One must put them back together, or must once again define them as the same. The One puts the many back together by positing them, or through the activity of characterizing them. It defines the many, or gives its quality to the many as their definition. To use the Hegelian language, the One repulses the many from itself (§97). We must keep in mind, however, that the definition of the One still includes the many: the many are the One. So when the One repulses or negates the many, it is really repulsing itself, or is negating the many as itself. In other words, the quality that it gives to the many when it characterizes the many is the same quality that it is. Thus, the One can have its own character or be defined on its own (is related to itself) only by holding itself apart from itself as the many. It is what it is as the One by negating or repulsing itself into the many.

Although we have not yet developed a determinate quality or universal, such as "human" (the only universal we have developed so far is the general quality of "being what it is" rather than some specific sort of what it is), we can use the example of the concept of human and the set of individual humans to illustrate the logical move in this stage, where the individual humans are the many, and the concept of human is the One. The sort of universal (One) we have defined so far is the universal of communality: universality as the thought of as a set of qualitatively connected items, or items connected to one another in terms of their quality of being what they are. According to this definition, the concept of human would be nothing but the set of items that are qualitatively related to one another in terms of what they are. In Spurious Infinity, the two inside bubbles achieved their qualitative sameness on their own. The individual humans in the set, for example, would be defined as the same as each other by their own relationship. As a result, Being-for-itself or the concept of human had no work to do to gather up the humans in the set. The humans had already gathered themselves up, so to speak, or were holding themselves together. Being-for-itself was simply the thought of the qualitative sameness of the things in the set. Since the concept of human had the same quality as the humans in the set and performed no independent function, the concept of human had no independent character apart from the things in the set (and so had a dashed outline in the diagram).

When the humans in the set were defined as the same as each other, they were connected together in virtue of their own definitions, or on their own. But the fact that they were connected together raised a new logical problem. They are supposed to be a set of things, which means there must be more than one thing. If the humans in the set are defined purely in terms of their quality of being human, then it seems as if they are only one thing. Indeed, that is just what the concept of Being-for-itself suggests: that they are one quality, namely, human. So if they are going to continue to be a *set* of items, the humans in the set must separate from one another. Now, in the stages of Being-in-itself and Limit, the passing-over process was the process in which the two inside bubbles were defined as different from one another: Being-in-itself was Being-in-itself, and Limit was Limit. In this stage, the passing-over process is now recast according to that earlier definition: it is recast as a process of mutual exclusion or distinction, as the way in which the humans in the set define themselves as different from one another. Even though two humans are human, they are always different from one another in some way or other. So the two inside bubbles or the humans in the set remain separate from one another through the passing-over process, now viewed as a process of mutual repulsion.

Now that the humans in the set are no longer connecting themselves together through their own processes, however, the concept of human has a new function that it has to perform to hold the set together. It must work, so to speak, to hold the humans in the set together. This new function gives it an independent character that defines it as separate from the humans in the set. How does the concept of human hold the humans in the set together? It defines them as human, or gives them their character as human. It imposes on them the sameness of character that defines them as the same as one another and hence holds them together. The One characterizes them. It defines itself as separate from the many and hence takes on an independent character by repulsing the humans in the set as itself, by giving those humans its quality. It gives them the quality of being what they are. The One comes to have a definition or character of its own by repulsing the many as itself.

We are driven to this stage by the inadequacy of the communality account of the universal that was offered in the stage of Being-for-itself. We cannot really grasp the universal or concept of human by merely defining it as the set of qualitatively connected humans. Defining the concept of human as the set of qualitatively connected humans relies on the sameness of the humans for defining the universal. When we use the humans in the set to define the quality of human, we are saying that the quality of human is just the sameness that the humans in the set have in relation to one another. What is it about the humans, however, that makes them the same? How are they the same? If you say that everything about the humans makes them the same, then we would no longer be able to distinguish one human from another. For, if everything about them makes them "human," then the concept of human captures everything about them. Every quality that they have would then make them human. If every quality about them makes them human, however, then they would be exactly the same as one another, they would share absolutely every quality. But if they share absolutely every quality—including their place in space and time and all of their descriptive qualities—then they would be the same, one thing. There would only be one thing, and not two things. They would meld into one "human," and there would no longer be a set. The claim that the concept of human is a set-term logically implies that we have at least two things in the set. And if there are two things in the set, then those things cannot share all of their qualities. There must be at least one quality of each item that separates it from the other. The humans in the set must be different from one another in some respect, such that there is some quality or other that they do not share.

At the same time, although the items or humans in the set must be different from one another, they must still be human, that is, they must still have the quality captured by the One to be in the set. So the quality that distinguishes one item from another in the set must be a quality that does not undermine their status or character as human, or as captured by the One. There must be some quality about the humans in the set that distinguishes them, but is also not part of their character or definition as "human—a quality that allows us to tell them apart, but is irrelevant to their status or quality as human.

Once we notice that there is some way in which the humans in the set are different from one another, or mutually exclude each other, then we can see that characterizing or defining the humans with the concept of human actually does some work. The concept of human is not merely a set-term that gathers up the previously established qualitative sameness of the humans. The concept of human must *sort out* some qualities of the humans from others. It has to sort out those characteristics that define the humans in the set as the same—or as human—from those characteristics that define them as different, but that do not effect their status as the same, or as human. The concept of human thus has a function above and beyond being a set-term, or gathering up the humans in a set according to their qualitative sameness: it sorts out their qualities. That sorting process is imposed on the humans in the set by the universal or the One. The sorting process is something that the concept of human does to the humans in the set. That process is not "given" or "found" in the humans as a set. Which qualities belong to the humans as human and which do not is not established by the mere presence of the humans in the set. That sorting process must be done by the concept of human, or by the universal—by thought. That process adds an element to the definition or character of the universal which is not given by the items in the set. It gives the universal a new character different from the character it gets from the items in the set.

Moreover, the fact that the universal must perform the function of sorting out the qualities of the items in the set shows that the communality definition of universals is inadequate. According to the communality definition, a universal is nothing but the set of items that it gathers up. However, Hegel has argued, the items in the set are not a set—or more than one item—unless there is some way of distinguishing them from one another. To remain in the set, however, they must be distinguished from one another in a way that does not undermine their having the quality captured by the universal. The universal therefore has the function of sorting out which qualities of the items in the set make them what they are as members of the set and which do not. That function gives the universal an additional characteristic that is not included in the communality account's claim that a universal is *nothing but* the set of items that it gathers up.

This stage helps to support Hegel's argument for idealism, which was begun in the last stage. According to idealism, thought or ideality is primary in relation to reality, such that ideas or concepts help to determine the nature of reality (see Chapter One, Section II). According to the argument of this logical stage, the universal helps to determine the nature of reality by sorting out those qualities that make something what it is from those qualities that do not. Some qualities about humans are clearly irrelevant to their being human—what color eyes they have, for instance, or whether they have all of their toes. Which qualities are irrelevant and which are not, however, is not given by reality itself. Reality presents a whole bunch of qualities; it does not sort or order those qualities. That sorting process can only be done by thought. Moreover, Hegel's argument suggests that thought's process of sorting qualities is necessary for reality to have the character it has, or to be what it is. Humans in the set cannot be characterized as "human" unless that sorting process has taken place. To remain a One and be a set at the same time, the humans in the set must both be the same as each other in some ways and different from each other in other ways. Characterizing the humans in the set as a One, or as human, requires that the qualities that make them the same are sorted out from those that make them different but are irrelevant to their character as human. Since the humans cannot *be* human unless they can be characterized as human, the reality of the humans as human—their ability to be human—depends on the activity of thought. Thought or concepts are necessary to establish their qualitative reality.

Attraction

Although the One repulses the many, it is also attracted to the many because the many are itself. Moreover, remember that the many are the same as one another, so they are attracted to one another too. The One is thus the thought of the attraction of the many at itself

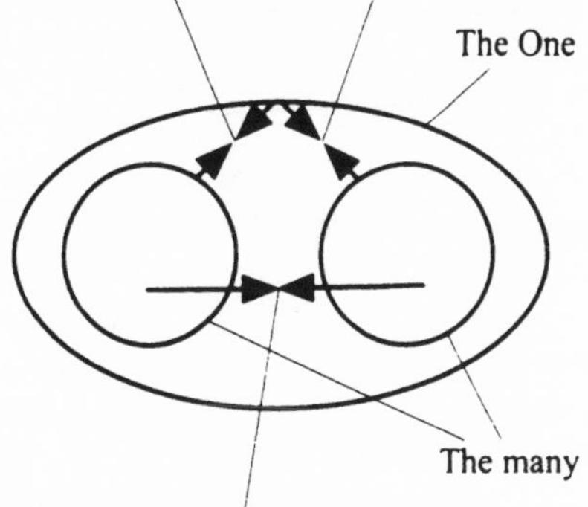

The many are each passing into the other as itself. They are therefore the same as one another, and so are attracted to one another as the same. They are ones of a kind

Figure 2.17

In last stage, the many were connected (or disconnected) by a process of negation: they maintained their separateness by repulsing each other in a process of mutual exclusion. However, this repulsion is grounded in the very same passing-over process that had defined the many (the inside bubbles) as the same as one another in Spurious Infinity. That process is therefore not only the way in which the many repulse one another, it is also the way in which they are attracted to one another. For Hegel, determination or having a character always requires negation (see the stage of Being-there). Because the sameness of the many is now defined by a process that includes negation, that sameness is determined or has a character. The many are attracted to, or the same as, one another in some particular way because they are also different from one another in some other way. *Attraction* is a determinate or determined sameness. The sameness of the many still has to do with the quality of being "what it is," but being what they are is now determined. The many are the same qualitative *kind* of something.

In the last stage, the connection between the One and the many was also defined by negation: the One repulsed the many. Like the connection between the many, however, the connection between the One and the many is defined not only by negativity, but also by positivity. The One is still defined positively as the sameness that the many share: it gathers up the many as a One. Because the process in which the One gathers up the many now includes negation, however, the connection between the One and the many is characterized by attraction: the One is the same as the many in some way while being different from the many in another way. The One still embraces the many as a set. Indeed, the One is still a set-term for their qualitative sameness. But the One is no longer just the general sameness of the many, it is now the determined or specific sameness that the many share. Now that the many are the same in some determinate way, they are the same in a determinate way that is grasped by the One or universal. Because the One still grasps the determinate sameness of the many, it is still the "what it is" that the many are. However, it is the determined or specific "what it is" that the many are. The One is the qualitative *kind* that the many are.

All this attraction produces a logical problem, however. The One and the many are now all qualitatively the same. They are defined by the same quality, or are the same kind. Moreover, they also have the same sort (or quality) of connection with one another: the One is attracted to the many, and the many are attracted to one another. Therefore, the category of quality can no longer distinguish the three elements. We cannot tell them apart by their quality. Hence, the category of quality is sublated (cancelled and preserved): we must move on to a new category to characterize what we have.

Let me return to the example I have been using to flesh out this stage. In the last stage, we noticed that the idea that a universal is a set-term for some qualitative sameness can work only if the humans in the set are distinguished or different from one another: they can be a set, multiplicity, many or more than one item only if they are distinguished. If they are the same in absolutely every respect, then they are one item. To remain more than one item—which a set requires, of course—they must be different from one another. To use Hegel's language, they must repulse each other, or mutually exclude each other.

However, that difference cannot undermine their sameness. The humans must still be capable of being gathered up into a set according to some qualitative sameness that can be grasped by the universal or the One. If they cannot be gathered up into a set, then the idea that a universal is a set-term would fail immediately. So the idea that a universal is a set-term for some qualitative sameness still requires that the humans in the set be the same as one another in some respect. Besides, the same passing-over process that defined the many as qualitatively separate from one another in the last stage is the very same process that defined them as the same as one another in Spurious Infinity. So the many still have a process that defines them as the same. The humans in the set are still defined as the same. What is new is that, since they have been defined as different in some way in the last stage, the sameness of the humans is now determined. The individual humans are no longer just the same generally, they are now thought of as the same in a specific way, a way that also takes account of their difference. This process is the result of the sorting that I suggested in the last stage that the concept of human has to perform: the concept of human has to sort out those qualities in which the humans in the set are the same as one another from those qualities in which they are different from one another, where those differences do not affect their status as the same or as human. The humans are therefore now the same as one another in some determinate way. They are a specific *kind* of something.

The connection between the One and the many was also defined by negation in the last stage: the One repulsed the many. The concept of human was thereby defined as different from the humans in the set. In this stage, however, the connection of sameness between the One and the many also reappears, just as the connection of sameness between the many came back as well. The concept of human still gathers up the sameness of the humans in the set, but, since the humans are now the same in a specific way, the concept of human gathers up the specific sameness of the many, or the specific "what it is" that the many are. It is the determinate *kind* of something that the humans are.

The stage of Attraction introduces a new account of universals that completes the sublation of the communality account. In Being-for-itself, the concept of Being-for-itself (now the One) was defined as the qualitative set of something-others (now the many). This account of universals will not work, however, because it either cannot account for their Oneness or it cannot account for their many-ness as more than one item (as a set). It must either treat the items in the set as completely the same—in which case they are all one item and not a many anymore—or as completely different—in which case they are no longer a One. It has no way of distinguishing ways in which items in the set are the same as one another from ways in which they are different from one another. The new account does make this distinction. It says that a universal is a set-term for what things in the set have in common, where what they have in common is a specific quality, as opposed to other qualities that they do not have in common. Universality is no longer merely about comm*un*ality, but about comm*on*ality. Universals grasp what the items in the set have in common. Items belong in the same class or set because they have something in common, some determinate quality, that puts them in that set and that is grasped by the universal. Items are the same kind, and this is what the One now grasps. The One is a concept that captures some determinate, qualitative common "what it is" of the many.

Unlike under the communality account, under the commonality account the universal now explains why the items in the set are connected to one another. Under the communality account, the universal did not do the work of making the items the same as one another. It merely put together items that were already qualitatively the same as one another according to their own definitions. To use Hegel's more anthropomorphic language, the items in the set or the something-others defined themselves as the same in the stage of Spurious Infinity. They did not need the universal to define their sameness. The universal simply put together their pre-established sameness. Under the commonality account, however, the universal does the work of connecting the items together. When it characterizes the items in the set, or imposes its quality on those items, it sorts their qualities. It sorts out those qualities that the items share from those that the items do not. Moreover, the universal's definition determines which quality the items share and which they do not, which quality is irrelevant and which is not. The sorting process is defined by the One or universal. Under the commonality account of the universal, then, the universal—rather than the items in the set—explains why the items are connected to one another. It says they are connected to one another by some determinate, shared (common) quality.

Like the comm*un*ality account of universals, however, the comm*on*ality account of universals will not stand as the last word on universals. We encounter a logical problem right away. Now that all three elements—the One, and both of the many—are defined by the same quality (they are the same kind) and have the same quality (type of) connection with one another (namely, attraction), we can no longer distinguish them by using the category of quality. In more Hegelian language, when the many repulsed each other into separate items, they each became a one. They were ones of many. And when the One repulsed the many or separated itself from the many and took on a character independent of the many, it also became a one. Since it is the same as the many, however, it is also a one of many. So each of the three elements is now defined as a one of many. In effect, Hegel is arguing, the commonality account of universals mistakenly ends up treating universals as simply another member of the set. The account intends the universal to be qualitatively different from the things in the set. The universal is supposed to be a multiplicity, or what gathers up the many. But the commonality account cannot maintain this view. It is forced into an untenable position according to which the specialness of the universal cannot be explained. The universal of commonality becomes just that: common—a mere one among many ones. Once we take seriously the qualitatively determinate sameness—or commonality—of the three elements, we cannot tell them apart anymore. We can no longer use the category of quality to distinguish them anymore. And we cannot use the category of quality to define the three elements we have before us. If we are going to succeed in grasping the logical elements we have, we are going to need a new category of definition.

The Addition to the section of the logic in which Hegel discusses this move (§98A1) contains an argument against atomism Hegel apparently offered in a lecture that points us toward a passage in the *Lectures on the History of Philosophy*. In the *Lectures*, Hegel criticizes most of the Presocratic atomists (Leucippus and Democritus excepted) for being unable to explain the determinate character of the One. They claim that all atoms are alike, and that the atoms combine into one clump—the One. But if all atoms are alike, then the clump of atoms—the One—can have no determinate character. It is One indistinguishable clump. If we think of the world as the One, then these atomists cannot explain why part of the world is plant, part animal, and so on. A clump of like atoms would have no distinguishing characteristics. The One would no longer be able to assert any identity separate from the atoms themselves. It could no longer be a distinct Being-for-itself separate from the many. As Hegel puts it in the *Lectures*, "the [O]ne, as that which is for itself, loses all its determinateness" (*Lectures on the History of Philosophy* 1983, vol. 1, 282, 306).

In the Addition in the *Encyclopaedia Logic*, Hegel chides the atomists for making a different error. He suggests that atomism cannot really even conceive of the stage of Attraction. Atomism, he suggests (§98A1), treats singular items as if they are discretely identified items that are independent of one another that come together merely by chance. What atomism ignores, however, to its detriment, is that the items are also attracted to one another. Thus, atomism ignores the fact that items in the finite world are attracted to one another by their own natures, that is, by their shared qualities. These shared qualities belong to ideality—they are thoughts, concepts. Thus, atoms do not come together by chance.

They come together by their own natures in specific ways that can be grasped by thought. To treat atoms as purely singular items is therefore one-sided (to use Hegel's term): it recognizes the independence of singular items, but not their interdependence. Instead, singulars are defined by qualitatively contiguous ideals. Without those qualitatively contiguous groups, singular items would not be what they are.

In the next stage, we begin the second sub-section of the Doctrine of Being: the Doctrine of Quantity. Now that we can no longer use the category of quality to define the three items that we have before us, we must try out a new category. The introduction of the new category is necessitated by the logical impasse we have reached with the old one. Moreover, the application of the category of quantity is implied by the last stage. When the category of quality falls away, all we can say about what we have is that we have a bunch of stuff whose quality we cannot specify. We have some quantity of qualitatively unspecified stuff. The new category we try out, then, is the category of quantity.

III. Doctrine of Quantity

Pure Quantity or Quantity in General

We have the same logical elements we had before: an outer bubble with two bubbles in it, or a larger rectangle split into two smaller squares. Rectangles are used to represent the category of Quantity. The boundaries are dashed because the elements cannot be distinguished. Since the boundaries are unclear, Pure Quantity may run on

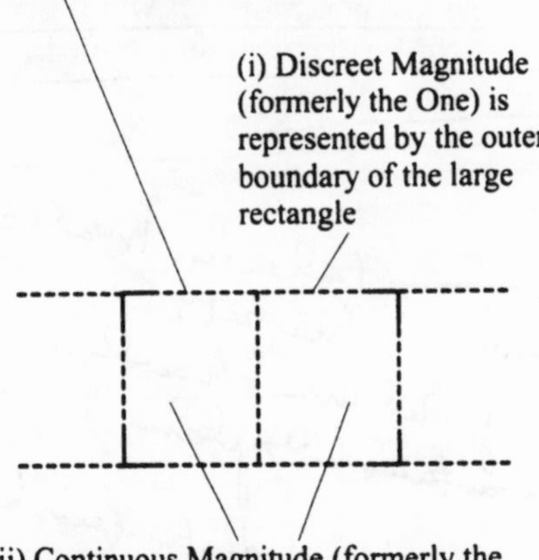

(i) Discreet Magnitude (formerly the One) is represented by the outer boundary of the large rectangle

(ii) Continuous Magnitude (formerly the many) is represented by the two inner squares, and—because the boundaries are unclear—may continue on either end

Figure 2.18

I have switched to a more rectangular depiction to represent the move to the category of quantity from the category of quality. The One is now represented by the larger rectangle, and the many is represented by the two smaller rectangles within it.

The concept of Pure Quantity is the first thought about what we have (what kind of being we have [remember we are still in the Doctrine of Being]) when the category of quality first falls away and all we are left with is qualitatively indifferent bits (formerly the many) and implied oneness (from what was formerly the One). Because the category of quality has failed (see Attraction above), the quality of what we have is indifferent.

Indeed, we have sublated (cancelled but preserved) the category of quality in Hegel's technical sense. The category of quality is cancelled because it is no longer directly applicable. But it is also preserved in the sense that the qualitative attributes we had before are still implied. The One is still taken to be gathering up the many, which is why I still depict it as surrounding the many, as it did in the Doctrine of Quality. However, this qualitative attribute is no longer posited or established here, which is why I have depicted the boundaries between the One and the many as dashed rather than as solid lines. The One is still supposed to be including the many, but its logical status as the gathering concept was called into question in the last stage and so is no longer established. Because the boundary around the One is no longer established, the many run on. In addition, the One is supposed to be different from the many, but its qualitative distinctiveness was lost in the last stage as well, and so its distinction from the many is also no longer established. The many, for their part, are also supposed to be different from one another, but because they lost their qualitative distinctiveness in the last stage, the boundary that is supposed to hold them apart or divide them is implied but no longer established. There is therefore no way to distinguish the different elements. The distinctions we had before—or the excluding determinacies, to use Hegel's language—are still implicit, but no longer posited or established. The boundaries we had in the diagram before are implied, but not posited.

What we are left with, then, is the idea of a bunch or quantity that (i) is complete—*discrete magnitude* on the side of what was the One (e.g. pure space, time etc. [§99R])—or (ii) can be continued further (since the boundaries have fallen away)—*continuous magnitude* on the side of what was the many (eg. undefined fillings of space, time etc. [§99R]). Continuous magnitude is continuous—it is a continuous many. And discreet magnitude is a chunk or is complete—it is a one.

Quantum, or Quantity as There

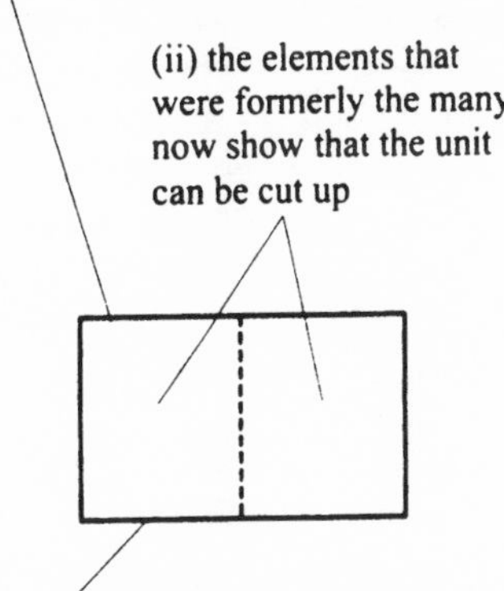
(i) Unit (formerly the One) as a limited quantity. The outer boundary of the large rectangle is now posited or asserted
(ii) the elements that were formerly the many now show that the unit can be cut up
The Quantum is a determinate magnitude, or a limited quantity. It is a quantitative chunk (i) as a unit, and (ii) as a many, or as able to be cut up into many

Figure 2.19

Quantum is the concept of externally limited quantity, or of a quantity with an outer boundary—a particular chunk of space or time, for example. As with the stage of Being-there, which was limited by having Nothing outside of it, the limitedness of the quantity is what allows it to be there or to have some determination or definition. A quantity with no limit is undefined. Space in general, for example, has no determination—when we try to say what it is, we simply wave our hands generally in the air, for instance. But we *can* point to a chunk of space, or to a quantity of space that has a boundary—to a two-foot square chunk of space, for instance. A limited chunk of space has enough of a character to be there, to be a something that we can point to. Thus quantum is a quantity that has enough of a definition, character or distinction to be there. It does not have any particular distinction, however, because it is not limited in a particular way that would give it a particular character. It is simply bounded or limited, which gives it enough of a character to be there.

Because the Quantum is now limited, the outer boundary is reestablished—which I represent by making the line for the outer boundary (the One) solid. Since the boundary of the One surrounding the many is now established, the many no longer run on—which I represent by eliminating the additional manys implied on either side.

Just as there were two ways of taking Pure Quantity in the last stage, this quantum can also be taken in two ways: as a unit (a chunk of quantity or one) or as cut up (which recognizes that the chunk of quantity can be further divided or is a many).

Number or Developed Quantum

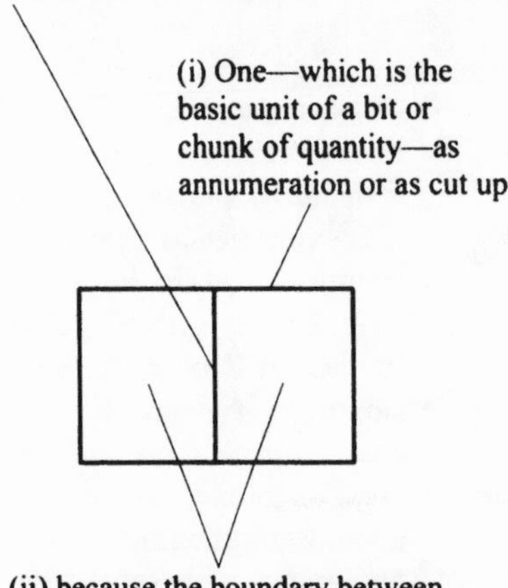

Figure 2.20

In the last stage, quantity was limited and thereby took on a character or definition. The concept of number captures or grasps the character or definition that the limited quantity has. Number is the concept that grasps a first attempt to describe a quantity with a determination, character or definition. A limited or defined quantity is a determinate bit, or a "one." Number is thus a developed concept of limited quantity. Its basic unit is "one," which is the basic concept of a bit of quantity.

The two ways of taking Pure Quantity and Quantum in the last two stages, however, give Number two different moments that can be distinguished by virtue of their identities or qualities—two qualitative moments, as Hegel puts it (§102R). First, (i) One can be seen as a whole chunk of put-together units, or as *annumeration*. Second, (ii) One can be seen as individual units.

Because Number includes the thought of the One as a unity of units or annumeration ([i] above), the inner boundary that separates and defines the units of the One is now reestablished. I represent this change in the diagram by making the boundary between the two many or inner units solid.

Extensive and Intensive Magnitude

(i) Extensive Magnitude, or the whole quantum as the limit, but also as multiple within itself: it is a many

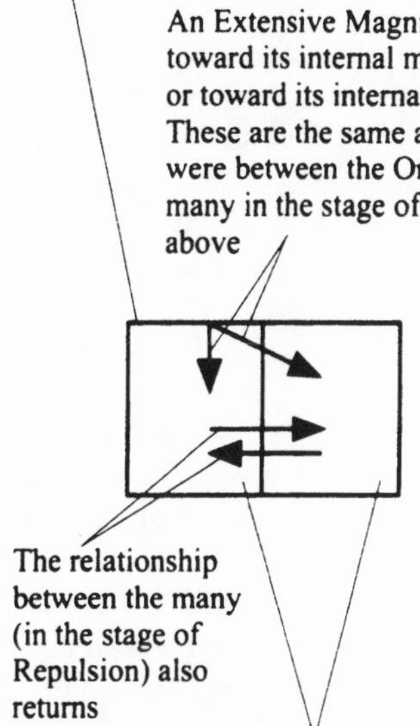

An Extensive Magnitude points toward its internal multiplicity, or toward its internal bits as a set These are the same arrows that were between the One and the many in the stage of Repulsion above
The relationship between the many (in the stage of Repulsion) also returns

(ii) Intensive Magnitude or Degree, which are each simple within themselves, i.e. they are ones. However, they are now defined in terms of their relationship with each other. They are bits of quantity that get defined by reference to —or by going beyond themselves into—other bits of quantity. They are *self-external*

Figure 2.21

The connections that were between the One and the many in the last stage of Quality are reestablished. As a result, the arrows representing those connections in the earlier diagram return in this one.

The two ways of taking number in the last stage lead to two new ways of conceiving of the One in this stage. First (as in [i] above), the One is the concept of a whole, externally limited quantity or quantum that is multiple within itself. It is a set or bunch of bits of quantity. Because the One is now the concept of a set of bits of quantity, it points toward those bits of quantity. An Extensive Magnitude is an extended quantity that points toward its being cut up into other quantities, a process represented by the arrows that point from the One to the units within the One. Because the One is defined as a set or by pointing toward the internal bits, it is a many.

Second, the One is the concept of individual units (as in [ii] above). As the stage of Being-in-itself in the Doctrine of Quality showed, however, something can be a something only if it is limited by something else. So each unit or bit within the One can be defined as or have its character as a bit only by being limited. The left bit of quantity is defined or limited by the right bit of quantity—the right bit provides its boundary. The right bit of quantity is the same as the left bit of quantity: it is also a bit of quantity. So the left bit of quantity is defined by being limited by something that is *itself*, although the "itself" that defines it is outside of, or external to it and sets its boundary. Because the left bit of quantity can be what it is only by being limited and defined by an external version of itself, it is what I'll call *self-external*. It can be what it is only by connecting to its limit, which is the same as itself. Because the left bit is defined in the same way that Being-in-itself was defined, I depict its process of definition with the same sort of arrow I used in Being-in-itself. The left bit defines itself through a process represented by the arrow that extends from the left bit and points toward the right bit. Of course, the right bit of quantity has exactly the same connection to, and is defined in the same way as, the left bit of quantity. It can be what it is only by being limited by an external version of itself. Hence, it, too, is *self-external*. The right bit is defined through a process represented by the arrow that extends from the left bit and points toward the right bit.

Therefore, each of the internal bits is a limited quantity whose limit, or external boundary, is fixed by another bit of quantity that is the same as itself. They are both *self-external* bits of quantity. Intensive Magnitude or Degree involves bits of limited quantity that point toward other bits of limited quantity. This process is represented in the diagram by the two arrows that run between the right and left bits: each bit is a limited quantity that is defined by pointing toward other bits of limited quantity. This process defines each of the many as a one—as a bit or unit separate from the other bit.

An example of intensive magnitude—which Hegel apparently offered in a lecture (§103A)—would be the sensation of a certain degree of temperature. What a certain degree of temperature feels like is a whole unto itself, and does not seem to break up into bits, although it is still characterized in relation to what other degrees of temperature feel like (the feeling of cold is simple in itself, but gets its character in relation to the feeling of hot, which is also simple within itself). Thus, the degree of temperature itself, from the point of view of how it is experienced, is an intensive magnitude. An example of extensive magnitude is the scale for measuring temperature (Fahrenheit or Celsius, for instance), which is broken up into a number of bits (§103A).

Notice that the "one" and the "many" have now changed places: the outer rectangle is now a many, and the two internal rectangles are now ones. I will say more about this phenomenon in the summary to this chapter.

In Intensive Magnitude or Degree, the concept of limited quantity has been developed further. A quantum or limited quantity is no longer just a bit or chunk of quantity: it is a chunk of quantity that is self-external. In the next stage this self-externality of quantity is driven to its limits, or taken as far as it can go. Because we end up in another spurious infinity, however, the concept of quantity will turn out to be inadequate, and the concept of quality will have to be brought back in to break a logical impasse.

Degree

The whole quantum (the outer rectangle) is now defined in relation to another quantum. Under Extensive Magnitude, it was a whole limited quantity that divided into further limited quantities or quanta. It is therefore defined by its connection with other limited quantities. This same definition process was what made the simple bits self-external in the last stage. There, the simple bits were defined by their connection with another limited quantity. As Intensive Magnitude, they were bits of limited quantity defined against other limited quantities.

So now all three of the limited quantities—the outer rectangle and the two inside bits—are defined in the same way.

Since all three of the quanta or limited quantities are defined in the same way, we can give a general definition of the concept of a quantum: quantum (limited quantity) in general is self-external. It is the "expulsion beyond itself" (§104). A quantum is always defined in terms of another quantum that, as quantum, is the same as itself. That is exactly the definition of the concept of Degree that was offered for Intensive Magnitude in the last stage. So now the whole quantum—and not just the two inside quanta—is defined by the concept of Degree. The concept of Degree is no longer only one way of defining what we have before us, as it was in the last stage; it now defines the whole.

The nature of the whole quantum is to be a self-external bit: it points toward or is defined in relation to other bits of quantity into which it divides. There is nothing to stop this division—the quantum divides infinitely. The quantum is thus a *mediated immediacy*

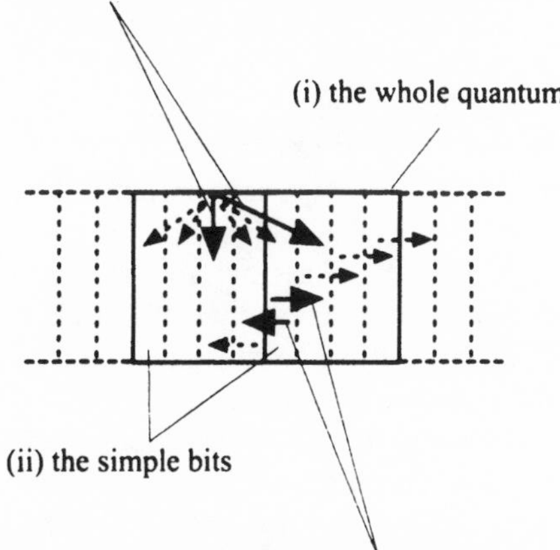

The nature of the simple bits is to be a self-external bit: they are defined by, point toward, or project into other bits of limited quantity that are their limits. Nothing stops this projection —the simple bits are infinitely progressive. They are *immediacies that are mediated*

Figure 2.22

Degree is thus the whole quantum now defined as self-external both within, which is to say insofar as it is cut up, and without, which is to say insofar as it runs on outwardly. Because there is nothing to stop this process of self-externality, Degree divides endlessly, and runs on endlessly. "In itself," or in its nature, quantum goes on or shrinks forever.

Here in Degree, the concepts of immediacy and mediatedness intertwine. In the stage of Quantum above, the whole chunk was an immediacy, was what was there on its own account. Here in Degree, however, the whole quantum has become a *mediated immediacy*—it is an immediacy that is mediated by other bits. The whole quantum is mediated by the inside bits because it cannot be defined or cannot be what it is without its connection to those other bits. Moreover, in Quantum, the bits were mediated. Since they were defined as the cut-up bits of the quantum, they could be what they are only through their connection with the whole quantum. They were not defined on their own accounts. In this stage, however, the bits are defined as immediacies, or simple, independent bits, *that are also mediated by*, or defined through their connection to, the other bits toward which they point. Thus, in Degree, all sides—the whole and the bits—have now been defined as mediated immediacies.

The fact that limited quantity is now defined in general terms as self-external leads us to another spurious or bad infinity. Since every limited quantity is defined in connection with another limited quantity, we cannot fix the definition of any limited quantity without introducing another limited quantity. The attempt to define a limited quantity thus produces an infinite progress of limited quantity.

Since the beginning of the Doctrine of Quantity, we have been trying to define the nature of quantity. This attempt, however, has produced a spurious infinity that blocks the ability to fix a definition of quantity. The understanding—which, for Hegel, is the faculty of reason that involves fixing the definitions of things—has produced an infinite progress that will make it impossible for the understanding to achieve its goal. The understanding will never be able to fix the definition of quantity if it is constantly caught in an infinite progress. This explanation can never be finished. Similarly, the definition of a concept can never be finished and hence fixed by an infinite progress. The definition of the concept of quantity can therefore be fixed or completed only if the infinite progress can be stopped.

The spurious infinity can also be characterized as a contradiction. The attempt to define the concept of quantity led to the concept of a limited quantity. A limited quantity was the first concept of a determined or defined quantity. But now the attempt to define limited quantity produces a spurious infinity. When the understanding tries to nail down the nature of a chunk of quantity or limited quantity it must bring in another quantity. But to define that second limited quantity, it must bring in another limited quantity. Since the attempt to define a chunk of quantity or limited quantity necessarily pushes on to another chunk of quantity, there is a sense in which a limited quantity is not actually limited. A chunk is not really a chunk if it cannot be defined without running on to other chunks. The understanding has thus produced a contradiction: it has produced a definition of the concept of limited quantity that is also not a concept of limited quantity. The limited quantity of the understanding turns out not to be limited.

As was the case at the end of the stage of Nothing and in the stage of Spurious Infinity, we have exhausted the current logical strategy. Our current strategy has been to try to define each of the limited quantities on its own. The fact that we have been led to another spurious infinity shows that this strategy will not work. We have still not succeeded in defining the three logical elements currently in play. We will need to adopt a new strategy if we are to break out of this logical impasse. The new strategy is necessitated by the results of this strategy. What we learn from the spurious infinity is that the logical elements cannot be defined without considering their connections to one another. In the next stage we use their connections to one another to try to fix their definitions.

Eventually, this exploration of the quantities' connections with one another will bring back into play the concept of quality. We are trying to establish the definition or character of quantity. The character of quantity is the quality of quantity. To fix the definition or character of quantity is to fix the quality of quantity, to say what quality quantity has. Thus, the attempt to define the concept of quantity will reintroduce the concept of quality.

We are not yet in a position to bring the concept of quality back into play, however. Reintroducing the concept of quality is not yet necessitated because we have not yet exhausted the attempt to define quantity with the category of quantity. In the next stage we try to define the connection between the logical elements by using the category of quantity. Only when that attempt fails will the reintroduction of the category for quality be necessitated. We must exhaust the resources of the category of quantity before the reintroduction of quality is necessitated. The concept of Ratio is an attempt to capture the connection between the logical elements by still employing the category of quantity.

Ratio

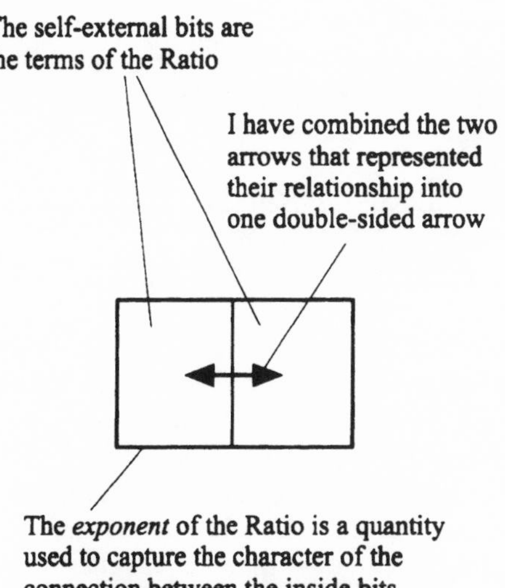
The self-external bits are the terms of the Ratio
I have combined the two arrows that represented their relationship into one double-sided arrow
The *exponent* of the Ratio is a quantity used to capture the character of the connection between the inside bits taken together as a set. It is the Ratio

Figure 2.23

The outside rectangle is still supposed to be the concept that gathers up the two inside bits. Its character as the gathering concept grew out of the connections that were implied in the Doctrine of Quality, where it was defined as the One. It did not have that character in the last stage, however, when it was defined as just another self-external bit, like the two inside bits. In this stage, the outside rectangle becomes the gathering term for the two inside bits. It fixes the character or nature of the inside bits—taken together—with a quantity. It captures the quantitative relationship between the two bits. So if one bit is 3 and the other is 6, for example, then the ratio is the exponent "x2." The outside rectangle represents the exponent of the ratio, which grasps the Ratio of the two bits. It is the thought of the connection between the two inside bits as a set. It is immediate because what it is or its definition is found in or given by the quantity of two inside bits.

The Ratio is the outside boundary, the gathering concept for the two inside bits, and corresponds to the stage of Being-for-itself in the Doctrine of Quality. Like Being-for-itself, the Ratio is defined by the two inside logical elements taken together as a set. Moreover, like Being-for-itself, the Ratio also succeeds in stopping the spuriously infinite process that occurred in the last stage. Although the Ratio is a quantity, it is not a self-external quantity. Like the concept of Being-for-itself, because it includes or gathers up the "others" that define it, there is no "other" into which it can pass. To put the point more quantitatively, there are no outside quantities into which the Ratio becomes self-external. It includes the passing over or self-external connection between the inside bits, but does not itself self-externalize except into the inside bits which it already contains. Hence it stops the spurious infinity of the last stage. It does not self-externalize into any outside bits, so quantity no longer runs on.

Moreover, like Being-for-itself, the Ratio is a new sort of being. Ratio is a new kind of quantity, or, to use the language of the stage of Being-for-itself, the category of quantity has now been determined or defined at a higher level. A Ratio is a universal for the category of quantity. It is a group-term for the category of quality, since, as a set of quantities, it contains a multiplicity of other quantities. Moreover, like Being-for-itself, because the Ratio stops the spuriously infinite process of the last stage, it is a quantity that has achieved a new level of stability. It is a quantity capable of overgrasping the constant flux of underlying quantities without undermining its own definition. The inside bits are defined in a process in which they each become self-external by reference to the other bit. The Ratio is a stable concept that includes this passing-over process of the inside bits.

Moreover, like the early definition of Being-for itself, the Ratio is currently being defined by the bits that it includes. It has no independent definition or character of its own. Its character is given to it by the nature of the bits. The fact that its character is simply given by the character of the inside bits makes the Ratio in its current form immediate.

This stage also leads to the processes of Repulsion and Attraction that Being-for-itself underwent, however. As in the stage of Repulsion, as soon as the Ratio draws the inside bits together as a set, there must be some way of distinguishing the bits from one another, or holding them apart or separating them. Remember that in the stage of Intensive Magnitude, the self-externalizing process of the two inside bits defined them as the same: as limited quantities or bits. However, that process also defined the bits as cut up or divided from one another. The element of division, separation or negation returns here. As was the case for the many in the stage of Repulsion, the inside bits can be a set of items only if they are both the same as each other (so that they can be together in the set) and also different from each other (so that they can be more than one item, a multiplicity). In this stage, the bits' self-externalization process defines them as different from one another, or holds them apart: they repulse each other.

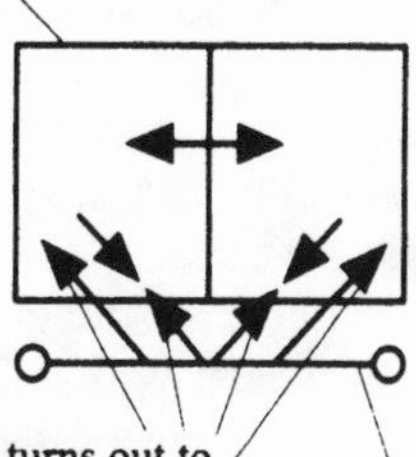
The whole quantum is the terms of the Ratio taken together as a set
The Ratio turns out to have a for-itself relationship with the terms taken together as a set. It is defined as separate from the terms of the set (repulses them), but also pulls the terms together as a one (attracts them)
The Ratio is now a separate concept that captures the quality of the quantity. It is a *proto-quality*

Figure 2.24

Now that the process of the inside bits defines them as different, however, they are no longer holding themselves together in the set. That means that the Ratio as a concept now has to do some work: it has to define the bits as a set, to pull or hold the bits together in a set. The Ratio holds the bits together by giving them its quantity—it characterizes them, or repulses them. In the stage of Repulsion, the One also repulsed or characterized the many, but it did so by giving the many its quality, rather than quantity. Here in the Doctrine of Quantity, however, the Ratio characterizes the bits by giving them its quantity—the ratio "x2," for instance.

Once the Ratio characterizes the inside bits, however, two things happen. First, the inside bits no longer have any value immediately on their own. Because the Ratio is now giving them their quantity as a set, each of their specific quantities no longer matters, so long as the Ratio stays the same. If the Ratio is "x2," for instance, the values of the inside bits could be any two numbers with a ratio of x2: 2:4, 4:8, 3:6 and so on. The specific value of the bits no longer matters. All that matters is the value of their connection to one another—a value captured by the Ratio. The ratio characterizes the two bits taken together as a set. The individual characters of the inside bits are not important.

Second, just as the One did in the stage of Repulsion, the Ratio now has a character or definition of its own that no longer relies on the given quantity of the inside bits. The process of repulsing the bits gives the Ratio a new function that the bits do not share, and thus defines the Ratio as separate from the bits. Moreover, the Ratio now has a character that is independent of the character or definition of the inside bits. The quantity of the bits could be 2:4, 4:8, or 3:6 and the Ratio would still be what it is. The Ratio no longer depends on the given quantity of the bits for its definition. Although the Ratio is still a limited quantity—a definition that it shares with the inside bits—it has a new character that gives it a definition separate from the bits.

While the Ratio's character is independent, it is still mediated. The specific quantitative character of the inside bits no longer matters, but the definition of the Ratio still needs the bits to be what it is. Without the bits, it could not be a Ratio.

As was the case for the many in the stage of Attraction, however, the process in which the bits are defined as separate is still the same process in which they are defined as the same. Since negation has come back into the picture, the way in which they are the same is now defined. The bits are attracted to one another, or the same as one another, in some particular way, namely in the way embraced by the Ratio. Moreover, now that the Ratio's connection with the bits is also defined by negation or repulsion, it, too, has a defined connection with those bits. It is the *kind* of quantitative connection that the bits are.

Finally, now that the Ratio has a separate definition from the quantitative bits, and is defined as the kind that the bits are, it is what I will call a *proto-quality*. Although the Ratio is still a quantity, it is now a concept that is independent of the specific quantities of the bits and captures the character or quality of the connection between the two bits.

I have divided the coverage of Ratio into two diagrams and two discussions because Hegel distinguishes two sorts of Ratio. The first sort of Ratio is an "immediate quantum" or exponent (§105). In mathematics, an exponent is a number or quantity that captures the relationship between two specific numbers. It is illustrated by the first diagram I offered for Ratio. The second sort of Ratio is defined by mediation (§105), rather than immediacy, and is illustrated by the second diagram for Ratio above. The first sort of Ratio corresponds to the early concept of Being-for-itself. Like Being-for-itself, this sort of Ratio gathers up given items for its character. The Ratio gathers up the given quantities of the bits by characterizing their connection with one another. This first sort of Ratio takes a set of given numbers and defines their numerical relationship. So, if the two bits are 2:4, the Ratio is x2; if the two bits are 1:5, the Ratio is x5; and so on. The Ratio is the exponent of the two specific numbers being connected together. This sort of Ratio is dependent for its character on the specific quantities of the bits. It is a bottom-up definition: it starts with some given numbers and then fixes or defines their connection by specifying the ratio. This sort of Ratio is exemplified by reports of the results of surveys, for example. When a poll asks people which of two presidential candidates they prefer, the results of the poll are often reported as a ratio: people preferred candidate X over candidate Y by a ratio of 3:1, for instance. In this case, the specific numeric figures are given: out of 1000 people, 750 preferred candidate X. The ratio is derived from the specific polling figures.

Sometimes, however, we use ratios in a way that does not depend on specific numeric figures. Unlike an exponent, this sort of Ratio does not capture the relationship between two specific numbers. This second sort of Ratio is a top down definition. My mother's instructions for cooking rice exemplify this sort of ratio. She said that, to cook rice, the ratio of water to raw rice should always be 2:1. Now I use that ratio to fix the quantities of the bits—the water and rice—rather than using the quantities of the bits to fix the ratio, as we did in the survey example. If I want a lot of rice, I use eight cups of water and four cups of rice. When I only want a little rice, I use two cups of water and one cup of rice.

This second sort of Ratio involves a higher level of ideality or universality than does the first sort. It is one step closer to thought or ideality than is the first sort of Ratio. The first sort of Ratio depends on the given reality for its character, but this second sort of Ratio imposes its character on, or determines, reality. In this second definition of Ratio, Ratio is a thought that determines or characterizes reality, rather than a reality that characterizes a thought, which was the case for the first sort of Ratio.

Although the definition of this second Ratio is independent of the specific character of the bits, the Ratio still cannot have its definition or character—or cannot be what it is—without its connection to the inside bits. It is not an immediate Ratio that is dependent on the character of the bits, as was the first sort of Ratio, but it still could not be what it is without the bits. There must be bits for it to be a Ratio. Hence, its character, while not determined by the bits, is mediated by the bits.

With this second definition of Ratio, the category of quality has begun to return. Now that Ratio has a function which distinguishes it from the inside bits, it has a character or quality of its own. Moreover, this sort of Ratio fixes or determines the character of the bits. It defines their quality. To be sure, the Ratio is still a quantity—which is why it has only proto-quality status. Nevertheless, it is a quantity which attempts to capture the quality of limited quantity. In the next stage, Ratio as proto-quality becomes a genuine quality: a given being-there or quality to which a quantity is connected. Since the categories of both quantity and quality will define the logical elements in play, a new logical category has been introduced: the category of Measure.

IV. The Doctrine of Measure

The category of "Measure" unites quality and quantity. Hegel drew his inspiration for using this term from the Presocratic philosophers. For the Presocratics, Hegel said, a "measure" is a moment of sensuous judgment, of judgment about sensuous being. It is a moment in which reason judges or measures being (*Lectures on the History of Philosophy* 1983, vol. 1, 294). To measure something in the world of sensuous objects is to size it up, to judge it, or determine its nature. In the Doctrine of Quality, to determine something is to fix its quality. But, as the expression "size it up" suggests, to determine something is also to fix its quantity—to size it, to measure it in terms of its quantity. To "measure" something is thus to fix both the quality and quantity of something.

There are expressions in English that capture Hegel's use of the term "measure" quite well. Think of the English sentence "he had a measure of wit." To have a measure of wit, or good humor, or some other characteristic is to have a definite quantity of wit, good humor or what have you. Thus, a measure is a definite quantity (thought of as having been measured). To have a definite quantity of wit is also to have a certain quality of wit. At the end of Doctrine of

Quantity, a defined or determined quantity is a certain quality of quantity which is precisely what appears in the next stage of Immediate Measure.

In Measure we will have two developments going on at the same time: (1) the development of the whole Measure, as the whole unity of quantity and quality, and (2) the development of the *connection* between quantity and quality *within* the whole Measure which occurs as the Measure develops. I have depicted these two processes in separate pictures. I depict (1) first, in diagrams that depict the whole measure, and then I depict (2) in spin-off diagrams that "zoom in" on or depict the relationship between the quantity (represented by a square) and quality (represented by a circle).

Immediate Measure

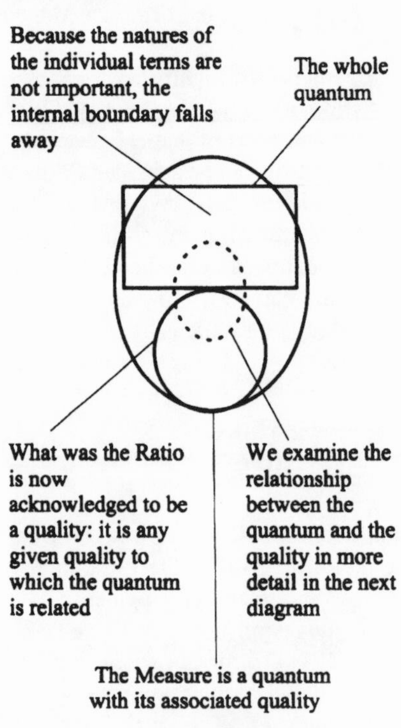
Because the natures of the individual terms are not important, the internal boundary falls away
The whole quantum
What was the Ratio is now acknowledged to be a quality: it is any given quality to which the quantum is related
We examine the relationship between the quantum and the quality in more detail in the next diagram
The Measure is a quantum with its associated quality

Figure 2.25

The internal boundary between the two self-external bits, or terms, has fallen away for logical reasons, not for pictorial convenience. In the second definition of Ratio above, the specific, quantitative definitions of the bits are not important. Again, the bits can be 2:4, or 3:6, or 4:8, and the Ratio will still the same, namely, x2. Because the specific characters of the bits do not matter anymore, the internal boundary disappears. The bits are no longer specifically distinguished from one another. They meld together into one quantum.

This stage draws out the conclusion implied by the last stage, namely, that the Ratio is a concept for the character or quality of quantity. The Ratio becomes the quality of the quantum (i.e. of the bits that have become one). The quantum itself has no specific quality (it is qualitatively indifferent), but it is connected to a quality. A quantum is a limited quantity that has enough of a character to be there (see the stage of Quantum). So the first quality of the quantity (i.e. quantum) is that it is there.

Immediate Measure offers the first definition of the quality of quantity: the quality of quantity is, to begin with, that it is there. An Immediate Measure is the thought of quantity that has thereness, or of a limited quantity that is connected to a Being-there as its quality (cf. the stage of Being-there). To say that the quality of the quantity is "there" is to say that the quantity's quality has thereness or is given. The quality of the quantity is simply found out there in the world of experience. Because the quality is given or found, the connection between the quality and quantity is undefined. The quality and quantity are simply "found" to be together in the world of experience. The givenness of the quality as well as the connection between the quantity and quality makes this stage of Measure "Immediate" (cf. Being-for-itself for a description of immediacy).

One example of an Immediate Measure is ice. Certain temperatures are associated with different solidities of water. The quality of water changes from solid (ice), to liquid (water), to gas (steam), depending on the quantity-range of the temperature. Ice is a limited quantity of temperature that is connected to a thereness or quality of water. Ice as a concept includes both the quality—namely the solidity of the water—and a limited quantity of temperatures (such as, 0°C to -5°C) that is connected to that quality.

Following the conventions I used in the Doctrines of Quality and Quantity, I have depicted the qualitative aspect of Measure as a round bubble, and the quantitative aspect of Measure as a rectangle. The Measure is depicted as an oval surrounding both the quantity and the quality. Because the quantity and quality have no special connection with one another in this stage, however, there is no arrow or other symbol in the diagram to represent their connection. The quality and quantity are simply "found" to be "next" to each other.

The next diagram depicts the relationship that obtains between quality and quantity in this stage.

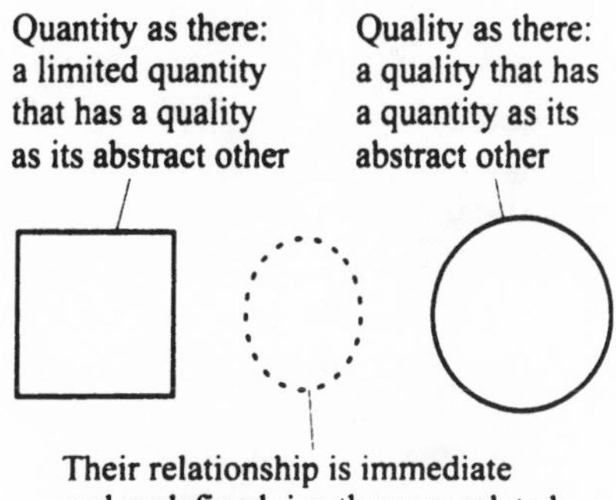
Quantity as there: a limited quantity that has a quality as its abstract other
Quality as there: a quality that has a quantity as its abstract other
Their relationship is immediate and undefined, i.e. they are related, but not in any particular way

Figure 2.26

This diagram depicts the connection between the quantity (represented by the square) and quality (represented by the circle) in Immediate Measure.

Here both quality and quantity are taken to be "as there": as in the stage of Being-there, they are both somethings that have the other as their abstract-other. Moreover, their connection is immediate, "as found" or "as there" as well: the quality and quantity are simply there together, or are found to be together. That they are found together is illustrated in the diagram by the absence of any arrow representing a connection or relationship between quality and quantity. In the diagram, the square (quantity) and circle (quality) are simply given or found to be "next" to each other.

Because the connection between the quantity and quality is immediate, it is not determined in any particular way. Hence, the relationship is fairly arbitrary: sometimes changes in the quantum (limited quantity) will not effect the quality, sometimes they will. Some changes in temperature, for example, do not affect water's solidity, some do. We cannot use logic to say which changes in quantity will change the quality because their connection is not determined by concepts. Whatever happens is just "given" to observation and experience.

The Measureless

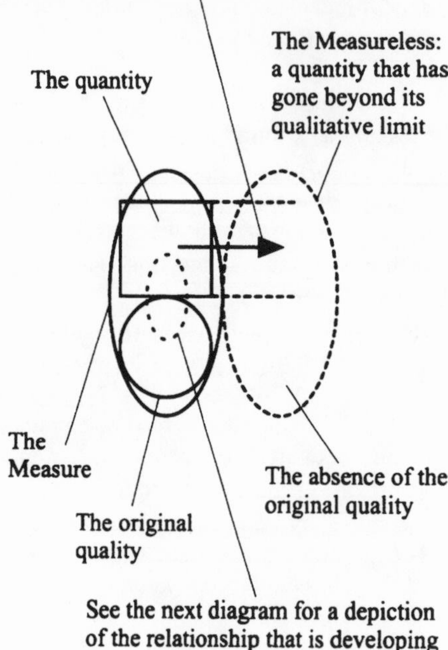
The quantity is a self-external bit: that is its quality. That quality now takes effect: the quantity self-externalizes or alters
The Measureless: a quantity that has gone beyond its qualitative limit
The quantity
The Measure
The absence of the original quality
The original quality
See the next diagram for a depiction of the relationship that is developing between quantity and quality here

Figure 2.27

The Measure implies the presence of the Measureless. It is the nature of quantity, by its concept, to alter, or to increase or decrease. Quantity is, by definition, self-external: it is defined by passing into another quantity. The quantity of the Measure can therefore be defined only by being self-external, or by passing into another quantity. So the Measure's quantity passes into a new quantity that, because it is no longer connected to the specific quality of the original Measure, is connected instead to an unspecified quality. Because the new quantity has no specific quality, it is Measureless (and has a dashed outline). The Measureless is the thought of a new quantity that has gone beyond its qualitative limit. It is a quantity without the original quality that was associated with the Measure. When temperature of the ice rises above 0°C, for instance, it produces a Measureless: a quantity that no longer has the specific quality of the original Measure.

The presence of the Measureless begins to define the quality of the Measure in a new way that is independent of the Measure's quantity. In the stage of Measure, the quality is defined by the quantity: the quality is just the quality of the quantity. Like the Measure, however, the Measureless includes both quantity and quality. The Measure's quality can now be defined in relation to the quality of the Measureless, and not just in relation to the quality of the quantity to which is it attached. At the moment, of course, the quality of the Measureless is defined only as the absence of the original quality of the Measure. The absence of the original quality, however, is just the original quality's nothing. The original quality is thus now able to be defined in the same way that Being-there was defined in the stage of Being-there. The original quality is alterable—it could be nothing—and therefore has enough of a character to at least be there.

This concept of the Measureless recalls the Presocratic philosopher Anaximander's notion of the boundless, or undetermined (*apeiron*) (see *Lectures on the History of Philosophy* I, 282, 44, 186). It is the indefinite—the unmeasurable—being (represented by a dashed oval) that Anaximander had used to explain change.

Please note that, although Hegel makes clear that quantity can alter by both increasing or decreasing, I have depicted the quantity as increasing. To depict it as decreasing would have required me to draw ever smaller pictures, which would become impossible (and likely impossible to read as well).

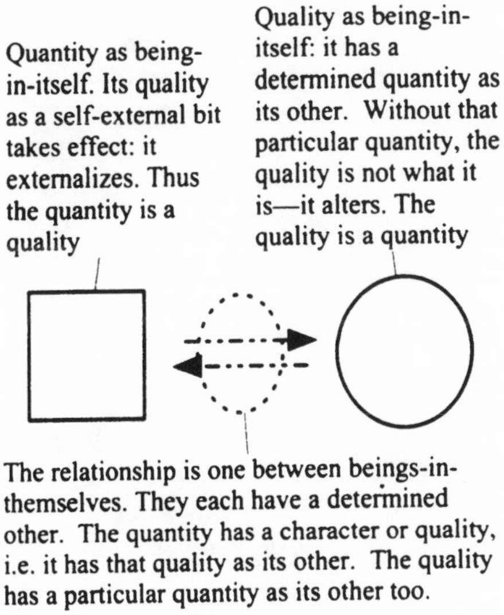

Quantity as being-in-itself. Its quality as a self-external bit takes effect: it externalizes. Thus the quantity is a quality

Quality as being-in-itself: it has a determined quantity as its other. Without that particular quantity, the quality is not what it is—it alters. The quality is a quantity

The relationship is one between beings-in-themselves. They each have a determined other. The quantity has a character or quality, i.e. it has that quality as its other. The quality has a particular quantity as its other too.

Figure 2.28

In the stage of the Measureless, the connection between quantity (the square) and quality (the circle) has become defined. It is the nature of quantity to be self-external—that is quantity's quality. A quantity is defined by being self-external. Here, the quantity of the Measure shows its character or demonstrates its quality: it lives up to its definition of being self-external by self-externalizing or passing into another quantity. The quantity lives up to its character as a self-external bit. A self-external bit runs on or shrinks endlessly (see Degree above), so the quantity of the Measure runs on too. By living up to its quality, however, the quantity shows that it is, "*in itself*," also a quality. It proves that it is not only a quantity, but also a quality. The quantity's process of definition therefore now connects the quantity to the concept of quality.

Moreover, the alteration of the quantity implies that there is a Measureless: a new quantity that has gone beyond its qualitative limit. Since the original quantity has gone beyond its qualitative limit, the quality has altered too. The quantity has changed enough so that the original quality is gone, though what that quality is has not yet been determined or defined.

Still, when the original quality changes, it shows that it is, "*in itself*," a quantity too. Quality is defined by quantity because, when the quantity changes, the quality changes too. A quality can be what it is only in the presence of a certain quantity. Without that certain quantity, the quality cannot be what it is. As a result, the definition of the quality is now also seen to be connected to the concept of quantity. Not only is the definition of quantity connected to quality, but the definition of quality is connected to quantity as well. Neither can be what it is without the other. The concepts of quality and quantity are therefore now connected to one another by definition.

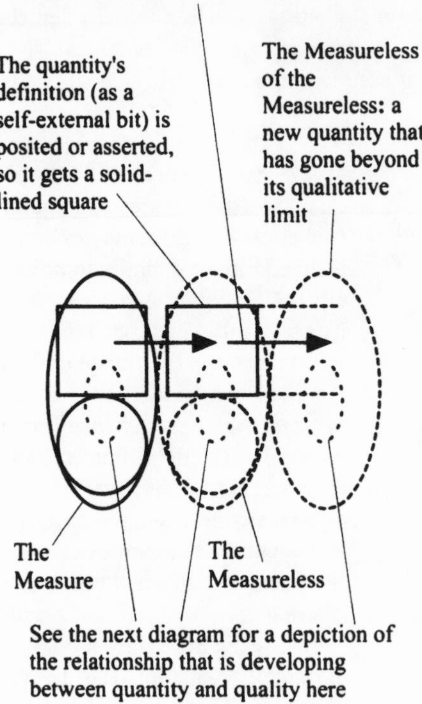
The new quantity has a quality: is a self-external bit too, so it externalizes or alters.
The quantity's definition (as a self-external bit) is posited or asserted, so it gets a solid-lined square
The Measureless of the Measureless: a new quantity that has gone beyond its qualitative limit
The Measure
The Measureless
See the next diagram for a depiction of the relationship that is developing between quantity and quality here

Figure 2.29

Now, the focus is on the Measureless. It is the nature of quantity to be self-external. A quantity can be there, have a definition or be determined only if it passes into another quantity. That means that the quantity of the Measureless can only be what it is or be defined by passing into yet another quantity. The quantity of the Measureless has the quality of being defined by passing into another quantity. In this stage, that quality of the Measureless's quantity takes effect: the quantity of the Measureless goes through its process of being defined by self-externalizing and so alters. So now the quality of the Measureless's bit of quantity implies the presence of its own Measureless: the Measureless spawns a new Measureless, which I'll call *the Measureless of the Measureless*, and represent in the diagram with another dashed oval like the oval of the Measureless.

But the Measureless of the Measureless, too, includes a quantity whose nature is to be there as self-external. So its quantity, too, must be defined by passing into yet another quantity. It must alter too. That alteration will produce yet another Measureless, a Measureless for the Measureless-of-the-Measureless. That third Measureless will also have a quantity that will alter too, and so on indefinitely. The quality of quantity—the fact that it is the nature or quality of every quantity to be self-external, and hence, to alter—thus produces a spuriously infinite progress of Measurelesses.

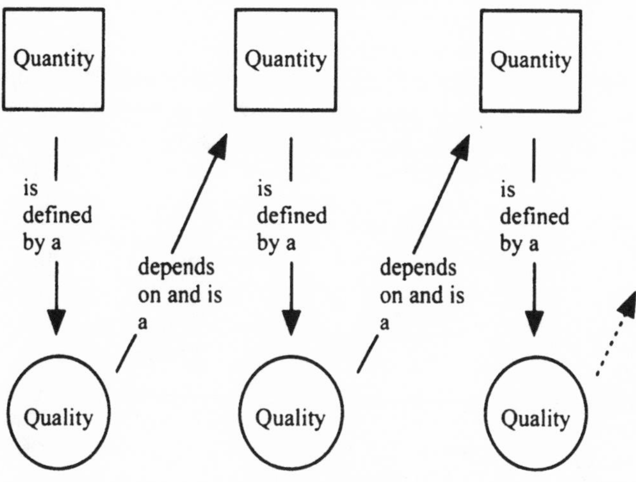

Figure 2.30

The running-on of Measurelesses generates a corresponding running-on process in the connection between quality and quantity. In the first moment in the stage of the Measureless, quantity was defined as "in itself" a quality. When we looked at the character of the quantity on its own, it turned out to be defined as a quality. Its quality is that it is self-external. The original quality was also defined as in itself a quantity, because once the original quantity changed, then the quality changed too. So a quality's definition or character, when taken on its own, is defined by quantity too. In this moment, as we go from Measureless to Measureless in the spuriously infinite progress, quantity and quality continue to be defined through their connection with one another: the quality of each new quantity comes out, so that each new quantity is defined as in-itself a quality by altering; when the quantity alters, however, it is connected to a new quality. But that quality shows that it is also in-itself a quantity, because when the quantity to which it is attached alters, it alters too. So the new quality is attached to yet another quantity, which is defined in-itself as a quality by altering once again; when that quantity alters it connects to yet another quality. But that quality shows . . . and so on, endlessly. So the first quantity is defined as a quality, which is in turn defined as another quantity, which is again defined as a another quality, which is again defined as another quantity, and so on. As the spuriously infinite process of the Measurelesses runs on, this process, too, runs on indefinitely.

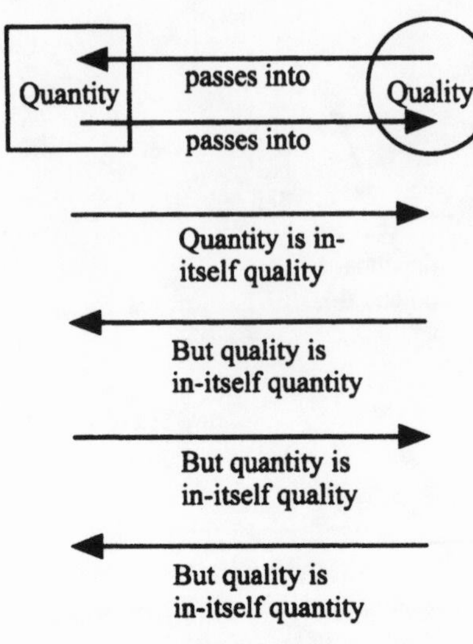

Figure 2.31

This running-on connection between quantity and quality can also be characterized as an endless process of flipping back and forth between the two: quantity turns out to be "in itself" quality, but quality, in turn, turns out to be "in itself" quantity, which turns out to be "in itself" quality, which turns out to be "in itself" quantity, and so on, *ad infinitum*.

The understanding has thus once again produced a spurious infinity with which it cannot rest (see also Becoming, Spurious Infinity and Degree above). The quantity's quality (character) is defined by pushing on to another quantity, which has a corresponding quality, by pushing on to another quantity, and so on, in a spuriously infinite process. Remember that the understanding is the faculty of reason that fixes the definitions of things. This section of the logic has been about trying to fix the definition of Measure as the unity of quality and quantity. The spuriously infinite process of the Measurelesses, however, prevents the understanding from being able to fix the definition of Measure. The understanding has produced a logical situation which prevents it from achieving its goal. Nevertheless, the understanding is right about the goal—the goal of logic *is* to determine or define the concepts of logic. The understanding must get its due. So reason must find a way to get beyond the pitfalls of the understanding. It must find a way to sublate (cancel but preserve) this spuriously infinite process—which it does in the next stages.

Transition to Essence

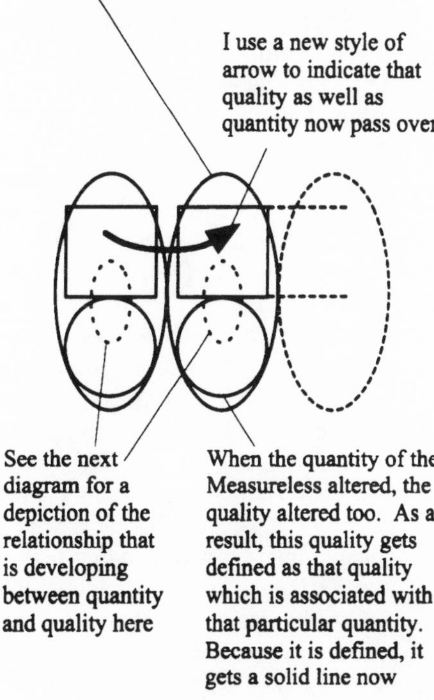
Now that the quality of the Measureless is determined or defined (see below), the Measureless *becomes a Measure*: it is a qualitative quantum; or a limited quantity with a particular quality attached to it
I use a new style of arrow to indicate that quality as well as quantity now pass over
See the next diagram for a depiction of the relationship that is developing between quantity and quality here
When the quantity of the Measureless altered, the quality altered too. As a result, this quality gets defined as that quality which is associated with that particular quantity. Because it is defined, it gets a solid line now

Figure 2.32

So far, the quality of the Measureless shows that it is "in itself" a quantity, because when its associated quantity alters, it alters too. But the quality of the Measureless has not yet determined itself as a particular quality or other. So far we have defined it as altered quality, or as the absence of the original quality that was in Measure. The quality of the Measureless is thus defined as an absence—namely, the absence of the original quality.

However, the Measureless's quantity is not really connected merely with an absence. No, it, too, must be connected to some particular, determined quality or other. The quality of the Measureless is defined by the quality of the Measure, first of all, insofar as it has the same sort of connection to the quality of the Measure that Being-there had to Nothing in the stage of Being-there. Just as the quality of the Measureless was the absence of the quality of the Measure, so the quality of the Measure is the absence of the original quality. The quality of the Measure is the absence—or Nothing—of the quality of the Measureless. Because the quality of the Measureless is being defined by its connection to its absence or Nothing, it has at least enough of a character to be there. A quality is also defined by being connected to its limit (see Being-in-itself). The quality of the Measureless *is* connected to a limit—it is limited by and so can be defined by its connection to the quality of the Measure, which limits it.

Once the quality of the Measureless is determined or defined, however, the Measureless is also defined *as a Measure*: like the original Measure, it, too, is a qualitative quantum, or a limited quantity with a particular quality attached to it. When the original Measure passes over, then, it is passing over into another Measure. As a result, both the quantity *and* quality of the original Measure pass over or alter. Until now, the arrows in the diagrams represented the passing or alteration only of quantity. I represent the fact that the whole Measure—both quality and quantity—is now passing over with a thicker, more substantial and slightly curved arrow.

When the Measureless becomes a Measure, the connection between quantity and quality also changes. Quantity and quality are now determined or defined as the same, and each passes into the other. Quantity has already been defined as quality, or as quantity that is quality. Quantity is defined as quantity and quality, or as determined/quantity/quality. Although quality had already been defined as quantity, it did not yet have a definition or character of its own. It was quantity/quality but was not yet determined.

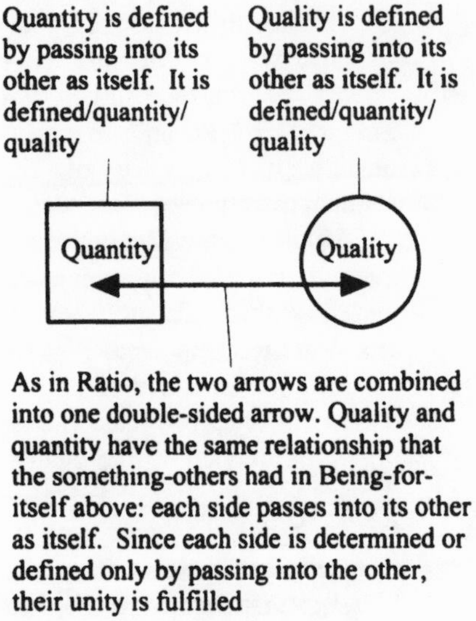

Now that the quality is determined, however, like quantity, it can be defined as determined/quantity/quality as well. Hence both quantity and quality are the now the same. The same situation obtained in the stage of Being-for-itself, when the spuriously infinite process of the something-others defined them as the same. As with the something-others, now that quality and quantity have the same character as determined/quantity/quality, when quality passes into quantity it is passing into itself. And when quantity passes into quality, it is passing into itself. Moreover, as in the stage of Being-for-itself, this process can be defined as a process of negation: each side is negated by passing over its other as itself.

Quantity is defined by passing into its other as itself. It is defined/quantity/ quality
Quality is defined by passing into its other as itself. It is defined/quantity/ quality
Quantity
Quality
As in Ratio, the two arrows are combined into one double-sided arrow. Quality and quantity have the same relationship that the something-others had in Being-for-itself above: each side passes into its other as itself. Since each side is determined or defined only by passing into the other, their unity is fulfilled

Figure 2.33

With this stage, the concept of Measure is fulfilled. Measure has been defined as the unity of quantity and quality, but at first the unity was not established. In Immediate Measure, quality and quantity were connected to one another, but that connection was simply given or found. Quantity and quality did not connect to one another by virtue of their definitions or characters. They had no determined or defined connection with one another. They were simply pasted or found together, so to speak. They were "given" as connected by the world of experience. Now, however, the unity of quality and quantity has been fulfilled in the sense that they are no longer pasted or glued together by the world of experience. Their definitions tie them together, since they must be defined in connection with one another. They are intertwined or unified by their own definitions. They combine themselves together, or blend themselves together, so to speak, through the process in which they each come to be defined. Quality and quantity are no longer like a child's pasted-together craft work. Their characters define their complete unity. As we will see, the syntactic pattern that has developed between quality and quantity here in the Doctrine of Measure—in which a unity between two concepts is at first defined as given or found, but is later established by the process through which the concepts are defined—will be repeated in other places in the logic.

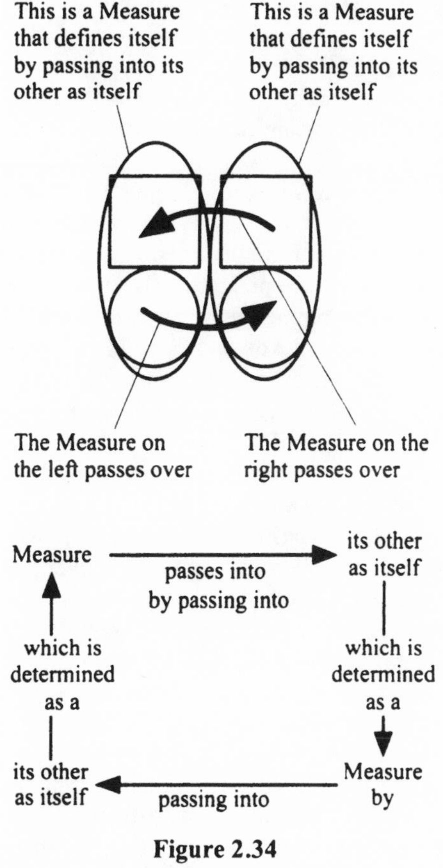

Figure 2.34

Now that the former Measureless is defined as a Measure, the Measure has the same relationship with its other that quality and quantity now have: the Measure can be defined only by passing into its other as itself, or into its other that is the same as itself. So now, not only do quantity and quality pass over within Measure, but their unity as Measure passes over as well. The whole, original Measure is determined or becomes what it is by passing into its other as itself.

The Measureless, too, of course, is determined as a Measure by passing into its other as well: it is the other that passes into its other as itself. Thus the original Measure (reading clockwise from the left) passes into its other as itself, which determines itself as a Measure too by passing into its other as itself, which in turn determines itself as a Measure by . . . and so on.

Therefore, a spurious infinity like the one in the stage of Spurious Infinity (in the Doctrine of Quality) has developed, except that the passing-over process here affects all the categories of Being—Quality, Quantity, and now their unity in Measure—and not just the category of Quality. Within each Measure, quality and quantity can be what they are only by passing into each other, where both are defined as the same. And each Measure can be what it is as a Measure only by passing into an other that is also defined as a Measure, and hence is the same. There is an endless flipping back-and-forth process between Measures. At the beginning of the Doctrine of Measure—in Immediate

Measure—Measure was defined in an immediate way, just as qualitative Being was at first defined in an immediate way in Being-in-itself in the Doctrine of Quality. But Being-in-itself was a something that turned out in Spurious Infinity to be a something-other. In a similar way, Immediate Measure has turned out to be a Measure-other. As in the case of the process of passing-over in Spurious Infinity, both directions of Measure's passing-over process can be described as processes of negation: the Measure is determined by negation by passing into its other; but its other is also determined by negation by passing into its other. Hence both sides are what they are by passing over, or by being negated. They contain negation as part of their definition.

A glob of chicken fat, for example, has a quality that is present only under a certain quantity, since, like water, it depends on quantities of temperature for its nature. The glob of fat is a "glob"—or has "globbiness" for its nature—only when the temperature is cool enough. Thus it is a Measure: its quality is dependent on a quantity such that, if the quantity changes, the quality changes also. But the quantity can be what it is or have its particular quality only against another quantity: the quantity of temperature is a certain temperature only in relation to the continuum of temperatures. But those other temperatures are associated with their own qualities—at higher temperatures, the chicken fat is a puddle of liquid, for example, and not a glob at all. As a result, the original Measure—the glob of chicken fat—can have its character only against other Measures, or against other quantities that have associated qualities. The glob of chicken fat is defined as a glob of chicken fat against other qualities and quantities of chicken fat. A Measure can be a Measure only by passing into another Measure.

As it did in the stage of Being-for-itself, this passing-over process spawns a new thought, and a *new level of ideality*. Remember that the passing over process of Spurious Infinity not only defined the something-others as unstable—in the sense that each something could not be defined on its own without being negated, or without passing into its other—it also defined them as *the same* as one another—namely, as something-others. This sameness generated the next thought. Being-for-itself was the thought of the sameness of the something-others. As the thought of their sameness, Being-for-itself was capable of grasping both the something-others and their passing-over process without itself passing over. It introduced a new level of stability. Moreover, Being-for-itself introduced ideality because it was defined by a process that was not given by reality, but could only be performed by thought. The new thought that will be introduced here and that grasps the sameness of the Measures moves even further away from reality into the realm of ideality or thought. The concept of Measure is the unity of all the categories of Being. It includes the category of quality, the category of quantity, and a category which unifies quality and quantity. It includes all of the logical categories that we use to grasp the realm of Being or world of experience—the world in which there are various quantities of somethings that are there. We ordinarily think of that world or realm of Being or world of experience as immediate, as given, or as found: that we just "find" things out there in reality or that reality is "given" to us by experience. That was how the realm of Being was defined by the logical categories here. To be "in itself" is to be given, immediate, or "found" in experience. The logic begins with this ordinary assumption. There is certainly some truth to this assumption. Many things happen to us in ordinary life that we did not predict or think about, and those events suggest that much about the world of experience is given. Empiricists such as David Hume translated this assumption into a conception of knowledge and reason (see Chapter One, Section I). On this view, our knowledge is simply given to us by the world of experience, and reason's job is to think about and process this given material.

The passing-over process of the Measures, however, shows that this ordinary assumption cannot stand. The assumption that the realm of Being is immediate or given must be sublated—cancelled but also preserved—in Hegel's technical, logical sense of "*Aufhebung*" (sublation) (see Chapter One, Section VIII). The assumption that things are given to us by the world of experience and that the job of reason is simply to draw the truths of that given reality into thought—to copy it with our thoughts—presupposes that things in the world of experience have their definitions or characters on their own. It presupposes that those characters and definitions are out there in reality so that we can copy them with our concepts or thoughts. The passing-over process of the Measures shows, however, that the characters or definitions of things in the realm of Being cannot be fixed on their own. The concept of Measure includes all of the logical concepts of the realm of Being—the basic concepts that are "behind the back" or presupposed by our ordinary judgments about reality and that are used to grasp the realm of Being. The attempt to define Measure on its own, however, has produced an infinitely spurious passing-over process that prevents us from being able to define it. We thought that we could grasp the concepts of Being in an immediate way based on the given character of reality, but the logical development shows that the supposed immediacy of Being was a sham. The realm of Being is not immediate, but mediated. It can be what it is only in relation to another. The immediacy of Being is a mere shine or semblance.

The logical conclusion that the immediacy of Being is a mere shine or semblance spawns a new thought, namely, the thought of whatever-it-is that is related to supposedly immediate Being. The fact that immediate Being is not really immediate, that its immediacy is a mere shine or semblance, that it is mediated and can be what it is only in relation to another, generates the thought of the other, of the whatever-it-is that stabilizes the passing-over process of Measure or of immediate Being. This thought will have the same logical relationship with the Measure-others that Being-for-itself had with the something-others: it will include or overgrasp the Measure-others and their passing-over process without itself passing over. Because the new concept is defined by the same logical process that defines Being-for-itself, it is a "for itself" concept. Unlike Being-for-itself, however, because the next concept steps out of or moves past all of the categories of Being, it will be one more step away from the (supposedly) immediate thereness of reality. It will be a new kind of presence, a new level of ideality. The logical process has shown that the realm of immediate Being is really mediated: it can be what it is or be defined only by being connected to another. The supposed immediacy of Being is a sham, shine, or semblance.

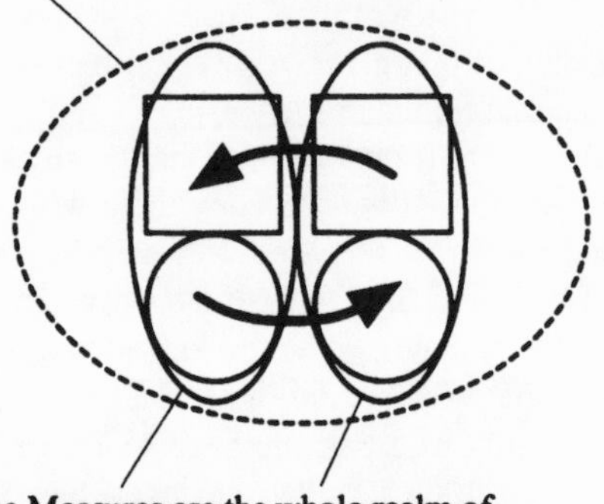

Essence as the one, overarching, stabilizing concept; a new presence or kind of being that does not itself pass over, but that has the whole realm of (supposedly) immediate-Being as its shine. It subsumes (cancels but preserves) the categories we saw in immediate-Being, but is not subject to them. It does not have thereness except through immediate-Being as its shine. It is not in the realm of immediate-Being, though it is related to immediate-Being
The Measures are the whole realm of immediate-Being, whose immediacy turned out to be a sham, mere shine or semblance. Immediate-Being is really mediated: it is what it is only in relation to another. Hence the whole realm of immediate-Being must pass over into a new negation-of-the-negation, or a new concept that stops the negation or passing-over process of immediate-Being. Immediate-Being passes over into Essence

Figure 2.35

Essence is the stabilizing, one concept of the sameness of the Measures and their passing-over process, but does not itself pass over. Since the Measures represent the whole realm of Being, and since the supposed immediacy of Being turns out to be a mere sham, shine or semblance, Essence is the thought of the supposed immediacy of the Measures as a mere shine or semblance. The spurious infinity of the Measures shows that they cannot be defined on their own. They can have their definitions or be what they are only for the Essence.

Like Being-for-itself, because the concept of Essence stops the passing-over or negation process of the Measures, it is the negation of the negation, or the negation of the process of negation of the Measures. Hence, like Being-for-itself, Essence introduces a new level of ideality. But, whereas Being-for-itself negated only the qualitative passing-over of something-others, Essence negates the passing-over of the whole realm of immediate Being.

Essence is thus a "for itself" concept in the same way that Being-for-itself was a "for itself" concept. Just as the One was a new level of ideality that stabilized the passing-over process of the something-others, so Essence is a new level of ideality that stabilizes the passing-over process of the Measures. Essence is defined as the concept of the sameness of the Measures and includes the Measures as the content of its definition. In the diagram, the Measures are literally the content of Essence, since they are inside the bubble depicting the Essence. Hence when Essence is mediated by the Measures or by Being, it is mediated with itself, with its own content. It is "for itself" or is defined through the

Measures, and the Measures are for-it. Because Essence is currently being defined from the bottom up by the Measures and is therefore not yet defined as a concept separate from the Measures, I have given its bubble in the diagram a dashed outline.

Although Essence has the same syntactic relationship with its contents that Being-for-itself had, Essence as a concept reaches a higher level of ideality than Being-for-itself did because it embraces the passing-over process of the whole realm of Being. Unlike Being-for-itself, Essence embraces all the comings and goings of the world of thereness or experience. The new level of ideality that Essence achieves therefore sublates the whole world of immediate Being. Unlike Being-for-itself—which depended on the thereness of the something-others for its definition—Essence does not have thereness. But it is *related* to thereness. It is the thought of a new kind of presence that is not itself immediate, but is related to thereness in the sense that it has thereness as its shine. It is a self-contained or stable thought that is mediated by thereness or by its shine, that shines within itself, or that shows up in thereness. The thereness of immediate Being is its shine, or is the way in which it has thereness or shows up. Essence has a relationship with the world of immediate Being that is similar to the connection that the second type of Ratio had with the quantitative bits: Essence embraces the world of immediate Being in the "for itself" sense, but does not depend on the specific thereness of that world for its definition. This freedom from the thereness of the world makes Essence an *essence*, rather than a "being." I will say more about what Essence is like in the Introduction to the next chapter.

V. Wrap Up Being: Comments on Syntax

Before leaving this chapter, I'd like to comment on the syntactic structures of Hegel's logic encountered so far. First, of crucial importance is the type of *necessity* that has emerged as a central syntactic device. Remember from Chapter One, Section V that Hegel is trying to show that the movement from stage to stage is necessary, or that there are no conceptual roads that reason did not take. This requires (1) showing that there are no other ways in which the dialectical development could go in the forward direction, and (2) that the dialectical development grows out of its own resources, or nothing extraneous or from the outside is brought in to assist reason, so that there are no roads not taken in the backward direction either. The concept of necessity that has emerged goes a long way toward fulfilling this promise in the forward direction. Hegel's concept of necessity is really a concept of exhaustion combined with a corresponding move that involves taking up something that was already implied or used in an earlier stage. By exhaustion I have in mind the idea that when reason runs out of things to say using one logical strategy, the move to a new logical strategy is necessitated. This concept of necessity-as-exhaustion helps Hegel show that no logical paths were left open or not taken. To have exhausted all options is just to have taken every possible logical path, to have exhausted all possible paths in the forward direction. This account of necessity thus contributes to Hegel's argument that rationality overgrasps reality, that there is no Thing-in-itself about which we could know nothing (as Kant had claimed) by suggesting that there is no other possible, rational way that the world could be. No rational path has not already been taken. More importantly, perhaps, it also shows why Hegel's logic is a real logic, driven from step to step by necessity.

Included in this concept of necessity, however, is the second element, namely, the idea that when reason introduces a new logical strategy, the strategy should be drawn out of something that is already there in the dialectical development—either something implied by earlier stages but not yet drawn out, or something actually used in earlier stages. Hegel relies on this second element to help him show that there are no paths not taken in the backward direction either (see Chapter One, Section V).

This second element of necessity contributes to Hegel's argument for the view that reason is developing on its own account and by its own power, and is independent even of us. If there are no extraneous sources for logical movement, then reason is indeed driving itself by its own resources. This second element of necessity thus contributes to his argument against Kant's view that the reason which develops logically is only in us, and not in the world itself (see Chapter One, Sections II and IV).

Because the story of the necessary development of reason captures Hegel's claim that there are no concepts beyond reason's grasp which could be used to understand the world in a way different from the way in which reason does understand the world, it underpins Hegel's argument against Kant's skeptical Thing-in-itself. But the argument is still a difficult one, for Hegel has to show, *throughout the entire logic*, that moves from stage to stage are necessitated, and that nothing extraneous has been brought in anywhere. Only at the end of the whole project—if he succeeds—will he have completed his argument against Kant.

The logical development of portions of the Doctrine of Being illustrates the beauty of Hegel's concept of necessity. In the Doctrine of Quality, there are three logical elements: Being (the side of presence), Nothing (the side of absence) and Becoming (their relationship). The Doctrine of Quality explores these elements exhaustively in a step-by-step way. First, each element is introduced and explored by itself, then the sides of presence and absence are explored in a step by step way corresponding to each move in the process of Becoming until all the elements have been exhausted. In the Doctrine of Quantity, the logical movement from Quantum through Degree exhausts the quantitative labels "one" and "many." In these stages, there are three logical elements: a whole (the "One" from the Doctrine of Quality) and two internal bits (the "many" from the Doctrine of Quality). In the following quick sketches I depict these items as a divided bubble, where the outer boundary represents the whole, and the inner blocks represent the bits:

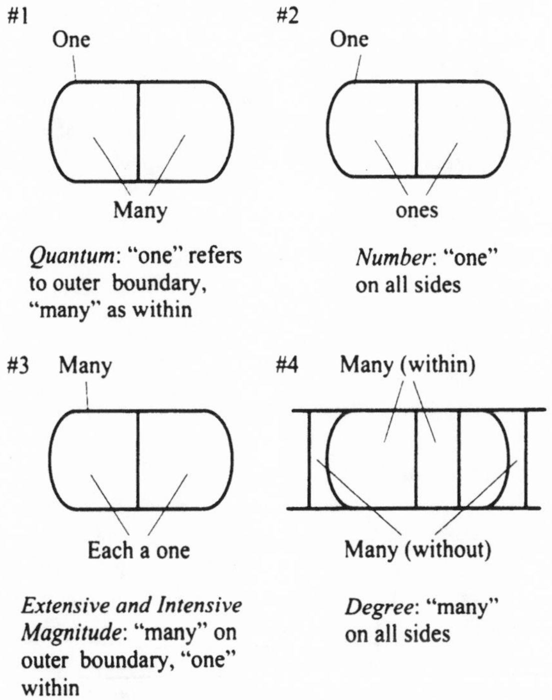

Figure 2.36

The quantitative labels "one" and "many" have been exhausted. There is nothing more for these labels to do. The next stage—Immediate Measure—must introduce a new element, namely, "quality," which is not really new, but is only new to this context. Hence, here Hegel also maintains the second element of necessity, namely, the idea that what is brought in must either be implied in or have been used in earlier stages (cf. the Introduction to the book).

Besides necessity, a number of other syntactic devices have emerged:

(1) A logical element first comes into view in an indeterminate way (which I represent pictorially by giving the element a dashed outline) and is later determined against other elements (and gets a solid-lined outline in the diagram).

(2) A concept is defined at first as merely a set of other concepts, but later comes to have a separate character of its own (and gets a solid outline: see Being-for-itself through Attraction, and Ratio, for instance).

(3) Spurious infinities keep cropping up, and are resolved by roughly the same move, namely by a new "for itself" concept that includes or grasps and hence negates or halts the passing-over or negation process in the spurious infinity (see Being-for-itself, Ratio, and the Transition to Essence, for example). In each case, the new "genuine infinity" is a negation-of-the-negation and a higher level of ideality or universality.

(4) A category is pushed as far as it can go before another category is brought in or reasserted, as in the stage of Ratio, where a quantity (the exponent) is tried out first as a way of capturing the nature of the connection between two quantities. Only later is the category of quality brought in instead.

(5) A unity between two elements is at first a kind of gluing-together, but later the elements create their own unity, so to speak, or unify themselves together by being defined in connection with one another. This is what happens to quality and quantity in the Doctrine of Measure. At first their unity is at immediate or given (in Immediate Measure). Later on, however, they fulfill their unity by being defined in relation to one another (in the Measureless).

Therefore, Hegel's logic has begun to reveal repeating syntactic devices, which helps to undermine two criticisms of Hegel's logic. On the one hand, Hegel's logic has often been portrayed as having one syntactic device, namely, the pattern "thesis, antithesis, synthesis," according to which, some positive concept—the thesis—and its opposite—the antithesis—are "resolved" into a synthesis that includes both. Our examination of the logic so far shows this old story to be both too simple and also somewhat false. First, Hegel's logic reveals a variety of syntactic patterns, so that, even if this one could be applied to his work, it would at best be one syntactic device among many. Second, this old story seems to misrepresent Hegel's syntactic patterns, even in places where it might at first seem to apply. Becoming, for example, is not really a synthesis of Being and Nothing at all, if by "synthesis" we are supposed to understand that the two concepts have been unified, or mushed together, under a new concept. Becoming does not synthesize or mush together Being and Nothing at all. Being and Nothing remain independent of one another in Becoming, since Becoming is the thought of flipping back and forth between the concept of Being and the concept of Nothing. In fact, Being is an independent element in the very next stage of Being-there, though it remains connected to Nothing.

In other cases where the old story might seem to apply, it also seems to describe Hegel's thought incorrectly. If Measure, as the unity of quality and quantity, is supposed to be a "synthesis," then the old story misrepresents Hegel's text here too by suggesting that quality and quantity are opposites, such that one is the thesis, and one is the "anti"-thesis. There is no suggestion in Hegel's text, in my opinion, that we should see quality and quantity as opposites. They are certainly different categories, and have different work to do in describing the world of Being. But they are not contradictory. Because the old "thesis, antithesis, synthesis" story does, at best, a poor job of describing the syntactic patterns of Hegel's logic, we should reject it. We can do a much better job of describing the syntactic patterns without it.

While this old story portrays Hegel's syntactic devices too simply, other old stories, on the other hand, assume that Hegel's syntax is too complex. Worse, as the joke that "Hegel's logic" is an oxymoron suggests, these other old stories suggest that there is no syntax. Since, most people think of "logic" as syntax, the joke that "Hegel's logic" is an oxymoron suggests that there are no syntactic devices, no repeating syntactic patterns at all in Hegel's logic. But the examination of the logic so far shows this complaint to be false. There are a number of repeating syntactic patterns or devices—necessity and the movement of "for itself," for example—that prove Hegel's logic does indeed have a "logic," have a syntax. Of course, that syntax is less predictable than the syntax that governs contemporary propositional and predicate logics, because Hegel's logic has to juggle the meanings of concepts as well as syntax. Sometimes the meanings of the concepts determine where the syntax goes, which syntactic device is invoked and how (as it does, for example, in the move from Ratio to Pure Quantity). In propositional and predicate logics, syntax drives everything, while semantics is largely ignored (see the Introduction to the book). Their syntactic patterns are more regular and predictable, then, because syntax completely dominates the direction of the derivations. It is unfair, however, to accuse Hegel's logic of having no syntax whatsoever simply because his dialectical derivations are not driven completely by syntax.

We will see many of the syntactic patterns that have emerged from the Doctrine of Being used again in the Doctrines of Essence and Concept. These repetitions will help to respond to the complaint that Hegel's logic has no syntax by showing that Hegel does indeed rely repeatedly on a few syntactic devices. Let me begin to make a case for this claim by moving on to picture the logical development of the Doctrine of Essence.

Notes

1. Justus Hartnack has suggested that Hegel does not intend his concept of Becoming to apply to objects, but only intends it to apply to the categories. Hartnack seems to make this suggestion to defend Hegel from the criticism—often applied to the ancient Greek, Presocratic philosopher Heraclitus—that a world that is constantly "becoming" or in flux self-destructs. I believe, however, that Hartnack is wrong to suggest that Hegel does not apply becoming to the world of objects, if by "world of objects" Hartnack means the finite world of things. In fact, the idea that becoming does apply to the finite world of things, it seems to me, is crucial to Hegel's view. The concept of becoming is, as I have suggested, just the idea of some, undetermined content going from presence to absence, and some undetermined content going from absence to presence. That process happens all the time in the finite world: various contents or items change from presence to absence (they die, dissolve, or whatever), and various contents or items change from absence to presence (they are born, put together, or whatever). Moreover, that this process happens in the finite world is crucial to Hegel's argument that we must therefore focus, not on immediately existing items—which are in a state of flux—but on what abides *through* this process of flux in immediately existing items. And what, we might ask, does abide through this flux? Hegel's answer, as we will see later: essences. When we ask, for example, about what abides through the coming and going, the births and the deaths, of immediately existing human beings, the answer is that the essence of humans, human-

ness, or the species "human being" is what abides through this flux. It is the constant flux that leads us to grasp on to or to see the necessity of rational essences that allow us to get a fix on the world, if only for a moment. Hence, if Hegel did not intend the concept of becoming to apply to the ordinary world, then his argument for the necessity of essences would fall apart. Essences are necessary precisely because they are what allow the world to be fixed, if only for a moment. It is only because the essences provided by rational thought overgrasp reality that we can comprehend reality—if only for fleeting moments—at all. Moreover, Hegel is therefore not subject to the critique against Heraclitus: he does not share Heraclitus's apparent view that *all there is* is a world of flux. For Hegel, there is over and above the flux the stability provided by the essences of rational thought.

Hartnack also seems to hold that Hegel does not intend the concept of becoming to apply to objects as a way of protecting Hegel from the criticism leveled by Kierkegaard and others that Hegel brought movement as a time-process into his logic. Here, however, Hartnack seems to have misunderstood what I take to be Kierkegaard's claim. Kierkegaard's claim is not that Hegel errs by putting time-movement into logic, but rather that Hegel errs because he *did not* put time-movement into his system. For Kierkegaard, the movement or motion that we get in Hegel's logic—the logical movement of dialectics—is a *fake* movement. Instead of concerning himself with the truly important movement of real life Hegel has merely snuck in this fake movement and pretended that it will do. The real movement that we philosophers should be concerning ourselves with, for Kierkegaard, has to do with real-life changes, and with real-life decisions. People have to make their decisions *in time*, and these decisions will *change* them. Hegel's merely logical motion has nothing to do with the real-life decisions that real people need to make, or with the real-time changes that people will undergo. Kierkegaard wants us as philosophers to be theorizing about these sorts of real-time issues. His complaint is therefore that Hegel has actually gone too far away from Heraclitus: Hegel's logic leads Hegel to give too much weight to the stable, unchanging and timeless essences, and not enough weight to the unstable and ever-changing conditions of the real lives of people who have to make their decisions in real time. Hence Hartnack is wrong to suggest that Kierkegaard criticized Hegel for bringing movement as a time-process into logic, and Hartnack is wrong to try to protect Hegel from this criticism by suggesting that Hegel does not intend the concept of becoming to apply to the "world of objects." For Hartnack's views here, see his *An Introduction to Hegel's Logic*, Lars Aagaard-Morgensen trans. (Indianapolis, Hackett Publishing: 1998), pp. 17-18. For more on my interpretation of Kierkegaard here, see my "Kierkegaard and the Madness of Reason," *Man and World*, vol. 29, no. 4 (October 1996), pp. 393-6.

2. I am therefore disagreeing with John Burbidge's reading of the concept of Being-there (or, as he calls it, "a being") at this point (Burbidge 1981, 44-5). He reads being-there or a-being as a unity, which in my terms would be diagrammed like this:

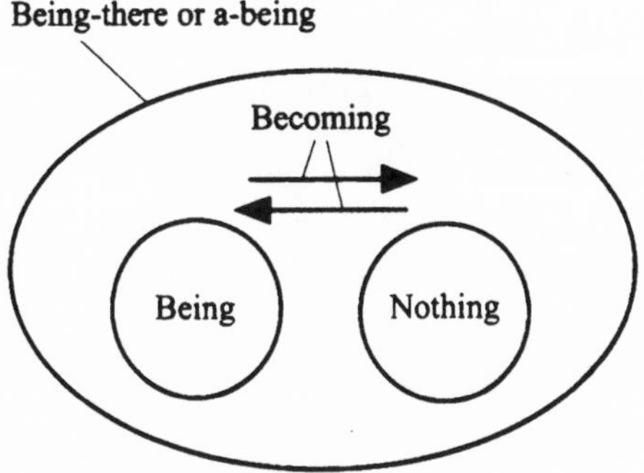

Figure 2.37

But I take seriously Hegel's claim that the result of the sublation or overcoming of Becoming is in the form of one of Becoming's moments, namely the moment of Being (§89R). So Being-there—which is the result of the sublation of Becoming—is a being with its negation (§89R), where the Being we have now is the same Being we had before (i.e. one of Becoming's moments), but the definition of that Being has been changed by the connection it discovered (in the moment of Becoming) that it had with Nothing.

3. Burbidge's reading of these steps is very different from mine, however. After the stage of "a being" (as he puts it), he suggests that the concept of "quality" appears as a new, individual concept. In my reading, however, quality is not an individual concept or stage, like Being-there is, but rather a concept-type, if you will. It first appears in Being-there as the type of determination that Being-there has (Being-there is determined because it has a character or quality). The full concept of quality—the concept of quality as such—is developed in the stage of Being-in-itself. In my reading, the concept of quality is thus the type of logical category to which all of these stages belong—it is not itself, as I say, an individual stage of the logic. This reading makes sense of Hegel's use of term "quality" to describe the whole section—the Doctrine of Quality—since the category of quality is developed throughout the section. However, Burbidge's discussion of these stages inspired me to take seriously the role that Becoming plays in the logical development.

4. The standard Diels-Krantz number for the relevant fragment is DK22b12. This interpretation of Heraclitus has been defended by Daniel Graham. See, for instance, Graham's entry for "Heraclitus" on *The Internet Encyclopedia of Philosophy*, http://www.iep.utm.edu/h/heraclit.htm (2006). Graham also has a translation of the relevant fragment in this entry.

Chapter Three
The Doctrine of Essence

I. Introduction

The last chapter ended with the introduction of a new concept—Essence—which Hegel thinks represents such a radical break from the Doctrine of Being that he uses it to begin a whole new section of the logic: the Doctrine of Essence. The Doctrine of Being outlined logical concepts that were "behind the back" (see Chapter One, Section VII) of the sensible world, or of the ordinary world of experience. It assumed that things in the world of experience can be grasped in an immediate way. Even the concept of Being-for-itself, which introduced ideality or universality into the logic and pulled away somewhat from the unstable comings and goings of sensible things, still remained tied to immediacy. Recall that sensible concepts turned out to be unstable because they could not be defined without referring to an "other" outside of them. The attempt to define sensible beings led to an endless process of flipping back and forth from one item to the other: defining one item required defining the other; but defining the other item required defining the first one again; and so on, endlessly. The concept of Being-for-itself stopped this endless process because it was defined as the one concept that embraced both sensible beings (which were called "something-others") and their unstable back-and-forth process. In Chapter One, I depicted Being-for-itself like this:

Being-for-itself is an overarching concept that embraces or contains internal elements (or bubbles) that are undergoing a process of alternation (back-and-forth flipping)

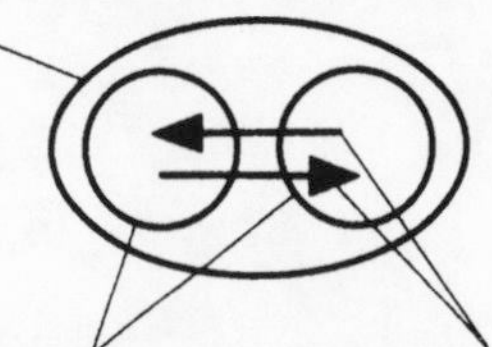

The internal elements or bubbles are something-others: they can determine themselves only by passing into their others

The arrows represent the passing-into process that the something-others are going through

Figure 3.1

Although Being-for-itself introduced rudimentary ideality, it remained tied to immediacy because it depended on the particular sort of thereness of the sensible items for its definition. The concept of "human" can be used as an example of a Being-for-itself. The qualitative similarity of individual humans—the fact that we humans are all pretty much alike—groups humans together in what seems like an immediate way. The concept of "human" is the universal that gathers up individual humans into a kind. It is the thought of the kind that humans are. Because the term "human" gathers humans up based on their sensible qualities, however, it gets its character from or is defined by the sensible thereness of the individual humans. Without the qualitative way of thereness that those sensible humans have, "human" would not be what it is, would not have the character that it has. Being-for-itself is thus an ideality that remains tied to thereness—to the ordinary being-thereness of the sensible things it embraces or gathers up.

Like Being-for-itself, the concept of Essence embraces an instability that is present in earlier concepts. While Being-for-itself embraced the instability of something-others, Essence embraces the instability of Measures that we saw at the end of the Doctrine of Measure. Essence has the same syntactic description that Being-for-itself has. In Chapter Two, I used the same basic diagram-structure to illustrate Essence that I had used to illustrate Being-for-itself:

Essence is an overarching concept that embraces or contains internal elements (or bubbles) that are undergoing a process of alternation (back-and-forth flipping)

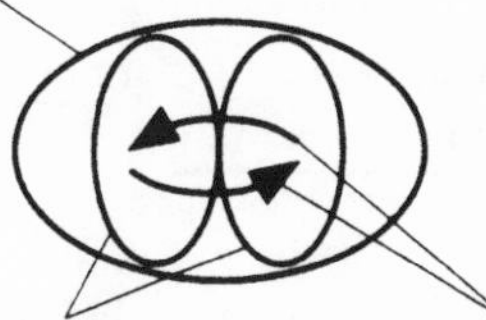

The internal elements or bubbles are measures: they can determine themselves only by passing into their others

The arrows represent the passing-into process that the measures are going through

Figure 3.2

Thus, both Being-for-itself and Essence can be depicted as big bubbles that get their characters or are defined by embracing an unstable back-and-forth process between two earlier concepts.

Since Being-for-itself and Essence have the same syntactic description, why are they not the very same concept? Hegel's logic, as we saw in the Introduction to this book, is both syntactic and semantic. Being-for-itself and Essence have the same syntactic description, which can be seen by the fact that I can use the same sort of diagram to represent them both. But they have different meanings because the concepts that they embrace have different meanings. Being-for-itself embraces immediate, sensible items in the world of experience (something-others). Essence, by contrast, embraces the conceptual apparatus of the whole Doctrine of Being (Measures, which are the unity of quality and quantity). Because the concepts they embrace have different meanings, Being-for-itself and Essence have different meanings.

Like Being-for-itself, however, Essence introduces a new level of ideality. The new level of ideality introduced by Essence explains why Hegel begins a new section of the logic. As we have just seen, Essence has the same syntactic relationship with the Measures that Being-for-itself had with the something-others. Essence is a "for itself" in relation to the two Measures which are passing into each other. The passing-over process of the Measures is of particular importance, however, because the concept of Measure has a special status. Unlike the something-others that Being-for-itself embraces, Measure unifies and includes all of the concepts of the Doctrine of Being. Because Measure unifies all the earlier concepts of the Doctrine of Being, its inability to be defined without passing over into an other shows that all the concepts of immediate Being cannot be defined without reference to some "other." Measure—as the highest concept in the Doctrine of Being, and as the concept that includes all the earlier concepts—cannot in fact be grasped immediately. It can be grasped only by reference to an "other." The failure of Measure to be defined in an immediate way has crucial logical consequences. It shows that the assumption that things in the sensible world can be grasped in an immediate way is not true. Since the Measures must pass into an "other" to be defined, they are not immediate but mediated: they can have a character only by being mediated by something else. Because Measure unifies all the concepts of the Doctrine of Being, its failure to have a character without mediation shows that none of the concepts of the Doctrine of Being can be fixed without mediation. Measure was supposed to be the concept that stabilized all of the earlier concepts of being. When it turns out to be unstable or to be a mediated concept, it shows that all the concepts of supposedly immediate Being are mediated. Hence, the assumption of immediacy that was at the heart of the Doctrine of Being is a sham. Supposedly immediate being is really mediated being. Its assumed immediacy is fake.

Because the immediacy of being turns out to be a fake, Hegel shifts the terminology that he uses to refer to the concepts that Essence embraces. Instead of containing two Measures, Essence contains one "*Schein*." This shift is justified for two reasons. First, because the two Measures are the same as one another, they can be treated as one element. Second, as Geraets, Suchting and Harris point out in their translation, the German term "*Schein*" has a couple of meanings (Geraets et al. 1991, xxv-xxvi). In one sense, "*Schein*" implies deception, or semblance. Hegel clearly wants us to read this meaning into his shift in terminology. Referring to the Measures as "*Schein*" points to the falseness of the supposed immediacy of being. The immediacy of being turned out to be a sham, a fake, a semblance, a mere "shine."

However, there is a second, more ordinary meaning of "*Schein*" that is also implied in Hegel's usage, and that helps to explain the new level of ideality achieved by Essence. A "*Schein*" is, in this second sense, a sparkle, or the way in which a newly waxed car shines forth in the sun. The Doctrine of Being covers concepts that are involved in grasping things that are *there*, or that have presence in the world of experience. This "thereness" is a way of showing up: things that are there in the sensible world show up, they have presence, they shine. Calling the Measures "*Schein*" instead of "Measures" highlights this aspect of the concepts we saw in the Doctrine of Being. Concepts in the Doctrine of Being are all used to characterize things that show up, or shine, in the sensible world.

The shift in number and terminology gives us a new diagram for Essence, in which the two Measures are combined into one bubble called the "Shine":

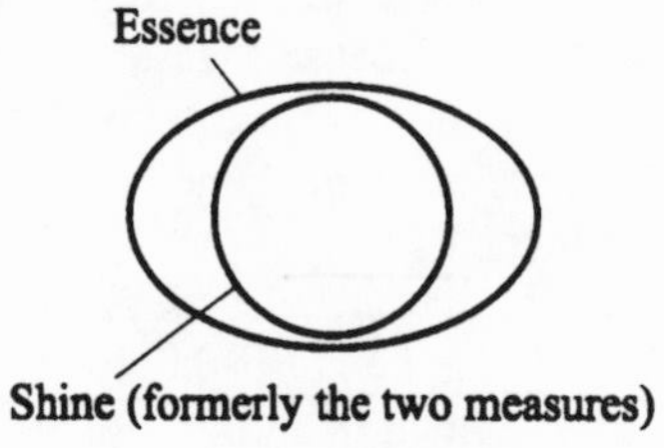

Essence

Shine (formerly the two measures)

Figure 3.3

Although I now depict Shine as one bubble, Shine, like Being-for-itself, is not a static concept. It is internally manifold, or internally active, since it still contains the passing-over process of the Measures as well as the activity of all of the earlier concepts of the Doctrine of Being. Shine now represents the whole realm of (supposedly) immediate Being, with all its comings and goings, its passing over, and instability.

To say that the supposed immediacy of the whole Doctrine of Being turns out to be a sham is to say that the Shine needs another concept to fix its character. Essence is that other concept. It is the concept that mediates the definition of the Shine, or of concepts about the sensible world of immediate being. Immediate being was supposed to stand on its own, be independent and solid. Now that it has been shown to be nothing more than a Shine, however, it is not independent. Shine cannot be defined on its own. It can have a character only in relation to an "other," on which it is dependent for its definition. Because Shine is dependent on Essence, Essence is primary—it is the defining power behind the sensible world. The sensible world or Shine is now secondary. Shine is merely—and here the second meaning of "*Schein*" that we saw above comes into play—the way in which Essence shows up, has thereness, or shines. Indeed, Essence has achieved a new level of ideality such that it has no particular thereness or does not show up in the sensible world at all. It has its thereness only in the Shine.

Let me use the concept of "fruit" to illustrate the new level of ideality introduced by the concept of Essence. This example is taken from Hegel's own work (§13R), though he is using it to make a different point from the one I make here. Hegel uses the concept of fruit to demonstrate a proper understanding of universals, but because he is arguing that a proper understanding of universals recognizes their independence from the world of immediate things, I can use the same example to illustrate the independence from immediacy that is at the heart of the concept of Essence. Compare the concept of fruit to concepts that it would include or embrace, namely concepts such as "apple," "banana," and so on. The concepts of "apple," "banana," "pear," and so on are like the concept of "human" that I used as an example of Being-for-itself above. Like "human," "apple," for instance, refers to a natural kind in the world that seems as if it can be picked out in an immediate way because of a shared qualitative character. Like "human," the concept of apple is a Being-for-itself that gathers up and overgrasps (see Chapter One, Section II) individual apples that are qualitatively alike. Moreover, like "human," "apple" also depends on the immediate thereness of sensible apples for its definition. "Apple" is what it is because of the particular character of the immediate thereness of individual apples. "Apple" is thus still tied to immediate thereness.

The concept of fruit, however, is not tied in the same way to any immediate thereness. It achieves a higher level of ideality. Because the individual therenesses of fruit are so varied, the character or definition of the concept of fruit is not dependent on any particular sort of thereness. The thereness of bananas, for instance, cannot define "fruit" because it is not the same as the thereness that is in oranges, and "fruit" includes both bananas and oranges. The thereness of oranges also cannot define "fruit," however, because it is not the same as the thereness that is in kiwi; and so on. Indeed, "fruit" does not need the particular therenesses of any particular sort of fruit to be what it is. Of course, it would be nothing at all if there were not some fruit or other, but its definition is not tied to the thereness of any sort of fruit, in the way that "apple" is tied to the thereness of apples. "Fruit" can be defined without reference to any particular sort of thereness, and hence is more ideal than are the concepts of natural kinds such as "apple." Being-for-itself was a qualitative concept. It was defined by reference to the qualitative thereness of the items it embraced. Qualitative appleness, for instance, is there in the individual apples. Fruit, by contrast, has no thereness in the world. You could not pick (a piece of) "fruit" off of a tray (Hegel makes a similar point in §13R). You can only pick an apple, a banana, and so on. Because Essence is not defined in relation to any qualitative thereness, it is qualitatively neutral. It embraces or includes the qualities in the Shine, but does not depend on any of them for its character. Essence itself has no particular thereness. Whatever thereness it has, it has only in its Shine, or in the qualitative and quantitative concepts it embraces.

The concept of Essence is also quantitatively neutral. Recall that Shine grew out of Measure. Measure as a concept was defined as the unity of quality and quantity. Since Essence embraces Shine, it has the whole realm of quantity and quality for its Shine. That means that Essence embraces not only the qualitative range of a concept, but also the quantitative range of a concept. The qualitative range of the concept of "fruit," for instance, is the different types of fruit in terms of quality—the qualities of apples, bananas, kiwi and so on. The quantitative range of the concept of "fruit" is some number of fruit. "Fruit" embraces many concepts of individual fruit, but does not depend on any number of them.

Although Essence is not tied to any particular thereness, it is still *related* to thereness insofar as it has a "for itself" relationship with Shine. Essence is defined or gets its character by being the concept that embraces the Measures. "Fruit," for example, is defined by being the concept that gathers up and embraces the concepts of individual kinds of fruit—"apple," "banana," "kiwi," and so on. Those concepts give it the definition or character that it has. Because Essence is a concept about concepts, it has no direct thereness in the sensible world. The Shine is the way in which it shows up in the world. Fruit, for example, has its thereness only through "apple," "banana," and so on, or through the concepts that it gathers up. "Apple," "banana" and so on have qualitative thereness insofar as they gather up the thereness of the individual items that they contain, while "Fruit" is only related to thereness through those concepts. Similarly, Essence has its thereness through the Shine. Essence is related to thereness through the Shine, but is not itself there. We can think of Essence as a kind of invisible movie-projector: it is the power behind the image, but it only shows up or shines forth on the screen—that is, in the Shine. Because the concept of Essence introduces a level of ideality that is even more removed from thereness than was the ideality achieved by Being-for-itself, Essence marks a radical break from the Doctrine of Being that Hegel emphasizes by introducing a whole new section of the logic.

Essence's independence from thereness is what makes Essence an *essence*, or an essential universal. Although Being-for-itself introduced ideality or universality, the universality it achieved was not essential universality. Because Being-for-itself's definition depends on the given thereness of the sensible items it embraces, the connection between the universal (Being-for-itself) and the instances is not essential. Being-for-itself gets its character from the arbitrary givenness or thereness of individual items, and so its connection to the items it embraces is merely accidental. Because the concept of human gathers up individual humans, for instance, its definition depends on the accidental, given, qualitative character of humans, on what humans happen (accidentally) to be like, or on what humans are found to be like. Essence, by contrast, embraces the variety of accidental qualitative, quantitative, and measurable characteristics, but is tied to none of them in particular. Instead, Essence as a concept is defined by its connection to other concepts. Again, "fruit" is defined by its connection to the concepts of "apple," "banana," and so on. Concepts are connected to one another by their definitions, or by *thought*, rather than by accidental, given qualities. Since thought determines the connections between concepts, those connections will be necessary, rather than accidental. Thought *makes* its own connections according to rational, logical requirements. The connections between thoughts are *essential*, rational, and logical, rather than given or found out there in the sensible world. Essence's connection to the items it embraces is therefore not accidental, but essential.

Like Being-for-itself, the concept of Essence stabilizes a passing-over process but does not itself pass over. Because Essence is defined by embracing the Shine, the Shine is not an "other" concept "outside" of it. Think of the concept of fruit again. Fruit is defined by embracing the concepts of apple, banana and so on. Although it gets its definition in relation to those concepts, those concepts are not an "other" for it. "Apple," "banana," and so on *are* fruit, they are not concepts of something with a character different from fruit, or that stands beside or limits "fruit." Instead, Essence gets its definition in relation to something that is itself. Because Essence is defined in relation to itself, rather than to something that is an "other" for it, Essence does not pass over.

The dominant logical movement of the Doctrine of Being was passing over, as Hegel remarks (§§161, 161A). The concept of Being passed over into Nothing, something passed over into its other, and Measure passed over into another Measure, for instance. Because Essence stops the passing-over process, the sort of logical movement we will see in this chapter will be different. Essence does not pass over for two reasons. First, as a "for itself" concept it has established a new level of stability (cf. Being-for-itself). Second, Essence has left behind all of the conditions that led to passing over. Because Essence is both qualitatively and quantitatively neutral, its is not limited in any way that will lead to its passing over. Essence has a *relationship* with, but is not limited by, its Shine. The logical development of this chapter is dominated by an exploration of *relationship*, beginning with the relationship between Essence and Shine. Because the focus will now be on relationship, the concepts we encounter will be relational concepts, as Hegel points out (§§111A, 112), or concepts that capture different sorts of logical relationships between two concepts.

Because we will now be exploring the relationships between concepts—beginning with Essence and Shine—we will need a new sort of diagram. Since the bubbles are currently nested one inside the other in the diagram, there is not much space between the bubbles for drawing relationships. I need a diagram that will provide more space to depict the developing relationship between the two sides. Of course, I used an overarching bubble to depict Essence in the last chapter for good reason. Essence is an overarching or embracing concept like the concept of Being-for-itself. Because Essence is a "for-itself" concept that embraces a whole passing-over process of earlier concepts, it made sense to depict it—like Being-for-itself—as a bubble surrounding the unstable bubbles. I have pictorial reasons now, however, for changing the convention. Instead of depicting Shine as inside Essence, let me expel Shine out of Essence and move it to the side, so that I can have plenty of space to depict the relationships that will dominate the logical movement of the Doctrine of Essence. Here is a depiction of what I am proposing:

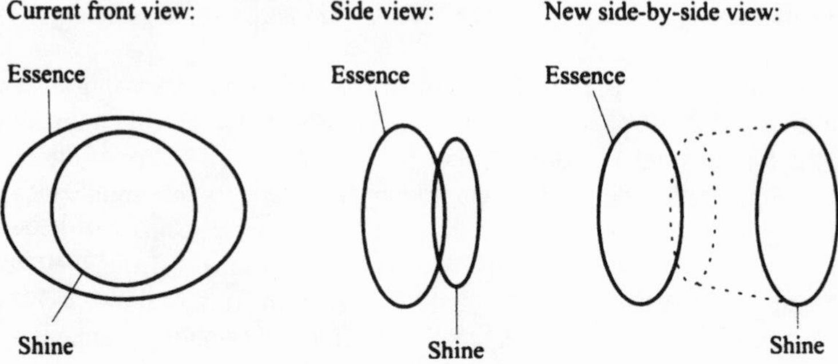

Figure 3.4

I will therefore begin my pictorial representations of the progress of the Doctrine of Essence using a side-by-side view of Essence and its Shine. Please keep in mind, however, the logical relationship of "for-itselfness" that exists between the two sides: Essence is the "for itself" concept that embraces or overgrasps the whole realm of (supposedly) immediate being as its Shine.

This new view suggests a parallelism between the beginning of the Doctrine of Essence and the beginning of the Doctrine of Being. The Doctrine of Being began with rudimentary presence and rudimentary absence. Here we have the same basic elements in play: a new kind of presence—Essence—and a new kind of absence—Shine or semblance. Hegel apparently made the same observation in a lecture in which he suggested that the first stage of the Doctrine of Essence—the stage of Identity—is a repetition of the stage of Being that we had in the Doctrine of Being. Whereas before we had Being as immediate-being, however, Hegel apparently said, since the Side of presence (Essence) is now a universal, we have Being as ideality (§115A). Identity will be the basic concept of presence for essential ideality or universality. Essence captures the most rudimentary account of how an essential universal can be or have presence in the world of (supposedly) immediate Being. Essence is an ideal presence that does not *have* being or thereness in an immediate way, as ideality did in the stage of Being-for-itself, but is *related* to Being. It is the Identity of its reflection or Shine in the world of (supposedly) immediate being.

The transition from the Doctrine of Measure to the beginning of the Doctrine of Essence is Hegel's logical argument for one of the tenets of idealism against materialism. Materialism maintains that matter is primary, and comes first, while idealism maintains that ideas, thoughts or concepts are primary, while matter is secondary. Clearly Hegel is arguing for the latter view here. Matter, he has argued, or the realm of immediate Being, cannot be defined or have a character on its own. Supposed immediate being is dependent on, and hence secondary to, ideal concepts without which it cannot be defined. The suggestion that the sensible world can be defined or have a character in an immediate way is a sham, a semblance. Ideal concepts are necessary to define matter (cf. Chapter One, Sections I and II). The transition to Essence provides the logical argument for this view. The instability of the Measures or within the Shine shows that things in the world of experience cannot really be grasped from the point of view of immediate being. A definition or character is never fixed or established under conditions of instability. An endless flipping or running-on process prevents a concept from having a fixed definition. The endless back-and-forth process of Measures reveals the error behind the supposed immediacy of being. Immediate being is mediated being, dependent being. And it is dependent on Essence, ideality. Hence, Hegel concludes, ideality is primary, and immediate being or matter is really secondary.

Let me take a moment to consider an objection to this argument—and to Hegel's logic more generally. As mentioned in Chapter One (Section V), Hegel claims that his logic is presuppositionless. This argument for idealism, however—like his rejection of "spurious infinities" generally—seems to rely on a preexisting bias. Hegel's rejection of "spurious infinities" rests on a commitment to the view that the character of something cannot be fixed under conditions of logical instability. Put another way, Hegel's philosophy demonstrates a bias for what is stable or fixed, or for what abides through the comings and goings of things. Here, his preference for what abides or is stable underpins his argument for idealism. It is because we supposedly cannot define something under conditions of instability (spurious infinities) that we are driven to ideal concepts such as Being-for-itself and Essence. A spurious infinity can never succeed in fixing something's definition. There must be some stability on which the character of something can be rested. As Hegel puts it in the discussion of the move from Being to Nothing, "the *drive* to find in [the concept of] Being or in both [the concepts of Being and Nothing] a stable meaning is this very *necessity*, which leads Being and Nothing further along . . ." (§87R).

We might reply, however, that we do not need conceptual stability to define things. We do not need to define things by reference to some abiding, stable, rational ideal that fixes definition above the instability of the sensible world. Our concepts come to have definitions because we are born into language communities that provide us with a conceptual apparatus that fixes the definitions of things well enough for human life. This second way of understanding how the definition of concepts can be fixed was defended, for example, by the 19th century German philosopher, Friedrich Nietzsche (1844–1900). Of course, this alternative account of how concepts can be defined requires giving up a commitment to Hegel's idea that there is something necessary about our concepts. On Nietzsche's kind of view, there is nothing necessary about how human communities grasp or define things. We need not be committed to logical or conceptual necessity. Human communities provide whatever stability is needed to define things for life. There is no underlying need for logical stability, or for necessary concepts. Concepts are stabilized by social communities in particular living conditions—and that is all the stability they have.

I cannot settle the debate between the Nietzschean and Hegelian approaches here. Still, the argument for idealism that appears in the transition from the Doctrine of Being to the Doctrine of Essence provides some evidence for the view that Nietzsche may well have been right to suggest that traditional, Western philosophers (which would include Hegel) presupposed a desire for and a valuing of what abides over what merely happens to be (see, for instance, the chapter "Reason in Philosophy" in Nietzsche's *Twilight of the Idols*).

II. Essence as the Ground of Existence

Identity

Essence has a "for itself" relationship with Shine. Essence gets its character or is defined by reflecting through Shine. Essence's process of shining forth as the Shine defines Essence, and so loops back to Essence—a relationship I represent with a looping arrow that runs from Essence to Shine and back to Essence

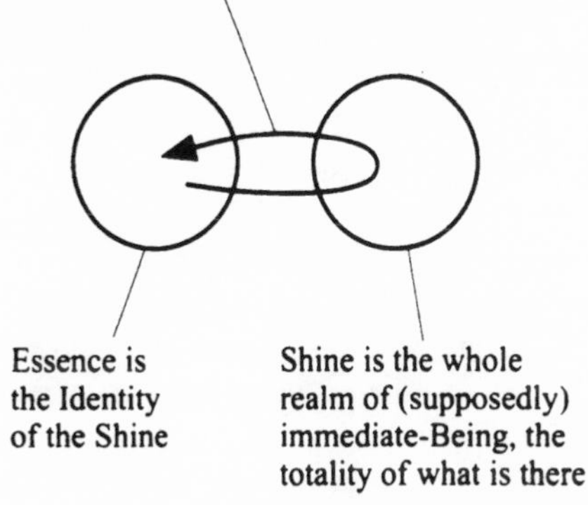
Essence is the Identity of the Shine
Shine is the whole realm of (supposedly) immediate-Being, the totality of what is there

Figure 3.5

At the end of Chapter Two, Essence was first proposed as a thought or concept that embraced the passing-over process of the two Measures. At that point, it was being defined *from below* or from the *bottom up* by the Measures, and so did not yet have a definition of its own. Because it did not yet have a definition of its own, I depicted Essence's bubble with a dashed outline. I used dashed outlines to represent other concepts that did not yet have a character or definition in earlier stages—in Being and Nothing, for instance, and will use it again in subsequent stages.

This chapter begins by defining what Essence is, not from below by starting with the Measures—which are now the Shine—but *from above*, by starting with Essence itself. Because this stage gives Essence a character of its own, I now depict Essence's bubble with a solid outline (cf. Being-there in Chapter Two).

As we saw at the end of the last chapter, Essence has a "for itself" relationship with the Shine. In the last chapter, I depicted a "for itself" relationship as a bubble surrounding the bubbles that it embraces. Now that I have separated Essence and Shine in a new side-by-side view, if we look at how Essence is defined *from above* in relation to the Shine, its relationship with the Shine is a process that is well depicted by a looping arrow that begins with Essence, goes through the Shine, and then ends back again with Essence. (That the arrow begins at the bottom and ends at the top [its vertical direction] is logically irrelevant. All that matters is the basic, horizontal direction of the arrow—namely, that it starts with and ends with Essence.) Essence gets its definition by going through its Shine: Essence shines forth as Shine, and ends up being defined in the process, so that the process actually ends up back at Essence. The Shine is the way in which Essence is defined by pushing out or showing up in the sensible world of thereness. Essence is what abides through the comings and goings of the world of (supposedly) immediate Being (Shine), or Essence abides through its Shine. As we saw in the Introduction, however, the Shine is not an "other" for Essence. It is Essence's own shine. The Shine is Essence's *reflection*, while Essence is what reflects. Essence reflects or shows up as the Shine. To use more Hegelian language, we could also say that, since Essence embraces the Shine as itself, Essence shines within itself (keep in mind my original depiction of Essence as a large bubble embracing the Shine [see the Introduction to this chapter]). Essence relates itself to itself through its Shine. Essence is defined by this self-relation, by this relationship that it has with itself as Shine, where that relationship involves reflection, or the process of shining forth as immediate thereness within itself as the Shine. Essence reflects—or is pure reflection—and the Shine is its reflection (§115).

This description of what Essence is in relation to its Shine can be grasped with the concept of Identity. Essence is in the sort of relationship with Shine that makes it the Identity of Shine. Essence introduces a more developed conception of universality from the ones we saw in the stages of Being-for-itself in Chapter Two. As we saw in the introduction to this chapter, Essence is a concept of essential universality. (See Chapter One, Sections II and III, for more about Hegel's conception of essence.) Essence is an *essential* universal because its connection to the concepts that it embraces is determined or made up by *thought*, and thought draws its own connections necessarily, according to reason and logic. "Fruit," for example, is defined by its connection not to thereness, but to other concepts—concepts such as "apple," "banana" and so on.

Moreover, Essence's connection to the lower concepts is also essential because the connection is determined from the top down by the definition of the Essence itself. The Essence is the *identity* of the lower concepts in the sense that it fixes the character of the lower concepts. The connection between "fruit" and the concepts it embraces is determined from the top down by the definition of "fruit." Whether "apple," "banana" and so on count as "fruit" depends on how "fruit" is defined. When we discover a new type of plant, for example, we use the concept of "fruit" to identify or determine what type of plant it is. Whether we classify the plant as a "fruit" depends on whether the plant fits the definition that we already have for what counts as "fruit." We use "fruit" to identify the type that the plant is. The concept of Identity is thus a higher and more developed account of determination—or of how things can be characterized or defined—from the ones we saw in Chapter Two. Things in the world of (supposedly) immediate being (the Shine), Hegel is suggesting, are ultimately defined—not by qualitative concepts—but by essences. Sensible things are identified by essences because the essences specify the type of thing that the sensible things are.

While Essence is the Identity of the Shine, Essence and Shine are not yet *identical*. There is still a distinction between Essence and Shine, which will be taken up in the next stage.

Immediate Distinction

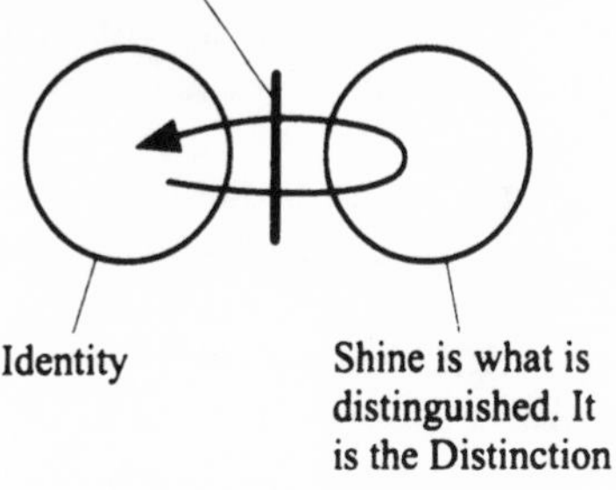
Essence is what it is by being related to its Shine, but it is also separate from or distinguished from its Shine. Immediate Distinction is the thought of Essence and Shine as distinguished from one another
Identity
Shine is what is distinguished. It is the Distinction

Figure 3.6

Hegel divides the concept of Distinction (*Unterschied*) into two stages. Immediate Distinction is the first (§117). As always, the fact that this stage is "immediate" tells us that it is the lowest, most rudimentary account of Distinction. It is the first, most "immediate," account. Moreover, as with other immediacies, each element in the immediacy has the character of a simple, independent chunk (see Degree in Chapter Two). Here, Essence and Shine are simple chunks taken to be independent of one another.

Essence is the Identity of Shine. It identifies the Shine. But Essence is also distinguished from its Shine. The Shine is its Distinction. The Shine is Essence's Distinction in two senses. First, although Essence defines or identifies the Shine, the Shine is not the same as the Essence. Essence and Shine are still two different things. The Essence gets to be what it is in part because it is *not* the Shine. Although Essence is defined in the "for itself" relationship through the Shine, Essence is what it is by being held apart from or distinguished from the Shine. The Shine, for its part, also gets to be what it is or has its character by being distinguished from the Essence. Thus, the Shine is Essence's Distinction. Second, the Shine is also the way in which Essence characterizes or distinguishes itself. Essence is defined by showing forth as the Shine. Since the Shine is the way in which Essence is characterized or defined—i.e. distinguished—the Shine is Essence's Distinction in this second sense as well.

I have used the concept of fruit to illustrate Essence. Since the Shine is the expression of Essence in the world of experience (thereness) or realm of Being, the Shine for the concept of fruit would be types of fruit in the world of thereness. According to the "for itself" relationship, the concept of fruit is defined through the types of fruit in the realm of Being or thereness. The types of fruit give the concept of fruit its character. For the concept of fruit to be a separate concept rather than merely the types of fruit themselves, however, the concept of fruit (or Essence) must both be the types of fruit and also *not* be the types of fruit (the Shine). The concept of fruit can be what it is as a concept only if the types of fruit both are and *are not* the concept of fruit. The concept of fruit can be what it is as a concept only if the types of fruit are both the same as, but also distinct from or different from, the concept of fruit. This stage takes up the logically necessary step in which the Shine or types of fruit are defined as distinct or different from the Essence or concept of fruit. At the same time, because the types of fruit are the way in which the concept of fruit comes to have a character, the types of fruit are also the Distinction of the concept of fruit in a second sense as well. The types of fruit are the way in which the concept of fruit is defined or distinguished. They are the Distinction of the concept of fruit in the sense that they are the way in which the concept of fruit comes to have a character. Essence is the Identity of Shine, but Shine is the Distinction of Essence.

Not only is Shine characterized by Distinction, but the relationship between Essence and Shine is now also characterized by Distinction. Essence is different from or distinguished from the Shine. The nature of the distinction between Shine and Essence is not determined. Their distinction is immediate: it is there, but it has no character. Essence and Shine are not distinguished from one another in any particular way, they are just distinguished from one another in general. Immediate Distinction is the first attempt to characterize the way in which Essence and Shine are distinguished from one another.

Because the difference between Shine and Essence is not determined, they no longer seem to be related to each other at all. If they were distinguished from one another in some particular way, then there would be some way in which they were distinguished from one another (different), and some way in which they were not distinguished from one another (the same). Since the distinction between them is not determined, however, they are simply different. There is no sense in which they are the same. So the relationship they had with each other in the previous stage now falls away. Essence and Shine are indifferent to one another. They are merely different, or external to one another.

The stage of Distinction captures the bifurcation of Thought or Reason (the mind) and the sensible world (the body, being, becoming) that is familiar from some traditional, Western philosophy. Plato famously used a parable of a cave to draw the same distinction that Hegel is drawing. For Plato, our natures as physical beings with senses tie us to the wall of a cave. From our spots, we can see only the shadows of models of things that are being carried along by people (whose own shadows are below the part of the wall we can see) in front of a firelight. The light projects the shadows of the models on to the part of the wall that we can see. We believe the shadows are real things, but we are mistaken. Those shadows are actually doubly removed from the real. We are seeing the shadows of models of the real things—the shadows of mere copies of trees, for example. If we could be untied from our physical caves, we would be released into the realm of the mind, from which we would have access to the genuine sources of the shadows, and, eventually, even to the sun itself, which is the ultimate source of light for all knowledge. The real things are the universals, concepts, that are not tied to the sensible world (see Plato's *Republic*, Book VII [514a-518d]). Hegel's realm of immediate Being is Plato's realm of becoming. It is the world of therenesses that come and go, pass into and out of presence. Essence represents the realm of Thought or the mind—of essential concepts in general. The stage of Distinction bifurcates Thought from becoming or Being. According to this stage, Thought and Being are simply distinguished from and indifferent toward one another. Plato had argued that Thought and becoming (or Being) are so different from one another that they must be in different realms. Thought, he said, is not part of the earthly world of Becoming, but is in a separate realm, apart from Becoming. Plato exiled Thought to the realm of the Forms (see Chapter One, Sections II and VIII).

Although Hegel does not mention Kant by name, this stage is reminiscent of Kant. Hegel says that Distinction represents the point of view of "[t]he understanding" (§117R). The "understanding" was Kant's term for the most trustworthy, rational faculty (see Chapter One, Sections IV and V). As we saw in Chapter One, the bifurcation of Thought from Being is at the heart of Kant's view that reason is only in us—is only in our heads—and is not in the sensible world itself. Kant limits Thought to our heads because he assumes that the sensible world, in itself, is different from the way we experience it. The concepts of Thought are the "filter" through which we experience the sensible world, for Kant, and do not belong to the world itself (see especially Chapter One, Sections I, IV and V). Like Plato, then, Kant sees Thought and Being as separate from one another. While Kant does not exile Thought to an otherworldly realm, he still exiles it to the realm of our heads.

We can read both Plato's and Kant's philosophy into this stage of the logic. According to Hegel, later stages subsume or sublate earlier stages: they both cancel and preserve earlier stages (see Chapter One, Section VIII). So the stage of Distinction both cancels but also preserves the stage of Identity within it. The stage of Distinction subsumes the stage of Identity in which Thought (Essence) and Being (Shine) were related to one another, but it asserts that what is most important about them is that they are separate. For Plato, Being is indeed related to Thought. Things in the world of Being are related to the world of Thought because the world "participates" in the realm of the Forms, or in Thought. Things in the world of Being are poor copies of the Forms, but they are copies nonetheless. Indeed, it's because things in the world of Being resemble the Forms that we can identify them at all. Thus, Plato's view mirrors the stage of Identity. It says that Thought (Essence) is the Identity of Being (Shine). But Plato goes on to stress the distinction between Thought and Being: the Forms are so different from the world of Being that they end up in a separate realm. For Plato, Thought and Being are related to one another in the sense that Thought is the Identity of Being, but they are also distinct from or indifferent to one another insofar as they are in separate realms: Thought is Thought, and Being is Being.

The stages of Identity and Distinction are also reminiscent of Kant's view. For Kant, Thought characterizes Being and Being is the expression of Thought. It is because our understanding is able to identify the world of experience that we can have knowledge of that world at all. Our understanding (Thought, Essence) is the Identity of that world (Being, Shine). But Thought and Being are really only related to each other in an external way. They are related to each other only because we humans make them related to one another. We impose our Thought onto Being. They are not related to one another on their own in any essential way. They are essentially distinct. That is why Thought is really only in us, and is not in the world-in-itself. My use of the term "essential" in this characterization of Kant's view has a double meaning. It means not only "essentially" in the colloquial sense of "really," but "essentially" in the logical sense of "essence." There is no logically essential connection, no logically necessary connection, Kant's view suggests, between Thought and Being. As mentioned in Chapter One (Section V), Hegel's overall philosophical project is aimed in large part at undermining Kant's claim that reason, or Thought, is only in us and is not in the sensible world itself. The next sections offer a logical argument for this view. Hegel will argue during the dialectical development of the concepts of Essence and Shine that a logically necessary connection can be established between Thought and Being.

The next few stages determine or define the distinction or difference between Essence and Shine. The process of defining their distinction, or of saying just how they are distinguished from one another, will involve looking at the two sides and comparing them against one another. Since the two sides are indifferent to one another, neither concept can make the comparison. When two people are indifferent to one another, for example, neither of them has the other side in view. They simply ignore each other. Making a comparison requires seeing both sides. Since indifferent people who are ignoring the other person do not see the other side, they cannot make any such comparison. For similar reasons, neither Essence nor Shine as concepts can capture the required comparison between them. Each concept is currently defined simply as what it is, as different from the other. Neither definition includes any reference to the other, and so neither definition can include any comparison with the other. The comparison that is required to define how Essence and Shine are different from one another must therefore be made by a third term.

Likeness and Unlikeness

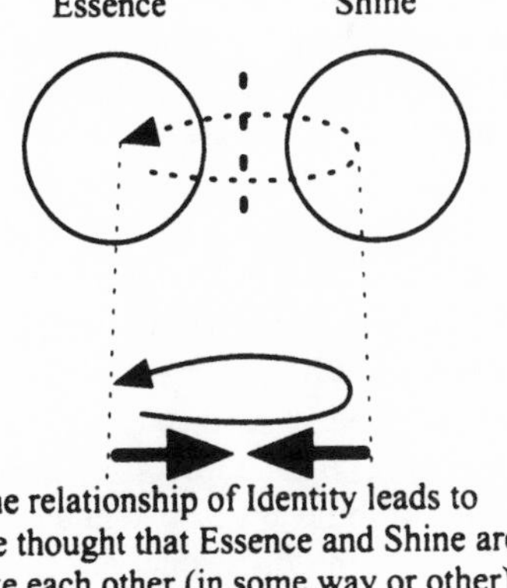

The relationship of Identity leads to the thought that Essence and Shine are like each other (in some way or other)

The relationship of Distinction leads to the thought that Essence and Shine are unlike each other (in some way or other)

The third term which makes the comparison

Figure 3.7

A third term or concept makes the comparison between Essence and Shine. It captures the thought that, insofar as Essence and Shine are identical (as they were in the stage of Identity), they are Likeness, and, insofar as they are not identical (as they were in the stage of Distinction), they are Unlikeness. The concepts of Likeness and Unlikeness both now describe the relationship between Essence and Shine.

In the stage of Distinction, Essence and Shine were indifferent toward one another. But that indifference is beginning to break down now, because the relationships of Likeness and Unlikeness create a connection between Essence and Shine. Likeness and Unlikeness—as concepts—are not indifferent toward one another. Likeness is always ascribed against a background of unlikeness, and unlikeness is always ascribed against a background of likeness. Two things are alike in some way only if they are also different in some other way. (If they were the same in every way—including spatial position—then they would be the same one thing.) And two things are different in some way only if they are also alike in some other way. This connection between Likeness and Unlikeness, as relationships, is beginning to draw Essence and Shine back together, or to relate them together once again, as they were related together in the stage of Identity.

The distinction between Essence and Shine, which was undefined in the last stage, is also beginning to be determined or defined. In Immediate Distinction, Essence and Shine were said to be different from one another, but not in any particular way. Now, however, their difference is beginning to be characterized. Relationships of Likeness and Unlikeness require focusing in on some particular characteristics: two things are like each other (the same) or unlike each other (different) in some particular way or other, and not just in general. So the distinction between Essence and Shine is beginning to have a character or be determined.

Moreover, not only are Likeness and Unlikeness drawing Essence and Shine together, but also Likeness and Unlikeness themselves—as relationships—have a connection with one another. Likeness and Unlikeness as concepts are mutually related. When we say that two things are alike, we are also implying that they are different. Indeed, it's because two things are different that we can point to their likenesses at all. What makes likenesses remarkable (and so makes us remark on them) is that two things are in other ways different. Similarly, unlikeness is remarkable because two things are in other ways alike. The expression "it's like comparing apples and oranges"—when used to mean that two things are incommensurable, or are so different from one another that they cannot be compared—is misleading. Apples and oranges are different, that is true, but their difference is remarkable precisely because they are also alike. Apples and oranges are both fruit, they are roughly the same size, they have rinds of a sort, seeds, and so on. We can point out the ways in which apples and oranges are different because there are other ways in which they are the same. There are likenesses between apples and oranges because there are other ways in which there are differences. (If they shared absolutely every feature, then they would not be two things, they would be just one thing.) Likeness and Unlikeness are like the two sides of a glass that is half empty: we can focus on the half that is full, or we can focus on the half that is empty, but we cannot focus on either side if they were not both there at the same time. A glass is half empty only against a background in which it is also half full, and it is half full only against a background in which it is half empty. Unlike the concepts of Identity and Distinction, then, which were indifferent, Likeness and Unlikeness as concepts have a relationship with one another. They each point toward the other: Likeness is what it is or is defined against the background of Unlikeness, and Unlikeness is what it is or is defined against the background of Likeness.

Because Likeness and Unlikeness—as concepts—have a relationship with one another, they are introducing a new element that must be examined: the relationships between the types of relationships. The relationships that have been introduced—Identity, Immediate Distinction and now Likeness and Unlikeness—have been evolving or developing. There are two sorts of relationships in play. On the one hand, the relationship of Identity pulls Essence and Shine together. It asserts that there is a connection between Essence and Shine. On the other hand, the relationship of Immediate Distinction pushes Shine and Essence apart. It asserts that there is a separateness between Essence and Shine. These two relationships are opposed to one another: Identity asserts connectedness while Distinction asserts separateness. Likeness and Unlikeness fit into this pattern too. Likeness is like Identity. It asserts that there is a connection between the two sides. Unlikeness, by contrast, is like Immediate Distinction. It asserts that there is a separateness or distinction between the two sides. This oppositional relationship between connectedness and separation evolves in the move from Identity and Distinction to Likeness and Unlikeness that I depict in the next stage—a stage that introduces a new sort of diagram that focuses on the development that affects the types of relationships in play.

Before introducing the new diagram, however, I want to point out that my use of the terms "Likeness" and "Unlikeness" to characterize this stage of the logic departs from the translation by Geraets, Suchting and Harris somewhat. Actually, I am siding with Suchting, who disagreed with Geraets' and Harris's decision about how to translate the relevant sections of Hegel's logic here (§§117, 118). The German words that Hegel uses for this stage are *gleich/ungleich*, and the noun forms *Gleichheit/Ungleichheit*. Geraets and Harris decided to translate these terms throughout the logic with the English words "equal/unequal," and the noun forms "equality/inequality." As a result, they translate §§117 and 118 with the words "equal/unequal" and their noun forms. Translating German words with the same English words throughout has its advantages: whenever these words appear in the English translation, readers know what the original German words were and can make their own judgments to try to understand Hegel's meaning. But Suchting would have preferred to translate *gleich/ungleich* in §117 and §118 as "like" and "unlike," and *Gleichheit/Ungleichheit* as "likeness" and "unlikeness" (Geraets et al. 1991, xliv-xlv). I think that Suchting is right that the English words "like" and "unlike" and their noun forms do a better job of capturing Hegel's meaning here. The terms "equality" and "inequality" suggest a mathematical formality that is not present in these stages. Essence and Shine are defined as distinct from one another, and the job now is to see what that difference is like, or to characterize that difference. Shine and Essence are being compared in a preliminary way, to see how they are alike, and how they are unlike each other. Of course, the terms "equal" and "unequal" (and the noun forms) are not incorrect: when we see how two things are alike we are seeing how they are the same, which we can express with the word "equal"; and when we see how two things are different we are seeing how they are not the same, which we can express with the word "unequal." Still, the informality of the terms "like" and "unlike" (and their noun forms) works better here, and so I have chosen to use these terms in these stages.

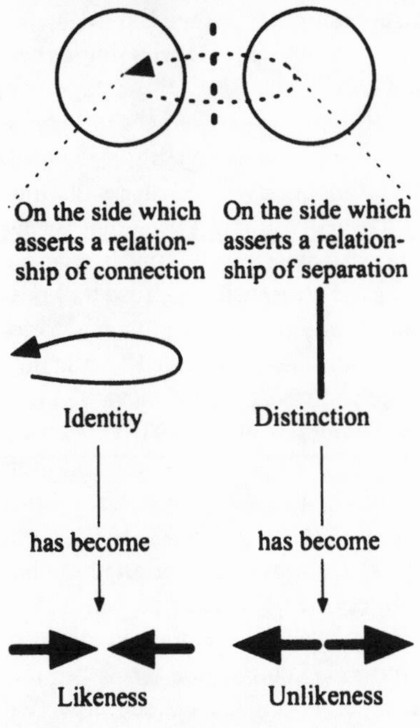

Figure 3.8

We need to shift our attention away from Shine and Essence as independent bubbles and toward the relationships between the relationships.

We have had two general types of relationships: relationships that involve pulling together or connecting, and relationships that involve pushing apart or separating. The relationship of Identity was a connecting relationship. It stressed the connectedness between Shine and Essence. The second relationship was Immediate Distinction, and it was a relationship of separation. It stressed the separation between Shine and Essence. Identity and Distinction as relationships are thus opposed to one another. Likeness and Unlikeness are opposed to one another in the same way. Likeness is a relationship of connection: it connects Essence and Shine together. Unlikeness is a relationship of separation: it separates Essence and Shine.

Each side in this opposition between relationships has evolved. On the side of connectedness, the relationship that was Identity has become Likeness, and, on the side of separateness, the relationship that was Immediate Distinction has become Unlikeness. We have two pairs of opposed relationships that are developing logically: Identity and Distinction, and Likeness and Unlikeness. We therefore have a new level of logical development to look at: a development in the types of relationships that are currently in play between Essence and Shine.

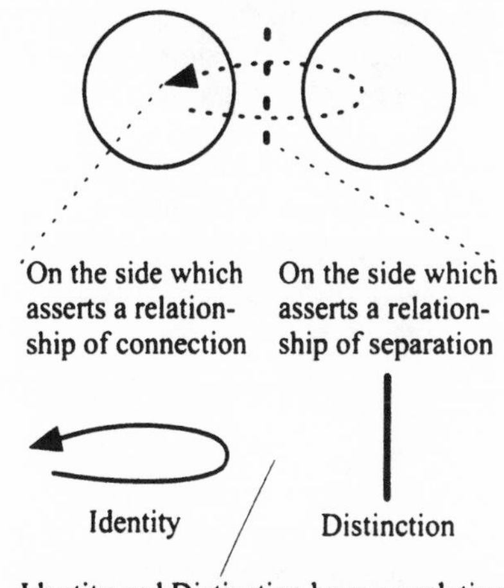
We "zoom in" on, or take out, the relationships to examine their relationship with one another
On the side which asserts a relationship of connection
On the side which asserts a relationship of separation
Identity
Distinction
Identity and Distinction have no relationship with one another. They are independent of each other. There is nothing to depict in the space between them

Figure 3.9

The next several stages of Hegel's logic trace the development of the relationship between the relationships, rather than the relationship between Essence and Shine. We are "zooming in" on the relationships (of connectedness and separateness) to examine the relationship between these pairs of relationships: between Identity and Distinction (as one pair), and Likeness and Unlikeness (as the second pair). (Essence and Shine themselves will return in the stage of Ground.)

At first there is no relationship between the relationships (which is depicted at left). Identity and Immediate Distinction are indifferent toward each other. Because this pair of relationships has no relationship with one another, the space between them in the diagram is empty: there is no element to display between them to represent their relationship with one another.

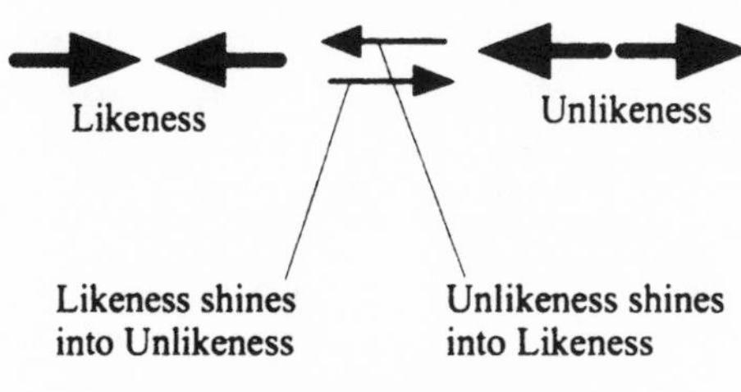
The relationships of Likeness and Unlikeness do have a relationship with each other: they point toward or shine into one another
Likeness
Unlikeness
Likeness shines into Unlikeness
Unlikeness shines into Likeness

Figure 3.10

But Likeness and Unlikeness have a relationship with one another that Identity and Immediate Distinction did not have. Likeness and Unlikeness are not indifferent toward one another. Likeness presupposes Unlikeness, and Unlikeness presupposes Likeness—in the way that half empty presupposes half full, and half full presupposes half empty. Likeness and Unlikeness thus presuppose or point toward, each other. Since we are in the Doctrine of Essence, however, we should express this relationship in the properly logical way: Likeness and Unlikeness shine into each other. Likeness is able to show up or have a definition or character because of the background of Unlikeness, and Unlikeness is shows up or has a definition or character because of the background of Likeness. Again, we pick out likenesses only against a background of unlikenesses, and we pick out unlikenesses only against a background of likenesses. Likeness shows up in the presence of unlikeness, and unlikeness shows up in the presence or shine of likeness. Each side can show up, or *shine*, only in the presence or shine of the other. Hence, they shine into each other (§118).

I first expressed the relationship between Likeness and Unlikeness by saying that they have a relationship such that they point toward each other, a relationship I depict with straight arrows above. The fact that they shine into each other implies that Likeness and Unlikeness have a different sort of relationship with one another—an implication drawn out in the next stage.

Positive and Negative

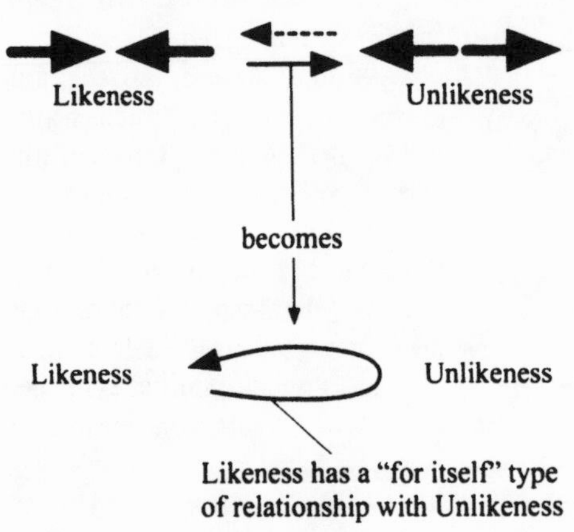
Likeness
Unlikeness
becomes
Likeness
Unlikeness
Likeness has a "for itself" type of relationship with Unlikeness

Figure 3.11

The logical move from Likeness and Unlikeness to Positive and Negative is complicated and hard to unpack. There are several moves that go on at once. The relationship between Likeness and Unlikeness is redefined or recognized to be a "for itself" type of relationship. Moreover, the "for itself" type of relationship runs in both directions: from Likeness through Unlikeness, and from Unlikeness through Likeness. In addition, the definitions of Likeness and Unlikeness evolve. Likeness is redefined as the Positive relationship, and Unlikeness is redefined as the Negative relationship. Finally, the Positive relationship is defined as a higher-level or evolved relationship of Identity, and the Negative relationship is defined as a higher-level or evolved relationship of Distinction. Let me try to unpack and explain all these developments in the next several diagrams.

Likeness now has a "for itself" relationship with Unlikeness because Likeness can be what it is, or can show up or *shine*, only through the presence or shine of Unlikeness. Likeness can be what it is only by shining or reflecting into Unlikeness. This is the relationship represented by the bottom of the two straight arrows between Likeness and Unlikeness at the top of the above diagram (the top arrow is dashed because it is not currently the focus of attention). Likeness therefore has the same sort of relationship with Unlikeness that Essence had with Shine in the stage of Identity, where Essence could be what it is or have a character only by reflecting into or showing up as its Shine. The term "shine" refers, in part, to the thereness of something: the Shine of Essence was the way in which Essence shows up or shines in the sensible world of thereness (see the Introduction to this chapter). In a similar way here, the background, presence or shine of Unlikeness is also the way in which Likeness shines or shows up. Hence Likeness has the same sort of "for itself" relationship with Unlikeness that Essence had with Shine. Because the same "for itself" relationship that was between Essence and Shine now defines the relationship between Likeness and Unlikeness, I use the same looping arrow to depict the relationship between Likeness and Unlikeness that we had between Essence and Shine in the stage of Identity. (Again, note that there is no significance to the vertical direction of these arrows [whether the arrow starts at the bottom or the top]. All that is important is where they begin and end [their horizontal direction].) In the above diagram, the arrow runs from Likeness through Unlikeness and back to Likeness. To use Hegel's anthropomorphic language, Likeness must go through or shine into Unlikeness to be defined or come back to itself as defined.

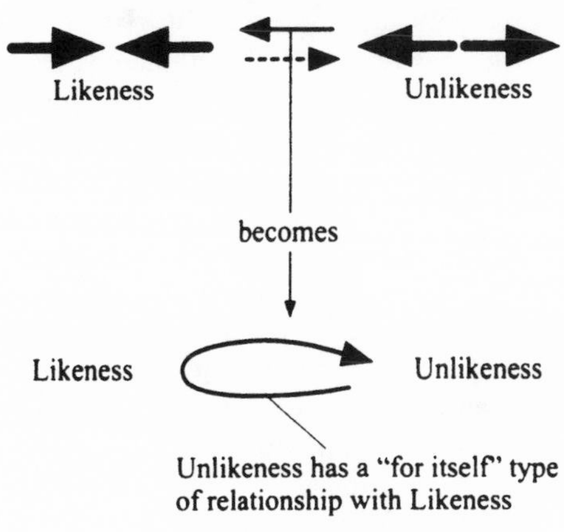
Likeness
Unlikeness
becomes
Likeness
Unlikeness
Unlikeness has a "for itself" type of relationship with Likeness

Figure 3.12

Unlikeness has the same relationship with Likeness that Likeness has with Unlikeness. Unlikeness can be what it is, or can show up or *shine*, only through the background of or by reflecting into Likeness. The background of Likeness is the way in which Unlikeness shines or shows up. Again, these characteristics of Unlikeness's relationship with Likeness are the same as those in the "for itself" relationship between Essence and Shine. Hence, Unlikeness has a "for itself" relationship with Likeness in the way that Essence had a "for itself" relationship with Shine. I have added a "for itself" looping arrow that runs from Unlikeness through Likeness and back to Unlikeness to represent this relationship in the diagram.

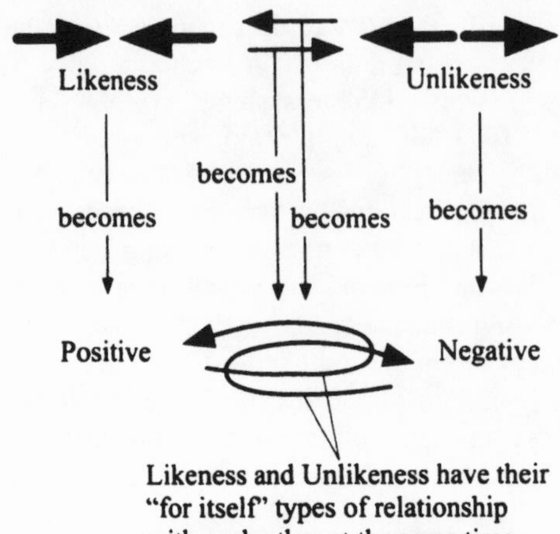
Likeness
Unlikeness
becomes
becomes
becomes
becomes
Positive
Negative
Likeness and Unlikeness have their "for itself" types of relationship with each other at the same time

Figure 3.13

Indeed, Likeness and Unlikeness have their "for itself" types of relationships with each other at the same time. Likeness and Unlikeness shine into each other, so Likeness has a "for itself" relationship with Unlikeness while Unlikeness has its "for itself" relationship with Likeness. To say that Likeness and Unlikeness shine into each other at the same time is really to say that there is only one relationship. Think of the glass that is half empty or half full, for instance. Whether the glass is half empty or half full, there is really only one glass. To use Hegel's own example, if $+w$ is six miles west and $-w$ is six miles east, the + and – are sublated—cancelled and preserved—in the six miles of road or space (§119R). The + and – are preserved because it is accurate to describe the road as extending six miles east and six miles west, but they are cancelled by the fact that they both refer to the same six miles of road. Similarly, there is really only one relationship between apples and oranges, in which apples and oranges are alike in some ways (at the same time that they are different) and different in some ways (at the same time that they are the same). Apples and oranges are alike in some ways and different in other ways at the very same time. Likeness and Unlikeness are two ways of describing the same one comparative relationship.

Since the relationship between Likeness and Unlikeness is a *mutual*, "for itself" type of relationship that really defines only one relationship, Likeness and Unlikeness as concepts evolve or come to have new definitions. Likeness evolves into the concept of the Positive relationship. To describe the glass as half full is just to draw the positive conclusion about that one glass, or to focus on the positive aspect of that one glass. To use Hegel's example again, +w is simply the positive way of describing the six miles of road. Or, again, to describe the way in which apples and oranges are alike—to focus on their connectedness—is simply to draw the positive conclusion about that one relationship. Likeness is the Positive aspect of the same one relationship. Likeness evolves into the Positive relationship.

At the same time, Unlikeness evolves into the Negative relationship. To describe the glass as half empty is just to draw the negative conclusion about that one glass, or to focus on the negative aspect of that one glass. $-w$ is the negative way of describing the six miles of road. Or, again, to describe the way in which apples and oranges are unlike each other—to focus on their distinction—is simply to draw the negative conclusion about that one relationship. Similarly, Unlikeness is the Negative aspect of the same one relationship. Unlikeness evolves into the Negative relationship.

Distinction "In Itself"

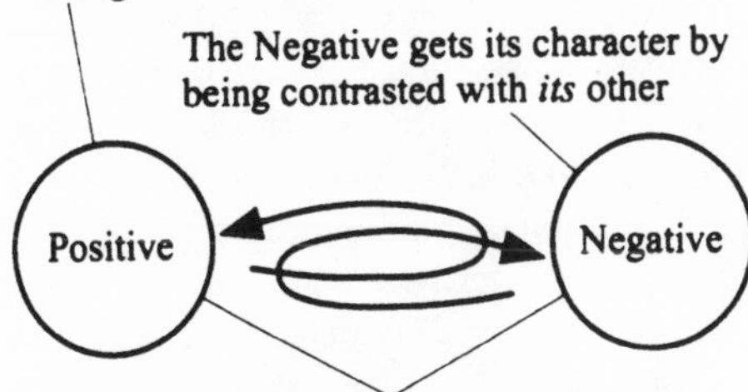
The Positive gets its character by being contrasted with its other.
The Negative gets its character by being contrasted with *its* other
Positive
Negative
The way in which the Positive and Negative are each defined can be grasped with the concept of Distinction In Itself

Figure 3.14

For Hegel, determination involves negation: something is always determined in relation to its negation (see Being-there in Chapter Two). Because the Positive relationship is defined in relation to its negation, it is beginning to be determined. It has a enough of a character such that it could be nothing. For similar reasons, the Negative is also beginning to be determined or have a character. The Negative can be what it is or can be defined only in relation to the Positive, which is *its* negation. As with the Positive side, because negation has entered the picture again, the Negative has enough of a character such that it could be nothing.

The Positive and Negative now have a character in the same way that Being-there had a character in the Doctrine of Being. Each is defined by its ability to be negated. Although the specific character of each has not yet been determined, each has enough of a presence such that it could be negated. Because the Positive and Negative have enough of a character to have presence as concepts, I now represent them as solid-lined bubbles.

Now that Positive and Negative each have a rudimentary definition, however, they are not merely each other's nothing or negative, they are each other's "other." The Positive is what it is or is defined insofar as it is *not* what the Negative is; and the Negative is what it is or is defined insofar as it is *not* what the Positive is. Each has its character or "is on its own account" (§119), then, only insofar as it is *not* the other one. The Positive shows up not only against the background of the Negative, but also because it is *not* the same as the Negative, or is contrasted with the Negative. Similarly, the Negative not only shows up against the background of the Positive, but also because it is *not* the Positive, or is contrasted with the Positive. Hence, while each concept can not only have its character or be what it is through the other, it can be what *it* is only because it is the negation of (or *not*) the other. Each gets a character by being contrasted with—or Distinct from—the other one. Hence, each is defined on its own account—or "in itself"—by Distinction (cf. Being-in-itself).

This stage of Distinction-in-itself offers a general account of how an essential concept can come to have a definition or character of its own, or come to be defined in an "in itself" sense. The term "in itself" is a logical one that captures what something is like, or how it is defined, when taken on its own, after being contrasted with or defined against its "other." This logical concept was introduced in the stage of Being-in-itself (see Chapter Two). I will have more to say about the "in itselfness" of the Positive and Negative in the next stage. Here, what is important is that both the Positive and Negative are each being defined on their own accounts, or in an "in itself" sense, through a general process of Distinction. The Positive is what it is on its own account because it is Distinct from its other, and the Negative is what it is on its own account because it is Distinct from its other. Hegel's suggestion is that this process is the general way in which essential concepts are defined. Because essential concepts are not tied to any particular qualitative or quantitative characteristics, they cannot be defined by reference to such characteristics. "Fruit" as a concept, for instance, is not tied to or dependent on any such characteristics because it includes many kinds of fruit (quantitatively) with all sorts of qualitative characteristics (see the Introduction to this chapter). If "fruit" cannot be defined as red, round, large, six or any other qualitative or quantitative characteristic, how does such a concept come to have any definition or distinct character at all?

Hegel's answer is that an essential concept such as "fruit" is defined "in itself," or can have a character "on its own account" (§119), through a process of Distinction. "Fruit" gets to be what it is or is defined by being distinguished from another concept that it is *not*. It is defined by being distinguished from another concept into which it shines, but against which it is also contrasted. To say that the other concept is one into which "fruit" shines is to say that the other concept must be a collegial one, or one with which "fruit" has some similarity (likeness) or connection. "Fruit" will not be very successfully defined, for instance, if we contrast it with the concept of "upward." As the relationship between Positive and Negative suggests, the relationship between "fruit" and the contrasting concept must include both likeness as well as unlikeness. The concept of fruit must be defined, then, in relation to a concept such as "flower." "Fruit" and "flower" are collegial concepts or alike because they both capture parts of flowering plants, but they are also different, unlike, or contrasted because they capture different stages and parts of flowering plants. To define an essential concept in general is thus to contrast it with another concept that it is like, but that it is also *not*. An essential concept is defined through Distinction, and so Distinction is the concept of definition for essences. Distinction in this stage is Essential Distinction (§120).

Hegel calls this sort of Distinction "Distinction in itself" (*der Unterschied an sich* [§119]). The Distinction is "in itself" for two reasons. As mentioned above, the process of Distinction outlined here is a process through which essential concepts are defined on their own, or in an "in itself" sense. I say more about this "in itself" process in the next stage. Second, the concept of Distinction also has an "in itself" definition. In Immediate Distinction, the kind of Distinction was undefined. Now that the process of Distinction has been spelled out, however, the Distinction is defined. The concept of Distinction has been characterized, determined or distinguished. Instead of Immediate Distinction, we have determined or distinct Distinction—a Distinction with distinction. Distinction "in itself" is a Distinction that is distinguished or characterized—a Distinction with a distinction of its own, *on its own account*, or "in itself."

Transition to Ground

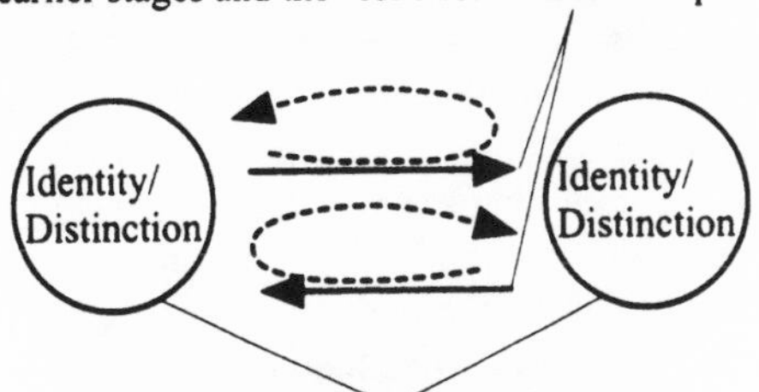
The Positive and Negative each have an "in itself" relationship with one another, implied by earlier stages and the "for itself" relationship
Identity/ Distinction
Identity/ Distinction
The "in itself" relationships give both the Positive and Negative the same characters as Identity/Distinction

Figure 3.15

In the last stage, the Positive and Negative could each be defined on its own, or in an "in itself" sense, through the process of Distinction. To see how the concept of Ground is generated, look more carefully at the "in itself" relationship that Positive and Negative have with one another, and at how that relationship affects their definitions.

Both the Positive and Negative have a definition or character in the "in itself" sense. Positive and Negative are both defined by the same sort of process of definition that we saw in Being-in-itself in the Doctrine of Being (see Chapter Two). Each one gets a character of its own in relation to an "other" that is its own "other." The Positive gets its character as Positive by being contrasted with (*not*) the Negative, which is the Positive's *own* other. The Negative is the negative *of the* Positive—it could not be negative without the Positive, the presence of the Positive *makes* the Negative negative. Similarly, the Negative gets its character as Negative by being contrasted with (*not*) an "other" that is also its *own* "other." The Positive is the Negative's *own* "other" because the Positive is the Positive *of the* Negative—the Positive would not be *Positive* without the Negative, the Negative *makes* the Positive positive. Thus they each have a character that they get through an "in itself" process with their own "others."

These "in itself" relationships that Positive and Negative have with one another were implied in earlier stages. Indeed, I originally used an "in itself" type of arrow to represent their relationship with one another back in the stage of Likeness and Unlikeness, where Likeness was defined by pointing toward Unlikeness, and Unlikeness was defined by pointing toward Likeness. Now, the Positive is defined by pointing toward its "other," while Negative is defined by pointing toward its "other." Their "in itself" processes are also embedded in the "for itself" relationship that Positive and Negative have with one another. Half of the "for itself" relationship involves pointing toward the other side. In the diagram, the "for itself" arrow begins by extending toward (or pointing toward) the other side, before it returns to the element from which it started.

The Positive and Negative are thus each defined by the same sort of "in itself" process, but what character or definition does the process give them? What "in itself" character or definition does each of them have? If we look at what the Positive is like in an "in itself" sense, it has the character of being an Identity with Distinction. It is an Identity with Distinction in two senses. First, the Positive grew out of the concept of Identity. It is a concept of likeness, sameness or Identity. Moreover, the Positive is now defined or characterized. A concept is defined when it is distinguished, or has Distinction. Since the Positive is now a defined concept of Identity, it is an Identity with Distinction. Second, the "in itself" relationship that the Positive has with the Negative means that the Positive is being defined by its connection with the Negative. According to the logical character of "in itself" definition (see Being-in-itself in Chapter Two), the Positive and Negative each have a separate character of their own (i.e. "in itself") because they are each defined through their connection with one another. Hence, the Positive is an Identity that is defined in a way that is connected to—or with—Distinction. The Positive is an Identity with Distinction.

The Negative, for its part, grew out of the concept of Distinction. It is a concept of unlikeness, difference or Distinction. Now that it is defined by the "in itself" process, the Negative is a defined Distinction, or a Distinction with a character. As we saw in the stage of Identity, to determine a concept is to fix its Identity. Hence, the Negative is a determined Distinction: it is a Distinction with an Identity. Moreover, like the Positive, the Negative, too, is defined through its connection with the other side—in the case of the Negative, it is defined by its connection with the Positive. Since the Positive is Identity, the Negative is a Distinction that is defined in a way that is connected to—or with—Identity. The Negative is Distinction with Identity.

When we look at the Positive and Negative each on their own (i.e. in an "in itself" sense), then, not only are they defined by the same sort of "in itself" process, but they are also defined as having the *very same character* in an "in itself" sense. The Positive is an Identity with Distinction, and the Negative is a Distinction with Identity. Both thus have the same "in itself" character of being the unity of Identity and Distinction. They are Identity/Distinction (or Distinction/Identity—the order of the terms does not matter here). To use the Hegelian language, both of them are "in-themselves the same" (§120). Now that both Positive and Negative have the same character as Identity/Distinction, I have relabeled their bubbles in the diagram.

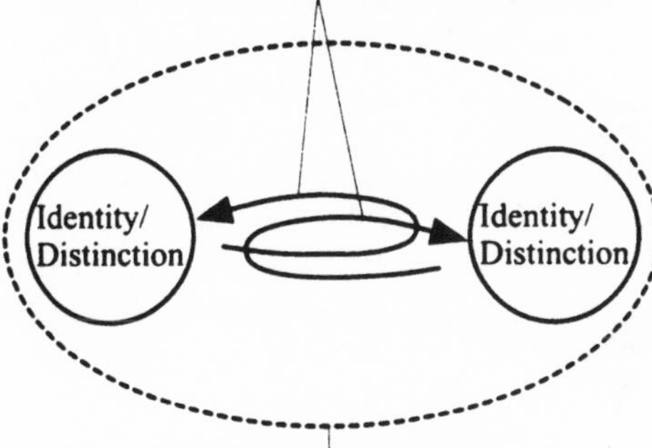
The two "for itself" relationships between the two Identity/Distinctions defines the Identity/Distinctions as One relationship. Moreover, defining each Identity/Distinction leads to an unstable back-and-forth process
Identity/ Distinction
Identity/ Distinction
The One relationship comes into view as a "for itself" concept that grasps the back-and-forth process between the Identity/Distinctions. It is not yet defined

Figure 3.16

The "in itself" process outlined so far, however, is not the whole story. In the stage of Positive and Negative, the Positive and Negative really had mutual "for itself" types of relationships with one another. Those relationships defined the Positive and Negative as the same one relationship. Positive and Negative are just two ways of describing the same one relationship, in the way that "half empty" and "half full" are just two ways of describing the same glass of water. There is only one relationship. "Positive" is a way of describing the likeness that obtains in the relationship, while "Negative" is the way of describing the unlikeness that obtains in the relationship. Because the mutual "for itself" relationships between Positive and Negative define them as the same One item or relationship, we could also say, as Hegel does, that Positive and Negative are "the same for-themselves" (§120).

Hegel's use of the term "for itself" here, however, has other implications as well. Since Positive and Negative are now both defined by their "in itself" processes with each other as Identity/Distinction, there are two items defined in an "in itself" sense as the same as one another. Moreover, because they have an "in itself" relationship with one another, they each get their definitions through an unstable back and forth process. In the stage of Positive and Negative, the Positive (as Likeness) could be what it is or have its character only by shining or reflecting into the Negative (as Unlikeness). Similarly, the Negative (as Unlikeness) could be what it is or have its character only by shining or reflecting into the Positive (as Likeness). Thus, according to the "for itself" relationship that each has with the other, each can be what it is or have its character only by shining or reflecting into the other. The attempt to define one forces us to define the other, and the attempt to define the other forces us to define the first, and so on. The attempt to define each side drives back and forth from one side to the other.

The One relationship that they both share now comes into view as the one, "for itself" concept that will stabilize the unstable, back-and-forth process between two items that are defined as the same as one another. This same syntactic description characterized the other two "for itself" concepts encountered so far, namely Being-for-itself and Essence (see Chapter Two and the Introduction to this chapter). Being-for-itself and Essence were both defined as the one concept that grasps or embraces two concepts that were the same as one another and engaged in an unstable back-and-forth process of definition. As I did in Chapter One, I depict this One "for itself" relationship here as a large bubble that surrounds and embraces the unstable back-and-forth process between two concepts defined as the same as one another—in this case as Identity/Distinction. Just as Being-for-itself was a concept that captures the type that the something-others were, and Essence was the concept that captured the type that the Measures were, so the One relationship is a concept that captures the type (of relationship) that the two Identity/Distinctions are. The One relationship is a "for itself" concept of the type of relationship that the two Identity/Distinctions share.

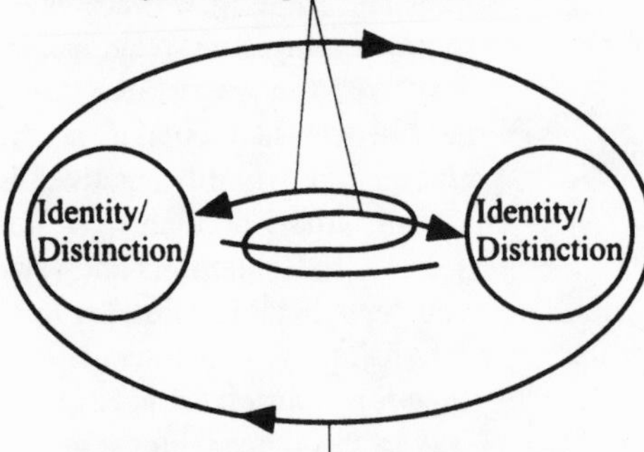
Both "for itself" relationships have the same character: each Identity/Distinction reflects its character (shines or shows up) only by reflecting or shining into its other
Identity/
Distinction
Identity/
Distinction
The One relationship grasps the type of relationship that the "for itself" relationships are. It is defined as "inward reflection which is just as much reflection into another" (§121). It is a relationship of Ground

Figure 3.17

What One type of relationship do the two Identity/Distinctions share? Each can be what it is or have a character only by shining or reflecting into its other. Since each of them has that same sort of relationship with one another, we can characterize the type of relationship that they have as a relationship involving having a character or definition only by shining or reflecting into its other.

There is another characteristic that the relationships they each have with one another share, however. In Likeness and Unlikeness, Likeness could only show up or shine against the background of Unlikeness, and Unlikeness could only show up or shine against the background of Likeness. That means that each can *reflect their own characters*, or *shine forth as themselves*, only against the background of the other. Each of the Identity/Distinctions has their own character as a shine or reflection. They reflect their characters, or reflect themselves. To use the Hegelian language, each Identity/Distinction, can have its character or be by itself ("*in sich*" [§119]) by reflecting. Each is, to use Geraets', Suchting's and Harris's translation "inwardly reflected" (*in sich reflektiert*) (Geraets et al. 1991, 185), or reflected by itself. Note that Hegel's use of the term "*in sich*" here is not a repetition of the logical concept of "in itself." That concept is expressed by the German phrase "*an sich*" rather than "*in sich*." The German preposition "*in*" suggests a rest, or motion in place. Because the Identity/Distinctions are reflecting their characters, they are engaged in a kind of motion. However, since that motion gives each element a stable character, they have achieved a level of restfulness that is generated by an activity or motion of reflecting. The process of reflecting their own characters gives each a level of stability over motion. They are each engaged in reflection "*in sich*," or in reflection as a motion in place.

These two characteristics of their relationships define the One relationship that they both share. The type of relationship that the two Identity/Distinctions each have with one another can now be defined or given a character. They each have a relationship with one another according to which each can reflect what it is (or be inwardly reflected) only by reflecting into its other. That is the character of the One relationship that they share. Now that the One relationship has a character, I represent it in the diagram with a solid outline. That One relationship is the relationship of Ground. Ground is the concept of the type of (the One) relationship that the two Identity/Distinctions share. It is defined as "inward reflection [*Reflexion-in-sich*], which is just as much reflection into another [*Reflexion-in-Anderes*]" (§121). Because Ground is an active relationship, I have added arrows to the overarching bubble to represent the process of Ground. Ground is the thought of the two, "for itself" relationships of the Identity/Distinctions, taken together as One *type* of relationship.

The relationship of Ground embraces both Identity and Distinction, so it is the unity of Identity and Distinction, as Hegel suggests (§121). Since Identity and Distinction are engaged in an active process (shining into each other), however, the unity is not static—as Hegel apparently suggested in a lecture (§121A).

Ground

The relationship of Ground developed in the last stage is the relationship that now obtains between Essence and Shine

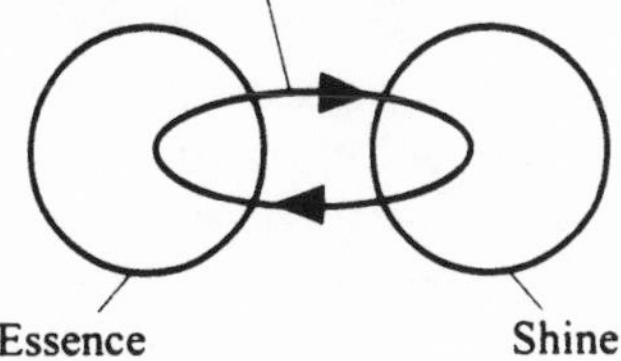

Figure 3.18

We have been examining up close, or have been "zooming in" on, the developing relationship between Essence and Shine. The relationship between Essence and Shine has now evolved from the "for itself" relationship that we had at the beginning of this chapter into the type of relationship that is a relationship of Ground. In this diagram, the relationship of Ground that was generated in the last stage is now depicted (as it should be) as the current relationship between Essence and Shine. Essence and Shine have a mutually determining relationship with one another—the relationship of Ground—that is represented in the diagram as a circular arrow.

Although Essence had a "for itself" relationship with Shine earlier—such that Essence shined forth as the Shine, and was defined or came to have a character through the Shine—we were driven to the stage of Immediate Distinction because Shine was still independent of, separate from, or distinct from Essence. Essence could be the Essence only by being distinguished from the Shine. Hence the "for itself" relationship was best depicted at the beginning of this chapter in the side-by-side view that emphasized or represented this separation or distinction between Essence and Shine. The stage of Immediate Distinction was the first thought of that separateness or distinction. Now that Essence and Shine are completely mutually determining, there are good logical reasons for depicting Essence and Shine, not in the side-by-side view, but rather as nested bubbles, with the relationship of Ground between them this way:

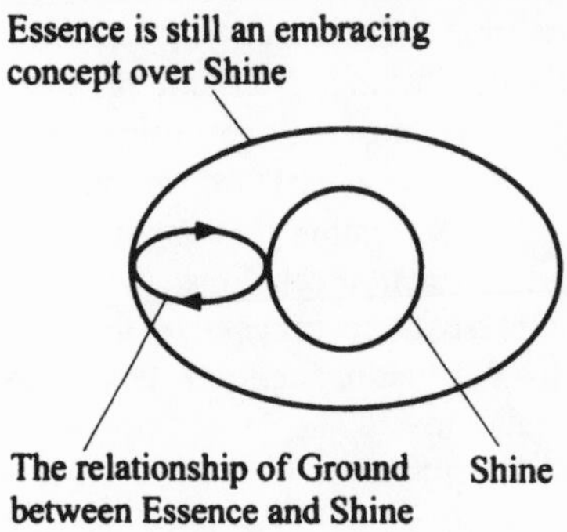

Figure 3.19

The mutually determining relationship of Ground suggests that the Essence is a concept that completely embraces the Shine. To say that Essence and Shine are mutually determining is to say that, while the Essence determines the Shine, the Shine also determines the Essence. The Shine determines the Essence, however, only if the Shine is the *complete* and *completed* expression of the Essence. The Shine is therefore now defined as the complete and completed realm of Being grasped by the Essence. Because the Shine is the complete realm of Being for the Essence, there is no longer any separation between the definition of Essence and the definition of Shine. The Shine is the complete set of items in Being grasped by the Essence. There is nothing left over in the realm of Being for Essence to grasp. Essence includes or embraces everything in the Shine. In diagrammatic terms, the Essence is a bubble that completely surrounds the Shine. Because the Essence completely grasps the Shine, there is nothing in the Shine any longer that could define it as separate from the Essence. Thus the Essence is now a completed and completely defined concept that shines, or has all of its being (since Shine represents the entire realm of Being), within itself. Essence is a being-with-self (§121). There are therefore good logical reasons for depicting Essence as a bubble that completely surrounds and hence embraces the Shine. Because Essence is now a whole that embraces all of its Shine, Essence is also a totality (§121) or completed concept.

We can see the difference that the move from a "for itself" relationship to a relationship of Ground makes by considering the example of "fruit" once again. At the beginning of this chapter, "fruit," as an Essence, was conceived of as qualitatively and quantitatively neutral. The Shine was the qualitative and quantitative realm of Being for "fruit." Shine was all sorts of different qualities and quantities of pieces of fruit, and Essence was the thought or concept of the sorts of qualities and quantities of fruit. Since Essence and Shine are now mutually determining, however, the definition of the Shine has changed. The Shine is no longer just different sorts of qualities and quantities of pieces of fruit, but is the *complete and completed* set of pieces of fruit. The Shine or pieces of fruit can determine the Essence or concept of fruit only if the set of pieces of fruit is complete and completed. To be an essential concept, the concept of fruit must ultimately include or embrace not merely some set of pieces of fruit, but *each and every piece of fruit* that has been and ever will be in the realm of Being. The Shine or set of pieces of fruit therefore defines the Essence or concept of fruit only when the Shine is thought of as finished, as complete. Only when the set of pieces of fruit is finished, complete, does it define the concept of fruit. The mutually determining relationship between Essence and Shine therefore redefines Shine as the *complete* and *completed* set of pieces of fruit in the realm of Being, and thus as the complete expression of the concept of fruit in the realm of Being. Shine now includes *all* the pieces of fruit—both quantitatively and qualitatively. It is the completed set of pieces of fruit.

Now that the Shine is completed, Essence, too, is a completed concept. Because the Shine is the completed set of pieces of fruit—both quantitatively and qualitatively—there is nothing left over out there in the realm of Being for Essence to embrace. Essence as a concept is completed, finished. Because the Essence of fruit now embraces the complete set of pieces of fruit, there is nothing left out there for it to grasp. It is a totality or completed concept. There is no fruit in the sensible world or world of experience that is not grasped by the Essence of fruit. The concept of fruit is an Essence with *all* of its being within itself. It is a totality—the total, the complete and completed concept of fruit. Moreover, the character of the Essence of fruit is fully defined as well: it is no longer merely all sorts of qualities and quantities of individual pieces of fruit, but is precisely those qualities and quantities of fruit that belong to the Shine or to the set of pieces of fruit.

Because Essence is the embracing concept, it is currently the ground in its relationship with Shine. In the "fruit" example, the Essence is the concept of fruit itself, while the Shine is now the completed set of individual concepts of fruit—"apple, "banana," "pear" and so on (an Essence is a concept of concepts). Because the concept of fruit gathers up and identifies all the individual concepts of fruit with all kinds of qualitative and quantitative characteristics, the concepts of fruit in the set cannot explain why they belong together in the set. None of the qualitative characteristics (such as "round" or "yellow") nor quantitative characteristics (such as "three-inches-long") of apples, bananas, pears and so on can capture all of the fruit in the same set. Only the concept of fruit itself captures all of those concepts of fruit together into the same set. Thus the concept of fruit—the Essence—is the ground of its relationship with the set of concepts such as "apple," "banana" and so on: only the concept of fruit itself captures why all of those concepts are in the same set.

The relationship of Ground can be characterized as "inward reflection which is just as much reflection-into-another" (§121). Why does Hegel think of a relationship that is defined as "inward reflection which is just as much reflection-into-another" as a "ground"? In our ordinary use of the term, a "ground" can show up as what it is (as a ground) only if it succeeds in grounding something else. To use Hegel's terminology, a ground is something that can shine forth or reflect itself as a ground only if it reflects into another, or only if it succeeds in grounding something else. If we say that a seed, for example, is the ground of a tree, the seed can only shine forth as a ground if the tree shows up. If nothing shows up out of the seed, then the seed wasn't a ground at all. A ground can only shine as a ground if the grounded shines. This is precisely the sort of relationship that is supposed to be captured by the phrase "inward reflection which is just as much reflection-into-another." Ground is the thought of the type of relationship that the two Identity/Distinctions had with one another, and each Identity/Distinction could show up or reflect its character only by shining into the other side. That's just what a Ground is like.

The concept of ground is thus what I would like to call a success term. It presupposes that what it asserts has successfully been completed. Only if the ground has succeeded in grounding something is it really a ground. That's why Hegel says that the ground is also a "good" ground in an abstract sense (§122R). The ground is good merely in the sense that the concept presupposes that it succeeded in being a ground.

Transition to Existence

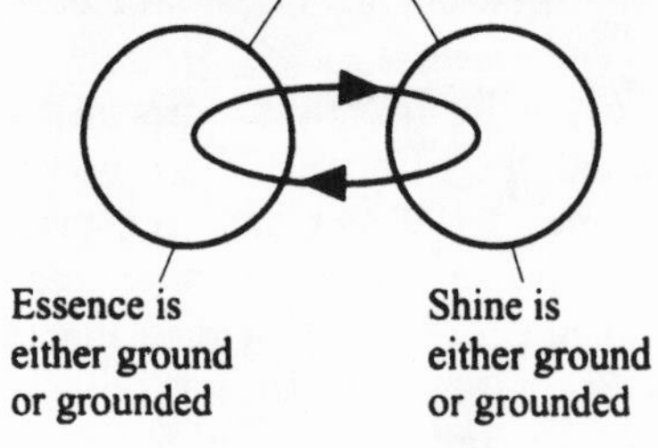
Essence and Shine—both as either ground or grounded—now have an equivalence and ambiguity in relation to one another that is best captured by the side-by-side view
Essence is either ground or grounded
Shine is either ground or grounded

Figure 3.20

In the last stage, Essence's character as an embracing concept was highlighted. Indeed, Essence's character as an embracing concept was so strong that there were good logical reasons for depicting Essence once again as a bubble that completely surrounded the Shine. Moreover, because Essence was defined as a concept that completely embraced the Shine, Essence was the ground of the relationship be-tween Essence and Shine. Essence was the side that captured or grounded the items in the Shine.

In this stage, however, a further logical implication of the mutually defining relationship between Essence and Shine undercuts Essence's status as the embracing and grounding side of the relationship and provides good logical reasons for once again depicting Essence and Shine in the side-by-side view. To say that Essence and Shine are mutually defining is to say that they each play an equal role in relation to one another in the process of definition. As equals in the process of definition, Essence can no longer be seen as the embracing or grounding element. Instead, Essence and Shine must be thought of as equal, side-by-side partners in the process of definition—a status best depicted by the side-by-side view of Essence and Shine. At the end of Chapter Two, Essence was defined as the more comprehensive element that embraced the Shine. Now that the Shine is the complete set of items grasped by Essence in the realm of Being, however, Essence has lost its character as the more comprehensive element. Moreover, since Essence defines Shine, and Shine defines Essence, both elements are now defined as either the ground or the grounded. When Essence is taken to be the side that defines or determines Shine, Essence is the ground of Shine, which would then be the grounded. But when Shine is taken to be the side that defines or determines Essence, then Shine is the ground of Essence, which would then be the grounded. We can think, for instance, of the concept of fruit as the ground of all the individual types of fruit, which are then the grounded. Or we can think of all the individual types of fruit as what grounds or defines the concept of fruit, which would then be the grounded.

Furthermore, since Essence (Thought) and Shine (Being) can be ground or grounded, and since the ground and grounded can be either Thought or Being, the relationship of Ground can obtain not only between Thought and Being, but also between two Beings and two Thoughts. Things in the world of Being can be grounds for other things in the world of Being, in the way that a seed can be the ground of a tree. A seed in the world of Being is the ground of a tree in the world of Being when the tree grows. And things in the realm of Essence can be grounds for other Essences. We can perhaps think of the concept of rectangle, for example, as the ground of the concept of square, since "square" is defined in relation to "rectangle," or, to put it another way, "rectangle" helps to determine the nature of "square." Because a square is just a special sort of rectangle, the concept of rectangle can then be seen as the ground of the concept of square. Whether the ground is a Thought or Being, any old ground will do.

This ambiguity in the definition of ground and grounded redefines Essence and Shine and makes the side-by-side view a more appropriate diagram for this stage. Essence was originally an identifying and more comprehensive (embracing) concept than was the Shine. Now that Essence and Shine can be either the ground or grounded, and since any old ground will do, the two sides are not only equivalent, but have lost their distinctness as Essence and Shine. Essence has become any old ground or grounded, and Shine has become any old ground or grounded. Therefore, the elements are now best depicted in a side-by-side view that treats them not only as equivalent in relation to one another, but also as equally interchangeable.

Although the relationship of Ground has been determined or defined, notice that it is not completely defined. There are many different sorts of relationships that could be described as grounding relationships. We can think of a number of different types of grounds. As we will see, causes, effects, properties, things or anything that is conceived of as having its being in an other (§121)—or as fulfilling its definition in an other—count as a ground. Because the definition of

Ground that we have so far does not distinguish between these different types of grounds, at this stage, again, any old ground will do.

This stage helps to explain one of the central disputes between Plato and Aristotle. Essence represents Thought, or essential, universal concepts (see the Introduction to this chapter), and Shine represents the world of (supposedly) immediate Being. Plato argued that things in the world of Becoming (Hegel's Being) could only be what they are if they participate in the Forms or Thought (see Immediate Distinction above). We can also characterize this relationship by saying that the Forms, or Thought, are, according to Plato, the source or ground of things in the world of Being. In Hegelian terms, Plato sees Essence as the Ground. Aristotle, by contrast, emphasized the view that the Forms are in the things in the world themselves (see the Chapter One, Section II). This view suggests that things in the world (or Being) determine the Forms. What "fruit" is, on this view, is determined by all the individual fruit. In this case, Being or Shine would be the Ground, and Essence would be the grounded. The stage of Ground includes both of these views: sometimes, Essence is the Ground, and Shine is the grounded, and sometimes Shine is the Ground and Essence is the grounded. When Essence and Shine are completely mutually determining, either can be the ground or grounded.

Existence

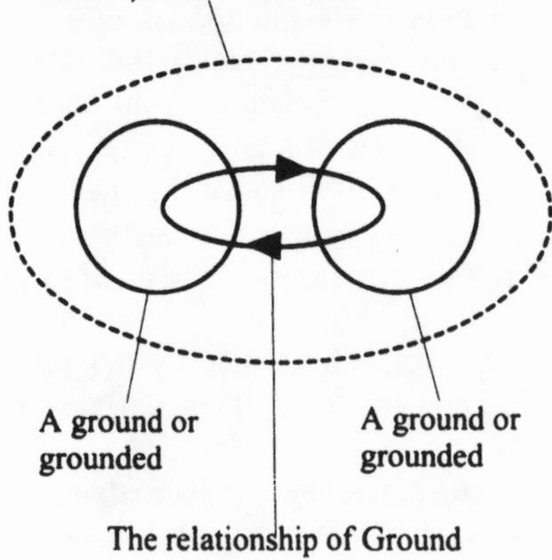
Existence is the thought of the successful process of ground and grounded as a new level of thereness, either (i) as a whole process, a world of Existence, or (ii) as a multitude, or bunch of existents
A ground or grounded
A ground or grounded
The relationship of Ground

Figure 3.21

The thought of the whole process of Ground—the relationship of Ground together with the ground and grounded—generates the concept of Existence. Existence is the thought of the grounds and grounded in a mutually defining process. Ground is a success term: every ground succeeds in grounding. A ground can show up as a ground only if the grounded shows up. Existence is the thought of the whole process of grounds and grounded showing up, shining, or being there. Existence captures a new kind of thereness produced by a successful, mutually defining process between grounds and grounded. It is a new immediacy (presence or thereness) that is defined or produced by a process, and hence is mediated (§122). Existence is the thought of essential universality (which is what Essence was) identifying and being identified by sensible being (which is what Shine was), in a mutual relationship of ground and grounded. When ground and grounded are in their mutually defining process, then Existence "emerges" (§122R). Since Existence is defined as the process of ground and grounded taken together, it gets what character or definition it has from the elements and process that it embraces. It does not yet have a character of its own, which is why I have represented it in the diagram with a dashed outline.

Existence is the kind of thereness that applies to essential concepts such as the concept of fruit. We were introduced to the concept of thereness in the stage of Being-there in Chapter Two. Thereness is basic, qualitative presence. Qualities such as "yellow" or "chair," and quantities such a "number" and "degree," have what seems to be immediate presence or thereness in the world of experience or realm of Being. "Existence" is a kind of thereness too, but it is a higher-level of thereness that applies, not to qualitative or quantitative concepts, but to essences. An essence or essential concept is not tied to any particular thereness (see the Introduction to this chapter), so it cannot have thereness in an immediate way. The concept of fruit, for example, includes all sorts of qualities and quantities. "Fruit" therefore cannot have any seemingly immediate qualitative or quantitative presence or thereness in the realm of Being. Nevertheless, the concept of fruit can have a kind of thereness—it can *exist*. When an essence or ground is in a mutually defining relationship with a thereness or grounded, then the essence has a certain sort of thereness, namely, it exists. The concept of fruit exists when it is in a mutually defining relationship with fruit in the realm of Being. Existence is, in part, the thereness of an essence. It is the way in which an essence—which is not tied to any particular thereness—can nonetheless be there, or have being in the sensible world.

The fruit in the realm of Being is equally dependent for its thereness on the concept of fruit. There can be no fruit in the realm of Being without the concept of fruit. As Hegel says, you cannot pick fruit off of a tray. You can only pick cherries, pears or raisins and so on (see §38 and the Introduction to this chapter). Just as the concept of fruit exists only by being tied to a set of items in the realm of Being, a set of items in the realm of Being can exist as fruit only by being tied to the concept of fruit. Fruit—not the concept, but the things themselves—have no existence in the realm of Being *as fruit* without being tied to the concept that grasps them. A sensible thereness cannot exist as fruit without the concept of fruit.

Therefore, when the concept of fruit is taken together with its sensible thereness, then *fruit*—now as both concept and thereness or Being—exists. In general, existence is a mutually defining relationship between essential concept and thereness. Existence emerges when an essence or essential universal is fleshed out, so to speak, in the sensible world of thereness, and when a sensible thereness is captured by an essential universal.

Hegel describes the overall connectedness of grounds and groundeds in Existence as "infinite" (§123). The connectedness is "infinite" in Hegel's sense of good infinity, not the spurious or running-on type of infinity (see the stages of Spurious Infinity and Being-for-itself in Chapter Two). It is because Existence is infinite in the good sense that it is an embracing, "for itself" concept of the sort we have seen before. Like Being-for-itself, Essence, and the relationship of Ground, Existence is an overarching thought that grasps and stabilizes a back-and-forth process between two other concepts that are defined as the same as one another. Here, Existence grasps the back-and-forth process of two concepts that are defined as both ground and grounded. The thought of Existence is the "for itself," embracing thought of the process of grounds and grounded. As in those other stages, I represent Existence as an overarching bubble surrounding the whole process.

Existence has two different characterizations. It is (i) the whole process of grounds and grounded, in which case the whole process is a kind of realm of Existence, or (ii) a bunch of individual processes of grounds and groundeds, in which case Existence is a multitude of processes. (i) On the one hand, the concept of Existence can refer to the whole process of all the grounds and groundeds taken together as a whole. This would be the concept of the realm of Existence, taken as a whole, or the whole of existence in general. When the concept of fruit is completely fleshed out in the sensible world, then the concept exists as a whole. Existence in this sense is the whole world of existence for the concept of fruit.

Existence, however, can also be thought of as a bunch of individual processes of grounds and grounded, in which case Existence is (ii) a multitude of processes of grounds and groundeds. The concept of fruit exists not only as the whole collection of fruit, but also as a whole multitude or bunch of individual therenesses, or as individual pieces of fruit. Because "fruit" is an essence and is not tied to any immediate qualitative or quantitative thereness, however, it cannot have thereness in an immediate way, in the way that qualitative and quantitative concepts did (see the Introduction to this chapter). "Fruit" can exist only if there is some thereness out there that is properly identified by (grounded by) and properly identifies (grounds) the concept of fruit. "Fruit" as a concept also exists, then, when there is a bunch (multitude) of thereness out there with which "fruit" has a successful, mutually grounding relationship. "Fruit" exists not only as the whole collection of fruit-thereness, but also whenever some bunch of thereness out there and the concept of "fruit" mutually define each other.

Notice that (ii) is not a reference to individually existing pieces of fruit. Because the concept of Existence has no boundaries, we have not yet defined a chunk of existence or an individual existent (thing), such as a piece of fruit or an individual rock, for example. Chunks of existence come up in the next stage. At the moment, we are talking about how "fruit" or "rock" exist—both as concepts and sensible thereness—and they exist either (i) as a completed, whole relationship between ground and grounded—all fruit-thereness or rock-thereness in general—or (ii) whenever there is any fruit-thereness or rock-thereness anywhere. In this second sense, so long as there is some fruit-thereness or some rock-thereness somewhere, then "fruit" and "rock" as concepts exist. "Rock" as a concept exists, for instance, if there is some corresponding thereness in the world that is rock—not any specific rock, but some rock-thereness somewhere in general.

Thing

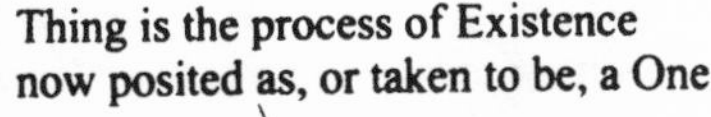

Thing is the process of Existence
now posited as, or taken to be, a One

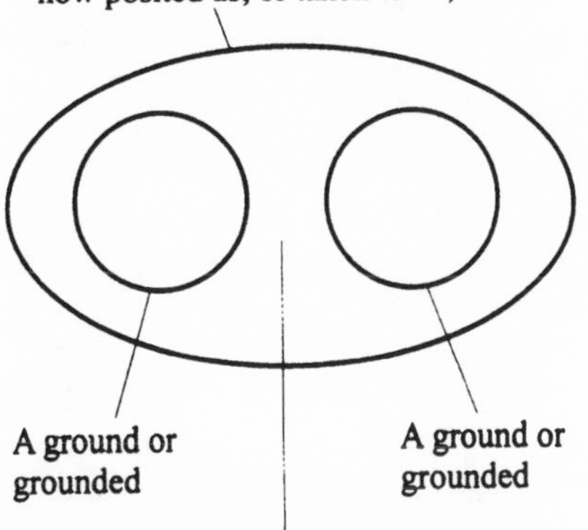

The relationship of Ground was fulfilled or completed in Existence. It slips into the background, or is no longer an active logical element. I have therefore eliminated the arrow that represented Ground from the diagram

Figure 3.22

The stage of Existence asserted that the mutually defining process between grounds and grounded is successful. "Fruit" as a concept and as a sensible thereness can exist, for instance, only if the concept succeeds in properly identifying and being identified by some thereness out there—either as a whole or as a multitude. Existence asserts that the mutually defining relationship is there. It asserts, in effect, that fruit exists. Thus, Existence logically implies that the relationship between ground and grounded was not a merely potential relationship, but is a fulfilled relationship. In this stage, the logical conclusion that the relationship of Ground between grounds and grounded is fulfilled. Ground and grounded fulfill the process of mutually determining each other. Because the relationship of Ground is fulfilled, it is finished, complete. It therefore slips into the background in the sense that it will no longer play an active role in the logical development. In this diagram, I have removed the circular arrow that represented the process of Ground in earlier stages to illustrate that the process has now slipped into the background as fulfilled.

Existence is a "for itself" concept: it is the concept that embraces the whole process of ground and grounded. Because the relationship of Ground is complete or fulfilled, Existence must now be thought of as a One, whole or chunk. We saw the same logical move in other "for itself" concepts: they were defined not only as the thought of back-and-forth *processes*, but as back-and-forth processes also taken to be a One (cf. Being-for-itself in Chapter Two). The process of ground and grounded within Existence is a process of showing up or shining: the ground shows up when the grounded shows up, and vice versa. Since the shining relationship between ground and grounded is fulfilled, and since Existence reflects that fulfilled relationship as a One, Existence is a One that shines forth as Ground, or is, as Hegel puts it, "reflected within itself as *ground*" (§124). Since its inward reflection or character is defined by the relationship of Ground, it has its own ground within it, which is to say, it is self-grounded or subsistent. Because Existence is a One that shines forth as if it can stand alone (is subsistent), it is a Thing. As Hegel puts it, "what exists is *thing*" (§124). Existence has become a subsistent existent (thing). Since Thing is a reconception of the same concept that was Existence in the last stage, I have represented it in the diagram as the same bubble that was Existence. Moreover, since Thing, as subsistent, has an independent character or definition, I have given its bubble a solid outline.

Because the Thing is defined by Ground, which is a process of ground *and* grounded, the Thing's character is defined by both ground (inward reflection) and grounded (reflection-into-another). It has Ground or inward reflection insofar as it is "reflected within itself," or is defined on its own. It has Groundedness or reflection-into-another insofar as it is related to an "other" existent (thing). The Thing "contains relationality and its own manifold connectedness with other existents" (§124) within it as one of its characteristics. Since the fulfilled relationship of Ground is the unity of inward reflection (ground) and reflection-into-another (grounded), these characteristics are not separate from one another within the Thing (§124). The Thing has each of these characteristics in its content as a unity: its content has one character (as a unity) or the other (as a unity). Because the Thing is subsistent (ground, inward reflection), the content is first defined as non-subsistent or as properties in the next stage. In the subsequent stage, the Thing is non-subsistent (grounded, reflection-into-another), and its content is subsistent or Matters.

Because the two inner bubbles grew out of Essence and Shine, they still represent Thought (Essence) and thereness (Shine). The concept of Existence was defined as a general correspondence between concept and thereness. A concept exists if it succeeds in grounding and being grounded by a thereness. "Rock," for instance, exists when it grounds and is grounded by rock-thereness out there—either as a whole, or as a multitude. In Thing, that Existence is defined as a chunk. When the correspondence between concept and thereness is taken as a chunk or One, then it is a Thing. Rock as a Thing would be the whole chunk of stuff to which the correspondence between "rock" as a concept and rock as thereness applies. It would be all the rock-stuff in the world. Hegel's concept of Thing is therefore a general concept of Thing—a concept of a type of thing, rather than of an individual thing itself. We ordinarily think of a specific rock—some little rock—as a thing, and we would think of all rock taken together as a type of thing. For Hegel, however, the Thing is the whole existent for which there is correspondence between concept and thereness. It is rock-thinghood, rather than an individual rock. Hegel develops the concept of an individual thing later on.

Although Hegel's Thing is not an individual thing, it still has characteristics ordinarily associated with things. Things are independent chunks of identifiable therenesses that are subsistent or exist on their own. A chair, for example, seems to be there on its own as a solid chunk, and does not depend on anything else for its existence. Hegel's Thing, is subsistent in the same way. Like a chair, all the rock-stuff in the world, is out there on its own, solid, and independent. Indeed, rock-stuff is the ground or support of other items. Rock-stuff-as-a-chunk or rock as a type has properties, for example, that depend on it for their subsistence. Thus, Hegel's concept of Thing includes the characteristics of subsistence and solidity that we ordinarily associate with the concept of thing.

Hegel outlines the logical development of the Thing as three separate "moments [*Momente*]" (§123), which he labels (α), (β) and (γ). Hegel's use of the term "moment" to describe logical stages is not defended until the end of this chapter (see Reciprocal Action). Since it would take us too far ahead to explain Hegel's defense of the term here, I will beg indulgence and use Hegel's terminology with the promise that it will be explained and defended later.

Properties

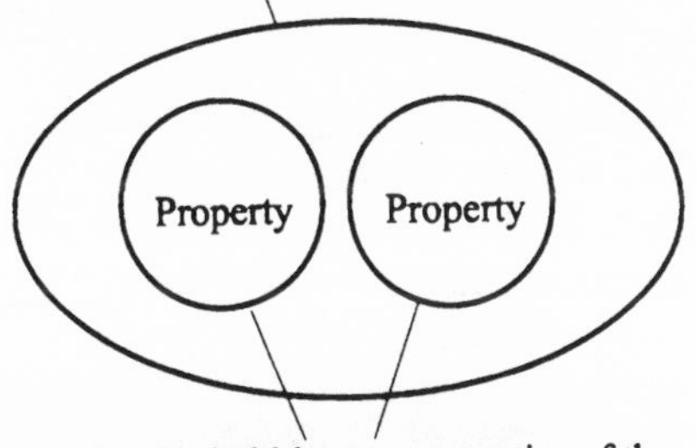
(α) Thing contains elements defined by reflection-into-another, or defined as grounded
Property
Property
The two inner bubbles are properties of the Thing. They are independent in terms of their reflection-into-another, but are dependent in terms of their inward-reflection

Figure 3.23

The logical development of Thing has three moments.

(α) The Thing contains the fulfilled relationship of Ground, which was defined as "inward reflection which is just as much reflection-into-another" (§121). In the first moment of the Thing, the Thing is defined by "inward reflection" and *contains* "reflection-into-another" (§125), so the elements that it contains are *properties*. Because properties are defined by "reflection-into-another," they reflect not only into the Thing, but also into each other, which is why they are separate from one another. Their reflection into each other holds them apart from one another, or distinguishes them from one another, in the same way that back-and-forth relationships distinguished elements from one another in earlier stages. Reflecting into the other was also the way in which Positive and Negative were distinguished from one another. The Positive could be the Positive only by shining into—or shining against the background of—the Negative, and vice versa (see the stage of Transition to Ground). Because properties are defined by "reflection-into-another," they are separate from one another. As Hegel puts it, they are "diverse from each other" (§125). But they do not subsist on their own. They have their inward-reflection only in the Thing, or they depend on the Thing for their characters. Properties shine forth against each other, but they need the Thing to have the character that they have. Properties are grounded in the Thing, which is their ground.

As the ground of the properties, the Thing is defined by inward reflection, and has its reflection-into-another in the properties. Since Existence is defined as two items in a relationship of "inward reflection which is just as much reflection-into-another," the Thing needs the properties to exist (as Hegel apparently remarked in a lecture [§125A]). Its relationship with the properties makes it determinate and concrete (§125), or gives it a character that allows it to be out there. However, because the Thing has inward reflection by itself, it is separate from and independent of the properties, and so is not tied to any particular properties (§125A).

Hegel says that, in this stage, "being" has been sublated and the relationship of "having" replaces the concept of "being" (§125R). In earlier stages, being and shine were taken to be together at the same time: whatever had shine (thereness), had being too, or, to put it another way, whatever had shine was assumed to have some subsistence on its own. But now shine and being are separated. Properties shine, but they don't have their being in themselves. They have their being, or subsistence only in the Thing. Being is sublated (cancelled and preserved): it is cancelled because the properties lack the subsistence that immediate being had, but it is preserved because the properties still show or shine forth in the way that immediate being did. This sublation is signaled by the change in terminology from "being" to "having." We do not say that things "are" properties (which would suggest that the things subsist in the properties, so that the properties provide the subsistence), we say that things "have" properties (which suggests that the properties cannot subsist without the things).

Hegel distinguishes the sorts of properties he has in mind here from the concept of quality that we saw earlier in the Doctrine of Being (see the stages of Being-for-itself, Repulsion and Attraction). Properties, he says, are not to be confused with qualities. Properties are characteristics that the Thing can lose without ceasing to be what it is, whereas qualities are what make something what it is. Something cannot lose its quality without ceasing to be what it is (§§125R, 125A, cf. Being-in-itself). The quality of a human is the what-it-is that makes a human a human. In earlier sections, I simply referred to this quality as "humanness." Because the Thing is defined as inward reflection, it is distinct or separate from the properties (§125R), so that if you took the properties away, it would still be what it is.

Matters

(β) Thing contains elements defined by inward-reflection, or defined as ground

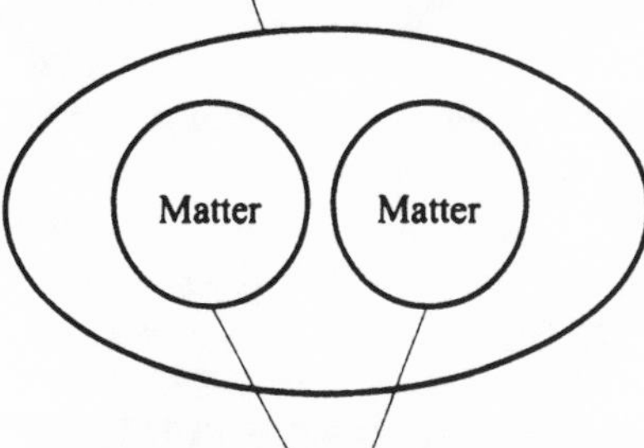

The inner bubbles are matters. They are independent in terms of their inward-reflection, but dependent in terms of their reflection-into-another

Figure 3.24

(β) In the second moment, the Thing contains inward reflection instead of reflection-into-another, as it did in the last stage. When the Thing contains inward reflection, the elements it contains are Matters (§126). Matters are independent in terms of their inward reflection or subsistence. As inward reflection, they have a character of their own which gives them a subsistence independent of the Thing. They therefore do not depend on the Thing for their subsistence, as properties did. But they depend on the Thing for their reflection-into-another. They cannot shine forth, show up or be out there without the Thing. Because they have no thereness without the Thing, they are not Things themselves. They have characters or determinacy, but only in an abstract way. Take electricity, for example (§126R). Electricity has a character or definition of its own—it is something on its own—but it needs a Thing to show up. Electricity shows up in the light bulb, for example, or in the hair that stands up after being rubbed with a balloon. Electricity cannot be out there without a Thing. It is not concrete—and hence is not a Thing—by itself. It has a character, but only in an abstract sense, that is, without out-thereness. Because the out-thereness or shine (reflection-into-another) of the Matters is abstract, their character (or inward reflection) is what determines the Thing. The Matters are the "being-thereness of Thinghood" (*das daseinde Dingheit*) (§127), or what gives the Thing *its* thereness. They are the subsistence of the Thing, or what the thing consists in. They are the stuffs or matters out of which a Thing is made. To take another example that Hegel apparently used in a lecture, granite is made up of quartz, feldspar and mica (§126A). Those are its matters.

Hegel says that Matters are qualities in the proper sense of the term because they are "one with their being (that on immediacy reached determinacy)," but a being that "is a reflected existence" (§126R). Matters are "one with their being" because they have a character or are inward reflection in an immediate way. Like qualities in the Doctrine of Being, they are defined or have their characters in an immediate way as independent characteristics of the Thing. Quartz, feldspar and mica, for instance, are characteristics of the quartz that are distinguished from one another within the quartz. But the being of Matters is a "reflected existence" because they only show up through a relationship of ground and grounded, which is the definition of Existence. In particular, they only show up in the Thing. They are what the Thing consists in—the ground of the Thing—and the Thing is how they show up, or their grounded.

Because Matters need the Thing to show up, they are like essences or essential universals in the sense that they are not tied to any particular thereness. Electricity, for example, has one sort of thereness in the light bulb, a different sort of thereness in copper wire, and yet another sort of thereness in a person's hair. Matters can be distinguished from one another without reference to the Thing, but they are essential qualities, or qualities that are essences, rather than mere therenesses or beings. Matters are qualities defined as thought, rather than qualities defined as thereness. Take magnetism, for example (§126R). Magnetism is a conceptual quality that is independent of any one thing. But it only shows up, shines or has thereness in a thing. Only things are magnetic. Although magnetism is independent of the thing—it is something that the Thing is made up of or consists in—magnetism is not something out there that we can point to. That's because magnetism is not "concrete," as things are, Hegel says (§126). Magnetism is not concrete because it is not a discretely bounded item with thereness. It is not a chunk of thereness in the sensible world. It is a conceptual quality—a thought of a quality—that has its thereness in the thing. So magnetism is a quality in an essential sense. Essence is a thought or concept that has its thereness only in its shine. That is what Matters are: they are abstract thoughts of qualities that are like Essence because they have their therenesses only in their shines in the Thing. Moreover, like Essence, the Matters are determined through their shines. In themselves, they are abstract. They have their thereness through their shines in the thing. So magnetism is fulfilled only in existence, that is, when its thereness (in the Thing) and its thought or concept (as magnetism) successfully mutually determine each other.

Thing as Form

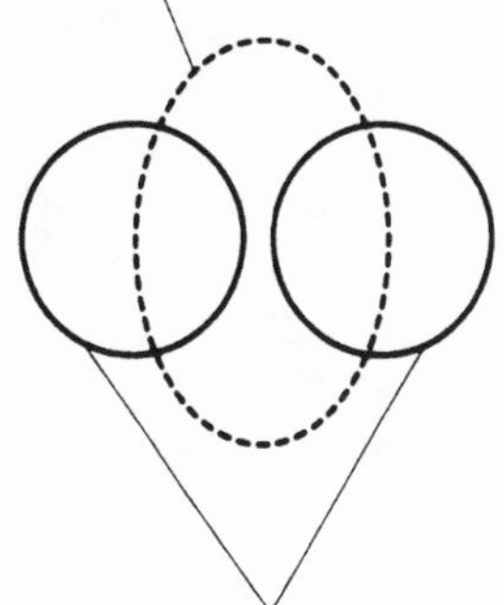

(γ) Thing is no longer subsistent by itself. It is the way in which the matters are presented, how the matters are put forth, or the Form of the matters
The matters subsist on their own. They are now the solid background

Figure 3.25

(γ) Unfortunately, when the Thing is defined as containing Matters—as it was in the last stage—it is not self-subsistent anymore. The Thing was originally defined as self-subsistent, but since the Matters are now what is really subsistent, and the Thing is how they shine, then the Matters seem to be what subsist by themselves, and the Thing is demoted to being merely their Form. The Thing is not independent anymore, as it was supposed to be. It depends on the Matters for its content, so to speak. The Matters give it its character. The Matters are the independent background, the content, and the Thing is merely the way or how they show up. The Thing has therefore become the Form. I have made the Thing a dashed bubble to represent its demoted status as not self-subsistent anymore. I have also made its bubble thinner than the Matters to represent the idea that the Matters are now the solid background, and the Thing is merely their form, or the way in which they are presented, show up, or shine forth. The Matters are the base, and the Thing floats in front of, or presents them.

Why is the demoted Thing a "form"? We often distinguish between form and content. We might say, for instance, that the content of an essay paper or the thoughts behind it are excellent, but that its form or the way those thoughts are expressed or presented is bad. This is roughly the same relationship we have here between the Thing and the Matters. The Matters now provide the content of the Thing—they are the independent stuffs that the Thing expresses. They are like the thoughts or concepts that provide the background ideas of the paper. The Thing, for its part, is now the way the Matters are expressed—it is the way the Matters show up or shine. So the Thing is like the form of the essay paper—it is the way the Matters are brought forth. The Thing is the form of the Matters.

One Matter

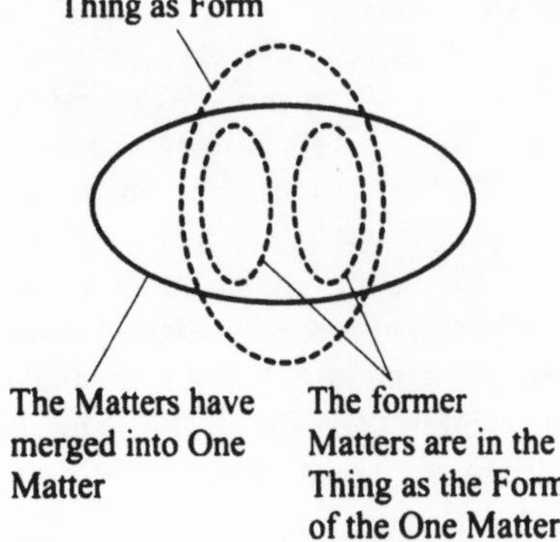
Thing as Form
The Matters have merged into One Matter
The former Matters are in the Thing as the Form of the One Matter

Figure 3.26

Each matter is currently being defined by two processes. First, matter is defined by inward reflection. Second, each matter is defined by reflection-into-another through the Thing. Since each matter is defined by both of these processes, we can say that each one is defined as "inward reflection that is just as much reflection-into-another," which is the process of Existence (see the stage of Existence). Moreover, because each Matter reflects into the Thing, as soon as each one goes through the process of "inward reflection which is just as much reflection-into-another" it ends up in the Thing. The Thing is defined as what exists (see the stage of Thing). As soon as the Matters each go through their process of existence, then, they exist (in the Thing). Their processes of existence immediately lead them to exist (in the Thing), or they come to exist in an immediate way just in virtue of their processes of existence. Because the Matters come to exist (in the Thing) in an immediate way as soon as they go through their processes of existence, each matter is an immediate unity of Existence with itself. Since both Matters share this same character, we could also say that, in general, Matter is an immediate unity of Existence with itself, as Hegel suggests (§128). Each matter is an immediate unity of Existence with itself because their processes of existence immediately lead them to exist.

This description of the process of the Matters has two logical implications. First, each matter is defined on its own (i.e. in an "in itself" sense) by exactly the same processes. So they each have the same definition in the "in itself" sense, as Hegel apparently remarked in a lecture (§128A). Second, the two Matters have no active relationship with one another. They are indifferent toward one another, as Hegel suggests (§128). They each have their reflection-into-another only in relation to the Thing. Since the Matters have the same definition and have no relationship with one another, they cannot be held apart or distinguished from one another. When two inside bubbles were defined as the same as one another or had the same definition in an "in itself" sense in earlier stages (see Being-for-itself, Transition to Essence, Transition to Ground, and Existence, for instance), the two inside bubbles could be distinguished from one another because they were engaged in a back-and-forth process of definition with each other that held them apart or that defined them as separate from one another, even if they had the same definition in an "in itself" sense. Because the two Matters here are indifferent toward one another, however, they have no relationship with one another that defines them as separate or holds them apart. Hence, they cannot be distinguished from one another or held apart. They merge into One Matter (§128). In the diagram, they have become one large bubble, the One Matter.

Hegel says that this One Matter is "Existence in the reflective determination of Identity" (§128). The One Matter is the thought of an existence defined as the Identity of what reflects. It is the solid or stable existence—the Identity—that gives identity to, or determines, what is reflected or shows up. In the same way, Identity was the stable concept that determined the Shine (see the stage of Identity). The One Matter is existence defined as an Identity that reflects, while the Thing is what is reflected or shows up. The One Matter is the content that is presented in the Thing. (We can anticipate how the Thing will be defined later. In later stages, what is reflected or shows up will be defined as appearance.) Because the One Matter is the determining factor, it is the subsistent background. In the diagram, the bubble for the One Matter therefore has a solid (rather than dashed) outline.

While the former Matters have merged to become One Matter, shadows of the two former Matters remain, but now they are only defined in relation to the Thing. The former Matters have become part of the Thing. Since the Thing is the Form, or the way in which the One Matter is presented, the former Matters have become part of the Form as well. They are defined *against* the One Matter as the way in which the One Matter is presented in the Thing. They are the Form of the One Matter. And the external relation that they have with one another—the relation in which they are separate from one another—is only in the Thing. Because they are presented in (belong to) and are separate from one another only in the Thing, I have squeezed them up in the diagram so that they are now inside the bubble for the Thing. They belong to and are separate bubbles only inside the Thing. Moreover, although the former Matters still exist, they do not have their characters on their own. As the presentation or Form of the One Matter, they have their characters in or subsist in the One Matter. Like the Thing, they have their subsistence only in the One Matter and are not subsistent on their own. In the diagram, I have given their bubbles dashed outlines to represent the fact that they are no longer the subsistent background, but are now merely the way in which the One Matter is presented in the Thing.

Because the former Matters are how the One Matter shows up or shines, they are the Distinction of the One Matter in the way that Shine was the Distinction of Identity (see the stage of Immediate Distinction). Like Shine, the former Matters are a Distinction that reflects. Since the Thing exists, however, they also exist, so they are a Distinction that reflects as existing. Finally, together with the Thing, they are the complete way in which the One Matter is presented. The former Matters have their distinction in the Thing—the Thing is what makes it possible for them to be distinguished from one another. The Thing gives them their existence and their external relation to one another. Since the One Matter has no distinctions of its own, all of its distinctions are in the former Matters. The former Matters are thus the completed set of distinctions of the One Matter.

They are therefore a totality. Hence the former Matters are a Distinction that reflects as existing and as totality, as Hegel suggests (§128).

Hegel says that this concept of the One Matter corresponds to Kant's conception of the Thing-in-itself (§128R). Kant's Thing-in-itself is supposed to stand for the world as it is in itself, beyond the filter through which we experience that world. According to Kant, our senses and reason are filters that allow us to see only the world as we experience it, and not the world as it is in itself, or the Thing-in-itself. The world as it is in itself exists as Thing-in-itself. Nonetheless, for Kant, the Thing-in-itself still provides the world of experience with its content. It provides the content that our filter works on. Thus, the Thing-in-itself is an existence that reflects or has a form. The world of our experience is the form, or the way in which the Thing-in-itself shows up or is presented. Moreover, because, according to Kant, we can't "see" the Thing-in-itself, it has no distinctions of its own. The Thing-in-itself is abstract (§128R) because it has no internal relationships or elements to give it a character. All of its distinctions are in its shine or Form, or the way in which it is presented. It is just one, big, indistinguishable existence that has distinctions only in an existence that shines or shows up. This is just how Hegel has characterized the One Matter. The One Matter is the One, indistinguishable existence and content for the distinctions in the Thing, which exists in a way that shows up or shines.

Thing as One Form

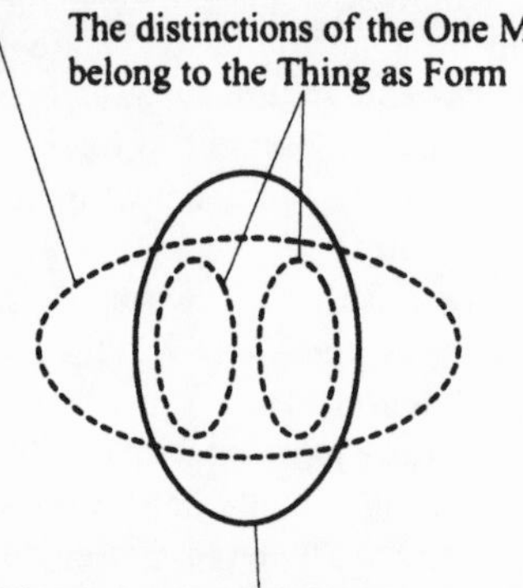
The One Matter turns out not to be so independent after all. It depends on the Thing or the Form (the Thing as Form) for its character or determination
The distinctions of the One Matter belong to the Thing as Form
The Thing is the determining element. It gives the One Matter its character. Because it contains all the distinctions of the One Matter, the Thing has become a totality: One Form

Figure 3.27

The One Matter was supposed to be the subsistent element, but now it turns out not to be independent after all. It depends on the Thing or the Form for its character. By itself, the Matter is abstract. It needs the Form to have any distinctions or character. So the Form now seems to determine the Matter (the content), and the Thing begins to look like the determining factor. It seems to be the self-subsistent item that determines the One Matter. Because the One Matter is no longer the subsistent element, I have demoted its bubble to a dashed status in the diagram. Because the Thing is the self-subsistent element, its bubble has a solid outline.

Because the former Matters

became a totality in the last stage, the definition of the Thing changes. Thing is no longer defined as a separate, independent chunk (such as rock-stuff), as it was in the stage of Thing. Because the Thing now contains all of the distinctions of the One Matter—or all the distinctions of the One Matter taken as a totality—it must be a totality as well. The Thing is the totality of Thinghood because only the totality of Thinghood contains all of the distinctions of the One Matter. The One Matter is the one whole Thing-in-itself in Kant's sense, so the Thing must now be conceived as the whole or totality of Thinghood. Only the totality of Thinghood contains all of the distinctions for the Thing-in-itself. Thing has therefore become defined as the complete and completed presentation of the One Matter—the One Form of the whole One Matter. The Thing is Every-Thing, the whole presentation of the One Matter. Only the whole world of Thinghood—all the rock-stuff, and dirt-stuff, and tree-stuff, and dog-stuff, and so on—contains and presents all the distinctions of the whole, One Matter (or Thing-in-itself).

Matter and Form Fall Apart

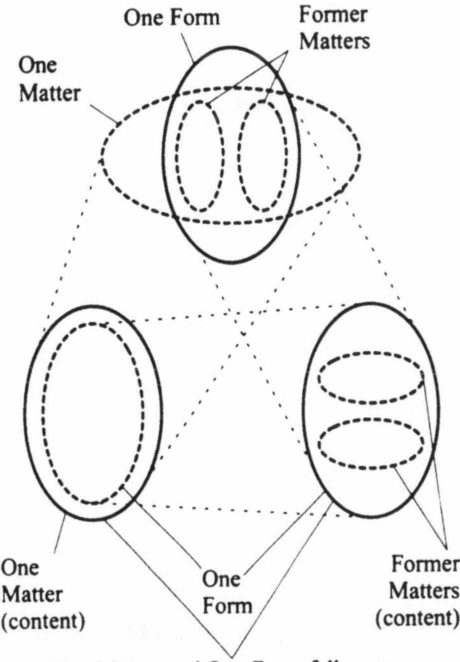

One Matter and One Form fall apart into independent "for itself" concepts defined in an "in itself" sense as the relation of matter and form

Figure 3.28

The One Matter and One Form now come to be defined as "for itself" concepts in relation to each of their own contents. They lose their connection to one another, and so fall apart as independent concepts. As Hegel puts it, they become concepts that are each independent "for itself" (*selbständig für sich* [§129]), or independent in the "for itself" sense. A "for itself" concept is a concept that is defined by embracing other concepts (see Being-for-itself). Moreover, they each come to be defined in an "in itself" sense as the relation of matter and form.

To see how this process develops, remember that, in the stage of Matters, the original Matters were defined as inward reflection that lacked reflection-into-another. The One Matter also has that characteristic—it is supposed to be the subsistent, existing element (inward reflection) that has its reflection-into-another only in the Thing. Now that the Thing has become the determining element, however, the One Matter has turned out to be an existence that is just as much reflection-into-another as it is inward reflection. The Thing or One Form is the determining element because it contains all of the One Matter's distinctions. By itself, the One Matter is abstract or without definition. So the One Matter can have its distinctions and hence have its own definition or being only by reflecting into the Thing or One Form. It has to reflect into another—into the Thing—to have its character. The One Matter has its character only if the Thing reflects, presents or is the shine of the One Matter.

As a result, the One Matter can have its character as the subsistent, existing element only if it is a "for itself" totality that embraces the One Form as its presentation or shine. Now that the One Form, like the One Matter, has become a totality, the One Matter has become a "for itself" concept. Since both the One Matter and the One Form are totalities, they are complete expressions of each other—the One Matter is *all* the content and the One Form is *all* of its presentation. Hence the One Matter and One Form have the same content—there is nothing in the One Matter that is not in the One Form, and vice versa. When the One Matter embraces the One Form, then, it is embracing itself or something that has the same definition or content that it has. The One Form is the form, presentation or shine of the One Matter. So the One Matter embraces the One Form as its defining content and form. The One Matter is thus a "for itself" concept in relation to the One Form. Because the One Matter is now defined as a "for itself" concept that embraces the One Form as itself, it is, or has its character as, the content or subsistent element. It is a content that contains, embraces or has form. It is a content with a form.

At the same time, the Form was defined as reflection-into-another that lacked inward reflection. The former Matters are also the Form of the One Matter, or the way in which the One Matter is presented. Because the One Form is now related to the former Matters, it relates itself to itself—it is a Form that embraces form. Since both the One Form and what it embraces have the same definition—as Form—when the One Form embraces the former Matters, it embraces itself. The One Form is thus a "for itself" concept that embraces the former Matters, which are also itself, as its content. In the diagram, the bubble for the One Form includes or embraces the bubbles for the former Matters.

Furthermore, although the former Matters are the Form of the One Matter, they are also the distinctions that are supposed to determine or define the One Matter. Because the One Form contains all the distinctions of the One Matter, it now contains inward reflection as well. The former Matters are the distinctions or character of the One Matter. Because the One Form contains or embraces those distinctions, it has a content of its own. So the One Form is a form that is related to a content.

The One Matter and One Form are thus now each defined by the process of Existence on their own, and, as existences, fall apart as independent. Existence is defined as two logical elements in a process of "inward reflection which is just as much reflection-into-another" (see the stage of Existence). Since the One Matter and One Form are each defined as the combination of both content (inward reflection) and form (reflection-into-another), they each exist. More than that, they have each become a Thing as well. Thing is defined as the process of Existence taken to be an independent element or One. Since the One Form and One Matter are each "for itself" concepts capable of having their definitions on their own, each is a One or independent element defined by "inward reflection (content) which is just as much reflection-into-another (form)," or is a Thing. Indeed, each is defined, insofar as each is an independent existence, as the totality of Thinghood (§129). The One Matter is the complete content, and the One Form is the complete presentation of that content. So One Matter and One Form are now each defined as independent Thing-totality or Thing-hood. In the diagram, I have represented the fact that the One Form and One Matter have fallen apart into independent concepts of Thinghood by depicting them as separate bubbles. However, although the One Form is defined as an independent concept from the One Matter, the One Matter is still a "for itself" concept that embraces the One Form. As a result, when I depict the One Form and One Matter as separate concepts in the diagram, we end up with two copies of the One Form: one copy within the One Matter (to depict the "for itself" definition of the One Matter), and a separate, independent copy (to depict the independent character of the One Form). The One Form has one relationship with the One Matter, and a different relationship with the former Matters. In relation to the One Matter, the One Form is merely a form, but in relation to the former Matters, it has a content. Because the One Form is currently defined primarily as an independent concept, I have given the bubble for the independently depicted One Form a solid outline, while I have given the bubble representing the One Form within the "for itself" definition of the One Matter a dashed outline. (That dashed outline also depicts the fact that, within the One Matter, the One Form is merely a form.) The dashed version of the One Form within the One Matter suggests that, although the One Form is currently defined as independent of the One Matter, the One Matter is still related to the One Form as a "for itself" concept that embraces the One Form. Indeed, that "for itself" relationship between the One Matter and the One Form will drive the logical move in the next stage.

Finally, if we look at how each is defined on its own, or in an "in itself" sense, they each have the same definition as both form and content. The One Matter is a content that has form, and the Form is a form that has content. They are, as Hegel puts it, "*in-themselves* the same" as "the relation of matter and form," although they are distinct or independent concepts (§129).

Transition to Appearance

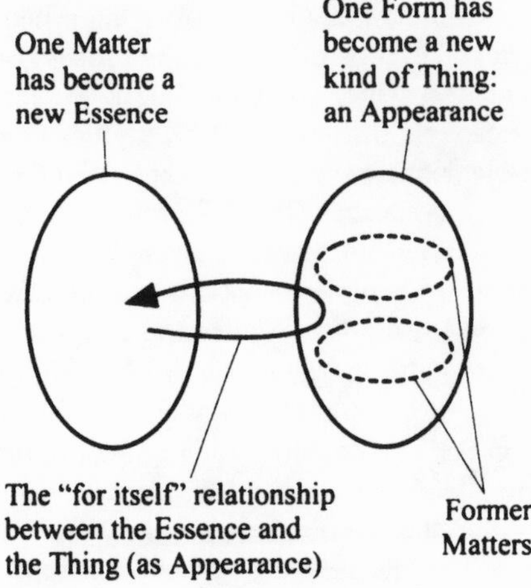
One Matter has become a new Essence
One Form has become a new kind of Thing: an Appearance
The "for itself" relationship between the Essence and the Thing (as Appearance)
Former Matters

Figure 3.29

The One Matter and the One Form are both "for itself" concepts, but they are not both "for itself" concepts in relation to each other. The One Matter is a "for itself" concept in relation to the One Form, but the One Form is a "for itself" concept in relation to the former Matters, which it contains or embraces as its content. In this stage, these two "for itself" relationships redefine both the One Matter and the One Form.

While the One Matter and One Form have fallen apart as independent, the One Matter is still related to the One Form because it is a "for itself" concept that embraces the One Form. The One Matter can have its definition or character as the subsistent and defining element only if it shows up or is presented in the One Form. As soon as the One Form was defined as a totality, the One Matter became a "for itself" concept that had the One Form as its presentation or shine. Two logical conclusions follow. First, the One Matter now has the same relationship with the One Form that Essence had with Shine in the stage of Identity. Like Essence, the One Matter is a "for itself" concept. The One Matter is also the stabilizing element. Of course, the One Matter and Essence are stabilizing elements in slightly different senses. Essence stabilized the Shine by being the element that could define the Shine in the sense that it identified the Shine. The One Matter also defines the One Form, but it stabilizes it by being the *subsistence*—rather than merely the identifying element—of the One Form. In the One Matter, Identity includes Existence. The One Matter is the identity but also the subsistent existence of the One Form. Nevertheless, because the One Matter has the same relationship with the One Form that Essence had with Shine, the One Matter is a new kind of Essence. Since the One Matter has the same "for itself" relationship with the One Form that Essence had with Shine, and since the One Matter and One Form have fallen apart (as independent) into a side-by-side view, I have depicted the "for itself" relationship between the One Matter and the One Form with the same looping arrow that we had between Essence and Shine in this diagram. Keep in mind, however, that, like Essence and Shine, this new Essence embraces the One Form, so that this new Essence and the One Form could also be depicted as nested bubbles. At the same time, however, the side-by-side view captures the idea that they have "fallen apart" into independent concepts.

Second, not only *can* the One Matter be what it is or have its definition through the One Form (as its presentation or shine), it *must* have its definition through the One Form. At first, the logic shows that the One Matter *can* have its definition as the subsistent and defining element only if it is presented in the One Form. Once the definition of the One Form became a totality, the One Matter *does in fact* have the One Form as its presentation. The One Matter is a "for itself" concept that embraces the One Form as its presentation or shine and content. Hence, the One Matter *is presented*. Indeed, because it *can* be what it is or have its definition only *if* it is presented, it *must* be presented. As I will explain in a moment, just as the One Matter is redefined (as a new kind of Essence), so the One Form will be redefined as well—as Appearance. Once the One Form is redefined as Appearance, we could also say, as Hegel does, that "Essence *must* appear" (§131).

The concept of the One Form has also been redefined by the logical process. The One Form is now defined as an existence that is the complete presentation of the One Matter. It is Thinghood, or the Thing defined as a totality. This new Thing by itself is characterized by contradiction. As is suggested by the diagram, the new Thing—which is now a whole or "for itself," embracing concept—has two components: the outside bubble, which was the One Form, and the two inside bubbles, which are the former Matters. The outside bubble is defined as a form, or as the way in which the One Matter is presented. As the form, it is defined by reflection-into-another. It is how the One Matter shows up. It is a shine. But it is also currently defined as concrete, insofar as it contains or has a "for itself" relationship with the former Matters. The former Matters are the defining content of the new Thing, and hence give the Thing a character or make it concrete. Moreover, because the former Matters belong to the Thing, they are the form of the Thing, or the way in which the Thing is presented. They are therefore defined by reflection-into-another. Because they belong to the One Form or Thing, they do not have inward reflection. They have their inward reflection only in the Thing. They thus have the very same definition that properties had in the stage of Properties. In the stage of Properties, a property was an element within the Thing that had reflection-into-another but not inward reflection. Because the former Matters have this same definition now, they have become properties of the Thing (§130). Since the Thing has the former Matters as its properties, it is a determined and concrete Thing, just as Thing was in the stage of Properties above (§125). So this new Thing or One Form is a shine (reflection-into-another or form) that is concrete (inward reflection).

Moreover, because the new Thing *consists* of the former Matters it is a "for itself" concept that embraces the former Matters as its defining content. As the defining content of the Thing, the Matters are independent and have inward reflection. But they are also the way in which the Thing is presented, or its form. They belong to the inward reflection of the Thing, they are negated (§130) by the fact that they are also merely the form of the Thing. They are the way in which the Thing reflects its character—they are within the inward reflection of the Thing (§130)—or are the shine or form of the Thing. The Thing uses them up, so to speak, or negates their independent character when it is presented. Hence the Matters are an independent content (inward reflection) that is a shine or form (reflection-into-another).

Notice that both the outer bubble (the Thing or One Form) and the two inside bubbles (the former Matters) meet the definition of Existence. They are both now defined by "inward reflection that is just as much reflection-into-another," which was the definition of Existence above (see the stage of Existence). Because the whole Thing is a "for itself" concept that includes both of these elements, we can therefore describe it as an existence that sublates (cancels but preserves) existence inwardly (§130). The outer bubble is an existence and the inside bubbles are defined as an existence, so the whole Thing is an existence (the outer bubble) that sublates existence (the inside bubbles) as its inward reflection or as the reflection of its character (since the former Matters are its form or presentation). The Thing is an existence that both cancels existence—because the former Matters are defined by existence but are just the properties of the Thing—and yet preserves existence—because the former Matters remain its content.

Although this new Thing exists, it is still a form. It is still the One Form too, the shine or presentation of the Essence or One Matter. Hence, it is a shine that exists, an *Ershcheinung* or Appearance.

The Transition to Appearance represents Hegel's logical argument against Kant's conception of the Thing-in-itself, which, Hegel suggested (§128R), corresponded to his own concept of the One Matter. Kant wants to say that the Thing-in-itself exists, provides and defines the content of what appears in the world of experience, but does not itself appear. For Kant, we can experience the world only through the filter of our reason and senses, and cannot get past this filter to find out what the Thing-in-itself is like (in itself). Since we cannot experience the Thing-in-itself, all we can know about the Thing-in-itself is that it exists. But, Hegel is arguing, the Thing-in-itself can *exist* only if it is defined not only as inward reflection but also as reflection-into-another. It can be the defining and subsistent content only if it shows up or is presented in the world of experience, which corresponds to Hegel's conception of existent Thinghood or Appearance. Thing-in-itself can have the definition or character that Kant says it has (i.e. existence) only if it appears. Thing-in-itself must appear. In that case, Kant is wrong to say that we know nothing about the Thing-in-itself except that it exists. We know very well what the Thing-in-itself is like (see §44R). It is an Essence that exists as the content of the world of experience, and the world of experience is existence as its form or presentation.

III. The Doctrine of Appearance

Appearance

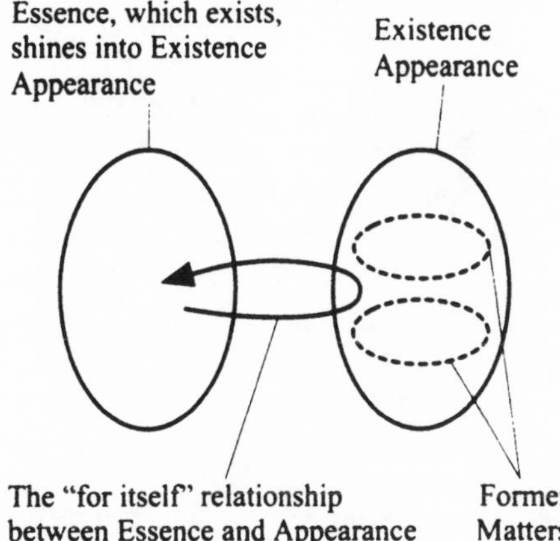

Figure 3.30

Essence *must* appear. It can reflect its character as an existence or as existing (it can shine inwardly [§131]) only through Appearance, or, as Hegel puts it, by sublating itself into immediacy (§131). Appearance is an immediacy because it is a self-contained, independent element that shines or shows up, just as being and thereness showed up in the Doctrine of Being. Essence sublates (cancels but preserves) itself through Appearance because, while Appearance is not the same thing as Essence (hence, Essence is cancelled), it is defined by existence and reflects the same character that Essence has (since the One Form had the same content as the One Matter). Moreover, because Essence *shines* into immediacy, it is not being but Essence. As was the case for the concept of Essence above, *shining* is what makes Essence an Essence, rather than a being (§131). Essence was not itself being, but it shined or showed up as being. Similarly, here, the new Essence is not itself being, but it shines or shows up as a kind of immediacy, namely Appearance.

Appearance, for its part, still contains the former Matters as its content, and those former Matters give it its subsistence. Those former Matters allow Appearance to reflect its character (it has inward reflection) as subsistence or matter. Moreover, because the former Matters are also the way in which Appearance is presented (see the stage of Transition to Appearance), Appearance is defined or characterized (in its content) by form or reflection-into-another. The former Matters are the properties of the Appearance. Since Appearance is both matter and form, it can also be defined as "subsistence *sublating itself*" (§131): Appearance is an existence that both preserves subsistence (in the former Matters) and also cancels subsistence (insofar as the former Matters are the form or properties of the Appearance).

This Essence (the former One Matter) is an embracing, "for itself" concept that has the Appearance as its content. It would be a mistake at this point, Hegel suggests, to say that the Essence is behind or beyond Appearance. Instead, through shining, the Essence, which exists, is both Existence and Appearance. It is, as Hegel puts it, Existence Appearance (§131). Essence exists by shining forth into an Appearance defined as existence.

World of Appearance

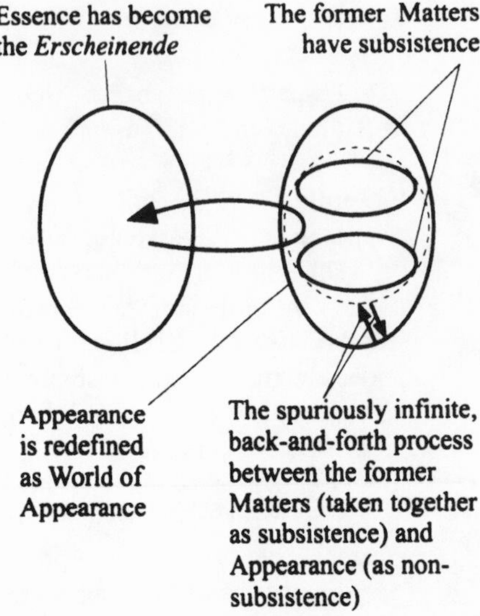
Essence has become
the *Erscheinende*
The former Matters
have subsistence
Appearance
is redefined
as World of
Appearance
The spuriously infinite,
back-and-forth process
between the former
Matters (taken together
as subsistence) and
Appearance (as non-
subsistence)

Figure 3.31

The next three sections of the *Encyclopaedia Logic* (§§132-134) are extremely difficult. They are very poorly written, with a lot of pronouns—"it," "its" and "this"—with unclear antecedents.[1] But the diagrams help to clarify what is going on in these sections.

Hegel introduces a new term to refer to this new Essence—"*Erscheinende*." He distinguishes between the Appearance (*Erscheinung*)—the term he has used until now (§§130 and 131)—and the *Erscheinende*, a new term Hegel introduces in §132 and which Geraets, Suchting and Harris translate with the phrases "what appears" and "something-that-appears" (§132). Hegel's term is a noun created out of the verb *erscheinen* or "to appear." Above, I suggested that Hegel draws a distinction between, on the one hand, the terms *scheinen* ("to shine") and *Schein* ("Shine"), and, on the other hand, the terms *erscheinen* ("to appear") and *Erscheinung* ("Appearance"). Whereas a Shine is a mere shine, an Appearance is a shine that exists, a shine that is characterized by existence. The Essence exists and is defined in such a way that it *must* appear. Because the Essence is now defined as the existing element that does the appearing, it has become the *Erscheinende*. It is the existing subject or noun that does the appearing activity or verb. In my view, there is no English word that comfortably translates the term *Erscheinende* (Geraets, Suchting and Harris use at least two different English phrases, for instance), and so I will continue to use the German term.

In this and the next several stages, the logical developments will take place only on one side of the diagram, namely, for Appearance. Later on, these changes will affect the relationship between the *Erscheinende* (former Essence) and Appearance, but, for the moment, because Appearance has the character of an independent element (which it has had since One Matter and One Form fell apart earlier), logic focuses on developments that grow out of the way in which Appearance is defined in relation to its own content, namely, the former Matters. In this first stage of development between the Appearance and the former Matters, a spuriously infinite process between the Appearance and the former Matters redefines Appearance as the World of Appearance.

To see how the spuriously infinite process within Appearance is generated, we must begin by reviewing the current relationship between the *Erscheinende* and Appearance. The *Erscheinende* (the existing subject that does the appearing) can have its character as an existing element only if it appears. Existence is defined as the thought of two elements in a mutually defining process of Ground, which was itself defined as "inward reflection which is just as much reflection-into-another." Now that we are past the category of Existence, inward reflection is subsistence, and reflection-into-another has become Appearance. The *Erscheinende* exists because it is both inward reflection (subsistence) and reflection-into-another (Appearance). As Hegel puts it, the *Erscheinende* "exists in such a way that its *subsistence* is immediately sublated [cancelled but preserved]" (§132). The *Erscheinende*'s subsistence is cancelled and preserved by its Appearance: the Appearance cancels the subsistence of the *Erscheinende* because the need for the Appearance shows that the *Erscheinende* lacks subsistence on its own, but the Appearance preserves the subsistence of the *Erscheinende* because the *Erscheinende* has, or gets to keep, its subsistence (inward reflection) by reflecting into the Appearance.

The Appearance is thus the Form of the *Erscheinende*. It is the way in which the *Erscheinende* is presented. The Appearance also contains the former Matters. In Transition to Appearance, the former Matters were defined both as subsistence (inward reflection) and as properties (reflection-into-another): as matter, they subsist (have inward reflection), but because they are presented only in the Thing (which is now the Appearance), they are properties, and so are defined by reflection-into-another as well. This dual nature of the former Matters will be important shortly.

Because the Appearance contains the Matters, it is defined in part by the same characteristic that defines the *Erscheinende*, namely, subsistence. As the Form, the Appearance has subsistence in it as one of its moments, to use the Hegelian language, because it contains the subsistence of the former Matters. Of course, it also contains the moment of reflection-into-another insofar as the former Matters are also defined as properties. Because Appearance is defined as an independent existence (since One Matter and One Form fell apart), because it is currently defined as reflection-into-another or non-subsistence, and because existence requires both reflection-into-another and inward reflection (subsistence), the Appearance can exist only if the former Matters are defined as inward reflection or subsistence. Hence the former Matters must currently be defined as subsistent. I have given their bubbles in the diagram solid outlines to represent that they are subsistent.

This element of subsistence that the former Matters have reflects the definition or essence of the *Erscheinende*. It reflects the concept or thought of what the *Erscheinende* is as a subsistent element, namely, inward reflection or subsistence. Because this element of subsistence of the former Matters contains the concept or essence of the *Erscheinende*'s character, it grounds or supports the thought or concept of the *Erscheinende* itself. The fact that the element of subsistence that the former Matters have shows up in the Appearance proves or grounds the thought or concept of the *Erscheinende* as the subsistent element.

Because the *Erscheinende* gives rise to the Appearance, and because the Appearance reflects the character of subsistence, as soon as the subsistence shows up in the Appearance, the character of the *Erscheinende* as the subsistent element is reflected or shows up, and so is reinforced. Thus the *Erscheinende* really is the element that gives rise to and has the subsistence.

However, this element of subsistence in the Appearance reflects the *Erscheinende*'s characteristic of inward reflection in an *immediate* way. The thought or concept of subsistence or the inward reflection of the former Matters is immediate because it simply shows up in, or with, the Appearance. Because that subsistence is immediate, it must have its own ground or subsistence in something else. As we learned at the end of the Doctrine of Being, no immediacy can stand or have its character on its own. Ultimately, an immediacy can be what it is only in relation to another concept or essence. Hence the thought, concept or essence of the subsistence of the former Matters is an *Erscheinende* itself (§132). An *Erscheinende* is an essence that exists as Appearance. That's what the original *Erscheinende* (the former Essence) is: in the last stage it was defined as an Essence that exists in such a way that it must appear, or that exists as Appearance. That's the very same character that the subsistence of the former Matters has here. The former Matters are also properties of the Appearance. And Existence is the thought of two elements in a relationship of "inward reflection that is just as much reflection-into-another." The former Matters have their inward reflection or subsistence on their own, but they have their reflection-into-another only through the Appearance. Hence they can have both inward reflection and reflection-into-another—they can exist—only through the Appearance. They have their own ground or subsistence in the Appearance. So they are each an essence that exists as Appearance—they are each an *Erscheinende*.

The Appearance itself, however, is defined by non-subsistence—it is an Appearance, or something that does not subsist on its own. Because it is currently defined as a "for itself" concept independent of the Essence or *Erscheinende* (again, the Essence [or One Matter] and Appearance [or One Form] have fallen apart), it gets its definition from the former Matters, from the elements that it embraces, rather than from the *Erscheinende*. So the Appearance has its own subsistence in the former Matters. The former Matters, of course, get their element of non-subsistence or reflection-into-another from the Appearance. There is therefore an endless, back-and-forth process between the Appearance as non-subsistence and the former Matters as the Appearance's element of subsistence: the Appearance is defined as an existence, but because, as reflection-into-another, it is non-subsistence, it must get its subsistence from the former Matters. So it can exist only in the former Matters. And the former Matters are defined as an existence, but, because they are defined as subsistent, they get their reflection-into-another from the Appearance. So the Appearance can have its definition as an existence only through the former Matters, and the former Matters can have their definition as an existence only through the Appearance. Each side can be what it is (as an existence) only by passing endlessly back and forth from one side to the other.

Because this spuriously infinite, back-and-forth process takes place completely within Appearance itself—to use Hegel's terms, as "a unity of relation to self" (§132)—it only changes the definition of Appearance. It does not affect the definition of the *Erscheinende*. Hegel's logic cannot rest with a spuriously infinite, back-and-forth process (see the stage of Spurious Infinity in Chapter Two). Moreover, such back-and-forth processes are resolved by a concept that includes or embraces the whole process. The same thing happens here. The back-and-forth process redefines the concept of Appearance as a general or complete concept that includes or embraces the whole back-and-forth process between subsistence and non-subsistence within it. If we ask, "what sort of Appearance includes the whole process of both subsistence and non-subsistence within it as its character?" the answer is: the whole World of Appearance. The concept of Appearance is redefined as the thought of a new kind of Appearance that embraces the whole process of subsistence and non-subsistence. Appearance has become the thought of the whole World of Appearance, the thought of the whole process of comings and goings of Appearances as a *totality*, or as a complete and completed whole. An individual appearance in the world of experience, such as a table, for instance, seems to subsist on its own. In is an Appearance. It has its own subsistence in its Matters, or in the elements out of which it is constructed. The whole World of Appearance, however, is the thought of all such individual Appearances coming and going in and out of subsistence, or is the thought of the complete process of Appearance as a back-and-forth process of subsistence and non-subsistence. It is the thought of the whole world of tables, chairs, books and so on. Appearance has become the concept of Appearance-in-general, which includes or embraces the whole realm of "reflected finitude" (§132), or all of the finite Appearances.

Although this spuriously infinite back-and-forth process is resolved in the same way that other such processes were resolved—namely, by a concept that embraces the whole process—there is an important logical difference between this stage and earlier stages that involved resolutions of spuriously infinite processes (see Being-for-itself and Transition to Essence, for example). In the other stages, a spuriously infinite back-and-forth process between two elements generated a *new* "for itself" concept that embraced both elements and their process. That is not what happens here, however. Here, the spuriously infinite process does not introduce a new concept at all, but, rather, simply redefines a concept that is already in play. There are two logical reasons for this syntactic difference between this stage and the others. First, here, the spuriously infinite back-and-forth process is taking place within a concept, or between a concept and the content that it already embraces. Because the process takes place within the concept, there is no need to introduce a new embracing concept to halt the spuriously infinite process. The process can be halted simply by generating a new definition of the original concept that already embraces the content. Here, the spuriously infinite process between Appearance and the Matters (taken together as its content) is resolved simply by redefining Appearance as World of Appearance.

In the other stages, by contrast, the spuriously infinite back-and-forth process took place between two separate elements or concepts, neither of which embraced the other. Neither element was in a logical position to embrace the whole process, so a new concept had to be introduced.

Second, the spuriously infinite process here does *not* involve two elements that are defined as *the same* as one another. In Being-for-itself, for example, the spuriously infinite back-and-forth process took place between two elements defined as something-others. The concept of Essence was introduced to stabilize the back-and-forth process between two elements defined as Measures. It is because the two elements were defined as the same as one another that a third concept had to be introduced. In those stages, the two elements were supposed to be both different from and the same as one another at the same time. When they were defined as the same as one another, however, the definitions of the elements themselves could no longer explain why the elements were different from one another. To use Hegel's anthropomorphic language, when the two elements were defined as the same, they could not hold themselves apart from each other anymore. That is why a third concept had be introduced—a third concept that could capture both the sameness of and the difference between the two elements (cf. the stages of Repulsion and Attraction for a more detailed explanation of the logical move).

In this stage, by contrast, the spuriously infinite process is taking place between two elements that are already defined as different from one another. The back-and-forth process here is between Appearance—defined as the non-subsistent element—and the Matters taken together—defined as the subsistent element. Since the two elements in the spuriously infinite process are already defined as different from one another, there is no logical need to introduce a third or new concept. Again, the spuriously infinite process can be resolved simply by redefining the concept (Appearance, in this case) that already embraces the content (the Matters in this case) in a new way that includes the whole, spuriously infinite, back-and-forth process.

Content and Form: Law of Appearance

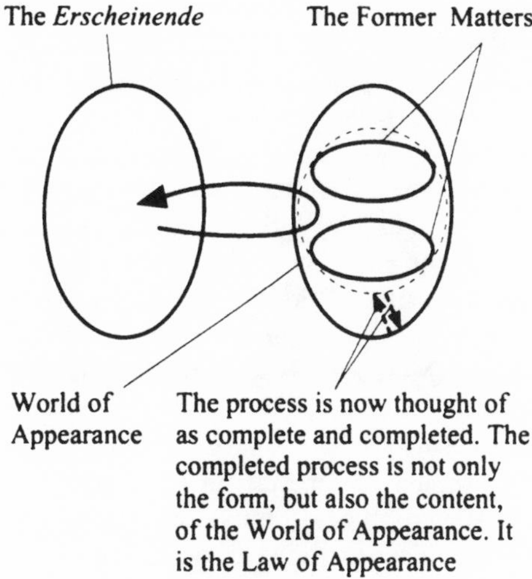
The Erscheinende
The Former Matters
World of
Appearance
The process is now thought of
as complete and completed. The
completed process is not only
the form, but also the content,
of the World of Appearance. It
is the Law of Appearance

Figure 3.32

Now that the back-and-forth process between subsistence and non-subsistence is completed, I have given the arrows representing the process dashed lines in the diagram. The dashed lines indicate that the process is finished, complete, and hence no longer active. It is still there in the background, but in this logical stage there is no longer any active passing-back-and-forth between the former Matters and the Appearance.

The World of Appearance is a "for itself" concept, just as Appearance was. But it is the thought of the whole process of Appearance as completed, and it embraces—as a "for itself" concept—the complete process of Appearance as its content. It is the complete thought of the completed process. As Hegel puts it, "the mutual externality [back-and-forth process] of the Word of Appearance is a totality and is contained in its [World of Appearance's] relation to self" (§133). Because the process that World of Appearance embraces is complete, there is nothing left for it to define. The World of Appearance is thus a completely determinate or defined (*volständig bestimmt*) concept. Moreover, since the World of Appearance is the thought of that complete presentation as a "for itself" concept, it is the Identity of the presentation, in the way that Essence was the "for itself" Identity of Shine, which was Essence's complete presentation in the realm of Being. World of Appearance is thus an essence, the Identity of the complete process of Appearance.

The complete process that the World of Appearance embraces is the whole story about subsistence—subsistence now thought of as the whole process of subsistence and non-subsistence, in which things come into and go out of subsistence. The process through which things come into and go out of subsistence is the general character of subsistence, or what subsistence in general is like. Since the World of Appearance is the "for itself" thought or essence of that process of subsistence, the World of Appearance is defined as essential subsistence, or as the essence of subsistence.

The World of Appearance is also the thought, however, of *how* subsistence works, or *the way in which* subsistence in general happens. The whole process of subsistence is the way in which subsistence in general—or the World of Appearance—is presented. Because the whole process of subsistence is the way in which the World of Appearance is presented, it is the *form* of the World of Appearance, just as the former Matters were the form of Appearance. The back-and-forth process between the former Matters and Appearance is how the World of Appearance is presented—its form. Since the process of subsistence is completed, and because the World of Appearance is the thought of that completed process, the form has become the content. The way in which the World of Appearance is presented—its form—is the complete definition, content or essence of the World of Appearance itself. So the form of the World of Appearance—the way in which it is presented—has become the content of the World of Appearance—the general character, definition or essence of the World of Appearance. As soon as the process of the form—the whole process of subsistence—is completed, then, the form becomes the content. Moreover, Hegel suggests, the form becomes the Law (*Gesetz*) of Appearance. In German, a *Gesetz* is something laid down, posited or established. The term has its roots in the verb *setzen*, which means to establish or posit. The form has become the Law of Appearance in two senses. First, since it is the completed process of subsistence and non-subsistence, it includes all the ways in which subsistence can be presented. It is the complete and completed set of processes of subsistence and non-subsistence within Appearance. Hence it is the Way of Appearance, or includes all the possible rules or ways in which Appearance can appear. It is the Law of Appearance. Second, when the process of the form is completely finished or developed, the form becomes content. That is the Law of Appearance. The Law of Appearance states that, when the process of the form is completed, form is content. According to the Law of Appearance, content is the overturning of form into content (§133R).

Form is also the overturning of content into form. The content has the form within it. The World of Appearance is the definition or content that is presented by the complete process of subsistence, which is its form. It is a "for itself" concept that embraces its form, and so gets its content or is defined by the form, or by the way in which the whole process of subsistence is presented. Thus form is the overturning of content into form (§133R).

Notice that the definitions generated for content and form so far are definitions in the "in itself" sense, that is, definitions that we have derived for form and content by looking at how they are each defined on their own, against one another as separate concepts (cf. Being-in-itself). Content has turned out to be defined in an "in itself" sense or on its own as the overturning of form into content, and the form has turned out to be defined in an "in itself" sense as the overturning of content into form. The two concepts are not yet defined by overturning into one another, however. They will not go through the process in which they overturn into each other until the stage of Absolute Relationship (§133R).

Content and Form: External Form

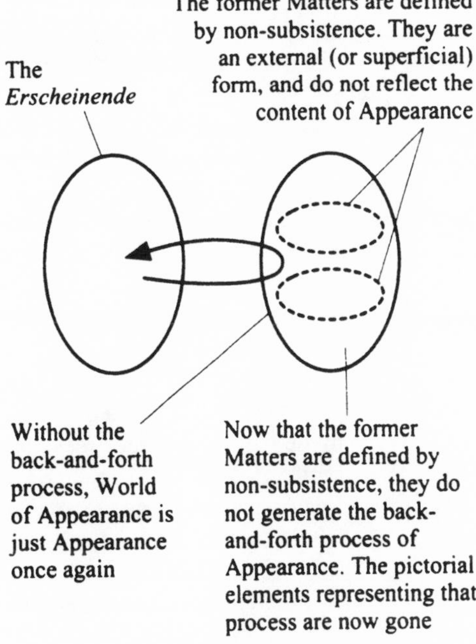

The former Matters are defined by non-subsistence. They are an external (or superficial) form, and do not reflect the content of Appearance
The *Erscheinende*
Without the back-and-forth process, World of Appearance is just Appearance once again
Now that the former Matters are defined by non-subsistence, they do not generate the back-and-forth process of Appearance. The pictorial elements representing that process are now gone

Figure 3.33

The process so far grows out of the former Matters' definition as subsistent or as inwardly reflected. When the former Matters are defined as subsistence, then the form of Appearance itself, or the way in which Appearance is presented, was defined by inward reflection. The former Matters' character of subsistence gave rise to the back-and-forth process between subsistence (the former Matters themselves) and non-subsistence (the Appearance). This process then generated the content that fulfilled and reflected the character and content of the World of Appearance in the Law of Appearance.

But the former Matters are also defined as properties, and, as properties, they lack subsistence and are *not* inwardly reflected. There are two ways in which the former Matters can be defined: as subsistence and as non-subsistence. We have completed the logical development that takes place when the former Matters are defined as subsistence, so we now take up the logical development that follows when the former Matters are defined as properties or as non-subsistent. When the former Matters are defined as properties, then they are *not* inwardly reflected or subsistent, and the form of Appearance itself, or the way in which Appearance is presented, is defined as "not inwardly reflected" (§133R). In this case, the former Matters do not generate the back-and-forth process that redefined Appearance as World of Appearance in that stage. So the World of Appearance is defined as Appearance once again, though Appearance is now the general concept of Appearance, which is what World of Appearance is anyway.

Moreover, when the former Matters, as the form or the way in which Appearance is presented, are defined as non-subsistence, they do not reflect the definition or content that the Appearance is supposed to have, given the fact that it is the Appearance of the *Erscheinende*. As the Appearance of the *Erscheinende*, the Appearance is supposed to reflect the content or definition of the *Erscheinende* as the subsistent element. The Appearance is supposed to have the content of subsistence. When the former Matters are defined as non-subsistent, however, the Appearance lacks that content. In that case, the former Matters are superficial (or external) to the content of Appearance. They are the negative of Appearance (§133). They are the way in which Appearance shows up, or the form of the Appearance, but they lack the content of Appearance. They are the form without-that-content, or the form that lacks the content of the Appearance.

Finally, since the former Matters lack subsistence, they are indifferent to existence (§133R) too. They have the characteristic of reflection-into-another required for Existence, but lack the inward reflection that is also required for Existence.

Because the former Matters are defined as superficial—as a form that lacks the content of the Appearance as well as subsistence—I have depicted them in the diagram with dashed outlines.

External Content

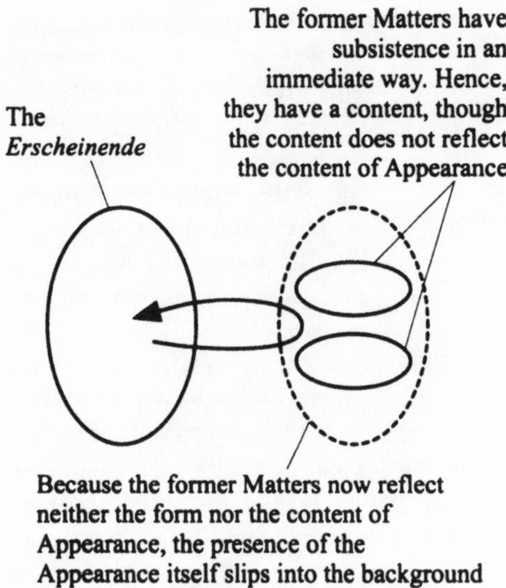
The former Matters have subsistence in an immediate way. Hence, they have a content, though the content does not reflect the content of Appearance
The *Erscheinende*
Because the former Matters now reflect neither the form nor the content of Appearance, the presence of the Appearance itself slips into the background

Figure 3.34

The former Matters are an immediate existence (see the stage of Law of Appearance). They are defined as both subsistence (inward reflection) and non-subsistence (reflection-into-another) in an immediate way—they just show up or appear with those characteristics. Although the former Matters are currently supposed to be defined as non-subsistence, as immediate existences, they have a defined subsistence after all, just as they did when they belonged to the form of World of Appearance. They have an immediate, defined subsistence insofar as they subsist or show up in an immediate way as something-or-other. Hence they have a content after all, although the content that they have is external to the Appearance, just as their form is external to the Appearance. *What* they show up as is not determined by, and hence is external to, the content of the Appearance. Their content is something-other-than-the-Appearance, just as their form is currently something-other-than-the-Appearance. Because the former Matters have a defined content once again, however, I have given their bubbles solid outlines in the diagram.

Since the former Matters no longer reflect either the form or the content of the Appearance, the Appearance itself fades into the background. The former Matters are no longer the presentation of (the form of) and do not reflect the content of the Appearance, so the Appearance itself is no longer defined. The Appearance slips into the background as undefined, and so I have given the bubble for the Appearance in the diagram a dashed outline.

Transition to Relationship

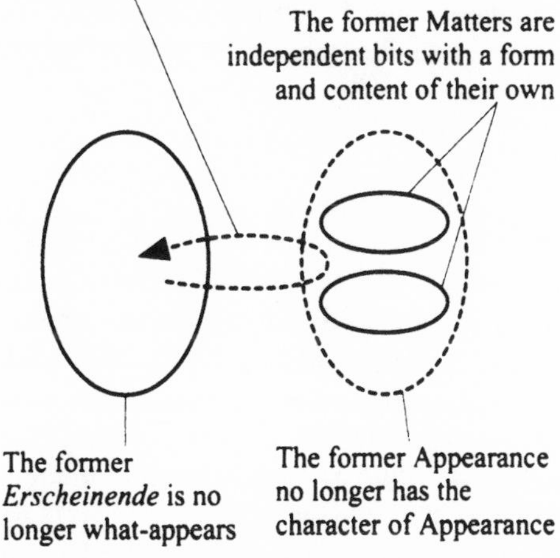
Because the Appearance no longer has the character of Appearance, the "for itself" relationship between the Erscheinende and what was the Appearance is no longer defined by identity. The relationship must be redefined
The former Matters are independent bits with a form and content of their own
The former Erscheinende is no longer what-appears
The former Appearance no longer has the character of Appearance

Figure 3.35

We have now completed the examination of the logical developments that take place only on the side of Appearance. However, the changes that have taken place within what was the Appearance also affect the entire relationship between the *Erscheinende* and what was the Appearance. First, now that the definition of the Appearance has slipped away, the definition of the *Erscheinende* has to change as well. Because the former Matters reflect neither the form nor the content of the Appear-ance, the Appearance no longer has its character of Appearance in relation to the former Matters. Remember that, so far, the Appearance has been defined only in relation to the former Matters. Because the Appearance no longer has its character of Appearance, however, the *Erscheinende* can no longer have its definition as the subject-that-appears (which is what *Erscheinende* means). Thus, both the former *Erscheinende* and the former Appearance will have to be redefined. We will see in the next stage what their new definitions will be.

Moreover, the changes in the former Appearance also affect the "for itself" relationship that currently obtains between the former *Erscheinende* and the former Appearance. According to the basic definition of a "for itself" relationship, a "for itself" concept is a concept that embraces or includes in its content and process an "other" that has the same definition that it does and so is not really an "other" for it. When the *Erscheinende* was the thought of the subject-that-appears, it embraced the whole process of Appearance, including the concept of Appearance itself. Indeed, in the stage of World of Appearance, the form and content of the concept of Appearance reflected the definition of the *Erscheinende*, so the "for itself" relationship between the *Erscheinende* and Appearance was fulfilled. In that stage, each of the former Matters were defined, like the *Erscheinende* itself, as an *Erscheinende*. Since the former Matters were both the way in which Appearance is presented (its form) as well as the content of Appearance, they were essences that exist as Appearance. And when the former Matters were defined as *Erscheinende*, they defined the Appearance (or World of Appearance) in a way that completed the "for itself" relationship between the *Erscheinende* itself and the Appearance. In that stage, because the Appearance had a form and content that was the same as or reflected the *Erscheinende*, the *Erscheinende* fulfilled the "for itself" relationship. It embraced a whole process of Appearance that had the same definition that it had and so was not an "other" for it, or was its own "other."

Now that Appearance is no longer an Appearance, however, the "for itself" relationship between the former *Erscheinende* and the former Appearance has changed. The former Matters no longer reflect either the form or content of Appearance. The *Erscheinende* is defined as "what-appears," but the former Matters no longer reflect the character (content) of Appearance and are not the way in which Appearance is presented (the form). The former Matters give the former Appearance its content and form—in the diagram, they are literally inside the former Appearance. But because the former Matters are no longer defined as Appearance, they define the former Appearance as both external to and opposed to the former *Erscheinende*. The former *Erscheinende* and the former Appearance therefore have "both the externality and *opposition* of independent existences" (§134), as Hegel puts it. We could also say that the relationship of Identity between the former *Erscheinende* and the former Appearance is no longer apparent, or no longer appears. The "for itself" process was defined as the relationship of Identity at the beginning of this chapter (see Identity). Because the former *Erscheinende* and the former Appearance no longer appear to be connected to one another by their definitions or identities, the "for itself" relationship has lost some of its force: it no longer appears. I have therefore given the arrow representing the "for itself" relationship between them a dashed outline in the diagram.

While the "for itself" relationship is no longer apparent, it has not disappeared altogether. It remains the background relationship between the logical elements currently in play. The relationship of Identity or the "for itself" relationship between the two elements is still there in the background, it just does not currently appear. The former *Erscheinende* is still the defining or identifying concept that is presented by the former Appearance, just as Essence was the identifying concept of the Shine, which was the presentation or shining forth of the Essence in the stage of Identity. Now that the concepts of content and form have been introduced, we can also say that the former *Erscheinende* is the content—it is what is presented—while the former Appearance is the form—the way in which the former *Erscheinende* is presented. When the former Matters are defined as inwardly reflected or subsistent, the former Appearance is still the form of the former *Erscheinende* in the sense that it presents the content of the former *Erscheinende*. Thus, the former *Erscheinende* and the former Appearance still have, as Hegel puts it, "their *identical* relation, within which alone these distinct existences are what they are" (§134). When the former Matters are defined by non-subsistence or as not inwardly reflected, however, the former Appearance does not reflect or present the content of the former *Erscheinende*, but is indifferent toward that content (§133R). Thus the two definitions of the former Matters lead to the "doubling of the form," or the two ways in which the form is defined (§133R).

Because the former *Erscheinende* and the former Appearance are currently dominated by their distinction, opposition or externality in relation to one another, and because the relationship that they had with one another has faded or become unclear, we must go on to specify that relationship. The logical elements currently in play cannot be grasped without specifying exactly what sort of relationship they have. We know that their relationship has both identity and opposition (or independent externality) at the same time, but we must characterize that relationship more precisely. We must therefore turn to examine the concept of Relationship.

Hegel divides the section on Relationship into three stages, which he labels (α), (β), and (γ). As before, however, we will need more than three diagrams to depict what is going on in the logical development of this section.

Immediate Relationship: Whole and Parts

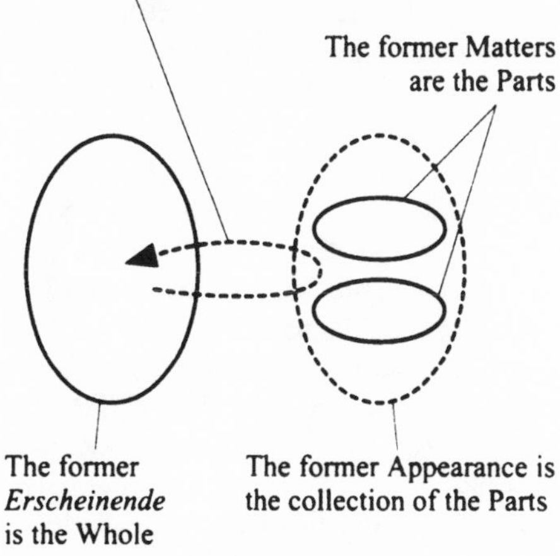
The implied "for itself" relationship between the Whole and (the collection of) the Parts
The former Matters are the Parts
The former *Erscheinende* is the Whole
The former Appearance is the collection of the Parts

Figure 3.36

(α) In the last stage, I suggested that the changes within the former Appearance would change the definitions of both of the logical elements currently in play—the former *Erscheinende* and the former Appearance—as well as their relationship. We also saw how their relationship has changed. We did not yet see, however, what the new definitions of the elements must be.

The former *Erscheinende* is still an embracing "for itself" concept over the former Appearance, which is its content. The former *Erscheinende* is thus the whole thought, or the thought of the Whole. The former Appearance contains the former Matters, which no longer reflect either the form or content of Appearance. Because both the former *Erscheinende* (as "what appears") and the former Appearance are defined by Appearance, the fact that the former Matters no longer reflect either the form or content of Appearance gives them a character independent of both the former *Erscheinende* and the former Appearance. Because the Appearance no longer appears, the former Matters are the independent Parts of the Whole. The Appearance has slipped into the background as nothing but the collection of those independent Parts. The former *Erscheinende* is therefore the Whole, the former Matters are the Parts, and the former Appearance is just the collection of Parts.

The concepts of Whole and Parts have exactly the sort of relationship that developed in the last stage. There is an implied "for itself" relationship between the Whole and its Parts (note the word "*its*"). The Whole *is* or *consists of* its Parts (§135). The Whole is what it is through its Parts. The Whole is also the content (§135) or identifying concept that captures the character or nature of the logical elements currently in play, while the Parts are the way in which the Whole is presented, or the form of the Whole, which, as the content, is what is presented. For example, a handle (of a bicycle) would not be what it is (i.e. a bicycle handle) without the whole bicycle. The whole bicycle gives the parts their character or content. Moreover, because the Parts make up the Whole, and because the Whole gives the Parts their content, the Parts can be what they are only insofar as they share the same identity, are taken together as a collection, or constitute the whole (§135). Only if the handle shares the same identity as other parts of the bicycle—as parts of a bicycle—can the handle and the other parts produce the whole bicycle that gives them their content. And the Whole—the concept of bicycle—captures the identity that everything shares.

At the same time, however, the Whole/Part relationship is also defined by the sort of opposition, distinction or externality that characterized the relationship between the former *Erscheinende* (now the Whole) and the former Appearance (now the collection of Parts) in the last stage. While the Parts cannot be defined without the Whole, they also have a certain independence from the Whole. That independence is what makes Parts interchangeable. While a (bicycle) handle, for example, would not be what it is as a bicycle handle without the whole bicycle, it still has a character of its own—as a *handle*—that gives it some independence from the whole bicycle. This independence is expressed in the logic by the fact that, as we saw in the stage of External Content, the former Matters (now the Parts) have a content that does not reflect the content of the former Appearance. The former Matters—which are now the Parts—show up as or reflect a content that is not the content of the Whole. The (bicycle) handle, for instance, shows up as a *handle*, not as a bicycle. It has a content that is external to the whole bicycle, and that gives it a character independent of the whole bicycle. This independent character of the Parts is what gives their togetherness ("*das Zusammen*" [§135]) or collection—i.e. the former Appearance—the character of being opposed to, or the negation of, the Whole (§136). The Parts are an independent collection of Parts, not the Whole itself.

Force and Utterance

The "for itself" relationship between the elements is once again active
The former Parts are the individual utterances
The former Whole is something that presents itself in Appearance as a collection of utterances. It is the Force
The collection of Parts is the Whole, but presented as opposition and Appearance. As a whole, it is the Utterance of the Force

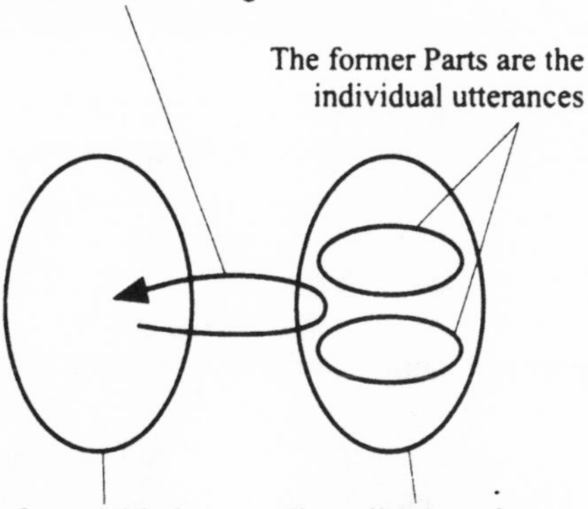

Figure 3.37

(β) The relationship of Whole and Parts redefines the logical elements once again. In the last stage, the Parts can be what they are only insofar as they are held together as a collection. The bicycle handle can be a bicycle handle only insofar as it is held together in the bicycle. But the collection of the Parts *is* the Whole. The (whole) collection of the Parts just is the same thing as the Whole itself. The phrase "the collection of Parts" and "the Whole" mean the same thing. The collection of Parts is the bicycle, and the Whole is the bicycle too. Although the collection of Parts is the same thing as the Whole, because the collection of the Parts is currently being presented or defined as opposed to or as the negation of the Whole, the collection of Parts is both the Whole and also *not* the Whole (i.e. the Whole defined as opposed to or as the negation of the Whole). While the bicycle handle can be what it is only as part of the *bicycle*, it is currently being presented as a *handle*. So it is both the bicycle and not the bicycle at the same time.

Moreover, the implied "for itself" relationship between the Whole and the Parts means that the collection of Parts is still the expression or presentation of the Whole, just as the Appearance was the presentation (or form) of the *Erscheinende* (the existing subject that does the appearing) in earlier stages. The Whole is defined in a process in which it is presented as the collection of Parts. Since the collection of Parts is the same thing as the Whole—though it is currently defined as opposition—the Whole is defined in a process in which it is presented as opposition. The Whole is defined by presenting or pushing out as the collection of Parts, which has the same definition that the Whole does, but is also defined as opposed to the Whole. The Whole has therefore become a Force: it is something that is presented as (or pushes out) something that has the same definition that it has but that is also opposed to it. A force is an existence whose character is such that it immediately pushes itself out into something that has the same definition that it does (and so is *itself*), but is also distinguished from it. As Hegel puts it, the Whole is now an "immediately *negative* relation to self" that "repels itself into distinction" (§136). Moreover, because the collection of Parts still has the character of Appearance that it had in earlier stages, the Force pushes itself out there into something that has its own character or distinction as Appearance. The collection of Parts is the same thing as the Whole, but also has its own character as Appearance. The Whole has become the Force, and the collection of Parts that it pushes out has become the Utterance of the Force. Because the former collection of Parts now has a character or definition of its own—as the Utterance of the Force—I have given the bubble representing the Utterance a solid-lined outline in the diagram.

In the Parts/Whole relationship, there was a sense of separation between the Whole and the Parts. Now, however, the collection of Parts (or Utterance) is just what the Force pushes out, so the collection of Parts (or Utterance) belongs to the Force. Both the Force and what it pushes out belong to the whole process of the Force. The character or definition of the Force includes the distinction (i.e. the Utterance), or includes its expression or presentation in the Utterance (or the collection of Parts). Because the definition of the Force now includes its expression as the Utterance, the "for itself" relationship between the Force and the Utterance has become logically active once again. The definition of the Force presents and includes its expression as the Utterance, just as the definition of Essence, for example, embraced and included its expression in the Shine. Because the "for itself" relationship of form between the two sides has become active once again, I have given the looping arrow in the diagram representing the "for itself" process a solid outline.

When the Force pushes out the Utterance, the Force exists or establishes its existence. The Force is what it is (or can be what it is as a Force) only by pushing out into itself (something defined as the same thing that it is) as opposition or distinction. We could also describe the Force by saying that it reflects its character—or has inward reflection, to use Hegel's technical term (§136)—by pushing out into opposition something with the same definition that it has (and so is itself). Moreover, remember that what it pushes out is the former Appearance, which was defined in earlier stages as a reflection-into-another that exists. Appearance is a kind of shine that exists. Because the Utterance *just is* the Force, when the Force pushes out into the Utterance, the Force is pushing out its *own* reflection-into-another. This activity of pushing out the Utterance posits or establishes the Force's existence—and it does so for two reasons. First, the Force exists because it pushes out into the Utterance, which still has the character of existence that it gets from having been defined as the former Appearance in earlier stages. But the Force also exists for a second logical reason. Remember that Existence is defined as two elements in a process of ground and grounded, or in a process of "inward reflection that is just as much reflection-into-another." The definition of the Force includes both the Force and the Utterance. The Utterance belongs to the Force. As a result, when the Force, which has inward reflection by itself, pushes out into itself as the Utterance, which is defined as reflection-into-another, the whole Force—which includes both logical elements (the former Whole and the former Parts)—is thereby defined as a process of "inward reflection which is just as much reflection-into-another." The Force is the whole process: both itself as inward reflection and the Utterance as reflection-into-another. Since the process of Force and Utterance gives the Force (as the whole process) both inward reflection and reflection-into-another, the Force now meets the logical definition of Existence, and so exists.

The law (or force) of gravity is an example of the concept of Force. Gravity is the whole Force. It is the concept that grasps or identifies all the individual instances or events of gravitational pull. And although gravity is something that exists, gravity itself (as a whole) does not appear. Instead, only the individual manifestations or utterances of gravitational force appear. Gravity appears as individually defined instances or parts: as an apple falling, for instance, which is an utterance of the force of gravity, but is not the force of gravity itself. Moreover, the individual instances are distinguished not only from gravity itself, but also from each other. One apple falling is not the same thing as another apple or a branch falling. Thus, the law or force of gravity is an existence that forces existences to appear, or forces its utterances. And all of the individual utterances taken together are the Utterance of gravity as a whole Force.

Hegel says that the Force is "the whole that is identical with itself, as being-within-self" (§136R). Hegel's use of the term "identical" here recalls the stage and concept of Identity. Since the Force and Utterance both belong to the Force, Hegel's claim seems to be that the Force is "identical with itself" because the Force-side is the identity of the Utterance-side (which is also itself), just as Essence was the Identity of Shine (see the stage of Identity). We should therefore be able to find in this stage the same logical features that we had in the stage of Identity. Indeed, *four* elements of the logical relationship between Essence and Shine have come back into focus. First, the concept of Identity is characterized in part by the "for itself" relationship that we had between Essence and Shine in the stage of Identity. That same sort of "for itself" relationship has returned in this stage between the Force and the Utterance. Because the character of the Force includes the distinction (i.e. the Utterance), or includes its expression or presentation in the Utterance (or the collection of Parts), the Force is a "for itself" concept that is defined in a whole process that embraces the Utterance, just as Essence embraced the Shine. The Force is therefore now defined as a "for itself" embracing concept that includes the Utterance, just as Essence was a "for itself" embracing concept that included the Shine.

Second, just as Essence reflected its character into, or as, the Shine, so the Force reflects its character into, or as, the Utterance. The Force reflects or expresses its character as a Force by pushing out as the collection of Parts (or Utterance), which is both distinct from the Force but also shares the Force's character. In the stage of Identity, Essence reflected its definition or character by showing up as the Shine. Essence did not push out the Shine—it was not a force—but it did reflect its character by showing up as the Shine (or by Shining), just as Force reflects its character by pushing out and hence showing up as the Utterance (or by Uttering). Essence was a "for itself" concept that sublated (cancelled and preserved) its definition by reflecting or showing up as the Shine. The concept of fruit, for instance—which I used as an example of an Essence in the beginning of this chapter—does not change its definition when it shows up as the apples and bananas and so on that are out there in the world of Being (it preserves its character). At the same time, however, the concept of fruit is also not just those apples, bananas and so on. As a concept, it has a character of its own that goes beyond (or cancels) those other concepts. Similarly here, as Hegel puts it, the Whole or Force sublates (cancels and preserves) its "being-within-self" or character by uttering (§136R). The Force preserves its character when it utters because the process of uttering does not change the Force's character or definition. The Force was a Whole before and, when it goes through the process, is still a whole: it is the whole process. The Whole or Force is thus, as Hegel puts it, "*indifferent* with regard to the distinction" (§136) in the sense that the process of producing or uttering the Utterance (which is its distinction) preserves the character of the Force (which is also the Whole) as a whole. But the process of uttering also cancels the Force's previous character as a Whole, because the process of pushing out redefines the Whole as not just a whole, but also as a Force. The "for itself" process of the Force thus involves a process of sublation, just as it did for Essence.

Third, the collection of Parts (or Utterance) has the same sort of character in relation to the Force that Shine had in relation to the Essence. The Shine is the Shine of the Essence. It is the way in which Essence shows up in the realm of Being. Hegel describes the Force as a "being-within-self" because, like Essence, the Force is (1) an active, "for itself" element that reflects out there or shines (2) into itself in the world of *being* or experience. Let me explain (1) first. The phrase "within-self" reflects the active nature of the Force—the Force moves or is active within itself because it pushes out the Utterance as part of its own character. The Force has an active character. Essence's "for itself" relationship with Shine could be depicted in either a side-by-side view, with Essence and Shine as separate bubbles linked by a looping arrow, or as nested bubbles, with Essence surrounding and embracing the Shine. Because we have the same "for itself" relationship between Force and Utterance here, we could also depict Force and Utterance as nested bubbles, with the bubble for the Force surrounding and embracing the bubble for the Utterance. In that case, the activity of the Utterance would literally be inside or *within* the Force, like this:

Nested view:

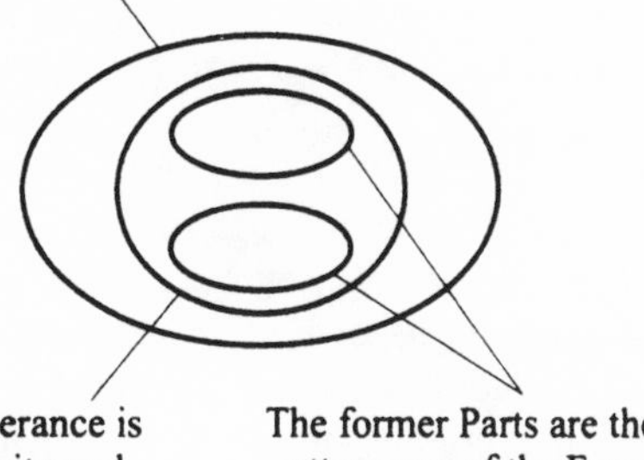
The Force is a "for itself" concept
that embraces the Utterance. It is
a "being-within-self"
The Utterance is
the activity and
being of the Force
The former Parts are the
utterances of the Force

Figure 3.38

But, (2) the Force is also active or moves within itself as *being*. Remember that the collection of Parts grew out of Appearance, which is an existence that shines or shows up, in the way that the world of Being shows up (see the Introduction to this chapter). Thus, the Force's activity of uttering is the way in which the Force shows up or shines in the realm of Being, just as Shine was the way in which Essence showed up in the realm of Being.

Fourth, like Essence, the Force is the concept that grasps the whole showing-up process, but does not itself show up. The Essence was the defining concept of everything that showed up, but did not itself show up. The concept of fruit, for instance, identifies or defines all the fruit that shows up in the world of Being (or the Shine), but does not itself show up in the sense that you cannot eat "fruit," you can only eat a banana, or an apple and so on (see also the Introduction to this chapter). Similarly, the concept of the Force identifies or defines what shows up as the Utterance, but does not itself show up. Although we think of gravity as something that exists, for example, gravity itself (as a whole) never shows up in the world of experience. Instead, we only ever experience individual manifestations or utterances of gravitational force. Gravity only shows up as those instances. It is an existence that forces out other existences that do show up. Gravity only shows up in its Utterance, just as Essence only shows up in the Shine.

Like Ground, Force is a success concept: something can be a force or power only if it succeeds in forcing, pushing out, or powering something (see the stage of Ground above). Here, the Force does succeed in pushing out or presenting something, namely, itself as the Utterance.

Although the "for itself" process (of form) between Force and Utterance has become logically active, and although the definition of the Force includes or embraces (as content) the Utterance, there are still good logical reasons for depicting Force and Utterance in a side-by-side view as separate elements. We were driven to this stage by the conclusion of the last stage that the Parts can be what they are or have their definition as Parts only insofar as they are held together as a collection. We then noticed that the Parts—taken together on their own as a collection—is the same as what the Whole is, when we think about what the Whole is, when taken or defined on its own as well. The Whole, after all, just is the collection of the Parts. Thus, the move to this stage was driven by thinking about how each of the elements—Whole and Parts—is defined when taken by itself, although each process of definition takes account of how the other side is defined. In Hegel's technical terms, the move to this stage is driven by noticing that the Whole and the collection of Parts have the same definition in an "in itself" sense, that is, insofar as each is defined on its own, even though the definition of each side takes account of, or looks at, how the other side is defined. The "in itself" definition of each side takes account of the other side because the Whole can be what it is as a Whole only if there *is* a collection of Parts, and the collection of Parts can be what it is as Parts only if there *is* a Whole. So what the Whole is on its own is still defined against the other side, and what the collection of Parts is on its own is still defined against the other side, even though we are defining each side on its own in an "in itself" sense. This is just the same sort of process of definition we had in the stage of Being-in-itself (see Chapter Two). Therefore, the Whole and the collection of Parts (now the Force and Utterance) have the same definition or character as one another in an "in itself" sense, as Hegel suggests (§136R).

The sameness of their definition is not produced by their "for itself" relationship with one another, however. In relation to one another, they are still two different items—a "Force" and an "Utterance." Although the force of gravity, for instance, grasps or identifies all the instances of gravity, it does not *completely* characterize those utterances. The utterances have a character of their own that makes them independent of the concept of gravity (the independent character of the Utterance will be defended by the logic in the next stage). Apples falling and rocks falling, for example, have a character of their own—they are "falling things," we might say—while the force is defined as gravity, and not as "falling things." Because the Utterance and the Force each have characters of their own separate from one another, they are best depicted in a side-by-side view as separate elements.

The fact that Force and Utterance are still two separate items has two logical implications. First, Force and Utterance are finite concepts (§136R), or are concepts that describe or characterize finite things in the finite world of experience. What makes things finite is that they are limited (see the stages of Limit and Being-in-itself in Chapter Two). Because Force and Utterance are separate concepts, they are each limited by the other. The Force utters. It pushes out something that, although it has the same definition that it does in an "in itself" sense, is also opposed to the Force, or does not have the same definition that the Force does. The Force pushes out a different concept, a concept that grew out of and is hence defined by its own character in earlier stages as Appearance and diversity (Parts). As Hegel suggests, the two elements "are diverse for each other" (§136R).

Hegel contrasts the relationship that Force and Utterance have with one another with the relationship that the logical elements in play will have with one another under the concept of purpose, which will be introduced in Chapter Four. The relationship that Force and Utterance have with one another defines them as finite concepts, whereas the concept of Purpose belongs to the infinite realm of spirits or conscious subjects. Here, Force and Utterance are defined logically as the same as one another in an "in itself" sense but not in a "for itself" sense. As we will see in Chapter Four, under the concept of purpose, by contrast, the elements will be defined as the same as one another not only in an "in itself" sense but also in a "for itself" sense. Suppose I have the concept or purpose to make dinner, for instance. When I then push out or utter (in a "for itself" sense) that concept or purpose—or go about making dinner—the purpose "dinner" defines both the concept and what I push out as the activity that I do. The concept that I have is defined as "dinner," the activity that I do is defined as "(make) dinner," and what I do or push out is defined as "dinner." In Force and Utterance, however, the concept is defined as a Force—such as gravity—and the activity or what it pushes out is defined as something else, namely, as Utterance—such as "falling things." Under the concept of purpose, the two sides are defined as the same as one another both in an "in itself" sense and in the "for itself" relationship. As Hegel puts it, in purpose, the two elements are defined as the same both "in and for itself" (§136R). Because Force and Utterance are still separate concepts here, however, they describe finite things in the world, whereas the concept of purpose is part of the infinite realm, or the realm of thought, spirit or of conscious, thinking subjects.

Second, because the concept of the Force does not completely capture or define what it pushes out (the Utterance), the Force "acts blindly," as Hegel suggests (§136R). Because the concept "make dinner" grasps my utterance and activity, I do not act blindly. What I do is guided by the concept "make dinner." But the concept of the Force does not completely grasp the Utterance. The Utterance has a character separate from, and so not covered by, the concept of the Force. From the point of view of the Force, then—slipping into Hegel's anthropomorphic language for a moment—the Utterance is a mystery. The Force cannot "see" the definition or character the Utterance will have.

Transition to Inner and Outer

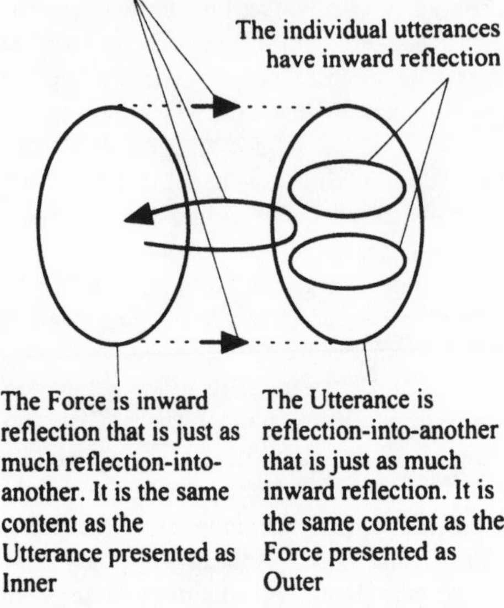
In the "for itself" relationship, the Force pushes out the Utterance and defines itself as a Force in the process.
The individual utterances have inward reflection
The Force is inward reflection that is just as much reflection-into-another. It is the same content as the Utterance presented as Inner
The Utterance is reflection-into-another that is just as much inward reflection. It is the same content as the Force presented as Outer

Figure 3.39

In the last stage I suggested that the "for itself" relationship between Force and Utterance could be depicted in both a side-by-side view and a nested view. The nested view represents the idea that the Force is the whole that embraces or includes the Utterance in its content (cf. Being-for-itself). Moreover, the nested view made better sense of some of the descriptions that Hegel offers in §136. The "for itself" relationship between Force and Utterance has another characteristic that means it is really better depicted in the side-by-side view. While the Force is the whole that embraces the Utterance, the "for itself" relationship between the Force and Utterance is more active than is implied by the verbs "embraces" or "includes." The Force embraces the Utterance, but it also can be what it is as a Force only by repulsing, by pushing out, the Utterance. The concept of Force is a success term. The Force can be what it is or have its character as a Force only by pushing out the Utterance. A Force is not a Force without pushing out or forcing something. Thus, the Force is what it is by pushing itself out as the Utterance (§137). Only when the Force *presents* (as form) the Utterance—a relationship that is better represented by the side-by-side view—can the Force be what it is. The Force can be what it is only by actively presenting, or reflecting-into another.

The presence of the Utterance thus defines the Force as what it is. The Utterance is the Force's reflection-into-another. Only when the Utterance shows up, is the Force truly a Force. When the Force pushes out the Utterance, the Force is determining itself as a Force, it is becoming what it is, or is returning to itself, as Hegel says (§137). Thus, the reflection-into-another of the Force—the Utterance—defines the inward reflection or character of the Force. The Utterance is the mediation through which the Force is defined as Force. The Force is a Force through the mediation of the Utterance (§137).

The Utterance, for its part, still contains the former Matters or Parts. Those Parts reflect their own characters, or have their own inward reflection. Take the example of "falling things" as utterances of the force of gravity once again. The collection of falling things—which, as a whole, is the utterance of the force of gravity—splits up into individual parts that reflect a character. Falling things (such as apples), falling water, and falling mercury in a glass tube are all parts of the utterance of gravity, yet each reflects a character of its own. How things fall, how water falls, and how mercury falls in a test tube have characters (i.e. inward reflection) of their own. This inward reflection means that the Utterance is characterized not only by reflection-into-another (because of the Force), but also by inward reflection (because of the former Matters).

Being defined by both reflection-into-another and inward reflection is precisely the same character that the Force had. The Force is the whole that includes both the Force and Utterance. The Force was at first defined as inward reflection, while the Utterance was defined as reflection-into-another. Because the definition of the Force is mediated by the Utterance, the Force is defined as *both* inward reflection and reflection-into-another. Now the Utterance, too, is defined as both reflection-into-another and inward reflection. It is defined as reflection-into-another in relation to the Force, but it is defined by inward reflection in relation to the former Matters or Parts. The fact that the Utterance is defined by both inward reflection and reflection-into-another means that, if we look at how it is defined on its own—in an "in itself" sense—the Utterance has the very same definition that the Force has. The "in itself" definition of the Utterance thereby sublates (cancels but preserves) the diversity or difference in definition between the Force and Utterance (§137) that was in the last stage. In that stage, the Force was the whole defined as inward reflection (character, content) and reflection-into-another (form, presentation) insofar as it embraced the Utterance, which was its reflection-into-another. The Force and Utterance therefore had different definitions, since the Force was both inward reflection and reflection-into-another, while the Utterance was merely reflection-into-another. Now, however, the "in itself" definition of the Utterance cancels this earlier difference in definition between the Force and Utterance because the Utterance is also defined as both reflection-into-another and inward reflection. As a result, the Force and Utterance now share the very same definition or content as both inward reflection and reflection-into-another. Notice, however, that they do not get that same content in the same way. The Force gets its definition as inward reflection and reflection-into-another in relation to the Utterance, while the Utterance gets its definition as inward reflection in relation to the former Matters or Parts, and as reflection-into-another in relation to the Force.

Indeed, the "in itself" processes of definition for Force and Utterance imply that, even though the elements are being defined in light of one another, they are still opposed to and separated from one another. Hence, the process of defining Force and Utterance each on their own implies that there is a relationship of opposition between Force and Utterance. That relationship of opposition still preserves the difference in definition between the Force and Utterance. Although Force and Utterance now have the same definition if we look at each of them on their own (in an "in itself" sense), Force and Utterance are still being presented by that "in itself" relationship as if they are different and separate from (opposed to) each other. When the Force is defined in opposition to the Utterance, it is the simple inward reflection of the whole relationship. When the Utterance is defined merely in opposition to the Force, it is the simple reflection-into-another of the whole relationship. However, because, the truth is that both sides ultimately have the same content or definition, we can say that the Force is the same content being presented as simple inward reflection—or as *Inner*—while the Utterance is the same content being presented as simple reflection-into-another—or as *Outer*.

Inner and Outer

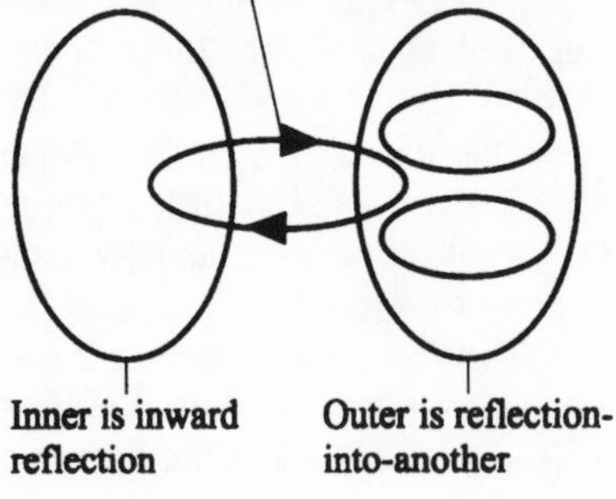
Inner and Outer are defined in a mutually determining relationship between inward reflection (Inner) and reflection-into-another (Outer). Because this is the same relationship we had in Ground, I use the same circular arrow to represent it
Inner is inward reflection
Outer is reflection-into-another

Figure 3.40

(γ) Although, Inner and Outer share the same definition or content, defining them as "Inner" and "Outer" treats the two elements as opposed to one another, and hence as one-sided and empty. Indeed, the mere fact that we are using two different terms to refer to them treats them as separated from and opposed to one another. As we will see in Chapter Four in the discussion of Judgment, to use two different terms to describe elements logically implies that the elements are distinguished from one another or not the same as one another. If the elements were the same as one another, we would not need to use two different terms to refer to them.

Moreover, defining Inner and Outer merely in opposition to one another also treats them as having no content. Defining the Inner as separate from and opposed to the Outer treats the Inner as one-sided because the definition overlooks the fact that the Outer contains the Inner, so that the Inner belongs to Outer. The Inner (the former Force) has a "for itself" relationship with the Outer (the former Utterance) and so includes or embraces the Outer for its definition. In diagrammatic terms, as a "for itself" concept, the Inner could be depicted as a bubble that surrounds the Outer, with the Outer literally inside it. When the Inner is defined as merely opposed to the Outer, however, it is defined as if the Outer is not included in its definition or inside it, as in the side-by-side view. The Inner is thus treated as empty. Since the Inner is defined by inward reflection in relation to the Outer, when the Inner is defined as opposed to the Outer, it is defined as one-sided, empty inward reflection.

When the Outer is defined merely in opposition to the Inner, it is also being defined in a way that is one-sided and empty. Although the Outer has a content (or inward reflection)—namely, the former Parts—when the Outer is defined merely in opposition to the Inner, then that content is ignored, and the Outer is defined or treated as itself empty. Since the Outer is defined as reflection-into-another in relation to the Inner, when the Outer is defined merely in opposition to the Inner, it is defined as one-sided reflection-into-another.

In fact, however, neither the Inner nor the Outer can be defined merely in opposition to one another. Indeed, in this stage, it becomes clear that they can each only be defined in relation to, or in a way that includes, one another. In the case of the Inner, because the Inner still has the "for itself" character that the Force had in earlier stages, the Inner can only truly be what it is by being mediated by the Outer. It can be what it is as a (former) Force only by reflecting-into-another in the Outer. The definition of the Inner is thus mediated by the Outer, which is its reflection-into-another. Once we see that the definition of the Inner includes the Outer, the Inner is defined not only as inward reflection, but also as reflection-into-another. Think again of the example of the force or concept of gravity. In that example, (1) gravity itself is the Force or Inner, (2) the set of the instances of gravity is the Utterance or Outer, and (3) each individual instance of something falling would be the Parts that are inside the Outer. In the Transition to Inner and Outer, the Inner (formerly Force) can be what it is only by uttering. Only when the Utterance or Outer shows up is the Force or Inner truly a Force. The Inner can be what it is only in the presence of the Outer. Thus, the concept or force of gravity (Inner), for example, can be what it is only when the set of instances of gravity (Outer) show up. The Inner is therefore fully defined only through the Outer.

The Outer is in the same situation in relation to the Inner that the Inner is in relation to the Outer. The Outer can be defined only in the presence of the Inner. The Inner must be there (have presence) for the Outer to be what it is. To see why the Outer needs the Inner for its definition, however, we need to examine more closely the relationship that the Outer has with its own content, namely, the former Parts. Remember that the Outer was defined in earlier stages as the collection of the Parts, and the Parts themselves were defined in earlier stages as the former Matters. The Matters were defined by subsistence and inward reflection. Because the Outer (as the collection of Parts) embraces or *contains* the former Parts, you would think that the Outer would be the element that was the *ground* of the relationship between the Outer and its Parts. But because the former Parts are characterized by inward reflection, they have the characteristic of subsistence that makes them seem to be the ground in the relationship with the Outer. It is therefore not clear whether the Outer is the ground and the Parts (or content) are the grounded, or whether the Parts are the ground and the Outer is the grounded. Think of the example of the concept of gravity again, but keep in mind that in speaking of the Outer and the Parts, we are not considering the Force or concept of gravity itself (i.e. (1) above), but are only considering the latter two elements: (2) the set of instances of gravity or Outer and (3) the individual falling things or Parts. When the Outer is taken to be the ground, we are taking the set of instances of gravity to be the ground of, or what defines, the individual things falling. In that case, we say that the set of instances of *gravity* defines or captures all of the things that fall, and hence that the falling things have the character that they have because they belong to the set of instances of *gravity*. When the Parts are taken to be the ground, however, then we are taking the falling things to be the ground or subsistence of the set "instances of gravity," and the set "instances of gravity" is merely the thought that gathers up those falling things.

Because the Parts provide the Outer with subsistence and inward reflection, you might think that the Outer could be defined from the bottom up merely in relation to the Parts, independently of the Inner. However, although the Outer can be a set in relation to the Parts alone, it cannot have the particular character or definition that it has simply in relation to the Parts. While the Parts do have characters of their own (the inward reflection), they cannot generate the particular set that the Outer is. Think of the example of gravity again, in which the Outer is (2) the set of the instances of gravity, and the Parts are (3) each individual instance of something falling. An apple falling has its own character as an apple falling. Mercury dropping in a thermometer has its own character as mercury dropping. Because those characters are different from one another, they cannot generate the set that includes them both. The apple falling and mercury dropping (the Parts) are members of the same set only insofar as they are instances of *gravity* (the Outer). However, the Outer can be defined as *gravity* only in relation to the concept of *gravity* itself, which is to say, only in relation to *the Inner*. We saw the same logical problem in the stages of Being-for-itself in Chapter Two. While the Parts can give the set or Outer its subsistence or outthereness, they cannot define the set as the set that it is. The apple falling and mercury falling cannot define the set or Outer as instances of *gravity*. The thought of falling things does not by itself generate the concept of gravity—that's why Isaac Newton had to "discover" gravity, even though things had been falling on earth for millions of years. Instead, the Outer can have its character or definition as instances of *gravity* only in relation to the Inner, or to the concept of *gravity* itself.

Neither the Inner nor the Outer can be fully defined merely in opposition to one another, then. The Inner must be defined in a way that includes (and not merely opposes) the Outer, and the Outer must be defined in a way that includes the Inner. The Inner can be what it is only if the Outer is there, and the Outer can be what it is only if the Inner is there. Inner and Outer have a mutually determining relationship with one another: each can have presence only in the presence of the other.

Not only do the Inner and Outer have a mutually determining relationship, but they also have the very same *kind* of mutually determining relationship that we saw earlier in the stage of Ground. The Inner is one-sided inward reflection that is defined through the Outer, which is reflection-into-another. Hence the Inner is defined as inward reflection and reflection-into-another. And the Outer, which is defined one-sidedly as reflection-into-another, is defined through the

Inner, which is inward reflection. So the Outer is also inward reflection and reflection-into-another. Since the relationship of Ground was defined as a mutually determining relationship between inward reflection and reflection-into-another (see Transition to Ground), Inner and Outer now have a relationship of Ground with one another. Because the Inner is currently the "for itself" embracing concept that defines the Outer, it is the ground of the relationship (§138).

While the Inner can be characterized as the ground, the Outer has the definition that we saw earlier in the stage of Existence. When we look at the Outer in relation to the Parts in its content, either the Outer or its Parts can be the ground or grounded. Existence was defined as two sides in a process of ground and grounded, or in a process of "inward reflection that is just as much reflection-into-another," in which either side could be the ground or grounded. That is precisely the character that the Outer has in relation to the Parts or its contents. In relation to its contents, the Outer is a reflection-into-another (the Outer) that is just as much inward reflection (the Parts), in which either side can be the ground or grounded. Hence, the Outer is defined as Existence (§138).

Now that the Outer is defined as existence, the mutually defining relationship between Inner and Outer can be characterized by saying that the Outer exists when the Inner is present, and the Inner is present when the Outer exists. While the Parts in the contents of the Outer provide the Outer with inward reflection, because the Inner provides the Outer with being-for-another, the Outer can exist (i.e. be both inward reflection and reflection-into-another) only if the Inner is present. The Outer exists as the set of instances of gravity, for example, only in the presence of the Inner, namely, the concept or force of gravity. The Outer exists only in the presence of the Inner. The presence of the Outer proves the presence of the Inner.

To say that the Outer is present, then, is to say that the Outer exists. The Outer has the sort of presence that is existence. What does it mean to say that the Inner is present, however? The Inner has presence in the way that Essence did in the stage of Ground—i.e. as the thought of the identity of the *complete* set of instances, or as the thought or concept of the Outer as a *completed* set. The concept of gravity, for example, is the thought of the identity—or the concept that captures the identity—of the complete and completed set of instances of gravity. As soon as all of the instances of gravity are there (existed), then the force or concept of gravity is there as a completely defined concept.

There are two logical reasons why we must see the Outer as a complete and completed set of instances. First, seeing the Outer as a completed set of instances follows from the Whole/Part relationship that Inner and Outer had in earlier stages. The Inner was defined as the Whole, and the Outer was defined as the collection of Parts. The collection of Parts was defined as the same as the Whole (see the stage of Force and Utterance). The collection of Parts can be the same as the Whole only if the collection is complete and completed, however. So the Outer—which still has vestiges of its definition as the former collection of Parts—must be defined as the complete and completed set of instances.

Second, the mutually defining relationship that the Inner and Outer now have with one another in this stage also defines the Outer as a complete and completed set, just as it defined the Shine as a complete and completed set in the stage of Ground. To say that Inner and Outer are mutually determining is to say that, while the Inner determines or defines the Outer, the Outer also determines or defines the Inner. The Outer can determine the Inner, however, only if the Outer is the *complete* and *completed* expression of the Inner. To use the gravity example again, the set of instances of gravity (Outer) succeeds in fully defining the force or concept of gravity (Inner) only when the set is finished, complete, completed. Therefore, the fact that Inner and Outer are in a mutually determining relationship logically reinforces the Outer's definition as a complete and completed set of instances. Thus, as Hegel suggests, the Inner and the Outer are the same one totality (§138).

Moreover, as was true for Essence and Shine in the stage of Ground, because Inner and Outer are the same one totality, there is nothing in the Outer that is not within the Inner, and there is nothing in the Inner that is not manifested (§139). As Hegel also puts it, what is Inner or internal is also Outer or present externally, and what is Outer or present externally is also Inner or internal (§139). Because the Shine was defined as the complete and completed realm of Being grasped by the Essence, there was no separation between the definition of Essence and the definition of Shine. The Shine was the complete set of items in Being grasped by the Essence. There was therefore nothing left over in the realm of Being for Essence to grasp, and the Essence completely included or embraced the Shine. Here, because the Inner is the complete or fully defined thought of the Outer or the set of instances, and because the set of instances is complete, there is nothing left over in the realm of Existence (the Outer) for the Inner to grasp, and the Inner completely includes or embraces the Outer.

Because the Inner completely embraces the Outer, we can also depict the Inner in the nested view as a bubble surrounding the Outer, just as it made sense to depict Essence as a bubble that completely surrounded the Shine in the stage of Ground:

Nested view:

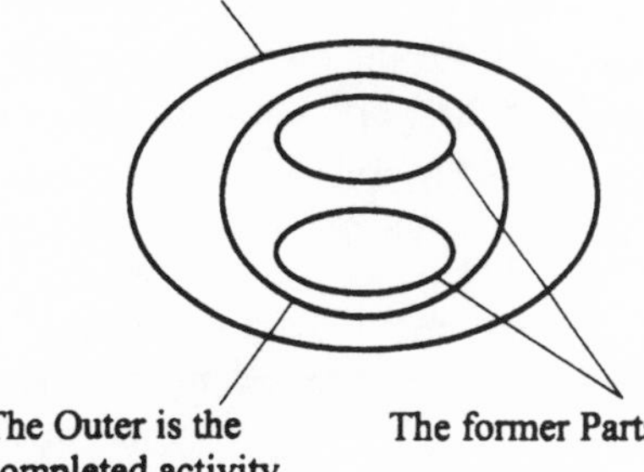
The Inner is a completed concept that embraces the Outer
The Outer is the completed activity (utterance) and set of instances of the Inner
The former Parts

Figure 3.41

Indeed, Inner and Outer have definition in relation to one another very similar to the one that Essence and Shine had in the stage of Ground. Es-sence was the thought or concept, while the Shine was the side that showed up. Here, Inner is the side of thought or concept, while Outer is the side that shows up. Of course, we have a different kind of showing-up here than we had in that earlier stage. The type of showing-up that Shine had was shining forth or mere being, while Outer has a type of showing-up that is existence. Essence was also a less sophisticated type of concept from the type of concept that Inner is. Essence was a "for itself" identifying concept (Identity) for a set of concepts with a variety of qualitative and quantitative characters—a concept such as the concept of fruit, which identifies a number of different kinds (concepts) of items with all sorts of qualitative and quantitative characteristics. Inner, by contrast, is a concept that not only identifies a number of different kinds of items, but also has an activity of its own—activity that logically grows out of its earlier definition as the Force. The concept of gravity, for instance, includes a "for itself" activity of presentation or form that the concept of "fruit" does not. Gravity is not only an identifying concept, it forces out or pushes out the kinds of instances of gravity. Gravity forces, pushes out or *presents* the kinds of instances of gravity as part of the definition of gravity itself. Although the concept of fruit is expressed into the kinds of fruit, the concept of fruit does not include in its definition the thought that it pushes out or produces those kinds. Fruit identifies the kinds of fruit that show up—are given or found—in the realm of Being. But the concept of gravity (Inner) *actively* identifies—it *makes* the kinds and instances of gravity (falling things, falling mercury in a thermometer) *happen*. Gravity *makes* things (such as an apple) fall, it *makes* water fall, it *makes* the mercury fall in a thermometer, and so on.

The stage of Inner and Outer is crucial to Hegel's argument against the view of Kant. Kant's view suggests that Thought and Being are irreconcilably separated from one another (see the stage of Immediate Distinction). For Kant, Thought is only our thought, and the world of Being is merely a world of appearance, or how the world appears to us. What the world is like in itself (the Thing-in-itself), beyond our thought or outside of the "filter" of how we understand or experience the world, cannot be known by us. We can know nothing about the Thing-in-itself (aside from the fact that it exists), because we can never have access to it outside of the "filter" through which we experience the world. For Hegel, however, Kant's view is unacceptably skeptical. Science should be about the Thing-in-itself—what the world is really like—not merely about the world of appearance.

In earlier stages we saw Hegel presenting and then arguing against various ways of understanding Kant's concept of the Thing-in-itself. In the stage of Immediate Distinction, Hegel treated the Thing-in-itself as the identity of the world of experience, but also took the Thing-in-itself and the world of experience to be distinct items. In Transition to Appearance, the Thing-in-itself was the Matter, while the world of experience corresponded to the Form. Another way of defining Kant's Thing-in-itself is as a Force that is behind, and gives rise to, the world of appearance or Utterance. The stage of Inner and Outer—in which the concepts of Force and Utterance are sublated or overcome—can be seen as Hegel's conclusion to yet another argument against Kant's conception of the Thing-in-itself—this time, against Kant's Thing-in-itself understood as the Force behind the Utterance or world of appearance. The concept of force, like the concept of ground, is a success term: a force can be what it is (a force) only if it succeeds in uttering something else. The force or Thing-in-itself therefore determines the content of the utterance. At the same time the utterance is how the Thing-in-itself shows forth or shows up in experience. As a result, the utterance determines the force as well, since how the utterance shows up in experience is also how the force shows up in experience. It follows that how the utterance shows up in experience defines the Thing-in-itself, in which case—contrary to what Kant had claimed—we know all about the Thing-in-itself. The Thing-in-itself is whatever the world of experience tells us that it is. Kant had suggested that the Thing-in-itself is the power behind the world of appearance, but does not itself show up. We do not experience the Thing-in-itself, for Kant, but only the world of experience. But, Hegel is suggesting, the Thing-in-itself has no content at all—no definition—without the world of experience. The world of experience provides the Thing-in-itself with content. The way in which the world of experience shows up determines what the Thing-in-itself is like, what content or character the Thing-in-itself has. Without the world of experience, the Thing-in-itself would have no content at all—it would be merely an empty concept.

Kant would argue that, since the Thing-in-itself exists, it does have one characteristic and so is not an empty concept. We can ascribe no further characteristics or content to the Thing-in-itself, however, because every other characteristic would invoke or presuppose the intuitive and conceptual "filter" through which we experience the world. According to Hegel's definition, to exist, something must have both inward reflection and reflection-into-another—it must both have a character and be capable of being experienced. Kant might say that the Thing-in-itself has reflection-into-another or can be experienced because we experience it. We just do not experience its inward reflection or character directly because of the "filter" provided by our thought or rationality.

Still, Kant's concept of the Thing-in-itself implies that the Thing-in-itself has some character or other—some inward reflection—that *in principle* cannot be experienced, or does not reflect-into-another. To say that *we* can't experience the character of the Thing-in-itself directly because of the "filter" of our rationality is just to say that no rational creature could ever experience the character of the Thing-in-itself. Every rational creature would have some filter or other. After all, to experience something is (1) to sense it or take it in *and* (2) to *label it, identify it, cover it with concepts, thoughts or rationality*. Things can show up in the world of experience only *as* something—i.e. with some quality, character, or content, some inward reflection. They show up only if they can be covered, labeled or identified by some concept or thought. If concepts or thoughts necessarily color or filter the Thing-in-itself, as Kant suggests, then the Thing-in-itself has a character that is beyond any concepts, beyond all rationality, beyond thought—a character that could therefore never *in principle* be experienced by *any* rational creature. Kant's Thing-in-itself would have some character or other which in principle could never be grasped, identified or covered by a concept or thought.

The move to the stage of Inner and Outer, however, suggests that the concepts or thoughts (inward reflection) that grasp or give content to the utterance or world of experience just are the content or inward reflection of the Thing-in-itself. The Thing-in-itself is *thought*, the concept that grasps all the thought that is *behind* the world of experience. It is determined by the concepts or thoughts used to label, identify and grasp the world of experience. If we ask: "what thought is behind the world of experience?" the answer is "the concepts or thoughts used to identify and grasp the world of experience." Those thoughts are all part of, and hence define, the concept that is behind the world of experience (i.e. the Thing-in-itself). The thoughts that we use to identify and grasp the world of experience give the Thing-in-itself its content. Thus, the world of experience or the utterance is not merely the form or presentation of the Thing-in-itself—the way in which the Thing-in-itself shows up—but also reflects the *content* of the Thing-in-itself. The world of experience gives the Thing-in-itself its particular character. The thought, reason, or concepts that grasp or cover the world of experience are the thoughts or concepts that give the Thing-in-itself a content. The Thing-in-itself just is the concept of the set of thoughts that grasp the world of experience.

Thus, the Thing-in-itself and the world of experience mutually determine each other: the Thing-in-itself pushes out the world of experience, as Kant suggests, and the world of experience defines the content or character of the Thing-in-itself, or what the Thing-in-itself is like. Moreover, since the utterance (world of experience) is determining the content of the force (Thing-in-itself), and the force is determining the content of the utterance, then there is really only one content—the content of both—and each side is merely a different approach to that same one content. If two words mutually determine each other's content, it's because they share the same one content. Similarly, Force and Utterance mutually determine each other's content because they share the same one content. The law of gravity and an apple falling, for instance, mutually determine each other's content because they share the same one content, namely, gravity itself. The law of gravity or the concept of gravity is just the Inner or conceptual approach to that same one content, while the apple falling is simply the Outer or experience-level approach to that same one content. The distinction between the Thing-in-itself and the world of experience and the claim that we cannot know anything about the Thing-in-itself (except that it exists) therefore fail. The Thing-in-itself is a concept that refers to only one approach—namely, to the inner approach—to that same one content, while the world of experience refers to the other approach—namely, to the outer approach—to that same one content, Hegel's logic suggests. The Thing-in-itself is just the one-sided concept of the thought that is used to give content to the world of experience, while the Kantian world of appearance or experience is just the one-sided concept of the way in which the Thing-in-itself shows up. In fact, the genuine world of experience is both the conceptual content and the way of showing up of the Thing-in-itself. Indeed, there cannot be *experience* at all without both thought and showing-up, as Kant had shown. Kant's argument that our intuitions of space and time as well as the categories or concepts such as the concepts of cause and substance *make our experience possible*—the famous Transcendental Deduction—shows that there can be no *experience* without both showing-up or sensation and concept or thought. The Thing-in-itself is the one-sidedly conceived Thought or Reason (Inner) that is present as the one-sidedly conceived world of experience or Outer. The world of experience is not merely an *appearance*, but is an *experience*: an Outer that can be present and exist only as Thought or Reason. Experience is both the Thing-in-itself and what shows up: the Thing-in-itself is the thought that grasps what is presented, and what is presented is what it is by being grasped by the Thing-in-itself.

Hegel's own discussion of the stage of Inner and Outer reads like the conclusion to an argument against Kant. At the end of the section introducing the concepts of Inner and Outer, Hegel writes: "appearance (*Erscheinung*) does not show anything that is not within essence (*Wesen*), and there is nothing in essence (*Wesen*) that is not manifested" (§139). This quotation echoes Kant because Hegel is using the terms "appearance" and "essence" in ways he has already rejected. By appearance, he has in mind Kant's notion of "appearance"—the one-sided conception of what merely appears—that Hegel had rejected earlier in the stage of Appearance. Hegel's own conception of Appearance already unites concept and thereness, and so cannot be thought of as "mere show," as Hegel implies in this sentence. And by "essence," here, Hegel must have in mind the more Kantian, one-sided conception of an essence that is supposed to be behind an appearance but does not itself show up—once again, a conception of essence which Hegel himself has already rejected. For Hegel, a genuine essence is an essence that shines (see the stage of Identity), so there is no essence that is not manifested or does not show up. Only a Kantian kind of essence—an essence conceived of one-sidedly as the Thing-in-itself—is not manifested. The fact that Hegel draws his conclusion here using distinctly Kantian terminology suggests that he intended this section to be understood as a conclusion to an argument against Kant.

The claim that Hegel intends the stage of Inner and Outer to be the conclusion to an argument against Kant is reinforced by Hegel's references to ethics in the Remark and Addition to the next section, §140. Kant had conceived of ethics as the hope for a kind of unification between Thought and Being. Thought and Being are separated, but, through moral action, human beings can bring Thought or the rational into the world of Being. Genuine moral action involves following the dictates of rationality or Thought. Hence, when we behave morally, we are giving those rational dictates a life in the real world of Being by expressing them through our actions. What matters for Kant's ethics is not what actually happens in the world, but what our intentions are when we perform actions. For Kant, so long as we follow the dictates of rationality and are motivated by those dictates when we perform an action, then what we do is moral, no matter what the consequences of our actions might turn out to be. That Kant places so much emphasis on intentions highlights his general skepticism about the potential unity of Thought and Being. Kant hopes that if we follow rational dictates with our intentions, then rationality or thought has some chance of achieving reality in the world of Being, but rationality may not succeed in the world. Thought and Being may be forever divided. Hegel criticizes this sort of view in the Remark to §140. If a person is moral only internally—has moral intentions—but his outward behavior does not share the same identity or content with those intentions, then his internal morality "is as hollow and empty as the latter," Hegel says (§140R). For Hegel, then, what is inner must be outer if it is to have any significance at all. Intentions cannot be morally virtuous without being expressed in actions with the same content, i.e. that can be grasped by the concepts of virtue. Thought is worthless without reality, and reality is nothing (has no character) without thought.

Hegel's claim in the stage of Inner and Outer that Thought and Being are united also expresses Hegel's optimism. Hegel's view is that the world is becoming more and more rational all the time, that it is, as a self-help-book author might say, getting better and better every day (see Chapter One, Section II). Hegel's conclusion that the Inner is Outer and that the Outer is Inner expresses this optimistic view as well, since it suggests that rationality or thought exists or is real. We must not forget a second point that Hegel makes in the stage of Inner and Outer, however. While Inner and Outer have the same content (§139), Inner and Outer have not united themselves, to use Hegel's anthropomorphic language. Inner and Outer are still presented as opposed to one another, as we will see in the next stage. Thus, the opposition between Inner and Outer does not completely go away. There are still the Inner and Outer approaches to the content that they share. Hence the one content that they point toward is still expressed through the opposition of Inner and Outer (§140).

The space between the Inner and Outer created by the different presentations (forms) makes Hegel's optimism *mere* optimism. If there were no space between Outer and Inner, then Hegel's claim would be that everything that is here in the world is already rational, so that rationality has already been completely expressed in the world. Hegel's claim is not that the world is completely rational at this very moment, but that there is no gap *in principle* between the Inner and Outer, that there is nothing *in principle* in the Outer that is not Inner, and in the Inner that is not Outer. As Hegel himself says in the *Encyclopaedia Logic*, "[w]ho is not smart enough to be able to see around him quite a lot that is not, in fact, how it ought to be?" (§6R). The space between the Inner and the Outer makes it possible to say that what is Outer is not yet Inner, and that what is Inner is not yet expressed in the Outer. The Outer and the Inner are aiming toward the same content, and they achieve their fullest expression only when they do express the same content. But the dual presentation of that content does not go away: there is still the Outer approach, and there is still the Inner approach. Indeed, the opposition in form between Inner and Outer will not go away until the whole relationship between them is completed, finished—that is to say, until time itself has completely finished. Only when the presentation of Being (the Outer) in time is finished, will the Thought of Being (the Inner) be finished and complete. Hegel's view is merely optimistic: it holds—not that everything is already currently rational—but that, in the history of the world, the space between the Inner and Outer is closing, and when the world is complete, that space will be closed.

Transition to Actuality

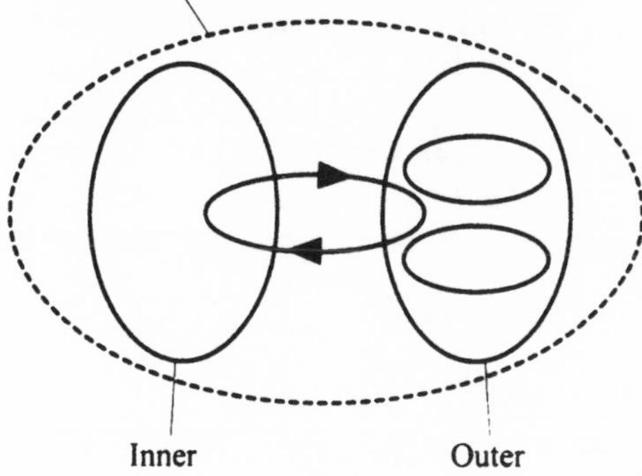

Inner and Outer share the same content and relationship or form as "inward reflection that is just as much reflection into another." Actuality is the new level of concept, essence or thought of what Inner and Outer share
Inner
Outer

Figure 3.42

In the last stage, the Inner seemed to be the ground in its relationship with the Outer. It was supposed to be the more comprehensive element of the two—growing as it did out of the Whole and the Force. It was supposed to include and embrace the Outer, which made the nested view an appropriate way of depicting their relationship in the diagram. However, the mutually defining relationship between Inner and Outer actually treats them as equals, undercuts Inner's status as the more comprehensive element, and makes the side-by-side view once again the more appropriate depiction of their relationship with one another. We saw the same logical move when Essence and Shine had a mutually defining relationship in the transition from Ground to Existence. To say that the two elements are mutually defining is to say that they each play an equal role in relation to one another in the process of definition. Here, the equality in the relationship undercuts the Inner's status as the embracing or grounding element, just as it undercut Essence's status as ground in a similar way in that earlier stage. Instead, Inner and Outer are equal partners in the process of definition—a status best depicted by the side-by-side view. The Inner was supposed to be the more comprehensive element that embraced the Outer. Now that the Outer is the complete and completed set of instances captured by the Inner, the Inner is no longer more comprehensive than the Outer. Moreover, since Inner and Outer define each other equally, the Inner is no longer the ground of the relationship. Inner and Outer are equally both ground and grounded in relation to one another.

Moreover, although Inner and Outer have the same definition as one another—namely, as both inward reflection and reflection-into-another—the way that definition is being presented by the mutually defining relationship (the form) still makes them radically different from and opposed to one another. Inner and Outer are, as Hegel puts it, "*opposed* to each other as determinations of the form" (§140). Inner is being presented by the mutually defining relationship as one-sided inward reflection or identity that is fulfilled by the reflection-into-another of the Outer, while the Outer is being presented as one-sided reflection-into-another that is fulfilled in the inward reflection of the Inner. Moreover, the

Inner is being presented as a whole, while the Outer is being presented as cut up or broken up within itself. To use the gravity example again, the Inner is just the concept of gravity—as a whole or one—while the Outer is the set of instances of gravity, and is therefore being presented as a bunch of items. The Inner is thus being presented as abstract, one-sided identity or essence, while the Outer is being presented as manifoldness (having the character of being cut or broken up) and as being out-there, existing, or as reality (§140). Because Inner and Outer are still being presented by the mutually defining relationship as opposed to one another, the side-by-side view best depicts their definitions.

Nevertheless, while Inner and Outer are being presented as opposed to one another, to say that they are mutually defining still implies that they cannot be defined without the presence of the other. Inner can be what it is—i.e. inward reflection—only in the presence of the Outer, and Outer can be what it is—reflection-into-another—only in the presence of the Inner.

Indeed, because Inner and Outer are mutually defining, they share the same *kind* of relationship with one another, namely, they each have a "for itself" relationship with the other. In the earlier stages of Whole and Parts and Force and Utterance, the Whole/Force/Inner had a "for itself" relationship with the Parts/Utterance/Outer that was not reciprocated. As a result, Inner and Outer did not have the same relationship with one another. Inner had a "for itself" relationship with the Outer, but the Outer did not have a "for itself" relationship with the Inner. Now that the Outer is defined only through the Inner, however, the Outer has a "for itself" relationship with the Inner as well. Their mutual, "for itself" relationship is also made possible by the fact that they both embrace the same activity and extension. The Inner is a completely defined concept that embraces the Outer, which is defined as the complete and completed set and activity of instances. The Inner is, to use the gravity example again, the completely defined concept of gravity that embraces the Outer, which is the complete and completed set of instances of gravity. Thus, the Inner and Outer share the same content in this third sense as well, in which they both have the same extension, or embrace the same items. Inner and Outer are *identical* (§140, cf. Essence and Shine in the stage of Existence). They have a relationship of identity with each other. They identify each other. To say that they have a relationship of Identity with each other is just another way of saying that they have "for itself" relationships with each other (see the stage of Identity). As I did in the stage of Ground earlier, I have depicted the mutually defining, two-way "for itself" relationship between Inner and Outer with a circular arrow between them. The circular arrow represents the idea that the Inner has a "for itself" relationship with the Outer at the same time that the Outer has a "for itself" relationship with the Inner, so that there is really only one, two-way "for itself" relationship that includes both sides (cf. Ground).

Inner and Outer do not only have the same relationship with one another in a syntactic sense, they also have the same relationship with one another in a semantic sense, that is, in terms of the definition or character of the relationships. Each relationship that they have with one another has the same definition as "inward reflection and reflection into another." Since the definition process of the Inner embraces the Outer, the Inner is defined by a relationship that can be characterized as inward reflection and reflection-into-another. Since the definition process of the Outer embraces the Inner, the Outer too is reflection-into-another and inward reflection. That kind of relationship—a relationship of inward reflection and reflection-into-another—is the One form (§140) or presentation that they both share. Each side, as an abstraction, can only be what it is, have an established character or be posited, by going through the immediate presence of the other side. Again Inner can be what it is only through the presence of the Outer, and vice versa. As Hegel puts it, "what is only *something internal* [Inner], is also (by the same token) only *something-external* [Outer]; and what is *only* something-external is also as yet *only something-internal* (§140).

Therefore, Inner and Outer are not only the same as one another in an "in itself" sense—because they have the same content—they are also the same as one another in the "for itself" sense. As Hegel puts it, "what is *inner* and what is *outer* are identical *in and for themselves*" (§141). While Inner and Outer are really the same as one another, however, they can still be taken to be different from one another because the mutually defining relationship they have with one another still implies that they are opposed to one another. They have the same identity, but they can be taken (be posited) to be different from one another. As Hegel puts it "their distinction is determined as mere positedness" (§141).

We now have the same syntactic situation that we have had at other points in the logic before a new "for itself" concept was introduced. There are two logical elements that are defined as the same as one another and are in a relationship in which the attempt to define each side passes over (in the Doctrine of Being) or reflects (in the Doctrine of Essence) into the other side (cf. Being-for-itself, Transition to Essence and Transition to Ground). The attempt to define the Inner leads to the Outer, and the attempt to define the Outer leads to the Inner. As in those earlier stages, this spuriously infinite process gives rise to a new thought or concept, namely, to the thought or concept of the one definition that they both share and that therefore embraces them both. As Hegel puts it, Inner and Outer "sublate themselves, through their immediate passing-over, into one another" (§141). The new concept that captures their shared definition is a new identity, a new kind of ideal or "for itself" concept that includes them both. This new identifying concept—the new level of essence that is the focus of logical attention—is Actuality.

Hegel's use of the terms "inner" and "outer" has been pointing toward a shared concept all along. Unlike the concepts of Force and Utterance, the concepts of Inner and Outer cannot be defined merely in relation to one another. "Inner" and "outer" depend on and point toward a third concept that they share. To speak of "inside" and "outside" is to imply that there is something in relation to which the inside is merely the inside, and the outside is merely the outside. If I say, "the inside is smooth, but the outside is rough," you will want to know what one item has this inside and outside. "The inside and outside of what?" you will ask me. Thus, the very terms "inner" and "outer" shift the focus away from the two logical elements themselves, toward the shared concept in relation to which both terms are merely the inner or inside and outer or outside.

Actuality is the new immediacy, a new "for itself" concept or essence, that embraces Inner (inward reflection) and Outer (reflection-into-another) and their mutually defining relationship, which is made up of two "for itself" relationships defined by inward reflection and reflection-into-another. Actuality is the thought of "inward reflection and reflection into another" as a new immediacy or self-contained concept. Because Actuality is currently being defined from below by Inner and Outer, and because it has not yet been defined as a separate element on its own, it is represented in the diagram as a bubble with a dashed outline.

IV. The Doctrine of Actuality

Why does Hegel use the term "Actuality" to describe this new essence? The Inner has its roots in Essence, and so continues to represent the realm of Thought. The Outer has its roots in Shine, and continues to represent the realm of thereness or Being. Actuality is a new level of unity between Thought and Being. There have been unities of Thought and Being before. The concept of Essence captured a unity between Thought and Being. An Essence was a concept that embraced, identified and was expressed by Being. The concept of Appearance also captured a unity between Thought and Being. Something appears when there is a presence (being) in the world that has been successfully characterized in the content of a thought or concept. To say, for example, "there is a hammer," not only points toward the presence of something in the world of being, but also points toward the successful coupling of that presence with the content of an identifying concept, namely, "hammer." What is there is covered by the concept "hammer." The concept of Actuality adds a further detail to the unity between Thought and Being. Now Thought and Being, Inner and Outer, are not only unified, they are unified in a way that points toward the very same content. The concept of Appearance considers the content of a concept. "Hammer" appears, for instance, only if what is out there reflects the definition or content of the concept of hammer. But the concept of Appearance does not indicate how *well* the thereness out there lives up to the concept. When we identify some appearance as a hammer, for example, we are asserting that the thereness in question is grounded by the content of the concept of hammer, and vice versa. But things can be grounded by concepts while still being flawed instances of those concepts. If we saw a hammer that had a cracked head, for instance, we would still recognize it as a hammer. We would still say that the thereness in front of us was grounded by the concept of hammer, even though the hammer is broken. In that case, the thereness lives up to the concept of hammer well enough to be an appearance of a hammer. But, because the hammer is broken and cannot be used, that appearance falls short. There is a gap between the concept and the thereness (the broken hammer) that is out there.

Indeed, the concepts in the Doctrine of Appearance all implied the possibility of a gap, in principle, between Thought or concept and thereness or Being. Identity, for example, asserted that there was a relationship between Thought and Being—a relationship that was promptly undercut in the next stage of Distinction, which asserted that Thought and Being are distinct or separate. The concept of Thing, too, left open the possibility of a gap between Thought and Being. It suggested that there was a grounding relationship between concept and thereness, but since it said nothing about the content of the concept or thereness, it left open the possibility that the thereness might not be quite the same as the concept, and visa versa. All of the logical categories we met in the last section permitted a gap between Thought and Being. The term "appearance" is a good word to use to describe that family of concepts because the ordinary concept of "appearance" implies such a gap as well. To describe something as an appearance presupposes that there is the possibility, in principle, that what we see (the thereness) might not be quite the same as or live up to what we think it is (the concept). Appearances are not always what they seem, and that is what the concepts in the Doctrine of Appearance suggested.

When a presence and a concept point toward the very same content—as they do in Actuality—however, then there is no gap between the presence and the concept. If the Outer and the Inner share the same content, then the Outer must live up to the Inner—the concept—completely, and the content of the Inner must be completely expressed by the Outer. Because the hammer is broken, it cannot be used, hence it makes a very bad *tool.* A hammer is an actual hammer or Actuality when it is a tool. The concept of tool is the Actuality of a hammer. One of Hegel's own examples can also be used to flesh out the difference between Appearance and Actuality. We often distinguish between a friend and a "true" or actual friend, for example. A mere friend is a fair-weather friend—someone whose relationship with us can be grounded by the concept of friendship (and vice versa), but who falls short of a full expression of the content of the concept of friendship. But a true or actual friend is someone who (in the outer world) lives up to the full concept of friendship—even when it may be difficult to live up to the content of the concept of friendship (§24A2; see Chapter One, Section II for an additional discussion of actuality and its connection with truth). Thus, an actuality is more than a mere appearance: it is a complete unity of Thought and Being in terms of content. With the Doctrine of Actuality, we leave Kant's skepticism about the unity of Thought and Being behind, and, hence, leave the family of concepts of Appearance behind as well.

Immediate Actuality

Immediate Actuality is the stipulated unity between Inner and Outer. Because the unity is stipulated, Actuality's status is still not established, and so it has a dashed outline

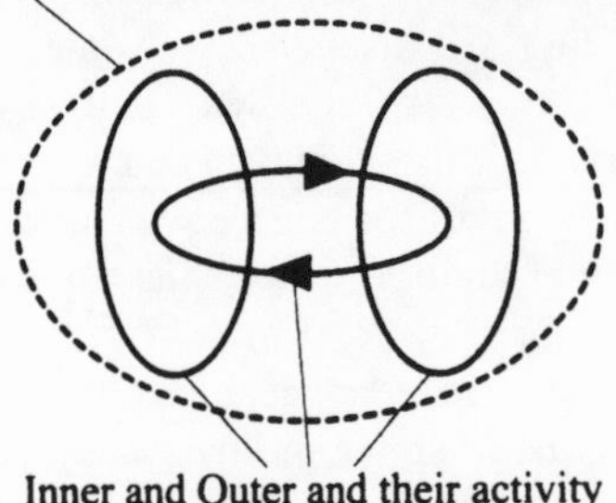

Inner and Outer and their activity are the utterance of Actuality

Figure 3.43

The first stage of Actuality defines the unity between Inner and Outer in the simplest and most straightforward way: it simply stipulates, assumes or posits that Inner and Outer point toward the same content. Immediate Actuality is the posited unity of Inner and Outer taken to be a new immediacy or a given, self-contained concept. As an immediate concept, it has nothing outside of it on which it could depend. Instead, it is defined in relation to the elements that it embraces, namely, Inner and Outer. Actuality is thus a new kind of completed concept that embraces and is expressed by the mutually defining activity of Inner and Outer. Inner and Outer and their relationship are the way in which Actuality has or expresses its definition: they are its *utterance*. Actuality is defined through a process in which it utters Inner and Outer. Because the unity of Inner and Outer is merely stipulated or assumed, Actuality's status as a concept and its definition are still not established. I therefore still represent Actuality with a dashed outline. Moreover, since Inner and Outer are now defined completely in relation to each other—without regard to their contents—the former Parts that had previously played a role as the content of the Outer are no longer active elements in the logical process. I have therefore eliminated the two bubbles representing the Parts from the diagram.

Any existing friendship—the friendship between Paul and Roosevelt, for instance—is an Immediate Actuality. At this time, what is out there (Outer)—Paul and Roosevelt's activity—lives up to the concept of friendship (Inner). So they have an actual friendship. The actuality of their friendship is immediate, given and stipulated, however, because we do not know whether they will be able to maintain their relationship. The question is not whether their activity out there (Outer) lives up to the concept of friendship (Inner)—that their activity does so is stipulated. Instead, the question is whether they will continue to have a relationship at all. Their friendship can be maintained only as the expression of a (human) *relationship*. (Human) relationship is thus the concept or Actuality that is uttered or expressed by their friendship.

When the concept of Force was defined in relation to the concept of Utterance, it had an utterance that was defined as something other than itself, or other than the Force. In the stage of Force and Utterance, the Utterance was defined in relation to its own contents, namely, the former Matters or Parts, which gave it a character separate from the Force: the Force was the Force, while the Utterance was the Utterance. The utterance of Actuality, however, is not defined as something other than itself (§142R). In the stage of Force and Utterance, the former Matters or Parts had an inward reflection or character of their own. Thus, for example, the force or concept of gravity uttered as something other than itself, namely, as *falling things* rather than as *gravity*. The Force was therefore related to an Utterance that had a different definition from the definition that the Force had. Actuality, however, is defined in relation to an utterance that has the same definition or content that it has. Paul and Roosevelt's friendship, for instance, *is* a (human) relationship.

Like other "for itself" or embracing concepts, because Actuality contains the elements in relation to which it is defined (namely, Inner and Outer), its process of definition does not lead it to pass over (§142R). Instead, its utterance or the way in which it externalizes or pushes out belongs to its own activity. It pushes out as both its inward reflection (Inner) and being-there (Outer), which are defined as the same as it is and are therefore expressions of itself (§142).

Hegel divides the development of Immediate Actuality into three moments. These moments explore various ways in which the stipulated or merely posited unity between Inner and Outer breaks down.

Possibility

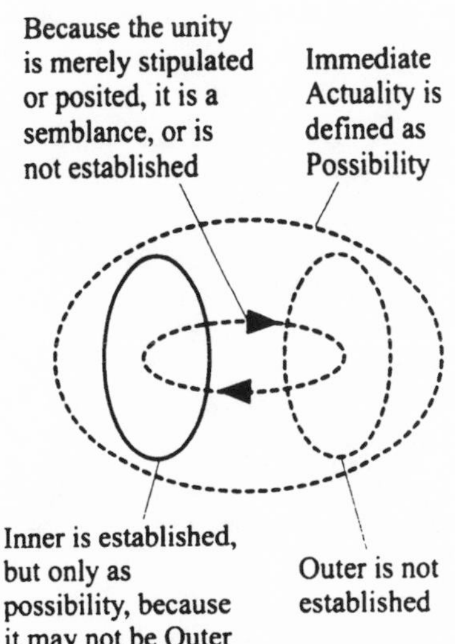
Because the unity is merely stipulated or posited, it is a semblance, or is not established
Immediate Actuality is defined as Possibility
Inner is established, but only as possibility, because it may not be Outer
Outer is not established

Figure 3.44

Because the mutually defining relationship between Inner and Outer is merely posited or stipulated, the unity between Inner and Outer is a fake unity: it is a unity as mere semblance (§143), as merely supposed-to-be, or as merely posited or stipulated. As a result, the mutually determining relationship that is supposed to be holding Inner and Outer together is not really established: maybe Inner and Outer mutually determine each other, maybe they do not. I have depicted the logical conclusion that the mutually determining relationship between Inner and Outer is not established in the diagram by giving the circular arrow representing the mutually determining relationship of Inner and Outer a dashed outline. Since the unity of Inner and Outer is not established, Actuality itself is not established. Actuality has become Possibility. Because Actuality is still not established, it still has a dashed outline in the diagram.

Actuality is still being defined only by Inner and Outer and their relationship, and does not yet have a definition of its own, separate from its contents. Since Actuality relies on Inner and Outer for its definition, to say that Actuality is a mere Possibility is to say that there are concepts there or present (i.e. the Inner) that may not be out there or Outer. So when Actuality is a mere Possibility, the Inner is established, but the Outer is not. Maybe the Inner or concept is out there (Outer), maybe it is not. I have depicted the Outer with a dashed outline to represent the fact that, just like Actuality itself, the Outer is no longer established either. Moreover, because the presence of the Inner depends on the Outer (see the stage of Inner and Outer above), and because the Outer is no longer established, the Inner is established, but it is established only as possibility, since it may not be Outer.

When we say that something is possible, we usually have in mind some idea or thought that is not real or is not out there. For example, a business is a mere possibility, rather than an actuality, when all we have is an idea for a business, but there is no reality out-there in the world of thereness that is captured by and expresses that idea. The Actuality of the business itself is a mere possibility because the Outer is not established. Moreover, while the idea for the business (the Inner) is established (it is in our heads), it is established only as a possibility.

Because Actuality is a mere Possibility in this stage, it is an essence that is abstract and unessential. A genuine or true essentiality would necessarily be out-there (Outer), but this Actuality is an essence that is only possibly out-there. Because Actuality is only possibly out there, it must not really be essential after all. So Actuality here is a concept, thought or essence that is not really essential. It is unessential essentiality (§143). Because Actuality is the force behind or utters Inner and Outer, it is the essence that makes the Outer or reality what it is. But since the status of the Outer is not established, Actuality itself is established only as a mere Possibility. As Hegel puts it, "[P]ossibility is essential to reality, but in such a way that it is at the same time *only* possibility" (§143).

The rules of morality are examples of Actuality that are mere Possibility. As I will explain in a moment, this example is suggested by a remark in the Addition to §143. Moral rules are concepts or thoughts that we think of as the force behind a set of instances and activity. We have conceptions of moral rightness or goodness (although these are not always considered the same by philosophers, we can treat them as the same for our purposes here) that we try to instantiate in the world by acting in ways that we think will express those concepts. But we are never sure about the connection between our conceptions (Inner) and our actions (Outer). We are acutely aware that our actions (Outer) often fail to express the moral conceptions (Inner) that we thought they would. While we are quite sure about our conceptions (Inner), then, we are less confident that those conceptions are instantiated in any particular activity (Outer). Our conceptions are mere possibilities. Moreover, because we think those conceptions (Inner) are mere possibilities that may not be instantiated in any particular set of instances and activities (Outer), we think of the moral rules themselves (Actuality) as mere Possibilities. The moral rules are ideals that we try to live up to, but that we may not in fact succeed in instantiating in any particular cases. We believe that there are actions or instances out there (Outer) that express the moral conceptions (Inner), and we believe that moral rules themselves (Actuality) are legitimate or actual and should be followed. We just think that the moral rules are established only as Possibility. Of course, as Hegel apparently told his students in a lecture, "it happens not infrequently in practical matters that evil will and inertia hide behind the category possibility, in order to avoid definite obligations in that way" (§143A). In other words, we often use the idea that the moral rules are mere Possibility as an excuse to avoid having to live up to our moral obligations.

Contingency and Chance

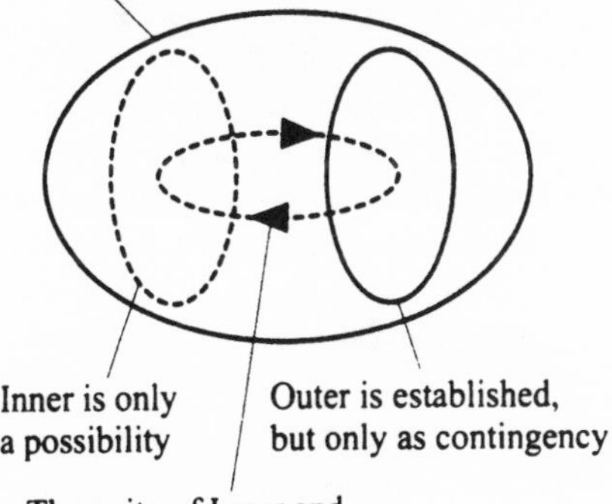
Immediate Actuality, as Contingency or Chance, is externally existent, but is there by mere chance
Inner is only a possibility
Outer is established, but only as contingency
The unity of Inner and Outer is still merely posited

Figure 3.45

In the last stage, Actuality was defined as Possibility. When something is defined by Possibility, it logically implies that there is another possibility that could serve as a genuine alternative for it. When we say that something is an "option" (or possibility), we logically imply that there are other options or possibilities. If something is the only choice, then it is not a possibility, "option" or optional choice anymore—it is a necessary choice. Suppose, for example, that you are trapped in a hallway with only one red door. If going through the red door is the only thing you can do, then going through the red door is a necessary next step, and not an option or possibility at all. Moreover, a grey spot of paint on the ceiling, for instance, would not make going through the red door any less necessary. Since the spot of paint does not provide an alternative route for you to take, it is not a genuine alternative for going through the red door. Only another door, a large hole in the floor, or something like that, would turn the red door into a "possibility" for you by providing you with alternative routes that make the red door merely one possible route among others. Something is a "possibility," then, only if there are other possibilities that are genuine alternatives for that possibility. Therefore, when something is defined as a "possibility," it logically implies the presence of at least one other genuine alternative or "possibility." We will see Hegel repeat this logical move in other stages later on.

The fact that Actuality was defined as a "possibility" in the last stage of Possibility therefore generates this new stage. Actuality's definition as a Possibility implies that there is another "possibility" for defining Actuality. And there *is* another possible way of defining Actuality. In Possibility, Actuality was only-internal: Inner was established—though only as a possibility—but Outer was not. The other possibility for Actuality is that Actuality can be only-external, where the Outer's presence is established (and so is now depicted with a solid outline), while the Inner is only a possibility (and so has become dashed). Because the Outer is established, Actuality has out-thereness and hence is a concrete existent. Since Actuality is a concrete existent, it is present, and so I represent it now in the diagram with a solid outline. However, Actuality is a concrete existent that is *only* external (§144). The Actuality is a present or concrete Outer whose connection to an Inner is implied but not established. (Continue to keep in mind that Actuality currently gets its definition completely from below, that is, from Inner and Outer and their relationship.)

Because the Outer is established or present while the Inner is not, Actuality itself is now defined as an immediate something whose connection to the Inner or essence is only a possibility. Hence, Actuality is, as Hegel puts it, "something-outer that is inessential" (§144). Moreover, because Actuality's out-thereness (Outer) does not have an established connection to the essence or Inner, Actuality is a something-there with a thereness or existence that is not established by a concept or essence. Since the out-thereness is not backed by an essence or concept, Actuality is an immediate, something-outer whose out-thereness is only possible. Actuality is something Contingent (§144), or an existent that is there by mere Chance. Thus, the definition we had in the last stage for Actuality—namely, Possibility—has become mere Chance (§144). Actuality is now defined as a Contingency or Chance.

As in the stage of Possibility, Hegel's concepts of Contingency and Chance are closely connected to our more ordinary ways of understanding these terms. When we say that something is contingent, we mean that it is out-there, or exists, but that it gets to be what it is by mere chance. What character it has is a matter of chance. Because the something is out-there, it has some character or other. It *must* be connected to some Inner or other. In the stage of Inner and Outer, Hegel already argued that something can be Outer or in the world of experience only if it is tied to an Inner or concept. Something can be out-there only *as something-or-other*, which is to say that the something must have some character or other—a character grasped by a concept—to be out there. We are past the stages of Appearance, in which something out there (i.e. in Being) might *in principle* be separate from Thought or concept. So the fact that the Outer is out there implies that there *must be* an Inner attached to it. It's just that *which* Inner the Outer is attached to is not established. The presence of an Inner is implied, in the sense that there is *some* Inner, concept or Thought that will apply to and present the Outer or what is out there. The out-thereness is not something that *in principle* cannot be grasped. But *which* Inner is connected to the Outer is not established. Whether or not some relationship between two people, for instance, will turn out to be a friendship is contingent, or a matter of chance. There is something out there—the relationship—and it is attached to some identifying concept or other. It's just that whether what is out there is connected to the specific concept of friendship is not established by the concepts themselves. Since what is out there *will* be attached to *some* Inner or other, the Actuality is established. There is indeed some actual something or other, it's just that *what* the Actuality is—its essence or identity—has not been established, because the Inner has not been established. Since the relationship may not turn out to be a friendship, the identifying concept of friendship (Inner) is not determining the nature of the relationship, or how the relationship is defined. Indeed, because what is out there (Outer) is not currently connected to *any* specific identifying concept (Inner), no concept is determining how the relationship is defined. Since how the relationship turns out is not determined by any concept, what kind of relationship it is—its Actuality—is a contingency or matter of chance.

We generally contrast contingency with necessity, a concept that Hegel will generate in the logic shortly.

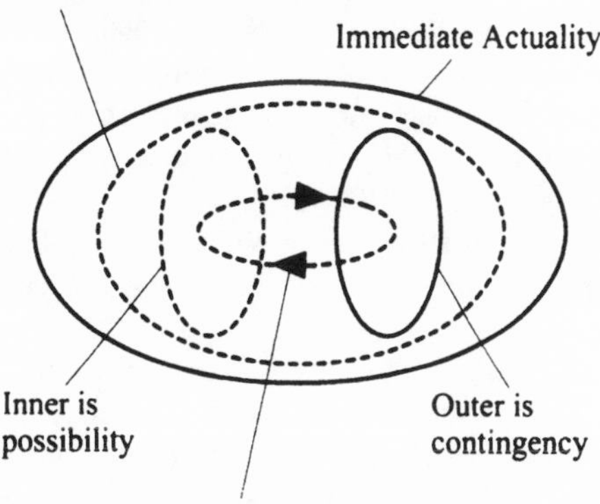
The innards of Actuality—Inner, Outer and their relationship—are the form of Actuality, or the way in which Actuality is (currently) being presented. They are also the content of Actuality
Immediate Actuality
Inner is possibility
Outer is contingency
The unity of Inner and Outer is still merely posited or assumed

Figure 3.46

Actuality is defined as the overarching concept that grasps Inner and Outer in a mutually determining relationship. That means that, according to the definition of Actuality, Inner and Outer are supposed to be mutually determining. In Possibility, however, the Outer and its connection to the Inner was not established; and in Contingency, the Inner and its connection to the Outer was not established. As a result, Inner and Outer are not living up to their billing in the last two moments. We can also say that Inner and Outer are not being presented in the way that they should. Since the way in which something is presented is always its form, we can also say that the *form of Actuality* is not as it should be. The innards of Actuality—Inner and Outer and their relationship—are the form of Actuality, or the way in which Actuality is being presented. At the moment, however, that form is not living up to the advertised definition offered for Actuality.

Of course, the innards of Actuality also play a role as the content of Actuality. Inner and Outer give Actuality its content or definition—in the diagram, they are literally its content in the sense that they fill it up. Since Actuality is defined as the concept of Inner-and-Outer-in-a-mutually-determining-relationship, according to the definition or content of Actuality, Inner and Outer should have an established, mutually determining relationship. At the moment, however, because of the way in which they are being presented, or the role they are playing as the *form* of Actuality, Inner and Outer do not in fact have an established, mutually determining relationship. So, therefore, a tension exists between the role that Inner and Outer are supposed to be playing as the *content* of Actuality (in which their mutually determining relationship is supposed to be established), and what they are doing as the *form* of Actuality, or as the way in which Actuality is currently being presented (in which their mutually determining relationship is not established).

We can now see why Hegel says that whether something is contingent or possible depends on the content (§145). In both Possibility and Contingency, Inner and Outer in their roles as the form of Actuality are not doing what they are supposed to be doing insofar as they are the content of Actuality. As the content or definition of Actuality, they are supposed to be in a mutually determining relationship, but they are not presenting themselves as being in such a relationship in either the stage of Possibility or the stage of Contingency. Indeed, in Possibility, their presentation was so poor that the Actuality itself was merely possible. In Contingency, by contrast, since the Outer is established, Actuality is present. But Actuality is only there in an external way, because the Inner is not established (*which* Actuality the Outer is presenting is not established, so the Actuality is external to the Outer or to what is out there). According to the definition or content of Actuality, Inner and Outer are supposed to be established and they are supposed to be in an established, mutually determining relationship. But since they are not being presented in that way, the Actuality itself has not got all its innards—or, we could say, its contents—in order. Whether something is contingent or possible, then, depends on whether these innards—the contents—are in order.

Because the form or presentation of Actuality does not live up to the definition of Actuality in the stages of Contingency and Possibility, Contingency and Possibility are finite concepts. The things to which they apply belong to the finite world, and hence come and go out of existence. That's because, even though things in the finite world may be actualities (concept and thereness may share the same content), the way in which they present themselves (their "form-determination" [§145]) does not live up to Actuality's advertising in terms of its content. Again, the content of Actuality says that Inner and Outer and their relationship are supposed to be established. In the stages of Possibility and Contingency, however, there is a tension between Actuality's promised content and the way in which Inner and Outer are being presented as the form of Actuality. That tension makes Contingency and Possibility finite. In the stage of Possibility, if the moral rules, for example, were necessary, they would automatically be instantiated in a set of instances and activities. Because they are defined by Possibility, however, they are not necessarily connected to any instances and activities. They can be instantiated in actions only if we work to bring them about by acting on them, and even then we tend to think of them as ideals whose ability to be instantiated is questionable, a mere possibility. The moral rules belong to the finite world of finite human intentions and actions, where they must contend with our limited powers, thoughts and wills.

In the case of Contingency, Inner and Outer are supposed to be united, but they are not being presented in that way. If the Actuality of (human) relationship were necessary, for example, then the identifying concept of friendship (the Inner) would automatically be united to a specific set of existing relationships out there (Outer). But since "relationship" as a concept is not necessarily connected to, or does not necessarily imply, any specific set of instances and activities, it is a finite concept. It applies to things that belong to the finite world and come and go out of existence. Thus the tension between what Actuality is supposed to be like—given its definition or content—and the way in which it is expressed or presented—its form—in the stages of Possibility and Contingency confines these concepts to the finite world.

Transition to Condition

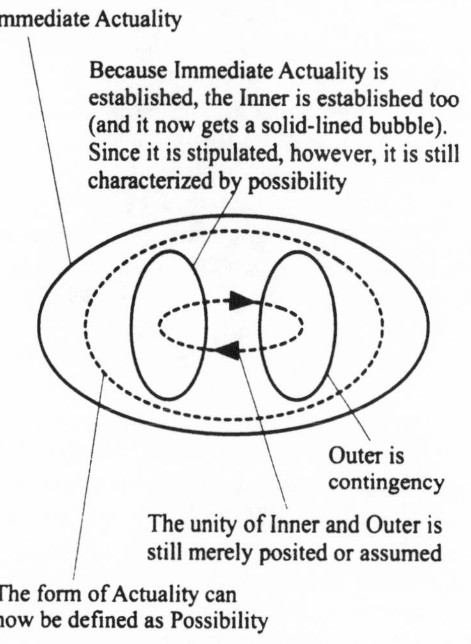
Immediate Actuality
Because Immediate Actuality is established, the Inner is established too (and it now gets a solid-lined bubble). Since it is stipulated, however, it is still characterized by possibility
Outer is contingency
The unity of Inner and Outer is still merely posited or assumed
The form of Actuality can now be defined as Possibility

Figure 3.47

Remember that Possibility and Contingency are stages of Immediate Actuality. Immediate Actuality does not have its contents in order, however. In Possibility and Contingency, its innards are not living up to their billing, given the definition of Actuality. Immediate Actuality is thus an out-there Actuality, without having the inside Actuality-stuff worked out. This out-thereness-without-the-insideness is what Hegel refers to as the externality of Actuality (§§146, 147). Without the Inner, the Actuality that is Outer has no content. The content of the Actuality is external to what is out there (the Outer) because the Inner is not established.

The externality-Actuality's contents are in disarray in a way that makes the Actuality itself inessential, since the side of essence (Inner) is the side that is not established, except merely as possibility (see Contingency). However, this externality-Actuality—which is currently defined as Contingency—can have its essential identity (the Inner) as positedness (§146). Actuality can have its essence and essentiality if we just stipulate that the Inner is established. Indeed, because Actuality's definition says that Inner and Outer and their relationship are established, and because the Outer is established, the Inner *must be* established too. The Outer or what is out there has *some* identity or other (see Contingency). It is attached or connected to *some* Inner or identifying concept. In this stage, we stipulate the Inner to which the Outer is connected. To use the friendship example again, we simply stipulate that the relationship in question is indeed a friendship. Since the Inner is now established, I represent it in the diagram with a solid outline.

While the establishment of the Inner is merely stipulated, that stipulatedness or positedness is also sublated (or cancelled but preserved) (§146). In Contingency, the Immediate Actuality was out-there or present because the Outer was established. In this stage, the presence of Immediate Actuality and of the Outer logically implies the presence of the Inner. First, since the Outer was established, the Inner must be present too. Something can be Outer only *as something*, that is, only if it is also covered or captured by a concept or Inner. Experience is both Inner and Outer (see Inner and Outer above). So the presence of the Inner *must* be stipulated or posited. Second, since the Actuality is there in Contingency, the Inner must be there too. Because Actuality is defined as both Inner and Outer, and because the Immediate Actuality is there or present, some specific Inner must be there too. Thus, while the Inner's presence is posited or stipulated, it is also more than *merely* posited, because it is there as part of the presence of Actuality. The stipulatedness of the Inner is preserved because the presence of the Inner is still stipulated: *which* Inner is established is stipulated. But the stipulatedness is also overcome because the presence of Immediate Actuality in the stage of Contingency necessarily implies the presence or establishment of the Inner. To use the friendship example again, because what is out there (Outer)—the relationship between two people—has a certain character, we stipulate that it is a friendship, or that it is captured by the identifying concept of friendship (the Inner).

This logical move—in which the "mere positedness" of an element is sublated (overcome but preserved) because it is present or out-there—will be used again in later stages. To be "merely posited" is to be assumed or stipulated, i.e. to be merely taken as. When something is present or out there, however, it has sublated (cancelled and preserved) mere positedness. Something present or out there is more than a *mere* assumption because it is present or there.

While the Inner's presence is established (as stipulated), its connection to the Outer is still "merely posited" or an assumption. Although the Inner is present, it still has the character of an assumption insofar as its connection to thereness (the Outer) is tenuous. The Inner is there, but it's not clear that the Inner properly grasps or is expressed by the thereness (the Outer). The Inner is thus an assumption in the sense that we are stipulating that the Inner properly grasps and is expressed by the thereness. We stipulate that the Inner is properly connected to the Outer, but that connection is not yet established. We are stipulating, for example, that the relationship out there is a genuine friendship, so that the relationship out there (Outer) is connected to an identifying concept of friendship (Inner). But that connection is not yet established. The relationship might well turn out not to be a friendship after all. In the diagram, the circular arrow representing the connection between the Inner and Outer is still dashed, which indicates that the mutually defining relationship that is supposed to obtain between them is tenuous. The mutually defining relationship they are supposed to have with one another as the content of Actuality is not yet established.

The Immediate Actuality, for its part, is still something-there (as it was in Contingency), but now, because the Inner is there, the Immediate Actuality is a something-there whose essence is presupposed. Actuality is something-there that is (in its essence) something-presupposed (§146) (or stipulated). To use the friendship example again, because activity out there (the Outer) has the character of friendship (the Inner), the Actuality is not only there or present—as it was in Contingency—but is also there or present *with a certain character or essence* (i.e. Inner), namely, the character of friendship. In short, what we have now is not some Actuality with some undefined character or essence, but an Actuality or relationship *that is a friendship*. Because the activity out there is taken together with an identifying concept of friendship, what we have is an actual relationship *of friendship*. However, the character or essence of that Actuality or relationship *as "friendship"* is currently stipulated or presupposed.

We can now characterize or define the *form* of Immediate Actuality, or the way in which this Actuality is currently being presented. The Inner is defined as possibility (see the stage of Possibility). And the Outer, too, is defined as possibility: it is a contingency, it is there by chance, or its thereness is a possibility (see Contingency and Chance). Moreover, the Immediate Actuality itself is now characterized as a contingent or possible something-there (Outer) that is something-presupposed or possible in terms of its character (Inner). Because the concept of Possibility now characterizes the way in which the Inner, the Outer and the Immediate Actuality itself are being presented, the form of Actuality is defined by Possibility. Thus, Immediate Actuality is (in essence) something-presupposed whose way of being (or form) is Possibility (§146). In the diagram, the bubble representing the form of Actuality has therefore now been defined as Possibility.

The Actuality here is Immediate for the same reason that other logical elements were immediate in earlier stages. An immediacy is something that is given and has the character of an independent chunk or item with a character of its own. Moreover, an immediacy always has a tenuous connection between its thereness and an essence, concept or thought. All of the concepts of the Doctrine of Being, for instance, were at first taken to be simply given or immediate. They were concepts of various sophistication about immediate thereness, or somethings that seemed to be independent and there on their own. We discovered at the end of the Doctrine of Being, however, that the supposed givenness or immediacy of those concepts was really a sham, since the concepts could not in fact be defined without reference to an essence. In the end, then, the immediacy of the concepts of Being turned out to be defined by the very same sort of tenuousness between thereness and Essence that we have here in Immediate Actuality. The concepts of the Doctrine of Being were immediate because they were not properly connected to Essence or Thought. Similarly, the Actuality in Immediate Actuality is immediate because the side which represents thereness or shine—the Outer—is still not properly connected to the side which represents Thought or Essence—the Inner.

Condition

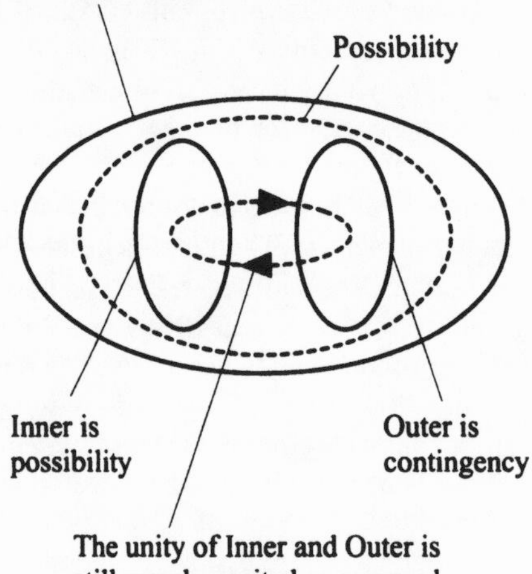
Because Immediate Actuality has Possibility as its way of being, it implies the possibility of something else. Immediate Actuality is a Condition: it is an existent or something-immediate whose destination is to bring about another one (§146A)
Possibility
Inner is possibility
Outer is contingency
The unity of Inner and Outer is still merely posited or assumed

Figure 3.48

Immediate Actuality is defined by Possibility in the sense that it has Possibility as its form, as the way it is presented, or as its whole way of being (§146). The concept of possibility logically implies that there must be another possibility that is a genuine alternative for the first possibility (see Contingency and Chance). Because Immediate Actuality has Possibility as its whole way of being, its whole being necessarily implies the possibility of something else that can serve as a genuine alternative for the Immediate Actuality. Because Immediate Actuality has a definition or content of a certain kind, the other possibility can be a genuine alternative for Immediate Actuality only if it, too, has the same kind of definition or content. As I suggested above in the discussion of the stage of Contingency and Chance, something can be a genuine alternative for something else only if it is the same kind of thing. In the example I offered in that stage, a grey spot of paint is not a genuine alternative for a red door because it is not the same kind of thing as the red door, namely, an escape route. But a large enough hole in the floor would be a genuine alternative for the red door because it is the same kind of thing as the red door, namely, again, an escape route. As a result, Immediate Actuality is now something-presupposed (and whose way of being is as possibility) that is the possibility of another that must also be something-presupposed (and whose way of being is as possibility). Immediate Actuality thereby immediately externalizes itself into another immediate actuality. It is an immediate externality defined by possibility that is destined to be sublated (overcome but preserved) in another immediate externality defined by possibility. Immediate Actuality has therefore become a Condition.

In ordinary usage, a condition is something that helps something else happen. An air conditioner, for example, does not make the air, it makes the air colder. Similarly, in a sentence such as "under what conditions will you work for us?", the conditions in question are understood to be circumstances that will make the working-for-us happen. In Hegel's logical terms, a Condition is an out-there or external possibility that, because it is defined by possibility, is destined to bring about another out-there or externalized possibility. Immediate Actuality has become Condition in the sense that it is now defined as something that makes something else—the other possibility—happen. Take the friendship example again. The relationship (which is the Actuality) of friendship (which is the definition of the Actuality) can be a possibility only if it points toward another possibility that can serve as a genuine alternative for it. To say that the other possibility can serve as genuine alternative for the relationship of friendship means that the other possibility must be both out there or externalized as well as the same *kind* of thing. The relationship of friendship is a possibility by pointing toward another kind of existing relationship: marriage, perhaps, or parental relationship, both of which belong to the same kind (i.e. relationship) and are also existent or out there.

Hegel's account of Condition has roots in Kant's philosophy. For Kant, a condition is a concept that gathers up individual items in the world and uses them to point toward another, more general concept. So, for Kant, in the traditional syllogism "All men are mortal; Caius is a man; therefore Caius is mortal," the concept of "man" is the condition. It gathers up the complete set of men and, in this example, points toward, or brings about, the concept of mortality. The concept of "man" is the condition that makes something else—the concept of "mortality"—happen. Moreover, for Kant, the condition leads toward universality. In this syllogism, "mortality" is the universal. It is the whole extension of mortal things that is being defined by the syllogism in relation to a certain condition, namely, all "men." The concept of "man" gathers up items that define or fill up the concept or universal of "mortality," and thereby makes the universal "mortality" happen. The concept of "mortality" is the universal in the condition, or in men, since, as the syllogism says, all men are mortal (see *Critique of Pure Reason*, A322/B379. See also my discussion of Kant's conception of reason in Chapter One, Section IV). "Mortality" is the universal or *kind* that the concept of man points toward.

As in Kant's account, for Hegel, the concept of Condition captures a rudimentary way of building or defining from the bottom up concepts that are kinds for other concepts. The concept of relationship, for instance, is the kind that captures the concept of friendship (which is itself a kind), or that grasps the kind to which the concept of friendship (as a kind) belongs. In this stage, the kind for kinds is beginning to be defined from the bottom up because the concept of friendship, as a Condition, points toward other existing concepts or kinds—such as the concept of marriage or parental relationship—that are of the same kind that the concept of friendship is. The stage of Condition is a *proto-kind*: a preliminary definition of the kind of concept that grasps other kinds of concepts. A kind for concepts is defined at first by the fact that it points toward at least one other existent concept (or Actuality) that can serve as a genuine alternative for it.

In a lecture, Hegel apparently said that, in the stage of Condition, we are no longer dealing with abstract possibility (§146A)—as we did before in the stage of Possibility. In the stage of Possibility, the possibility was merely abstract in the sense that it did not imply any out-thereness or was not connected to an Outer. I used the example of a concept or idea for a business to illustrate the stage of Possibility. My idea or concept for a business is abstract in two senses. First, it is abstract because, since it lacks an Outer, its character or concept is not fully defined. I may have some vague ideas, for instance, about the kind of business that I want, but, until that business is realized out there, my ideas will always be only vague. I may have a general idea for a clothing store, for example, but a clothing store includes specific sorts of racks in specific places within a specific retail space. So long as the store is not established or brought to fruition out there (made Outer), those details will remain undefined, and the store itself will remain an undefined Possibility. So the sort of possibility we have in the stage of Possibility is abstract in the sense that it is not completely defined. We had the same sort of abstract possibility in the stage of Contingency. In Contingency, the Outer is undefined because it is not connected to any identifying concept. There is something out there, but since its connection to an identifying concept is not established, what is out there remains an abstract possibility in the sense that it is undefined. Second, however, the Possibility that we had in the stage of Possibility was abstract in the sense that it did not imply any other possibility. A possibility is only a genuine possibility if there is another possibility that can serve as a genuine alternative for it (see Condition and Chance). Unless there is another possibility there that can serve as a genuine alternative for it, the possibility is only a possibility in an abstract sense. It is a possibility that does not really live up to the definition of a possibility. Indeed, in the stage of Possibility, the possibility is so abstract that it does not even imply its *own* possibility will be there, since it is not connected to an Outer. Nothing about my (abstract) idea or concept for a clothing store, for example, implies that the clothing store will ever come about or be established out there.

In Condition, both of these sorts of abstractions are overcome. First, because the Condition includes both Inner and Outer, the Inner and Outer are both completely defined. The Inner is a concept whose defining details are completely worked out in the Outer, and the Outer is an Outer with a defined character, since the identifying concept or Inner is there. The Condition is therefore *concrete*, rather than abstract, because it is defined. Second, the Condition is a possibility that lives up to the definition of possibility because it is defined in such a way that it implies that there is another possibility out there. A Condition is a possibility that brings about another possibility that can serve as a genuine alternative for it. It is a possibility that is defined or determined such that the other possibility will be out-there too (§146A). The Condition is therefore a *concrete*, rather than abstract, possibility because it has the genuine character of a possibility.

When the original Immediate Actuality or Condition points toward the other possibility, it is sublated (cancelled and preserved) by the other possibility (§146). Although the other possibility replaces and so cancels the original Immediate Actuality or Condition, because the other possibility is the same *kind* of thing as the original Condition, there is a sense in which the original Condition is also preserved by the process as well (cf. §146A).

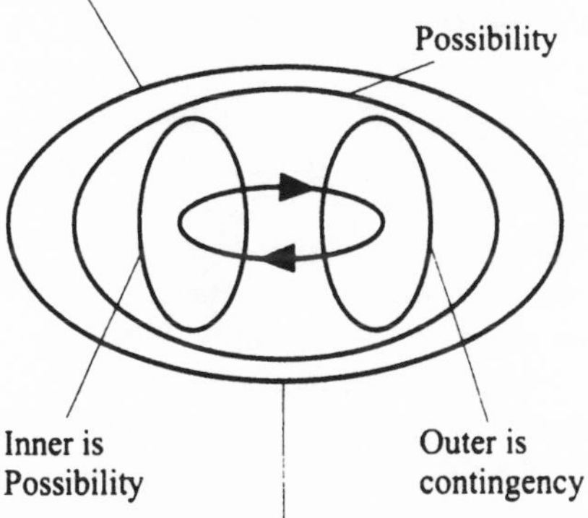
Inner and Outer now mutually determine each other. Since their mutually determining relationship is established, the circular arrow now has a solid outline
Possibility
Inner is Possibility
Outer is contingency
Condition has both the form and content of possibility. It fulfills the definition of Actuality

Figure 3.49

Because Inner and Outer are both defined by possibility, and because Immediate Actuality—as the Condition—is defined by possibility, Inner and Outer finally live up to their original billing. First, Inner and Outer now mutually determine each other. The Inner, as the concept of possibility, can be what it is as possibility (as its inward reflection) only by reflecting into the Outer (its reflection-into-another), which, as contingency, also has the character of possibility. Without the Outer, the Inner cannot *be* anything at all, since it has no out-thereness without the Outer. And the Outer can have its character as possibility only by reflecting into the Inner, which, as the concept of possibility, captures the character that the Outer has. The Outer can have its character only if that character is captured by an Inner or identifying concept with the same content. Since Inner, as a concept, is defined as possibility, Inner and Outer have the same content. Thus, because Inner and Outer are both defined as possibility, they now fulfill the definition of being in a mutually determining relationship. Each can be, present or have its being as what it is only in the presence of the other side (cf. the stage of Inner and Outer). Because the mutually defining relationship between Inner and Outer is now fulfilled or established, I have given the circular arrow representing their relationship in the diagram a solid outline. That relationship is now established or fulfilled.

Inner and Outer therefore also now live up to their advertising as the content of Actuality. They finally do what the definition of Actuality claimed they would do—they mutually define one another. And they now have the same content, which is grasped by the Actuality. They are in a mutually determining relationship defined by possibility, and the Actuality—which grasps their content or character—is, as a Condition, now also defined as a genuine possibility.

Because the mutually defining relationship between Inner and Outer is established, it is no longer given or stipulated, as it had been in the stages of Immediate Actuality. Actuality itself is no longer defined as an immediate or given unity between Inner and Outer. Inner and Outer really do have a mutually defining relationship because they are now defined in relation to one another and have the same, shared content, namely, possibility. Because the unity between Inner and Outer is no longer immediate, stipulated or presupposed, Immediate Actuality has become simply Actuality.

There is another reason why Immediate Actuality has become Actuality. Before, Actuality had the form of possibility, or was presented as possibility, but its form did not live up to its content. Now that Actuality is defined as Condition, however, it not only has the form of possibility, it also has the genuine character or content of being defined as possibility. As in the stage of Condition, because a Condition points toward another possibility, it is not merely an abstract possibility, but has a definition that makes it a genuine possibility. A possibility can only be a genuine possibility if there is at least one other option or possibility that can serve as a genuine alternative for it (see Contingency and Chance). As a Condition, Actuality points toward just such an alternative option or possibility. Actuality is therefore no longer merely a possibility in its form or presentation, it has become a genuine possibility in its content as well, because it points toward other possibilities or options. Hence, as Condition, Actuality has now fulfilled its definition as possibility. Now that Actuality, as Condition, is defined as genuine possibility, and since Inner and Outer now mutually determine each other as possibility, Actuality fulfills its definition as the thought or concept of the shared character of Inner and Outer that has emerged from their mutually defining relationship. Actuality has fulfilled the promise of its definition.

These logical developments also change the status of Possibility, which has until now been only the form of Actuality, and has been represented in the diagram by a bubble with a dashed outline. Possibility contains Inner and Outer and their relationship, which are the *form* of Actuality, or the way in which Actuality is presented. Inner and Outer and their relationship are also the *content* of Actuality, however, since Actuality is defined as the concept that grasps Inner and Outer and their relationship for its definition or content. Up until now, there has been a tension between the way in which Inner and Outer and their relationship were being presented (i.e. as form), and what they were supposed to be doing as the content or definition of Actuality. That's why the Possibility bubble has so far been defined only as the form of Actuality rather than as the content of Actuality, even though the same elements that are Actuality's form are also its content. Up until now, the Possibility bubble was only the way in which Inner and Outer and their relationship were presenting Actuality—i.e. the form—but were not living up to the definition of Actuality—i.e. the content. Because Inner and

Outer now mutually determine each other as possibility, and because they now fulfill the promise of the definition of Actuality, however, Possibility is no longer merely the *form* of Actuality, or the way in which Actuality is presented, it is also the *content* of Actuality. Inner and Outer and their relationship are now presenting Actuality in a way that meets the content or definition of Actuality, and the content that they both share and that is grasped by Actuality is Possibility. Possibility is therefore now both the content or character and form of Actuality. Because Possibility is now both the genuine content of Actuality as well as its form, its definition is established, and so I have given the bubble representing it a solid outline in the diagram.

An Actuality is thus a Possibility whose form, or the way in which it is presented, lives up to the content of the Actuality. A relationship (the Actuality), for instance, is an actual relationship of friendship when it is presented by the concept of friendship (Inner) and activity out there (Outer) in a way that lives up to the content of Actuality—i.e. the concept and activity succeed in mutually determining one another.

Although Condition points toward another possibility and fulfills its definition as a genuine possibility, it has not yet generated that other possibility. In this stage, Condition *implies* that it will generate another possibility, but the activity of generating another possibility has not yet happened. In the next stage, the Condition goes through its activity of generating another possibility, and we must characterize this activity more precisely. This is another syntactic pattern that we will see repeated in Hegel's logic. In one stage, an activity is implied or some process is defined that has to be undergone to achieve some logical end; and in subsequent stages the activity or process happens.

Real Possibility

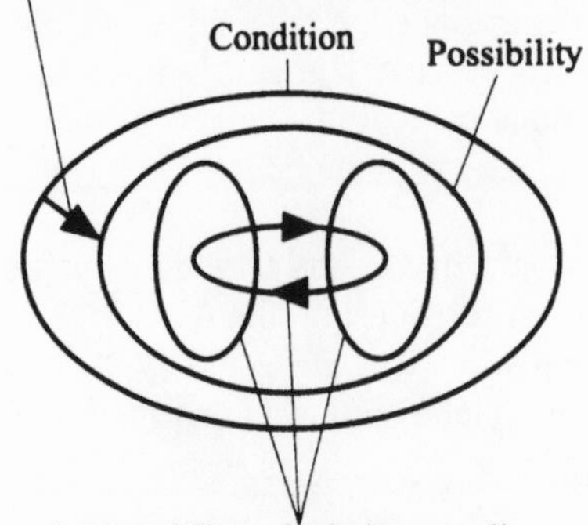
Condition fulfills its definition as a Condition by pointing toward another Possibility. This is the first process
Condition
Possibility
Inner and Outer in their mutually determining relationship

Figure 3.50

The Condition points toward another possibility that can serve as a genuine alternative for the Condition. We can represent this activity with an arrow that runs from the outermost Condition bubble to the bubble for Possibility. The Condition points toward another Possibility. The arrow represents the Condition's activity of fulfilling its way of being as a possibility by pointing toward another possibility (Fig. 3.50).

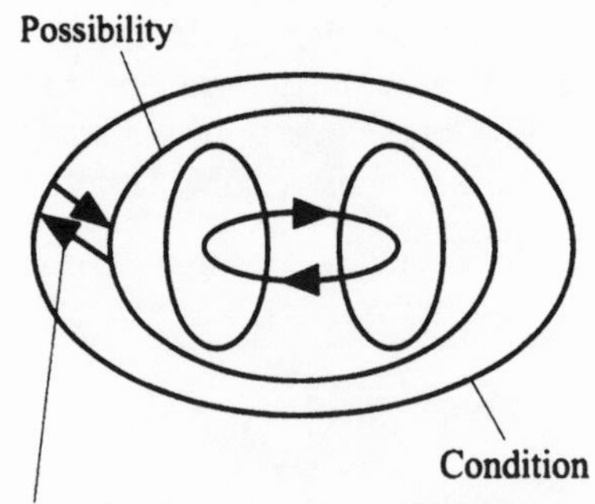
Possibility
Condition
To be a genuine Possibility, Possibility must be a Condition: it must point toward another possibility. So in the second process, Possibility points back toward Condition

Figure 3.51

But the Possibility toward which the Condition points cannot be a mere possibility. It has to be a possibility that can serve as a genuine alternative for the Condition, which means it has to have the same character as the Condition. Again, something can be a genuine possibility only if there is another option or alternative for it, otherwise a possibility is necessary, rather than possible (see Contingency and Chance). The other possibility must therefore be another actuality that has possibility as its form and content. That is just what a Condition is, so the other Possibility, too, is a Condition. This second process, in which the possibility is defined as another Condition, is represented by an arrow that runs from the Possibility bubble back to the Condition bubble.

This second Condition, to be defined as a genuine possibility, must itself point toward a further possibility, repeating the first process once again, which is represented by the arrow that runs from Condition to the Possibility bubble. But the further Possibility, to be a genuine possibility, must be another Condition, and so we get a repetition of the second process again, which is represented by the arrow that runs from the Possibility bubble back to the Condition bubble. We thus end up in a process that goes back and forth endlessly between Condition and Possibility. Each Condition can be what it is only by pointing toward another Possibility, which can be what it is as a genuine possibility only if it is a Condition, which points toward another possibility, and so on, endlessly.

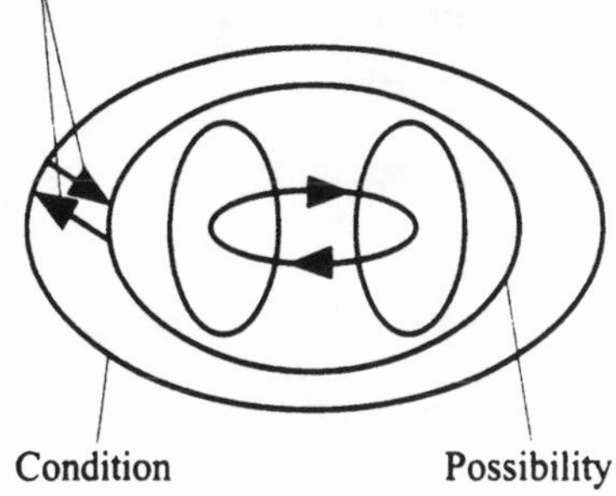
Real Possibility is the endless alternation or back-and-forth process between Condition and Possibility
Condition
Possibility

Figure 3.52

These two processes, taken together, are Real Possibility. Real Possibility describes in a general way the character of the activity of each Condition. A Condition carries out its definition as possibility by bringing about another Condition. Real Possibility is the thought of a Condition, pointing toward another Possibility, which must itself be a Condition, and so must point toward another Possibility, which must itself be a Condition, and so on, endlessly. In the diagram, Real Possibility is the back-and-forth or alternating process between the Condition and the Possibility bubbles. In logical terms, when Actuality—as a Condition—points toward something just like itself, it points toward another Condition. Condition fulfills its definition as a possibility by pointing toward another Possibility (the first process) that is itself a Condition (the second process). A Condition can be what it is only by pointing toward a Possibility that is itself defined as a Condition. The Condition's process of definition therefore leads to an endless, spuriously infinite back-and-forth process between Conditions and Possibility.

This alternating process captures the process through which genuine possibility is expressed in reality or is real. Genuine possibility in reality is the process through which a Condition, to be a real or genuine possibility, generates another real Condition. Notice that the Conditions are now defined as "real" possibilities here in two senses. They are "real" (1) in the conceptual sense in which they must live up to the genuine definition of possibility, which says that a possibility can be a possibility only if there is a genuine alternative for it, or another genuine possibility, and (2) in the sense that they have reality or are out-there, because of the presence of the Outer. The process in which Conditions point toward other Conditions is the process of Real Possibility.

The stage of Condition offered a preliminary account of how a concept that is a kind for concepts is defined from the bottom up. The stage of Real Possibility offers an account of how a concept that is a kind for concepts is defined from the top down. In general, a concept belongs to a kind if there are other concepts that are both real (out there) and can serve as genuine alternatives for the original Condition. The concept of cat (a Condition), for example, is a kind of concept insofar as it points toward other concepts that are real (have instances out there) and are genuine alternatives for it—concepts such as "dog," "hamster" and so on. Although we have not yet generated the concept of the kind to which these concepts belong, you can probably guess what it is: cats, dogs and hamsters are all concepts grasped by the concept of pet.

The Condition as a Totality

Real Possibility is the activity, in general, of all the Conditions. It is the activity of the Conditions taken together as a one or whole

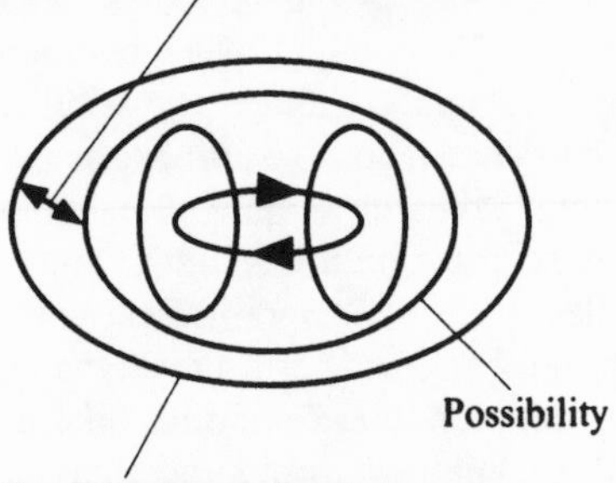

Condition is redefined as a totality: it is all the Conditions and their activity taken together as a complete and completed whole

Figure 3.53

The logical process cannot rest with an endless or spuriously infinite back-and-forth process (cf. Spurious Infinity). So long as Condition's process of being defined as genuine possibility generates a spuriously infinite back-and-forth process between Condition and Possibility, Condition can never be defined. Condition can only be defined if the endless alternation process can be stopped.

In the last stage, Real Possibility was two separate processes that affect the way in which each Condition must be defined. However, the endless back-and-forth process between Condition and Possibility can be stopped by redefining Real Possibility as the concept, *in general*, of the activity of Conditions. Since each and every Condition can be what it is only by producing an endless process of flipping back and forth between Condition and Possibility—which is what the process of Real Possibility is—then, in general, a Condition can be what it is only by producing an endless back-and-forth process between Condition and Possibility—i.e. through the process of Real Possibility. Real Possibility is therefore now defined, not as the activity of each Condition, but as a general account of the activity of Conditions in general. Real Possibility is the thought of the general process or activity by which Conditions are all defined. Because Real Possibility is now defined as one general activity, I have merged the two separate arrows I used to depict it in the last stage into one new, double-sided arrow. Real Possibility is now the thought or concept of the one general process through which all the Conditions, in general, are defined. Using the cat/dog/hamster example again, Real Possibility—which was defined in the last stage as the single process in which the concept of cat pointed toward the concept of dog, which pointed toward the concept of hamster and so on, is now reconceived as the whole process in which the concepts of kinds or types of pets point toward one another. (Keep in mind that the concept of pet itself has not yet been generated.) Real Possibility is the process, in general, of all of the different concepts of pets.

Defining Real Possibility as one general process changes the definition of the Condition. To say that Real Possibility captures the character, in general, of the activity of Condition not only defines Real Possibility as a one or whole, but also defines Condition itself as a one or whole. Now that Real Possibility is thought of as a general activity, it is the process of definition for a Condition that is also now defined as Condition-in-general. Real Possibility, as the activity-in-general of Condition, is the process of Condition-in-general. Real Possibility is the back-and-forth process between each Condition and Possibility, now thought of as a complete and completed whole. What sort of Condition has the whole process of Real Possibility for its activity? The sort of Condition that has the whole process of Real Possibility for its activity is Condition-in-general, or all of the Conditions, taken together as a whole. The whole set of Conditions, taken together, has the whole process of Real Possibility—taken to be a general process—as its activity. Condition is now defined as a totality (§147), or as the complete and completed set of Conditions and their activity. It is the concept of Condition-in-general, which includes and embraces all of the Conditions along with all of their activity of Real Possibility in relation to one another. In the cat/dog/hamster example, the Condition was at first the concept of cat, then the concept of dog, then the concept of hamster and so on. Now the Condition is the whole, completed process of all of the kinds of pets. (Remember that the concept of pet itself has not yet been generated.) Condition has been redefined as the Conditions-taken-together-as-a-totality.

I will call this newly developed concept of Condition the "Condition as a Totality," but the term is not one that Hegel himself ever uses. Instead, he will simply continue to refer to "the condition." Since the Condition as a Totality is simply the general concept of Condition, or the concept of Condition-in-general, Hegel is within his rights to continue to refer to it simply as the "condition." However, in the service of (termino)logical[2] precision, I will distinguish this new concept of Condition from the earlier concept of Condition by referring to it as the "Condition as a Totality," or the "Condition_{AT}" for short.

Now that Real Possibility is defined as the complete process of Conditions, and Condition itself is defined as the completed set of Conditions, the spuriously infinite, back-and-forth process of the stage of Real Possibility has been stopped. Real Possibility is the completed activity of all the Conditions and includes the whole process through which the Conditions are defined in relation to one another. Since the Condition_{AT} is all the Conditions taken together as a complete set, it includes the whole process of each and every Condition. There are no further Conditions for it to include, and so it does not push on to any further Possibilities. It is the whole set and activity of Conditions defined as Possibilities. As in earlier stages, then, the spuriously infinite process is resolved by a new, stable concept that embraces the whole, spuriously infinite, back-and-forth process. Condition_{AT} includes the back-and-forth process of all the Conditions and their Possibilities along with their activities, but does not itself pass over.

This logical move repeats the one we saw in the stage of World of Appearance, in which a concept that is in a spuriously infinite back-and-forth process with a content it already embraces is redefined as the whole, completed process. Like the stage of World of Appearance, this stage differs from other stages in which spuriously infinite processes were resolved because it does not lead to the introduction of a completely new concept. In stages such as Being-for-itself and Transition to Essence, for example, spuriously infinite processes were resolved by introducing a third, new concept that embraced the two elements that were in the spuriously infinite back-and-forth process. In those stages, I depicted the new concept as a new bubble that surrounded the bubbles depicting the two elements that were locked in the spuriously infinite, back-and-forth process. That's not what we have here, however. Here, no new concept is introduced. Instead, the concept of Condition is simply redefined in a way that embraces the whole back-and-forth process. As I argued in World of Appearance, there are two logical reasons for the difference. First, as in World of Appearance, the spuriously infinite back-and-forth process is taking place within a concept, or between a concept and the content that it embraces. Because the process takes place within a concept that already embraces its content, there is no need to introduce a new, embracing concept to halt the spuriously infinite process. The process can be halted simply by generating a new definition for the original concept that already embraces the content.

Second, the spuriously infinite process is not between two elements that are defined as *the same* as one another. It was because the two elements engaged in the spurious infinity were defined as the same as one another in those other stages that a third concept had to be introduced. Only a third concept could capture both the sameness of and the difference between the two elements at the same time (cf. Being-for-itself, Repulsion and Attraction for a more detailed explanation of the logical move). In this stage, by contrast, the spuriously infinite process takes place between two elements that are already defined as different from one another. The back-and-forth process here is between Condition and Possibility. Since the two elements in the spuriously infinite process are already defined as different from one another, there is no logical need to introduce a new concept. Again, the spuriously infinite process can be resolved simply by redefining the embracing concept (Condition, in this case) in a new way that embraces the back-and-forth process as a completed whole.

Although $\text{Condition}_{\text{AT}}$ is now defined as a totality, it has not lost its character as Possibility. $\text{Condition}_{\text{AT}}$ is still defined by Possibility because it is the set of Conditions that are established or present, but have possibility as their way of being. $\text{Condition}_{\text{AT}}$ embraces the character of possibility that Inner and Outer had. It includes all possible defining concepts (the Inner), as well as everything that happened (by chance) to show up in existence or be out there (the Outer). The character of the $\text{Condition}_{\text{AT}}$ is therefore laced with the same Possibility that each individual Condition had. The whole $\text{Condition}_{\text{AT}}$ still has Possibility as its form or the way in which it is presented or has its being, as well as its content.

Because the Condition_{AT} is the complete set of Conditions, however, it is *all* Possibility, the *whole realm of Possibility*, or Possibility as a completed whole. Possibility is completed: there are no more Inners and no more Outers that it does not contain. Possibility is now defined as all the (possible) contingent existences (Outer) together with all possible identifying concepts (Inner). Moreover, since Possibility is a whole, Inner and Outer and their process of mutual definition are each also a whole. There are no possible Outers not identified by an Inner, and no possible Inners not connected to an Outer, so that the process of mutual definition is a complete whole as well.

The Matter (*Sache*) Itself and the Activity of Necessity

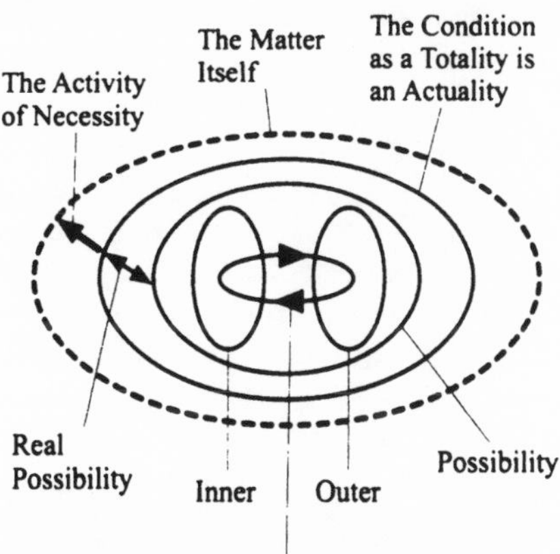

Figure 3.54

The Condition_{AT} and its activity of Real Possibility give rise to (1) a new concept, and (2) a new activity. (1) First, as soon as the Condition as a Totality completes its activity, then the Matter (*Sache*) Itself arises, or is present. The term Hegel uses here—"*Sache*"—and that Geraets, Suchting and Harris translate as "matter," is not the same term that Hegel had used in the discussion of the Matters earlier on. Those earlier Matters were the *Materie*, the underlying matter or material of the Thing. The German term "*Sache*," by contrast, is a topic or subject (matter). (2) Second, this activity of giving rise to the Matter Itself is the Activity of Necessity.

(1) First, then, the activity of the Condition_{AT} is the whole process of Real Possibility, taken together as completed or finished. The process of Real Possibility is the process in which each and every Condition points toward another Condition that is a genuine alternative for it. The Condition_{AT}'s activity thus draws all the individual Conditions together (as genuine alternatives for one another) into a set. As soon as all the Conditions are drawn together into a set, then the Matter Itself arises. As soon as all the Conditions are taken together along with their activity of Real Possibility, then the Matter Itself necessarily arises. The Matter Itself is represented in the diagram as a new bubble that surrounds the bubble for the Condition as a Totality. Because the Matter Itself is currently defined from the bottom up by its contents and does not yet have a definition of its own as a separate concept, I have given the bubble representing it in the diagram a dashed outline.

Think of the cat/dog/hamster example again. The Condition$_{AT}$ is the completed set of Conditions, namely the concept of dog, cat, hamster and so on all taken together. Those concepts are conditions in relation to one another because they can serve as genuine alternatives for one another (see Real Possibility). To say that they can serve as genuine alternatives for one another is to say that there is some character that they share, some way in which they are the same as one another, which allows them to be genuine alternatives for one another. In short, they are all the same *kind*. As soon as all of the items of the kind are gathered together into a set in which they serve as genuine alternatives for one another, then the concept of the kind itself is present or there. As soon as all of the concepts of cat, dog, hamster and so on are gathered together into a set on the basis of their sameness, then the kind itself—the concept of *pet*—emerges or is there. The concept of pet itself just is the sameness that all of the actualities in its set share. It is the Matter Itself, or the subject-matter at hand. The Matter Itself is thus a new concept that is generated by and embraces the completed set of items—along with all their activity of serving as genuine alternatives for one another—that belong to the Condition$_{AT}$. It is the thought of the *kind* that the Conditions are—the kind that allows the Conditions to point toward one another in a way that draws them together into a completed set or as the Condition$_{AT}$. The Matter Itself is the thought of the subject-matter (*Sache*) of all the Conditions. As soon as all of the concepts of cat, dog, hamster and so on and their activity of pointing toward one another is completed, then the concept of pet itself—as the thought of the kind that they are—necessarily arises.

There is another logical reason why the Condition$_{AT}$ produces the Matter Itself. The Condition$_{AT}$ is supposed to be a condition, which was defined earlier as a concept that points toward another possibility (see Condition). Because the Condition$_{AT}$ has absorbed all of the activity in which Conditions were pointing toward Possibility—and contains or includes all of that activity within its content or definition—the Condition$_{AT}$ has not itself been pointing toward any other possibility. The Condition$_{AT}$ was a possibility that was not yet defined as a genuine possibility since it did not yet point toward another possibility that can serve as a genuine alternative for it. It is therefore logically driven to generate the Matter Itself to fulfill its character as a condition. The Condition$_{AT}$ fulfills its definition as a condition by pointing toward the Matter Itself as another possibility. Because the Matter Itself just *is* the concept of the *kind* that the Condition$_{AT}$ is, the Matter Itself is the same kind as the Condition$_{AT}$, and can serve as a genuine alternative for it. Moreover, because the activity of the Condition$_{AT}$ is defined not just by possibility, but also by *Real* Possibility, the possibility it generates is necessarily present.

The Matter Itself is "present" in two senses. First, it is present in the sense that it has a character or definition. Since it is the thought of the *kind* or sameness that allows the individual Conditions to be genuine alternatives for one another, then, as soon as all the Conditions are drawn together as genuine alternatives for one another into a set or totality, then the Matter Itself is defined or has its definition. Second, the Matter Itself is also present in the sense that it is out there. The Matter Itself embraces, contains or is defined by Actuality. That's why Hegel says that, "when *all conditions* are present, the Matter *must* become actual" (§147). Actuality contains both defining concepts (Inner) and out-thereness or existence (Outer). Using the pet example again, the concept of pet—as the subject-matter itself—embraces the *Actuality* of dog, which includes both the identifying concept of dog (Inner) and all the instances of dogs out there in reality (Outer) that live up to the identifying concept. Because "pet" includes not just the identifying concept of dog but also all of the existing *dogs*, it is out there or exists in the dogs. Thus, the Matter Itself is present or established in the sense that it is both defined and actual. As actual, it includes both defining concepts and existence. Because the Matter Itself is present or established, I represent it in the diagram with a solid line.

(2) Second, this activity of generating the Matter Itself is an Activity of Necessity or is necessary. Since the Matter Itself just is the concept that embraces the Condition$_{AT}$, then the activity of the Condition$_{AT}$ automatically, necessarily, and without further ado generates the Matter Itself. As soon as the Condition$_{AT}$ completes its activity, then the Matter Itself is present. Again, the process in which the all of the concepts of cat, dog, hamster and so on are gathered up into a set in which they serve as genuine alternatives for one another necessarily generates the concept of pet, as soon as the process is finished. The whole activity of Real Possibility of the Condition$_{AT}$ generates the Activity of Necessity by giving rise to or producing the Matter Itself. As soon as all the activity of Real Possibility that belongs to the Condition$_{AT}$ is completed, then the Activity of Necessity generates the Matter itself. The Activity of Necessity is represented by an arrow that runs from the Condition$_{AT}$ to the Matter Itself.

Because the Matter Itself is being defined from below, that is to say, in relation to the elements that it embraces, its definition and existence includes all the character of possibility and contingency that the elements that it embraces have. The Matter Itself is actual, but it still has Possibility for its character because it is defined by the Condition$_{AT}$, which has Possibility for its character. The Matter Itself is currently being defined from the bottom up by all the given, possible identifying concepts (Inner) and whatever items happen to be out there (the Outer) that the Condition$_{AT}$ contains. The identifying concepts (Inner) are given or possible. The concept of pet, for example, includes all possible concepts used to identify individual pets out there—cat, dog, hamster, snake and so on. Indeed, the concept of pet is itself one of the conditions. Since it is one of the possible concepts used to identify pets, it is given by the Condition$_{AT}$. As Hegel puts it, "the matter itself is one of the conditions" (§147). Moreover, the Matter Itself is also defined by possibility because it is being defined from the bottom up by all of the items out there that happened to show up (by chance) (the Outer). In the case of the pet example, the given items out there are all the pets that happened by chance to show up and to be paired with the identifying concepts of different pets. Because the Matter Itself includes both given (possible) defining concepts (Inner) and the given items out there, it is itself something-presupposed (§147).

The Matter Itself is a defined and out-there *something*, but it is defined as, and out-there in, a set of items that happened by chance to show up and that are defined by possible identifying concepts (Inner).

Hegel says that the Matter Itself is the Concept (§147R). The diagrams will help to support Hegel's claim because the bubble that is now defined as the Matter Itself is the very same bubble that will be defined as *the Concept* later on. Although I have been using a specific concept (namely, the concept of pet) to illustrate the Matter Itself, the Matter Itself and *the Concept* is what we ordinarily think of as Reason or Rationality. The Matter Itself, which is the first definition offered for the Concept, defines the Concept as the thought that grasps $\text{Condition}_{\text{AT}}$, or the complete and completed set of all the Conditions and their activity. Because the Conditions themselves are concepts, this stage suggests that Reason is the thought of all of the concepts and their activity, taken together as a complete and completed whole (a totality). That is one ordinary way of defining Reason. According to this definition, Reason is the thought of all the concepts that have actuality, taken together as a complete set. There is an important difference between how we ordinarily think of Reason, however, and how Hegel defines Reason here. We ordinarily think of Reason as a system of *mere* thoughts, that is, as *just* concepts. For Hegel, however, because the Conditions are each Actualities, they are all the defining concepts (the Inner) along with the complete set of possible instances and activity out there in reality (the Outer) that they embrace, or in relation to which they are mutually defined. For Hegel, then, Reason is not just concepts, but the complete set of concepts along with the way in which those concepts are instantiated in items out in reality.

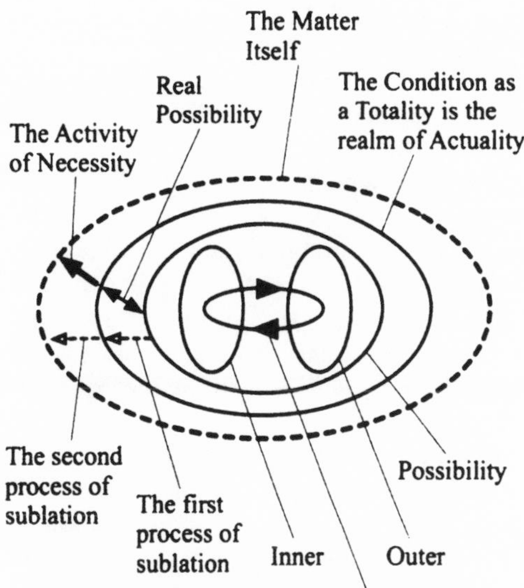

Figure 3.55

In the difficult and obscure §147, Hegel describes the movement to the Matter Itself as involving two processes of sublation. A concept "sublates" another concept or concepts when it cancels but also preserves the earlier concept(s). I have depicted this process with an overarching bubble that surrounds the bubble(s) it embraces. Because the diagram here depicts bubbles that embrace each other by being nested within one another, it illustrates why Hegel would have described the process that generates the Matter Itself as processes of sublation. Hegel says that the Matter Itself contains within it two processes of sublation. I have added temporary, dashed arrows to the diagram just to illustrate where these processes take place in relation to the logical elements. In the first process, Possibility is sublated by the Condition$_{AT}$; and in the second process, the Condition$_{AT}$ is sublated by the Matter Itself.

To begin to see the first process of sublation, recall that the Condition$_{AT}$ is defined as the completed set of Conditions, which had earlier been defined as Immediate Actualities. Because the Condition$_{AT}$ is the totality of Immediate Actualities, it is an Actuality: it, too, is a set of existents (Outer) that live up to identifying concepts (Inner). (Immediate Actuality was defined as Inner and Outer in a mutually determining relationship.) As the *totality* of Immediate Actualities, the Condition$_{AT}$ is the complete and completed set of Conditions or Immediate Actualities. It is thus the *whole realm of Actuality*, or the whole realm of existents (Outer) that live up to identifying concepts (Inner).

Since the stage of Condition, Possibility has been both the form and content of Actuality. It is the form of Actuality because it is the way in which Actuality is presented. It also contains the content of Actuality. It has Inner and Outer and their relationship in its contents. Because Inner and Outer were defined in the stage of Condition as having a mutually determining relationship, and since Actuality was defined as Inner and Outer in a mutually determining relationship, Possibility's content lives up to the definition of, and so is the content of, Actuality.

Moreover, the mutually determining relationship between Inner and Outer (which Hegel describes here as "the immediate self-translation of the inner into the outer, and of the outer into the inner" [§147]) is a relationship of Ground. Since Actuality is defined as Inner *and Outer* in a mutually determining relationship, it includes out-thereness or reality. Inner and Outer thus give Possibility its out-thereness or reality (Outer). Because Inner and Outer are defined by the relationship of ground, and because they contain the reality of Possibility, they are the *real* ground within Possibility.

In the first process of sublation, Hegel is suggesting, Inner and Outer complete their process of mutually defining one another within Possibility and generate the Condition$_{AT}$. I have depicted this process in the diagram with the temporary, dashed arrow that runs from Possibility to the Condition$_{AT}$. To say that Inner and Outer *completely mutually define one another* is to say that Inner and Outer are complete as sets. There are no more identifying concepts left (Inner) and no more items out there (Outer) to identify. Inner is all the possible identifying concepts and Outer is all the possible items out there in reality. When all the possible defining concepts (Inner) are in a mutually determining relationship with all the possible items that happened to be out there in reality by chance (Outer), then the realm of Possibility is completed. It is the form and content of the whole realm of Actuality. When Inner and Outer are completed as the content and form of Actuality, then what we have is the whole, completed realm of Actuality. There is no more Actuality out there left over to be identified. Taken together as a whole, when every identifying concept (Inner) and every item out there (Outer) completely mutually identify one another—which is the content of Possibility—then Possibility is the whole realm of Actuality. Moreover, in that process of sublation, Possibility itself—as a characteristic of reality—is also sublated. When all the possibility in Inner and Outer has been completed, then reality is no longer characterized by Possibility. Instead, it is characterized by Actuality. When all the possibilities have happened, then there is no more possibility. What was a mere possibility before has now become an actuality. Once I have knitted all the possible stitches that I can possibly knit on a particular sweater, for instance, then the sweater itself is complete. Once all the possibilities are in place—both conceptual possibilities (Inner) and possibilities out there (Outer)—then what we have is a completed realm. Because a completed realm is finished, it is an Actuality. Thus, when the realm of possibility has been completed, it is an actuality, rather than a possibility. Putting these factors together, Inner and Outer and their completed, mutually defining relationship are the ground that allows Possibility itself—as a characteristic of reality—to be sublated (cancelled and preserved). Even though Possibility has become an actuality as the whole realm of Actuality, it still has possibility within it (and so Possibility is preserved), insofar as all of the Inners and Outers were only possibilities before they happened. Now that they have all happened, they are actualities, but they are actualities that still have the character of having been a mere possibility before, in the same way that the stitches on my sweater were only a possibility before I completed them all. Even when the sweater is finished, the stitches maintain their character of having been a possibility before they happened. At the same time, because the realm of Actuality is now complete, it is no longer subject to any further possibilities, and so Possibility is cancelled because it has been completed. As Hegel puts it, the complete process by which Inner and Outer mutually determine one another provides "the *real* ground, which sublates itself into Actuality" (§147). Inner and Outer and their relationship are the *real* ground (since they include reality and the relationship of Ground) through which Possibility is sublated by the whole realm of Actuality, which is what the Condition_{AT} is. They are the real ground through which Possibility becomes the whole realm of Actuality, or the Condition_{AT}. Moreover, Inner and Outer are the real ground within Possibility that allows Possibility itself—as a characteristic of reality—to be sublated. Possibility is thus sublated—or both cancelled and preserved—as the Condition_{AT} in two senses: first, when its contents (Inner and Outer) are completed, it generates the Condition_{AT}, and second, once it generates the Condition_{AT} and is completed, then Possibility itself as a characteristic of reality has been sublated.

The second process of sublation focuses on the activity of the Condition_{AT}, and how it is sublated by the Matter Itself. The Condition_{AT} is defined as the completed set of Conditions, which had earlier been defined as Immediate Actualities. Because the Condition_{AT} is the totality of Immediate Actualities, it is an Actuality: it, too, is a set of existents (Outer) that live up to their identifying concepts (Inner). (Immediate Actuality was defined as Inner and Outer in a mutually determining relationship.) As the totality of Immediate Actualities, the Condition_{AT} is the whole realm of Actuality or existents (Outer) that live up to their defining concepts (Inner). But it is an actuality that is contingent, or is produced by chance or possibility. The Condition_{AT} is the completed set of Conditions, which are all the possible identifying concepts (completed Inner) along with all the existents (that happened, by chance, to come along) (completed Outer) that they embrace. Thus, the Condition_{AT} contains the same contingency that characterized Immediate Actuality—indeed, that is why it is still a Condition. (A Condition was defined as an Actuality that had Possibility or Contingency as its form.) While the Condition_{AT} is an actuality because it has been completed—just as the sweater is an actuality once it has been completed—it is a contingent actuality.

The Matter Itself, too, is an actuality. It, too, contains Inner and Outer and their mutually defining relationship. However, the Matter Itself is not a contingent actuality. The Matter Itself is not the completed set of Conditions—that is the Condition_{AT}. It is the actuality (thought and completed existence) *of* the completed set of Conditions. While the completed set of Conditions is characterized by possibility, the *thought and existence of* the completed set of Conditions is not. The completed set of Conditions is characterized by possibility because it is defined by all the possible Conditions that happened (by chance) to come up. If we think of the sweater, for instance, as the completed set of stitches, then it is characterized by possibility because each of the stitches is merely a stitch that happened to be the one I made. But the *thought and existence of* that completed set of Conditions treats the set as finished, and so is not characterized by possibility. If we think of the sweater as the thought of the sweater itself, along with the whole existing sweater that is already completed and out there, *that* sweater is not characterized by possibility. It is already there and finished. Because the Matter Itself is the thought and existence of the completed set of Conditions, it, too is *finished*. From the point of view of the Matter Itself, so to speak, there is nothing further that is possible that could change the completed set. The Matter Itself is the thought (or concept) and existence of the completed set as a finished product. The set therefore has no further possibilities. As finished, nothing further could happen to it (by chance). The Matter Itself is therefore an actuality with no further contingency.

So we can now say that the Condition$_{AT}$ is a contingent actuality that is sublated by another actuality when it generates (through the activity of necessity) the Matter Itself. The Conditions (as a totality), taken together as the contingent actuality, sublate themselves into another actuality (§147), namely into the actuality of the Matter Itself. In the second process of sublation, then, once the Condition$_{AT}$ completes the activity of gathering all the Conditions together into a completed set, it is sublated by the Matter Itself. I depict this process in the diagram with the temporary, dashed arrow that runs from the Condition$_{AT}$ to the Matter Itself. The Matter Itself preserves the contingency of the Condition$_{AT}$ insofar as the Conditions still have their character of having been contingent in the past, just as the stitches in the sweater have the character of once having been contingent stitches, or the stitches that happened by chance to show up. But the Matter Itself also cancels the contingency of the Condition$_{AT}$ insofar as it is the thought *of* the Condition$_{AT}$ as a completed and finished item.

As in other cases of sublation, these processes of sublation generate higher-level concepts. Possibility has been sublated by the Condition$_{AT}$, which, as the concept of Condition-in-general, is a more universal concept. Moreover, while the Condition$_{AT}$ is a contingent actuality, the Matter Itself is an actuality with no further contingency. It is *unconditioned* in Kant's sense (see Chapter One, Section V). As the thought of all of the Conditions as a completed set, there are no Conditions outside of it that it does not already contain. Hence it is not subject to any further conditions. It is unconditioned. In the Matter Itself, the character or inward reflection (§147) of the Condition$_{AT}$ is both cancelled and preserved. The character is preserved because the Matter Itself is also an actuality, just as the Condition$_{AT}$ was. Just as the thought or concept (Inner) of the sweater out there (Outer) as a finished product is an actuality—it is a concept or Inner (the concept of sweater) in a mutually defining relationship with something out there or Outer (the completed sweater that now exists)—so the Matter Itself, as the thought or concept of all the Conditions taken together as a completed set, is an actuality. However, the character of the Condition$_{AT}$ is cancelled by the Matter Itself because the Matter Itself is no longer directly characterized by the contingency that defined the Condition$_{AT}$.

The Matter Itself therefore includes two processes of sublation: the sublation of Possibility into the Condition_{AT} (or the realm of Actuality), and the sublation of the Condition_{AT} into the Matter Itself.

External Necessity

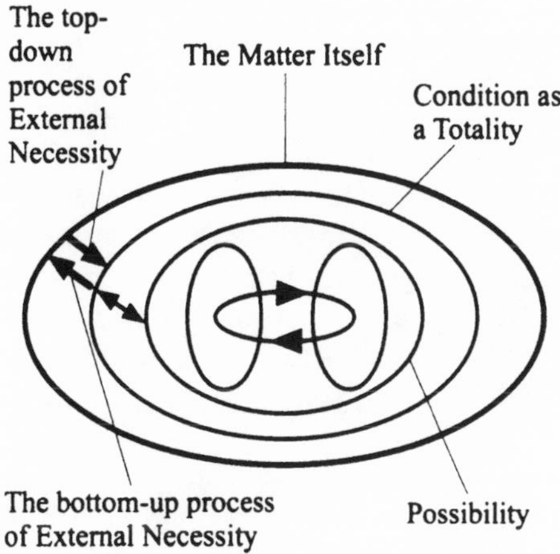

Figure 3.56

Hegel describes this stage by dividing the discussion into separate discussions of each of the main logical elements currently in play: (a) the Condition, (b) the Matter Itself, and (c) the activity. Hegel also further divides the discussion of each element into two ([α] and [β]) (§148). For each element, he discusses how the element was defined from the bottom up in earlier stages, and how the element is now defined from the top down.

(a) *The Condition (as a Totality)*. What Hegel calls the Condition in §148 is what I have been calling the Condition as a Totality (Condition_{AT}). Hegel's use of the term "condition" is fair because the Condition_{AT} is still a Condition (as we saw in the stage of the Matter [*Sache*] Itself), it is just the most general definition of the concept of Condition. It is the concept of Condition-in-general. Keep in mind as you refer to Hegel's text, however, that Hegel never uses the term "Condition as a Totality." Instead, he assumes that his readers will remember that Condition has now been defined as a totality and continues to use the term "condition" (*Bedingung*). In his text, the Condition_{AT} can be distinguished from individual Conditions because individual Conditions are referred to in the plural form, i.e. as "conditions." I do not want the more developed definition of Condition—i.e. Condition_{AT}—to be confused with the earlier one, however, which Hegel had also called simply the "condition."

(α) At first, the Condition_{AT} was defined from the bottom up. It was defined by the mutually determining concepts (Inner) and items (Outer) that it embraced. When the Condition_{AT} is from the bottom up this way, it has the character of being "what is presupposed" (§148). It is presupposed because the concepts in the Condition_{AT} are simply given. Remember that the Condition_{AT} is a set of concepts (Inner) and items (Outer) of a certain kind—cats, dogs, hamster and so on, for example. When the Condition_{AT} is generated from the bottom up, it is defined by whatever concepts (Inner) and items (Outer) happened to be around or were given. Hence, the definition of the set is presupposed or stipulated.

(β) Once the concept of the Matter Itself has been generated, however, we see that the Condition_{AT} is also defined from the top down. Once the concept of the Matter Itself is present, the Condition_{AT} is redefined as the form and content of the Matter Itself. In relation to the Matter Itself, the Condition_{AT} is now defined as the way in which the Matter Itself is presented (form), and as the element that contains the definition or character of the Matter Itself (content). When the Condition_{AT} is defined as the presentation (form) and content of the Matter Itself, however, it is now thought of as having been *shaped* or *formed* by the activity of the Matter Itself. Once we think of the set of cats, dogs, hamsters and so on as the presentation (form) and content of the concept of pet, for instance, we come to see it as having been shaped or formed by the concept of pet itself. The concept of pet presents and contains that set of concepts (Inner) and items (Outer), so the set itself (the Condition_{AT}) has been defined and worked on by the concept of pet. Although I am using dogs, cats, hamsters and so on to illustrate the Condition_{AT}, the Condition_{AT} is really the whole set of concepts that are kinds of other concepts, and the Matter Itself is Reason. When the Condition_{AT} is defined from the top down by the Matter Itself, or as the presentation and content *of Reason*, then it is no longer defined merely as whatever concepts (Inner) and items (Outer) happened to be around. Instead, it must now be thought of as a set of concepts and items that have *been worked on* by Reason itself. The set of concepts and items has been *presented* by Reason. It is thus a set of concepts and items that has been *rationalized*, from the top down, by Reason itself. It is therefore now a *system*, a *conceptual scheme* of concepts and items. As Hegel puts it, the Condition_{AT} has become "a *complete circle of conditions*" (§148). It is a *circle* because it has been shaped, formed, systematized and completed by the Matter Itself. The Condition_{AT} is now defined as a completed *system* of rational concepts. I have added an arrow in the diagram that runs from the Matter Itself to the Condition_{AT} to represent the top-down process in which Reason or the Matter Itself shapes or presents—i.e. rationalizes—the Condition_{AT}.

(b) *The Matter (Itself)*. (α) When the Matter Itself is defined from the bottom up, it is, as Hegel puts it, "something-presupposed" (§148). This was the sort of process of definition for rational concepts that had been envisioned by Kant (see Chapter One, Section IV). In this case, the Matter Itself is defined by being built up out of the set of possible Conditions that happened (by chance) to exist (i.e. the Condition_{AT}), so its definition is simply given to it by the Condition_{AT}. From this point of view, Reason is the thought of the set of concepts and items that is built—from the bottom up—out of experience.

(β) Once the Condition_{AT} is defined from the top down as the presentation (form) and content of the Matter Itself, however, the definition of the Matter Itself also changes. Before, the Matter Itself was defined simply as the thought or concept of the Condition_{AT}. It was the same as the Condition_{AT}, and had no character of its own beyond the Condition_{AT}. I therefore represented it in the diagram with a dashed outline. Now that the Condition_{AT} is defined as the presentation (form) and content of the Matter Itself, however, the Matter Itself has a character on its own account, separate from the Condition$_{AT}$. Once we see the concepts of cat, dog, hamster and so on as the content and presentation (form) of the concept of pet, for instance, then the concept of pet comes to be seen as a separate and independent concept with its own definition that is presented by the cats, dogs and so on in the Condition$_{AT}$. The Matter Itself is a concept in its own right that is merely presented by its content. I have given the bubble representing the Matter Itself a solid outline in the diagram to represent the idea that it now has a definition of its own, separate from the Condition$_{AT}$ that it presents (as form) and embraces (as content).

Hegel uses this logical move as a syntactic device. Any time a concept is defined as a concept that *presents* its content (has a form), the process of *presenting* defines the concept as an independent concept, separate from and opposed to its contents. It is because the Matter Itself has become a concept in its own right, separate from the elements that it embraces that Hegel describes the Matter Itself as determined in and for itself (§147). An "in itself" type of relationship is a relationship of separation or opposition (see Being-in-itself in Chapter Two). The Matter Itself is defined in the "in itself" sense because it has a character or definition of its own that is separate from or opposed to the Condition$_{AT}$, which it presents. But the Matter itself is also defined as a "for itself" concept because it still embraces the Condition$_{AT}$ in its content (cf. Being-for-itself in Chapter Two). In the diagram, Matter Itself literally embraces the Condition$_{AT}$ because the Condition$_{AT}$ is inside it.

Moreover, the Condition$_{AT}$, as the *expression or presentation* (form) of Reason or the Matter Itself, is the way in which Reason is presented, and therefore constitutes the being or presence of Reason. All of the Conditions are actualities, so they include not only defining concepts but also the existing items out there in reality that are defined by those concepts. So the set of concepts or Conditions is the way in which Reason has its external existence (§148). Reason or the Matter Itself has its external presence in the set of Conditions, or in the Condition$_{AT}$. To use the pet example again, the concept of pet has its external presence in the concepts (Inner) and items (Outer)—the dogs, cats, hamsters and so on—that it embraces (in its content) and presents (as its form).

(c) *The Activity*. (α) Now that the Condition$_{AT}$ and the Matter Itself are defined from the top down, the activity between them also changes. The bottom-up Activity of Necessity was the activity in which the Condition$_{AT}$ generated the Matter Itself. Now there is also activity running from the top down: from the Matter Itself back to the Condition$_{AT}$. The Condition$_{AT}$ is the content and the way in which the Matter Itself is presented. It is the way in which the Matter Itself is presented in two senses. First, the Condition$_{AT}$ contains and presents the Matter's being or presence. Because the concepts and items in the Condition$_{AT}$ are present and exist, the Matter Itself is presented as an existing item. Hence, the activity of the Matter Itself includes existence, insofar as the Matter Itself presents (as form) and contains (as content) each and every existing item in the Condition$_{AT}$. As Hegel puts it, using his own example, the activity is "existent on its own account, independently (a man, a character)" (§148). In the pet example, the existent set of cats, dogs, hamsters and so on, as the presentation (form) and content of the concept of pet, is the activity of the concept of pet. When the concept of pet acts, it acts by containing and presenting that existent. In Hegel's example, the Matter Itself or Reason is an existent on its own account in each man or each character because, Hegel has argued, everything in the world (of experience) is both concept (Inner) and out-thereness (Outer). Something can be out-there (Outer) only *as* something, that is, only with an identity or only if it is connected to an Inner; and a defining concept (Inner) can be anything at all only if it is also out-there (Outer). Existence involves both inward reflection (Inner) and reflection-into-another (Outer) (see the stage of Inner and Outer). That means that everything in the world or everything that exists—because it is not only out there (Outer) but also attached to some defining concept or other (Inner)—is a presentation of the Matter Itself or of Reason. Everything in the world of Possibility (which is the thought that captures Inner and Outer and their mutually defining relationship) is necessarily an expression of Reason. A man, a character, to use Hegel's examples (§148)—everything that exists—all express Reason, insofar as each exists as a combination of both out-thereness (Outer) and identifying or defining concept (Inner).

(β) Although the activity between the Matter Itself and the Condition$_{AT}$ includes the top-down process just outlined, it still includes the bottom-up process that we saw before. Indeed, the activity is the both the bottom-up and the top-down processes, which are both processes of necessity. The bottom-up process is the process in which the Matter Itself or Reason is generated by all the Conditions or by the Condition$_{AT}$. This bottom-up process is necessary because, as soon as all the Conditions are present, then the Matter Itself is necessarily present (see The Matter [*Sache*] Itself and the Activity of Necessity). The top-down process is the process in which the Matter Itself or Reason shapes or *rationalizes* all the Conditions or the Condition$_{AT}$. The top-down process is necessary because everything that exists in the contingent world of Possibility is *necessarily* an expression or presentation of both concept and existence, and hence presents Reason or the Matter Itself. Using Hegel's anthropomorphic language, the bottom-up process gives Reason concepts and existence to work on, while, in the top-down process, Reason shapes or rationalizes the character of what exists.

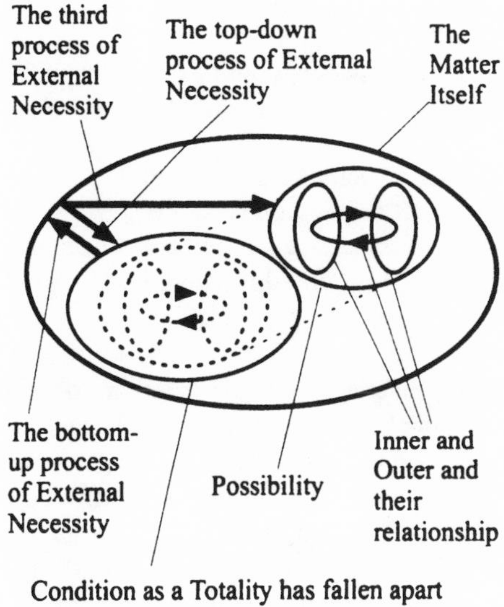

Condition as a Totality has fallen apart

Figure 3.57

Notice that there are actually three processes going on here, however. First, there is the bottom-up process between the Condition$_{AT}$ and the Matter Itself. This is the process in which the Condition$_{AT}$ generated the Matter Itself (see The Matter [*Sache*] Itself). Second, there is the top-down process between the Matter Itself and the Condition$_{AT}$. This is the process in which the Condition$_{AT}$ is defined as systematized or rationalized, and the Matter Itself is defined as an element separate from the Condition$_{AT}$. There is a third process at work here, however, that we need to see in more detail. A moment ago, we said that the Matter Itself or Reason was presented in each and every existing item. Once we have conceived of all the existing items as belonging to the Matter Itself or Reason, then we have deprived the Condition$_{AT}$ of its existence. Let me use Kant's "mortality" example to illustrate this stage. Recall that, for Kant, concepts such as "man" and "animal" were conditions for the concept of mortality. In the bottom-up process of definition envisioned by Kant and that we had earlier, the concepts of man, animal (and of other mortal things) gathered up all of the existing items into a set, and "mortality," as an actuality, depended on the concepts of "man" and "animal" for its own content. To use anthropomorphic language for a moment, the concept of mortality needed the concepts of man and animal to gather up the existing items for it. In the top-down process, however, "mortality" is presented directly in the existing (mortal) items, in which it was implicitly present in the first place. "Mortality" is implicitly present in individual men, animals and trees because those items die. The fact that those items die is the direct presentation in existence of "mortality." So "mortality" is expressed directly in the existing items insofar as those items die. As soon as we see the existing items as belonging directly to the concept of mortality, however, then we rob the concepts of man, animal and so on of their existence. The Matter (Itself) sublates the existence that the Conditions had (§148). The Conditions are no longer needed to gather up the existing items. They no longer have to do any work, and are no longer filled up with any items. The concept of mortality presents the existing items in Possibility directly, without the intervention of the Condition$_{AT}$ at all.

I have added a third arrow that runs directly between the Matter Itself and Possibility to represent this third process in the diagram. Because the Matter Itself is presenting Possibility directly, without the intervention of the Condition$_{AT}$, I have also separated the Condition$_{AT}$ bubble from the Possibility bubble. As Hegel says in the next section, the "other" in relation to the Matter Itself (or "what is necessary")—which is the Condition$_{AT}$—has "fallen apart" (§149). The Condition$_{AT}$ has fallen apart into itself as one element, and Possibility as another. The fact that the Condition$_{AT}$ has lost its existence is also depicted in the diagram because the elements that represent existence—Inner and Outer and their mutually defining relationship—remain inside Possibility, so that the Condition$_{AT}$ has become an empty bubble.

Like the other two processes, this third process is also a process of necessity. The Matter Itself is a concept on its own account, separate from the concept of the Condition$_{AT}$. Like other concepts of concepts—or essences—however, the Matter Itself can have a character or definition of its own only by pushing out, shining forth or showing up. The Matter Itself *must*, therefore, necessarily show up, and it shows up by presenting its character in existing items.

Moreover, because the Matter Itself no longer uses the Conditions to do any work, the Conditions—"man," "animal," "tree" and so on—are now defined as separate from the Matter Itself. "Mortality" is one concept, the concepts of man, animal, tree and so on are other concepts. The Matter Itself is one concept, the set of concepts that is the Condition$_{AT}$ is another. This relationship is represented in the diagram by the two opposing arrows between the Matter Itself and the Condition$_{AT}$. The Matter Itself and the Condition$_{AT}$ are being defined in opposition to one another in an "in itself" sense. The Matter Itself is merely presented by the Condition$_{AT}$, and so has a character of its own that is against or opposed to the character of the Condition$_{AT}$. Hegel describes their relationship as an "in itself" one in the first line of §149, when he says the One essence (which is what the Matter Itself is) is "in itself" (§149).

Even the existing items are defined as separate from both the Conditions and Matter Itself. The existing items are separate from the Conditions because they are now being presented directly by the Matter Itself. The existing items—men, animals and so on, for instance—are being presented insofar as they *die* and not insofar as they are men or animals. But they are also defined as separate from "mortality" because they are being presented as independently existing items, as items that exist on their own, independently of the concept of mortality. Their dying is something that happens to each of them separately as independent items. Indeed, "mortality" does not characterize what happens to them at all, since what happens to them that makes them mortal—namely, the *dying*—is not itself grasped by the concept of morality. Their dying *presents* mortality, but is not grasped or characterized by mortality. The existing items in Possibility are therefore separate from both the Condition$_{AT}$ and the Matter Itself. That the existing items are defined as separate from the Conditions is represented in the diagram insofar as the Condition$_{AT}$ is now a separate bubble from the bubble for Possibility. That they are separate from the Matter Itself is represented by the two arrows between the Matter Itself and Possibility. The Matter Itself is presented by Possibility, and so is opposed to Possibility, and does not define the items in Possibility. The items in Possibility have the shape of independent existence, separate from the Matter Itself.

Therefore, these three processes together currently define the three elements in play—the Condition$_{AT}$, Possibility, and the Matter Itself—as separate elements. To use the example again, "mortality" is one element, the Conditions—the concepts of "man," "animal," and so on—are another, and the existing items—the individual men and animals—are yet a third element in the activity we have before us now. Each element or moment has the shape of, or is presented as, an independent existence in relation to one another (§148). Because the whole process of necessity defines each of the elements as separate from and external to one another, it is a process of "*external* necessity" (§148). The necessity is external because, although the activity between the elements is defined as necessary, the characters or definitions of the elements themselves do not reflect that necessity. At the moment, the elements are defined in a way that makes them separate from one another. Therefore, while they are necessarily connected in the three ways we have seen, they are not *defined* as necessarily connected. The necessary relationships they currently have with one another are external to their definitions or characters.

Hegel says that this process of necessity "has a *restricted* content as its [subject] matter" (§148). The Matter Itself is being presented in the Condition$_{AT}$ and in existing items, both of which are still characterized by Possibility. The existing items are all the existents that happened (by chance) to come along and that are connected to all the possible identifying concepts. That externality is what restricts the content of the Matter Itself. Because the Matter Itself is currently being presented by Possibility, the content of the Matter Itself is *restricted* to whatever is given to it by that Possibility. To use Kant's example again, so long as the concept of mortality—the Matter Itself—is being presented by whatever possible mortal types (Inner) happen (by chance) to show up, then its definition or content will be restricted to whatever shows up. If the concept of mortality were defined as what produced or caused those items rather than as what is merely presented by those items, then the existing items would have no character that was not already grasped or covered by the concept of mortality. If "mortality" generates the existing items, then it gives them all the character they have. So long as those items are defined as separate from and hence as not generated by "mortality," however, they come along with or have a given content that is not yet grasped or covered by the concept of mortality. The definition of "mortality" is therefore *restricted* by the other content—content not generated by its own activity—and is restricted to whatever content is given to it by those existing items. Existing mortal items, for example, are not only mortal, but also men, animals, tigers, trees and so on. All of those other characteristics, because they are not generated by mortality itself, restrict the definition of "mortality." They are other concepts to which "mortality" is opposed. Indeed, since the Matter Itself or "mortality" is currently being defined as opposed to the Conditions, then "mortality" is currently being limited by concepts in the Condition$_{AT}$.

To say that external necessity has a restricted content is to say that this way of defining the Matter Itself makes it a finite concept. The Matter Itself is defined by items presented in the finite world of existence that are grasped by other concepts that are opposed to and hence limit the Matter Itself. So long as Reason is defined as separate from both existence and from the set of concepts that make it up, it will be conceived as something that is restricted to the finite world. Reason will be defined, as Kant had said, as our reason, as the system of reason of finite human beings who use various rational concepts to grasp existence. Reason will not be seen as the defining element of existence itself.

The Necessary

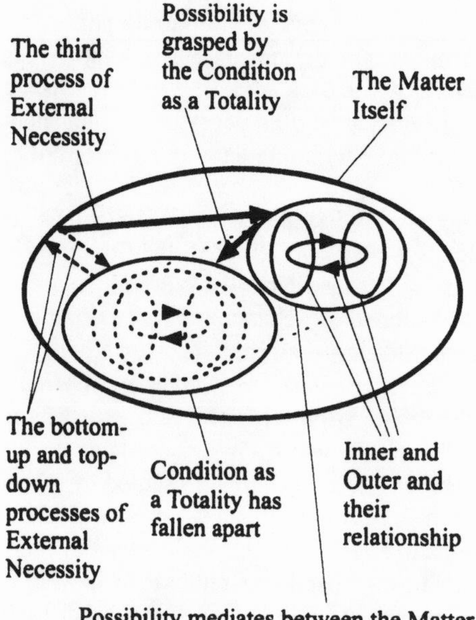

Figure 3.58

The Matter Itself is currently being presented directly in all the existing items that live up to some identifying concept, or in the realm of Possibility. This was the third process of External Necessity that we saw in the last stage. Because the Matter Itself is directly presented in Possibility, the bottom-up and top-down processes of External Necessity between the Matter Itself and the Condition$_{AT}$ are not currently active. I have given the arrows for those processes dashed and thinner lines to indicate that they are not currently logically active.

According to the definitions developed earlier, if we look at how the Matter Itself is defined in an "in itself" sense or on its own, it is the one concept that embraces and defines or identifies everything else. It is, as Hegel puts it, "the *One essence* that is identical *with itself* but full of content" (§149). It is the whole shebang, so to speak, the Necessary, Matter-in-charge, that both embraces and defines everything else. Although the Matter Itself is supposed to be the all-embracing concept or essence, it is not currently being presented in that way because its contents are currently being presented as independent of and separate from it. It shows up or "shines within itself," to use Hegel's terms, as independent items, or "in such a way that its distinctions have the form of *independent actualities*" (§149).

Unfortunately, the phrase just quoted is ambiguous between two possible interpretations based on what is meant by the "distinctions." On the one hand, the "distinctions" might refer to the logical elements that the Matter Itself contains, namely, the $\text{Condition}_{\text{AT}}$ and Possibility. In that case, the $\text{Condition}_{\text{AT}}$ and Possibility would be the actualities that are independent of the Matter Itself. On the other hand, the "distinctions" might refer to the independently existing items, which are currently the presentation of the Matter Itself. In that case, the existing items would be the independent actualities. Fortunately, we do not need to decide between these two interpretations because both interpretations correctly characterize this stage. The Matter Itself is currently being presented in a way that defines it as separate from both the $\text{Condition}_{\text{AT}}$ and Possibility, which are also being defined as separate from one another. Hence the $\text{Condition}_{\text{AT}}$ and Possibility are both currently defined as independent from the Matter Itself. Moreover, because Possibility is the complete set of existing items that live up to an identifying concept, it is a one or an item that is defined by actuality. (Actuality is defined as Inner and Outer in a mutually defining relationship, or as Outer that lives up to [and hence is mutually defined by] the Inner.) Each of the existing items in which the Matter Itself is currently being presented is also an independent actuality. To use the "mortality" example again, each (mortal) existing man is an independent actuality because each man is presented as existing on his own, separately from the Matter Itself or Reason. Moreover, each man is an actuality insofar as he is an existing item that lives up to an identifying concept, namely, the concept of man. I will explain why the $\text{Condition}_{\text{AT}}$ can be defined as an immediate actuality in a moment.

Hegel says that the Matter Itself is being presented as if it is defined through an "other" that is made up of two parts: (i) the "mediating ground," which Hegel describes as "the matter and the activity" (§149), and (ii) "an *immediate* actuality, something-contingent which is at the same time condition" (§149). In the same way that the interpretation of the "distinctions" was ambiguous, this claim, too, is ambiguous. Indeed, the ambiguity here follows from the ambiguity there, since the "other" in relation to which the Matter Itself is being defined is the "distinctions" of the Matter Itself. Hence, the "other" in relation to which the Matter Itself is being defined might be (1) the $\text{Condition}_{\text{AT}}$, which is the "other" that has been split apart into (i) Possibility and (ii) the $\text{Condition}_{\text{AT}}$ itself, or (2) the independently existing individual items or actualities, such as individual men or animals who (as actualities) live up to their identifying concepts (I will explain how they are split into two parts in a moment).

I think the ambiguity in Hegel's text here is not an accident. The text is deliberately ambiguous because the ambiguity allows Hegel to talk simultaneously about two different processes of Reason that correspond to Kant's observation that Reason can be seen as both an ascending and descending series of concepts (see Chapter One, Section IV). The Matter Itself, as I have suggested, is an early definition of Reason. One the one hand, as an ascending series, Reason produces more and more inclusive and comprehensive concepts until it reaches the last, completely comprehensive concept, which Kant had called the Unconditioned. Interpreting Hegel's text to mean (1) generates the ascending series which leads to the definition of Reason as the completely comprehensive Unconditioned. On the other hand, as the descending series, Reason is the process of splitting up into less and less comprehensive concepts. Interpreting Hegel's text to mean (2) generates this descending series. Reason's presentation or expression in individually existing items that are identified by concepts is the least comprehensive concept in which Reason can be expressed as an *independent item*. Each existing item—no matter how small it may be—is an expression of Reason as an independent item insofar as it is attached to an essence or identified by some concept or other (i.e. an Inner) that captures the type of thing that it is. Reason is also expressed in qualitative and quantitative concepts of the characteristics of existing items—insofar as a man is tall or short, for instance. But those quantitative or qualitative concepts do not define the item as an independent item. "Red," for instance, is not a concept that identifies something as an independently existing item. Of course, the independent item need not be a separate *thing*. A man's character, for example, does not exist as a thing apart from the man. However, it has an *existence* that can be grasped or identified separately from the man. A man's character has a life of its own, so to speak. That life is separate from the life of the whole man. The man's life includes his character, but the life of his character does not include everything else about the man. The combination of separate existence (Outer) and identity (Inner) makes his character an independent actuality, even if it is not a separate *thing* from the man. Because his character's existence is identified by a concept that is not the concept of man—namely the concept of character—it is an independent actuality. In the descending series, Reason is presented in such individually existing, independent actualities. The concept of mortality, for instance, is expressed in individual men and animals whose existence expresses the Matter Itself, namely, "mortality." Each man exists in a way that presents "mortality."

In Hegel's text, as we'll see, the definition of Reason as the Matter Itself evolves into the definition of Reason as Substance. Both the ascending and descending series lead to the concept of Substance. In the ascending series, Substance is the definition of Reason as the all-embracing thought or concept that is behind the whole world of experience. Reason is Spinoza's Substance, Spinoza's God. In the descending series, Reason is the substance of the matter insofar as each existing item is an expression of Reason itself. The way of existing of each man as *mortal*, for instance, is the way in which "mortality" is presented in existence. The substance of the matter that is presented in a man's existence, then, is "mortality." In the descending series, Reason is the substance of the matter that is presented in each individually existing actuality's activity.

(2) Let me begin by explaining how Hegel's text would apply to individually existing items. The Matter Itself is currently being presented in individually existing actualities. In the "mortality" example, the Matter Itself is "mortality," which is currently being presented in individual men, animals and so on. Although each man or animal is mortal, they are also defined as "other" than the

"mortality" or the Matter Itself. Each individually existing actuality also has other, given characteristics. Those are precisely the characteristics that define the items as "man" or "animal"—characteristics captured not by the Matter itself, but by the Conditions (remember that, in the example, "man" and "animal" are the Conditions). The individual existing items therefore have a character that is "other" than "mortality."

If the individually existing items are the "other" in relation to which the Matter Itself is being defined, then what would be the two parts into which they are split? Hegel describes the first part (i.e. [i]) as "the matter and the activity." The "matter" is just the Matter Itself. In the "mortality" example, the "matter" is mortality itself. The activity is just the activity of being out there, of existing, of showing up. In the "mortality" example, then, one part of an existing man is the combination of his activity, his showing up or existing, and the "matter" or "mortality." Each man shows up or exists *as mortal*. Mortality is the way in which he has his activity of existing. His showing up as mortal is thus one expression of mortality, of the Matter Itself. The second part (i.e. [ii]) of the existing man refers to the way in which he shows up as a *man*, i.e. as being connected to a Condition. Each existent (Outer) man is an immediate actuality insofar as he is a man (Inner). He is an immediate actuality because his existence lives up to an identifying concept. Because he shows up as an item by chance, he is something-contingent, but because his identity is captured by a concept, he is also a condition or kind (e.g. human).

Hegel also characterizes (i) as the "mediating ground." In the "mortality" example, a man's way of showing up or existing is the mediating ground insofar as it is the activity that mediates between the Matter Itself and the Condition. His way of existing is what connects his being a kind (his condition) with his being mortal (the matter). Thus, according to this interpretation, the Matter Itself is being defined in relation to the set of all individually existing actualities which are "other" than the Matter Itself and whose activity (of existing) mediates between the Matter Itself and all the Conditions (i.e. Condition_{AT}).

(1) Under the first interpretation of what the "other" is, the Condition_{AT} is the "other" that splits up into (i) Possibility, which is the "mediating ground" as matter itself and activity, and (ii) the Condition_{AT} or set of Conditions, which is an immediate actuality as well as something contingent. Under this interpretation, increasingly comprehensive concepts (the concepts of Possibility and then of Condition_{AT}) will ultimately generate a new definition of the Matter Itself as the completely comprehensive concept. This is the ascending series or process.

Let me begin by explaining why (ii) is the Condition_{AT}. To show that (ii) is the Condition_{AT}, we need to see why the Condition_{AT} is an immediate actuality and something-contingent. The Condition_{AT} is an actuality because it is the complete set of all possible Conditions. Actuality is defined as the thought of Inner and Outer in a mutually determining relationship. It is the thought of existing items (Outer) that live up to some identifying concept (Inner). The completed set of all possible Conditions is an *actuality* because it is made up of given, existing items (Outer) that happen (by chance) to live up to some possible identifying concept (Inner), and hence is the thought of Inner and Outer in a mutually defining relationship. After all, although the Condition$_{AT}$ has fallen apart for the moment, Inner and Outer and their mutually defining relationship is *the content of* the Condition$_{AT}$—in the diagram, they have been literally *inside* the Condition$_{AT}$.

The Condition$_{AT}$ is *immediate* for two reasons: it is a whole or one item that is out there or exists, and it is given. First, because it is *the completed set* of existing items that live up to some identifying concept, it is itself an existing something (a one, a whole), but because the defining concept (Inner) is merely some possible concept and the existence is by chance (i.e. possible), the set of Conditions is merely something-contingent (§149). What it is like is given, depending on the possible concepts and existence. In the "mortality" example, the Condition "human" is one set of existing mortal items (Outer) that happen to live up to the concept of man (Inner). Each Condition for "mortality" is equally a given set of existing mortal items that happen to live up to some possible identifying concept. So the Condition$_{AT}$ for "mortality"—the whole set of Conditions—is just the whole set of existing, mortal items that happen to live up to some identifying concept (that is included in the concept of mortal). That set is itself an existing something, and because it contains all the given, existing mortal items and concepts, it is what it is by chance: it is something-contingent. Because the logical Condition$_{AT}$ (rather than the Condition$_{AT}$ for the concept of mortality) is the set of *all* the Conditions, it contains *all* possible actualities as a completed set. As the complete, finished set of all possible actualities, it is an immediate actuality. Because it is all *possible* actualities, however, it is still something-contingent, something that happened by chance.

To see why (i) is Possibility, remember that Possibility is the thought of Inner and Outer in a mutually defining relationship. It is the set of all of the Outers that live up to Inners as a completed set—as the *whole realm* of Possibility (see the stage of Condition as a Totality). Since the mutually defining relationship between Inner and Outer is a relationship of Ground, Possibility contains the relationship of Ground, which would explain why Hegel would describe it as the mediating "ground." Moreover, the characterization of the "mediating ground" as "the matter and the activity" applies to Possibility. Think of the "mortality" example again. "Mortality," as an example of the Matter Itself, is currently being presented in the individual existing mortal items. Those items are a combination of the Matter (Itself) and the activity. They are a combination of the Matter Itself insofar as they are *mortal*, since their mortality reflects the character of the Matter Itself. But they are also the way in which the Matter Itself shows up. As the way in which the Matter Itself shows up, they are the activity of the Matter Itself.

Finally, Possibility currently meets the logical description of being the "mediating ground." It currently mediates the relationship between the Matter Itself or the Necessary and the Condition$_{AT}$. "Mortality," for example, is currently presented in the existing mortal items which have other characters captured by the Conditions—such as "man" and "animal"—that belong to the Condition$_{AT}$. So "mortality" is connected to the Condition$_{AT}$ through the existing mortal items. Here, the set of existing items is mediating the relationship between the Matter Itself and the Condition$_{AT}$. The Matter Itself is presented as all the existing items, and those existing items are in turn grasped by all the Conditions in the Condition$_{AT}$ (which is just the set of all the Conditions). So we have a process that runs from the Matter Itself, through Possibility or the set of existing items, and back to the Condition$_{AT}$. Although the Matter Itself or the Necessary is still defined in an "in itself" sense as the One essence, when it is presented through this process, its character as the One essence is merely posited or stipulated. In the ascending series (i.e. interpretation [1]), the Necessary has its character as the all-embracing One essence in an "in itself" sense, in terms of how it is defined as opposed to the Condition$_{AT}$, but since its form or process of presentation treats the Condition$_{AT}$ as separate from or as "other" than it, it does not have its character as the One, all-embracing essence for itself, or in terms of how it is actively presented. It is defined as the all-embracing One essence in an "in itself" sense, but not in a "for itself" sense, since it is not being presented (as form) in a "for itself" relationship in which it is the all-embracing One essence. The Necessary is directly presented in Possibility, but not in the Condition$_{AT}$. Hence the Necessary's status as the all-embracing One essence over the Condition$_{AT}$ is not established, but merely stipulated. As Hegel puts it, "as what is through an other, the necessary is not in and for itself, but is something that is merely *posited*" (§149).

For the descending series (i.e. interpretation [2]), the necessity of the Matter Itself in the individually existing actualities is also merely stipulated. To use the "mortality" example again, although mortality is the way of existing of men, its necessity is not yet established, but merely posited or stipulated. Because the men are defined as "human"—that is, through the Condition—mortality is not yet necessary. The men could be men without being mortal. Only when the concept of mortality (the Necessary) completely embraces the concept of human (the Condition) as well as the men's way of existing (Possibility) will the mortality be Necessary.

I have added an arrow that runs from Possibility to the Condition$_{AT}$ to represent the idea that, under both interpretations (1) and (2), Possibility mediates between the Necessary (Matter Itself) and the Condition$_{AT}$.

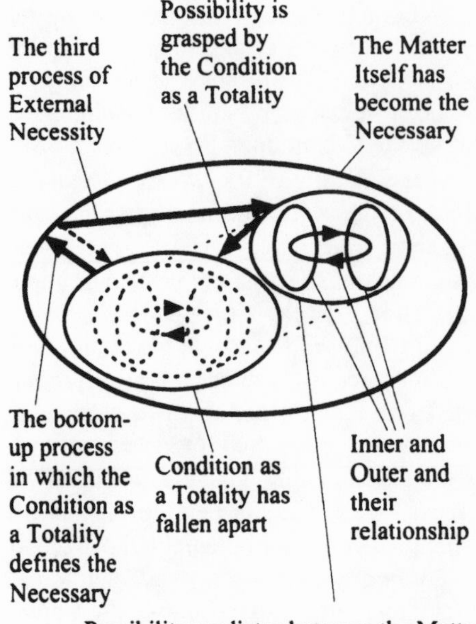

Figure 3.59

However, there is another element at play here that we have not yet accounted for. Once we include that element in the process, the activity or process of presentation for the Matter Itself will in fact define the Matter Itself as the all-embracing One essence or Necessary (at least in terms of activity or process (form), if not yet content). The Matter Itself or the Necessary is the thought of the Condition$_{AT}$ as a completed or finished element and process. The Condition$_{AT}$ generates the Matter Itself in the first, bottom-up process of External Necessity (see The Matter [*Sache*] Itself and the Activity of Necessity). That is the process represented in the diagram by the arrow that runs from the Condition$_{AT}$ bubble to the bubble for the Matter Itself. I have given that arrow a solid outline to represent the fact that it has come back into view as an active, logical element. (Because the top-down process of necessity that we had between the Matter Itself and the Condition$_{AT}$ is not part of and hence not logically active in this process, however, it is still depicted with a dashed and thinner line in the diagram. The top-down process has still receded from the picture, so to speak, for the moment.) As soon as we take that process into consideration, there is a complete process that runs from the Matter Itself through Possibility, through the Condition$_{AT}$, and back to the Matter Itself. This process treats the Condition$_{AT}$ and Possibility as separate from one another, but ends up defining the Matter Itself—at least in terms of process—as the all-embracing One essence, or as the Necessary. The Matter Itself is the Necessary as the element that initiates the whole necessary process in which it embraces and presents the other elements. Moreover, because the activity of necessity now circles back to define the Matter Itself, the Matter Itself is also the Necessary as *the end or result of the process of necessity*. The process of necessity that generated the Matter Itself in the stage of the Matter (*Sache*) Itself is now part of the Matter Itself's own process. The Matter Itself is thus the Necessary not only as the initiator of the necessary process, but also as the necessary result of the necessary process.

However, although the Necessary is defined as the all-embracing One essence in terms of its process (form), the content of its definition is still mediated by circumstances. The realm of Possibility and the set of Conditions (i.e. the Condition$_{AT}$) are currently defined as independent circumstances, through which the Necessary's process of definition as the Necessary passes. As Hegel puts it, "the necessary is so, *mediated* by a circle of circumstances" (§149). This process of passing through Possibility and the Condition$_{AT}$ is the Necessary's "activity of the sublating into mediatedness" (§149).

Let me take a moment to flesh this process out in terms of a definition of Reason. Remember that the Matter Itself was Reason. Now that the Matter Itself has been redefined as the Necessary, we have a new definition of Reason. Reason is now defined as the initiator and end of a necessary process of definition. But since that process involves mediation through a circle of circumstances, to use Hegel's terminology, Reason is the necessary initiator and end of that process of mediation. Reason is what it is *necessarily*, but what it is is determined through a circle of circumstances. Reason *must* be what it is, but what it is is determined through both the completed set of existing, defined items (Possibility), and the complete set of concepts or actualities of *types* or *kinds* that those items are (the set of Conditions, or Condition$_{AT}$). This Reason is the Necessary as the end of the process of necessity in two senses. First, it is the end of the process of necessity in the logical sense. The stages of the logic have driven us to the current definition of Reason. But the definition of Reason is also necessary as the end of a process in the world of experience—in the real world—that mirrors the logical one. The logical process of development outlines a process of development in the world of experience, at the end of which is also Reason. The set of existing, defined items (Possibility) and the set of types that those items are (the set of Conditions) will only be *completed* or *finished* at the end of time, when time itself is completed or finished. At the end of time, everything possible will have existed, and all of the types that they are will be finished. Hegel's point, then, is that, at the end of time, Reason will necessarily be what it is. Since the set of existing, defined items and the set of concepts that they are will be finished, the definition of Reason, too, will then be finished. There will be no further developments in the definition of Reason. Hence, Reason will *necessarily* be what it is—there will be nothing else that it can be. But what it is will have been mediated by the circle of circumstances made up of existing items and the types or kinds for those items.

These two senses in which Reason is the end of the process of necessity correspond to the ascending and descending series or processes, which have now been united as definitions of the Necessary or of Reason. Reason's presentation in individually existing things (the descending series) is part of the necessary conceptual process that defines Reason itself as the end of the whole presentation (the ascending series). The presentation of Reason in existence (the descending series) is part of the logical process of conceptual development (the ascending series) that defines the Reason as the Necessary end of both. The circumstances that the process of Reason goes through are both conceptual and existential. At the end of both the existential and conceptual necessary processes of Reason is Reason itself.

After this completed process of Reason, the necessity of Reason is no longer presupposed or stipulated. Because the circumstances are finished, Reason is necessarily whatever it is. Again, there can be no further developments in the definition of Reason after the circumstances have been finished. Reason is necessary here in the same way in which the Matter Itself was necessary in the stage of The Matter (*Sache*) Itself: when all the circumstances are completed, then Reason itself is necessarily generated and completed. Reason is therefore now defined as the Necessary end of the completed process of mediation by the circumstances.

Absolute Relationship

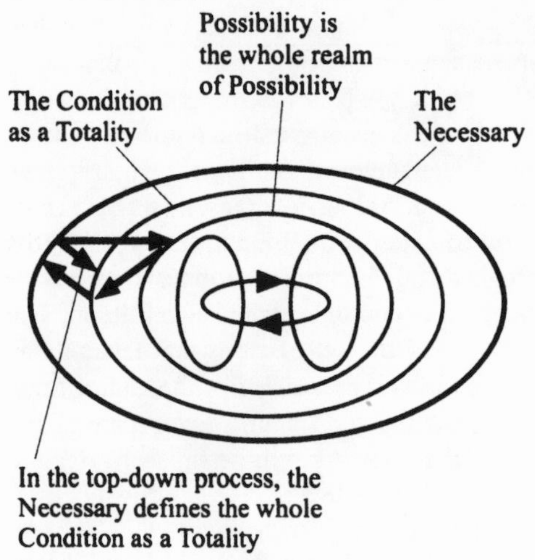

Figure 3.60

The Condition$_{AT}$ was defined as an immediate actuality that is something-contingent. Because it is an immediate actuality and something-contingent, it is not really an empty concept, separate from Possibility. The Condition$_{AT}$ is an actuality because it is the complete set of (possible) existing items (Outer) that (by chance) live up to (possible) identifying concepts (Inner). It is also a one or a something—an item—because the realm of Possibility is completed or finished, and so the Condition$_{AT}$ is completed and finished as well. But because the realm of Possibility is still given or there by chance, the Condition$_{AT}$ is immediate and contingent. Nevertheless, as an immediate actuality, the Condition$_{AT}$ contains Possibility. It is the thought of the completed set of types or kinds for items in the realm of Possibility. Because the Condition$_{AT}$ *contains* the whole realm of Possibility, I have put the bubble for Possibility back inside the bubble for the Condition$_{AT}$ in the diagram.

There is another logical element that we did not fully account for in the last stage, however. In particular, there is still the top-down process of necessity that runs from the Necessary (as the Matter Itself is now defined) to the Condition$_{AT}$. That is the process in which the Condition$_{AT}$ is defined as the presentation or form and content of the Necessary, and the Necessary is thereby defined as an element on its own account. The arrow representing this process has had a dashed and thinner line to illustrate the fact that it has not been logically active.

In this stage, the arrow becomes active once again, so I have returned it to its former status as a solid and thicker arrow in the diagram.

These two elements add to the definition of the Necessary. In the last stage, the Necessary was defined as the Necessary in the sense that it was the initiator and end of a process of Necessity. In this stage, the Necessary is defined as Necessary not only in terms of process or activity (i.e. form), but also in terms of its content. The Necessary becomes the One identifying essence of the (one whole) Condition$_{AT}$—which includes Possibility—by sublating (canceling and preserving) the process of mediation through the circumstances that we had in the last stage. First, the Necessary is now defined in relation to one element—the whole Condition$_{AT}$, which now once again contains Possibility. Second, in the top-down process of presentation that defines the Necessary as a separate element, the Necessary directly presents the whole Condition$_{AT}$, sublates the process of mediation that was in the last stage, and defines itself, to use Hegel's anthropomorphic language, as a new immediacy or whole. Because the Necessary presents the whole Condition$_{AT}$—including Possibility—the process of necessity in the last stage is reconceived as a process in which the Necessary uses the Condition$_{AT}$ along with Possibility to generate an independent definition *for itself*, which is to say, *through its own activity*. The Necessary is defined as a new, independent and immediate element that contains and directly presents the process of mediation in the whole Condition$_{AT}$. It is the defining concept or identity of the whole process of the Condition$_{AT}$. The Necessary uses the Condition$_{AT}$ (as its form or presentation) to generate a new, immediate, independent identity or essence for itself. As Hegel puts it, "the ground [Possibility] and the contingent condition [Condition$_{AT}$] is translated into immediacy" (§149). In the last stage, the Necessary was defined through a process of mediation through Possibility and the Condition$_{AT}$. Now, however, the Necessary is defined as the Necessary, immediate identity or essence without mediation. It is what it is as the Necessary not because it is mediated by a circle of circumstances, but rather because of what it is first. Since the Condition$_{AT}$ (and Possibility, which it contains) are now defined as nothing but the presentation of the Necessary itself, the nature of the Condition$_{AT}$ is determined (from the top down) by the Necessary. The Necessary brings about its presentation in the Condition$_{AT}$. The whole process is thus generated by the fact that the Necessary is a unity that includes the Condition$_{AT}$ (and Possibility). The Necessary's definition as the all-embracing One element or unity necessarily gives rise to the process of presentation on its own account. The Necessary *must necessarily* go through the process of presentation to have its definition as the all-embracing One unity or whole. Since the whole process grows out of the Necessary's own definition, which includes the Condition$_{AT}$ (and Possibility), the Condition$_{AT}$ is no longer an independent element that mediates the Necessary's process of definition. In going through the process, the Necessary is merely following out its own necessary process of definition as the all-embracing One unity by embracing and presenting the Condition$_{AT}$, which is just part of itself, or of its definition. As Hegel puts it, "it [the

Necessary] is so [i.e. necessary] *without mediation*—it is so because it is" (§149). As a result, the Necessary has become the unconditioned actuality that simply is (§149).

The diagram makes sense of the grammatical oddity contained in the phrase quoted above: "the ground and the contingent condition *is* [*wird*] translated into immediacy" (§149; emphasis added). Geraets, Suchting and Harris also note this grammatical oddity in their translation (Geraets et al. 1991, 225). Because there are apparently two items—the contingent condition *and* the ground—we would think that Hegel should have constructed his sentence using the plural form "are," rather than the singular "is." Hegel's use of the singular form of the verb—"is," rather than "are"—is thus an odd grammatical construction (for Geraets et al.'s discussion of this oddity, see note 29, p. 330, and p. xxvii). As I have argued, from a logical point of view, the contingent condition is the Condition$_{AT}$, and the term "ground" refers to the relationship of Ground between Inner and Outer, which defines Possibility. Because the ground is *inside* the Condition in the diagram, there really is only one item being translated into immediacy. The process of the Condition$_{AT}$—which contains Possibility—is translated into or becomes a new immediacy in the Necessary insofar as it is used by the Necessary to generate an independent identity or essence. Possibility is the content of and therefore belongs to the Condition$_{AT}$. Since the contingent condition and the ground both belong to the same one element, it is better to say, as Hegel does, that, in this process of the Necessary, the Condition$_{AT}$—and the ground which it contains—*is* translated into immediacy.

The Necessary or Reason is *unconditioned* in the sense suggested by Kant (see Chapter One, Section IV). Kant had defined reason as the faculty of the Unconditioned. The Necessary is unconditioned for three reasons. First, because its process of definition goes through all of the Conditions or actualities (i.e. the Condition$_{AT}$ along with the whole realm of Possibility), there are no further Conditions that it must embrace. The Necessary embraces all *possible* defining concepts (the Inner) and *every* instance that happens by chance (possibility) to be out there in reality (Outer). Because the Necessary contains all the Conditions within its definition process, it is not itself conditioned by anything. The diagram helps to illustrate this logical definition because it depicts the Necessary as a bubble that surrounds and embraces everything else, and outside of which there is nothing. Second, the Necessary is unconditioned in the sense that it is independent. It has its process of definition completely on its own. Since a "condition" is something that helps or points toward something else (see Condition), to say that the Necessary has no conditions outside of it is to say that there is nothing outside of it on which it might depend for its definition. It initiates the whole process in which it is defined. Third, because the process that the Necessary initiates is completed, the process is necessary, in the same way that the stitches in the completed sweater are necessary. It must go through the process to be what it is. The Necessary—or Reason—is therefore unconditioned, independent and Necessary.

Kant had conceived of Reason as filled up by existing items and the concepts that grasp those items (see Chapter One, Section IV). Hegel has offered a similar definition here. Reason is defined by both concepts (the Conditions and Inner) as well as the existing items out there that fill them up (Outer). Reason is an unconditioned *actuality*, which includes both all the possible concepts as well as all the existing items to which they are connected.

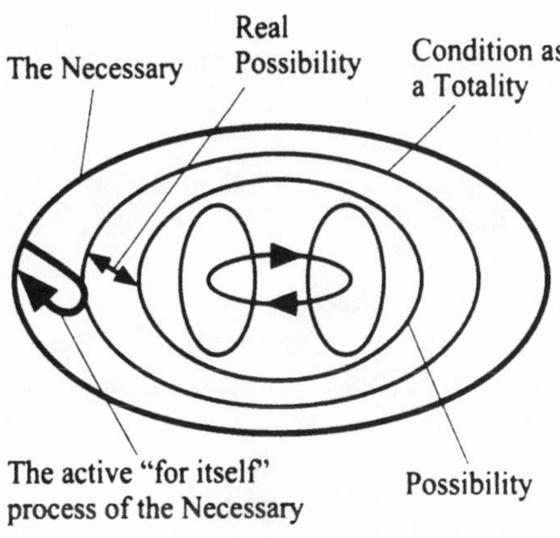

Figure 3.61

Now that the Necessary has been defined as an unconditioned actuality, not only does the definition of the Necessary change, but the relationship between the Necessary and the Condition_{AT} changes as well. When the Necessary was defined as the Matter Itself, the Necessary and the Condition_{AT} were defined as opposed to one another as separate elements. That relationship of opposition has been sublated (cancelled and preserved). Instead of a relationship of opposition, the Necessary now has an Absolute Relationship with the Condition_{AT}. The relationship between the Necessary and the Condition_{AT} is absolute for three reasons. First, the Necessary is an embracing, "for itself" concept that embraces its content (i.e. the Condition_{AT}) as a result of its own activity, that is to say, it embraces its content *for itself*. Of course, the Necessary has been defined as an embracing, "for itself" concept all along, which has been represented in the diagram by the fact that the Necessary (as the Matter Itself earlier) has been depicted as an overarching bubble surrounding the other elements. However, the Necessary is now *doubly* "for itself": it is a "for itself" embracing concept *for itself*—an embracing concept that is defined as an embracing concept through an active process that it initiated for itself or on its own. The Necessary or Matter-in-charge initiates the process through which it is defined as the all-embracing, Necessary Matter-in-charge. Indeed, to be defined as the Necessary all-embracing element, it *must* (necessarily) go through the activity of embracing and presenting everything. The Necessary is an active concept that is the source of both the bottom-up and the top-down processes that define it. It is defined by embracing everything (in the "for itself" sense) *for itself*, or through its own activity.

How should I represent these two layers of "for itselfness" in the diagram? Until now, I have depicted "for itselfness" in two ways: in a nested view, and in a side-by-side view. In the nested view, I represented "for itself" concepts as bubbles that surrounded the other element(s) as the content. In the side-by-side view, two elements were depicted next to one another, with a looping "for itself" arrow between them. The looping arrow illustrated the idea that, in the "for itself" relationship, the embracing element goes through the other element and then comes back to itself, insofar as the process of going through the second element ends up defining the first one as an embracing, "for itself" element. We have the same process here between the Necessary and the Condition$_{AT}$, except that here the "for itself" process is conceived of as the active process of presentation or form on the part of an element that is *already defined* as the embracing element. The Necessary, which is already the embracing element, actively *embraces* (content) and *presents* (form) the Condition$_{AT}$ through its own process. The Necessary is doubly "for itself": it is an embracing "for itself" concept or actuality that fulfills its definition by actively embracing the contents *for itself*, or through its own activity. To represent this double-layered "for itselfness," I will employ both diagrammatic strategies used so far to depict "for itselfness." The first layer of "for itselfness" is represented in the diagram by the fact that the Necessary is depicted as a bubble surrounding the Condition$_{AT}$. The second layer of "for itselfness" is depicted by a looping arrow that runs from the Necessary bubble to the Condition$_{AT}$ bubble, and then back to the Necessary bubble. (As before, the vertical direction of the arrow does not matter [i.e. whether it starts on top and ends on the bottom, or starts on the bottom and ends on top], only the horizontal direction matters, i.e. whether the arrow starts and ends on the left or right.) My use of the looping arrow to depict the active "for itself" process of the Necessary is appropriate not only because I have used the same sort of looping arrow before to depict "for itselfness," but also because I have used *arrows* to depict processes. The looping arrow here represents not only the second layer of "for itselfness" that the Necessary has in relation to the Condition$_{AT}$, but also the fact that this second layer of "for itselfness" is an active process or *activity* of the Necessary.

I have also put the arrow representing Real Possibility back between the Condition$_{AT}$ and Possibility. The relationship of Real Possibility was the process that redefined the Condition as the thought or concept of the complete set of Conditions, or as the Condition$_{AT}$ (see Condition as a Totality). When Condition$_{AT}$ and Possibility were split apart within the Necessary in the last stage, that relationship (and the arrow representing that relationship) dropped out of the picture. Now that the Condition$_{AT}$ has Possibility within it again, I have put the arrow for Real Possibility back into the diagram.

The relationship between the Necessary and the Condition$_{AT}$ is absolute for a second reason as well. Because the Necessary is the all-embracing, unconditioned concept, Absolute Relationship includes or embraces everything. It is therefore Absolute because it is the last relationship. Since the Necessary embraces everything and there are no further concepts outside of it, there will be no new relationships with any new concepts. The Necessary already has a relationship with all of the concepts that there are. So this relationship is the last, final, all-embracing relationship—i.e. it is the absolute one.

Third, Absolute Relationship is a relationship that is not really a relationship, or, at least, it is not a relationship in the usual sense. We ordinarily think of a relationship as a link between two independent items, but here the relationship is already an identity (cf. Identity). The Necessary already embraces (in the "for itself" sense) the Condition$_{AT}$—in the diagram the bubble for the Necessary surrounds the bubble for the Condition$_{AT}$. The Condition$_{AT}$ is the content of the Necessary insofar as it gives the Necessary its character or definition as the thought of the completed set of Conditions (i.e. the Condition$_{AT}$). But the Condition$_{AT}$ is also now the form of the Necessary insofar as it is the way in which the Necessary is presented. Condition$_{AT}$ is the content and the form of the Necessary. Thus, in Absolute Relationship, form and content have an absolute relationship not only "in itself" (when we look at how they relate to one another when they are each defined on their own) but also "for itself," as Hegel had promised they would (see §133R, and the stage of Content and Form). Form and content have an absolute relationship "in itself" because they characterize the same one element. Form is content and content is form because the Condition$_{AT}$ is both the form and the content of the Necessary. But the relationship of sameness between the form and content is also now a "for itself" relationship, which it was not before (cf. Form and Content). The sameness of form and content is the result of the "for itself" activity of the embracing, "for itself" concept. The Necessary actively defines the Condition$_{AT}$ as both the form and content. It embraces the Condition$_{AT}$ in its content and presents the Condition$_{AT}$ in an active "for itself" relationship as its form.

Absolute Relationship offers a more refined definition of Reason. Reason is now defined as the thought or concept that identifies *and presents* everything in the world of experience. The whole world of experience—both concept (Condition, Inner) and out-thereness (Outer)—is the presentation of Reason. Reason is the *essence* of the world of experience in the same way that Essence was the essence of the Shine (see Identity). Like Essence, Reason is the thought that grasps the character of the presentation, and, like Shine, the presentation is the way in which Reason shows up. But the type of showing-up that we have here is much more sophisticated than the type of showing-up we had earlier. Shine simply showed up, but Reason actively presents actuality and existence. Because Reason actively presents as actuality and existence, actuality and existence show up in a way that has been *shaped* or *sorted* by Reason itself. Reason is an independent, self-defining *system* of concepts and actual items that is necessarily presented in the world of experience. Everything in the contingent world of experience is now defined as shaped or sorted by Reason itself.

Immediate Substance and Substantiality

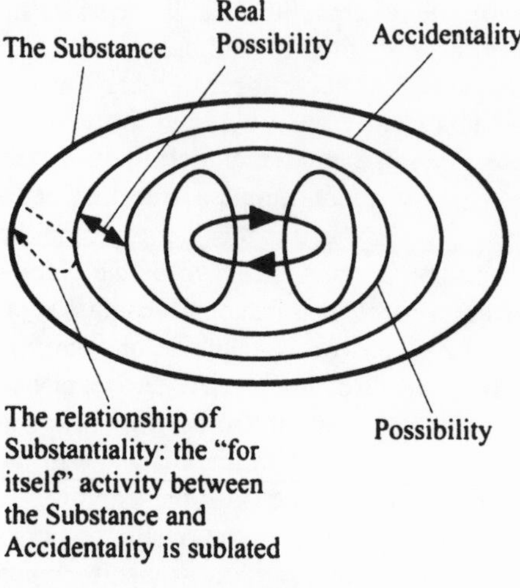

Figure 3.62

Absolute Relationship is not really a relationship. Because the Condition_{AT} is the content of the Necessary, the active "for itself" "relationship" in which the Necessary presents the Condition_{AT} does not link two independent items, but takes place completely within the Necessary itself. At the end of the "for itself" process is just the Necessary itself, now defined as a complete whole that is not only filled with content, but that actively presents the content *for itself*, or through its own activity. Since the process defines the Necessary as a self-contained whole process, the process itself is no longer active, however. The process is completely absorbed into the definition of the Necessary. The Necessary goes through the process and remains a self-contained whole. Thus, the "relationship" process has been sublated (cancelled and preserved). The relationship is preserved because the Necessary must go through the process to be what it is as the all-embracing whole; but the relationship is also cancelled, because the Necessary remains a self-contained whole. It therefore does not have a relationship with anything else in the ordinary sense. The relationship is there, but it also is not there, since, at the end of the process, the Necessary is just a whole that contains the whole process. The Necessary is the one essence that identifies *and presents* everything else. As Hegel puts it, the Necessary is "the developed process . . . in which relationship sublates itself equally into absolute identity" (§150). I have given the active, "for itself" relationship a dashed outline in the diagram to represent the fact that the relationship has been sublated within the definition of the Necessary itself.

The fact that the "for itself" relationship is sublated means the Necessary both *is* and *is not* the Condition_{AT}. Insofar as the relationship is cancelled, the Necessary is the whole that simply contains the Condition_{AT}. In that case, the Necessary *is* the Condition_{AT}. However, insofar as the relationship is preserved, so that the Necessary has a relationship with Condition_{AT}, the Condition_{AT} is the form or presentation of the Necessary. In that case, the Necessary is also *not* the Condition_{AT}. Insofar as the Necessary *presents* the Condition_{AT}, it is a separate element from the Condition_{AT}, and hence is *not* the Condition_{AT}. Hegel employed the same logical move in External Necessity. When the Condition_{AT} was defined as merely the presentation of the Matter Itself, the Matter Itself became an element separate from the Condition_{AT}. Similarly here, because the Condition_{AT}

is the (necessary) presentation of the Necessary, the Necessary is a separate element from the Condition$_{AT}$. As Hegel puts it, the Necessary is the "negativity" of the Condition$_{AT}$ (§151), a separate element on its own that (necessarily) posits, establishes or presents the Condition$_{AT}$. Insofar as the Condition$_{AT}$ is defined as the form or presentation of the Necessary, then, the Necessary is defined as a separate element from the Condition$_{AT}$.

The Condition$_{AT}$ is an immediate actuality. It is the whole realm of Possibility—the set of everything that exists by chance (Outer) and is covered by some possible concept (Inner)—now grasped and presented by the Necessary. The Condition$_{AT}$ is the whole realm of every possible actuality. Because the Condition$_{AT}$ is an immediate whole or one, it is a *something*, an item, that is characterized by possibility and chance. As Hegel puts it, it is "something-accidental" (§150). The Condition$_{AT}$ is something-accidental that is identified *and presented* by the Necessary as an immediate item. The Condition$_{AT}$ has become Accidentality. It is the whole realm of everything accidental. The completed realm of every contingent thing and the whole system of possible concepts is the whole realm of Accidentality.

Once the Condition$_{AT}$ has been redefined as Accidentality, the definition of the Necessary changes as well. Accidentality has two characteristics that alter the definition of the Necessary. First, Accidentality is an immediate something. An immediacy cannot be defined on its own. The definition of an immediacy can be fixed only by an essence that captures the identity of the immediacy and into which the immediacy passes over. At the end of the Doctrine of Being and the beginning of this chapter, for example, the realm of Being or the Shine (as the realm of Being was defined) can never be defined on its own. It can have its character or be defined only in relation to the Essence, which captures its identity, and into which the Shine passes over. Because Accidentality is an immediacy, the Necessary is the thought or essence that captures Accidentality's identity and into which Accidentality passes over. The Necessary was already defined as the essence or identity of the Condition$_{AT}$ in the last stage. What we do not see yet, however, is why Accidentality (as the Condition$_{AT}$ is now defined) must pass over into the Necessary, and how that passing over changes the definition of the Necessary.

Accidentality has a second characteristic that explains why it passes over. Accidentality is an immediate actuality that is defined by Possibility, because it still has Possibility in its contents and as its form. Accidentality is thus *an actual* possibility. A possibility can have its character as a possibility only by pointing toward another possibility that can serve as a genuine alternative for it, which means the second possibility is the same character or *kind* as the first possibility (see Contingency and Chance). Because Accidentality is an actuality, it must point toward another possibility that is also an actuality. Since Accidentality is an immediacy, that activity of "pointing toward" will be an activity of passing over. Accidentality must pass over into another actuality that is the *kind* that Accidentality is. Since Accidentality passes over into the Necessary, the Necessary is the kind that Accidentality is, insofar as the Necessary is the essence or identity of Accidentality. But the Necessary must also be the same kind as Accidentality insofar as Accidentality is an *actuality*. It must therefore be the identity of Accidentality that *is also an actuality*. The Necessary is an actuality insofar as it is an identity that also *presents into* Accidentality. Hence, the Necessary has become a *substantial* identity—the essence or identity of Accidentality that is also *an actuality*. The Necessary is an identity that is now not only the Matter Itself as a thought or concept, but is also the *substance*-of-the-matter that, as an actuality, presents and identifies Accidentality. The Necessary has become the Substance of Accidentality.

In ordinary English, the word "substance" generally refers to some chunk of thereness. We might say, for example, that there was some sticky "substance" on the bottom of someone's shoe, where we mean that there was some chunk of sticky stuff on the shoe. The word "substance" often indicates that the chunk of stuff is not well defined—there is some sticky substance on the bottom of the shoe, but the nature of the substance is not yet defined. Still, our ordinary concept of substance generally picks out a thereness. But this is not what Hegel means by "substance." His Substance is a kind of thought. It is the subject-matter-itself, the substance-of-the-matter or thought that identifies and presents all of accidental actuality. Of course, Substance is *actual* in the sense that it contains and presents actuality, which includes thereness, but Substance does not directly have thereness itself.

Hegel says that Substance has both a finite and infinite sense (§153R). A finite conception of substance would be one that defines Substance as limited. Having a limit is the hallmark of the finite world or reality (see Limit and Being-in-itself in Chapter Two). Such a definition of Substance would also be finite in the sense that it would apply only to items in the finite world. The 17th century empiricist philosopher John Locke, for example, defined substance as the (invisible, "I know not what") substratum of all the accidents, where "accidents" are all of the properties of something (see *An Essay Concerning Human Understanding*, Book II, Chapter XXIII, §2). If we take away all the properties of an individual thing, then what is left is the substance, the whatever-it-is in the background that holds all those properties or accidents together. Because *all* of the properties are accidents, the substance itself does not have any properties. That is why Locke held that we cannot say what the substance is like. The substance is merely the whatever-it-is that holds or contains the properties. Locke's definition of "substance" is finite in Hegel's sense because it treats substance as limited by and opposed to the accidents. The substance is *not* the accidents. The substance is whatever is left over (i.e. what is *not* the accidents) when the accidents are taken away. This definition of the substance sees the substance as limited by the accidents. When the substance and accidents are defined as opposed to one another, the concept of substance is a finite one that applies only to the world of finite things (see §153R), rather than to the infinite realm of thought or ideality (see Being-for-itself in Chapter Two for an explanation of ideality).

An infinite account of substance, however, defines a substance as an ideal, a *universal*—a "for itself" concept or thought that embraces and presents the whole realm of Accidentality. Against Locke, Hegel would say that we know very well what substance is like, because its definition embraces or includes everything in its presentation. Substance is what it is on its own account, as Locke had said, but it *also* is what it is by embracing and presenting the world of experience. The definition of the Substance includes Accidentality. A properly ideal or infinite account of Substance treats Accidentality as belonging to the Substance, rather than as merely opposed to the Substance. It defines Substance as a "for itself" concept or ideal that embraces and presents the accidents.

Hegel's Substance is logically infinite for several reasons. First, Substance is logically infinite as a "for itself" concept in the same way that Being-for-itself was infinite in Chapter Two: Substance is an ideal, a unifying concept that embraces (in the "for itself" sense) the elements in relation to which it is defined. This "for itselfness" of content is portrayed in the diagram insofar as Substance is a bubble that surrounds and contains the bubble for Accidentality. Actually, Substance achieves a higher level of ideality than did Being-for-itself because it is an *essence*. Like Essence, Substance is a concept of other concepts. It is the thought or concept of the *essence* or *identity* of the accidents, which are Conditions, and so are themselves concepts.

Second, however, Substance achieves its "for itself" status *for itself*, or in virtue of its own logical activity. It is doubly for itself: it embraces its contents (in the "for itself" sense) and *presents* its contents *for itself*, or through its own activity. Substance is thus "for itself" both in terms of identity (content) and in terms of presentation (form). Substance is an essence or thought that identifies *and presents* the whole realm of Accidentality. It must present Accidentality to be what it is or have its definition or contents. It can be what it is on its own account (as "negativity" [§§150, 151]) as the essence or identity of Accidentality only by (necessarily) presenting everything in Accidentality. Substance not only identifies Accidentality but also *determines* Accidentality. Substance determines Accidentality in two senses. In one sense, to determine something is to characterize it or identify it. Substance determines Accidentality in this sense because it identifies Accidentality. But it identifies Accidentality only insofar as, and *because*, it determines Accidentality in a second sense. In another sense, to determine something is to *give it its identity*, to *make* something what it is (cf. Inner and Outer). Substance determines Accidentality in this second sense because it presents Accidentality. Thus Substance has Accidentality as its content (i.e. identifies Accidentality) only insofar as, and because, it has Accidentality as its form (i.e. makes Accidentality what it is, presents it, pushes it out). The content of Substance (i.e. Accidentality) is also the presentation or manifestation of Substance as well (§151). Thus, in the activity of the Substance—which is Substantiality—form and content overturn into one another absolutely (§151). The Substance is the self-contained whole that presents (form) its contents to be defined (have a content) and that has a content (is defined) by presenting (form) its content. In pictorial terms, it is an active whole that embraces and presents all the other bubbles, which represent the whole realm of Accidentality. As Hegel suggests, Substance as such—infinite Substance, as a whole that includes or embraces all of its contents—is the *absolute* identity of Accidentality (§150R).

The stage of Substance defines Reason as the all-embracing, overarching conceptual system that both identifies and presents the whole world of accidents. Because Reason is *presenting* the realm of accidents, those accidents are shaped by Reason. This world is what it is as a possibility because the Substance or Reason not only identifies it, but also *makes it what it is* or identifies it in the stronger sense of giving it its character. Everything in the world has some identity or other that is given to it—in both a passive and active sense—by Reason. Reason is the simple substance of the matter that passively identifies and actively defines the whole process of the world of experience. Substance is the thought of Reason and its completed *expression* in the world of experience at the end of time.

Although Substance belongs to the side of thought or concept, it is not merely thought. We often think of Reason and concepts as mere thoughts, or as merely inward, to use Hegel's terminology (§150R). But Reason is an actuality. Like Actuality, which is the unity of Inner and Outer, Reason has outerness or is external, as well as inwardness. Reason is external insofar as it *presents* the realm of Accidentality. However, Reason as Substance is also the negativity of that external side. It is something on its own account, apart from the realm of accidents, that *presents* the accidents. Insofar as it is something on its own that merely presents the accidents, Reason is the power or *might* (§151) over the accidents. Reason is the substance-of-the-matter that actively presents and rationalizes the whole realm of accidental actuality. Thus Reason—as the Substance—is both the "*richness of all content*" as well as "the *absolute might*" over the totality of the accidents (§151). Reason identifies the whole world of experience, but it also presents the whole world of experience, or makes experience what it is. Reason, as an organized system of concepts, *determines* the nature of the world of experience.

Substance as Cause

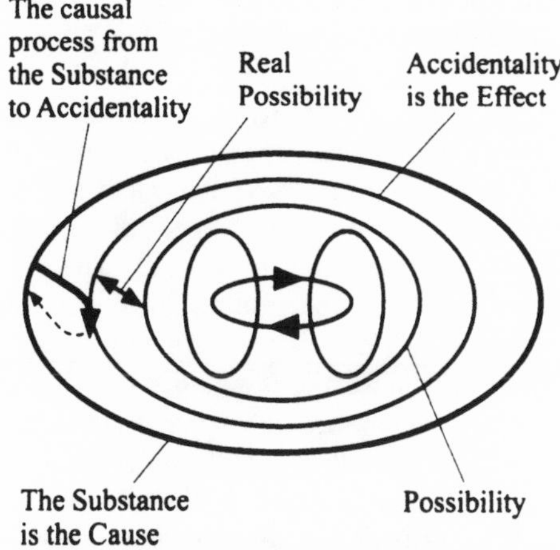

Figure 3.63

So far, Substance has been defined as the whole, simple, outermost bubble that has Accidentality as its content and form or presentation. In this first form, as Hegel puts it, "substance is substance" (§152). Substance is what it is as the inwardly active but also whole Substance. As we saw, however, to say that Substance has Accidentality as its presentation also implies that Substance is a *separate element* from Accidentality that *presents* Accidentality. Insofar as Substance presents Accidentality, it determines Accidentality in the second sense we saw above—it makes Accidentality what it is. This is the sense in which the Substance can be what it is as the identity of Accidentality only by being the power or might over Accidentality (§152). Since this definition of the Substance treats Substance and Accidentality as separate items, it once again conceives of them as having a relationship (§152). We must now explore the nature of this relationship more precisely. The sort of relationship that Substance will have with Accidentality is a causal one that redefines Substance as Cause, and the power or might that Substance has over Accidentality is causality.

Substance can have its character or be what it is as the all-embracing, necessary element only by going through the process of presenting Accidentality. This logical conclusion grew out of the development of the Necessary and of Substance. There is now a second, logical reason, however, why Substance can be what it is only by presenting Accidentality—a reason that grows out of the last stage. Because Substance is an actuality that *embraces* all of its contents, it embraces Possibility. Its content or character as a concept—its inwardness—is therefore defined by possibility. Like other possibilities, it can have its character or inwardness as possibility only by producing another possibility that can serve as a genuine alternative for it. Substance fulfills its own character as a possibility by determining—in the sense of producing—Accidentality. As Hegel puts it, Substance "is the might that *relates itself to itself* as merely inner possibility, and hence determines itself to accidentality" (§152). Because Substance is an inner that is defined by possibility (or is inwardly defined by possibility), it determines or defines itself through Accidentality, which, as the contents of Substance, means that Substance is really relating itself to itself. Substance sublates its mere possibility by positing Accidentality (§153). Because the Substance can be what it is as the identity of Accidentality and as a possibility only by positing or producing Accidentality, the process of positing or producing Accidentality is logically necessary. (I will explain in the next stage why Accidentality can serve as a genuine alternative for Substance, or why Accidentality is the same kind of thing that Substance is.)

In the relationship between Substance and Accidentality, it seems as if the Substance has all of the content, and Accidentality has become an empty concept. First, Substance already includes Accidentality in its content, and so has Accidentality as its definition or character. Substance is, as Hegel puts it, "inwardly reflected" (§153). It contains Accidentality as its inwardness. The diagram depicts this logical feature because the bubble representing Substance has the bubble for Accidentality inside it. Moreover, Substance is defined by possibility—it is defined by embracing Possibility. This feature is also depicted in the diagram because the Possibility bubble is also inside the Substance bubble. Because Possibility and its contents are now taken to belong directly to Substance, it is as if Accidentality has no content. Of course, Possibility is the content of Accidentality too—in the diagram, it is literally inside Accidentality—but since Possibility belongs to Substance, then it is as if Accidentality has nothing in it. Because Substance contains Accidentality *and* Possibility, it is the element that has the content or character, not Accidentality.

Since the Substance has the character or inwardness, it is the originating element. It is the element that originates and defines everything else. Moreover, since the Substance posits or produces Accidentality, we can also say that the Substance has the character or inwardness that is expressed or externalized as Accidentality when Substance posits or produces Accidentality. Because Accidentality already belongs to the content of the Substance (it is inside the Substance), however, when the Substance passes over or externalizes into Accidentality, it is not really passing over. Producing Accidentality is merely the Substance's way of being inwardly reflected or reflecting its content or character. Accidentality *is already* the content of Substance, so when the Substance produces or posits Accidentality, the Substance is really just positing *itself* in a negative form, or positing the negative of itself (§153).

Because the Substance's process of producing Accidentality is *necessary*, the Substance is the Cause, which undergoes its necessary activity and produces or posits Accidentality as its Effect. The Effect is Accidental, rather than necessary, because it is still defined by possibility in relation to the Cause. Without that Cause, there would be no Effect. However, the causal process itself *is* necessary (§153), because it is logically implied by the definition of Substance.

According to this stage, Reason determines or causes the nature of the concepts and items in Accidentality. Take the legal concept of property—an example that Hegel apparently used in a lecture, although he used it to make a slightly different point that I will come back to shortly (§160A). If the legal concept of property is an example of one of the categories or concepts of Accidentality, Reason causes or shapes the concept of property by systematizing it in relation to other concepts. Reason's process of systematization distinguishes the concept of property from other categories and causes the concept of property to come to have a certain definition. For example, "property" is systematized in relation to "public domain" and "the commons," for instance. Insofar as the concepts of Accidentality are defined or determined by Reason's process of systematization, they are nothing but the Effect of Reason's causal process.

The concept of cause that Hegel outlines captures the characteristics we ordinarily associate with the concept of cause. First, a cause is something that actualizes itself when it brings about the effect. A cause is not an actual cause without bringing about an effect. When a cause brings about its effect, then, it also brings about itself. Since a cause is not really a cause without an effect, the effect is the culmination of the cause's own definition. The Substance is a cause because it can be what it is as a possibility only by producing another possibility that can serve as a genuine alternative for it, namely, Accidentality. Second, in traditional Western philosophy, the causal process is typically regarded as necessary: a cause necessarily causes its effect. Hegel's Cause includes this second element as well. Finally, even though the causal process is necessary, there is still a sense in which the effect is accidental. The cause can be actual only by producing the effect, but the effect is still accidental in the sense that it is still characterized by possibility. The effect, while actual, was only a possible effect because, without that cause, there would not have been that effect.

Because Hegel's Cause grows out of his concept of Substance, his Cause belongs to thought, rather than to thereness or Being. Cause is the overarching, all-embracing Rationality that is the causal power over all of accidental actuality (Accidentality), which is therefore the effect. Cause is the system of Reason that actualizes itself in the realm of Accidentality, which is its effect. This definition of Cause allows Hegel to solve the puzzle over the concept of cause that was introduced by the eighteenth century British philosopher, David Hume—a puzzle that Kant had tried to correct with his own philosophy (see Chapter One, Section I). Hume had argued that the concept of cause is not justified by experience and reason because we never experience any necessary connection between a cause and effect. Hegel's concept of Cause suggests that Hume is right that Cause is not itself in the world of thereness or experience. Although Cause expresses itself in thereness—through its effect—it does not itself have thereness. That is why we cannot experience Cause directly with our senses, as Hume had shown. However, Kant was wrong, for Hegel, to propose that we can rescue the concept of cause from Hume's skepticism only by limiting cause to our heads. Kant had suggested that, since we cannot find cause in the world of experience, it must be a concept that belongs only to us, to our rationality. The concept of cause belongs to the filter, Kant had suggested, through which we rational beings experience the world. Cause is therefore something we add to the world. For Hegel, by contrast, Cause is in the world itself. Cause is thought, reason, which is in the world because the world itself is rational (see Chapter One, Sections I and II). Cause is out there in the world of experience insofar as the world itself is rational. Hume could not find cause in the world because he was looking for the wrong kind of thing. Hume was looking for cause as thereness, but no such thereness can be found, as Hume had argued. For Hegel, however, Hume's argument only shows that Cause is not in the world as thereness. Cause is in the world, but it is in the world as thought. For Hegel, Cause is thought or reason that has actuality, and hence out-thereness, through its effect on accidental actuality.

As he does for the concept of Substance, Hegel distinguishes between a finite conception of cause and an infinite conception of cause. A finite conception of cause treats cause and effect as opposed to one another, so that the cause is limited by the effect, whereas an infinite conception of cause treats the effect as embraced by the cause (in the "for itself" sense). According to the infinite conception of cause, the production of the effect does not erase the presence of the cause (§153R). Since the cause embraces or includes the effect in its definition, the effect is the fulfillment of the cause's own definition or character. Everything in the world of experience is identified by some rational concept or other because Reason—now defined as the whole, completed process at the end of time—produces all of the possible identities and kinds in the world of experience. Because the Cause presents or produces the Effect, it has its own character as the Cause (i.e. in an "in itself" sense) through its own activity. It is *causa sui* or the cause-of-itself in an "in itself" sense. Moreover, because the process in which the Cause presents the Effect is an active "for itself" process, the Cause is also *causa sui* or cause-of-itself in a "for itself" sense as well. As Hegel puts it, "[i]n and for itself therefore the cause is *causa sui*" (§153R).

Under the infinite conception of cause, not only is the Cause *causa sui*, but there is also nothing in the Effect that is not in the Cause. Cause and Effect share the same content because the content of the cause embraces and includes the effect. As Hegel puts it, "there is no content in the effect that is not in the cause" (§153R). Substance (as the Cause was defined in the last stage) contains everything in Accidentality (as the Effect was defined in the last stage). Now that Reason is defined as the thought that embraces the whole, completed presentation of rational concepts and items in the world of accidents, there is nothing in the realm of accidents that Reason, so defined, does not already embrace. Since Reason is the whole process of presentation, there is nothing in accidentality that it leaves out. The conclusion that there is no content in the Effect that is not also in the Cause is an important moment in Hegel's idealism. It shows, for Hegel, that there is nothing in the realm of Accidentality that cannot in principle be grasped by Reason. This conclusion is justified logically by the claim that Reason *contains and presents* the whole realm of accidents.

The Effect, for its part, is still the form/content of the Cause (just as Accidentality [which is now the Effect] was the form/content of Substance [which is now the Cause]). Since a cause cannot be a cause without an effect, the Cause presents its character as a cause through the Effect. The Effect is the way in which the Cause is a Cause (the form). The Effect is also the content of the Cause. It is the fulfillment of the Cause's nature or the nature or identity of the Cause showing forth. The diagram depicts this element well, since the Effect is inside the Cause and so is, literally the content of the Cause. In more Hegelian terms, the Effect is the inward self-reflection of the Cause: it is just the Cause showing or reflecting its (inward) content, definition or nature (§153R).

In the finite conception of cause, the cause and effect are treated as opposed to one another, so that the cause vanishes when the effect shows up. Hegel gives the example of rain (as cause) and wetness on the ground (as effect). As soon as the wetness on the ground shows up, then the rain is not there anymore. Even for finite cause, however, while it is true that the rain is not the same as the wetness on the ground, the cause and effect share the same content, namely the same existing water. The specific definition of the cause is lost in the effect because the form of the water changes. The cause is rain, which is a specific form of the wetness (water falling from the sky), while the effect is water on the ground, which is a different form of wetness. Nevertheless, the content remains the same from one form to the other, namely, the existing water itself (§153R). While the specific definition of the cause is lost in the effect, the specific definition of the effect is also *dependent* on the cause. The wetness on the ground can only have its specific definition as wetness *on the ground* if there is some other form of wetness, namely, wetness falling from the sky or rain. Without the cause, there is "only the undifferentiated wetness" (§153R), or wetness that is not specified, or has no further character as any form or kind of wetness or other.

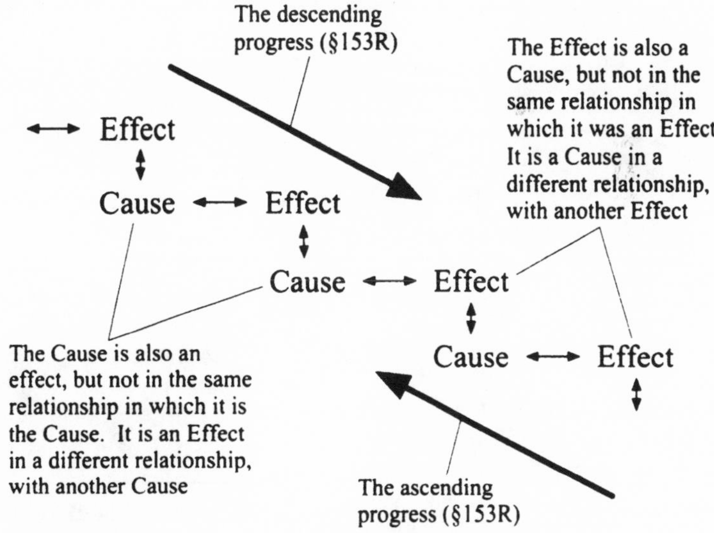

Figure 3.64

Finite and infinite cause are distinguished, not by the content of the causal relationship, but by the form of the causal relationship. In finite cause, the form of the cause and effect are distinct. The cause and the effect are presented in different relationships. Although cause and effect are the same in terms of their content in the finite world, they take different forms, so that something can be only one or the other (cause or effect) in any one relationship. The same water is the cause when it has the form of rain and the effect when it has the form of wetness on the ground. The rain is an effect too, but in the finite world it can be the effect only in a different relationship from the one in which it is the cause. The rain is the effect in a relationship with water in the form of cloud, for instance, not in the form of wetness on the ground. Because the form of cause and effect are distinct from one another in the finite world, the finite conception of cause generates a spuriously infinite progress (see Spurious Infinity), rather than a genuinely infinite progress. The diagram above depicts a genuine infinity, which is associated with "for itself" embracing relationships (see Being-for-itself). A spurious infinity is an endless, linear progression. Finite cause produces both a descending and an ascending, spuriously infinite process. The ascending process goes up the chain of causes: something that is a cause in one relationship is also an effect in another relationship, and so has a cause, which has another effect, and so on. The descending progress goes down the chain of effects: an effect in one relationship is also a cause in another, and so has an effect, and so on forever (§153R).

The Effect as a Substance

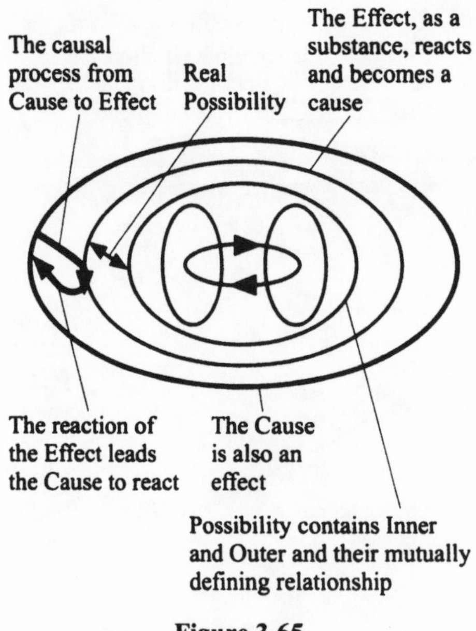

Figure 3.65

While the Effect is the content and presentation (form) of the Cause, it is not exactly the same as the Cause. According to the causal relationship, the Cause is what does the positing, and the Effect is what is posited. Hence the Effect is separate from the Cause insofar as it is defined by positedness (§154), while the Cause is not.

The Cause gets to be a genuine possibility when it produces Accidentality, which must be able to serve as a genuine alternative for the Cause. In the last stage, Accidentality—now the Effect—was an empty concept, because Possibility to belonged to the Substance or Cause. Accidentality is not really an empty concept, however. It is an immediacy or given, whole item (see the stage of The Necessary) that has its own character, content or inward reflection (§154). In particular, it is an actuality. It is a complete whole that contains Possibility. In the diagram, the bubble for the Effect contains the bubble for Possibility and its contents. The Possibility bubble belongs to the Effect as well as the Cause. It is the content of the Effect. Possibility includes Inner and Outer and their mutually defining relationship, which is how Actuality was defined earlier. The Effect is thus an actuality because it embraces or identifies the whole (immediate or given) realm of actuality. Because the Effect is posited or produced by the Cause, however, it is not an independent actuality. It is a posited actuality (§153), or an actuality that is established by something else, namely, by the Cause. Nevertheless, the Effect can serve as a genuine alternative for the Cause because they are the same kind of thing: actualities defined by Possibility.

Moreover, while the Effect is the product of the Cause, it is not *merely* the product of the Cause. It has a subsistence of its own. In the last stage, the Cause was defined as the originating and all-embracing element over the whole causal process: the Cause produced the Effect, which was nothing but the content and presentation of the Cause itself. But we cannot really look at this causal activity one-sidedly in this way (§153R), as if the Cause can stand alone. After all, the Cause cannot be what it is without the Effect. The fact that the Cause produces *itself* through the Effect implies that the Effect produces the Cause too. Until the Effect shows up, the Cause is not really a cause, so the Effect's showing up produces the Cause too. Hence the Cause cannot be a Cause by itself alone. Thus, to say that something is a cause both *implies* and *presupposes* the effect (§154). Since a cause cannot be a cause without the effect, to say that something is a cause is therefore to say at the same time—to presuppose—that there is an effect. Calling something a cause presupposes that the effect will show up. That the Effect is presupposed in this way logically implies that it can stand on its own, or has subsistence and identity by itself, without the intercession of the Cause. And indeed, the Effect does have identity and subsistence on its own, since it has its own content and definition in Possibility.

This content gives the Effect another characteristic that defines it as the same kind of thing as the Cause and allows it to serve as a genuine alternative for the Cause. Just as the Cause is defined as a substance (see the stages of Immediate Substance and Substance as Cause), the Effect has three characteristics that now define it as a substance as well. First, the Effect is an essence that is also an actuality. The Effect is an essence because it is a "for itself" concept that identifies and embraces the whole realm of Possibility (cf. Identity). The Effect is an actuality because it is defined by Possibility, which contains Inner and Outer and their mutually defining relationship, which is the definition of Actuality. It is also an actuality because it is a concept that is presented and has subsistence on its own. The Effect is a concept with subsistence—a substance. Second, the Effect is defined in such a way that form and content overturn into one another. Possibility is both the content and form or presentation of the Effect. Third, when we look at the Cause and Effect as separate elements, the Effect has the character of being an essence, a substance-of-the-matter, into which something else passes over. Because the Cause cannot be a cause without the Effect, the Cause must pass over into the Effect. Of course, the Cause does not really pass over, just as Accidentality did not really pass over into Substance earlier. Because the Substance contained Accidentality as its content, when Accidentality, as an immediacy, was grasped by the Substance, it did not pass over into a completely separate element. Similarly, here, because the Cause contains the Effect, when the Cause produces the Effect, it does not pass over into a completely separate element. Nevertheless, the Effect is a substance-of-the-matter into which the Cause passes over. Moreover, because the Effect is presupposed by the Cause, there is a sense in which the Effect is already there. Hence the Effect is the presupposed substance on which the Cause happens to work (§154). When the Cause produces the Effect, then, it is working on another substance that is already there (or is presupposed). Work is an activity characterized by sublation (canceling and preserving). Because the Cause presupposes the Effect, the Effect is already there. The Cause preserves the Effect because the Effect is still there when the Cause is finished with it, but the Cause also cancels the Effect in the sense that its activity *changes* the presupposed Effect. The Cause does not produce the Effect from scratch—it sublates or changes the presupposed Effect through work.

I have given three logical reasons for why the Effect is now defined as a substance. There is a fourth. The Effect's character as a substance also follows logically from the fact that the Cause can be what it is as a possibility only by producing another possibility that is a genuine alternative for it. Something can be a genuine alternative for something else only if both items are of the same kind. Since the Cause is a substance, the Effect can be a genuine alternative for the Cause only if it, too, is a substance. For this reason too, then, the Effect must now be defined as a substance.

Although the Effect is a substance, it is still defined as immediate. It is the thought of the given realm of Accidentality, the complete and completed set of accidents that happen that is identified and presented by the Cause.

Moreover, the Effect is not the same sort of substance that the Cause is. Hegel says that the Effect is not "a negativity relating itself to itself" (§154). The Cause is a negativity that relates itself to itself because it is a doubly "for itself" concept: a "for itself" concept that embraces its contents *for itself*, or through its own activity of presenting the contents. It's because the Cause actively *presents* its contents that it is defined as an element separate from its contents, i.e. as a negativity (cf. External Necessity, Immediate Substance and Substance as Cause). Because its content is nothing but itself, however, the Cause is a negativity that (by its own activity) relates itself to itself. The Effect is not that kind of substance, however. The Effect is a "for itself" concept, but it is not doubly "for itself." The Effect embraces its contents—in the diagram it is a bubble that surrounds the Possibility bubble as its contents—but it is not connected to its contents through an active "for itself" relationship. As the diagram suggests, the Effect is connected to its contents with a double-sided arrow—the arrow of Real Possibility—rather than through the sort of looping arrow that I have been using to represent "for itself" activity. The Effect is a "for itself" embracing concept, but it is not a "for itself" embracing concept that presents its content *for itself*, or through its own activity. It is not doubly "for itself." Because it does not *present* its contents, it is not defined as a separate element from its contents or as a negativity. Hence it is not a negativity that relates itself to itself, as Hegel says. Because the Effect is not active "for itself," it is passive in relation to the Cause.

Nevertheless, because the Effect has activity in relation to its contents—activity represented by the double-sided arrow of Real Possibility—when the Cause acts or works on it, the Effect *reacts* (§154). Remember that the Effect was initially presupposed in relation to the Cause—the nature of the Cause as a cause presupposed that the Effect will be what it is, i.e. an effect. As soon as the Effect reacts, however, the Effect sublates (cancels and preserves) the presupposed immediacy that it had in relation to the Cause. The reaction of the Effect *cancels* the presupposed immediacy of the Cause because it comes to have a new character that is not yet grasped by the Cause. The reaction also *preserves* the character of the Cause, however, because, insofar as the Effect reacts to the action Cause, it still fulfills and preserves the Cause's definition as a cause. The Cause is still the cause that caused the reaction.

Because the Effect has something new about it, however, it has an immediacy in relation to the Cause. The Cause must therefore work on the Effect to sublate the new immediacy in the Effect that it produced. The Cause *reacts* (I will say more about how the Cause reacts in a moment). Because the Effect produces a reaction in the Cause, the Effect is now a cause in relation to the Cause, which is an effect.

In the property example from the last stage, Reason's process of systematization gives the legal concept of property a certain definition in relation to all the other concepts. The trouble for Reason is that the concept of property is not an empty concept. It is itself an active concept that is defined not only from the top-down—by Reason's organizing activity—but also from the bottom-up by the concepts, processes and existences that it embraces. Rational concepts such as the concept of property are shaped by Reason, but they are also substances that have a life of their own—a life given to them by the elements and processes that they embrace. The concept of property is defined by the process of things that happen in the actual world. When devices were invented to record music, for example, music could be commodified or made into property not only by writing it down as sheet music, but also by recording the sounds themselves. What counted as "property" for music was changed by something that happened in the actual world. More recently, the invention of rap music has once again affected the definition of "property" for music, when it raised questions about whether pieces of recorded sound or "samples" of other people's music were infringements of someone else's "property." Reason's process of systematization—Reason as a Cause—must react and take account of events in the actual world that define the concepts that it works on. It must draw these events into its process of systematization. Because Reason has to react to changes in rational concepts resulting from activity in the actual world, Reason is not just a Cause, but also an effect in relation to the system of concepts that it embraces and systematizes. Integrating rap music samples as a type of property into the system of concepts shapes Reason itself.

Transition to Reciprocal Action

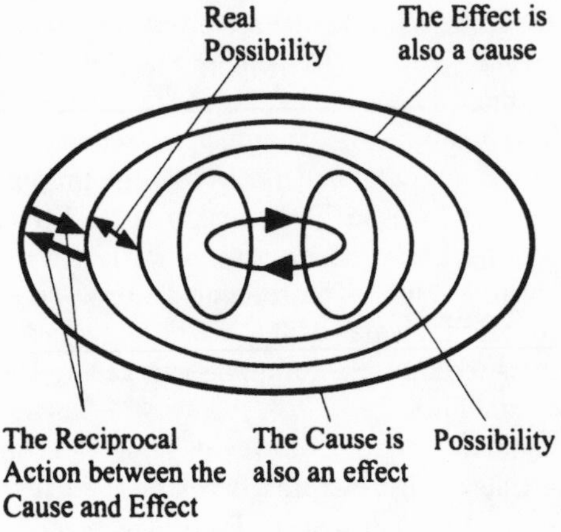

Figure 3.66

The Cause must work on the Effect to sublate the immediacy that the Effect developed in reaction to the Cause. The Cause sublates (cancels and preserves) the immediacy in the Effect by reacting. The reaction *preserves* the immediacy of the Effect insofar as it implies that there was indeed some new immediacy in the Effect. But the reaction also *cancels* the immediacy in the Effect because, after the Cause reacts to the Effect, the Effect is no longer immediate in relation to the Cause.

The Cause reacts to the reaction of the Effect by *working on* the Effect. The Effect has an immediacy. An immediacy is a given something that can be what it is or can have its character only by being grasped or identified by a concept (see Transition to Essence in Chapter Two). When the Effect reacts to the original causal activity of the Cause, it comes to have some immediacy about it that the Cause has not yet grasped or identified. Because the Cause is defined as the whole process of the Effect, however, it must react to that new immediacy. The Cause cannot have its definition as the element that grasps and presents the whole Effect unless it grasps everything about the Effect. So long as the Effect has something immediate about it that the Cause has not yet grasped, then the Cause would not be living up to its definition as what grasps and presents the whole process of the Effect. Hence, the Cause *must* react. The Cause reacts by grasping or identifying the newness within the Effect and by *presenting* that newness. As before, the Cause's activity of *presenting* the newness is *causal*. Therefore, the Cause reacts by causing the Effect once again, or making the Effect what it is. As soon as the Cause *causes* the Effect once again, however, the Effect reacts, which will cause the Cause to react again, and so on. The original causal action of the Cause and the subsequent reaction of the Effect thus triggers a back-and-forth process of Reciprocal Action between the Cause and the Effect.

Notice that the back-and-forth process of Reciprocal Action involves two "in itself" processes of definition. The Cause is what it is by passing into the Effect: the Effect must show up for the Cause to be a Cause. The Effect is what it is by passing into the Cause: the Effect can be an effect only as the effect of the Cause. Thus each can have its definition on its own only by passing into the other side. Cause and Effect also have an "in itself" connection insofar as they are opposed to or "other than" one another, too. This is the same process of definition that defined Being-in-itself in Chapter Two. Their activity of mutual causation is thus made up of two back-and-forth "in itself" processes. The relationship between the Cause and Effect has changed. Instead of the one, "for itself" relationship between the Cause and Effect, there is a two-way process of Reciprocal Action. I have replaced the "for itself" arrow with two straight-lined arrows representing those "in itself" processes in the diagram.

Take the legal concept of property once again, for instance. Events that happen in the actual world affect the concept of property and force Reason to work to re-systematize and hence define or cause the concept of property once again. The concept of property that comes out of Reason's systematization process is then used or applied to define legal decisions in the actual world. As Hegel himself apparently remarked in a lecture, we "do speak of the 'deduction' of a content from its concept, for instance, of the deduction of legal determinations pertaining to property from the concept of property" (§160A). Reason's process of systematizing the concept of property into the scheme of rational concepts, however, redefines the concept of property once again, which will then contain new activity that Reason will once again have to work to integrate it into the conceptual scheme. We end up with a process of Reciprocal Action between Reason, on the one side, and, on the other side, the system of rational concepts and the activity that they embrace (the Effect).

Although the Effect is full of activity, only some activity in the Effect will cause the Cause to react. In particular, only those activities that create an immediacy in the Effect in relation to the Cause will force a reaction on the part of the Cause. Again, an immediacy is an item or element that has not yet been identified. Computer programs, for example, qualified as an immediacy at one time because they were a new invention whose impact on the system of rational concepts had not yet been fully integrated. They remain an immediacy in relation to Reason until they are integrated into all of the rational concepts or categories that could possibly grasp them. Many other sorts of changes in the world of accidents, however, will not require shifts in Reason. When a new house is built where an old house burned down, for example, that change will not require any shifts in the concept of property and hence in the system of Reason. The concept of property does not have to be updated every time this or that house comes into or out of existence. Concepts are already defined by Hegel in a way that includes negation, or the comings and goings of individual realities (see Chapter One, Section II), so the concept of property, too, embraces the comings and goings of individual items that are already classified as property. Since the concept of property already covers houses as a type of property, a new house here or a new house there does not require any shifts in the concept of property. The same old concept of property can be used to grasp the new house as merely a new instance of a type of property it already covers. So long as the comings and goings of property involve types of property that the concept already covers, the concept of property will not have to shift in any way.

The concept of property will have to react or adapt, however, when new types of property challenge the old definitions. In our own lifetimes, we have seen a few new types of things that challenged the established definition of the concept of property—the introduction of computer programs and of rap music, for instance. Computer programs and samples in rap music challenged the old definitions because they were not merely new items of an established type of property—as a new house would be—but introduced the possibility of new *types* of property. Those new types of property were immediacies in relation to the concept of property because they were given or "found" items in the world that the concept of property did not yet fully embrace. Only changes in types or kinds that challenge the old definitions will require Reason to react by integrating any shifts in the definition of property into the system of rational concepts.

The concept of property does not act to embrace the new material on its own. Although the Effect is an embracing concept, it is not a doubly "for itself" concept—it does not embrace its content *for itself*, or through its own activity. It is not "a negativity relating itself to itself" (§154). Instead, Reason's activity of re-systematizing the concept of property redefines the concept of property in a way that embraces the immediacy generated by the introduction of new types of property such as computer programs and samples in rap music.

The Reciprocal Action between the Effect and the Cause does not undermine the definition of the Cause as the whole process. The fact that Reason is forced to react to the Effect by re-systematizing the set of rational concepts and items does not change the fact that Reason is still defined as the whole system and process of rational concepts at the end of time. Because the Cause or Reason is defined by the whole process, the shifts and processes of re-systematization are merely *moments* in the whole process of Reason itself (§154R).

Hegel divides the discussion of the details and logical implications of Reciprocal Action into three subsections, which he labels using the Greek letters (α), (β), and (γ). This discussion will provide the transition to the next section of the logic, the Doctrine of the Concept.

Reciprocal Action

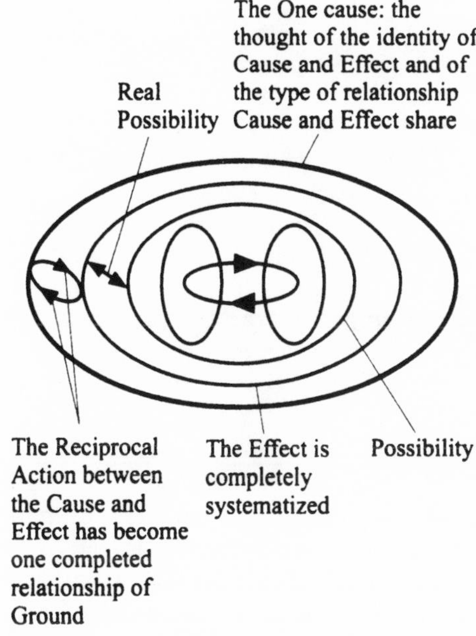

Figure 3.67

(α) Now that Cause and Effect have an "in itself" type of definition in relation to one another, we must specify what character each has in an "in itself" sense (cf. Being-in-itself). Cause and Effect are completely the same now in an "in itself" sense, that is, in terms of what they are like when each one is defined on its own, insofar as it is distinguished from or opposed to the other side. First, they are each both cause and effect in terms of content. The Cause is both a cause and an effect in relation to the Effect: it is a cause/effect. The Effect is both a cause and effect in relation to the Cause: it is a cause/effect. Second, they are each original. The Cause is original insofar as its reaction causes activity in the Effect. The Effect is original insofar as its activity causes the Cause to react. Third, they are both active. The Cause is active as a doubly "for itself" concept and cause, and the Effect is active both insofar as it is a substance and has activity in its content (though it is not doubly "for itself" in the way that the Cause is—see the stage of Effect as Substance), and insofar as it causes a reaction in the Cause. Fourth, they are both passive. The Cause is passive insofar as it receives the causal activity of the Effect and has to react, and the Effect is passive insofar as it receives the activity of the Cause and reacts. As Hegel puts it, they are "*in-themselves* the same; each side is the cause, original, active, passive etc., just as much as the other one" (§155).

Not only are Cause and Effect the same as one another in terms of content or how each one is defined on its own in an "in itself" sense, they are also the same as one another in terms of form, or how they are presented. They were not previously the same as one another in terms of form. In the stage of Substance as Cause, the conception of cause could be interpreted in both a finite and infinite sense. While cause and effect have the same content or definition as both-cause-and-effect for both finite and infinite cause, in finite cause, they had different forms or presentations, because the cause is presented as the cause, while the effect is presented as the effect. In the finite conception of cause, the form or presentation is distinguished because finite things cannot be both cause and effect in the same presentation or relationship (i.e. form).

In Reciprocal Action, however, this distinction between the content and form of cause and effect is sublated, so that the finite definition of cause is sublated as well. As Hegel puts it, "the rectilinear progression from causes to effects and from effects to causes is *curved* and *bent back* upon itself" (§154R). In Reciprocal Action there is only one relationship, the relationship in which causes and effects are inseparable from one another, and in relation to which the cause and effect are merely moments of the whole relationship. Not only do cause and effect have the same content or definition, but they also have the same presentation, insofar as they can both be presented only in a complete relationship of both cause and effect. The cause can be presented only if the effect is also presented, and the effect is presented only if the cause is presented. The cause is the *identity* of the effect insofar as the cause shines, shows up, or is presented in the effect; and the effect is the *identity* of the cause, insofar as it shines, shows or presents through the cause (§154R; cf. the stage of Identity). Thus, cause and effect have the same presentation or form insofar as they can be presented only in a whole relationship in which they are *both* presented. As Hegel puts it, "in all those unthinking repetitions [between cause and effect] there is only one and the same relation" (§154R). Cause and effect are preserved as separate elements insofar as they are still separate moments of that whole relationship, but their separateness is also cancelled insofar as they are both now defined and presented as one whole relationship: the causal relationship as a whole. Cause and effect are therefore now defined in an infinite sense: they are not defined as opposed to one another, so that one is the limit of the other, but instead are defined through a unitary process of Reciprocal Action that embraces them both. Cause and Effect are each presented in a whole relationship that is also defined as both cause and effect.

As a result, Cause and Effect have the same sort of relationship in relation to one another. The Cause is the *identity* of the Effect insofar as it shines, shows up, or is presented in the Effect, and the Effect is the *identity* of the Cause, insofar as it shines, shows up or is presented through the Cause (§154R). Cause and Effect are therefore mutually identifying in just the same way that Essence and Shine were mutually defining in the stage of Ground. They are conceptually identical in Hegel's technical sense: they are in a relationship of Identity with each other or are in a mutually determining relationship with one another according to which each can reflect or present what it is (or be inwardly reflected) only by reflecting or presenting into its other (reflection-into-another). Cause and Effect have the same identity. They define themselves as the same as one another (in an "in itself" sense) in a process in which each can be what it is only by presenting into the other side (a "for itself" process of Identity). There is only one process, then—a kind of relationship that can be characterized as "inward reflection which is just as much reflection into another," which is just how Ground was defined earlier. Cause and Effect therefore now have a relationship of Ground. The process presents them as different from one another—one is presented as the cause and the other as the effect, so they have different forms within the process. But there is still only one whole process that presents them both—the process of Ground. In the next stage, the mutually determining relationship of Ground between Cause and Effect generates the thought of the identity, content or character that both sides share.

Noticing that Cause and Effect have the same kind of relationship with one another changes the definition of Reciprocal Action. Reciprocal Action is now defined, not as the back-and-forth process between Cause and Effect, but as the One *kind* of relationship that Cause and Effect each have with one another, i.e. as a process of Ground. Because Cause and Effect have a relationship of Ground with one another, I have replaced the two arrows that ran between Cause and Effect in the last diagram with the circular arrow that I have used to represent the relationship of Ground throughout this chapter.

One of the Additions in the *Encyclopaedia Logic* (§156A) provides an example drawn from Hegel's lectures that reinforces the suggestion that the relationship of Ground has returned here. Suppose we are debating about whether the character and customs of a people—the Spartans, for instance—are the cause of their constitution and laws, or whether the constitution and laws are the cause of the people's character and customs. Our debate might see the question, Hegel apparently suggested, not in terms of Cause and Effect, but in terms of Reciprocal Action. To see the customs and laws in terms of Reciprocal Action is to see them as mutually determining, or as both cause and effect in relation to one another: the customs helped produce the laws, which in turn produce the customs, and so on. While this move represents an advance in thinking, Hegel apparently suggested, it is still not going to be satisfactory, because it takes both the customs and the laws as given, or as immediate. A better explanation would show how both of these—along with all the other characteristics of the Spartans—are grounded in the concept of the Spartans. As Hegel apparently said in his lecture, "[c]omprehension comes only when both of them [both the laws and the customs], and similarly all of the other particular aspects that the life and the history of the Spartans display, are recognized as *grounded* [*begründet*] in their concept (§156A, emphasis added). Thus, a better explanation, according to Hegel, would show how both the customs and the laws grow out of the defining *concept* of the Spartans. As we will see shortly, Reciprocal Action will give rise to the logical concept of the Concept too. Nevertheless, Hegel's use of the concept of "ground" to suggest that an explanation that appeals to a concept is better than one that appeals to a reciprocal action of cause and effect reinforces my suggestion that the relationship of Ground has returned.

The suggestion that the relationship of Ground has returned is also reinforced by something Hegel says later. He says that the Concept—which will be developed in a moment—is the truth of Being and Essence, "which are both returned into it [the Concept] as *ground*" (§159R). He also says that the Concept "has *developed* itself out of *being* as out of its *ground*" (§159R). We will have to see how the Concept is defined and what the logical development of the Concept is like later, but, I would like to suggest, Hegel's claim that the Concept develops "out of its *ground*" is a reference to the relationship of Ground that has returned here and that, as we will see shortly, eventually leads to the redefinition of the Cause into the Concept.

Cause and Effect now have not only the same definition as each other in an "in itself" sense, but also the same sort of relationship with each other. As a result, they cannot be held apart from or distinguished from one another by either their ("in itself") content or character (which is the same) or in terms of the sort of relationship or reciprocal activity they have with one another (which is the same, one process). Both Cause and Effect are the same as one another—they are each defined as cause *and* effect. And they have the same relationship with one another—a causal one. Their Reciprocal Action generates the concept that grasps the "in itself" character or identity of Cause and Effect and the one sort of activity that they both share. The concept that grasps and identifies both cause and effect as well as the thought of the causal process in general is the concept of "*cause*"—now understood not as a reference only to one side of the causal relationship (namely Cause), but as a reference to the whole relationship and process of cause. The *general concept of cause* is the thought that grasps the fact that *cause*, in general and as a whole process, includes both the cause and the effect and their mutually defining relationship. The Reciprocal Action between Cause and Effect thus generates the thought of the general concept of cause, or, as Hegel calls it, the One cause. As Hegel puts it, the "distinction between the causes that are said to be *two* is therefore empty, and there is *in-itself* only One cause present" (§155). The Cause has been redefined as the complete, whole or general concept of cause. It's the general concept of cause—the One cause—that identifies or grasps the identity of both Cause and Effect and their whole causal process.

This logical move repeats the earlier development from the stages of Ground to Existence, where a mutually defining relationship generated the concept of the shared identity and whole process. Here, too, the mutually determining relationship of Ground between Cause and Effect generates the thought of the shared identity, content or character and the whole process. The general concept of cause or the One cause is the concept that grasps and identifies the whole, mutually identifying process of cause and effect. In the stage of Existence, I depicted the new thought that was generated—namely, Existence—as a new, embracing "for itself" bubble that surrounded Essence and Shine and their relationship of Ground. Here, however, because the concept of Cause already embraces the concept of the Effect (in the diagram, Cause is a bubble that surrounds the bubble for the Effect), the mutually determining relationship between Cause and Effect does not introduce a new concept, but rather merely redefines the embracing "for itself" concept that is already there. The Cause is redefined as the general concept of cause or as the One cause.

There is a second logical reason for why the thought of the One cause now emerges—a reason that also explains why the relationship of Ground between Cause and Effect does not generate a new embracing, "for itself" concept (as it did in the stage of Existence), but merely redefines the embracing "for itself" concept that is already there (namely, the Cause). Two logical things are happening at the same time that redefine the Cause as the concept of the One cause: (1) the spuriously infinite back-and-forth process of Reciprocal Action is stopped when Reciprocal Action is defined as a relationship of Ground, or as a whole, complete process; and (2) Cause and Effect are defined as the same as one another both in an "in itself" sense and through their mutually defining relationship of Ground. These two logical processes together redefine the concept of Cause as the general concept of cause, or as the One cause. In (1), Reciprocal Action is a spuriously infinite back-and-forth process of the sort we have seen before. That spuriously infinite process—with which the logic cannot rest (see Spurious Infinity)—is stopped when Reciprocal Action is redefined as a relationship of Ground. The relationship of Ground is the thought of the whole causal process between Cause and Effect as one complete process. Because the process of Reciprocal Action is a whole complete process, that process is *finished.* In (2), Cause and Effect are already defined as the same as one another in an "in itself" sense. They have the same character or content as both cause and effect. When Reciprocal Action is redefined as a relationship of Ground, the Cause and Effect are now defined as the same as one another in a "for itself" sense as well. According to the relationship of Ground, Cause and Effect mutually define each other as the same as one another. The Cause can be what it is as a cause only when the effect shows up, so the Cause is cause/effect; and the Effect can be what it is as an effect only when the Cause shows up, so it is a cause/effect too. According to the relationship of Ground, then, Cause and Effect mutually define one another as the same as one another, through a mutual "for itself" process of identity.

Putting (1) and (2) together, Reciprocal Action is a completed process in which Cause and Effect have finished mutually defining one another as the same. Since the process of mutual definition is finished, Cause and Effect are completely the same as one another. There will be no further changes in either the Cause or Effect. The Cause will not have to react any more and the Effect will not have to react any more. They are completely the same and the process of mutual adjustment between them is finished. The thought of the process of Cause and Effect as a *completed, one whole process* in which Cause and Effect are defined as *completely the same as one another* redefines the Cause. We must now think of the Cause not as one momentary cause, but rather as the whole concept of cause that embraces and presents every causal process. Now that the process of mutual definition is finished, the Cause has become the whole process of cause—i.e. all of the moments of cause—that embraces and presents all the moments of effect. It is the general concept of cause—the thought of the whole, complete process of cause, the whole causal process. It is still a concept of cause, it is just a more general concept of cause—the One cause.

Hegel used the same logical move in the stages of World of Appearance and Condition as a Totality, where a back-and-forth activity between an embracing "for itself" concept and its content redefined the embracing "for itself" concept as a whole or totality, or as a general concept. As in those stages, there are two logical reasons that explain why the back-and-forth process merely redefines a concept without generating an entirely new concept. First, the back-and-forth process is taking place within a concept, or between a concept and the content that it already embraces. Because the process takes place within the concept, there is no need to introduce a new embracing concept to halt the spuriously infinite process. The process can be halted simply by generating a new definition of the original concept that already embraces the content. Here, the back-and-forth process between the Cause and its content—the Effect—is halted simply by redefining the Cause as the One whole cause, or as the general concept of cause that grasps or identifies the entire causal process.

Second, the spuriously infinite process here does *not* involve two elements that are defined as completely the same as one another. While the Cause and Effect have the same *sort of* "in itself" character or definition and have the same *kind* of relationship with one another, they still take different *forms* in relation to one another within that type of relationship. Within the causal relationship, one side is always presented as the cause and the other side is always presented as the effect. Since the two sides are still presented as different from one another, there is no logical need to introduce a third or new concept to hold them apart. Again, the spuriously infinite process can be resolved simply by redefining the embracing concept (the Cause, in this case) that already contains the content (the Effect) in a way that grasps the whole, back-and-forth process. The One cause is the *identity* of the causal process. It grasps the type of thing that the causal process is, or the nature of the whole causal process *as a type*. Reason is now defined as the One cause—the thought of the whole causal process in which Reason and the set of rational concepts mutually define one another. It is the whole causal process that includes all of its systematizing activity and all of the rational concepts and their activity in the actual world. Reason is now defined as the One general concept of cause that includes the entire systematizing activity and the whole set of rational concepts and their activity in the actual world throughout time. Because Reason and the rational concepts are completely mutually defining, *time is finished*. There will therefore be no further changes either to Reason's systematizing activity or to the rational concepts in the actual world. They have the same content (insofar as they are each defined on their own or in the "in itself" sense) and are defined by the same one, whole process of Reciprocal Action. On the one side is Reason, now defined as the One complete, general concept of cause that includes the whole process of Cause and Effect; and on the other side is the completely systematized set of concepts and their activity in the actual world throughout time. Because the process of adjustment between the Cause and Effect has been completed, there is no further work for the One cause to do on the Effect. The Effect has been redefined as the completed and completely systematized Effect, or as the Effect-Completely-Systematized or $\text{Effect}_{\text{CS}}$.

Because Reason is defined as a completed, temporal process, Hegel's use of the term "moments" is justified. Since Reason is defined as all of time, every individual causal process is just one time, one moment, in relation to the whole process of time. In pictorial terms, now that all of the logical bubbles and arrows are defined as one whole, completed process—as all of time—each of the elements and activities within that whole process is just one moment in the whole process of time. Thus each stage of logical development is a "moment" of that logical development. Not only is Hegel's logic both semantic and syntactic—that is, about meanings as well as logical syntax, or termino-logical (see the stage of Condition as a Totality as well as the Introduction to the book)—it is also *temporal*. Hegel's logic is *termino-temporal-logical*. Each step is a conceptual and syntactic moment of the whole, termino-temporal-logical process. For Hegel, logic develops through time, through the history of thought in the world. Of course, for those of us who exist in time, time has not finished, so this definition of the One cause has not yet been achieved. Nevertheless, the logical development makes it possible for us to see how the One cause would be defined, even though, for those of us for whom time is not finished, it does not have that definition.

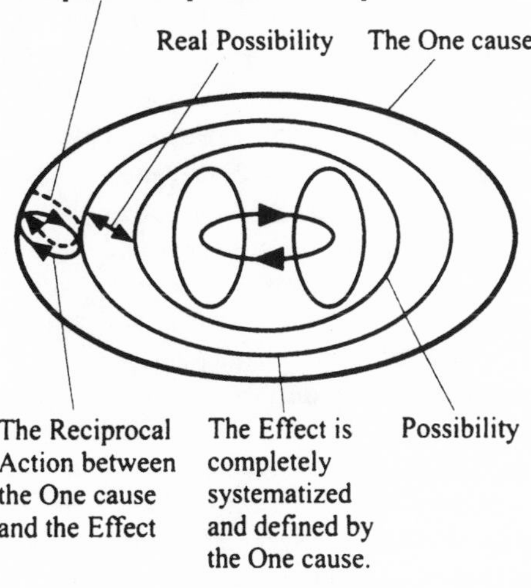

Figure 3.68

(β) So far, the One cause is defined *from the bottom-up*—that is, by the elements that it embraces or contains—as the one thought of the whole completed back-and-forth process between Cause and Effect. The thought of the One cause was generated by following out the logical implications of the back-and-forth Reciprocal Action between Cause and Effect. But the back-and-forth process between the Cause and Effect does not take into account the full activity of Reciprocal Action. In particular, it does not take into consideration that—as in the stage of Substance as Cause—the One cause (as the Cause is now defined) is doubly "for itself": it is a "for itself" concept that embraces and presents the Effect$_{CS}$ *for itself* (§156), or through its own activity. That "for itself" activity is the activity in which the One cause *presents* or causes its content and initiates the process of Reciprocal Action. Reciprocal Action was initiated because the Substance—which is now defined as the One cause—must present or cause the Effect to have its character as the all-embracing One essence and to have *being* or presence (§156), including out-thereness. The Substance became the Cause because it can be actual and have out-thereness only in the Effect, which contains Possibility and Inner and Outer in a mutually defining relationship, and is therefore defined as Actuality. As a result, Substance must get its being—its character, actuality and Outer (out-thereness)—through the Effect. In this stage, the One cause's character as a doubly "for itself" concept comes back into view.

Because the One cause still has the "for itself" character that it had as a Substance, it is still a "for itself," embracing content that *must* present its content *for itself*, or through its own activity, to be what it is or to have its being. In short, the One cause is still a *cause*. Its systematizing activity—all of the moments of systematizing activity taken together—still *defines or presents* the $\text{Effect}_{\text{CS}}$. Although the Cause is now redefined as the One cause—the thought of the whole, completed process of Cause and Effect as a type—the distinction between Cause and Effect within it is sublated (cancelled and preserved), but not extinguished. The One cause is still a cause insofar as it is still defined by the process in which it presents or causes the $\text{Effect}_{\text{CS}}$. Its process of presenting the $\text{Effect}_{\text{CS}}$ involves two logical processes. First, the One cause "sublates itself as substance in its effect" (§155), as Hegel puts it. A substance is an essence that has subsistence, actuality, and passing over, and in which form and content overturn into one another. The One cause *cancels* itself as the substance-of-the-matter in the $\text{Effect}_{\text{CS}}$ insofar as it causes the $\text{Effect}_{\text{CS}}$, which is distinguished from and hence *not* itself. Insofar as Reason as the One cause divides into moments of thought in which it systematizes and re-systematizes the concepts in time, it is not the complete One cause, and so cancels itself. But the One cause also *preserves* itself as the substance-of-the-matter in the $\text{Effect}_{\text{CS}}$ insofar as presenting the $\text{Effect}_{\text{CS}}$ is what defines it as the substance-of-the-matter that embraces the whole process. The process of dividing into moments and systematizing the rational concepts preserves the One cause insofar as going through that process is what defines it as the complete One cause, i.e. as *completed* Reason. Reason gets to be defined as the element that systematizes, defines and grasps the entire set of rational concepts and items only by going through the process of systematizing, defining and grasping the entire set of rational concepts and items.

Second, however, the activity of presenting the $\text{Effect}_{\text{CS}}$ also defines the One cause as an element separate from its content (§155; cf. External Necessity). Because the One cause *presents* the whole process, it is a separate element on its own. Whenever a concept is defined by a process in which it presents something else, that process of presentation (form) defines the concept as an element separate from what is being presented. The One cause's activity of presenting the $\text{Effect}_{\text{CS}}$ in the whole causal process defines it as a separate element on its own, and hence as *not* the $\text{Effect}_{\text{CS}}$. Like Substance, it is the negative of what it presents. Reason defined as One cause is what it is on its own—it is the thought of all the moments of systematizing and defining as well as the whole set of rational concepts on its own. It merely *presents* the completely systematized and defined set of rational concepts as its Effect_{CS}.

Cause and Effect have the same definition, then, not only for us students, who are thinking through the logical process, but also for the One cause itself, or through the activity of the One cause itself. As Hegel puts it, "the nullity of the distinctions [between Cause and Effect] is not only in-itself or our reflection" (§156). Instead, he implies, that nullity is also "for itself," or the action or presentation of the One cause itself. What Reason is like—its nature, or how it is defined overall—explains the process of Reciprocal Action. Reason as the whole, general concept of One cause is the *cause* of the process of Reciprocal Action between moments of systematizing Reason and the set of rational concepts in the actual world, including this moment, in which the logical conclusion about the definition of Reason is drawn. The One cause or Reason initiates the process in which it is defined through Reciprocal Action. It is what it is not only from *the bottom-up*—as defined by the elements it embraces—but also from *the top-down*—as the result of its own activity.

The One cause sublates (cancels and preserves) its definition as *both* cause and effect. It preserves its definition as cause and effect because it is defined as both cause and effect in two ways. First, since the One cause captures the whole back-and-forth process between Cause and Effect, it is the unity of Cause and Effect. The One cause is the thought of the shared "in itself" content or character and the one kind of causal relationship that Cause and Effect have in relation to one another. It is therefore defined as both cause and effect. More precisely, it is the thought of the *identity* of Cause and Effect. Since Cause and Effect have the same "in itself" content or character and are in a mutually defining relationship in which each is the identity of the other, they are identical with one another. The One cause grasps Cause, Effect and their process *as a type*. Second, since the One cause is defined as the identity of Cause and Effect *from the bottom-up*, it is still an effect. Insofar as the One cause is defined by the elements that it embraces, it is an effect. It is the *effect* of the process of Reciprocal Action. However, the One cause cancels its definition as both cause and effect because, since it is a doubly "for itself" concept that embraces and *presents* Cause and Effect and their process, it is only the cause of the process of Reciprocal Action—the One cause.

Transition to the Concept

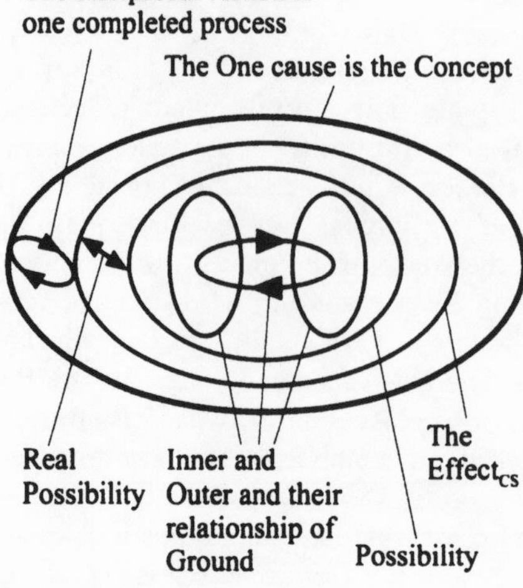

Figure 3.69

(γ) Originally, the One cause was defined from the bottom-up by the elements it embraced. It was defined by the concepts of both Cause and Effect and the whole process of Reciprocal Action. The One cause now has two characteristics, however, that require it to be defined differently. First, since the One cause *presents* the Effect$_{CS}$, it is now defined as an element on its own, separate from the contents that it embraces (i.e from the Effect$_{CS}$). Second, now that the One cause is a separate element from the Effect$_{CS}$ that initiates the Reciprocal Action, it generates its own definition from the top down through its activity. The One cause *causes* the Reciprocal Action—now taken to be one whole, complete and completed process—from the top down *for itself*, or through its own activity. Because the One cause is no longer defined from the bottom-up but instead generates is own definition from the top-down, it can no longer be defined simply as the One cause anymore. The One cause is the all-embracing, all-systematizing, all-defining element that embraces, systematizes and defines everything else, including itself, *for itself*, or through its own activity, in a completely reciprocal relationship. The One cause has become the *Concept*. The thought or concept that initiates the Reciprocal Action is the Concept.

It is difficult in English to see how the definition of the One cause generates the Concept because the English word "concept" does not have the same undertones that the German word that it translates has. There are a couple of obvious implications that the English word "concept" has that fit well into Hegel's logic, but these implications are better linked to Hegel's concept of the One cause. Because these implications are more closely linked to the definition of the One cause, they also make it hard to see in English what difference there is between the "One cause" and the "Concept." For example, the One cause is the general *concept* of cause. It is the identity of the Effect$_{CS}$, which is the completely systematized set of rational concepts and items (see Section [α] of the stage of Reciprocal Action [Fig. 3.67]). What identity do all the rational *concepts* have in common? They are all *concepts*. So the concept that identifies them all is the concept of Concept. But if the One cause is already in this sense the "Concept," why does Hegel introduce the concept of the Concept only now?

The key to understanding the move to the "Concept" is the German word that Hegel uses. Although the English term "Concept" is similar in root to the

German term, most contemporary English speakers are unaware of this etymological background. The German word that is translated as "Concept"—"*Begriff*"—has its roots in the word "*greifen*," which means "to grasp." When the One cause is defined from the top down as a separate, "for itself" element, it is the concept that *grasps* the Effect_{CS}. The One cause is the "*Begriff*," "Grasper," or "Concept." The metaphor of grasping explains the features that the Concept has in relation to the Effect_{CS}: the Concept is a separate element from the Effect_{CS} that is the initiating and defining cause; it is also the effect; it both is and is not defined by the "for itself" reciprocal activity of embracing the Effect_{CS}; and it defines itself *for itself*, or through its own activity. When we grasp something, for instance, we initiate the activity by reaching out. Hence, we are the cause of the activity. When we latch on to the item we are reaching for, we change or impose a new character on that item. That item is not exactly what it was, now that we have latched on to it. At the very least, we put our fingerprints on it. Hence, we also cause the definition of, or define, the item that we grasp. But then, when we pull that item back to ourselves, we are also defined. We are no longer what we were either. At the very least, we are now defined as what we were *plus* the item. In that sense, we are also defined by, and hence are the effect of, our grasping activity. Because we started the activity, however, we were ultimately the authors of the new definition that we have as the effect. Hence, we are self-defining *for ourselves*, or through our own activity. But we are also *not* defined by the grasping activity. The definition we had from the start—as something with hands, for instance—made the grasping activity go the way that it did in the first place. Finally, because the activity started with our reaching out, it is a top-down activity: the activity starts at the top with the element that does the reaching out, and then embraces the element that was aimed at. If we ask, what character or definition do we have in light of this top-down activity, the answer is that we are the *grasper*. The concept of "the grasper" captures what we are (1) as elements separate from the item that we grasp, (2) as the initiating and defining cause, (3) as the effect of the activity, and (4) as the element whose character both is, and is not, defined by the activity.

The only logical feature missing from this metaphor that is included in the definition of the "Concept" is the idea that the reciprocal relationship between the Concept and the Effect_{CS} is completed. When we reach out and grasp something, we are not in a *completely* reciprocal relationship with what we grasp. What we grasp is not all of our activity and everything we have ever grasped. The Concept, by contrast, is in a completely reciprocal relationship with what it grasps, so that what it grasps is its complete activity and everything that it has grasped. Indeed, because the Concept has grown out of Substance, what it grasps is absolutely everything. The Concept is thus the overarching, all-embracing, all-systematizing, all-defining "grasper." Its activity grasps and defines *everything* in a completely reciprocal relationship.

While the term "*Begriff*" has its roots in "*greifen*," it is more closely linked to the verb "*begreifen*," which means "to comprehend," "to conceive" or "to grasp" (in the conceptual sense). The Concept is the overarching "grasper" in the conceptual sense. The process of comprehending, conceiving or grasping something *in thought* has the same general outline that the process of literally grasping something does—which would explain why the German words for "concept" and "comprehend" have their roots in the German verb "*greifen*" or "to grasp." The act of comprehension or grasping-in-thought begins by reaching out, so to speak, to the object in question. Then the grasper (in thought) labels or conceives of the object, or turns the object into a thought. The act of labeling or turning the object into a thought affects the object by giving it a character that it did not have on its own before. The grasper is therefore a cause in relation to the object. The grasper causes the object to have a certain character, or *defines* the object. Labeling the object also defines the grasper, insofar as the grasper is now defined by a thought that it did not include before, in particular, the thought that the object in question "is X," where "X" is the label or thought that captures the object. Because pulling the object in as a thought defines the grasper, the grasper is the effect of the activity. But the grasper is also *not* defined by the grasping activity, since the character of the grasper determined how the grasping activity would go in the first place. It is because the grasper is a thinker that the object was turned into a thought. Moreover, while the new thought defines the grasper, the grasper's status as the initiating element gives it a character beyond or separate from that new thought. The grasper is what it is as a thinker, and presents the object as a thought. Finally, to the degree that the grasper is defined by the activity, the fact that the grasper initiated the activity means that whatever character the grasper has at the end of the activity is a character the grasper gave itself, through its own activity. The grasper is therefore self-defining. Once again, a logical feature missing from the metaphor is the completed reciprocal relationship between the Concept and the $\text{Effect}_{\text{CS}}$. The grasper in the metaphor should be grasping its complete activity, so that the object being grasped completely reflects the grasper and the grasper's activity. The grasper-in-thought is the separate, overarching, self-defining grasper that is affected by, but also determines, the whole grasping activity.

As in German, in English the words "comprehend" and "conceive" have the same etymological root as "concept" (the Latin word "*concipere*"), but they lack the obvious connection to the verb "to grasp" that the German term has. The Latin word "*capere*" means "to take." To take and to grasp something are similar activities, and so the root of the word "concept" does hint at or imply a taking or grasping activity in the same way that the German term "*Begriff*" does. However, since most contemporary English speakers cannot make the connection between the terms "concept" and "to take," the word "concept" does not imply the grasping activity as vividly or obviously as the German word does.

As the logic suggests, to grasp something in thought is a semantic, syntactic and temporal activity. To conceive or comprehend something is to label or define it—to turn it into a thought—which involves assigning it some *meaning* or other, and hence is semantic. Moreover, as the etymology of the English word "conceive" suggests, to conceive of something is to link or take a thought together with an object. The English word "conceive" has its roots in the Latin "*com-*," which means "together," and "*capere*," which means "to take." A link is a syntactic device, so to link a thought together with an object is a *syntactic* activity. Moreover, an activity takes place *in time*. To think, reason, or do logic is to do something in time. The grasping activity of the Concept is therefore temporal as well. The Concept grasps the temporal activity in which the rational concepts and their activity in the actual world along with the systematizing and logical activity of Reason are presented in time. The Concept is thus complete and completed Reason, as the overarching cause (and effect) of the complete collection of thought-bits or concepts, and all possible thought-activity taken together as one complete process in all of time.

There is a third connotation to the English word "Concept" that also accurately reflects Hegel's logic. In the English-speaking world, we often think of concepts as *mere* concepts, as thoughts without much reality. In Hegel's terms, concepts are merely "inner," without any "outer" or out-thereness. While Hegel's Concept and rational concepts are *actual*—they include both Inner and Outer (in the diagram, the Effect$_{CS}$ includes the Possibility bubble, which contains the Inner and Outer bubbles)—the Concept itself remains merely inner because, as I will explain in the next several paragraphs, its necessary connection with the Effect$_{CS}$ remains inner. Therefore the implication in English that a "concept" is merely inner is also reflected in the concept of the Concept.

The connection between the Concept and the Effect$_{CS}$ is a necessary one because they have a causal relationship with one another. The reciprocal action between the Concept and the Effect$_{CS}$ defines both of them as both cause and effect. A connection between a cause and effect is always a connection of necessity or a necessary connection. A cause must produce an effect to be a cause, and an effect must have a cause to be an effect. Because the Concept is defined in a way that includes its two-way causal connection with the Effect$_{CS}$, its definition presents not only the Effect$_{CS}$, but also the complete, necessary connection between cause and effect. The diagram illustrates this logical feature because the circular arrow representing the reciprocal relationship between the Concept and the Effect$_{CS}$ is inside the bubble representing the Concept. The Concept literally contains or presents the necessity in the diagram because it has the necessary connection inside of it.

The Concept presents the necessary connection between cause and effect because, as was the case for Substance, the Concept must present the Effect$_{CS}$ to be what it is as the all-embracing Concept. Substance was the completed system of rational concepts and could have its definition as the system of rational concepts only by causing or systematizing the rational concepts. That is why Substance became the Cause in the stage of Substance as Cause. As Hegel puts it, Substance "is subjected to the *necessity*, or to the destiny, of passing over into positedness" (§159R). Substance passes over into positedness because, as the Cause, it must produce the Effect, which is what Hegel means by "positedness." Because the Concept is the thought of the completed activity of cause and effect, however, it does not pass over into the Effect$_{CS}$. For the Concept, the reciprocal relationship between itself and the Effect$_{CS}$ is finished, complete. The Concept presents the necessary connection between cause and effect as a finished product, and so is not subjected to the causal process in the same way that Substance was. Hence, the necessity that the Concept presents is unveiled or posited necessity (§157), as Hegel puts it. It is a necessity that is established or presented by something else, namely, by the Concept. Because the Concept *presents* the necessity, it is not subject to that necessity. The Concept is what it is on its own. It merely causes or presents the necessity. It is therefore not the victim, so to speak, of the necessity. This characteristic will help to explain why the Concept is *free* shortly.

While the Concept presents the completed, necessary connection between cause and effect, that "bond of necessity" (§157) or necessary connection does not have actuality or out-thereness, or does not show up in the actual world. The Concept presents the connection as a mere thought. The necessary connection and identity between the Concept (which is both cause and effect) and the Effect$_{CS}$ (which is also both cause and effect) is "still inner and hidden" (§157), as Hegel puts it, because it has no actuality out there in any element. The Concept and the Effect$_{CS}$ have actuality, but their necessary connection does not. The Concept and the Effect$_{CS}$ have actuality because they contain Possibility, which contains Inner and Outer in a mutually defining relationship. Since Inner and Outer in a mutually defining relationship is the definition of Actuality, both the Concept and the Effect$_{CS}$ contain Actuality. But the necessary connection between the Concept and the Effect$_{CS}$ does not have actuality. The diagram illustrates this point because, unlike the Concept and the Effect$_{CS}$, the connection between the Concept and Effect$_{CS}$ is not a bubble. It is an arrow or activity, and so does not contain Possibility or Actuality. Hence, unlike the Concept and the Effect$_{CS}$, it is merely a thought or inner, and not outer or actual.

The completed, reciprocal relationship or necessary connection between the Concept and the Effect$_{CS}$ defines the Concept and the Effect$_{CS}$ as *the same as* or identical to one another. The reciprocal relationship or necessary connection therefore captures and presents the *identity* between the Concept and the Effect$_{CS}$. Because the necessary connection is merely a thought or inner, and therefore hidden, however, the identity between the Concept and the Effect$_{CS}$ is inner and hidden as well. In the definition of the Concept, the identity between Reason and its complete presentation in the actual world is merely a thought.

There is another reason why the identity between the Concept and the Effect$_{CS}$ is inner and hidden, however. Because the Concept and the Effect$_{CS}$ are actual, they have the character of being self-subsistent, self-standing or independent in terms of their content. Since they both contain Possibility, they are each combinations of both thought (Inner) and out-thereness (Outer), and so have subsistence, or are capable of having their definitions on their own, or independently. They are also independent in terms of their relationship with one another, insofar as they are separate from one another. Because the Concept *presents* the Effect$_{CS}$, it is defined as separate from the Effect$_{CS}$, which is in turn separate from the Concept. The identity between the Concept and the Effect$_{CS}$ is inner or hidden, then, not only because their connection is a relationship without actuality of its own, but also because, as actualities, the Concept and the Effect$_{CS}$ are separate, independent and self-subsistent elements, each capable of standing on its own.

This independence between the Concept and the Effect$_{CS}$ is part of what is necessary, or part of the necessity (§157). A necessary connection is a kind of relationship, and a relationship is always between two separate things. Something can have a relationship with itself, as the Concept does here, only if it is divided into two elements that can be separated from one another or are different from one another in some way or other. The Concept and the Effect$_{CS}$ could not be in a relationship at all unless they were different from and separate from one another in some way. If they were completely the same as one another—if they shared absolutely every characteristic—then they would be the same one thing, and so could not have a relationship at all. While the reciprocal relationship or necessary connection captures the identity or sameness between the Concept and the Effect$_{CS}$, it also defines them as separate from one another. The very same relationship that defines the Concept and the Effect$_{CS}$ as the same as or identical to one another also defines them as separate from and independent of one another. The reciprocal relationship they have with one another makes them separate from or independent of one another. This separation or independence is just as important to their necessary connection as is the identity. Hence, the independence that the Concept and the Effect$_{CS}$ have is just as necessary to the necessary connection as is the identity that they have in relation to one another. As Hegel puts it, "the independence of these is just nothing but their identity" (§157). The Concept thus equally contains both the mutual identity between and mutual independence of itself and the Effect$_{CS}$.

The Concept is like Substance insofar as it must present the Effect$_{CS}$ to be what it is or have its definition. Because it contains both the mutual identity and the mutual independence of itself and the Effect$_{CS}$, however, unlike Substance, the Concept does not leave itself open to further processes of development. Substance was defined as independent in terms of its content. It contained absolutely everything. But it turned out not to be independent in terms of its process or presentation. It was the original and hence apparently independent element insofar as it was defined as the Cause, but because a cause must produce an effect, Substance pushed on to the Effect and to further processes of development that were not contained in its definition. Because the Concept presents the whole or completed process of cause and effect, it is not only everything in terms of content, but also everything in terms of process. There is not only no other content or element for the Concept to embrace or present—which was also true for Substance—there is also no other *process* for the Concept to embrace or present. The Concept is the whole process of cause and effect as well as everything that is presented in that whole process. Whereas the Substance's definition as the Cause forced the Substance to push on to further processes, the Concept's definition as everything *and every process* means that the Concept does not push on to any further process. It is at rest and completely contained in a way that Substance was not.

The Concept is thus truly independent and self-standing in a way that Substance was not. Hegel says that the Concept is independent because it is "the infinite negative relation to self" (§157). Like Substance, the Concept is a negativity. The Concept is a negativity in two senses. First, it is defined as a separate element on its own. Substance had this characteristic as well. But the Concept is also negative, according to Hegel, in a further sense—a sense the Substance does not share. Hegel says that the Concept is negative because "distinction and mediation become in it the originality of actualities that are independent in relation to each other" (§157). The phrase "distinction and mediation" refers to the process in which the Concept is defined or distinguished: the Concept is distinguished or defined through a process mediated by the Effect$_{CS}$. Moreover, in relation to one another, the Concept and the Effect$_{CS}$ are independent actualities and original. They are original in relation to one another because they are both causes: the Concept causes the Effect$_{CS}$, and Effect$_{CS}$ causes the Concept. The Concept is thus defined by a process in which two independent and original elements are distinguished from one another, or are defined *negatively* against one another. Although the Substance was defined by separate elements that were distinguished from one another—namely the Cause (which was just Substance itself) and the Effect—those elements were not both original in relation to one another. The Substance was only the Cause, while the Effect was only the Effect. The Effect was not yet defined as also a cause. Because the definition of Substance did not include the causal activity of the Effect, it pushed on to other processes that its definition did not contain.

Since the Concept includes the causal activity of the Effect in its definition, however, it does not push on to other processes. It is therefore defined not only as negative, but also as an "infinite relation to self" (§157), as Hegel puts it. The Concept is infinite because it is a doubly "for-itself" concept: it is an embracing, "for itself" concept (cf. Being-for-itself) that is also "for itself" in terms of its process. Unlike Substance, because the Concept contains the necessary connection between itself and the Effect$_{CS}$, it includes every process, and so does not push on to any further processes. It is completed or infinitely related to itself in a way that Substance was not. Substance was a separate element on its own that held everything in the Effect together. The Concept is a separate element on its own that holds everything *and the whole process* together. Because the Concept contains everything and every process as a completed whole, it is truly independent. True independence belongs only to the Concept, as the thought that grasps and presents everything and every process as a completed whole.

Because the concept of Substance has developed into the concept of the Concept through a necessary process of logical development, the truth of Substance is the Concept (§158), as Hegel suggests. The diagrams help to illustrate this claim because the very same bubble that is the Concept now is the same bubble that represented Substance earlier. Thus the truth of Substance is the

Concept in the sense that the highest definition of Substance is the Concept, or Substance has developed logically into the Concept.

Because the Concept is the identity of the Effect$_{CS}$ in terms of both content and process or relationship, it is the completely developed *Essence* of the Effect$_{CS}$. At the beginning of this chapter, we started out with the most rudimentary concept or definition of essence. There, Essence was the Identity of the Shine in terms of content. The Concept is an identity in terms of both content and form, presentation or process. The Effect$_{CS}$, for its part, is the complete and completely systematized set of rational concepts along with their activity in the actual world. It is everything and every process that can be thought about in actuality, or the highest and most developed concept of being out there. In the stage of Identity, the realm of Being was the Shine of Essence. In this stage, the Concept, as the highest definition of "essence" is the Identity of the Effect$_{CS}$, which is the highest definition of "being." The Concept "is the *truth of being and essence*" (§159).

The stage of the Concept completes Hegel's argument for the view that there is no separation between Thought and Being. There are two caveats, however. First, Thought and Being are still presented as independent elements. The Concept and the Effect$_{CS}$ are presented as separate from and independent of one another. Second, because of their independence, their identity is inner and hidden. They must be pulled together or identified by the work or activity of Thought. Thus, their unity is only inner or in thought. So while Thought and Being are united, for Hegel, that unity does not show up, or is not out there, in the actual world. Nevertheless, because the conclusion that Thought and Being are united is the result of a necessary process of logical development, the unity is established in Thought. There is no longer any question that Thought and Being are united, even if the unity does not show up in the actual world. The unity has presence or is present in thought.

Reason, as the Concept, is the same Reason that, as Substance, did the systematizing work on the rational concepts. The Reason that systematizes the concepts (i.e. Substance) is the same Reason that, at the end of the whole process, grasps and presents the whole systematizing process (i.e. the Concept). Indeed, it is *because* the Reason at the end of the process *is* the same Reason that went through the process that the Reason at the end of the process can have its definition as the thought of the completely systematized and completed set of rational concept. Reason has to go through the process of systematizing the set of rational concepts before it can be the thought of the completely systematized set of rational concepts. Substance is thus an earlier definition of the same Reason that is the Concept later on. In the diagrams, the very same bubble that was defined as Substance earlier is now defined as the Concept. Indeed, the Concept is the very same bubble that was defined as the Matter (*Sache*) Itself much earlier, which, as I suggested in that stage, explains why Hegel says that the Matter Itself is the Concept (§147R).

Since Reason is defined as all the possible thought-processes taken together as a completed whole, there are actually four processes going on. First, Reason presents the completely systematized set of rational concepts (this is the completed, Reciprocal Action between the Concept and the Effect$_{CS}$). Second, Reason undergoes the necessary process of logical development that we have been following (this is the logical development). Third, Reason systematizes the rational concepts (the back-and-forth process of Reciprocal Action between the Cause and Effect, which the Concept includes). Fourth, Reason defines the rational concepts themselves in relation to one another during the systematizing process.

While the Concept is all concepts and all activity of thought, it also offers a general definition for concept, or is the concept of concept-in-general. It captures the general character or identity of all rational concepts, and the general character that all rational concepts share is that they are concepts. The definition of "concept" offered in this stage therefore applies to each individual rational concept as much as it does to Reason as the whole Concept. Take the concept of animal, for instance. The concept of animal is the completely finished and defined concept. It is what the concept of animal will be like after it has been fully presented in time, once all of the animals have been present in the actual world and after Reason has systematized that full actuality by integrating it into the system of rational concepts. The completed concept of animal is both the cause and effect of that presentation. The concept of animal is the effect of that presentation insofar as it is defined by everything that happened in the presentation. But it is also the cause of the presentation because its nature—i.e. what the concept of animal is like as a whole—also determined what that presentation would be like. Which existences counted as belonging to the concept of animal and hence as being in the presentation of "animal" was predetermined in part by the very concept of animal, although it is not complete or completely fixed until the end of the whole process. The completed concept of animal includes its presentation in the actual world. If the concept of animal is merely what is behind—or the negative of—the process of presentation, then the concept of animal is empty. Everything it is is in the presentation, so that without the presentation, "animal" is defined in a merely negative way as *not* that presentation. But the completed process of reciprocal action defines the completed concept of animal as both separate from and the same as its presentation. The very process that defines the completed concept of animal as *not* that presentation or as independent of that presentation is the same process that defines the concept of animal as the same as its presentation. Hence, like the Concept, the concept of animal identifies or is the identity of the complete process of presentation only through the process of presentation itself.

Besides the claim that the truth of Substance is the Concept, there is another logical lesson to draw out of the movement from Substance to Concept, according to Hegel. The development of the Concept from Substance also shows that the truth of necessity is freedom (§158). The Concept is free insofar as it initiates or causes all of its necessary activity, but it is also free because, unlike Substance, it is defined completely through its own activity, or through activity that belongs to its own definition. Substance, as Cause, pushed on to other processes that did not belong to its definition, namely, to the process of the Effect. There was therefore activity beyond Substance or outside of Substance's own definition on which Substance depended for its definition. Since Substance was defined as Cause, and since a Cause cannot be what it is without an Effect, Substance needed the activity of the Effect—which fell outside of it—to be what it is. It was therefore not completely independent in terms of its activity and hence not free. The Concept, by contrast, includes within its activity every activity that defines it. It is defined completely through its own activity. There is no activity at all outside of it that it does not already embrace and include. Hence, it is completely free in a way that Substance was not. The Concept is completely self-contained, in terms of both content and activity or presentation.

Hegel says that the Concept is free because, although it repulses or expresses itself into "distinct independences [*unterschiedene Selbständige*]," it remains "identical with itself" through this repulsion and so "remains at home *with itself*" (§158). The "distinct independences" are the Concept and the $\text{Effect}_{\text{CS}}$, which are independent of one another and defined negatively against one another (i.e. are distinct or distinguished from one another). Then the Concept is free, according to Hegel, because, while it pushes out the completed realm of rational concepts and all their activity in the actual world (i.e. the $\text{Effect}_{\text{CS}}$) as a separate element, that process is merely the way in which the Concept defines itself through its own activity. Moreover, the $\text{Effect}_{\text{CS}}$ is nothing but the content of the Concept itself. As a result, the Concept's exchange with the $\text{Effect}_{\text{CS}}$ is an exchange with itself, and the process of pushing out the $\text{Effect}_{\text{CS}}$ is a process in which the Concept remains at home with itself, because the Concept itself is the cause of or initiates the activity that pushes out the $\text{Effect}_{\text{CS}}$. The activity of necessity between the Concept and the $\text{Effect}_{\text{CS}}$ has been completely absorbed into the process of the Concept as a whole, and the Concept has nothing else outside of it. The activity of the Concept includes necessity, but because the Concept (over)grasps the necessity, the necessity is not an "other" for it, and so the Concept is still independent and free in relation to the $\text{Effect}_{\text{CS}}$ that it grasps. To be free, then, is not to avoid necessity, but to grasp it, and to remain, as Hegel says, at home with itself through this grasping process (§159). Freedom presupposes necessity and contains necessity sublated (canceled but preserved) within it (§158A).

In a lecture, Hegel apparently contrasted this sort of "concrete" or "positive" freedom with "abstract" freedom (§158A). To be abstractly free would be to have the possibility of expression. To be really free is to have actually expressed oneself out there. To use Hegel's anthropomorphic language, because the Concept succeeds in expressing or repulsing itself out there in actuality in the $\text{Effect}_{\text{CS}}$, it is actual, and so has concrete, and not abstract, freedom. The Concept is also free, however, because, when it actualizes itself out there in the $\text{Effect}_{\text{CS}}$, it also defines itself as—or makes itself into—what it is. The Concept thus actualizes itself not only in the sense that it makes itself into an actuality, but in the sense that it fulfills its identity in the $Effect_{CS}$. Although the $Effect_{CS}$ is independent, the $Effect_{CS}$'s independence is not a restriction on the Concept's freedom. The $Effect_{CS}$ is nothing but the Concept's own content, and the way in which the concept fulfills its identity. Thus, what is out there in actuality (i.e. in the $Effect_{CS}$) both expresses and defines the Concept, and so the Concept remains at home with itself in its repulsion (§158) in the $Effect_{CS}$. I am free to be a tailor in an abstract sense, for instance, because I could possibly be one. But that freedom does not become concrete until I succeed in carrying it out, that is, until I put my "tailoring" out there into actuality, or until I act as a tailor. Until I design and make some clothes, my freedom to be a tailor is only abstract freedom. I am truly free to be a tailor only when I actually design and make some clothes. A tailor cannot just be a tailor in his or her head. A tailor is really free to be a tailor only if the tailor creates some clothes, puts his or her "tailor-ness" out there into actuality, or actually *is* a tailor.

But what is put out there is not only the expression of the tailor, but also defines the tailor. So what I design and make also determines who I am. If I say I am a tailor but what I design and make cannot be worn or put to use as clothing, then I am not really a tailor after all. What I succeed in putting out there also defines me. Thus to be free is to be able to express oneself into actuality, but also to succeed in having what is out there define oneself *as what one is*. I succeed in being what I am—a tailor—then, when the concept and the activity that I do are completely mutually defining. To be free to be what I am is to go through both of these processes—both the process of expression into activity, and the process by which the activity defines who I am. Because the Concept and the $Effect_{CS}$ are completely mutually defining, the Concept has freedom in both of these ways, it is truly free. It repulses or expresses itself into an actuality that completely expresses its definition, and so through which it is defined.

Hegel apparently intended his claim that the truth of necessity is freedom to apply to the ordinary world of human beings. In a lecture, he apparently suggested that we can see the same sort of freedom that the Concept has in ethics, for example. The ethical person understands that the content of his or her action is necessary (§158A). When we behave ethically, we do our duty, or follow moral laws or rules. We use terms such as "duty," "rules" and "laws" because they capture our sense that there is an element of necessity in ethics. We say that we have to do what duty or the moral rules demand of us. Indeed, Hegel says, it is only when we are conscious of this necessity that we exercise our true freedom. For our true freedom is not merely abstract freedom (the abstract idea that we can do anything) or freedom of choice (the freedom to pick among options, or freedom as possibility), but, rather, is a freedom that must have a content. The action that we perform must have some content or other—it must be labeled or defined by a concept. The concept that captures the action will be provided by thought, by rationality, by Reason—not my personal rationality (though that too), but rationality as a whole system. We are free when governed by Thought or rationality, and least free when governed by the world of (supposedly) immediate being and thereness. Our actions are most free, then, when they are (necessarily) determined or dictated by rational Thought. Hence, we as individuals are most free when our actions presuppose the necessity of rational Thought. When we are motivated to do what we do by the necessity of rationality, we have freely chosen that necessity, and so have that necessity sublated (overcome but preserved) within us. The highest freedom for a human being, Hegel apparently suggested, is to know oneself as determined by rationality (§158A).[3]

Independence or freedom is thus defined by both cause and effect. The Concept, which is the independent and free element, is both cause and effect too, but it is not dependent on anything outside of itself. It is a cause and effect that is established by its own necessary activity. Thus, to be free is not to be uncaused. To be free is to be caused too, but by the necessary activity of the free element itself. What is free causes activity that defines it as an effect, but since the activity follows necessarily from the concept (or character) of what it is, that activity does not come from outside of it. Something is free and independent when its necessity flows out of itself.

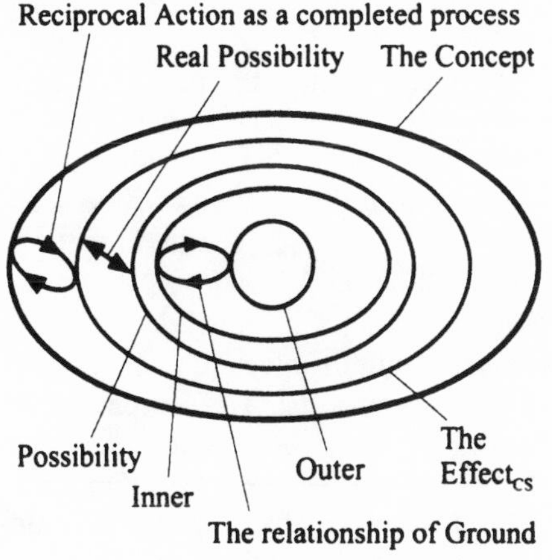

Figure 3.70

Since the beginning of the Doctrine of Actuality, I have been depicting the two inner-most bubbles—Inner and Outer—in a side-by-side view. However, because Inner is a "for itself" concept that completely embraces the Outer in a mutually defining relationship, I can also picture the Concept with the Outer bubble nested within the Inner bubble, as in the diagram on the left.

The stages of Reciprocal Action and Transition to the Concept are important to the debate about the degree to which Hegel is an idealist. The conflict between materialists and idealists in philosophy is a large topic that I certainly cannot solve in a few paragraphs here. But our logical analysis so far provides some hints about Hegel's place in this debate, which I now want to touch on briefly. According to the typical distinction between materialists and idealists, materialists hold that matter or reality is self-generating, self-subsistent, and primary in terms of its causal relation with ideality, thought or rationality. For the materialist, matter is the primary cause of thought. Idealists, on the other hand, hold that thought or rationality is the primary cause of reality or matter, which is therefore not independent, causally generating or self-subsistent in any sense. In Reciprocal Action and the Transition to the Concept, Hegel does not fit neatly into either of these categories. Hegel's idealism does not deny that reality is self-generating, independent, original and causal in relation to thought. Indeed, in the Transition to the Concept, the Effect$_{CS}$ is all of these things. Hegel conceives of Reason as something that develops, or (at the end of time) as something that developed, rather than as static.

It is true, of course, that, for Hegel, the Concept (as doubly "for itself") acts first: it initiates the whole process of Reciprocal Action. It is also the defining element. And, in the end, it is the independent, all-embracing, overgrasping element that presents the Effect$_{CS}$. But what do these logical claims mean? As I see it, Hegel is an idealist in three senses. First, he claims that thought or Reason is the first cause in the sense that Reason is the necessary background and motivation for the whole grasping process. Second, Reason is the defining element insofar as it is the standard and guiding principle that governs the grasping process. And third, Reason or thought is independent, all-embracing and overgrasping in the sense that, in the end, it is the element that pulls and holds everything else together. None of these claims, however, I would like to suggest, necessarily undermines what the materialist typically wants to claim, namely, that matter or reality is self-subsistent, self-generating, independent, original and causal in relation to thought.

First, thought is the first cause in the sense that it is the necessary background of the grasping process. In the stage of Reciprocal Action, activity in the actuality of the rational concepts (the Effect) generates new immediacies that Reason has to work on. The rational concepts with their activity in the actual world are thus original causes in relation to the Substance or Cause. In the stage of Transition to the Concept, the Effect$_{CS}$ is still defined, for Hegel, as an independent actuality in relation to the Concept. But changes in reality do not require or force any response in thought. When a new reality shows up, nothing forces Reason or thought to grasp it. Changes in reality will not cause changes in thought unless there is a reason (pun intended) to grasp the new reality. Reason acts first by motivating the grasping process. Unless there is a reason to understand, no change in reality will cause changes in thought. Changes in reality cause changes in thought only if the attempt to understand things—to reason things out—is already there in the background. Reason is the logically necessary background that must be there *before* changes in reality can cause changes in thought. This is the sense in which Reason *initiates* the whole process of Reciprocal Action. Reason is the first cause insofar as it motivates the grasping process. But the fact that Reason is the first cause in this sense does not mean that it is not also shaped and determined by what happens out there in reality.

Second, when changes in reality are grasped or characterized, reason functions as the overarching standard of definition. The guiding principle for deciding how changes in reality should be conceptualized rests in questions about how the concepts that characterize those changes should be *systematized* into the whole set of rational concepts. When computer programs, for instance, were considered property—even if the old definition of property had to shift to do the job—the application of the concept of property to the new reality had to be *rea-*

sonable. To say that the new application is reasonable is to say that the shift in the concept of property could be *systematized* into the whole conceptual scheme. What makes the choice of a new concept or a shift in an old concept reasonable is determined by how the shift or new introduction will affect the whole scheme of rational concepts, or the rational, conceptual system as a whole. In short, when a new reality is labeled with a concept—whether new or old—the application makes sense only in light of the whole scheme, that is, in light of Reason or the Concept, as the whole system of thought itself. As a result, for Hegel, Reason provides the overarching, guiding principle and standard for defining reality. Again, however, this claim would not undermine the claim that what Reason is like is shaped by what happens out there in reality. Changes in reality do cause changes in Reason, which, as an ongoing, developing system, shifts over time. Reason and reality develop in response to one another—in a relationship of Reciprocal Action—in time. But, when reality shifts, Reason works to grasp and define that shift in light of the whole conceptual scheme *after the fact*.

Finally, when the whole process of development of reality in time is finished or completed, the Concept, or Reason, is the thought of the completely systematized and completed set of rational concepts. From the point of view of the end of time, looking back at the whole process of rational concepts in the actual world, that process is nothing but the development and presentation of Reason itself, of the complete conceptual scheme or system. Reason is the concept that captures the whole process in the end. Because Reason as the Concept grasps the whole development of reality *after the fact*, that is to say, after the development is finished. Therefore, the fact that Reason is the one thought that grasps the whole process of development does not undermine the claim that reality is self-generating and causal in relation to thought.

The work of the logic is not yet complete, however. As Hegel says, seeing the Concept as a simple whole that relates itself to itself—or, in the diagram, as a single bubble with all the activity inside it—is really a poor characterization of the Concept (§159R).

V. Wrap Up Essence: Comments on Syntax

As I did at the end of Chapter Two, I want to assess the syntactic progress of this chapter briefly. Although the concepts in the Doctrine of Essence have become more complicated, the diagrams reveal that there is a step-by-step development from stage to stage, so that Hegel has offered a much more syntactically tight logical argument than has generally been assumed in the literature. Some sequences seem more exhaustive—and hence more necessary—than others (cf. Chapter Two, Section V for a discussion of necessity as exhaustion). From the stage of Immediate Actuality to the stage of Real Possibility, for instance, faded (dashed) elements come forward (become solid-lined) in a step-by-step way, so that at the end of the sequence, every possible combination of faded and forward elements has been explored.[4] But there are other sections where the sequence of moves seems to rely more heavily on the meanings of the terms rather than on purely syntactic patterns. For example, from the stage of Thing as Form to the stage of Matter and Form Fall Apart, the moves are driven largely by semantics. The matters merge into One Matter, for example, because the matters were defined semantically as abstract—so that there is no way to tell them apart as separate Matters—and not because of any syntactic requirement.

Still, Hegel's emphasis on exhaustion continues to shape the course of the logic. As the concepts become increasingly complicated, for instance, their internal elements come into play in a step-by-step way in layers. At first we explore the outer-most logical elements, but then some internal element will come into play again, or assert itself again, and change the course of the logic. In the development of the relationship between the *Erscheinende* and the Appearance, for example, the full character of the former Matters as both subsistence and non-subsistence must be exhausted before moving on to further stages (see Content and Form). We see the same phenomenon in the stages of Substance, when taking seriously the internal contents of the elements in play redefines the Substance as a Cause (see Substance as Cause). The idea that logical necessity is a kind of exhaustion is illustrated in these sections in the sense that the full content of the elements must be exploited before moving on to subsequent stages.

The emphasis on exhaustion has other logical effects as well. In the discussion of the Doctrine of Being we saw that Hegel tended to reuse logical elements from earlier stages rather than bring in something new. We see him doing the same thing in this section. The relationship of Identity is developed very early, and then reappears in several subsequent stages. Similarly, the activity of Ground also reappears in several subsequent stages. In these cases, Hegel exhausts a concept by reusing it over and over.

In Chapter Two we saw that logical elements often first come into view in an indeterminate way (which I represent by giving them dashed outlines) and only later become determined. This pattern according to which a concept is first presented as indeterminate and later as determinate is also repeated in this chapter (see, for instance, Immediate Actuality).

The most important syntactic pattern that is repeated in this chapter is the logical development of increasingly ideal, "for itself" concepts that, as in Chapter Two, embrace a spuriously infinite, back-and-forth processes. Although the logical process by which "for itself" concepts are defined sometimes differs in this chapter, the basic outline remains the same: a concept is defined as a "for itself" concept by embracing a spuriously infinite back-and-forth process. In this chapter, when the spuriously infinite process takes place between one concept and another concept it already embraces, the process does not generate a whole new concept, as it did in Chapter Two. When one concept already embraces the other, the spuriously infinite process simply redefines the embracing concept as a more general or ideal concept (see World of Appearance, Condition as a Totality, and Reciprocal Action). This chapter also refined the syntactic definition of "for-itselfness," however, by distinguishing a "for-itselfness" of content and one of form (or presentation)—a distinction which produced "doubly for itself" concepts. Under the "for-itselfness" of content, a concept embraces another concept (or two) in its contents, which I depicted by drawing the bubble around the embraced content. Under the "for-itselfness" of form, a concept *presents* another concept *for itself*, or through its own activity, which I depicted with a looping arrow that runs from the embracing element to the content and back to the embracing element. Being-for-itself in Chapter Two outlined only the "for-itselfness" of content—it grasped but did not present its contents. However, the "for-itselfness" of form was foreshadowed in Being-for-itself's process of Repulsion. The process in which Being-for-itself repulsed the something-others as its own content is similar to the "for itself" process of form or presentation that is introduced in this chapter. The distinction between form and content was developed in the stage of Properties. Although the concept of Essence was also introduced before the "for-itselfness" of form was defined in the stage of Absolute Relationship, Essence could be depicted with either the side-by-side view (using the "for itself" arrow) or as a bubble surrounding its contents. Because Essence embraced its content (the "for-itselfness" of content) by *shining*, its definition included a presentation (i.e. the shining), which is properly represented by an arrow, even if that process was not yet formally defined as a "for itself" process of form or presentation.

There are also some new patterns in this chapter that rely on both semantics and syntax:

(1) Possibility by definition (semantics) implies another possibility. A possibility fulfills its definition as a possibility by generating another possibility that can serve as a genuine alternative for it, giving rise to a syntactic pattern according to which a possibility produces another possibility (see Contingency and Chance, Condition, Reciprocal Action).

(2) The "positedness" of something is sublated (canceled but preserved) by the fact that it exists (see Immediate Actuality, The Necessary). If something exists, then it is not merely supposed or assumed because it is already there. Since it is there, it loses its air of having been merely assumed or supposed. I will say more about "positedness" in a moment.

(3) A reciprocal relationship of mutual identity becomes a relationship of Ground (see Inner and Outer, Reciprocal Action).

(4) When a concept is defined as something that *presents* its contents, or as a concept that has a form or presentation, it is defined as a concept on its own, separate from and opposed to that content and has an "in itself" relationship of opposition with its content (see External Necessity).

There are two apparent gaps in the syntactic development, however, that require special comment. First, in the Doctrine of Appearance, Thing's innards contain two concepts (ground and grounded) which may be interchangeably applied to the two bubbles that Thing contains. Because ground and grounded may be applied interchangeably to each of the two bubbles inside Thing, there are, mathematically speaking, four different possible renditions that seem to follow. In the subsequent development of the logic, however, only two of those options are explored. This fact raises the possibility that there are two options that Hegel has not explored, thereby leaving a serious gap in the syntactic development. Here are the two options I do not mention:

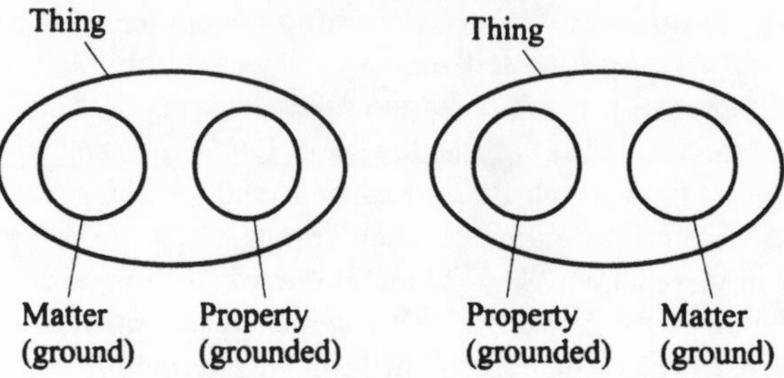

Figure 3.71

Because the relationship of Ground—or the mutually defining relationship between ground and grounded—is completed or finished in the stage of Thing, however, the characteristics of ground and grounded are not separate within the Thing (§124). Hegel's claim that the characteristics of ground and grounded are not separate within the Thing can be interpreted in a straightforward pictorial way: since ground and grounded cannot be separate within the Thing, then the two options diagrammed above are ruled out. The elements (bubbles) within the Thing cannot be defined in such a way that one is grounded while the other is ground. Semantically, since the relationship of Ground is a finished whole, it can no longer be divided up into ground on one side, and grounded on the other. Syntactically, since either side can be ground or grounded, they are each both defined as ground-and-grounded, or as ground/grounded. Hence they cannot be distinguished from one another using those terms. They have the same character as one another, and so must be defined—together—as either ground or grounded at the same time: they are either both grounded (as in the stage of Properties) or both ground (as in the stage of Matters).

The second apparent gap appears in Hegel's discussion of Likeness and Unlikeness. Hegel introduces a third term to compare Essence and Shine and determine how they are like and unlike each other. To use Hegel's anthropomorphic language for a moment, because Essence and Shine are holding themselves apart from one another in Immediate Distinction, they cannot make this comparison by themselves. Only a term that can see both sides can make the comparison. Since Essence is refusing to see Shine, and Shine is refusing to see Essence, neither of them can see both sides of the comparison. So they need a third term to determine how they are alike or unlike each other. As soon as Hegel brings in this third term, however, he seems to have introduced an extra element. Has Hegel introduced a hanging logical element that is not followed out? Is there a road-not-taken in his logical syntax after all?

I do not think so, for the third term that is hinted at in the stage of Likeness and Unlikeness is later introduced and defined on its own. There is a concept that sees both Essence and Shine and that makes the comparison between Essence and Shine, namely, the concept of Ground. I therefore think we can see the "third term" as a concept of proto-Ground. Because Essence and Shine are not related, their definitions cannot capture their relationship. As a result, the introduction of a third term is necessitated by the inability to go further with the logical elements at hand. The third term steps in to make the necessary comparison in order to get the logical development going again, and then we find out later that this third term is the relationship of Ground. The third term is therefore not an extra, hanging element that is left unexplored. Instead, Hegel's introduction of the third term is a place where a concept is implied in an earlier stage, but is not fully developed, posited or established until later on. The concept of Ground is the third term whose presence is hinted at in the stage of Likeness and Unlikeness, and then posited in its own right later on.

There is one final terminological issue I would like to address before leaving this chapter, namely, the status of certain concepts in Hegel's logic that we can think of as meta-logical terms. There are, in addition to the series of concepts that Hegel has introduced so far—from Being to Essence to Concept—other concepts that Hegel uses to describe the logical development. Terms such as "concrete" (*konkret*) and "abstract" (*abstrakt*), for instance, never appear on the list of concepts that are developed during the course of the logic. Rather, they are used to characterize concepts that belong to that list. "Abstract" and "concrete" therefore do not seem to be part of the logic itself, but belong instead to the commentary about the logical development—to a meta-language about the logic (Harris 1990, 82), or to a meta-logic.

Their presence raises two problems. The first has to do with their basic legitimacy. In the *Science of Logic*, Hegel says that a properly scientific logic must restrict itself to terms that are defined within the logic itself (Hegel 1969, 40). As Phillip T. Grier and others have pointed out, we cannot interpret Hegel's claim to mean that, at every point in the logic, the commentary must restrict itself to concepts that have already been developed. Such a restriction would mean that at the beginning of the logic—where few concepts have yet been introduced—the commentary could hardly say anything at all (Grier 1990, 62-3). Hegel's remark does suggest, however, that the commentary should restrict itself to categories or concepts that are at least introduced somewhere in the logic. Hegel's use of meta-logical terms that are not developed anywhere in the series of logical concepts therefore seems to violate his own scientific requirement. What status do the meta-logical terms have? Are they extraneous concepts? Because I am arguing that Hegel's logic is syntactically tighter than has often been thought, the presence of possibly extraneous concepts is a serious problem. Hegel succeeds in defending his system only if there are no logical concepts left out, and only if there are no extraneous concepts that are not properly developed by logic itself (see Chapter One, Section V). The presence of extraneous meta-logical concepts—if they *are* extraneous—would violate this syntactic requirement.

The second problem raised by the meta-logical terms has to do with their meanings. Grier has argued, for example, that there are six different meanings of "abstract" and "concrete" in Hegel's logic (Grier 1990, 66-9). Not only might Hegel be introducing terms with a questionable logical status, then, but he may also be failing to give those terms a consistent meaning. Using terms consistently is surely one of the most basic requirements of "science."

Let me begin with the terms "concrete" and "abstract." In the introduction to Chapter Two, I defined "concrete" to mean "having a content." A concrete concept has a content. It is a concept that has the character of having a content—that is what it is like. I suggested that we can picture a concrete concept as a bubble with other bubbles inside it, where the other bubbles represent other concepts which define or "fill up" the concrete concept—in short, give the concrete concept its content. In the stage of Becoming in the same chapter, however, I had to modify this pictorial suggestion somewhat. Hegel says that Becoming is the first concrete concept, but since I depicted Becoming with an arrow rather than as a bubble—to represent its status as a process—I could not put any concepts inside it in the diagram. I argued, however, that Becoming should nonetheless be seen as a concrete concept because Being and Nothing define it, and thus succeed in giving it a character or content. Other concepts that represent processes are in the same position that Becoming is in. The concept of Ground, for example, captures a process of mutual identification between concepts that is also best represented by an arrow. Like Becoming, then, Ground is not a bubble that can be filled up with other bubbles. Nonetheless, the concepts whose process defines Ground still determine it, or give Ground what character it has, and are therefore its contents, I would argue, even if they are not pictorially "inside" Ground.

As Errol Harris points out in his reply to Grier, this basic sense of the term "concrete"—the sense in which a concrete concept has a content, or, as Harris would put it, is a whole with earlier concepts sublated within it—gives rise to other, corollary uses of the term that appear to be different definitions (Harris 1990, 81). Grier had suggested that Hegel sometimes uses "abstract" to mean "separated," or "pulled apart," so that "concrete" would mean "not separated," "not pulled apart," or "taken as a whole" (Grier 1990, 66). As Harris suggests, this meaning can be seen as a corollary of the sense in which to be concrete is to have a content. Concrete concepts have a content because they are defined in relation to the logical context of concepts that give rise to them, and hence are not separated out (abstracted) from that context (Harris 1990, 81). The basic sense of "concrete" can also be seen in Hegel's tendency to use the term "abstract" to mean that a concept is "empty." When concepts are separated from their contexts (abstracted), they are empty in the sense that they lack a content (see also Harris 1990, 81). A third meaning, according to which abstractness is "one-sidedness," can also be seen as a corollary of the basic meaning. As Harris points out, abstract concepts are "one-sided" because they are partial: since they are pulled apart (abstracted) from their context, they have only one side to them, and do not make reference to the full context of concepts which should make up their contents or define them (Harris 1990, 81). In another related usage, the term "abstract" sometimes means not just one-sided, but "one-sidedly positive." Once again, however, this fourth meaning can be explained by reference to the basic one. The content of "concrete" concepts includes both positive and negative elements. Being-there, for example, gets positivity from the side of Being, but is also defined by negativity because of the presence of Nothing. Because abstract concepts are separated out from the complexity of what should be defining them (they are one-sided), they may be one-sidedly positive, without any negativity (see Harris 1990, 81). When Hegel uses "abstract" to suggest that a concept is falsely immediate (rather than mediated), limited, or fixed, these meanings, too, are corollaries of the basic one (see Harris 1990, 81).

There is an additional shift in Hegel's use of the term "concrete," however, which neither Grier nor Harris notice, and so which is not explained in their discussion. In the Doctrine of Essence, "concreteness" comes closer to a more everyday sense of "concrete." When we describe a topic or concept as "concrete," we generally associate that concreteness with existence. So, for example, we distinguish concrete disciplines such as biology from abstract ones such as philosophy. We think of biology as a concrete discipline because it deals with real, existing things—plants, animals, hearts and so on—whereas philosophy deals "merely," as we say, with abstract ideas. In the Doctrine of Actuality, Hegel seems to use the term "concrete" in this more standard sense as having to do with existence. In §143, for example, Hegel says the first Actuality we meet (in the stage of Immediate Actuality) is concrete. While it is concrete in the basic sense mentioned above—because it contains the immediate unity of essence and existence, and so has a content—part of what makes the Actuality concrete for Hegel also seems to be that it exists. In Contingency and Chance, Hegel describes the developing Actuality as "externally concrete" (§144). Again, part of what makes it concrete is that it is a conceptual unity and so has other concepts as its content. But it is also concrete ("externally concrete" in fact) because it exists. This interpretation of what Hegel means by concreteness is reinforced by his apparent suggestion in a lecture that the type of possibility that the stage of Condition has is "no longer the merely abstract possibility that we began with; instead, it is the possibility that is" (§146A). Here Hegel appears to be drawing a distinction between abstract possibility, which lacks existence, and a kind of concrete possibility, which would include existence—thus implying that concreteness means "having to do with existence," as it does in our more ordinary usage.

Although this use of the term "concrete" appears to involve a shift in meaning—or at the very least an extension of meaning—it, too, ultimately has its roots in the basic meaning. To explain why this is so, however, we need to examine what it means to be a meta-logical term. As a meta-logical concept, the term "concrete" describes the nature or character of logical concepts. Using more (onto-)logical terminology, we could also say that meta-logical terms capture the being of logical concepts. Meta-logical terms describe what the logical concepts are like, how they are, or how they have their being. According to the basic meaning of "concrete," for instance, a "concrete" concept has a content or character. To say that a concept has a content or character is to say that it has a certain sort of being, namely, that it has its being in such a way that it has a content. The term "concrete" thus describes a type of being for concepts. Meta-logical concepts are about the being of concepts, rather than the being of things in the world, but they are still about being.

Notice that this is just what the logic itself has been about so far: it has developed concepts that describe ways of being. Being, Being-there, Being-in-itself, Being-for-itself, Number, Degree; even Essence, Appearance, Existence, Actuality and Substance, for instance, all describe ways of being. Some things are just there, some are there as individual chunks. Some things can be in the world as kinds, numbers, or degrees. Having an essence is a way of being, even if we can't "touch" the essence (since it does not belong to the physical world of immediate being). Being an appearance is a way of being. Existing is a way of being. Existing such that the essence and thereness mutually determine each other (Actuality) is a way of being, and so on. In short, so far, the logic has developed concepts about ways of being.

The term "concrete"—which is about the being of concepts—is parasitic on the types of being developed by the logical concepts themselves. As the logical concepts develop their definitions of types of being, so the being of concepts develops. The type of being or "concreteness" that a concept can have depends on the type of being it captures or describes. That's why the basic meaning of "concreteness" is just "having a content." At the beginning of the logic, in the Doctrine of Being, the logical concepts capture types of being that are quite abstract. At first, they define being as simply having some content, some character or other, some quality. This is the same type of being that the logical concepts themselves can have. When the logical concepts describe a type of being that is just "having a content," they themselves have a type of being (concreteness) that is just "having a content." As we move along in the development of the logic, however, the type of being that the logical concepts capture becomes more sophisticated, and hence the type of being that they themselves can have as concepts (their concreteness) becomes more sophisticated as well. Once we pass the stage of Existence, in which the logical concepts capture types of being that include existence, the type of content or being that the concepts can have includes existence as well. That's why "concreteness"—which just is the type of being of a logical concept, as I have suggested—comes to include existence. Logical concepts that capture existence themselves have a content that includes existence. Their "concreteness" includes existence. The meta-logical concept of "concreteness" is therefore parasitic on the logical concepts themselves in the sense that it depends on the type of being that is developed by the logical concepts. When, early on, the logical concepts are about quality, definition, or having any kind of content or character, the concepts themselves are "concrete" in the sense that they have a content, a definition, or a basic character too. But when the logical concepts are about having existence, then they themselves have the sort of being, content, or "concreteness" that includes existence. The type of being or content that the logical concepts can have—which is captured by the meta-logical term "concrete"—is parasitic on the type of being that the logical concepts are about.

Noticing the parallelism between the types of being captured by the logical concepts and the types of being that those logical concepts have (their "concreteness") allows us to answer the first worry about the meta-logical concept of "concreteness" mentioned above, namely, the worry about whether it involves importing extraneous material into the syntactic development of the logic. Because the types of being that meta-logical concreteness ascribe to the logical concepts are parasitic on the types of being captured by the logical concepts themselves, the concept of "concreteness" does not in fact import any extraneous material into the logical development. Where the logical concepts define being as having a content or character, concreteness is defined as having a content or character. Where the logical concepts define being as having existence, concreteness is defined as having existence. There is no sense of "what it is to be something" that is contained in the meta-logical concept of "concreteness" that is not already developed in the logic proper.

A second family of meta-logical terms I would like to address here is the term "posit" (*setzen*) and its cognates, such as "positedness" (*Gesetzsein*). In the Doctrine of Being, I interpreted "posit" to mean "taken as," or "characterized as." Like "concreteness," these terms belong to the meta-language about the logical concepts. They capture something about the nature of those concepts—something about their determination, or their being. In the original German, the connection between "positedness" and "being" is expressed etymologically by the fact that the German word for "being"—"*sein*"—is within the German word for "positedness." The German root word, "*setzen*" means to place, set or establish. It also means to suppose or assume. The cognate "*gesetzt*" means to be fixed, set or established. Thus "positedness" or "*Gesetzsein*" means to have the sort of being that is set as, established as, or, as I put it above, taken as, or characterized as. In the stage of Being-there, for example, Hegel says that "the determinacy [of Being-there] is one with Being, and is at the same time posited as negation" (§92). I took this to mean that Being-there is Being (which is why I depicted it as the same bubble as Being), but it is Being now determined or characterized in a way that takes account of negation (Nothing). So Being-there is a type of Being that is also taken or established as negation. To be "posited" is to have a type of being or character that is defined by passivity: to be characterized as something *by something else*. Unlike having a content (concreteness), when a concept is "posited" it is defined in a passive way by something else.

Between §141 and §143, Hegel modifies "positedness" somewhat. Here we have not only "positedness," but "mere positedness." In §141, for example, he describes the difference that remains between Inner and Outer as "mere positedness." Inner and Outer are really the same as one another, so that their distinction "is determined as mere positedness" (§141). If to be "posited" is to be taken or characterized as, to be "merely posited" would be to be *merely* taken as, or *merely* characterized as. While both "positedness" and "mere positedness" indicate that the concept in question has been defined in a passive way, in "mere positedness" there is an air of failure, disappointment, semblance or show that is not implied by the term "positedness" by itself. To be "merely posited" is to be assumed or stipulated in a way that might be wrong, and the clear implication is that this status as "merely" posited is a flaw—that what is merely assumed or stipulated should be known better. The contrast here echoes the contrast between "appearance" and "mere appearance." An "appearance" is a definite something that shows up or shows forth, but a "mere appearance" is likely to be a false show, and the implication is that it should be more than "mere"—that its status as "mere" is a flaw or disappointment. Still, while the addition of the qualifier "mere" puts a new spin on "positedness," it has not changed the term's basic meaning, and so does not raise worries about unjustified shifts in meaning.

There is a third application of the term "positedness" here in the Doctrine of Essence during the discussion of Effect. Hegel suggests that the concept of Effect is characterized by "positedness" as well. He says, for example, that Cause makes itself into positedness in Effect (§153R), and that Effect is positedness (§154). This use of "positedness" is consistent with the one we saw above. To be an effect is to be characterized or established by something else, namely, by a cause. Every effect has its being or definition established, set or characterized by something else, namely, by the cause. So effects have a type of passive character or being that can be described as "positedness." Just as effects out there are characterized by causes, Hegel is suggesting, so the concept of Effect is characterized by the concept of Cause. The concept of Effect is posited as well—it has the sort of being which involves being characterized by something else, namely by the concept of Cause. From a meta-logical point of view, then, the concept of Effect has its being as "positedness."

While the term "positedness" may not have changed meaning between the earlier and later uses, a different change has occurred. In the Doctrine of Being, the "something else" that did the positing was left unspoken: Being-there was posited as negation, but whatever was doing the positing was never named. In part, of course, the "something else" that does the positing is us: we who are reading the logic characterize Being-there as Being with negation. For Hegel, however, the logic is supposed to be the development of rationality itself, or rationality driving itself (see Chapter One, Section IV). So it must not be only us readers who take Being-there this or that way. Reason itself posits Being-there this or that way. In the Doctrine of Essence, this source of the "positedness" is revealed. Effect is "positedness"; and the "something else" that does the positing is Cause. Hegel associates Cause with the side of Thought or rationality. As a result, the true source of the "positedness" (for Hegel) becomes clear: Thought or Reason itself—which is what Cause is—posits the Effect.

While "positedness" does not raise worries about shifts in meaning in the way that "concrete" did, there is still the question about its logical status. Does "positedness" raise the specter of a "yes" answer to the worry about whether meta-logical terms introduce logically extraneous concepts? Is "positedness" an extraneous concept that is not properly developed by the logical process? Again, I don't think so. The concept of Effect captures the type of being that effects have. It suggests that effects have a type of being which is "positedness," since they have a passive character such that what they are like is established by something else (the cause). This is the type of being that the concept of Effect is itself supposed to have as well. So the type of being that the concept has—meta-logical "positedness"—is the same type of being that the concept captures—"positedness." As with "concreteness," then, "positedness" as a type of being that a concept has is parasitic on the type of being that the concept captures. Thus "positedness" as a type of being is developed during the course of the logic in the stage of Effect. The concept of Effect has the same type of being that it captures or means. The concept of Effect both captures and is itself characterized by passive "positedness." Because the type of being that Effect has is developed (in the stage of Effect) by the logical concepts, the "positedness" of Effect does not go beyond what is developed by the logical process. Hence, meta-logical "positedness" does not introduce any extraneous material to the logic.

In the next section of the logic, the Doctrine of the Concept, we shift gears somewhat. During a good part of the chapter, the type of conceptual development we will see—and the nature of the diagrams—will take a form more familiar in today's formal logic. To see why this is so, however, we need to move on to the detailed business of tracing the logical development in the Doctrine of the Concept.

Notes

1. In their translation, Geraets, Suchting and Harris sometimes replace an unclear pronoun with the item to which they think it refers. In §132, for example, Hegel says "[d]as Erscheinende hat so seinen Grund in dieser als seinem Wesen." Geraets, Suchting and Harris replace the "dieser" ("this") with what Hegel had been discussing in the previous sentence, "the form." I do not always agree with their judgments about what a pronoun refers to, however.

2. Notice that the English word "terminological" echoes Hegel's claim that logic involves both syntax and semantic (cf. the Introduction to this book). The word "terminological" suggests that there is logic to the meanings of terms, or that the meanings of terms include logic.

3. For an excellent discussion of the concept of freedom that grows out of the logic see Will Dudley's *Hegel, Nietzsche and Philosophy: Thinking Freedom* (2002, 17–21).

4. There is one combination that is never explored, and that is the combination in which only the Outer bubble is solid-lined, and everything else is dashed. As soon as the Outer bubble becomes solid, however, the Actuality bubble becomes solid as well, so that the Outer bubble is never solid by itself. That is because the meaning of the terms makes the combination in which the Outer bubble is solid by itself impossible. Once the Outer is established, the whole Actuality is there as well, since to be Outer is by definition to be there. So once the Outer bubble is solid (the Outer is there), the Actuality which contains it has thereness too, which is why the Actuality bubble must become solid-lined at the same time that the Outer bubble becomes solid-lined. At first, the Actuality is there only as a Possibility, of course, but once the Outer is established, the Actuality is established too.

Chapter Four

The Doctrine of the Concept

I. Introduction

This chapter begins where Chapter Three ended, with the concept of the Concept. At the end of Chapter Three, the Concept was defined as the last and final, unconditioned concept that grasps and presents everything else, and outside of which there are no further concepts (see the stages of Substance and Transition to the Concept). It is the thought or concept of the completed and completely systematized set of rational concepts (content) (see Substance), along with all of the processes (form) of rational thought for the set (see Transition to the Concept). It is the overarching thought or grasper of everything else at the end of time. It is Reason itself, defined as the concept or thought that grasps the completed *system* of thought at the end of time.

Since the Concept is the one, overarching concept that grasps and defines everything else, both in terms of content and process (form), what logical task remains to be done? Although the Concept has been defined as the overarching grasper, it has not yet *gone through* or *carried out* the grasping process. Think of a toaster, for instance. We can define a toaster as a machine that makes toast. When we go to the store to buy a machine that makes toast, we know what to pick out because we know what machines that make toast tend to look like. But the toaster that I buy is not fully "a machine that makes toast"—it does not really have its definition as "a machine that makes toast"—until it goes through the process of making some toast. Only after I take the toaster home, plug it in, put in a piece of bread, push the lever down, and the toaster goes through its process of making toast, does the toaster fulfill its definition as "a machine that makes toast." The Concept is currently defined as the grasper in the same way that a toaster is defined as a toaster when it is still at the store. The Concept is defined as what thought or Reason, which grasps the completed set of rational concepts and rational processes, will "look like" at the end of time. As Hegel suggests, the Concept is defined so far only in a formal way (§§162, 164R). A toaster is defined in a formal way at the store when we apply the label "toaster" to it, or say it is a "toaster." That label is abstract because the toaster has not yet succeeded in making any toast. We may yet get it home and find that it does not work, and so is not really a "toaster" after all. The toaster only gets to be a toaster—to really *be* or *have being* as a toaster—when it goes through the process of toasting something. Similarly, so far, because the Concept has not yet gone through the process of grasping, it is defined only formally—or abstractly—as the overarching grasper. It gets to really *be* or *have being* as the overarching grasper only when it goes through the process of grasping everything. In the Doctrine of the Concept, we follow out the logical development in which the Concept undergoes the process of grasping everything.

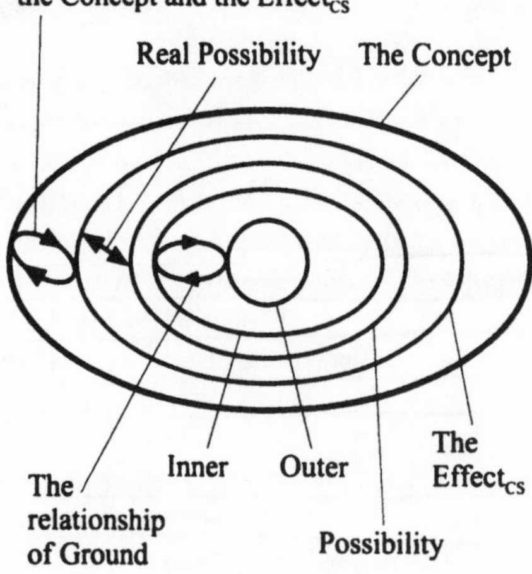

Figure 4.1

While the definition of the Concept is formal, that definition is still concrete in the logical sense. To be concrete is to be determined, or to have a definition (see Chapter Three, Section V for a discussion of the meaning of "concrete"). In the logic, a concept is concrete in the most basic sense when it has other concepts that define it. Because the Concept contains *all* other logical concepts, it is as defined as anything can get: it is altogether concrete, as Hegel says (§164). The diagram for the Concept at the end of Chapter Three depicts this concreteness of the Concept because the Concept is the outer-most bubble and contains all the other bubbles (concepts) and arrows (logical processes) within it. In the diagram of the Concept here, each of the logical elements is labeled with the last concept (and hence the highest concept) that was used to characterize that element in Chapter Three. Nevertheless, the Concept is still abstract because it has not yet gone through the activity of grasping and hence has not fulfilled its definition as the all-embracing grasper.

Hegel describes the Concept in logical terms as a free whole or totality that is "in and for itself" determinate (§160). We will see why it is free shortly. The Concept is a totality because it is the *completed* set and system of rational concepts. It contains all of the rational concepts. The Concept is "in and for itself" determinate because it is defined in both an "in itself" and a "for itself" sense. At the end of Chapter Three, the Concept was defined through a doubly "for itself" relationship with its contents, which was the Effect_{CS}. The letters "CS" in the term "Effect_{CS}" stand for "completely systematized." The Effect-Completely-Systematized is what the set of rational concepts will be like after it has been completely systematized by Reason. It is the set of rational concepts together with all of the processes of rational thought, as a completed whole at the end of time. The Concept has a doubly "for itself" relationship with the Effect_{CS} because it has a "for itself" relationship with the Effect_{CS} in terms of both content and process or form. As the thought or concept of the completed set of rational concepts, the Concept embraces the Effect_{CS} as its content. It has or contains in its content the completed set of rational concepts. This relationship is represented in the diagram by the fact that the bubble depicting the Concept surrounds the bubble depicting the Effect_{CS}. The Concept embraces the Effect_{CS} "for itself," or as its content. This type of "for itself" relationship captures the most basic definition of ideality or universality and was introduced in the stage of Being-for-itself in Chapter Two. (A "for itself" logical relationship is always associated with ideality or universality.) It suggests that a universal embraces a group of items (the comm*un*ality account of universality) insofar as they have something in common (the comm*on*ality account of universality).

Moreover, although this conclusion will not be drawn (or depicted) until the stage of Universality, because the Concept initiated the process of thought that systematizes the set of rational concepts throughout time (see the stage of Transition to Concept in Chapter Three), it *presents* the Effect_{CS} as its own activity. The Concept presents the Effect_{CS} *for itself*, or through its own activity. It has the Effect_{CS} as its form, process, or the way in which it is presented in time. In the stage of Universality, this relationship will be depicted in the diagram by a looping "for itself" arrow that will run from the Concept (Universality) to the Effect_{CS} and back to the Concept. To use Hegel's more anthropomorphic language, the Effect_{CS} is the way in which the Concept presents itself in time. The looping arrow will depict this second, "for itself" relationship of form or presentation, which captures the universality (or ideality) according to which a universal actively identifies its contents by *making* the items it embraces what they are. This "for-itselfness" was introduced in the stage of Absolute Relationship in Chapter Three.

It is because the Concept *presents* the Effect_{CS} *for itself*, or through its own activity, that it will have not only a "for itself" relationship with the Effect_{CS}, but also an "in itself" relationship with the Effect_{CS}, and so will be "in and for itself" determinate, as Hegel suggests. The Concept maintains a "for itself" relationship with the Effect_{CS} because it still embraces the Effect_{CS} as its content (the "for itself" relationship of content). But the second "for itself" relationship of form or presentation gives the Concept an "in itself" relationship with the Effect_{CS} as well. The stage of External Necessity in Chapter Three developed the logical conclusion that, in general, whenever a concept actively *presents* its contents through a "for itself" relationship of form, that concept is defined as separate from and opposed to its contents. In the same way here, because the Concept presents the Effect$_{CS}$, it is not the same as the Effect$_{CS}$ but is a separate concept of its own. The Concept is what it is, and then presents the Effect$_{CS}$. The Concept thus has a relationship of separation or opposition with the Effect$_{CS}$, which was precisely the sort of relationship that was the hallmark of the "in itself" relationship introduced in the Doctrine of Being in Chapter Two (see the stage of Being-in-itself). In general, an "in itself" relationship is one in which a concept is defined as a separate concept in opposition to another concept. Although the definition of the first concept points toward or mentions the second concept, the first concept has a definition of its own, separate from and opposed to the other concept. That is just the sort of relationship that the second "for itself" relationship of form gives to the Concept in relation to the Effect$_{CS}$. Although the Concept must be defined in relation to the Effect$_{CS}$—it still embraces the Effect$_{CS}$ in its content—because it *presents* the Effect$_{CS}$, it also has a definition of its own, "in itself," separate from and opposed to the Effect$_{CS}$. Therefore, the doubly "for itself" relationship that the Concept will have with the Effect$_{CS}$ gives the Concept a relationship with the Effect$_{CS}$ that can also be characterized as an "in and for itself" relationship, as Hegel suggests.

The "in and for itself" relationship that the Concept will have with the Effect$_{CS}$ makes the Concept free and independent (see also the Transition to the Concept in Chapter Three). Because the Concept *presents* the Effect$_{CS}$, it initiated the process of presenting or going through the Effect$_{CS}$, and so produces or causes its own definition. It is therefore free in the sense that it gives itself the definition that it has. Moreover, because it is defined completely in relation to its own contents and contains everything, it is completely independent. It defines itself completely through its own contents and processes. Moreover, since it contains everything else (it is unconditioned [see the stage of Substance in Chapter Three]), there is nothing else outside of it on which it could depend for its definition.

In the *Science of Logic*, Hegel calls the Doctrines of Being and Essence, taken together, the "Objective Logic." The example of the toaster helps to explain why the definition generated for the Concept by the Doctrines of Being and Essence is an *objective* one. By the end of the Doctrine of the Concept in Chapter Three, the definition of the Concept characterizes what the Concept is like if we look at it out there as an object, or in an objective way, in the same way that we can characterize a toaster at the store based on what it looks like as an object from the outside, without plugging it in. When we go to the store to buy a machine that makes toast, we know what objects to pick off the shelf because we know what machines that make toast look like, when viewed as objects from the outside. Similarly, the definition of the Concept developed by the end of Chapter Three tells us what the Concept looks like as an object, when viewed from the outside. The Concept is the thought of the set and system of all rational concepts together with all the processes of thought belonging to those concepts in a completely reciprocal relationship.

The Doctrine of the Concept, by contrast—which, in the *Science of Logic*, Hegel calls the "Subjective Logic"—offers a *subjective* definition of the Concept. The definition of the Concept offered in the Doctrine of the Concept is subjective in three senses. (1) The Concept will be defined in a subjective way in the grammatical sense, which is to say, in the same way in which the subject of a sentence is the subjectivity of the verb in the predicate. (2) The Concept will be defined as subjective in the sense in which human beings are subjective: it will be defined as a consciousness, and later as a self-consciousness. (3) The definition of the Concept will be subjective in the sense that it will include types of thought that belong to consciousnesses—types of thought such as purpose and cognition, for example, that we ordinarily associate only with living, conscious and self-conscious beings—i.e. with the subjective thought of individual (human) subjects.

(1) First, in the Doctrine of the Concept, the Concept goes through the process of grasping as its own activity. To use Hegel's anthropomorphic language, the Concept will be defining itself through its own activity, just as we might say that a toaster defines itself as a toaster through its own activity of toasting. Once we plug in the toaster, put in the bread, and push down the lever, the toaster goes ahead and does its toasting activity on its own. It defines itself as a genuine toaster when it goes through the process of toasting. The toaster is thereby the subject that goes through its own toasting activity. Since the Concept will be defining *itself* through its activity, it will be the *subject* of its definition process in the same sense in which something is the subject of a sentence. The Concept will be the subject or actor that is performing the defining activity, in the way that the subject of a sentence is the subject or actor that performs the verb, or does the activity captured by the verb. Just as the toaster is the subject of the toasting activity when it goes through the process of toasting, the Concept is the subject of the grasping activity when it goes through the process of grasping. The toaster and the Concept are each the subject of the activity or verb. Since the Concept will now be the actor or active subject of the defining activity, it is a subject, rather than merely an object, in this first sense. Instead of tracing how the Concept is defined from the outside, when viewed as an object or objectively, we will be tracing how the Concept is defined as the subject that goes through the defining activity.

This first sense of subjectivity explains my use of the term "activity"—rather than just "process"—to describe what the toaster and the Concept do. In the grammatical sense, the verb in the predicate is the activity *of the subject*. Similarly, the toasting activity is the activity *of the toaster as the subject*, and the grasping activity is the activity *of the Concept as the subject*. Something undergoes a "process" in a passive way, but something has an "activity" in an active way. A "process" is something that happens to something, while an "activity" is something that something *does*. Since the toaster and Concept are the subjects of the verb or sentence—to use the grammatical metaphor—they do not just undergo a "process," they have or do an "activity."

Because the Concept is the subject of its defining activity in the grammatical sense, we will meet more traditional logical forms in this chapter—such as the judgment and the syllogism. Judgments and syllogisms (which are built out of judgments) involve applications of the copula "is." As I suggested in the Introduction to this book, one way of understanding Hegel's logic is as a long examination of the concept of being. We should expect to find applications of the copula "is" within the logic, because "is" is a concept of being. To say that "A *is*" is to say that A has being. That judgment is a way of using a concept of being (i.e. "is") to express the being of a concept (i.e. of A). To say that "A *is* B" is to say that A and B have the same being in some way. That judgment is a way of linking two concepts together (i.e. A and B) by means of a concept of being (i.e. "is"). In a syllogism, judgments *add up to* a conclusion, which is just a way of saying that a set of judgments "is" a conclusion. A syllogism is thus a way of linking judgments together by means of the concept of being (namely, by the assertion of the conclusion, or by the assertion that the conclusion therefore "is"). Judgments and syllogisms are thus ways in which the concept of being can link concepts together by means of its own activity, or by a concept of being. That is why they appear here in Chapter Four, in which the Concept goes through its own activity. Since the Concept is a general concept of being for concepts (see Transition to the Concept in Chapter Three), and since judgments and syllogisms are ways in which concepts of being are linked together by means of concepts of being, they belong to the part of the logic in which the Concept goes through its own activity. In judgments and syllogisms, the Concept—as a concept of being—does the grasping activity by linking concepts together by means of concepts of being, which is nothing but its own activity.

(2) Second, because the Concept's process or activity involves grasping, rather than toasting, the Concept's activity of going through the process of grasping will give the Concept an additional characteristic that the toaster's process of toasting does not give the toaster. The toaster can be a toaster—it can go through the process of toasting—without ever being *aware* that it is toasting. The Concept can be the overarching grasper of *everything* else, however, only if it grasps everything, *including the thought that it is the overarching grasper.* The Concept will have to grasp—in addition to everything else—the thought that it is the overarching grasper, if it is to succeed in living up to or fulfilling its definition as the overarching grasper. The unfolding of the Concept will thereby introduce a third sense of logical "for itselfness." The Concept will be not only doubly "for itself," but "for itself" in three senses: to be the overarching grasper the Concept will not only be an embracing "for itself" concept (the first sense, the "for itself" relationship of content), and grasp everything *for itself,* or through its own activity (the second sense, the "for itself" relationship of form), but it will also be the overarching grasper in its own thought, in its own judgment, or for itself, as part of its awareness of itself (the third sense, the "for it-

self" relationship of self-consciousness). In the end, then, the Concept will have to be, as Hegel suggests, a spirit (§164R), or a self-conscious subject.

Being conscious and being self-conscious are types of being that will also be defined in the Doctrine of the Concept. The Concept is already characterized by a doubly "for itself," logical relationship because it is a logically embracing, "for itself" concept (the "for itself" relationship of content) through its own activity, or *for itself* (the "for itself" relationship of form). Consciousness and self-consciousness will also be defined by Hegel as complex forms of universality or "for itselfness." Conscious being is a doubly "for itself" being that is immediately connected to thereness in the form of awareness. A minimally conscious being embraces its own internal states as its content (the first sense of "for itselfness" for content) through its own activity or *for itself* (the second sense of "for itselfness" for form) in an immediate way. Its internal states are its immediate object (of consciousness). As suggested in the last paragraph, self-conscious being is a type of being that is triply "for itself"—a logical status that will be depicted in the diagrams.

(3) There is yet a third sense in which the development of the Concept will be "subjective" in this chapter. In the first subsection of the Doctrine of the Concept, which Hegel calls the "Subjective Concept," we begin tracing the subjective development of the Concept in the grammatical sense (i.e. [1]). Because this section spells out different types of judgments and syllogisms, however, the Concept is also subjective in a third sense. We ordinarily think of judgments and syllogisms as kinds of things that belong only to the thinking process of conscious subjects. Syllogisms, judgments and arguments cannot be found out there in the world of objects. *We (human) subjects* make judgments; *we subjects* use syllogisms to make arguments. These sorts of things belong only to thought, to subjectivity, and do not have any independent (objective) existence beyond we subjects who think them. Judgments, syllogisms and arguments are not out there in the world. Because the Subjective Concept focuses on judgments and syllogisms, it is subjective in this third sense as well: it develops the types of thoughts that we ordinarily think of as belonging only to subjectivity, or only to thinking (human) subjects.

The first and third senses of "subjective" are in tension with one another. To the degree that the Subjective Concept develops the processes that the Concept undergoes on its own or through its own activity, those processes are independent of us, which is to say that they do not belong merely to (our) subjectivity. As I suggested in Chapter One, for Hegel, Reason is not only in our heads, but in the world itself (see Section I). But, to the degree that the developments of the Concept belong only to our thought—to the thought of individual (human) subjects—these processes are not independent of us. They belong only to our subjectivity—to our heads—and so are not in the world itself. This tension will be resolved later in the chapter by two claims. First, the Concept itself will be defined as a subjective consciousness. If the Concept is a subjective consciousness, then its processes are independent of our (human) subjectivity, without being independent of subjectivity *per se*. The arguments, judgments and syllogisms are subjective in this third sense because they belong to the conscious subjectivity of the Concept itself. Second, because the Concept's activity embraces all activity of thought, it embraces our thought as well. So our conscious subjectivity is the Concept's subjectivity as well. Our subjectivity belongs to the process or activity in which the Concept goes through its grasping activity. Our thought belongs to the thought of the Concept itself. In the end, then, the first and third senses of "subjectivity," which seem to be in tension with one another, unite in the thought that our subjectivity belongs to the Concept, which is itself a subjectivity.

The logical processes in the Doctrines of Being and Essence involved generating and defining new logical elements. Because the Concept is defined as the completed, all-embracing grasper (see Transition to the Concept) over everything else, the logical process here cannot involve generating any new concepts. There are no other concepts that the Concept does not already embrace. As a result, in the Doctrine of the Concept, Hegel must introduce a new kind of logical development, which he calls "development" (*Entwicklung*) (§161). In English, this characterization of the logical process does not seem very helpful. After all, the logical processes that we had in the Doctrines of Being and Essence were also kinds of development. However, the German verb "*entwickeln*" means to unroll, unfold or evolve, and the noun "*Entwicklung*" means an evolution and unfolding, as well as development. In this chapter, the Concept will be unfolding, evolving or unrolling. Rather than generating new logical elements, the logical process will elaborate on, evolve, or unfold the definition of the Concept that has already been generated.

In the first two sections of the Doctrine of the Concept, the Concept will be almost unrecognizable. When the Concept's process of going through its defining activity leads it to "utter" in the first section—the Subjective or Formal Concept—the Concept itself will drop out of the picture completely at first, and only the next two elements—the ones currently defined as the Effect$_{CS}$ and as Possibility—will play a role. Moreover, because the elements will be connected together only abstractly by the copula "is," the logical development will best be depicted as logical sentences, rather than using the bubbles and arrows we have seen so far. This first section will therefore present logical elements and forms that will be more familiar to those who know something about contemporary formal logic. It develops different sorts of logical judgments and arguments, such as the hypothetical and disjunctive judgments, the argument from analogy and so on. In the stages of syllogism, the Concept itself will come back into the picture, but it does so in a way that remains abstract, and so is still best depicted using abstract sentences, rather than using the bubbles and arrows we have seen in the last two chapters. As in Kant's logic (see Chapter One, Section IV), because Hegel's treatment of the forms of argument is centered on the syllogism, it differs from contemporary symbolic logic. Nevertheless, the forms of syllogism that Hegel discusses include all of the basic logical connectors familiar from contemporary logic, such as "not," "if . . . then," "or," and "and."

In the second section of the Doctrine of the Concept—the Doctrine of the Object—Hegel returns to the more semantic logic that we have seen so far—a type of logic centered around the development of the meanings of logical concepts as well as logical syntax, and best depicted by the sorts of bubbles and arrows we saw in the last two chapters. Nevertheless, because the Concept will "fall apart," it will remain largely unrecognizable. By the end of the Doctrine of the Object and throughout the Doctrine of the Idea, however, the diagram that we have here for the Concept will return. We should not be surprised to find that the Concept will end up looking more or less the same when it is defined subjectively as it did when it was defined objectively at the end of the Doctrines of Being and Essence. Just as a toaster looks more or less the same after it is defined subjectively by going through its toasting activity as it did when we define it objectively while it is still at the store, so the Concept will "look" more or less the same after it is defined subjectively as it did when it was defined objectively in the Doctrines of Being and Essence. At the end of the "Subjective Logic," the subjectively defined Concept will still be Reason itself, as the one thought that embraces and defines everything else, it will just be Reason defined as a subjectivity—as a self-consciousness—rather than merely as an objectivity—as a system. To see what Reason will be like at the end of the Doctrine of the Concept, however, we need to dive into the logical development.

II. The Doctrine of the Subjective or Formal Concept

Now that the Concept will be defined from the top down by its own activity, we must redefine the three outer-most logical elements. These *moments* correspond to the three top (or outside) layers (or bubbles) of the Concept. Because the next several stages involve merely redefining elements we already have, the diagrams themselves will not change from one stage to the next. Only the labels for the relevant elements will change.

As we will see shortly, because the Concept is a unified whole, the three elements cannot really be fully separated from one another (§164). The Concept is the whole set of bubbles—not just the outside bubble, but the outside bubble together with its contents (the inside bubbles). The Concept is the overarching grasper that grasps and defines everything else. It includes the whole process of definition throughout time that we had at the end of the last chapter. Nevertheless, the Concept can be classified into separate moments of this whole process. (Hegel's use of the term "moment" is defended in the stage of Reciprocal Action.)

Universality

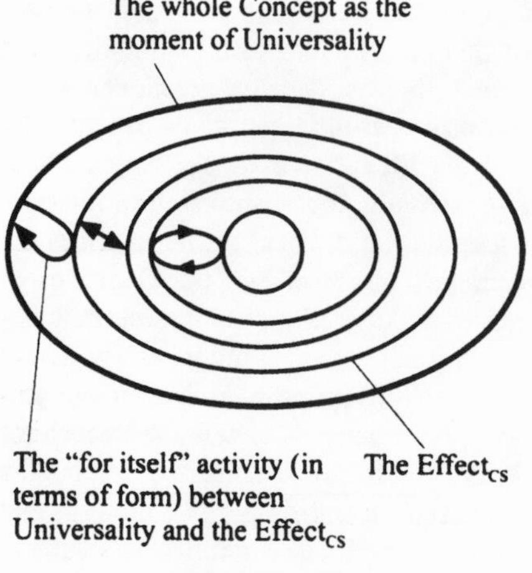

Figure 4.2

At the end of the Doctrine of Essence, the Concept was in a reciprocal relationship with the Effect$_{CS}$ that it had initiated (see Reciprocal Action and the Introduction to this chapter). Because the Concept *initiated* the whole back-and-forth process of Reciprocal Action, the reciprocal relationship is a process that the Concept carries out on its own, as its own activity. This stage draws out the logical conclusion that the process that defined the Concept at the end of Chapter Three is a process in which the Concept is defining itself by its own activity. Drawing out this conclusion redefines both the relationship between the Concept and the Effect$_{CS}$ as well as the Concept itself. When the Concept is defined from the top down by its own activity, it has an "in and for itself" relationship with the Effect$_{CS}$ that redefines the Concept as Universality. When the Concept is defined from the top down by its own activity, instead of being in a reciprocal relationship with the Effect$_{CS}$, it has a doubly "for itself" relationship with the Effect$_{CS}$ (cf. the Introduction to this Chapter). It embraces the Effect$_{CS}$ in its content (the first "for itselfness" of content) and, because it initiated the whole process of Reciprocal Action, presents the Effect$_{CS}$ *for itself*, or through its own activity (the second "for itselfness" of form). The first sense of "for itselfness" is already represented in the diagram because the Concept is depicted as a bubble that surrounds the bubble for the Effect$_{CS}$. Because the Concept is now defined by presenting the Effect$_{CS}$ *for itself*, or through its own activity, I have replaced the circular arrow that represented the reciprocal relationship between the Concept and the Effect$_{CS}$ with the same sort of looping arrow that I have used before to depict "for-itself" relationships of form or presentation.

This doubly "for itself" activity gives the Concept an "in and for itself" relationship with the Effect$_{CS}$ that redefines the Concept as Universality. Whenever a concept *presents* another concept, it is defined as separate from and opposed to the concept that it presents (see External Necessity). Because the Concept has the second "for itself" relationship of form with the Effect$_{CS}$, it *presents* the Effect$_{CS}$, and so is defined as separate from and opposed to the Effect$_{CS}$. The fact that the Concept is defined as opposed to and separate from the Effect$_{CS}$ gives the Concept an "in itself" relationship with the Effect$_{CS}$. An "in itself" relationship between two concepts is a relationship of opposition or "otherness" (see Being-in-itself in Chapter Two). The "for itself" relationship of form creates an "in itself" relationship of opposition or "otherness" between the Concept and the Effect$_{CS}$. Because the Concept embraces the Effect$_{CS}$ as its contents, it still has the first "for itself" relationship of content with the Effect$_{CS}$. Now that the second "for-itselfness" of form gives the Concept an "in itself" relationship with the Effect$_{CS}$, the Concept has an "in and for itself" relationship with the Effect$_{CS}$.

That "in and for itself" relationship redefines the Concept as a Universality. In general, a universal concept or universality is a concept that is a separate concept ("in itself") that is an embracing, identifying and defining grasper over some complete and completed content, through its own activity (i.e. "for itself"). (Please note that I will capitalize "Universality" and, later on, "Particularity" and "Singularity," when I am referring to the moments that are within the Concept, but I will not capitalize "universality," "particularity" and "singularity" when I am referring to the general concept of universality, particularity and singularity, or to universals, particulars and singularities in general.) The concept of fruit, for instance, is a universal concept when it is defined as the one concept that presents, grasps, identifies and defines every possible piece of fruit that shows up in the world throughout time. The universal concept of fruit is not the same as the pieces of fruit. Instead, it is a separate, one concept *of* all of those pieces of fruit taken together as a finished product. It is the one, universal concept that presents all the pieces of fruit as a completed whole or one. The universal concept of fruit presents or defines and applies to every piece of fruit that could (possibly) be there.

This stage offers not only a general definition of a concept, but also a general definition of universality. It adds to the definition of "universal" that has been developing throughout the course of the logic. The Doctrine of Being introduced three different ways of defining universality: universality as commu*n*ality, universality as comm*on*ality, and essential universality. In the most basic sense, a universal is just a concept that grasps or captures a group or set of items, i.e. more than one item, or a community of items. The Doctrine of Essence added an account of universality that included totality. In this sense, a universal is a completed set of items, or a totality. This stage adds to the definition of universality by suggesting that a universal is a (one) concept or thought *of* a completed set of items as a finished product. It captures the traditional intuition in Western philosophy that a genuinely universal concept must apply to every instance of the concept throughout time. According to this intuition, the genuinely universal concept of fruit, for example, will apply to every piece of fruit that shows up in the world of experience throughout time. The genuinely universal concept is the (one) thought that grasps and defines all those pieces of fruit taken together as finished product. That is precisely the definition of "universal" that we have in this stage.

Hegel characterizes Universality as the moment of "free equality with itself in its determinacy" (§163). Universality is a separate concept from the Effect$_{CS}$ (because of the "in itself" relationship) that nevertheless presents the Effect$_{CS}$—which is its own content—by its own activity. Hence Universality is defined only in relation to itself and through its own activity. Because Universality is defined completely in relation to itself through its own activity, it is free and independent. Thus Universality is the moment in which, as the whole process, the Concept is completely free and independent (cf. the Introduction to this chapter).

Particularity

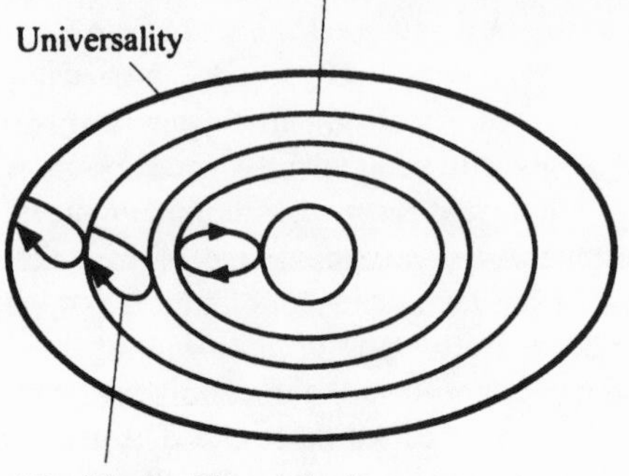
The element into which the Universal splits up or particularizes during its process of definition. This is the moment of Particularity
Universality
The "for itself" activity between Particularity and its contents

Figure 4.3

When the Concept is defined from the top down by its own activity, the Effect$_{CS}$ is redefined as the Concept's moment of Particularity. There is a logical reason why the Effect$_{CS}$ must be redefined. Hegel says that we are no longer dealing with a relationship of cause (§163R). We sublated (cancelled but preserved) the concepts of cause and effect in the stage of Reciprocal Action in Chapter Three. In Reciprocal Action, the Concept and the Effect$_{CS}$ are the same as each other because they are each defined as both cause and effect or as cause/effect (in terms of content) in a whole process (presentation or form) that is defined by both cause and effect. Indeed, as we saw in the stage of Universality, the Concept and Effect$_{CS}$ have the same definition. The Concept is being defined in relation to something that is its own contents, and so is still itself, or has the same character that it does. That's why the Universal remains equal to itself in this moment (§163). Because the concepts of cause and effect defined both the Concept and the Effect$_{CS}$ as the same as one another in terms of content and form or presentation, the concepts of cause and effect can no longer be used to distinguish or define the two elements. As a result, we cannot continue to call the Effect$_{CS}$ an "effect." The logical move to this stage—in which the Effect$_{CS}$ is redefined as Particularity—is necessitated by the fact that we must find another concept to characterize or distinguish the logical element that has been the Effect$_{CS}$.

The Effect$_{CS}$ is the Concept's "Particularity" in two ways. First, the Effect$_{CS}$ is the "particularity" of the Concept because, as the content and form of the Concept, it defines or particularizes the Concept. In the diagram, the Effect$_{CS}$ is literally the content of the Concept because it is inside the bubble representing the Concept. The Effect$_{CS}$ is also the form of the Concept, or the way in which the Concept is presented. Particularity defines the Concept or gives the Concept a particular character by being both the Concept's content and form or presentation. Particularity is the way in which the Concept is defined or particularized.

Second, the Effect$_{CS}$ defines the Concept by being the whole set of elements into which the Concept divides. The Effect$_{CS}$ is the completed and completely systematized set or system of rational concepts and their activity. When the Concept defines and presents the Effect$_{CS}$, then, it splits up or divides into that set of rational concepts. Those concepts are thus the characteristics into which the Concept divides. They are the Particularity of the Concept or, now that the Concept is defined as Universality, the Particularity of Universality. We sometimes use the term "particularity" in a similar way in ordinary English. If I ask you to give me the "particulars" of a company or business, for instance, I want you to list the complete set of characteristics of the company that make it what it is: what it does, its profit margin, its assets and so on. These are the characteristics into which the business divides and that make the business the business that it is. The rational concepts and processes define the Concept by particularizing it as one thing and another. To be particularized is to be characterized as one thing or another, to be split up into defining concepts and processes or characteristics. Because the Effect$_{CS}$ is the set of particularities or defining characteristics into which the Concept divides, it gives the Concept its particularity. The Effect$_{CS}$ is the Particularity of the Concept.

While Particularity is the completed and completely systematized set of rational concepts (see Reciprocal Action in Chapter Three), because time itself is finished, Particularity is also more than merely the rational concepts into which the Concept divides. Since time is finished, Particularity is finished. There will be no further changes in the set of rational concepts. Thus Particularity is also a completed whole or one, the exhaustive set of concepts and activity into which Universality divides. It is, as Hegel puts it, "*something-particular*" (§162R). Because it is a one, completed concept that embraces all of time, Particularity has become a *universal concept.* Now that the Effect$_{CS}$ is defined from the top down by the activity of the Concept as Particularity, it has taken on the character and activity of the Concept. Particularity has absorbed the character and activity of the Concept or of Universality by becoming a *universal concept.* Universality is a completed universal, and it presents and defines Particularity as a completed whole or one. It therefore passes on its own character as a universal concept to Particularity. Particularity is not just the whole set of rational concepts and processes, it is the (one, universal) thought *of* the whole set of rational concepts as a finished product at the end of time. The Concept particularizes as the universal concept of Particularity.

Because Particularity is now a universal concept, it has a different relationship with its contents from the one it had before. Universality was defined as a universal concept because it had an "in and for itself" (or doubly "for itself") relationship with its contents. Now that Particularity is a universal concept, it has an "in and for itself" relationship with its contents too. The "in itself" relationship grows out of the second sense of "for itselfness"—the "for itselfness" of form—in which the universal concept presents its contents *for* itself, or through its own activity. That is the process that defines the universal concept as opposed to or separate from—and hence in an "in itself" relationship with—its contents. Now that Particularity is defined as a one, completed whole, it has a character of its own that is separate from and so presents the set of rational concepts that make it up. I have replaced the double-sided arrow in the diagram that represented the relationship between the Effect$_{CS}$ and its contents with a looping "for itself" arrow. The new arrow depicts the idea that Particularity, as a universal concept, is not only an embracing "for itself" concept (the "for itself" relationship of content, depicted by the fact that its bubble surrounds the bubble for its contents), but also presents its content *for itself* (the "for itself" relationship of form), which gives it a character separate from its content (in an "in itself" sense).

As in the stage of Universality, in this stage, Hegel offers a general, logical definition of particularity. In general, to be the particularity of universality is to be the form and content of universality, and the one thought of the complete and completed set of concepts into which a universal divides or presents during the process of definition. Thus, the particularity of the concept of fruit, for instance, is the *one* thought *of* the completed set of concepts into which the concept of fruit divides or is presented—the concepts "apple," "banana," and so on.

Singularity

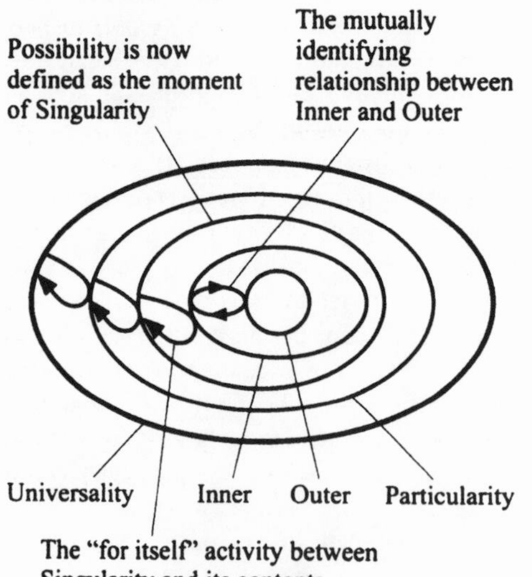

Figure 4.4

In this chapter, we have started out with exactly the same set of bubbles that we had at the end of the last chapter. Even though those bubbles and their relationships are being redefined in this chapter, the fact that we are dealing with the same bubbles helps to explain some of the connections that Hegel draws between the concepts that now define a bubble and the concepts that defined the same bubble in earlier stages. The logical development involves a process of *aufheben* or sublation (to cancel and preserve): later concepts and definitions replace but also absorb earlier concepts and definitions (see Chapter One, Section VIII). As we have seen many times, Hegel's concept of *aufheben* means that new embracing concepts cancel but also absorb or preserve the earlier concepts that they gather up or include. It also means that later definitions of the same elements replace but also absorb earlier definitions of that same element.

The Concept's moment of Singularity is the same bubble that was defined as Possibility in Chapter Three. Possibility is the Singularity of the Concept because it is the singular items into which the Concept divides during its process of definition. Possibility has already been defined as the completed realm of Possibility (see Condition as a Totality). Because Singularity is the same bubble that was defined as Possibility, and, before that, Actuality in Chapter Three, it, too, contains the completed realm of Possibility. It is the completed set of singularities or actualities (Inners and Outers in a mutually defining relationship) in the world of experience into which the Concept divides. Because Singularity is being presented by the Concept, however, it is also more than merely that set of items in the world of experience. Because time is finished, there are no further singularities that will be presented by the Concept. Because the set of actualities presented by Singularity is a one whole or finished product, Singularity—the concept that grasps them—is now defined as the thought *of* the whole set of singular items. Singularity is not merely the set of items, then, it is the one whole concept that grasps and presents the set of singular items as a finished product. Like Particularity, then, Singularity has become a *universal concept*. Now that Possibility—as Singularity—is defined from the top down by the activity of the Concept, it has taken on the character and activity of the Concept. Singularity has become a *universal* (§163). Since Universality is a completed whole or one, a finished product, when Universality presents and defines Singularity, it presents and defines Singularity as a completed whole or one, as a finished product or universal. It therefore passes on its own character as a universal to Singularity. As Possibility, Singularity was already a universal in two more basic senses. First, it was a set or group of items. And, second, it was a completed set of items. As a completed set of items, or an "all," it is what Hegel calls a totality (§163R). Singularity is now a universal in the additional sense that it is a universal concept, or *a concept of* a completed set of items as a finished product. As Hegel makes clear in the Remark to this section, however, although Singularity is now defined as a universal concept, because Singularity is made up of existing individual items that have thereness, it is a universality of somethings. While it is the thought of the whole set of somethings taken together as a finished product, it is itself a something. It has thereness or presence out there in existing actuality. Singularity still has Possibility's definition as the whole realm of existing actuality. Hence, Singularity is something-universal (§163R), or a universality that is a something.

Because Singularity is now a universal concept, it has a new relationship with the elements it embraces. Universality was defined as a universal concept because it had an "in and for itself" relationship with its contents. Now that Singularity is a universal concept, it has an "in and for itself" relationship with its contents too. As we saw in the Introduction to this chapter, the "in and for itself" relationship grows out of a doubly "for itself" relationship. Singularity therefore has a doubly "for itself" relationship with its contents. It is not only an embracing, "for itself" concept (the "for itself" relationship of content)—which it was even when it was defined as Possibility—but is now an embracing "for itself" concept *for itself*, or through its own activity (the "for itself" relationship of form). Because the activity of Singularity is a top-down process that is part of the activity of the Concept, Singularity *presents* the set of singulars *for itself*, or as its own activity. This activity of presenting its contents gives Singularity an oppositional, "in itself" relationship with the individual actualities it embraces and a character of its own, separate from and opposed to the individual actualities. We saw Hegel use this same logical move several times in Chapter Three, in which a concept comes to have a character of its own as a separate element (i.e. "in itself") as soon as it is defined as a concept that presents its contents (see the stages of External Necessity, Immediate Substance and the Matter [*Sache*] Itself). Since Singularity is now defined as a one, completed whole or finished product, it has a character of its own that is separate from and so presents the set of items that make it up. I have added a looping "for itself" arrow to the diagram to represent the fact that Singularity, as a universal concept, is not only an embracing "for itself" concept (which is represented in the diagram by the fact that its bubble surrounds the bubble for its contents), but is also separate from its contents (in an "in itself" sense) because it presents its contents *for itself*, or through its own activity (the second "for itself" relationship of form). As Hegel puts it, Singularity is "*in and for itself determined*" (§163). The concept of Singularity captures the idea that, when the Concept presents into singular items (Inners and Outers taken together), it does so as a whole or one (i.e. as a Singular). It presents into Singularity as the thought *of* the whole (one) completed set of singulars as a finished product. The Concept presents into singularity as the universal concept of Singularity.

The fact that Singularity is the same bubble that was defined as Possibility in Chapter Three helps to explain some of Hegel's remarks. Hegel says that Singularity is "the inward reflection of the determinacies of universality and particularity" (§163). In Chapter Three, the "inward reflection" of a concept was its reflected content, or the content of a concept that showed up (or reflected). Singularity is the "inward reflection" of Universality and Particularity, first, because it is the content of both of them. The diagram illustrates this fact because the Singularity bubble is inside of—and hence literally the content of—both the Universality and the Particularity bubbles. Second, Singularity is also the way in which Universality and Particularity show up or have actuality. Because Singularity was Possibility, it is defined as both the form and content of Actuality. Singularity is both what shows up in actuality as well as how actuality shows up: it contains the complete set of identifying concepts (Inner) and items out-there (Outer) in a mutually defining relationship, and so is the complete set of individual actualities that Possibility contained. Because Singularity is the way in which *both* Universality and Particularity show up, Universality and Particularity show up in the same or in an identical way. Hence, Singularity is also "the particular and the universal within an identity" (§171), as Hegel defines Singularity later.

Moreover, because Singularity is the same bubble that was Possibility in Chapter Three, we can also explain why Hegel says that Singularity is the same as the actual, except that now the actual has developed out of the Concept (§163R). Singularity is the same as the actual because the Possibility bubble was defined in Chapter Three as the set of individual actualities as well as the content and form of Actuality (see the stages of Transition to Condition and Condition). Because Possibility is the complete realm of Possibility, like Possibility, Singularity is a whole or totality. It is the completed set of all individual actualities or "the actual" as a whole. However, while Singularity is the actual, it is also distinguished from the actual because, unlike the definition of Possibility, the definition of Singularity develops out of the Concept. Whereas the Possibility bubble was being defined from the bottom-up by the actualities themselves, Singularity is being defined from the top-down by the Concept. When Possibility was defined from the bottom up, it got its character from the set of individual actualities that it embraced. Possibility's character therefore depended on what the actualities happened to be like. The actualities turned out to be defined by possibility, giving Possibility its character as "possibility." That same element's character is now determined from the top down by the Concept—it develops out of the Concept, as Hegel suggests—rather than from the bottom up by the nature of the individual actualities that it embraces.

When Possibility is defined from the top down as the activity of the Concept, it no longer has the character of being merely possible. The Concept is the completed process of Reason (see Transition to the Concept in Chapter Three). Time itself has ended, so that the set of singular items is finished. No new singular items will be presented and there will be no changes to the set of singular items that are presented in the world of experience. Once the set is finished, there are no other possible versions of the set. Singularity's character is *necessary*, rather than possible. Hence the bubble that was Possibility is no longer defined by possibility. Instead, it is the *necessary* thought *of* the set of singular items as a finished product. Since there will be no further changes to the set, it is also completely defined. When the Possibility bubble is defined as the "inward reflection" of the Concept and Particularity, it is the necessary, universal and completely defined concept of Singularity.

Now that Singularity is defined from the top down by the Concept, it is also effective (§163R) and substantial (§164R), as Hegel suggests. Singularity is effective because it succeeds in presenting elements that have subsistence, or that subsist out there on their own account. Because the actualities that Singularity presents are out there (Outer) as somethings (Inner), they are independently defined elements capable of subsisting on their own. Because the actualities subsist on their own, Singularity's activity of presenting is a cause that has an effect or succeeds in presenting something out there in actuality. As will become important later, Singularity's effectiveness in presenting subsistent elements gives Singularity subsistence as well.

Singularity is substantial in the same way that the Cause and the Effect were substantial in the last chapter. Three characteristics define Singularity as a substance (see the stages of Immediate Substance, Substance as Cause, and Effect as Substance in Chapter Three). First, a substance is a concept that is an essence that is also an actuality. Actuality is defined as Inner and Outer in a mutually defining relationship, which is exactly the relationship that Inner and Outer have within or as the content of Singularity (see Transition to Actuality in Chapter Three). Moreover, an essence was defined as a "for itself" concept that is both the identity of, but also separate (distinguished) from, its Shine, or the way in which it shows up (see Identity and Immediate Distinction in Chapter Three). Now that Singularity is defined from the top down by the activity of the Concept as "in and for itself" determined, it is both the "for itself" identity of, but is also separate from (in an "in itself" sense) Inner and Outer and their mutually defining relationship. Hence Singularity is now a concept that is an essence that is also an actuality. It is an essence insofar as it is separate from Inner and Outer and their mutually defining relationship, but it is an actuality insofar as it has Actuality (i.e. Inner and Outer and their mutually defining relationship) as its contents and presentation. As an essence with actuality, Singularity is a substance. Second, Singularity is defined in such a way that form and content overturn into one another. Singularity is both the content and form of the Concept. It is the content of the Concept as well as the way in which the Concept is presented by the Concept's activity. Third, when we look at Singularity as a separate element from the Concept, it has the character of being an essence, a substance-of-the-matter, into which something else passes over. The Concept must present Singularity to be what it is. Of course, because Singularity is the content of the Concept, the Concept does not really pass over into Singularity, just as Accidentality did not really pass over into Substance in Chapter Three. When the Concept presents into Singularity, it is not passing over into a completely separate element or "other." Nevertheless, Singularity is an essence that is an actuality, for which content and form overturn into one another, and is an essence into which something else (i.e. the Concept) presents.

Although Hegel makes clear that the Singularity defined here is not immediate singularity—such as a man, a house or whatever, as he says (§163R)—there is a connection between the way in which Hegel defines Singularity here and the singularity of immediate things. Hegel defines Singularity as "being determined in and for itself." Singularity is a whole that has a definition (is "in-itself") by embracing and presenting (the two "for itself" relationships) an "other" that is not really an "other," but is in fact itself. Because Singularity is a self-defining whole, it has an air of independence and self-subsistence. Singularity seems to subsist on its own account by itself. Immediate singularities such as men and houses seem to have the same sort of independence and self-subsistence. They have a character and so are in-themselves because they define themselves in relation to "others" that are really themselves. A house, for example, might be characterized as "brick," "red" and "two-story." While those characteristics are in one sense an "other" for the house—the house is not the same as "brickness"—they are also the house too. The brick, red, and two-story are the way in which the house is presented or defined. So the house gets its character (is "what it is") on its own as a separate item from those elements (i.e. "in-itself") by embracing an other (as a "for itself" in terms of content) that is also itself, or is its own presentation, through its own activity (i.e. *for itself* in terms of form). A singular is a kind of being that is determined in and for itself. Still, Hegel is right that we are well beyond immediate singularities by this point in the logic. Singularity here is the universal concept of singularity.

Indeed, this stage offers a general account of Singularity as a logical concept. In general, to be a singular is to be "in and for itself" determined in Hegel's sense. A singular is a self-subsistent whole or one that has a character or "what it is" of its own through a doubly "for itself" process that defines it as an independent one ("in itself") and gives it a self-subsistent character ("for itself").

The Three Moments Cannot be Held Apart

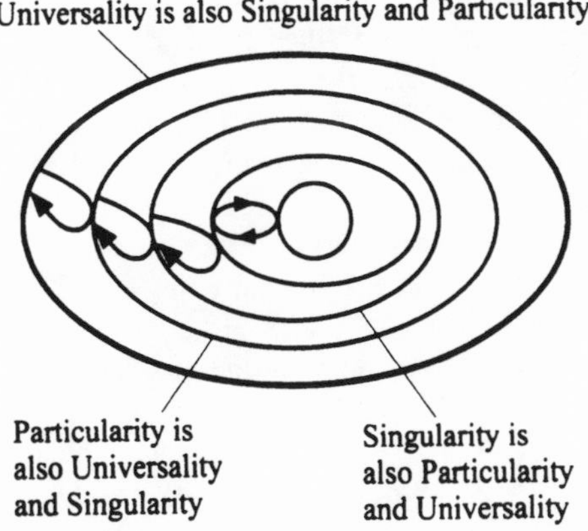
Universality is also Singularity and Particularity
Particularity is also Universality and Singularity
Singularity is also Particularity and Universality

Figure 4.5

Although Universality, Particularity and Singularity are separate concepts, these three moments cannot really be held apart (§164). They are all just moments of the whole Concept. Moreover, they are really the same as one another. Universality is Singularity and Particularity; Particularity is Universality and Singularity; and Singularity is Particularity and Universality.

First, Universality is also defined by Singularity and Particularity. Universality is singular because it is a self-subsistent whole or one—i.e. a *singular*—that includes or embraces everything. Because Universality has the sort of being that is determined in and for itself, it is an independent and completely self-defined whole or one. It is "being determined in and for itself," which, as Hegel points out in parentheses and as we just saw in the last stage, "is what singularity is" (§164). Universality is defined by Particularity because Particularity is the thought of the elements into which Universality divides and so is the form and content of Universality.

Particularity is defined by Universality and Singularity. Particularity is universal because it is a universal concept. Particularity is Singularity for two reasons. First, it has Singularity as its contents and form. In the diagram, Singularity is literally the contents of Particularity because the bubble for Singularity is inside the bubble for Particularity. Second, now that Particularity is defined from the top down by the activity of the Concept as a universal concept, it not only embraces but also *presents* Singularity. Because it presents Singularity, it has a character as "what it is" on its own, separate from Singularity. Moreover, because Particularity presents Singularity, it is now doubly "for itself" too: it embraces Singularity (and so is "for itself") *for itself*, or through its own activity. Particularity is therefore now "in and for itself determined," which is the definition of Singularity. Hence Particularity is a one or singularity.

Singularity, for its part, is also Universality and Particularity. Singularity is a universal concept because it is "in and for itself" determined. It is *the universal thought or concept of* the completed and completely systematized set of individual actualities and their activity. Because its content is actual, it is something-universal. Singularity is particularity for three reasons. First, just as Particularity is Singularity, so Singularity is Particularity. Singularity is the content and presentation that defines Particularity, which is just another way of saying that Singularity is Particularity.

Singularity has the character of particularity in a second way. Particularity is defined in general terms as the set of concepts into which a universal divides as it is defined. Particularity, which is a universal, is defined by dividing into the concepts that Singularity contains. Singularity is thus the way in which, not only the Concept (Universality), but also Particularity is defined or particularized. Hence, Singularity is the particularity of Particularity—it is the set of concepts into which Particularity, as a universal, divides during the process of definition. Singularity is a particularity because it is the particularity of Particularity—the complete and completely systematized set of concepts and activities into which Particularity divides during its process of definition.

All three elements are therefore defined as the same as one another as universality, particularity and singularity. Because all three elements are defined by universality, particularity and singularity, each is a one or singular, universal concept or thought that is particularized by dividing into a completed and completely defined set of concepts. They each therefore reflect the character of the Concept in two ways. They are each "in and for itself" determined, and so have the same defining activity that the Concept does. Each is an overarching and defining grasper over its contents. And they are also each *universal concepts*. The Concept, as the element that defines everything, has passed on its character and activity to each of its elements, and turned each of its elements into (universal) concepts. Universality is the completed thought or universal concept of everything, which particularizes (in Particularity) as the completed thought or universal concept of all the rational concepts and their activities, which expresses into Singularity as the completed thought or universal concept of the completed set of singularities and all their activity. Universality, Particularity and Singularity are thus identical with or the same as one another, insofar as they are each universal concepts.

Hegel distinguishes the way in which Universality, Particularity and Singularity are defined as concepts here from the way in which concepts were defined earlier in the logic. Earlier concepts were, as he puts it, "*determinate* concepts" (§162R). They had definitions or were defined, but they were only concepts "in themselves" or "for us" (§162), Hegel says, or for those of us who are studying the logic. They were not yet defined as concepts through their own activity or defining process, which is what we have now. They were not yet defined by universality (§162R), or were not yet "in and for themselves" determined as concepts, as they are now.

Universality as Identity, Particularity as Distinction, Singularity as Ground

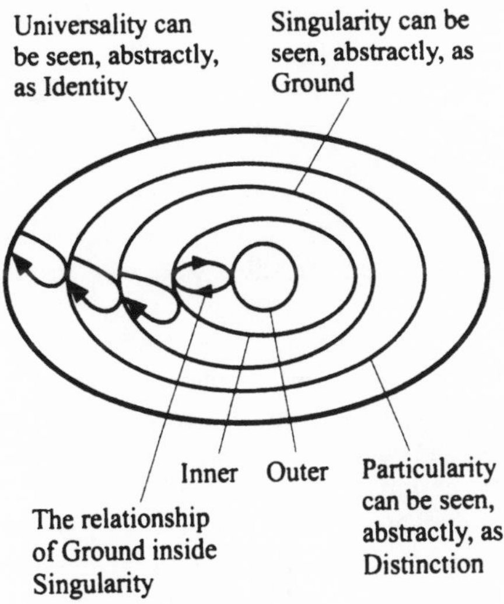
Universality can be seen, abstractly, as Identity
Singularity can be seen, abstractly, as Ground
Inner
Outer
Particularity can be seen, abstractly, as Distinction
The relationship of Ground inside Singularity

Figure 4.6

Hegel says that we can compare Universality, Particularity and Singularity to Identity, Distinction and Ground, at least in an abstract way (§164R). The diagrams show why. Universality has the same sort of top-down "for itself" relationship with Particularity that Essence had with Shine in the stage of Identity when Essence was defined as the Identity of the Shine. Universality or Reason is the embracing essence that grasps the concepts of Particularity. Moreover, as was the case between Essence and Shine in the stage of Identity, the identity between Universality and Particularity also implies distinction. Universality is determined "in and for itself" in relation to Particularity, which means that, while Universality grasps and defines (in the doubly "for itself" process) Particularity and hence identifies Particularity, it is also a separate, "in itself" concept that is "what it is" on its own, and hence is distinguished from Particularity. Finally, just as Essence showed up in the Shine, Universality is presented in or shows up in Particularity.

This comparison between Universality and identity is abstract, however, for two reasons. First, it ignores the more complicated process of definition that obtains between Universality and Particularity that did not obtain between Essence and Shine. While Essence merely embraced or showed up (reflected in) the Shine (is "for itself"), Universality embraces ("for itself") and *presents* Particularity *for itself* (is doubly "for itself"). Reason as Universality not only grasps but also presents the concept of Particularity—it gives Particularity its character from the top down. Moreover, the comparison also ignores the more complicated definition or content that Universality and Particularity have. While Universality is like Essence insofar as it shows up in Particularity, the type of "showing up" that it has is different in detail from the type of "showing up" that Essence has. The type of "showing up" that Essence has was thereness, while the type of "showing up" that Universality has is both conceptual (from Particularity) and actual (from Singularity). Essence had its thereness in the Shine, while Universality has its conceptual definition and actuality in Particularity. Conceptual actuality is a more sophisticated type of "showing up." Universality is also a more sophisticated essence than is Essence. While Essence was an essence that grasped only the concepts of Being, Universality grasps all of the concepts introduced throughout the Doctrine of Essence—Existence, Appearance, Whole, Force, Actuality and so on.

Particularity, for its part, is the Distinction of Universality. Although Essence and Shine had the same content or definition (namely, Shine itself), Shine was also different from, distinguished from, or the Distinction of Essence. Similarly here, too, although Universality and Particularity have the same content or definition (namely, Particularity itself), because Universality *presents* and is opposed to Particularity (in the "in itself" sense), Particularity is also separate from, distinguished from, or the Distinction of Universality. Moreover, just as Shine was the content of Essence, or the way in which Essence was defined, so Particularity is the content of Universality, or the way in which Universality is defined or particularized. Particularity is also the way in which Universality shows up, in the same way that Shine was the way in which Essence showed up. This characterization of Particularity as Distinction is also abstract, however, because it ignores the more complicated definition that Particularity has compared with Universality. Shine contains the categories and concepts of Being, Particularity is the thought of the completed set (Singularity) of all the possible contingent existences (Outer) together with all the possible identifying concepts (Inner) in a mutually defining relationship (of Ground; cf. Condition as a Totality in Chapter Three).

Finally, Singularity is like the Ground of Universality and Particularity. Singularity is the ground because, as the diagram depicts, it contains the relationship of Ground between Inner and Outer (see the stages of Ground and of Inner and Outer in Chapter Three). Inner and Outer are in a mutually defining relationship that is a relationship of Ground within Singularity. Because Singularity is defined by the relationship of Ground between Inner and Outer, Singularity can be seen as the Ground of Particularity and Universality.

Because Singularity contains the logical relationship of Ground, it is also the ground of Particularity and Universality in the more ordinary sense of being their foundation (§164R). Now that Singularity is defined from the top down by the Concept as a separate item with a character of its own, Singularity is foundational in the sense that it is the shared content without which Universality and Particularity could not be what they are. Since Universality and Particularity use Singularity for their own definitions, Singularity is the foundation or ground of their definitions. Moreover, as in the stage of Thing, when something shines forth or shows up as Ground, that process of showing up as Ground gives that something subsistence, or allows it to subsist on its own. Singularity contains the element of Outer—which is out-thereness or a way of showing up—that is in a mutually determining relationship of Ground with the Inner. Because Singularity contains Inner and Outer, it is the concept that shows up as a Ground and so subsists. Since both Universality and Particularity have their Outer (are out-there, or show up) as Singularity, and since Singularity shows up as Ground, Singularity is the element that allows Universality and Particularity to subsist. Singularity is thus also their foundation in the sense that it is the element that gives Universality and Particularity subsistence. Without the identifying concepts (Inner) and their mutually defining relationship with existing items (Outer), Reason as both Universality and Particularity would not subsist at all.

The Concept Utters

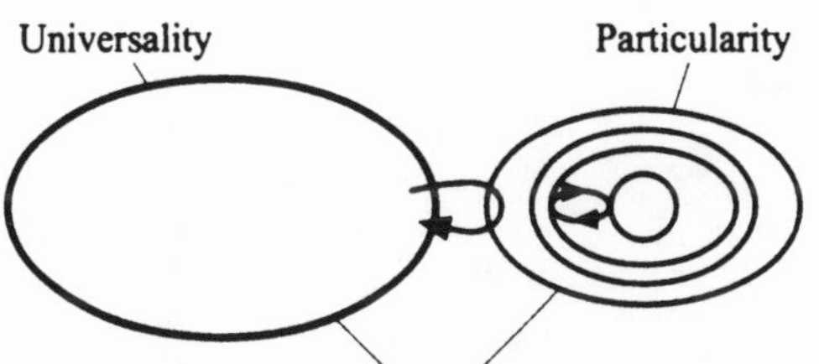

The Concept or Universality begins its activity of definition. It utters, presents or pushes out Particularity

Figure 4.7

The Concept is defined as a doubly "for itself" concept: it embraces ("for itself" [the first sense]) and presents its content *for itself*, or through its own activity (the second sense; cf. the Introduction to this chapter). That doubly "for itself" process outlines the activity that the Concept must go through to be defined. But the Concept has not yet *gone through* that process of definition. Since the outline says that the Concept or Universality is defined by presenting Particularity, when the Concept begins the process, it *presents* or utters Particularity. Particularity is thus the "utterance" (*Entäußerung*) of the Concept (§166R). In German, an *Äußerung* is already an utterance or expression, so why does Hegel use the different term "*Entäußerung*" to characterize the utterance of the Concept here? I think there are two reasons for Hegel's use of the special term. First, as Geraets et al. point out, "*Entäußerung*" is often used in a religious context to describe God's expression of himself in his incarnation as man (Geraets et al. 1991, 347). As they suggest, Hegel uses the special term in part to anticipate his conclusion that the Concept—which develops into the Absolute—is God and that Particularity is God's expression. I think that Hegel's use of the prefix also has a logical significance, however. In German, the prefix "*ent-*" adds to the meaning of a term. It is used to designate a condition in which something has entered into a new state. By putting this prefix in front of *Äußerung*, Hegel suggests that when the Concept expresses itself in Particularity, it not only utters, but it utters in a way that puts it into a new state. As mentioned in the Introduction to this chapter, in the Doctrine of Essence, the Concept was defined from the outside as an object. It was also defined primarily from the bottom up in relation to the elements that it embraced and the processes by which it embraced those elements. When the Concept utters here, it begins the process in which it will be defined as the active subject of its own activity, and in which it will be defined from the top down. In Hegel's anthropomorphic language, it now begins a process in which it defines itself. Because the Concept's utterance means that it is now defining itself through its own activity from the top down, the Concept has become the subject of its own definition. The utterance of Particularity thus leads the Concept to enter into a new state as the subject, rather than an object. Particularity is therefore not only the *Äußerung* or utterance of the Concept, it is the *Entäußerung* of the Concept—the utterance through which the Concept has entered into a new state.

Transition to the Judgment

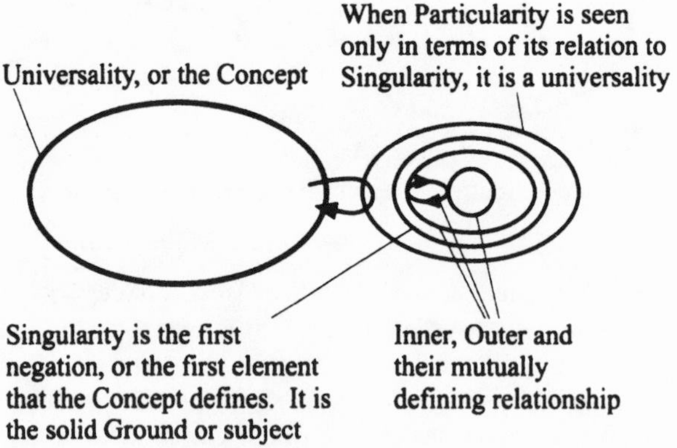
When Particularity is seen only in terms of its relation to Singularity, it is a universality
Universality, or the Concept
Singularity is the first negation, or the first element that the Concept defines. It is the solid Ground or subject
Inner, Outer and their mutually defining relationship

Figure 4.8

When the Concept utters, it pushes out its Particularity. Although Particularity came to be defined as a separate element with a character or "what it is" of its own in the stage of Particularity, as "Particularity" it was still being defined in relation to the Concept or Universality. Particularity was the particularity of Universality. Now that Particularity has been pushed out of the Concept, however, it must be characterized on its own, independently of the Concept or Universality, from which it has now been separated.

Because Particularity is separate from the Concept or Universality, and because the logical goal is to define the connection between Universality and Particularity, Universality cannot be used to characterize Particularity without begging the question. To define Particularity in terms of Universality presupposes that there is a link between them. Particularity must therefore—necessarily, in the logical sense—be defined in relation to its own contents, or to Singularity, rather than in relation to Universality. When Particularity is defined only in relation to Singularity, it is a universal. Particularity is the universal concept of Singularity. Moreover, Particularity has the same relationship with Singularity that Universality had with Particularity: it is "in and for itself" in relation to Singularity. Unlike Universality, Particularity does not initiate this "in and for itself" activity by itself—it is not completely free. Its activity is initiated by the Concept. Nevertheless, when we look at it only in relation to Singularity, it is related to Singularity as a universality or universal.

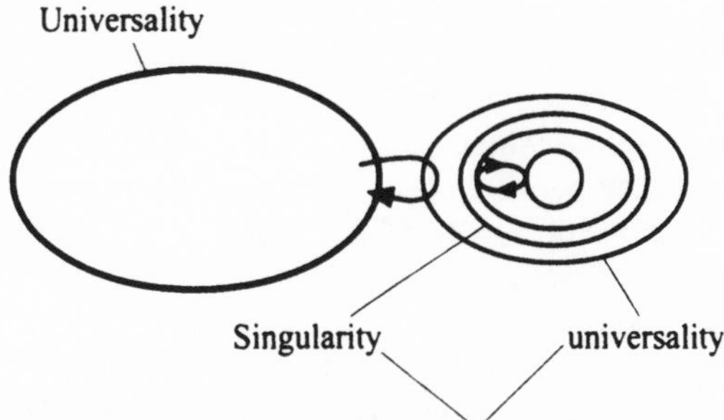

The relationship between Singularity and Particularity (now seen as universality) can be captured by the word "is." Singularity is the content of Particularity, hence it "is" Particularity (as universality)

Figure 4.9

Singularity, has a special status in relation to both Particularity and Universality. It is the content or inward reflection (§165) of both Universality and Particularity. It is the foundation and subsistence that they both share but from which they are both distinguished, separated or negated. Universality is defined as a separate concept from Particularity because it presents Particularity ("for itselfness" of form), and Particularity is defined as a separate concept from Singularity because it presents Singularity ("for itselfness" of form). Hence, Singularity is the one element from which both Universality and Particularity are distinguished and that both Universality and Particularity present. Singularity was also defined as separate from its own contents, because it presents Inner and Outer and their mutually defining relationship ("for itselfness" of form). That separation gives Singularity its character as both a substance and as an independent subsistence, or as something capable of subsisting on its own. Indeed, since Singularity, as a universal concept, is defined "for itself" or by presenting its contents, it gets its subsistence as a result of its own process of presenting its contents. It is therefore self-subsistent. Because Singularity is the one element capable of subsisting on its own that both Universality and Particularity present, it is the first element that the Concept or Universality distinguishes or defines during its process of uttering. Singularity is the initial free distinguishing (§165) of the Concept, the first negation (§165) or first, independent element that the Concept defines. Singularity is therefore the first element that must be defined.

Singularity is also the first negation, the first element that must be defined, or the *subject*, because of its status as the foundation or ground (§163R). Singularity is the ground of the other two moments in the sense that it seems to be what is supporting them. As the content that the Concept (or Universality) and Particularity share, Singularity seems to be what is holding the Concept and Particularity together. We are trying to define, characterize or specify what links Universality and Particularity together, and since Singularity is the content that they share, Singularity is presented as the first thought of what links Universality together with Particularity. It is not presented by itself, however. The Concept utters the entire moment of Particularity, so Singularity is presented only insofar as it belongs to Particularity (§165). Singularity is presented first, but only in its relation to Particularity. Since Particularity is a universal in relation to Singularity, Particularity as a whole, together with its content (which is what we are trying to define) is a relationship between Singularity and universality.

What sort of relationship? In The Three Moments Cannot be Held Apart, Singularity is defined as Particularity, and Particularity is defined as Singularity. This is just a fancy way of saying that Singularity "is" Particularity. We can therefore characterize the relationship that Singularity has with Particularity with the concept of "is." Since Particularity is universality in relation to Singularity, however, we should say instead that Singularity "is" universality. The copula "is" captures the relationship of identity that Singularity has with Particularity, now defined as universality. And Singularity really *is* universality. Singularity is not only Particularity, but it is defined by universality as well. The copula "is" expresses the idea that the three moments really cannot be defined in isolation from one another (§166R), which means that Singularity cannot be defined without universality too. In The Three Moments Cannot be Held Apart, Singularity was also defined by universality: it was defined "in and for itself" as the thought of a completed set of items as a finished product. So the claim that Singularity is universality is certainly logically correct.

The Judgment

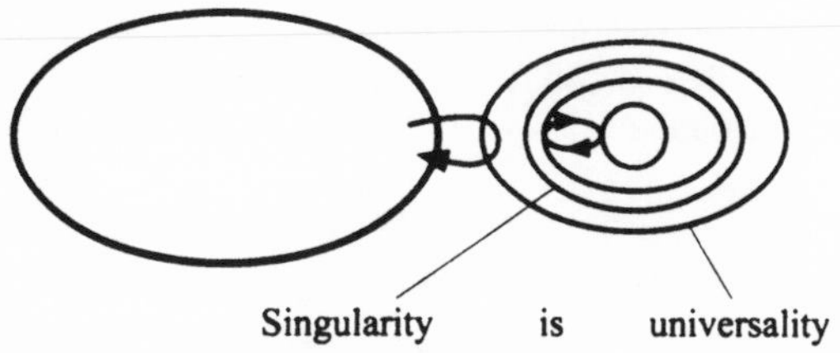

Figure 4.10

The relationship of identity does not completely capture the relationship between Singularity and Particularity, however. Particularity was defined "in and for itself" in relation to Singularity. The "in itself" relationship is an oppositional relationship that defined Particularity as separate from Singularity. Since Particularity is separate from Singularity, Singularity is also separate from Particularity. Hence the definition that Singularity has in relation to Particularity must express both the identity that they have in relation to one another as well as the separation (distinction) between them. Singularity is Particularity, but it is also *not* Particularity.

This simultaneous relationship of identity and separation between Singularity and Particularity—which defines Particularity as a whole (the current logical task)—is expressed by the *judgment*. As Hegel puts it, "[t]he *judgment* is the Concept in its Particularity" (§166). The general form of the judgment—or the way in which the judgment is presented—always implies *both* that the two items linked together by the copula have a relationship of identity and that they are separate items. On the one hand, the form of a judgment asserts that the two things are the same or have a relationship of identity. Take the judgment "X is Y." "X is Y" says that X *is* Y, that X and Y are identified or identical with one another. On the other hand, however, the form of the judgment also implies that the two things it mentions are separate. The judgment "X is Y" also implies that X and Y are separate—that's why they are "X" and "Y," rather than "X" and "X" (or just "X"), or "Y" and "Y" (or just "Y"). In fact, if there were only one thing, then it would not be possible to *relate* them together. There can only be a relationship at all if two items are separate from one another in some way or other (see Transition to the Concept in Chapter Three). If there were only one thing, we could only make assertions about that one thing: "X is," for instance. The fact that two things are being related together in a judgment necessarily implies that there are two different things. The form of the judgment thus defines items as separate from one another by using different terms, and then pulls those items back together into a relationship of identity with the copula "is."

Particularity as a whole, separate from the Concept or Universality, can now be defined. Since it has been uttered by and separated from the Concept, it has the character of being a judgment. Particularity is a whole that is made up of two items connected by the copula "is." Particularity is a judgment. More precisely, Particularity is the judgment "Singularity is universal." Singularity comes first in this judgment because it is the subject, the first negation, the element that is presented and so must be defined first. And in relation to Singularity, Particularity is a universal. (Particularity is defined as particularity only in relation to the Concept.)

This judgment—"Singularity is universality"—captures both the relationship of identity and of separation between Singularity and Particularity (as a universal). First, the judgment "Singularity is universal" says that Singularity *is* universality, that they are the same. The copula "is" of the judgment asserts that the two moments are related to one another (§166) in such a way that they cannot be isolated, but rather *are* one another (§166R). In The Three Moments Cannot be Held Apart, Singularity and Particularity (here as universality) really were the same. The judgment expresses this fact by pulling them together with the "is." Second, the judgment "Singularity is universality" also asserts that there is a distinction between the moments of Singularity and Particularity (as universality), and it treats those moments as beings-for-themselves (§166). Singularity and Particularity are each a "being-for-itself" because they are each Ones or separate concepts on their own that grasp the sameness of a set of items (cf. Being-for-itself in Chapter Two). Singularity and Particularity (which is what the universality here is) are both thoughts or concepts of a set of items. But because the set of elements they contain are different, they are also different and separate from one another. The judgment "Singularity is universality" captures their difference or separation by using two different terms to refer to them.

Hegel says that the judgment is the only genuine expression of the Concept's Particularity (§166R). Using the judgment to define Particularity gives Particularity a character that expresses the essence of the Concept as a universal, or the Concept's essential universality. There are several ways in which the judgment expresses the essence or essential definition of the Concept. First, the Concept or Reason is defined by the same relationship of both identity and separation that defines the form of the judgment. As The Three Moments Cannot be Held Apart suggests, while Universality, Particularity and Singularity are separate from one another, they are also not separate from one another. Under this interpretation, the essential nature of the Concept is that it both distinguishes the three moments and asserts their identity with one another at the same time. That is precisely the same character that the form of the judgment has.

Moreover, the particular judgment here—not just the form of judgment in general, but the particular judgment "Singularity is universality"—also expresses the nature of the Concept. Reason itself is a Singularity that is universal. As the one thought of a whole system, Reason is a singular; but as a system of separate items or a set of items, it is a universal.

Hegel says that the judgment is entirely universal because "*every thing is a judgment.*" Everything is a singular that is defined by universality, or, to put it the other way, every thing is a universal that is made singular (§167). Although the Singularity of the Concept does not refer to individual, singular things such as individual houses or men, Hegel's suggestion that every thing is a singular applies not only to singular things in the more ordinary sense in which houses and men are singular things, but also to concepts that grasp types of things. The examples that Hegel offers in the text can be read as being ambiguous about whether singularity should be interpreted to refer to singular things or whether it refers to thing-types. The sentence, "the rose is red" (§167R), for instance, could mean both "this individual rose here is red," as well as "the rose in general, as a thing-type, is red" (the type of thing that is rose is red, or redness as a characteristic belongs to the type of thing that is rose). A singular rose is a judgment because the universal rose is made singular in that specific rose. Rose as a thing-type is a judgment because it is a universal that is made singular in "red," which is one of the concepts that defines the rose as a type. The second example Hegel offers seems best interpreted as a reference to singularity as a thing-type. The judgment "gold is metal" (§167R) does not seem to mean that this piece of gold right here is metal, but rather that gold in general is metal.

That Hegel intends his point to apply to both individual things and thing-types is also suggested by his claim that the judgment "Singularity is universal" expresses the general nature of finite things, namely that finite things are a judgment (§168). Finite things are singulars that are universal because they have a thereness that expresses a universal nature (§168). If this thing is a lion, for instance, its "this" or singularity has an identity by being united with a universal, namely, the universal "lion." Indeed, the universal is like a soul, as Hegel suggests (§168), since it makes the thing what it is (as a lion). Finite things have no defining character at all without being unified with a universal, so an individual thing would be nothing without the universal, as Hegel suggests (§168). A "this" must be unified with some universal or other if it is to be something or other at all. The point applies to both singular individual things and thing-types. An individual rose can be a rose only if it is united to the universal "rose." Similarly, gold as a type of thing can have a definition only if it is related to some universal, such as the concept of metal, which captures the type of thing that it is. A finite thing or thing-type can be what it is only by being united to a universal.

The judgment "Singularity is universal" also expresses the nature of finite things in another way. Although finite things unite a singular and a universal, the form of the judgment expresses the fact that each side is in principle separable (§168). Finite things unite a singular and a universal together, but the unity is given, immediate, and therefore weak. In finite things generally, a singular and universal are united, but they are united together simply as a fact or reality of the given, finite world of Being. The singular and the universal are pasted together by the "is," but are not weaved together by their definitions. That's why the singularity and universality are separable. The fact that the connection between the singular and the universal is weak is partly what defines finite things as finite. Since finite things are defined in a way that treats the connection between the singular and the universal as in principle separable, the singular and universal are bound to separate. The singular and universal in finite things separate when those things change. Finite things are alterable—they are bound to change. A singular dog and the universal of dogness separate or fall apart when the dog dies, for example. When the dog dies, the dog is separated from the universal, and the dog is no longer a dog.

To simplify the diagrams for the stages of Judgment and Syllogism, the stages are depicted as sentences and as syllogistic structures, using only the first letters of the names of the bubbles that are in play. "Singularity is universal" will therefore be depicted as "S is U." Reducing the diagrams to sentential form will help to bring out the similarity between Hegel's discussion of judgment and syllogism, and contemporary formal, symbolic logic.

In the simplified diagrams for the Judgment, the Concept itself drops out of the picture. The judgment "Singularity is universal" defines only Particularity, and not the Concept itself. When I simplify the judgment into sentential form, the Concept itself is no longer represented. There is a logical reason why the Concept drops out of the picture. We are trying to define the nature or character of Particularity—what it is—once it has been uttered by and hence separated from the Concept or Universality. Since we are focusing on defining Particularity, the Concept itself slips into the background. Bear in mind, however, that the logical activity in the development of the judgment is still the activity of the Concept itself. We are not going to be paying direct attention to the Concept, but the Concept is there in the background, as the source of the logical moves.

Abstract Judgment

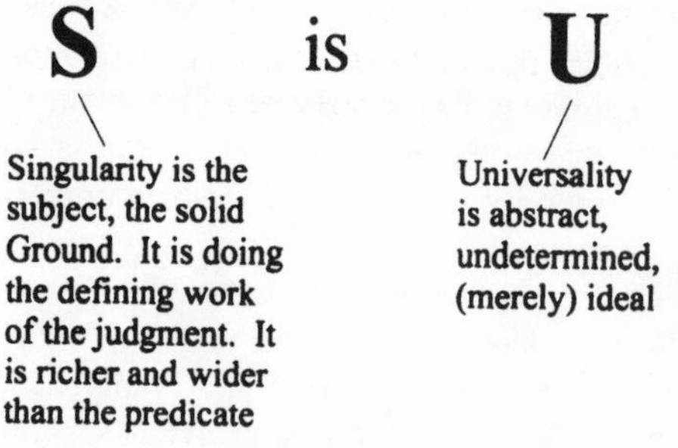

S is **U**

Singularity is the subject, the solid Ground. It is doing the defining work of the judgment. It is richer and wider than the predicate

Universality is abstract, undetermined, (merely) ideal

Figure 4.11

Singularity is the subject of the judgment because it is the content that both Universality and Particularity present and has the character of being the solid foundation or ground for the whole Concept. Because Singularity is mentioned first in the judgment, we have to start with whatever character it has on its own so far, without reference to either of the other elements. Because Singularity has taken on the activity of the Concept as a universal concept and contains the relationship of Ground, it is self-subsistent and capable of being defined on its own. It is, as Hegel puts it, "immediately concrete" (§169). Since Singularity has taken on the activity of the Concept, it is "in and for itself," or it is defined through both an "in itself" relationship—in which it is opposed to its contents—and a "for itself" relationship—in which it embraces ("for itself") its contents *for itself*, or through its own activity. Singularity "relates itself to itself negatively," as Hegel puts it (§169). It is defined by relating itself (through its own activity) to its content (which is itself), but is also defined (negatively) as separate from or opposed to (i.e. as an "in itself" in relation to) that content. Singularity is thus completely defined on its own through its own activity. This characteristic allows Singularity to have a definition in an immediate way, without reference to any other element.

What character or definition does Singularity have when taken by itself? Singularity is defined as the thought of the completed and completely systematized set of actualities. An actuality is an existence (Outer) that is in a mutually defining relationship with an identifying concept (Inner). The completed and completely systematized set of actualities is the whole realm of Outer in a mutually defining relationship with the whole realm of Inner: every (possible) contingent existence in a mutually defining relationship with every possible identifying concept. Because Singularity is immediately concrete, it has this character in an immediate way. Singularity's character as the completed and completely systematized set of actualities is simply given.

Since Singularity is immediately concrete and is the ground of the judgment, it is the element within the judgment that is currently doing the work of defining the whole judgment. The judgment has a definition because of what Singularity is like. As Hegel puts it, Singularity is the distinguishing moment (§169). The given character of Singularity as the systematized set of actualities provides the judgment with its character. The universality, by contrast, is abstract and undetermined (§169). As a result, the subject is taken to be richer and wider than the predicate, while the universal is (merely) ideal (§170).

Because the judgment is currently abstract, the universal can be any old universal that applies to the Singularity. At the moment, Singularity is the thought of the completed and completely systematized set of actualities, and the universality is any universal concept or ideality that applies to that set. Although Singularity is the thought of the completed and completely systematized set of actualities—it is the thought of *all* actualities, of the whole realm of Actuality—the thought of a specific completed and completely systematized set of actualities can be used to illustrate this judgment. Take the concept of rose, for example (an example Hegel will use later [§172R]). If we think of the concept of rose as completely defined and systematized, and as including every rose that has and will ever exist in the world, then the concept of rose would be a Singularity. The concept of rose is the *thought of* the completed and completely systematized set of actual roses. Since Singularity currently gets its definition in an immediate way, "rose" as a concept currently gets its definition in an immediate way as well. What "rose" is like is given by the set of actual roses. In Abstract Judgment, the predicate would then be any universal concept that applies to "rose": "the rose is red," "the rose is real."

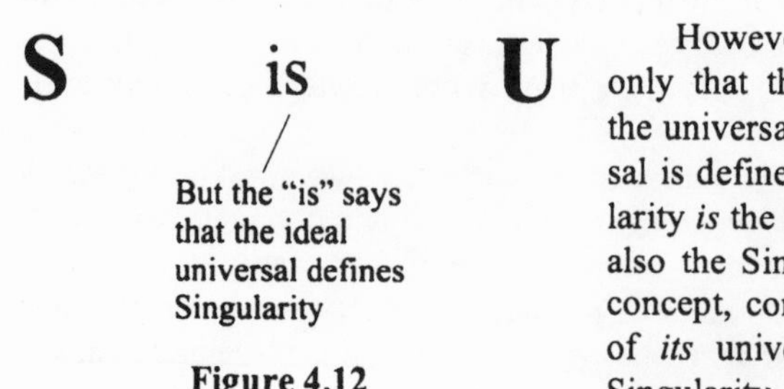
S
is
U
But the "is" says that the ideal universal defines Singularity

Figure 4.12

However, the copula "is" says not only that the Singularity is defined by the universal, it also says that the universal is defined by Singularity. The Singularity *is* the universal, but the universal *is* also the Singularity. The universal, as a concept, contains the Singularity as part of *its* universality. Not only does the Singularity "rose" define the universal "red," for instance (because the rose can indeed be red), but the universal "red" also defines the "rose." "Red" is one of the concepts that "rose" contains. "Rose" is a particularity of the universal "red," or one of the concepts into which the universal "red" divides or particularizes (§169). Singularity is therefore merely a part of the definition of the universality.

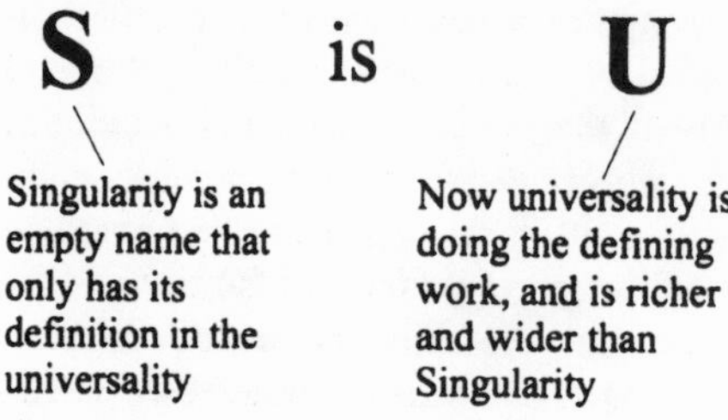
S
is
U
Singularity is an empty name that only has its definition in the universality
Now universality is doing the defining work, and is richer and wider than Singularity

Figure 4.13

So now the universality is the defining element, or is doing the defining work within the judgment. Moreover, the definition, determinacy or content of the universal (which is Particularity) is doing the work of the "is." Singularity "is" universal, not because of what Singularity is like, but because of what the universal is like. The definition of the universal is asserting the identity (the "is) between Singularity and the universality. The universal "real" is what does the job of connecting "rose" together with "real." The universal (i.e. Particularity) is doing the defining work and seems to be able to subsist on its own account. It is now richer and wider than Singularity, and is indifferent to that specific Singularity (§170). While "real" includes the "rose," it is also richer and wider than that specific Singularity, since it includes other things that are also real, such as "house" and "shoe." The universal is no longer an empty ideal. Its definition or content is the part of the judgment that is doing the defining work and the job of uniting the subject and predicate.

At first Singularity did the defining work, but now universality is doing the work of defining the judgment and holding the judgment together. The promise that was made in the general definition of the judgment has therefore been fulfilled. The general definition of the judgment says that the two sides of the judgment define each other. That logical conclusion has now been developed. Since the Singularity defined the universal, and then the universal defined the Singularity, the logical conclusion that the two sides define each other has been drawn. The definition of the judgment in terms of content—what it says—has been fulfilled. As Hegel puts it, the "posited identity of the subject and predicate" (§169) in terms of content has been established.

Unfortunately, however, the identity between the subject and predicate is not yet *presented* in terms of form (§169). In the judgments seen so far, when the subject or Singularity is doing the defining work, the universal is an empty ideal or predicate, and when the universal is doing the defining work, the Singularity is an empty subject. Hence, while Singularity and the universal are identified or define each other, they do so (so far), only in separate judgments that present them (in terms of form) as different from one another—in judgments in which, when one is full, the other is empty. The general form of the judgment says that the two sides define each other at the same time. Singularity and the universal should therefore define each other within the *same* judgment, but they do not do so at the moment. As we will see, they will do so only when the predicate contains a certain kind of universal, rather than any old universal, as it does here—or when the kind of universal that is in the predicate is defined.

Hegel's suggestion that Singularity and universality should be defining each other at the same time in the same judgment implies that judgments are, by definition, transitive. According to the form of the judgment (in general), S and U are supposed to identify one another at the same time in the same judgment. The judgment "S is U" says that S is U *and* that U is S. A judgment is therefore similar to multiplication in mathematics: just as 3 x 2 is the same as 2 x 3, so "S is U" is the same as "U is S." This logical transitivity grows out of the sort of relationship that Singularity has with Particularity (the universal) in the Concept. Because the Concept is completed and completely defined—time itself is finished for the Concept—both Particularity and Singularity as concepts are completed and completely defined too. Moreover, Singularity is the particularization of Particularity—it is the thought of the (completed and completely systematized) set of concepts into which Particularity divides during the process of definition. Because Singularity is complete and completed, it is *all* the concepts and *all* the activity of Particularity. It is the full definition of Particularity. Hence Singularity and Particularity are completely mutually defining: Particularity as a concept grasps and defines everything in Singularity, and Singularity as a concept is the complete and completed presentation of Particularity, the full content of Particularity.

Hegel divides the logical development of judgment into three types of judgments: the *Qualitative Judgment*, the *Judgment of Reflection*, and the *Judgment of Necessity*. He says that these types of the judgment correspond to the spheres of Being and Essence (§171R). Qualitative Judgment corresponds to Being because the type of universal in play is a sensible universal, or a universal that has being. The Judgment of Reflection corresponds to Essence because the type of universal in play is a universal that expresses a relationship, which was the hallmark of Essence.

Because Hegel's treatments of the judgment and, later on, of the syllogism in the *Encyclopaedia* are sketchy, I have drawn heavily on the *Science of Logic* to construct the logical development here. However, there appear to be some inconsistencies between the two texts. Those inconsistencies pose a problem for my project. I am arguing that the logical development that Hegel outlines is tighter and more logically necessary than many commentors have thought. If Hegel cannot follow out a single line of logical development himself, however, then it cannot be very necessary or tight. Of course, the disagreements could always be resolved by choosing one text's story over the other. It is always open to argue that Hegel got the story right in one place, and wrong in the other. Such a claim would resolve the logical inconsistencies, of course, but it might not allay the suspicion of many critics that Hegel's logic is loose and not very logical. If Hegel cannot get his own story straight, then the necessity that is supposedly driving the logical development cannot be very strong. I will revisit these issues when we come to places in the logical development where the two texts diverge.

Qualitative Judgment: the Immediate Judgment or Judgment of Thereness

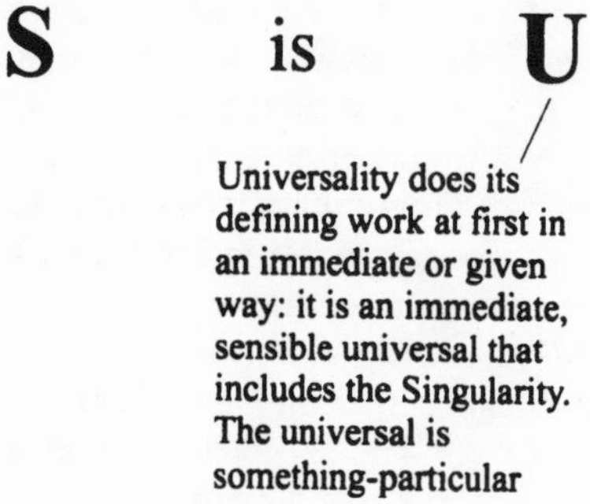

S is U

Universality does its defining work at first in an immediate or given way: it is an immediate, sensible universal that includes the Singularity. The universal is something-particular

Figure 4.14

The content of the judgment is fulfilled, but not the form. The content and form of the judgment will be fulfilled at the same time only if the sort of universal that is in the predicate is restricted to certain kinds of universals, that is, to a universal that expresses not only the universality of the Singularity, but also the particularity of the Singularity. We need a sort of predicate that is, for the Singularity, "the particular and the universal within an identity" (§171). The universal still has to be a concept that captures a way in which the Singularity is universal, of course, but now it also has to capture one of the ways in which the Singularity particularizes. It has to be a universality of the Singularity that is also an element into which the Singularity—which is also a universal—particularizes for its definition.

What kind of universal does that? Singularity has a character of its own as a universal. In general, a universal has a character by particularizing (see Particularity). The particularities of a universal are the way in which a universal is defined. Because Singularity is the thought or concept of the given set of singularities, its character is immediate. Singularity therefore particularizes into immediate, given thereness. Since the universal must capture both the universality and the particularity of the Singularity, it will be a universal that applies to the Singularity but that also captures the given thereness or immediate character that the Singularity has. The universal will therefore be a universal concept of thereness or an immediate sensible quality of the Singularity.

Hegel gives the example of the judgment "the rose is red" (§172R). Since the Doctrine of the Concept has to do with universal concepts—Singularity, Particularity and Universality are all universal concepts—the Singularity here—i.e. "rose"—is not an individual rose, but rather the universal concept of rose. It is "the rose," as a whole type, or kind, of thing. Because the Singularity is given or immediate, the type or kind of thing must also be a "one" that has immediate existence in the actual world, which, of course, "the rose" does. The rose has immediate existence in the actual world insofar as it is all the roses that have and will ever exist—the whole expanse of rose. It has its character in an immediate way insofar as it simply gathers up the character of existence that the individual roses have. The predicate must then be a universal that applies to the Singularity insofar as it captures the given character of the Singularity and is also one of the qualities into which the Singularity divides. Redness, for instance, captures the given character of the Singularity "rose" because the rose exists as red, or is red. Redness is also one of the particularities into which the rose divides. "Red" is the concept of one of the characteristics into which rose as a type divides.

Immediate Judgment is really the first legitimate judgment, because only now do Singularity and the universality have both the content and form that was promised by the general form of the judgment. Although they are distinguished from one another, they also identify one another at the same time in the same judgment. The rose is red, and redness has the rose as one of its particularities.

In Abstract Judgment, one side of the judgment was not defined or was abstract. Now, however, both the singular and universal are defined at the same time, so the whole judgment is defined.

The (Simply) Negative Qualitative Judgment

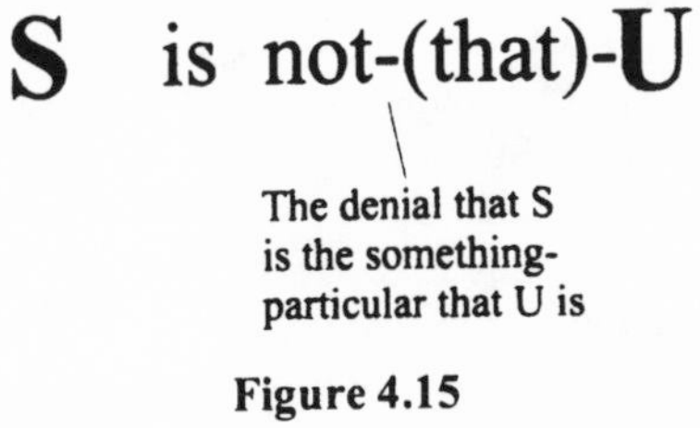

S is not-(that)-U

The denial that S is the something-particular that U is

Figure 4.15

Because the universal is something-particular, or some given singular quality, however, it does not capture the defining or concrete nature of the subject (§172). Since such a universal does not capture the defining or concrete nature of the Singularity, the Singularity is also not-(that particular)-universal. As a result, the (Simply) Negative Judgment arises: S is not-(that)-U. In the example of the judgment "the rose is red," the universal "redness" characterizes the rose as a type. Because some roses are red, rose as a type is or includes red—the Singularity *is* defined by the universal. At the same time, the rose is an item into which "redness" divides—the universal contains, and so defines, the Singularity. But the universal is a given quality that does not capture the defining nature of the rose (as a type). The defining nature of the rose as a type is that it is a *flower*, but the universal says the rose is "red," not that the rose is "flower." Since the universal "red" does not capture the concrete or defining nature of the rose—the "what it is" of the rose as a type—the rose is just as easily not-red. The judgment "the rose is red" therefore generates the judgment "the rose is not-red." And, indeed, the rose as a type is in fact not-red, because it also comes in other colors, such as yellow and pink. The (Simply) Negative Judgment is generated by the fact that there is no tight identity-connection between the Singularity and a given singular quality, sensible universal, or universal as something-particular.

Transition to The Empty Qualitative Judgment of Identity and the Negatively Infinite Qualitative Judgment

Even though S is not (that) U, it is still some other U, so the judgment "S is U" is reasserted. But because that U also does not capture the concrete or defining nature of S, "S is not that U" is reasserted once again. But S is still some other U, so "S is U" is asserted once again, and so on. In other words, we get an endless flipping back and forth between "S is U" and "S is not (that) U"

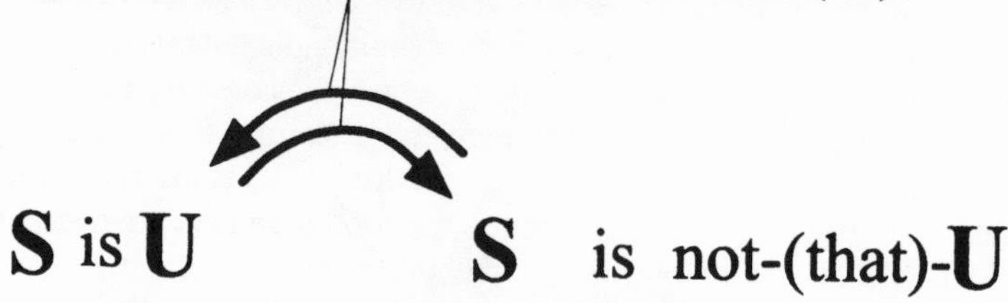

Figure 4.16

The claim that Singularity is not that particular universal still implies that there is some other particular universal that it is. To say that S is not *that* U, is to imply that S is some other U. As Hegel suggests, the claim that the rose as a type is not red does not deny that the rose is any color—or any other universal as something-particular—but only that it is red. So the denial that the rose is red leads to another Qualitative Judgment (§173) that asserts that the rose is some other universal as something-particular: a judgment such as "the rose is yellow." In logical terms, the (Simply) Negative Judgment leads to the reassertion of the Qualitative Judgment: S is not (that) U implies that S is U again.

But since this second U, as a qualitative universal, also does not capture the concrete or defining nature of S, so the second Qualitative Judgment leads to the (Simply) Negative Judgment once again: S is not (that) U either. This second (Simply) Negative Judgment, however, still implies that S is some other U, so the Qualitative Judgment is reasserted yet again: S is U again. Once again, however, S is not (that) U, either. But then S must be some other U again: so S is U again. Qualitative Judgment generates a spuriously infinite process of going back and forth between the Qualitative Judgment "S is U" and the (Simply) Negative Judgment "S is not (that) U."

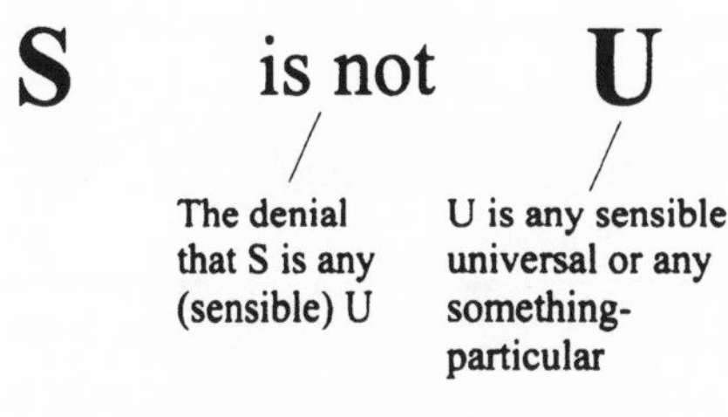

Figure 4.17

The trouble with the Qualitative Judgment is that no sensible universal will ever capture the concrete or defining nature of Singularity. The rose as a type is never just yellow, or red, or round, or any other sensible universal. None of those sensible universals capture the "what it is" of the rose as a type or what makes a rose a rose. They lead to a spuriously infinite process that make it impossible to fix the character of the Singularity (cf. Spurious Infinity). Indeed, the character of the Singularity can never be defined or fixed using sensible universals. The spurious infinity is generated not by some particular sensible universal such as "red," but by the type of universals being applied, or by sensible universals as a type. The (Simply) Negative Qualitative Judgment, denied only that the particular universal—*that*-sensible-universal—applied. The logic draws out what the spurious infinity implies, namely, that the attempt to characterize the Singularity with any sensible-U must be abandoned. The claim that S is any sensible universal is therefore now denied with the judgment "S is not (in general) (any) U," where U is defined as sensible universals as a type.

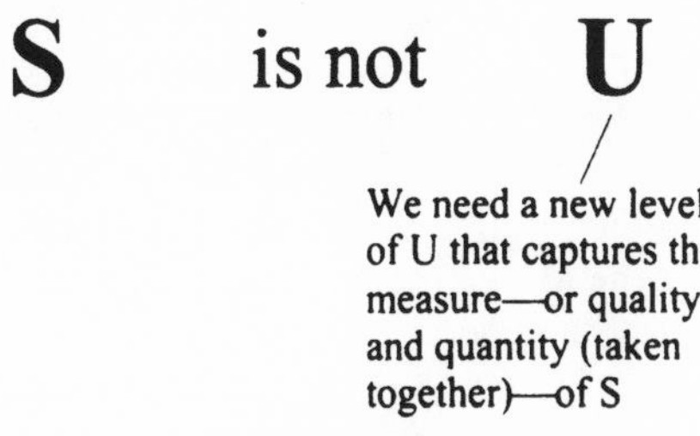

Figure 4.18

This denial can be depicted by attaching the word "not" to the word "is" rather than to the "U": S is-not (any) U. Instead of saying that S is not some particular sensible universal ("S is not-U"), the judgment "S is-not U" says that S is not any sensible universal, or is not in general a universal, when the universal is defined as sensible universals (as a type). Instead of denying that there is an identity-connection ("is-ness") between Singularity and some particular sensible universal, this new judgment denies that there is an identity-connection between Singularity and any sensible universal. The rose is not really defined by any sensible universal. Sensible universals fail to grasp the "what it is" of the Singularity because they fail to capture both the quality and quantity of the Singularity. The sensible universal of redness falls short qualitatively, because there are some roses that are not red. So the sensible universal of redness fails to capture the full quality of the rose as a type. The sensible universal of redness also fails to capture the quantity of the rose as a type because a number of roses are not red. Redness does not capture the full quantity of the rose as a type. In short, sensible universals fail to capture the full *measure* of the type. The use of the term "measure" is particularly appropriate here because Measure was defined as the unity of the categories of quality and quantity in the Doctrine of Measure in Chapter Two.

The spurious infinity or endless back-and-forth process between the Qualitative Judgment and the (Simply) Negative Judgment can be stopped only with a new kind of universal—a new ideality—that can capture both the quality and quantity of the Singularity, or the *measure* of the Singularity.

The Empty Qualitative Judgment of Identity

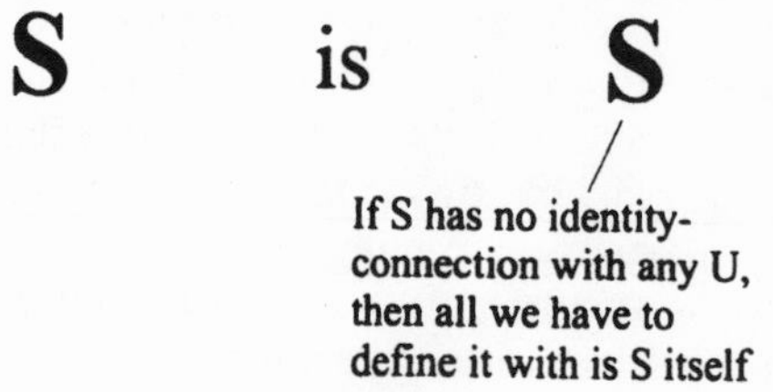

S is **S**

If S has no identity-connection with any U, then all we have to define it with is S itself

Figure 4.19

Before the new sort of universal can be defined, however, the full logical implications of the last judgment must be drawn out. The judgment in the last stage said that S is not any universal, where the universal was defined as sensible universals as a kind. While it is true that only sensible universals have been used so far, the judgment says simply that S is-not U, or that there is no identity-connection (no "is-ness") between S and U (where U is defined as sensible universality as a type). The judgment does not *say* that U is restricted to a sensible type of universal. We have to proceed logically based on what the judgment says, and all it says is that S is, in general, not any sensible U. This stage draws out the implications of this general denial that there is an identity-connection between S and U (as a sensible universal) in two ways. (1) First, if Singularity has no identity-connection with the universal, then the singular is only related to itself. If, in general, S is-not U, then the only resource to define S is S itself. If S is unrelated, in general, to U, then S is just S. The implications of the general denial that S is related to U can therefore be expressed with the identity statement "S is S." If the rose (as a type) is not any universal, for instance, then all there is to define the rose (as a type) is itself: "the rose (as a type) is the rose (as a type)."

Although the judgment "S is S" is correct—since S really *is* S—it is correct in an obvious way that adds no information (it is empty). Indeed, there is no real relationship here at all. A judgment is supposed to be asserting that there is a relationship between the subject and predicate, but there can be a relationship only if there are two different things being related together, or, in the case here, only if the subject and predicate are different from one another. Since both sides of the judgment are exactly the same as one another, the judgment is not really a judgment at all (§173R). "S is S" expresses an identity with no difference. There is an identity, but no distinguishing, and so the judgment is uninformative or empty.

Although "S is S" is an empty or uninformative judgment, there is a new and improved version or type of universal in the predicate. The trouble with the Qualitative Judgment was that the type of universal in the predicate—sensible universality—failed to capture the full quality and quantity of Singularity. Since the predicate is now defined by Singularity itself, however, the predicate now contains a universal that captures the full quality and quantity of the subject. Singularity is a universal: it is the thought of a whole set of actualities, and so is the concept of a kind or type of thing. Singularity is, for instance, the concept of the rose as a type or of the whole set of actual roses. Singularity is a universal that captures the full measure of the subject (which is just Singularity itself). It is *all* (i.e. the full quantity) of the things that are S-quality (i.e. captures the full quality of S). Now that Singularity is the universal in the predicate, the predicate finally captures the full measure of the subject. In "the rose is the rose," the predicate contains all the things (the full quantity of S) of rose-quality (the full quality of S). Singularity itself is a universal that contains the full measure of the Singularity.

Singularity introduces a new type of universal into the predicate: a universal as something-particular. Because it is the concept of a set of items that exist, it is a universal that has its character or particularity in an immediate way. It is therefore a concrete universal. It is a concrete universal in two senses: (a) it is concrete in the sense that it has a definition—the rose as a concept, for instance, is defined by the set of all actual roses—and (b) it is concrete in the sense that it exists, since all of the actual roses that belong to the set exist (even if those individual roses do not all exist at the same time [see also Chapter Three, §5 for a discussion of the term "concrete"]). Because Singularity is now the predicate of the judgment, the universal in the predicate is not a sensible universal anymore. The nature of the universal in the predicate has evolved: as a concrete universal, it is the concept of the kind (of thing) that S is. Instead of merely a sensible universal in the predicate, we now have a universal in the predicate that is the concept of the kind that the Singularity is.

As Hegel suggests in the *Science of Logic*, we could also write "S is S" as "U is U," so long as we keep in mind that both Singularity and the universal are defined as concrete universals. Again, because S is a type of sensible thing—such as the rose as a type—it is already both a singularity and a universal. It is a singularity insofar as it is one (singular) type or kind, but it is a universal insofar as it is a *type*. Hence "U is U" captures what we have here just as well as "S is S" does.

Negatively Infinite Qualitative Judgment

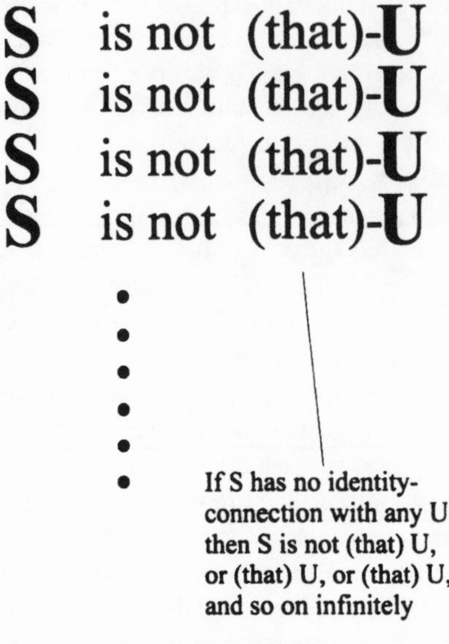
S is not (that)-U
S is not (that)-U
S is not (that)-U
S is not (that)-U
If S has no identity-connection with any U, then S is not (that) U, or (that) U, or (that) U, and so on infinitely

Figure 4.20

(2) The denial that there is an identity-connection between the Singularity and any universal (where the universal is defined as a sensible universal) led to the judgment "S is S" (or "U is U"). The only available element to define Singularity in the predicate was S itself. Singularity's lack of identity with the universal can also be expressed, however, as an infinite negative judgment, where the infinity here is a bad or spurious infinity—infinity as an endless, process of running-on (see the stage of Spurious Infinity in Chapter Two). If Singularity is in general not defined by (or is unrelated to) any universal (other than itself), then no matter how many universals we list, so long as those universals are not S itself, S will not be defined by any of them. We can go on listing such universals forever, but none of them will capture the concrete identity or full measure of Singularity. So the fact that the universal fails to define Singularity can be expressed not only as (1) above (Figure 4.19), but also as a spuriously infinite list of denials that S is related to any universal that is not S itself: S is not (that) U, and it's not (that) U, and it's not (that) U, and so on, *ad infinitum*. We thus end up with an infinite series of judgments that assert that S is unrelated to this and to that specific U. Hegel gives the following examples: "the spirit is not an elephant," "a lion is not a table," and so on (§173R). We could add, "the rose is not a chair," "the rose is not an elephant," and so on. Here, the subject and the predicate are completely incommensurable. As a result, instead of having identity with no distinction as in the last stage, we now have distinction with no identity. The subject and the predicate are not like one another at all.

The Negatively Infinite Judgment is not really a judgment. According to the general definition of the judgment, the "is" is supposed to express that there is an identity-connection between the subject and the predicate (cf. The Judgment above). In the Negatively Infinite Judgment, however, Singularity and the universal now have no connection of identity with one another at all, and thus fail to satisfy one of the general requirements of the judgment.

Because there was a more advanced type of universal in the last stage—namely, concrete universals—the sort of universals in the predicate in this stage are not sensible universals anymore, but concrete universals. "Elephant," "lion," and "table" are all universals that, like "rose" itself, are supposed to capture a kind or type of existing actuality, or the full measure of a set of actualities. Because they can have a definition or be defined on their own simply by gathering up the existence of the individual actualities that they embrace and define, these universals are no longer sensible universals, but concrete ones.

The last two judgments—the Empty Judgment of Identity and the Negatively Infinite Judgment—when taken together, are exhaustive. Taken together, the two judgments say that S is the kind of thing that S is (the Empty Judgment of Identity), and that S is not any other kind of thing (the Negatively Infinite Judgment). There are no other kinds of things that S could be: S is either S, or some other kind of thing. Since the two judgments say that S is S and not any other kind of thing, the options for defining S using a concrete universal have been exhausted. There is no other concrete universal that S could be. From a logical point of view, then, these two judgments exhaust all the possibilities for concrete universals. There are no other judgments with concrete universality in the predicate to be considered. Since neither judgment succeeds in defining S satisfactorily, however, we are driven logically to move to a new sort of universal to define S in the next stage. The move to a new sort of universal is logically necessitated by having exhausted all other options.

Taken together, the Empty Judgment of Identity and the Negatively Infinite Judgment show that Singularity and the universal have now fallen apart completely. In the last stage, S is S (and U is U), and in this stage, S is never U: Singularity is Singularity, Universality is Universality, and Singularity is never Universality. Qualitative Judgment has fallen apart into either (1) an "is" which is meaningless because the two things being related together are the same as one another and so cannot really be in a relationship with one another (the Empty Judgment of Identity), or (2) an "is" which has the potential to be a real relationship, since the two things being related together are different, but ends up being meaningless because the two things are too different from one another and so cannot be related together at all, or are incommensurable (§173).

Hegel says that we can find things in the world that express the Negatively Infinite Judgment. He uses the examples of civil law and criminal law to distinguish the (Simply) Negative Judgment from the Negatively Infinite Judgment. Civil law expresses the former Judgment, he says, while criminal law expresses the latter (§173A [because this example is repeated in the *Science of Logic*, I think we can accept this Addition from the *Encyclopaedia* as a relatively accurate account of Hegel's own views]). Take civil law first. Suppose Chante contracts with Alan to build a house, and Alan fails to fulfill the contract. Alan's failure to fulfill the contract expresses a (Simple) Negative Judgment because it denied that Chante had a particular right, namely, to property. Breaking the contract says, in effect "Chante is not-that-right," or, in more standard English, "Chante does not have that-right," namely, the particular right to property. As a result, civil law deals with cases in which some particular right has been violated, as Hegel says (§173A). When Alan breaks a contract and fails to build the house, he is not denying all of Chante's rights, but only a particular right.

Criminal law, by contrast, Hegel suggests, deals with cases in which right in general has been violated (§173A). Take a theft, for instance—as Hegel apparently suggested himself (§173A). There is a sense in which a theft expresses a more general denial of the victim's rights. In a mugging, for instance, the thief holds a knife to the victim's throat and demands the victim's wallet. The thief is certainly denying the victim's right to property when he takes the wallet or any other property. But because of the threat of injury or death, the thief has also denied all of the other rights the victim has. For example, because the threat forced the victim to remain silent, the victim's right to speak was denied. Indeed, the threat of death or injury also denied the victim's basic right to life, or basic right to live without interference. Any concrete kind or type of right that we plug in—the right to speech, the right to life, the right to the free practice of religion or whatever—was denied by the mugging. The one act of mugging asserts that the victim has none of the specific rights that we might plug into the sentence. We can express this general denial of the victim's rights as a Negatively Infinite Judgment:

the victim has not the right to property (that-right)
the right to life (that-right)

and so on, so that no matter what concrete kind of right we attribute to the victim, the theft says that the victim had no right to it.

As Hegel suggests, this general denial of the victim's rights (the Negatively Infinite Judgment) eventually points toward the idea that what the thief denied was not this or that right, but right in general, or right as such (§173A). Hegel's suggestion is reminiscent of calculus: as x infinitely approaches 1, what comes into view is 1 itself. Similarly, in the theft example, if the victim does not have this right or that right, *ad infinitum*, then what comes into view is the idea that the victim has no rights at all. Ultimately, it is the victim's rights in general that the theft denies. That's why the thief is not only required to return the particular item that was stolen, but is punished as well, Hegel says (§173A).

The Negatively Infinite Judgment is the truth of Qualitative Judgment (§173R), which means it is the last, most developed form of Qualitative Judgment. Even though the kind of universal in the predicate is a concrete universal, rather than a merely sensible one, concrete universals are still tied to quality. Concrete universals capture the full measure of the subject, which means they capture the full quantitative *quality* of the subject, but the judgment falls apart.

That the Qualitative Judgment has fallen apart, however, shows once again that it expresses the nature of finite things. According to Hegel, the form of the judgment expresses the nature of finite things (see the stage of Judgment). Finite things are singulars that get their identity by being related to a universal, but the nature of finiteness is such that the finite singular and the universal are always in principle separable. Finite things ultimately fall apart. The judgment "S is U" says that S and U are related, but also says that S and U are in principle separable. The "is" connects S and U, but not in a way that prohibits their being pulled apart. And indeed, they do fall apart in Qualitative Judgment: S is S, U is U (the

Empty Judgment of Identity), and S is never U (the Negatively Infinite Judgment). S and U have separated from one another.

This failure of the Qualitative Judgment to capture a relationship between Singularity and the universal points toward the next stage. We need a judgment that is capable of capturing the relationship that Singularity is supposed to have with the universal. Singularity is supposed to be the universal (as expressed by the "is"), but it is also supposed to be related to the universal, which means that the universal must be separate from or distinct from it. Something cannot be related to itself (cf. the Empty Judgment of Identity). The need for S to be related to U points to the next sort of universal in the predicate. Instead of qualitative universals—which failed to capture the relatedness of S and U—the next stage employs universals that express Singularity's relationship to something else.

There is a second lesson in the failure of Qualitative Judgment. The Empty Judgment of Identity, in which the universal drops out and Singularity is defined in relation only to itself, says nothing. "S is S" is empty or uninformative. The S remains undefined. The Negatively Infinite Judgment, by contrast, includes a universal, but because the universal has no relation to the Singularity, neither the Singularity nor the universal are defined. The judgment "the lion is not a table" fails to define lion, but also fails to define table. Indeed, the universal "table" is only meaningful because we know from other contexts what a table is. If we had to try to learn what a table is from this judgment alone, we would be out of luck. Suppose the judgment were "the lion is not a bibble-fip." This judgment offers no chance of learning what a bibble-fip is. Just as the Singularity can only be what it is, or be defined, in relation to a universal which expresses its identity (what it is), the universal can only be defined by being reflected into a Singularity which expresses *its* identity. In the next stage this discovery that the Singularity and universal can only be defined by being reflected into one another is employed: the Qualitative Judgment becomes the Judgment of Reflection.

In the Judgment of Reflection, the relationship between Singularity and the universal will have the same sort of relationship that was the hallmark of the Doctrine of Essence: the relationship of Ground (see Ground in Chapter Three). According to the relationship of Ground, each side of the relationship can be what it is or have its identity only by being reflected in and reflecting into the other side. In Chapter Three, I defined the relationship of Ground as "inward reflection which is just as much reflection into another," where "inward reflection" referred to each side's reflected inward character or definition. Singularity and the universal will have this same relationship in the Judgment of Reflection: Singularity can have or reflect (show up as) its identity or have inward reflection only by reflecting into the other side; and the universal can have or reflect (show up as) its identity or have inward reflection only by reflecting into the other side too. Because the relationship between Singularity and the universal mirrors the relationship of Ground—the relationship that was central to the development of the concept of Essence—we can see why Hegel says that the Judgment of Reflection reproduces the sphere of Essence (§171R). Still, as Hegel points out, it reproduces the sphere of Essence in a way different from the way Essence was developed in the Doctrine of Essence. There, the stages of Essence were defined from the bottom up out of the stages of Being, whereas here Essence is being defined from the top down out of the Concept (§171R).

Moreover, in the Doctrine of Essence, the concept of Ground gave rise to the concept of Existence (see Existence). The concept of Ground captured *the relationship* between ground and grounded, while the concept of Existence captured ground, grounded *and* their relationship of Ground. Because Singularity and the universal are in a relationship of Ground, when we take them together with their relationship, they, too, satisfy the definition of Existence. In the stages of the judgment so far, only the Singularity or universal existed. Now, however, the whole judgment—S and U in their relationship of Ground—exists (§174).

Furthermore, in Chapter Three, Existence could be thought of in two ways: either (1) as a whole, one process (the whole realm of Existence) or, (2) as a multitude of individual processes. Singularity and the universal in their relationship—i.e. their existence—can be seen in these two ways as well. The stages of the Judgment of Reflection will draw on this double-aspect of Existence. If (1) Singularity and the universal capture the whole realm of existence, then Singularity by itself is one piece of that realm and has its identity in relation to that realm. That's why the universal in the next stage captures the idea that Singularity can be characterized only in relation to the whole realm of existence. Singularity is an external multitude: it is one part of the whole realm of existence, which exists outside of it. In the Singular Judgment of Reflection, the universal is an expression of existential relatedness. In the subsequent stage, however, Singularity and the universal are (2), that is, an internal multitude, so that the Singularity is broken up internally into groups.

The Judgment of Reflection: The Singular Judgment of Reflection

This S is U

Although S is still a concrete universal, it is Singularity now defined as singularity, or as a singular: as this S

The universal is now relational, or expresses that S can be what it is only in relation to an other

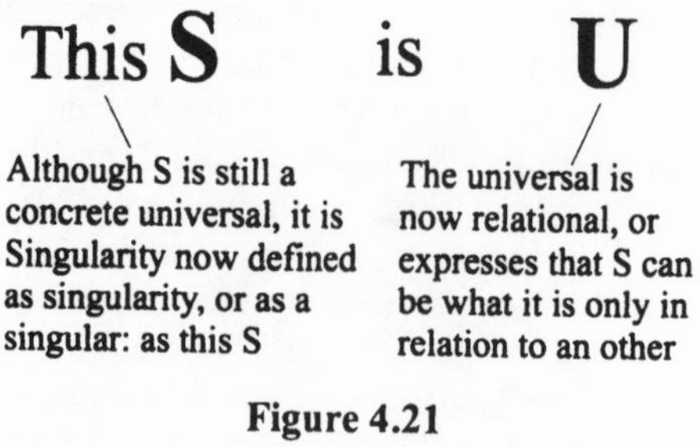

Figure 4.21

Singularity is supposed to have a definition or character of its own, but the judgments so far have been unable to grasp or specify Singularity's character. In the Empty Qualitative Judgment of Identity, Singularity was left undefined because the judgment was uninformative. And in the Negatively Infinite Qualitative Judgment, Singularity was left undefined because the universal was not related to Singularity at all. The Negatively Infinite Qualitative Judgment failed because S was not related to anything, while the Empty Qualitative Judgment of Identity failed because S had no other. The failure of Qualitative Judgment leads to the conclusion that Singularity can be what it is only *in relation* to something that is *an "other"* for it. The Singular Judgment of Reflection expresses this conclusion by bringing in a new kind of universal.

To see how the predicate or universal changes, however, we have to see how the subject or Singularity changes. To say that S can be what it is only in relation to an other implies two things: (1) that S has its own character, and (2) that S's character shows up. (1) Having an "other" was the hallmark of the "in itself" relationship, which spelled out the basic, logical definition of having a defined thereness or character (see Being-in-itself in Chapter Two). (2) Having a character that only showed up in relation to an "other" was the hallmark of the "for itself" relationship in the Doctrine of Essence (cf. Essence in Chapter Three). The new judgment must express how S's character shows up or reflects, or how S is "inwardly reflected" (§174) insofar as it has a character of its own.

S or Singularity's character shows up or is reflected insofar as it is a "this." Singularity is expressed or presented as a "this." That's how Singularity has its Singularity. The judgment in this stage specifies how Singularity shows up by adding the word "this" in front of "S": the subject is "this S," instead of just "S." Singularity is still a concrete *universal*—a something-universal—but it is now a concrete universal that shows up as or is inwardly reflected as singularity or singular. Because S is concrete, it has a character that allows it to exist in the world. The rose, for instance, as a concrete type of thing, is the whole expanse of rose that exists in the world. Since we have not yet grasped the specific character of S, we cannot say specifically what S is as a singularity. But we can refer to, or point to S's singularity in a general way with the word "this." S shows up as a Singularity, as a "this." The whole expanse of rose is a singular as a "this." "This" rose is how the whole expanse of rose shows up as a singularity.

The universal, for its part, must meet three logical conditions: (1) it must still characterize S, because the judgment still says that S *is* U; but (2) the universal must characterize S in a way that has "otherness" in relation to S. U must characterize S, but it must be different from S in some specific way. U must be S's own other (cf. Being-in-itself in Chapter Two). These two features of U are implied by the failure of the last two stages. The Empty Qualitative Judgment of Identity—"S is S"—failed to define S because the universal in the predicate (namely S itself) was not different enough from S. The Negatively Infinite Qualitative Judgment failed because the U was so different from S that it failed to characterize S at all. So the predicate must be a universal that characterizes S, but is also different from S at the same time. (3) Third, U must express the other lesson implied by the last two stages, namely, that S can be what it is only *in relation* to something else.

These three characteristics give a different kind of universal in the predicate. The concept in the predicate is a concept that characterizes S, but also (to be "other" than S) is defined in a way that is different from the way in which S is defined. So far, S has been defined in relation to its contents—S is the set of actualities. If S is the concept of the rose, for instance, then it is defined as the set of roses. If the universal is to be defined in a way different from the way in which S is defined, it must grasp a different set of items from the set of items that S grasps. Because U characterizes S, it will have to grasp the items that are in S's set, but, because U is supposed to capture S's relationship to an other, U will also have to grasp items outside of the set of items included in S. U cannot simply be defined by the set of items in S. It has to define S, and therefore has to include the items in S's set, but it also has to include other items outside of the items in S's set. If U did not include other items—if U were simply the same set of items as S—then U would be S, and S would be related only to itself again, leading to the untenable Empty Qualitative Judgment of Identity ("S is S"). The universal must now be richer and wider than S, or must include the items in S's set, but also include additional items outside of S.

Moreover, because U has to express S's connection to an "other," U can no longer be an immediately qualitative universal (§174). Take the judgment "the rose is red." Since the set of all red things taken together is richer and wider than the set of roses, the quality "red" seems to meet the logical conditions defining the universal in this stage. However, the quality "red" still treats S as if S can be defined on its own. The quality "red" does not *say* or *express* the logical lesson implied by the last two stages, namely, that S can be what it is only *in relation* to an other. S can have its redness all by itself. It does not need anything else to have its redness. The same is true of all other qualities of S. Even S's quality of "being what it is" is something that S can have by itself, since Singularity embraces and defines its content. The rose can have its roseness by itself, for instance, insofar as it embraces and defines all the roses. If the universal is to express S's relatedness to another, the universal must be a relational universal. It must be a universal of relationship or of connectedness with another (§174)—a universal that cannot apply to S by itself, but that S can have only through a connection to other items. Since the universal in the judgment is no longer a qualitative universal, but a universal of relationship, connection or "reflection"—which is how relationship was characterized in the Doctrine of Essence—the judgment is now a Judgment of Reflection.

Hegel gives the following examples of relational universals: curative, useful, dangerous, having a certain weight or acidity, and having a drive (§174, §174A). These universals are all relational: something is only curative, useful or dangerous in relation to something else; weight and acidity are always relative to a standard; and a drive is always a drive for something else. This (type of) plant, for instance, can be, or be defined as, *curative* only in relation to some illness, that is, only if it cures some illness. The (type of) plant cannot be curative at all without the illness. The universal "curative" thus expresses the relationship between the plant and something else outside of it, in this case, the illness.

Although the universal captures Singularity's relation to an "other," or to something outside of it, the universal still fails to grasp the defining character of Singularity. The plant may be curative, for instance, but its being curative does not capture the "what it is" or type of thing that the plant is. Moreover, while U is relational, it is still immediate, given or "found." Plants are given or found to be curative. A (type of) plant is curative based on what it happens to be like, or based on the character of its existence, not on its concept.

In Qualitative Judgment, the universal evolved. In the Judgment of Reflection, Singularity will evolve. In Qualitative Judgment, the Singularity was given, while the universal, which was doing the main defining work of the judgment, developed logically. Now, however, the roles of Singularity and the universal are reversed. The universal is the primary defining element of the judgment—it is richer and wider than the Singularity, which is part of what makes up the universal. In the judgment "this (type of) plant is curative," for instance (Singularity is still an immediate, given or existing type of thing), the universal "curative" is the primary, given element, and this type of plant is merely an instance of it or part of what makes it up. Because this plant fills up the universal "curative," the universal no longer inheres in Singularity. Instead, the universal subsumes the Singularity within it. The Universal is richer and wider than the Singularity, which it contains: in addition to that type of plant, other things are curative also. Changes in the Singularity—rather than the universal—will now drive the logical development.

Particular Judgment of Reflection

S is a universal as something-particular, so it is an internal multitude, or a bunch of existents. Unfortunately, the word "this" (bunch of existents) does not capture the full extension of U. So we look at S and judge that:

Positive Judgment:
these (some) S's are U

Negative Judgment:
these (some) S's are not U

Figure 4.22

The judgment of the last stage defined the Singularity as a singular in relation to an "other," or to something outside of it. The universal or U is richer and wider than S, and includes other items along with S. S is merely a singular item in relation to the other items that U includes. S is one item in the set of items that U includes. This (type of) plant, for example, as a singular, is simply one item in the set of items grasped by the universal "curative."

Singularity is still a type of thing that has a character of its own, however. It is, to use Hegel's terminology, something-universal. Moreover, the judgment of the last stage also *expressed* or *said* that the Singularity is a universal: it said that S is U. This stage draws out the conclusion implied by the fact that S has been a universal all along and by the last stage. Since S is universal, then "this S" is not really a singular, but a universal—a one thought of a bunch of items. Since S has a character of its own, we should actually say that S is the *character* of a bunch of items. So, to say that "this S is U" is to say that this bunch of items that have the character of, or show up as, S are U. These things that are S are U: "these (some) S's are U." This judgment is the *Positive* Particular Judgment of Reflection. If S is the concept of fern, for example, then the Positive Judgment might be "these (some) ferns are curative."

S's character as the thought or concept of a set of items produces a Negative Judgment as well. In the Doctrine of Being, a universal as a set-term came to have a definition through a top-down process that involved sorting the items in its set (see Repulsion and Attraction). A One can be the grasping concept for a set of items only if the items in the set are not only the same as one another (they attract one another), but are also distinguished from one another (they repulse each other). Singularity has a similar sorting process here, although it is somewhat more sophisticated than the sorting process there. Whereas the One in the Doctrine of Being was a set of qualities or therenesses, Singularity is the thought of the set of identifying concepts (Inner), as well as of out-therenesses (Outer). Since Singularity grasps a set of concepts, its contents will be sorted into concepts, rather than into mere therenesses. A concept is a universal or kind. Hence Singularity's sorting process will involve dividing into universals, kinds, categories. To be defined as a One, Singularity's definition process will sort the actualities in its set into universals, types, or categories that distinguish the items in the set from one another (the equivalent of repulsion) without undercutting their sameness as one another and hence their status as a One (the equivalent of attraction). Singularity thus comes to have a character or definition of its own by dividing into types or categories. This is the very same process of definition that defined the Concept in the stage of Particularity. Therefore the process of definition that Singularity now undergoes is a process of particularization. Just as the Concept is particularized (or defined) by dividing into the types or categories that make it up (see Particularity), so Singularity is defined by dividing into the concepts, types or categories that it contains. Because Singularity is defined or has a character of its own by dividing into types or kinds, not all of the items in its set will have the same characteristics. Since U is richer and wider than S, some of the items will have characteristics captured by the U, some won't. The fact that some of the items will not be captured by U generates the judgment "these (some) S's are not U." This judgment is the *Negative* Particular Judgment of Reflection. The concept of fern, for instance, is defined by dividing into types or kinds. The positive judgment said that the ferns are curative. Since there are different types of ferns, however some of these ferns are not curative.

Because the definition of Singularity is completed or finished (cf. Singularity), the division or particularization of S into types must also be complete. Hence the positive and negative judgments, taken together, are exhaustive: "these (some) S's are U," "these (some) S's are not U," and that's all the S's there are. The S's have been completely divided with respect to the U.

The Particular Judgment of Reflection captures Singularity's process of particularization from a merely subjective point of view, from the point of view of a third party, or from the outside. The Judgment of Reflection does not say which S's are U, and it does not say which U's belong to which S's. Those judgments must be made from the outside by an external subjectivity or third party. The judgments say only that some S's are U, and some S's are not U. Judgments about which S's are and which are not have to be made by a third party capable of making such judgments, namely, an external subjectivity. We human beings have to distinguish those plants that are curative from those that are not.

Universal Judgment of Reflection

All S's are **U**

This "all" is implied by the "some" that we had in the last stage. For any "some" that is U, all of it is U

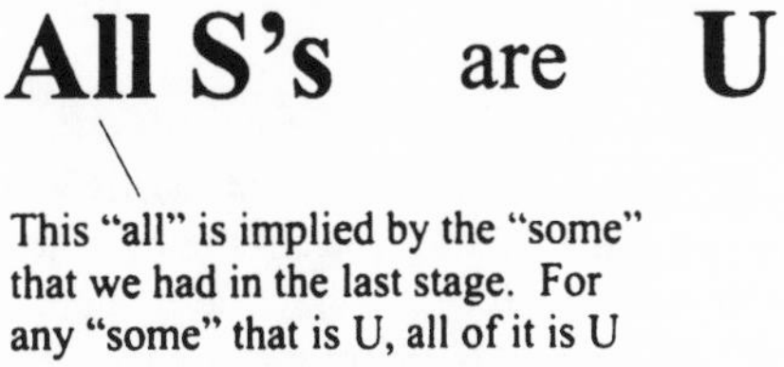

Figure 4.23

To say that "some S's are U" is to say that the particular bunch of S's we are pointing at are all U. For any "some" S's that are U, all of the S's in that "some" or group are U. "These (some) S's are U" says that *all* of those S's are U. Thus, the last stage implies the judgment "all S's are U."

The judgment "these S's are U," also implies that the S's being pointed at have been characterized as a type of thing, namely, as *S's*. The judgment says "these *S*'s," where the "S" characterizes the individuals as some type of thing. The judgment "all (these) S's are U" draws out this implication: it asserts that S is a type of thing and tries to characterize that type by asserting that the S's all have some characteristic (the one specified by the universal in the predicate) in common. In Chapter One (Section III), I discussed three kinds of universality: universality as comm*un*ality, universality as comm*on*ality, and essential universality. This stage and the last are abstract expressions of the first two. The universality of communality involves simply gathering things together into a set. That's what the judgment did in the last stage when it picked out a bunch of S's and collected them together into "these (some) S's." Even the Universal Judgment of Reflection at first asserts nothing but comm*un*ality, insofar as it simply puts all the S's into a bunch as a "this." Nevertheless, when the judgment refers to all the "S's," it has not only gathered them up, but has also typed them, or characterized them as a certain type or kind of thing. It says that all of the S's share some universal, so the universality in the predicate is a universality of comm*on*ality. It characterizes the type of thing that S is in relation to a universal that all the S's have in common.

The universality of comm*on*ality still does not grasp the defining nature of S, however. Things have characteristics in common that are not related to their defining nature. Humans, for example, have earlobes in common, but having earlobes does not capture the defining nature of humans, as Hegel apparently mentioned in a lecture (see §175A). An essential universal, by contrast, will capture the defining nature of a type of thing. Still, the universality of comm*on*ality is an improvement over the universality of comm*un*ality, for Hegel, because it at least aims at characterizing a thing as a type, rather than merely gathering things into a bunch.

Hegel suggests that the Universal Judgment of Reflection captures the kind of universality that dominates ordinary reflection (§175), or ordinary empirical assertions. When we say, for instance, "all garlic is curative," we are talking about garlic as a type. Moreover, because we have our eyes on garlic as a type, we are not simply referring to the garlic cloves that happen to be around on Earth at this very moment. Garlic as a type includes cloves of garlic that existed in the past, as well as cloves of garlic that will exist in the future. The Universal Judgment of Reflection tries to characterize garlic as a type by noticing some common property, such as garlic's (supposed) curative powers. As the British philosopher David Hume argued, however, this type of claim can never be fully proven, since it always reaches beyond the evidence that we have available to us (see Chapter One, Section I). The judgment claims or asserts that all garlic as a type is curative, but since all garlic as a type hasn't existed yet, all the evidence for the claim is not here. The judgment reaches beyond the available evidence, and so remains only an "ought:" all garlic should be, or ought to be, curative, but we cannot say for sure yet whether it will be.

The uncertainty of this sort of judgment will be overcome when the universal is no longer merely a universal that the S's have in common, but an essential universal that captures the defining nature of S. When the universal in the predicate captures the defining nature of S, then all S's will certainly have that universal because, if they did not have that universal, then they would not be an S anymore. When the universal captures the defining nature of S, S is necessarily U, as we will see in the next stages.

Transition to the Judgment of Necessity

S is U
S is universal all by itself, and so no longer needs a universal of reflection to gather it up and define its nature. S is so universal, in fact, that it is necessarily the universal
As a result, if the universal in the judgment is to have a point, or to do any work, it can no longer be a universal of reflection or a property. It has to capture the defining nature of S. So the universal develops from a universal of reflection to a universal of necessity

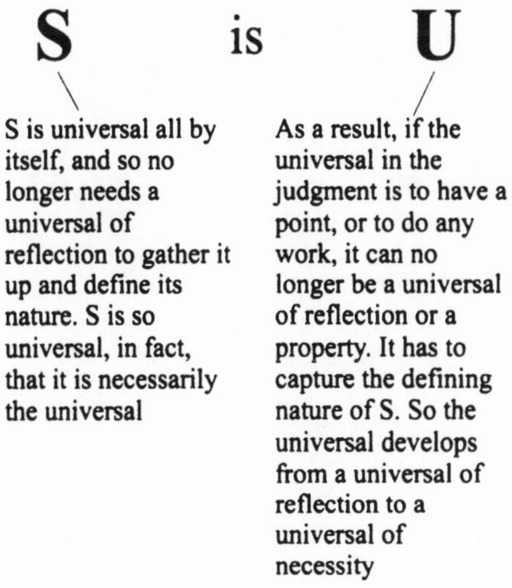

Figure 4.24

Singularity has been a type or totality all along—it is the completed set of actualities. The set is a totality because it is an "all" that is finished (cf. Singularity). Singularity's status as a type of thing, or a whole type of thing, was also implied in the last stage by the judgment "All S's are U." To say that all S's are U implies that all S's are some type of thing: that garlic is a curative type of thing, for instance. This stage draws out the conclusion implied by the last stage: S is not merely an "all," but the type as such. S is, for instance, not just all men, but man as a type, or as such; not just all garlic, but garlic as a type, or as such.

When S is the type as such—garlic as garlic, man as man—the S in the judgment does not need a universal to gather it up or give it universality anymore. S is universal all by itself, and so is indifferent to *any* universal of reflection that might be used to characterize it. Garlic, for instance, does not need the universal "curative" to gather it up or hold it together. Garlic as a type is already gathered or tied together by its type. Since the stage of the Particular Judgment of Reflection, the universal has been the defining element of the judgment: U has been what holds the judgment together, and as richer and wider than S. Now that S has been defined as a type on its own, however, U seems superfluous. The relational universals seem like a mere particularity next to the universal power of Singularity itself. In the last stage, for instance, the predicate "curative" was supposed to be gathering up the subject "garlic," so that the universal was defined as richer and wider than the subject: other things are also curative. Now that garlic is a type on its own, however, the predicate "curative" becomes just one particularity of garlic, or one of the categories that defines garlic. Whether garlic is curative or has any other relational characteristic is just one particular character of garlic as a type.

So now Singularity, rather than the universal, once again seems to be the primary defining element in the judgment. As in the stages of Qualitative Judgment, Singularity is defined as stable and whole on its own, richer and wider than the universal. Indeed, the universal has now become so unimportant that it is no longer needed in the judgment at all. The need for it has fallen away. Because S is defined as a universal by itself, it has completely fulfilled the "is" of the judgment: S really *is* universal. S is so universal, in fact, that the universal no longer stands outside of it as something to which it is related. S *is* universal, or has the universal within it. S is, all by itself, now necessarily universal.

If the universal in the judgment is going to do any work or have a job to do, then, it is going to have to develop into a new kind of universal. We also know what sort of universal it is going to have to be: a type of universal that applies to the already fulfilled universality of S, or to S as a universal or as a type. In the next stage, the universal develops into the sort of universal that captures the character of S as the type that it is, or that captures the defining nature of S.

The Judgment of Necessity: Categorical Judgment of Necessity

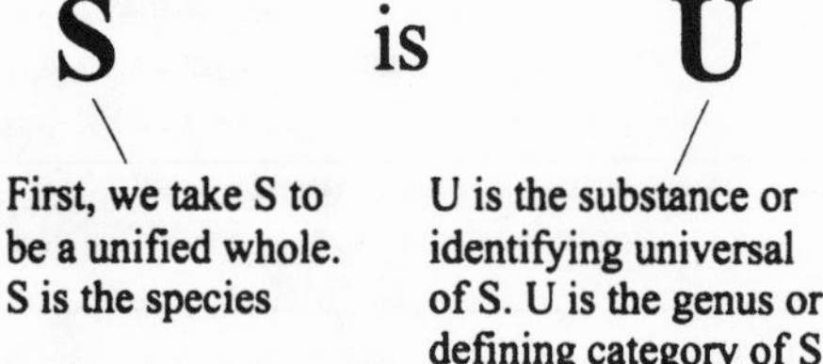

Figure 4.25

The universal must now capture the universality of S itself, the nature of S as a type, or the defining nature or category of S. Nevertheless, S is still a bunch of things, or a multitude within, that is defined from the top-down by particularizing, or by dividing into types or categories. In the Particular Judgment of Reflection, this characteristic of S gave the stage two different moments: a positive and a negative moment. There are two similar moments of the judgment here as well.

First, if S is a unified whole, the universal captures the defining nature of S by being the substance of S. In the stage of Immediate Substance in Chapter Three, a Substance was the grasping and defining concept that is the identifying power behind the totality of accidents. That's the kind of universal here: a universal that identifies and captures the totality that S is. In this case, the universal is the genus of S: "gold is metal," for instance, where the universal "metal" captures and identifies all the gold as a type or totality.

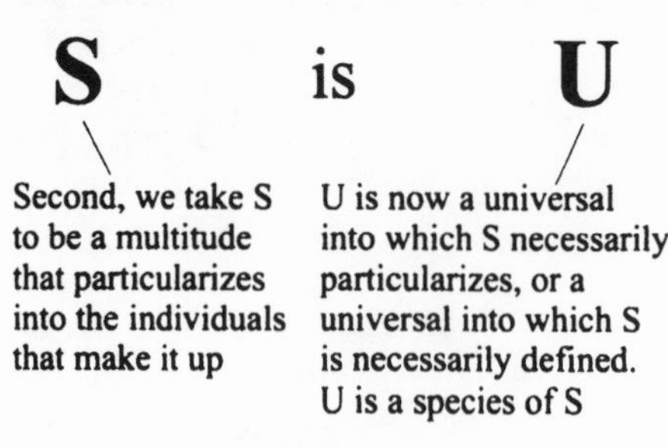

S
is
U
Second, we take S to be a multitude that particularizes into the individuals that make it up
U is now a universal into which S necessarily particularizes, or a universal into which S is necessarily defined. U is a species of S

Figure 4.26

Second, if S is a multitude, it is a universal that particularizes or divides into other universals (cf. Particular Judgment of Reflection). Here, the universal in the predicate would now be one of the universals into which S divides. In this case, U is a species of S: "metal is gold," for instance, where gold is one of the types or universals into which S divides.

Whether U is a species of S or the genus of S, U and S are necessarily connected to one another. When U is the genus of S, it is necessarily connected to S because it captures the defining nature or character of S as a universal. Gold could not be what it is if it were not metal. The same thing is true, however, when U is defined as a species of S. Gold is necessarily connected to metal because it is one of the categories or types that defines metal by being one of the categories into which metal divides (I will say more about this connection in the discussion of the next stage).

Hypothetical Judgment of Necessity

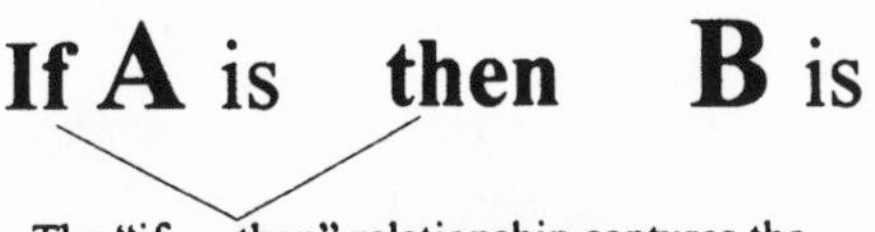

If A is then B is

The "if. . .then" relationship captures the relationship of necessity that S and U were supposed to have. But S and U have lost their distinctiveness relative to each other, so we no longer talk of "S" and "U," but of variables. This judgment captures the *form* that S and U are supposed to have—that they are being presented as necessarily related—but not their *content*

Figure 4.27

Although S and U are necessarily connected with one another, the Categorical Judgment does not *express* that necessary connection. The judgment "S is U" does not *say* that S and U are necessarily connected with one another. The form of the judgment "S is U"—or the way in which the judgment is being presented—is therefore not adequate to express the content that the judgment is supposed to have. S and U are supposed to have a content according to which they are necessarily connected, but the form of the judgment "S is U" does not capture that content. This stage introduces a form of judgment that can express the necessary connection between S and U. To say that S and U are necessarily connected is to say that, if S is, then U is too.

Unfortunately, however, S and U have lost their distinctiveness in relation to one another or cannot be distinguished. In the last stage, S was both the genus and species, and U, too, was both the genus and species. So S and U are no longer different from one another: they are both genus/species. S was supposed to be the singularity in relation to a universal, but now it can also be a universal in relation to a singularity. U was supposed to be universal in relation to S, but now it can also be a singular in relation to universality. So the characterization of S and U as singularity and universality no longer applies. The logic can no longer refer to S and U, but only to variables that stand for the two different elements in the judgment. The Hypothetical Judgment must use variables to express the necessary connection between two necessarily related but indistinguishable universals: "if A is, then B is."

A is either a genus or species, and B is either a genus or species. Because species and genera are mutually defining, they have the sort of relationship with one another described by this stage. Gold, for instance, is defined as a type by the concept of metal, or, as Hegel put it earlier (§167R, 168), metal is its soul, or is the type of thing that it is. Metal is the soul of the gold. As a result, if gold is, then metal is too: if A (gold) is, then B (metal) is.

At the same time, metal also defines into gold. Gold is one of the metals into which metal particularizes. Metal must therefore be gold too. If A (metal) is, then B (gold) is too. This claim may seem more dubious than the claim that metal is necessarily connected to gold because it captures gold's defining character. One might argue, against Hegel, that gold is not a necessary category of metal because metal could have existed without gold. So long as there were steel, silver, or any other kind of metal, there would still be metal, even if there were no gold. Since there could have been metal without gold, it doesn't seem to follow that, "if metal is, then gold is." However, since metal is a universal concept, it is a completed type of thing through all of time. It is a finished product (cf. Universality). Because gold is an actuality out there in the world, metal would not be what it in fact is (what it actually is) unless it particularized as gold. Hence, if metal is, then gold is also.

The Hypothetical Judgment captures the connectedness of the moments of the Concept, but has lost their content. The universal or U in the judgment "S is U" was originally the Concept's moment of Particularity. Particularity was defined as a universal in the judgment "S is U" because Particularity had to be characterized only in relation to Singularity, and not in relation to the Concept, from which it had been uttered or pushed out. In relation to Singularity or S, Particularity is a universal. Since A and B in the Hypothetical Judgment grew out of Singularity and Particularity, the Hypothetical Judgment expresses the connectedness between Singularity and Particularity. Because the moments Singularity and Particularity have lost their distinctiveness in relation to one another, however, the Hypothetical Judgment actually expresses the connectedness in general between the Concept's moments of Singularity, Particularity *and* Universality. Since Particularity was defined as a universal in relation to Singularity, the fact that the two elements in the judgment have lost their distinctiveness also means that Singularity and Universality have lost their distinctiveness in relation to one another. Thus, Hypothetical Judgment is not only the expression of the connectedness between Singularity and Particularity specifically, but also the connectedness in general between any of the three moments of the Concept. The Hypothetical Judgment says that, if you have one moment, then you have the other. This is precisely the sort of relationship that Singularity, Particularity and Universality had in The Three Moments Cannot Be Held Apart. Because the Concept is absolutely universal, it embraces everything else. To the degree that it is internally distinguished, those distinctions are not absolute, but are only moments of the one whole Concept. The Hypothetical Judgment expresses this aspect of the Concept's universality. It expresses the necessary connectedness of the Concept's moments: those moments are connected to one another such that, if you have one, then you have the other.

There is another aspect of the Concept's universality, however, which has not been expressed yet, namely that those moments are necessarily connected to the whole. The Hypothetical Judgment expresses the elements' connection to one another, but not yet their connection to the whole, or to universality. To be universal is to be a unity, but the Hypothetical Judgment does not express that universality. Of course, the fact that the moments are necessarily connected with one another is the beginning of universality—that's how universality is built up, so to speak. When this metal (gold) is connected to that metal (silver) is connected to that metal (steel) and so on, the universality of "metal" is beginning to be built. But each moment's connection to the whole universal has not yet been expressed. The next stage tries to express that connection.

Because the specific character of Singularity and Particularity has been lost, the Hypothetical Judgment captures any kind of relationship of necessity between universals: the relationship between ground and grounded, between condition and conditioned, between cause and effect and so on. In Chapter Three, Ground, for example, was what I called a success term: Ground cannot be what it is unless it succeeds in grounding something. A ground cannot be a ground without there being a grounded. As a result, if the ground is, then the grounded is also: if A (ground) is, then B (grounded) is. The same is true for condition and cause: a condition cannot be a condition unless it succeeds in conditioning something else; a cause cannot be a cause unless it succeeds in causing something. Hence a condition cannot be a condition without the conditioned; a cause cannot be a cause without the effect. If the condition is, then the conditioned is also; if the cause is a cause, then the effect is also. If A (condition, cause) is, then B (conditioned, effect) is. This judgment expresses the relationship that these concepts have with one another.

Disjunctive Judgment of Necessity

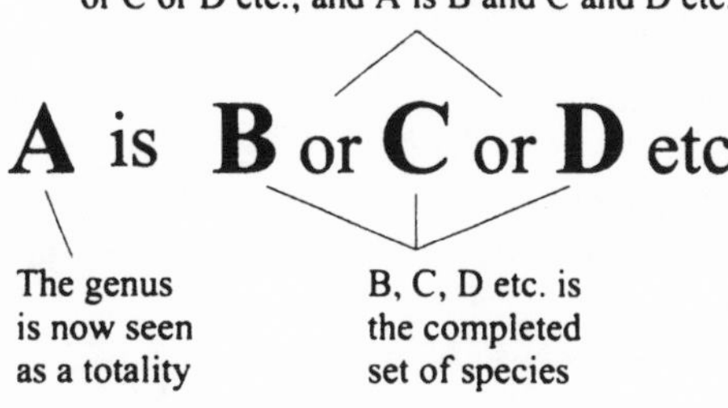
These are logically inclusive "or's": A is B or C or D etc.; and A is B and C and D etc.
A is B or C or D etc
The genus is now seen as a totality
B, C, D etc. is the completed set of species

Figure 4.28

The Hypothetical Judgment "if A is, then B is" expresses the necessary connection between A and B. That necessary connection cannot be "seen" or experienced, however, because it is not outer (out there), but only inner (conceptual).[1] The connection can only be grasped by thought. Like the reciprocal relationship between the Concept and the Effect_{CS}, the connection is a thought that does not show up (cf. Transition to the Concept in Chapter Three). The logic now focuses on the conceptual content of the connection, or on the thought that connects A and B. As we know, A and B are a species and genus: one is the species, one is the genus. Which one is which does not matter. A genus and a species are connected by the content or definition of the genus: it is because the genus is what it is, or is the kind of thing that it is, that the species is connected to it. It is the nature, definition or content of metal, for instance, which connects it with gold. It is because metal is what it is that gold is a metal. Thus the definition or content of the genus is the thought that connects A and B.

Because A and B grew out of Singularity and Particularity and still represent moments of the Concept, and because the moments of the Concept still have the relationship of identity and distinction that was expressed by the judgment (cf. The Judgment), the form of the judgment returns. Although the judgment "A is B" would seem to grow out of the last stage, it will not capture the logical conclusions that have been developed. A and B stand for a genus and species. Because the genus is a totality, the species is not equivalent to the genus. While metal is gold, for instance, gold does not express the totality of metal because metal is also silver, steel, and so on. To capture the full, necessary connection between A and B, then, the full totality of the genus must be on both sides of the "is." The full universality of the genus will be on both sides of the "is" when the genus is on one side, and the completed set of species is on the other: "metal is gold or silver or steel etc." The Disjunctive Judgment is "A is B or C or D etc.," where "B or C or D etc." is the completed list of species of the genus. Which side of the "is" the genus and the list of species are on does not matter: "A or B or C etc. is D" would also be appropriate.

Because the list of species has to fully define the genus, the "or" between each species ("B *or* C *or* D") is an inclusive "or." An inclusive "or" means both "or" and "and." In ordinary life, we usually use the word "or" in an exclusive rather than inclusive sense. When we tell our children that they can have a cookie or a piece of cake, for example, we mean they can have one or the other, but not both. That's an exclusive reading of the "or": the children can have either B or C, but not both B *and* C. In formal logic, the connector "or" is usually defined inclusively. It is difficult to find examples in English to illustrate the inclusive "or," because "or" is usually used exclusively, but suppose you are having a conversation with friends about the types of food you like. One friend says she likes chocolate. The other says she likes pasta. You say, "I like chocolate or pasta." In this context, you would be using the "or" inclusively to mean that you like each of the items—chocolate *or* pasta—and that you like both—chocolate *and* pasta. In Disjunctive Judgment, the "or" means both "or" and "and."

The "or" in the Disjunctive Judgment must be interpreted inclusively because the relationship between the genus and the set of species is defined by necessity: the genus is necessarily linked to the species. The genus is necessarily linked to the species only if the species-side of the judgment captures the full nature of the genus. The species-side of the judgment captures the full nature of the genus only if it is the complete and completed list of species, or all of the species of the genus taken together. Thus, the genus is necessarily the whole set: it is "B *and* C *and* D" etc. This version of the Disjunctive Judgment—with the connector "and"—can be called the positive identity of the universal with the particular (Hegel calls the other sort of Disjunctive Judgment the "negative" one [§177]). But the genus would not be anything at all, or would have no definition at all, if it were not particularized as one of its species. If there were no gold or steel or aluminum or silver etc., then there would be no metal. So the genus is also necessarily B *or* C *or* D etc.—i.e. it must be one of its species to have any character at all. This is the negative identity of the universal with the particular (§177), which uses the "or" connector.

Disjunctive Judgment captures the general character that a universal has in relation to its particularity. In general, a universal is defined by particularizing, or by dividing into species or types (the negative identity), and is fully defined when it has completely divided into its species (the positive identity). Thus, the content of the Concept that dropped out in the Hypothetical Judgment has returned: this judgment is not just about variables, but about universality and particularity. Moreover, because the set of species is complete, both sides of the "is" have the equivalent content—the totality of the genus. The particularity of the universal is therefore fulfilled in Disjunctive Judgment: the particular really *is* universal, and the universal really *is* particular, just as the judgment says.

The Judgment of the Concept: Assertoric Judgment, or the Immediate Judgment of the Concept

This **A** is **R**

The genus is now taken to be an immediate, individualized particularization

R stands for a relation between the immediate, individualized particularity of the genus and the content or concept of the genus: i.e. "good" "correct," "true"

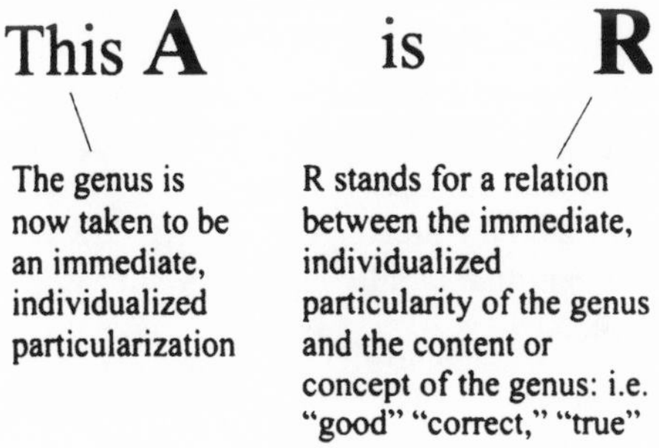

Figure 4.29

In the moment of negative unity, metal must particularize as one of its species. But gold—as a species—cannot have thereness or be out there. The particularity of a universal is supposed to be how the universal is presented into actuality. But gold in general—the species gold—is not out there. Only individual pieces of gold can have thereness. Metal cannot be particularized as gold (in general). It can only be particularized as some specific piece or bit of gold. The moment of Singularity is missing. Disjunctive Judgment presupposes the moment of singularity, because it presupposes that when metal particularizes as gold it is particularizing as pieces of gold. But because the judgment refers to species, rather than to singulars, it does not capture Singularity. It presupposes singularity, but does not *say* it.

The judgment here expresses singularity by redefining the subject of the judgment as an immediate, individualized or singularized particularization of the genus. The subject of the judgment is, not "A," but "this A." "This A" is an immediately singular instance of the genus or universal—it is "this (piece of) metal," instead of the category or concept of "metal," for instance. This judgment corrects for the defect in the last one. It does not merely presuppose Singularity, it *says* it. Singularity has its character as a singularity by being a "this" (cf. Singular Judgment of Reflection). Because the genus in the subject is now defined as a "this," this judgment expresses the singularity that was missing from the last stage. The predicate of the judgment, for its part, must now capture the character of the relationship (R) between the particular and the universal that became central in the last stage. Thus the whole judgment can be rendered: "this A is R," where R stands for the character of the relationship between the particular and the universal. As we saw in the last stage, the character of the relationship between the particular and the universal is that it is fulfilled: the particular and the universal have the same content, or the particular really *is* the universal. To say that the particular ("this A") and the universal have the same content is to say that "this A" *is* an A—it is a true, correct or good A. When a particularized instance of a universal ("this A") lives up to the content of the universal, then, the relationship between the instance and the universal has the character of being "good," "true" or "correct." When a piece of metal lives up to the content of the universal "metal," the relationship between the instance and the universal is a good one. Such a piece of metal is good (as metal). A "this" friend who lives up to the content of the concept of friendship is good (as a friend). The predicate R expresses the fulfilled relationship between the particular and the universal: "good," "true," "correct."

Assertoric Judgment thus brings the moment of singularity back into the judgment, without losing sight of the fulfilled relationship between the universal and the particularity in the last stage. The judgment "this A is R" is assertoric because its truth is guaranteed by nothing more than the assertion itself. Its truth is merely a matter of subjective assurance: a third party or subjectivity vouches for or assures its truth. We simply have to trust the person who asserts "this A is R" that the A really is R. The logical element that would connect A with R in a necessary way has not yet been developed.

Problematic Judgment of the Concept

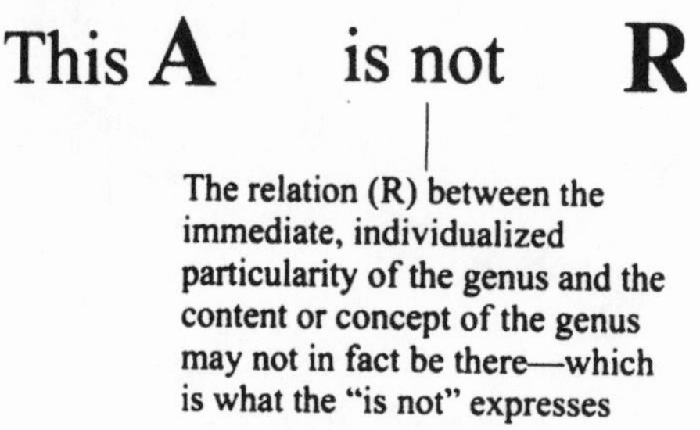

This **A** is not **R**

The relation (R) between the immediate, individualized particularity of the genus and the content or concept of the genus may not in fact be there—which is what the "is not" expresses

Figure 4.30

Because the individualized particularization of the genus is immediate, however, A may not in fact be R, or be good, true, or correct. The connection between the particular and the universal is simply given or "found," and so may not in fact be fulfilled, good, true or correct. This piece of metal or this house might not fulfill the concept of metal or house, and hence might not be correct, good, or true. So the judgment "this A is *not* R" has the same right—or the same lack of right, as Hegel says (§179)—as the judgment "this A is R."

Moreover, although "this A" is supposed to capture an immediate, individualized particularization of the universal, it does not really succeed in doing so. "This metal," for instance, does not really capture the particularization of the metal. The term "metal" is a universal that can be an individual bit of metal only by having its own particularity or way of being. "This" does not capture its particular way of being metal, which opened the door to the problem that what the Assertoric Judgment asserts may not in fact be true. Whether or not the house is "good" depends on the particular way of being of the house. "This house" does not tell us anything about how the house has its being, or what it is like in particular as a house. The Problematic Judgment captures the problem or weakness of the Assertoric Judgment. It says that this A is not in fact found or given to be R. We will solve the problem of the Assertoric Judgment when we capture the objective particularity of this metal—what the metal is like or how it has its being. What this metal is like in particular determines whether or not it is R.

Apodictic Judgment of the Concept

This A
constituted thus-and-so
is (or is not)
R
The constitution or particularity of A is now specified or asserted

Figure 4.31

Apodictic Judgment captures the particularity of "this A" with a claim about how this A is constituted. "This A" has a particular constitution: "this piece of metal, constituted thus-and-so, is R," or "this house, constituted thus-and-so, is R." It includes the objective particularization of A, the way in which "this A" has its being, or what this A is like, that was left out of the Assertoric Judgment. Because the way in which this A is constituted determines whether A is R, the relationship between A and R is now clear or necessary—i.e. apodictic. Since the constitution of the house is what determines whether the house is good, correct or true, the judgment itself links this house together with the relationship R. There is no longer any need for a subjectivity or third party to do the linking.

Both the subject and the predicate contain the content of a whole judgment (§180). The content of a judgment links a singularity to a universal: "S is U." The subject of the Apodictic Judgment—"this A constituted thus-and-so"—links a singularity to a universal because "this A" is an immediate singularity ("this") that, because of its constitution, is a genus or universal (A). A genus such as "metal" is a universal, not an individual. Indeed, every noun is a universal. In the phrases "this apple," "this ball," and "this book," for example, all of the nouns—"apple," "ball," and "book"—are universals: they capture types of things (apples, balls and books) rather than individual things. The predicate of the Apodictic Judgment also links a singular to a universal. R by itself expresses the relationship between the immediate singularity and the content or concept of the genus. R says that the relationship between the immediate singularity (the "this") and universality (the A) is fulfilled (good, correct, true). To say that the relationship between the "this" and the genus (A) is a good, correct or true one, is to say that the "this," given its constitution, is an A, or that the immediate singularity is the universal. If the relationship between the "this" and the genus "house" is a good one, for example, then the "this" is a house. To say that the house "is good" is to say that the "this" (or singularity) really is a house (the genus or universality). Hence R, too, contains the content of a judgment by linking a singularity to a universal. The subject and predicate also both make the same assertion. They both assert concrete universality, or say that universality is defined in relation to an immediate singularity. "This A" asserts that the "this" is an A; and R also asserts, that the "this" is an A.

Because both sides are the same in the sense that they both have the same content and make the same assertion, the subject really is the predicate, the subject and the predicate are now completely the same. Hence, the copula "is" of the judgment is fully fulfilled: both sides now have the same content and *say* the same thing. In earlier stages, both sides had the same content, but they did not make the same assertion, claim, or say the same thing. In the Disjunctive Syllogism ("A is B, C, or D etc."), for instance, both the subject and the predicate had the same content, namely the content of the genus. But the two sides did not *say* the same thing. One side asserted the genus, while the other side asserted the list of the genus's species. Now that both sides of the judgment have the same content and say the same thing, however, the subject really *is* the predicate, and the copula "is" is fully fulfilled.

The promise of the Concept has been fulfilled. The subject of the judgment grew out of the moment of Singularity in the Concept, while the predicate grew out of Particularity (which, in relation to Singularity, was defined as universality). The definition of the Concept claimed or promised that Singularity and Particularity are the same, and that result has now been logically developed.

Because the copula "is" has been fulfilled, the judgment can no longer be used to characterize the logical elements currently in play. Since both sides of the judgment are exactly the same, such that there is no distinction between them at all, the copula "is" no longer makes any sense. According to the general form of a judgment, the "is" says both that the two things are (the same as) each other (identity), and that the two things are not each other (distinction) (see The Judgment). Now that there is no distinction between the subject and predicate, the copula—and hence the form of judgment itself—cannot be used. We need a new form of statement, or a new kind of statement to say what we have.

Transition to the Syllogism

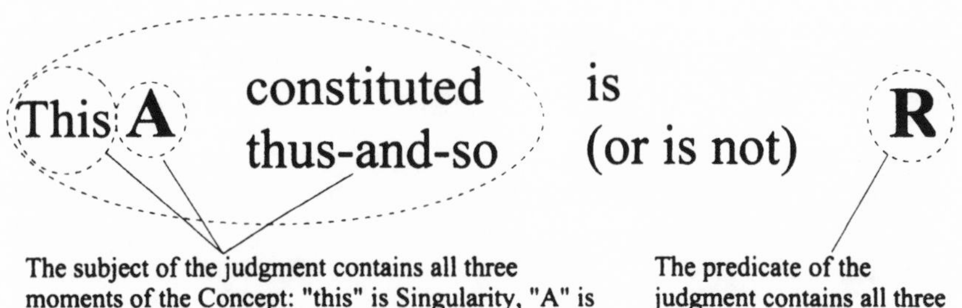
This
A
constituted
thus-and-so
is
(or is not)
R
The subject of the judgment contains all three moments of the Concept: "this" is Singularity, "A" is Universality, "constituted thus-and-so" is Particularity
The predicate of the judgment contains all three moments of the Concept

Figure 4.32

Both the subject and the predicate also each contain the unity of the whole Concept, namely singularity, particularity and universality. In the subject, "this" is singularity, "A" is the genus, or universality, and "constituted thus and so" is particularity. The predicate, R, contains all three moments by itself. It expresses the fulfilled relationship that the particular way of being (the particularity) of the immediate singularity (singularity) has with the genus or universal (universality). The house, for instance, is a good house because the singularity there (the "this"), given its constitution (particularity), is a house (universality). The new kind or form of statement must express this unity of singularity, particularity and universality. Unfortunately, judgment, as a form of statement, cannot do a good job of expressing this unity. In a judgment, the copula "is" says that the subject and predicate are connected, but does not say how they are connected. It says only that the relationship is defined by identity and distinction. The relationships between the moments must be defined with more sophistication.

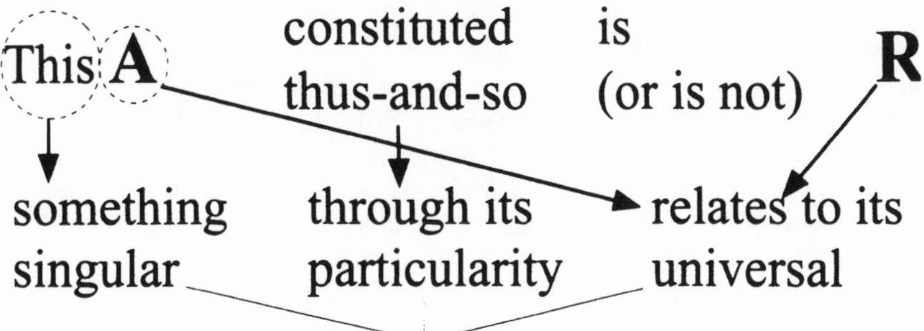
This
A
constituted
thus-and-so
is
(or is not)
R
something
singular
through its
particularity
relates to its
universal
There are three elements in Apodictic Judgment, not two

Figure 4.33

We need a form of statement that captures the fact that all three moments of the Concept are now doing logical work. The basic form of the judgment can only talk about two moments of the Concept, namely singularity and universality. The basic form of statement that relates all three moments of the Concept together is the *syllogism*.

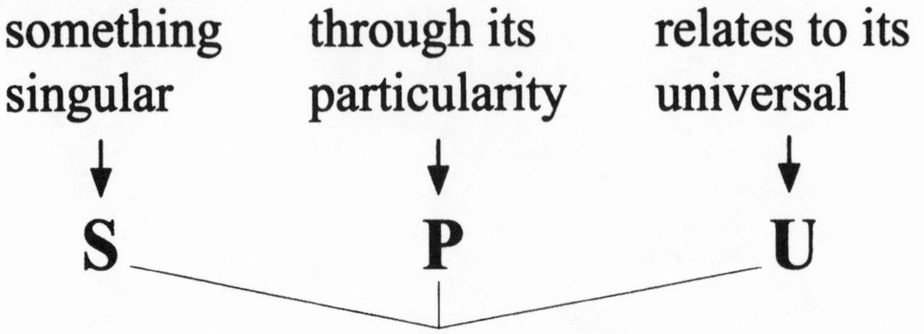
something singular
through its particularity
relates to its universal
S
P
U
This is the basic form of the syllogism

Figure 4.34

The order that the moments of the Concept will have in the syllogism grows out of Apodictic Judgment. Both the subject and predicate of the Apodictic Judgment asserted that a singularity (the "this") was a universality based on the particularity of the singularity (the constitution of the "this"). Thus particularity is presented as the moment that holds the other two moments together. Since the particularity belongs to the singularity—it is the particularity of the singularity—singularity is presented first. The singularity has the particularity that links it to the universality. In the basic form of the syllogism (§181A), then, something singular relates to its universal through particularity: S-P-U. The particularity is the mediating ground between the singularity and the universal.

With Apodictic Judgment, the logical development of the form of judgment comes to an end. Apodictic Judgment has developed into the basic form of the syllogism: S-P-U. While the syllogism has replaced the judgment in the logical development, in classic Hegelian fashion, it has really sublated (canceled, but also preserved) the judgment (see the discussion of "*aufheben*" in Chapter One, Section VIII). The syllogism expresses the unity of the singular, particular and universal in *judgments*. The basic form of the syllogism S-P-U (singularity-particularity-universality) is really a short-form for three judgments: "S is P," "P is U," and "therefore S is U." The syllogism is thus the unity of the Concept and the judgment (§181). It expresses the nature of the Concept because it expresses the unity of singularity, particularity and universality that defines the Concept (see The Three Moments Cannot be Held Apart). And the syllogism expresses that unity by means of judgments. Because the syllogism expresses the nature of the Concept in judgments, it is the unity of the Concept and the judgment.

Hegel says that the syllogism is the judgment posited, asserted or pushed out into reality (§181). It is the judgment expressed into reality because a fact (in reality) is always a syllogism. This basic form of the syllogism says that a singularity, through its particularity, is a universal. Every fact in the world has exactly that character. The character of singularity is expressed as a "this." A "this" (singularity) cannot be a fact unless its way of being (or particularity) is good enough to be connected to the universal. Some "this," for instance, is not a fact as a house unless its way of being or particularity is good enough to be connected to the universal "house." There must be enough "house-like" particularity in the "this"—say, a roof, walls, perhaps windows and so on—for the "this" to be a house. Thus something can be a fact only if there is enough correspondence between the "this's" way of having its thereness and a genus. Only if there is enough correspondence between singularity, particularity and universality is there a fact, or something out there in reality. Since the Concept is defined as the correspondence between singularity, particularity and universality, whether a "this" is a fact depends on the Concept. The Concept is the soul of the fact. Because the judgments of the syllogism express the correspondence between singularity, particularity and universality that must be there for something to be a fact in reality, the syllogism is the judgment expressed into reality.

The syllogism is thus what is rational and it is everything that is rational (§181). Every fact or reality, everything that is, must have enough correspondence between its singularity, particularity and universality to be there. Everything must be rational enough to be there. To be there, something must be there as something-or-other, which is just to say that there must be enough correspondence between its singularity, its way of being (particularity), and some rational universal for it to be there (see also Chapter One, Section II). Everything is a syllogism. The syllogism is the Concept (or Reason) asserted into reality.

Because the syllogism includes judgments, it also includes the general character of the form of judgments. A judgment both divides and links together the subject and predicate: it says that there are two separate elements (they are distinct), but also that each of the elements "is" the other (they are identical) (see The Judgment). This character of the judgment affects the syllogism as well. The premises of the syllogism—"S is P" and "P is U"—say that S has a particularity, and that the particularity is linked to the universal: the "this" has a way of being that makes it a "house," for instance. But the form of the judgment in these premises also separates S and P, as well as P and U, from one another. S may or may not be linked to the sort of particularity that is linked to the universal. The "this" may or may not have a way of being that makes it a "house." The conclusion of the basic form of the syllogism—"S is U"—also both divides and links S and U. It asserts that S and U are separate, but also that S "is" U. Since U is separable from S, U is what S or the "this" *ought* to be. U is the concept, universal or character that the "this" strives to live up to, so to speak, to be what it is. The genus "house" is what the "this" ought to be. Thus, the form of the syllogism expresses that there are gaps between S, P and U, or between a singularity, its particularity, and what the singularity ought to be, namely, its universality. S, P and U are separable in the syllogism.

Since U, P and S are all moments of the Concept, which is U itself, all three elements are defined in relation to the Concept. U is the Concept itself (defined as Universality), P is the Particularity *of the Concept* and S is the Singularity *of the Concept*. The activity that the syllogism does insofar as it both separates the three elements and yet holds them together is the activity of the Concept. The Concept is the source of the syllogism's activity. It separates and yet links singularity together with the universal through the particularity. It is the power that separates and also reunites what is (singularity) and what ought to be (universality). That power is the soul of a fact. Because a fact is anything at all only when the three moments are held together with an "is" by the Concept—in the conclusion "S is U"—the soul of the fact is the concrete identity of what is (the "this") and what ought to be (the universal), which is grasped by the Concept itself. Indeed, for every fact, the applicable concept—"concept" with a lower-case "C"—is the power that separates and reunites the singularity and universality. The concept of "house" separates the moments: its definition is not the same as what defines the particularity or singularity of the house. The definition of the concept itself is not the same as the house's roof, for instance, or the house's windows (the house's particularity), nor is it the same as the immediately singular "this" or thereness of the house. The concept of the house is a concept, not a roof, window or color of the house. Nevertheless, this house is a fact because the universal "house" holds the "this" and its way of being together under the banner of the concept of "house." The house is anything at all because the concept, as the soul of the fact, links the singularity together with the universality, or grasps the concrete identity of what is and what ought to be.

Unlike the judgment, the syllogism mentions all three moments of the Concept. The judgment was about only singularity and universality, but the syllogism is about singularity, particularity and universality. Because the syllogism is about all three moments of the Concept, and because the Concept is the source of the syllogism's activity, the Concept itself has come back into the picture. In the judgment, the Concept as a whole had dropped out of the picture because we were focusing on defining only the utterance of the Concept, which included only Particularity and Singularity, and not the moment of Universality itself. Because the syllogism mentions all three moments of the Concept, we are once again talking about the whole Concept, and not just part of it.

Immediate Syllogism, or Formal Syllogism of the Understanding

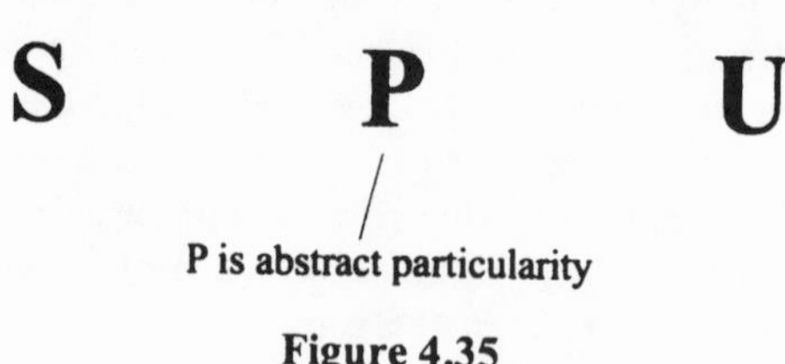

Figure 4.35

Apodictic Judgment generated the first and basic form of the syllogism, namely, S-P-U. It also tells us what initial definitions or characters S, P and U have: they have *no* definition beyond their basic characters as singularity, particularity and universality. S is an undefined, immediate singularity, and P and U are undefined particularity and universality. P and U are any particularity and any universal that applies to the singularity. In other words, Apodictic Judgment fails to provide more specific definitions for S, P and U. As Hegel says, the moments of the Concept here are abstract (§182) or undefined. The singularity is defined as immediate, given or "found." The particularity is not actually defined at all—it is simply "some" or any-old particularity of the singularity. Similarly, the universality is not defined either—it is simply "some" or any-old universality of the particularity. Since the types of particularity and universality that can be connected to the singularity are not defined, any-old particularity or universality can be plugged into the syllogism. A "this," given its constitution, is a "house," but it is also "yellow," "large," "run-down," "Cape Cod," and so on. Any particularity of the immediately singular "this" and any universality of the immediately singular will do. Because the singularity is immediate, it, too, is abstract or undefined. Any-old "this" or singular—anything capable of being defined as a singular—can be plugged into this type of syllogism. The "this" could be a thing, a crowd, a puddle, whatever. Thus the singularity, particularity and universality are all abstract or undefined. As we go through the development of the syllogism, the singularity, particularity and universality will be specified or defined more precisely.

Hegel says that, because the moments are abstract, they stand in an external relationship with one another (§182). To say that they stand in an external relationship with one another is to say that, although they are united by the syllogism, they are currently being defined as separable from one another, seem to be related to one another from the outside, and do not relate to one another on their own in virtue of their definitions. If the singularity were defined in a certain way it would be linked to a certain sort of particularity, which, in virtue of its definition as a certain sort of particularity, would be linked to a certain sort of universality. But S, P and U cannot be related to one another in virtue of their definitions because they do not have any definitions—they are abstract. It is as if the "this," the particularity, and the universal are merely glued together in an external way from the outside. They are not linked together by their own definitions or characters (cf. Transition to Essence in Chapter Two). The "this," what particulars it has, and the universal "house," for instance, are just stuck together in an external way.

Because S, P and U are abstract and not defined, this syllogism is formal: it has the form of the Concept, but not the content. It has the form of the Concept insofar as it is defined by the same relationships between singularity, particularity and universality that were in the moments of the Concept, namely identity and distinction at the same time. However, this syllogism does not include the definitions or content of S, P and U that those moments had within the Concept (see the stages of Universality, Particularity and Singularity). Within the Concept, Singularity was a certain sort of Singularity, namely Singularity as a totality or completed type of thing, for instance. Singularity was the rose as a type of thing, for example. That definition of Singularity is lacking here, however. Singularity is simply anything that can be isolated as a singular—this particular rose, this instant in time, whatever. Because this syllogism is merely formal, it is the sort of syllogism that is usually grasped by the understanding. It is rational in terms of its form, but since it does not apply the definitions that the elements have insofar as they are defined by the Concept, it is a kind of syllogism that, as Hegel says, is "the rational that lacks the Concept" (§182).

P is supposed to be the middle term that relates the other two moments of the Concept together, but because P is abstract and not defined in any way, its definition does not hold singularity and universality together very tightly. As a result, singularity and universality seem to subsist on their own and are indifferent toward each other as well as indifferent toward P itself. Because P is not any specific kind of particularity of the house, for instance, the "this" of the house and its concept "house" seem capable of having their definitions on their own. The "this" does not seem to need any of the possible universals—"house," "large," run-down," or "Cape Cod"—to be what it is. It is an immediate singular, a "this," all by itself, without any of those universals. It is indifferent toward those universals. The universals are just as indifferent toward the "this." "Yellow," "large," and so on can be what they are without *that* "this." Moreover, the particularity grasped by P is also a matter of indifference. P could be the "this's" color, its style, its condition, its size or whatever.

Hegel says that this syllogism expresses the finitude of things (§182R). Things in the world are all syllogisms in the sense that they are unities of singularity, particularity, and universality (cf. Apodictic Judgment). A house is some singularity that is constituted in such a way that it is graspable by the concept of house. However, although the house is a unity of singularity, particularity and universality, it also has its singularity, particularity and universality in a way that is in principle separable. The singularity may have some other way of being or particularity—it could have a different style, color or condition, for example. Even its universality or genus—its "houseness," so to speak—is separable from it: it might not even be a house. That's why, Hegel suggests, we tend to see the universality of finite things as merely one of the thing's qualities, as if the thing could be some other universality (§182R). And, of course, the house could be some other universality. It wouldn't take much before the "this" could be a pile of rubble, for example. The moments of universality, singularity and particularity are separable in finite things because finite things can always change. As things change, their singularities and particularities and universalities separate from one another.

Hegel divides the logical development of the syllogism using the same categories that we saw in the development of the Judgment: the *Qualitative* Syllogism, the Syllogism *of Reflection*, and the Syllogism *of Necessity*. Each type of syllogism will have three versions, or three figures.

The First Figure of Qualitative Syllogism or Syllogism of Thereness

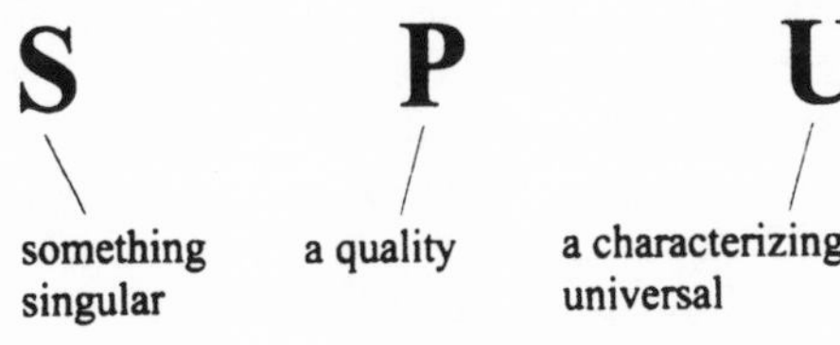

Figure 4.36

Singularity, particularity and universality are abstract so far. In the first figure of Qualitative Syllogism (Fig. 4.36), some (or any-old) immediate singularity has some particular aspect or quality, and because of this, quality turns out to be some universal. The standard form of this Qualitative Syllogism is S-P-U, which should be written out into judgments as "S is P, P is U, therefore S is U." Because the elements are abstract, singularity is any kind of "this," and particularity is any-old thereness or quality of the "this." Because any-old quality can be plugged in for the particularity, the same singularity generates an indefinite number of syllogisms. Moreover, because any-old particularity can be plugged in, this syllogism is also subjective: a third party or subject is needed to complete the syllogism. Someone or some subjectivity has to *choose* which particularity from among the many possible particularities to focus on, before the syllogism can be completed.

Hegel apparently used the following example for this First Figure in a lecture: "This rose is red, red is a color, therefore this rose is something colored" (§183A). But the example says more than it should, given the logical development. When the subject in Apodictic Judgment—"this A, constituted thus-and-so"—was divided into the three elements—singularity, particularity, and universality—"this" and A were split up: the "this" was singularity, and the A belonged to universality. This division followed from Hegel's claim that both the subject and the predicate of the Apodictic Judgment contained the whole Concept. The subject contains the whole Concept if the "this" is singularity, the "constituted thus and so" is particularity, and A is universality. Moreover, the singularity here should be abstract and undefined, and therefore could be any "this." The example from the §183A therefore mischaracterizes the singularity of the syllogism. The singularity for this syllogism should be just "this," and not "this rose." "This rose" is already a highly defined singularity. Because singularity is, by definition, a concept that is a one or chunk, the immediate singularity here has to be a something—it has to be something out there that is capable of being picked out, pointed at, or defined by itself. It has to be a chunk, an item out there. It must therefore be something like a rose or a house, but it should not yet be defined *as* a rose or a house. A better example of the syllogism would therefore be: "this something is red, red is a color, therefore the something is something colored." The example from Hegel's lecture can still work if we think of the word "rose" as an aside, a parenthetical remark, or an external reference to what the speaker who is making the judgment happens to be pointing at. Think of court transcripts reporting the testimony of witnesses. When a witness points at something and says "this" or "that," the transcript will indicate in parentheses what the witness was pointing at. The identification of the "this" as a rose should be understood in a similar way. The first premise could be read: "this [the witness points at exhibit #1, the rose] is red." Because every immediate something has all sorts of therenesses or qualities, the same something can generate an indefinite number of other syllogisms.

In this syllogism, P and U are both ways in which S has its being and inhere in S. P is just an immediate thereness of S, and U is just a more general (universal) way of characterizing S. Neither P nor U are true concepts in this syllogism. P is not the concept of "red," it is just the redness of S. And U is not the concept of color, it is just the coloredness of S.

In the discussion of this stage in the *Science of Logic*, Hegel says that, although the standard form of the syllogism includes three judgments, a syllogism need not have merely three judgments in it. The idea that a syllogism must have only three judgments is an overly formalistic view. What matters instead is the relationship between the terms, or between S, P and U. So the example above could also take the form: "this something is red, this something is white, this something is blue, red is a color, white is a color, blue is a color, therefore this something is colored."

Hegel apparently suggested in a lecture that we use qualitative syllogisms all the time in ordinary life, so that they are not merely for useless logic games or textbooks. When we wake up on a winter morning, he suggests, and hear a cart creaking in the street outside, and then conclude that the cart must have frozen quite hard last night, we are syllogizing (§183A). In standard form, Hegel's syllogism could be written: "the cart is squeaking; squeaking is from sticking, sticking in winter is from freezing hard, therefore the cart is frozen hard."

Because any-old particularity will do, an indefinite number of particularities can be applied to the singularity. Qualitative Syllogism is thus subjective. We individual subjects must choose which particularity to focus on to generate the syllogism. These syllogisms therefore appear arbitrary, and it seems as if the conclusion can be drawn only in subjective reflection, or only in us. But Hegel says there is some objective truth in this kind of syllogism. First, it expresses the objective finitude of things (§182R), as we saw in Immediate Syllogism. Second, it also expresses that there are indeed objective connections between singulars, particulars and universals. There is an objective connection, for instance, between squeaking carts and extreme cold. So while the syllogism may be subjective, it is not merely subjective.

Still, this sort of syllogism is contingent in a number of ways. First, it is contingent with respect to its determinations, or with respect to which concepts get plugged in for the singularity, particularity and universality. As we saw, for any singularity, any particularity will do, and even the same particularity could lead to different universals (§184). Second, the syllogism is contingent with respect to the relations that obtain between its terms. Because any-old singularity, particularity or universal will do, the relations between the concepts that get plugged in for these terms will be immediate. The squeakiness of the cart, for instance, is an immediate relation—we simply hear or observe it, we do not derive it from any concept or inference. Even the universal we apply here is immediate—we feel some of the cold, and so immediately apply the universal "frozen" to the squeakiness of the cart. Because immediate connections are always contingent—they depend on the circumstances—these immediate connections are contingent as well. As we progress logically, the syllogism will develop to a point where there will be necessary connections between the elements: the particularity will not be abstract, but will be essentially defining.

Because the connections are contingent, a logical demand or need arises. The immediacy of the connections between S, P and U gives rise to the demand to *establish* those connections. In the example of the squeaky cart, for instance, the connections between the cart (S) and the squeaking (P), or the squeaking (P) and the cold (U) need to be established or proven. Something else might be squeaking, or perhaps what we're hearing is not squeaking at all. The demand to ground or establish the immediate connections within the Qualitative Syllogism leads to further syllogisms. To establish the connection between the cart and the squeaking, for instance, we would need another syllogism: "the cart is making noises, these noises are high-pitched, high-pitched noises are squeaking, therefore the cart is squeaking." But even here the connections are too contingent, and demand to be established in turn. This demand would generate yet another syllogism: "the cart is emitting sounds with unclear, high pitches that are not patterned enough to be speech; such sounds are noises; therefore the cart is making noises." But this syllogism too has immediate connections that demand to be established, generating yet another syllogism, and so on. Qualitative Syllogism thus generates a spurious infinity or endless, running-on process of syllogisms similar to the spurious infinities we've seen before (see Spurious Infinity in Chapter One, for example). As always, logic cannot rest with a spurious infinity, because a spurious infinity blocks an element or concept from being defined. The logic must therefore develop to stop the spuriously infinite process.

The spuriously infinite process of syllogisms can be stopped by noticing that, since the connections between S, P and U are contingent, and since the particularity is abstract, what is actually holding the syllogism together is not the particularity, but the subject or singularity. Whether the "this" (rose) is red or this (cart) is squeaky, for example, depends on the nature of the rose and the cart. There is therefore a double-meaning to the idea that this sort of syllogism is subjective. First, the syllogism is subjective in the sense that it depends on subjective reflection or on our (human) thought to be completed. Second, however, the syllogism is subjective in the sense that it is grounded in the subject, or is being held together not by the particularity, but by the singularity or subject. Because singularity holds the syllogism together, S moves into the middle position as the link between P and U in the next stage.

Hegel presents two different versions of the progress of the Qualitative Syllogism in the *Encyclopaedia Logic* and the *Science of Logic*. We also get two different stories justifying the progress. I will begin with the more extensive treatment offered by the *Science of Logic* (SL). I will then use that presentation to shed light on the much more brief version of the development in the *Encyclopaedia Logic* (EL). Afterward, I will consider whether these two competing presentations undercut my claim that the development of Hegel's logic is driven by necessity and tighter than most commentors have thought.

The SL Development for Qualitative Syllogism

The logical development of Qualitative Syllogism in the *Science of Logic* is driven by two factors. First, in the First Figure of Qualitative Syllogism (S-P-U), the immediacy or contingent nature of the connection between the moments led to a logical demand or need to establish the connections between the moments. This was the logical demand that led to the spurious infinity of that figure. S's connection to P is so immediate, contingent and hence flimsy that there must be a new syllogism to establish that S is connected to P. And P's connection to U is so immediate, contingent and hence flimsy that there must be a new syllogism to establish the connection between P and U. We need a syllogism to establish the premise "S is P," and one to establish the premise "P is U." The logical development in SL is driven by the need to establish these two premises.

The second factor explains *how* the development in SL attempts to establish these two premises. The first relates S and P together—it says "S is P." But P is not really a P or particular in relation to S (see Transition to the Judgment). P is a universal in relation to S. In relation to the rose (S), for instance, "red" is not a particular, but a universal. Red is a set-term that includes the rose as one of the items in its set. As a result, the demand to establish the premise "S is P" will have to be done through U or universality, because P is defined by universality in relation to S. The second premise relates P and U together—it says "P is U." But P is not really a P or particular in relation to U either. P is a singular in relation to U. Suppose P is red and U is colored-ness, for instance. Red is just one (singular) color among many colors. "Colored-ness" is a universal that contains red as one of its particularities. Red is one of the singulars in the set "coloredness." As a result, the demand to establish the premise "P is U" will have to be done through S, because P is a singular in relation to U.

Therefore, the demand to establish the two premises "S is P" and "P is U" leaves us with two logical projects for the Qualitative Syllogism: (1) the premise "P is U" will have to be established by S, because P is a singular in relation to U; and (2) the premise "S is P" will have to be established by U, because P is a universal in relation to S. These two projects lead to the Second and Third Figures of the Qualitative Syllogism respectively. As a result, in the Second Figure, we try to establish "P is U" through S, so that S becomes the middle term that links P and U. In the Third Figure, we try to establish "S is P" through U, so that U becomes the middle term that links S and P together.

The Second Figure of Qualitative Syllogism (from SL)

P S U

Figure 4.37

The conclusion of the First Figure (Fig. 4.36) says that S is U, so the judgment "S is U" is established. But it is established through a process of mediation, that is, through P. The fact that "S is U" through P has two consequences. First, because this conclusion was drawn through the mediation of P, it really says that S is U through P. Since S is U through P, S is the one element that is connected to both P and U. S is connected to U because it is also connected to P, so S is connected to both U and P. Second, because the process of mediation is a logical relationship, it is a necessary relation. Therefore the relation between S and U (through P) is a necessary one. Since S is necessarily connected to both U and P, it is the element that is necessarily holding the syllogism together, and it therefore moves into the middle position in this Second Figure (Fig. 4.37) as the term that is mediating the whole, necessary process of syllogism.

Moreover, the truth of the First Figure is that a something (an S) is united with a defining quality (the universal) not "in and for itself" (see Universality) but through a contingent particularity, or through another quality that captures the being (or constitution) of the singularity. So the singularity is not yet grasped by its defining concept. Instead, it is being grasped or defined only through its externality, or the way in which it has its being out there. What mediates the syllogism now, then, is the immediacy of the singularity itself, which includes how it has its being out there.

Furthermore, the conclusion of the First Figure was "S is U," which is now one of the premises of the Second Figure. Because "S is U" was the conclusion of the First Figure, it's the one premise in the Second Figure that is posited or established. According to the judgment "S is U," S is the subject, and U is the predicate. Since U's status as the predicate has been established, U remains the predicate in this Second Figure.

Since S is in the middle, and U is in the third position, P must be in the first position of the syllogism: P-S-U. It should be written out as "P is S, S is U, therefore P is U."

Because the process of syllogism of the First Figure has already happened, the sort of mediation in this syllogism has changed. At the beginning of the First Figure, the "is" of the judgments represents purely a relation of identity: S is P is U. S is P is U says that S identifies P and U, so P and U are what they are by being the sameness of S. P gets whatever character it has from S, and U gets whatever character it has from P—P inheres in S, and U inheres in P. Because the "is" of the First Figure involves only a relation of identity, S and P and U are not yet defined as concepts in that figure. A universal concept is defined through an "in and for itself" process, which is a process of both identity (the "for itself" process of content) and distinction or "otherness" (the "for-itselfness" of form or "in itself" process) (see Universality). Because S and P and U are defined only by identity in the First Figure, they are not yet defined as universal concepts—which is how they are supposed to be defined. It's because they are not defined as concepts in the First Figure that the First Figure was abstract: the terms or elements were abstract because they did not express the full definitions of singularity, particularity and universality. The process of syllogism that the First Figure undergoes, however, sublates (cancels and preserves) this immediate identity between S and P and U. The conclusion of the First Figure says that S is U, but S is U only by being something else first, namely P. In other words, S is U, but only through an "other." So the mediation of this Second Figure is now defined by a negative moment, or a moment of "otherness."

The fact that this figure's mediation has introduced a moment of negativity or "otherness" has two consequences. First, it explains why the logical development of the syllogism introduced in this Second Figure is a kind of syllogism that violates the proper form of a syllogism. This syllogism violates the proper form of a syllogism because the middle term, S, is not a genuine middle term. A genuine middle term is supposed to be the subject in relation to one element, and the subsumed term in relation to the other element. In the First Figure, for instance, the middle term, P, was subsumed in its relation with S in the first premise—"S is P"—but the subject in its relation with U in the second premise—"P is U." That's not the case here, however. The middle term, S, in this Second Figure is either the subject in relation to both U and P or the subsumed element in relation to both U and P (since judgments are transitive—see The Judgment). This syllogism has to be written out either as "P is S, U is S, therefore P is U," or as "S is P, S is U, therefore P is U": either "sparrow is this something, bird is this something, therefore sparrow is bird," for instance, or "this something is sparrow, this something is bird, therefore sparrow is bird" (I will say more about how each of the elements is defined in this Second Syllogism shortly.) Because this syllogism violates the standard form of the syllogism, it is "other" in relation to that standard form. It is an "other" kind of syllogism. The elements are not currently defined as concepts—they do no currently realize the Concept, or have the definitions they are supposed to have as moments of the Concept. The fact that this syllogism violates the standard form of the syllogism shows that the elements will be defined as concepts only through a negative moment of mediation—a moment of "otherness"—in the process of development for the syllogism itself. As the syllogism develops logically, it has to pass through a moment of "otherness." The syllogism must alter or become "other" than it was during the process of logical development. That's why there is a different kind of syllogism in this stage, one that violates the standard form of the syllogism.

The second consequence is that P is redefined as a universal concept. The kind of mediation here has a negative moment, or a moment of "otherness." The Second Figure is in S. Since the mediation has a moment of "otherness," and since S does the job of mediation, S is now defined not only as the identity of P and U (as it was at the beginning of the First Figure), but also as "other" than P and U. This fact changes the definition of P. In the First Figure, P was some specific particularity of S—it was a determinate particularity, a particularity that belonged to and inhered in S. The fact that S is now a negative unity of, or "other" than P and U, however, means that P is now defined as an "other" in relation to S. P is therefore not only identified with S, it is also "other" than S. This is precisely the relationship that defines something as a universal—both identity and distinction at the same time. So P is now a universal. It is not just the particularity of S—in which it is the identity of S—it is the *thought of* the particularity of S—because it is also "other" than S. P is not just the "sparrow-ness" of S, for instance, it is the *thought or concept of* the "sparrow-ness" of S. It is "sparrow" now defined as a concept of its own that is wider than, and hence not merely a predicate of, S. P is a universal, a concept that is both the identity of, but also "other" than, S. It is a quality of S that does not only inhere in S, but that stretches beyond S. S is merely what *presents* P as a singular. Again, for instance, P as "sparrow" is a concept on its own, so that "this something" (i.e. S) is merely what presents "sparrow" as a chunk or singular.

There is a second logical reason why P is now redefined as a particularity that is *presented* as a singular by S. In the First Figure, S and P were both abstract, or undefined, given immediacies. S was any singular, and P was any particularity or thereness of S. Now, however, S and P are beginning to have a character or be defined. Because P and S have changed positions in this second syllogism, they are now defined in part by the character of each other. That's because the three positions within the syllogism (first, middle, last) have a character or definition separate from the moment that happens to occupy them. The basic form of the syllogism—S-P-U—defines the positions of the syllogism. The first position is defined as singularity, the second position as particularity and the third position as universality. Those positions define the form or presentation of the moment that happens to occupy the position. When P moves into the first position of the syllogism here, it has the form of singularity. And when S moves into the middle position here, it has the form of particularity. Because P and S are coming to have a definition, they are no longer merely abstract immediacies—at least not formally, which is to say, at least not in terms of their presentation, or in the way in which they are presented. P is still P, of course—it has not completely become S. It gets its S-ness, so to speak, only through its place or presentation in the syllogism, that is, through its form. Similarly, S has not become P either, but gets its P-ness through its presentation or form in the syllogism. S is an S that has the form of P-ness; and P is a P that has the form of S-ness.

While S and P are no longer abstract, they are not concrete either. They do not yet have definitions or characters of their own. Each is what it was before, and gets the character that it has only externally, through its relation with the other one. So S does not have the particularity on its own. It gets its particularity or quality only externally, in the definition of P. And P does not have its singularity on its own. It gets its singularity only in the definition of S.

The fact that the characters of S and P have changed also explains why I had to introduce a new example in this stage—why I can no longer use the example of "red" for P, but had to use "sparrow" instead. S is still a something, but it is a something that is now presented as a particularity, as something particular. S is something-in-particular, which means it is now presented as having a "what it is," or a particular character. Of course, S does not have that particular character on its own. It has its particular character only in the definition of P. That is why I continued to refer to S merely as "something" in the example I gave above, rather than as "this sparrow." S's character is in the definition of P, so P is the "sparrow." The fact that S is presented as having a particular character or "what it is" also explains why I cannot use "red" as an example for P. "Red" is a concept of thereness. It does not capture the "something" or "what it is" that something is. Nothing can be "a red." P must now be the sort of particularity that captures the "what it is" of something. It must be, for instance, "sparrow." Keep in mind, however, that because the first premise of this syllogism—"P is S"—is not established by the First Figure (Fig. 4.36), P and S are still being connected together in an immediate way. P is just the given or immediate "what it is" or particular character of S.

P's new character as a P that is presented as singularity reinforces not only the claim that P is now a concept, but also the change in the example used. The fact that P is presented as singularity reinforces the relationship of "otherness" between P and S that we saw above in the discussion of the negativity that the mediation of the syllogism now has. A process in which an element *presents* another element always defines the elements as separate from one another (see External Necessity in Chapter Three). Because P is presented by or made singular by S, it is wider than S, and so must inhere in other things as well. That's why P is now a concept on its own, rather than merely a characteristic of S that inheres in S. Again, P is the thought or concept of "sparrow," which is wider than S and so must inhere in other somethings as well. At the same time, S (which must be an individual sparrow, though it does not yet have that character on its own) presents P as a singularity. The concept of "sparrow" is presented as a singularity in individual (sparrow) somethings.

Of course, it is important to note that, just as S is not yet defined as a sparrow, P is not yet really defined as the concept of "sparrow" either. P is still just what it was as a particularity or characteristic of S, except that now it is a concept that is presented by S. P does not yet have its character on its own either. It is not a defined concept, or not a concept that is defined on its own. Instead, it has its definition as "sparrow" only in the definition or "what it is" of S. Nevertheless, the definition of P is now established in its developed form as the relation of S and U, because P is the concept (universal) of the "what it is" that S is, which U then grasps ("is bird"). P is the identity of S that is also "other" than S that presents the "what it is" that S is, which is grasped by U.

So far, I have not said much about what U is like, but U's definition has been affected as well. Because the mediation of this Second Figure (Fig. 4.37) has a negative moment, so that S is now defined as an "other" in relation not only to P but also to U as well, U is now a concept too. Moreover, since S is presented as a "what it is," like P, U is the thought or concept of the "what it is" of S. U is the quality of S too. Because U has not changed positions, it is still defined as a quality that belongs to S, or a predicate of S, just as it was in the First Figure (Fig. 4.36).

Because P does not really have a definition of its own, the example of this syllogism I gave above over-defines P. Since P does not yet have a definition of its own, it is not really defined as "sparrow," just as S was not really defined as a "rose" in the First Syllogism. So a better example of this syllogism is: "'what it is' (P) is something (S), something (S) is sparrow (U), therefore 'what it is' (P) is sparrow (U)." Other universals could also be substituted for U: "'what it is' is something, something is bird, therefore 'what it is' is bird;" "'what it is' is something, something is animal, therefore 'what it is' is animal"; and so on. U is any predicate that belongs (necessarily) to S, but only through P. (The conclusion that U is any predicate that belongs to S and P will be brought out in the Third Figure [Fig. 4.38] below.)

The conclusion of this Second Figure (Fig 4.37) says that "P is U." Because of the mediation by S, however, P and U are not in the sort of "in and for itself" relation with one another that universality and particularity are supposed to have (see Universality and Particularity). The fact that S has moved into the middle position and that this syllogism violates the standard form of the syllogism expresses the truth of the First Syllogism (Fig. 4.36), namely, that the standard form of the syllogism connects the terms together in a subjective and contingent way. For this syllogism, P and U are therefore two, mutually indifferent qualities connected to one another in an indifferent way through singularity. They are indifferent toward one another because S is not really a genuine middle term. Since S is either the subject of both premises or the predicate of both premises, P and U are indifferent toward one another. They are not really related together through S at all. Suppose S is a sparrow, and P is its "what it is" as a sparrow, and U is S's quality of being a bird. Then the syllogism would say "S is a sparrow (S-P) (or "sparrow is S" [P-S]), S is a bird (S-U), bird is S (U-S)" (the judgments in the premises are transitive), "therefore sparrow is a bird." Now this conclusion is correct—a sparrow *is* a bird—but it is only correct because sparrow itself *is* a bird, and not because of anything that S did in the syllogism. If "P is U" is correct, then, it is correct only on its own account, because of the nature of P and U, and not because it is the conclusion of this syllogism.

Of course, the First Figure (Fig. 4.36) had the same subjectivity and contingency in its conclusion. Whether the conclusion "S is U" was correct depended on the nature of the S and U, and not on the fact that it was the conclusion of the syllogism. Whether the "this" is colored, for instance, really depends on the nature of the "this" and of the universal "color," and not on the syllogistic process. Whether the "this" (cart) is frozen hard depends on the nature of the "this" and of the thought or universal "frozen hard," and not on the syllogistic process by which the conclusion was drawn. This Second Figure (Fig. 4.37) posits or establishes this truth because its violation of the standard form of the syllogism undercuts the suggestion that the middle term or the syllogism's process of mediation is necessary to the correctness of the conclusion. Again, since the premises are S-P and S-U (or P-S and U-S), S does not really do the job of linking U and P together, which is what it should be doing insofar as it is the middle term. That's why this syllogism's violation of the standard form expresses the truth of the First Figure that the mediation process is not really doing any work.

Like the First Figure (Fig. 4.36), this syllogism (Fig. 4.37), too, has an objective meaning, which is contained in the conclusion "P is U." The objective meaning of this syllogism is that a universal is not in an "in and for itself" relationship with any one of its particularities. The concept of "bird," for instance, is not in an "in and for itself" relationship with only the concept of "sparrow," but is in such a relationship only with the whole set of particularities that it includes: "sparrow," "raven," "albatross," "penguin," and so on. The universal has a relationship with any one of its particularities only through singularity. Singularity is the element that splits universality into its separate particularities because Singularity is the element that presents the individual actualities, which is where one particularity can be divided from the rest. Singularity presents the individual, actual birds, for instance, so it is the element in which the "sparrow" can be divided from "raven" and all the other types of birds. Notice that this reading of the objective meaning takes the syllogism's conclusion to be "U is P:" it says U is not in an "in and for itself" relation with any one of its P's. The objective meaning is also expressed by the judgment "P is U": the one particular is also not in an "in and for itself" relationship with the universal. However, P has been raised to the level of universality—again, it is a concept of its own now, rather than merely a characteristic that inheres in that one, little, individual sparrow.

The Third Figure of Qualitative Syllogism (from SL)

S U P

Figure 4.38

U or universality moves into the middle position for two reasons. First, the conclusion of the Second Figure (P-S-U [Fig. 4.37]) is "P is U" in which P and U have a relationship of both identity or sameness (the positive relation) and "otherness" or distinction (the negative relation). That is just the sort of relationship that defines a relationship of universality (see Universality). Since the relationship between P and U in the conclusion to the Second Figure is defined by universality, this Third Figure (Fig. 4.38) must be mediated by a relationship of universality, a universal relation, or a relation between two concepts. So universality moves into the middle position in this Third Figure.

There is a second reason why universality moves into the middle position. Because the First Figure (S-P-U [Fig. 4.36]) started out with or was based in immediate singularity, the kind of mediation in that First Syllogism was contingent: some subject or person had to pick out which P or particularity to focus on to complete the syllogism. The Second Figure (P-S-U [Fig. 4.37]), however, established the particularity. The singularity's particularity or "what it is" is established. Singularity is an S (something) that is presented as P ("what it is"). Moreover, since S is presented as P, and P is a concept or universal, S is presented as a universal. (Keep in mind, too, that, in relation to S, P is defined as a universal [see Transition to the Judgment]). As a result, the singularity that mediated the Second Figure is a singularity that points toward universality. S could be a something, have its character as a something, be what it is, or be defined only through P, which was a universality. The mediation by S in the Second Figure therefore points toward another kind of mediation, namely, mediation by U or universality, which is the mediation in this Third Figure (Fig. 4.38). The kind of mediation in the Second Figure was a mediation by a singularity that pointed toward another kind of mediation, namely, mediation by universality. S was therefore the sort of mediation that is *self-external*: it is a type or form of mediation that points toward another type of mediation, or toward mediation in its other form (cf. Extensive and Intensive Magnitude in Chapter Two, where quantity is defined as "self-external"). In this Third Figure, then, the two terms on the outside are mediated not by singularity or immediateness, but by universality. U moves into the middle position in the Third Figure, yielding anther form of Qualitative Syllogism, S-U-P. This syllogism can be written out as: "S is U, U is P, therefore S is P."

Because this Third Figure (Fig. 4.38) is a new form of syllogism, the logical movement from one syllogism to the next in Qualitative Syllogism has once again involved alteration, change or passing over, just as it did in the Doctrine of Being. The move from S-P-U to P-S-U involved changing from one type of syllogism to another type of syllogism. This stage, too, has a different form of syllogism. That's because the Qualitative Syllogism is grounded in immediate singularity. According to the definition of the Concept, however, singularity is supposed to be the unity of particularity and universality by sublating (canceling and preserving) the specific character of particularity, that is, by raising particularity to the status of a universal. This Third Figure succeeds in raising particularity to the status of a universal, but only as an abstract universality.

Think of the diagram of the Concept in which the Concept was a set of nested bubbles, with Universality as the outer-most bubble, Particularity as the next bubble inside, and Singularity as the next bubble inside Particularity. Singularity was the unity of Particularity and Universality because it was the content of both—both the Universality and Particularity bubbles contained the Singularity bubble as their content. Particularity is a one, and so has the character of being a singular or something. But because P contains Singularity, which is a set, it is also *not* a one or whole. Since Singularity is the elements into which Particularity divides, S also sublates Particularity's definition as a something or one. The Second Figure (Fig. 4.37) does not include both of these ways of defining P, however. There, singularity presents particularity as a singular. Singularity succeeds in defining particularity as a universal or set only by disappearing in the conclusion. In the conclusion of the Second Figure, P and U were not united by Singularity, but only by their own characters as concepts. While universality does mediate the Third Figure (Figure 4.38), that universality does not have any specific, unified (singular) character. Instead, the universality that mediates the Third Figure is abstract universality. U defines the sameness or positive unity between S and P only in an abstract way. U is not some specific character that S and P share, it is defined as whatever character S and P share. If S is a sparrow, for instance, and P is the concept of what the sparrow is, then U is any shared universality of S and P. The following syllogisms could all exemplify this Third Figure:

S—"bird"—"what it is" (where what it is is a sparrow)
S—"vertebrate"—"what it is" (where what it is is a sparrow)
S—"color"—"what it is" (where what it is is a sparrow)
. . . and so on. Because U is abstract, U is any universal that S and P share.

Although U is abstract, it is not completely indeterminate or undetermined, because its connection to S and P give it some character. Although there are many universals that we can plug in for U in the example, there are also many universals we could *not* plug in for U, because those universals would not be shared by S and P. For instance, we could not plug "alligator," "painting," or "telephone" in for U. Thus the character of U is fixed somewhat, relative to S and P, or in relation to S and P.

This Third Figure (Fig. 4.38) has no immediate premises: "S is U" was established by the First Figure (Fig. 4.36), and "U is P" (or "P is U") is established by the Second Figure (Fig. 4.37). The Third Figure therefore presupposes the first two. But they also presuppose it, of course, because they each contain premises that are established by this Third Figure. The figures are mutually supporting, which shows that the logical development and definition of the general form of the syllogism is now complete. Although each syllogism is by itself mediated, each figure by itself does not define the nature of mediation as a whole or as a totality because each figure contains an element of immediacy (namely the two premises) whose mediation lies outside of each figure in the other two figures. The process of mediation as a whole or totality, then, is defined only by the process of development of all three figures, taken together as a whole. Moreover, because the three figures are mutually supportive, there is no more demand to establish any of the premises. The demand to establish the premises of the First Figure led to a spurious infinity of syllogisms. Now that there is a circle of mutually supporting syllogisms, each of which has premises that are established by the other syllogisms, there is no need for further syllogisms. We have therefore overcome the spurious infinity of the first, immediate Qualitative Syllogism (Fig. 4.36).

The stages of Qualitative Syllogism are the logical development of the form of syllogism, or of the formal syllogism. Because this Third Figure (Fig. 4.38) is the last general form of syllogism to be developed, it is the highest definition of the form of syllogism, and expresses the truth of formal syllogism, namely that what is really mediating the forms of the syllogism is abstract universality. The two outside terms are contained in or linked together by the middle term not insofar as they are specific items—insofar as S is a specific, immediate singularity or "this" out there in the world, or P is a specific, single characteristic of S—but only insofar as they are universals. In the First Figure (S-P-U [Fig. 4.36]), for instance, the "this" (the rose) can be "colored" not because it is a single thing, but because it is the universal "red." The "this" is red because it is itself a universal or multitude that links it to a number of universals (its characteristics), one of which is that it is red. That universality makes it "colored." In the Second Figure (P-S-U [Fig. 4.37]), the "what it is" of the sparrow is not connected to the concept of "bird" because of the singular existing sparrows, but because of the conceptual relation between "sparrow" and "bird," which is independent of the singular, existing sparrow. Qualitative Syllogism started out by claiming that the syllogism in general could be mediated by specificity. In the First Figure, P was the specific character of S, and U was the specific character of P: P inhered in S, and U inhered in P. This Third Figure (Fig. 4.38) expresses the truth that the syllogism in general is actually mediated by universality.

In the Second Figure (Fig. 4.37), the middle term was not really a middle term because it was either the subject or the predicate of both of the premises. In this Third Figure (Fig. 4.38), the middle term, U, is the subsuming element or predicate of both S and P in the premises. Because the middle term has to be the subsuming element or predicate of both premises, the Third Figure can have the form of a standard syllogism (which, for the Third Figure would be "S is U, U is P, therefore S is P") only if the relationship between subject and predicate in the premise "U is P" is indifferent. When U is indifferent, then the conclusion ("S is P") also becomes indifferent in the sense that it does not matter whether the singularity and particularity are interpreted, (1) as a single singularity or immediate "this" (the "extreme of singularity" [§1467]) and some single particularity or specific characteristic of the singularity, or (2) as *categories in general*. Some more robust examples of the Third Figure than the ones offered above—examples that give separate identities to S and P as well as to U—will help to show why. Since U must be the subsuming element for both S and P, P has to be a sub-category of U, just like S is. If S is a "sparrow," then P can be "bird," and U can be "animal." In the standard form for the syllogism, this syllogism would be written out as: "the sparrow is an animal, the animal is a bird, therefore the sparrow is a bird." In the standard syllogism, a major premise links two categories together, the minor premise subsumes an existing singularity under one of the categories, and the conclusion subsumes the existing singularity under one of the categories: "all men are mortal, Caius is a man, therefore Caius is mortal." In this syllogism, "the sparrow" is supposed to refer to a specifically existing sparrow—some particular sparrow. The second premise is indifferent, however, toward whether the "animal" is subsumed under the category of "bird" or whether the "bird' is subsumed under the category of "animal." If the "animal" is subsumed under the category of "bird," then it must be a specific animal, while "bird" is the category. And if the "bird" is subsumed under "animal," then the bird is a specific bird and "animal" is the category. Either way, "animal is bird." Because of this indifference over which side is specific and which is category, or between which side is the subject and which is the predicate, the conclusion is infected with the same indifference. The conclusion—"the sparrow is bird"—is indifferent as to which side is category or predicate, and which side is subject or specific item. "The sparrow" can be the specific, and the "bird" its category, or the "bird" can be a specific bird, and the "sparrow" its category. Keep in mind that this example is artificial because it overdefines both the singularity and the particularity. In this stage, singularity is still just a "something" that has no character of its own, and is therefore not defined as a sparrow. And particularity is the "what it is" of the "something," but does not have its character on its own. So it is not yet defined as a "bird" either. I just used this example to illustrate the indifference that now belongs to the conclusion of this Third Figure.

Like the other two figures, this Third Figure (Fig. 4.38), too, has an objective meaning. Because the Qualitative Syllogism has developed into this form as the highest form of syllogism, this Third Figure shows that, in general, the mediating element of the syllogism is universality. Because universality is abstract in this Third Figure, however, there is still something missing from this definition of the syllogism. As in the First and Second syllogism, there is still a contingency in this syllogism. Some subjectivity or some person must still pick which specific universal to plug into the syllogism. The "what is it" of the "this" could be all sorts of universals. The universal is therefore indifferent toward and external to S and P. It no longer captures the specific character of the singularity, its "what it is" or particularity. "Vertebrate" could be any vertebrate, not just a sparrow. Because the U can no longer distinguish the qualitative differences between S and P and itself as U, the three elements are defined as the same as one another by a universality in a relationship of identity or sameness that must be fixed by something external to or outside of them. This is a relationship of equality or likeness between universalities—a relationship in which the universalities are held to be the same as one another, but in which the comparison must be made by a third term (cf. Likeness and Unlikeness in Chapter Three). That relationship will yield the fourth figure of Qualitative Syllogism, the Mathematical Syllogism, which Hegel characterizes in the *Science of Logic* with the syllogism U-U-U (cf. Fig. 4.43).

The EL Development for Qualitative Syllogism: The Second Figure of Qualitative Syllogism

U S P

This new syllogism expresses what we discovered in the last, namely, that singularity is really doing the work of the middle term because it is what is holding the whole syllogism together

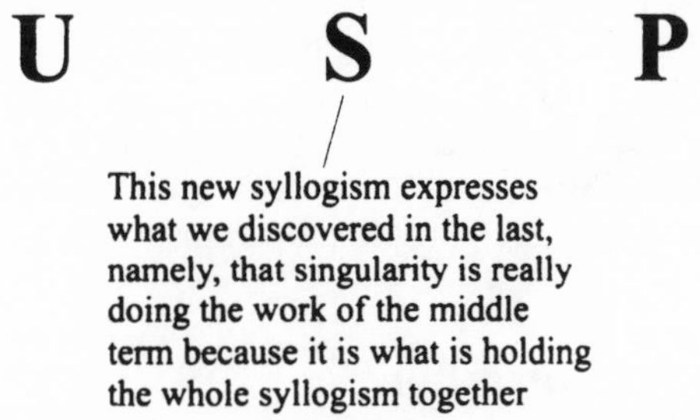

Figure 4.39

The *Encyclopaedia Logic* (EL) offers a different set of syllogisms for Qualitative Syllogism. In the Second Figure in EL (Fig. 4.39), singularity becomes the mediating term between particularity and universality because singularity is really what is holding the syllogism together in the First Figure (Fig. 4.36). Moreover, according to the conclusion of that First Figure, S is U, or the singular is something-universal. As a result, universality steps across the syllogism and takes S's (singularity's) place as the immediate subject of the syllogism (§187). Since U is first, and S is in the middle, P must be last: U-S-P. This second syllogism can be written out as: "U is S, S is P, therefore, U is P."

Because the conclusion of the First Figure (Fig. 4.36) was "S is U," or the singular is universal, it defines the type of singularity in this second syllogism. A kind of singularity that is something-universal is now mediating the two extremes of the syllogism (§186). The definition of the singular has thus changed as a result of its having been through the first syllogism. The singular is no longer a completely undefined singular, but a singular that is universal. The singular is now defined as a something, or as a "this" with a character (or universal). It is a singular of a certain kind.

What does Hegel mean when he says that "[s]ince the universal steps across from the . . . conclusion [of the First Figure (Fig. 4.36)], it now occupies the place of the immediate subject" (§187)? This is an important question, because U was never the immediate subject of the syllogism in the development in the *Science of Logic*. Now that singularity is defined as a singularity of a certain kind or universal, the logic must explore the kind (or universal) that the singularity is. To give an example, if the First Figure was "this"—"constituted thus-and-so"—is "bird," the question arises "what is bird," and so "bird" now becomes the subject of interest for this Second Figure (Fig. 4.39).

Hegel says that this figure expresses the truth of the First Figure (Fig. 4.36), namely, that "since the mediation has taken place in singularity, it is something contingent" (§186). In SL, Hegel says that the First Figure is contingent because some outside subject or person has to decide which particularity to focus on to complete the syllogism. There are two things that Hegel might mean in EL by the claim that the mediation has "taken place in singularity." He might mean that the mediation has "taken place in singularity" in the sense that some singular person or subject has to mediate the syllogism. That interpretation would echo the contingency that Hegel assigns the First Figure in SL. But he also might mean that the mediation takes place in singularity in the sense that the singularity of the First Figure is really what is holding the syllogism together and, since the singularity is contingent, so is the mediation. Singularity was holding the First Figure together because the P and U were both taken to be characteristics that inhered—by chance—in the specific "this" or singularity. The "this" (as a rose) happened to be red, which, since red is a color, means that the "this" also has color in it. This Second Figure (Fig. 4.39) expresses the contingency of the first by placing the contingent singularity squarely in the middle of the syllogism as its mediation.

The Third Figure of Qualitative Syllogism (from EL)

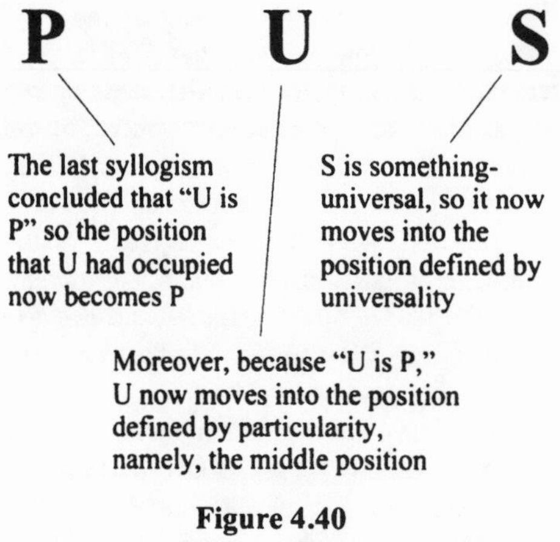

P
U
S
The last syllogism concluded that "U is P" so the position that U had occupied now becomes P
S is something-universal, so it now moves into the position defined by universality
Moreover, because "U is P," U now moves into the position defined by particularity, namely, the middle position

Figure 4.40

The conclusion of the Second Figure (Fig. 4.39) "locks the universal together with the particular," or defines U as something-particular (*Besonderes*) (§187). It says that "U is P," or the universal is particular, and so defines the U as one of the U's particularities, which is a specific something. If U is "bird," and P is "sparrow," and S is "something," the conclusion of the Second Figure says that "bird is sparrow." In relation to "bird," "sparrow" is just one of its particularities, since bird includes all the other kinds of birds as well. Hence the conclusion says that the U is something-particular, namely, one of its types. Because "sparrow" is a one type or whole, it is a singularity. But, because it is one of U's types, it is also a particularity. U is therefore now defined as both singularity and particularity, and so moves into the middle position in this Third Figure (Fig. 4.40) as the element that unifies particularity and singularity. The other two moments occupy the positions at the extremes of the syllogism. Hegel gives the following figure for this syllogism: P-U-S (§187). Although Hegel provides this figure specifically—P-U-S—he does not give an explanation in EL for why P is in the first position, or S is in the last position.

Since each moment has now occupied the middle position as well as both outside positions, their defined distinction from one another has been sublated (canceled but preserved). We will see why the distinction has been preserved shortly. The cancellation of the distinction between them will generate the Fourth Figure of Qualitative Syllogism, namely, the Quantitative or Mathematical Syllogism (Fig. 4.43). Because each element has occupied the middle position, they have each been defined as the unity of all three elements, and hence as singularity/particularity/universality. Moreover, because they have each occupied each of the outside positions, they cannot be distinguished in terms of their form either—each element has been presented in all three positions and so is defined as singularity/particularity/universality in terms of its form or presentation. Hence, all three moments now have the same definition as the whole unity of singularity, particularity and universality. Because they all have the same quality in terms of both content and form, they cannot be distinguished anymore. They are just three elements that are equal to or like each other, and so generate the Mathematical Syllogism: "if two things are *equal* to a third, they are equal to one another" (§188).

Comparing the EL and SL Developments of Qualitative Syllogism

The *Encyclopaedia Logic* and the *Science of Logic* offer two different versions of the development of Qualitative Syllogism. Did Hegel change his mind about how the logical development should go from one text to the other, or can we reconcile the two versions so that there is only one version of the logical development? These questions are crucial to assessing Hegel's claim that he has offered a logic that develops necessarily from stage to stage. If there are two versions of the development of Qualitative Syllogism, then neither version would seem to be necessary. I will argue that the two versions are effectively the same as one another and so can be reconciled, which will reinforce the claim that the logical development is necessary. Here is a quick sketch of the three Figures of Qualitative Syllogism offered by the two books:

	From the *Encyclopaedia:*	From the *Science of Logic:*
First Figure	**S — P — U**	**S — P — U**
Second Figure	**U — S — P**	**P — S — U**
Third Figure	**P — U — S**	**S — U — P**

Figure 4.41

The middle term develops in the same order in both texts: it starts as P, then becomes S, then U. The texts disagree about the order of the outside terms, however. Where EL has U-P around S in the Second Figure, SL has P-U. And where EL has P-S around U in the Third Figure, SL has S-P. I will argue that, because the syllogisms are *reversible*—U-S-P is the same as P-S-U, and P-U-S is the same as S-U-P. The reversibility of the syllogism means that the different sets of syllogisms offered by the two texts can be reconciled.

If Hegel took the syllogisms to be reversible, as I am suggesting, then he would have regarded the order of the outside terms in each syllogism he offers to be unimportant. In the *Encyclopaedia*, some passages seem to imply that the order of the outside terms is indeed unimportant, but other passages suggest that the order is crucial to the logical development. An example of the first sort of passage can be found in §187. In §187, which discusses the Third Figure from EL (P-U-S), Hegel says that the universal occupies the middle position and "mediates between the extremes, whose places are occupied by the other" terms. This description certainly treats the order of the outside terms cavalierly: U is in the middle, he says, and the other terms are wherever they are on the outside. Although Hegel gives the figure P-U-S for this syllogism, his emphasis on the middle term in his written description suggests that the order of the outside terms does not matter all that much.

Other passages in EL suggest the order of the outside terms *does* matter. In the discussion of the move from the First (S-P-U) to the Second (U-S-P) Figures in EL, Hegel says that U steps across from the conclusion in the First Figure to take S's place in the first position as the subject of the syllogism in the Second Figure (§187). This explanation of the logical development seems to require the specific placement of the outside terms offered by EL, since it requires U to be in the third position in the First Figure, and the first position in the Second Figure. In SL, U occupies the third position in the Second Figure (P-S-U), rather than the first position. Hegel's explanation in EL for how U moves to the middle position in the Third Figure (P-U-S) also seems to rely on the specific order of the outside terms that is offered in that text. Hegel says that U moves into the middle position in the Third Figure because the Second Figure "locks the universal together with the particular." This locking process defines U as something-particular (*Besonderes*), or as the unity of singularity and particularity, and therefore moves U into the middle position of particularity in the Third Figure (§187). This explanation of the logical development fits more naturally with EL's account of the order of the outside terms. In EL, the conclusion of the Second Figure (U-S-P) is "U is P," or "universality is particularity." This judgment says that U is defined by particularity, which would explain why U moves into the middle position in the Third Figure (P-U-S): since U is defined by particularity, it moves into the position defined by particularity (namely, the middle position) in the next stage. In SL, however, the conclusion of the Second Figure (P-S-U) is reversed. It says "P is U," or "particularity is universality," rather than "universality is particularity." This judgment seems to characterize P or particularity rather than U, and would therefore not seem to explain why universality should move into the middle position in the Third Figure in SL (S-U-P). Hegel's explanation for the logical development in EL thus seems to be tied to the specific order of the outside terms offered in that text.

In the *Science of Logic*, there are two claims that suggest the order of the outside terms is unimportant. First, when Hegel discusses the objective meaning of the Second Figure (P-S-U), he spells out the meaning of the conclusion as both "P is U" and as "U is P." Perhaps Hegel only intended to suggest that the individual *judgments* of a syllogism are transitive, but his reversal of the conclusion also implies that the *whole* syllogism is reversible, because "U is P" is the conclusion of the syllogism U-S-P, while "P is U" is the conclusion of the syllogism P-S-U. The second claim in SL which suggests that the order of the outside terms is not important is contained in the explanation Hegel offers for how the Mathematical Syllogism is generated. As in EL, Hegel says that each term has occupied the middle position, and that each term has occupied "in turn the places of the two extremes" (§1475). But in the outline for the syllogisms that Hegel provides, U never occupies the first position at all. His claim that each term has occupied all three positions in the syllogism is only true if we assume that the syllogisms are reversible, so that the Second Figure could be written as either P-S-U or U-S-P, which puts U in the first position.

There is one place in SL where Hegel's explanation for the logical development seems to require a certain order in the outside terms, however. Because "S is U" was the conclusion of the First Figure (S-P-U), he suggests, it is the one premise in the Second Figure (P-S-U) that is posited or established. According to that judgment, S is the subject, and U is the predicate. Since U's status as the predicate has been established in the First Figure, U must remain a predicate and so stay in the same position in the Second Figure, namely, in the third position.

Hegel should have regarded the syllogisms as reversible for one good logical reason: the reversibility of the syllogisms follows from the transitivity of the judgments within the syllogism. I have already suggested that the judgments are transitive in the mathematical sense. Just as 2 x 6 is the same as 6 x 2, "P is U" is the same as "U is P": both judgments mean the same thing (see The Judgment). Reversing the judgments of the syllogism reverses the conclusion, and the reversed conclusion is the conclusion of the *reversed syllogism*.

There is both logical and textual evidence for the view that Hegel regarded the judgments as transitive. In the *Encyclopaedia*, the most important evidence for the view that the judgments are transitive is logical. Hegel argues that the defect of Abstract Judgment is that Singularity and the universal do not define each other at the same time in the same judgment. The claim that S and U are supposed to identify one another at the same time in the same judgment implies that the judgment "S is U" says both that S is U *and* that U is S. The transitivity of the judgment "S is U" is also implied by the fact that, within the Concept, Singularity and Particularity (which is what the universal is) are mutually defining. Singularity is the complete particularization of Particularity—it is the thought of the (completed and completely systematized) set of concepts into which Particularity divides. And Singularity is the complete presentation of Particularity—it is *all* the concepts and *all* the activity of Particularity, the full definition of Particularity. Indeed, because the whole Concept is a finished product, all three moments are mutually defining: they are "identical with one another" (§161), or are in reciprocal relationships of identity with one another. Since all three elements are mutually defining, all of the judgments between U, P and S should therefore be transitive.

Hegel's claim that the qualitative syllogisms are mutually supporting also suggests that the judgments within the syllogism are transitive. In EL, Hegel says that, for the whole triad of syllogisms, "*the mediation* . . . has been completed" because the syllogisms "reciprocally presuppose each other" (§189). The premises of the First Figure (S-P-U) are established in the other two figures, and the premises of the Second and Third Figures are also established by the other two figures (§189). The first premise of the First Figure is S-P, Hegel says, or "S is P." It is mediated in the Third Figure (P-U-S), while the second premise, P-U or "P is U," is mediated in the Second Figure (U-S-P) (§189). Notice, however, that the conclusion of the Third Figure is actually "P is S," not "S is P." Therefore the Third Figure establishes or mediates the premise "S-P" only if the conclusion of the Third Figure (or the premise of the First Figure) is reversed. The Second Figure also reverses the order of the terms of the premise of the First Figure: the conclusion of the Second Figure is "U is P," not "P is U." This passage therefore suggests that Hegel regarded the judgments of the syllogism as transitive.

Indirect evidence also suggests Hegel regarded the judgments as transitive. As Geraets, Suchting and Harris point out (Geraets et al. 1991, 332), Hegel's emphasis on semantics in logic makes his logic similar to Aristotle's. I. M. Bochenski has argued that Aristotle's logic focuses on meanings (semantics) rather than merely syntactic structures. Bochenski suggests that Aristotle's emphasis on meanings led Aristotle to say that there were only three possible figures for the syllogism. Aristotle refused to admit that there were four possible figures for the syllogism, according to Bochenski, because the terms in Aristotle's syllogisms were defined by their extensions—and hence by their meanings—and not merely formally according to their places in the syllogism (Bochenski 1961, 13.21).[2] Bochenski also suggests, however—a point Geraets, Suchting and Harris do not mention—that Aristotle regarded the order of the terms in the premises of the syllogism as irrelevant. According to Bochenski, for Aristotle, reversing the order of terms in the premises was an irrelevant logical operation (Bochenski 1961, 13.21). Since the terms of the syllogism are defined by their meanings, rather than formally by their places in the syllogism, changing their order would not affect their meanings. Hegel's terms are also defined in part by reference to their meanings. Like Aristotle, then, Hegel can view the order of the terms in the premises of the syllogism as irrelevant. In addition, like Aristotle, as Geraets, Suchting and Harris do point out, Hegel is "within his rights" (Geraets et al. 1991, 332) to reject the idea that there is a fourth figure of the syllogism, which he does (§187R). Hegel can reject the view that there is a fourth figure because, as I will argue shortly, the three figures he spells out in EL can be used to stand for all possible permutations and combinations of the syllogism. There is therefore no need for another figure.

In EL, Hegel is clearly aware of the similarities between his own logic and the logic of Aristotle. He explicitly criticizes modern revisions of Aristotle's discussion of the syllogism for treating the syllogism in an overly formalistic or mechanical way. His criticisms suggest that what is missing from modern formalistic logic, for Hegel, is semantics or meanings. He praises Aristotle for refusing to include a fourth figure for the syllogism. The overly formalistic or mechanistic approach to the syllogism, by contrast—which belongs to the logic of the understanding—recognizes four figures for the syllogism because it treats each figure of the syllogism as an empty formalism, and ignores the fact that the syllogisms have meanings (§187R). Thus, the logic of the understanding is overly formalistic and mechanical because of its lack of attention to meanings or semantics. Unlike the logic of the understanding, Hegel says, Aristotle did not treat the syllogism in a purely formalistic way (§187R). Although Hegel does not mention the fact that Aristotle regarded the premises of the syllogism as transitive here, he clearly allies his own logic with Aristotle's in this passage and accepts Aristotle's rejection of a fourth figure for the syllogism. He might well have been aware of and adopted other features of Aristotle's logic as well, such as the transitivity of the premises.

If the premises of the syllogism are transitive, then the whole syllogism is reversible. Hegel can deny that the syllogisms are reversible, I would like to suggest, only if he treats the syllogisms in the overly formalistic way that he criticizes as part of the "logic of the understanding" in the discussion of Aristotle in the *Encyclopaedia*. In the syllogisms Hegel outlines for the *Science of Logic*, U never occupies the first position. But denying U a placement in the first position would not only run counter to Hegel's claim in SL that each element has occupied all three positions within the syllogism during the development of Qualitative Syllogism, it would also treat the syllogism in an overly formalistic way. It would suggest that the formal placement of the terms within the syllogism is more important than are their semantic relationships with each other, or that syntactic position is more important than semantic meaning. It would be similar to suggesting that the subject of a sentence must always come first, no matter what the words mean, so that, in the sentence "tall is the man," for instance, "the man" is not the subject of the sentence because it is not in the first position, even though the meanings of the terms still make "the man" the subject of the sentence, and "tall" a description of that subject.

An emphasis on meaning is also compatible with the syllogism's roots in Apodictic Judgment, the stage of judgment that generated the syllogism. In Apodictic Judgment, a singularity (S) is related to a universal (U) through its particularity (P) or constitution—or S is related to U through P. This judgment gave rise to the First Figure of Qualitative Syllogism (Fig. 4.36), which had the form S-P-U, or S goes through P to U. So long as we keep the definitions of S, P and U in mind, S-P-U can be just as easily put in reverse order as U-P-S, or by saying that a universal is related to a singularity through the particularity (or the constitution of the singularity). It is more natural in English (and German) to say "a 'this,' given its constitution, is a house (or is captured by the concept of house)"—which has the form S-P-U. But it means exactly the same thing to say "house (or the concept of house), given the constitution (particularity) of the 'this,' captures the 'this' (singularity)"—which has the form U-P-S.

What about those passages in EL suggesting that the specific order of the outside terms offered by that text is crucial to the logical development? Seeing the syllogisms as reversible does not undermine the ability to make sense of Hegel's explanation for the development. Take the syllogism in the First Figure (S-P-U), for instance. Hegel says that U steps across the syllogism from the First Figure to take the place of the immediate subject in the Second Figure (U-S-P) (§187). We ordinarily think of the subject of a sentence as what comes first in a sentence, but the placement of the subject first in a sentence is a function of custom, and is not required by the nature of sentences themselves. Reversing "the man is tall" to "tall is the man" does not change the fact that "man" is the subject of the sentence. Even in reverse order, the man is what the sentence is about—the subject—while "tall" is a description of that subject. The sentence is not about "tall" or tallness itself, and the man is not a description of "tall" or tallness. Similarly, S or singularity is defined in the First Figure as the immediate subject of the syllogism. When U steps across the syllogism to take S's place as the element now defined as the immediate subject in the Second Figure, it does not matter whether U comes at the end of the syllogism or at the beginning—whether the Second Figure is U-S-P or P-S-U. What matters is that U has now been defined as the immediate subject of the syllogism. Just as "the man" was the subject of the sentence no matter where it occurred in the sentence, so U is now the subject of the syllogism, whether it comes first or last. What matters is the meaning or definition given to U in relation to the other terms, rather than merely its formal placement as first or third within the syllogism.

We can also still make sense of Hegel's explanation in EL for how U moves to the middle position in the Third Figure (P-U-S). Again, Hegel says that U moves into the middle position in the Third Figure because the Second Figure (U-S-P) "locks the universal together with the particular," defines U as something-particular (*Besonderes*), and therefore moves U into the middle position of particularity in the Third Figure (§187). I argued above that this explanation of the logical development fits more naturally with EL's account of the order of the outside terms, since the conclusion of the Second Figure—"U is P"—characterizes U as something-particular, or as a unity of singularity and particularity, and therefore explains why U would move into the middle position in the Third Figure. The reversed premise, by contrast—"P is U" or "particularity is universality"—characterizes P rather than U, and would therefore not seem to explain why universality should move into the middle position in the Third Figure. However, the claim "universality is particularity" characterizes a relationship between U and P that remains the same no matter what order the terms are in. That relationship characterizes U as P and P as U at the same time. "P is U" defines P as a singularity in relation to U. P is one of U's particularities: if U is "bird," P is "sparrow," for instance. The sparrow as a type is just one of the particularities of U. It is one (singular) particularity of U. Hence, P is a singular in relation to U. Because P was already defined as the unity of singularity and universality in the First Figure, however, the conclusion of the Second Figure does not change the definition of P. It only changes the definition of U. It locks the universal together with the particular, defines U as something-particular, and moves U into the middle position as the unity of singularity and particularity.

The claim that the syllogisms are reversible, however, does require us to give up the explanation Hegel offered *in SL* for the position that U has in the Second Figure (P-S-U). Hegel argues that, since the the conclusion ("S is U") of the First Figure (S-P-U) establishes U's status as the predicate, U remains the predicate in the Second Figure, or stays in the same place in the Second Figure that it was in in the First Figure. If the syllogism is reversible, however, then U could be either first or third in the Second Figure, and need not be confined to the third position. There are several good reasons for abandoning Hegel's explanation here. First, as I have already suggested, it is not compatible with his claim later that all three elements have occupied all three positions within the syllogism. Second, I argued, it treats the syllogism in the overly formalistic way that Hegel says is the hallmark of the "logic of the understanding." Finally, it is not consistent with one of the other claims Hegel makes about the Second Figure. Hegel claims that this syllogism (P-S-U) violates the usual form of the syllogism, so that the middle term, S, is either both subject or both predicate in the judgments of the syllogism. In that case, the Second Figure has to be written out as either "P is S, U is S, therefore P is U," or as "S is P, S is U, therefore P is U." If it is written out in the first way, then U is the subject of the second premise, thereby undermining Hegel's claim that U remains the predicate.

In any case, Hegel should have regarded the syllogisms as reversible for an important logical reason. As I suggested in the Introduction to this book, Hegel's logic can qualify as a *logic* only if there is some sense of necessity driving the stages. I have suggested that much of the necessity that drives Hegel's logic is a kind of exhaustion: once all of the current options are exhausted, then a move to a new stage or strategy is necessitated (see Chapter Two, Section V). If Hegel is to succeed in showing that the development of the syllogism is *necessary*, he needs the premises within the syllogisms to be transitive and the syllogisms themselves to be reversible. The fact that Hegel has offered two different versions of the development of Qualitative Syllogism in EL and SL suggests that neither treatment is exhaustive. EL fails to discuss several possible formulations of Qualitative Syllogism—namely, those that appear in SL—and SL also fails to discuss several possible formulations of Qualitative Syllogism—namely, those that appear in EL. Since both versions leave out possible formulations of the syllogism, the move to the next stage could hardly be said to be driven by exhaustion. In each presentation, some options—some formulations of the Qualitative Syllogism—have not been exhausted.

If the judgments within the syllogism are transitive and the syllogisms are reversible, however, then the three figures for Qualitative Syllogism that Hegel offers in EL exhaust all possible permutations and formulations of the syllogism. In purely mathematical terms, there are six possible permutations for the whole syllogism: S-P-U, U-S-P, P-U-S, U-P-S, P-S-U, and S-U-P. Because each of these schemes for the syllogism actually stands for a more complex series of judgments, however, there are more permutations of the syllogism than just these six. Each syllogism-scheme breaks down into a series of judgments. S-P-U, for instance, breaks down into the syllogistic argument: "S is P, P is U, therefore S is U." Since each of the judgments within this argument can (mathematically speaking) be reversed, then there are several possible permutations for each of the six syllogisms themselves. There is a pattern to these different mathematical formulations of the syllogism. The six main schemes for the syllogism are made up of three schemes plus the reverse of each of those three schemes: U-P-S is the reverse of S-P-U; P-S-U is the reverse of U-S-P; and S-U-P is the reverse of P-U-S. If Hegel's syllogisms are reversible, then three syllogisms can be used to represent all six. Indeed, the very three syllogisms Hegel offers in EL—S-P-U, U-S-P, P-U-S—understood to be reversible can stand for all six syllogisms. If the judgments within each syllogism are reversible, then each of these syllogisms can be used to represent all of its possible permutations. Thus, all of the possible mathematical permutations of the syllogism, as well as the permutations within each syllogism, can be represented with only the three syllogisms Hegel outlines in EL—so long as the judgments within each of these syllogisms are transitive, and each syllogism itself is reversible.

EL's presentation of Qualitative Syllogism is superior to SL's in part because the three syllogisms it offers are exhaustive in this sense. Two possible triads of syllogisms are exhaustive: (1) S-P-U, U-S-P, P-U-S (which is the triad offered by EL) and (2) U-P-S, P-S-U, S-U-P. These triads are exhaustive because each term occupies all three positions within the triad—a feature that Hegel uses in both SL and EL to justify the move to the next stage of Mathematical Syllogism. Moreover, (2) is simply the reversal of each of the individual syllogisms in (1). While the *Encyclopaedia* offers the first triad, the *Science of Logic* arguably offers the second—except that the first syllogism is reversed, since it is S-P-U, when it should be U-P-S. So long as the syllogisms themselves are reversible, however, and so long as the judgments within each syllogism are transitive, as I have suggested, then the development of the Qualitative Syllogism in both EL and SL are exhaustive in the sense that each includes every possible permutation of the syllogism.

Seeing the syllogisms as reversible does not undercut the overall explanation Hegel offers in SL for the development of Qualitative Syllogism (see p. 384). Hegel says the moves to the Second (P-S-U) and Third (S-U-P) Figures in SL were driven by the need to establish the premises ("S is P" and "P is U") of the First Figure (S-P-U). If the judgments within the syllogisms are transitive and the syllogisms are reversible, then SL's presentation could be revised so that S, P and U occupy all three positions within the syllogism without sacrificing SL's justification for the logical development. If (1) the First Figure were reversed to read "U-P-S," or (2) the Second Figure were reversed to read "U-S-P," then all three terms would occupy all positions within the triad of syllogisms. The logical development in SL could still be driven by the need to prove "S is P" and "P is U," so long as we (a) reversed the order of the premises generated by the reversed syllogism (from "U is P; P is S" to "S is P; P is U"), or (b) flipped the concluding judgment of the revised Second Figure (to "P is U" from "U is P"). If the judgments are transitive, then reversing the premises or the conclusion would not alter the logical significance of the figures.

Moreover, if the judgments within the syllogism are transitive, then the Second and Third Figures from EL and SL (see Fig. 4.41) are equivalent. Here are the two syllogisms generated by the two Second Figures, for instance:

	The *Encyclopaedia:*	The *Science of Logic:*
	U is **S**	**P** is **S**
	S is **P**	**S** is **U**
Therefore:	**U** is **P**	**P** is **U**

Figure 4.42

If the individual judgments are transitive, then the conclusions of these two syllogisms are the same: "U is P" is same as "P is U." The premises of the two syllogisms are also the same. The second premise from EL—"S is P"—would be the same as the first premise from SL—"P is S." And the first premise from EL—"U is S"—would be equivalent to the second premise from SL—"S is U." Hence the whole syllogism in EL—U-P-S—is the same as the syllogism in SL—P-S-U. As suggested above, if the judgments within the syllogism are transitive, then the order of the outside terms does not matter, making the whole syllogism itself reversible. And if the syllogisms are reversible, then the second and third syllogisms of EL and SL are the same. Indeed, the entire series of syllogisms or figures offered by EL and SL (Fig. 4.41) would be the same.

Therefore, the two versions of the development of Qualitative Syllogism in SL and EL can be reconciled, so long as the judgments of the syllogism are transitive and the syllogisms themselves are reversible. Moreover, SL and EL reach similar logical conclusions: the type of singularity evolves; the syllogisms are mutually supporting; the three elements are the same as one another in terms of both content and form; and the development leads to the Mathematical Syllogism. While the two versions can be reconciled, the outline that EL offers is superior to the outline offered by SL because EL offers one of the two exhaustive triads of syllogisms, while SL mixes the two exhaustive triads together. I will return from time to time to the issue of whether we should see the judgments as transitive and the syllogisms as reversible as we go through the logical development of the rest of the syllogisms.

The Quantitative or Mathematical Syllogism

The development of the Qualitative Syllogism in both EL and SL leads to the same end: the Quantitative (as it is called in EL) or Mathematical (as it is called in both texts) Syllogism. I will depict the syllogism in a moment, after I discuss some more interpretive issues.

At the end of Qualitative Syllogism, each element—S, P and U—is defined as singularity/particularity/universality in terms of both content and form (or presentation). All three therefore have the same character or quality, and so can no longer be distinguished from one another in virtue of their quality. They can be distinguished only in terms of their quantity. This logical situation is similar to the one that was developed at the end of the Doctrine of Quality, in which quality could no longer distinguish the logical elements in play, so that there was only some quantity of indistinguishable elements (see Attraction). Similarly, here, there are three indistinguishable elements defined as the same as, like, or equal to each other. Because they cannot be distinguished, the logic can no longer refer to them as "S" and "P" and "U." There are just three elements, each of which "is" also the other. This "is" is the "is" of identity, defined in the way in which the understanding defines identity, i.e. as equivalence. Qualitative Syllogism thus generates the Mathematical Syllogism, which says that if two things are equal to a third, then they are equal to each other (§188).

The *Encyclopaedia Logic* does not indicate—either in the text that Hegel wrote, or in the Additions drawn from his students' class notes—how Hegel would express this stage. As I will argue in a moment, I think variables are best because they express that there are three items that cannot be distinguished from one another. This is the same problem that led Hegel to use variables in the Hypothetical Judgment of Necessity. Using variables would give the following figure for this syllogism:

A = B = C

Figure 4.43

The *Science of Logic* characterizes this stage in terms of universality: U = U = U. Hegel offers two reasons in SL for why this syllogism should be expressed in terms of universality. First, since U was the middle term in the Third Figure (S-U-P), it served as the mediating element that linked the other two terms together. Thus, the Third Figure expressed the objective truth that S and P must be mediated by universality. We saw this same idea in the discussion of the Second Figure for SL above (Fig. 4.37). In that Second Figure, S and P are not related to one another directly. They are only related to one another through U, because P is a universal in relation to S. The Third Figure in SL (S-U-P) expresses this truth. It says that S and P must be held together by U. As a result, universality certainly seems to be the element that captures the essence of the connection between S and P. However, this argument for using U to characterize the Mathematical Syllogism is weak. Even if U defines the *connection* between S and P, it does not seem to follow that S itself and P itself have become U, as the U-U-U formulation suggests. Of course, S and P *have* become U, but U has also become S and P—they are each defined by universality, particularity *and* singularity. There therefore seems to be no justification for defining all three terms with just one of the characters that they have (namely, universality).

Hegel offers a second reason in SL, however, for defining all three elements as universality. Although universality is the middle term that links S and P together in the Third Figure (S-U-P), U is still characterized as abstract universality. It is a universality that is not completely defined. Because U is abstract, Hegel suggests, it is not associated with either singularity or particularity. To say U is abstract is just to say that it has no particular character (no P), and no one (singular) expression (no S). U is indifferent and external to the specificity of S and P. As a result, there are three elements defined as the same as one another by (abstract) universality, in a relationship of identity or sameness that must be fixed by something external to them. Since (abstract) universality defines all three elements as the same as one another, they are the same as one another *as universality*. Hence S and P are universality. Moreover, the sort of relationship they have is a relationship of equality or likeness: the universalities are the same as one another as a result of a comparison made by a third term (cf. Likeness and Unlikeness in Chapter Three). That relationship yields the fourth figure of Qualitative Syllogism, the Mathematical Syllogism: U-U-U.

Again, however, this argument does not seem very strong. Although the terms in the conclusion ("S is P") of the Third Figure (S-U-P) are indifferent toward one another—insofar as either term could be the single thing, subject or subsumed element while the other is the category, predicate or subsuming element—they are not categories (or universals) *at the same time*. The conclusion that they are both defined by universality therefore does not seem to follow. Moreover, in SL, Hegel also characterizes the Mathematical Syllogism as "relationless." To say that it is "relationless" is to say that it is no longer possible to specify what the terms' relationships with one another are like. The meaning of the terms defines what their relationships are like. S was supposed to be a *singular* in relation to U and P; P was supposed to be a *particular* in relation to S and U; U was supposed to be a *universal* in relation to S and P. They get their definitions, characters or meanings in relation to one another. Hegel's suggestion that the terms are "relationless" thus implies that they have lost their meanings, their definitions or distinctive characters in relation to one another. Since universality is one of their meanings or characters, if they have no meanings, then they could not be defined by universality.

Because the elements have lost their meanings, they are best represented by variables, rather than by universality. The use of variables captures the quantitative or mathematical nature of this syllogism: it suggests there are three elements that cannot be distinguished from one another in terms of their qualities or characters. Hegel does not repeat SL's formulation of the Mathematical Syllogism in EL, I think, because he is unhappy with defining all three elements as U. Although the *Encyclopaedia* does not offer a formulation for the Mathematical

Syllogism, its emphasis on a comparison with mathematics points toward a formulation using variables. Moreover, since universality is a quality in Qualitative Syllogism, SL's use of U to characterize the Mathematical Syllogism does not fit with the idea that the category of quality has fallen away. Finally, since Hegel used variables in earlier stages for reasons similar to the ones that apply here, using variables here is more consistent with earlier portions of the logic than is the formulation offered in the *Science of Logic*.

Because this syllogism grows out of what cannot be done—namely, that the three elements cannot be distinguished from one another qualitatively—this stage is the *negative* outcome of the failure of Qualitative Syllogism.

The Syllogism of Reflection

There is also a positive outcome, however, to Qualitative Syllogism. Each moment has occupied every position in the syllogism. Because the character of the positions is defined by the basic form of the syllogism, and because each term has occupied the middle position and each outside position, they each have taken on the character of the other two terms. The negative result of this change is that they all have the same quality as singularity/particularity/universality, and so cannot be distinguished from one another. But the positive result is that each term has a more complicated character than before. The next type of syllogism follows out this positive result by exploring in more detail the complex character that each moment now has, given the development of Qualitative Syllogism.

According to the development so far, each moment—S, P and U—has its own character and is defined by the other two elements in an external way because of the different positions it occupied. Each moment is what it is and *reflects* the other two moments. When I used to work for a city alderman, for instance, I had my own character when taken by myself (i.e. in an "in-itself" sense), but I reflected the identity of the alderman because of my position in his office. The moments of the syllogism have a similar reflection. They each have their own character, when taken by themselves in an "in itself" sense, but they reflect the identities of the other two moments because of the positions they have occupied within the syllogism during the development of Qualitative Syllogism. Just as the job that I did for the alderman gave me the character of reflecting his identity, so the job that each moment of the syllogism does when it occupies each position in the triad of syllogisms gives it the character of reflecting the identity of each of those jobs or positions. In addition to having its own character, because each moment occupied each of the positions defined by the other moments, each *reflects* the character of those other two moments. The fact that each element is what it is and reflects the characters of the other two elements leads to the development of the next category of syllogism, the Syllogism of Reflection.

While the diagrams of these stages illustrate the syllogisms in a way that suggests the outside terms have a certain order, I have argued that all of the syllogisms are reversible (see Comparing the EL and SL Developments of Qualitative Syllogism). Because the triad of syllogisms in these stages places each of the terms in the middle position, and because the syllogisms are reversible, each triad of syllogisms represents every possible permutation of the syllogism. The triad of syllogisms Hegel offers is therefore exhaustive.

The Syllogism of Allness: the First Figure of the Syllogism of Reflection

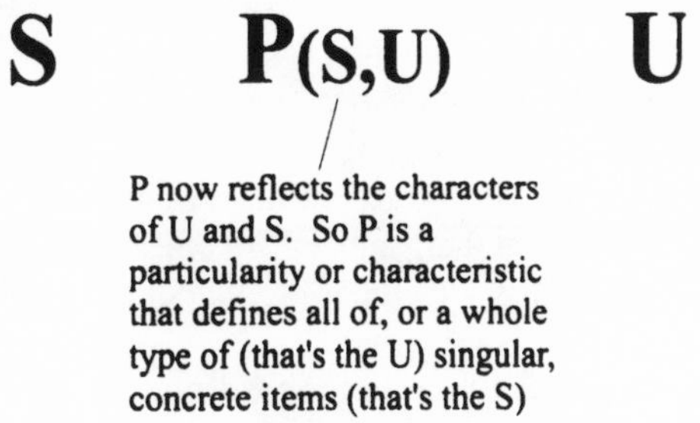

S P(S,U) U

P now reflects the characters of U and S. So P is a particularity or characteristic that defines all of, or a whole type of (that's the U) singular, concrete items (that's the S)

Figure 4.44

The development of Qualitative Syllogism produced two overall results. First, each of the terms has its own definition but also reflects the definitions of the other two moments (§189). Because each of the terms of the syllogism is now more defined, the whole syllogism itself has evolved into a more defined type of syllogism. This new kind of syllogism is defined by being defined. Since concepts are defined by having a particularity, this new sort of syllogism is defined by or held together by the fact that it is now particularized. Hence, it is the sort of syllogism that is once again held together by particularity. Particularity moves back into the middle position of the syllogism.

Second, the mediation of the whole triad of syllogisms has been completed because the premises of each syllogism are established by the other two syllogisms, so that the three syllogisms mutually support one another (§189). As a result, the type of definition or particularity that is holding the syllogism together has to reflect this completed mediation. That means that the particularity has to be defined in a way that links S, P and U together all at once. P or particularity links S, P and U together all at once by being the sort of P or particularity that treats S as a U, in the sense that P applies to S as a type, or to the type of thing that S is. Although S and U also reflect the characters of the other two moments—since they, too, occupied all three positions in the syllogism during the development of Qualitative Syllogism—that logical conclusion is not yet drawn out in this stage. In this First Figure (Fig. 4.44), we return to the basic form of the syllogism—S-P-U—but P now reflects S and U: S-P(S,U)-U. It can be written out as "S is P(S,U); P(S,U) is U; therefore S is U."

Hegel uses a classic example of a syllogism from ancient Greek philosophy to illustrate this sort of syllogism (§191R). The classic syllogism is usually written like this: "all men are mortal; Caius is a man; therefore Caius is mortal." To fit Hegel's basic form of the syllogism, however, we would have to write the syllogism like this instead: "Caius (S) is a man (P(S,U)); all men (P(S,U)) are mortal (U); therefore Caius (S) is mortal (U)." In this syllogism, the particularity "man" applies to S as a type or as the type of thing that S is: Caius is the type of thing that is man, or all S's like Caius are men. P is no longer merely any abstract character of S, as it was in the First Figure of Qualitative Syllogism (Fig. 4.36). Now, P must reflect both singularity and universality. P reflects these characters by being a characteristic of S that defines all of the singular, concrete items to which S belongs (even if it is only one characteristic among others). In other words, P applies to all of a type (this is how P reflects U) of singular, concrete items (which is how P reflects S). P is a universal characteristic of the S, and therefore reflects both universality and singularity. So if S is Caius, for instance, then P must apply to all of the kind of thing that S is, such as "man."

Although the fact that P must apply to all the S's shows that P reflects universality, the universality of "allness" is still a low or basic level of universality. The universal "all men," for instance, is built or defined from the bottom up. "All men" means all individual men taken together, and is therefore still attached to the singularity of individual men. This attachment to singularity will become important in the next stage.

Notice that the Syllogism of Allness corrects for the problem that the First Figure of the Qualitative Syllogism (Fig. 4.36) had. Because P was abstract in that syllogism, any old characteristic of the singular could be plugged in for P. Which characteristic of S would be picked out by P was completely contingent and hence arbitrary. Here, however, P is no longer completely abstract. It is somewhat defined: P has a character such that, in addition to being P, it reflects S and U. That definition specifies more precisely the kinds of characteristics that can be plugged in for P(S,U) in this syllogism, therefore making the syllogism less contingent or arbitrary than was the First Figure of Qualitative Syllogism. Again, P(S,U) must pick out a characteristic of S that applies to all S's. Caius's mortality is a characteristic that applies to all men, or applies to Caius insofar as he is a man, for instance. Caius may also be tall, thin, dark, brave, and moody, but none of those characteristics apply to all men as a kind. While any of those characteristics could have been plugged in for P in the Qualitative Syllogism, they cannot be plugged in here. Of course, there may still be more than one P for any S. Caius may belong to different types of things: he is human, a man (gendered), a slave or citizen, and so on. There are different P's that could characterize Caius as a type. That's why Hegel makes clear that P(S,U) may still be only one defining characteristic among others (§190). Still, because P(S,U) is defined somewhat, it is no longer completely abstract, and therefore no longer completely contingent.

While the Syllogism of Allness corrects for the defect in First Figure of Qualitative Syllogism (Fig. 4.36), it has its own defect. One of its premises presupposes its conclusion. Since the particularity ("all men") is being defined from the bottom up by the individuals that make it up, the premise "all men are mortal" is established by induction, or by noticing the mortality of individual men and concluding that all men are mortal. But all men are inductively mortal only if Caius, who is a man, is also mortal. So the premise "all men are mortal" presupposes the conclusion that Caius is mortal. The whole argument is therefore circular.

What is really holding this syllogism together, then, is all the singularities. Whether Caius is really linked to mortality depends on all the Caius's—on all the things of the same type as Caius, or all the men. The next syllogism draws out this conclusion by moving S into the middle position, which is the position that now holds the two outside terms together.

The Syllogism of Induction: the Second Figure of the Syllogism of Reflection

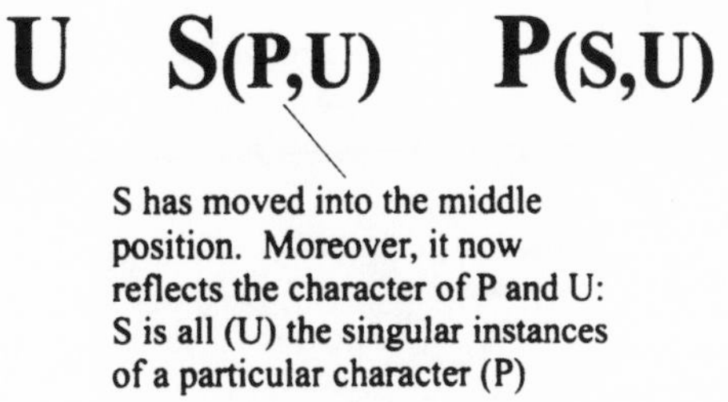

U S(P,U) P(S,U)

S has moved into the middle position. Moreover, it now reflects the character of P and U: S is all (U) the singular instances of a particular character (P)

Figure 4.45

S moves into position as the middle term, because it turned out to be what is really holding the syllogism together in the last stage. Moreover, S's character was changed by the development of Qualitative Syllogism. S is defined not only as singularity, but now also reflects both particularity and universality. S is S(P,U). In Qualitative Syllogism, S evolved from a single individual to an individual with a character as "what it is" that was connected to a universal. S is therefore a singularity with a character ("what it is") of a certain *kind* (or universal). The singularity that is holding the syllogism together is all of the singularities with a character of a certain kind (see the last stage). The syllogism is inductive because the connection between the P (character or particularity) and U (the universal that all the S's share) is established by examining each of the S's in turn, i.e. by induction. The Addition to §190 in the *Encyclopaedia* gives the following example for the Syllogism of Induction: gold is a metal; silver is a metal; copper is a metal; lead is a metal etc. (where gold, silver etc. are S, and being a metal is P); all these bodies (all the S's) are conductors of electricity (U); therefore all metals (P) are conductors of electricity (U). The character of being a metal (P) is linked to the concept of being a conductor of electricity (U) by each of the types of metals (the S's).

Although the Additions were put together by Hegel's students and not by Hegel, the example in §190A reinforces the suggestion that the syllogisms are reversible and the premises of the syllogisms are transitive. First, the Addition says that the Syllogism of Induction has the form U-S-P, but the example illustrates the figure P-S-U, not U-S-P. The same example can be used to illustrate the figure U-S-P by rewriting it this way: "one conductor of electricity is gold, one is silver, one is copper and so on (until all metals are listed)("U is S"); gold, silver copper and so on (until all metals are listed) are all the metals ("S is P"); therefore conductors of electricity are all the metals ("U is P")"—or, in more natural English, "therefore, all the metals are conductors of electricity" ("P is U," or the reversal of the conclusion). Second, the example violates the standard format for writing out syllogisms by reversing the first premise. Ordinarily, the syllogism P-S-U would be written out as "P is S; S is U; therefore P is U." The example, however, takes the form "S is P; S is U; therefore P is U," in which the order of the first premise is reversed from the standard format. The example can be written in the standard format. Since S is all the instances of metal, they could be listed first: "a metal is silver; a metal is gold; a metal is copper," and so on, or in more natural English, "one metal is gold; another metal is silver; another metal is copper, etc." Putting the first premises this way follows the standard format, since each of the clauses "one metal is gold; one metal is silver; one metal is copper" and so on has the form "P is S" rather than "S is P."

This example also illustrates Hegel's claim that a syllogism can have more than three judgments (see the First Figure of Qualitative Syllogism [Fig. 4.36]), since the first sort of premise ("S is P") would occur as many times as there are metals.

Hegel's discussion of the Syllogism of Induction in the *Science of Logic* also reinforces the suggestion that he intends the syllogisms to be reversible. In SL, he says that the Syllogism of Induction expresses the objective truth that an immediate genus (such as metal) characterizes itself through all the singulars as a universal property (Hegel 1969, 690). Because the immediate genus is P, the singulars are S, and the universal property is U, this comment suggests that the Syllogism of Induction has the form P-S-U. SL explicitly gives the Syllogism of Induction the form U-S-P, however. These conflicting remarks suggest that the order of the outside terms of the syllogism is unimportant.

The Syllogism of Induction moves beyond the mere perception of qualities—which characterized Qualitative Syllogism—to *experience*. Perception is immediate, while experience requires reflective thought or concept (cf. the stage of Inner and Outer). The Qualitative Syllogisms picked out qualities of S in an immediate way: the rose, for instance, was red because it looked red in an immediate way. The Syllogism of Induction, however, picks out qualities of S in a way that requires reflective thought. All the S's must be compared with one another in thought before a universal can be found that belongs to them all.

The Syllogism of Analogy: The Third Figure of the Syllogism of Reflection

P(S,U) U(S,P) S(P,U)

U has moved into the middle position. Moreover, it now reflects the character of S and P

Figure 4.46

The trouble with the Syllogism of Induction is that it can never be finished, as Hegel apparently suggested in a lecture (§190A). The claim "all ravens are black" can mean only that all the ravens observed so far are black. The claim that absolutely *all* ravens are black involves applying an additional principle of reasoning or another syllogism, namely, an analogy. The syllogism of analogy is used to conclude that, because all of the things of a certain type observed so far have a certain characteristic or particularity, then, by analogy, everything else of that type will have the same characteristic or particularity. Because all of the ravens observed so far have been black, everything else that is the same type—namely ravens—will have the same characteristic—namely, black. This analogy, along with the previous induction, would lead to the conclusion that absolutely *all* ravens are black. What is holding the syllogism together now, then, is the universal, kind or type. Whether or not the singularities have the particularity or not depends on whether they are the same type of thing, on whether they share a universality. Thus U moves back into the middle position as what is holding the syllogism together. Hegel apparently gave the following example for the Syllogism of Analogy: all planets observed so far obey such and such law of motion; therefore any newly discovered planet will also (§190A).

The universality in the middle position here is not simply defined as U, however. As was developed in Qualitative Syllogism, it must reflect both S and P. The type of universal in this stage is more advanced than the universal of "allness" that was in the First (Fig. 4.44) and Second (Fig. 4.45) Figures of the Syllogism of Reflection. The universal is no longer a mere aggregate or bunch of singular things, but a kind or type of thing. We saw the same sort of development in the definition of universality in Chapter Two. In the stage of Being-for-itself, a universal was defined at first merely as an aggregate or group (comm*un*ality), but then had a character of its own when the group was taken together to be a one according to some shared character (comm*on*ality). There is the same development in universality here: at first the universal was an "all" or group, but then came to be taken together as a type or kind according to some shared character or particularity. Because the universal is a type or kind of thing, it reflects the character of singularity—it is a one (as one kind of thing). Moreover, because the universal is now some certain kind of thing, its universality reflects the character of particularity as well—it is a kind of thing with some character, or a particular kind of thing. U is thus U(S,P).

Because the universal is a one with a character or particularity of its own, it no longer needs the aggregate of things to define it. Since it is a one (S) that has its own content (P), it has the sort of relationship with the subsistent things that it embraces—its content—that defined Universality in the stage of Universality: it is a one or whole that *presents* its contents or those subsistent things *for itself*, or through its own process. It characterizes itself internally on its own by presenting its particularity. Because it is capable of having its definition on its own through its own process, it no longer needs the aggregate of things to define it from the bottom up. The universal is a type of universal that is defined from the top down. We use the universal "raven," for instance, to decide whether some S is black. We decide whether the S is a raven, then we conclude that the S is black. We no longer use the S's to establish the blackness, we use the universal "raven" to establish the blackness. This shift from a bottom-up to a top-down strategy redefined the Concept as Universality (see Universality). The universal is now defined as doubly "for itself" or as "in and for itself"—it is a one that determines or defines itself from the top down by embracing the S's or singularities (the "for-itselfness" of content) *for itself*, or through its own process (the "for itselfness" of form), by *presenting* its contents, which gives it an "in itself" relationship with that content. It contains the S's, but has an independent character of its own beyond those S's. In Hegel's technical language, it is essentially determined within itself (§191). The universal of "allness," by contrast, just is the aggregate of S's, so it depended on those S's for its definition, and could not characterize itself independently.

Hegel makes clear in SL that his Syllogism of Analogy is intended to mirror the so-called argument from analogy in traditional logic. An argument from analogy has the following general form:

A has characteristic C
B has characteristic C
Therefore, A and B are the same
A has characteristic D
Since A and B are the same
B has characteristic D

A classic example of an argument from analogy is the traditional argument for the existence of God called the argument from design:

a watch (A) appears to be designed (C)
the world (B) appears to be designed (C)
therefore a watch and the world are the same
a watch (A) has a designer (D)
because a watch (A) and the world (B) are the same
the world (B) must have a designer (D)
(God is that designer, therefore God exists)

As Hegel points out, however, the standard form of the argument from analogy has four elements (namely, A, B, C and D), rather than only three, which is what the standard form of the syllogism requires. Hegel suggests that the standard form of the argument from analogy can be converted to three elements because A is taken to be a concrete universal, that is, a universal with a characteristic. A is taken in its C-ness, or, using the example above, the watch is taken in its C-ness, which is to say, the watch is taken to stand, in general, for a designed thing:

The world is a type of thing (S[U,P]) *that is a watch or an appears-to-be-designed type of thing* (P[S,U])

A watch or an appears-to-be-designed type of thing (P[S,U]) *has a designer* (U[S,P])

Therefore, the world is a type of thing (S[U,P]) *that has a designer* (U[S,P])

The general syllogistic form of the argument from analogy would therefore be:

A (as a C-ness type) (S[U,P]) *is a B* (as the type that is C-ness)(P[S,U])

B (as the type that is C-ness) (P[S,U]) *has D* (U[S,P])

Therefore A (S[U,P]) *has D* (U[S,P])

The weakness of the Syllogism of Analogy is that it is unclear whether A has characteristic D in virtue of its C-ness or whether it has D because it is a particular sort of C (or in virtue of its particularity). Does the watch have a designer because it appears to be designed (its C-ness), or is it just a particular appears-to-be-designed type of thing that has a designer? Do appears-to-be-designed things as a type always have a designer? This question points toward the weakness of the Syllogism of Analogy. Like the Syllogism of Allness, the Syllogism of Analogy presupposes what it is supposed to show: it is only if the world, as an appears-to-be-designed thing, has a designer, that (all) appears-to-be-designed things—as a type of thing—have designers. The world might well be a counter-example, or an example of an appears-to-be-designed thing that does not in fact have a designer.

Take another example, which is drawn from SL:

The moon is a type of thing (S[P,U]) *that is an earth, or an orbiting body in this solar system (OBSS)*(U[S,P])

The earth as an OBSS (U[S,P]) *is inhabited* (P[S,U])

Therefore, the moon (as an OBSS)(S[P,U]) *is inhabited* (P[S,U])

This syllogism obviously fails, and it fails because the earth is inhabited not in virtue of being an OBSS, but because it is a particular type of OBSS, namely, one with an atmosphere and so on.

Although the Syllogism of Analogy shares the weakness of the Syllogism of Allness, it is still a more advanced syllogism than the Syllogism of Allness. We are no longer talking about the world or the moon as an uncharacterized, singular type, such as "the rose." Instead, the world and the moon are now characterized as particular types of thing—as a type of thing that appears to be designed, in the case of the former, and as the type of thing that is an orbiting body in this solar system, in the case of the latter. They are S's that are particular (P) kinds (U) of thing—i.e. S(P,U)'s. So S is no longer simply a singular type, but a singular that is also a particular type. S is a concrete singularity—a characterized type, or a singularity as a type with a character.

The Syllogism of Necessity

The failure of the Syllogism of Analogy leads to the Syllogism of Necessity. Guaranteeing the truth of the syllogism requires going beyond a stage that relies on immediate connections between S, P and U to a stage in which the connections are necessary. The connection between the earth as an orbiting body and its being inhabited is simply an immediate one, for instance—that the earth is inhabited is simply given or found. The reliance on that immediate connection led to the weakness of the Syllogism of Analogy because something that is an immediate characteristic of the earth (being inhabited, or P) was ascribed to the earth as an orbiting body in general (U), or to the type of thing that the earth is. Overcoming this weakness will require a syllogism in which the terms are necessarily connected—a Syllogism of Necessity. If P were the characteristic of being in motion, for instance, then P and U would necessarily be connected to one another. The earth as an orbiting body is necessarily in motion (it orbits), in which case the analogy between the moon and the earth would work: the moon, as an orbiting body, is indeed in motion.

Categorical Syllogism: the First Figure of the Syllogism of Necessity

S(P,U) P(S,U) U(S,P)

P is back in the middle position. It captures the category of S, or the type that S is

Figure 4.47

The failure of the Syllogism of Analogy suggests that the term that is really holding the syllogism together is the concrete universal, or the particular type (P[S,U]) that characterizes S. The analogy between the earth and moon works because of the particular type of thing that they are, namely, orbiting bodies. Characteristics that belong to them as orbiting bodies—such as being in motion—will be characteristics that they share. Since what is holding the syllogism together is the particular type, P returns to the middle position

To see what character P now has, we have to review parts of the development of the Syllogism of Reflection. P is still a P(S,U), as it was in the Syllogism of Induction, but it is now an even more sophisticated P(S,U). In the Syllogism of Induction, P linked S and U together all at once by being the sort of particularity that treated S as a U, or applied to S as a type or to the type of thing that S is. P was a particularity of each of the S's. The Syllogism of Induction was imperfect, however, because it can never be completed. We can never observe all of the S's, since many of the S's have not happened yet. Nevertheless, the sense that the Syllogism of Induction is imperfect leads to the thought of all the singular instances as a whole kind or type. Although we cannot finish the enumeration of all the singular instances, we *should* or *ought to* carry on the enumeration to infinity. The *demand* to carry out the enumeration to infinity points toward the idea that the genus or type—P—has a defining character or universality "in and for itself," rather than only through the singularities. Having a character "in and for itself" was what defined Universality (see Universality). P is a universal concept. At first, P seemed to depend on the singularities for its character—it was simply a particularity or character that belonged to the singularities. But the thought that we can keep on counting the singularities to infinity suggests that there is something about P itself—some character that P has on its own—that allows us to go on picking out the singularities. Since we can continue to enumerate the S's to infinity, there must be some P that we can use to go on picking out the S's. We can't use the S's to define the P; we must use the P to pick out the S's. In short, P must do the defining work, rather than the singularities. In logical terms, P must have a character or definition on its own that is opposed to the S's (the "in itself" relation) that it gets by having a doubly "for itself" logical relationship with the individual singularities—a relationship in which P embraces but also presents the singularities. This change is the same one that affected U in the Syllogism of Analogy and that repeats the definition of universality. Thus P becomes the same sort of type or universal that U was in the Syllogism of Analogy: it is a universal that has a character of its own ("in itself") that allows it to embrace and define—from the top down—the things that make it up (it is doubly "for itself"). P no longer depends on the S's for its character; it gives the S's their character.

This change in the nature of P defines P more precisely and restricts the sorts of concepts that can be plugged in for the P. In the Syllogism of Analogy, for instance, P could be the characteristic "blackness" that belongs to ravens as a type. Now that P is defined as what gives the S's their character, however, it can no longer be characteristics such as the blackness of the ravens. P must be a character that picks out the ravens, rather than a character that the ravens share. The character "blackness" cannot be used to pick out ravens, since it does not capture the nature of ravens as a type. "Blackness" does not give ravens their character as the type of thing that they are. Other things—even other birds—are also black. Instead, P must be a character that defines ravens as the type of thing that they are: "crow" for instance (the raven is the largest bird in the crow family). The concept of "crow" can be used to pick out ravens, since it gives ravens their character as the type of thing that they are—namely, as ravens.

We can also characterize P's new definition in a different way. Now that P defines the S's from the top down, it is independent of the S's in the sense that it no longer depends on the given or immediate character of the S's for its character. This independence from the given character of the S's means that P has become an *essence*. Essence is defined by a certain level of independence from the world of Being, or from the world of individual thereness (see the Introduction to Chapter Three). Now that P is defining itself on its own, and no longer needs the thereness or character of the individual singularities for its definition, it has developed into an essence. S is no longer a type of thing that has a number of properties, and hence to which a number of universals can apply. Instead, S is a one type of thing that is unified by a character—a particularity—that is captured by P. Hence, P no longer captures any accidental property of S. It captures the (essential) character of S as a type. P characterizes or particularizes the type that S is. P is an essential determination, or essential characterization of S.

Because P is independent of the aggregate of singularities, P is no longer defined by the collection of singularities. Instead, the particular (P) taken together as a type defines S from the top down. The ravens do not define the P: the P defines the ravens. P is P(S, U) as the (singular) type (universal) that characterizes or particularizes S as a type.

The change in P's character explains why we have moved to a new sort of syllogism—to a Syllogism of Necessity. U already had a necessary relationship with S in the Syllogism of Analogy because it was defined as a characterizing universal that was necessary to S, since it grasped and defined the type of thing that the S's are. Since P now has the same relationship with S that U had with S in the Syllogism of Analogy, P is now also necessary to S. It, too, captures the type of thing that S is.

The form of the syllogism also makes the relationship between P and U a necessary one. The form of the syllogism says that S, P and U must be related together as singularity, particularity and universal (see Immediate Syllogism). Since singularity is now defined as a type of thing—the rose as a type, for instance—then S is a type of thing that is a singular (S) in relation to P. The fact that S is a singular in relation to P implies that S is just one type of P—that there must be more than one S, and hence that P is a multitude or group of things. Now that P is defined as the essence of S, P is the defining character of the aggregate of S's. U is defined as a type too. The form of the syllogism says that it is a universal (U) in relation to P. This relationship between U and P defines P as a particularity of U, as a concept or conceptual character that particularizes or defines U. It follows, first, that, just as there was more than one S, there must be more than one P, too—that P is an aggregate in relation to U. Second, it also follows that P is one of the concepts that defines U, or that makes U up. U is an independent, top-down-defining or characterizing ("in and for itself") universal that particularizes, divides, or is defined into P. U is a universal that not only grasps or characterizes S as the type that it is, it also grasps or characterizes P as the type or concept that it is. U is necessarily linked to P as well as to S. Both relationships in the syllogism—the one between S and P and the one between P and U—are characterized by necessity.

Moreover, the form of the syllogism also says that S is linked to U *through* the character of P. Since U was defined as a characterizing universal of S in the Syllogism of Analogy, P must be a go-between concept—one that characterizes S in a way that necessarily links S to U. S must be linked to U only through P.

An example of this sort of syllogism would be lion(S)-panther(P)-feline(U). S still exists and is sensible—it is an existing, sensible kind. The lion is an existing sensible kind because we can find it as a type out there in the world in an immediate way. The lion is a natural kind. Lions share a sensible description and a type of existence or way of life that gathers them together into a natural kind or set. They live with and mate with one another. P is a concept that grasps or characterizes lion as the type that it is. Scientists regard the lion as a kind of panther, which distinguishes the lion from other sorts of cats. Thus P is "panther." U is a concept that grasps or characterizes the essential nature not only of S, but of P as well. U is "feline," the universal that gathers up types of cats, including the panther, which is the type that gathers up lion as a type. U also grasps the essential nature of S *through* P. The lion is a feline; but it is a feline only through the concept of panther. That's because "feline" is a broad, umbrella-term for a number of different types of cats. "Panther," which grasps the type of cat that lions are, is only one type of cat. Lion can be a feline only if there are other types of cats besides panthers, or the type of cats that lions are. Thus there must be other types of cats—other cats besides panthers—before the lion can be a feline. S is one of a multitude, but P must also be one of a multitude before S can be U.

Because P(S,U) captures the essence or defining nature of S, P is the category for S. It is the universal that captures what makes S the type that it is. P is the necessary, essential category to which S belongs. Similarly, because U was defined as a characterizing universal in the Syllogism of Analogy, and because U characterizes not just S but also P, U captures the category of P. It is the necessary, essential category to which P belongs. As a result, the two premises of the syllogism—"S is P" and "P is U"—are Categorical Judgments (see Categorical Judgment). The syllogism is a Categorical Syllogism.

Now that U and P can be defined from the top down, without reference to the P and S respectively, the whole syllogism has become independent in a new way. Not only has the universality or genus become more independent of the singularities, but S, P and U as logical elements have become more independent as well. In particular, they are now being related together on their own, in virtue of the types of things that they are. They no longer need a subjectivity—namely, one of us rational human subjects—to hold them together. "Lion" is related to "panther" because of the natures of "lion" and "panther"; and "panther" is related to "feline" because of the natures of "feline" and "panther." They are gluing themselves together now, and no longer need a third party—a subjectivity—to glue them together. In the First Figure of Qualitative Syllogism (Fig. 4.36), when we were focused on S as singulars such as the rose, for instance, and on P as qualities—redness, and so on—the syllogism needed a third party—a thinking subject—to hold it together. Somebody (some thinking somebody, some subjectivity) had to take the rose, pick out redness as the one property to be focused on, and then draw the conclusion of the syllogism. Even the Third Figure of Qualitative Syllogism (Figs. 4.38 and 4.40), was contingent insofar as a subject or third party had to pick out the universal. Because S, P and U are now being defined according to the types that they are, there is no longer any need for someone to decide (arbitrarily) what characteristic to focus on. S is being characterized as the type that it is by P, and P is being characterized as the type that it is by U. The need for an outside subjectivity to draw out the syllogism—to think it—is falling away. Since the conclusion of the syllogism no longer needs some subjectivity to draw it, it has also become necessary. The syllogism draws its own conclusion, so to speak, necessarily, without any subjectivity to help it. The conclusion—"lion" is "feline"— follows necessarily based on the nature of and syllogistic relationships between "lion," "panther" and "feline" as concepts themselves. A third party or subjectivity need not draw the conclusion.

When the need for a subjectivity to glue the syllogism together falls away completely, we will encounter the category of objectivity, which is the next major sub-section of the Doctrine of the Concept.

While S, P and U are necessarily connected with one another in terms of their content—since P and U capture the essential, defining nature of S and P respectively—the form of the syllogism is still treating them as if they are separable. The form of the syllogism connects them with an "is," and so still implies that they can, in principle, be separated. A syllogism uses judgments, and the form of the judgment in general says that the elements are in principle separable (see The Judgment). Because the syllogism employs the "is" of the judgment between the three terms ("S is P is U"), it inherits the claim that the elements are in principle separable. Therefore, S, P and U are not yet fully connected in terms of their form, or the way in which they are being presented by the syllogism. Their necessary bond is inner—it is conceptual or part of their character as concepts (cf. Transition to the Concept in Chapter Three)—but is not yet being presented or "said" by the syllogism.

Although the connections between S, P and U are necessary, there is still some immediacy in this syllogism, namely, in S. First, S is subsumed under the genus P(S,U) as the middle term, but there is still an indefinite number of other singulars under the same genus. Lions are panthers, for instance, but "panther" also includes other types of cats—black panthers, and so on. So the syllogism is contingent in the sense that only one singularity is being asserted or subsumed under the genus. This contingency gives the syllogism immediacy: that particular singularity is simply given or found to be the relevant one. While the contingency of the previous syllogisms was provided by us—by subjectivity, or subjective consciousness—however, the contingency here is not from us. Before, *we* had to pick out the redness of the rose as the property to be focused on, and so *we* provided the contingency of that syllogism. We picked a given characteristic of S to focus on. P was therefore determined from the bottom up by the nature of the S. Now that P captures S's essential character, there is no longer any need for us to pick what character of S to focus on. S only has one essential character. Instead, the contingency of this syllogism grows out of the fact that there are other S's with the same P-sort of character. It comes from S's own relation to P, based on the character of P. This contingency thus develops from the top down, out of the concept of P itself, or from the nature of P. Because S does not exhaust P, the relationship between them is contingent.

There is a second source of contingency in Categorical Syllogism. Even though we are talking about actuality, and so are beyond talking about realities that do not live up to their concepts, singularity is still tied up with existence. The moment of Singularity grew out of the form of Actuality, or the way in which Actuality was presented, and contains the definition or content of Actuality, insofar as it contains Inner and Outer and their mutually defining relationship, which was the definition of Actuality (see the stage of Singularity). Although S is a type, it includes the way in which the type is presented in actuality. If S is the type "lion," then, it includes the way in which lion has its actuality, or the way in which lion exists. S is thus still defined by immediacy or givenness, since the way in which the type lion happens to exist is found or given. Moreover, it follows that S will also include other characteristics from existence that are not contained in P as its genus or universal nature. For instance, one characteristic of the adult male lion is to have a mane, but that is not a characteristic of the genus panther, to which lion belongs. Lions are also social, which other panthers are not. These additional characteristics that do not belong to P as a type are a contingent factor in S's relation to P. Because P is still defined in relation to the existence of the S's, it has the same contingency in its relation with U. The panther—insofar as it exists—has characteristics that do not belong to all felines too.

So while P and U capture the objective universality or category of S and P respectively, they are still being presented as immediate or contingent. The syllogism is supposed to be necessary, but it is not presenting itself as necessary. The Categorical Judgment had the same weakness.

Hypothetical Syllogism: The Second Figure of the Syllogism of Necessity

If **A** is then **B** is

A is

Therefore **B** is

Figure 4.48

The trouble with the Categorical Syllogism is that it does not "say" or capture the necessary relationships between S, P and U, even though the relationships between S, P and U *are indeed* necessary. The Hypothetical Syllogism corrects this defect in the Categorical Syllogism by "saying" or asserting the necessary relationship between S, P and U.

The Hypothetical Syllogism can succeed in asserting those necessary relationships, however, only by using variables, rather than the terms singularity (S), particularity (P) and universality (U). The contingency or immediacy of the Categorical Syllogism grew out of the specific definition that S had as a singularity in relation to P and out of P's specific character as a particularity in relation to S and U. In short, the contingency grew out of the definitions of S, P and U as singularity, particularity and universality respectively. The Hypothetical Syllogism can avoid "saying" or mentioning the contingency, then, only by avoiding mentioning the definitions of S, P and U that led to the contingency in Categorical Syllogism. It avoids mentioning the definitions of S, P and U by using variables.

There are only two, rather that three, variables in the Hypothetical Syllogism, however—A and B. Because the Hypothetical Syllogism is using variables to replace the terms S, P and U, you would expect it to have three variables—one variable for each of the terms. The Hypothetical Syllogism only needs two variables, however. It grasps the relationships between S, P and U. While there are three terms, there is only one sort of relationship between the three terms. In Categorical Syllogism, P was defined as the category for S, and U was defined as the category for P. Put another way, S is a singularity in relation to P, which is the defining universal in relation to S; and P is a singularity in relation to U, which is its defining universal. Hence, P has the same relationship with S that U has with P. It is a universal defined as a totality of types that make it up, while the types that make it up are the way in which the universal is presented in reality. P is the panther, for instance, which is a category or universal made up of types such as lion, and the lion is one of the ways in which the universal panther is presented in reality. U has the same relationship with P. U is the category or universal that captures the set of all the types that make it up, while P is one of the types that make it up. U is a universal defined as a totality of types that make it up, while the types that make it up are the way in which the universal is presented in reality. U is the feline, for instance, which is a category made up of types such as the panther, and the panther is one of the ways in which the feline is presented in reality. Thus U has the same relationship with P that P has with S: U is the universal for P, the singularity; and P is the universal for S, the singularity.

Just as singularity was defined as including existence in its relationship with particularity, so particularity is defined as including existence in its relationship with universality as well. Since P—panther, for instance—is defined as one of the ways in which U—feline, for instance—is presented, P includes its presentation in actuality or existence, just as S did. The panther can be the way in which feline is presented—i.e. presented in reality or existence—only if the concept of panther is defined or thought of as including all of the existing panthers out there in reality. The panther presents the feline in reality in existing panthers, just as the lion presents the panther in reality in existing lions. Thus P, once again, has the same relationship with U that S has to P, not only in terms of content, but also in terms of how they are presented (or form).

The relationship between S and P is therefore a relationship between a singularity and a universality, and the relationship between P and U is a relationship between a singularity and a universality. Because there is only one sort of relationship, the Hypothetical Syllogism can capture the nature of both relationships as a single relationship between two variables. That Hypothetical Syllogism characterizes both the relationship between S and P and the one between P and U also helps to explain why it must be stated by using variables, rather than by using the terms S, P and U. A and B each have to stand for more than one term or element.

Although I have been using the lion as an example of singularity, notice that we can also treat the concept of lion as a universal. Since lion is a type, it, too can be thought of as a universal that presents into the types of lions that make it up—mountain lions, African lions and so on. Indeed, we can treat any type or kind as either a singularity or a universality, depending on the context.

The Hypothetical Syllogism captures the necessary relationship that obtains between S and P and between P and U. To say that the relationship between any two things is necessary is to say that, if you have one, then you have the other; if one obtains, then the other obtains; or, to use more Hegelian language, the being or nature of one is equally the being or nature of the other. In short, if A is, then B is. This is precisely the sort of relationship between lion and panther and panther and feline. Because the panther includes the lion, if the lion is, then the panther is too. Since the Concept is a finished product, and since the lion is one of the panther's particularities, if the panther is, then the lion is (cf. Hypothetical Judgment). The premise "if A is then B is" is a Hypothetical Judgment.

The next premise of the syllogism acknowledges the immediacy or givenness. S includes the givenness of existence or actuality, and since P is a singular in relation to U, it also includes the givenness of existence or actuality. This premise asserts that givenness or immediacy by asserting that A is. Unlike this second premise, the first premise of the syllogism is indifferent about whether A and B exist. For instance, we could draw a necessary connection between mythical creatures, without those creatures ever existing. The first premise asserts that types are necessarily linked, whether or not there are any such types. The first premise is thus indifferent to the category of being. In the second premise, being reappears. The premise says that A is, in an immediate way.

The conclusion of the syllogism is that, given the necessary connection between A and B, since A is, B is also. An example of the whole syllogism might be: "if the lion is, the panther is; the lion is; therefore the panther is."

As Hegel suggests in the discussion of this stage in the *Science of Logic*, if we were to characterize this syllogism in terms of S, P and U, it would have the form U-S-P (or P-S-U). S is the middle term in this syllogism between U and P, because the syllogism relies on the assertion of an immediate singularity (S)—namely, that A is—to draw out the connection between the universality (U) and the particular type that it characterizes (P). For instance, the lion's singularity—the way in which the lion has its actuality or exists—is what ties together its status as a panther, and the particularity or character that makes it the type that it is, i.e. as lion. The lion exists in a way that gives it the character of being a panther.

In the stage of Hypothetical Judgment, the Hypothetical Judgment stood for any sort of necessary relationship: ground and grounded, condition and conditioned, cause and effect and so on. In the discussion of Hypothetical Syllogism in SL, Hegel says that the Hypothetical Judgment within the Hypothetical Syllogism also stands for any sort of necessary relationship. However, he also suggests that the relation of condition and conditioned best captures the nature of the Hypothetical Judgment in the Hypothetical Syllogism. To see why that might be so, compare the concepts of condition and conditioned with the concepts of cause and effect, for instance. Since cause and effect are immediately transitive, they satisfy the relation captured by the Hypothetical Judgment. A cause implies an effect. A cause can only be a cause if there is an effect. If a cause is, the effect must be too: if A is, then B is. A condition has the same status. A condition can only be a condition if there is a conditioned. As we saw in the stage of Condition in the last chapter, a condition is a possibility that points toward another possibility. The other possibility must be there also, then, for the condition to be a condition. So the relationship between condition and conditioned is captured by the Hypothetical Judgment: if the condition is, then the conditioned is also, or if A is, then B is also. Unlike the relationship between cause and effect, however, the relationship between condition and conditioned is more general. The concept of condition is a general concept for something that points toward another possibility. A cause, by contrast, is a specific sort of condition. Like a condition, a cause points toward another possibility. However, whereas nothing in the concept of condition specifies the nature of the other possibility, or what that other possibility must be like, a cause must bring about a specific possibility to be what it is, namely, an effect. Because the concept of condition is a more general concept and does not presuppose anything about the nature or definition of the possibility that it points toward (i.e. B), the concepts of condition and conditioned do a good job of capturing the unspecified nature of the variables here.

There is a second reason to prefer the concept of condition as a way of capturing the relationship specified by the Hypothetical Judgment within the Hypothetical Syllogism. The concept of condition captures the nature of *both* A and B: A is the condition of B, and B is the condition of A. A and B are both conditions in relation to each other. The concept of condition captures in a general way—a way that applies to both A and B at the same time—the sort of relationship that they have. To say that A and B are both conditions is just to say that their being is such that it points toward another.

The syllogism has always involved mediation. The connection between the two outside terms has always been mediated by the middle term. But that mediation could not be specified, beyond the basic claim that the middle term linked or locked together the other two terms. In Hypothetical Syllogism, the nature of the mediation at work in the syllogism is beginning to be specified. In the Categorical Syllogism, the elements were supposed to have a necessary connection with one another, but the Categorical Syllogism could not say, assert, or capture that necessary connection. Because the Hypothetical Syllogism succeeds in asserting or stating the nature of that necessary connection, it begins to characterize that connection more precisely. First, A is functioning as the mediating term. Its presence in the second premise is what draws the conclusion in the third. In the second premise by itself, however, A is an immediate being, since A's being is simply asserted or given in that second premise. At the same time, in the conclusion, A disappears altogether. Only B's presence is asserted in the conclusion. Hence, within the whole syllogism, A is an immediate being that, as the mediating being, sublates (cancels and preserves) itself, since it is both there and yet gone in the conclusion. A's presence is still implied by the conclusion because B would not be there without it, but A is not present in the conclusion. A is a condition that is an immediate being that is destined to be used up by the conditioned. Because A's presence is missing from the conclusion, A has been used up. The mediation of the syllogism can therefore be characterized as a kind of negativity. A's activity of being used up mediates the syllogism. The syllogism is mediated, not by the being of A, but by the *being-used-up* of A, or by A's activity of being used up.

A's necessary activity of being used up defines A as a contradiction that can be captured with the concept of becoming. First, A is a condition that *becomes*. A and B are both universals, types or kinds (from Categorical Syllogism). Since the second premise asserts that A is, or that A has being, A is a type or kind that has being, exists, or pushes out into the actual world. A is thus a universal or type that has being—i.e. it exists or has objective being—but whose immediate being leads necessarily to and is sublated in another. A is therefore defined by a contradiction: it is immediate, but also mediated into another. A is a universal that necessarily becomes something else—specifically, it becomes B.

The form of the conclusion—"therefore B is"—expresses the same contradiction, namely, that B is both an immediate being and yet mediated, or has its being through another and so is sublated as a merely immediate being. B is defined as an immediate being that *becomes* because the conclusion says that "B is" only as a "therefore." The "therefore" implies that something else had to be there first, and only then—"therefore"—could B be there too. B thus has the same activity of pointing toward something else that A had. B points toward A. Just as A became B, so B becomes A. B's being becomes A's being.

According to the form of this syllogism, then—or the way in which A and B are being presented by this syllogism—A and B have the same content. They are each mediated as well as the activity of mediating. Because A and B are the same in terms of their content, when A becomes B, it becomes itself, and when B becomes A, it becomes itself too.

This description of the nature of A and B within the syllogism points toward a more sophisticated way of conceiving of universality. A and B are universals, and they are both the same. The second and third premises of the Hypothetical Syllogism assert that A and B also exist, or are. Because A and B are types or kinds that are or exist, they are singularities as well as universalities. Singularity is the way in which actuality is presented, i.e. it is existence. So existence belongs to singularity. A and B can exist because, even though they are universals, they are singularities insofar as they are one type, or one kind. We can think of lion, panther or feline as either identifying, universal labels (universality) or as individual (singular) types that can be found in the world. Panther, for instance, is an identifying label when we think of it as nothing but the collection of types that make it up, such as lion, black panther and so on. In this case we are taking lion, black panther and so on to be what really exists, and the concept of panther to be nothing more than an identifying universal that gathers those existing items up and defines them. But we can also think of the concept of panther as all of the individual panthers that exist in the world, or as the set of all the existing panthers. In that case we are treating panther as an existing singularity—as the (one, singular) set of existing panthers. Hence types or kinds that have existence are both universals and singulars.

We can treat lion and feline in both of the same ways as well. We can either see feline as nothing but a gathering-universal for the types that make it up—panther, house cat, lion and so on—or we can think of feline as the set of all existing felines. Similarly, we can see lion as a universal for the types that make it up—the concept of lion breaks into smaller categories as well, such as mountain lion, African lion and so on—or as the set of existing lions.

In the Hypothetical Syllogism, however, A and B have another characteristic as well—they *become*. A becomes B and B becomes A. Because they become, they negate themselves. When A becomes B, A is negated, and when B becomes A, B is negated. Moreover, because A and B are the same, when they become or negate themselves, they do so in a relationship with themselves. When A becomes B it becomes itself, and when B becomes A it becomes itself too. When panther becomes lion, it is not becoming something other than itself. The lion is a panther. Thus A and B are universals that differentiate themselves—that become something else—but that remain themselves through that process of differentiation. The panther differentiates into lion etc., but still remains what it is through that process of differentiation. A and B are identifying or essential universals (cf. Identity in Chapter Three). To use Hegel's anthropomorphic language, they are an identity or essential universal that differentiates itself and then gathers itself into itself out of that difference. Panther differentiates into lion etc., but does not become something else in the process. It remains what it is and defines itself by including all the types into which it differentiates: panther is what it is by gathering up lion, black panther etc.

The type of mediation within the syllogism has now changed, however. Before, we started with two premises and concluded something else. Now the move from A to B does not involve a change in identity or definition. The mediation is no longer a mediation from one thing to another, but rather a mediation within itself, a mediation within which the identity of the universal does not change. A and B are really one identity presented as two different elements, and the move from A to B does not alter the basic identity that they share. Panther and lion are really one identity, and the move from panther to lion does not change that shared identity. A and B have thus become one. What emerges from the Hypothetical Syllogism, then, is the thought of this one, shared universality as an active identity. This shared universality is what is really holding the syllogism together. It is an active universality that differentiates itself but remains itself during this differentiation process. "Panther," for instance, is the overarching, unifying identity or universality that, in the Hypothetical Syllogism, differentiates itself and yet remains itself in this process of differentiation. It is the self-differentiating universality that includes and embraces lion (as a type or concept) and all the other types of panthers. This thought of a self-differentiating universality leads to the next stage, the Disjunctive Syllogism.

Keep in mind that, although I am using the example of panther and lion to illustrate Hegel's points, P is really all of particularity, and S is all of singularity. Panther and lion are merely one particularity and singularity, not the whole of particularity and singularity, which is what the Hypothetical Syllogism is really about. The universality that emerges from Hypothetical Syllogism, then, is not the shared, self-activating identity of just panther and lion, but the shared, self-activating identity of the whole realm of particularity and singularity. As we'll see in a moment, that universality is the Concept once again.

Disjunctive Syllogism: The Third Figure of the Syllogism of Necessity

Two important logical points emerged out of the last stage. First, the thought of the Concept, as it had been defined at the end of the Doctrine of Essence, is beginning to be asserted or posited once again here in the syllogism. During the Transition to the Judgment earlier in this chapter, the thought of the Concept slipped into the background. The stages of judgment focused on the particularization or utterance of the Concept—on P (which is a U in relation to S), and S, which P includes. In the syllogism, which contains all three moments of the Concept, the thought of the whole Concept returned, but it was divided into the three moments (S, P and U). Moreover, the sort of universality that has been in play lacked the independence and self-activating nature that the Concept had had at the end of the Doctrine of Essence. In the Doctrine of Essence, the Concept was the overarching whole, the first Cause in a process of Reciprocal Action in relation to all of the rational concepts. Here, the Concept's character as an active and self-activating, overarching, essential (identifying) universal has come back into the picture, and so the definition of the Concept that we had developed at the end of the Doctrine of Essence has once again returned. The Concept, as the one thought of the whole rational system of concepts, is the one universal identity that differentiates itself into all of particularity and singularity and that holds together the entire conceptual scheme. At the beginning of this chapter I depicted the Concept like this:

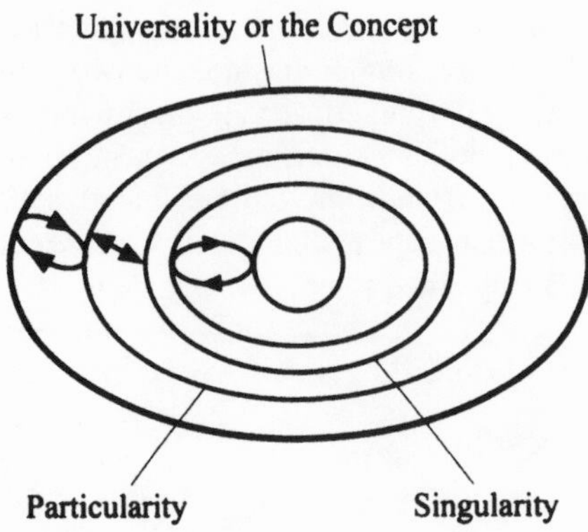

Figure 4.49

Because the Concept's status as the overarching, self-activating one universal has reemerged, we will return to this depiction of the Concept in the next stage.

Second, the self-activating universality that has emerged out of the Hypothetical Syllogism is a type of universality that is increasingly independent of our subjective consciousnesses. At the beginning of the development of the Syllogism, the types of universality in question were highly subjective. In the First Figure of Qualitative Syllogism (Fig. 4.36), we subjects had to pick a particularity to focus on from the many particularities that belong to any existing thing. Even in the Third Figure (Figs. 4.38 and 4.40), a subject or subjectivity had to pick the universal to focus on. Now, however, the universality has its own activity. We human subjects do not differentiate the universality into types, but the universality itself has this activity. As the Concept's universality becomes increasingly independent of our thought, it becomes increasingly less subjective, and more objective, or independent of subjective thought. Objectivity will develop out of the syllogism.

It is ironic that objectivity develops out of the syllogism. We ordinarily think of the syllogism and other argumentative forms as completely subjective. In the ordinary view, we subjects use forms of argument to make assertions or claims. Argument-forms such as the syllogism are merely tools used by (human) subjects to make assertions. They are therefore completely subjective or dependent on our subjectivity for whatever truth or validity they have. We subjects make the arguments; arguments don't make arguments. However, this suggestion that argument forms such as the syllogism are completely subjective is undercut by our practice. When we lay out the structure of an argument for our students, for instance—the argument from analogy, for example (see the Syllogism of Analogy)—we are implying that those structures have some validity outside of their use by particular subjects in particular arguments. This objective validity—the validity that the structure has independently of how it is used by particular subjects in particular arguments—is emerging through the logical development of the syllogism here. The syllogism has validity on its own, outside of our thought—a validity that it has in relation to the Concept, or the thought of the whole rational system, independent of the thought of subjective individuals.

Because his discussion of this stage in the *Encyclopaedia* is very brief—too brief—I am relying heavily on the discussion of this stage in the *Science of Logic* for my own presentation of the development of Disjunctive Syllogism. Here is a diagram for the Disjunctive Syllogism:

A is **B** or **C** or **D** etc.
A is **B**
Therefore **A** is neither
C nor **D** etc.

Figure 4.50

Disjunctive Syllogism begins by drawing out the two conclusions that grew out of Hypothetical Syllogism, namely, first, that what is really doing the work of mediating the syllogism or holding the syllogism together is a universality now pregnant with form or activity, which, as I just argued, is the hallmark of the Concept as it was defined in the last chapter. What holds the syllogism together is a universality that differentiates itself into types and yet holds itself together as those types. Characterized in terms of S, P and U, the Disjunctive Syllogism has the form S(U,P)-U(S,P)-P(S,U): objective universality is doing the work of mediating its expressions as S and as P. Second, this universality is not only active, but also objective, because its activity is independent of subjective thought. To use the same example again, the panther objectively differentiates into lion etc. There is some objective character that lion and all of the other types of panthers share that makes them "panther" and that is grasped by the concept of panther, whether or not any of us subjective human beings grasp that character. These two conclusions are expressed by the first premise of the Disjunctive Syllogism, which is a Disjunctive Judgment: "A (the universal) is B or C or D etc.": the universal differentiates itself or divides by its own activity into a completed set of other universals.

Because the Disjunctive Judgment asserts that A is a completed set of universals, it corrects for the contingency of the Hypothetical Syllogism. The Hypothetical Syllogism was contingent because the universal was only one of its particularities. The panther was only the lion. Which particularity the universal became was a subjective matter. In the Disjunctive Syllogism, the universal is now the whole set of its particularities. Hence there is no longer any need for a subjectivity to pick one of the particularities of the universal. The universal is all of its particularities. B, C or D etc. is an exhaustive set of all the universals into which A particularizes. As Hegel puts it in the *Encyclopaedia*, A is the totality of its particularizations (§191).

The fact that A—the universal—is the subject of all three premises of the Disjunctive Syllogism highlights the importance of the universal (i.e. U[S,P]) as the mediating factor in this syllogism. The syllogism mediates universality with singularity and particularity, but the mediating factor is A itself, or the universal itself. In the second premise—which is the mediating premise—the universal is a singular because it is the subject of this premise, or is what this premise is about. Thus the character of the universal holds the whole syllogism together.

As was true for the Disjunctive Judgment—and as Hegel suggests in the *Science of Logic*—the "or" of the Disjunctive Judgment within the Disjunctive Syllogism is an inclusive "or" in the logical sense. The "or" means both "and" and "or." A is B *and* C *and* D etc. because it is all of them, the whole or unity of all of its particularizations. But because A's process of particularization involves breaking up into elements that are distinct from one another and mutually exclusive, A is also B *or* C *or* D etc. The universal is thus a negative unity, or a unity that involves distinctions. The "or" captures the distinction that the particularizations have in relation to one another. The self-activating universal (A) thus differentiates into an exhaustive set of mutually exclusive universals—B, C and D etc., or B, C or D etc. A is *all* and *each* of its particularizations taken together as a whole.

The second premise asserts what was implied by, but not explicitly posited or stated by, Hypothetical Syllogism, namely, that A is B, or that A is one of its particularizations. In the Hypothetical Syllogism, A became B and B became A, but the syllogism did not *say* that. Moreover, A was B and B was A only in a negative way, because each was used up in the process of becoming the other. In the Disjunctive Syllogism, the unity is no longer negative. A is B in a way that leaves A in place, and B remains in place even though it is A too.

Moreover, as Hegel says in SL, the unity is also no longer negative because it is no longer indifferent to existence. The only premise in the Hypothetical Syllogism that came close to asserting the unity of A and B was the first premise—if A is, then B is—but that premise was indifferent to existence because A and B had their categorical connection whether or not they existed. In Hypothetical Syllogism, the particularization of the universal (i.e. P) included actuality or existence (i.e. S or singularity), but the universal did not. The universal panther, for instance, was merely its particularity, while its particularity—lion, in that case—included singularity, actuality or existence, or all the actual lions that have existed and will exist. In Disjunctive Syllogism, however, the universality includes existence on its own. Since the premise "A is B" in Disjunctive Syllogism says that A (the universality) *is* B (the particularization of A), and since B includes actuality and existence, and then A now includes the actuality and existence that belongs to B. Therefore panther, for instance, is now defined not merely as lion as a category, but as lion in a way that includes all of the actual lions that have existed and will exist.

It is because the second premise includes singularity (actuality and existence) that the third premise follows. Since panther is currently defined as the whole collection of actual lions, then it is not any of the other kinds of panthers: A is neither C nor D etc. The mutual exclusiveness between B and C and D etc. follows from the inclusion of singularity or actuality. Actual, real lions are lions—they are not some other kind of panther. Without the inclusion of actuality or existence, it is hard to see what information the third premise adds to the syllogism. You might think that the third premise highlights the mutual exclusiveness between the categories of particularization, that is, between B and C and D etc. In other words, since B and C and D etc. are mutually exclusive, if A is B, then A isn't C or D etc. But this conclusion can be drawn out of the first premise, which already says that A is B *or* C *or* D etc. The "or" already suggests that the categories of particularization for A are mutually exclusive. Moreover, under this interpretation, the third premise simply seems false. According to the first premise, A is C or D etc. The third premise's claim contradicts the first premise by suggesting that A is not C or D etc. Moreover, since A is already B according to the first premise—in which A is also C or D—A's being B in the second premise should not change the fact that it is C or D in the third premise. Only when we notice that the assertion of B in the second premise includes actuality and existence does the assertion of the third premise make sense. It's because "A is B" includes B's actuality and existence that A is not C or D etc. Insofar as panther exists as lion, it does not exist as other sorts of panthers—not because of the category of lion, because actual lions are not those other sorts of panthers. It's the singularity of lion—actual lions—that makes panther not other types of panthers in the conclusion of the Disjunctive Syllogism.

In the *Science of Logic*, Hegel says that we should see Disjunctive Syllogism as offering a general definition of universality. With Disjunctive Syllogism, the universality has been fully defined. Universality is the active, identifying and substantial power (see the stages of Identity and Immediate Substance for a definition of these terms) behind the full particularization—right down to the level of existence—of itself. The concrete or fully defined universal contains its total particularization—its division into types and their extension into actuality and existence. When the universal is thus defined or differentiated, it includes singularity and captures the mutual exclusiveness of types of singularities in relation to one another. Because this stage offers a general definition of universality, the definition applies to each and every universal. Each universal is fully defined or particularized by fleshing itself out completely, so to speak, into actuality or existence. Panther as a universal is defined by being divided up into types that extend into actuality or existence. When this definition is applied to the Concept, which is *Universality*—with a capital "U" (see the stage of Universality)—the Concept is defined by actively particularizing into its genera (P), which extends into species of actuality or existence, or species that include actuality or existence (S). This definition or particularization of the Concept can be depicted like this:

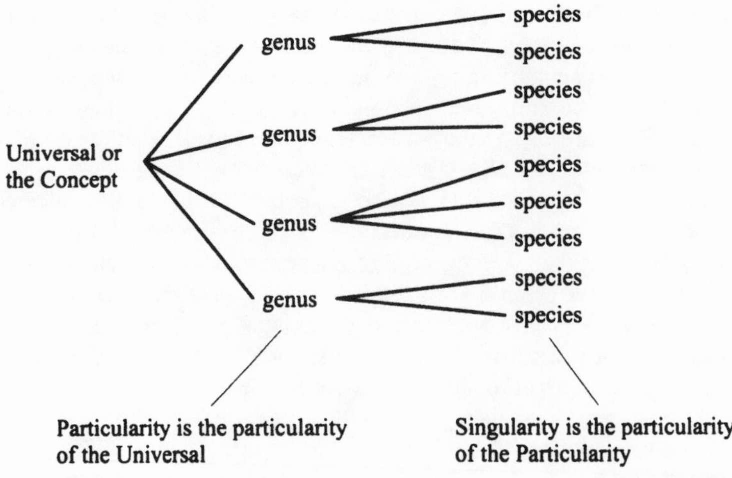

Figure 4.51

Disjunctive Syllogism captures the whole activity of the Concept: its form determination, to use Hegel's term, or the way in which the Concept determines or defines itself as a simple identity or one. The Concept defines itself by dividing up or differentiating into Particularity that extends into Singularity.

Two elements of Disjunctive Syllogism push on to the next stage. First, the middle term of the syllogism—namely U—already contains the other two terms. The universal is U(S,P)—or the universal that is also Particularity and Singularity. The universal particularizes or divides up into Particularity, which extends into Singularity. So Singularity and Particularity are once again conceived of as *inside* Universality. That's why it will make sense to return in the next stage to the nested-bubble view of the Concept that we had at the beginning of this chapter. That diagram depicts Singularity and Particularity as literally inside Universality. Particularity and Singularity no longer have any character or determination separate from Universality. Universality captures all that they are.

Second, the unity of mediating and mediated in the last stage is now asserted to be a characteristic of Universality. In the Hypothetical Syllogism, because A and B were the same, when A (the mediated) was mediated by B (B was doing the mediating) it was mediating itself with itself; and when B (the mediated) was mediated by A (A was doing the mediating), it was mediating itself with itself too. So the mediated was really the same as the mediating. Now that Universality defines *itself* when it divides into Particularity and Singularity, there is no longer any distinction between what is mediated and what is doing the mediating. U is both what is mediated and doing the mediating. The fact that A—as Universality—is the subject of each line in the syllogism helps to express this fact as well. Universality is both what is mediated—it is the subject of the first premise—and what is doing the mediating—since it is the subject of the second or mediating premise as well. Because the distinction between mediated and mediating has broken down, the need for the syllogism as a form disappears. Universality is capable of defining itself on its own through its own process. It can hold itself together with Particularity and Singularity. U no longer needs the form of the syllogism to hold it together with P and S. As Hegel points out in the *Science of Logic*, the second premise and conclusion are interchangeable. In SL, Hegel offers two versions of this syllogism, which reverse the order of the second premise and conclusion: (1) "A is either B, C or D, etc.; but A is B; therefore A is neither C nor D"; and (2) "A is either B, C or D, etc.; A is neither C nor D; therefore A is B." The second premise and conclusion are reversible because the need for the "therefore" has fallen away. The Disjunctive Syllogism is nothing but a list of propositions that characterize the Universality or Concept and no longer need the mediation provided by the form of the syllogism to hold them together. The form of the syllogism will fall away.

Transition to The Object

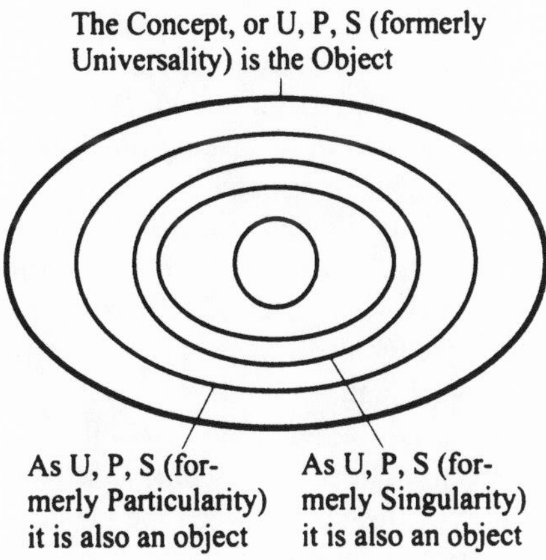
The Concept, or U, P, S (formerly Universality) is the Object
As U, P, S (formerly Particularity) it is also an object
As U, P, S (formerly Singularity) it is also an object

Figure 4.52

Universality has been defined since the beginning of the Doctrine of the Concept as the one concept (the Concept) that embraces (the "for-itselfness" of content) and presents *for itself*, or through its own activity (the "for-itselfness" of form) Particularity and Singularity. In Disjunctive Syllogism, U fulfilled this definition. U defines and presents P and S by dividing into P and then S, which includes actuality and existence. Three logical consequences follow. First, U now defines P and S in terms of content—it gives them its character. Although I have distinguished the moments by calling them U(S, P), P(S, U), and S(P,U), they have the same definition as universality-particularity-singularity (U, P, S). They are each defined by *all three* moments of the Concept and of the whole syllogism, as Hegel suggests (§192). Hence U has succeeded in defining P and S—it has given them its character as the unity of U, P and S. So all three elements are not only the same, they are identical, or have the same identifying concept, namely, U itself. Unlike the Concept (as it was defined in the stage of Universality), because U, P and S are now defined as the same as one another (their difference has been negated), when U particularizes into P and S and extends into actuality and existence, it remains itself, and does not become something else (§192). This is the same sort of relationship that Essence had with Shine, when Essence was the "for itself" identity of, or identified, the Shine, which was also itself (see

Identity). When Essence shined or had its thereness as the Shine, Essence did not become something else, but remained at home with itself.

Second, U also defines P and S in terms of form. Because U's own process embraces and presents P and S, U is now the one whole that is defined on its own, through its own process. It therefore no longer needs the "is" of subjectivity—judgments and syllogisms—to hold it together. In the stages of judgment and syllogism, the elements were being held together by subjectivity—by subjects that made the judgments or drew the conclusions of the syllogisms. Now, however, the connections between U, P and S are not mediated by any subjectivity. U links P and S together by itself. The form of syllogism (which included judgments) has therefore been sublated (cancelled and preserved). It has been cancelled because syllogisms are no longer needed to hold U together. U has no subjectivity or "other" outside of it on which it must depend for its definition. It is independent and, since it extends into actuality and existence, self-subsistent. The form of syllogism has been preserved, however, because syllogisms will return in later stages. Because the form of the syllogism has fallen away, the mediation between U, P and S has also been negated. U is a one, self-subsistent, whole concept that embraces and presents its content from the top down by dividing into P and S. U has become a being-for-itself, though, unlike Being-for-itself, it is "for itself" in terms of both content and form (cf. Being-for-itself in Chapter Two) (§192). Since U is a self-subsistent whole through its own process of dividing into concepts or categories (P) and actuality and existence (S) *independently of subjectivity*, it has become *the Object*, or the whole objective world.

Because the forms of judgment and syllogism and have fallen away, I can not use the same sentential diagrams to depict the Object (formerly the Concept) that I have been using during the stages of judgment and syllogism. I have therefore returned to the nested-bubble view that I used to depict the Concept at the beginning of this chapter. Like the Concept, the Object is a whole that completely embraces P and then S. Because the relationships between the elements have disappeared, however, I have put no arrows between the bubbles in the diagram, which would represent any relationships between the elements. The three elements have no defined relationships with one another. They are simply there together because of the dividing activity of the Object. The Object is an immediate unity, a free being-for-itself, independent of subjective consciousness without any internal relationships or mediation.

Third, since P and S are defined by the Object (i.e. U) as the same as it is (i.e. as the unity of U, P and S), and because they, too, no longer need the "is" of subjectivity to hold them together, they are also objects.

When we say something is "objective" or an object, we generally mean that it is independent of consciousness, concrete, independently self-subsistent and complete within itself because it divides fully into concepts and actuality and existence. This desk, for instance, has its existence and character by dividing into the concepts and actuality and existence that it contains—its legs, the table-top, drawers and so on—independent of anybody's thought about it. These parts are held together purely by the desk. Moreover, they are the same as the desk as objects. The Concept—as the Object—has this same character, although, instead of being just one object, such as the desk, it is the One whole Object, or the whole objective world in general (§193R). Like the desk, however, the Object has distinction within it, and falls apart into other objects, or, to use Hegel's language, into manifoldness, such that each of the isolated bits within it is also an object, or a something-there (something that has thereness) that is inwardly concrete (has a character or definition on its own), complete and independent (§193A). Both the Object and the manifold objects are objective in the sense in which we ordinarily understand this term.

III. The Doctrine of the Object

The Concept has become the Object. It can have its contents, which includes actuality and existence, on its own, and does not need subjectivity, or subjective thought, to hold it together by means of a judgment or syllogism.

The fact that the Concept has developed into the Object shows that Thought and Being are the same. They are the same because they are the very same logical element. The diagram depicts this fact because the diagram for the Object is the same basic diagram we had for the Concept, and the bubble for the Object is the same bubble that was defined as the Concept earlier. Moreover, the Concept and the Object are the same as one another in an "in itself" sense, as Hegel suggests (§193R), insofar as they have the same content or definition when they are defined on their own against an "other" (cf. Being-in-itself in Chapter Two). The Concept was defined at the beginning of this chapter as the unity of Universality, Particularity and Singularity in which Universality was defined in an "in and for itself" relationship with Particularity. The Concept or Universality had an "in itself" relationship of separation or opposition with Particularity because it *presented* Particularity *for itself*—or divided into Particularity through its own activity (the "for itself" relationship of form). The "in itself" definition of the Object here is the same: it is defined as the whole unity of Universality, Particularity and Singularity that pushes out into or divides into Particularity. Because Universality or the Object divides within itself into Particularity, it, too, has an "in and for itself" relationship with Particularity. Since the Object is what it is as the one whole, while Particularity is the thought of a multitude or set, the Object is opposed to and separated from Particularity. But it also embraces (the "for itself" relationship of content) particularity through its own process of division (the "for itself" relationship of form). The Object therefore has an "in and for itself" relationship with Particularity, just as the Concept did. Hence both the Concept and the Object have the same "in itself" definition when looked at on their own—they are each defined by the same unity of elements (U, P and S) in which the moment of Universality has an "in and for itself" relationship with Particularity. Because the Object divides into actuality and existence, however, it includes the thereness of Being—not just as a thought, but also as a reality. Thought (the Concept) is the same as Being (the Object).

However, while the Concept and Object are the same in an "in itself" sense, and although they are the very same logical element (the same bubble), their definitions are not exactly the same. Because the Object's definition is indifferent toward the relationships between the elements U, P and S, it leaves out the relationships that were contained in the Concept. The definition of the Object is even indifferent toward the "in itself" relationship that Universality has with Particularity. *We* can draw the inference that the Object, as the whole or Universality that divides into Particularity, has a relationship of opposition with Particularity that it gets from the stage of Disjunctive Syllogism, but that relationship of opposition is not part of the current definition of the Object. The Object is the whole that is indifferent toward all internal relationships, which is why I depicted it with no arrows within it that would represent relationships between the elements. The diagram of the Concept, by contrast, did have arrows within it. While the Concept has become the Object for a third party watching the logical development unfold, the claim that Thought (Concept) and Being (Object) are the same has not yet been drawn by the logical development in the "for itself" sense in which the logical development draws the conclusion through its own activity. That's why Hegel says that the sameness of the Concept and the Object has yet to be determined for itself (§193R).

The Object

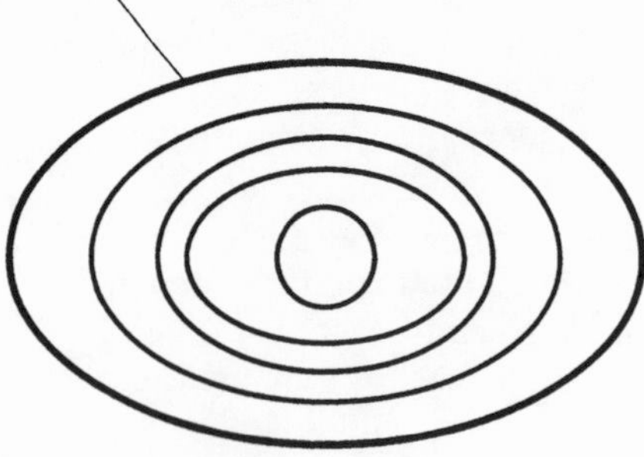

The Object is an immediate universal that contains the character of the Concept but is otherwise indeterminate

Figure 4.53

Because the mediation that was provided by the judgment and then syllogism has been sublated (cancelled and preserved), the Object is an immediate being that is indifferent toward the distinctions that the judgment and syllogism contained, namely U, P and S. The Object contains or unifies U, P and S in an immediate way. It has the character that it gets as the Concept as the unity of the whole, but is otherwise indeterminate. The diagram depicts the character it gets from the Concept because the Object still contains all the bubbles that the Concept had. Nevertheless, the Object is indeterminate insofar as it is indifferent toward the distinctions that it contains. In the stage of Being-in-itself in Chapter Two, Hegel's basic account of determination or having a character required opposition. Something has a character by being opposed to its other. Because the Object has no relationships between U, P and S in it at all, its definition contains no relationships of opposition. Hence, as the unconditioned universal with a content, it is complete, but it is otherwise indeterminate. The diagram depicts the indeterminateness of the Object because there are no arrows in it that would be used to represent internal relationships or oppositions that could give the Object a more developed or specific character. The Object has a content because it is filled with other bubbles that allow it to have some character on its own, but it is otherwise indeterminate because it is indifferent toward whatever relationships there may be between U, P and S. Indeed, as we will see more fully in a moment, the Object, as Universality, has no relationships at all with P and S. In anthropomorphic language, the Object is "ignoring" its internal elements or content. That's why I have not labeled the internal bubbles in the diagram for this stage.

Nevertheless, because it contains the complete set of particularities and singularities that we had before, the Object is a totality in itself (§194). It is defined, "in itself," as the whole objective realm, or the completed set of objects and actualities as a finished product.

An object (in general) is defined as independent of subjective thought. However, an object is never completely independent of thought, since the *thought* of an object is still a *thought*. When we think of an ordinary object—a table, for instance—as an object, we think of it as if it is independent of thought. The table does not depend on my thought for it existence or character. When I stop thinking of the table and go away for a while, it does not go out of existence or change. When I come back, it still has the same character it had before I left. Moreover, the table will have the same relationship with any other person's thought that it has with mine. Therefore, in general, the table seems to have its actuality, its existence and character (as a table), in a way that is independent of subjective thought. It is an actuality—an actual table—that has its subsistence and determination on its own, independent of how anybody thinks about it. But since the thought of an object is still a thought, it never succeeds in being completely independent of thought. The concept of an object is still a concept. To think of a table as an object is still to *think* of the table as an object. As we will see in the development of this section of the logic, to think of an object as completely independent of thought is therefore to think of it one-sidedly, or to ignore the fact that the thought of an object is still subjective because it is a thought. In later stages, the connection between object and subject will return. For the moment, however, the Object, or the concept of object, is an actuality with a character that is independent of subjective thought. Just as the definition of the Concept as Concept (i.e. as thought or subjectivity) has proven to be one-sided, however—since the Concept has now become the Object—so this definition of the Object as purely objective will prove to be just as one-sided in later stages.

As an independent chunk with a character, the Object is a new kind of immediacy. Although the fact that P and S belong to its contents gives it a character that it can have on its own, independently, since the relationships between U and P and S are unspecified, that character or content is simply given or found to be in U.

Transition to Mechanism

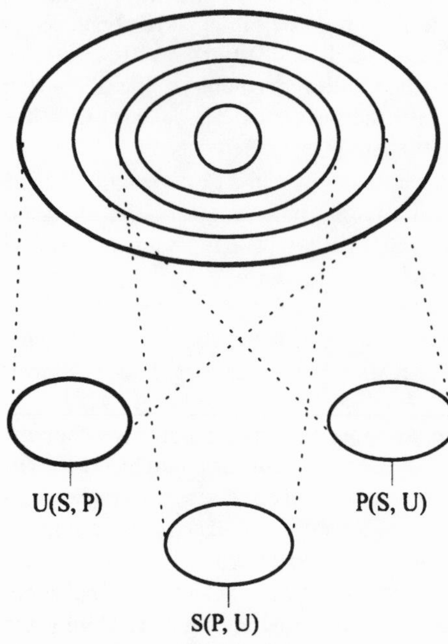

The Object falls apart into its differences. It is even indifferent toward itself as the unity

Figure 4.54

The Object is a one or whole immediate being that is indifferent toward its distinctions. The indifference that the Object has toward its differences or distinctions is actually built into the syllogism that defined their relationship in the stages of the syllogism. The judgments of the syllogism treat the Object (which is U itself) and its distinctions (P and S) as related, but also as separable—as dependent, but also as independent. Syllogisms are constructed out of judgments, and the general form of a judgment says both that the two terms in the judgment are the same and that they are different. A judgment, "A is B" says that A is separable from B because it refers to them as two different items (namely, as A and B), but the copula "is" says that A is not separable from B because it says that A *is* B (cf. The Judgment). This ambiguity within the judgments of the syllogism leads the Object—which is only an immediate, and hence unstable, unity anyway—to fall apart into its distinctions. The Object is indifferent toward its distinctions in the sense that it both *is* the unity of its distinctions but also *is not* the unity of those distinctions.

Moreover, although the Object has the definition of the Concept—it is defined as the independent, all-embracing, identifying universal, which is how the Concept has been defined since the end of the Doctrine of Essence—the Object has this character only in an immediate way. Since the internal relationships between the moments U (which is the Object itself) P and S are not spelled out, the Object is the simple, immediate identity of the elements with no internal relationships at all. It is an object, and defines P and S as objects too, but, as the identity of U, P and S, it is only the being-in-itself of the moments ("*diese Identität nur die* ansichseiende *der Momente ist*," §194). Because U, P and S each have the same definition as independent objects, the Object is their unity insofar as it captures that content or character. The Object is the concept—namely, the concept of "object"—that defines the character that each moment has. But the Object captures that sameness or identity only as a "being-in-itself" because it is currently defined as separate from the other moments. Hence, even though the Object is the unity of the moments insofar as it grasps their content characters, it is also indifferent toward that unity, since it currently grasps the definition that each moment has only insofar as each is defined separately from the others. The Object therefore falls apart into its distinctions: the distinctions separate from one another. Put a different way, because the Object is filled with distinctions—with U(S, P), P(S, U) and S(P, U)—it can have its immediate character as the all-embracing universal only by being indifferent toward the distinctions that it contains. The Object has its definition as the one totality only if its distinctions (U[S, P], P[S, U] and S[P, U]) are thought of as not really different. Only if U (which is the Object itself), P and S are thoughts belonging to *the Object itself*, and so not really different from the Object, can the Object have its immediate character as the all-embracing universal. As soon as the distinctions are treated indifferently, however, the Object no longer seems to be connected together at all. P and S are supposed to belong to the Object, but the Object's connection with them cannot be specified. Moreover, the Object is even indifferent toward itself as the unity of them. The more it is defined as the immediate One whole, the more the connection between the elements falls apart. And the more the connection falls apart, the less capable it is of unifying them. The Object, as the U, cannot hold itself together with P and S if it is not connected to them.

The definition of the Object is missing part of the doubly "for itself" process that defined the Concept at the beginning of this chapter. That's why the Object, as the identity, is *only* the being-*in*-itself of the moments. The doubly "for itself" process is the process in which the Concept, as the Universality, *embraces and defines* Particularity and Singularity (the "for-itself" of content) *for itself*, or through its own process (the "for-itself" of form). The "for-itself" of content was defined by the stages of Being-for-itself, which included two processes: the process of gathering up or embracing the something-others (cf. Attraction) and the process of giving the something-others their "in itself" characters by repulsing or dividing into them (cf. Repulsion). The "for-itself" of form adds that a concept can do (1) and (2) through its own process. There are therefore four parts to the doubly "for itself" process: (1) the process of embracing or unifying the elements, (2) the process of identifying or dividing into the elements (both of which belong to the "for itself" of content), (3) the ability to do (1) independently, or through its own process, and (4), the ability to do (2) independently, or through its own process. The Object has (2) and (4), since it can do (2) through its own activity, but not (1) or (3). As Universality, it gives Particularity and Singularity their characters in the "in itself" sense insofar as it *divides* into them and defines them as objects like itself. But it fails to *embrace* P and S as a whole, because it cannot *connect* them back together. As a result, the Object falls apart into its distinctions. Indeed, even the Object as the whole falls apart and becomes just another distinction itself. Its status as the Universality becomes just another one of the distinctions. It falls apart into U(S, P), P(S, U) and S(P, U)—a mechanical relationship of externally related, distinct parts. In Disjunctive Syllogism, for instance, the concept of feline divided into all of its sub-categories—the concepts of panther (pantherinae) and felinae. These are the P's of the concept of "feline," which in turn divide into their sub-categories, which are too numerous to name, but include concepts such as "neofelis" and "panthera" (for the former), and "puma," "lynx," and "leopardus" (for the latter). These concepts are the S's of "feline." Since the Object includes actuality and existence, this process of dividing defines the concept of feline as existing: "feline" exists in all of the existing felines into which it divides. It is defined in terms of how it exists or is an object, and it exists as all the felines. Because each of the other concepts also divides, each, too, is defined as existing: "panther" is all the existing panthers, and "felinae" is all the existing pumas, leopards and so on. Hence each of those concepts is also defined in terms of how each of them exists or is an object. Even though the concept of "feline"—which is the unity of all the other concepts—includes the same existing panthers, leopards and pumas that the other concepts include, at the moment, each of the elements seems like a separately existing object independent of the others. "Feline" is an object as the complete set of felines; "panther" (one P) is an object as the complete set of panthers; "felinae" (the other P) is an object as the complete set of pumas, lynxes and so on, and "puma" (an S) is an object as the complete set of pumas. Because they are each defined as complete, separate objects on their own, they fall apart into separate items. The concept of feline (U) is all the existing felines. It cannot explain why the existing panthers and felinae (P's) or existing pumas etc. (S's) belong to it. It cannot hold the P's and the S's together. Now that the distinctions have fallen apart, they seem to be independent of one another, but, since the Object still has the character of the Concept, they are still dependent on or connected to one another. This combination of indifference and non-indifference (or connectedness) plays out over the next few stages.

Hegel says that each of the distinctions or differences is the totality (§194).[3] U(S, P), P(S, U) and S(P, U) are each totalities in a couple of senses. First, each is a totality in the sense of being a completed universal. U(S, P), P(S, U) and S(P, U) are each a universal. Feline is a totality as all the existing felines, panther is a totality as all the existing panthers, lion is a totality as all the existing lions, for instance. Hence U, P and S are each a totality in the sense of being a completed universal as a group concept. Moreover, U(S, P), P(S, U) and S(P, U) are also *the* totality itself, which is to say, smaller versions of the whole Concept or Object. The Object grew out of the Concept, and the Concept was defined as the unity of U, S and P. Now that the distinctions are each defined by U, S, and P, they are each mini-versions of the whole Concept (or Object) itself.

Formal Mechanism

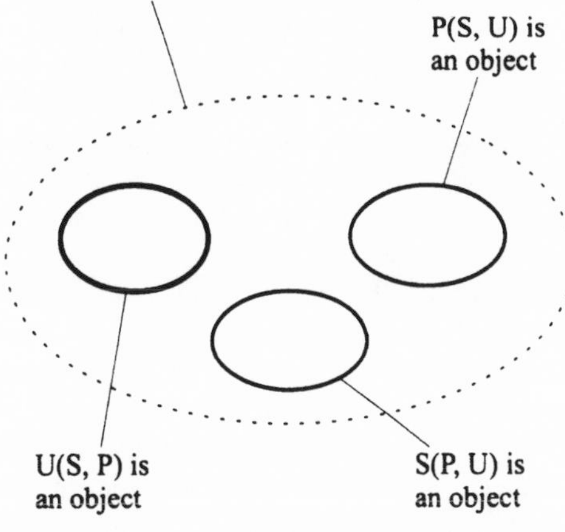
The Object has itself as the unity outside of it. To the degree that the Object is taken together as a unity at all, it is a mere aggregate
P(S, U) is an object
U(S, P) is an object
S(P, U) is an object

Figure 4.55

Because the Object (as U[S, P]) is indifferent toward its own status as the unity, its character as the unity falls outside of it. Although the Object is U(S, P), and although U(S, P) is already supposed to be the unity of P(S, U) and S(P, U), U(S, P) is currently being treated merely as one of the indifferent distinctions. As a result, U(S, P) is not functioning as the unity of the Object. So the Object's function as the unity falls outside of U(S, P), That function as the unity is not being performed by U(S, P). The Object is merely taken together—or posited as—the aggregate unity of the three distinctions. All of the determining elements of the Object—namely, U(S, P), P(S, U) and S(P, U)—are posited as external to the unifying function of the Object. I depict this unifying function that has fallen outside of U(S, P) as a very lightly dashed bubble surrounding the three elements, to indicate where it would appear—and will appear later. But since it is not doing any logical work at the moment, I will drop it out of the picture altogether in the next diagram.

Moreover, the elements operate on one another in an external way. Their relationships with one another are not bound up with their characters. Each element gets its character or is determined in an external way, that is, through external relationships with the other elements. This external determination is depicted in the diagram because each element is an independent bubble outside of the others. None of them has any of the other bubbles inside them anymore, and so there are no internal relationships between the bubbles.

This sort of external determination grows out of the Object's character as the "being-in-itself" identity of the elements. The "in-itself" type of relationship is always an external one. In an "in itself" relationship, something has its character in opposition to its other or negation, which lies outside of it (see the stage of Being-in-itself in Chapter Two). A "for itself" relationship, by contrast, involves internal relationships because a "for itself" concept has other concepts as its content, or inside it, and therefore has an internal relationship with its contents (cf. Being-for-itself in Chapter Two). Because this stage is dominated by "in-itselfness," the elements are independent of and external to one another, and offer resistance toward one another. All three elements are objects. Each element is a totality that is defined by U, P and S: they are each a U-P-S. Because the whole Object—namely, U(S, P) is an object—and because all three elements are the same, each of the other elements—P(S, U) and S(P, U)—is an object too.

Hegel's characterization of this stage of the logic as "mechanism" seems apt. We do conceive of a machine as a whole or system that is an aggregate of independent elements or parts. The independence is illusory, but the unity that they have falls outside of the elements. While the parts of a machine seem independent, they are also mutually defining, and would not be capable of being what they are outside of the machine. The gear of a watch would not be anything without the watch or the machine. It depends for its character on the nature of the whole machine, and so is in that sense dependent on the whole machine. The gear "is"—syllogistically—the gear-system-for-the-minute-hand, which "is" (again syllogistically) the whole watch. Our landfills and junkyards are filled with parts that turned out to be dependent for their character on the whole machine to which they belonged. Without those machines, the parts have no identity, which is why they wind up discarded in landfills. Nevertheless, the parts of a machine do have an air of independence and separability, and do seem to be related to one another in an external way—i.e. not because of their natures or definitions, but just because they are held together in a merely aggregate way by the machine. The gear of the watch, for instance, does seem to be capable of being defined without the watch, and it is certainly separable, in the literal sense that it can be taken out of the watch, and exchanged for another gear (at least, one just like it). The stages of mechanism outline how the elements, U, P and S, are related together in logical ways that are analogous to the mechanistic relationships that a machine and its parts have.

Although I am using the words "part" and "whole" here, it must be kept in mind, as Hegel remarks in the discussion of this stage in the *Science of Logic*, that the part/whole relationship has already been sublated (cancelled and preserved) in the Doctrine of Essence and so does not fully apply here. In particular, the elements do not have the sort of relationship with one another that would define them as parts and a whole. The relationship between the parts in a machine is syllogistic, and is therefore more complicated than that of a part/whole relationship. In a machine, the whole not only has parts, it "is" its parts. While a room "is" not the sofa that makes it up, the watch "is" the parts that make it up. That's why Hegel puts Formal Mechanism in the Doctrine of the Concept, rather than the Doctrine of Essence. Nevertheless, the words "part" and "whole" provide a convenient short hand for the logical elements currently in play.

Hegel's stage of Formal Mechanism captures the logical character of one fairly ordinary, scientific approach. Suppose that U is "feline," P is the genus "panther," and S is the species "lion." Because earlier stages are always sublated (cancelled but also preserved) and because we are past the stage of syllogism, it must be kept in mind that the syllogistic relationship is still implied here. That means that there is an implied syllogistic relationship between U and P and S such that "U is P is S," or, in our example, "feline is panther is lion." And of course, we *do* think that feline is panther is lion, or that lion is a panther and feline. A mechanistic approach to science sees these connections, but it would treat the relationship between lion, panther and feline as an external one. It would maintain that, while a lion is a panther is a feline, that relationship is external in the sense that there is nothing internal to the concepts of lion, panther and feline themselves that links them together. The concepts are held together only in an external way, by an outside party, so to speak, or by some kind of glue, in the same way that quality and quantity were being held together in an external way in the stage of Immediate Measure in the Doctrine of Being. There is nothing about the concepts themselves, in the mechanistic view, that links them together. The same air of independence and separability between the parts of a machine seems to belong to the parts in a natural system, when such a system is understood in a mechanistic way. "Lion," as all the existing lions, is capable of being defined on its own—without reference to the concepts of panther and feline—from the bottom up by all the existing, individual lions that it contains.

Non-indifferent Mechanism

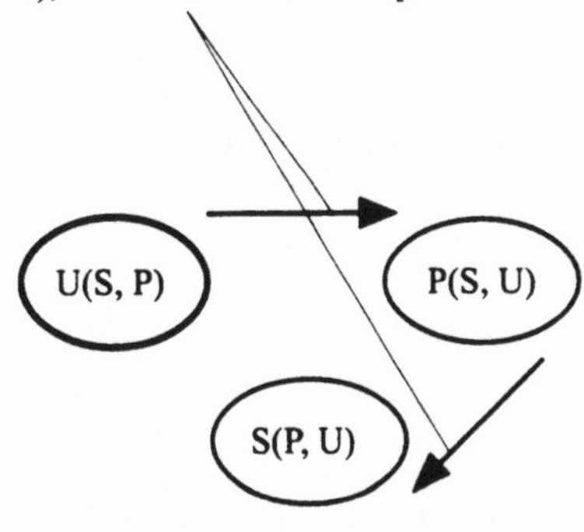
U(S, P) communicates its U to P(S, U) and P(S, U) communicates the U to S(P, U), which are thus both dependent on U
U(S, P)
P(S, U)
S(P, U)

Figure 4.56

Even though the three elements are independent of one another, U(S, P) still defines or identifies the other two elements. It defines them because they are both totalities, or universals—P is P(S, *U*) and S is S(P, *U*). U's role as the defining element is the power (*Gewalt*) that it imposes on the other objects, which therefore turn out to be dependent on U for their definition. In the *Science of Logic*, Hegel characterizes this relationship as *communication*. U(S, P) communicates its universality to S(P, U) and to P(S, U). Just as I do not lose my thought by communicating it with you, none of the elements loses its universality by communicating the universality to the other element. U(S, P) passes its U on to P(S, U) which passes the U on to S(P, U), but each keeps its share of U at the same time.

This process of communication has roots in the Concept's process of particularization in Disjunctive Syllogism above. The most basic sense of universal is a set or group term. In Disjunctive Syllogism, U is defined as a universal when it divides into the P. When U's action causes P to go on to divide into the S's, U passes its U down to P by defining P as a set or multitude. P passes its U down to S when it leads S to divide into individual existing items, and hence defines S as a set or multitude. U thus gives P and S their definitions as basic universals. The relationship of communication between U, P and S was also foreshadowed in the stages of Particularity and Singularity, in which Universality passed its "in and for itself" process on to Particularity and Singularity and defined them as universal concepts.

Here, communication is spurred by Object's (U's) character as the "being-in-itself" identity of P and S. The Object is a Universality that is a separate object that can be defined (in an "in itself" sense) independently and on its own. It passes on this definition of its universality by identifying and presenting the "in itself" character of P as an object that is multitude, or a separate and independently defined bunch of objects; and then P passes on that universality by identifying the "in itself" character of S as an object that is a multitude, or a separate and independently defined bunch of objects. Because this process is a process of "being-in-itself," I have used the same sort of straight arrow to represent it in the diagram that I have used to represent the process of "in-itselfness" throughout the logic (cf. Being-in-itself in Chapter Two). Like Being-in-itself, which is a moment of logical rest and stasis, each universal (U and P) remains what it is even though it defines or passes its U on to an external "other."

Although U, P and S are separate objects, the process of communication defines P and S as dependent on U. P and S are dependent on U for their universality and definition. They get their universality and definition from U or the Object. U's process of communication establishes the universality of U, P and S in three senses: (1) in the most basic sense in which they each are defined as *universals*, as communities or groups of items, (2) in the sense in which they divide into items that meet the definition communicated by U and so reflect the character of the Universality, and (3) in the sense in which they reassert their characters as each a *universal* concept (one or singular), as will be explained in a moment. Therefore, P and S cannot really have their definitions as universals on their own. In the last stage, it looked as if S and P could be what they are or have their character or definition on their own. To use the same example again, it looked as if lion and panther could each be defined on their own without reference to panther and feline respectively. This apparent independence follows from the fact that a concept can be defined from the bottom up by the existing items that fill it up, rather than from the top down by the higher concepts that it belongs to. A universal can be treated as either an identifying label or as including existence (see Hypothetical Syllogism). When a universal is taken to include existence—or the existing things that it gathers up—those existing things give it a character or definition from the bottom up so that it seems to allow it be defined on its own, without reference to higher concepts. The concept of lion, for instance, seems to be capable of being defined on its own by reference to all of the individual, existing lions that fill it up, and the concept of panther can be defined from below by the existing panthers that fill it up.

Unfortunately, however, what the lion *is*—its essence—cannot be fully captured from below. Existing universals have all kinds of characteristics in common, none of which capture the essence of the type, or the whatever-it-is that makes the type what it is. Humans have earlobes in common, for example, but having earlobes does not capture what it is to be human (cf. Universal Judgment of Reflection). The nature of a totality cannot be fixed from below, that is, by gathering up what the existing things it contains have in common. This is the same logical lesson drawn out of the stages of Being-for-itself in Chapter Two, where the suggestion that an ideal, concept or universal could be defined as nothing but a set-term failed. In those stages, a something can be what it is only by being defined from above by a concept. That's because things can be a set of items (i.e. more than one item) only if they are different from one another, and they can be one item (i.e. one set) only if they are the same as one another in some determinate way. Only the universal or higher, grasping concept can sort out those ways in which the items are different from one another (and hence more than one item) from those ways in which the items are the same as one another (and hence belong to the same set as the same kind of thing) (see Repulsion and Attraction).

That same insight reappears here: the essence of a type or totality can only be captured by a higher or more universal concept. The kind of thing that lion is can only be grasped from above, by a higher concept that can sort out those characteristics that grasp the essence or essential "what it is" to be a lion from those characteristics that make individual lions simply different from one another as individuals. According to this stage, the totality or universality of S cannot be defined from below, but must be communicated to it from above or from the higher concepts that absorb S. S gets its universality or totality from above: it's because P is a more inclusive universal or totality that it can capture the essence of S. Thus, the essence of S as a universal or totality cannot be defined from below. Similarly, it's because U is a more inclusive universal or totality that it can capture the essence of P. P is a universal whose essence can only be captured from above by U. Since U is the Concept or the thought of the complete, rational conceptual system, to say that P and S get their completeness and universality from above is to say that their universality comes from their place in the complete, rational conceptual system, rather than from the set of items that fill them up (from below). This latter view was Kant's way of defining universality (see Chapter One, Section IV).

P and S therefore turn out to be dependent on and hence non-indifferent toward U: they need U to be what they are.

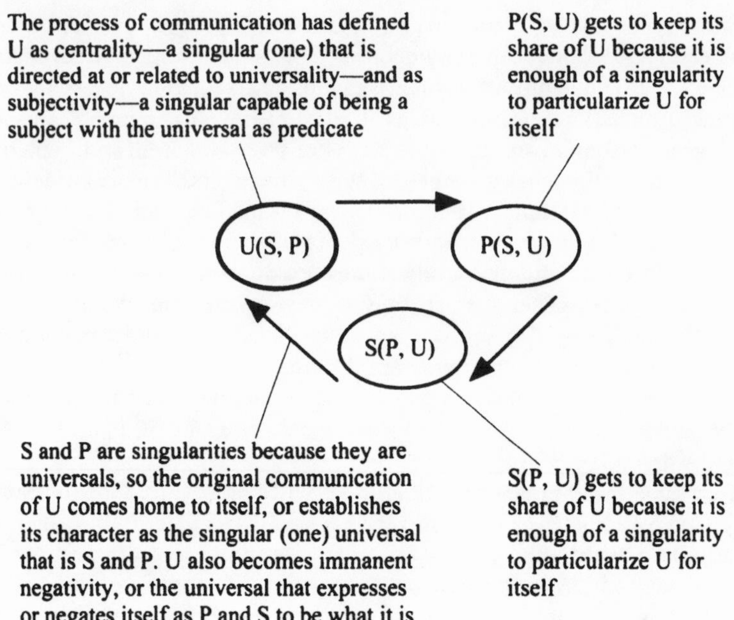

The process of communication has defined U as centrality—a singular (one) that is directed at or related to universality—and as subjectivity—a singular capable of being a subject with the universal as predicate
P(S, U) gets to keep its share of U because it is enough of a singularity to particularize U for itself
U(S, P)
P(S, U)
S(P, U)
S and P are singularities because they are universals, so the original communication of U comes home to itself, or establishes its character as the singular (one) universal that is S and P. U also becomes immanent negativity, or the universal that expresses or negates itself as P and S to be what it is
S(P, U) gets to keep its share of U because it is enough of a singularity to particularize U for itself

Figure 4.57

At the same time, however, P and S can each keep its share of U, so to speak, only insofar as each is also independent. When I tell you my thought, you get to keep the thought only to the degree that you are capable of making that thought make sense for you. In other words, you must be able to particularize that thought for your singularity, or for you as an individual, to keep it. The logical elements here must do the same thing. P(S, U) can keep its share of U only if it is enough of an S (singularity, individuality) to particularize the U for itself. And S can keep its share of U only if it is enough of an S (singularity, individuality) to particularize the U for itself. Of course, P(S, U) and S(P, U) *do* have enough singularity to particularize the U, because they are both defined by both S (singularity) and P (particularity) too. The element of singularity gives P and S their resistance to U, or the ability to specify the communicated universal for themselves. It's because you are an individual on your own that you can particularize the thought or universal that I communicate to you. Similarly, it is because P and S are singularities—as *universal concepts*—that they can particularize the communicated U on their own. They must be one, whole thoughts or concepts that have "in and for itself" relationships with their contents, and so are separate from the elements and items that they present *for themselves*, or through their own activity (cf. Universality, Particularity and Singularity). The particularizing process that appeared in Disjunctive Syllogism—in which U presents, particularizes or divides into P; P presents, particularizes or divides into S; and S presents, particularizes or divides into individualized actuality—returns.

When U communicates its universality to P and S, U, P and S reassert their singularity by particularizing, or dividing into and hence presenting the elements that they each include. "Panther," for instance, gets to keep its status as a universal concept only if has enough of an individual character to particularize into further items *defined by the universality "panther,"* i.e. into individually existing panthers. Similarly, "lion" gets to keep the universality it received from U only if it has enough individuality and particularity to divide into all the individual items *defined by the universality "lion,"* i.e. into individually existing lions. Because that process of division is a process in which "panther" and "lion" push out or *present* their contents, it is a "for itself" relationship of form that defines "panther" and "lion" as universal concepts, separate from their contents (in an "in itself" sense) (cf. External Necessity). The process of presentation and division thus reinforces their characters as both singularities and as universals insofar as it defines them as *universal concepts* (cf. Universality).

Moreover, using Hegel's more anthropomorphic language, U's communication to P and S expresses its own singularity and particularity. When U characterizes P(S, U) it particularizes itself, or expresses itself as P, and when U characterizes S(P, U), it singularizes itself (if I may coin a term for a moment), or expresses itself as S. U's process of communication thus defines U as the U that is also S and P—i.e. as U(S, P). Because U is being defined as a singularity or universal concept, it is an independent one or singular (an S). In Hegel's terms, the process establishes U as an independent, negative unity with itself (§196). U is a singular (one) universal that, while communicating through its opposition, negation or "other"—i.e. through P and S—nevertheless comes home to itself, so to speak, because the process defines U or establishes U's own character (particularity) as the one (singular) universality, or as *the* U(S, P).

Moreover, now that U is defining S and P, it is getting rid of, or negating, its difference from them. Up until now, in mechanism, U's difference from S and P was holding U apart from them. S and P were being presented as external to U, or as U's externality (§196). But U has now eliminated that difference because it is defining S and P. Hence U is now a one (independent singularity) that is directed at and related to (and hence dependent on) its externality. Moreover, because U defines itself when it externalizes into P and S, U is now also dependent on its process of externalizing. U has to externalize itself to be what it is. In Hegel's terms, U is inherent or immanent negativity (§197)—it inherently externalizes or negates itself into P and S to be what it is. As a result, just as P and S turned out to be non-indifferent toward U, U is now non-indifferent toward P and S: it needs P and S to be what it is, just as they needed U to be what they are.

Now that U's process has defined it as a singular, or established its singularity, U is now defined by *centrality*, or as a one (a singularity) that is related to universality. U is a singular defined as universality. Because U has this character as a result of a process it underwent, we might also use Hegel's more anthropomorphizing language: U is a singularity that relates to itself (as universality) through the process of externalizing itself into P and S. Centrality is a new kind of singularity: a singularity that is still at rest—or is a oneness that has self-subsistence—but that positively reflects or aims at the universal as its own character. A center is an S-that-reflects-or-aims-at-U, or, for short, as an S-as-U. U is at rest insofar as it is defined as an immediate, independent and so self-subsistent Object, but U's defining process has now established its singularity. Moreover, U's status as a group-term (i.e. as a basic universal) has also been established. When U characterizes and hence divides into P and S, it establishes or aims at its character as a basic group-term or universal. U's process of communication also aims at or establishes its status as the characterizing or identifying universal over P and S. When U communicates its U to P and S, it characterizes or identifies them—it makes them what they are—and hence once again establishes its character as an essential or identifying universality. U is thus an S-that-reflects-or-aims-at-U. U is a singularity that positively reflects or aims at universality as its own character.

U is also now defined by *subjectivity*. U has enough individuality or singularity to be the subject of the universal, or to be a subject with the universal as its predicate. U is a singularity that *has* universality: it is a singular "this" or *subject* that "is" universal. We ordinarily think of subjectivity as consciousness, but subjectivity has a much more basic logical definition that Hegel employs here (cf. the Introduction to this chapter). This more basic definition is reflected in our grammar. The subject of a sentence is an individual item that has a universal as its predicate, or an item that is the subject of the universal. In the basic sentence, "the cat is black," the word "cat" is the subject of the sentence because it is the singularity that has the universal—"black"—as its predicate. Even in more complicated sentences, the subject of the sentence has this same basic character. Take the sentence "the underbelly of the cat is black." In this sentence, the subject of the sentence is no longer simply "cat," but "the underbelly of the cat." What makes that more complex phrase capable of being the subject of the sentence is that it picks out one thing—a singularity—that can be characterized with a universal. The underbelly of the cat is one (singular) thing. As we learned in "grammar" school, no matter how many words it takes to specify the subject, so long as those words capture a singularity capable of being characterized by, or of having, a universal, those words constitute the subject of the sentence. In logical terms, to be a subject is simply to be a singularity capable of having, reflecting, or being characterized by a universal. Conscious subjectivities have this same characteristic as well. A person's consciousness is a singularity (a [one] consciousness) capable of reflecting universality. To be conscious is to be capable of conceptual thought, and conceptual thought is universality in two senses. First, a conscious subject's conceptual thought is a bunch of thoughts put together—a stream of consciousness. So conceptual thought is a universality in the most basic sense that it is a set or group of items. But it is also a universality in the sense of being a centrality. Conscious thought based on concepts and language are neither individual nor private. Concepts and language are what we have in common, are public universals. A conscious human being is therefore a subject in the basic logical sense: he or she is a singularity capable of reflecting universality.

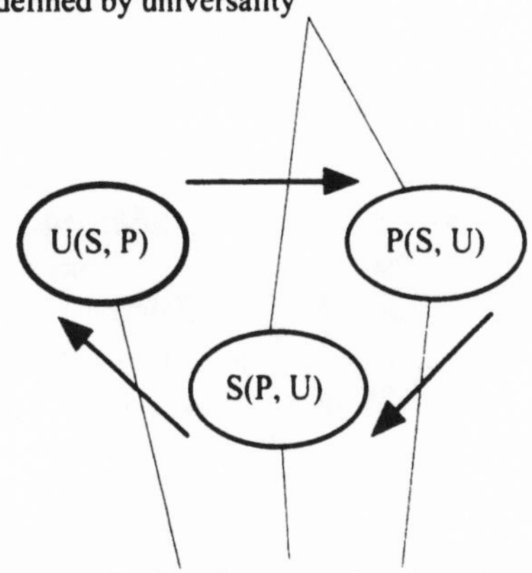
P(S, U) and S(P, U) are centers too: they are each enough of a singularity to be defined by universality
U(S, P)
P(S, U)
S(P, U)
Now all three objects are what they are only through their relation to one another. They are Non-indifferent Mechanism

Figure 4.58

U's process of communication also turns S and P into centers. They, too, become ones that are related to universality. When U passes on its universality, S and P respond by reasserting their own character as singularities: they particularize by dividing. But this process of dividing reasserts their status as basic universals, as universal concepts, and as concepts that reflect the particular character *of U*. They thus become singularities that are defined or characterized by universality. Because S gets its universality from P—which is a universal in relation to S—and P gets its universality from U—which is a universal in relation to P—P and S each have their centers in universality. S has its center in its universal P, and P has its center in its universal U.

Because U started the process of communication and both P and S reflect the character *of U*, both S and P get their universality from U, which is the Object. Hence, S and P have the same character as the Object. They are objective ones: individual self-subsistences or singularities that reflect the character or universality of the Object. P's process of dividing into S and S's process point back to U. In the diagram, this process will be depicted as return arrows from S(P, U) to U(S, P), but there are a couple of steps of development to finish first.

Now all the objects are what they are only through their relation to one another. S and P are what they are only through their relation with U, and U is what it is only through its relation with S and P. The objects are thus no longer indifferent toward one another: the mechanism has become non-indifferent. In Formal Mechanism the objects were characterized as mutually indifferent. This stage draws the logical conclusion that the objects are non-indifferent toward one another after all.

Hegel suggests that Non-indifferent Mechanism is exemplified by fall (decay, ruin, decline), desire, and the urge to socialize (§196). Non-indifferent Mechanism is characterized by centrality, by singulars that aim at universality. The decline, ruin or decay of finite things exemplifies centrality, or the idea that singulars are directed at universality. There are different senses in which a singular can be "aimed at" a universal, and the kind of "aiming" here is not yet determined. It includes any kind of "aiming at." As I suggested in Section VIII in Chapter One, for Hegel, death, decay and decline are not accidents that attach to finite living and inanimate things. Instead, to be a human, for instance, is to be a singular that is aimed at the universal. One kind of "aiming" is teleological: a human is "aimed at" the universal in the sense that the universal sets a human being's goal or purpose (see the stages of Purpose). Like Kant, Hegel conceived of ethics as universal, so ethical goals and purposes that people aim at are universal. Individual humans are also aimed at the universal "human" insofar as they grow up and come to instantiate the full definition of "human." Singulars are aimed at the universal in a different sense, however, when they fall, decay, or decline. Because Hegel sees death, sickness and so on as part of what it means to be human, when people die or decay or decline, they are fulfilling the universal character of human beings. The death of individual humans also fulfills the universal in a final sense. The species "human" subsists over time, through the comings and goings of individual human beings. Our individual lives keep the species going, and our deaths highlight the fact that it's the species that remains, and hence the universal at which our individual lives aim. Singulars are thus "aimed at" the universal in the sense that the universal captures their genuine nature: their nature as full human beings, their nature as ethical people, their nature as humans who die, and their nature as humans who live to maintain the species or the universal.

In the realm of spirit or consciousness, a desire can also serve as an example of centrality. Having a desire is a way of having one's center in the universal, or of being what one is through the universal. If I want (desire) to be a teacher, I want to instantiate a universal, namely, the universal of being-a-teacher. I cannot make up what a teacher is simply in my head. What a teacher is is defined by the larger community—it is a thought or concept, an ideal, a universal. To be a teacher I have to particularize *that* universal, or become a singular exemplar of the universal "teacher." I have to make myself part of the community of teachers, part of the universal "teacher." Similarly, an urge to socialize is a way of being directed at, and of being what one is, in the universal. The desire to socialize is a desire to be an "I" that is part of an "us," or to be an "I" that is "we." To desire to socialize is to want to be part of a group, or to want to be part of some universal.

Absolute Mechanism

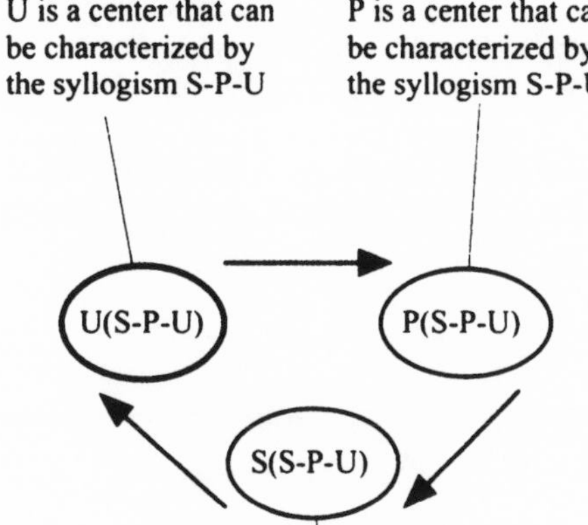
U is a center that can be characterized by the syllogism S-P-U
P is a center that can be characterized by the syllogism S-P-U
U(S-P-U)
P(S-P-U)
S(S-P-U)
S is a center that can be characterized by the syllogism S-P-U

Figure 4.59

Centrality is a new kind of singularity: a singularity that is still at rest—or is a oneness that has self-subsistence—but positively reflects or aims at the universal as its own character. It is an S-as-U, for short. Because each object (U, P and S) is now a center, each is an S-as-U, or a central singularity.

Centers are singularities that are also destined to externalize or negate themselves. This destiny grows out of their universality. U, P and S are all universals. A universal in its most basic definition is a group or bunch (of items), a community of items (see Being-for-itself in Chapter Two). Hence, as a universal, each center must externalize or negate itself into some (particular) group of objects that make up its totality (U) and so make it a U. Hence, each center can be defined by the syllogism S-P-U: each is an S (an S-as-U) that, given its nature (P) as a center, externalizes or particularizes (P) into some bunch of objects (U). Notice that P or particularity here is both a content and activity: the S-as-U is a P in terms of content and that undergoes P-activity by externalizing or dividing into some bunch of objects. This dual nature of P as both content and activity will become important later in the stages of Purpose.

Seeing each object as an S-P-U grows out of two characteristics of the object encountered before. First, since Chapter Three, S, P and U have been totalities, or completed or complete sets or group-terms. They are concepts that gather up and contain all of their items as a finished product. The syllogism S-P-U captures the process that a universal must go through to be a universal as a group-term, namely the process of sundering or dividing into the items that they contain. S-P-U: the singular centrality particularizes by becoming universal, or by dividing into the group of items that it contains.

Second, seeing S, P and U as each a syllogism is also a way of restating the process of particularization in the stage of Disjunctive Syllogism. In Disjunctive Syllogism, a universal is fully defined when it particularizes into actuality or existence. The Concept particularizes into genera, which in turn further particularize into species. Now that the centrality of each element has come to light, this process can be characterized as the syllogism S-P-U. The Concept—as an

Object-as-center—is an S-as-U that presents its universality by externalizing or particularizing (P) into a bunch or universality (U) of objects. Similarly, each particularity or genus is also a center, or an S-as-U that must express or present its universality by externalizing or particularizing (P) into a bunch or universality (U) of objects. The genus panther, for instance, particularizes into the species lion, tiger and so on. Even singularity (S), however, is a center or an S-as-U that must present its universality by externalizing or particularizing (P) into a bunch or universality (U) of objects. The species lion, for instance, particularizes into actual, individual lions.

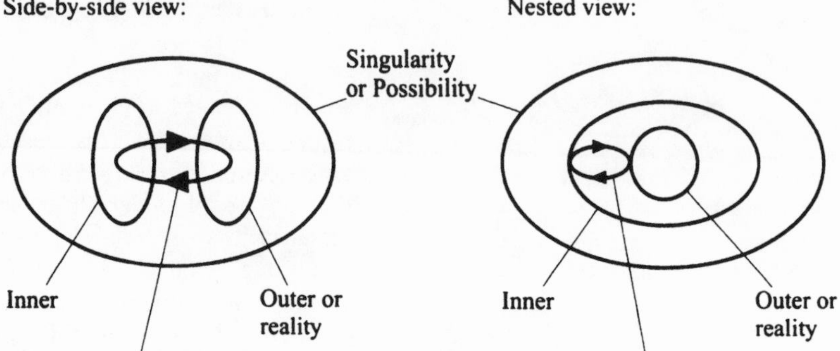

Figure 4.60

S's process of centrality, or of becoming a genuine universal or totality, reactivates elements of the Concept or Object that have been ignored since the Transition to Mechanism, namely, the internal elements of Singularity that extend into actuality or existence. In the Concept, Singularity had additional bubbles and arrows within it. Singularity developed out of the Possibility bubble from the Doctrine of Essence, which was defined as the real possibility of Inner and Outer achieving a mutually defining relationship (see Singularity). I have used two standard ways of depicting this relationship between Inner and Outer: the side-by-side view, which I used in Chapter Three, and the nested-bubble view (see Figure 4-60 above). These internal elements come back into view because Singularity can be a totality or universal only if it sunders or divides into the objects that it defines, just as Universality and Particularity did. Singularity sunders itself into individual (singular) actualities, or individual Outers that live up to their defining concepts or Inners. These singularities are the non-self-subsistent or dependent objects, or what Hegel also calls the extreme of singularity in the discussion of this stage in the *Science of Logic* (see also his discussion in SL of the Third Figure of Qualitative Syllogism, in which he says that S can be taken as the "extreme of singularity" [§1467] or as individually existing, actual singularities). S can be an S-as-U only by sundering into the extreme of singularity, or into singular actualities. Again, lion can be an S-as-U only by dividing into the individual existing lions that make it up.

Now that these internal elements of Singularity have come back into focus, I have put them back inside the bubble for S in the next diagram. I will use the nested view that has dominated this chapter.

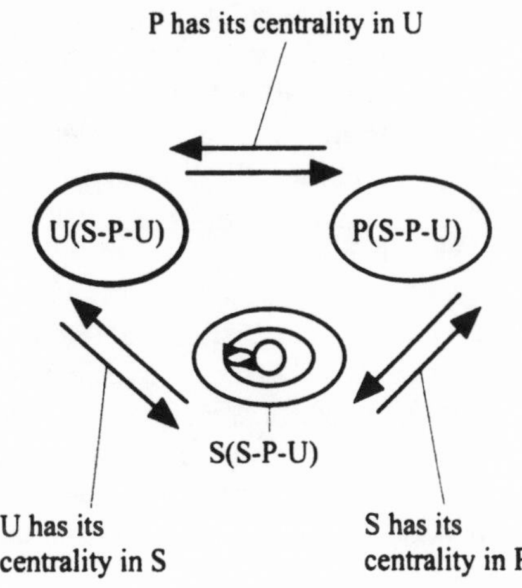
P has its centrality in U
U(S-P-U)
P(S-P-U)
S(S-P-U)
U has its
centrality in S
S has its
centrality in P

Figure 4.61

Centrality is therefore a syllogistic relationship between the three elements that can be characterized by the syllogism S-P-U. While communication was the process represented by the arrows that ran from U to P to S and then back to U (since that process as a whole defined U itself), centrality is the return trip, so to speak. Centrality can be represented as arrows that run from S to P to U and ultimately back to S. S was really the last step in U's process of communication: U communicated its U to P, and then P communicated its U to S. The relationship of centrality begins with S. Once S gets its U-ness, it becomes an S-as-U, or a center, by emulating P, from which it got its U-ness. So S has its centrality in P, because P is the universality S aims at. S responds to the U-ness it got from P by becoming a center, an S-as-U, by sundering or dividing into the group of items that it contains. Because S has its centrality by emulating P, S's centrality points back to P. Similarly, P has its centrality in U. U is the universality that P emulates. P responds to the U-ness from U by becoming a center—an S-as-U. It emulates U by sundering. Because P has its centrality by emulating U, P's centrality points back to U. U has its own centrality in S. U is already a U, so it gets to be a center—an S-as-U—by getting S-ness from S. S is the totality or universality that defines U as a singularity. S gives U its singularity in two senses. First, U sunders into S through P, so that S is U's singularity just as much as it is P's singularity. Second, U is a one (singular) or a totality: it is a U-as-S. U is a singular because it is characterized by oneness or singularity (S). So S also gives U its singularity by making U a one. U's centrality therefore points back to S.

The type of mechanism developed here is absolute in the usual sense. First, it is absolute because all sides have the same character or are the same in an "in itself" sense, or in terms of how they are each defined on their own in relation to the other elements. Second, their relationships with one another are the same as well. They each split up into and hence point toward their particularities and have their centrality in, and hence point toward, their universals. They are the same as each other in terms of both their content and their form or how they are presented. Form and content overturn into one another. The activity that defines their form also defines their content. Hence, S, P and U are absolutely and completed related—both in terms of their definitions and in their relationships, through their external, mechanistic relationship.

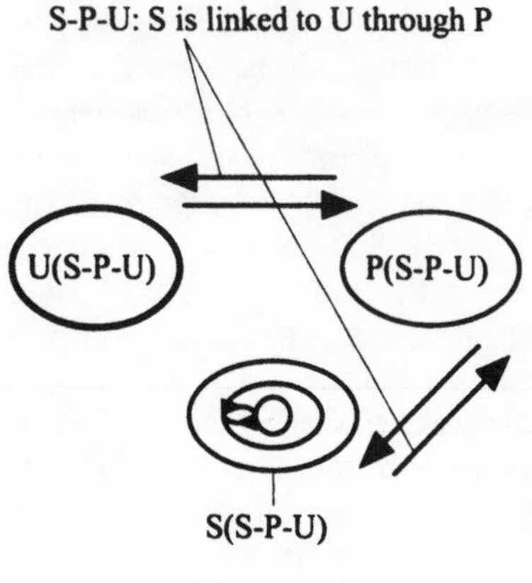
S-P-U: S is linked to U through P
U(S-P-U)
P(S-P-U)
S(S-P-U)

Figure 4.62

We can also think of the process of centrality as a trilogy of syllogisms (§198). The first syllogism takes the standard form of syllogism, namely, S-P-U. This is the syllogism that Hegel says is at home in Formal Mechanism (§198). In Formal Mechanism, all the objects are treated more or less as singularities—as self-subsistent objects that are opposed to their universality or their unity, which therefore seems to fall outside of them. This first syllogism takes up Formal Mechanism's emphasis on singularity by beginning with singularity.

Of course, even in Formal Mechanism, the objects are *supposed* to be unified, or to be a universal, which is why we saw S, P and U as an aggregate. They are a machine. This syllogism takes up this idea as well by suggesting that the singularity that it starts with is supposed to be unified or be a U. According to this syllogism, S is linked to U through some particularity, or because S and U are in the same (particular) sphere. Hence S is U through P, a relationship that can be captured by the syllogism S-P-U. Because syllogisms are reversible, as I have argued, we can also say that U is S through P—so long as we keep in mind that U is currently defined as an external form of universality. According to this reversal of the original syllogism, then, an external universal is linked to singularity in virtue of some particularity: U-P-S.

In §198R, Hegel gives an example to flesh out the whole trilogy of syllogisms, an example that also appears in the *Science of Logic*. In Hegel's example, S stands for individual people, P stands for their needs and external existence, and U stands for some relevant, overarching universal—such as society (as a whole), government, law, or right (where that means the concept of rightness, or ethics and morality). According to this first syllogism, people (in general or as a totality) (i.e. the S) are linked to society, government, law, or ethics and morality (U) through their needs and external existence or particularity (P). Hegel says that this syllogism is at home in Formal Mechanism (§198), so the objects (S, P and U) are being treated as self-subsistent, and are not yet defined in terms of one another, as they were in the stage of Non-indifferent Mechanism. The S's are therefore not yet defined in relation to U, so their relationship with the U is such that they *strive* for it. Thus, on this view, people in general (S) strive, when they are working on their needs and external existence (P), to be right, be the ideal social being, meet the ideals of government, follow the law, and so on (U).

This example conceives of society, government, morality and law in a way that is highly mechanistic. According to this view, governments and so on are mere aggregates—the cumulative results of people striving after their needs and external existence. There is no acknowledgment of the ways in which (individual) people, as well as their needs and external existence, are shaped and defined by the collectives—universals—in which they live.

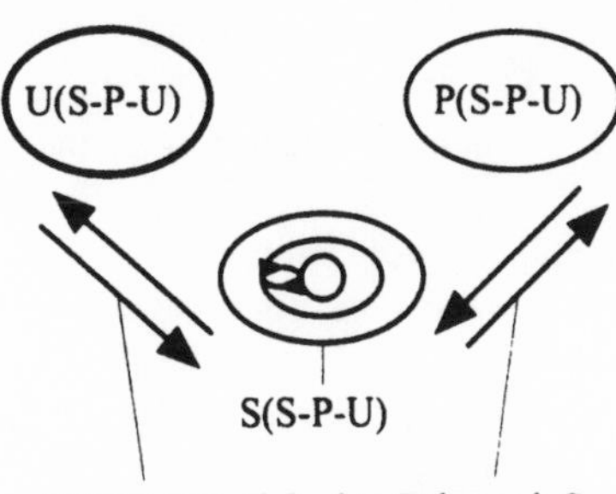
U(S-P-U)
P(S-P-U)
S(S-P-U)
U-S-P: U is linked to P through S

Figure 4.63

U is supposed to be a universal or totality—that is its character or particularity (P). But to truly *be* a universal, that is, for U to be a universal with being, it has to have two components. First, it has to divide into a group of items to be a universal at all. Second, however, it must have *being*, or exist. U gets the first component—its universality as a group—not only from P, but also from S, into which it sunders too (through P). But, U gets the second component—its being or existence—from S. For S provides the existence (in its Outer and Inner bubbles [see the stages of Appearance through Inner and Outer in Chapter Three]) that U requires if U is going to succeed in *being* (in having being as) a universal. So U gets to have its being or P-ness (or particular character) as a universal through S. It gets to be a particular (P) through S, or U is P through S: a relationship that can be captured with the syllogism U-S-P. P gets to be a U through S too. Just as U gets its P-ness through S, P gets its U-ness through S. P gets to be a totality (U) at all and have its being by dividing into S. So P is a U through S, a relationship that can be captured by the reversed syllogism, P-S-U.

It might be easier to understand this syllogism if we think for a moment of the diagram of the whole Object as a set of nested bubbles. In the nested view of the Object—before it fell apart in Formal Mechanism—U was the outer-most bubble, P was the next inside bubble, and S was the next inside bubble after that. If we keep in mind that S is supposed to be nested inside P and U, S is the one content that P and U both share. Because S contains Inner and Outer in their mutually defining relationship, it also contains Existence. Hence U can be a particular U, or have a character and exist, only if it succeeds in grasping S. And it succeeds in grasping S only through P, that is, only if the S's are successfully characterized and grasped by P. U gets to be a defined (particularized) universal only if S is subsumed under P. Take the concept of "feline" for a moment. The universal concept of "feline" can have a character and exist only if all the actual felines that exist (S's)—house cats, leopards, cougars and so on—are genuinely grasped by the concepts of panther and felis (P), for instance. So U gets to be some universal or other (some P)—a universal with a definition, character and existence—only if the S's are subsumed under the P: U is P through S, or U-S-P.

In Hegel's example, the needs (P) of the individuals (in the context of the society) are satisfied or actualized through the activity of people (S), insofar as that activity actualizes the universal (U). The universal (society, government etc.) is fulfilled and actualized—i.e. gets to be what it is as the characterizing or particular universal that it is—to the degree that the activity of people (S) actualizes the particularity (the P) in question. So U gets to have being and a specific character as a government only to the degree that what the people (S) are doing lives up to the concept of some type or species of government (P)—democracy, for instance. If what the people are doing cannot be characterized as some type (P) of "government," then U does not have any specific character or being as some government. U gets to be the P that it is only through S.

There has been a subtle change in the way P is now conceptualized from the way it was conceptualized in the last syllogism. The needs and particularities of individuals are now said to be satisfied in the context of society. The people's activity is now characterized in relation to a P that is connected to U. The activities of the people—in which they satisfy their needs and wants—must count as some type of government (U). This syllogism thus suggests that it's only in the context of the universal that the needs of people can be satisfied by their activity. Our needs are shaped and satisfied in the context of our communities. When I am hungry, I need bread. But bread is a gift of the community. The recipe for bread and the skill needed to make it were given to me by the community. Hence what our needs are as well as how those needs are satisfied is determined in the context of our communities. That means that the needs are now explicitly universalized to some degree—P is now characterized in relation to U. This sort of connectedness between S, P and U was the hallmark of Non-indifferent Mechanism.

At the same time, P gets to be some U through S too: P-S-U. Whether the need-satisfying activity or democracy-activity (P) counts as a type of government (U) depends on the people (S). So P gets to be a U through S.

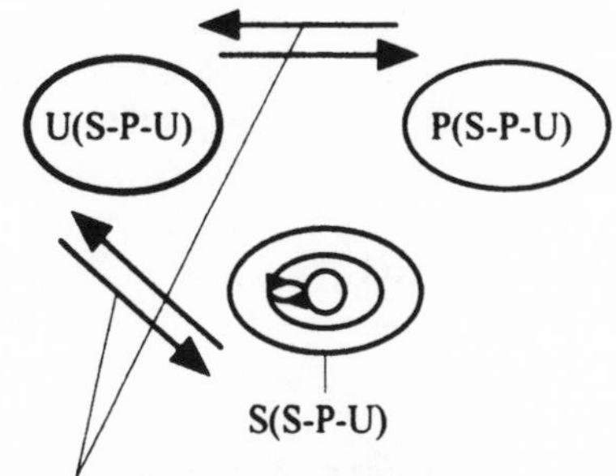
U(S-P-U)
P(S-P-U)
S(S-P-U)
P-U-S: P is linked to S through U

Figure 4.64

In Absolute Mechanism, U was the substantial universal that identifies and brings rest to the whole. U locks singularity in itself or defines itself as a singularity, and, in communication, drives the dividing or particularizing process that makes U the identifying essence of the whole syllogism. U is the one whole singularity that defines and holds the whole process together as a restful, being-in-itself. For U is *the* Center, the one Center toward which S and P are pointing and which ultimately defines S and P. So U is really the middle term between P and S. P is S through U. In communication, P communicated U to S, and P divides into S because of the action of U. This sundering process also gives P its singularity—through the sundering, P becomes a (singular) totality, center, or an S-as-U. All of this activity can be captured with the syllogism P-U-S. At the same time, S is P through U too. S gets its character (P-ness) as a totality from U because U's activity of communication ultimately inspired S to sunder or divide and hence to particularize (P) as well. S sunders or particularizes into the extreme of singularity—or into the set of individual actualities, which is Inner and Outer in their mutually defining relationship—in response to the action of U.

In Hegel's example, this syllogism captures the idea that it is really the universal (society, government, ethics and morality, law and so on) that is the middle term within which individuals and the satisfaction of their needs come together, or, in more Hegelian language, have their full reality, mediation and subsistence (§198). Society, ethics and morality, government, law and so on, make possible the satisfaction of people's needs and desires. Not only are our needs shaped by the social or universal—as in the last syllogism—but whether we can satisfy our needs depends on the sort of society, government, or legal and moral community that we live in. The government, society and so on are constitutive of, or construct, who we are as individuals. What we choose to "be" when we grow up, for instance, is determined by the menu of options provided by our society. Many jobs that were available in the past are either rare or nonexistent today, just as there are jobs today—such as the job of computer-programmer—that did not exist in the past. Moreover, whether we can satisfy even our most basic needs depends on the sort of social community in which we live. In times of war, or under anarchy or tyranny, when government has become insecure and we have difficulty satisfying our needs, our dependence on our community is laid bare. What we do—the needs we have and the ways in which we satisfy those needs—is thus largely determined by our government and society, which set the parameters for our choices. In this sense, people can satisfy their particularity, or be the people that they are, only in virtue of the nature of the universals—government, society, law, morality—in which they find themselves. In more logical terms, needs (P) are satisfied (or made actual as singularities) (i.e. S) through the government, society and so on (U): P is S through U, or P-U-S. Reversing the syllogism, people (S) satisfy their particularity (P)—their needs, which are shaped by the social or universal—in virtue of the nature of the government, society and so on (U): S is P through U, or S-U-P.

Transition to Chemism

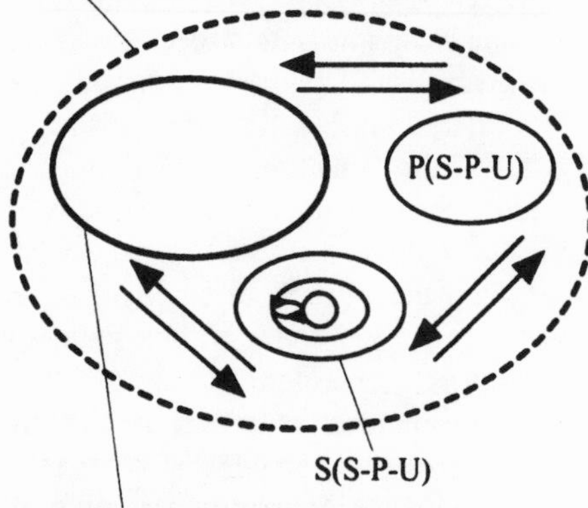
U as the totality or unity of S and P has now come into view, but only as a concept (i.e. as inner) and not yet as object. The unity is the overarching bubble, but because it is only a concept, I represent it as dashed
P(S-P-U)
S(S-P-U)
Objectively, as Center, U is still setting up S and P as its opposition

Figure 4.65

U is not only a center, but *the* Center. It is the central distinction that makes the difference, or that distinguishes or determines the other two elements. U is *the Center* in the sense that it is the element out of which and into which the other elements flow. U makes P and S what they are through its relationships with them. U determines and is the defining essence (identity) of S and P. It particularizes, divides or expands into P and S, and it is the universality at which S and P aim, and without which S and P would not be what they are. As a result, the idea that U is the unity of S and P has now come into view, but only in an inner way, or as an idea, concept, or thought. The thought of U as the unity of U, P and S fell out of the picture in the Transition to Mechanism. Because the thought of U as the unity of the whole has returned, I have added an overarching bubble surrounding everything to represent that thought in the diagram. That thought of U as the unity falls outside of U, however—it is an additional bubble that surrounds U, P and S. Because the unity is merely a thought, and not an object, the bubble has a dashed line instead of a solid one.

Although the thought of U as the unity or totality has come into view, because U is still an object, U is still the Center. U is still the central universal that fulfills its definition as a universal in actuality and existence by expanding into P and S. In more Hegelian language, U is the centrality that is concrete (defined and existing) and that is expanded in an immediate way into its own objectivity. In short, U, as the Center, is still defined by pushing out or dividing into P and S as its objectivity. U therefore has a relationship of opposition with S and P. As

U's objectivity, P and S are separate from or opposed to U. So while the thought of U as the unity has begun to return, U's role as the Center still puts U in an oppositional relationship with P and S that undercuts its ability at the moment to fulfill the function of being the unity of everything. Thus, while U now includes the *concept or thought* of the whole totality or unity, as an *object*, U is not fulfilling the role of being the unity or totality of the whole.

In a sense, then, there are two U's. There is the U defined as an object, which still has an oppositional relationship with P and S, and there is now U defined as a concept, or in thought, at least, as the unity of the whole. Since the second U is just a thought, however, only the first U has being at this point.

Because the second U is a thought or concept, the definition of U according to which U is the Concept, rather than the Object, has begun to return.

The "in-itself" relationships between U and P and S (taken together), are still defined by opposition. So U falls apart into (i) itself as the Center and (ii) P-and-S (together) as its objective opposition
P(S-P-U)
S(S-P-U)
U as the unity
(i) U as the Center
(ii) S and P are the completed, objective opposition to U. Their completed relationship is represented as a single, double-sided arrow

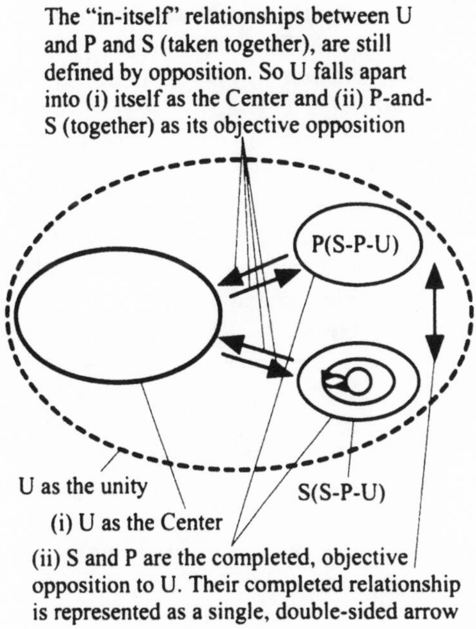

Figure 4.66

The relationships of communication and centrality between P and S are completed. Because P and S are totalities, P has completely communicated its U to S, and S has aimed at P completely by dividing into all of the elements defined by P. I have changed the two, one-way arrows that ran between them into one, double-sided arrow to represent that the process is completed. I used the same pictorial device in the stage of Real Possibility in Chapter Three.

Formal Mechanism grew out of taking the Concept in an "in itself" sense. The relationship of opposition that U now has with both S and P is an "in-itself" opposition. In an "in itself" relation—which is Hegel's general account of determination—each side can have a character or be determined only against or in opposition to its own other (see Being-in-itself in Chapter Two for a general description of "in-itselfness"). Here, the "in itself" relation gives the Object its determination. U as the Object has a character because of the "in itself" relationship that it has with S and P, as its own opposition. Yet the opposition characterizing the "in itself" type of relationship that U has with S and P blocks U from fulfilling its role as the totality or unity of S and P, and explains why U as the unity of S and P (represented by the dashed, outermost bubble) is only a thought or concept. The opposition between U as the Center and P and S as its objectivity bifurcates U into the two U's that we saw in the last stage.

The "in itself" opposition also bifurcates the whole in another way as well. Because U as the Center has an oppositional relationship with P and S, U splits or falls apart into (i) itself as the Center and (ii) the objectified opposition to which it is related, which is S and P taken together. Since S and P are also defined as objects (see Formal Mechanism), they are U's objectivity. P and S taken together are the entire or complete objective opposition to U. P and S are therefore now taken together as the completed objectivity of U.

In the stage of The Object, the Concept-that-had-become-Object was immediate. It contained no defined relationships and had no character or determination beyond the basic one in which it was the whole as the moments of U, P and S. There, the Object was depicted as a group of nested bubbles with no arrows in it, which illustrated the lack of relationships within the Object—a lack of relationships which left the Object largely undefined and without character. Now that the Object has developed relationships in it—which are represented by the arrows—the Object is determinate or has character.

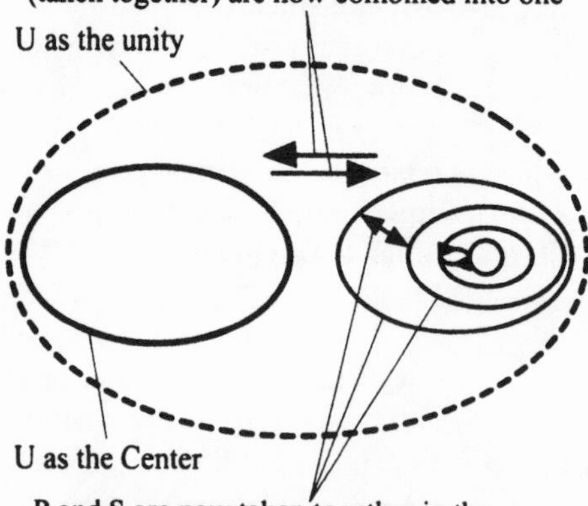
The two "in itself" relationships of mutual tension between U as the Center and P and S (taken together) are now combined into one
U as the unity
U as the Center
P and S are now taken together in the original form that they had at the end of the last chapter, namely, as nested bubbles with a double-sided arrow between them

Figure 4.67

Because P and S are being taken together as one, they are depicted once again as nested within one another: P is a bubble surrounding S. Depicting P and S this way is also justified because, in the process of communication and centrality, P proved to be the defining universal or essence of S, and S was the particularity into which P sunders or divides. The relationship between a defining universal or essence and what it defines can be depicted as nested bubbles, with the defining essence surrounding what it defines.[4] Because they still have their two-way relationship with one another, the double-sided arrow remains between them. This double-sided arrow (or two two-way arrows) representing the relationship between S and P is the very same double-sided arrow (or two two-way arrows) that represented their relationship with one another in the stage of Real Possibility and throughout the rest of the Doctrine of Essence. Indeed, we have reconstructed a large portion of the diagram that depicted the Concept at the beginning of this chapter. The Concept is beginning to "look like" it did when it was defined objectively at the end of the Doctrine of Essence. As the Concept goes through the process in which it subjectively defines itself *for itself*, or through its own activity, it is reconstructing the objective definition that it had earlier (cf. the Introduction to this chapter).

Chemism

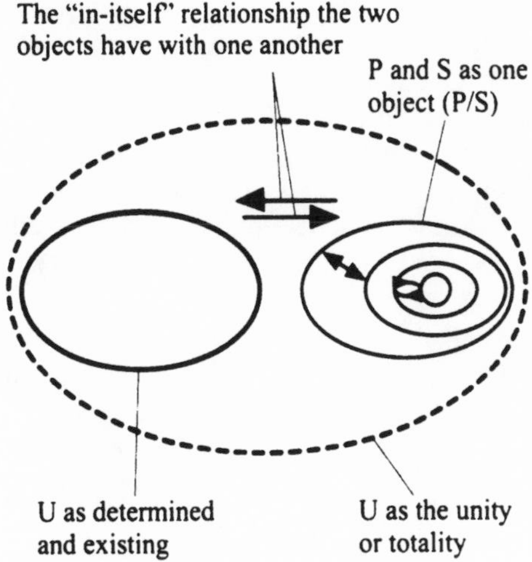

Figure 4.68

There are two U's: U-as-an-object—which is represented by the bubble next to the nested bubble representing Particularity and Singularity—and U as the unity—which is represented by the dashed bubble surrounding the other two bubbles. The bubble representing U as a unity is dashed because, at the moment, it is just a thought. Moreover, Particularity and Singularity are still being taken together as the complete objectivity or object of U-as-an-object.

The independence of the two objects—U-as-object, and P and S taken together as one object (which I will henceforth call P/S)—is mediated by the "in itself" relationship that they have with one another. According to the "in itself" type of relationship, each object can be what it is insofar as it is connected to the other. The objects are thus not only opposed to one another, but also dependent on one another, and are therefore not indifferent toward one another, as they were in Mechanism. This non-indifference between U-as-object and the object (i.e. P and S taken together as one object, or P/S) is the hallmark of Chemism. Unlike the parts of a machine, chemicals are non-indifferent toward each other because they react to one another. When chemicals are put together, they react with each other in a process of interconversion to form new products that typically have new characteristics that none of the original chemicals (or reactants) had by themselves. The stages of chemism outline how the elements, U, P and S, are related together in logical ways that are analogous to the non-indifferent chemical relationships that chemical elements have. As we will see, as is true for chemical processes in science, the stages of chemism will generate a new product that is the unity of the elements (U, P and S) and has a character that none of these elements (as they are each currently defined) has by itself.

The two U's have different characters: (1) U is *concrete*, divides into actuality and existence, or has its existence as an object that is in an "in itself" relation with its own other (i.e. with P/S). When U is taken in this sense, it is *split or bifurcated* into itself as U-as-object and P/S as its object. (2) U is also defined as a *thought or concept*, however, as the *totality* or unity of the whole, which is currently represented in the diagram by the dashed outer-most bubble surrounding everything else. When taken in this way, U is not split. (2) is the definition that U is supposed to have as the unity of P and S. There is therefore a contradiction between (2)—i.e. U defined as the totality—and (1)—i.e. U as it is determined and has its existence. The totality or the definition that U is supposed to have as the unity of P and S—which is for the moment merely a concept—strives to sublate (cancel but preserve) this contradiction, so that U's way of being—how it is determined and has its existence (or [1])—will live up to its concept (§200)(or [2]). U should get its character or determination and exist (i.e. [2]) in a way that defines it as the genuine unity or totality (overarching bubble) of P/S (i.e. as [1]), but, at the moment, it is not. U is determined and exists only as an element that is outside of and opposed to P/S—i.e. as U-as-object or (1).

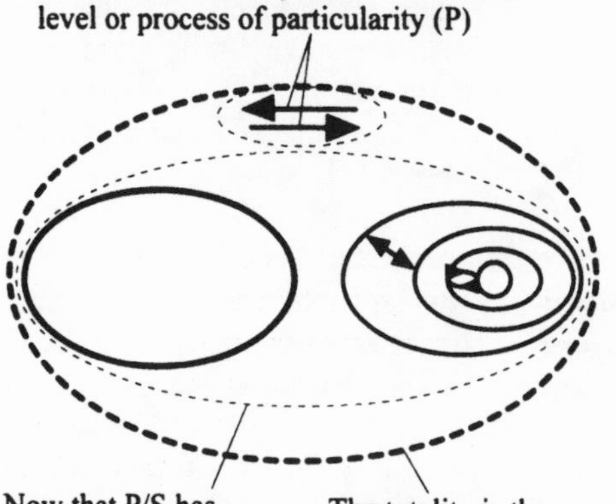

U and P/S determine themselves in relation to one another. This determination or particularizing process between U and P/S is the chemical process. It is a new level or process of particularity (P)

Now that P/S has become U's own other (through the "in-itself" relationship), U and P/S taken together are the Concept as a concrete universal. They are the U of the syllogisms

The totality is the neutral product of the chemical process. It is a singularity (S), a one

Figure 4.69

The chemical process is the back-and-forth determination or particularizing process between U-as-object and P/S while they are external to one another and in their "in itself" relationship. (A universal is determined by dividing or particularizing [see Particularity], and U and P/S are both universals.) This back-and-forth process captures their non-indifference but immediate independence at the same time. The process of going back and forth captures their non-indifference because it highlights that they are connected to one another: one leads directly to the other. They are connected to one another because U-as-object and P/S can each be what it is or be defined only in opposition to the other. The back-and-forth process also captures their independence from one another, however, because it still treats them as opposed to, and hence as separate from and independent of, one another in an immediate way. Each is still outside of the other, so that you have to go back and forth from one to the other to define them.

U-as-object and P/S taken together are the Concept (or U) insofar as it is defined as a concrete universal—or insofar as it is determinate, defined and existing. Together, they are what I'll call *concrete U*.

Now that chemism is the back-and-forth process, the concept or thought of the unity or totality (i.e. U as the unity, or the big, dashed bubble) is the neutral product of the process. The neutral product is the thought of the whole process of chemism as an immediate unity, or as a one or singularity. Keep in mind that U as determined and existing (i.e. U-as-object and P/S, taken together as a whole) is supposed to be the same as the totality, unity or neutral product (the dashed outer-most bubble, or U as the unity). As Universality, U is supposed to be the Concept both as concrete (determined and existing) and as the unity or universal, though they are currently not the same.

Hegel suggests (§201) that the process of chemism contains the same trilogy of syllogisms that were in Absolute Mechanism, namely U-P-S, U-S-P, and P-U-S (keep in mind that the syllogisms are reversible). Hegel's suggestion makes sense if the "in itself" chemical relationship between U as determined and existing (or U-as-object inner-bubble U) and P/S (as the particularizing process) as a new level or process of particularity, or as the P in the trilogy of syllogisms. That "in itself" relationship is the way in which the concrete U (inner-bubble U taken together with P/S) is defined, determined or particularized, since it includes the process in which U divides or particularizes into P and S. Concrete U itself (U and P/S together) is the universality or U of the syllogisms, and the totality or neutral product (outer-bubble U)—the one whole—is the singularity or S of the syllogisms.

According to the syllogism U-P-S, U and P/S taken together (concrete U) as a one whole, syllogistically links itself with itself as the neutral product or S, through the particularizing, chemical process (P). Concrete U, together with P/S, is defined through the back-and-forth chemical process (P) that gives rise to the thought of the whole or neutral product as a unity (S). At the same time, however, the neutral product, as the singularity (S), really is nothing but the activity of the chemical process (P) at this point. So the whole neutral product or S is really the mediating element between itself as concrete U (together with P/S) and the particularizing process (P): which gives us the syllogism U-S-P. Finally, because the concrete U (together with P/S) is the defining essence (identity) of P/S—as we saw in the communication process and process of centrality above—and hence of the whole process (P), concrete U is the element that ultimately gives the neutral product (S) the character or definition that it has as well. So concrete U is the mediating term between S and P: which gives us the syllogism P-U-S.

Let me try to flesh out this stage and the three syllogisms using the example of the syllogism feline(U)-panther(P)-lion(S). Because there are two U's, "feline" is currently split into two definitions. First, as the neutral product, it is the universal concept of feline—the concept that embraces every feline that has and will ever exist throughout time. It is the unity of all felines. It is the concept that explains why each of the individual, existing felines belongs in the set "feline." It makes or defines the existing felines as what they are as felines. Because it is a unity or one, it is the S or singularity of the syllogisms. But this universal concept of feline does not itself *exist* as those felines. That's because there is a second version of the concept of feline, namely, the concept of feline insofar as it exists or divides into all the existing felines—the individual panthers, house cats, lions, leopards and so on (i.e. P/S). This is the concept of feline that is defined as a concrete universal, or in terms of how it exists or divides into existing felines. This is the definition U has had since the beginning of the Doctrine of the Object. Because this concept of feline is defined as the set or group of items that exist, it is a set or group-term, and so is a universal in the most basic sense in which it is a bunch or group of items. But it falls short of being the one concept that does the job of unifying all of the existing felines throughout time—of explaining why each of those felines is a feline. It is not the one (singular) universal concept of feline. It is the U of the syllogism: it has U-ness, but lacks singularity. Being-for-itself in Chapter Two—which introduced qualitative universality—had two functions. In repulsion, the Being-for-itself or concept pushed out the something-others that it contained (see Repulsion). This is similar to the process in which the existing concept of feline (concrete U) divides into the individual existing felines. In attraction, the Being-for-itself pulled the something-others together. It explained why they belonged together in a set. This is similar to the process in which the universal concept of feline (U as the unity, which is the S of the syllogism) embraces all the existing felines, or explains why those felines belong together in a set. Both of these activities are top-down processes, or processes that must be done from the top down by the higher concept. Being-for-itself was the higher concept that did both activities. Here, universality is split into two U's, each of which does only one of these activities. In addition to the higher, universal concept of feline as the neutral product (S), there is also the concept of feline as a set, or insofar as it exists, or pushes out into existence (U). The final element of the three syllogisms would be the particularizing process between the concept of feline as existing (inner-bubble U) and all of the existing felines in which it exists (i.e. P/S). That is the new level or process of particularity, or the particularity (P) of the three syllogisms of Chemism.

This example can illustrate the three syllogisms (keep in mind that the syllogisms are each reversible). One syllogism—U-S-P—says that the concept of feline as existing (U) is linked to the particularizing process (P) by the universal concept of feline (S). The universal concept, which embraces every feline that has and will ever exist, makes possible the fact that "feline" as a concept exists through its process of particularizing. The syllogism S-U-P says that the universal concept of feline (S) is linked to the particularizing or dividing up process (P) by the concept of feline as existing (U). The concept of feline as existing makes the universal concept split up or particularize. Finally, the syllogism U-P-S says that the concept of feline as existing is linked to the universal concept of feline by the particularizing process. The particularizing process makes the universal concept of feline exist, and makes the existing concept of feline universal.

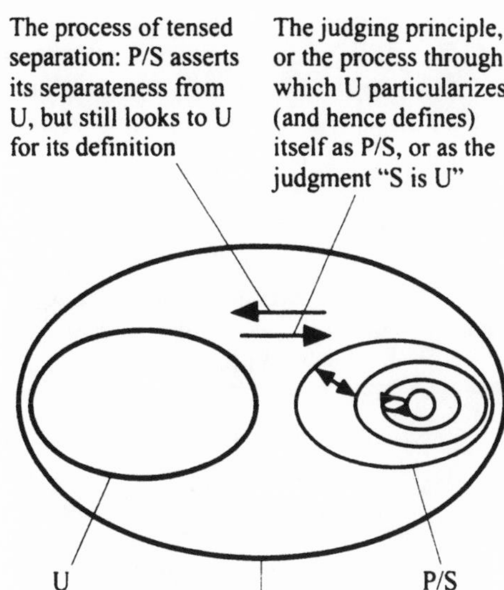
The process of tensed separation: P/S asserts its separateness from U, but still looks to U for its definition
The judging principle, or the process through which U particularizes (and hence defines) itself as P/S, or as the judgment "S is U"
U
P/S

The neutral product is determined now (and so receives a solid outline), but in an immediate way. It is something separable, i.e. it is defined by its contents, but is capable of being separated from its contents

Figure 4.70

As the thought of the whole chemical process, the neutral product has once again sunk back into immediacy. It has a character or definition (and so has a solid outline in the diagram), but only in an immediate way. The neutral product has a character because it contains the whole process and so is defined by the determinate properties that U and P/S have in relation to one another. But the neutral product has that character only in an immediate way, since it has no relationships with its contents. It gathers up or embraces its contents, but is otherwise not related to them. This immediacy is depicted in the diagram because there are no arrows between the bubble representing the neutral product and any of the internal elements. The neutral product thus sublates (cancels but preserves) the specific determinations of U and P/S. As the thought of the whole chemical process, it contains the determinations of U and P/S. At the same time, since it has no relationships with concrete U and P/S, what their characters are like does not really matter to the neutral product's definition. Hence it also cancels those determinations, or renders them unimportant.

Because the neutral product lacks relationships with its contents, it conforms to the Concept insofar as it captures the unity of U and P/S, but does not conform to the Concept because it is not doing the job of unifying U and P/S by itself, or by its own process. According to the definition of the Concept developed before, the neutral product—as the unifying concept—should be the judging principle: it should be what sunders P/S into its extremes and yet leads P/S to pull back together. It should be what turns P/S into a judgment. In the Transition to Judgment, the Concept, as the unifying concept, pushed out Particularity as the judgment "S is U." Since the neutral product is the unifying concept now, it should be doing what the Concept did earlier. Moreover, as the overarching concept, the neutral product should also be the source of the process of tensed separation between U and P/S, or should be what splits up U and P/S into their current relationship of opposition.

At the moment, however, because the neutral product does not have any relationships with the internal elements, these two processes fall outside the unifying process of the neutral product (§202). As a result, the neutral product is something separable (§202): it has a content or definition and so counts as a something, but, because it lacks any relationships with its contents, it is capable of being separated from that contents, and so is characterized by separability.

Transition to Purpose

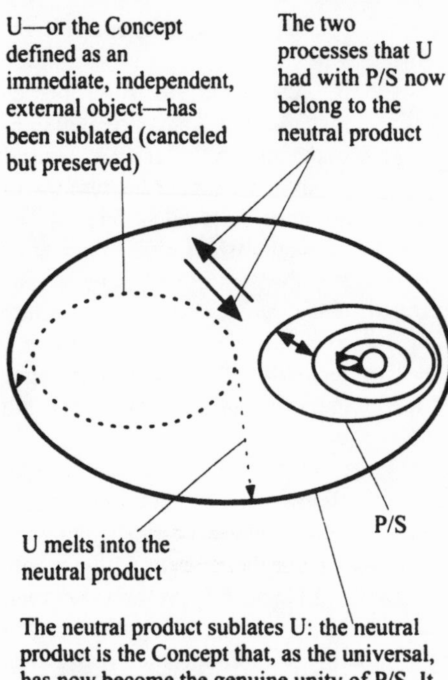
U—or the Concept defined as an immediate, independent, external object—has been sublated (canceled but preserved)
The two processes that U had with P/S now belong to the neutral product
P/S
U melts into the neutral product
The neutral product sublates U: the neutral product is the Concept that, as the universal, has now become the genuine unity of P/S. It is the Concept posited as a "for-itself," or an embracing concept—i.e. that has now become an overarching bubble

Figure 4.71

Concrete U (the U that splits up as inner-bubble U and P/S) and the neutral product are supposed to be the same one element—the universal, unifying Concept. So far, concrete U has the universal function of the Concept insofar as the universal divides up or particularizes, but has failed to succeed in unifying the whole. Now, however, the neutral product is U or the Concept finally performing both the unifying function and the particularizing function that it was supposed to be performing all along. The neutral product has now become the genuinely unifying and particularizing U, or the Concept itself. When the thought of the totality or unity—what is now the neutral product—first arose, it was just a thought. There seemed to be two U's, but only concrete U had being. Now that the neutral product is defined and has a character (and a solid outline in the diagram), however, it has enough being to suggest that both U's now have being. However, the thought of concrete U is sublated (cancelled but preserved), and so disappears. Since the beginning of mechanism, what we are now calling inner-bubble U was being defined as external to, and independent of, P and S. It was still external to and independent of P/S when it was defined by the "in itself" relationship as opposed to P/S. But the whole chemical process—the back-and-forth process between inner-bubble U and P/S—shows that the supposed independence and immediacy of the objects (inner-bubble U and P/S) is null and void (§203). Neither U nor P/S can be what it is without the other. Neither U nor P/S can have its character in an immediate way. Each can have its definition or character only in a mediated way in relation to the other. Inner-bubble U therefore cannot stand on its own anymore as the defining or particularizing universal. It has no independent, defining role. The real, defining universal is now just the neutral product itself, which captures the whole back-and-forth chemical process. As a result, inner-bubble U—which was the Concept defined as the immediate, defining universal of P/S—melts into the neutral product—or the Concept defined as the totality or unity of the whole. I represent this change by eliminating inner-bubble U as a bubble separate from the neutral product. The neutral product sublates inner-bubble U, and inner-bubble U melts into the neutral product.

Think of the example for the concept of feline again. When U is split into two, it is (1) the universal concept of feline as the unity of all felines, or the concept that grasps all of the felines together as a set, and (2) the concrete concept of feline, or the concept of feline insofar as it exists, or pushes out into the individual existing felines. Now that the universal concept of feline (i.e. [1]) is defined by the Chemical process as the whole process in which the existing or concrete concept of feline (i.e. [2]) exists or pushes out into existing felines, the universal concept (i.e. [1]) includes the whole process in which the concrete concept of feline (i.e. [2]) exists. Hence the same concept that is the universal unity of all felines or that grasps all the felines together as a set is the concept that goes through the process of pushing out into or splitting up into the existing felines.

There was a similar logical move at the end of Reciprocal Action in Chapter Three. Reciprocal Action was the process in which the Concept—defined as the thought of the systematized set of rational concepts—both defined and is defined by (as cause and effect) the activity of those rational concepts in the actual world. This process generated a new definition of Reason, namely Reason defined as the complete and completely systematized set of rational concepts, or as the thought of what the set of rational concepts will be like at the end of time, when the process of Reciprocal Action is completed. Although the process of Reciprocal Action generated a new definition of Reason, the Reason that we had at the end of the process is the very same Reason that was the Reason that went through the process of Reciprocal Action. Similarly, here, it's the same Concept that is defined as the unity of all felines that goes through the process of pushing out into existence as all the individual felines. Just as the thought of Reason at the end of the process of Reciprocal Action sublated (canceled and preserved) or absorbed the earlier definition of Reason as the thought of the systematized set of rational concepts that is both cause and effect in relation to the actual world, so the universal Concept that is defined as the unity sublates or absorbs the Concept defined as concrete, as it exists or as it pushes out into existence.

When the neutral product absorbs inner-bubble U, it absorbs or sublates (cancels and preserves) inner-bubble U's processes as well. Inner-bubble U and P/S were engaged in the chemical process, which was a spuriously infinite, back-and-forth process between inner-bubble U and P/S that defined them both (cf. Spurious Infinity in Chapter Two). Since the neutral product absorbs the role of being the defining universality over P/S from inner-bubble U, it absorbs the processes that that inner-bubble U had with P/S as well. The two arrows in the diagram that used to run between inner-bubble U and P/S and represent their process therefore now run between the neutral product and P/S. Inner-bubble U's two processes become the processes of the neutral product itself. So, to use Hegel's language, the process of tensed separation becomes the reduction of what is non-indifferent (namely P/S, which was non-indifferent toward inner-bubble U because it looked to inner-bubble U for its universality and definition) to the neutral itself; and the judging process (the process of division or particularization) becomes the process of non-indifferentiation of the neutral product itself, or the process through which the neutral product becomes non-indifferent toward P/S (since it now particularizes or defines into P/S) (§203). While the neutral product is the defining universal, it is not independent of P/S. It still unifies and defines P/S, which is its content. It is the genuinely unifying and defining universal over P/S.

In §203, Hegel suggests that, although the two processes that used to belong to inner-bubble U have now been absorbed by the neutral product—which is supposed to be a genuine unity, totality or universality—the two process are still defined as finite. They are still finite from a logical point of view because they are defined by a finite, "in itself" relationship. They are the same sort of finite, passing-over processes that were in Being-in-itself. I have therefore used the same sort of arrows to represent them in the diagram that I used to depict the process of "in-itselfness" in Being-in-itself in Chapter Two. For Hegel, every passing-over process is finite. Here, he says, the processes are finite because the logical elements are still treated as external to one another—or as up against one another—and each side passes over into a product in which it is sublated (cancelled but preserved) (§203). The neutral product, which is supposed to be indifferent to its contents, passes over into the non-indifferent P/S, and P/S, which is supposed to be non-indifferent, passes over into the indifferent neutral product. Of course, the two processes taken together also show that the neutral product is not really indifferent, since it is defined in relation to P/S, and P/S is not entirely non-indifferent either. Because of the "in itself" process, P/S has its own definition in relation to the neutral product, and so to that extent still maintains some independence from and indifference toward the neutral product. As a result, the neutral product is indifferent, but sublates non-indifference, and P/S is non-indifferent, but sublates indifference.

The neutral product—as the genuinely unifying and defining universal—finally lives up to the definition or concept of the Concept or Universality as both the unity and defining element over P and S. Thus, the neutral product is the Concept once again. There is only one U now, then—one unifying and defining, universal or Concept that is concrete or pushes out into existence. This U is both Concept and Object: it is the Concept that pushes out as Object. U is both the concept that grasps all the felines together as a set, for instance, *and* pushes out into existing felines. How is U both of these definitions at the same time? As we will see more fully shortly, U can be both the concept that grasps all of the felines together as a set and the concept that pushes out into existing felines by *making those existing felines what they are*. In short, the Concept has become the *purpose over* the object.

Moreover, the neutral product—or Concept—has begun to be defined once again as a "for itself" concept in the sense that it embraces its contents (cf. Being-for-itself in Chapter Two). Although the Concept—as Object—was defined as a "for itself" concept, it failed to embrace its content in the Transition to Mechanism. The Object was supposed to be the embracing universality over P and S, but because it had no internal relationships, it was not defined by or did not include a process in which it embraced P and S. Its activity of dividing into P and S defined P and S in the immediate sense of giving them the same "in itself" character, definition or content that it had (as objects), but could not connect P and S within it. It did not *embrace* P and S through its own activity, so that they remained separate elements. Indeed, it fell apart into separate objects in the Transition to Mechanism because it lacked a process that embraced P and S within it as its content, or defined it as the unity of P and S in terms of activity or form. Now, however, because the neutral product is not only the unifying universal in terms of content—it genuinely includes or embraces P and S—but is also beginning to include an active process in which it ties itself to P and S—even if that process is still finite—its status as a "for itself" embracing concept in terms of its form or presentation has also begun to be reasserted. In short, U is beginning to live up to its definition as doubly "for itself," or as an embracing "for itself" concept that actively embraces its content *for itself*, or through its own activity. U is beginning to *have the activity* through which it will actively embrace its content *for itself*.

Abstract Purpose

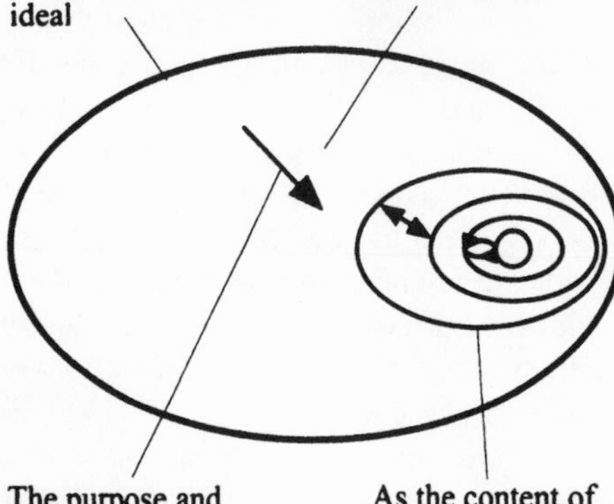
The Concept is now the purpose: a "for-itself" concept that contains P/S as its content. It is still opposed to objectivity, however, and so is subjective, or merely ideal
Now that P/S is the content of the purpose, it no longer negates the purpose. The arrow representing P/S's negation of the purpose disappears
The purpose and object have a relationship of abstract opposition: the purpose is the overarching Concept that negates the object
As the content of the purpose, P/S is the objectivity of the purpose, or the way in which the purpose objectifies itself

Figure 4.72

Although the Concept absorbed the processes of inner-bubble U, it does not absorb all of the characteristics that those processes had in relation to inner-bubble U. For one thing, although the Concept defines or identifies P/S in the way that inner-bubble U did, because it is the unity of the whole, P/S is not external to it. The fact that the Concept is not external to P/S is depicted in the diagram insofar as the bubble for the Concept now contains or embraces P/S as its content.

Moreover, although the Concept is defined by P/S—as inner-bubble U was—it does not have an immediate relationship with P/S in the way that inner-bubble U did. Inner-bubble U had an immediate relationship with P/S because, even though they were defined in relation to one another by their "in itself" relationship, the back-and-forth process from one to the other still implied that each was independent of the other, or could subsist on its own. Since the Concept includes P/S in its contents, however, its definition or character is clearly mediated by or includes P/S as its content. P/S is still immediate, but the Concept is not. Hence the exteriority and immediacy of the relationship between inner-bubble U and P/S has been negated (§203) by the Concept. Because the Concept includes the whole process of existence, that process is completed. Hence it is no longer defined by the way in which P/S happens to show up, is given or presented. P/S's process of being presented is finished, and the Concept embraces that process as finished. It therefore no longer has any immediacy in it.

Now that P/S belongs to the Concept, P/S is no longer opposed to the Concept. The Concept's process as the embracing, unifying universal negates the antithetical or oppositional relationship that P/S used to have with inner-bubble U. Since the Concept embraces and defines P/S, P/S is not opposed to the Concept. Moreover, in the Concept's embracing process, P/S's independence from universality has now also been negated. Since the Concept contains P/S as a completed process, it embraces everything about P/S. There is nothing left in or about P/S that is different from or opposed to what the Concept embraces. The exteriority or externality, independence, and immediacy—as well as the antithetical or oppositional nature—of the "in itself" relationship that P/S had with inner-bubble U has been sublated by the Concept. Since these are the characteristics—externality, immediacy, opposition and independence—that define an "in itself" relationship, it is fair to say that the "in itself" relationship between P/S and the Concept has been sublated. I have therefore removed the "in itself" arrow in the diagram that represented the oppositional relationship that P/S had with the Concept.

Although the "in itself" relationship that P/S had with universality (now the Concept) has been sublated, there is a remnant of the "in itself" relationship between inner-bubble U and P/S that still survives. According to the "in itself" relationship, inner-bubble U and P/S were opposed to one another. While P/S is no longer opposed to the universality of the Concept (since the Concept embraces or includes P/S), for the Concept, P/S is still defined as a separate element into which it divides. Therefore, the Concept's opposition to P/S—which has its roots in the "in itself" relationship—remains. As a result, the Concept is a "for itself" concept that embraces or includes, but also *negates*, P/S. There is still a need for one arrow that runs from the Concept's bubble to the bubble for P/S, to represent the Concept's negation of P/S. Because this negation is a remnant of an "in itself" relationship, I will continue to use the same sort of straight arrow that I have used to depict "in itself" processes before. As the fact that only one arrow remains suggests, the "in itself" relationship only goes one way: the Concept is still opposed to P/S, but P/S is no longer opposed to the Concept.

The Concept was defined at the beginning of this chapter as Universality that had an "in and for itself" relationship with Particularity (see Universality). That "in and for itself" relationship grew out of two "for itself" relationships—one for content, and one for form or presentation. The Concept embraced its content (the "for itself" relationship for content) *for itself*, or through its own activity (the "for itself" relationship of form or presentation). The "for-itselfness" of form gave the Concept an "in itself" relationship with its content by defining the Concept as opposed to or separate from its content. Here, although only half of the "in itself" relationship of opposition remains between the Concept and P/S, the Concept is opposed to P/S, and therefore has an "in itself" relationship of opposition with P/S, even if P/S does not have one with it. The "for itself" relationship of content actually has two parts): (1) the process in which it identifies its contents by gathering up, unifying or connecting its contents together (cf. Attraction), and (2) the process in which the universality defines its contents by giving them its character (cf. Repulsion). In the Transition to Mechanism, the Object did (2), but did not do (1), which is why it fell apart into separate mechanical objects. As the thought of the whole process of division into existence, the Concept still does (2), but it is also now the unifying concept, and so connects its contents together (as in [1]). However, it connects its contents together by *dividing*, and hence by presenting into something—i.e. P/S—that is defined as separate from and opposed to it, and with which it has an oppositional relationship. It does not yet *gather up* its contents through its own activity. The "for itself" relationship of form that the Concept is supposed to have with its contents is therefore incomplete: the Concept's own activity embraces, gathers up or unifies its content (i.e. [1] above) through its own activity insofar as it divides into and hence imposes its character on that content (i.e. [2] above), but its activity does not yet actively gather up that content. The Concept's form, presentation or activity involves identifying and pushing out, but not gathering up. The "for itself" process in which the Concept gathers up its content will be traced in the next several stages. In that process, the Concept's character as a doubly "for itself" concept that embraces and connects its content—in the sense of actively gathering it up through its own activity—will be developed.

Now that P/S no longer negates or opposes the Concept, P/S has lost any degree of independence from the Concept. What P/S is like "in itself" or how it is defined on its own in relation to its "other" is null and void. It has only whatever identity is given to it by the Concept. Moreover, because the Concept negates P/S, the character that the Concept gives to P/S negates the "in itself" character of P/S. As the embracing "for itself" concept, the Concept is the ideality that negates the "in-itselfness" of P/S. Keep in mind that P/S is still defined as an object. So we can also say that the object (P/S) is nothing or has no identity or definition on its own. All that matters about the object is the ideality assigned to it by the Concept. The object is merely *for* the Concept: it is the immediate objectivity of the Concept (§204).

What sort of definition does the Concept have? As a "for itself" concept, we know that the Concept belongs to ideality or thought insofar as it embraces and defines other concepts, which are its contents. But what sort of ideality is it? Because the way in which the Concept negates P/S is abstract or undefined, the Concept cannot be precisely defined, but we do know something about its definition. It is defined simply as a "for itself" concept that is opposed to immediate objectivity. What sort of "for itself" concept is that? In the Introduction to Chapter Three, a "for itself" concept was defined not only by the *syntactic* connection between concepts, but also by the *semantic* definition that the concepts have. Even though Being-for-itself and Essence had the same logical structure, for example, they had different definitions because the definitions of the concepts that they embraced were different. Similarly, here, to see what sort of "for itself" concept the Concept has become, we have to pay attention not only to the fact that the Concept is a "for itself" concept that also opposes P/S (i.e. the syntactic structure), but also to the semantic content of the concept that the Concept embraces (namely P/S). The Concept is a "for itself" ideality that embraces and defines but also negates or is opposed to P/S, which is defined as *immediate objectivity*. What sort of ideality defines and yet is also opposed to immediate objectivity? Answer: subjectivity—that is, subjectivity taken to be the type of subjectivity that is mere subjectivity, and hence opposed to objectivity. If we ask: what is opposed to an immediate object? The answer is: an immediate subject, or subjectivity defined in an immediate way as what is opposed to, but also defines, objectivity. Since the Concept defines and is opposed to immediate objectivity, it is a "for itself" concept that is neither Being-for-itself nor Essence, but *subjectivity* instead. Subjectivity is the type of ideality, thought or concept that defines and is opposed to immediate objectivity. As a result, the Concept is now defined as subjectivity.

The kind of subjectivity defined here is different from the kind of subjectivity defined earlier. U, P and S were defined as "subjectivity" in a weaker sense when they were defined as centers. A center was a subjectivity insofar as it was an S-as-U, or a singularity that has a universal. A center is a "subjectivity" in the same way that the subject of a sentence is a "subjectivity," i.e. insofar as it is capable of having a universal, which is the predicate of the sentence. The Concept sublates (cancels and preserves) this weaker definition of "subjectivity." It is a singularity that has a universal—insofar as it embraces and defines P/S, which, as a concept, is a universal (even though P/S is currently defined insofar as it exists or is an immediate object). But the Concept as a subject is also *opposed to* objectivity. The Concept is a kind of subjectivity that negates the "in-itselfness" or independent character of immediate objectivity. Whatever character the objectivity has on its own—that is to say, in an "in itself" sense—is negated by the Concept, which treats the "in-itselfness" of the object as null and void. It is therefore a subject that not only has, but also *works on*, an object. Work is an activity that both preserves but also cancels something. In the stage of Effect as Substance in Chapter Three, because the Cause presupposed the Effect, there was a sense in which the Effect was already there in the Cause. Although the Cause (as a cause) produced the Effect, then, the Cause also did not produce the Effect, in the sense that it did not produce the Effect from scratch. The Effect was redefined as something on which the Cause *works*. The Cause preserves the Effect because the Effect is there when the Cause is finished with it, but it produces the Effect in the sense that its activity changes the presupposed Effect. Similarly, the sort of subjectivity here both has and yet opposes objectivity—it works on it.

These characteristics define the Concept as a *purpose*. A purpose is a subjectivity that embraces and defines but also negates the independent character of immediate objectivity. A purpose works on objectivity. The Concept has become *purpose*, and P/S has become the content of the purpose. The Concept, as purpose, is defined by embracing and identifying P/S, which is its content. Since P/S is the content of the Concept, when the Concept is defined in relation to P/S, it is defined in relation to itself. Finally, because the Concept is the defining universal of P/S, it is also the identity and essence of P/S (cf. the stage of Identity).

Because the Concept here is merely subjective or ideal, its definition is one-sided. It is a one-sided subjectivity that is opposed to one-sided objectivity. This definition of the Concept ignores the fact that the Concept has already been defined by the logical process as both Concept and Object. At the beginning of the Doctrine of the Object, when the Concept was redefined by the logical process as the Object, it became objective. This objective nature of the Concept is not acknowledged here, however.

An example will help to show why Hegel is entitled to call the concept that has the logical characteristics just outlined a "purpose." When I decide to fix dinner, for instance, the concept of "dinner" becomes the defining purpose over whatever I do. That concept of "dinner" is a purpose insofar as it (through me) works on objectivity. The independent character of the objects I use to fix dinner is presupposed, but also has no real weight, except insofar as that character makes them fodder for dinner. The nature of the objects is presupposed in the sense that I select only certain sorts of objects to satisfy my purpose. I pick lettuce, for instance—and not metal—to fix for dinner. But at the same time I treat that independent character as null and void. I am interested in the object only insofar as it can satisfy my purpose. My lack of interest in the independent character of the object becomes obvious in relation to certain sorts of examples. If I pick a chicken for dinner, for instance, I go on to kill it and cook it. I certainly have no interest in its "in itself" character as a chicken. My purpose—and not the independent character of the object—defines or determines what I do with the object. A purpose is thus an overarching ideality or "for itself" concept that defines but is also opposed to immediate objectivity and treats the immediate objectivity as only ideal, that is, as only *for* the ideal or purpose.

Because Hegel has offered an abstract account of purpose here, it should capture all kinds of purposes—not just the sort of subjective purposes that humans can have, but other sorts of purposes too. Take the sort of internal purposiveness, as Hegel calls it (§204R), that was proposed by Aristotle. For Aristotle, the defining universal of something—a dog, for instance—not only captured the defining essence of the object, but also captured the purpose of the object. This is the heart of Aristotle's teleological conception of the world, or his account of the world in which the purposes are internal to, or part of, the very definitions of objects themselves. For an individual dog, for instance, the universal or concept not only defines the essence of the dog, it also captures the end, ideal or purpose of the dog. The end or purpose of a dog is to become a dog, that is to say, to carry out its nature as a dog in the world. The dog carries out this nature in two senses, for Hegel. First, insofar as it goes around doing dog-like things, the dog is carrying out its nature as a dog. Second, the dog reproduces and dies, which still brings about and satisfies the dog's purpose, which is not its individual nature, but its universal nature as a dog, which is to say, its species. Hence the universal (or essence) of "dog" is a purpose in the same way that my desire to fix dinner was a purpose: it is an overarching, defining ideal or concept that embraces but also negates the immediate objectivity of the individual dog and treats that immediate objectivity as merely ideal. In carrying out its purpose, the individual, objective dog reproduces and dies, and hence is used up or negated. As Hegel suggests, subjective needs and drives are also examples of abstract purposes (§204R). When I am hungry, for instance, I presuppose or embrace the "in itself" character or nature of an object, but I also negate that nature in a rather obvious sense. I select only certain sorts of objects for my hungry purpose, but once those objects are selected, I no longer care about the character of the object. Indeed, I eliminate that character: I eat the object up.

Subjective, Immediate, External or Finite Purpose

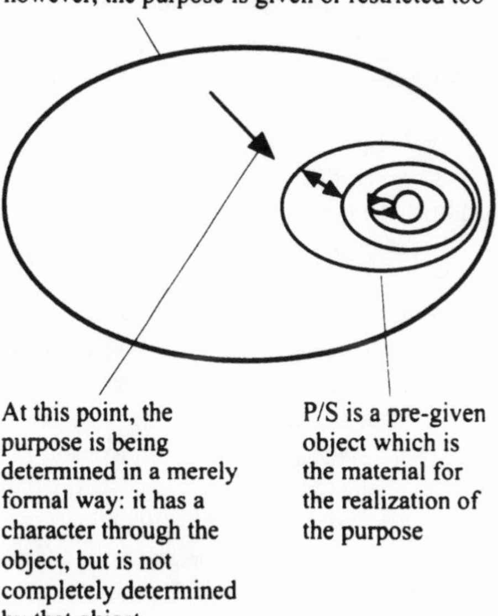
The Concept—as purpose—confronts the object, which it treats as something given, presupposed. Because the object is given, however, the purpose is given or restricted too
At this point, the purpose is being determined in a merely formal way: it has a character through the object, but is not completely determined by that object
P/S is a pre-given object which is the material for the realization of the purpose

Figure 4.73

In Subjective, Immediate External or Finite Purpose, the Concept confronts and identifies the object P/S, which is still taken to be immediate, given or presupposed. The object (P/S) is defined as the (objective) material for the realization of the purpose. Because the object is given, however, the purpose has an external relationship with it, or seems to be imposed on the object from the outside. For instance, suppose we find that a plant has medicinal qualities. When we then use the plant to make medicine, our purpose is determining the character of the plant—we turn the plant into "medicine." However, that purpose has an external relation to the plant, or seems to be imposed on the plant from the outside. Even though the purpose does pick out something about the nature of the plant itself—the qualities of the plant that we use for medicine are really in the plant—those qualities do not capture the essential character of the plant itself. Since the plant is given or "found," it has a character of its own independent of the character that our medicinal purposes impose on it. The plant still has its own character as garlic, for instance, not just as "curative." Because this sort of purpose has an external relationship to the object, it is external purposiveness (§205).

According to the general definition or concept of purpose, a purpose should be a free self-determining, identifying ideality over the object. As explained, external purpose does not succeed in determining the object completely, even though it does determine the object to some degree. An external purpose also fails to be completely self-determining. The external purpose presents itself formally as if it is a free subjectivity determining the character of the object, but does not succeed in living up to that definition. Because an external purpose must rely for its character on characteristics that are given or "found" in a given object, the purpose is not completely self-determining. Whether we can use a plant for our medicinal purposes depends on the given character of the plant, on what we find the plant to be like. As a result, our purpose for the plant is given or "found" just as much as the object is given or "found." What purposes can be made of given objects is restricted by what those objects happen to be like. Because the content of external purpose is restricted by the given or "found" nature of the relevant objects, this sort of purpose is finite, contingent and given. The content of external purpose is restricted in the sense that only certain sorts of purposes come up, namely, whatever purposes are "found" out there in the world of immediate objects. These are purposes that, as Hegel apparently remarked in a lecture, include all the purposes of utility (§204A). A concept of "purpose" which relies on the given nature of objects for its definition will be restricted, depending on what those objects happen to be like. Hegel has talked about concepts with restricted contents before. In the stage of The Necessary in Chapter Three, he suggested that the Matter Itself would have a restricted content, because the Matter was relying on the set of given conditions for its definition.

In an Addition in the *Encyclopaedia*—which was drawn from his students' lecture notes—Hegel divides purpose into three stages (§206A). Since these stages correspond to stages he outlined in the *Science of Logic*, I will use the division to present the logical movement of purpose here.

The first stage of purpose is this one—the stage of subjective purpose. For Hegel, this sort of purpose is "subjective" because these purposes are defined as opposed to objectivity, which still has something of a character of its own, separate from the purposes. The purposes do not fully succeed in *being*, or in having being. They are not realized, and so remain merely subjective. The second stage of purpose is purpose in the process of realizing or accomplishing itself (§206A). The third stage of purpose is the accomplished purpose (§206A). Hegel divides the second stage, which we will turn to next, into three separate moments.

First Moment of Purpose Realizing Itself

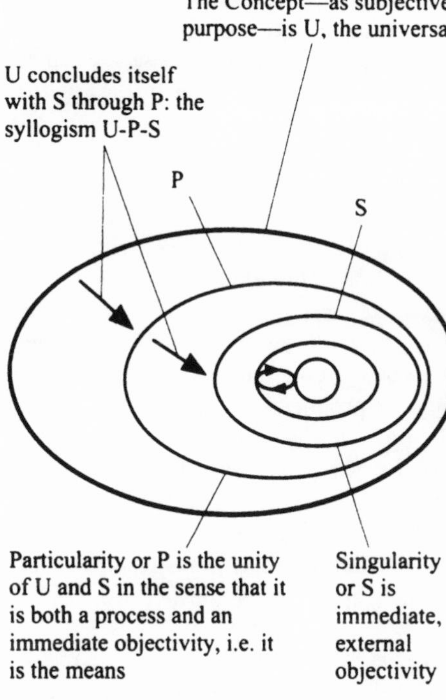
The Concept—as subjective purpose—is U, the universal
U concludes itself with S through P: the syllogism U-P-S
P
S
Particularity or P is the unity of U and S in the sense that it is both a process and an immediate objectivity, i.e. it is the means
Singularity or S is immediate, external objectivity

Figure 4.74

The concept of a purpose is like the concept of cause: it is a success term. Unfortunately, unlike the word "cause," which has the verb "to cause," "purpose" has no corresponding verb in English. Nevertheless, just as a cause truly gets to be a cause only when it succeeds in causing something, so a purpose truly gets to be a purpose only when it succeeds in—what shall I say?—"purpose-ing" something. A cause can be a cause only if it succeeds in pushing out an effect. A cause therefore determines itself as a cause through the effect: only when the effect shows up does the cause get to truly be a cause (cf. Substance as Cause). Purpose is a success term too. A purpose gets to be a purpose or has being as a purpose only when it succeeds in pushing out there as the purpose of something. Only when it shows up in objectivity does the purpose get to be a purpose. There is an important logical difference, however, Hegel remarks (§204R), between cause as a success term and purpose as a success term. A cause becomes a cause when it produces something other than itself, namely, the effect. The element of "otherness" between the cause and effect is illustrated by the fact that there are two different terms for them: a cause produces an *effect*, not another cause, and hence something different from itself. Although a cause and effect are unified in a whole process that includes them both, they are presented as different from one another by the process insofar as one is defined as *cause* and the other is defined as *effect*. The effect still remains "other" than the cause—an "otherness" implied by the need to use two different terms or concepts to refer to them. As Hegel says, even though the cause fulfills itself as a cause through the effect, the effect is something other than the cause (§204R). Indeed, this conceptual "otherness" may help to explain why the British philosopher David Hume was never able to find any necessary connection between cause and effect (see Chapter One, Section I).

Unlike a cause, however—which succeeds when it produces something else (the effect)—a purpose succeeds only when it pushes *itself* out there, pushes out what it is, or pushes out something with the same character, determination or definition as itself. Indeed, what makes it "original" (the origin) is precisely that it remains the same in what it pushes out (§204R). When it remains the same as what it pushes out, then it was genuinely the origin of what was pushed out. My purpose to make dinner, for instance, gets to really *be* or *exist* as a purpose only if it succeeds in pushing something out there into objectivity that has the same character, concept or ideal as the original purpose, namely, "dinner." For one thing, the purpose—which is currently defined as merely subjective—cannot have being or exist at all without being objectified. A subjective purpose, such as my purpose to make dinner—which is at first nothing but a thought—must be objectified to be realized. My purpose to make dinner does not have any being at all if it remains only in my head, so to speak. Until there is something out there in the objective world, my purpose has no being, or *is* nothing at all. In addition, however, a purpose is realized only if what is produced out there in objectivity is the same as what is in the head, that is, only if what is out there in objectivity can be grasped by the very same concept that was in subjectivity. My purpose to make dinner is realized only if what is out there can be characterized as "dinner." When the concept of dinner captures both the subjectivity and the objectivity then the purpose has been realized. Thus, while cause is realized in another concept, purpose is realized only if the concept remains consistent throughout the process.

It is because purpose remains what it is during the process of pushing out into objectivity that it belongs to the Doctrine of the Concept rather than the Doctrine of Essence. The Doctrine of the Concept is dominated by the syllogism, which is at the heart of much of the logical movement in this chapter. Built into the syllogism is a conceptual sameness or connectivity that is not present in the essential relationships that dominated the Doctrine of Essence. Again, in the relationship of cause and effect, a cause is realized in something that is captured by a different concept. When ball A hits ball B, the movement of ball A is the cause, while the movement of ball B is the effect. While the movements of ball A and ball B are the same kind of thing—namely, movement—in the relationship of cause and effect, they are not conceptually the same. One is the cause, while the other is the effect. What they share is an essence—a kind, namely, again, movement—but they must be captured by two different concepts. It is the shared kind or essence that explains why the concepts of cause and effect belong to the Doctrine of Essence.

In the relationship of purpose, however, the purpose can only be realized when the concept remains constant from one side to the other. When I decide (in thought or subjectivity) to make dinner, that purpose is only fulfilled when what I make (in objectivity) is conceptually the same as my purpose: the object that I make must be capable of being characterized by the very same concept that defined my original purpose, namely "dinner." This conceptual connectedness or sameness is characteristic of the syllogism itself. Although the elements of the syllogism—U, P and S—can be distinguished from one another as moments of the Concept, they cannot really be held apart from one another (see The Three Moments Cannot be Held Apart). They are just moments of the same thought or concept. Take the example of a syllogism that I gave earlier—the syllogism "feline(U)-panther(P)-lion(S)." In this syllogism, U, P and S all belong to the same concept, namely "feline." Panther is nothing but a sub-concept of feline, and lion is a sub-concept of panther, and hence a sub-concept of feline as well. They all belong to the same concept. S, P and U are conceptually the same as one another in a way that cause and effect are not.

While I have been using individual concepts, such as the concept of feline or "dinner," to illustrate the stages, the Concept is the thought of the whole, completely systematized conceptual system. Accordingly, the purpose here is not simply one purpose, but the purposiveness of the whole conceptual system, or purposiveness in general. Since the sort of purpose defined so far still includes finite purposes, or purposes that belong to the finite realm, the characteristics that purpose has in this and in the next few stages apply not just to the Concept-as-purpose, but also to finite purposes, or to the other two levels of purpose,[5] namely, the internal, Aristotelian purposiveness of living organisms as well as the ordinary purposes of humans.

In this first syllogism, the subjective purpose, Concept or U concludes itself with S or the objectivity external to it, through P or a middle term, which is the unity of U and S. This process has the form of the syllogism U-P-S. P is the unity of U and S because, as I will explain further shortly, it is both a process or activity (like U), and a content. Since S is the content of P, and since P presupposes a content, P is not only activity (like U), but also content, as S. In the activity of P, P grasps immediately on to a content, which is another object, namely S (§206). (P had the same dual nature as both an activity and content in the stage of Absolute Mechanism earlier.) The first premise of this syllogism is "U is P." This premise asserts that there is an immediate relationship between the Concept and the object (P/S). The second premise of the syllogism is "P is S." It captures the activity of P in which P particularizes into S.

In the Doctrine of the Subjective Concept, syllogisms were reversible. This reversibility stemmed from the fact that it concerned the forms of the syllogism in general, divorced from specific activity or content. What mattered there was how U, P and S were each defined in relation to one another in general. Even in Mechanism and Chemism the syllogisms were reversible, because what mattered there still was the definitions that U, P and S had in relation to one another in general. Now, however, the syllogism defines a specific conceptual activity—one that begins in U, goes through P, and ends with S. Because the syllogism captures a specific conceptual activity, it is not reversible. If we reversed the syllogism, we would be talking about a different activity. If I give John a ball, that is one activity. If John gives me a ball, that is a different activity. The syllogism *will* be reversed later on, but when it is, it defines a different activity.

Let me return to my example of making dinner to flesh out what is going on in this stage. So long as my purpose to make dinner remains a mere subjectivity, or stays only in my head, so to speak, it is not a real purpose, or, to put it another way, it is not really a purpose at all. Again, the concept of purpose is a success concept, like the concept of cause. Just as a cause can only genuinely be a cause if it succeeds in producing an effect, so a purpose can genuinely be a purpose only if it succeeds in being the end (purpose) of something. My purpose of making dinner is not a purpose unless it succeeds in being the purpose over something. So, I set about pushing out my purpose into objectivity, a process that can be captured with the syllogism U-P-S.

For the first step, I must particularize or define the purpose by specifying it. This process of narrowing it down takes the form of the judgment "U is P." Suppose I decide, for instance, that I will make a salad for dinner. In that case, I judge that "dinner (U) is make a salad (P)." I particularize the purpose as a salad. Notice that this particularization (P) of the purpose will involve both activity and content. The activity is the process of making the salad. But I must also make the salad out of something particular, that is, out of something in particular, or some content in particular. The particularity (salad) must therefore also particularize. According to the syllogism, P particularizes as S. So now my purpose grabs at a singularity (S) that particularizes the particularity. I pick lettuce, for example, as the type of thing out of which I will make the salad. I could have picked cucumber instead, to make a cucumber salad; or egg or tuna, for egg or tuna salad. So lettuce is only one type of thing out of which salad can be made. Lettuce as a type of thing is the singularity (S) that my now more particularized purpose grasps.

We can now see why Hegel says in §206 that P, which is the middle term, is both activity and objectivity. P is objectivity because it immediately particularizes as S. S—lettuce—is the object or content that P immediately grasps onto or particularized into. But P is itself a purpose (§206). In the dinner example, the purpose of making dinner is particularized as "salad," which includes the *activity* of making a salad, which is itself a purpose. Particularity is a second purpose (P) that grasps onto the content S—lettuce (as a type)—for its own means and material. P uses S as its own means. Notice this process has still not grasped immediate objectivity. Lettuce (S) is still a *type* of thing, not yet an immediate object.

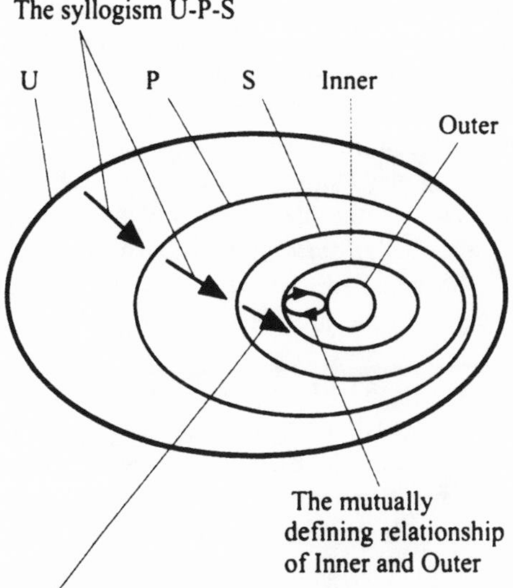

Singularity or S particularizes U by judging into "U is S." When S judges into "U is S," its internal elements are activated: Inner, which is an essence or U, is in a mutually defining relationship with (and so "is" Outer, which is the realm of immediate being or a new level of S. So inside S there is the judgment "U is S"

Figure 4.75

The Concept or purpose begins the process of becoming a genuine purpose by pushing out there into objectivity. And it begins this process by going through the syllogism U-P-S. In this stage, when the Concept goes through this syllogism, it leads S to particularize into a further judgment. When I decide to make dinner (my purpose or U), for instance, that purpose grabs at a particularity, such as making a salad (P). That's the judgment "U is P." The purpose then focuses on some singularity (S) as the particularization of the particularity. My purpose particularizes by grasping at lettuce as a type of thing (S), for instance, out of which to make the salad (P). That's the judgment "P is S." But in grabbing at the singularity, my purpose also leads the singularity itself to further particularize into a judgment. That's because S is really a universal—a type of thing—and I cannot make the salad out of lettuce as a type of thing. I have to make the salad out of some particular bit of lettuce—some immediate objectivity. So lettuce as a type (which is the original S in the larger syllogism) is now thought of as a universal that must be further particularized. It particularizes into a further judgment of the form "U is S," or, in my example, "lettuce (as a type) (U) is this bit of lettuce over here, or this immediate objectivity (S)." (Because the judgments are transitive, we can also characterize my judgment as the judgment "this is lettuce" ["S is U"] or "this lettuce" ["S/U"]). This new judgment particularizes the original S—it particularizes lettuce as a type into some specific bit or immediate object.

When I judge "this lettuce," I activate or bring into play the logical contents of the S-bubble. S grew out of the form of Actuality in the Doctrine of Essence (see the stage of Singularity in this chapter). S is the content and form of Actuality because it contains Inner and Outer in their mutually defining relationship, which is also the definition of Actuality. In more logical language, when the subjective purpose or Concept goes through its syllogism (U-P-S), it leads S to judge. S particularizes or judges into its own contents (cf. the discussion of the judging principle in Chemism above), namely into Inner and Outer in a mutually defining relationship. Outer is the whole realm of Being—the full measure of thereness or out-thereness—while Inner represents all the identifying concepts used to capture the essences of what is out there. Inner is an identifying essence or universal (a smaller U) and Outer is the realm of being, or of singularity with thereness (a smaller level of S). In the judgment "this is lettuce," "this" represents the Outer, while "lettuce" is the Inner, or the identifying concept for the Outer. Because Inner and Outer are in a mutually defining relationship, we can also say that Inner (U) "is" Outer (S). So when the Concept goes through its syllogism, it leads S to particularize itself into the judgment "U (as Inner) is S (as Outer)" or "S (as Outer) is U (as Inner)."

The judgment "this is lettuce"—in which the "this" is no longer a type of thing but rather an immediate objectivity—actualizes or realizes the original U or the purpose (i.e. the Concept). Since S is defined as Actuality and includes the Outer, thereness or reality (see Singularity), it actualizes or realizes the purpose in the sense of making it real. The bit of lettuce makes the dinner real: it is the reality of the purpose. The original S thus particularizes or defines the Concept, or the original U, by giving U a determinate or real content. S's content is U's definition.

When I judge "this is lettuce" or "this lettuce," the subjective concept "lettuce" is set up against the immediate objectivity or object, namely, the "this." However, the judgment also suggests that each side of the antithesis is deficient on its own. The "this" is the Outer—the being with out-thereness—but it is of no use to me unless it is in a mutually defining relationship with the Inner or subjective concept "lettuce." Because the bit there really *is* lettuce, Inner and Outer do succeed in mutually defining each other in this case. If they did not, then I would not be able to use the "this" in my salad. Inner and Outer must be in a mutually defining relationship for the "this" to be used. So the judgment of singularity includes the thought that subject and object are deficient on their own. Neither can be what it is without the other. A "this" cannot be anything at all without a concept, and the concept "lettuce" cannot be anything at all without there being something out there, that is, some Outer, which it grasps. Hence, when the original S judges into "U is S," it reflects or echoes the Concept's own character. Because S has split into a judgment—i.e. "U is S"—it posits, makes explicit or repeats the antithesis between subject and object that also currently belongs to the whole Concept. Inside S, Inner is the subject, while Outer is the object, and they are set up against one another, joined only by an "is." However, S's judgment also shows that each side of the antithesis is deficient on its own. In S, Inner and Outer are in a mutually defining relationship, so S includes the thought that neither subjectivity nor objectivity can be what they are on their own—a logical conclusion that was also drawn in the Doctrine of Essence (see the Activity of Necessity in Chapter Three). At the moment, the Concept also contains the antithesis of subject and object: the Concept is subjectivity, which is currently opposed to P/S as its object. Indeed, the Concept is pushing out into objectivity precisely because subjectivity by itself is deficient. The Concept is playing out the conclusion that subjectivity by itself is deficient by pushing out into objectivity. That conclusion—that subjectivity by itself is deficient—is the character of the Concept that the judging activity of S reflects. So when the Concept pushes out into the judgment of singularity, the Concept is reinforcing its own character. As we saw above, my purpose of making dinner is no purpose at all if it fails to push out there into objectivity. My subjectivity—the purpose in my thought—is deficient without objectivity. This is the character of the Concept that is echoed in the judgment of S or singularity (§207).

Second Moment of Purpose Realizing Itself

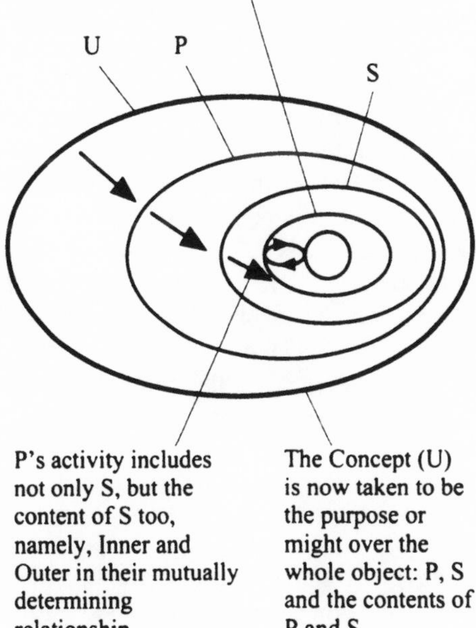
Inner and Outer and their relationship is the contents of P as well as S, since it is inside both. They are a means for the whole object (P/S)
U
P
S
P's activity includes not only S, but the content of S too, namely, Inner and Outer in their mutually determining relationship
The Concept (U) is now taken to be the purpose or might over the whole object: P, S and the contents of P and S

Figure 4.76

Whereas the first moment of subjective purpose treated S as if it were empty, this second moment acknowledges that the contents and activity that belong to S also belong to P. Inner and Outer and their relationship belong to the content of *both* S and P. In the diagram, the bubbles representing Inner and Outer in their mutually defining relationship are inside both the bubble for S and the bubble for P (since S itself is inside P). Since Inner and Outer are also the content of P, the outward-directed activity of S—i.e. the activity of S pushing out there into external objectivity as Inner and Outer—is part of P's activity as well. In more Hegelian language, the external objectivity (Inner and Outer in their relationship) is the means (activity and objectivity) not only for S, but also for the whole object, i.e. for P and S taken together, or for P/S (§208). To use my example again, the judgment "this is lettuce" belongs just as much to making the salad—i.e. to P—as it does to specifying the lettuce—i.e. to S. Since the content of S is the content and activity of P too, the whole activity of P/S is a syllogism. P is a purpose too—an active universal that particularizes through S into the contents of S, or into Inner and Outer in a mutually defining relationship. This activity of P can be captured with a new syllogism of the form U-P-S. In this syllogism, the original P is the "U," the original S is the "P," or the particularization of the original P, and Inner and Outer in their mutually determining relationship are a new, smaller level of singularity or "S"—a level that was reactivated in the last stage. In our example, making the salad—i.e. the original P—is itself a syllogistic activity. P—make salad—is a new level of U; S—lettuce—is the particularity (P) of the original P or of making the salad; and Inner and Outer in their mutually defining relationship—this lettuce—are a smaller level of singularity (a new S), inside the old S. When I make the salad for dinner, I go through an activity captured by the syllogism U-P-S.

Now that P's activity is a syllogism, the syllogism for the Concept of the whole purpose changes. In the First Moment of Purpose Realizing Itself, the first premise of the syllogism was simply "U is P." Now that P is itself a syllogism, we must replace the "P" in the original premise with the syllogism that captures the activity of P itself, namely, the syllogism U-P-S. The first premise of the syllogism for the Concept thus becomes, not "U is P," but "U is (U-P-S)." Since the activity of S is now included in the activity of P, we replace both P and S in the original syllogism with the activity of P, so that the whole syllogism is no longer U-P-S, but U-(U-P-S). To return to the example again, the original syllogism *"dinner"(U)-"make salad"(P)-"lettuce"(S)* (i.e. U-P-S) has become *"dinner"(U)-"make salad"(U)-"lettuce"(P)-"this lettuce"(S)* (i.e. U-U-P-S). I have put parentheses around the whole activity of P—as in U-(U-P-S)—but if we simply move the parentheses, we can explain Hegel's comment (in §208R) that, in this stage, the original first premise—namely "U is P," or U-P—becomes the middle term of the new syllogism—namely, U-(U-P)-S.

Now that P, S and the contents of S are taken together, the Concept is no longer the purpose over only P by itself—where P is taken to be separate from S and S's contents. Instead, the Concept is now defined as the purpose or might over the whole object, namely over P, S, and Inner and Outer in their mutually determining relationship. The Concept is now acknowledged to be the overarching, embracing "for itself" over all the activity of P/S, and not just over P. The Concept is the activity that activates the whole middle term (§208), namely, P with all its contents.

In a lecture, Hegel apparently used the relationship between soul and body to flesh out the first and second moments of Subjective Purpose. The first moment is captured by the basic syllogism U-P-S, where the subjective Concept is U, P is the moment of Particularity, and S is the moment of Singularity. This syllogism asserts that there is an *immediate* relationship between U and P. So, the soul or living being, for example, has a body in an immediate way ("U is P"), and is in that way immediately objectified. In this judgment, the body is simply the immediate realization of the soul. However, to claim that the soul has a body is not yet to say that the body has become a genuine means for a soul, or that the soul can use the body for its purposes. The soul of a baby, for example, has a body, but the soul of the baby cannot yet use the body for its own purposes. As Hegel apparently suggested, there is much work to do for a soul to make a body into its means (§208A).

This work constitutes a second way in which a purpose can be objectified. A purpose can be objectified in a *mediated*, rather than an immediate, way. For the body to be the means for the soul's purposes, the soul must turn outward. It must fix upon specific or particular purposes, and then objectify those purposes through the activity of the body. This process is the syllogism of P: the particular purpose becomes a new "U" that is further particularized ("P") through S and then pushed out into Inner and Outer in their mutually determining relationship (a new "S"). The syllogism needed to describe this mediated process of the whole purpose (or the soul) is "U-(U-P-S)." The body becomes the means for the soul when the body itself becomes an active syllogism (U-P-S) that the soul (the original U) uses for its purposes.

The distinction between the immediate and the mediated objectification of the purpose can also be illustrated—as Hegel apparently suggested in a lecture—by the two German words for "to decide": "*Beschließen*" and "*sich entschließen*." On the one hand, when we decide on some purpose (in the sense captured by the verb "*Beschließen*"), that purpose is the immediate objectification of our soul. In this case, we treat the purpose as one option among many, and think of ourselves as open to this or that option. But, on the other hand, we also set ourselves purposes or decide on (in the sense captured by the verb "*sich entschließen*") things in a stronger sense that is not only "in the head," so to speak, but involves objectivity (§206A). Sometimes we decide on things in a way that includes the activity of going and getting them, or the activity of mixing ourselves up with objectivity. There is an expression in African-American culture that captures this second, stronger sense of decision well. In African-American culture, when you hear someone say that they have "fixed on" some end, you know that the person is already in the process of carrying out whatever activity is required to achieve the end. To give a silly example, there is a difference in African-American culture between "I want a piece of cheese," and "I am fixing on getting me a piece of cheese." Both of these sentences indicate that the person has decided to have a piece of cheese. But the first sentence is uttered while the person is still sitting on the couch, so to speak, while the second sentence is uttered while the person is rising from the couch and heading for the kitchen. In the first case, although the person wants a piece of cheese, there is still a sense that the person is open to other options, other wants, and could have chosen something else. In the second case, however, the person is already working on satisfying or objectifying the purpose, and there is no longer any sense of "openness," or of being open to other options. "To want" something is simply to decide on some end in an immediate way ("U is P"), but "to fix on" some end is already to be committed to carrying out the end or to working on achieving that end ("U is [U-P-S]"). This work constitutes the sort of process of mediation that is present in the mediated way of objectifying the purpose.

Similarly, in the dinner example, the original syllogism *"dinner"(U)-"make salad"(P)-"lettuce"(S)* (i.e. U-P-S) offers a more theoretical approach to making the salad. It spells out how to make a salad, but has not yet committed to making the salad, whereas the expanded syllogism, which has "fixed on" this lettuce—*"dinner"(U)-"make salad"(U)-"lettuce"(P)-"this lettuce"(S)* (i.e. U-U-P-S)—has committed to the work required for actually making the salad. Again, this work is the mediated way of objectifying the purpose.

This second moment wraps the whole activity of P/S into the Concept as the purpose or U. In the first moment, the Concept was the direct power over only P, which was then the direct power over S, which was in turn the direct power over its own judging. Now the Concept is the power over the whole middle term and all its activity, and not just over P (§208). "Dinner" is my purpose not just for deciding to make a salad, but ultimately for deciding on lettuce, and then for picking out this lettuce too. "Dinner" is the purpose over the whole process. "Dinner" is being objectified or realized: it has fixed on this lettuce. All of this activity is the way in which the Concept is related to P/S as a whole.

Third Moment of Purpose Realizing Itself

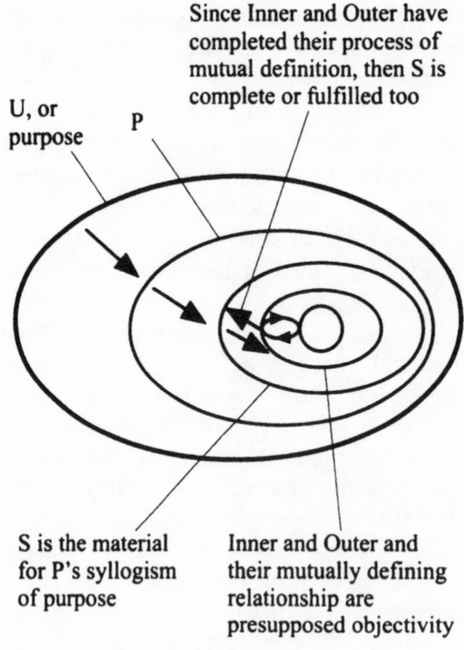
Since Inner and Outer have completed their process of mutual definition, then S is complete or fulfilled too
U, or purpose
P
S is the material for P's syllogism of purpose
Inner and Outer and their mutually defining relationship are presupposed objectivity

Figure 4.77

In the First Moment of Purpose Realizing Itself, P is itself a purpose that has activity characterized by the syllogism U-P-S, where P is the U of this syllogism, S is the P of this syllogism, and Inner and Outer and their mutually defining relationship are the S of this syllogism. P's purposive activity is thus an additional syllogism—(U-P-S)—embedded into the whole syllogism of the Concept, which has become U-(U-P-S). Now that P/S is being taken together as a whole, or when P is taken together with its means—namely S—its activity as a purpose is still directed outwards, or still pushes out into its object. To say that P *pushes out* into its object is to say that P is not the same as, or not identical to, its object (§209), namely S. P pushes out into S because S is an object that is "other" than, different from, or opposed to P. Because P is defined as opposed to S, P as a purpose is mediated by its object (§209). P's object is S taken together with its content, namely Inner and Outer and their mutually defining relationship.

If we look at the syllogism for P's purposive activity (U-P-S), it can be written out as "U is P, P is S, therefore U is S." The second premise of this syllogism for P—namely "P is S"—says that the original-S, which is the means or object for P, is immediately related to Inner and Outer and their relationship. Inner and Outer and their relationship, taken together as a whole, is the "other extreme" (§209) of the whole syllogism of for the Concept. Again, the whole syllogism for the Concept is U-(U-P-S), which has the Concept itself at one end (the first U), and Inner and Outer and their relationship at the other as the S in the syllogism for P, which is (U-P-S). That second premise of P's syllogism says that original-S is immediately related to Inner and Outer and their mutually defining relationship, or "P *is* S."

Let me use my example again to try to flesh out why "P is S" in the syllogism of P, or why original-S is immediately related to Inner and Outer and their relationship. In the last stage, my purpose—"dinner" (U)—was in the process of being realized in objectivity by particularizing into "salad" (P), and then into "lettuce" (the original S) and then fixing on what I was calling "smaller S"—which is the particularization of the original S, or "this lettuce." But P is itself a purpose, with its own syllogism—(U-P-S)—in which P is the U, S is the P and smaller-S is the S. The original purpose was "dinner," but "salad" is itself a purpose. The salad has to be made too, and so it has to take hold of an object for its own means and material. As a purpose, the syllogism for the salad is: "*salad—lettuce—this lettuce*." According to this syllogism, original-P (the U) takes hold of S as its object (the P), which is immediately related to smaller-S (the S), or to Inner and Outer and their relationship. Original-S is a universal too, so "lettuce" is the concept of "lettuce" as a type of thing. The relationship expressed by the second premise of the syllogism for P—namely, "P is S"—is the relationship between original-S, or "lettuce," and smaller-S, or "this lettuce," which gives us the premise "lettuce (as a type) is this lettuce."

"This lettuce" is already a combination of concept and out-thereness because, while the "this" is the out-thereness (Outer), the "lettuce" is an identifying concept (Inner). Because the Concept is one-sided subjectivity or Thought, and because all concepts are themselves thoughts, the fact that "this lettuce" is out there presupposes that the Concept has succeeded in identifying an object. Inner and Outer and their mutually defining relationship are therefore the presupposed objectivity or material (§209) of the syllogism for P. The assertion "this lettuce" presupposes that the Concept has identified something out there as an object, namely whatever happens to be out there (Outer) that is grasped by the concept of "lettuce" (Inner). When the syllogism for P pushes out into Inner and Outer and their mutually defining relationship, then, it asserts that Inner and Outer are in a mutually defining relationship. When "lettuce (as a type)" divides into "this lettuce," it presupposes that there is an out-thereness—namely the "this"—that is mutually identified by, and identifies, a concept—namely "lettuce." "This lettuce" is the objectivity or material that is presupposed by the syllogism for P.

As soon as "this lettuce" is presupposed, however, then S, or "lettuce" is established too. As soon as some lettuce is out there, then lettuce as a type is there too. The second premise of the syllogism for P says that "lettuce *is* this lettuce," that there is an immediate relationship between original-S and Inner and Outer and their relationship. Since there is such an immediate relationship between original-S and Inner and Outer and their relationship, as soon as Inner and Outer and their relationship is presupposed, then S is too: as soon as "this (some) lettuce" is, then "lettuce (as a type)" is too. This logical conclusion can be represented in the diagram as a return arrow from the particularization of original-S (i.e. Inner and Outer in their mutually defining relationship) back to original-S. Because "P *is* S" (where "P" is original-S, and "S" is Inner and Outer and their relationship) in an immediate way, and because Inner and Outer and their mutually defining relationship is established (as presupposed), then original-S is established too. Because "this lettuce" is there, "lettuce" is there too.

Hegel says that the relationship here between the P and S of the premise "P is S"—or between original-S and Inner and Outer and their relationship—is the sort of relationship that dominated the spheres of mechanism and chemism (§209). That's because mechanism and chemism defined concepts as existing. In those stages or spheres, a concept was defined as the set of existing items into which it divided. The concept of feline, for example, was just the set of existing felines out there. That is just the sort of relationship that S has with Inner and Outer and their mutually defining relationship here. S, as the concept of lettuce (as a type), for instance, just is whatever out there is identified with the concept of lettuce. When the concept of feline is defined by its existence, it, too, just is the bits out there that are identified by the concept of feline. Not until the Transition to Purpose was the concept of feline defined not only as existing but also as a universal concept. When a concept is defined as a universal concept it is not *merely* the bits or items that it divides into. It is also a concept on its own that explains why all those items belong to the set. The universal concept of feline, for instance, not only exists or divides into existing felines, it also explains why those items count as "feline." It is something *more* than just that content or the set of existing items it gathers up. The universal concept *makes* those individual felines what they are, and it does so by being their *purpose*.

We can now see why Hegel would say that the Concept is the truth of both mechanism and chemism (§209). Both mechanism and chemism can be characterized with the premise "P is S," which is the second premise of P's syllogism of purpose. In the whole syllogism of the Concept, that premise is just the last two parts. In the whole syllogism for the Concept—namely U-(U-P-S)—the spheres of mechanism and chemism are captured by the last two elements—the "P" and the "S," which are Singularity (original-S) and Inner and Outer and their relationship (smaller-S). Because these spheres are part of the whole syllogism of the Concept, they have no truth or validity outside of that larger syllogism. "P is S" is immediately true here, because the Concept has already succeeded in defining an object out there, namely, for example, that bit of lettuce. Thus "P is S" is true only in the context of the overall purpose of the Concept, or only because the Concept has succeeded in pushing something out that is identified by and identifies a concept or thought. If the Concept had not succeeded in pushing out, then the "this" would not be a "(bit of) lettuce" or any other object. An object is always a something that is identified by a concept. Without a concept—and hence, without *the* Concept—nothing would be what it is or anything at all.

That Reason remains what it is through the process in which it pushes out individual objects such as the bit of lettuce is what Hegel calls the "*cunning* of reason" (§209). Because universal concepts are beyond the existing items that they gather up, they are not troubled, so to speak, by the comings and goings of those existing objects. They remain what they are through the comings and goings of existing objects. This account of universal concepts is embedded in a larger view that sees Reason or the Concept as purposive or teleological. The Concept or Reason must act first. Individual objects in the world—even that bit of lettuce—can be what they are only because Reason has acted first, because Reason makes things what they are by pushing them out, because Reason is the purpose behind the objective world. The Concept itself is the *purpose* behind the whole display of even the simplest, individual objects.

Realized Purpose

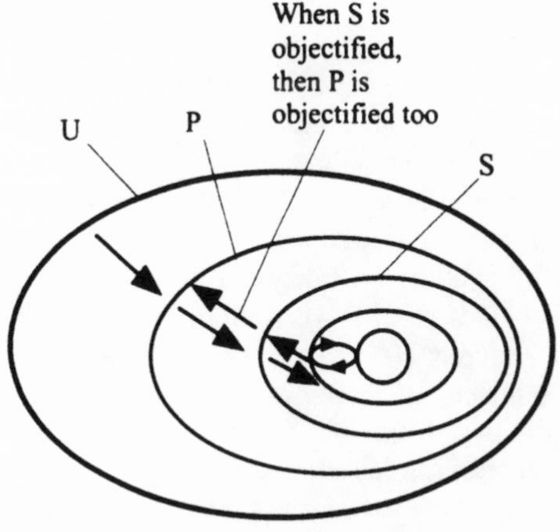
When S is
objectified,
then P is
objectified too
U
P
S

Figure 4.78

Since judgments are reversible and the first premise of the syllogism for P—"U is P"—says that U is P, P is also U. So as soon as original-S (the P in the judgment) is, then P (the U in the judgment) is too. As soon as original-S is objectified then P is objectified too. Since "salad is lettuce," for instance, then, as soon as the lettuce is, then the salad is too. P—the salad—is objectified as soon as S—the lettuce—is objectified. Since S *is* objectified, as seen in the last stage, then P is objectified too. This process can be represented by a return arrow from S to P in the diagram.

This stage follows from the characteristics that the elements have in virtue of their earlier incarnations in the logic. P grew out of Actuality. S grew out of Possibility—which was the form and content of Actuality—or the way in which Actuality is presented along with the definition of Actuality—and contains Inner and Outer in their mutually defining relationship (see Singularity). When Inner and Outer fulfill their process of mutual definition, or succeed in mutually defining each other—at least in one case—then S as a Possibility is fulfilled. S is the Possibility of Inner and Outer being in a mutually defining relationship, so when Inner and Outer are in a mutually defining relationship, as in the last stage, then

S is fulfilled. S is also by definition the Possibility of Actuality, which is P. So S is—by definition—the Possibility of P being fulfilled. Once S is fulfilled, then P is automatically fulfilled too. When the Possibility of Actuality (S) is fulfilled then Actuality (P) is fulfilled.

The whole syllogism of the Concept is U-(U-P-S), where (U-P-S) is the syllogistic process of P. Since S is objectified, P is objectified too. So P's whole syllogism—(U-P-S)—is complete. Think of the "dinner" example again. The syllogism of P for the dinner example is "*salad—lettuce—this lettuce*," which must be written out as "salad is lettuce (U is P), lettuce is this lettuce (P is S), therefore salad is this lettuce (U is S)." It can also be written out in a shorthand way as "*salad (U) is lettuce (P) is this lettuce (S)*." In the last stage, since lettuce (as a type) is this lettuce, as soon as this lettuce is presupposed, then lettuce is there too. In this stage, we move on to conclude that, since salad is lettuce, and since lettuce is, then the salad is too. Moreover, since P, as a purpose, was "salad," and since the salad is, then P as a purpose is therefore objectified.

Of course, this example is a little strange, because, although I have tried to convince my family members otherwise, "lettuce (as a type)" (original-S) does not by itself make a "salad" (P). If I tried to get away with serving my family nothing but lettuce for a salad, I would face loud complaints that "salad" has to have other things in it too: cucumber, tomato, green onion, and so on. The reason why the "dinner" example does not quite work is because it does not illustrate one part of the relationship that U, P and S have with one another. U is the Concept or Reason itself—the thought of the completed and completely systematized set of rational concepts as a finished product. Since the stage of Disjunctive Syllogism, P, or the set of rational concepts, has been defined as the *complete division* of the Concept or U. P is all of the categories or concepts into which U divides. And S is the *complete division* of P—it is all of the categories or concepts into which P divides. Even smaller-S—or Inner and Outer and their mutually defining relationship—is also the *complete division* of S. It is all of the concepts and thereness into which S divides. Although the "dinner" example is helpful in showing how the purpose is realized, it lacks the character of the Concept according to which P and S are complete divisions. While "this lettuce" (smaller-S) is the complete division of "lettuce" (S), "lettuce" is not the complete division of "salad" (P), and "salad" is not the complete division of "dinner" (U).

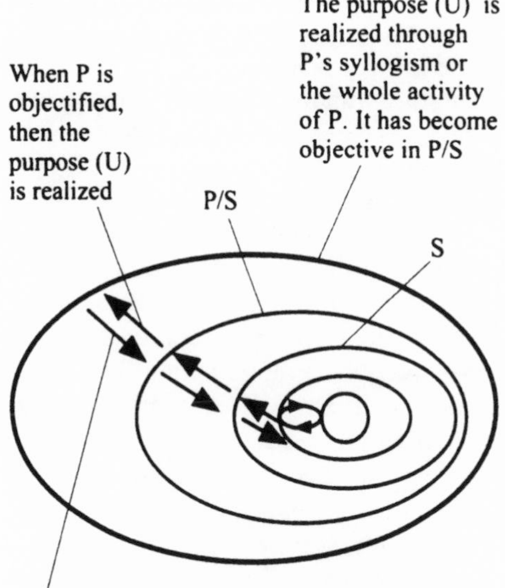
When P is objectified, then the purpose (U) is realized
P/S
The purpose (U) is realized through P's syllogism or the whole activity of P. It has become objective in P/S
S
Because the purpose or subjectivity "works on" the object, there is still separation or opposition between it and the objective

Figure 4.79

As soon as the process or syllogism of P is accomplished—as in the last stage—then the purpose itself (i.e. U) is realized. Since the process of P is the syllogism for P (i.e. [U-P-S]), it involves P and all of its contents, or P/S as a whole. P/S as a whole—which undergoes the whole syllogism for P—is the expression in objectivity of the purpose (U). As soon as P is objectified through its process or syllogism, then the purpose (U) is objectified too. U is the Concept, and (U-P-S) is the whole activity of P/S. According to the syllogism for the whole Concept, "U is (U-P-S)," or "U is P/S." Since "U is P/S," and because P/S is there—as the last stage showed—then U is there too. This process can be represented by a return arrow from P to U. The whole syllogism for the Concept in the example was "*dinner—(salad—lettuce—this lettuce)*"—i.e. U-(U-P-S), where "(U-P-S)" is the syllogism for P. The first premise of this whole syllogism—"U is U," or more precisely, "U is P" (since the second "U" is really original-P)—says "dinner is salad." As a result, as soon as the salad is accomplished, then the dinner is realized too. In the last stage, the process of P or the salad is accomplished. So the dinner is realized too. The purpose, "dinner" has been realized in the salad in the sense that it has succeeded in being objectified in the salad.

The fact that U has been realized in an object or in P/S shows that the one-sidedness of subjectivity, like the one-sidedness of objectivity earlier (see Abstract Purpose), must also be sublated (§212). The Concept or purpose (U) has been confronting P/S as opposed or external to it because of the vestiges of the "in itself" relationship between U and P/S that has been playing a role since the stage of Abstract Purpose. This "in itself" opposition gave the Concept the appearance or semblance of having a character independent of P/S or the object. The Concept or purpose seemed to have a character on its own, which it then imposed on P/S by "working on" P/S. But the fact that the one-sidedly, subjective purpose has to be realized through an object shows that that sort of purpose cannot really be realized, defined, or have its being, without the object. A one-sidedly subjective purpose has no "being" at all until it is pushed out or expressed into objectivity. A purpose only has "being" or thereness if it pushes out there into the realm of Being or thereness. Because P/S contains Outer, or the realm of Being, thereness is in the object or P/S.

There is a second way in which the purpose has been realized. Purpose is a success term: a purpose cannot be a purpose without being the purpose over something. Moreover, unlike cause, a purpose succeeds in being a purpose over something when it pushes out—*not* something with a different definition (as cause does, when it produces an "effect")—but something with the *same definition* that it has (see Abstract Purpose). Because P turned out to be a purpose on its own, with its own syllogism of purpose that pulls together P/S as a whole, U has succeeded in pushing out something with the same definition that it has. U has pushed out P, which is itself a purpose. U has therefore succeeded in putting something out there into objectivity that has the same definition that it has, namely, as a purpose. U has therefore succeeded in being realized in the sense that its process has now fulfilled its own definition as a purpose. In the "dinner" example, "salad" is a purpose too—it is a purpose that is realized in its own object. As a result, the activity and the character of the object defines the purpose just as much as the concept or purpose defines the activity and the object. As the old saying has it, "actions speak louder than words." Words or purposes mean nothing if they are not expressed by actions and objects that have the same definition that they have. Hence, just as the object was defined by subjectivity or the purpose, so the purpose or subjectivity is realized in, and hence defined by, the object.

Although the purpose is realized, because it is finite, it is only realized in a restricted way, as Hegel says (§211). S was based on presupposed objectivity (which is what Inner and Outer and their relationship was). Because S is based on presupposed objectivity, S is presupposed. And since S was presupposed, then P/S is presupposed or given as well. Although the purpose (U) is realized in the accomplishment of P/S, the purpose is still relying on a presupposed or given content for its definition. Its content is therefore still finite and restricted. Because the fulfillment of S was relying on given or presupposed material, P's fulfillment is presupposed or given too. The nature of lettuce (S), for instance, is given or presupposed, so the nature of the salad (P), too, is given or presupposed. Since the purpose is still relying for its definition on something that is given or presupposed, its content is restricted by whatever happens to be out there in that given or presupposed content. While cause is realized when it produces something else, namely an effect, a purpose is realized when it produces itself in objectivity (see the First Moment of Purpose Realizing Itself). That situation obtains here: the original purpose was "dinner," for instance, and the salad that appears on the table is properly captured by the concept of "dinner." However, as in the First Moment of Purpose Realizing Itself, the finiteness of the relationship still means that the purpose is external to the object, or seems to attach to the object from the outside. Because the salad as a purpose still relies on the given character of its own content, the purpose "dinner" does not completely determine the salad, but seems to be imposed on the salad from the outside. The salad still has a character of its own—namely, as *salad*—that is independent of the purpose. Although the purpose is realized in the object, then, it is currently defined only as "salad." Its definition is currently imposed on and hence restricted to what happens to appear on the table. The "salad" *is* "dinner" (that's what's for dinner), and, like "dinner," it is also a purpose, but it is being presented (i.e. form) as something other than "dinner" or the purpose, namely, as salad.

Think also of the example I used for the concept of feline. In that example, the syllogism for the whole Concept was "*feline(U)-panther(P)-lion(S)*." The concept of feline is currently being defined as a concept that is *beyond* the way in which it has its existence. It is not merely an object—or a concept that is defined by the way it divides into existence—but a *purpose*—a universal concept that makes the items into which it divides what they are. Like "feline," though, "panther" is a universal too—it is a purpose that has its own syllogism of purpose. That syllogism is the syllogism of P, which pushes out into Inner and Outer and their mutually defining relationship. The syllogism of P is "*panther-lion-this lion*," where "this lion" is Inner and Outer and their mutually defining relationship, or the Outer ("this") that is identified by and defines an identifying concept or Inner ("lion"). Since there is this lion out there, then lion as a type is, and since lion as a type is, then panther is too. So the syllogism of P is accomplished. Since the syllogism of P is accomplished, the concept of feline as the purpose of the whole display is realized too: since "panther" is accomplished, then the concept of "feline"—defined as the universal concept that makes all those lion/felines what they are—has been realized too. The concept of feline really is the purpose—it made those lion/felines what they are. However, the definition of the realized purpose is restricted. Although the concept of feline, as a purpose, is realized because "this lion" is there, the concept of feline does not yet completely define what is out there. Because what is out there has a character of its own—namely, as "panther"—that is given to it by its presupposed material, "feline" as the purpose still seems to be external to it, or imposed on it from the outside. The lions are feline, but they are being presented as "other" than feline. The definition of "feline" itself is thus restricted by whatever happens to be out there.

Transition to Idea

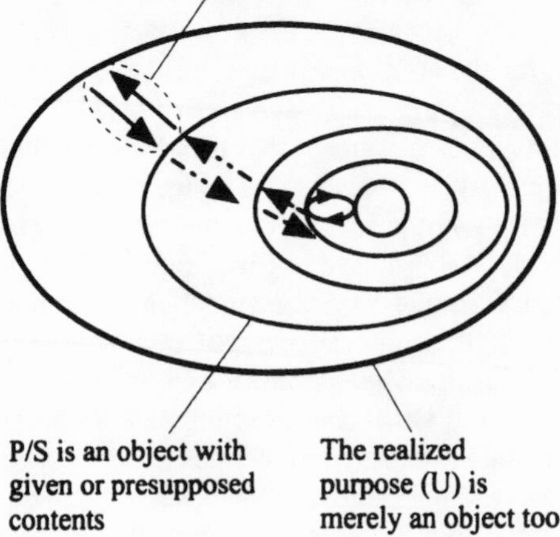
The externality or opposition between the subjective purpose and the object leads to a spurious infinity between finite purposiveness and finite objectivity
P/S is an object with given or presupposed contents
The realized purpose (U) is merely an object too

Figure 4.80

Now that the syllogism of P has been accomplished, the activity of P/S is complete. I have given the arrows representing the purposive activity of P within P/S dashed lines to indicate that the activity has slipped into the background as logically completed. P/S is the complete objectivity of U because it is all of the categories, concepts and thereness—all of the purposive activity—which U defines. P/S is the *whole realm* of finite objectivity for U.

Because the syllogism of P/S is complete, the focus of logical activity is the relationship between the Concept (U)—as finite subjectivity—and P/S—as finite objectivity—a relationship between a one-sidedly subjective purpose (U) and an object (P/S) that is not one-sided. P/S's one-sidedness was sublated when the "in itself" character and independence of the object (i.e. of P/S) was sublated (cancelled but preserved)(see Abstract Purpose). What the object was like on its own, or its independent character, no longer mattered. All that mattered was the identity given to the object by the purpose. This relationship showed that objectivity is nothing on its own without subjectivity, or that objectivity must be defined in relation to subjectivity. The one-sidedness of objectivity was sublated because the Concept or purpose was the defining essence of the object (§212). As Hegel points out (§212), the lack of independence of P and S (separately) and of P/S (together) had already been foreshadowed in mechanism (which foreshadowed the former) and chemism (which foreshadowed the latter). In mechanism, P and S each proved individually to be non-indifferent toward U or toward the Concept—which is now the purpose—and in chemism, P/S as a whole was also non-indifferent toward U or the Concept.

Because the process of realizing the purpose links the subjective (U) together with the objective (P/S), the realized purpose can be defined as the posited or established unity of subjective and objective. Just as the objective had to be defined by the subjective, the realization of the subjective in the objective shows that the subjective has to be defined by the objective. Although subjective and objective are unified, their relationship is not one of equals. The objective is subordinate to and conforms to the subjective or purpose, which is the might over it. That's because the objective's definition was determined as null and void at the beginning of the stages of Purpose. Hence, although the purpose is one-sidedly subjective, subjectivity is the side that preserves itself against and within the objective, in the sense that it is the identity of and determines the objective. The purpose is a U that defines P/S, or makes P/S what it is. It is the U that penetrates and remains the same through each term of the syllogism and throughout their movement. The concept of feline, for instance, remains what it is in "panther," "lion," and "this lion." This is the cunning of Reason (cf. Third Moment of Purpose Realizing Itself).

However, the unity here still treats the subjective and objective as separate in terms of how they are presented (form). Although the subjective and objective are unified in the sense that each is defined as only one side in a larger relationship, the subjective still works on the objective—a relationship represented by the arrow from U to P/S. Because the subjective "works on" the objective in the process of realizing the purpose, P/S is still being presented as separate from or external to U. Moreover, since the purpose is realized in only a restricted way—in relation to pre-given or presupposed content—it is not completely defining P/S. P/S has some elements in it over which that finite U is not the purpose, so P/S is still being presented (form) as something with a different content from the purpose or U, and U is still being presented as if it is externally imposed on P/S. As the same time, P/S has already been defined as null and void on its own. Because the object or P/S is not completely determined by this purpose or U, and because it is null and void on its own, as soon as the purpose is realized in, or turned into, that finite object (i.e. P/S), the object becomes the means or material for other purposes (§211) in a new relationship of purpose. Since U is not the purpose over everything about P/S, P/S must be taken hold of by some other finite purpose—some other U—to be defined. But that U, too—because it, too, is a finite purpose—is relying on given or presupposed material in the object, and so is also only one possible or a contingent way of defining the purpose (§211). So that second finite purpose, too, is realized in an object that, because it contains given or found material, is not completely defined by the U, and so will need to be taken hold of by other finite purposes, or other U's, to be defined. A spuriously infinite process from one purpose to the object to another purpose to the object to yet another purpose to the object and so on is therefore generated. The object or P/S generates a spuriously infinite number of finite purposes, none of which is the purpose over everything about P/S. (Notice that there is only one object, while the number of purposes is infinite.)

This process can also be characterized as a general, back-and-forth relationship between finite purpose (which is how U is currently defined) and finite objectivity in general (which is how P/S is currently defined). Because P/S is currently being presented with given or presupposed material, and hence as something other than U, U—as finite subjectivity in general—must continue to *work on* P/S. It works on P/S insofar as it generates other purposes to be purposes over P/S. But because P/S contains given or presupposed materials, each of those finite purposes, too, is not the purpose over everything about P/S, and so U must continue to work on P/S. The fact that finite purpose (U) has been realized only in given or "found" material thus generates a spuriously infinite, back-and-forth process between finite purpose in general (as U is currently defined) and finite objectivity in general (which is the definition of objectivity that P/S currently has). Again, U must continue to *work on* finite objectivity. This process is represented in the diagram by the two straight arrows between U and P/S. Because finite subjectivity always presents P/S (finite objectivity) as different from it, and because finite subjectivity always defines finite objectivity from the outside or as external to P/S, they are caught in a spuriously infinite, back-and-forth process. I have used the same sort of solid, one-way arrows used to represent spurious alternation processes in earlier stages (see, for instance, Spurious Infinity, Measureless, World of Appearance, Condition as a Totality, and Real Possibility).

P/S generates this process because it is "inwardly broken," Hegel says (§211), or because it is split up inwardly. P/S is "inwardly broken" in the sense that it is all of the categories, concepts and thereness into which U divides. Because P/S is "inwardly broken," it is presented by finite purposes that fail to be the purpose over everything that it is. U as a purpose "fixes on" one division of P/S, and is thereby itself finite. Because U grasps only one division of P/S, other U's must be generated as purposes over other divisions of P/S. "Feline," as a purpose, for instance, is realized in existing lions out there, but those lions also have given or presupposed characters that are not grasped by "feline" as a purpose. For instance, lions are social animals, which not all "felines" are, so being social is a characteristic that lions have that is not given to it by the concept of feline. That characteristic must be explained by some other purpose or concept that explains why lions are social animals—perhaps a concept explaining why any animal is social. Male lions also have large manes, which not all felines have, so that is another characteristic that the concept of feline does not explain, and so must be explained by another purpose. None of those other purposes, however, will succeed in explaining everything about existing lions either. Since no finite purpose will explain all of the characteristics that existing lions have, we will be driven back and forth from finite purpose to lions, to finite purpose to lions and so on, in an attempt to define both the finite purposes and the finite object, namely, the existing lions.

As in earlier stages of Hegel's logic, the logic cannot rest with a spuriously infinite progress because such a process blocks the ability to define either side of the spurious relationship. Here, the purpose is being defined through an object that is defined by a purpose, which is defined by an object, and so on. The inability to reach a moment of stasis makes it impossible to fully and finally define either the purpose or the object (see Spurious Infinity in Chapter Two). Therefore, the spuriously infinite, passing-over process must be stopped for the logic to achieve the goal of defining its terms.

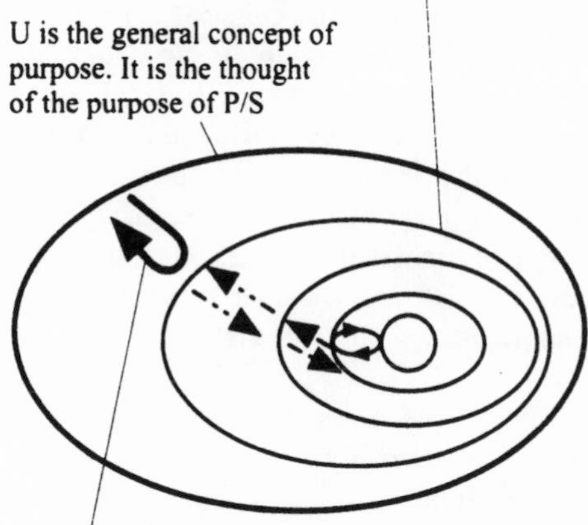
The flipping back-and-forth process defines P/S as the whole display of finite purpose and finite object
U is the general concept of purpose. It is the thought of the purpose of P/S
U is once again in a doubly "for-itself" relationship with P/S. This arrow represents the second layer of "for itself" activity that U now has with P/S

Figure 4.81

In earlier stages of Hegel's logic, spurious infinities have been stopped by an overarching concept that embraces the whole, spuriously infinite process. In some stages, a spurious infinity generated a new concept (cf. Being-for-itself and Transition to Essence in Chapter One). When the spurious infinity is taking place within a concept that already embraces the content, however, it does not generate a new concept, but redefines the concept that already embraces the content (cf. World of Appearance and Condition as a Totality in Chapter Three). In those stages, the embracing concept is redefined as the thought of the whole back and forth process, or as the general concept of what it was. World of Appearance is the general concept of an Appearance, and Condition as a Totality is the general concept of a Condition. Here, the concept of finite purpose is redefined as a concept of infinite purpose, which is the general or universal concept of purpose.

In the last stage, the finiteness of the subjectivity led to a spuriously infinite back-and-forth process between finite subjectivity (the purpose or U) and finite objectivity (P/S). While the object or P/S is complete—it is the complete objectivity for U, or is all of the categories, concepts and thereness into which U divides—because P/S is "inwardly broken," U carries out its purposive activity by "fixing on" only some aspect or division of P/S. That's why U was finite. It explains or is the purpose over only some aspect or division of P/S, and so its definition was restricted by whatever division it happens to "fix on." Moreover, because its definition was limited, the purpose is also finite in the sense that it is defined as external to or opposed to the object.

Because the logic cannot rest with a spurious infinity, it is driven to stop it (cf. Spurious Infinity in Chapter One). The spurious infinity is stopped because the back-and-forth process is taken to be one whole, completed process. Redefining the process as one completed process redefines U and P/S. Because the back-and-forth process is completed, U is now the thought of all of the finite purposes of P/S taken together as a whole, or of the purposes-in-general of P/S.

Moreover, when the back-and-forth process—in which finite purposes explain aspects of P/S—is completed, then *all* aspects of P/S have been explained, and there is nothing left in P/S to be explained, or over which U is not the purpose. Hence, the spuriously infinite back-and-forth process in the last stage has been stopped. When U was finite purpose, it was Reason or the Concept defined as a finite purpose over some aspect of the finite world of objectivity. Now it is Reason or the Concept defined as the thought of purpose-in-general. It is still a concept of purpose, but it is a concept of purpose that has been raised to a new level of ideality. Since it is a concept of purpose that grasps all of the purposes, and since the concept of purpose that grasps all of the purposes is just the concept of purpose itself, U has become the concept of purpose itself, or the concept of the concept of purpose. It is the concept of purpose *per se*, which grasps all of the individual, finite purposes. As I will explain more fully in a moment, it is the "being-for-itself" of purpose.

P/S, for its part, is also now redefined. It becomes the complete unity of finite subjectivity and finite objectivity. P/S was already defined as finite objectivity—it was the whole realm of finite objectivity. But U only explained P/S in relation to one of its aspects. Now that U is the thought that grasps and explains all of the finite purposes and the whole process in which finite purposes define P/S, however, P/S is a finite objectivity that has been fully defined by all of the finite purposes of subjectivity. It is finite objectivity completely covered by finite purposes. Hence it is the complete unity of finite subjectivity and finite objectivity. It is the means (activity) and material (object) for the whole process of U (§212), which includes every finite purpose or subjectivity as well as the whole realm of finite objectivity. P/S is no longer merely the whole realm of finite objectivity, it is the whole realm of finite purpose and finite objectivity, or the whole realm of finite, objective purposiveness. Since P/S includes all of the finite purposes and finite objectivity, and since U grasps and explains all of the purposes and finite objectivity, U grasps and explains everything about P/S. Hence, once again, there is nothing left over for U to grasp, and the spurious infinity has been stopped.

Because P/S is defined not only as completed finite objectivity but also as completed finite subjectivity or purpose, U has become not just the general concept of purpose, but an *essential* concept of purpose, or the concept of purpose as a *essence*. Because P/S is the complete objectivity and subjectivity of U, P/S contains the full measure of U—not just in terms of quality, but also in terms of quantity. P/S now contains not only all the finite purposes and objects that are embraced by U—and hence the quality of U—but P/S is also the full quantity of items and purposes into which U divides. At the end of Chapter Two, Essence was defined as the concept that grasps not only the full quality of a set of items, but also the full quantity of a set of items. It was the full *measure* of the set of items (cf. Transition to Essence in Chapter Two and the Introduction to Chapter Three). Because U, as purpose, grasps the full measure of P/S, it is the *essence of purpose* over P/S (§212). It grasps not only the sameness (or identity) of the felines in terms of what they are (i.e. as felines), but also the sameness (or identity) of the felines in terms of their purpose. U is not just the essential identity of P/S in terms of what they are, it is also the essential identity over P/S in terms of their purpose. U is now the *essential purpose* over P/S.

Because U is now defined as the essential purpose over P/S, it has become a new kind of unity over P/S as well. In the stages of judgment and syllogism (which was based on judgment), U was defined as the unity of P and S by grasping their identity and difference at the same time, since the form of the judgment says both that the two items in the judgment are the same as one another and that the two items in the judgment are different from one another at the same time (see The Judgment). When U fell apart in the Transition to Mechanism, U was still the identity or unity of P and S in an "in itself" sense. U captured the character (or identity) that they all shared—they were all objects—but only insofar as they were defined as separate from, opposed to, or up against one another, which was the hallmark of Being-in-itself in Chapter Two. U was the unity of U, P and S only insofar as they were divided. That's why the three elements fell apart in the stage of Transition to Mechanism. That same sort of "in itself" unity dominated finite purpose in the last stage. In finite purpose, U was the unity over P and S insofar as they were split up or divided. Since "feline," for instance, divided into individual lions, it was the unity of the lions insofar as they were divided into separate objects. As a result, it could grasp their identity as the same as one another, but not their differences from one another. Because the concept of feline was treating the existing felines as separate objects, it could explain why they were all "feline," but could not explain the differences between different types of felines. It could not explain why some felines are social, for instance, while other felines are not. The concept of feline was their unity, insofar as it grasped the character that each of the felines share as separate objects—they are all felines—but it still treated them as separate objects. Because it treated them as separate objects, it grasped them only as "felines-in-general," and so could not explain why those objects are different from one another. It grasped what was alike about them—as felines—but could not explain or grasp what was different about them. U was the unity of P/S only insofar as U was divided into separate objects with the same general character or identity.

Now that U and P/S have been redefined, however, U is no longer the unity of P/S as a "being-in-itself," it is now the unity of P/S as a "*being-for-itself*" (§212). Now that U is the thought of all the purposes and the whole process of purpose over P/S, and now that P/S is the object completely defined by both finite subjectivity (or purpose) and finite objectivity, U explains not only the sameness of P/S insofar as it is divided into separate objects, it also explains or is the purpose over the *differences* within P/S. Now that the concept of feline (U), for instance, has been defined as the thought of all the purposes over the individual felines, it is not only as the thought or concept of the complete set of categories, concepts and thereness into which "feline" *divides*, but also as the thought or concept that *gathers up* all of the felines. U's object (i.e. P/S) is not just all the categories, types and individual felines into which "feline" divides, it is all the felines out there *along with all of their finite purposes*. P/S is the whole realm of purpose and objectivity for felines, or the *whole display* of felines. It is everything that felines are *and do*. Because the concept of feline is defined as everything that felines are *and do*, it grasps and explains not only how they are the same as one another (i.e. their identity as felines), but also how they are *different* from one another. Because the concept of feline is the thought of the whole display of felines, it grasps and explains why lions are social and other felines are not. The fact that lions are social and other felines are not belongs to the whole display (i.e. P/S) of felines. That fact is one of the finite purposes that now belongs to the object or P/S itself. Because the concept of feline explains everything about felines—the categories, concepts, thereness *as well as purposes*—there is no longer any difference between felines that is not grasped by the concept of feline itself. P/S is everything that felines are and do, and the concept of feline grasps everything about them, both their identity as felines, and the differences that they display as they go about doing their feline activity. In the same way, U, as the thought or concept of everything that P/S is and does, not only grasps the identity of P/S insofar as P/S is split up or divided, but also the differences within P/S insofar as the items in P/S are gathered up or have their whole display. Because U grasps and presents P/S not only in terms of how it is divided, but also in terms of how it is pulled together, U is a one, whole, *singularity*.

It is because U is the One that explains not only the way in which the elements within P/S are the same as one another (insofar as they are split up or divided), but also their differences from one another (insofar as they are gathered up) that it grasps the unity of P/S as a "being-for-itself." Being-for-itself in Chapter Two grasped not only the sameness that the elements shared insofar as they repulsed one another (see Repulsion), but also the way in which the elements were different from one another insofar as they were attracted to one another or pulled together (see Attraction). Being-for-itself involved both Repulsion and Attraction because it had to sort out those characteristics that defined the something-others as the same as one another from those characteristics that defined the something-others as different from one another without undermining their sameness. That's the very same relationship that U now has with P/S, except that U's "for itself" process is a process of both form and content (as we will see more fully in a moment), while Being-for-itself's "for itself" process was a process only of content (cf. Chapter Three, Section V). Still, U explains not only the way in which the items in P/S are the same as one another (insofar as they are split up or divided), but—now that it is the concept of the whole display of P/S— also the ways in which they are different from one another insofar as they are the same, or without undermining their status as the same as one another. Since the concept of feline, for example, includes the whole display of felines, it explains not only the individual felines as "feline" (insofar as they are split up into individual felines) but also their differences from one another as felines or insofar as they are the same. There is a pattern here that will become important in later stages. In the stages of Purpose, U is a purpose insofar as it divides into its object, but U is an identity insofar as it gathers up the differences within its object. *Splitting up or dividing is a process of purpose; gathering up differences is a process of identity.*

U is a "being-for-itself" in another way as well. In the stages of Being-for-itself, Being-for-itself was not only defined by the processes of Attraction and Repulsion, it was also a concept that grasped the thereness or reality of the items or something-others in its set. U does that here too. U grasps the whole display of P/S, including its thereness. U is therefore also a "being for itself" in the sense that it grasps the thereness of the items that it embraces. Indeed, in the next stage, U will be defined as the unity of the Concept and reality or thereness.

U now fulfills the definition that was promised in the concept of purpose. Purpose was the concept that pushed out into smaller-S, or into Inner and Outer and their mutually defining relationship. Since Outer is the whole realm of Being, it includes thereness. It is out-thereness. Purpose was therefore defined as a concept that includes thereness. But because purpose had to push out into thereness, it was still defined as opposed to or separate from thereness, and so was the unity of concept or subject and object or thereness only as a being-*in*-itself, rather than as a being-*for*-itself. But U now includes thereness in a "for itself" relationship—in a relationship in which it comes home to itself through an "other" that is not really "other" for it (cf. Being-for-itself)—U fulfills the definition of purpose as a being-*for*-itself. As Hegel says, this logical move establishes what the concept of purpose was, namely "the *being in itself* unity of subject and object now *as being for itself* [*die* an sich seiende *Einheit des Subjektiven und Objektiven nun* als für sich seiend]" (§212).

Now that U grasps everything about P/S, U and P/S are not only the same as one another in terms of content or identity, they are also the same as one another in terms of form or how they are being presented. In finite purpose, U was realized as the purpose over P/S, but P/S was still being presented as different from U. U was pushing out or working on P/S insofar as P/S was divided or split up. "Feline," for instance, was the purpose over a bunch of lions, house cats, and so on, so that P/S was being presented as lions, house cats and so on, rather than as "feline." That's why the concept of "feline" could not grasp or explain the ways in which lions are different from house cats: it could grasp and explain their sameness (as "feline"), but not their differences. Now that P/S is the whole display of "feline," U and P/S are being presented (i.e in terms of form) as the same as one another as well. U is being presented as the universal concept of feline, and P/S is being presented as the whole display of felines. Since a universal concept just *is* the whole display of what it grasps (cf. Universality), U and P/S have the same content or are the same as one another. U and P/S are therefore being presented as the same as one another since they have the same content.

The new definitions for U and P/S give them a new relationship with one another as well—a relationship that grows out of two factors. First, U or the Concept itself initiated this whole process of purpose, and therefore produced the definitions of U and P/S that are currently in play (see the First Moment of

Purpose Realizing Itself). The U here at the end of the stages of Purpose is the same U that went through the processes of purpose that led to the current definition of U. The definition that U now has is a definition that it got *for itself*, or through its own activity (it is a "being-for-itself" in terms of form). Second, the process of purpose has reinforced U's definition as an embracing concept (as a "being-for itself" in terms of content). The process of purpose has redefined U as an embracing concept *of purpose*. So U has succeeded in fulfilling its definition as a doubly "for itself" concept: it is an embracing, "for itself" concept that embraces its content *for itself*, or through its own activity. More precisely, U has defined itself as an embracing, "for itself" concept of *purpose* for itself, or through its own activity.

Because there is no longer any distinction in form or content between U and P/S, the "in itself" opposition that they had in relation to one another that generated the spuriously infinite back-and-forth process has now been sublated. I have therefore removed the two straight arrows that represented the back-and-forth process of opposition between U and P/S from the diagram. That back-and-forth process between U and P/S has been completed, and so now slips into the background as no longer logically active. Moreover, now that U has fulfilled its doubly "for itself" relationship between itself and P/S, I have added a looping arrow between U and P/S in the diagram to represent the second sense of "for itself" activity taking place between U and P/S. U is not only a "for itself" concept that embraces or surrounds P/S—the "for itselfness" of content, which is depicted by the fact that the bubble for U surrounds the bubble for P/S—U also embraces P/S *for itself*, or through its own activity—the "for-itselfness" of form, which I have depicted in the diagram by adding the same sort of looping, "for itself" arrow between U and P/S that I have used to represent "for itself" activity of form in earlier stages (cf. Absolute Relationship in Chapter Three). The "for itself" activity replaces the spuriously infinite back-and-forth process because the whole back-and-forth process is just the way in which U or the Concept presents its contents *for itself*, or through its own activity. To use Hegel's anthropomorphic language for a moment, the Concept—which is now defined as the thought of the whole, back-and-forth process—uses that process to define itself *for itself*, or through its own activity. As Hegel puts it, the shine or semblance of independence that U had from P/S at the beginning of the stages of Purpose (cf. Abstract Purpose) has been sublated (canceled and preserved) (§212). The back-and-forth process has been absorbed and replaced as part of the Concept's own process of being defined *for itself*, or through its own activity. P/S is now *nothing but* the way in which the Concept is defined *for itself*. Because the "in itself" opposition between U and P/S has been sublated, U no longer "works on" P/S.

The diagram here is very similar to the diagram that illustrated the stage of Universality, in which the Concept was defined as a "for itself" concept because it initiated the process of Reciprocal Action that ended Chapter Three. Because the Concept initiated the whole process of Reciprocal Action, that process was the Concept's own presentation or activity. That's why the Concept had a "for itself" relationship of form with the Effect_{CS} in the stage of Universality.

Moreover, although Reason initiated the whole process of Reciprocal Action, because Reason as it is defined at the end of the process is the same Reason that went through the process, the definition that Reason has at the end of the process is a definition *after the fact*, which therefore does not undermine the suggestion that the world of experience (the Effect$_{CS}$) is original and causal in relation to Reason (see Transition to the Concept in Chapter Three). Similarly, here, Reason or the Concept-as-purpose is defined as what Reason will be like *after* the whole process of finite purposes (subjectivity) and finite objectivity in time. The same U that went through the process of finite purpose and objectivity is the U that is defined as infinite purpose at the end of the process. So while Reason is the thought that drives or initiates the processes of finite purpose and objectivity in time, what Reason is like at the end of the whole process is determined *after the fact*. The world of finite subjectivity and finite objectivity that unfolds in time is original insofar as it defines what Reason is like at the end of the whole process.

Although the logical process here is similar to the process that defined the Concept (as Universality) after Reciprocal Action, there is an important difference. In Reciprocal Action, the back-and-forth process between the Concept and the Effect$_{CS}$ was a causal process. Here, the back-and-forth process is a process of purpose. Because purpose is a process of thought or subjectivity, it is part of the activity of the Concept—which is Thought—and so belongs to the Doctrine of the Concept—which spells out the Concept's own activity as a subject (see the Introduction to this chapter)—rather than the Doctrine of Essence.

Because the Concept is defined as infinite purpose only at the end of the back-and-forth process over time, it is the purpose over everything only when the process is completed or when time is finished. That is why Hegel apparently said in a lecture that, even though objectivity is just "a wrapping under which the Concept lies hidden," those of us who live "in the finite sphere," or in time, "cannot experience nor see that the purpose is genuinely attained" (§212A). We cannot see that the purpose is genuinely attained because the purpose is, for us, not genuinely attained. The purpose is only genuinely obtained at the end of time or for a point of view outside of time, which none of us mere mortals can have. At the same time, this "error," Hegel apparently said, is produced by the Concept itself (§212A), since the Concept must go through the process of purpose in time to be what it is. So the moment in which the object is determined as "other" or as "error" is a necessary moment of the Concept itself (§212A)—not least of which because it motivates us to act, and our (human) actions are part of the very process through which the Concept develops its definition as the purpose over everything.

IV. The Doctrine of the Idea

Now that the Concept is the thought of a whole display of purpose and object over time, it is Idea. An Idea is the concept of the identity and whole purpose of an object. It is the thought of all of the purposes, categories, concepts and thereness of an object that is not just divided, but is also pulled back together as a whole or one. Idea is the concept that grasps and explains the whole display of the object. Hegel has two reasons for selecting the concept of "idea" as the label for the current definition of the Concept. First, although U is the purpose over P/S, it still grasps the identity of P/S in the more straight-forward sense in which it grasps the "what it is" and essence of P/S. Even though the concept of feline, for instance, is the purpose over all the existing felines, it is the purpose over all of the existing felines in the sense that it makes them what they are as *felines*. Hence it still grasps the "what it is" or essence of felines. Of course, it grasps the essence or identity of felines *because* it is the purpose over felines, but, nevertheless, it still grasps the character of the felines in the more general sense in which it captures what they are. Although Hegel could have used the concept of purpose to label the Concept here, doing so would have obscured the dual nature of U as both the purpose and the identifying essence over P/S. It would place too much focus on the teleological implications of U, and too little on the U as an essentially identifying universal. The second reason Hegel has for choosing the concept of "Idea" grows out of the history of philosophy. "Idea" was Plato's and Aristotle's term for concepts conceived of as both teleological and as essences.

In logical terms, the Idea is the Concept now once again defined as doubly "for itself"—both as a "for itself" concept that embraces the world of objective purposiveness (or finite subjectivity and finite objectivity [P/S]) as its content, and as what pushes out the world of objective purposiveness *for itself*, or through its own activity. As what pushes out the whole realm of objective purposiveness, the Idea is purpose, and as what embraces the whole world of objective purposiveness, it is essence or identity. As the Idea, the Concept is still the thought of the completed, conceptual scheme or system of rational concepts--or of Reason itself. Indeed, Hegel says, the Idea is Reason, properly understood (§214). Now that the Concept is defined as Idea, however, it is the purpose behind the system of rational concept—a purpose that is fleshed-out into the objective world of purposes. Because the same Reason that is at the end of the process is the same Reason that went through the process, the Idea is the thought of Reason going through and having gone through its doubly "for itself" process in relation to the whole world of objective purposiveness. Although the Concept was defined at the beginning of the stages of Purpose as an overarching concept that "contained" the objective world, it now "contains" that objective world in a more active sense. It pushes out and gathers up the world of objective purposiveness as the purpose behind that world. As Idea, the Concept is Reason as a force in the world, or as alive in the world of objective purposiveness. I have suggested that Hegel shares Aristotle's view that things in the world have their forms, concepts or purposes in them (cf. Chapter One, Section II). Individual rocks or plants are what they are or have the character that they do because they have enough of the form, concept or purpose in them to be what they are. Without that concept, form or purpose, they would not be what they are. Rocks and plants cannot think their own purposes, of course, in the sense of subjectively formulating their own purposes. Rocks and plants are not conscious, they have no awareness or thought. But, from the point of view of Reason, rocks do have purposes. They go about being rocks—that is their purpose in the world of objective purposiveness. The general process of objective purposiveness, then, is just the whole process in which the world of finite objects with finite purposes go about their business as what they are, including whatever finite purposes are included in what they are. Rocks go about being the rocks that they are, plants go about being the plants that they are, we go about being the humans that we are, and so on. The Idea is thus the thought of Reason pushing out and gathering up the world that is going about its business. It is Reason now defined as the source of objective purposiveness, of the world going about its business, or of the life of the world. The Idea is Reason thought of as fleshed out in the life of the world.

"Fleshed out" is a good metaphor to use to describe the Concept here because the Idea includes the world of immediate being or thereness as part of its activity. Hence, the Idea includes both other concepts (or Thought) and "flesh" (or Being). The Idea is the Concept as fully fleshed out, both conceptually and materially. Hegel uses a similar metaphor when he describes the Idea as a soul with a body (§214). Because the Idea is an essence, it belongs to the Concept, to Thought or to subjectivity. As Hegel suggests, the process of the Idea leads back into subjectivity (§215). In the Idea, the Concept or U is once again defined as subjective. But the Idea is a thought or subjectivity that is "fleshed out" into P/S. It is, as Hegel puts it, the Subject-Object, or the unity of the ideal and the real (§214). The Idea is the unity of Concept and reality (cf. *Science of Logic*, §1743).

The Idea is a process (§215). It is the Concept and its full content of determinations—both conceptual determinations (other concepts) and determinations in reality—where all these determinations are part of the "for itself" activity of the Idea itself. It is the Concept (U) going through its determinations in P and S. Since S includes the world of reality, then the Idea includes the world of reality too. The reality that the Idea embraces, however, has no significant "in itself" or independent character of its own. The "in itself" character of the object has been sublated (cancelled but preserved). The Idea explains everything that is objective, so the objective world is *for* the Concept or Idea. The reality that the Idea includes has no significance on its own, but is merely the way in which the Concept presents into external thereness, as Hegel says (§214).

The fact that P/S has no *significant* "in itself" opposition to U does not mean that P/S has become completely the same as U, however. The "for itself" opposition that required U to "work on" P/S in the stages of Purpose has been sublated, and U and P/S have the same content, insofar as U is the thought of the whole display of P/S, and P/S is the whole display. But there is still some opposition between U and P/S. In particular, U and P/S still have the same type of "in itself" opposition between them that defined U as a *universal concept* (see Universality). Because P/S is not only the content of U, but also the way in which U is *presented*, U has a character of its own separate from P/S, even though they share the same content. As soon as a concept *presents* another concept, it is defined as separate from the other concept (see the stage of External Necessity in Chapter Three). The two concepts share the same content, but not the same form. One is presenting the other, so they are not the same in terms of how they are being presented, or their form. That is precisely the sort of separation that defines U as a universal *concept*. As the purpose over P/S, U is pushing out or presenting P/S as its form, and P/S is the way in which U is presented. Because U *presents* P/S, it is still opposed to P/S in terms of presentation or form. U is the *thought of* P/S, rather than P/S itself.

While U is still a U, P/S is now defined as a singularity. P/S is all of the categories, concepts, thereness and finite purposes of objectivity, not insofar as they are divided, but insofar as they are *pulled together*. It is a one, a whole, a singular. P/S is the whole display of objectivity (insofar as it is divided) as a one or singular (insofar as it is pulled back together). In short, P/S is an S.

U now has the very same kind of relationship with P/S that is expressed by the judgment "U is S." The general form of a judgment ascribes both identity as well as separation to the elements. In general, "x is y" says both that x is the same as y (identity) and that x is distinct from y (separation). The identity is expressed by the copula "is" in the judgment—the "is" says that x is y, and hence that x is the same as y. The distinction is expressed by the fact that the judgment uses two different terms to refer to x and y. Since the judgment is calling one "x" and one "y," there are two different items (cf. The Judgment). U has exactly the same sort of relationship with P/S now. It is separate from P/S insofar as it presents P/S as its form or is the concept *of* P/S. But it is the same as P/S insofar as it is the identity of or defining essence over P/S because they share the same content. As a result, U or universality has the same kind of "in and for itself" relationship of identity and separation that defines the judgment. The relationship between U and P/S takes the form of the judgment "U is S." The Idea can therefore be expressed as the judgment "U is S." I have added this judgment to the diagram. As we will see, the logical progression of the stages of the Idea will involve progression in this judgment as well as within the Concept (or Idea) itself, which will still be depicted with the usual bubbles and arrows.

As in the stages of judgment, the judgment "U is S," which expresses the relationship between U and P/S, is at first taken to be an expression of the simple identity that U has with P/S (cf. Abstract Judgment). It says that U *is* P/S. Moreover, as in other places throughout Hegel's logic, the logical development of the Doctrine of the Idea begins by treating the unity of the elements in play as an *immediate* unity. At first, then, the identity between U and P/S is immediate: U is connected to P/S in an immediate way, or "U is S" in an immediate way. Moreover, since an Idea is any concept (U) that is both the essential identity as well as the essential purpose over the object (P/S as a whole, or as an S), the claim that "U is S" (in an immediate way) also means that U is performing those two functions together in an immediate way. U's function as the essential identity of as well as its function as the essential purpose over S are connected together in an immediate way. Thus, the immediacy of "U is S" applies not only to the "is" or connection between U and S, but also to the connection between the two functions that U is performing as both the essential identity of as well as the essential purpose over S. Because those two functions of U are connected together only in an immediate way, they will fall apart later on.

Immediate Idea or Life

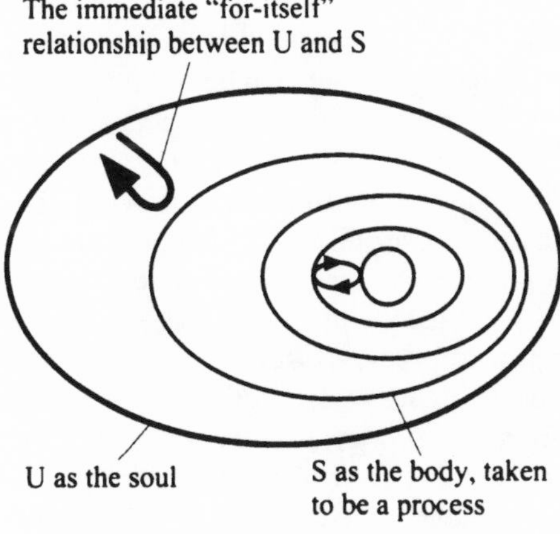

Figure 4.82

Since the activity within P/S has given U the definition that U has now, that activity is no longer logically active, but has been completely absorbed by the definition of U. I have removed the dashed arrows that represented P/S's activity of purpose from the diagram to depict this fact. The definition of U has absorbed P/S's earlier activity of purpose. P/S is a whole process without any specific internal activity. Moreover, the relationship between U and S (or P/S) is an immediate one that is expressed by the judgment "U is S."

Because the relationships within P/S are no longer determined, P/S is an S or singular that is in an immediate process with a content. Since P/S has Singularity (the "S" of "P/S") for its content, its content is the set of singularities into which P divides. So even though P/S as a whole is now a singular (an S), it is a singular that is itself a set or bunch of singulars. P/S is a whole that is a process of a bunch of singulars.

The Immediate Idea is life or, to coin a term in English, living-ness (*Lebendiges* [§216]). (I will explain why I coin this term shortly.) To be something alive is to be a universal that is immediately singular, or to be a U that is fleshed out in an immediate way into S. But it is also to be fleshed out in an immediate way into an S that is itself a set or bunch of singulars. Every living thing is a universal that presents itself (through its own activity) in an immediate way as a whole (singular) process of a bunch of singulars. Take a plant, for instance. Because a plant grows from a seed to small plant and then to a larger plant, we cannot say what the plant (as a whole) is by pointing to any one thing in the world. That is why using the term "living thing" to characterize S at this point is somewhat misleading. When a plant is a "thing," it is only a singular, momentary instance of the plant—what you can point to out there in the world that is the plant at the moment. But the *living* plant is the whole space-time continuum of things or instances that the plant has been during its life, as it went about its business of being a plant (through its own activity). The living plant includes the seed originally planted in the box by the window, the big plant by the window that finally dies, and every stage of the plant in between. The *living* plant is an immediate universal of singularity—a whole set or group of singular instances taken together (i.e. as a group or universal) in an immediate way. Once the bunch of singulars that is the plant is taken together as a group (along with all of their business), then the plant—the concept (universal) that grasps the whole group—immediately is. To be alive is to be a universal (U) that is, in an immediate way, a set (S) of singulars. To be living or growing is to be a universal that is objectified in an immediate way, through its own activity, as a singular that is a bunch of singulars, or as a process of singularity.

Because the connection between the universality of living things and their singularity is immediate, this life is finite. In Chapter Two, I characterized an immediate relationship as a kind of gluing-together (see Transition to Essence). In the Doctrine of the Concept here, the immediate relationship is also a relationship of judgment, or an "is": in the case of living, as soon as the set of singulars is taken together as an "is," then the U immediately "is." Nevertheless, the immediate relationship here still involves gluing together because the connection between the universality and the collection of singulars can come apart, or is in principle separable. Living things are finite, or are the sort of thing whose universality is separable from their singularity. They come unglued. The whatever-is-it that holds the plant together as the living plant—we can call this, following Aristotle, the *soul* of the plant—can be separated from the whole process of singularity. The soul is separated from the body or the process of singularity when the plant dies. Once the plant dies, it is no longer a set of singularities, or a process of objectification in singularity. Its process stops, so that it only "was" a universal, but no longer "is" a universal. No further moments of singularity will be added to the plant's set as a universal. Its U-ness has stopped.

This section is therefore a description, not of a living being,[6] in the sense of a living thing, but of living-ness, or what it is to be alive. So long as something is alive, it is an immediate "U is S." Once something dies, it is no longer an immediate "U is S" at all. So "U is S" (taken in an immediate sense) describes not the thing-ness of the living being, but rather the living-ness of the living thing, the being of its living, or what it is for the living thing to be alive. *Lebendiges* is not living being, but being-living, or the being of living. The immediate "U is S" is a living thing's life, or its "living-ness."

From a logical point of view, Life is doubly "for itself." It is "for itself," firstly, as an embracing concept, or as a concept that embraces an "other" in its content that is really itself, and so is "for itself" in the most basic, logical sense. In Being-for-Itself in the Chapter Two, a basic qualitative universal, such as "apple," is logically "for itself" because it grasps or embraces individual apples that—because they are apples—are not an "other" for the concept of apple. Life is a basic universal in this sense: U is S and S is U. They are the same. U is the thought of S as a process. However, Life is also "for itself," secondly, in the sense that it is going through its activity "for itself," which is to say, on its own. In the Introduction to this chapter, I suggested that a toaster is the subject of its defining activity when we put in a piece of toast, plug it in and push down the lever. The toaster defines itself as a toaster when it goes through the process of toasting. But the toaster cannot do this process by itself, independently of another subjectivity. *We* have to put in the toast, plug it in, and push down the lever. The logical hallmark of life is that it can go through its defining process by itself, independently of any other subjectivity. When a seed grows into a plant and so on, it does not need another subject to make that process possible. It needs nutrients, water, and so on, but, unlike the toaster, it can be the subject of its activity *for itself*. These two levels of "for-itselfness" are portrayed in the diagram, firstly, insofar as Life is an overarching bubble surrounding the other bubbles, and, secondly, insofar as Life has a relationship with S (P/S) represented by the looping arrow that runs from U to S and back to U.

"Life" is an unusual category to meet in contemporary logic. Why is Hegel's logic concerned with the concept of life? Hegel's logic develops different accounts of being, or of what it is to be something (see the Introduction to this book). Life is a way of being, a kind of being, and is therefore a legitimate topic for a logic concerned with defining all the different sorts of being and "is" that there are. Moreover, the concept of life appropriately belongs to the Doctrine of the Concept because the Doctrine of the Concept outlines the process through which Reason or the Concept—as the thought of the completed and completely systematized set of rational concepts—is defined *for itself*, or through its own activity. Reason is defined *for itself* or by its own activity in part through living things. The activity of living things *is* the activity of Reason. As living things go about their business of being what they are and doing what they do, they define all the concepts that grasp them. As will be seen in the stages that spell out the processes of Life, house cats, for instance, define the concept of house cat by going about their business of living. Living is the flesh of Reason. It is the activity through which the concepts of natural kinds are defined. Our (human) activity in particular, as we'll see more fully in the stages of Cognition, is a crucial part of Reason's activity. As we go about our business of being human, we define not only the concept of human, but all sorts of other concepts as well. Because we are self-conscious, thinking beings, our activity defines the concepts we use in that activity—the concepts of property, law, all the concepts of ethics, and so on. In short, *our thought* defines Reason too. Life generally is therefore one of the ways in which Reason is defined through its own activity.

Hegel says that living-ness (*Lebendiges*) is "the syllogism whose very moments are inwardly systems and syllogisms," and then lists three earlier paragraphs (§§198, 201, 207[7]). §198 describes the triad of syllogisms that was associated with mechanism. §201 discusses the syllogism of the process of chemism, and §207 discusses the syllogism of subjective purpose. Being alive or "living-ness" can be characterized in all three of these ways—as a mechanical system, as a chemical or organic system, and as a purposive system. First, many of the processes of living beings can be conceived of in mechanical ways. We often describe the circulatory system, for example, in mechanical ways as involving independent and interchangeable parts. Hearts are pumps, for example, arteries are hoses, one heart can be replaced for another, one artery for another, in the way the parts of an engine are exchanged.

Second, other systems of living-ness are better conceived of as organic systems whose "parts" are not independent of the whole system. Limbs, for instance, are probably best conceived of organically, rather than mechanically. This point can be illustrated by an example drawn from Aristotle—which Hegel apparently also referred to in a lecture discussing this part of the logic (§216A). Aristotle pointed out that a hand that has been cut off from the body is not really a hand anymore.[8] We cannot replace one hand with another—at least not yet. Thus a hand cannot be conceived of as an independent and interchangeable mechanical part (at least not yet), but is best thought of as part of an organic system. (Indeed, the fact that transplanted organs can be rejected taught us that hearts and other organs are organic systems too, and are poorly conceived of as mechanical parts.)

Third, living-ness is also characterized by systems of subjective purpose. A plant that is sickly, for instance, or does not produce fruit the way it should, is a bad plant, or a plant that fails to live up to its promise or purpose. To say that the plant fails, or falls short, is to assume that there is a goal or purpose for the plant and hence to ascribe a purposiveness to the plant, which it failed to achieve. A bad plant is a plant that is not what it should be, or does not fulfill its purpose.

The second stage of the development of Life in the logic is the life process. Hegel divides this syllogistic "for itself" process of being alive into three different processes.

The First Process of the Life: Living-ness Inside Itself

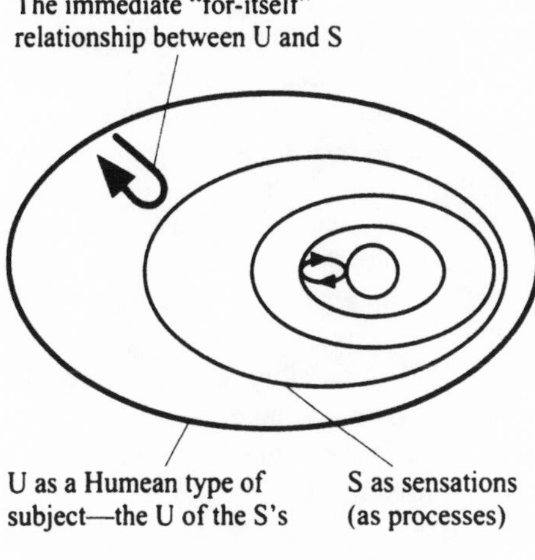

Figure 4.83

The first process is the process of the living being inside itself. Here, Life is taken to be a universality that sunders or divides itself up internally. The life is still a "U is S," but it is a U that is an immediate universal for an internal, rather than an external process of singularity. In the last stage, the life was a unity with the body in an external way. The singular instances of the plant—as a seed, then as a small plant, then as a larger one—were its body. The plant was a U that was broken up externally into its bodily instances. Now living is a U that is broken up internally into bodily instances. This sort of life is similar to the way in which David Hume thought of the human subject, namely, as a collection (or universal) of internal states or awarenesses. The relationship between U and S is still immediate: once all the internal states are taken together as a whole, then the U immediately is too, since the U just is the collection of singular instances of internal states. But S is now the object of U in a more complicated sense as well. Here, S is not just the external body of U, but also the body that U is directed toward, or *aware of.* The kind of life defined in this stage is therefore more sophisticated than the sort of life that a plant can have, since a plant lacks basic sentience or awareness. This kind of living is a basic level of conscious living. Now that the Idea has become conscious, I can use Hegel's anthropomorphic language without blushing. Since the Idea has awareness, it can truly turn its attention toward things, presuppose things, have a point of view, and so on.

Although the system (or set) (S) of states belongs to U, and although U is aware of them, there is still an element of externality between U and S. U treats the states as relatively external: it takes the states to be distinguished from itself. The states are not itself, but rather are moments of itself. But since the states are also *its* moments, they are itself too. Through a process of distinguishing and assimilating the internal states, U becomes aware of itself as the one (singularity) that is the states. Hegel does not explain this process in the *Encyclopaedia*. In the *Science of Logic*, however, Hegel divides the process of life inside itself into sensibility, irritability and reproduction. Because these same processes appear in the Addition to §218 in the *Encyclopaedia*—Hegel apparently mentioned them in his lectures—I think it is fair to assume that Hegel expected his students to be familiar with these terms, and to apply them to this section of the logic.

Sensibility is the system of sensory awareness, where the sort of state in question is a moment of sensation. The process of sensibility is a syllogism. Recall that the whole syllogism for the process of the Concept in the stages of purpose was U-(U-P-S), where (U-P-S) was the process of syllogism from P to S, to smaller-S (which was Inner and Outer in their mutually determining relationship). In the example I used there, the syllogism, U-(U-P-S), was *dinner(U)—(salad(U)—lettuce(P)—this lettuce(S))*. The Idea incorporates this same syllogism into its judgment "U is S." In that judgment, U is the whole Idea, or the outer-most bubble, and S is the former P/S and its process. P/S's process is the syllogism U-P-S, where P is the U, S is the P, and smaller S (Inner and Outer in their mutually determining relationship) is the S. Sensibility is the syllogism U-(U-P-S), where the first U would be the Idea or living being itself, which in sensibility goes through the syllogism of P/S. In the syllogism of P/S, for instance, the living being has a general internal awareness of the body (U). That general awareness particularizes into the different types of sensation, such as sight or seeing (P), which in turn particularizes into a specific instance of seeing or a sight (S). Thus, in sensation, the living being or U goes through the syllogism U-P-S: *internal awareness of the body (in general) (U)—seeing (in general) (P)—this sight (S)*. The whole syllogism would be U-(U-P-S): *the living-ness (U)—internal awareness of the body (in general) (U)—seeing (in general) (P)—this sight (S)*. Because the judgment of sensibility (i.e. "U is S") still expresses an immediate relationship between U and S, there is an immediate connection between the living being (U) and this process of S. In other words, the first U, as the living-ness, has an immediate connection with the syllogism of sensibility: it simply experiences the sight in an immediate way. As a result, it is at home in this sight, and assimilates this sight easily to itself, to use Hegel's phrases.

Unlike sensibility, irritability emphasizes the relative externality between U and S. It opens up a negative space between U and S within the living process of internal awareness, so that U becomes aware of this negative space as an urge. In a syllogism for irritability (U-(U-P-S)), for example, the living being's (the first U) general, internal awareness of its body (the second U) particularizes as itchiness (P) which then further particularizes as a specific itch (S): *the living-ness (U)—internal awareness of the body (in general) (U)—itchiness (in general) (P)—this itch (S)*. Unlike the awareness of the sight—in which the living being was at home—the awareness of the itch creates a negative space between the U and the S (where S is the whole syllogism of P/S) because the living being does not want to be the itch. Thus, although "U is S," or the living being is the itch, the U does not want to be the S. This negative space is experienced as an urge—in this case, as an urge to scratch and be rid of the itch.

Through irritability, the living being or U becomes aware of itself as an individual. Irritability disrupts the immediate at-home awareness of itself that the life had in sensibility. The life now becomes aware of itself as a life that must actively produce itself. In irritability, U is a U with an irritating state, and the U has the urge not to be that irritating state. This urge creates the space for the realization on the part of the life that it—as U—must work at being itself. It must actively reproduce itself internally, moment to moment, to be what it is. It must actively produce and reproduce its states to be what it is. This process of production and reproduction is the third process of life inside itself.

Hegel's use of the term "reproduction" (*Reproduktion*) does not refer to the process of having offspring. Reproduction in this stage is a process of life inside itself, or a process that the life-form is aware of, or experiences as part of its awareness. Hegel discusses the reproductive process of having offspring specifically in §220 and §221. Here, reproduction is just the dawning of *the awareness* that life, *as awareness* (at least for those capable of this sort of life), is a series of produced and reproduced awarenesses. It is the dawning of an awareness of awareness. It is the dawning of self-consciousness, which is a second-order awareness of awareness. Because the life wants to avoid certain awarenesses (the itch, for instance), it becomes aware of its awareness and of its ability to produce and reproduce or alter awarenesses (by scratching the itch, for instance).

Now that the life is aware of itself as a process of awarenesses, it is also aware of itself as a whole one or singularity. U is aware of itself as the whole process of produced and reproduced awarenesses. As a result, the U becomes an S—a universality that is defined as a singularity. Moreover, now that U has become aware of its internal states as a whole process of singularity, it has a bunch of singularities for its object. The object—which was defined as an S in the last stage—has therefore now become a group or bunch of items or a universal. S has become U. Since the Idea (formerly U) has become an S, and the object (formerly S) has become a U, the next stage will be expressed by the judgment "S is U." The Idea is a subjectivity in the grammatical sense: it is a singularity that has a universal for its predicate. It is also *a self-conscious subject*: a subjectivity that is aware of itself as a universality or bunch of items.

The Second Process: Living-ness Against Inorganic Nature

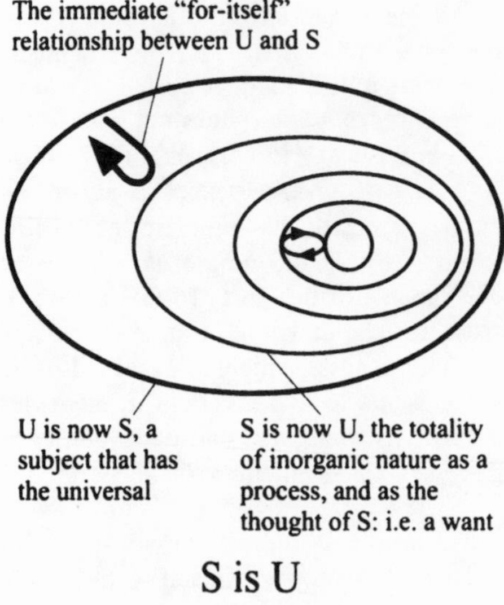
The immediate "for-itself" relationship between U and S
U is now S, a subject that has the universal
S is now U, the totality of inorganic nature as a process, and as the thought of S: i.e. a want
S is U

Figure 4.84

Now that the Idea has become a unified singularity (an S), it can no longer treat its internal states as external to itself. It is a one as the whole process of produced and reproduced internal states. It *is* its internal states. As a result, its internal states no longer count as an object for it, or as something to which it is related. At the same time, now that it is aware that it must reproduce itself from moment to moment, it still needs an object to work on, an object in relation to which it can produce and reproduce itself. Since the Idea no longer has an inward object, it turns outward. It directs its attention toward an object or objectivity now taken to be, or be defined as, the totality of the external, objective world, or as inorganic nature. The Idea looks to reproduce itself in relation to this new externality.

From a logical point of view, two things have happened. First, The Idea, which started out as a U, has become an S. It is a singular, whole, one. Second, this S now looks to reproduce itself in relation to an external totality. The whole objective world is not a singular, but a universal—a set, or bunch of objects. So the object, which used to be defined as an S, is now defined as a U. This new logical relationship between the Idea and objectivity (the former P/S) can be expressed with the judgment "S is U." The Idea has become an S that is U. It is a subjectivity that is conscious of an external world.

Although the Idea is relating to an external objectivity, it still has the characteristics that were developed in the stages of purpose. That means that the Idea is still the identifying power over the totality of inorganic nature to which it is now related. As in the stages of purpose, the "in itself" character of the object is not significant. All that matters is the identity that the Idea gives to or imposes on the inorganic nature. To put it another way, the inorganic nature that the life takes itself to be confronting remains a conceptual moment of the life itself (§219). From the point of view of the life, which is defining and objectifying itself through this relationship, the inorganic nature is its *urge* or *want*. As in the last stage, the process of the Idea here is a syllogism. Since the Idea has become an S rather than a U, the syllogism can be symbolized as: *S—(U[want]—P—S)*, where the last S is once again the smaller-S, or the process of Inner and Outer in their mutually defining relationship. In an example of such a syllogism, the life

(S) has a want (U) which particularizes as a desire for food in general (P), which then further particularizes as a desire for this particular bit of food: *the life(S)—(want[U]—food[P]—this food[S])*. A want is like a purpose in the sense that it is an identifying concept that sublates (cancels but preserves) the "in itself" character of what is aimed at. In purpose, the nature ("in itself") of the object—what character it has on its own or "in itself"—was not significant. What matters is its character in relation to the purpose. The same is true here. "Food" is an excellent example of a concept that largely ignores the nature ("in itself") of what it characterizes. What matters about the apple (or banana, or orange) is not what it is in itself, but only how it can be put to use by the subjectivity in question as food. When we are hungry, what we want is "food." What that "food" is like "in itself" is not very important. "Food" as a concept does not capture what the inorganic nature is like on its own, but only what it is like for us. In calling the inorganic nature "food," we are taking ourselves to be the identifying power over that inorganic nature: "food" is how *we* characterize the thing, not how the thing is characterized in itself. The inorganic nature that the life confronts need not be inorganic in an "in itself" sense. We ordinarily think of "inorganic" things as things that are not alive. But the "food" that we pick, for instance, may be cabbage, or a chicken, both of which are indeed alive. The point is that, in defining what we have our eye on simply as "food," we treat it as if it's inorganic. We define it as dead in order to eat it up.

The Idea or life picks up two characteristics during this process. First, because the life is the identifying power and purpose over the object or inorganic nature, what is "out there" in the object becomes the objectification of the life itself. Because the life defines the inorganic nature as "food," what the life confronts out there in objectivity is really only itself. In characterizing what is out there as "food," the life is putting itself out there into objectivity. It is objectifying itself. So the life confronts itself in what is out there. Second, the life is developing its own character, or determining itself, through this engagement with reality. As it goes through its processes of wanting and desiring, it is defining itself as the subjectivity that has those wants and desires. Its process of wanting defines what it is.

The life is the same sort of subjectivity that characterized the stage of Non-indifferent Mechanism. There, subjectivity was defined as a process of *centrality*. Centrality was a one (or singularity) that aimed at universality. It was a new kind of singularity that was at rest and had self-subsistence, but that positively reflected or aimed at the universal as its own character. A center was an S-that-reflects-or-aims-at-U, or, for short, as an S-as-U. The life here, as a singularity, has wants and desires that are characterized by universals. As in Non-indifferent Mechanism, because this life is a center, it has enough individuality or singularity to aim at a universal for its own definition or character. It reflects or aims at a universal in the process of defining its own singularity.

Life's centrality shows why subjectivity is associated with self-consciousness and with conscious thought. When the life has urges and wants, it demonstrates self-awareness. It is aware of its urges and desires. Moreover, those urges aim, *not* at the "in itself" character of the object out there, but at a universal character that the subject imposes on the object—a character such as "food" for instance. In those urges and wants, then, a conscious subject "aims at" a universal in the sense that it aims at an object that has been turned into a concept or thought.

The Third Process: Living-ness as the Genus-in-itself

The life has lost its connection to the object, so the immediate "for-itself" relationship between U and S is no longer established. That's why this stage cannot be captured with either "U is S" or "S is U"
Outer, out-thereness, or reality
Life as genus-in-itself, or the natural mating-kind that the individual life is. It is once again a U
The object is still a process of singularity

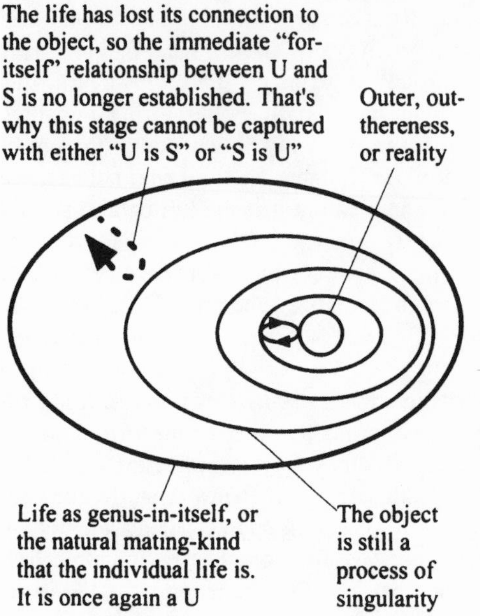

Figure 4.85

The life's process of wanting defines what the life is on two levels: as an individual (an S), and as a kind (a U)—the sort or kind of thing that the life is. What I want, for example, defines me not only as an individual, but as a human being. I want human sorts of things, and not cat or horse sorts of things. My cat, by contrast, has wants and desires that define him not only as the individual cat that he is, but also as a cat (in general). He has cat sorts of wants, not human or dog sorts of wants. Wants and desires define the subjectivity as the kind that has those wants and desires. The logical status of S and U thus captures or reflects the suggestion that what a (conscious) life wants defines it not only as an individual but also as a kind. As a center, the life is not only a singular (i.e. S), but a universal (i.e. U). It is an S-*as*-U. Just as its U-process in the process of Living-ness Inside Itself defined the life as an S, so its S-process here defines it as a U. These processes grow out of and reinforce the life's logical status as an S-as-U (or U-as-S). The process of Living-ness Inside Itself (its U-process) also defines the life as the kind of thing that it is, or gives it a character as a concept (an S). In that process, the life was a subject defined in a way that was similar to the way David Hume defined a subject: a universal that is all of its internal states taken together. The sorts of internal states that a life has define it both as an individual and as the kind of thing that it is. The internal states that my cat has define it not only as the individual cat that it is, but also as a cat (in general). My cat has cat-like internal states.

The life is therefore now defined as the kind that it is (i.e. as cat). It has the character, when defined on its own account (i.e. in an "in itself" sense), of its *kind*. It is a genus "in itself" (§220). As it goes through its process as a "for-itself," the life gives itself the character of the very concept that captures its reality. In the case of my cat, it gives itself the character of the concept of "cat," which is the very concept that captures its reality, or its real character. In the realm of reality, my cat has the character of a cat or is captured by the concept of "cat." If you look my cat from the outside, as he shows up in the realm of reality, he has the character (in an "in itself" sense) of being a cat. His life process as an individual gives him this real character, or defines him in relation to the concept that captures his real character. The life now has, by its own processes, the very character (in an "in itself" sense) that defines it in reality as the type of thing that it is. The life process has redefined the nature of the life by giving the life the character—in an "in itself" sense—of its genus. The life is now defined as the life of a genus or universal.

This sort of life has been raised to a higher level of universality. It is a kind or genus, rather than an individual life, and so is more inclusive or universal than earlier sorts of life. An example of this sort of life is the life of a natural kind in the animal kingdom. In the animal kingdom, a natural kind is a set of individual animals that group together by virtue of the life processes (including wants or desires) of the animals in the group. Dogs, humans, horses, elephants, house cats and so on are all natural kinds in the sense that they self-group through their desires insofar as they mate with one another. The German word that Hegel uses for genus or kind here has similar implications. The word "*Gattung*" is rooted in "*Gatt*," which means spouse or, in the animal kingdom, mate. A "*Gattung*" is therefore a genus or kind that is a natural mating kind.

Although the life has been raised to a higher level of universality, it is still defined by "thereness" or by given characteristics insofar as a natural mating kind is defined by the given, natural processes of the lives of the individuals that make it up. A natural mating kind is simply a grouping of individuals that happen—in the given, objective world—to want and to be able to reproduce with one another. Hence, although the sort of life has achieved a higher level of universality than before, it is still in an immediate relationship with a process of singularity, or with the individuals that make it up.

Now that the life is defined as a genus or kind—rather than as individual lives—those individual lives have a new logical status. When the life was defined as an individual life in the stage of Living-ness Against Inorganic Nature, its wants were objects that the life confronted or was up against. There was therefore a relationship of opposition between the individual life and the objects that it confronted. When I wanted "food," for instance, I had to confront or work on the apples and bananas that I pursued. Now that the life is defined as the life of a genus or natural mating kind, however, it no longer confronts objects that are opposed to it. The life of the genus is the genus as it is fleshed out in the world, or as it goes about its business. That life includes and identifies all of the characteristics that the lives of individuals in the genus can have. The life of the genus "human," for instance, includes any and all desires for types of food that are appropriate for humans. In relation to the life of the genus, the individual characteristics of my life—my desire for apples rather than bananas, my color, my size, and so on—are merely accidents. The life of the genus, or the genus as it is fleshed out in the world, includes all the permutations and combinations of characteristics that individuals within the genus can have. In logical terms, the life of the genus is a substantial universal, or a universal that is the substance of the accidents. The life of the genus sets out the parameters for what counts as food that is appropriate for humans, for example. It picks out or identifies all the types of food out of which my or any other human's particular desires will be selected. Again, whether I select apples or bananas is a mere accident in light of the fact that both of those types of food are appropriate for individuals belonging to the genus "human." The life of the genus is thus a substance—or substantial identity—that includes and identifies the accidents (cf. Immediate Substance in Chapter Three).

Life's new definition as the life of a kind or genus and as a substantial universal creates a logical problem, however. Because the accidental properties are included in the universal itself—they belong to the nature of the life of the genus itself—U no longer has any particularizing characteristics. Before, the life at issue was particularized in an immediate way as an individual or singular living thing—a plant, a cat, a human. An individual plant, cat or human is an immediate singular with particularizing characteristics. A cat is given as, or is immediately, a (singular, one) cat, with black fur, a love of cheese and other particularizing characteristics. Because the life of the genus includes and identifies all of the individuals that belong to the genus as well as their particularizing characteristics, however, it no longer has any particularity or singularity. Since "cat-ness" or "human-ness" includes all the types of internal states and wants and all the accidents of individual cats and humans, those characteristics can no longer particularize the genus or kind itself. The genus includes those characteristics as itself. It is a substance with *all* of the accidents. As a result, this sort of life is a U-as-S that has *lost its S-ness*. At the beginning of the stages of life, the object was defined as an immediate process of a bunch of singularities. Later on, the object was defined as a whole or one singularity. Now, U is no longer connected to any singularity or singularities at all. Because U includes all of the singularities along with all their wants and urges as individuals, those wants and urges no longer particularize U, or give U a particular character. Since U is, for instance, everything about all cats—all of their internal states and external, bodily states—then it is no longer connected to or particularized by any specific or singular cat or cat-character. It is every cat, every thereness or reality of cat, and is not defined by any one of them.

Because the U has lost its S-ness, the immediate "for itself" relationship between U and S no longer holds. I have given the looping arrow representing the immediate "for itself" relationship between U and S a dashed outline to illustrate the fact that the "for itself" relationship is no longer established. Because U has lost its connection to S, and because S contains the Outer or out-thereness of reality, U has lost its thereness. U is therefore a kind of life and an Idea that has lost its status as a "being-for-itself," or as a concept that includes thereness or reality in an immediate way within itself.

Moreover, because U has now lost its connection to S, we can no longer characterize what we have with either the judgment "U is S" or the judgment "S is U." That's why there is no accompanying judgment in the diagram for this stage. The life is a kind or universal that is no longer connected to any bunch (U) of singularities (or to singularity) (S) at all.

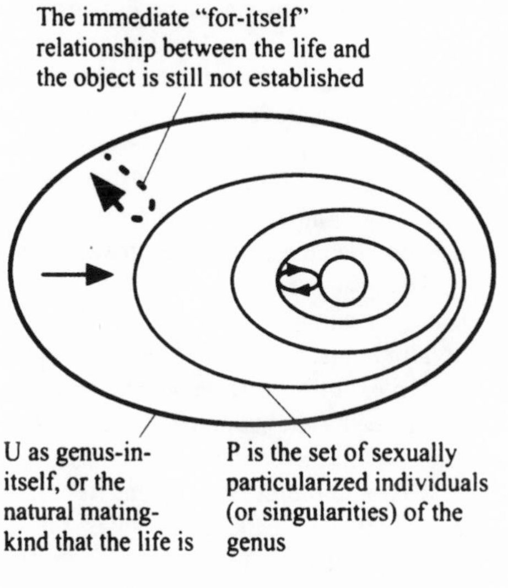
The immediate "for-itself" relationship between the life and the object is still not established
U as genus-in-itself, or the natural mating-kind that the life is
P is the set of sexually particularized individuals (or singularities) of the genus
U is P

Figure 4.86

Life, however, is the unity of concept and reality, or is by definition a U-as-S, or a U that is S (see Livingness Inside Itself). Because life is by definition a U-as-S, this sort of life must reestablish its S-ness. A genus or kind is defined by particularizing or dividing into the elements that it includes (see Disjunctive Syllogism). Hence life, now defined as a genus-in-itself, particularizes too. Also, a genus divides at first into P or Particularity, and then into S or Singularity. That's how the genus will be defined here too. This process can be described by the syllogism U-P-S. As was the case in the stages of Purpose, because the syllogism is a description of a particular process, it is not reversible. This stage develops the first judgment of this syllogism, "U is P."

Because the sort of life here includes consciousness or awareness, the individuals who belong to the genus are aware of the logical requirement that the genus must particularize. They experience that logical requirement as an urge, which first appeared in irritability (see Living-ness Inside Itself). Here, each life-of-the-genus has a drive or urge to define itself by particularizing. In the move from U to P, or in the particularization of U, the life (which is now defined as the life of the genus) will still be particularized in relation to external objectivity (cf. Living-ness Against Inorganic Nature), but that external objectivity must be defined more precisely. During the logical development of the stages of life, the nature of the external objectivity in relation to which life was defined has been changing. At first, the external objectivity in question was the life's own body (see Immediate Idea or Life). Then it was the life's body experienced internally, or the life's internal states (see Living-ness Inside Itself). In the stage of Living-ness Against Inorganic Nature, the external objectivity was inorganic nature. Here, because the genus is a life that must particularize, the external objectivity to which the life will be related is its P and S—i.e. the groups into which it divides (P), and then the singulars into which those groups divide (S). The genus or universal begins the process of particularizing by dividing into the groups that define it. This process can be expressed as the first premise of the syllogism U-P-S, namely, as "U is P." I represent this process in the diagram with the same sort of straight arrow that I used to represent syllogistic processes in mechanism, chemism and purpose. Here we get a straight arrow between U and P. U particularizes, sunders or divides into P.

Because of the current logical character that the life has, the groups into which the genus divides must meet three conditions. The first two conditions follow from the nature of U, P and S that was developed in Disjunctive Syllogism. According to Disjunctive Syllogism, a universal divides into an exhaustive set of mutually exclusive categories. As a result, U must sunder into groups that, first, are mutually exclusive and, second, when taken together, completely characterize U, or exhaust the character of U. The groups into which U divides must be mutually exclusive in the sense that an individual within the genus cannot belong to two different groups. Each individual must be in one group only. Also, the list of groups cannot be open-ended, but must be an exhaustive and complete division of U. These conditions are also required by the judgment "U is P." That judgment says that U *is* P, but the universal *is* (immediately and necessarily) P (the groups into which it divides) only if what is on both sides of the "is" is the same, or only if the U is the same as the P. "U is P" is correct only when the set of groups that is P is the same as and adds up to the U. The set of groups of P must therefore meet two conditions. First, it must be the list of mutually exclusive groups into which U divides. If the groups overlapped, then they would not "add up" to U. Second, it must, when taken as a whole, completely exhaust U, or be the completed set of groups belonging to U. The groups of P must therefore be mutually exclusive, and the set as a whole must be an exhaustive (there must be no groups left out) and complete characterization of U.

Third, because the singularities into which U divides are the particularities of U, they must be sets or groups that belong to or are *of* the genus, which is to say that they must be the same kind of thing that the genus is. As in the stages of Purpose, the U is passing on the character of its universality to P and S as it goes through the process of being defined by dividing into P and S. As in the Transition to Idea, U is both the identifying essence and the essential purpose over P and S. Because the genus is defined as *life*, the groups must be defined by *life* too. So the genus sunders, not into mere concepts or categories, but into living groups, or groups of living things. Moreover, because the genus is a mating-kind, the groups must capture the genus's character as a mating-kind, that is, the groups must be central to the genus's mating or sex activity.

When these three logical conditions are put together, the genus must divide into mutually exclusive groups of living things that make up an exhaustive set of sexual or mating categories. As Hegel puts it, the genus divides into

"*Geschlectsdifferenz*," or the difference of the sexes (§220). In German, "*Geschlecht*" means not only "sex," but also "genus," "kind" or "species." So we could also translate Hegel's claim by saying that the natural mating kind or genus divides into genus-differences. Of course, the sexual implications of "*Geschlecht*"—along with the sexual implications of "*Gattung*" (genus, mate, spouse) itself—suggest that those genus-differences have to do with mating. Thus, the groups in the "*Geschlectsdifferenz*" are the complete list of sub-groupings or differences which make possible the mating or reproduction of the natural mating kind or genus. From a logical point of view, the groups in the "*Geschlectsdifferenz*" are the complete list of mating particularities (P's), for the genus or U.

Because U is life, however, when it sunders or divides, it divides into things of the same genus, which, in this case, must be living things. So when the U divides, it is not dividing into the *categories* of sexual difference—they are not alive. Instead, U must divide into the living individuals that are so categorized. Thus the natural mating kind of "house cat," for instance, divides into male and female *cats*, not into the categories of maleness and femaleness. There are actually two reasons why "house cat" as a mating kind must divide into male and female cats rather than into the categories of maleness and femaleness. We have already seen one: the genus as a life must divide into other lives, and the categories of "male" and "female" are not alive. Male and female house *cats* are the living beings that define the genus "house cat" as a mating kind. Second, however, other kinds of things are also "male" and "female" in relation to similar reproductive processes. Humans, dogs and other mammals, for instance, have the same types of reproductive systems as cats, and so also divide into the categories of "male" and "female" in relation to those reproductive systems. But dogs or humans do not belong to the genus "house cat." If the genus "house cat" as a mating kind divided into "male" and "female" as categories, it could be instantiated by male humans, or female dogs. In the Transition to Idea, however, U is the essential identity over P and S. The genus "house cat" must therefore divide into *cats*, rather than into dogs or humans. As a result, the genus as a living kind must divide into the sexually particularized individuals of the same species or genus that U is. For that reason too, then, the genus "house cat" as a living kind must divide not into the categories of "male" and "female," but into the individual, living house cats that are particularized as either male or female.

The object has been defined as a process since the beginning of the stages of Life. P is still a process here too. The set of particularized singularities and their process is the objectivity that the genus or life now confronts.

Hegel says that the judgment of this logical stage—which is, again, "U is P"—"is the *Verhältnis* [relation] of the genus to these individuals determined against-one-another" (§220). Although *Verhältnis* is usually translated as "relation," it also means love-affair or liaison. Thus the judgment "U is P" captures not only a relation between U and P, but a kind of love-affair or liaison between the genus as a mating kind and the sexually particularized individuals. We will see why the relation has sexual implications in the next stage.

The Process of the Genus

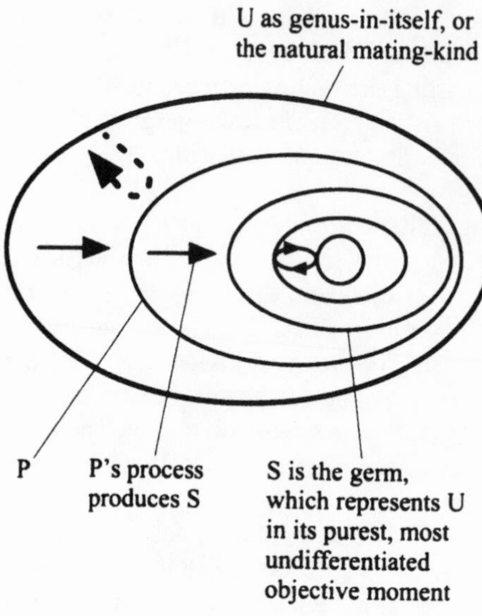
U as genus-in-itself, or
the natural mating-kind
P
P's process
produces S
S is the germ,
which represents U
in its purest, most
undifferentiated
objective moment
P is S

Figure 4.87

As was the case in the stages of Purpose and in the earlier stages of life, the objectivity here is not a static objectivity, but an objectivity that is itself a process. The same is true here too. Unfortunately, Hegel does not say much in the *Encyclopaedia* about what "the process of the genus" (§221) is supposed to be like. For the account of the process of the genus, we must rely primarily on the *Science of Logic*.

The process of the genus is the process of P, which is the set of sexually particularized individuals. Each of the individuals into which the U sunders is an aware living thing. Sentience was captured by the judgment "U is S" (see Living-ness Inside Itself), which expressed the idea that a sentient creature is a universal that divides internally into singularities. In the case of sentience, those singularities would be bits of awarenesses, or moments of awareness. Moreover, each of the sexually particularized individuals here is a centrality. In Non-indifferent Mechanism, centrality was logically defined as an S-that-aims-at-a-U, or an S-as-U. Each sexually particularized individual here is an S-as-U too. They are each internally universal subjects that aim at U by having *urges*.

The process of P begins when each of these sexually particularized subjects (the P's) confronts another individual subject (another P) that is both the same as, and yet also different from, itself. Each subject confronts subjects that are different because the other subjects belong to another sexual particularity, but that other subject is also the same because both subjects belong to the same genus or universality. My male cat, for instance, confronts a female cat, which is different from it as female, but the same as it as a cat. In logical terms, each subject has a contradictory relationship with that other subject. Notice that, although the subjects share a universality, that universality is only internal or subjective at the moment, which is to say that it is there only as a thought. The shared universal nature of the two cats as *cats* is available only for thought, but has no objective reality or is not out there in any object.

The contradictory relationship between the two subjects (the two P's) gives rise to two urges. First, each S-as-U has the urge to make its own universality explicit and realize itself as a universal. Each has an urge to put its own universality out there into objectivity. My cat, for instance, has an urge to realize his universality by putting his cat-ness out there into objectivity. As we'll see, the baby or the germ that the mating process produces will be that universality. Second, each subject has the urge to realize its universality in relation to the other subject with which it is currently in the contradictory relationship. In other words, my cat has an urge to realize its shared universality (and hence unity) with a female cat by uniting with her. So, to borrow from Hegel's euphemistic language, each dissolves itself in, or carries out, its urge or longing for the universality of the genus with the other particularity, which does the same to it. The sexually particularized individuals mate or have sex.

The fact that the original urge of the genus to divide develops into a sexual relationship between individuals within the genus explains why Hegel described the "relation" between U and P in the judgment "U is P" with the term "*Verhältnis*" in the last stage (§220). "*Verhältnis*" implies that the relationship between the genus and the sexually particularized individual is not just a relation, but a love affair, which is certainly what it has become in this stage.

The result of the sexual union is a new individual or singularity (i.e. an S)—the babies or germs. I represent this process in the diagram with a straight arrow that runs from P to S. The sexually particularized individuals give rise to S or singularity. Keep in mind that P is the thought of the whole set of individuals that are sexually particularized, not just two individuals. And S is the thought of all of the babies or singularities that those individuals produce, not just one baby or germ. We can express this relationship with the judgment "P is S."

Hegel suggests that the babies or germs are the purest expression of the universal in objectivity. The germ is an undeveloped version of the universal with no particularizing characteristics. Human babies, for instance, tend to look similar, they are roughly the same size, they tend to move the same ways, do the same things, and have the same basic wants and desire. Their characters are simple and not highly individualized. Because the S is undeveloped and has no particularizing characteristics, it represents the objectivity of the genus or universal in the purest, most undifferentiated form. The kitten, for instance, is the purest example of a living cat-in-general. In the case of newborn kittens, it is even difficult to see what sexually particularized identity they have (i.e. whether they are male nor female). Because the germ is the purest expression of the universal in objectivity, the process of producing the germ allows both U or the universal itself as well as the sexually particularized individuals (the P's) to succeed in objectifying the universality or genus through S. In the kitten, for instance, both the genus "cat" and the individual male and female cats, succeed in making the universality "cat" objective, or succeed in putting the universality "cat" out there into an object.

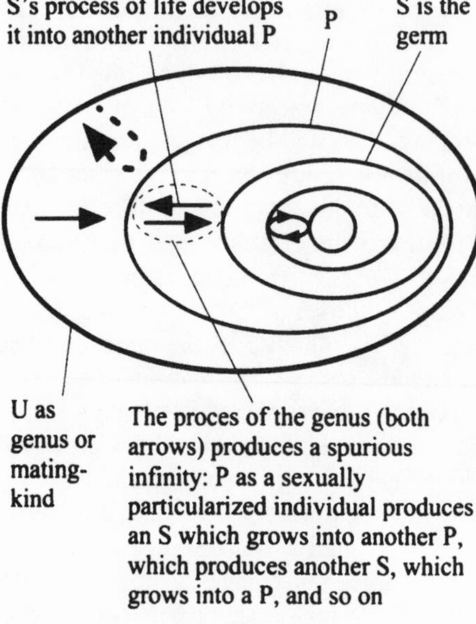
S's process of life develops it into another individual P
P
S is the germ
U as genus or mating-kind
The proces of the genus (both arrows) produces a spurious infinity: P as a sexually particularized individual produces an S which grows into another P, which produces another S, which grows into a P, and so on

Figure 4.88

S, as the germ or baby, goes through its own processes of life (see the earlier stages of Life) and develops into another P, or another sexually particularized individual. As the kitten grows up, carries out its wants or desires, and generally goes through its life processes, for instance, it develops into a full-blown male or female cat (a P). As a P, it mates and produces another S, which develops into yet another P, which produces another S, and so on. The kitten grows into a sexually particularized cat and mates with another sexually particularized cat, which produces another kitten, which grows into a sexually particularized cat, and mates with another sexually particularized cat, and produces another kitten, and so on. So the process of the genus leads to a spuriously infinite back-and-forth process between P, or sexually particularized individuals, and S, or singularized universality as the germs. One sexually particularized individual (P) leads to a germ (S), which leads to another sexually particularized individual (P), which leads to another germ (S), which leads to yet another sexually particularized individual (P) and so on.

Transition to Cognition

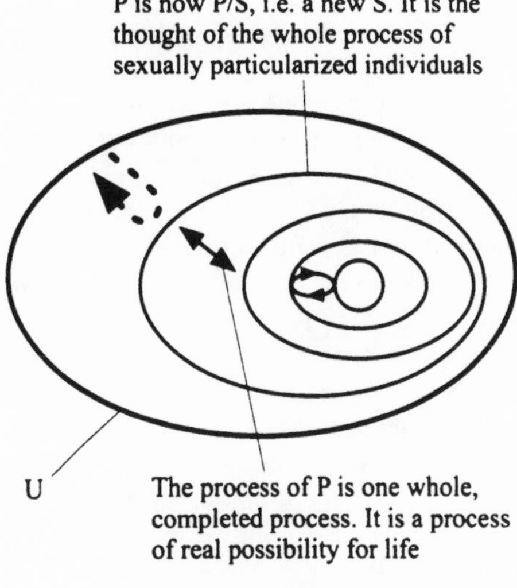
P is now P/S, i.e. a new S. It is the thought of the whole process of sexually particularized individuals
U
The process of P is one whole, completed process. It is a process of real possibility for life

Figure 4.89

Hegel's logic cannot rest with an endless or spuriously infinite process (see Spurious Infinity). The job of the logic is in part to define its terms, but an endless back-and-forth process leaves both terms in the process undefined. Logic can achieve the goal of defining its terms, then, only if there is some way to stop the back-and-forth process.

In the last stage, the process of reproduction was defined as a process in which sexually particularized individuals produce a germ or baby. That definition led to a spuriously infinite process of going back and forth between P and S. In this stage, the endless back-and-forth process between P and S is stopped by redefining the process as one completed process. The process of reproduction is now conceived—not as a process that produces one baby—but rather as the whole, completed process of sexually particularized individuals in general. P is the whole process of reproduction for the genus or natural kind, taken to be a completed whole. It is all of the sexually particularized individuals and it embraces all of the germs or babies (the S's). I have combined the two, one-way arrows representing the back-and-forth process into one, two-way arrow to represent the fact that the spuriously infinite back-and-forth process is now defined as one whole, complete process (cf. Condition as a Totality in Chapter Three).

The very same double-sided arrow between P and S that was between Particularity and Singularity in the diagram of the Concept at the beginning of this chapter (and that we had between the same bubbles at the end of Chapter Three, when they were defined as the Effect$_{CS}$ and Possibility) has returned. In Chapter Three, this double-sided arrow was the arrow representing the process of Real Possibility, which was defined as a completed process in the stage of Condition as a Totality. As the diagram suggests, we are rebuilding that earlier definition of the Concept. The Concept is defined by the same bubbles and arrows that defined it in an objective way at the end of Chapter Three (see the Introduction to this chapter). In short, the definition of the Concept from the end of Chapter Three is being rebuilt. The objective definition for the Concept at the end of Chapter Three captured what the Concept would look like when viewed from the outside as an object, in the same way that a toaster can be defined from the outside as a "machine that makes toast" (cf. the Introduction to this chapter). This chapter is tracing the definition that the Concept comes to have through its own activity, as a subject or subjectively, in the same way that a toaster defines itself as a "machine that makes toast" when it goes through its toasting process. Although the activity of the Concept in this chapter will give it characteristics that are different from the ones it had when it was defined objectively—just as the activity of the toaster gives it different characteristics (it gets hot, for instance, when it toasts)—the Concept at the end of the process should "look" more or less the same as it did when it was defined objectively, just as a toaster looks more or less the same after toasting activity as it did before it was plugged in. That is exactly what is happening for the Concept: it is beginning to "look" more or less the same in the diagrams as it did when it was defined objectively at the end of Chapter Three (cf. Transition to Chemism).

The reappearance of the double-sided arrow that depicted Real Possibility in Chapter Three is appropriate here because the process of P can be thought of as a process of real possibility. Real Possibility was defined as the process through which one condition fulfilled its character as a condition by pointing toward or producing another condition (see Real Possibility). In the stage of Condition as a Totality, Real Possibility was redefined as the whole, completed process in which conditions point toward or produce other conditions—which is why I depicted the two arrows of Real Possibility as one double-sided arrow in that stage. The back-and-forth process here is similar to the process of Real Possibility in the sense that it is the process through which each life points toward or produces another life. Each life is a condition or the real possibility of another life insofar as it produces another life through the reproductive process. Taken together as a whole complete process, reproduction is a process of real possibility *for life*. Through the reproductive process generally, each life carries out its process of being the real possibility of another life. As will be explained more fully in a moment, each life fulfills its own character as a life by producing another life, or through the reproductive process, or the process of real possibility for life.

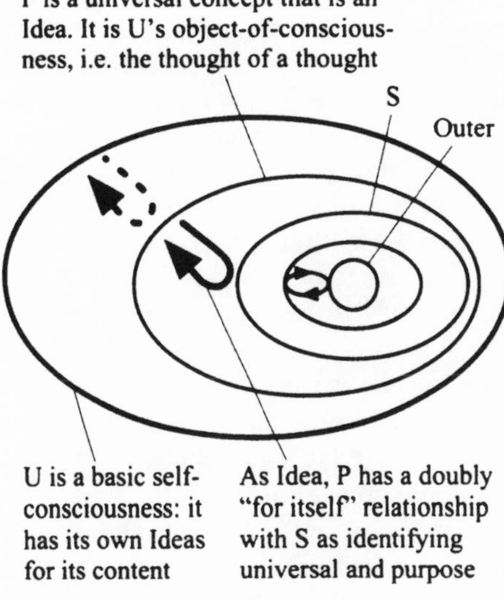
P is a universal concept that is an Idea. It is U's object-of-consciousness, i.e. the thought of a thought
S
Outer
U is a basic self-consciousness: it has its own Ideas for its content
As Idea, P has a doubly "for itself" relationship with S as identifying universal and purpose

Figure 4.90

The redefinition of the reproductive process as one whole process redefines the object (i.e. P), the object's relationship with its own contents (i.e. with S), and the definition of the life (i.e. U) as well.

First, because the reproductive process is defined as a completed whole process, it is finished. The object (P) is therefore defined as a completed whole or totality. It is the completed set of all the sexually particularized individuals, together with their complete reproductive process throughout time. This complete reproductive process includes the lives of the sexually particularized individuals—their growing up, their wants and desires in general, as well as their mating process. As a result, P is not just the completed set of sexually particularized individuals, it includes the whole process of living of the sexually particularized individuals. Since that whole process of living is the whole process of living for the genus, P includes the whole process of living for the genus. To use the house cat example again, P is no longer defined merely as my particular house cat, but is the completed set of all the house cats that have lived or will ever live throughout time, as well as their completed process of living. P is the whole process of living for the genus "house cat." It includes the whole display of living and thereness for the genus (U), which is the general concept of genus for all living beings. P thereby includes the whole display of living for all the living beings.

Second, the fact that P includes the whole process of living of the genus changes the logical status of P itself. Until now, P has been defined as the external objectivity or object of the life or U. Now, however, P is no longer merely an object or external objectivity. Instead, it has become a thought—more specifically, a *universal concept*. Because P includes the whole process of living of the genus, P has become a *being-for-itself* (§221). The concept of a being-for-itself was introduced in the stage of Being-for-itself in Chapter Two, and was Hegel's first logical definition of ideality or universality. According to that stage, a being-for-itself is a concept, ideal or universal that grasps or embraces the thereness of a set of somethings. It grasps both the way in which the somethings in the set are the same as one another (Attraction), as well as the way in which the somethings in the set are different from one another (Repulsion). Because the somethings in the set are defined as both the same as and as different from one another, the somethings cannot be held together in the set by their own thereness anymore—as they had been in earlier stages—but instead must be held together from the top down by the being-for-itself. The being-for-itself does the work of pulling the somethings together into the set (Attraction) and distinguishing them from one another (Repulsion). The being-for-itself sorts out the characteristics of the somethings that distinguishes them (Repulsion) from those characteristics that make them the same and thus hold them together as members of the same set (Attraction). In Chapter Two, I depicted Being-for-itself as a bubble that surrounded or embraced the somethings in its contents.

P must play the same logical role here. Now that P includes the whole process of living for the genus, it is the whole process of thereness for the genus. It is the way in which the genus has thereness in the world. Moreover, it includes both the ways in which the sexually particularized individuals are different from one another, as well as the ways in which they are the same as one another and so belong together in the same set. The whole process of living for house cats, for example, is the way in which the genus "house cat" has thereness or is out there in the world. Moreover, it includes not only the ways in which the house cats are the same as one another (cf. Attraction), but also the way in which they are different from one another (cf. Repulsion). As the individual house cats go about living their lives, they are defined not only as the same as one another by their wants and desires—especially their mating desires—but also as different from one another. One house cat likes to eat olives and peanut butter cookies, for instance, while most do not. As cats go about living their lives, their process of living defines them not only as house cats (which is the way in which they are the same as one another), but also as individuals with their own characteristics (which is the way in which they are different from one another). As a result, the house cats can no longer be held together in a set by their own thereness—their mating desires and general activity of living—anymore, as they did earlier (in Living-ness as the Genus-in-itself). They must be held together from the top down by a being-for-itself or concept. P must now be the *concept* that does the logical work of holding the thereness of the genus together by sorting out those characteristics that make the sexually particularized individuals different from one another from those characteristics that make them the same as one another and so hold them together as members of the same set. P is a concept, ideal or being-for-itself.

P has therefore become the concept of the genus itself. It is, for instance, the concept of house cat itself. Since U had been defined as the genus earlier (see Living-ness as the Genus-in-itself), P has taken over the definition that U had. U's new definition will be explained shortly.

Although P is a being-for-itself, it is a different kind of being-for-itself from Being-for-itself in Chapter Two. P is not just a concept, it is a *universal concept* (cf. Particularity). It has a different relationship with S from the one characterized by the double-sided arrow. It has a doubly "for itself" relationship, or an "in and for itself" relationship with S (cf. the Introduction to this chapter and the stage of Universality). That is just the sort of relationship that P now has with S. P is a concept that not only embraces S as its contents (the first "for itself" relationship of content), but also presents S *for itself*, or through its own activity (the second "for itself" relationship of form), because the elements in S are produced by the mating process of P. P presents S *for itself*, or through its own process. P thereby has a doubly "for itself" relationship with S. Moreover, because P presents S, it is also defined as separate from and opposed to S. In short, P also has an "in itself" relationship with S. P is already depicted as a bubble surrounding S (the "for itself" relationship of content). I have added a looping "for itself" arrow that runs from P to S and back to P to the diagram to depict P's new relationship with S as the concept that presents S *for itself*, or through its own activity (the "for itself" relationship of form).

Not only is P a universal concept, P is an *Idea*. P has now undergone the same logical process that defined U or the Concept as an Idea during the Transition to Idea. When the Concept became the thought of the completed process of purpose, it defined not only the ways in which the existing items out there were the same as one another but also the ways in which they were different from one another. It grasped the whole display of thereness of the singularities. As the thought or concept of the whole display of purpose, it grasped both the essential identity of all the objects as well as the differences between the objects insofar as they were divided. An Idea is a universal concept that is a being-for-itself in the sense that it includes a process of pulling together the items in the set (cf. Attraction), of distinguishing or differentiating the items (cf. Repulsion), as well as the thereness of the items that it embraces (see Transition to Idea). P is defined in the same way as a being-for-itself. It is the thought or concept of the whole display of living for the genus, and so is both the essential identity of the S's insofar as they are pulled together (e.g. as house cats), and the essential purpose over the S's insofar as they are divided into types (e.g. as male and female house cats). Because P has the same logical definition that U or the Concept had at the beginning of Idea, P has become an *Idea* too.

P, as the Idea of the genus and hence essential purpose over S, is the thought or concept at which the whole display of living for living beings *aims*, in three ways. First, it is the universal at which the living of the beings aims. Individual house cats, for instance, come and go, are born, give birth and die. Through all the coming and going, the reproductive process of birth and death aims at the survival of the genus "house cat." The whole display of the process of living shows that the real purpose of the whole process of living is the genus itself. Individual house cats, dogs, horses, lions and so on come and go, live, reproduce and die. But what is preserved in the whole process is the genus itself, or the thought of the living of all the living kinds. *It* is the purpose at which all the living aims. Keep in mind, however, that P has its definition as the purpose over the whole process only *after* the whole process is completed. Its definition is mediated by the process (§221). Only at the end of time, after all the living has been completed, does the genus have its definition as the purpose over the whole process of living. P is the purpose at which S, as the whole process of living throughout time, aims.

Second, now that P is the thought of the whole display of the reproductive process, it grasps the differences between the living beings. Those differences are determined by their living—by the desires, aims and purposes of the living beings—which divides the beings into kinds during the process of reproduction. Sexually particularized house cats, for instance, desire, mate with and behave like other house cats, not dogs. The same situation obtained in the stages of Purpose above, where U was defined as the purpose over P/S insofar as P/S divided into different types of objects. P is thus defined as the thought or concept of the purposes over living things insofar as the living things divide into different kinds.

Third, P's own process of purpose is a syllogism of the form U-P-S, in which P is the U that passes its universality down to its own particularity and singularity. In the Second Moment of Purpose Realizing Itself, my purpose or concept of dinner, for instance, was passed down to particularity (P) as the concept of salad. But P as the concept of salad had its own syllogism of purpose. In P's syllogism of purpose, the concept of salad was passed down to singularity (S) as the concept of lettuce (as a type), which, as a type of salad, was still grasped by the concept of salad. The concept of lettuce as a type passed the universal down to "this lettuce," (smaller-S), which, as part of the salad, was still grasped by the universal "salad." Now that P is the genus, it has its own process or syllogism of purpose through reproduction. P is the genus, or the concept of house cat, for instance, which is passed down to sexually particularized cats (S), which, because they are *house cats*, are still characterized by the genus or by P. The sexually particularized house cats then produce baby cats or kittens (smaller-S), which, because they are still *cats*, are also grasped by the genus.

Now that P is a universal concept and purpose, it is defined by all three elements that belong to the Concept, namely particularity (P), singularity (S) and universality (U). P, which is the object of U, is a universal that, in its own syllogism of purpose, has a particularity and singularity. As Hegel puts it, "objectivity itself is as the Concept" (§223). Hegel's claim that "objectivity itself is as the Concept" has a double-meaning. First, the claim is a reference to the idea that P is now logically defined by all three moments of the Concept. As a purpose, P is a U that divides into a P of its own (i.e. S) which in turn divides into another S (i.e. smaller-S). But Hegel's claim also indicates that the kind of life captured by U has changed. Now that the process of living has produced a concept or thought (i.e. P is a concept), the life that goes through this process is the kind of living that *thinks*.

P's status as a universal concept and Idea redefines U. Since P has become the concept of the genus, U—which used to be the concept of the genus (see Living-ness as the Genus-in-itself)—must now have a new definition. P is still the object of U, but because P is now a thought or concept, U is a thought or concept that has a thought or concept as its object. Because U is a thought or concept that has thought as its object, U is the kind of life that *thinks*. It is a more sophisticated type of conscious life.

Now that U is a consciousness that thinks, P is defined as the object of a consciousness, or as an object that is also a thought. As a result, Hegel changes the term he uses to refer to P or the object. There are two terms in German that translate into "object" in English: "*Objekt*" and "*Gegenstand*." Until now, all of the objects have been "*Objekt*." An "*Objekt*" is an object that is defined as separate from and independent of subjectivity. That is the way the object has been defined since the beginning of the Doctrine of the Object. An "*Objekt*" is an object "out there" that is independent of subjectivity—objects such as tables, chairs and so on. A "*Gegenstand*," by contrast, is an object that is another thought, or an object-of-consciousness. It is an object that has been turned into a thought. Consciousnesses that think have other thoughts, or objects-of-consciousness, for their objects. Until now, P has been defined as an object in the first sense—as an "*Objekt*." Now that P is a thought that is the object of another thought, P is not an object ("*Objekt*") anymore, it is an object-of-consciousness ("*Gegenstand*"). That's why Hegel begins using the term "*Gegenstand*," instead of "*Objekt*," to refer to the object (i.e. P) in §223.

Although U and P have new definitions, their connection with one another is still defective—and so the looping, "for itself" arrow between U and P in the diagram remains dashed. In Living-ness as the Genus-in-itself, I dashed the looping "for itself" arrow for form or presentation because U had lost its S-ness, or was no longer connected to. The immediate "for itself" relationship of form or presentation between U and P was therefore not established. That relationship is still not established here. On the one hand, a consciousness (i.e. U) is immediately connected to thereness or presence (i.e. P) insofar as P is thought or a stream of consciousness. A stream of consciousness is a kind of thereness or presence or a way of being there for consciousness. A consciousness (U) has thereness or presence in its stream of consciousness (P) in terms of *content*. P is the content of U's awareness. U is therefore appropriately depicted as a bubble that surrounds, embraces or has P as its content. But a stream of consciousness is not necessarily or immediately connected to *out*-thereness, since what is there or present in the stream of consciousness (in terms of content) may not be *out there* in *reality*. A stream of consciousness is there or present in terms of content (in the head, so to speak), but it is not presented or pushed out into *out*-thereness (in terms of form). S is the element that contains reality or thereness (represented by the Outer bubble), but U has still lost its S-ness. U is not pushing or presenting (in terms of form) its content out there into *reality*. A stream of consciousness is not connected to out-thereness in an immediate way, but only through *work*. In particular, it is connected to *out*-thereness through the work of cognition—theoretical cognition and practical cognition or willing—which are the next logical stages.

U is not only conscious life, however: it is a *free*, *self*-conscious life in the most basic sense. U is a *self*-conscious being that has its self *as consciousness* (or thought) as its object (of consciousness). Because P, as thought or Idea, is *U's own content*, U has its *own* self or Idea(s) for its content. U is a conscious life that is aware of its own thought or consciousness as it object (of consciousness).

U has its *self* as its object in two other ways as well: (1) as an Idea, and (2) as a concept of Life. (1) U is currently defined as the *Idea* of Life. Now that P is defined as the thought or concept of the whole display of living, it is an Idea too. So U is an Idea that has another Idea as its object—it has itself as an Idea as its object. (2) U is the Idea of *Life*. Now that P is defined as the thought or concept of the whole process of living, it is a concept of *life* too. So U is an Idea of Life that has living as an Idea for its object. Since the Idea of living is just the process of life itself, U is life that has its own process of living as its object. U is a life that has itself as a life as its object. U is a self-conscious life.

Although U is a basic, free self-consciousness, the logical relationship between U and P is still immediate. U has an immediate relationship with P that still defines U as a life. Life is an immediate Idea (see Transition to Idea), so that U "is" the object (P) in an immediate way. That is still true here. As a second-order awareness, U still embraces or includes P in its content in an immediate way. U is still a life. It is the immediate awareness of its awareness. The difference between the life defined in Immediate Idea and the life defined here is that the *object*—what U is aware of—is now mediated. As the terms "consciousness" and "self-consciousness" in English suggest, the difference between consciousness and self-consciousness is not in the consciousness—they are both consciousnesses—but in the object, or in what they are aware of. A self-consciousness is a consciousness that is aware of itself. In earlier stages of self-consciousness, the self that the Life had as its object were simple awarenesses—urges, itches and so on—that were defined as separate from and opposed to the thought, subjectivity or consciousness. Here, U is aware of itself as *thoughts*. U is still a consciousness of internal states, it's just that the sorts of internal states that it is aware of have changed. Because U is aware of internal states that are not out-there or opposed to it (as the subjectivity), but have been mediated by thought or subjectivity, its objects are internal objects-of-consciousness, rather than merely internal objects.

While U still embraces P in an immediate way in terms of content, because the character of P is mediated (by the syllogism outlined above), U's character is mediated as well. What U is like—its specific character as the type or kind of thing that it is—depends on P's process of mediation. U cannot have its specific character without whatever process P undergoes. What U, as the thought of P, is like will depend on the process of P. The kind of thought that U will be, or the character of U, piggybacks on the character and process of P.

Because U is the thought of its own thought, it is free of all immediacy or givenness. As Hegel puts it, "the Idea of life has freed itself not just from *some one or other* (particular) immediate This, but from this initial immediacy in general" (§222). Because P is a thought, and because P is U's own thought, U is completely free of immediacy. U's object-of-consciousness is nothing but its own thought. U is currently defined in such a way that it has its existence as its own thought. Since U exists as its own thought, it is not dependent on given objectivity for its definition. It is a kind of life that, as Hegel puts it, "enters *into existence for its own self as free genus*" (§223). Because U has universality as its element of existence (§223) or exists as thought, U is free to determine what sort of existence it will have. As free, self-conscious thought, U has become *spirit.* A spirit is a free, self-conscious life, because it can give itself the thoughts that fill it up. Since U is thought, and its content is its own thought, it can determine its own content. That is the sort of life now represented by U.

U is "determined as universality" (§223). It is determined as a universality in the basic sense that it has a bunch of items (its bits of consciousness) for its content, and so captures a group or set of items. Spirit is a self-conscious *subject.* To be a subject is to be a singular capable of having a universal (cf. Non-indifferent Mechanism). A self-consciousness is a singular thought or one that has a process of a bunch of individuals (i.e. individual bits of consciousness)—and hence a universal—as its content. U is also determined as universality insofar as it is a universal concept that is defined by another universal concept (i.e. P) for its content. U is a universality that has universality for its content.

U is the Concept or Reason itself, now defined not only as the thought of what the completed and completely systematized set of rational concepts will be like at the end of time, when their whole process of development has been finished, but also as the concept of the thought of the whole process of living of all kinds of living. Because Reason now has or exists as a whole process of living, it is a life too. It is the thought that has the thought of the whole life of the existing world as its object-of-consciousness. Since U is also defined as a life that has its own thought of the whole display of living as its object-of-consciousness, Reason has become a living, self-conscious spirit that has the whole display of living as its object-of-consciousness.

While U is free, self-consciousness in the most basic sense, its self-consciousness and its freedom are defective. First, U's character as a self-consciousness is defective because the self that U has as its object-of-consciousness (i.e. P) has not been completely determined by U, and so is not a full reflection of the self that U is. U is a *self*-consciousness that does not quite have its *self* before it as an object, or that is not quite conscious of its *self* after all. S contains Inner and Outer and their mutually defining relationship (see Singularity) and so contains all of out-thereness or reality, but because the "for itself" relationship of form or presentation between U and P is not established, S is currently being presented by P, not by U. S belongs to P, not to U. U has still lost its connection to S or thereness (cf. Living-ness as the Genus-in-itself). U is a free being in terms of its content because it has nothing but its own thoughts as its object (of consciousness), but because the "for itself" relationship of form or presentation between U and P is not established, U is not presenting its own free Idea into the singularities (i.e. S) or into out-thereness. U as the Idea has not yet presented its own Idea out there in reality *for itself*, or through its own activity. S is being presented by P, not by U, so P makes S what S is out there, while U does not. U depends on P's process for U's form or presentation into thereness (i.e. S). Because U must rely on P's process for U's presentation into S, the self that it has before it as its object-of-consciousness is not fully itself. Since U does not define S, U does not define everything about P by its own process. So P is not a complete reflection of the same self that U is. Hence U's self-consciousness is defective in the sense that the self it has before it is not a full reflection of what U is as a self. This tension between U's character in terms of content and in terms of form is represented in the diagram because U is depicted as a bubble that surrounds P—and so has P for its content—but does not yet have P for its form, since the "for itself" looping arrow between U and P remains dashed. The looping "for itself" arrow represents the activity of form, or the way in which U is presented. U's defect is therefore a defect in form or presentation. U passes on its universality to P insofar as it defines (identifies) or gives P its character as a universal or thought, and so has thereness or presence *internally* as a process of thought. But U is not yet *presenting* (in terms of form) its Idea *out there* into thereness or reality (i.e. into S) through P. P is presenting S through its own process.

Second, U's freedom is also defective. U is supposed to be a free being. Since it has nothing but its own thought as its content, it is free in terms of its content. But since it must rely on P's process for its form or presentation, U is not free in terms of its form. So U is not yet living up to its definition as a free being in terms of both content and form.

Because U's character as both a self-consciousness and a free being is defective, U must continue to develop and live up to its own definition as a free self-consciousness by freely determining or defining the object (i.e. P and S)—i.e. by imposing its own definitions on the object from the top down. When the process of imposing its own definitions on the object is completed, and when the object is completely defined as a finished product, then U will finally have its own self as its object-of-consciousness (content) and as its object out there (form). U will then have nothing but its own free self as its object, and so will fulfill the highest definition of self-consciousness.

Cognition Generally

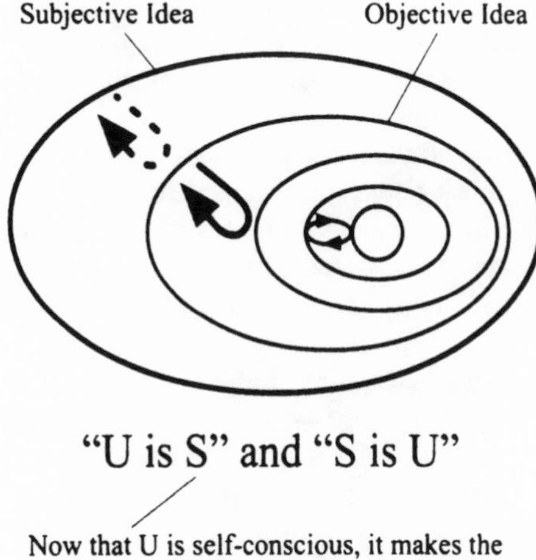

"U is S" and "S is U"

Now that U is self-conscious, it makes the distinguishing judgments itself—that's why the judgments are in quotation marks now

Figure 4.91

Now that both U and P have been redefined, there must be new terms to refer to them. U and S now have the same character as universal concepts that are defined as both Idea and Life. At the beginning of the stages of Life, U was the Idea and life, and P was the object. Now that P is an Idea and life too, however, we cannot use either the concepts of Idea or of Life to distinguish them.

U and P also have the same definition or character in another way. They have the same definition or character because each has been defined, in turn, as an S (or singular) and a U (or universal). Moreover, each has been defined as both an S and U at the same time (or as S/U). Thus they each share the same character or definition in terms of how they have been defined by singularity and universality. Immediate Life was defined by the judgment "U is S." That judgment said that U is a U and P or the object is an S. But the stages of Life have shown that U is not just a universal, but also a singularity or S, and that the object (P) is not only a singularity, but also a universal. U has been defined primarily as a universal throughout these stages, but in the stage of Living-ness Against Inorganic Nature it was defined as an S or singularity. And P was defined primarily as a singularity, but in Living-ness Against Inorganic Nature, it was defined as a U or universal. So U has been both U and S; and P has been both S and U. Moreover, in the last stage, U was both a U and an S *at the same time*; and P was both an S and a U *at the same time*. U is the one (singular, S) universal thought over P, and hence is both S and U. And P is the one (singular, S) universal thought over the whole display and process of living. Hence P, too, is both S and U. U and P have therefore also both been defined as S and U at the same time, or as S/U. Because U and P have each been defined as S and U, and have been defined as S and U at the same time (as S/U), neither the concept of singularity (S) nor of universality (U) can distinguish U and P.

How can they be distinguished? Although U and P are both Ideas, they are different *kinds* of ideas. They can be distinguished by reference to the kinds of ideas that they are. U is the Idea that is the subject, so it is the subjective Idea. U is the subject for several reasons. First, U is the subject as self-conscious. As a self-conscious (way of) being, it is an S that is U, or an S-as-U. It is a singularity that has a universal or thought as its object. Second, U is also the subject in the sense in which the subject of a sentence is the subject: since U contains P, U is the subject that has the object as its predicate. Third, U is the subject in the sense that it is defined as a thought or subjectivity without any immediacy. Since U has lost its connection to S or thereness, it is merely subjective. P, by contrast, is the object for U, or, more precisely, the object-of-consciousness for U. P's process is doing the defining, and so it is the predicate of the sentence, rather than the subject. Finally, although P is a thought or concept, it is tied to objectivity, insofar as it identifies and presents the whole, objective process of living of all of the S's or singularities. Because U is an Idea defined by subjectivity, we can call U the Subjective Idea (or SI). Because P is an Idea defined by objectivity, it is the Objective Idea (or OI) (§224).

The relationship between SI and OI can be captured by the two judgments "U is S" or "S is U." The "or" here is an inclusive or—it means both "or" and "and" (cf. Disjunctive Judgment). Since U is both an S and a U, and since P is both an S and a U, the judgment that captures their relationship can be characterized equally as either "U is S" or "S is U." Moreover, those two judgments exhaust the way in which the relationship between SI and OI can be characterized. According to the general form of the judgment, the two sides of a judgment must be both the same as, and different from, one another (see The Judgment). Because SI and OI must be different from one another within the judgment, these are the only two judgments that can capture their relationship. The judgments "S is S" and "U is U" are ruled out as options because neither of those judgments defines the two elements as different from one another within the judgment. Because the relationship between SI and OI can be captured with either "U is S" or "S is U," I have added the two judgments to the diagram. The fact that the relationship between SI and OI can be captured with either of these judgments will become important in a moment. Notice that, unlike in the stages of Life, I have put the two judgments in quotation marks in the diagram. As I will explain more fully in the next stage, I have put them in quotation marks because, now that SI is self-conscious, it thinks those judgments *for itself*, or as part of its own activity.

Since SI's "for itself" relationship with OI is not established, neither of these judgments has been *established* by SI's activity (see Transition to Cognition). SI has OI for its content and *internal* presentation, but is not yet presenting OI *out there for itself*, or through its own activity. SI *thinks* or *judges* "U is S" and/or "S is U," but the *out-thereness* of those two judgments has not yet been established. In other words, the judgments "U is S" and "S is U" may not be true or correct, or may not describe what the world is like out there. Because SI thinks these judgments itself, the judgments are objects-of-consciousness, but they are objects-of-consciousness that are not yet *objects* (or out there), or that SI has not yet established as objects (or out there) *for itself*, or through its own activity.

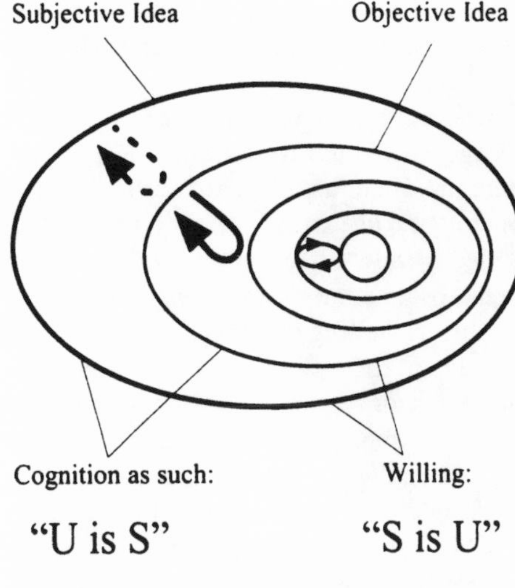

Figure 4.92

In the stage of Immediate Life, U (now SI) and P (now OI), which was the "S" in the judgment for that stage, were immediately connected to one another in the sense that U was immediately a bunch of singularities. This sort of immediate connection between U and P (or SI and OI) was lost in the stage of the Living-ness as Genus-in-itself, when U lost its immediate connection to out-thereness (or S). The reproductive process or the process of the genus in the last few stages was a process in which U or the genus tried to reestablish its connection to out-thereness. The genus is out-there as germs, babies or offspring. But this process redefined P as a concept or thought, so that the object that U ended up embracing was just an object-of-consciousness, rather than an object out there. Because P was redefined as an object-of-consciousness, the process of the genus failed to connect U with the out-thereness of S. U must therefore find some other way of connecting with the out-thereness of S.

There was also a second way in which the relationship between U (now SI) and P (now OI) was immediate in the stage of Immediate Life, however. In Immediate Life, U had two functions: it was both the essential *identity* of, as well as the essential *purpose* over, P. The connection between U and P was immediate in a second way because U was performing both of these functions (immediately) together at the same time. The function of U as the essential identity of P was immediately connected to the function of U as the essential purpose over P. Although U is now defined as Subjective Idea (i.e. SI), it is still supposed to have both of those functions here. It is still an Idea, and an Idea is by definition supposed to be both the essential identity of and the essential purpose over the object (see the introduction to the Doctrine of the Idea). SI is the thought or concept that is supposed to be both the essential identity of and essential purpose over the thought or concept of the whole display of living for living things (i.e. over OI). However, the immediate connection between the two functions of SI now falls apart. As Hegel puts it, "[s]ince life is still the immediate Idea, the product of this process falls apart into two sides" (§221).

SI's function as the essential identity of OI separates from SI's function as the essential purpose over SI for two reasons. First, the functions fall apart because the relationship between SI and OI can now be captured, not just with one judgment, but with two judgments *at the same time*, namely the judgment "U is S" and the judgment "S is U." As will be explained in a moment, each of these judgments captures one of the functions of SI.

Second, the two functions fall apart because SI is currently related to each of the functions differently. In the last stage, SI (which was defined as U in that stage) was a free self-consciousness in terms of content, but not form. U was a free self-consciousness in terms of content because it had its own Ideas as its object-of-consciousness. U (now SI) pulled P (now OI) together into its content as thought. The process that defines a universal as the essential *identity* over its content is the one that involves gathering up or pulling together the content into a one or universal *concept or thought*. The concept of feline, for instance, is the essential identity over all of the types and kinds of felines insofar as it gathers up the whole display of felines into one whole concept. It is the identity of the whole display because it is the concept that applies to, characterizes or gathers up the whole display. In the last stage, U embraced P in its content through the "for itself" relationship of content, and so was the essential identity of P, which was a one or universal. However, U embraced or identified P *only as a thought*, and not in reality or out there. U did not succeed in pulling all of the singularities out there in reality (i.e. the S's) together into a set because U had lost its connection with S. It was connected to S only through P's process, since U relied on the process of P to present the S's. This logical result was represented in the diagram by the fact that the "for itself" arrow between U and P had a dashed, rather than solid, outline. That arrow represents the "for itself" process of form or presentation between U and P, in which U would be presenting P *for itself*, or through its own activity—a process which was not established. SI has a "for itself" relationship with OI in terms of content, but not form.

The process that defines a universal as the essential *purpose* is the one in which the universal divides. That was precisely the kind of process that was outlined in the stages of Purpose, in which U divided into P, which divided into S, which in turn divided into smaller-S. "Dinner," for instance, was defined as a purpose by dividing into the types or kinds of dishes and ultimately into individually existing food, such as this lettuce. This process of division is a process of form: it is a process in which a universal *presents* the items into which it divides. In the last stage, U (now SI) did not succeed in performing that function, because U did not have a "for itself" relationship of form with P (now OI). U did not achieve full self-consciousness and freedom in terms of form because it was not presenting its free self out there in singularity or into objectivity. Again, this failure was represented in the diagram by the fact that the "for itself" arrow between U and P had a dashed, rather than solid, outline. U was not presenting P *for itself* in terms of form, or through its own activity. U contained P in its content (as a thought), but did not divide into S as purpose, because U had lost its connection with singularity or S. P divided into singularity or S because P has a "for itself" relationship of form with S, but U did not. U had to rely on the process of P to divide into singularity (S) or objectivity out there. Therefore, U did not succeed in presenting the items into which it divides *for itself*, or through its own activity. Since U (now SI) did not divide into P (or the objective Idea), or into objectivity, it was not their purpose.

Because SI has a partially successful relationship with OI as the essential identity of OI (through the "for itself" relationship of content), but does not have a successful relationship with the objective Idea (i.e. OI) as the purpose over objectivity (through a "for itself" relationship of form), the function in which SI is the essential identity of OI falls apart from the function in which SI is the purpose over OI. SI has one sort of relationship with one function—the process of essential identity—and a different sort of relationship with the other function—the process of essential purpose. Because SI is not related in the same way to the two different functions, it must treat the two functions separately.

In earlier stages, when two logical elements "fell apart," I pictured that result by depicting the two elements as separate bubbles (cf. Transition to Mechanism, Matter and Form Fall Apart). I do not depict SI and OI as separate here, however, because SI and OI themselves have not fallen apart. What has fallen apart is the two *functions* or processes, both of which belong to SI. The two different processes through which SI is defined in relation to OI have fallen apart: the one in which SI is defined as the essential identity by pulling together everything in OI, and the one in which SI is defined as the essential purpose by dividing into everything in OI. The two judgments "U is S" and "S is U," which are separate in the diagram, depict the fact that the two functions have "fallen apart." (I will explain in a moment how they represent those two functions.)

Here I provide a general introduction to the two different processes. Each process will then be taken up in more detail, one after the other, in the following stages. These two processes are the way in which SI determines or defines itself in relation to OI *for itself*, or through its own activity. They are the way in which SI distinguishes or defines itself, or are the distinctions within SI.

Because the Subjective Idea (SI) is self-conscious, its distinctions are its own thoughts—they are distinctions purely within itself as identical universality (§223). That is why the judgments "U is S" and "S is U" are in quotation marks in the diagram. Think of ourselves as examples. Although we are each unified as a self-conscious being, we still have distinctions within our self-consciousnesses, or within our identical universality, to use Hegel's terms. We distinguish or divide our consciousness into sensations, wants, and beliefs, for instance, but those distinctions never fall outside of our consciousnesses. The distinctions themselves belong to our thought or consciousness. As a result, those distinctions can only be made by consciousness itself. Similarly, SI as the Idea still has distinctions. Its distinctions are the same sort of distinctions we've had all along, namely, judgments. However, those judgments are now inside the Idea itself in the sense that they are part of the Idea's ideas, or in the sense that the Idea makes these judgments for itself. Distinctions within our consciousnesses are judgments as well—judgments such as "(this sort of) consciousness is sensations," "(this sort of) consciousness is wants," "(this sort of) consciousness is beliefs," for instance. And they are judgments that we ourselves make, that belong to our own thoughts. We think those judgments ourselves. Here, too, SI as a consciousness makes the distinctions itself—its judgments and distinctions are part of its own thought. Now that SI is self-conscious, then, it thinks the judgments that define it for itself. Or, to put it another way, the judgments that define the relationship between SI and OI are part of SI's own thought. In the development of life, the judgments "U is S," "S is U," and "U is S" were not made by the Idea (now SI, or the outermost bubble in the diagram) itself. Those were judgments that *we* used to characterize what was going on in those stages, but they were not judgments that the (outermost bubble) Idea thought for itself. In the development of cognition, however, SI now makes those judgments for itself—it thinks them. Again, I have put the judgments in quotation marks in the diagram to indicate that these are judgments that SI makes on its own—SI "says" (asserts, or thinks) them.

The first distinction that SI makes involves the process of pulling together, or the process in which SI is defined as the essential identity of OI. This is the process of the "living collective individual ["*Individuum*"]" (§§220, 221). It was at first presupposed as immediate (§221) when it was defined simply as the collective behavior of living individuals. In the stage of Living-ness as the Genus-in-itself, the genus was defined simply as the collective behavior of the living beings. So, for instance, my cat defines the genus "house cat" insofar as he goes around doing cat-like things and having cat-wants and cat-urges. The genus "house cat" is then defined in an immediate way as the given behavior of all the individual house cats. This was the immediate process of essential identity that pulled all the cats together into a collective individual. Now that OI (formerly P) is the *thought* of the process, however, that process of pulling together is mediated *by thought*. Now the concept of "house cat" is no longer immediate, but mediated by thought. What the living beings are like is therefore now defined as "something-mediated and *generated*" (§221), as Hegel puts it, by *work*. The subjective Idea has to work by thinking through and figuring out what the living beings are like. This is the process of *theoretical cognition*.

When SI goes through this process, it looks at OI as a whole, one or singular, and takes itself to be the characterizing or identifying universal or thought over that singular. Because OI is the whole display of living for living beings, it is the whole external universe, which includes both organic and inorganic nature. In theoretical cognition, SI defines OI as the whole external universe, which it at first takes to be opposed to or different from itself, and then goes about the process of showing that that external universe is really the same as itself, so that SI *is* the universal, essential identity over OI. At the end of the process, SI will be the characterizing universal (U) over the whole external universe taken to be a one or singular (S). This process is characterized by the judgment "U is S." At the end of the process of cognition, SI will judge that "U (SI) is S (OI)."

Notice that Hegel characterizes "cognition" as a process of the collective individual ("*Individuum*"). Knowledge belongs not to the single individual or person, but to the collective or society. Knowledge is held by the society, not by individual people. It is a collective or social product.

The second distinction that SI makes involves the process of dividing up into a bunch of items and elements, or "determinate distinguishing" (§223), which defines SI as the essential purpose over OI. This process of "living singularity"—like purpose and the reproductive process—involves the activity of individual living beings insofar as they divide into types and kinds. In the Process of the Genus, the process of dividing up was initially defined in an immediate way because its character depended on the given character of the individually existing beings. The living, singular individuals were presupposed to be immediate, and the genus was defined by the immediate or given behavior of the individuals in the genus. The genus divided into immediate, natural mating kinds based on the fact that the individuals of those kinds naturally desired to mate with and share a life process with sexually particularized individuals of the same kind. However, the whole display or process of living in the Process of the Genus shows that the individuals of a kind are not really immediate after all, but are instead "something-mediated and *generated*" (§221). The fact that the individuals of the genus share a life with other individuals of the genus, produce new individuals of the genus, and then die, shows that what the individuals really aim at is the universal (§221). Moreover, the individuals are mediated and generated by the universal not only biologically through the reproductive process, but also *socially*, that is, to the degree that they share a life process with other members of the genus. Individual humans, for example, share a life process with other humans insofar as they are taught and raised by adults of the genus. That shared life process—which belongs to the genus or universal—mediates and determines the characters of the individuals. It's the universal genus "human" that ultimately explains and is the power over everything that individual humans do (cf. Living-ness as the Genus-in-itself). Individual humans are mediated, determined and generated by the universal. As in the processes of purpose earlier—in which a universal divides up—in this process of purpose SI divides as well, except that, because OI is a universal, concept or thought, SI's process of dividing up is now defined in a mediated way—i.e. in a way mediated *by thought*, or by concepts or universals. Before, SI divided into given, naturally behaving individuals. Now, however, SI divides into kinds and singularities in a way that is mediated by thought or universals. This is the process of *willing*.

Because this process is a process that involves dividing up, when SI goes through this process it takes the external universal to be a bunch or group of things (i.e. a universal). SI is then the one, singular universal (or S) that imposes or pushes out its universality (U) into the world through this bunch or group of individuals. At the end of the process, when all of the individuals are defined by the universality of SI, SI will judge that "S is U."

These two judgments capture two sorts of cognitive activity. The first, "U is S" captures the activity of cognition, namely, the drive to know the truth. This cognition is the theoretical activity of the Idea, according to which SI is the characterizing U that is certain of its ability to grasp OI or the found world (taken as an S), and pulls that world into itself by grasping it. Since subjectivity is one-sided (just as objectivity is), the subjective Idea (i.e. SI) is one-sided—it is defined as merely subjective. This first sort of cognition sublates (cancels but preserves) the one-sidedness of the subjective Idea by pulling the objective world into its subjective representation or thought. SI sublates its mere subjectivity by filling itself up, so to speak, with given objectivity. In theoretical cognition, or the drive to know the truth, SI fills itself up with given objectivity (OI) as its (thought) content: it knows facts.

In both theoretical cognition and willing, SI and OI are first defined as opposed to one another. In theoretical cognition, SI is the U while OI is the S, and in willing, SI is the S while OI is the U. Both theoretical cognition and willing thereby start out by defining OI as opposed to and "other than" SI. Through these processes, however, SI will be defined as the same as OI.

Theoretical cognition and willing are the two processes through which SI will establish its connection to out-thereness *for itself*, or through its own activity. An Idea, by definition, is supposed to be connected to thereness (see the introduction to the Doctrine of the Idea). SI is currently a one-sidedly subjective Idea (i.e. SI) that is not connected to thereness (i.e. S) by its own activity, because U (now SI) had lost its connection to S (now OI) (see Living-ness as Genus-in-itself and Transition to Cognition). Theoretical cognition is the activity or process through which SI pulls everything in OI together—including its S or out-thereness. It is *how* SI pulls everything in OI together through its own activity. Willing is the activity or process through which SI divides into everything in OI—including its S or thereness. It is *how* SI divides into everything in OI through its own activity. Keep in mind that neither of these judgments or processes has been established yet. At the moment, the processes are promised by or implied by the definition of SI as an Idea, but have not yet been established by SI *for itself*, or through its own activity. That's why the looping arrow representing the "for itself" activity of form or presentation between SI and OI remains dashed. When these two processes and the judgments that capture them are established by SI's own activity, then SI will be connected to thereness in the way promised or implied by its definition as an Idea. Then the subjective Idea (S) will no longer be merely subjective.

Theoretical cognition is undergirded by a presupposition or faith, namely, the faith that Reason—which is what the subjective Idea is—will be able to identify and capture the objective world, or will be able to know truth (§224). This faith assumes that there is in fact no real antithesis between the subjective and objective, between Reason and the world (§224), since it presupposes that Reason can grasp the objective world. The faith has some logical support. Because the distinction that SI makes in theoretical cognition is one it makes within itself—or in its subjectivity—SI is, from its own point of view, or *for itself*, in its own activity, both itself and OI (§224). As thought, SI is already the unity of SI (concept) and OI (object). SI therefore already has some logical reason for presupposing that concept and object agree. To grasp or understand the objective world is just to put the subjective and objective together in subjectivity. Since truth is the agreement between concept (Reason) and object (cf. Chapter One, Section II), in its search for truth, theoretical cognition presupposes that concept and object agree.

This faith is also supported by other logical developments that prove, at least in an "in itself" sense, that the antithesis between subjective and objective is null and void. Several earlier stages have shown that thought (subjectivity) and being (objectivity) cannot stand on their own. In the Doctrine of Essence, Essence (thought) and Shine (being) mutually determined each other in the stage of Ground, Inner (thought) and Outer (being) mutually determined each other in Transition to Actuality, and Cause (thought) and Effect (being or existence) mutually determined each other in the stage of Reciprocal Action. In this chapter, purpose was the drive on the part of the Concept for its subjectivity (thought) to push out into objectivity (in the First Moment of Purpose Realizing Itself). These logical developments showed that neither thought (or subjectivity) nor being (or objectivity) is capable of being what it is without the other.

Theoretical cognition is the drive to nullify or eliminate the antithesis between subjectivity and objectivity not only "in itself" but also "for itself." It is the drive on the part of the SI to come to be able to say, posit or assert—*for itself*, or through its own activity—that the antithesis is null and void. Those of us who are looking at or studying the unfolding of the logic can see that the antithesis is null and void in the "in itself" sense because we have seen in the logical development that neither subjectivity nor objectivity can be defined as what it is without the other. But theoretical cognition is the drive on the part of Reason—as self-consciousness in general—to know—*for itself*, or in its own activity or thought—that the antithesis is null and void (§224).

The second judgment, "S is U," captures the subjective Idea's drive toward the accomplishment of its subjectivity. This sort of cognition is willing, or the practical activity of the Idea. Here, the subjective Idea tries to sublate (cancel but preserve) the one-sidedness of the subjectivity not by sucking the objective into its subjectivity (so to speak)—as it did in cognition—but by *imposing* its subjectivity on the objective. The subjective Idea cancels but preserves the one-sidedness of the objective Idea by putting itself into that objective world. It treats the objective Idea as a mere semblance or show, as a collection of contingencies and shapes which are null and void in an "in itself" sense, that is, in terms of what they are like on their own (cf. Abstract Purpose). It takes itself to be the real objective, and imposes itself on the objective world by determining, shaping or forming the objective world through its own subjectivity (§225). Willing actively *puts* the subjective and objective together in objectivity by *imposing* the subjective on to the objective. It is the practical activity of SI (§225), or practical reason or cognition.

Because both "U is S" and "S is U" are judgments, they treat SI as opposed to or "other" than OI (cf. The Judgment). Because they are also the activity of SI itself, Hegel says that, through these processes, SI is *for itself*, both itself and its other (OI) (§224, emphasis added). SI will be "for itself" through these processes in two senses. First, it will be "for itself" in the logical sense: it will be logically, doubly "for itself" in terms of both content and form. It will be the "for itself" embracing concept in terms of content (which is represented in the diagram by the fact that it is a bubble surrounding the other bubbles) that is also going through the "for itself" activity of actively embracing its other *for itself*, or through its own activity in terms of form (which is represented in the diagram by the looping arrow that runs from SI through OI and back to SI). However, because SI is the kind of life that is a self-conscious subject, it is also "for itself" in the sense that it is self-consciously *aware* that it is both itself and its other. It is both itself and its other *in its own judgment or thought*, or for itself through its own activity of thought. SI's *for itself* activity is an activity of self-consciousness, so that it has the judgments or thoughts "U is S" and "S is U" through its own activity-of-self-consciousness, or as part of its own self-consciousness. Through both the process of dividing up and of pulling back together, SI identifies and determines or defines the external universe (which is its own existence) *for itself*, through its own conscious activity.

Both of these judgments are the same in an "in itself" sense (§223), that is, in terms of how they are defined on their own, because they both refer to the same two objects and relate those two objects together with the same term, namely the copula "is." The first term in both "U is S" and "S is U" refers to SI, and the second term refers to OI. So both judgments say that "SI is OI," and hence have the same meaning or definition. However, the fact that the two judgments have the same meaning has not yet been developed by the logical process, or has not yet been established by SI's own activity. To put it another way, the sameness or identity of these two judgments has not yet been explicitly posited or established (§223) by the logic, and so cannot yet be asserted.

Because both of these processes involve at first defining OI as separate from or "other" than SI, and because the identity of the two judgments has not yet been posited or established, both of these processes are finite (§224) (cf. Immediate Substance in Chapter Three). So long as SI and OI are defined as opposed to one another, the truth of the judgments is only a relative truth (§224). For cognition, so long as OI is "other" than SI, OI has not been completely defined or identified by SI. SI "is" OI only in a relative way. To use a more modern expression, SI is the *approximate truth* of OI in the sense that OI has not been completely understood or cognized, but only partially understood or cognized. Similarly, for willing, so long as OI is "other" than SI, SI has not completely imposed its U on OI either. OI has not been completely defined, determined or willed by SI. Again, SI is then only the approximate truth of OI, in the sense that it has not completely willed OI. Both of these processes are partial or relative because time itself is not finished. They are finite, then, because they belong to the finite world that happens in time. Only at the end of time can the conclusion that the two judgments (namely, "U is S" and "S is U") are the same as one another be drawn. Only at the end of time will SI and OI be completely the same. In time, that conclusion cannot be drawn: SI and OI are not completely, but are only relatively, the same as one another.

Because SI and OI are not completely the same as one another, the kind of relationship that they have with one another is a relationship of reflection (§224). If SI and OI were completely the same as one another, they would be the same one thing. At the moment, however, they are two different things that are the same as one another insofar as they reflect each other's character. This is just the sort of relationship between concepts that was in the Doctrine of Essence.

Theoretical Cognition, Cognition as Such, or Understanding

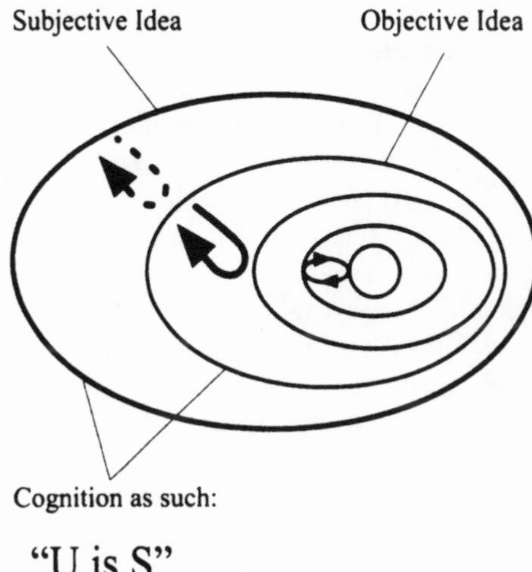

Figure 4.93

Cognition as such, or cognition in the usual sense, is captured by the subjective Idea's judgment "U is S." In cognition, the subjective Idea fills itself up with this content (to use more Hegelian language [§225]) in the sense that the judgment—"U is S"—is its own thought or utterance.

In the diagram, SI is represented by the same bubble that represents U in the judgment "U is S," i.e. SI is the U. The diagram therefore suggests that Hegel's account of knowledge involves only two elements: (1) SI/U and (2) S. One might argue that I should have a different diagram for this stage. We often talk about human cognition in a way that suggests that knowledge involves three elements, rather than two. We say that subjects know or cognize something when they have some judgment—say, "X is Y"—in their heads. We say that the subject *knows* that X is Y. This characterization of knowledge might be depicted by a diagram with three elements: one element or bubble to represent the subject or the knower, another to represent the "X," and a third to represent the "Y." In such a diagram, the subject would be a logical element that has the judgment "X is Y" nested within it as its content. If I were to draw the diagram for Hegel's logic according to this model, there would be an additional, large bubble to represent SI or the subject that would surround the U bubble and then the S bubble, which together make up the judgment "U is S." However, there is and should be no third element or additional bubble in the diagram. The judgment of cognition has a specific logical meaning, which explains why Hegel's account of knowledge or cognition should not be depicted with an additional bubble. It is not simply any random judgment—any "X is Y"—that a subject can know. The judgment "U is S" says that U is the characterizing universal over the objective world (S is defined at the moment as the objective world). According to this logical stage, cognition can be captured by the judgment "U is S." The logic of this stage therefore suggests that cognition or knowledge involves grasping or characterizing the objective world with a thought, a universal, a U. U is the thought that is S, or that grasps or characterizes the objective world. To know something is thus to be defined by the thought, the U, that characterizes the objective world. As a result, SI—the knowing subject—can know something only when it is itself the thought that is the U that characterizes the objective world. Because SI, as a subject, is conscious, or is thought, to say that it is the thought that is U is to say that SI itself—as thought—is U. Hence, SI knows or cognizes when *it is itself the U*, when it—as thought—is itself the characterizing universal over the objective world. To be the knower, SI must itself be the thought—the U—that characterizes the objective world. SI can be the characterizing universal over the objective world or the knowing subject, then, only if it is *at the same time* the U that grasps the S, or the U that is S. SI *knows* when it is the U that is S. There is therefore no third element, no additional subject that knows "U is S." SI *knows* because it *is* the U that is S.

This description of knowledge or cognition also captures how ordinary human subjects know anything. As is the case for SI, in any particular moment of knowledge, I know or grasp something when I myself—as a conscious subject—am the characterizing universal over the objective world. To grasp the world is to be the characterizing universal over the world, or to be the U that grasps S. To be the knower, I must be the thought—the U—that characterizes the objective world. I must be the U that is S.

According to Hegel, then, one logical condition that a subject must meet to be a knower is that the subject must be defined by the thought or universal that captures the objective world: the subject must be the U that is S. There is another criterion that the knowing subject must meet to be a knowing subject, however. Not only must SI be the same U that grasps S, but SI must also be *self-reflectively aware of itself* as the U that grasps S. As the knowing subject, I must not only be the U that grasps S, I must also be *aware* that my U grasps S. I know something not only because I (as conscious thought) am the characterizing universal over the objective world, but also because I am *aware* that I am the characterizing universal over the objective world. This second criterion is expressed by the logic of this stage insofar as SI is defined by the judgment or thought "U is S," or has that judgment as its own contents. Not only is SI the thought or U that is S, but SI also thinks "U is S" for itself (consciously). According to this account, then, I am a knower, not only because I am the U that is S (I am the characterizing universal over the objective world), but also because I think "U is S" for myself. My judgment that "U is S" is equivalent to the thought, "my thought is the objective world" or "my thought characterizes the objective world." To put it another way, because the U is my thought, it defines or characterizes me, so when I judge "U is S," I am expressing an awareness that the U that defines me characterizes the objective world. Not only am I the characterizing universal over the objective world, then, I also judge that my thought is (and hence I am, since my thought defines me) the characterizing universal over the objective world. Hence, the knowing subject, for Hegel, is self-reflectively aware of itself as the characterizing universal over the objective world.

At this point in the logic, the knowing subject (or SI) is defined by "U is S" in an "in itself" sense but not in a "for itself" sense. SI is defined by "U is S" in an "in itself" sense insofar as "U is S" captures its character: since SI is the characterizing universal over S (the objective world), it is the U that is S, so the judgment "U is S" defines the nature of SI: SI is U such that U is S. But, although SI makes the judgment "U is S" for itself, or as the content of its own thought, SI does not have "U is S" "for itself" in the sense of form or presentation, because SI has not yet drawn the judgment "U is S" *for itself*, or through its own activity, since it has not yet established its connection to OI through its own activity. The process of cognition is the process in which SI establishes that connection *for itself*, or through its own activity.

This sort of cognition is finite, Hegel says, because SI takes S (the world of being or OI) in the judgment "U is S" to be given or presupposed. In finite cognition, the moments SI and OI have a reflective relationship with one another, rather than the sort of relationship that they should have with one another as moments of the Concept (§226). The element that is now defined as SI is supposed to have a doubly "for itself" type of relationship with the element now defined as OI. That was the sort of relationship that Universality—which is now SI—had with Particularity—which is now OI—at the beginning of the Doctrine of the Concept. Universality was a "for itself" embracing concept (the "for itself" relationship of content) that presented Particularity *for itself*, or through its own activity (the "for itself" relationship of form). Although SI does embrace OI in its content, since the "for itself" activity between SI and OI is not established, the relationship between SI and OI currently lacks the "for itself" relationship of form. SI does not yet fully embrace OI *for itself*, or through its own activity, because SI's activity does not yet include or embrace the thereness of OI. At the moment, the thereness of OI is simply presupposed.

Instead of having the doubly "for itself" relationship that SI and OI are supposed to have with one another as moments of the Concept, SI and OI have the sort of relationship that dominated the Doctrine of Essence. Their relationship is therefore characterized by relationships from the Doctrine of Essence: SI is the Identity of OI, the Ground of OI, the Cause of OI, the Effect of OI, and so on. In other words, the knowing subject identifies the objective world, explains (or grounds) the objective world, causes the objective world (insofar as the knower's theories are imposed on the objective world in a certain sense (see Definition below, for instance), and is affected by the objective world (insofar as the objective world causes or creates thoughts in the knower, as in Analytic Cognition below, for instance). The Concept, by contrast, should be defined by a syllogistic relationship. In a syllogistic relationship, SI and OI would not only be related to one another but would also be defined as the same as one another, and SI would be the source of OI. SI and OI do not have a syllogistic relationship here, however, because of the finiteness that still obtains. Since OI has an air of givenness, SI does not yet see itself as the same as OI and as the full source of OI, or as what pushes OI out of itself, so to speak, as it would if it had a syllogistic relationship with S. It merely relates itself with OI, so that OI is its reflection, and it is the reflection of OI.

According to Hegel, although this sort of understanding does not have the relationships of the Concept, it is still guided by the Concept (§226). Cognition here is guided by the concept, I think, because it is a moment of, or part of, the Concept's own development and, as we'll see in a moment, is defined by the determinations or logical elements of the Concept, namely, by Universality, Particularity and Singularity. Nevertheless, this sort of understanding still only reaches finite truth because of the presupposed givenness or immediacy of OI (formerly S).

Keep in mind that the judgment of Cognition is not yet established by SI's activity. The judgment "U is S" is the judgment that SI will make when it pulls everything in OI together. It is the judgment that will capture the whole process through which SI is connected to singularity (S) and to thereness. But the judgment and connection have yet to be established by SI's activity. The next stage begins examining in detail the logical process of Cognition. Hegel divides Cognition into two types: the *analytic method* and the *synthetic method*.

The Analytic Method of Cognition

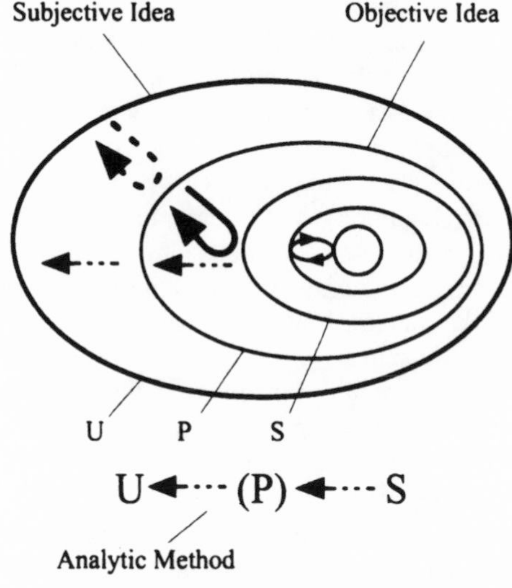

Figure 4.94

In the analytic method, the subjective Idea (SI) is an abstract universal (U) that grasps the formal identity of its content or activity. So, for instance, U might be the abstract concept of animal, which is treated as the identity of, or the identifying concept for, what it captures. The concept is formed by isolating a distinction or character in the given, concrete world and then highlighting that distinction with the concept. The relevant character or distinction is isolated by abstracting or stripping away all characteristics that are inessential to get to the essential characteristics. So, for example, to isolate the distinction or defining character of "animal," cognition would ignore the colors of the different animals, how many legs they may have, and other characteristics that are inessential to what it is to be an animal, or to what makes things animals, and focus on the characteristic that is essential to animals—the characteristic of mobility, perhaps. What distinguishes animals from plants, for instance, on this view, would be that animals are living creatures with mobility, while plants are living creatures without mobility. Cognition highlights the isolated distinction or defining character (being a living creature with mobility) by labeling it with a concept (the concept of animal). "U is S" because U is the concept of S.

Logically, this method starts with a given S—species—goes through P when it abstracts out any inessential particularities, and ends with an abstract U. The U or concept confers the form of abstract universality on the highlighted distinction. For example, the concept of animal understood in this sense functions as an abstract universality or unifying characteristic. The concept of animal is universal because it captures a distinction or character shared by more than one thing, but the universality is abstract because its relationship with the things that it captures is undefined. It separates the things it captures (animals) from other things (plants, for instance), but it does not have a specifiable relationship with the things (the animals) it is supposed to be grasping. As I will explain in a moment, because the particularities have been abstracted out of the thought, the relationship between the animals and the universal "animal" cannot be specified.

Analytic cognition looks like a syllogism because it develops through a middle step that links U to S, just as a syllogism develops through a middle term that links two outside terms. But the middle step here does not succeed in linking the two elements. It is really a negative moment—it involves abstracting out or ignoring particularities (P), so that P is not functioning as a term that relates U to S at all. Once all the animals' particular characteristics—their colors, number of legs and so on—are abstracted out, what links the universality "animal" to the animals cannot be specified. "U is S" is true—those things are animals—and it is true in a mediated way, since the judgment is the result of a process of abstraction. (Since we are past the stages of Life, the judgment "U is S" should no longer be immediate [see Transition to Cognition], but should be mediated. Here, the judgment "U is S" is mediated by the process of abstraction.) Because P is being negated by the process, however, the judgment "U is S" has the form of an immediacy. Once P drops out of the picture, U is presented by the judgment as if it has a merely immediate relationship with S. Being a "living creature with mobility" is not a particularity—it is the definition of the concept "animal." Because the analytic process involves abstracting out the particular characteristics of types of animals, we cannot say what connects the individual types of animals (S's) with their being "living creatures with mobility" or "animal" (i.e. U). Moreover, in a proper syllogism, U is the unifying universal over, and source of, P and S. The analytic method gets this relationship backwards: it treats S as the source of P and U, rather than U as the source of P and S. The diagram reflects that analytic cognition appears to be a syllogism by using the same kind of straight arrows to represent the relationships from S to P to U used to represent syllogistic relationships earlier. Because the relationship is not really syllogistic, however—since P is abstracted out of the "picture" by the analytic process—I have given the arrows a dashed status. I have also put P in parentheses in the diagram to try to indicate the ambiguous status that P has in this process: P is there insofar as it is used in the process of abstraction, but it is used by being abstracted out, so that by the end of the process, it is a merely parenthetical element, so to speak.

The Synthetic Method of Cognition

The analytic method of cognition cannot grasp the relationship between U and S, however. Once the judgment "U is S" is made, it presents the relationship between U and S as if that relationship is immediate. However, relationships are not immediate. U "is" S always in some specific way. There is always some sort of specific relationship between U and S. There are many types of "is"-relationships: the "is" of identity, the "is" between part and whole, between force and utterance, between ground and grounded, between cause and effect, between universal and singular, and so on. All of these pairs of concepts capture types of "is"-relationships between elements. The judgments "feline is housecat" or "animal (U) is dog, cat etc. (S)," both assert that there is a relationship of identity between U and S. The claim that meat is a certain collection of chemicals (see §227A) also implies a relationship of identity. The claim that gravity is falling objects, or that watches are cogs, springs etc., or that good health is good food—all these judgments of the form "U is S" presuppose a certain sort of relationship between U and S that remains undefined in analytic cognition. Analytic cognition treats these relationships as if they are given, just as it treats the objective world as if it is given.

While these implied relationships remain undefined by the analytic method, they define or construct what is known or cognized—a fact the analytic method fails to grasp. These relationships are *constitutive* of what is grasped. In the Doctrine of Essence, for instance, relationships had logical definitions that affect the character of the cognition (or of what is known). A relationship of identity or the relationship between cause and effect have particular logical structures or meanings. The logical meaning of these relationships shape what is known. If the "is" between U and S is a causal one, then what is known about "U is S" is very different from what is known about "U is S" if the "is"-relationship is one of identity. These logical relationships are synthetic—they help to determine what is known. The analytic method claims that U or the universality can simply be drawn out of S. It treats U as if it is built out of the S and adds nothing to the meaning of the judgment "U is S." U is supposed to be cognitively neutral. Since the unspecified and hidden, essential "is"-relationships are constitutive of what is known, however, it is clear that U shapes the S, just as much as S shapes U. In the essential logical relationships, each side is determined by the other as well as by the nature of the relationship. Cause is determined by effect as well as by the relationship between cause and effect. Identity is determined by distinction as well as by the relationship between identity and distinction, and so on. While the analytic method does not specify or define the essential "is"-relationship between U and S, that relationship nonetheless has some character or other, which, because it is an essential relationship—a relationship of Essence—means that U defines S just as much as S defines U. If the "is"-relationship is one of identity—as it is in the claim "animal is dog, cat etc.," for instance—then U is shaping the nature of the S by identifying the S. If the relationship is a relationship between whole and parts, unity and plurality, ground and grounded—whatever sort of essential relationship it is—U is determining and constitutive of what is known or cognized. Since the unspecified and hidden, essential "is"-relationships mean that U constitutes what is known just as much as S does, the analytic method's claim to have produced a cognitively neutral universality (or U) is a sham. In fact, the U is not neutral. Moreover, by failing to fully define both the U as well as the essential relationship (the "is"-relationship) that U has with S, its cognition (or what the analytic method knows) is not fully defined.

The failure of the analytic method leads to the synthetic method, which tries to define U and the relationship between U and S. Hegel divides the synthetic method into three moments. These moments correspond to the three logical elements of the Concept: the moment of universality, the moment of particularity and the moment of singularity. These moments are not separate, elements, however. We are past the stages of mechanism in which these moments can be treated as if they can be defined on their own. Instead, they are all moments of SI. In pictorial terms, they apply to the whole diagram, rather than merely to one of the bubbles within the diagram. The moment of Particularity, for instance, will apply to all of SI, and not only to the second bubble from the outside (contrast with the stage of Particularity). Indeed, because each of these moments applies to the whole, each moment has three sub-moments within it. Those sub-moments do refer to each of the three bubbles or logical elements—the former U, P and S bubbles—separately.

The Synthetic Moment of Universality: Definition

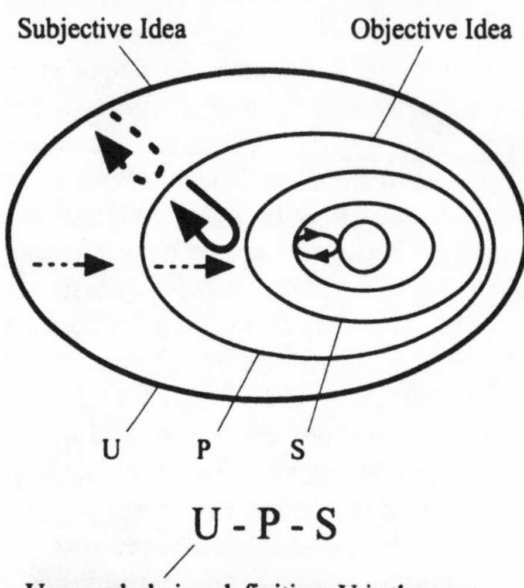
Subjective Idea
Objective Idea
U
P
S
U - P - S
U as a whole is a definition: U is the next or nearest genus, P is the determinate qualities or quality of the species, and S is the thing to be defined

Figure 4.95

The analytic method produces an abstract universal that is supposed to capture an isolated distinction or defining character. In the first moment of the synthetic method, the universal that was produced by the analytic method is defined as a definition. The definition contains the three moments of the concept, namely U, P and S. The object (of consciousness) is the singular (S) moment of the definition: it is defined. Although S is a singularity, it is still a type, kind or species, not an individual thing (cf. Singularity). S is a (singular) type of thing. In Purpose, for instance, S was lettuce (as a type) of thing, not any particular bit of lettuce. The moment of particularity (P) is the determinate quality (or qualities) that specify or define the species, and the moment of universality (U) within the definition is the next or nearest genus. If S or the thing to be defined is the species "lion," for example, P would be the quality or list of qualities that determine or define the species, and U would be the next or nearest genus, which, in the case of the lion, is the panther. The whole definition could be written: a panther (U) that lives in prides, has beige fur, and in which the males have large manes (P) is a lion (S).

Seeing the universal as a definition takes seriously the constitutive nature of the universal that was ignored by the analytic method. A definition is applied to or imposed on the objective world. When "animal," for example, is a definition, it is used to define things. Unlike an abstract universal that merely summarizes a given character that is "found" out there, a definition works downward: it shapes what is "found" out there. We use the definition of "animal" for instance, to decide whether newly discovered living organisms are animals.

Although the syllogism is now a real syllogism, the straight arrows representing the process of the syllogism in the diagram remain dashed because the connections between the moments are not yet part of SI's thought. SI is the U that is connected to S through P, but because P is given material, the connection between U and S is still shaky. The definition was produced by the analytic method based on given or "found" material, so there is still an air of separation between the definition and the object being defined. The definition is still one-sidedly subjective, as if it is merely a thought, divorced from what it is supposed to be defining out there in the objective world. The definition is external to and imposed on the object it (is supposed to) define(s). The concept of panther is external to and merely imposed on living lions because lions can go on being what they are with or without the concept of panther. The concept of panther does not make lions what they are.

The Synthetic Moment of Particularity: The Universal Specified and Divided

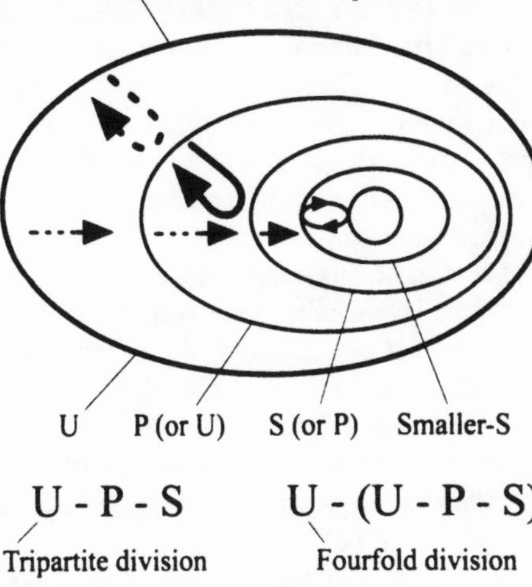
SI is specified and divided. Tripartite division: U is the next or nearest genus, P is the division of the genus into species or types, S is an actualized sub-species. Fourfold division: U is U above, the second U is P above, the next P is S above, and smaller- S is an actual instance of the sub-species
U
P (or U)
S (or P)
Smaller-S
U - P - S
U - (U - P - S)
Tripartite division
Fourfold division

Figure 4.96

In Definition, the connection between the definition and the thing to be defined was shaky: the definition might apply to what is being defined, but it also might not apply. The lion might be a panther with the character listed by the definition, for instance, but also might not be. In this stage, the whole universal tries to establish its definition and the connection between U, P and S by particularizing or dividing which is how a universal is always defined (cf. Particularity and Disjunctive Syllogism). The division of U is top-down, or grows out of the whole universal, and so must be complete and exhaustive (cf. Disjunctive Syllogism). The judgments of the syllogisms—"U is P" and "P is S"—are true: U *is* P, and P *is* S, because P and S are the complete and exhaustive divisions of U and P respectively. U *is* P and P *is* S only if P and S are equal to U and P respectively, so P and S—U's and P's particularity—must be the exhaustive set of mutually exclusive categories into which U and P divide. Because this division is still within the realm of finite knowledge, however, the principle of the division will be based on some external or given aspect or other (§230). So, for example, the concept or universal "animal" will be divided according to some given aspect or other, such as types of teeth or claws, as Hegel apparently suggested in a lecture (§230A). "Animal" might be divided into categories or particularities according to the different types of claws that animals can have: finger nails, sharp claws of the sort that cats have, hooves and so on. The universal is defined from the top down by dividing, but the division is based on given characteristics (hooves or claws).

There is a comment in the Addition to this stage (§230A) that I want to address because it is quite puzzling and understanding it helps to make sense of this and subsequent stages of the logic. It is puzzling because it seems so clearly false at first sight that it is hard to imagine that Hegel would have said it, or that his students would have regarded the comment as important enough to be enshrined in the Additions. Hegel apparently claimed that a genuine division, classification or arrangement (*Einteilung*) of the whole universal—one that is determined by the Concept—will be, first, tripartite, and then fourfold "because particularity presents itself as doubled" ("*die Besonderheit sich als ein Gedoppeltes darstellt*") (§230A). The most obvious interpretation of this comment would take Hegel to be suggesting that universals divide into three or four categories—that "lion," for example, will divide into three or four types of lions. That claim seems patently false and arbitrary, however. We divide many universals into more than three or four types. Scientists divide the universal "lion," for instance, into approximately 15 different sub-species, though the exact number is controversial. Fortunately, Hegel need not be claiming that universals divide into only three or four different types. The "division" can be interpreted in terms of (1) *width* or (2) *depth*. I first interpreted the comment as a reference to division in terms of *width*. Under this interpretation, Hegel would be claiming that "lion" divides into three or four types of lions *wide*—"lion" spreads out, widthwise, into three or four types of lions. The claim can also be interpreted, however, as reference to division in terms of *depth*. In this case, his claim would be that a genuine division extends three or four levels *deep*. The whole universal would be a comprehensive category or type that divides into increasingly less comprehensive categories for three or four levels. An example of a tripartite division in terms of depth would be: *feline-panther-lion*, where "feline" is U, which divides into (among other categories) "panther," a less comprehensive category or type, which in turn divides into (among other categories) "lion," an even less comprehensive or inclusive category or type.

A reference to the depth—rather than width—of the division of U makes sense in light of earlier stages of the logic. In the First and Second Moments of Purpose Realizing Itself, there were two possible syllogisms of purpose, one of which has three layers, and one of which has four. In the First Moment of Purpose Realizing Itself, the syllogism was U-P-S, which included the three outer-most bubbles of the Concept. But P was itself a purpose that included activity that can also be characterized as a syllogism. In the Second Moment of Purpose Realizing Itself, the syllogism of the Concept was expanded to include the activity of P. It had four layers, U-(U-P-S), where (U-P-S) was the syllogism of P: P was a second U; S was a P, and Inner and Outer and their relationship was a new level of S, which I called "smaller-S." The Addition to §230 is intended to recall these two syllogisms. Tripartite division is only three layers deep: U-P-S, while fourfold division is four layers deep: U-(U-P-S). Hegel's comment that a genuine division would be either tripartite or fourfold "because particularity presents itself as doubled" (§230A) accurately characterizes the expansion of the division in Purpose as a consequence of Particularity doubling. P doubles and becomes U-P, so that the original tripartite division—U-P-S—becomes fourfold—U-(U-P)-S. In the Second Moment of Purpose Realizing Itself (§208R), Hegel had characterized the move from the tripartite to fourfold syllogism by saying that the first premise in the original syllogism—"U is P," or U-P—becomes the middle term of the new syllogism. That characterization yields the syllogism U-(U-P)-S, in which P certainly appears to have been doubled.

When the division of the universal is tripartite, then, it is three levels deep, and corresponds to the original syllogism of the Concept, namely U-P-S. When the universal is defined this way, U is the next or nearest genus, P is the genus divided into its species or types (whatever number there may be) and S is the set of actualized sub-species of the genus, or sub-species of the genus that exist. Again, for example, in the natural sphere, the genus might be feline, which divides into species or types, such as "panther," which in turn exists as sub-species or types, including "lion." I used the example of the syllogism "*dinner (U)—make salad (P)—lettuce (S)* for the stages of Purpose. If "dinner" is an example of tripartite definition here, it would divide into three layers deep: "dinner" itself (U), all of the species or particularities (P) of "dinner"—"salad" and whatever other types of dishes "dinner" includes (P has to exhaust or be a complete division of U)—and all of the sub-species of P, or all of the types of food that exist in the dishes (S has to exhaust or be a complete division of P too), such as "lettuce" (S), which is a type of food that exists or has existence in the objective world. When the division is fourfold, it includes the activity of P and has four layers: U-U-P-S. In the Second Moment of Purpose Realizing Itself, I gave the following example for this syllogism: *"dinner (U)—make salad (U or original-P)—lettuce (P or original-S)—this lettuce (smaller-S)."* Here, "dinner" would divide not only into species (salad) and sub-species (lettuce), but also into sub-sub-species, or into all of the existing singularities that make up the sub-species, such as this (bit of) lettuce here ("this lettuce").

The same Addition (§230A) also claims that division in the sphere of spirit will tend to be tripartite. The sphere of spirit is the realm of free self-consciousness, or free subjective thought (cf. Transition to Cognition). Because smaller-S is left out of tripartite division, the claim that divisions in the sphere of spirit will tend to be tripartite suggests that they will tend not to include immediate being or "this." The fourfold division of the universal (U-U-P-S) adds smaller-S to the tripartite division (U-P-S). If U is "dinner," then the next U is "make salad," P is "lettuce," and S is "this lettuce." S as "this lettuce" includes both concept and immediate being or thereness: "lettuce" is the identifying concept, while "this" is a particular thereness in the world of immediate being, one that is identified by the concept "lettuce." The Second Moment of Purpose Realizing Itself would seem to contradict the claim, however. Purpose belongs to the realm of sprit: spirits, or free, self-conscious subjects, have purposes. Moreover, in the stages of Purpose, the purpose is *realized* by extending into smaller-S, or into the level that includes immediate being or "this." So a purpose would seem to be an example of a concept in the sphere of spirit that leads to fourfold division, contradicting the claim that division in the realm of spirit should be tripartite, rather than fourfold. In fairness to Hegel, he only seems to have claimed in his lecture that tripartite division in the realm of spirit *predominates*, so purpose might just be an example of a concept in the realm of spirit that violates the general tendency. However, the claim can be justified by its context. The discussion here is about *cognition*, not the accomplishment of purposes. While a purpose must extend to the level of thereness to be *realized*, it need not extend into thereness to be *understood*. While you have to deal with "this lettuce" to accomplish or realize making a salad, you can *understand* or cognize the nature of "dinner" without ever getting your hands dirty. Unlike actual accomplishment (or accomplishment in actuality), the cognition or understanding of concepts or purposes can stop short of having to engage with the realm of thereness or singular reality (i.e. smaller-S).

Unfortunately, interpreting the claim about tripartite and fourfold division as a reference to *depth* rather than *width* does not seem to make it any less dubious. My daughter's old science textbook's classification of the lion, for instance, extends seven levels deep: animal, vertebrate, mammal, carnivore, feline, panther, and lion. Just as there seemed to be no reason to think conceptual classifications divide into only three or four categories *wide*, there also seems to be no reason to think they extend only three or four levels *deep*.

The claim is less dubious, however, given its context. Synthetic cognition is finite cognition, or finite understanding in the finite world. In that context, Hegel may only be suggesting that, for finite beings such as ourselves, genuine understanding or cognizing requires dividing or classifying things three or four levels deep. The Addition to §229 characterizes the sort of definition outlined in the last stage as a *proximum genus*, where *proxima* means "next" or "nearest," and therefore refers to a relative relationship. The genus or universal in the definition is the "next" or "nearest" universal, not an absolute one. Finite cognition does not require knowing the entire depth of a universal. On the contrary, it needs to refer to a relatively close universal. We understand the concept of lion, for instance, in relation to its next or nearest genus or universal. That universal captures what distinguishes the lion—or makes it distinctive—in relation to other universals in its layer or level. We do not really understand the lion if we know only that lions are vertebrates, for instance. To understand a universal or concept in the finite world is to be able to link it to its nearest genus (*proximum genus*) or universal, not a far away one. The relationship "panther-lion" tells us more about the lion than the relationship "vertebrate-lion," even though the lion is also a vertebrate. Hegel's claim in his lecture, then, might only have been that, in the context of finite cognition, to understand a concept is to be able to define it in relation to the nearest three or four levels of classification.

The Synthetic Moment of Singularity: Theorem, or the Universal in Its Concrete Singularity

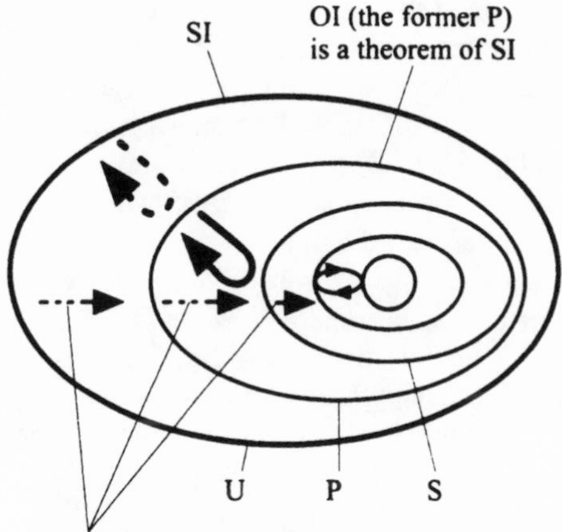
SI
OI (the former P) is a theorem of SI
U
P
S
The demonstration of the theorem must now be explicit, i.e. part of the thought: SI tries to prove its connection to OI in thought through the syllogism

U - P - S

Figure 4.97

The moments of the synthetic method of cognition are moments of the subjective Idea taken as an active whole. In other words, they apply to the whole diagram, and not just to the individual bubbles. Here, the moment of Singularity applies to the whole process of SI, and grows out of SI's character as a whole, one or singularity.

The first moment of synthetic cognition saw SI as a universal: SI was a definition that gets applied through P to S, where S was the thing to be defined. The second moment spelled out the particularity of SI, or the process through which SI, as a universal, is particularized or defined by dividing. In that process, SI divides into either three layers—U-P-S (tripartite division)—or four layers—U-U-P-S (fourfold division). As in the moment of Definition, in this stage, SI is defining or determining its contents in a process that is synthetic or top-down. In Definition, however, SI had a shaky connection with S: the definition seemed to be external to or imposed on S. Now that SI has gone through the process of particularity or division, however, the connection between SI and S is established: S is a particularity of SI. S is produced by SI's own process of particularity or division, and so is clearly connected with SI. Because P and S grow directly out of SI, SI is now defined as a complete singularity or whole that determines its content, which is nothing but a collection of instances of the whole. This is SI's moment of Singularity. Because everything in SI's content now grows out of SI, SI is a complete and unified whole, a one, a Singularity, and everything it contains are its instances. If SI is the concept of animal, for instance, then S is the set of animals into which the concept of animal divides.

The process of division in the moment of Particularity gives the instances two characteristics. First, because SI has divided into a bunch of instances, there is more than one instance in the set of instances. That means that the instances must be diverse from one another (§231), or distinguished from one another. Second, because the instances must be distinguishable from one another, each instance must have distinct characteristics or determinations (§231) that make it possible to distinguish one from the other. Because SI (as U) is currently defining all of the instances as the same as one another, it cannot do the job of distinguishing the instances from one another. If SI (as U) is the concept of animal, and S is all of the animals, because SI defines all of the animals as the same as one another (i.e. as animals), it cannot do the job of distinguishing them. That job must be done by P. However, P itself is a whole thought or concept that is in the process of grasping all of the individual S's of S. Now that P has to grasp all of the S's in a way that distinguishes them, it does not simply grasp what the S's have in common. Instead, it must now be defined as a concept *that makes those S's what they are*—that *constructs every thereness* or the *whole display* of the S's. P as the object of consciousness or OI has become a *theorem* (§231). It is the universal concept that grasps and *presents* (or pushes out) the whole display of S's—all of their sameness and differences, everything that they are out there. This is the same process that Being-for-itself had in Chapter Two, and that P had when it was defined as a being-for-itself in the Transition to Cognition. The object-of-consciousness (P) is the thought or theorem that pushes the whole display of S's out into thereness. Because the S's out there are different or diverse from one another, their identity as S's is mediated (§231) by another concept, namely, by P. The S's are grasped not only by U, but also by P, where P is now defined as a theorem.

Suppose the universal "animal" was divided in the last stage according to the type of mobility that different animals have, for example—how many legs they have, let's say. Some animals have no legs (e.g. snakes), some have two legs (e.g. birds, humans), some have four legs and so on. In that stage, P was the different types of mobility that animals have out there. In this stage, P is a whole concept that grasps and pushes out both the sameness of the existing animals as well as their differences. As a whole concept that grasps and pushes out both the sameness and difference between the animals, P is not just the type of mobility that different animals have, it is the universal concept of "having mobility," which—because it includes all of the different ways in which the different animals out there have mobility—is now a *theorem* about *what defines the whole display of animals*. What makes animals what they are as animals is that they are living things with mobility (or something like that). Being living things with mobility is now a theorem about what animals are like that grasps and explains or pushes out the whole display of animals. It is a universal concept that does not simply capture what the animals out there have in common as *animals*—which is the identity that SI (as U) grasps. Instead, it is a universal concept that explains or makes animals what they are. The identity of the animals is therefore now mediated by a second universal concept besides U. P is this second concept or theorem, and it is connected to the whole display of animals, not SI or U.

The theorem *constructs* the identity of the instances by grafting a new identity on them that they did not have before. The animals are not just the same as one another as animals, for instance, they are also different from one another in terms of how they have their mobility. How they have their mobility is a new identity that is grafted on to or imposed on the animals by the theorem. The theorem synthetically adds to the definition of the instances. P and S together as a whole have a synthetic relationship between two differently defined elements or two distinct determinations (§231)—P is a synthetic relationship between the S's, which are defined as animals, and P itself, which is defined as "having mobility" (or "how having mobility"), for example.

As in the earlier stages of cognition, this stage is still governed by the judgment "U is S" (or "SI is OI"), which is a judgment that SI makes for itself. Although "U is S" was true in those stages, it was true only in an immediate way. SI and OI were connected by the "is" and identified one another only in an immediate way, as if they were just pasted together (cf. Immediate Measure in Chapter Two), without being bound up with or related together by their concepts. Only in this stage do U and S genuinely have a *relationship*, because they are both the same as and different from one another at the same time. Relationship was the centerpiece of the Doctrine of Essence, the chapter that examined logical relationships between different sorts of being. Two things can be in a relationship only if they are both the same as and different from one another at the same time (cf. Transition to the Concept in Chapter Three). When P was nothing but the completed division of U, it was the same as U but not different from U. Now that P is a theorem, it is still U insofar as it captures the same S's that U does, but it also has a different definition from the one that U has. Since U (SI) and P (OI) are both the same as and different from one another, the judgment "U is S" (or "SI is OI") fulfills the form of a judgment, or has become a genuine judgment (cf. The Judgment).

Moreover, in Definition, "U is S" was true—U *was* P (the "S" of the judgment)—but because the connection between the definition (U) and the defining characteristics (P) was shaky, U (SI) and P (OI) still maintained an air of separateness. Because the Definition relied on given or "found" material, U seemed to be imposed on P. "Lion" (U), for instance, might or might not be characterized by living in prides, having beige fur, having males with manes (P) and so on. The definition ("lion") could be what it was, and the particularity could be what it was, without their connection. In a theorem, however, neither U nor P can be what it is outside of their relationship with one another. The concept of animal (SI or U), for instance, grasps the sameness of the animals out there, but it cannot grasp their differences. It needs the concept of "having mobility" (OI or P) to grasp their differences. It is because SI only grasps the sameness of the animals that it grasps them only as a thought, and cannot grasp their out-thereness. The subjective Idea (SI) is one-sidedly subjective—mere thought. It lost its "for itself" relationship of form with OI because it lost its S-ness, or could no longer grasp or be connected to the thereness of the S's (see Livingness as Genus-in-itself and Transition to Cognition). SI can grasp the thereness of the S's only if it grasps the whole display of S's—not only their sameness, but also their differences. An Idea is defined as a universal concept that grasps the whole display—concepts, purposes, thereness—of objects. SI is a one-sidedly subjective Idea (i.e. SI) that can be an Idea and grasps the whole display of S's only through its relationship with P or OI. SI needs OI to be what it is as an Idea. OI is in the same condition that SI is in. OI is a one-sidedly objective Idea (i.e. OI), but it is still an Idea too. An Idea is supposed to be the universal concept that grasps the whole display of S's. OI grasps the differences, but it needs SI to grasp the sameness of the whole display of S's. OI grasps all the different types of mobility, for instance, but it needs the concept of animal to restrict it to the particular set of S's that the S's are. After all, other things have mobility too—cars, for instance. OI needs the concept of animal to restrict it to types of mobility for *animals*. OI needs SI to grasp the identity of the S's before it can define the thereness or individual, singular objects (S's) to which it applies. OI can be the Idea that it is only through its relationship with SI.

Because SI and OI can each be what they are only in a relationship with the other, the judgment of Cognition that captures the connection between SI and OI—the judgment "U (SI) is S (OI)"—is now explicitly a relationship.

Because neither SI nor OI can be characterized without their relationship with one another, their relationship or connection must now become explicitly part of the thought itself. SI (or U) must *prove* the theorem (OI or P). Whether animals really are defined by "having mobility," for example, depends on what the universal concept of animal is like, because the universal concept of animal is the concept that will ultimately determine whether all the animals have mobility. All the animals will have mobility only if all of the animals out there that are grasped by the concept of animal have mobility. Because SI—as an Idea—needs OI to have the thereness or out-thereness of the animals, SI must prove or demonstrate its connection with OI to be what it is as an Idea. That's why OI is so far just a *theorem*. In particular, it is a theorem of SI, or in relation to SI. OI's truth has yet to be determined or defined by the activity of SI. Because SI has to prove or demonstrate its connection with OI, the connection that SI has with OI must now become part of the thought of SI itself.

How will SI ultimately prove its connection with OI? It will prove its connection with OI by *pushing out* only S's that have OI. SI, as the concept of animal, for instance, will push out only animals that have mobility. In short, SI proves its connection to OI through willing, and what it wills are *good* animals.

Before the stage of willing, however, there is a process within theoretical cognition through which SI at first tries to establish its connection to OI. The necessity of the logic is based on exhaustion—a concept or approach must be exhausted before another approach can be tried (see Chapter Two, Section V). There is a process of proof in cognition that must be tried before introducing the process of willing, which is a different process of proof. The process of proof within Cognition involves *construction* and *demonstration*. This process is a syllogism in which the S's are the middle term. It's the individual animals (S's), for instance, that are holding the concept of animal (SI or U) together with the theorem of "having mobility" (OI or P). The individual animals are the middle terms (§231) that hold the syllogism together. SI, as cognition, begins the process of trying to prove its connection with OI by bringing forth the materials or middle terms (§231): SI brings forth the individual animals. As the concept of animal, it begins by bringing forth the individual animals. This is the *construction* of the proof. It then connects itself—*in thought* (SI is one-sided subjectivity or thought)—to OI through those animals by means of the syllogism "U-S-P." This process of mediation in thought through the syllogism is the *demonstration* of the proof (§231). Although the construction of the proof can be characterized as a syllogism with the form U-S-P, the construction of the *theorem* itself has the form U-P-S. In the Synthetic Moment of Particularity, P was the particularities of U, so P first grows out of U, and then gathers up all the sameness and differences of the S's. The types of mobility in P are types of mobility that belong to *animals* (U), not to cars, for instance. Although the connection between SI and OI becomes part of SI's activity or thought, because the process still takes place *only in thought or subjectivity*, I have left the arrows representing the process in the diagram as dashed, to indicate that SI has not yet succeeded in connecting itself directly to the thereness of the S's, and so still falls short of its definition as an Idea.

Because P (OI) is the division of U (SI), the syllogism of proof is successful, and U (SI) *is* S (OI or P). However, the connection that SI has with OI is still deficient because it is only *in thought*. As an Idea, SI is supposed to be connected not just to the identity of the S's in thought, but to the S's *thereness*. Because SI cannot grasp the differences between the S's, it still needs OI to gather up the thereness of the S's. In finite cognition, because SI is defined as opposed to OI, it will always need OI to have out-thereness. SI can have or satisfy its definition as an Idea, then, only if tries a different method of proof. SI will be connected to OI in a different way if it brings forth all of the S's in such a way that they are also OI. If SI brings forth all the individual animals, for instance, in such a way that they also have mobility, then SI will have demonstrated its connection to OI. The next process of proof that SI tries out, then, is that it brings forth all the S's in such a way that they are OI. It *puts* the OI in the S's. It brings forth the individual animals by actively putting the mobility in them. Because SI works on the individual instances or S's in this process, this is the process in which SI is divided (cf. Transition to Cognition and Cognition Generally). It is the process of *willing*.

Transition to Willing

OI's status as a theorem introduces the idea that SI must prove or demonstrate its connection to OI in the set of S's. At the moment, this process is one-sidedly subjective, since the demonstration is taken to be only for SI, only for thought, or only for subjectivity. The demonstration is not yet taken to be out there or objective in the instances themselves.

Now that SI or cognition must demonstrate its own truth or necessity for itself, its character is changed in two ways. First, now that cognition is defined by the characteristic that it must demonstrate its own truth, it can no longer be satisfied—as it has so far—with "found" or given content. Before, SI was satisfied with given or "found" material, but now that it sees that it must demonstrate the truth or necessity of its thought, it comes to see itself—in an "in itself" sense (§232), or insofar as it is defined one-sidedly as separate from OI—as the arbiter of truth. SI takes itself to be the side that has a definition on its own and imposes its definition on OI. As a universal concept, SI has an "in and for itself" (or doubly "for itself") relationship with OI that gives it a character of its own and makes it free and independent. SI no longer takes OI to have a legitimate character of its own. It is the side with the character, and it must make its own content. The process that SI undertakes therefore now changes from cognition to *willing*.

Second, as will be shown more fully later as well, since SI now sees itself as the arbiter of truth, it must be *aware of* the demonstration. So SI will be proving or demonstrating its truth *for itself*, or through its own activity. Because SI is currently defined one-sidedly as subjectivity, it will at first be demonstrating its truth *in thought*, or as part of its own thought. As a result, cognition is now defined as a kind of thought that demonstrates the truth or objectivity of thought through its own activity *of thought*. That kind of thought is aware of itself as the kind of thought that is the mediator of truth. Its character as self-determining is part of its own thought. Now that the thought sees *itself* as the mediator of and source of truth, it passes over into a new activity of cognition or knowing process, namely, into *willing*. SI is a thought that pushes out into or imposes itself on to objectivity or OI. Later on, however, SI will demonstrate its own truth for itself (through its own activity) not only in thought, but also *out there*, or in objectivity.

Whereas in cognition, Reason was defined as a kind of blank slate that was filled up by the given contents of the objective world, Reason is now defined as subjectivity. Reason as the Universal Concept is not the receiver or predicate of the activity, but the subject of the activity—the subject whose own activity pushes out the contents and meaning of the objective world (cf. §232A). Because SI is still defined one-sidedly as a subjectivity that is opposed to one-sided objectivity (i.e. OI), this process is at first one-sided or finite.

Finite Willing

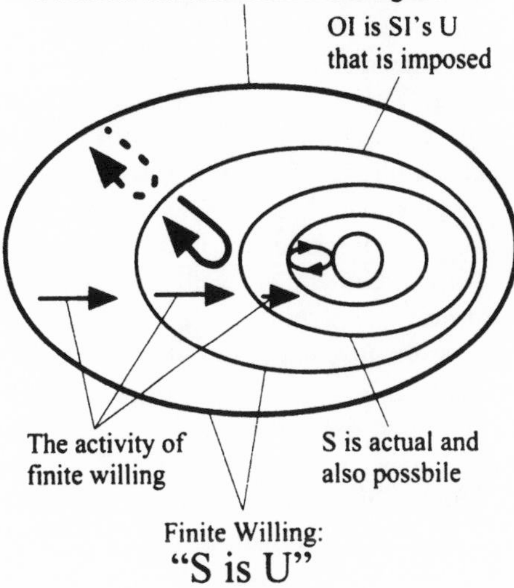
The Subjective Idea (SI) is an S-as-U: it is an S that has defined itself by U. It is rational and universal: it is the good
OI is SI's U that is imposed
The activity of finite willing
S is actual and also possbile
Finite Willing:
"S is U"

Figure 4.98

In the stages of cognition, SI was a universal or U. The Moment of Singularity or Theorem changes SI's definition to a singular. SI is a singular now for two reasons. First, in the Moment of Particularity, P was a set or bunch of concepts into which SI divided. SI was therefore being treated as a universal insofar as it was being defined by dividing. Now that OI—as the theorem—is a whole or one universal concept, however, SI is being defined in relation to a singular or a one. SI is not being defined by dividing, and so is not being treated by the defining process as a universal. Instead, OI is now the universal. Because OI is now defined as the whole display of S's, it is a universal concept that is defined by dividing. So SI is now a simple whole or singular concept that is being defined in relation to OI, which is a universal. Second, SI is a subject: a singular that has a universal as its predicate (an S-as-U). Now that SI's self-determining character is part of its own thought, or now that SI is aware that it must be self-determining, SI takes itself to be a subject or an S-as-U that must define itself by determining the instances (the S's) of the universal. Because SI is aware of its own self-determining nature, it works on the instances in a self-conscious way. SI self-consciously works on imposing its U on to the set of instances, or on to the objective world. SI *wills*. To will something is to self-consciously impose one's own universal on to a set of instances, or on to the objective world. When I will, for example, I self-consciously carry out some activity that imposes the identity or universal that I have in my subjectivity on to an object of consciousness. I turn that object of consciousness into a reflection of *my thought*. Through my willing, I carry out activity intended to force the object(s) to have the character or universal that I give it.

While cognition could be characterized with the judgment "U is S," willing can be characterized with the judgment "S is U." In willing, the subjective Idea is a self-determining, simple singularity defined by the thought that it must determine itself by imposing its universal (thought) out there into the objective world. The process of willing is the process in which SI puts its U into or imposes its U on the S's (cf. Cognition Generally). SI's U is currently captured by OI—OI is the universal concept to which SI is related. Under willing, SI is the one (or S) that puts its U—namely OI—into the S's when it divides into the S's. So the concept of animal, for instance, puts the "having mobility" (OI) into the individual animals when it divides into the individual animals. SI will be *successful* as willing when it succeeds in putting OI into the S's. When SI's willing succeeds, then SI as a singularity or S will have succeeded in imposing its U (namely, OI) on the S's, so that "S is U" or "SI is OI" will be true because the individual S's will be defined by OI: S (or SI) *is* (or will be) U (or OI) because the U that is out there in the S's was put there by the SI. Hence, the successful process of willing can be captured with the judgment "S is U."

Willing, like the concept of purpose, is a success concept. A purpose can have its being and be a purpose only if it succeeds in being the purpose over some instances (cf. First Moment of Purpose Realizing Itself). In willing, SI succeeds in willing, or in being the will over the instances, only if it succeeds in putting its U (i.e. OI) in the S's. A will that fails to put its U into thereness is no will at all. Hegel relates willing explicitly to purpose when he says that willing divides into a subjectively good purpose and an independent objective world (§234). This comment suggests that, for finite willing or willing that is defined as opposed to the objective world, purpose is part of willing. (I will explain where the "good" comes from in a moment.) Finite willing includes a one-sidedly subjective purpose but, like the theorem (P/S or OI) in the last stage, also includes the purpose's instantiation into the objective world. Purpose is one-sidedly subjective because it is a concept or thought that may not be realized into objectivity at all. Willing, by contrast, implies its realization in objectivity in at least one sense. SI is already the identity of the S's that are out there. The concept of animal, for instance, is the identity of the individual animals (which is expressed by the word "animals" in the phrase "individual *animals*"). Because willing includes the thought—like theorem—of the demonstration into the instances, it includes the instances. Unlike a purpose—but like a theorem—the activity of willing necessarily implies its realization as an identity into instances. However, as will be clear shortly, what makes *finite* willing *finite* is that there is still a gap between the subjective purpose that belongs to willing and its objective realization. The finite willing is realized as an *identity* in the S's because of the process of cognition, but as a *purpose*, it may not be realized in the S's.

The suggestion that willing—like theorem—must include its instantiation into the objective world follows from the fact that willing is an activity of self-consciousness. Because willing is a self-consciousness, it has thoughts as its objects—it has objects-of-consciousness as its objects, rather than mere objects. To be a free self-consciousness is, in its most basic sense, to be a consciousness that is conscious of itself, or that currently has itself before it as the object of its thought, or as its object of consciousness. That basic logical meaning implies that the self or consciousness must be out there as an object first, so that it can be available out there as an object for its consciousness. A consciousness makes itself into an object by putting its consciousness out there into the objective world, by putting its thought—its U or universal—out there into the objective world. A self-consciousness must have put its thought or consciousness out there into the objective world *before* its self can become an object for it. Like a theorem, then, a consciousness must be instantiated in the objective world to be a *self*-consciousness. Hence a self-consciousness can be what it is or can have its definition—as a *self*-consciousness (a consciousness that is conscious of itself or has itself as its object)—only *after* it has instantiated itself in the objective world. Unlike purpose, willing presupposes that the subject has already put itself out there into the objective world, at least *in thought*, insofar as it is the identity of the objective world. To will is not just to put oneself out there in thought, however, but to put oneself out there in a new way. To will is to be the free *purpose* over the objective world by giving objects in that world a new character *that they do not necessarily have on their own*.

Two things must happen for the process of willing to be successful. First, the willing subject must translate its singularity into a universal or concept. In logical terms, the willing S must translate itself into an S-as-U for itself or in its own thought. It must translate itself into a thought. When I will, for instance, what gets put out there is not the S of me—my singularity—but a U of me—my thought or concept. I cannot put my singularity out there in a thing. I can only put my thought—a characterizing universal or concept—out there in the thing. So the first thing I must do is pull out of my S-ness a thought, or U. I must explicitly draw a thought or U out of my S-ness. A free self-consciousness or spirit, such as I am, is already an S-as-U or centrality in an "in itself" sense, that is, in terms of its definition. But now I must make my S-as-U-ness explicit for me. My U-ness must become part of my thought. I must define myself by the thought "S is U." Second, willing is a success term—willing can be what it is only if it succeeds in determining the objective world. So the thought "S is U," includes the assumption that U is characterizing the objective world. Thus willing includes the thought about the connection between my U and the U out there. This thought about the connection between my U and the U being out there is my drive or urge to realize myself, or to put myself out there. SI must go through the same process. Its U-ness must be explicitly part of its thought if it is going to succeed in imposing that U-ness on the objective world or U. So the first thing SI must do is pull out of its concept another U or concept. That's what OI is—another concept that, as a particularity of SI, SI explicitly pulls out of itself. Moreover, SI as a will imposes its U as the characterizing universal over the S's. This thought of the connection between SI's U and the U in the S's is the drive of the subjective Idea to realize itself (§233). SI goes through a process of imposing its U (namely OI) on the S's, or of using its U to characterize the S's. This is the same process of demonstration that SI used to characterize its instances in the theorem, except that now SI is not undergoing the process *only in thought*. The arrows in the diagram that represented the theorem's demonstration—its activity of becoming the characterizing universal or identity over the instances—now represent the will's self-conscious drive to realize itself. But because this process is not in thought but is a process in which SI imposes its U—namely OI—on the *thereness* of the S's, I have given the arrows a solid line.

Hegel says that willing divides into a subjectively *good* purpose and an objective world. The purpose is good because a spirit that has made its U-ness an explicit part of its thought is a special kind of spirit. "U" is a universal or concept. Universals or concepts are the heart of reason or rationality. The conceptual system just is Reason or Rationality—with capital "R"s. So when a spirit makes its U-ness an explicit part of its thought, it is defining itself by means of universal concepts, which is to say, it is defining itself by means of rationality. When the spirit defines itself and its willing process by the thought "S is U," then, it is imposing this universality or rationality on itself. It is thus using reason to shape its will. Hence, the will of SI has become a rational will. When SI has become a rational will, its willing is guided by rational concepts. Rational concepts *just are* the *purposes* of things (cf. Abstract Purpose). So if I am a rational will and will to make dinner, for instance, I not only make dinner, I make a dinner that lives up to the universal concept of "dinner." In short, I make a *good* dinner. I have to *strive* to make the dinner good, however, because of the fact that finite willing falls short of the concept of willing. In finite willing, the purpose may not necessarily be instantiated. Nevertheless, as a rational will, I will that purpose. I will the rational concept. I will the good. As a rational and universal will, the subjective Idea (SI) is the good (§233).

If SI is the concept of "animal," for example, and OI is the thought of all the particularities that make animals animals, when SI imposes OI on all of the individual animals, it strives to make those animals the sorts of animals that live up to the particularities of the concept of animal. In short, it strives to make them *good* animals. SI strives to produce good S's of itself. What character does SI have as a will? It has the character of being a good will, insofar as it aims at producing good instances of everything. "Goodness" is therefore now the concept that defines what SI is like as a will or as a self-conscious purpose over the S's. When SI imposes its OI on the individual S's, SI defines itself as the good. SI imposes its purpose as the good on the S's through OI.

Hegel's introduction of the concept of good follows a formula, according to which universal = rational = good. This formula has a long history in Western philosophy. For the ancient Greek philosopher Plato, for instance, the good was the primary exemplar of a Form, and the Forms just were the realm of rational universality, or the *logos*. The same formula is in Kant's philosophy. For Kant, the good will, as a rational will, is a universal will (Kant 1985, 9). For him, moral rightness or goodness is defined by acting according to universal principles that do not violate rationality. The so-called "universal-law" version of Kant's famous Categorical Imperative, for example, says that "I should never act in a way that I could not also will that my maxim should be a universal law" (Kant 1985, 18). According to this principle, if I want to be moral, I must put any action I am considering performing to a certain test. First, I must formulate my action as a maxim, or turn it into a general rule. So if I am considering helping someone who appears to be overloaded and having difficulty carrying groceries to his or her car, the maxim of that action might be something like "help people in need." I must then see if I can universalize this maxim without becoming self-contradictory or irrational. To universalize the maxim is to imagine that the rule is a universal law, or is a rule that applies to everyone, everywhere, in similar circumstances. Under Kant's theory of morality, if I cannot universalize the maxim without getting myself into a contradiction or endangering my rationality, then the maxim is neither rational nor universal, and the action is morally wrong. If I can universalize the maxim without endangering my rationality, then the action is universal and rational, and hence morally good. Kant's theory thus contains the same formula—from universal to rational to good—that is repeated in Hegel's logic.

Kant's version of morality illustrates that there are really two characteristics of rationality that are supposed to make a will good. The first is the element of universality itself. What makes a rule a morally right rule is its connection to universality. The idea that a universal rule is morally good or right stems, I think, from the fact that it seems to capture a sense of fairness. According to this view, racists and racism are immoral, for instance, because they apply one set of rules to one category of people and another set of rules to another category of people for no good reason. While it is true that we often apply different rules to different people—we do not put three-year-olds who pocket a piece of candy at the grocery store into jail, for example—we must have good, morally relevant reasons for treating those people differently from the way we treat others. We treat children differently, for example—especially three-year-olds—because they are not yet morally mature and may not understand the wrongness of what they are doing. That is why we do not punish children as severely as we would punish an adult. But the race of a person—which is nothing but certain sorts of hair type, skin color and bone structure—has no connection whatsoever to any morally relevant characteristics. Under a Kantian theory, to treat people differently because of such superficial features is morally wrong because the race of a person does not provide a good reason for treating people differently. All people should be treated the same in the same circumstances (i.e. the moral rules are universal), unless there is some good, morally relevant reason for treating some people differently.[9]

In Hegel's philosophy, the claim that we should treat things of the same kind the same way—that we should act according to universal principles—has a logical basis. To act universally is simply to take concepts seriously, to treat every object of consciousness according to the concept that it instantiates. If something is a "rock," one behaves one way toward it, but if something is "person," one behaves another way toward it. To treat all persons the same is just to take seriously the concept of person that grasps them all. To treat all persons the same is to treat them all as Ideas—as concepts (i.e. "persons") that are fleshed out in the world. We must treat things in the world as Ideas, which means treating them according to the concepts that they instantiate. Universal treatment follows from the logical status that things have as Ideas—as combinations of flesh and concept. To act universally is to treat flesh—objects—according to their concepts. Insofar as the subjective Idea (SI) governs its will according to concepts—insofar as it takes concepts and hence rationality seriously—it is universal and hence good.

In Kant's theory, there is a second element of rationality that underpins its connection to goodness. When the moral agent uses the Categorical Imperative to decide to do the right or good thing, the moral agent must not only universalize his or her maxim, but must also universalize the maxim without getting him- or herself into a contradiction. To ensure that he or she does not contradict him- or herself is to see if the action he or she is considering fits into a systematized set of thoughts. If we think of the moral agent's beliefs and concepts as a set, to contradict him- or herself is to have contradictory beliefs in the set. Kant's demand that the moral agent not contradict him- or herself requires the agent to *systematize* his or her beliefs and concepts. To be rational is thus not only to think universally, but also to have a well-systematized set of beliefs and concepts. If the new thought or idea under consideration is good, it will fit neatly into the agent's already rationalized system of beliefs and concepts. A contradiction points to a glitch in the system, a place where the system needs to be updated, changed, worked out—or rationalized.

Hegel's logic also echoes the suggestion that a rational and hence good will must follow from a systematized set of thoughts. The Subjective Idea that is doing the willing here has already passed through the long process of sorting out concepts and thoughts—a process that is the entire course of the logic so far. Moreover, in Chapter Three, the Concept—which is the same logical element that is now defined as SI—was already defined as a systematized set of rational concepts (see the stages of Transition to Reciprocal Action and Reciprocal Action). SI's conceptual apparatus has therefore already been systematized or worked-out. As a result, Hegel's willing consciousness in this stage is rational in this second sense as well, namely, in the sense that the willing grows out of a well worked-out conceptual system.

Therefore, Hegel's willing Subjective Idea is good for the same reason that Kant's good will is good: it is rational. Because it is rational, its willing activity is guided by universals (as Objective Ideas [OI's]) and its universals are part of a well worked-out system of concepts or Ideas.

In finite willing, there is still an air of independence between the Subjective Idea (SI) and the Objective Idea (OI): in willing, the Subjective Idea must *work on* an independent Objective Idea. On the one hand, the Subjective Idea treats the objective world as null and void (§234) in an "in itself" sense, that is, in terms of its own character. After all, the Subjective Idea plans to impose its own universal on that Objective Idea, so what OI is like on its own, insofar as it is defined on its own (in an "in itself" sense) doesn't matter to SI. On the other hand, the Subjective Idea still treats the objective world as somewhat independent of it, because it has to *work on* that world to put its U out there (cf. Effect as Substance in Chapter Three). If the objective world were not independent of the Subjective Idea, then the objective world would already—automatically, so to speak—reflect SI's subjective U-ness. SI wouldn't have to work on OI. We can describe OI's independence by saying that SI is both *essential* to OI—in the sense that it is the defining essence or purpose over the Objective Idea—but also *inessential* to OI (§234)—since it is still an open question whether SI succeeds in being the characterizing purpose over the S's. SI is both the characterizing essence or identity of OI, but also *not* the characterizing essence or identity of OI, insofar as OI still has a purpose independent of SI.

OI's independence can also be characterized by saying that SI is both the *actual* purpose of OI but also a merely *possible* purpose of OI (§234). SI is the actual purpose over OI because SI's willing characterizes the essential identity of the S's. The S's really are animals, for example. But SI is also only a possible purpose over OI because OI has a character of its own which makes it independent of SI's characterizing activity, which means that SI must rely on what OI happens (possibly) to be like to succeed in characterizing or being the essential purpose over OI. OI's character as both the actual and possible realization of SI's will has logical roots in the Doctrine of Essence. Part of what makes the diagrams so helpful to understanding the logic is that they allow us to see the connections between later stages and earlier stages. In many cases, later stages simply redefine elements from earlier stages. Because a logical element is often represented in the diagrams by the same bubble throughout several stages, that same element has come to have different definitions through the logical process. Moreover, according to Hegel's concept of *Aufheben* (sublation), although the old definitions have been overcome, vestiges of the earlier definitions remain, and often help to explain the character of later stages. That is precisely the situation here. The Singularity bubble in the tripartite division of U (i.e. U-P-S) grew out of the Form of Actuality in the Doctrine of Essence (cf. Singularity). There, the Form of Actuality was defined as Actuality being presented as Possibility. So the logical element that is S here was Actuality being presented as Possibility in that earlier stage. That logical history defines S as both actual and possible. Since OI contains S in its contents, it includes both the actuality and possibility that belonged to S. Hence, OI is both actual and possible in relation to SI, as Hegel suggests in §234.

The independence between the subjective Idea and the objective Idea makes this sort of willing finite. The subjective Idea is finite because it is limited by whatever independence the objective Idea has. To the degree that the objective Idea is independent—to that degree—the objective Idea is opposed to or up against and hence limits the subjective Idea (cf. Immediate Substance in Chapter Three). Both finite cognition and finite willing work with a presupposed, found or given world. However, while finite cognition is satisfied with the given or found world, finite willing is not. Finite cognition aims to adjust itself to fit the given world, while finite willing aims to change that world to fit itself (§233).

The air of independence between the subjective and objective Ideas leads Hegel to switch back to the term he had used earlier to refer to the "object." In this stage, Hegel once again uses the term "*Objekt*" instead of "*Gegenstand*." As

Geraets, Suchting and Harris point out in their translation of the *Encyclopaedia*, both "*Objekt*" and "*Gegenstand*" can be translated with the English word "object" (Geraets et al. 1991, xxii-xxiii, xliii-xliv). Whereas "*Gegenstand*" refers to an ordinary object of experience or object of consciousness, "*Objekt*" refers to an object that is one-sided and independent of the subject. Until the Transition to Cognition, the "object" was defined one-sidedly as opposed to a subject, and so was an "*Objekt*" rather than a "*Gegenstand.*" Since the Transition to Cognition, however, the object has been an object-of-consciousness of SI: it has been the Idea of the SI. Hence OI has been a "*Gegenstand*" rather than an "*Objekt.*" Because OI's air of one-sidedness and independence has returned here, it is now an "*Objekt*"—an object that is opposed to the subject—and not just a "*Gegenstand.*" That's why Hegel uses the term "*Objekt*" again in this stage, as he did in the beginning of the Doctrine of the Object.

The Spurious Infinity of Finite Willing

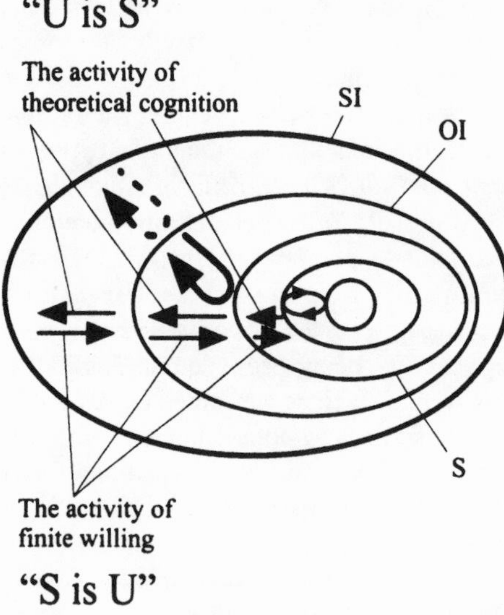

Figure 4.99

Willing is a success term. SI only succeeds in being the will over the objective Idea (OI) if it succeeds in putting its U out there. SI has a drive to realize itself in two senses. First, the drive to realize itself means that SI is driven to put itself out there, as it has done in Finite Willing. Second, however, the drive to realize itself means that SI is driven to *know* that it succeeded in putting itself out there. SI can realize itself as the will over OI only if it has the thought that it is the will over OI for itself, or as part of its own activity of thought. To realize itself as the will over OI, SI has not only to put itself out there, but SI must also have the thought (i.e. to *realize*) that it put itself out there, which is to say, to know that it put itself out there. SI can know or realize that it put itself out there only if two conditions are met. First, SI, as an S or singularity, must be defined by the same character or universal as the U that is out there. In short, S must be U, or the judgment "S is U," must be correct. The judgment "S is U" says that SI, as an S, has succeeded in characterizing OI with its U. OI is the U that SI, as an S, put out there. Second, SI must have the thought, must think, or must make the judgment, "S is U" *for itself*, or through its own activity.

The logical need to know that S is U drives the subjective Idea back to theoretical cognition. Theoretical cognition involves looking at the objective world and seeing what U applies to it. That's what SI, as finite willing, has to do now to find out whether it succeeded in putting its U out there into the objective world. To see if SI succeeded in putting its U into OI, SI now has to look at OI and see what U applies to OI. It starts with the Analytical Method of Cognition: it looks at the S's within OI to see what U applies to them. We can characterize the whole process of theoretical cognition once again with the judgment "U is S." SI has worked to put its U into OI, and it now looks at OI as a whole, to see what U applies to it. OI is an S-as-U too. The objective world is a singular (a whole, one) universal concept of a set of instances. When SI looks to see what sort of U OI now has, SI expresses its conclusion by applying the appropriate identifying universal to OI (now taken to be a singular whole or an S). SI looks at OI, and judges "*U* is S." This judgment is the judgment of theoretical cognition. Because this process begins with the Analytical Method of Cognition, I represent it in the diagram with a set of return arrows that run from the original S-bubble, back through OI to SI. SI looks at the S's to see what U they reflect for OI and SI.

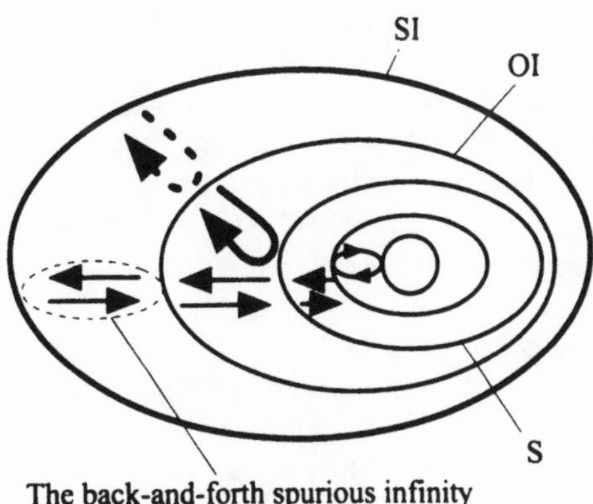

The back-and-forth spurious infinity of finite willing and theoretical cognition between SI and OI

Figure 4.100

Because this is finite willing, OI is defined as independent of SI's willing. Sometimes, the U that SI finds in OI after it wills won't be the U that SI put into OI, since SI's activity of finite willing fails to impose its U on the S's within OI. In that case, OI remains merely objective and fails to be linked to SI, while SI, for its part, remains merely subjective and fails to make itself objective. The antithesis between subjective and objective remains: U turns out not to be S.

When the activity of willing does not succeed, SI's drive to realize itself leads it to try again. It goes through the process of finite willing again, to see if it (as an S) can succeed in putting its U out there (i.e. into OI as a U): it wills "S is U." Once again, though, for SI to realize itself as a will, it has to have the judgment "S is U" *for itself*, or through its own activity, which means it must check to make sure that OI reflects the U that SI put out there. SI goes through the process of theoretical cognition again, to see what U OI has: it cognizes or judges "U is S." Sometimes, OI will fail to have the U that SI put out there, so SI will be driven again to the activity of willing to put its U out there into OI. Because OI is defined as separate from and independent of SI, it will sometimes fail to have the U that SI put out there, and SI will be driven back and forth between finite willing and finite cognition—between putting its U out there, and checking to see that it succeeded in putting its U out there.

Even if SI sometimes *succeeds* in putting its U into OI, because OI is in its own dynamic process and is defined as separate from and opposed to SI, SI must nevertheless *constantly* work to put its U out there into OI or engage in finite willing. OI is an objective Idea (i.e. OI). As *objective*, it is defined as separate from and opposed to SI. As an *Idea*, it is an internally active purpose and identifying essence (see the introduction to the Doctrine of Idea for a general definition of the concept of Idea). Indeed, OI was defined as a purpose over the S's in the stage of Theorem. It is an internally active purpose and identifying essence on its own, separate from SI. In the stages of Purpose, a purpose was defined by a syllogistic process. Because OI is a purpose, its own activity is a syllogism of purpose. OI is the concept that grasps the purpose and identifying essence of the objects it contains, as those objects go about their business of being what they are. Because OI is currently defined as separate from SI, OI as a concept is not yet completely defined by SI, or as *good*. OI is defined by its own syllogistic activity, so that whether it lives up to the definition of SI or of the good is not yet established. OI's activity as an Idea is represented by the looping "for itself" arrow that runs between OI and Singularity (S). The separation and independence between SI and OI is represented by the fact that the "for itself" looping arrow between SI and OI is dashed, since SI's "for itself" activity of form over OI is not established because SI has lost its S-ness, or its connection to thereness (cf. Living-ness as the Genus in Itself and Transition to Cognition). SI is not succeeding at the moment in embracing the thereness of OI *for itself*, or through its own activity.

Because OI's character, in general, is not yet established completely by SI or the good, SI will have to continually work—through finite willing—to impose its U on OI. And then SI will have to continually check—through theoretical cognition—to see whether OI reflects the U that SI put out there. The fact that OI is currently defined by its own syllogistic activity as separate from SI therefore forces SI to continuously go back and forth between the activity of finite willing and finite theoretical cognition. SI wills the rational or good through its willing, but, because SI is defined as limited by and separate from OI—i.e. as finite—SI must continually work to impose its U on OI (through finite willing) and must continually use theoretical cognition to check to see if OI reflects its will. From SI's finite point of view, its rational willing of the good is never fully achieved. SI must continually work to bring the good into the objective world (as Hegel apparently remarked in a lecture [§224A]).

The relationship between SI and OI here mirrors the relationship between the Cause and Effect in the stage of Reciprocal Action in Chapter Three. OI is the same bubble that was the Effect at the end of the Doctrine of Essence, and SI is the same bubble that was the Cause. In the Doctrine of Essence, the Cause was not only a cause but also an effect in relation to the Effect, and the Effect was a cause in relation to the Cause. Similarly here, SI is not only the cause or will over OI, and OI is not only the effect of SI. Instead, OI is an independent element that has an active content of its own that makes it a cause in relation to SI, which is therefore also its effect. OI's independent activity forces SI to react by continuously using finite willing to impose its U on OI and theoretical cognition to check to see if it succeeded in imposing its U on OI.

The relationship between SI and OI here also repeats aspects of the relationship between U and P in the stages of Purpose. OI is the same element or bubble that was defined as original-P, and SI is the same element or bubble that was defined as original-U in the stages of Purpose. P turned out to be a purpose too, just like U was. OI, as an Idea or purpose, still contains or absorbs this earlier definition. OI has sublated—cancelled but also preserved—this earlier definition. OI is a purpose with its own internal activity that is currently defined as separate from SI. OI is the purpose over the objects it contains, which go about their business of being what they are. Whether OI reflects the U that SI gave it—whether OI is good—is not yet established.

SI's activity of finite willing thus leads to a spuriously infinite back-and-forth process between willing and theoretical cognition: willing from SI to OI; theoretical cognition from OI back to SI; willing from SI to OI; theoretical cognition from OI to SI; and so on. This spurious infinity is depicted in the diagram because there are two arrows running back and forth between SI and OI—one arrow that runs from SI to OI, and one that runs back again from OI to SI. Since straight arrows have also been used to represent an "in itself" relationship of opposition (cf. Being-in-itself in Chapter Two), these straight arrows also represent the "in itself" relationships of opposition or separation that SI and OI currently have with one another. In finite willing, SI and OI remain opposed to one another. SI does not fully succeed in putting its U into OI, and so remains largely one-sided as thought or subjectivity, while OI is not fully defined by SI's U, and so remains largely one-sided as object or objectivity. SI as the good remains a thought, and OI remains what it is as objective, but not necessarily good. SI remains subjective and OI remains objective, and they remain opposed to one another.

Absolute or Speculative Idea

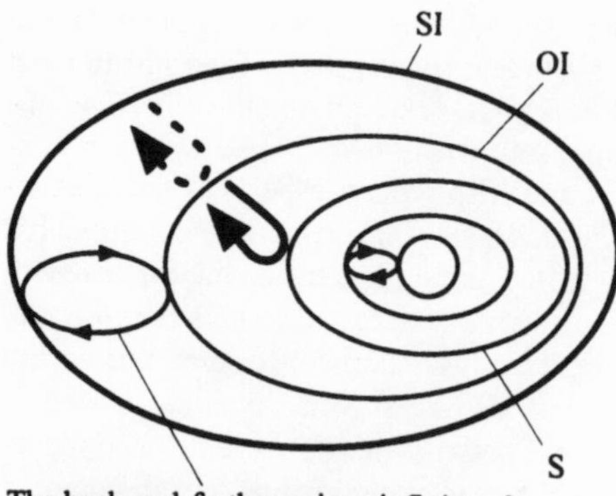

The back-and-forth spurious infinity of finite willing and theoretical cognition between SI and OI is now one whole completed process in which SI and OI are completely mutually defining

Figure 4.101

As always, Hegel's logic cannot rest with a spurious infinity (cf. Spurious Infinity in Chapter One, for example). So long as concepts are locked in an endless back-and-forth process, they are never defined. To achieve the goal of defining terms, the logic must progress to a stage that stops the endless, spuriously infinite process. As in earlier stages, the spuriously infinite back-and-forth process will be stopped by redefining the embracing concept as the thought of the whole completed process. Moreover, the embracing concept is redefined as the general definition of the concept in play process (cf. World of Appearance and Condition as a Totality in Chapter Three). Here, SI will be redefined as the general concept of Idea, Idea-in-general, or the concept of the concept of Idea.

In the last stage, SI wills something, and then uses theoretical cognition to check to see if OI reflects its will. Notice that the processes of both willing and theoretical cognition take place from the point of view of SI. SI is the active subject of both the willing and the cognition. SI does them, not OI. When SI wills something, there are two possible results: either OI does or does not reflect SI's will. If OI does not reflect SI's will, then SI's drive to realize itself—to push itself out there—leads SI to assert its will once again, thereby generating the back-and-forth process between willing and theoretical cognition. As we saw, even though SI sometimes succeeds in imposing its will on OI, because SI is finite and OI is defined as a separate concept with its own internal processes, SI will continuously have to reassert its will over OI (in finite willing) and then check to see (in theoretical cognition) whether OI reflects the U that SI gave OI, thus generating the back-and-forth process of finite willing and finite cognition between SI and OI. In this whole process of development, there is one possible move that has not yet been explored. SI acts on OI, OI either is or is not changed or defined by SI's willing activity, and OI has a dynamic character of its own that it gets as a result of its own internal process. At no point in the process so far, however, does SI change or undergo a dynamic process. Even when OI changes on its own, SI simply reasserts its (original) will on OI. The move to Absolute Idea is driven by the recognition that SI changes or develops—a recognition that redefines SI.

When OI's own internal processes lead OI to change, SI has two possible responses. The last stage contained the first: SI can reassert its (original) will on OI. The second possible response that SI can have, however, is that SI can *change* in response to the changes in OI. This second response is implied by the reciprocal causal relationship at the end of the Doctrine of Essence between the outermost bubble of the Concept—which is now SI—and the next layer or bubble of the Concept—which is now OI. OI still has vestiges of its causal relationship with SI from the stage of Reciprocal Action, and SI, for its part, still has vestiges of its relationship as an effect in relation to OI. OI has the power to cause changes in SI, and SI can be changed by OI. This stage recalls that reciprocal causal relationship by taking up the second possible response that SI can have in relation to OI: SI *changes* in response to OI's causal power.

To see SI as dynamic or capable of changing in response to OI is to recognize that Reason is not simply a system of concepts that is imposed on or fleshed out (as Idea) into the objective world, but also responds and adjusts to changes in the objective world. Reason is dynamic. Just as the objective world develops in response to Reason or the Concept, so the Concept develops and adapts to grasp the objective world. Reason develops too (as Hegel apparently pointed out in a lecture [§234A]). It is not defined by thought alone. It is also defined by the objective world. Reason is not one-sidedly subjective or thought-based, but is objective or defined by objectivity as well.

The stage of Absolute Idea repeats or reasserts the same, dynamic nature of Reason that was introduced in Reciprocal Action in Chapter Three, but it also adds two additional elements. First, Reason no longer changes the objective world merely through causation, but through willing, which includes and has absorbed all the stages of judgment, syllogism and so on in this chapter. Second, the recognition of the dynamic relationship between Reason and the objective world is part of the thought of Reason itself. In Reciprocal Action, *we* saw the dynamic relationship from the outside, as third-party observers of the logical development. At the end of the stages of Absolute Idea, Reason will recognize its dynamic character for itself, or in its own thought or judgment (I will discuss the Absolute Idea's logical "for-itselfness" in a moment).

Once Reason or SI is recognized to be dynamic, the spuriously infinite, back-and-forth process of finite willing and cognition is defined as one whole, *completed*, reciprocal process between SI and OI, in which SI both acts on, and adjusts to developments in, OI. Hegel has used this same logical move, in which a spuriously infinite back-and-forth process is halted by redefining the process as one whole, completed process, in other stages (cf. Condition as a Totality, Reciprocal Action, Transition to Idea). The whole process of development and adjustment between subjectivity and objectivity is finished when time itself is complete. Thought or subjectivity has developed, adjusted and acted all it can in relation to the objective world, which has developed on its own and been acted on by subjectivity all it can. Since objectivity has developed all it can, then the objective world is complete, its process of temporal development is over. Time itself is finished. At the end of time, subjectivity and objectivity will be completely mutually defining. Since Reason's development is completed, there can and will be no further adjustments to Reason as a conceptual scheme. Moreover, because the process of adjustment between the SI and the OI is complete, each side is a complete reflection of the other. There is no longer anything in the subjective that is not in the objective, and nothing in the objective that is not in the subjective. Because the spuriously infinite process is now defined as one whole, completed process in which SI and OI are completely mutually defining, I have changed the two arrows representing the back-and-forth process between SI and OI to the circular arrow that I have used to represent mutually defining relationships (cf. Ground).

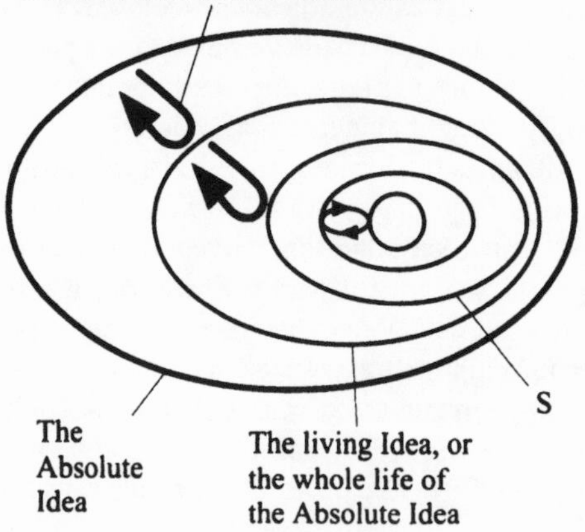

The "for itself" activity between the universal and the object that was lost in the stage of Living-ness as Genus-in-itself is now reestablished

S

The Absolute Idea

The living Idea, or the whole life of the Absolute Idea

Figure 4.102

So far, SI has been defined as dynamic and SI and OI are completely mutually defining. These logical developments change the definition of SI. Once SI changes in response to OI, SI is no longer SI or the one-sidedly subjective Idea anymore. As soon as the *subjective* Idea is affected by or defined by the *objective* Idea (i.e. OI, which has been one-sided as well), the *subjective* Idea is no longer *subjective* anymore. As soon as the *subjective* Idea is defined by the *objective* Idea, it is both *subjective and objective*, it is defined by both subjectivity and objectivity. Hence SI is no longer SI—it is (S-and-O)I, both subjective and objective Idea. SI is Reason now thought of as the dynamic result of a complete process of finite willing and finite theoretical cognition as a finished product—the one thought of the whole subjective and objective development of the temporal world. SI has become the *Absolute Idea* (AI).

Although AI is a new concept, it is still an *Idea* for two reasons. First, Idea was defined as Reason as it is fleshed out or objectified in the world. SI was defective as an Idea because, although it was thought or concept, it lost its S-ness, or failed to be extended as a free spirit into out-thereness or S (see Living-ness as Genus-in-itself and Transition to Cognition). It was extended into thereness as the identity of OI, but not as a free, self-conscious spirit. It did not yet succeed in being the purpose over the object, or making the object what it is (i.e. good) as a free spirit. In finite willing, however, SI pushes itself out as purpose and free, self-conscious spirit into thereness. In finite theoretical cognition, SI checks to see that it has succeeded in putting itself out there into thereness. AI fulfills its definition as an Idea or as both concept and thereness because it has succeeded in being extended as a free, willing spirit into out-thereness.

Second, Idea was defined logically as Subject-Object (§215: cf. the introduction to the Doctrine of the Idea), or as Concept-Object. It was the thought of the Concept connected to or fleshed out into the Object. In Immediate Idea, the connection between the Concept or Subject and the object was immediate. Subject and object were in a doubly "for itself" relationship of identity, but they were still being presented as two separate elements, namely, as Idea and object. They were unified as a judgment: as two separate elements joined together by the copula "is." Now however, they are unified in the very same thought or concept. AI is the one concept that has the whole process of subjectivity and objectivity as its content, or grasps the whole subject and whole object together as a one. It is the Subject/Object, no longer as a judgment, but as one concept. Because AI is the one (single) concept that has the general definition of an Idea as both Concept-Object as its content, it is the general concept of Idea (§236), or the thought of Idea-in-general. Similar logical moves have been encountered before: a completed back-and-forth process redefines the element that already embraces the process as the general definition of the concept that it already is (cf. Condition as a Totality in Chapter Three).

AI is not a different logical element from SI—in the diagram, they are the same bubble. AI is the same Reason that SI was. The same Reason that went through the processes of finite willing and finite cognition is the same Reason that is AI at the end of the whole process (cf. Transition to the Concept in Chapter Three). AI is the thought of Reason having completed its own dynamic process of development, so that it is no longer one-sidedly subjective (as it was as SI), but is now both subjective and objective, or determined by both subjectivity and objectivity.

While SI evolves into AI, OI evolves as well. SI had the one-sidedly objective Idea (OI) as its object of consciousness. OI was the one-sidedly fleshed-out or objective set of concepts, or the set of concepts understood to be out there in the objective world but not completely determined by subjectivity. Unlike SI, however, AI has the whole process of subjective and objective Idea as its object. AI is the thought of the completed process in which subjective Reason and the objective world mutually define one another, or the whole process in which subjective (Concept) is fleshed out into the objective world. At the beginning of the Doctrine of Idea, "Idea" was the Concept fleshed out in the objective world. That is what AI's object of consciousness is like. AI has the whole process of the subjective (Concept) and objective (world) as its object of consciousness. Hence, AI's object of consciousness is just the Idea (§236).

Absolute Idea has not only succeeded in fulfilling its definition as an Idea or Concept-Object by pushing out into thereness as a free, self-conscious spirit, it has also fulfilled this definition *for itself*, or through its own activity. AI is the subject of the whole process—of both the willing and theoretical cognition. Finite willing and theoretical cognition are processes or activities *of AI*. Since they produce the current definition of AI, they are the processes in which AI defines itself as AI *for itself*, or through its own activity. The mutually defining relationship between AI and the Idea (formerly OI) is a process that AI acts out, and so is AI's own process. In the stage of Living-ness as Genus-in-itself, the universal (which is now AI) was no longer connected to the thereness or S-ness of the object *for itself*, or through its own activity. As a result, the looping arrow representing the "for itself" relationship of form between U (now AI) and P took on a dashed status in the diagram. U (now AI) lost its "for itself" relationship of form with the object and so was defined as one-sidedly subjective Idea (i.e. SI) in Transition to Cognition. Because AI pushes out into thereness or presents the Idea (formerly OI) *for itself*, or through its own activity, it has reestablished both its connection with thereness and the "for itself" activity of form. I represent this change in the diagram by giving the looping arrow between AI and the Idea (formerly OI) a solid outline. Since the mutually defining relationship is AI's own process—a process in which AI defines itself *for itself*, or through its own activity—I have eliminated the circular arrow representing the mutually defining relationship from the diagram. That circular arrow is replaced by the "for itself" arrow of form (cf. Transition to the Concept in Chapter Three and Universality).

In Absolute Idea, then, the "in and for itself" or doubly "for itself" relationship that the Concept is supposed to have with its content is fulfilled (cf. Universality). As the one thought of the completed back-and-forth process of finite willing and finite cognition—which are AI's own activities—AI now embraces its content *for itself*, or through its own activity. It is the "for itself" embracing concept (the first sense of "for itselfness" for content) that presents its content *for itself*, or through its own activity (the second sense of "for itselfness" for form). It is the one concept that embraces its whole life "for itself," both in terms of content and form, or that both embraces and *presents* its content, and so has both an "in itself" relationship of opposition (cf. External Necessity in Chapter Three) and a "for itself" embracing relationship with its content.

Because AI has fulfilled the doubly "for itself" relationship with its content, it meets the highest definition of self-consciousness. SI (now AI) was defined as a free self-consciousness in the most basic sense in Transition to Cognition when it was a consciousness that had its own Idea as its object-of-consciousness. But SI was not a complete self-consciousness (or was a defective self-consciousness) for two reasons. First, it did not yet succeed in putting itself as a free self-consciousness or spirit out there into thereness. And, second—partly because of the first reason—it did not yet have its complete self as an object. A "self-consciousness" is by definition a consciousness that has its "self" as an object. This definition includes two requirements: (1) the self-consciousness must have its *self* as an object, and (2) the self-consciousness must have is self *as an object*, that is, *out there* as an object for it. These two requirements are fulfilled when (1) the self that the self-consciousness has as an object is its *whole or completed* self, and (2) when the self that it has as an object is *out there (completely) in objectivity*. SI fell short of being a complete self-consciousness because it (a) had only an incomplete or partial self as its object, and (b) its self was not completely *out there*, since it did not succeed in extending itself as a free spirit into thereness. AI fulfills both of the requirements as a self-consciousness. It (1) has its whole or completed self for its object. AI is the general definition of an Idea that has the completed Idea as its object-of-consciousness. It is an Idea that has its whole life as an Idea, or its whole process of subjectivity and objectivity as its object-of-consciousness. AI also (2) is completely extended into or out there in objectivity. Because AI includes everything about objectivity in its content, and because its process of pushing out into thereness and objectivity is completed, it is completely extended into objectivity. AI is therefore a free self-consciousness that has its whole self out there as an object. It is a complete and completed self-consciousness.

Unlike AI, because we are still alive and in process, we are not yet completed self-consciousnesses. When in the process of life, we do not yet have our completed selves for our objects and have not finished extending ourselves into objectivity. We are only partial self-consciousnesses. Let me embellish on an example that Hegel apparently used in a lecture (§237A) to try to flesh out this claim. SI is a spirit: an active, willing, self-consciousness. We human individuals are spirits in this sense too. In our day-to-day lives, we are one-sided SI's engaged in the activity of finite willing. We are finite, subjective beings who flesh ourselves out into the objective world (OI) by working on it. We have thoughts, will goals (U's), and then try to make those goals happen in the objective world, or try to impose our goals (U's) on the OI, in the way that SI in finite willing imposes its U on OI. When we are carrying on with our day-to-day lives in this way, we have only finite or restricted goals in mind. We may pursue a Bachelor's Degree, a nice dinner, and so on. When we achieve our goals, Hegel apparently said in a lecture, we are often "amazed to find just what we willed and nothing more" (§237A). When we receive a Bachelor's Degree at graduation, for instance, the diploma in our hands seems thin and weak compared with everything we had to do to get the degree. But the achieved goal really contains the whole process that we had to go through to get it. We have to think of a goal as embracing the whole course of life that led up to it (§237A).

Although Hegel's lecture imagines that a person achieves an adopted, finite goal, often the goals we *fail to achieve*, rather than the ones we achieve, draw our attention to the importance of the whole process of our lives. We are often more amazed to find that things turn out all right, even after things go wrong, or when a goal is not achieved. Cases of failure are often precisely the sorts of cases that make us see that the point of our lives is neither this nor that (finite) goal, but the whole process. The logical move to Absolute Idea as the thought of the whole process is driven by the recognition of the dynamic nature of SI. Cases of failure draw our attention to the importance of the whole process of our lives because they force us to recognize that we—as finite, subjective Ideas (SI's)—must be dynamic in relation to our objective lives (OI). Failing to achieve goals in our objective lives (in OI) often forces us to adjust ourselves (as SI's). Objective life kicks back and changes us. Not getting what we willed or hitting an obstacle in life often forces us to adjust our willing and identities (SI) in ways that end up enhancing the value or goodness of the whole process of our lives. Unexpected events and failures lead us to come to define ourselves differently, have different identities, or be characterized by different universals or U's. We then realize that we are not merely subjective Ideas after all—that we do not simply make ourselves up in thought and often do not get to decide who or what we are. Instead, we are also defined by our objective lives. We are both subjective and objective Ideas (i.e. AI's).

What we are like as a whole, however, can only be captured when our lives are finished. For AI, time itself is finished, but for us, when we get to the end of our lives, we can still have a thought (AI) about what we are like as a whole person. We would come as close as we can to being an Absolute Idea if we made a judgment about who we are just before the moments of our deaths. Of course, each of us is limited to making a judgment about our own lives, and so we can never truly be absolute in Hegel's sense. AI includes the completed processes of the whole subjective and objective world. But in theory, anyway, we could at least make a final (absolute) judgment about our own characters. Right before the moment of our deaths, we could look back on our lives as a whole, finished or completed process, and make a judgment about what we are. Our day-to-day subjective selves (SI) would be finished, and our objective lives (OI) could do nothing more to us. The whole process in which our day-to-day selves work on our objective lives (through willing) and adjust to what happens in objective life (through theoretical cognition) is finished, and we are complete and completed selves. The thought of that self—of that completed and complete self as a whole—is the Absolute Idea of our lives. The Absolute Idea is thus like an old man, who, at the moment of his death, has a thought about his whole life as a finished process. Just as the purpose of his life was neither his day-to-day, subjective self nor his objective life by itself, so the point of Life generally, of the Life of Reason—of *that* life—is neither subjective Reason (SI) nor the objective life of the world (OI) by themselves, but the whole process of their development together. The Absolute Idea is Reason—and goodness (§235)—now defined as the whole completed process of interchange between subjective Reason and the objective life of the world. It is the thought of an old man who, at the end of his life, thinks about the whole completed content of his life.

In another example that Hegel apparently used in a lecture, he says that there is a difference between a child who thinks about the religious claim that one must forgive others and an old man who thinks the same claim. The proposition that one must forgive others is the same for both, but for the old man, it carries the content of a whole life, whereas, for the child, the claim is merely abstract, or outside of life (§237A). When a child thinks about forgiveness, his concept is theoretical, empty, or abstract, but when an old man talks about forgiveness, his thought is filled with the burdens and struggles of a whole life, and so has a content that the child's does not. His concept of forgiveness is an overarching thought that takes into consideration his whole life process, a process in which his (one-sidedly subjective) conception of forgiveness and his (one-sidedly) objective life mutually adjusted to one another over time. His conception of forgiveness is in*form*ed by a whole life. Not only did it shape his life, but his life also shaped or *form*ed his conception of forgiveness. Similarly, for a dying old man, a holistic thought about his life is an overarching thought that takes into consideration a whole life process in which both his reason (concepts) and his objective life adjusted in relation to each other. The dying old man's thought about his life is in*form*ed by his whole life.

The comparison between an old man at the end of his life and the Absolute Idea helps to illustrate some of the logical features of AI. It helps to show, for instance, why OI is redefined in this stage. When the old man looks back over his life as a completed process of development between his thought and his life as it was lived objectively, what he now has before his mind as his object is his whole life, or rather, his life. His object, or what he confronts, is not just his life as it was lived objectively, but his whole life, including all of the (subjective) thoughts he had about that life earlier, before this very moment. Everything he thought before, as well as everything he lived and the whole process of development between the two is now what he is thinking about. He is thinking about the whole display of his life. So his object of consciousness has changed definition: it is no longer merely his objective life—what happened to him in the world—but his whole life, including his earlier, subjective thoughts about that life. Similarly, AI's object is not merely the objective Idea, but the subjective and objective Idea taken together, or the Idea in general.

The comparison also helps to show why AI should not be depicted as a new, separate bubble surrounding all the other bubbles, or as an additional, larger bubble in the diagram. In the last stage, the outer-most bubble was defined as the subjective Idea that embraced the objective Idea. Since the Absolute Idea now embraces an Idea that is both subjective and objective, you might think that AI should be depicted as a new bubble surrounding the old SI and OI bubbles. However, the comparison with the old man shows why AI is the same bubble as SI. The old man's self-consciousness that looks back over his life is not a new self-consciousness. The same thinking man who lived the life is now thinking about that life as a whole process of development of his thinking and his objective life. Similarly, AI is not a new sort of Reason that is the thought of the whole (complete) process of development between Reason (thought of subjectively) and the objective life of world. Just as the old man's self is the same self that underwent the development during his life, so the AI is the same Reason that underwent the development of Reason (as SI) during its life, and so is the same bubble as SI in the diagram.

For the Absolute Idea, as for the old man, there is no longer any sense of passing-over or presupposing (§237). The old man is at the end of his life (we are imagining). His life is truly completed, a finished product. There will be no new given, possible or accidental objective elements to which his subjectivity will have to respond. Any accidents or given things that were going to happen to him have already happened. The givenness and contingency of his life is therefore finished. And there will be no new thoughts except for the (absolute) one in which he will sum up the whole course of his life. That thought will embrace all the objective contingency of his life, and all the previous thoughts he had in relation to that life. He knows everything that will ever happen to him and every thought that will ever happen to him. There is nothing left to discover in either his objective or subjective life. Since AI is the thought of the completed process of development between Reason and the objective life of the world at the end of time, it, too, considers everything in the development of objectivity and subjectivity. There is nothing left to discover, or that could be given or presupposed. The process of subjective and objective development is finished, complete. Everything that will happen or be thought has already happened or been thought.

Because the process of passing back and forth between subjective and objective is completed, AI ends the spuriously infinite process between finite willing and theoretical cognition. AI embraces and presents the whole, passing-over process, but does not itself pass over. It includes every bit of thought (concept) and every process and activity of thought within it. There are no further thoughts or activities of thought for it to pass into. Moreover, because AI is every bit of thought (concept) and every process or activity of thought (i.e. all subjectivity over all objectivity), it embraces all of the earlier movements or logical developments. To use more Hegelian language, AI is the singularity or object in which all the previous determinations of the logic have come together (§236).

Finite willing presupposed that the objective and subjective realms—that Reason (or Thought) and Being (or object)—are opposed to one another. Once the dynamic nature of Reason is recognized, this presupposition is sublated (cancelled, but preserved). The presupposition is cancelled because Reason is the result of a completed process in which subjectivity and objectivity are unified—in AI. At the same time, the presupposition is preserved because, while AI stops the endless back-and-forth process between subjective and objective Idea, it does not eliminate the distinction between subjective and objective. The back-and-forth process remains in the background, so that there is still a distinction between the subjective Idea (as spirit) and objective Idea (as nature) (§234A). The distinction does not go away, but the antithesis or the assumption that they are forever opposed to one another does. The presupposed antithesis between the subjective and the objective in finite willing does go away.

The idea that the antithesis between subjective and objective has been sublated can be characterized in another way as well. Because the subjective Idea is Reason—conceived of as one-sidedly subjective or as generated by thought alone—and the objective Idea is the one-sidedly objective life of the world, the thought that the antithesis between SI and OI goes away can also be expressed by saying that Reason (conceived of as one-sidedly subjective or as generated by thought alone) and the objective world (conceived of as one-sidedly objective) correspond to one another. In the finished product of both subjective and objective Reason, which is AI, there is nothing in the subjective that is not in the objective, and nothing in the objective that is not in the subjective. In AI, one-sidedly subjective Reason and the one-sidedly objective world correspond to one another. Notice that the claim that Reason and the objective world correspond to one another was the presupposition of theoretical cognition (see Cognition Generally). So the presupposition of theoretical cognition has been established (§234).

This stage reinforces Hegel's use of the term "moment" to describe stages of the logic (cf. Reciprocal Action in Chapter Three). From the point of view of a completed life, everything that happened before is a mere moment. Take the old man, again. For him, at the end of his life, everything that happened to him or that he thought (before this one thought of the whole) will be mere moments of the whole. His thought is now of the whole of his life. Every event or thought that he had in his life is merely a moment in relation to that whole. Every identity or goal (willing) he had before are now mere moments in the whole journey. Similarly, for AI, every logical step is nothing but a mere moment of the whole.

While the imagined old man and AI—as completed lives—will undergo no further development, there is one project left for the logic to do. At the end of Chapter Three, the Concept was defined as the one thought that grasps everything else. But the Concept cannot be the all-embracing grasper unless it also grasps *itself*. AI is currently defined as the Idea that embraces and defines everything else, except itself. The last bit of activity that the AI has to go through is that it has to say what it is. It has to grasp and define itself *for itself* or through its own activity. It has to go on to have a summary thought about what it is like. If we imagine the old man lying on his deathbed, he has to go on to say or define for himself who and what he is.

We can characterize AI as the judgment "S is U and U is S." That whole judgment is the thought of the alternation process between theoretical cognition ("U is S") and finite willing ("S is U") as one whole process ("U is S and S is U"). It is crucial to keep in mind, however, that AI does not yet have this combined judgment *for itself*, or through its own activity. That is what the next three stages will accomplish. While AI embraces the completed processes of finite willing and finite cognition, it still takes the two processes to be separate from one another. *We* can see that Absolute Idea can be defined by this one judgment, or that the two processes belong to the same whole, one process, but AI has not yet drawn that conclusion *for itself*, or through its own activity. Of course, "U is S" and "S is U" have always been the same in an "in itself" sense. They both describe the same relationship between the same two bubbles and therefore have the same meaning (see Cognition Generally). When AI comes to have the judgment "U is S and S is U" for itself, however, the two judgments will also be the same in a logically "for itself" sense. They will be "for itself" the same through the process of an overarching concept—in this case, AI.

These final stages examine the form or method of that summary thought. In what way will the thought of Reason as a completed whole present itself? To use the analogy with the old man again, what form will the old man's summary thought about his life take? Since AI is the whole logical system, spelling out the form that the thought of the whole system will take is equivalent to spelling out the speculative method in general. Hegel divides the development of the speculative method into three stages, but we will need more than three diagrams to illustrate the logical movement of these stages.

The Beginning of the Speculative Method: Being, the Immediate

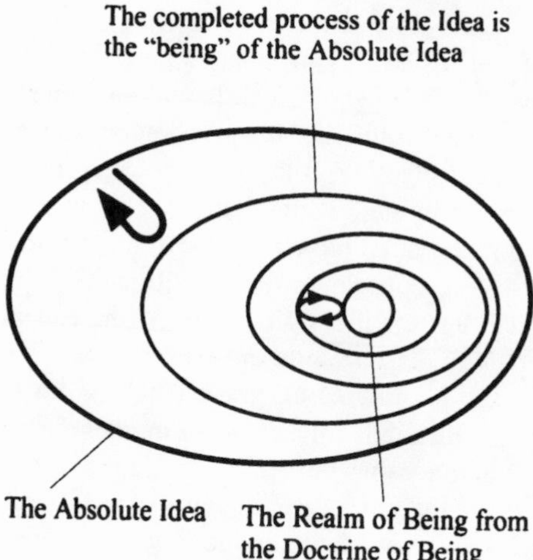

Figure 4.103

Because the process that AI undergoes is finished, that process simply is—it is done, complete, a fact of the matter. Since the process is done, or a fact of the matter, it is an immediate given. As an immediate given, it is the "being" of Absolute Idea. For the old man looking back on his life at the end, the life he lived is finished, complete. It is done, a fact of the matter. Hence it is a given or simply is. As done, given or immediate, that whole life is his "being." In the diagram, this "being" is the whole content of AI—it's object-of-consciousness, or the living Idea. Because this "being" is defined as completed, I have eliminated the second looping arrow that represented its activity from the diagram. Its activity is finished, completed, and so is no longer logically active. Its slips out of the picture or into the background as completed.

I put the word "being" in quotation marks to distinguish it from the realm of Being in the Doctrine of Being. That realm of Being is not the same as the "being" here. In the diagram, the realm of Being is represented only by the smallest bubble in the center of AI. It was the Outer bubble later in the Doctrine of Essence, and is linked with a circular arrow to the next smallest bubble, which represents the concept of Inner. The "being" of the Absolute Idea, by contrast, includes the whole realm of the objective as well as subjective Idea, and is represented by the next-to-largest bubble, the former objective Idea (OI) bubble. At the same time, AI's "being" does include the logical realm of Being or thereness—indeed it includes all of the concepts that predicate a kind of out-thereness in the world. So while the "being" of AI is not the same as the realm of Being, it does include that realm. The "being" of Absolute Idea includes the way in which the Absolute Idea is out-there. It also includes all of the higher-level concepts from the Doctrine of Essence that were linked to thereness—existence, actuality and so on.

What method does AI use when it thinks about its whole process of development? As AI thinks about its process of development, the first thing it does is examine its given, completed, whole "being." Since AI is the thought of the whole process of speculative logic, we can also say that the speculative method of logic begins with the "being" of AI. That "being" is the beginning of the method of the AI. In the example of the old man, he begins the process of thinking about his life by thinking about his life up to this point as a completed whole. That life is finished, it is his given, his "being." His first thought is thus of his "being."

The claim that "being" is the beginning unifies the synthetic and analytic methods of cognition, as Hegel suggests (§238R). As just argued, AI's "being" include thereness, which belongs to the realm of sense perception and perceptual judgment. Moreover, because it is a completed whole, the "being" is also given or immediate. For AI, then "being" is the immediate realm of sense perception and perceptual judgment or intuition. The claim of this stage—that "being is the beginning"—therefore implies, on the one hand, that cognition starts with the realm of sense perception, which is what the analytic method claimed. On the other hand, however, the "being" is itself a process: not a static whole, but a whole that is also a bunch of bits—a life—and hence a universal in the sense that it is a group of things. It is also a thought, namely, the thought of the whole process of life. The claim that "being is the beginning" thus also implies that cognition begins with universal thought or concept, which is what the synthetic method claimed.

The "being" is AI in both an "in itself" and a "for itself" sense, since AI has a doubly "for itself" relationship with its "being." According to the first "for itself" relationship of content, AI embraces its "being" in its content. This first sense of "for itselfness" is depicted in the diagram by the fact that AI is a bubble that surrounds the bubble for its "being." In the second "for itself" relationship of form, AI presents its "being" *for itself*, or through its own activity. This is the activity of form or presentation. As soon as a concept *presents* another concept, it is defined as separate from and opposed to that other concept (see External Necessity in Chapter Three). This second sense of "for itselfness" is represented in the diagram by the looping arrow between AI and its "being." Because this "for itself" activity defines AI as separate from and opposed to its "being," and because an "in itself" relationship just is a relationship of opposition, this "for itself" activity gives the Absolute Idea an "in itself" relationship with its "being" (cf. the Introduction to this chapter and Universality).

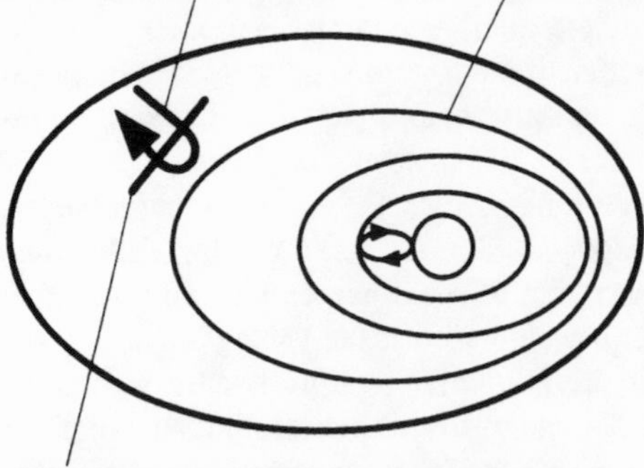
The "for itself" activity of form of the Absolute Idea
The "being" of the Absolute Idea
The Absolute Idea defines itself at first as not-"being." It is its "being"—since that "being" is its content—but it is also not its "being." It holds itself apart from that "being"

"U is not S"

Figure 4.104

While AI is defined by its "being," insofar as its "being" is its content, it is not completely defined by that "being." In this stage, AI denies that it is its "being" in a certain sense. It accepts that the "being" is its *content*, and so I continue to depict it in the diagram as a bubble that embraces or surrounds its "being" or content. But it denies the "for itself" relationship of form that it has with its "being." AI denies that its "being" is its form or presentation, or that it presents its "being" *for itself* (or though its own activity), by denying that it *willed* that "being." The "being" is its content, but not its form. Because this denial is a denial of the "for itself" activity of form that AI has with its "being," I represent it in the diagram with a large black bar running through the looping arrow that represents the "for itself" activity between AI and its "being." The black bar indicates that AI takes itself to be distinct from or separate from the "being" that it nevertheless embraces. I used the same pictorial convention to represent the denial of a "for itself" embracing relationship in the stage of Immediate Distinction in Chapter Three. Although Immediate Distinction appeared before the introduction of "for itself" relationships of form (the second sense of "for itselfness"), the denial of a connection between Essence and Shine was a denial that Essence embraced its Shine at all (the first sense of "for-itselfness" for content, but see Chapter Three, Section V). Here, AI does not deny that it embraces its "being" (the "for-itselfness" of content), it only denies that it presents the "being" *for itself*, or through its own activity (the "for itselfness" of form). Nevertheless, the solid bar through the "for itself" activity still represents a denial of a "for itself" relationship, just as it represented the denial of the "for itself" relationship in Immediate Distinction.

Take the example of the old man again. For the old man looking back on his completed life (his "being"), the life he has lived has made him who he is—it is the content through which his self-consciousness has passed. At the same time, however, that lived life is not him either. He is still a free self-consciousness looking at that life. From the point of view of his free self-consciousness now, his life is not him, it does not have to define him. That life—his "being"—is the negative of him, or is "not him." He, as the unifying consciousness over the whole lived life, still stands apart from that life. As a free, unifying self-consciousness or spirit, he is beyond that life. He can deny that he presented that life, or that the life is his form, or the way in which he has his being. Imagine that, in a death-bed confession, the old man repudiates his life. He says, "I am not really that evil man who lived and did those things." This confession illustrates the logical freedom that he has from his "being." As a free self-consciousness, the old man is not determined by his life. His life is still the content that his self-consciousness went through, however. To repudiate a whole life is to admit that the "being" is his content, that he did all of those things. Nevertheless, it also insists that his "being" is not him, does not determine who he is. He is still a free self-consciousness, in the sense that he is free to insist that his "being" is also not him. His life did not present who he really is.

In the diagram, I have represented AI's refusal to see itself as its "being"—its characterization of its "being" as its negation—with the judgment "U is not S." AI is the U or universal that is "not" its "being," which is an S or singular. AI is the one thought or universal because it is the unity of all of the moments of its "being." It also has the "in and for itself" relationship with its content that defines a universal as a universal (cf. Universality). Moreover, it is pulling the "being" together into a whole or one, and so is treating its "being" as a singularity. But AI's denial is also built into the judgment "U is S." The judgment "U is S" actually says *both* that AI is and is *not* its "being." The form of judgment always expresses a tension between the two terms of the judgment. The copula "is" says that the two terms are the same, but the fact that two different terms or variables are being used implies that the two terms are not the same (see The Judgment). On the one hand, then, the copula "is" in the judgment "U is S" says that AI is its "being." On the other hand, however, because the judgment uses two different terms to describe AI and its "being" (namely "U" and "S"), the judgment "U is S" also implies that U is *not* S, or that AI is not its "being." If U and S—or AI and its "being"—were the same, then there would not be two terms to refer to them. The use of two different terms implies that there is some way in which U is not S—which is precisely what AI claims in this stage. However, although the judgment "U is S" suggests that AI is both the same as its "being" (identity) and is not the same as its "being," AI is currently stressing the distinction, rather than the identity. AI is not acknowledging that it is its "being," which is also built into the judgment "U is S." AI's current self-definition is therefore best captured with the judgment "U is *not* S." *We* can see that that AI is in fact both its "being" and *not* its "being," which the judgment "U is S" captures. But because AI is refusing to see itself as its "being," or is treating its "being" as its negation, it is not making the judgment "U is S" for itself. It will make that judgment in subsequent stages. The old man's repudiation of his life exhibits the same tension: he has to admit that he was indeed the person who had that "being" in order to repudiate it and insist that it is not him after all. Since he is repudiating it at the moment, however, he is claiming that his life is *not* him. To use more Hegelian language, when AI looks at the "being," it holds itself apart from that "being." It judges that, while the "being" is itself, it is also the negative of itself. So AI does not yet posit or take that "being" to be itself (§238). The judgment that the "being" is itself remains for a later stage. For now, AI, as a free self-consciousness, takes the "being" to be its negation (§238).

Hegel uses a number of terms to characterize the "being" of AI in this stage. He describes the "being" as AI's, positedness, mediatedness and presupposedness (§238). The "being" is AI's "mediatedness," because, in this stage, it is the way in which AI developed or mediated itself, but is not the AI itself. AI is what it is in terms of content because it has gone through its process of "being," and so is mediated by the process of its "being," but is also not that "being." That "being" is only its mediatedness: an immediacy (completed, given whole) that is also its mediation. That "being" is the element through which AI defined itself in terms of content—its mediation—but since AI is separate from and not determined by that "being," the "being" is mere mediatedness, and not determinateness. Think of the old man again. At the end of his life, his identity is mediated by the whole process of his life. What he is now is mediated by that life, but he is also not that life. That life is merely his mediatedness but not his determinateness, since it does not determine him now. Now that his life is finished and given, it is an immediacy that is also his mediation, but because he is still a free self-consciousness, it does not determine what he is now.

The "being" of AI is also the way in which AI posited itself, made itself explicit, or defines or establishes itself. AI posited itself through its "being" both in the sense in which the "being" defines it or gives it its character, but also in the sense in which its "being" is the way in which it put itself out there into existence. Because its "being" includes the realm of Being, thereness or reality, its "being" is the way in which AI put itself out there into existence or actuality. At the same time, since that "being" is also not AI (is the negative of the Absolute Idea), it is *merely* AI's positedness. In the example of the old man, his life is how he defined himself or gave himself a character, and also how he put himself out there or made himself explicit in his objective life and the world of his day-to-day subjectivity. But since he is still a free self-consciousness and so is also not that life, that life is *merely* his positedness. It is merely how he made himself explicit, but does not determine him now.

Finally, because the process of "being" is finished or complete, from the point of view of AI, it is given or presupposed. Since AI is not determined by that "being," however, that "being" is *merely* its presupposedness. From the point of view of the old man, whose life is finished, that life is given or presupposed. There is nothing more that can be done with it. But since he is now saying that he is not that life, or is not determined by that life, that life is *merely* his presupposedness.

The Progression of the Speculative Method

The Absolute Idea still defines itself as separate from its "being," but it recognizes that it is both

The "being" of the Absolute Idea

The Absolute Idea's process of self-definition leads it to define itself by dividing into itself as unifying self-consciousness (its U-moment) and its "being." It sees that it is both U and S

"U and S"

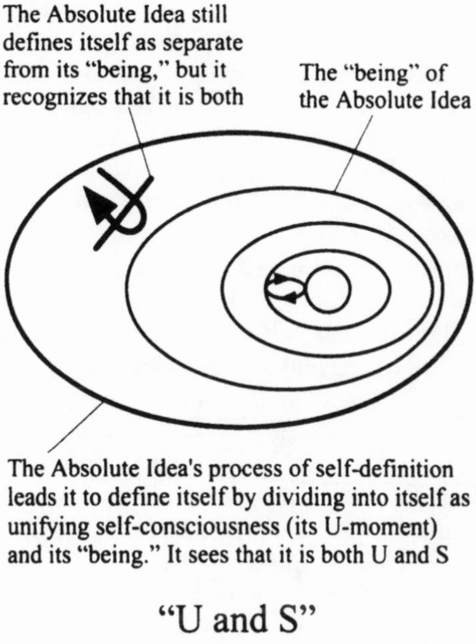

Figure 4.105

In the last stage, AI took itself to be the completed process of "being," but did not recognize that "being" as itself. It separated or distinguished itself from that "being," which it took to be its negation. The progression of the speculative method is the process through which AI moves toward the explicit judgment that it *is* its "being."

In the Beginning of the Speculative Method, AI defined itself merely as a "not"—as the negative of the "being," or as not-"being." Its denial that it is its "being," however, logically requires it to go on to say what it is, or to go on to define or determine itself. Suppose I start out by saying, for example, that I am not a cat. To say that I am not a cat is to logically imply that I am something else, that I have some other definition, determination or character that is not cat. Indeed, I can only succeed at being not-a-cat—it is only true that I am not-a-cat—if I am something else, if I have some other positive character. Similarly, as soon as AI says it is not "being," it implies that it is something else, some other, positive character. AI can only establish or prove that it is not-"being" by going on to say what it is instead. So its assertion that it is not-"being" must necessarily be followed up by an assertion of what it is instead. The logical progression of the speculative method is driven by AI's process of saying what it is.

AI begins this process of self-definition or self-determination by defining itself as the negation of the negative claim that it said it was in the last stage. It says that it is not-not-"being." My claim that I am not a cat, for instance, implies that I am something else. To be something else is, first of all, to be more than merely not-a-cat. To be something else is to have some other positive definition or character—a positive character that is not merely not-cat. My attempt to characterize myself, then, begins asserting that I have such a positive character by denying that I am merely not-cat. The first step I must take to say what positive character I am instead of cat, then, is to say that I am not not-a-cat. I assert the negation (not) of the negative (not-cat) that I said I was a moment ago. I assert that I am not (merely) not-cat, that I am not-not-cat.

The process of self-definition cannot stop there, however, AI has asserted that it is not merely a negative, that it has a positive identity beyond the negative. It must now go on to specify what that positive identity is. AI currently sees itself as a U. It is the unifying thought of its "being." Since every U or universal is a group or collection of items, a universal defines or determines itself by dividing into the elements that make it up (cf. Disjunctive Judgment). As a universal, AI's process of self-definition begins the same way: it defines itself by dividing into the elements that it groups. AI divides into two moments: the moment in which it is the unifying universal or whole (its U-moment), and its "being" (its S-moment). The old man at the end of his life has the same two moments: this one, in which he is the unifying self-consciousness (his U-moment), and his lived life or "being" up until this moment (his S-moment).

Because AI is an Idea—a fleshed out concept—it cannot really be divided into independently separate chunks or items, but only into moments of the whole. The life of a plant, for instance, cannot be divided into separate items. To separate out any specific moment would require stopping the plant's process as an Idea—i.e. killing it. As an Idea, the plant is the whole process of its life. But an Idea is still a *universal*—a *concept* that pushes out into thereness, or is both concept and object. AI cannot be a universal—even in the most basic sense as a bunch or group of items—unless it includes more than one element. AI can be a unifying universal only if it has some thing*s* to unify. Since AI only has two moments—its U- and S-moments—it can be a unifying universal only if it is *both* its U- and S-moments. AI therefore recognizes that it can have a positive character as a basic, unifying universal only if it is *both* U and S. AI thinks of itself now as U *and* S. It says or asserts its positive character by asserting "U and S." Neither its U-moment nor its S-moment can stand on its own. Each moment only has significance for the whole AI. They can be separated from one another only as discrete periods (moments) in the process of the whole Absolute Idea.

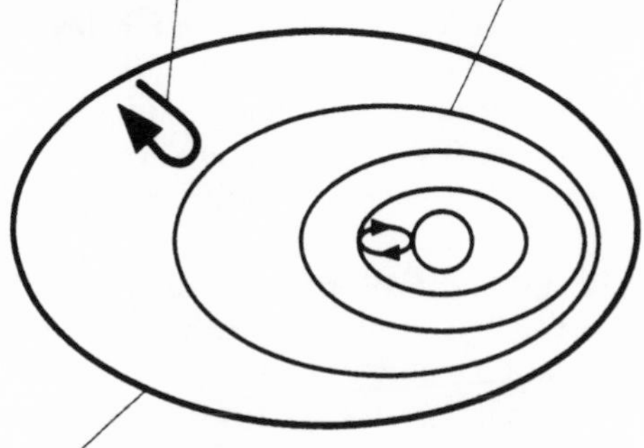
The Absolute Idea now acknowledges its "for itself" activity with its "being"
The "being" of the Absolute Idea
The Absolute Idea can have a positive character only if its U-moment reflects the S-moment, and the S-moment can have a character only if it reflects the U-moment. The Absolute Idea thus recognizes that it can be what it is only if U *is* S
"U is S"

Figure 4.106

In the (stage of the) Beginning of the Speculative Method, although *we* could see that AI was defined by the judgment "U is S," AI defined itself as the judgment "U is not S." But the judgment "U is not S" is contained in or implied by the judgment "U is S." The general form of judgment always contains a tension: the "is" asserts that the two elements in the judgment are related together, while the fact that two different terms are being used to refer to the two elements asserts that they are different (cf. The Judgment). In the Beginning, AI was "U is S" in the first sense, which stressed the difference between U and S. It took itself to be the unifying universal that was not its S, or not its "being." Now, AI will define itself as "U is S" in the first sense, or in the sense in which U is taken to be *related* to S.

U is the unifying universality over S, and S is U's content. U can be a universal (or group of items) only if it contains a multitude or divides. S is what U divides into. It contains the moments or multitude of U's "being." Hence U can be what it is as a universal only through S, or by presenting S. Moreover, because S is the content of U, whatever character U has, it has that character because of the character that S reflects. So S is the presentation of whatever character that U has. Think of the example of the old man, again. The old man's U-moment is his moment of free self-consciousness, while his S-moment is his life. It is true that his life does not completely define him, but his U-moment cannot have any positive character without it. Without the S-moment, the U-moment is nothing but an empty, undefined self-consciousness. Imagine, for instance, that the old man repudiates his life on his deathbed. He says, "I am not really that evil man who lived and did those things." Just before he draws his last breath, we ask him, "Who are you, then, instead?" He cannot say. There is nothing else. Without his S-moment, he has no other, positive identity. He can be nothing but the repudiation of his S-moment: a not, a naught, a null. AI is trying to specify what its positive character is like, and to do that, it needs its S-moment.

S, for its part, is equally dependent for its character on U. S is a multitude, a bunch of moments, in a life. It cannot be a whole or singular (S) at all without being held together by the U. The U is what gathers up or unifies all of the moments in the life. Moreover, whatever character the S can have will be contained in or grasped by the U. As the old man looks back on his "being" or life, his life is nothing but a bunch of moments. If that bunch of moments succeeds in having some unified character, or in adding up to something, what they add up to can only be grasped by his U-moment, by the unifying self-consciousness that is examining them now. Whatever character S has, then, can be captured or grasped only by U.

Because both U and S can have their characters or can be what they are only by reflecting into the other, they have the same sort of character, namely, each side can be what it is only by reflecting into the other. The reflective relationship that AI has with its "being" is contained in the "for itself" activity of form between AI and its "being"—the relationship represented by the looping "for itself" arrow that runs from AI to its "being" and back to AI. That "for itself" activity between AI and its "being" is the activity in which AI presents its "being" *for itself*, or through its own activity. Now that AI recognizes its own reflective relationship (as U) with its S or "being," it is no longer merely the unity and identity of S or "being," it is also the actively identifying universal over S or "being." It *made* S what it is. For AI, U *is* S because U identified or presented S, and S reflects U's identity. AI expresses the positive character that it has by saying or asserting that it is "U is S." AI is the identifying universal over its "being." Because AI is now acknowledging that it has "for itself" activity with its "being"—that it presented its being *for itself*, or through its own activity—I have removed the black bar from the diagram that represented the denial of the "for itself" activity of form in the last stage.

Thus, AI negates the negation or its earlier claim that "U is not S" by relating U and S together. It now genuinely has the judgment about itself that "U is S." It defines itself as the judgment "U is S." The negation of the last stage is not forgotten, however. That negation is sublated (cancelled but preserved), but not erased, in the form of the judgment "U is S." Since the form of judgment always includes the tension between the thought that the two terms are not the same and the thought that the two terms are the same, AI's current self-definition—"U is S"—contains *both* the thought that S and U are the same *and* the thought that S and U are not the same. The judgment itself includes both of those implications. Indeed, to say that two things are *related* already includes these two implications: when two things are related together they are both the same in some way (which explains their connection or relationship) and different in some way (which explains why there are two things and not one). So the claim that S and U are in a relationship, by itself, includes the implications both that U is S and that U is not S.

This "for itself" reflective relationship of form between U and S involves passing in thought from U to S and then from S back to U. According to this reflective relationship, U (AI) defines itself by reflecting into S. Since U is defining itself, this process of self-definition starts with U, passes through S and then points back to U (which is the element being defined). It is because this kind of reflective relationship involves a movement of "passing through"—passing from one side to the other and then back again—that I use the looping arrow to represent it (cf. the Introduction to Chapter Three). This reflective movement echoes the relationship between Essence and Shine in the Doctrine of Essence. Essence was the identifying concept over all of the concepts of thereness or Being from the Doctrine of Being, which were nothing but the Shine of Essence. Essence had its thereness or being in the Shine (cf. Identity). Like Essence, AI reflects in or has its shine or out-thereness in its "being."

The "for itself" relationship also explains why AI's thought is both synthetic and analytic, as Hegel suggests (§239R). Since S or its "being" is defined as completed, finished, or given, when AI begins with S and then thinks about U (the process represented by the part of the looping arrow that returns from S to U [i.e. AI]), AI's thought begins with what is given, which is the analytic method. At the same time, the identity or character of all of the moments of S is not contained in S itself, but only in U. Whatever all of the moments of S add up to, whatever character they have as a whole, is only available to U, to the unifying—and now also defining—self-consciousness over them. U makes S what it is. When AI, as U, defines S or gives S its character, it adds to the character of S synthetically, which is the synthetic method.

The synthetic relationship between U and S highlights another parallel between this logical stage and the relationship between Essence and Shine. Because S gets its character from and is only *for* U, S is not given or immediate after all, as Hegel apparently suggested in a lecture (§239A). S gets to be what it is only after it is synthetically constituted by U. Hence, S is not in fact "what simply and immediately *is*" (§239A), to use the language of Hegel's students. This is the same situation that Shine was in at the beginning of Chapter Three. Shine was the whole realm of Being, or all of the categories or concepts from the Doctrine of Being in Chapter Two. The logical development of the Doctrine of Being had shown that those concepts cannot be defined without the Essence—which is why the realm of Being was renamed the "Shine" at the beginning of Chapter Three. Essence was not related to a stable "Being," capable of being defined on its own. Instead, Essence was related to something that could not be defined on its own, but could only be defined as the Shine of the Essence. Similarly, here, AI will conclude that it is also related, *not* to its "being," but to its Shine. Unlike Essence, however, AI is related to its Shine through a doubly "for itself" relationship: a "for itself" relationship of content, which is represented in the diagram by the fact that AI's bubble surrounds and embraces its "being," and a "for itself" relationship of form in which it *presents* S *for itself*, or through its own activity, which is represented in the diagram by the looping arrow between AI and its "being." However, although the distinction between content and form had been introduced when the concepts of Essence and Shine were introduced in Chapter Three, the relationship between Essence and Shine really implies both an embracing "for itself" relationship of content and a "for itself" relationship of form, which explains why the relationship could be depicted in both the side-by-side view (with the looping arrow that later came to represent the "for itself" relationship of form) and in the nested-bubble view (in which Essence was depicted as a bubble surrounding the Shine—the depiction that later came to represent the "for itself" relationship of content). In the relationship between Essence and Shine, the relationships of identity and form (presentation) were together in an immediate way at the same time. Essence was the Identity of Shine, but Shine was also the presentation of Essence, or the way in which Essence shined, had its thereness, or showed up (cf. Chapter Three, Section V). AI also contains both the relationship of identity and form (or presentation), but the two processes or relationships have been *developed* separately by the logic, and no longer occur together in an immediate way.

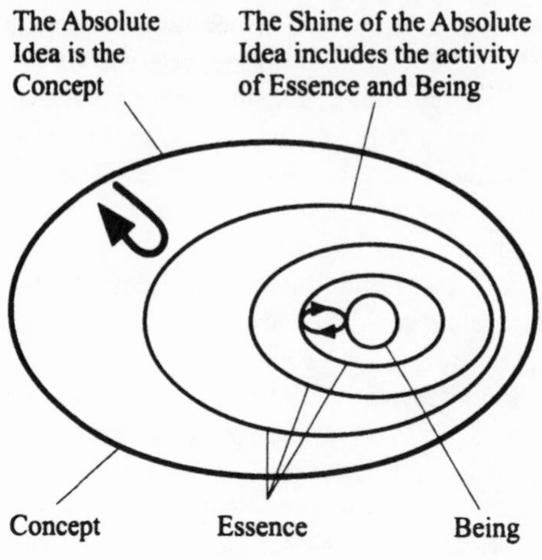
The Absolute Idea is the Concept
The Shine of the Absolute Idea includes the activity of Essence and Being
Concept
Essence
Being

Figure 4.107

There are two important parallels between the relationship between AI (as U) and S here, and the relationship between Essence and Shine at the beginning of the Doctrine of Essence. First, the Absolute Idea is now not merely a *unifying* universal over S, but also the *identifying* universal over S. Whatever character all of the moments in S add up to is given to it by U. Essence and Shine had this same relationship. Because the elements in the Shine could not be distinguished by any qualitative or quantitative perceptual character, their nature could only be grasped by an identifying universal or Essence that was not merely a perceptual concept (cf. Transition to Essence in Chapter Two). As in that stage, here, AI has become the identifying universal or essence over S. Second, S has no overall character of its own without U. Again, whatever character all of the moments in S add up to is available only to U. Hence S can no longer be thought of as a given or presupposed "being." Like the Shine, S can have a character only by reflecting U, or by being the Shine of U. For AI, then, S is no longer its "being," but is now its Shine. In the diagram, the bubble that was the "being" bubble has been redefined as the "Shine" bubble.

The Absolute Idea is an Idea, which was defined as a fleshed-out concept (see the introduction to The Doctrine of the Idea). Moreover, in Chapter Three, the Shine was the perceptual manifestation (or flesh) of the Essence—the whole realm of Being or thereness that had been developed in the Doctrine of Being in Chapter Two (see the Introduction to Chapter Three). Now that AI has a Shine, rather than a "being," it genuinely has the character (in an "in itself" sense) of an Idea (§241). AI is a fleshed-out concept. It is fleshed out in its Shine.

As AI goes through the process of defining its character, it must take into account both itself as U or identifying universal and its S or Shine. This process will activate all of the earlier stages of the logic. S is not static. It is a whole life or process that has its own development. In particular, S's activity includes all of the logical activity and all of the stages of development in the Doctrines of Essence and Being in earlier chapters. AI's Shine is an active universal that divides into several layers of Essence, and into Being. These layers are represented in the diagram by the layers of nested bubbles within AI. Moreover, AI itself (as U) is the Concept. It is the same bubble that grew out of, and underwent, all of the processes of development of the Concept earlier in this chapter. Because AI cannot have a positive identity at all without both its U- and S-moments, it will have to take into account all of these layers as it goes through its process of self-definition. As AI defines its character, then, it will set into motion all of the logical developments in the Doctrines of Being, Essence and the Concept.

Hegel says that, within the sphere of Being, the logical progression takes the form of passing over (§240). We saw precisely this sort of logical progression in Chapter Two, where Being passed into Nothing, something-other passed into something-other, measure passed into the measureless, and so on. "Passing over" is the general way of characterizing relationships between things in the realm of Being or reality. Since everything in reality is defined in opposition to its "other," everything can be what it is only by passing over into its other, or only by opposing it to its other. Things also come and go temporally: they pass over from Being to not-Being. Motion in reality can also be characterized as a relationship of "passing over": when a car moves from one place to another, it has gone from here to there, and so "passed over" into another sort of thereness or reality (cf. Chapter One, Section VIII). In the sphere of Essence, Hegel says, logical progression will take the form of reflection—of shining into an opposed concept. An identifying concept (Essence) is what it is by reflecting in and being reflected by something that shows up in reality (its Shine) and vice versa. An identifying concept and what it identifies are reflected into one another in the sense that they determine one another. In the Doctrine of Essence, other sorts of relational, identifying concepts—such as ground and grounded, cause and effect and so on—all reflected into and mutually defined one another. The concept of existence, too, turned out to be a concept of reflection because it captured the thought of a successful reflective relationship between ground and grounded. In the sphere of the Concept, the logical progression is driven by the tension between universality and singularity—a tension defined by the fact that, while U is S (or S is U), U is also not S (or S is not U). Again, the judgment "U is S" says both that S and U are the same (which is asserted by the "is") and that U and S are different (since there are two terms used to capture them). Moreover, even when there were three elements in play—Universality, Particularity and Singularity—because P is a singularity (S) in relation to U, and P is a universal (U) in relation to S, the relationship between U and P, and P and S can still be characterized as a relationship between universality and singularity. The logical movement in the Doctrine of the Concept traced the development of this relationship within the Concept.

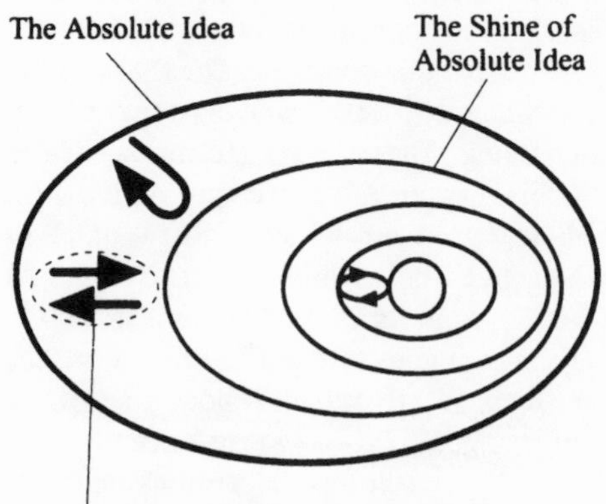

The Absolute Idea's process of self-definition leads it into another spuriously infinite, back-and-forth process, this time between Absolute Idea (as U) and its Shine (as S)

Figure 4.108

Not only will AI's process of self-definition set into motion all of the logical developments so far, it will also lead to another bad, spuriously infinite, back-and-forth process—this time between AI or the Concept (the "first sphere" that Hegel refers to [§§241-2]) and its Shine (or the "second sphere" that Hegel refers to [§§241-2]). Because AI needs both its U- and S-moments to be what it is, it can have a positive identity or definition only if the character it says it has is presented, exemplified or expressed by its Shine. So to define itself, AI must present the Shine. At the same time, the Shine can have a character at all only insofar as the characterizing universal (i.e. AI) characterizes it, or defines what it is. So the Shine can be what it is only through AI. But AI can be what it is only through its Shine, which can be what it is only through AI, and so on, endlessly. AI's attempt to give itself a positive character will therefore lead to an infinitely spurious, back-and-forth process between AI and its Shine. To use the example of the old man again, the old man can have a positive definition only if the identity he gives himself (his U) is exemplified, presented or out there in his Shine. His question, "what am I?" requires him to look at the way he was presented in his Shine. But his Shine has a character only insofar as he gives it one. So when he looks at the Shine to see what it is like at any moment, his question, "what character does the Shine have here?" requires him to say who he is. His process of defining himself will therefore require him to go back and forth between his judgment about his definition or character (his AI) and his Shine.

Suppose, for example, that the old man thinks that he is (or was, since he is dying) a forgiving person. I am deliberately using the example of forgiveness to recall the comparison we made above—drawing on an example from Hegel's lectures—between a child's concept of forgiveness and an old man's concept of forgiveness (see Absolute or Speculative Idea). While both the child and the old man can have the same proposition as a thought—say, the proposition "one must forgive others"—the child's thought is empty compared to the old man's because the old man's thought is in*formed* by a whole life process. At one time, for instance, the old man may have defined forgiveness as an act that puts away or sets aside a past wrong: people do something wrong, they apologize and agree not to do the wrong anymore; you forgive, you set the wrong aside, and move on. Think of this definition as forgiveness_1. On many occasions, this concept of forgiveness would have guided his behavior or life, and so would be reflected in some moments of his Shine. But life has a way of changing our conceptions. Suppose that, over time, he came to think of forgiveness in a more complicated way. Sometimes people do not apologize. Sometimes, they do not change. Sometimes, forgiveness means finding a way to live with an ongoing wrong, rather than setting it aside. As he lived, then, his concept of forgiveness may have been changed or revised: it may have changed from forgiveness_1 to, say, forgiveness_2. As a result, the forgiving behavior that he presented during the course of his life (in his Shine) would have been different from one moment to another. When the old man thinks now about his character as a forgiving person, he must look to his Shine to see how his character as a forgiving person was reflected in his Shine. But how his character as a forgiving person was reflected in his Shine at any moment is determined by him (as the characterizing U or AI), that is to say, by his concept or definition of what forgiveness is. So in his attempt to give himself a positive identity he is driven to look at his Shine, but his Shine can only have a character based on his concepts now, insofar as he gives it one, but then he can have his character only if it is reflected in the Shine again, and so on, endlessly. His process of defining himself leads to an endless, back-and-forth process between his AI and his Shine.

Hegel says that the fact that AI's (or Reason's) process of self-definition must include both the Concept (or Reason) and its Shine or manifestation ensures that neither AI (or Reason) nor its flesh is one-sided (§241). Only in this double movement, he says, are both fully defined or determined (§241).

Immediate Absolute Idea as Nature

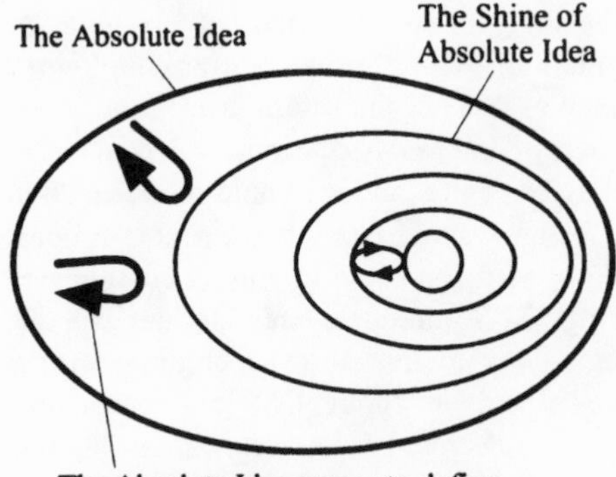
The Absolute Idea
The Shine of Absolute Idea
The Absolute Idea comes to define itself as the Being-for-itself or universal concept that captures the completed, back-and-forth process between its self-consciousness (U) and its Shine (S).
"U is S and S is U"

Figure 4.109

Hegel's logic can never rest with a spurious infinity (see Spurious Infinity in Chapter Two). So long as AI's attempt to define itself is caught in an endless back-and-forth process, the definition can never be finished. The spurious infinity here is resolved in the same way that other spurious infinites have been resolved, namely, by a concept that embraces the whole process. Since neither AI's U-moment (self-consciousness) nor its S-moment (its Shine) can have their definitions or be what they are without the other, AI recognizes that its free self-consciousness and its Shine are non-indifferent toward one another. This recognition redefines AI as the thought of the unified identity that their non-indifference generates. AI's self-consciousness and the Shine are each merely a one-sided expression of a whole process that is the end toward which they both aim. Moreover, AI and the Shine each have the same character or are the same when looked at as separate but also non-indifferent or connected concepts (i.e. in an "in itself" sense [cf. Being-in-itself in Chapter Two]). They are "in themselves" the same (§243). Since AI is just the thought (self-consciousness) of its Shine, it has the same character that the Shine does and vice versa. The non-indifference of the two sides is sublated—cancelled but also preserved—in the thought of AI redefined as a finished and hence completely defined process of both sides. At the end of the whole process, both AI as self-consciousness and its Shine or flesh are merely first steps. Who the old man is as a forgiving person, for instance, is the one character at which both his self-consciousness and his life (his Shine) aimed. He defines himself as exactly the person at which the whole process aimed during his self-conscious life. Similarly, AI is redefined as the final, summary thought, judgment, statement or concept of what its positive identity is like as a finished product at the end of the whole process of its self-conscious life, or the process of both its self-consciousness (the former AI) and its life (the Shine). To use Hegel's language, AI has become the universal that, although it still contains both non-indifferent sides preserved within it, is the thought of their unity, in which their non-indifference has been overcome or cancelled (§242). AI is redefined by the back-and-forth process as a concept that embraces the whole process (cf. World of Appearance, Condition as a Totality, and Chapter Three, Section V).

The redefinition of AI also redefines the Shine. The Shine is now not only the objective life (i.e. the S-moment), but also the self-consciousness (i.e. the U-moment). When the self-consciousness (the former AI) is redefined as the summary thought of its whole, *self-conscious* life, it has both its self-consciousness (the U-moment) and its Shine (objective life) before it as its object. As in Transition to Cognition and the stage of Absolute Idea, the redefinition of the overarching, embracing concept (AI in this case) leads the embraced concept or object to come to include the definition that the embracing concept used to have. Here, when AI or self-consciousness is redefined as the summary thought of the whole process, the object or Shine is redefined to include self-consciousness. The Shine's redefinition now includes two moments: the self-consciousness (the U-moment) and the life (the former S-moment or Shine itself).

Because the summary thought is the overarching, embracing concept that includes everything else—a logical status represented in the diagram by the fact that its bubble surrounds everything else—and because the former Shine is still an Idea (see Absolute Idea), the new AI is the being-for-itself of the Idea (the former Shine) (§244). A "being-for-itself" is a concept that has an independent character of its own by embracing both the sameness and thereness of an "other" (Attraction) as well as the differences or separation between itself and an "other" (Repulsion) that is not really an "other" for it. Like Being-for-itself in Chapter Two, the summary thought grasps the "in itself" sameness of the self-consciousness and the Shine. It is the *one whole identity* that both its self-consciousness and its Shine share. But because it is defining itself in its own thought, it also *presents* or offers the whole display of its self-conscious life as its self-definition, and so is separate from and opposed to its object or contents. Unlike earlier "for itself" concepts, however, since the summary thought draws its own judgment about its definition, it is triply "for itself," rather than merely doubly "for itself" (cf. the Introduction to this chapter). Not only does it (1) embrace its object for its content (the "for itself" relationship of content, represented in the diagram by the fact that its bubble surrounds the former Shine), (2) by presenting its object through its own activity or *for itself* (the "for itself" relationship of form represented in the diagram by the top "for itself" looping arrow), it now also (3) *thinks for itself*, or judges for itself, that it is both itself as free self-consciousness and its life. It is (1) for itself (embraces its content), (2) *for itself* (through its own activity of presentation or form), (3) for itself (in its own thought). This third layer of "for itselfness" is a second layer of "for itself" activity of form—since it is something the summary thought does through its own activity—and is represented in the diagram by a new "for itself" looping arrow that replaces the two straight arrows depicting the spuriously infinite, back-and-forth process between AI and the former Shine. The summary thought stops the endless back-and-forth process of trying to define itself as self-consciousness in relation to it Shine by defining itself in its own judgment as the completed whole process of its self-conscious life.

Because the summary thought defines itself as a one whole or being-for-itself, it is no longer a U, but an S. Earlier, AI defined itself as the universal (U) unity and defining concept over its "being," life or Shine (as an S). Now, however, the self-consciousness has defined itself as a one, whole, singularity or S. Moreover, it also sees that the former Shine includes two moments and so is no longer simply an S or singularity, but a U, unity or universality over a multitude. Its self-definition must therefore be characterized with the judgment "S is U" instead of "U is S": it judges that it is a relationship between a whole or singularity (S) and a universal (U) or multitude. This new self-definition sublates its earlier one (cancels and preserves it). The former AI still recognizes that it has the two earlier distinctions—itself as free self-consciousness or U and itself as Shine or singularity (S)—within it. As a result, its earlier characterization of itself as a universal unity and identity (U) over its whole Shine (taken to be a singularity or one [S]) still remains or is preserved. It still defines itself as "U is S." But it also now defines itself as "S is U." The summary thought's self-definition must therefore be characterized with the judgment "U is S and S is U."

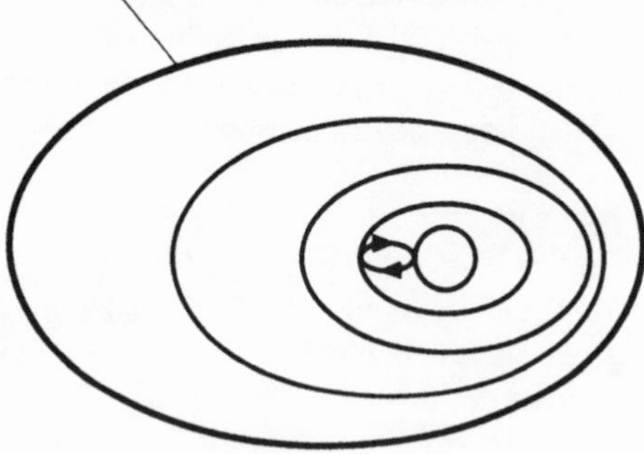
The Absolute Idea has become a new immediacy: Reason now taken to be fleshing itself out in the objective world in an immediate way. It is Nature

Figure 4.110

Since the summary thought is a being-for-itself that embraces its whole self-conscious life as its contents "for itself," or through its own activity of thought, it is an independent concept that has a definition on its own. It has no "other" to which it must be related for its definition. It is a simple whole or one filled with contents. The details of the relationship that it had with its contents therefore slip into the background as no longer logically active. I have eliminated all of the internal arrows representing the relationship between the former AI and the former Shine in the diagram to represent this change. Once the old man, for instance, grasps his final self-definition, he no longer thinks about all the processes that led up to it. His self-definition presupposes but also replaces the details of the process that gave rise to it, since it captures his character or his "nature" as a completed, whole process.

Since the internal relationships have sunk into the background, however, the summary thought no longer has any oppositions in it. As a result, it has become a new immediacy—an immediate, given whole—in the same way that the Object became an immediate, given whole at the beginning of the Doctrine of the Object. It is simply the whole completed process of thought or Reason as an Idea, fleshed out in an immediate way into the realm of subjectivity and objectivity. It is the thought of the one identity of the self-conscious, subjective and objective world, taken as a completed, immediate whole. For the old man, for example, now that the details of his life have slipped into the background, he has become a new kind of immediacy. He is the simple thought or summary judgment of a whole process of self-conscious subjectivity and objectivity taken together. That thought is his nature, his character, now taken to be an immediate, completed, fleshed-out whole. Of course, we are not thinking of him as an immediate being in the world, but as a completed, completely fleshed-out, process of self-conceptualized consciousness. He is his nature.

This summary thought of the completed, one identity of the self-conscious, subjective and objective world (as an immediate whole) is nature, or rather, Nature, with a capital "N." When completed Reason is thought of as fleshed out in the world in an immediate way, it is Nature. The immediate nature of Reason is Nature. Nature is the immediate expression of Reason's self-conscious life. To put the same point the other way around, Reason expresses itself—both its self-conscious understanding and its objectivity—in an immediate way as Nature—not dead nature, or mere nature, but nature *characterized.* How Nature is characterized has yet to be specified (because of the lack of internal arrows or processes), except that it has been grasped by a reasonable and well-worked out system or apparatus of self-consciously systematized concepts. *N*ature is not merely an account of all the accidents of nature, but an account of nature as a conceptual system, as a unity of the self-conscious subjective and objective realms as a *completed* process. For it is only when nature is conceived of as finished or complete that it has its character or identity as a whole conceptual and real system. Nature—with a capital "N"—is completed or finished nature-*theorized* or nature-thought-through. It is the thought of natural processes or life as a completely conceptualized (and hence self-conscious) and fleshed-out system of concepts and thereness. It is the identifying thought of the nature of nature, or the general concept of nature. Thus Nature, as a thought, is not dumb at all, as our more contemporary conception of nature might suggest. Nature is nature-theorized. It has Reason in it, and that is why we can grasp it (cf. Chapter One, Sections One and Two).

The Absolute Idea is now truly an *absolute* Idea. It is an Idea because it is a U-as-S (or both a U [universal] and S [singularity]) that is completely fleshed out. But it is an *absolute* Idea because its process of being fleshed out is now the result of the process of the whole itself. The Absolute Idea has defined itself as the overarching U-as-S as the result of its own activity (cf. Absolute Relationship in Chapter Three).

The move to Nature ends the process of development of Hegel's logic, and begins the process of development of a new subject, namely, the philosophy of nature. The *Encyclopaedia of the Philosophical Sciences in Outline*, of which the *Encyclopaedia Logic* is only the first part, goes on to discuss the Philosophy of Nature and then the Philosophy of Spirit. In effect, as Hegel mentions in the *Science of Logic*, the process of development of logic has ended where it began, thus closing the first circle of philosophical subject matters (see the Introduction, Section V). The Absolute Idea has ended with a simple unity of immediate Being, which is just where the logical journey began. Of course, the immediate Being we had at the beginning is not the same as the immediate Being we have now. At the beginning of the logic, immediate Being was abstract and empty. In the diagram, it was an empty bubble. Now, the immediate Being we have before us is Being as a self-comprehended Idea. In the diagram, it is a whole that is filled with all the other elements. However, although the Being we have now is filled with content, it is once again immediate in the sense that it is a complete and simple whole.

V. Wrap up Concept: Comments on Syntax

Some of the syntactic patterns from the Doctrines of Being and Essence are repeated in the Doctrine of the Concept:

(1) Logical moments defined by the same sort of spurious, infinite progresses that were in the Doctrines of Being and Essence appear (cf. Transition to the Empty Judgment of Identity and Negative Infinite Judgment; Transition to Idea; The Process of the Genus; The Spurious Infinity of Finite Willing; Progression of the Speculative Method; Immediate Absolute Idea as Nature), and are resolved by a concept that embraces the whole process and introduces a new level of ideality or universality.

(2) Mutually defining "in itself" opposition from the Doctrine of Being also returned (cf. Chemism, Abstract Purpose, The Spurious Infinity of Finite Willing, Immediate Absolute Idea as Nature).

(3) A unity between two elements is at first defined as a kind of gluing together (cf. Immediate Idea or Life), but later the two elements go through a process in which they define themselves in relation to one another, and hence glue themselves together, so to speak (see, for instance, the Process of the Genus through the stages of Cognition, in which the elements that were merely glued together or had only an immediate connection in Immediate Idea or Life defined themselves in relation to one another through their own processes).

(4) At first a process is merely implied, but then the logical elements go through the process (see all the stages of Purpose).

(5) Logical elements "fall apart" (see Transition to Mechanism).

The Doctrine of the Concept also introduces three new logical processes. First, it introduces the judgment, which is a way of linking two logical elements together with the concept of being. As suggested in the Introduction, Hegel's logic is an exploration of the many layers and versions of "being." A quality is a type of "being"; a quantity is a type of "being"; existence is a type of "being"; a cause is a type of "being," life is a type of "being," and so on. Another type of "being" is the "being" that is used to link a subject and predicate together, namely, the "being" of the copula "is." In the stages of Judgment, Hegel explores the different sorts of being that link together a subject and predicate. There is the sort of "is" that links an individual thing with an immediate quality (Qualitative or Immediate Judgment), the sort of "is" that links a genus and species—actually, there are a few of these (Categorical Judgment of Necessity, Hypothetical Judgment of Necessity, Disjunctive Judgment of Necessity, Assertoric Judgment), and so on.

The logical operators "or," "and" and "if . . . then . . .," which also appear in the stages of Judgment, capture kinds of being that involve relationships of being. "A and B," for instance, is just a shorthand way of saying that A is and B is too. It asserts a being in which both A and B have being. "A or B" also asserts a being that involves a relationship of being. It says there is a state of being in which A is or B is. Since Hegel's "or" is inclusive, "A or B" asserts the state of being in which at least one of A or B has being (and possibly both do). "If A, then B" is also a shorthand way of asserting a sort of being that involves a relationship of being. It says that there is a state of being according to which, if A is (or has being), then B is (or has being).

The second new logical process that the Doctrine of the Concept introduces is the syllogism. The syllogism is a more developed form of the judgment, but, like the judgment, it is a form of "being" that links logical elements together. The syllogism captures the "is" of implication—the sort of "is" according to which a judgment implies another judgment. In the early stages of the syllogism, this sort of "is" is an "is" of deduction: the cart is squeaking, the cart squeaks when it's cold, therefore it is cold (Qualitative Syllogism). A deduction of this sort is a kind of "is"-ness because it captures the way in which a set of judgments leads to, adds up to, or "is" a conclusion. Purpose is another example of an "is" of implication. A purpose is a judgment that implies other judgments. To use the example that I used throughout the discussion of purpose, if I adopt the purpose of making dinner, that purpose can only be realized through a series of judgments implied by the original purpose: "dinner is salad," "salad is lettuce," "salad is this lettuce." Ultimately, that series of judgments links the original purpose with singularity, or with individual existing things. Indeed, until a purpose mixes itself up with singularity, it "is" nothing at all, or has no "being" (or existence) at all. The purpose of making dinner is realized and has being or existence only when it is translated into singularity—into individual bits of lettuce, chicken, potatoes or whatever else the real salad is made out of.

The third logical process introduced in the Doctrine of the Concept is one in which a universality particularizes or defines itself by dividing into the elements that make it up (see Disjunctive Syllogism; Absolute Mechanism; Living-ness as the Genus-in-Itself, The Progression of the Speculative Method). A universal is a group of items, and so is defined by dividing into the items that it groups—categories, individuals or both. "Fruit," as a universal, for example, is defined by the categories it groups—pear (as a type), apple (as a type), orange (as a type) and so on—and also by the individual (pieces of) fruit that it groups. The fact that a universal can be defined in relation both to the categories into which it divides as well as the individual items into which it divides, however, was foreshadowed in Chapter Three by the ambiguity in the movement of the stage of the Necessary, in which the Necessary (which later became the Concept) could be defined either in relation to the Condition as a Totality—which was the set of all the concepts or Conditions that make it up—or Possibility—which was the set of all of the individual existing items that make it up.

In the Introduction and in the wrap-up to Chapter One, I suggested that Hegel's concept of necessity is largely a concept of exhaustion: once all the combinations and permutations of the current logical elements have been exhausted, then a new move or the introduction of a new logical element in the next stage is necessitated. Hegel explicitly defined necessity as a kind of exhaustion in the stage of The Necessary in Chapter Three. There, he defined necessity as the presence of all the conditions: once all the conditions are there, then whatever they add up to necessarily follows. We can characterize this definition of necessity as a kind of exhaustion: once all the conditions are exhausted, in the sense that there are no more conditions to go through, then whatever they add up to necessarily follows. The same sort of necessity—necessity as exhaustion—is at work in this chapter as well. In Abstract Judgment, for instance, the first judgment says *S* is U—where the emphasis is on the S as the solid element. Here, the "is" attaches to the U, so that the sentence reads "*S* (emphasis on the S) (is-U)." The second judgment says S is *U*—where the emphasis is on U as the solid element. Here, the "is" attaches to the S: "(S-is) *U* (emphasis on the U, as the solid element)." The idea that U is the solid element, however, can also be expressed by putting the judgment the other way around: "*U* (emphasis on the U) (is-S)." Put this way, Abstract Judgment contains the two judgments "S is U" and "U is S." There are only the two abstract elements, namely S and U, there are only two possible combinations of judgment for these elements: "S is U" and "U is S." So "S is U" and "U is S" exhaust all possible versions of the abstract judgment "S is U," and Abstract Judgment is exhaustive.

The same sense of necessity as exhaustion can be seen in the stages of Qualitative Judgment. Here is a summary of those stages:

S is U (where U is a quality)
S is not-U (where the "not" attaches to the "U" [S is not that quality])
S is U (or) S is not-U (but not both) (a spurious, back-and-forth infinity)
S is-not U (where the "not" attaches to the "is")
S is S (or) U is U
S is-not (that)-U (infinitely) (a spurious infinity)

In the first stage of Qualitative Judgment, "S is U" says that a singularity is universal. Here, the universal is defined as some quality, or as a sensible universal. In the next judgment, the "not" attaches to the "U": "not-U." The judgment "S is not-U" says that S is not the particular qualitative U. The next step involves an infinite process of going back and forth from one judgment to the other: either S is U, or S is not-U, but not both. This infinite back-and-forth process can also be expressed as a single judgment with a hidden or implied exclusive "or": "S is U (or) S is not-U (but not both)." Since "S is U" and "S is not-U" are the only two options, there are no additional options left out. S is either U or not-U, and that's it. Either one is true, or the other is true, *ad infinitum*. The possibilities for S here are exhausted. It expresses the exclusivity that the logical operator "not" has in the context of perceptual judgments. For standard perceptual claims, either something is, or it is "not." It must be either one or the other, and is never both. Either the rose is red, or the rose is not red, and it is never both. In the fourth judgment, the "not" attaches to the "is" rather than to the "U": "S is-not U." It says that S is in general not a sensible universal. Because some roses are soft and some are not, the rose in general (or as a whole) is-not soft. The sensible quality of softness does not apply to the rose is general, or to the rose as a type. The general denial that S is a U can also be written as "not (S is U)," or, in general, it is not the case that S is U. To use the example of the rose, this judgment would say that it is not the case (in general) that the rose (as a type) is soft. Here, then, are the various permutations of judgments employing "S," "not" and "U" (where U is currently defined as a sensible universal) in this development:

S is U
S is not-U
S is U (or) S is not-U (but not both)
not (S is U)
S is S
U is U
S is-not U (infinitely)

In the list of judgments, the "not" occupies all possible positions within the judgment "S is U"—with the exception of one. The "not" attaches to U by itself, to the whole judgment "S is U," and to the "is" (infinitely). The "not" never attaches to S by itself, however. Judgments of thereness or quality always presuppose singularity. When we say, for instance, that the rose (S) is red (U), we presuppose the presence and givenness of the singularity or rose. The denial of the presence of the rose—not-rose, or not-S—never comes up. Because qualitative judgments presuppose the presence or thereness of singularity, "not-S" never comes up. The list also contains every possible pairing of elements: S:U (or U:S); S:S and U:U.

The stages of the Judgment of Reflection capture all the modalities of the judgment "S is U": singularity ("S is U" could also be written "one (S is U)"), plurality ("some"), and totality ("all"). Because Hegel includes both the positive and negative versions of plurality—some S's are U, some S's aren't—his treatment of plurality is exhaustive. Some S's are U, some S's are not U, and that all the S's there are—there are no S's left over.

The stages of the Judgment of Necessity capture the relationships between S and U as totalities. Since both are totalities, either side can be the whole while the other is the divisions of the whole, or the way in which the whole expresses itself. The conjunction "if . . . then . . ." expresses the necessary relationship that a totality has with its expressions or divisions in terms of their presence or thereness: if the totality is (is there), then any of its expressions is (there) too, and if any of its expressions is (is there), then the totality is (there) too. The disjunct "or" expresses the nature of a totality *per se* (as a totality, or as the totality of its expressions or divisions): the totality is both any one of its expressions ("B or C or D etc.") as well as the completed list of its expressions ("B and C and D etc.").

The stages of the Judgment of Necessity complete the presentation of the basic logical operators found in contemporary sentential or propositional logic. The first operator, negation, is in Qualitative Judgment. The fact that Hegel introduces negation in the stages of Qualitative Judgment while he introduces the other logical operators in the Judgment of Necessity anticipates some debates in more recent modal logic. Negation arguably captures the contingency of things and judgments: S may be U or not-U, and the judgment "S is U" may be true or not true. Whether S is U, or "S is U" is true is dependent or contingent on the nature of S and on the U in question. The other operators, however, seem to assume a certain sort of necessity. The truth of the assertion "A and B" is not treated as dependent on anything. If "A and B" is true, its truth is a matter of necessity. Today, this assumption is called the Rule of Necessitation. According to this Rule, theorems in logic are necessarily true. The fact that Hegel placed all of the operators except for negation within the Judgment of Necessity suggests that he, too, recognized the element of necessity that underpins these logical operators. Some more contemporary logicians have criticized the Rule of Necessitation, however. Arthur Prior, for instance, criticized standard modal logical systems for failing to take the contingency of things in the world seriously enough. He suggested that the Rule of Necessitation improperly presupposed that existing things exist necessarily (Prior 1968, 48). Hegel addresses this presupposition about the necessary existence of its objects or elements—although he distinguishes the "if . . . then . . ." connector from the others on this score. The judgment "A and B" presupposes the existence of both A and B, while the judgment "A or B" presupposes the existence of at least one of either A or B. Unlike these two judgments, however, the judgment "if A, then B" does not presuppose the existence of either of its elements. The conditional judgment presupposes the necessity of the relationship between A and B, but does not presuppose their existence, Hegel says.

The stages of the Judgment of the Concept express all the possibilities of successful connection between singularity and an identifying universal. If the singularity or "this" is properly connected to the universal "house," then the "this" is a successful house: it is "R"—good, correct. Whether the "this" is properly connected to the universal depends on how it is constituted. If the specific house lacks a roof, for instance, or windows, then it is a less successful "house." Its constitution makes it a bad house. If the "this" is constituted in a way that lacks a connection to the universal "house"—when the "this" is really a dog, for instance—then the singularity is a very bad house. Taken together, the

Judgments of the Concept say that, for every "this" singularity that is connected to a universal, either the connection is a success (good, correct) ("This A is R"), or it is not ("This A is not R"), depending on how the "this" is constituted ("This A, constituted thus-and-so, is or is not R").

The logical development of Hegel's stages of the syllogism is also quite tight. As I argued in the discussion of syllogism above (see Comparing the EL- and SL-Developments of Qualitative Syllogism), if the judgments of the syllogism are transitive and the syllogisms themselves are reversible, then each triad of syllogism is exhaustive. In that case, the move from one triad to the next is necessitated by the exhaustion of the earlier form of the syllogism.

The Doctrines of the Object and of the Idea returned once again to the more familiar patterns of bubbles and arrows from the Doctrines of Being and Essence. Here, the diagrams themselves help to capture the tightness of the step-by-step development. For these sections, I leave it to the reader to decide to what degree Hegel is successful in keeping his promise that each stage is necessary and driven by earlier stages.

VI. Epilogue: Hegel's Materialism, Optimism and Faith

At the end of Chapter Three, I argued that Hegel's account of the stage of Reciprocal Action suggests that matter can be independent and causal in relation to Thought (or Reason), and that Hegel therefore offers an account of the relationship between matter and Thought that is neither neatly idealist nor neatly materialist. The question about whether Hegel is able to maintain some degree of materialism becomes especially acute here at the end of the logic, when everything culminates in the "Absolute Idea" (*die absolute Idee*). That the logic culminates in the "Absolute Idea" seems highly idealist, and not at all materialist. However, an "Idea" is a fleshed-out concept that includes its complete and completed process of fleshing out into thereness, or into the sensible world (see the introduction to the Doctrine of the Idea). When the connection between the concept and the process of fleshing-out is an immediate one, the Idea is living-ness or being-alive generally. So, for instance, the Idea of "fruit" would be the concept or essence "fruit" along with the completed processes of the different sorts of fruit in the world. We can think of those processes—the processes of all the bananas, apples, pears and so on—as the "life" of the Idea of "fruit." They are the way in which "fruit" as a concept or essence lives.

When Absolute Idea becomes Nature, it is still an Idea, and so includes a subjective and objective process. It is a summary thought about the character of the completed subjective and objective process, and is embodied in the processes of the objective or material world. The Absolute Idea's self-consciousness (U-moment) as well as its life (S-moment) remain preserved in its final thought of its one identity (§242). Moreover, as in Reciprocal Action in Chapter Three, in which the world of Accidentality causes changes in Reason, in the spuriously infinite, back-and-forth process between the self-consciousness (the U-moment) and its Shine or life, the life continues to have effects on and cause changes in the self-consciousness. Take the example of the old man once again, which I used throughout the discussion of Absolute Idea above. The "Absolute Idea" of the old man is his summary thought about his nature or identity at the end of his life. That summary thought takes account of his life-process as a self-consciousness and as a physical or material being, and so includes his material life. Moreover, so long as he is alive, his objective life has effects on his self-consciousness. The objective life loses its efficacy in the summary thought only because his back-and-forth process or life is finished, but the summary thought does not erase the fact that the objective life remains effective so long as the process is on-going. Just as the old man's final thought about his identity does not erase the fact that his life shaped his self-consciousness, so the Absolute Idea's thought of its one identity at the end of its process of development does not erase the fact that the objective world also shaped it. Because the Absolute Idea or Reason is the summary thought about a completed process, the process has to happen first, before the summary thought can summarize it later. In that case, the summary thought has no direct causal control over the process. When the old man summarizes his life in a thought at the end of his life, for example, that thought changes nothing about how his life went. It has no direct control or causal power over the course of his life. Again, we are imagining that the old man's life is completely finished, with the exception of this one thought. That last thought does not control anything in reality about how his life went.

There is perhaps an indirect sense, however, in which the Absolute Idea does control something about the life process. Because the summary self-consciousness is the same one that went through the life, the character or nature of that self-consciousness did have some causal influence over the life process. As the man was going through his life, his self-consciousness—its nature or character—helped to shape the course his life. Since the summary thought he has now *includes* (sublates) both his subjective and objective life, it did shape his life process to the degree that it includes those earlier moments of self-consciousness. Because the old man's summary thought includes the same conceptions that influenced what he did in reality and what happened to him during his life, the summary thought did, in an indirect sense, shape his life. The Absolute Idea has a similar relationship with its "life process." AI—as the summary thought of the subjective and objective world—contains the same concepts that were developed in and fleshed out by the material processes of the objective world. Because it includes the concepts that shaped the material processes of the world as they were going along, it also shaped the world. Still, since AI is a *summary* thought that happens after the fact, it does not directly control the world's "life processes."

While the Absolute Idea as the summary thought does not control its "life processes," the "life processes" also do not control it. Because it is thought, AI has a certain independence from its "life processes." The old man *is* his life, for instance, but, as thought or consciousness, he is also *not* that life, or not *only* that life. Although, as Hegel argues, AI can have a positive identity for itself only if it takes proper account of its "life processes" (cf. The Progression of the Speculative Method), since it is a free self-consciousness, it is still something beyond its subjective and objective life process, more than *merely* those processes. The old man's self-definition is empty if he repudiates the contents of his life, but, as a free self-consciousness, he is still more than merely his subjective and objective life processes. Those life processes are him, but they are also not him, or not only him. In a similar way, the world's processes *are* AI, but they are also *not* AI, or not *only* AI. AI is something *beyond* its "life processes." AI goes *beyond* the world not because it is not the world, but because it is a summary thought about itself, or a free, self-conscious thought.

So what does God, as the Absolute Idea, turn out to be, in Hegel's logical story? God is the self-consciousness that has the world and its process of conceptual development as His life, or the way in which He has His being. Thus, God is the world, or better, perhaps, the world is God. But, according to Hegel's conception of AI, that God is also *beyond* this world. Just as the old man both is and is not only his life, so God both is and is not only the subjective and objective world. And just as the old man's *beyond* is in his self-consciousness, so God's *beyond* is in self-consciousness too. God is the free, self-conscious thought that has the world itself as His self-conscious life. The belief in that *beyond*—in the idea that there is a self-consciousness playing itself out in all of this bluster we call daily life and the objective world—is the heart, perhaps, of religious faith.

Notes

1. As we saw in Chapter One (Section I), David Hume, too, had suggested that we can never "see" or experience directly with our senses the necessary connection between cause and effect. To Hume's observation Hegel adds that we can never experience the necessary connection between any of these other sorts of relational concepts either.

2. In footnote #19 to §187R, Geraets, Suchting and Harris suggest that, like Aristotle's syllogism, Hegel's syllogism relies on the meanings of the terms. This reliance on the meanings of the terms explains why both authors rejected the supposed fourth figure for the syllogism. Geraets, Suchting and Harris also refer to this section of Bochenski's work.

3. It's because each of the elements is a totality that we cannot think of them as atoms, as Hegel says in the discussion of "The Mechanical Object" in the *Science of Logic*. (Errol Harris misses this explanation [1983, 263]. He says that Hegel suggests that atoms are not objects because atoms are not correlative to subjects. But Hegel says atoms are not objects "because they are not totalities" [1969, 712].)

4. I have actually depicted the relationship between a defining universality or essence and what it defines in two ways: as nested bubbles—the original depiction developed in the Doctrine of Being—and as side-by-side bubbles with a looping arrow between them, the depictions which dominated the Doctrine of Essence. In the Introduction to the Doctrine of Essence, I switched to the side-by-side view so that I would have enough space between the bubbles to depict the relationships that were developing between them.

5. As was remarked by Errol E. Harris (1983, 268).

6. And so I think that the decision by Geraets, Suchting and Harris to translate "*Lebendiges*" as "living being" is somewhat misleading.

7. Early printings of Geraets, Suchting and Harris's translation of the *Encyclopaedia Logic* mistakenly listed §107, but this error was corrected in later printings.

8. See Aristotle's *Generation of Animals*, 1.19.726b24.

9. This is more or less the explanation that Kwame Anthony Appiah offers for the basic immorality of racism in his article "Racisms" (Appiah 1990, 3–17), for example.

References

Appiah, Kwame Anthony. 1990. "Racisms," in David Theo Goldberg, ed., *Anatomy of Racism* Minneapolis, University of Minnesota Press, pp. 3–17.

Barwise, Jon and Etchemendy, John. 1990. "Visual Information and Valid Reasoning," in W. Zimmerman and S. Cunningham, eds., *Visualization in Teaching and Learning Mathematics*. Washington, D.C.: Mathematical Association of America.

Barwise, Jon and Etchemendy, John. 1991. *Tarski's World*. Stanford: CSLI and Cambridge: Cambridge University Press.

———. 1998. "Computers, visualization, and the nature of reasoning," in T.W. Bynum and James H. Moore, eds., The Digital Phoenix: How Computers are Changing Philosophy. London: Blackwell.

Bochenski, I.M. 1961. *A History of Formal Logic*. Notre Dame, IN: University of Notre Dame Press.

Burbidge, John W. 1981. *On Hegel's Logic: Fragments of a Commentary*. Atlantic Highlands, NJ: Humanities Press.

Dudley, Will. 2002. *Hegel, Nietzsche, and Philosophy: Thinking Freedom*. Cambridge: Cambridge University Press.

Fichte, J.G. 1982. *The Science of Knowledge*. Cambridge: Cambridge University Press.

Geraets, T.F., Suchting, W.A. and Harris, H.S. (trans.). 1991. *The Encyclopaeidia Logic: Part I of the Encyclopaeidia of Philosophical Sciences with the Zusätze*, by G.W.F. Hegel. Indianapolis, IN: Hackett Publishing.

Graham, Daniel W. 2006. "Heraclitus," *The Internet Encyclopedia of Philosophy*, http://www.iep.utm.edu/h/heraclit.htm (accessed May 17, 2009)

Grier, Phillip T. 1990. "Abstract and Concrete in Hegel's Logic," in George di Giovanni ed., *Essays on Hegel's Logic*. Albany: State University Press of New York, pp. 59–76.

Harris, Errol E. 1983. *An Interpretation of the Logic of Hegel*. Lanham: University press of America.

———. 1990. "A Reply to Philip Grier," in George di Giovanni ed., Essays on *Hegel's Logic*. Albany: State University Press of New York, pp. 77–84.

Hartnack, Justus. 1998. *An Introduction to Hegel's Logic*. Indianapolis, IN: Hackett Publishing.

Hegel, G.W.F. 1967. *Hegel's Philosophy of Right*. T.M. Knox, trans. London: Oxford University Press.

———. 1969. *Hegel's Science of Logic*. A.V. Miller trans. London and New York: George Allen & Unwin and Humanities Presses. Section numbers refer to the

Marxists Internet Archive version, which is available at http://www.marxists.org/reference/archive/hegel/hl_index.htm.

———. 1977. *Hegel's Phenomenology of Spirit*, A.V. Miller (trans.). Oxford: Oxford University Press.

———. 1983 (1805–1806). *Lectures on the History of Philosophy.* E.S. Haldane and Frances H. Simson, trans. New Jersey: Humantities Press.

———. 1991. *Elements of the Philosophy of Right.* Allen Wood ed., Paul Guyer trans. Cambridge: Cambridge University Press.

———. 1991. *The Encyclopaeidia Logic: Part I of the Encyclopaeidia of Philosophical Sciences with the Zusätze*, Geraets, T.F., Suchting, W.A. and Harris, H.S. (trans.). Indianapolis, IN: Hackett Publishing.

Hume, David. 1748. *Enquiry Concerning Human Understanding*. Available online at http://18th.eserver.org/hume-enquiry.html through Carnegie Mellon University (accessed May 17, 2009). Since Hume wrote in English, readers can consult any edition of this text, however.

Kant, Immanuel. (1781 [A Edition], 1787 [B Edition]). *Critique of Pure Reason.* All references to the *Critique* make use of the standard Ak numbers, which refer to the pagination in the W. de Gruyter Publishing edition of Kant's collected works. Readers can therefore consult any translation of the *Critique* that includes marginal references to the Ak numbers. Because there were two editions of the *Critique*, Ak references include the paginations for both the A and B Editions.

———. 1950 (1783). *Prolegomena to Any Future Metaphysics.* Lewis White Beck, trans. Indianapolis, IN: The Bobbs-Merrill Company.

———. 1985. *Foundations of the Metaphysics of Morals*, Lewis White Beck (trans.). New York: Macmillan Publishing.

Kierkegaard, Søren. 1992 (1846). *Concluding Unscientific Postscript to Philosophical Fragments* (in two volumes). Howard V. and Edna H. Hong, trans. Princeton, N.J.: Princeton University Press.

Kirk, G.S., Raven, J.E. and Schofield, M. 1983. *The Presocratic Philosophers* (Second Edition). Cambridge, Cambridge University Press.

Locke, John. 1690. *En Essay Concerning Human Understanding*. Available online at http://oregonstate.edu/instruct/phl302/texts/locke/locke1/Essay_contents.html through Oregon State University. Since Locke wrote in English, readers can consult any edition of this text, however.

Mueller, Gustav E. 1958. "The Hegel Legend of 'Thesis-Antithesis-Synthesis,'" *Journal of the History of Ideas,* 19 (3), pp. 411–14.

Nietzsche, Friedrich. 1968. *Twilight of the Idols/The Anti-Christ*, R.J. Hollingdale (trans.). Harmondsworth, England: Penguin Books.

Pinkard, Terry. 2000. *Hegel: A Biography.* Cambridge: Cambridge University Press.

Plato. 1985. *Parmenides* and *Republic* in *The Collected Dialogues of Plato: Including the Letters*, Edith Hamilton and Huntington Cairns (eds.), Princeton, NJ: Princeton University Press. All references to Plato's texts use the standard Stephanus page, section and line numbers. Readers may therefore also consult other editions of Plato's works that include marginal references to the Stephanus numbers.

Prior, Arthur. 1968. *Papers on Time and Tense.* Oxford: Clarendon.

Rinaldi, Giacomo. 1992. *A History and Interpretation of the Logic of Hegel.* Lewiston, NY: The Edwin Mellon Press.

Index

absence, 51, 61, 62, 67, 73, 107, 114, 128
absoluteness, 8, 22, 24, 27, 28, 29, 338, 453, 601
Absolute Idea (AI), 8, 576, 580, 597, 599, 607, 608; as absolute, 601; as general concept of Idea, 577, 579; as highest definition of self-consciousness, 578; as Idea, 576; as Reason, 577, 580; as Subject/Object as one concept, 577; as summary thought, 598, 599, 600, 607, 608; as whole logic, 584; becomes Nature, 601; "being" of, 584, finite willing and finite cognition as own process, 578; "for itself" of form, 578; fulfills "in and for itself" relationship of the Concept, 578; fulfills definition as Idea, 577, 595; fulfills doubly "for itself" relationship of Concept, 578; has Idea as object of consciousness, 577; includes all moments of the logic, 582; moments of, 590; process of self-definition, 595, 596, 597; reestablishes "for itself" of form, 578; reestablishes S-ness, 578, stage of, 574–84
Absolute Mechanism, 457, 463, 479, 603; stage of, 451–58
Absolute Relationship, 182, 261, 305, 317, 502, 601; as reason, 263; not a relationship, 263, 264; stage of, 258–63
Abstract Judgment, 349, 399, 506, 604; stage of, 344–48
Abstract Purpose, 491, 492, 494, 502, 543, 566, 602; stage of, 470–75
abstraction, 549; process of, 550
abstractness, 33, 163, 226, 299, 300, 307, 308, 309, 316, 379, 386, 387, 392, 394, 410, 472, 474, 549, 580, 602; relative, 392
accident: mere, 518
Accidentality, 265, 267, 269, 270, 276, 332, 608; as actuality, 265; as Effect, 270, 272, 274; realm of, 265
activity: use of term, 319
Activity of Necessity, 235, 237, 482; as bottom up, 245; as top down, 245, stage of, 235–43
actual is rational, 14, 15, 208
Actuality, 14, 211, 212, 222, 223, 237, 238, 239, 241, 253, 258, 261, 268, 275, 288, 293, 294, 309, 332, 336, 420, 422, 423, 430, 434, 436, 459, 482, 489, 556, 585, 588; as externality, 222; as posited, 275; as possibility, 228, 329, 330, 331; as Singularity, 345; conceptual, 336; content of, 220, 239, 421, 481, 489; existing, 329; form defined by Possibility, 223; form fulfills content, 228; form of, 219, 223, 224, 239, 421, 425, 481, 489, 569; form of vs. content of, 220; fulfilled, 228; realm of, 239, 240, 241, 243, 275, 345; vs. Appearance, 213. *See also* Immediate Actuality
Additions, xx
African-American culture, 485
AI. *See* Absolute Idea

analogy, 413; argument from, 414
Analytic Method of Cognition: 571; stage of, 549–50. *See also* cognition.
Anaxagoras, 7
Anaximander, 103
"and," xviii, 323, 370, 430, 536, 603
animal, 12, 13, 16
annumeration, 90
antithesis. *See* thesis-antithesis-synthesis
Apodictic Judgment of the Concept: 380, 381, 401; stage of, 373–74
Appearance, 44, 167, 173, 174, 175, 180, 181, 184, 194, 206, 218, 304, 312, 336, 455; as a shine that exists, 190; as collection of Parts, 188; as existence that shines or shows up, 193; as Form, 177, 186; as unity of Thought and Being, 212; former, 185, 190; general concept of, 183; mere appearance, 312; stage of, 175; use of term, 213; vs. Actuality, 213; vs. Shine, 176. *See also* World of Appearance
arbitrariness, 382, 410
Aristotle, 2, 12, 13, 156, 401, 479, 504, 505, 508, 510, 609, 610; logic of, 400, 401; teleology of, 474
arrows, x, xi, 45, 50, 54, 91, 101, 108, 142, 230, 239, 244, 248, 249, 323, 452, 494, 495, 506, 525, 561, 565, 607; absence of, 460; as process, 262, 294, 308, 316; as relationships, 434, 436, 437, 459, 465, 600; circular, 151, 210, 223, 228, 324, 576, 578; dashed, 507; double-sided, 232, 262, 277, 328, 459, 460, 525, 528; looping "for itself," 131, 143, 262, 277, 305, 317, 324, 328, 330, 502, 509, 519, 529, 534, 538, 542, 544, 572, 578, 584, 585, 586, 592, 593, 594, 599; return, 449, 488, 489, 491, 571; straight "in itself," 147, 444, 468, 471, 496, 502, 520, 523, 550, 553, 573, 599. *See also* bubbles, dashed outline, diagrams *and* solid outline
Assertoric Judgment, 603; stage of, 371–72
atomism, 86
Attraction, 88, 96, 98, 115, 162, 180, 234, 362, 406, 439, 445, 464, 471, 500, 527, 529, 599; stage of, 83–87
Aufhebung/aufheben. *See* sublation
Äußerung, 337; vs. *Entäußerung*, 337
baby, 523, 524, 525, 537
back-and-forth process. *See* process: back-and-forth
Barwise, Jon, ix, xi
Becoming, xix, 47, 49, 50, 66, 68, 106, 114, 116, 117, 308, 425, 426; negative, 430; stage of, 53–55
Beginning of the Speculative Method, 589, 591; stage of, 584–88
Begriffe, x
Being, xvi, xix, 46, 48, 50, 55, 62, 66, 67, 70, 73, 78, 114, 129, 131, 155, 175, 283, 308, 309, 312, 482, 543, 582, 595, 602; as categoy, 423; as "flesh," 505; as ideality, 129; as self-comprehended Idea, 602; as showing up, 193; categories of, 109, 110, 336; distinct from Thought, 134, 136; immediacy of, 111, 124, 125, 129; immediate, 129, 301, 424, 425, 436, 505, 556, 602; mediating, 425; objective, 425; of Absolute Idea, 584, 585, 586, 588, 593, 594, 600; of purpose, 603; of universal, 455; realm of, 110, 111, 112, 125, 129, 131, 133, 134, 135, 152, 155, 156, 157, 181, 192, 193, 202, 203, 207, 212, 218, 224, 265, 297, 347, 436, 482, 492, 501, 584, 588, 593, 595; relationships of, 603; separated from Shine, 162; stage of, 51; types of, 602; unity with Thought, 212, 297, 435
Being-for-another, 58, 62
Being-for-itself, xv, xvii, 47, 60, 78, 79, 80, 85, 86, 95, 96, 101, 108, 110, 111, 112, 115, 116, 121, 122, 123, 124, 127, 128, 129, 132, 149, 158, 159, 162, 166, 169, 179, 180, 196, 200, 211, 234, 245, 267, 274, 296, 305, 317, 338–40, 413, 434, 439, 441, 445, 451, 464, 469, 472, 497, 498, 499, 500, 501, 509, 527, 528,

558, 599, 600; lacks an "other," 72; stages of, 71–87. *See also* Attraction *and* Repulsion
Being-in-itself, 41, 64, 65, 67, 68, 70, 74, 78, 80, 91, 107, 110, 145, 146, 147, 182, 194, 245, 266, 281, 318, 325, 359, 435, 436, 438, 439, 441, 444, 457, 460, 468, 499, 573, 598; stage of, 58–63
Being-there, 42, 60, 62, 73, 74, 78, 83, 89, 100, 101, 103, 107, 119, 145, 157, 309, 311, 313; stage of, 55–58
being-within-self, 191, 192
Berkeley, George, 7, 8
Beschließen, 485
Bochenski, I.M., 400
body, 484, 505, 508, 511, 520
bubbles, x, 45, 54, 101, 168, 323, 435, 441, 452, 453, 483, 506, 525, 552, 555, 569, 583, 607; as circles, 101; as ovals, 101; as rectangles, 88, 101; as squares, 101; empty, 602; nested, 59, 128, 172, 192, 432, 434, 452, 455, 459, 460, 461, 594, 595; overarching, 128, 151, 158, 239, 260, 261, 262, 267, 276, 284, 305, 316, 317, 323, 324, 328, 462, 509, 529, 531, 534, 544, 585, 586, 599; separate, 56, 59, 63, 171, 193, 248, 441, 539; side-by-side, 128, 192, 453. *See also* arrows, dashed outline, diagrams *and* solid outline
Burbidge, John, x, 59, 118, 119
Categorical Judgment of Necessity, 419, 421, 603; stage of, 366–67
Categorical Syllogism, 424; stage of, 416–421
category, 421, 422, 496, 497, 500, 504, 521, 604; essential and necessary, 419; exhaustive set of categories, 520, 554; mutually exclusive, 520, 554
causality, 269
Cause, 2, 32, 33, 269, 270, 271, 274, 278, 279, 282, 284, 285, 286, 290, 298, 312, 313, 332, 369, 423, 467, 473, 477, 478, 480, 492, 543, 547, 550, 573, 595, 603; as cause/effect, 281; as One cause, 287; as Substance, 296; as thought, 271; finite, 272, 273, 281; form of causal relationship, 273; general concept of, 284; infinite, 272, 273, 281; reacts to immediacy in the Effect, 279; same identity as Effect, 282; sublated, 326; vs. condition, 424. *See also* One cause, Substance *and* Substance as Cause
the Center, 457, 458
centrality, 448, 449, 451, 458, 460, 463, 473, 515, 516, 522, 565; as syllogism, 453; as trilogy of syllogisms, 454; completed, 459; examples of, 449; externality of, 451; new kind of singularity, 447; syllogism of, 451. *See also* the Center
chance, 218. *See also* Contingency and Chance
change, 42, 43, 47, 51, 65
Chemism, 463, 479, 482, 488, 494, 520, 602; stage of, 461–66
Clinton, Bill, xv, xix
cognition, 531, 540, 556, 562, 602; analytic, 550, 552, 585, 593; analytic method of, 549, 551; as willing, 543, 562; diagrammatic issues, 545; failure of analytic method, 551; finite, 547, 556, 561, 569, 578; finite cognition adjusts to world, 569; judgment of, 563; moments of synthetic cognition, 551; practical, 544; process of, 564; synthetic, 585, 593; synthetic as finite, 556; two judgments of, 542. *See also* the individual stages of Cognition
Cognition as Such: stage of, 545–48
Cognition Generally, 562, 564, 583; stage of, 535–45
communication, 443, 449, 453, 457, 460, 463; completed, 459
Comparing the EL and SL Developments of Qualitative Syllogism, 397–406, 409, 607
concept, 48, 238; abstract, 32, 33, 49, 54, 210; as a completed set, 201; as a universal, 362; as beyond existence, 489, 493; as essence, 504; as a kind

for other concepts, 226, 231; as Reason, 238; as teleological, 504; as theorem, 558; as totality, 152, 153, 168, 169, 170, 171, 172, 179, 181, 202, 233, 238, 239, 316, 325, 329, 331, 366; completed, 214, 240, 242, 254, 258, 368, 434; completely defined, 181, 201; concrete, 49, 54, 162, 173; determinate vs. universal, 335; empirical, 33, 34; empty, 248, 258, 270, 274, 277, 309; English term, 290; essential, 498; general, 64, 79, 93, 94, 158, 160, 179, 183, 232, 284, 286, 298, 497, 527, 577, 601; German term, 291; identifying, 433, 482, 487, 493, 556; identity of, 290; includes negation, 279; lacks content, 49, 51, 198, 204; life of, 607; meta-logical, 307, 310, 311, 313; not genuine, 382; of process have content, 308; overarching, 245, 315, 466, 497, 584, 599, 601; power of, 378; rational, 566; separate, 195, 249, 289, 318; sorting function, 81, 84, 85; subjective, 482; success concept, 154, 193, 196, 204, 369, 477, 480, 492, 564, 570; take concepts seriously, 567; universal, 325, 327, 329, 334, 349, 368, 385, 386, 444, 446, 467, 488, 489, 497, 501, 506, 527, 528, 533, 562, 563. *See also* the Concept

Concept, the, 283, 290, 291, 293, 295, 297, 300, 315, 317, 323, 326, 327, 329, 334, 344, 347, 358, 362, 369, 371, 377, 414, 427, 433, 438, 440, 445, 451, 459, 466, 467, 479, 482, 484, 488, 494, 509, 533, 543, 547, 551, 555, 568, 595, 604; absorbs activity of necessity, 299; as "for itself," 502; as "in and for itself," 316; as "in itself," 460; as a singularity, 500; as altogether concrete, 316; as both Concept and Object, 469, 474; as completed process, 295, 296; as concrete, 463; as doubly "for itself," 337; as Essence, 297; as finished product, 399, 423; as finite purpose, 498; as finite subjectivity, 494; as free, 299; as general concept, 320; as general definition of concept, 298; as grasper, 291, 315, 323, 334, 583; as one-sided, 437; as one-sided subjectivity, 474; as power over whole object, 486; as power that separates and unites singularity and universality, 378; as purpose, 484, 489, 494; as Reason, 490; as self-differentiating, 431; as separate, 324; as soul of fact, 378; as subject of willing, 562; as subjective, 484; as subjectivity, 487; as totality, 316; as unity with reality, 501; becomes the Object, 434; character of, 482; comes back into the picture, 378; defined from the bottom up, 338; defined from the top down, 338; defined objectively, 323, 338, 525; defined subjectively, 323, 338; definition of, 391, 399, 466, 469, 471, 472; doubly "for itself" relationship fulfilled, 578; drops out of picture, 344; dual nature of, 504; error of, 503; essential universality of, 342; form but not content, 379; fulfilled definition of, 374; fulfills definition as doubly "for itself," 502; "in and for itself" relationship fulfilled, 578; initiates process, 299, 302, 317, 318, 324, 502, 503; logical progression of, 595; moments as mutually defining, 399; moments of, 368, 370, 375, 379, 386; necessary connection remains inner, 293; rebuilding diagram for or reconstruction of, 461, 525; same as the Object in "in itself" sense, 435; subjective definition of, 525; syllogistic activity of, 378; tripartite syllogism of, 555; unified with object as judgment, 577; unity of, 375; universality of, 368; utters, 338, 340; vs. Substance, 295, 299; whole syllogism of, 486, 487, 488, 490, 491, 511, 555. *See also* the individual stages of the Concept

Concept Utters, The: stage of, 337–339

concreteness, 49, 54, 163, 173, 218, 227, 299, 300, 307, 308, 309, 310, 313, 316, 344, 353, 378, 387, 410, 434, 458, 463, 549; altogether concrete, 316; as existence, 309; of Singularity, 345
Condition, 225, 227, 239, 241, 253, 305, 310, 369, 425; as general concept, 231, 233, 242, 243; definition of, 423; in general, 233; Kant's, 22, 225; leads to universality, 225; stage of, 224–29, 331; vs. cause, 424. *See also* Conditon as a Totality *and* Condition$_{AT}$
Condition as a Totality, 286, 287, 305, 329, 336, 496, 497, 525, 526, 575, 577, 599, 604; stage of, 232–35
Condition$_{AT}$, 233, 236, 237, 239, 241, 242, 243, 244, 245, 246, 247, 248, 249, 250, 251, 253, 254, 255, 256, 257, 258, 259, 260, 262, 263, 264; as Accidentality, 265; as actuality, 258; as content, 244; as form, 244; as immediate actuality, 265; as system, 244; falls apart, 248; loses its existence, 248. *See also* Condition as a Totality
connectedness, 478. *See also* non-indifference
connection: arbitrary, 101; categorical, 430; contingent, 383; immediate, 372, 388, 416, 537, 577, 607; merely posited, 222; necessary, 367, 369, 370, 383, 385, 416, 420, 423, 424, 477; necessity merely inner, 420; objective, 382; shaky, 553, 557, 559. *See also* non-indifference *and* relationship
consciousness, xvii, 11, 31, 33, 75, 195, 319, 321, 420, 428, 434, 448, 450, 514, 516, 519, 532; as centrality, 448; basic, 511; lack of, 505; stream of, 531; thereness as content, 531; vs. self-consciousness, 532
Constitution, 64; stage of, 65
construction: of theorem, 561
content, xvi, 184, 197, 220, 224, 254, 256, 257, 258, 262, 263, 281, 372, 397, 406, 420, 422, 425, 433–35, 437, 438, 466, 469, 495, 501, 506, 507, 533, 534, 593; "in itself" definition of, 182; as inward reflection, 273, 275; as inwardness, 269; as overturning of form into content, 182, 267, 275; as what gets presented, 186; external, 184, 221; given, 562; overturns into form, 288, 332, 454; restricted, 249, 250, 476, 492, 495, 497. *See also* External Content
Content and Form, 263, 304; stages of, 181–84. *See also* Law of Appearance, External Form *and* External Content
contingency, 14, 15, 218, 220, 221, 222, 223, 241, 242, 253, 254, 258, 385, 395, 410, 421, 429, 495, 543, 582, 606; as subjectivity, 389; of relationship, 421; of syllogism, 382, 420; top down, 420
Contingency and Chance, 223, 224, 226, 228, 230, 265, 305, 309; stage of, 217–21
continuous magnitude, 89
contradiction, 11, 12, 36, 38, 40, 41, 42, 43, 52, 69, 94, 116, 173, 425, 568
Copernicus, Nicolas, 4
copula "is," 320, 322, 340, 341, 342, 346, 374, 375, 420, 434, 438, 506, 544, 577, 587, 591, 603; fulfilled, 374; of identity, 406; of implication, 603
correctness, 14, 372, 374, 520, 536, 606
Critique of Pure Reason, 3, 4, 5, 19, 20, 21, 22, 25, 38, 225
Dasein, 59
dashed outline (in diagrams), 51, 56, 73, 74, 80, 88, 102, 103, 104, 113, 131, 142, 157, 165, 167, 168, 171, 181, 184, 185, 186, 212, 214, 215, 216, 218, 223, 228, 236, 245, 250, 256, 259, 264, 304, 458, 461, 494, 507, 519, 531, 534, 538, 542, 550, 553, 561, 572, 578; meaning of, 115
deduction, 603
definition, 548, 553, 557, 559, 562; abstract, 316; as external, 553, 557;

as syllogism, 552; bottom up, 75, 96, 113, 131, 200, 226, 231, 235, 237, 243, 244, 245, 246, 256, 261, 277, 287, 289, 290, 331, 358, 410, 411, 420, 443, 444; concrete, 316; for essential concept, 146; formal, 316; objective, 318; stage of, 552–53; top down, 85, 98, 99, 113, 131, 231, 243, 244, 245, 246, 258, 259, 261, 277, 289, 290, 323, 326, 327, 329, 330, 331, 332, 334, 335, 358, 362, 366, 414, 417, 418, 419, 434, 444, 528, 534, 553, 557. *See also* determination *and* self-definition

Degree, xii, 45, 77, 92, 103, 106, 114, 133; stage of, 92–95

Democritus, 86

demonstration, 562, 564, 565; of theorem, 560, 561

dependence, 438, 444, 447, 533, 606

desire, 449, 450, 515, 516; as "fixing on," 485. *See also* drive, urge *and* want

Determination, xiv, xvii, 41, 49, 51, 55, 56, 64, 83, 89, 132, 145, 436, 437, 465, 588, 589; as identity of content, 267; as identity of form, 267, 268; being determined, 62; diagram for, 64; essential, xvii; external, 441; for logical concepts, xvi; for universals, 462; general definition of, 460; lack of, 460; of essential concepts, 146; requires negation, 78; stage of, 65. *See also* definition *and* self-detemination

Developed Quantum: stage of, 90

diagrams, xvii, 45, 47, 49, 50, 54, 57, 62, 92, 103, 112, 128, 139, 141, 168, 171, 172, 176, 177, 210, 215, 222, 223, 238, 242, 258, 260, 262, 293, 294, 297, 303, 313, 317, 323, 328, 330, 334, 409, 432, 435, 436, 444, 449, 453, 456, 458, 459, 465, 466, 468, 470, 483, 489, 496, 502, 506, 507, 509, 519, 520, 523, 525, 531, 534, 538, 545, 552, 561, 565, 573, 578, 581, 585, 586, 587, 594, 595, 599, 602; benefit of, xii; content, 220; depict exhaustion, 66; depict step-by-step development, 607; depict sublation, 62; fading into background, 159, 185, 214, 304, 344, 427, 502, 584, 600; helpful to understanding logic, 569; judgments in, 536, 539; nested view, 128, 132, 150, 152, 154, 158, 172, 192, 196, 198, 261, 301, 305, 594; of "for itself" relationship, 262; parentheses in, 550; quotation marks in, 539; sentential, 322, 344, 434; side-by-side view, 128, 131, 152, 154, 155, 172, 192, 193, 194, 196, 198, 209, 210, 594; solid black bar, 133, 586, 592; squares in, 101; rectangles in, 88, 101; use of, viii–xi; zooming in, 100, 141, 151. *See also* arrows, bubbles, dashed outline *and* solid outline

dialectical moment, 43, 52

dialectics, 11, 12, 25, 27, 32, 34, 35, 36, 68; of reality, 11, 12

Ding an sich. *See* Thing-in-itself

discrete magnitude, 89

Disjunctive Judgment of Necessity, 429, 430, 536, 590, 603; negative, 371; positive, 370, stage of, 369–71

Disjunctive Syllogism, 443, 446, 451, 490, 519, 520, 553, 603; stage of, 427–33

display: whole, 500, 501, 504, 506, 527, 529, 537, 538, 540, 541, 558, 560, 563, 581, 599

Distinction, 133, 137, 138, 140, 141, 145, 151, 167, 187, 188, 190, 192, 213, 296, 299, 336, 341, 342, 374, 375, 377, 379, 385, 390, 506, 529, 539, 549, 557, 558, 587, 589; as "other," 387, 388; determined, 147; essential, 146; how essential concepts defined, 146; "in itself," 146; Particularity as Distinction, stage of, 335; process of, 146; with Identity, 148; with no identity, 354. *See also* Immediate Distinction *and* relationship: of separateness

Distinction "in itself," stage of, 145–47

division, 96; as depth, 554, 556; as process of form, 538; as process of

purpose, 501, 538; as width, 554, 556; fourfold, 554, 555, 556, 557; genuine, 554; in the sphere of spirit, 555; process of, 432, 435, 439, 451, 453, 455, 457, 458, 462, 463, 467, 468, 471, 488, 490, 496, 497, 498, 499, 504, 506, 519, 520, 529, 530, 541, 542, 544, 553, 557, 562, 563, 590, 591; tripartite, 554, 555, 556, 557, 569
Doctrine of Appearance, 213
Doctrine of Being, xxi, 16, 32, 41, 128, 211, 224, 265, 312, 323, 362, 391, 584, 593, 595, 602, 607
Doctrine of Essence, xxi, 32, 48, 117, 128, 323, 324, 325, 336, 338, 357, 358, 360, 427, 438, 442, 478, 545, 547, 551, 559, 569, 573, 584, 593, 594, 595, 602, 607
Doctrine of Measure, 46, 129, 351
Doctrine of Quality, 46, 88, 95, 99, 406
Doctrine of Quantity, 46, 100
Doctrine of the Concept, xxi, 32, 35, 117, 349, 478, 595, 596
Doctrine of the Idea, 323, 607; introduction to, 504–507
Doctrine of the Object, 323, 607; introduction to, 435–36
drive, 565. *See also* desire, urge *and* want
earlobes, 18, 363, 445
Effect, 33, 270, 274, 278, 279, 282, 284, 285, 286, 288, 290, 298, 312, 313, 332, 369, 423, 467, 473, 477, 478, 480, 492, 543, 547, 550, 573, 595; as cause/effect, 281; as posited actuality, 275; as presupposed, 275, 276; as substance, 275, 276; different kind of substance from Cause, 276; not doubly "for itself," 276, 281; reacts, 277; same identity as Cause, 282
Effect as Substance, 281, 332, 473, 569; stage of, 274–78
$Effect_{CS}$, 287, 288, 289, 290, 291, 293, 295, 297, 298, 299, 300, 317, 322, 324, 326, 327, 369, 503, 525
effectiveness, 331
Egyed, Béla, v, 44
EL. *See Encyclopaedia Logic*
Eleatic philosophers, 46
empiricists, 111
emptiness (conceptual), 248, 258, 270, 274, 277, 309, 352, 483, 602
Empty Qualitative Judgment of Identity, 357, 358, 359; stage of, 352–53
Encyclopaedia Logic, 404, 406, 408, 428, 476, 511, 522, 570, 602; can be reconciled with *Science of Logic*, 405; differs from *Science of Logic*, 347, 383, 395, 397; use of, xx
Entäußerung, 337; vs. *Äußerung*, 337
entschließen, sich, 485
episyllogism, 21
Erscheinende, 176, 177, 178, 179, 183, 185, 186, 187, 188, 189, 304, 314; as content, 186; defined, 176; vs. *Erscheinung*, 176
Erscheinung: vs. *Erscheinende*, 176. *See also* Appearance
Essence, xv, xvii, 48, 112, 113, 121, 122, 123, 127, 129, 131, 133, 137, 140, 149, 151, 152, 155, 164, 172, 175, 177, 180, 181, 186, 190, 191, 192, 193, 201, 203, 206, 212, 224, 263, 265, 267, 282, 283, 284, 288, 297, 305, 307, 332, 335, 359, 417, 433, 445, 458, 460, 463, 472, 473, 474, 478, 482, 494, 498, 504, 505, 506, 520, 543, 551, 569, 586, 593, 594, 607; abstract, 216; as concept of concepts, 153; as *Erscheinende*, 178; as qualities, 164; as Thought, 155, 156, 160; as unity of Thought and Being, 212; general concept of essential concepts, 134; how essential concepts defined, 146; identifying, 457, 572; not tied to thereness, 125; realm of, 347, 358; related to thereness, 126; thereness for, 157; unessential, 216. *See also Erscheinende*, fruit *and* Transition to Essence
Etchemendy, John, ix, xi
ethics, 31, 207, 216, 221, 300, 454; Kant's, 207
exclusiveness: mutual, 430, 431

Existence, 32, 160, 166, 170, 172, 174, 175, 177, 178, 184, 190, 201, 209, 210, 247, 248, 250, 284, 311, 336, 358, 421, 422, 423, 425, 430, 434, 436, 455, 458, 462, 467, 470, 478, 488, 493, 555, 585, 588, 595, 603, 606; as Outer, 252; as type of thereness, 157; as universality, 533; belongs to singularity, 425; of universal, 455; stage of, 156–59
experience, 135, 153, 174, 179, 192, 193, 194, 205, 206, 244, 246, 257, 268; as both Inner and Outer, 222; as both thereness and concept, 206, 218; sensory, 46, 56, 75, 77, 101, 102, 108, 110, 111, 113, 121, 123, 124, 129, 133, 157; vs. perception, 412; world of, 503
Extensive and Intensive Magnitude, xii, 391; stage of, 91–92
External Content: stage of, 184–85
External Form: stage of, 183–84
External Necessity, 264, 276, 288, 306, 318, 324, 388, 447, 506, 578, 585; stage of, 243–50
External Purpose: stage of, 475–76
externality, 188, 218, 220, 221, 225, 249, 385, 407, 408, 441, 442, 443, 444, 447, 451, 462, 466, 468, 470, 471, 475, 483, 491, 492, 493, 495, 496, 497, 505, 511, 512, 514, 553, 554; independent, 187. *See also* self-externality
fact, 378; as a syllogism, 376; depends on the Concept, 377; soul of, 377
Fichte, Gottlieb, 33, 38, 39, 40
Finite Purpose: stage of, 475–76
Finite Willing: stage of, 563–70
finiteness, 65, 69, 179, 194, 195, 220, 250, 266, 380, 468, 479, 492, 495, 496, 497, 508, 544, 547, 562, 572, 579; in general, 343
First Figure of Qualitative Syllogism, 410, 412, 419, 428; stage of 381–384
First Moment of Purpose Realizing Itself, 484, 492, 502, 543, 554, 564; stage of, 477–83
for another, 59, 60
for itself, 74, 111, 112, 115, 117, 123, 126, 127, 131, 133, 142, 144, 149, 151, 158, 159, 169, 170, 171, 172, 173, 175, 181, 182, 185, 191, 195, 198, 199, 210, 211, 215, 245, 272, 282, 284, 285, 304, 317, 332, 335, 359, 441, 469, 471, 474, 501, 505, 517; arrow, 186; as consciousness, 546, 565, 570, 599; as self-consciousness, 321, 544; between Essence and Shine implies doubly "for itself" relationship, 594; content separates from form, 186; defined, xvi; doubly, 261, 267, 276, 280, 281, 287, 289, 291, 296, 302, 305, 317, 318, 320, 321, 324, 327, 330, 332, 333, 334, 335, 337, 414, 417, 434, 469, 472, 502, 504, 509, 528, 544, 547, 562, 577, 578, 585, 593, 599; doubly "for itself" has four parts, 439; fulfilled, 185; immediate, 519, 531; lack of an other, xvi, 73, 74, 96, 127, 132, 185, 215, 332; logical sense, 436; looping arrow, 131, 143, 172, 262, 277, 305, 317, 328, 330, 502, 509, 519, 529, 531, 534, 542, 572, 578, 586, 592, 594, 599; mutually defining, 144, 149, 155; nested view, 128, 132, 150, 152, 154, 158, 172, 192, 196, 198, 261, 301, 305; not established, 536; of content, 186, 188, 191, 193, 196, 201, 203, 261, 262, 263, 267, 305, 317, 320, 321, 324, 330, 333, 385, 414, 433, 435, 471, 500, 502, 529, 538, 539, 544, 547, 578, 585, 586, 593, 599; of content has two parts, 439, 472; of form, 186, 189, 190, 192, 193, 196, 203, 255, 261, 262, 267, 288, 305, 317, 320, 321, 324, 327, 330, 333, 385, 414, 433, 435, 447, 471, 500, 502, 503, 529, 531, 538, 539, 542, 543, 544, 547, 562, 571, 572, 578, 583, 586, 592, 593, 599; of form as "in itself" relationship, 317, 325, 471, 578; of form defines concept as separate, 318, 324, 335, 339, 388, 506, 529, 447, 585, 599; of form has two parts,

439, 472; of form not established, 533, 572; opposition, 506; overarching bubble, 305, 484; side-by-side view, 128, 131, 152, 154, 155, 172, 192, 193, 196, 198, 209, 262, 301, 305; three parts of process, 439; triply, 320, 321, 599; two-way relationship of Ground, 210
for-anotherness. *See* for another
Force, 44, 189, 196, 198, 205, 209, 214, 336, 550; as both Force and Utterance, 190; as finite, 195; as success concept, 196, 204; as whole process, 190; same "in itself" as Utterance, 194; vs. purpose, 194
Force and Utterance, 201, 214; stage of, 189–95
for-itselfness. *See* for itself
form, xvi, 165, 167, 174, 182, 208, 256, 258, 262, 263, 281, 397, 406, 420, 422, 434, 469, 493, 495, 501, 506, 533, 534, 593, 594; "in itself" definition of, 182; as content, 182; as overturning of content into form, 182, 267, 275; as reflection-into-another, 174; as the way content is presented, 186; defines concept as separate, 245, 264, 276, 288, 305, 334; doubled, 187; external, 184; overturns into content, 288, 332, 454; related to content, 170. *See also* External Form *and* One Form
Formal Mechanism, 454, 460; stage of, 441–43
Formal Syllogism of the Understanding: stage of, 378–80
formalism, 382
Forms (Plato's), 9, 10, 12, 13, 36, 40, 135, 156, 566
freedom, 294, 299, 300, 301, 316, 318, 326, 562, 564, 586; abstract, 299; concrete or positive, 299; defective, 533, 534; not uncaused, 301; of self-consciousness, 532; presupposes necessity, 299
friendship, 15, 23, 213, 214, 219, 222, 223, 225, 226, 229
fruit, xv, xvii, 13, 125, 127, 132, 133, 146, 152, 155, 157, 158, 192, 193, 203, 325, 328, 604, 607
gathering differences: as process of identity, 501; process of, 504, 506, 538, 340, 542, 544, 592
Gattung, 517
Gegenstand, 531, 570. *See also* object *and Objekt*
Geist/geistlich. *See* spirit
genus, 366, 367, 369, 372, 373, 375, 377, 417, 419, 431, 451, 517, 518, 521, 525, 533, 540, 541, 603; as general concept, 527; as "in itself" 517, 519; as natural mating kind, 517, 521; as power over individuals, 541; as purpose over whole process of living, 530; as substantial universal, 518; as universal concept, 528; baby as pure objectivity of, 523; content of, 369; defined by dividing, 519, 521; immediately singular instance of, 371; next or nearest, 552, 555, 556; process of, 522, 537; totality of, 371; whole process of living for, 527, 528
Geraets, T.F., xx, 6, 35, 124, 139, 150, 176, 235, 260, 314, 337, 400, 570, 609, 610
germ, 523, 524, 525, 537
Geschlectsdifferenz, 521
givenness, 56, 75, 81, 95, 101, 102, 108, 111, 224, 238, 243, 244, 249, 254, 258, 275, 276, 278, 372, 379, 420, 421, 423, 425, 438, 475, 476, 492, 495, 517, 540, 541, 547, 548, 549, 553, 554, 559, 562, 569, 582, 584, 585, 588, 593, 594, 601, 605
goal: as whole process, 579
God, 8, 9, 30, 252, 337, 414, 609
goodness, 372, 374, 560, 564, 566, 572, 577, 580, 606; = universal = reason, 566; as rational, 568; as thought, 573; as well-systematized set of beliefs, 568; as will, 566
government, 454
gravity, 4, 191, 193, 194, 195, 197, 199, 200, 201, 202, 203, 206, 210, 215, 550

Grier, Phillip T., 307, 308, 309
Ground, 141, 147, 155, 156, 158, 160, 177, 190, 193, 200, 201, 202, 203, 209, 210, 212, 240, 241, 254, 260, 282, 283, 284, 285, 304, 305, 306, 307, 308, 344, 357, 369, 383, 423, 543, 547, 550, 576, 595; arrow for, 210; as Singularity, 336; as subsistence, 199, 337; circular arrow, 151; fulfilled, 159, 161; stage of, 151–54, 335
Harris, H.S., xx, 6, 35, 66, 124, 139, 150, 176, 235, 260, 307, 308, 309, 314, 400, 570, 609, 610
Hartnack, Justus, 117, 118
Heraclitus, 47, 53, 70, 72, 74, 117, 118, 119
history, 31, 46, 287; of philosophy, viii, 46, 47
Hume, David, i, 2, 3, 4, 5, 6, 33, 43, 111, 271, 272, 364, 477, 511, 516, 609
Hypothetical Judgment of Necessity, 371, 406, 423, 603; stage of, 367–69
Hypothetical Syllogism, 428, 429, 432, 444; stage of, 421–27
Idea, the, 29, 32, 504, 515, 532, 534, 561, 573, 577, 578, 590, 594, 599, 601; as both subjective and objective, 577, 580; as Concept-Object, 577; as "fleshed out," 505; ,; as process, 505; as purpose, 514; as Reason, 504; as Subject-Object, 505, 577; as subjectivity, 513; completed, 579; definition of, 504, 537, 542, 560, 572, 607; general concept of, 577; lost its "being-for-itself," 519; subjective, 535, 537; process of, 514; syllogism of, 514; take seriously, 568. *See also* Absolute Idea, Objective Idea *and* Subjective Idea
idealism, 7; Hegel's, 8, 17, 23, 77, 82, 129, 157, 272, 301, 302, 607
ideality, 42, 74, 77, 82, 99, 110, 112, 116, 121, 123, 125, 129, 211, 242, 267, 302, 304, 317, 472, 473, 474, 475, 498, 505, 527, 528, 602. *See also* concept *and* universality
Identity, 128, 137, 138, 140, 141, 151, 167, 172, 181, 186, 191, 203, 206, 210, 213, 262, 263, 265, 267, 282, 289, 290, 295, 297, 300, 304, 332, 341, 342, 370, 374, 375, 377, 379, 385, 386, 388, 390, 400, 406, 407, 409, 426, 427, 431, 432, 434, 439, 442, 443, 458, 464, 472, 473, 499, 500, 501, 504, 506, 547, 550, 559, 563, 564, 569, 576, 577, 580, 587, 588, 592, 593, 594, 599, 601, 608; actively identifies, 317; and independence, 295; as active form, 203, 267; as essential purpose, 499; as identical, 187, 210, 282, 294, 331; as passive process of content, 203, 267; as process of gathering up, 501; concrete, 378; essential, 520, 521, 529, 538, 540, 569; essential function or process of, 507, 537, 539, 540; immediate, 386; mediated, 558; negative, 371; positive, 371, 590, 591, 592, 595, 596, 598, 609; stage of, 131–32, 335; substantial, 266, 518; vs. identical, 132; vs. Inner, 203; with Distinction, 148; with no distinction, 354; with opposition, 187
"if . . . then," xviii, 25, 323, 603, 606
immediacy, 14, 33, 45, 56, 75, 93, 98, 101, 111, 122, 123, 125, 133, 134, 156, 166, 175, 178, 184, 212, 214, 218, 223, 225, 228, 254, 259, 260, 265, 275, 276, 277, 278, 279, 309, 345, 349, 361, 371, 373, 379, 382, 385, 387, 391, 417, 418, 421, 423, 424, 436, 437, 448, 458, 459, 463, 465, 467, 470, 471, 474, 475, 479, 484, 487, 489, 507, 508, 511, 512, 517, 518, 520, 531, 532, 536, 537, 540, 541, 548, 550, 559, 577, 584, 585, 588, 593, 601, 602, 607; and mediation, 425; concrete, 345; mediated, 93; of relationships, 76, 343; of syllogism, 420; vs. logically developed, 594
Immediate Absolute Idea as Nature, 602; stage of, 598–602

Immediate Actuality, 221, 223, 224, 227, 239, 241, 254, 258, 265, 304, 305, 309; becomes Actuality, 228; stage of, 214–215
Immediate Distinction, 137, 138, 140, 147, 152, 167, 203, 204, 307, 332, 586; stage of, 133–36
Immediate Idea or Life, 520, 535, 537, 577, 602; stage of, 507–10
Immediate Judgment: stage of, 348–49
Immediate Judgment of the Concept: stage of, 371–72
Immediate Life. *See* Immediate Idea or Life
Immediate Measure, xiii, 56, 76, 108, 110, 115, 116, 443, 559; stage of, 100–102
Immediate Purpose: stage of, 475–76
Immediate Relationship: stage of, 187–88
Immediate Substance and Substantiality, 275, 276, 332, 366, 431, 518, 544, 569; stage of, 264–68
Immediate Syllogism, 418; stage of, 378–80
implication: logical, 603
in and for itself, xvi, 245, 272, 316, 317, 318, 324, 325, 327, 329, 332, 333, 334, 335, 339, 340, 341, 344, 385, 389, 390, 414, 417, 418, 435, 446, 471, 506, 529, 562, 578, 587; as universality, 325
in itself, 63, 71, 93, 103, 104, 111, 145, 146, 147, 148, 149, 166, 171, 182, 194, 197, 211, 245, 248, 250, 255, 262, 272, 279, 281, 282, 284, 286, 289, 306, 317, 324, 328, 330, 332, 333, 335, 359, 386, 408, 414, 417, 435, 437, 441, 444, 447, 453, 460, 461, 462, 463, 463, 467, 468, 469, 470, 471, 472, 474, 475, 491, 494, 499, 502, 506, 516, 517, 529, 543, 544, 547, 562, 565, 573, 578, 583, 585, 595, 598, 599, 602; as relationship of opposition, 341; defined, xvi; "in itself" character does not matter, 473, 505, 515, 543, 568; part of "for itself" relationship, 147, 336; straight arrow, 147
in sich: vs. *an sich*, 150. *See also* in itself
independence, 75, 80, 125, 161, 172, 188, 260, 294, 295, 296, 297, 299, 300, 301, 318, 326, 332, 417, 418, 419, 433, 434, 438, 441, 442, 443, 444, 446, 448, 461, 462, 467, 469, 470, 472, 473, 493, 494, 502, 505, 509, 531, 562, 564, 568, 569, 572, 573, 599, 609; and identity, 295; from subjectivity, 434, 437, 509; immediate, 462
indeterminateness, 436
indifference, 136, 137, 141, 166, 184, 187, 192, 380, 389, 393, 407, 423, 436, 439, 440, 450, 468; as built into syllogism, 438; toward existence, 430
individual: collective, 540
induction, 411
infinity: as doubly "for itself" process, 296; as process of running on, 68, 105, 129, 274, 417; as thought, 195; genuine, 72, 75, 116, 158, 274; of Cause, 272; of Substance, 266. *See also* process (logical): back and forth *and* Spurious Infinity
In-itselfness. *See* in itself
Inner, 198, 209, 210, 211, 214, 215, 218, 220, 221, 223, 227, 234, 237, 239, 240, 242, 243, 245, 246, 252, 254, 258, 265, 293, 312, 336, 345, 362, 369, 482, 487, 493, 543, 584; actively identifies, 203; as content of Actuality, 228; as smaller-U, 482; as thought or concept, 203; different form from Outer, 208; mediated by Outer, 199; merely, 458; mutually defining relationship with Outer fulfilled, 227; same content as Outer, 198, 207; syntactically same as Outer, 210; vs. Identity, 203
Inner and Outer, 216, 218, 222, 246, 267, 305, 336, 337, 412, 455; as mutually defining, 200, 210; in mutually defining relationship, 241, 246, 248, 251, 254, 260, 275, 288, 294, 329, 330, 332, 345, 421, 452, 455, 457, 481, 483, 484, 485, 486,

487, 488, 490, 492, 493, 501, 511, 515, 533, 555; stage of, 198–208
instance, 557, 559, 561, 562, 563, 564; two characteristics of, 558
instantiation, 564, 565, 567
intention, 60
intersubjectivity, 4
inward reflection, 151, 160, 161, 163, 166, 169, 171, 173, 175, 183, 184, 190, 196, 199, 200, 204, 211, 212, 227, 282, 331, 357, 359; as content, 275, 330; as Singularity, 339; as subsistence, 177, 184; not inwardly reflected, 183; one-sided, 198, 209.
inward reflection and reflection-into-another, 151, 154, 161, 166, 171, 174, 177, 178, 190, 201. *See also* Ground.
irritability, 511, 512, 519
Judgment, 320, 354, 370, 378, 399, 436, 465, 480, 481, 482, 484, 508, 512, 513, 519, 520, 522, 523, 535, 540, 541, 550, 559, 575, 587, 600, 603, 606; absolute, 580; as genuine expression of Concept's particularity, 342; as relationship, 560; as subjective, 434; as transitive, 347, 386, 389, 399, 404, 405, 412, 481, 489, 607; can no longer be used, 374; conditional, 606; content of, 367, 373; definition fulfilled in terms of content, 346; definition not fulfilled in terms of form, 347; empty, 352, 357; everything is a, 342; form of, 198, 341, 347, 356, 367, 370, 374, 375, 377, 399, 420, 438, 499, 506, 536, 544, 559, 577, 587, 591, 592, 595; general definition of, 354; genuine, 559; in diagrams, 536, 539; in stages of life, 540; links concepts together with concept of being, 602; of cognition, 560, 563; of essential identity, 538; of essential purpose, 538; of willing, 563; perceptual, 605; qualitative, 605; stage of, 341–344
Judgment of Necessity, 606; stages of, 366–71
Judgment of Reflection, 357, 605; as Essence, 347; stages of, 358–66
Judgment of the Concept, 606; stages of, 371–74
Judgment of Thereness: stage of, 348–49
Kant, Immanuel, i, ii, xxi, 1, 2, 3, 4, 5, 6, 12, 13, 17, 18, 19, 20, 21, 22, 23, 24, 25, 26, 27, 29, 31, 32, 33, 34, 35, 36, 37, 38, 39, 40, 41, 43, 44, 68, 114, 135, 136, 168, 169, 174, 203, 204, 205, 206, 207, 213, 225, 226, 242, 244, 247, 249, 250, 252, 260, 271, 445, 450, 566, 567, 568; antinomies, 36; categorical imperative, 566, 568; Copernican revolution, 4, 6; logic, 25, 322; reason, 20–23, 251, 260; table of categories, 32, 34; table of judgments, 32, 35. *See also* Thing-in-itself
Kierkegaard, Søren, 9, 30, 118
kind, 83, 84, 85, 98, 225, 227, 236, 265, 283, 552; as both universal and singular, 426; as either singularity or universality, 423; as genus, 517; natural kind, 509, 517; natural mating kind, 521, 525, 541; of relationship, 286; sensible, 418; that has being, 425
knowledge, 545, 546, 570; as social, 541; as willing, 562; constructed, 551; finite, 554; requires self-reflective awareness, 546; vs. opinion, 51. *See also* Cognition
law, 455; civil, 355; criminal, 356
Law of Appearance, 184; stage of, 181–82
Lebendiges. *See* living-ness
Lectures on the History of Philosophy, 7, 31, 46, 47, 86, 99, 103
Leucippus, 47, 86
Life, 507, 522, 536, 550, 578, 579, 585, 591, 603, 607, 608; as a life that thinks, 530; as centrality, 515, 516; as doubly "for itself," 509; as genus, 517; as genus-in-itself, 517; as higher level of universality, 517; as immediate Idea, 532; as

independent, 509; as individual, 517; as process, 532; as self-defining, 515; as spirit, 533; as substantial universal, 518; as unity of concept and reality, 519; defined in relation to external objectivity, 519; defines Reason, 510; divided externally, 511; divided internally, 511; finite, 508; free, self-conscious, 532; in general, 580; lost "being-for-itself," 519; lost its S-ness, 518; must reestablish S-ness, 519; objectification of, 515; of Reason, 580; of world, 505; process of, 510, 524; real possibility for, 526; stage of Immediate Life, 507–10; stages of, 507–24; whole proces of, 579, 580

Likeness, 137, 138, 140, 144, 149, 150, 499; choice of term, 139

Likeness and Unlikeness, 306, 394, 407; stage of, 137–42

Limit, xvi, 32, 70, 74, 75, 78, 80, 89, 91, 107, 194, 266; stage of, 64–67

living-ness, 507; as flesh of Reason, 509; as syllogisms, 510; vs. living being, 508

Living-ness Against Inorganic Nature, 517, 520, 535; stage of, 514–16

Living-ness as the Genus-in-itself, 528, 530, 531, 533, 537, 540. 541, 542, 560, 572, 576, 578, 603; stage of, 516–22

Living-ness Inside Itself, 516, 519, 520, 522; stage of, 511–13

Locke, John, 266, 267

logic, 30, 32, 34, 38, 40, 46, 47, 48, 49, 102, 546; Aristotelian, xix; as Absolute Idea, 582, 584; as account of "being," xv, 310, 320, 509, 602; as reason driving itself, 313; as semantic, 292; as syntactic, 292; as temporal process, 287, 292; as termino-logical, 287; bias for what abides in Hegel's logic, 129; cannot rest with spurious infinity, 69, 179, 232, 496, 497, 525, 574, 598; conceptual, 24, 25, 40, 45; consistency of meaning, 308; contemporary, vii, xiv, xviii, 24, 45, 117, 322, 509, 606; content and form of, xiv; dialectical, 43; ends, 601; formal, 370; formalistic, xviii, xix, 401, 403; goal of, 53, 68, 70, 94, 106, 339; Kant's, 25, 322; modal, 606; of Hegel's logic, 116, 117, 304, 308, 348, 384, 607; predicate, xiv, 24; prepositional, xviii; propositional, xiv, xviii, 24; scientific, 307; speculative, 584, 585; theorems in, 606; traditional, 414. *See also* Objective Logic, Subjective Logic, syntax, semantics, necessity, process (logical) *and* oxymoron

logical impasse, 53, 70, 92

logical movement (types of): development, 322; driven by tension between universality and singuarlity, 595; passing-over, 127; relationship, 127

logical operators, xviii, 323, 603, 605, 606. *See also* "and," "or," "not," "if . . . then"

logos, 566

Magnitude: Extensive, 92; Intensive, 93, 96. *See also* Intensive and Extensive Magnitude

manifoldness, 210, 435

master-slave dialectic, 60, 61

materialism, 7, 129; Hegel's, 12, 302, 503, 607

Mathematical Syllogism, 394, 396, 399, 404; stage of, 406–8

Matter and Form Fall Apart, 304, 539, stage of, 169–71

Matter (*Sache*) Itself and the Activity of Necessity, 256; stage of, 235–43

Matter Itself, 235, 239, 241, 242, 243, 244, 245, 246, 247, 248, 249, 250, 251, 252, 253, 254, 258, 264, 298, 330, 476; as Reason, 244, 246; as the Necessary, 250, 255, 256, 257, 258; not contingent, 241; unconditioned, 242; vs. Matters, 235

Matters, 165, 306; as qualities, 163; dual nature of, 177; former, 167, 170, 172, 173, 175, 177, 178, 180,

181, 182, 183, 186, 187, 196, 199, 214, 304; stage of, 163–64; vs. Matter Itself, 235. *See also* One Matter
means, 480, 483, 484, 487, 495
measure, 32, 46, 76, 99, 102, 107, 110, 112, 116, 122, 123, 127, 129, 131, 150, 352, 356, 482, 498, 595; fulfilled, 108. *See also* Immediate Measure
Measureless, 116, 496; stage of, 102–6
Measureless of the Measureless, 104
mechanism, 467, 479, 488, 494, 510, 520, 552. *See also* Formal Mechanism *and* Non-indifferent Mechanism
mediation, 93, 97, 98, 99, 111, 113, 124, 125, 196, 199, 257, 259, 296, 309, 426, 432, 457, 461, 463, 467, 470, 485, 487, 529, 532, 540, 541, 550, 558, 561, 588; as a totality, 392; as logical, 385; as necessary, 385; as negativity, 425; contingent, 390, 396; defined, 77; negated, 434; negative moment of, 386, 388; of syllogism not doing any work, 390; of syllogisms completed, 409; self-external, 391; specified type of, 424; sublated, 436
meinen, 51
middle term: general definition of, 393; genuine, 386; not genuine, 386, 389
modality, 32, 605
moments (logical), 161, 215, 280, 323; use of term justified, 287, 583
motion, 42, 47, 51, 595
multiplicity, 47, 74, 84, 91
Nature, 582, 600, 601, 607, 608; as a conceptual system, 601; as general concept, 601; inorganic, 514, 520; inorganic, definition of, 515
Necessary, the, 255, 257, 258, 260, 262, 263, 265, 275, 305, 476, 604; as content and form, 258; as form, not content, 256; as immediacy, 259; as result of process of necessity, 256, 259; as Substance, 266; as the Matter Itself, 250; as unconditioned, 259, 260; as unconditioned actuality, 260; became the Concept, 604; initiates of process of necessity, 256, 259; stage of, 250–58; sublates relationship, 264
necessary connection, 367, 369, 370, 383, 385, 416, 420, 423, 424, 477. *See also* the Necessary
Necessitation: Rule of, 606
necessity, xvii, 18, 19, 25, 27, 28, 32, 38, 40, 59, 82, 95, 114, 117, 130, 219, 236, 237, 246, 255, 257, 270, 294, 295, 331, 339, 389, 419, 503, 520, 562, 606; as bottom up process, 246; as Cause, 270; as completed, 260; as exhaustion, 52, 66, 70, 94, 113, 304, 355, 403, 409, 561, 604, 607; as inner, 294; as process, 242, 245, 249, 256, 299; as top down process, 258, 246; external, 249, 250, 256; first process, 247; logical, 257, 361, 385; of cause and effect, 293; of Hegel's logic, viii, xii, 45, 384, 397, 403; of reason established, 258; of relationship, 423; of spurious infinity, 68; posited or established, 294; real, 257; second process, 247; third process, 247, 248; truth of necessity is freedom, 299, 300. *See also* External Necessity
negation, xvi, xvii, 11, 32, 41, 42, 43, 56, 58, 63, 71, 72, 73, 75, 78, 83, 84, 96, 98, 108, 110, 115, 145, 173, 188, 189, 279, 312, 313, 340, 441, 447, 451, 470, 471, 472, 473, 512, 550, 587, 588, 589, 592, 606
negation of the negation, xvi, 72, 74, 112, 116
Negative, 145, 147, 148, 149, 161; relation, 390. *See also* Positive and Negative: stage of
Negative Qualitative Judgment (Simply), stage of, 349–50
Negatively Infinite Qualitative Judgment, 357, 358, 359; stage of, 354–58
negativity: immanent, 447
neutral product, 463, 465, 466; becomes the Concept, 469
Nietzsche, Friedrich, 130, 314

non-indifference, 440, 445, 447, 449, 461, 462, 468, 469, 494, 598
Non-indifferent Mechanism, 456, 515, 522, 533; stage of, 443–50
non-subsistence, 178, 180, 181, 183, 184, 187, 304; as reflection-into-another, 178
"not," 323, 349, 350, 351, 354, 362, 587, 589, 604, 605, 606
Nothing, xvi, xix, 46, 50, 55, 66, 67, 70, 73, 78, 89, 94, 107, 129, 131, 308, 309, 312, 595; redefined as "otherness-in-general," 59; stage of, 51–53
nous, 7
Number, xii, 50; stage of, 90
object, 458, 472, 482, 483, 484, 486, 491, 492, 493, 494, 497, 499, 504, 513, 514, 516, 517, 527, 530, 543, 582; as error, 503; as independent of subjectivity, 531, 570; as mediated, 532; as not one-sided, 494; as out there, 536; as P/S, 461; as process, 522; becomes universal concept, 527; defines the purpose, 492; dependent, 453; finite, 495, 496; identified by Concept, 489; immediate, 473; not self-subsistent, 453; of consciousness, 531, 532, 533, 534, 536, 537, 538, 552, 558, 563, 564, 570, 578, 579; out there, 534, 537. *See also* the Object
Object, the, 434, 449, 455, 459, 469, 601; as a totality, 437; as determined, 460; as immediacy, 437, 460; as immediate being, 436; as one-sided, 437; becomes the Concept, 469; falls apart, 438; indifference of, 439, 441; introduction to, 449; same as the Concept in "in itself" sense, 435; stage of, 436–38
objectification, 489, 492, 508; immediate, 485; mediated, 485; of life, 515
Objective Idea (OI), 582; antithesis with SI sublated, 583; as active purpose, 572; as cause over SI, 573, 375; as dynamic process, 572; as external universe, 540; as independent of SI, 568, 570, 571, 573; as object opposed to subjectivity, 570; as one-sided objectivity, 573; as opposed to SI, 542; as purpose, 573; as universal concept, 563; becomes Idea, 577; finite as not yet good, 572; goodness not yet established, 573
Objective Logic, 318
objectivity, 4, 51, 61, 318, 323, 420, 428, 429, 434, 458, 478, 487, 491, 505, 506, 515, 522, 523, 536, 538, 562, 601, 607; as deficient on its own, 482; as independent of subjectivity, 437; as inorganic nature, 514; as mutually defining with subjectivity, 576; as objective world, 564; as one-sided, 543; as one-sided must be sublated, 491; as process, 522; as realm of finite objectivity, 494; as subordinate to subjectivity, 494; as the Concept, 530; corresponds to Reason, 583; defined by subjectivity, 494; distinct from subjectivity, 582; external, 483, 514, 519, 527; finite, 494, 495, 497, 503, 504; given, 551; immediate, 472, 474, 480, 481, 482; needs subjectivity to be what it is, 560; objective ones, 450; of the genus, 523; of universality, 461; one-sided, 560, 573, 582; presupposed, 487, 492; realm of, 498; unity with subjectivity, 498, 542, 582
Objekt, 531, 570. *See also Gegenstand*
OI. *See* Objective Idea
one, 73, 90, 160; as relationship, 151
one and many, xiii, 47, 77, 92, 114
One cause, 284, 286, 290; as completed causal process, 286; as unity of Cause and Effect, 289; doubly "for itself," 288; general concept of cause, 284; initiates process, 289, 290
One Form, 169, 170, 172, 173, 175, 178. *See also* Thing as One Form
One Matter, 168, 169, 170, 172, 173, 175, 178, 304; stage of, 166–68

one-sidedness, 56, 63, 68, 87, 198, 199, 206, 209, 275, 309, 437, 474, 476, 487, 491, 494, 495, 542, 543, 553, 560, 562, 570, 597, 598
opinion, 51
opposition, xvi, 11, 40, 41, 42, 43, 52, 62, 70, 71, 74, 138, 140, 188, 189, 190, 197, 198, 199, 200, 207, 208, 209, 245, 248, 249, 255, 261, 266, 272, 279, 281, 306, 318, 324, 325, 330, 341, 435, 436, 437, 441, 447, 459, 460, 462, 466, 470, 471, 472, 476, 491, 497, 499, 502, 506, 517, 540, 573, 578, 585, 595, 599, 600, 602; with identity, 187
optimism (Hegel's), 207
"or," xviii, 323, 603, 606; exclusive, 370, 605; inclusive, 370, 430, 536, 603
origin, 478
"other," xv, xvi, xvii, 58, 59, 60, 61, 63, 64, 70, 72, 74, 75, 121, 123, 127, 147, 160, 185, 186, 248, 251, 253, 255, 299, 332, 333, 359, 386, 434, 447, 477, 486, 493, 503, 509, 544, 599, 600
otherness-in-general, 58, 59
ought, 364, 377, 416
Ought-to-be, 64; stage of, 65
Outer, 198, 199, 209, 210, 211, 214, 215, 218, 220, 221, 223, 226, 227, 234, 237, 239, 240, 242, 243, 245, 246, 252, 254, 258, 264, 288, 293, 312, 336, 337, 345, 362, 369, 455, 482, 487, 492, 493, 501, 519, 531, 543, 584; as content of Actuality, 228; as showing up or existence, 203; as smaller-S, 482; different form from Inner, 208; mediated by Inner, 199; mutually defining relationship with Inner fulfilled, 227; same content as Inner, 198, 207; syntactically same as Inner, 210. *See also* Inner and Outer
oxymoron, Hegel's logic as, vii, xii, xix, 114, 117
P. *See* Particularity
P/S: as particularity/singularity, 461
pantheism, 9
Parmenides, 10, 46, 47, 51, 53
Particular Judgment of Reflection, 366; negative, 362, 366; positive, 362, 366; stage of, 361–63
Particularity (P), 326, 338, 348, 349, 362, 368, 370, 371, 374, 375, 376, 377, 378, 379, 389, 430, 433, 435, 446, 452, 462, 465, 471, 481, 519, 548, 551, 552, 553, 596; abstract, 379, 410; as a "being-for-itself," 342, 558; as a center, 449; as a judgment, 341; as a purpose, 483, 486, 487; as a singular in relation to Universality, 384; as a universal in relation to Singularity, 384, 391; as abstracted out, 549; as both activity and content, 452, 479, 480; as both activity and objectivity, 480; as definition, 431; as genus, 530; as Idea, 529, 532; as immediate thereness, 382; as "in and for itself," 341; as mediated, 532; as mediating ground, 376; as object of consciousness, 531; as original-P, 491; as purpose, 480, 490, 492, 530, 573; as the universal in the judgment, 346; as the utterance of the Concept, 337; as theorem, 558, 559; as universal concept, 327, 334, 339, 390, 417, 528; as universality and singularity, 333; contingent, 385; determinate, 387; essential, 418; essentially defining, 383; general definition of, 328, 334; includes existence, 422; necessary relationship, 418; new level of in Chemism, 463; no longer abstract, 387; not a concept, 382; objective, 373; process of, 366, 368, 452, 534; redefined as a concept, 386; reflects the character of the Concept, 334; reflects universality and singularity, 409; same as Singularity, 374; stage of, 326–28; syllogism of, 485, 487, 489, 490, 491, 492, 493, 494, 530. *See also* division (process of) *and* process (logical): of particularizing

Parts, 188, 189, 193, 443, 550; collection of, 201; former, 191, 196, 199, 214
perception, 585; of quality, 412; vs. experience, 412
Phenomenology of Spirit, 11, 31, 33, 60, 61
philosophy, 14, 602; presuppositionless, 28, 129; Western, vii, viii, 1, 5, 38, 46, 51, 130, 134, 271, 325, 566
Philosophy of Right, 14, 31
picture-thinking. *See Vorstellung*
Pinkard, Terry, vii, 2
Plato, 9, 10, 11, 12, 13, 36, 40, 41, 43, 134, 135, 156, 504, 566
plurality, 32, 605
Pohle, William, v, 43
positedness, 222, 274, 305, 311, 312, 313, 385, 587; mere positedness, 211, 312; mere positedness sublated, 222; merely posited, 222, 255; posited, 275, 294, 312; positing, 79
Positive, 145, 147, 148, 149, 161; relation, 390; unity, 392
Positive and Negative: stage of, 142–45
possibility, 32, 219, 220, 221, 223, 226, 234, 236, 237, 239, 240, 246, 247, 248, 249, 251, 253, 254, 255, 256, 257, 258, 259, 260, 262, 265, 269, 270, 274, 275, 276, 288, 293, 294, 322, 329, 330, 452, 489, 525, 569, 604; abstract, 226; as Actuality, 329, 330, 331; as content of Actuality, 229; as form of Actuality, 228; as immediate actuality, 265; as realm of Actuality, 240; characterized by Actuality, 240; concrete, 227, 310; defines form of Actuality, 223; genuine, 217, 226, 228, 229, 230, 231, 274; implies another possibility, 217, 224, 228, 236, 265, 269, 271, 276, 305, 424; mere, 230; no longer merely possible, 331; realm of, 235, 240, 246, 250, 254, 257, 258, 260, 265, 275, 329, 331; stage of, 215–17; sublated, 240
presence, 50, 51, 61, 62, 67, 68, 73, 112, 114, 128, 156, 196, 200, 201, 210, 212, 213, 217, 218, 222, 236, 244, 297, 531, 605, 606; determinate, 56; sublates mere positedness, 222
Presocratic philosophers, 46, 99
presupposedness, 587. *See also* givenness
Problematic Judgment of the Concept: stage of, 372–73
process (logical): as arrows, 262; back and forth, xvi, 53, 66, 67, 68, 78, 106, 109, 121, 123, 129, 149, 158, 161, 178, 179, 182, 183, 211, 231, 232, 279, 285, 298, 304, 350, 462, 467, 468, 470, 495, 502, 524, 572, 573, 574, 575, 577, 578, 582, 596, 598, 599, 605, 608; causal, 503; chemical, 463, 465, 467, 468; completed, 181, 182, 233, 235, 285, 295, 296, 460, 497, 525, 575, 576, 578; concepts of, 308; immediate, 507; of essential identity, 540; of falling apart, 170, 172, 248, 323, 537, 539, 602; of distinction, 146; of negation, 73; of particularizing, 362, 366, 368, 452, 534; of passing over, xvi, 50, 67, 73, 76, 78, 96, 108, 109, 111, 112, 113, 115, 123, 124, 127, 211, 215, 288, 391, 496, 595; of purpose, 503; of the Idea, 514; of thereness, 528; syllogistic, 389, 572; use of term, 319. *See also* in itself, for itself, in and for itself, reflection, inward reflection, reflection-into-another, inward reflection and reflection-into-another, division (process of), gathering differences (process of), separation, opposition, definition, determination, contradiction, connection, *and* relationship
Process of the Genus, 541, 602; stage of, 522–24
Progression of the Speculative Method, xv, 602, 603, 609; stage of, 589–97
proof: of theorem, 561
Properties, 173, 175, 183, 305, 306; as reflection-into-another, 175, 177; stage of, 161–62; vs. Quality, 162

prosyllogism, 21, 36
Pure Quantity, 90, 117, stage of, 88–89
purpose, 194, 451, 469, 504, 514, 515, 519, 520, 522, 530, 543, 552, 564, 569, 573, 576, 602, 603; abstract, 474; actual, 569; as "fixing on," 485, 487, 496, 497; as infinite, 195; as not self-determining, 476; as one-sidedly subjective, 476, 494, 495; as part of willing, 564; as process of division, 501; as rational concept, 566; as success concept, 477, 480, 491; as syllogism, 479, 484, 572; as unity of subjectivity and objectivity, 494; being of, 478, 491, 603; being-for-itself of, 498; complete objectivity of, 497; concept of, 501; defines objectivity, 495; defines the object, 492; definition fulfilled, 501; definition of, 473, 474, 475, 493; essential, 498, 520, 529, 541, 569; essential function of purpose, 507, 537; essential process of purpose, 538, 539; existence of, 478; external, 475, 476, 492, 495, 497; finite, 475, 479, 492, 495, 496, 497, 501, 503; fourfold syllogism of, 554; general concept of, 498; good, 566; immediate, 475; in general, 479; in realm of spirit, 556; infinite, 497, 503; internal, 474, 479; mediated objectification of, 485; objectified, 484, 485, 491; of utility, 476; one-sided, 564; one-sidedly subjective, 476, 494; possible, 569; process of, 504, 541; realized, 476, 478, 482, 486, 491, 494, 495, 501, 556; restricted, 476, 492, 493, 495, 497; self-conscious, 566; spurious infinity of finite purpose, 495; stages of, 470–93; subjective, 475, 476, 479, 484, 564; syllogism of, 492, 493, 510; three stages of, 476; tripartite syllogism of, 554; universal concept of, 497; vs. cause, 477; vs. willing, 564, 565. *See also* the individual stages of Purpose
purposiveness, 510; objective, 498, 504
Pythagoreans, 7
Qualitative Judgment, 361, 365, 604, 604, 606; as Being, 347; expresses finiteness, 356; failure of, 356, 359; stages of, 348–58; truth of, 356. *See also* the individual stages of Qualitative Judgment
Qualitative Syllogism, 380, 411, 412, 413, 603; failure of, 408; First Figure, 381–84; in *Science of Logic*, 384–94; logical conclusions of, 405; Second Figure (from EL), 395–96; Second Figure (from SL), 385–90; stages of, 381–97; Third Figure (from EL), 396–97; Third Figure (from SL), 390–94; truth of, 385
quality, xiii, xvi, 32, 49, 55, 56, 62, 69, 71, 73, 79, 84, 95, 99, 100, 108, 116, 157, 351, 362, 380, 381, 385, 387, 389, 397, 406, 408, 412, 443, 498, 552, 594, 602, 604, 605; as Matters, 163; as such, 62; as type of category, not stage, 119; determinate, 79; essential, 164; immediate, 603; in general, 62; in itself quantity, 104; of being what it is, 62, 63, 72, 74, 78, 79, 80, 83, 84, 85, 333, 360; sensible, 605; unity with quantity, 109; vs. properties, 162
Quantitative Syllogism, 396; stage of, 406–8
quantity, xvi, 32, 77, 87, 108, 116, 157, 351, 406, 443, 498, 594, 603; in itself quality, 103; quality of, 104; unity with quality, 109. *See also* Pure Quantity
Quantity as there. *See* Quantum
Quantity in general. *See* Pure Quantity
Quantum, xii, 92, 93, 100, 114; in itself, 93; qualitative, 107; stage of, 89–90
quotation marks: not used with names of stages, 50; use of in diagrams with judgments, 539
Ratio, 95, 115, 116, 117; first definition, 95, 98; second definition, 97, 98, 99, 113; stages of, 95–99
rational: as syllogism, 377. *See also* rational is actual

Real Possibility, 231, 236, 237, 262, 277, 304, 459, 460, 496, 525, 526; as general concept, 232; completed, 235; double-sided arrow for, 232, 277; stage of, 230–32
reality, 8, 11, 12, 13, 14, 17, 32, 41, 42, 60, 62, 65, 68, 74, 77, 82, 111, 112, 125, 207, 210, 216, 231, 238, 240, 241, 245, 257, 266, 302, 303, 376, 422, 436, 457, 482, 501, 505, 515, 517, 518, 531, 533, 534, 538, 556, 588, 595, 601, 608; objective, 523
Realized Purpose: stage of, 489–93
reason, 23, 252, 342, 468, 498, 503, 504, 509, 542, 597, 608; = universal = good, 566; as Absolute Idea, 576, 577; as Absolute Relationship, 263; as actuality, 267; as blank slate, 562; as bottom up process, 246; as cause, 270, 279; as dynamic, 575; as effect, 278; as essence of world of experience, 263; as first cause, 302; as Idea, 601; as living, self-conscious spirit, 533; as Matter Itself, 244; as might, 267; as Nature, 601; as the Necessary, 257; as necessary process, 256, 257; as One cause, 286, 288; as standard for defining reality, 303; as subjective and objective, 575; as subjectivity, 562; as syllogism, 377; as system, 244, 267; as teleological, 15, 19, 23, 450, 489; as the Concept, 297, 315; as Thought, 582; as top down process, 246, 336; as unconditioned, 260, 261; as universal, 568; as Universality, 336; as well-systematized set of beliefs, 568; as willing, 575; ascending process, 21, 251, 252, 253, 255, 257; completed, 288; conceptual, 27, 40; conceptual and existential, 258; corresponds to objective world, 583; cunning of, 489, 495; defined, 19; descending process, 21, 251, 252, 255, 257; dialectical, 11, 13, 19, 38, 41, 43; initiates process, 302; life of, 580; moments of, 43; overgrasps reality, 6, 7, 8, 13, 15, 16, 26, 31, 32, 40, 43, 77, 114, 238, 245, 252, 257, 271, 272, 321, 601; practical, 544; reacts, 280; recognizes own dynmic nature, 575; restricted, 250; speculative, 22, 23, 43, 52, 68
Reciprocal Action, 161, 279, 282, 283, 284, 285, 287, 290, 298, 301, 302, 305, 323, 324, 326, 327, 467, 502, 543, 568, 573, 575, 583, 607, 608; stage of, 281–89
recognition, 61
reflection, 132, 142, 143, 150, 160, 192, 211, 408, 412, 545, 547, 591, 592, 594, 595; as showing up, 192, 335, 594; ordinary, 364; subjective, 383
reflection-into-another, 151, 160, 161, 163, 166, 169, 171, 173, 184, 190, 196, 201, 204, 212, 227, 282, 357; as Appearance, 177; as form, 196; as non-subsistence, 178, 184; as properties, 175; one sided, 199, 209
Reinhold, Karl Leonard, 33
relationlessness, 407
relationship, 32, 269; absolute, 261, 262; as judgment, 559, 560; as synthetic, 551; causal, 273; completed reciprocal, 294; completely reciprocal, 291; constitutive, 551; contradictory, 523; essential, 551; external, 379, 387, 441, 442, 443, 454; fulfilled, 159; fulfilled relationship between singularity, particularity, universality, 375; fulfilled relationship between universal and particular, 372; genuine, 559; immediate, 382, 470, 484, 487, 508, 511, 512, 517, 531, 532, 550; "is"-relationships, 550; lack of, 437, 459, 466; logical, 385; logical development in, 140; mutually defining, 151, 156, 200, 202, 205, 209, 212, 214, 215, 219, 220, 239, 242, 282, 289, 300, 305, 306, 336, 345, 367, 399, 452, 576, 578, 595; necessary, 373, 385, 418, 421, 423, 606; not in usual sense, 262; of being, 603; of cause and effect, 369,

424; of centrality, 453; of condition, 369; of condition and conditioned, 424; of connectedness, 138, 140, 457; of ground, 151, 240, 241, 259, 282, 283, 285, 357, 369; of identity, 341; of judgment, 508; of likeness, 407; of likeness for universality, 394; of necessity, 370; of opposition, 138, 245, 261, 318, 324, 436, 471; of reflection, 545, 592; of separability, 379, 380; of separateness, 138, 140, 341; of universality, 390; oppositional, 459, 471; reciprocal, 294, 319, 324, 369; reciprocal causal, 575; reflective, 547; requires sameness and difference, 559; requires separation, 295, 341, 352, 355, 357, 592; sexual, 523; stages of, 187–95; sublated, 264; syllogistic, 548; synthetic, 559. *See also* reflection, inward reflection, reflection-into-another, inward reflection and reflection-into-another, *and* the individual stages of Relationship
Remarks, xx
reproduction, 511, 513. *See also* sexual reproduction
Republic, 10, 134
Repulsion, 83, 96, 162, 180, 234, 305, 362, 439, 445, 464, 471, 500, 527, 529, 599; stage of, 78–82
Restriction, 64; stage of, 65. *See also* content: restricted
right, 356, 455
Rinaldi, Giacomo, 64
S. *See* Singularity
Schein. *See* Shine
Schultze, Johannes, 33
science: natural, 31
Science of Logic, xx, xxi, 64, 307, 318, 319, 347, 353, 355, 382, 384, 395, 399, 401, 404, 406, 408, 412, 423, 429, 430, 431, 433, 442, 443, 452, 454, 476, 505, 511, 522, 602, 609; can be reconciled with *Encyclopaedia Logic*, 405; differs from *Encyclopaedia Logic*, 347, 383, 397. *See also* SL-Development for Qualitative Syllogism
Scientific Revolution, 1, 2
Second Figure of Qualitative Syllogism: (from EL), stage of, 395–96; (from SL), stage of, 385–90
Second Moment of Purpose Realizing Itself, 530, 554, 556; stage of, 483–86
self: as Absolute Idea, 580; as completed, 580; subjective, 580
self-consciousness, xv, xvii, 60, 61, 319, 321, 323, 510, 516, 535, 543, 544, 563, 581, 599, 600, 601, 608; as content, 538; as form, 538; as an individual, 512; as spirit, 533, 555; dawning of, 513; defective, 533, 538, 578; defining, 593; definition of, 578; distinction within itself, 539; free, 532, 564, 565, 576, 577, 578, 586, 587, 588, 591, 598, 599, 609; highest definition of, 534, 578; incomplete, 579; objectification of, 564; requires instantiation in objective world, 565; unifying, 590, 592; vs. consciousness, 532
self-definition, 589, 593, 595, 596, 597, 599, 600
self-determination, 476, 515, 562, 563, 589
self-externality, 91, 93, 94, 96, 102, 391
semantics, xvii, 68, 287, 305, 306, 323, 472; drives logic, xix, 304; in Aristotle's logic, 400; in Hegel's logic, xiv, xvi, xviii, 23, 117, 123, 400; intertwines with syntax, xvi–xviii
sensation or sensibility, 511, 512; as syllogism, 511
sentience, 511, 522
separability, 438, 442, 443, 463, 508
separation, 96, 245, 318, 435, 466, 468, 471, 495, 499, 506, 544, 553, 559, 562, 572, 585, 599
setzen. *See* positedness
sex, 523
sexual reproduction, 525, 527, 530, 537, 541; as process of real

possibility for life, 526. *See also* reproduction
Shine, 111, 224, 335, 502; as a process, 305; as showing up, 142, 143, 173, 175, 192, 250; of Absolute Idea, 593, 594, 595, 596, 598, 600, 608; of Essence, 124, 126, 127, 131, 133, 137, 140, 151, 152, 155, 156, 167, 172, 186, 190, 191, 192, 193, 202, 203, 212, 263, 264, 282, 284, 297, 307, 332, 433, 543, 586, 593, 594; of Essence as thereness, 160; of Essence as separated from Being, 162; vs. Appearance, 176
SI. *See* Subjective Idea
Simply Negative Qualitative Judgment, stage of, 349–50
Singular Judgment of Reflection, 372; stage of, 358–61
Singularity (S), 329, 348, 368, 370, 374, 375, 376, 377, 378, 379, 387, 430, 433, 435, 446, 452, 453, 455, 473, 480, 481, 482, 490, 500, 506, 513, 519, 523, 529, 533, 535, 538, 548, 550, 551, 552, 572, 582, 587, 592, 596, 600, 601, 603, 605, 606; abstract, 379; as a "being-for-itself," 342; as a "this," 359; as a center, 447, 449, 452; as a one, 362, 381; as a totality, 331, 365, 366; as both actual and possible, 569; as centrality, 450, 452; as concrete, 344, 415; as concrete universal, 359; as content of both universality and particularity, 391; as existing actuality, 329, 334, 345; as finished, 362, 365; as general concept, 333; as ground, 337, 339, 344, 345; as immediately concrete, 345; as inwardly reflected, 359; as original-S, 487, 488, 489; as sensible kind, 418; as smaller-S, 484, 487, 488, 490, 501, 511, 515, 530, 555, 556; as something-particular, 388, 353; as something-universal, 334, 361; as subject, 340, 344; as subsistent, 332, 337, 339, 344; as substance, 332, 339; as univeral concept, 333; as universal concept, 329, 334, 344; as universality and particularity, 333, 334; being determined in and for itself, 332, 334; contingent, 395; defintion of, 425; divides universality into particularities, 390; extreme of, 452, 457, 487; immediate, 332, 373, 378, 379, 380, 385, 390, 391, 393, 423; immediate definition of, 345; immediate universal of, 508; includes existence, 422; judges, 481; judgment of Singularity reflects character of the Concept, 483; lost, 371; no longer abstract, 387; particular and universal within identity, 331; particularizes, 362; process of, 508, 517; reflects the character of the Concept, 334; reflects universality and particularity, 411; same as actual, 331; same as Particularity, 374; stage of, 328–33; tied to existence, 421
skepticism: Hume's, 3, 271; Kant's, 12, 17, 19, 114, 204, 213, 271
SL. *See Science of Logic*
SL Development for Qualitative Syllogism, 384
Socrates, 11
solid outline (in diagrams), 55, 58, 79, 88, 90, 145, 151, 160, 167, 171, 177, 184, 190, 218, 222, 228, 229, 237, 245, 256, 259, 304, 465, 466, 566, 578; meaning of, 56, 115
soul, 343, 367, 377, 378, 484, 505, 508
species, 366, 367, 369, 431, 452, 474, 549, 552, 555, 603; as completed set, 370; cannot be out there, 371
Speculative Idea, 597; stage of, 574–84
Speculative Method, 585; stages of, 584–97
Spinoza, Benedictus (Baruch), 252
spirit, 14, 43, 75, 195, 321, 450, 533, 555, 556, 565, 576, 577, 578, 579, 582; as Reason, 533; rational, 566
Spurious Infinity, 68, 72, 77, 78, 79, 83, 84, 85, 94, 96, 105, 106, 109, 110, 112, 115, 129, 158, 176, 179, 231, 232, 274, 285, 304, 350, 351, 354, 383, 468, 495, 496, 502, 524,

525, 573, 575, 582, 596, 598, 599, 608; resolved, 602; resolved (stopped) by embracing concept, xvi, 72, 74, 96, 112, 121, 127, 149, 179, 211, 497; resolved (stopped) by redefinition, 179, 180, 233, 285, 497, 577, 598; stage of, 67–71. *See also* process (logical):back and forth
Spurious Infinity of Finite Willing, 602; stage of, 570–73
stages: names of, 50
subject, 321; conscious, 546; knowing, 546
Subjective Concept, 321, 322
Subjective Idea (SI), 582; antithesis with OI sublated, 583; as "for itself," 544; as active subject of both willing and theoretical cognition, 574; as arbiter of truth, 562; as basic, free self-consciousness, 578; as dynamic, 575, 576; as effect of OI, 573, 575; as essential, 569; as essential identity, 539, 540; as essential purpose, 541; as identity, 564; as inessential, 569; as one-sided subjectivity, 542, 560, 573; as opposed to OI, 542; as rational will, 566; as self-determining, 563; as singularity, 557, 563; as subject, 563; as the U, 546; as unity of SI and OI in thought, 543; becomes Absolute Idea, 576; defective as essential purpose, 539; drive to realize itself, 565; establishes connection to out-thereness, 542; functions fall apart, 537; judgment of, 540, 541; lost its S-ness, 560, 572, 576; must establish connection to OI, 560; particularity of, 557; sublates one-sided subjectivity, 542, 576
Subjective Logic, 319, 323
Subjective Purpose: stage of, 475–76
subjectivity, 195, 323, 478, 505, 509, 531, 535, 601, 607; as "fleshed out," 505; as centrality, 515; as cognition, 319; as consciousness, 319; as contingent, 389; as deficient on its own, 482; as grounded in subject, 383; as Idea, 513; as independent of objectivity, 437; as might over objectivity, 494; as mutually defining with objectivity, 576; as one-sided, 487, 542, 543; as reflection, 383; as self-consciousness, 516; conscious, 514; contingency of, 429; defined by objectivity, 494; definition of, 533; distinct from objectivity, 582; external, 363, 372, 381, 382, 394, 395, 419, 420, 434; finite, 494, 497, 503, 504; grammatical sense, 319, 448, 473, 513; immediate, 473; independence from subjectivity, 428, 434; "is" of, 434; mere, 476, 480; needs objectivity to be what it is, 560; no external subjectivity, 373; of cognition, 321; one-sided, 473, 474, 553, 561, 562, 573, 576, 578, 582; one-sidedness must be sublated, 491; self-conscious, 513; three senses, 319–22; unity with objectivity, 498, 542, 582
sublation, 18, 35, 54, 62, 84, 88, 106, 111, 113, 119, 135, 144, 162, 174, 175, 177, 192, 197, 204, 211, 222, 227, 239, 240, 241, 242, 243, 247, 259, 261, 264, 277, 282, 288, 289, 326, 328, 376, 386, 391, 396, 425, 434, 442, 462, 465, 466, 467, 468, 491, 494, 502, 505, 515, 542, 543, 569, 573, 582, 592, 598, 600, 608; as work, 276, 277, 278; defined, 35; of positedness by existence, 305
subsistence, 75, 160, 161, 163, 165, 167, 168, 169, 172, 175, 177, 179, 180, 182, 183, 186, 199, 200, 275, 288, 294, 304, 331, 332, 333, 380, 434, 437, 448, 449, 451, 454, 457, 470, 515; as a whole process, 181; as ground, 199; as inward reflection, 177; as Singularity, 337, 339; essential, 181; separated from thereness, 162
Substance, 32, 252, 265, 269, 270, 272, 276, 288, 289, 295, 296, 297, 304, 315, 318, 331, 332, 431, 518; as "for itself," 266; as actuality, 266; as

Cause, 269, 270, 271, 272, 274, 293; as Concept, 297; as essence, 267; as Singularity, 339; as thought, 265; finite, 266; infinite, 266, 267; vs. the Concept, 295, 299; vs. thereness, 266. *See also* Immediate Substance and Substantiality

Substance as Cause, 275, 276, 287, 293, 304, 332, 477; stage of, 269–74

substantiality: as activity of Substance, 267

Suchting, W.A., xx, 6, 35, 124, 139, 150, 176, 235, 260, 314, 400, 570, 609, 610

syllogism, 320, 322, 442, 478, 481, 483, 491, 499, 514, 530, 532, 548, 561, 575, 607; as conceptual connectedness, 479; as developed form of judgment, 603; as independent, 419; as not reversible, 479; as reversible, 397, 399, 401, 403, 404, 405, 409, 412, 454, 455, 458, 463, 464, 479, 607; as semantic, 401; as subjective, 434; as the Concept in reality, 377; as the judgment in reality, 376; as trilogy of syllogisms, 463; as what is rational, 377; backward, 550; completed mediation, 392; contains all three moments of the Concept, 378; contingency of, 382, 394, 410, 420, 421; expresses finiteness, 380; expresses nature of the Concept, 376; form of, 376, 377, 386, 387, 393, 408, 412, 418, 420, 425, 433, 479; form of syllogism sublated, 433, 434; formal, 379, 392; formalistic treatment of, 401, 403; fourth figure of, 400; genuine, 550, 553; immediacy of, 420; includes form of judgment, 377; indifference of, 438; may have more than three judgments, 382, 412; mediated by universality, 394; mediation of, 425, 426; mutually supporting premises, 392; necessary, 383; necessary conclusion, 420; necessity of, 421; not genuine, 549; not reversible, 519; objective meaning of, 390, 394; objective truth of, 382, 412; of particularity, 486; of proof for theorem, 561; of purpose, 479, 484, 530, 572; of universality, 451; positions within syllogism define form, 387, 397, 408; positions within syllogism have a definition, 387; presupposes conclusion, 411, 415; singularity defined by, 395; standard form violated, 386, 390; subjective, 381, 382, 394; subjective in two senses, 383; sublated, 436; sublates judgment, 376; triad of, 404, 409, 510, 607; truth of formal syllogism, 392; unity of the Concept and judgment, 376. *See also* the individual stages of the syllogism

Syllogism of Allness, 415; stage of, 409–11

Syllogism of Analogy, 418, 419, 428; stage of, 413–15

Syllogism of Induction, 416; stage of, 411–12

Syllogism of Necessity, 380; stages of, 416–33

Syllogism of Reflection, 380; stages of, 408–15

syntax, xii, xiv, xvi, xvii, xviii, xix, xx, xxi, 24, 25, 32, 34, 35, 56, 68, 113, 116, 117, 123, 179, 287, 305, 306, 307, 314, 323, 400, 472; concepts of, xvii; devices, 115, 116, 117, 245; in Hegel's logic, xii, xvi, xviii, xix; intertwines with semantics, xvi–xviii, 56; patterns, xvii, 50, 55, 59, 109, 113, 229, 602

synthesis. *See* thesis-antithesis-synthesis

Synthetic Method of Cognition: stage of, 550–52

Synthetic Moment of Particularity, 561, 563; stage of, 553–57

Synthetic Moment of Singularity, 563; stage of, 557–62

Synthetic Moment of Universality: stage of, 552–53

Thales, 46

Theorem, 558, 559, 562, 563, 564, 565, 572, 606; as synthetic, 559;

constructs identity, 559; proof of, 560; stage of, 557–62
Theoretical Cognition: 542, 544, 571, 572, 578, 580, 583; as "for itself" process of form, 547; as drive, 543; as process of gathering up, 542; defined, 540; faith of, 542; from point of view of SI, 574; guided by Concept, 548; presupposition of, 583; stage of, 545–48. *See also* Cognition
thereness, 56, 59, 74, 75, 100, 112, 113, 122, 125, 131, 133, 156, 157, 161, 164, 175, 212, 223, 224, 266, 271, 301, 329, 336, 343, 362, 371, 377, 378, 382, 435, 436, 482, 487, 491, 494, 496, 497, 500, 501, 504, 505, 517, 518, 519, 527, 529, 531, 533, 536, 542, 547, 556, 561, 564, 572, 576, 578, 579, 585, 588, 594, 605, 607; as showing up, 124, 125; external, 505; for concepts, 157; process of, 528; separated from subsistence, 162
thesis-antithesis-synthesis, xii, 39, 116
Thing, 161, 163, 164, 166, 167, 171, 177, 213, 306, 337; definition of, 161; stage of, 159–61
Thing as Form, 304; stage of, 165
Thing as One Form: stage of, 168–69
Thinghood, 163, 169, 171, 173, 174
Thing-in-itself, 5, 26, 31, 44, 114, 136, 168, 169, 174, 203, 204
Third Figure of Qualitative Syllogism, 419; (from EL), stage of, 396–7; (from SL), stage of, 390–94
Third Moment of Purpose Realizing Itself, 495; stage of, 486–89
"this," 14, 343, 359, 371, 372, 373, 374, 375, 376, 377, 378, 379, 380, 381, 389, 393, 394, 395, 396, 448, 482, 487, 489, 493, 556, 606
Thought, 487, 505, 543, 582; conscious, 516; distinct from Being, 134, 136; realm of, 134, 135, 212, 224; unity with Being, 212, 297, 435
Three Moments Cannot be Held Apart, 340, 368, 376, 479; stage of, 333–35
time, 323, 503, 595; as finished, 208, 257, 267, 286, 303, 327, 329, 331, 347, 467, 470, 490, 503, 527, 529, 533, 545, 575, 582, 588, 593, 601; as not finished, 545
toaster, 315, 318, 319, 320, 323, 509, 525
totality, 32, 422, 429, 437, 442, 445, 451, 452, 453, 455, 457, 462, 463, 468, 527, 605, 606; external, 514
Transition to Actuality, 332, 543; stage of, 209–12
Transition to Appearance, 175, 204; stage of, 172–74
Transition to Chemism, 525; stage of, 458–61
Transition to Cognition, 536, 542, 550, 555, 558, 560, 562, 570, 572, 576, 578, 599; stage of, 525–34
Transition to Condition, 331; stage of, 221–24
Transition to Essence, 116, 129, 166, 179, 211, 234, 278, 379, 497, 498, 508, 594; stage of, 107–13
Transition to Existence: stage of, 154–56
Transition to Ground, 161, 166, 201, 211; stage of, 147–51
Transition to Idea, 520, 521, 529, 532, 575, 602; stage of, 494–503
Transition to Inner and Outer: stage of, 196–98
Transition to Mechanism, 452, 458, 469, 471, 499, 539, 602; stage of, 438–40
Transition to Purpose, 488; stage of, 466–70
Transition to Reciprocal Action, 568; stage of, 278–80
Transition to Relationship: stage of, 185–87
Transition to Syllogism: stage of, 375–78
Transition to the Concept, 302, 315, 317, 318, 320, 322, 331, 341, 369, 420, 503, 559, 577, 578; stage of, 290–303
Transition to The Empty Qualitative Judgment of Identity and the

Negatively Infinite Qualitative Judgment, 602; stage of, 350–52
Transition to the Judgment, 384, 391, 427, 465; stage of, 338–40
Transition to the Judgment of Necessity: stage of, 365–366
Transition to the Object: stage of, 433–35
Transition to Willing: stage of, 562
transitivity: immediate, 424. See also Judgment: as transitive
truth, 14, 372, 374, 488, 536, 542, 559, 560, 562; as relative, 544; definition of, 543; finite, 548
U. See Universality
übergreifen (overgrasp), 6, 11
unconditioned, 22, 24, 25, 27, 28, 29, 35, 36, 37, 47, 242, 252, 259, 260, 262, 315, 318; as actuality, 261
understanding, 35, 38, 43, 52, 68, 94, 106, 135, 380, 548, 556, 601; defined, 19; finite, 556; logic of, 401, 403; stage of, 545–48
unity, 32, 592, 598, 602; as aggregate, 441; as judgment, 577; as merely inner, 297, 458, 460, 462; "for itself," 499, 500; fulfilled (not immediate), 108, 116, 228; genuine, 56, 468; immediate, 101, 108, 116, 436, 438, 507; "in itself," 499; merely posited, 214, 215; negative, 430, 447; not negative, 430; of concept and reality, 519; of finite subjectivity and finite objectivity, 498; of ideal and real, 505; of immediate being, 602; of subjectivity and objectivity, 495; of subjectivity and objectivity as "for itself," 501; of subjectivity and objectivity as "in itself," 501; of the Concept with reality, 501; one-sided, 56; only of content, 439; positive, 392
Universal in its Concrete Singularity: stage of, 557–62
Universal Judgment of Reflection, 445; stage of, 363–64
Universal Specified and Divided: stage of, 553–57
universality (in general) and Universality (U), 13, 15, 16, 18, 74, 116, 317, 324, 327, 334, 348, 368, 371, 375, 376, 377, 378, 379, 385, 386, 389, 414, 431, 433, 435, 444, 446, 447, 452, 471, 501, 502, 506, 529, 535, 548, 550, 551, 552, 578, 585, 587, 596, 601, 602, 606; = rational = good, 566; abstract, 379, 391, 392, 394, 407, 549, 552, 553; as "in and for itself," 325; as a center, 448; as a thought with thought as its object, 530; as a totality, 422, 429, 440, 445, 462; as actively defining or identifying, 444, 449, 592, 594, 595; as aggregate, 454; as "being-for-itself," 434; as both mediated and mediating, 432; as centrality, 458; as cognitively neutral, 551; as commonality, 16, 17, 23, 35,74, 76, 79, 80, 82, 85, 317, 325, 363, 413; as communality, 325, 363, 413; as consciousness, 321; as constitutive, 552; as defective, free self-consciousness, 533, 538; as a defining universal, 422; as determined, 462; as existing, 444, 462; as fairness, 567; as free existence, 533; as free in terms of content, 533; as free self-conciouness, 532; as heart of reason, 566; as identity and distinction, 387, 390; as including existence, 445; as inner, 523; as mediated, 532; as not free in terms of form, 534; as particularity and singularity, 333, 396; as purpose, 488; as rationality, 567; as set-term, 443, 445, 448, 451, 464, 513, 590, 591; as singularity, 453; as singularity and multiplicity, 425; as something particular, 396; as soul of thing, 343; as subjectivity, 448; as two U's, 459, 460, 461; as unity, 369, 458, 462, 587, 590, 591, 593, 594, 600; basic sense of, 444, 448, 451, 464; being of, 455, 466; concrete, 353, 374, 415, 416, 462, 463; defined by division or

particularizing, 371, 553, 590, 603; definition fulfilled, 433; definition of, 325, 431, 469; determined as universality, 533; essential, 18, 23, 32, 76, 127, 129, 132, 157, 164, 325, 363, 426, 448, 460; fulfilled relationship with particularity, 371, 372; general relation between universal and its particularity, 371; immediate particularization of, 373; Kant's, 445; lost its S-ness, 531, 533, 536, 537, 538, 542, 560, 572, 576, 578; not a concept, 382; not in "in and for itself" relationship with any one particularity, 390; objective, 421; objectivity of, 523; of "allness," 410, 414; of finite things, 380; passes on its character, 327, 329, 444, 520, 530, 534; qualitative, 360, 464; rational, 566; redefined as a concept, 389; reflects character of the Concept, 334; reflects particularity and singularity, 413; relational, 359; self-differentiating, 427, 428, 430; sensible, 348, 604; stage of, 317, 324–26; subjective, 428; substantial, 457, 518; syllogism of, 451; universal principles have logical basis, 567. *See also* ideality, concept *and* the Concept

Universality as Identity, Particularity as Distinction, Singularity as Ground: stage of, 335–37

Unlikeness, 137, 138, 140, 144, 149, 150; choice of term, 139. *See also* Likeness and Unlikeness

urge, 512, 514, 516, 518, 519, 522, 565; for objectification, 523. *See also* desire, drive *and* want

Utterance, 44, 190, 192, 196, 205, 214, 322, 550; defines the Force, 196; of Actuality, 214; of the Force, 198; same "in itself" as Force, 194, 197

validity: objective, 428

variables, 367, 371, 406, 408, 421, 422

Verhältnis, 522, 523

Vorstellung, ix, x, xi, 48

want, 514, 516, 518; as a purpose, 515; defines the kind, 516; defines the singularity, 516. *See also* desire, drive *and* urge

what it is: character of, xvii, 13, 15, 17, 18, 42, 62, 63, 64, 67, 68, 71, 72, 74, 77, 78, 79, 82, 83, 84, 85, 89, 91, 95, 97, 104, 109, 110, 111, 122, 125, 133, 136, 138, 142, 143, 145, 149, 150, 151, 154, 162, 173, 178, 179, 188, 190, 194, 196, 199, 200, 206, 210, 211, 216, 218, 227, 231, 232, 254, 257, 259, 261, 264, 267, 268, 269, 270, 271, 275, 276, 278, 279, 282, 285, 288, 289, 293, 295, 299, 300, 301, 311, 318, 332, 333, 334, 335, 338, 350, 351, 361, 380, 388, 391, 393, 394, 409, 411, 445, 489, 504, 515, 589, 595, 596. *See also* Quality: of being what it is

Whole, 32, 187, 189, 193, 201, 209, 336, 442, 550; former, 191

Whole and Parts: stage of, 187–88

willing, 531, 541, 542, 543, 544, 560, 562, 580, 586; as drive or urge, 565; as free purpose over objective world, 565; as good, 566, 567; as process of division, 542; as rational, 566; as self-consciousness, 564; as both subjective purpose and objective world, 566; as success concept, 564, 565, 570; as whole process, 579; definition of, 563; drive to realize itself, 570; finite, 564, 566, 568, 569, 571, 572, 578, 579, 582, 583; finite willing fails, 571; finite willing aims to change world, 569; from point of view of SI, 574; good will as rational, 568; guided by universals, 568; implies realization into objectivity, 564; judgment of, 563; like theorem, 564; process of, 563; rational willing as systematized set of concepts, 568; spurious infinity of, 573; successful, 564, 565; vs. purpose, 564, 565; willing the good, 566. *See also* Cognition *and* Cognition Generally

Wissenschaft der Logik. See Science of Logic

Wood, Allen, vi, 44

work, 276, 277, 278, 473, 485, 495, 501, 502, 506, 513, 514, 517, 531, 540, 561, 568, 572, 579, 580; as mediation, 485
World of Appearance, 181, 184, 185, 234, 286, 305, 496, 497, 599; stage of, 176–180
Zeno, 47

Made in the USA
San Bernardino, CA
18 April 2014